Studies in Macroeconom[ic History]

SERIES EDITOR: Michael D. Bordo, *Rutgers Uni[versity]*

T0289615

EDITORS: Forrest Capie, *City University Business School, U.K.*
Barry Eichengreen, *University of California, Berkeley*
Nick Crafts, *London School of Economics*
Angela Redish, *University of British Columbia*

The titles in this series investigate themes of interest to economists and economic historians in the rapidly developing field of macroeconomic history. The four areas covered include the application of monetary and finance theory, international economics, and quantitative methods to historical problems; the historical application of growth and development theory and theories of business fluctuations; the history of domestic and international monetary, financial, and other macroeconomic institutions; and the history of international monetary and financial systems. The series amalgamates the former Cambridge University Press series *Studies in Monetary and Financial History* and *Studies in Quantitative Economic History*.

Other books in the series:

Howard Bodenhorn, *A History of Banking in Antebellum America* [0-521-66285-0; 0-521-66999-5]

Michael D. Bordo, *The Gold Standard and Related Regimes* [0-521-55006-8]

Michael D. Bordo and Forrest Capie (eds.), *Monetary Regimes in Transition* [0-521-41906-9]

Michael D. Bordo and Roberto Cortés-Conde (eds.), *Transferring Wealth and Power from the Old to the New World* [0-521-77305-9]

Trevor J. O. Dick and John E. Floyd, *Canada and the Gold Standard* [0-521-40408-8]

Barry Eichengreen, *Elusive Stability* [0-521-44847-6]

Barry Eichengreen (ed.), *Europe's Postwar Recovery* [0-521-48279-8]

Michele Fratianni and Franco Spinelli, *A Monetary History of Italy* [0-521-44315-6]

Mark Harrison (ed.), *The Economics of World War II* [0-521-62046-5]

Kenneth Mouré, *Managing the Franc Poincaré* [0-521-39458-9]

Larry Neal, *The Rise of Financial Capitalism* [0-521-45738-6]

Lawrence H. Officer, *Between the Dollar–Sterling Gold Points* [0-521-45462-X]

Angela Redish, *Bimetallism* [0-521-57091-3]

Aurel Schubert, *The Credit-Anstalt Crisis of 1931* [0-521-36537-6]

Norio Tamaki, *Japanese Banking* [0-521-49676-4]

Mark Toma, *Competition and Monopoly in the Federal Reserve System, 1914–1951* [0-521-56258-9]

David C. Wheelock, *The Strategy and Consistency of Federal Reserve Monetary Policy, 1924–1933* [0-521-39155-5]

Elmus Wicker, *Banking Panics of the Great Depression* [0-521-66346-6]

Central Bank Cooperation at the
Bank for International Settlements, 1930–1973

This book covers the history of the Bank for International Settlements (BIS), the first-born among international economic institutions, from its founding in Basel in 1930 to the end of the Bretton Woods system in 1973. While the focus is on cooperation among the main central banks for the stability and efficiency of the international monetary system, this book also offers an institutional history of the BIS. The first chapters explore the foundation of the BIS, its role in the financial crisis of 1931, the London Economic Conference of 1933, and the following years when central bank cooperation was reduced to mostly technical matters. Considerable attention is devoted to the much-criticised activity of the BIS during World War II. The book then deals with the intensive central bank cooperation for the re-creation of Europe's multilateral payments in the 1950s and for the support of the Bretton Woods system in the 1960s. The last chapter is devoted to the involvement of central banks in the first timid steps towards European monetary unification and to the eurodollar market.

Gianni Toniolo is Professor of Economics at the Università di Roma Tor Vergata (Italy) and Research Professor of Economics at Duke University. A former Professor of Economics and Chair of the Economics Department at the University of Venice, he has held visiting positions at All Souls College and St. Antony's College, Oxford; Hitotsubashi University, Tokyo; the University of California at Berkeley; and the University of Connecticut. He is also a Research Fellow of the Centre for Economic Policy Research in London and a member of the European Academy. Professor Toniolo is the author of several books on European and Italian economic growth from 1800 to the present and on the history of financial markets and institutions with special reference to central banking, including *The European Economy between the Wars* (1997, with C. H. Feinstein and P. Temin) and *An Economic History of Liberal Italy, 1850–1918* (1990). He is the editor of 17 books, including *Patterns of European Industrialization: The Nineteenth Century* (1991, with R. E. Sylla), *Central Banks' Independence in Historical Perspective* (1988), and *Economic Growth in Europe Since 1945* (Cambridge University Press, 1996, with N. Crafts). Professor Toniolo is co-editor (with P. Ciocca and G. Federico) of *Rivista di Storia Economica*.

Central Bank Cooperation at the Bank for International Settlements, 1930–1973

GIANNI TONIOLO

*Università di Roma Tor Vergata,
Duke University, and CEPR*

with the assistance of
Piet Clement

CAMBRIDGE
UNIVERSITY PRESS

CAMBRIDGE UNIVERSITY PRESS
Cambridge, New York, Melbourne, Madrid, Cape Town, Singapore, São Paulo

Cambridge University Press
32 Avenue of the Americas, New York, NY 10013-2473, USA

www.cambridge.org
Information on this title: www.cambridge.org/9780521845519

First published 2005
This digitally printed version 2007

A catalog record for this publication is available from the British Library.

Library of Congress Cataloging in Publication data
Toniolo, Gianni, 1942–
Central Bank Cooperation at the Bank for International Settlements, 1930–1973 / Gianni Toniolo.
p.   cm. – (Studies in macroeconomic history)
Includes bibliographical references and index.
ISBN 0-521-84551-3 hardback
1. Bank for International Settlements – History. 2. International finance – History – 20th
century.   I. Title. II. Series.

HG3881.5.B38T66   2005
332.1´55´0904 – dc22   2004061758

ISBN 978-0-521-84551-9 hardback
ISBN 978-0-521-04370-0 paperback

Contents

Figures and Tables

Foreword

In 2005, the Bank for International Settlements, the world's oldest international financial institution, celebrates its seventy-fifth anniversary. The central bankers who gathered around the BIS meeting table in Basel, Switzerland, for the first time in May 1930 shared a vision that endures to this day. They created an institution that provided them with valuable services in international banking and research while serving also as a meeting place where they could discuss monetary policy issues amongst peers and cooperate effectively whenever necessary. The BIS has played this dual role of service provider and meeting forum for central banks ever since its foundation 75 years ago, and it continues to do so while moving forward to meet new challenges.

In 1980, on the occasion of its fiftieth anniversary, the BIS asked Paolo Baffi – a long-serving BIS Board member, former governor of the Bank of Italy, and outstanding economist – to write the history of the Bank. Unfortunately, Baffi died while his work on the BIS was still at an early stage. The idea of having the Bank's history written was revived under the impulse of my predecessor Andrew Crockett. In 1999, the BIS entrusted this task to Gianni Toniolo.

The book covers the years 1930 to 1973: from the foundation of the Bank until the end of the Bretton Woods monetary system. In writing the BIS's history during this period, Professor Toniolo has made extensive use of the Bank's archives. He also greatly benefited from close and productive collaboration with Piet Clement, Head of Library, Archives & Research Support at the BIS and himself an experienced historian.

In this book, Gianni Toniolo has succeeded in disentangling the sometimes complex and technical issues that are at the core of central banking, placing them in their broad historical context. At the same time he has provided a clear and often compelling narrative that makes this book accessible and worthwhile to layman and specialist alike.

It is a good thing to look back once in a while. By gaining a better understanding of the past – its successes and its setbacks – we are able to make a more balanced judgment of the present and, it is hoped, to look with more confidence to the future. Moreover, for an international organisation such as the BIS, it is a healthy and instructive exercise to have its past performance evaluated by an external expert such as Professor Toniolo, who has really steeped himself in the Bank's history. It goes without saying that the author's views do not necessarily reflect those of the BIS or of its member central banks. Having said that, I believe that Gianni Toniolo's review of more than four decades of central bank cooperation at the BIS offers a sober judgment and provides many thought-provoking insights.

In my view, the book's most important message is that, in the interconnected world of the twentieth and twenty-first centuries, international cooperation (even if does not always yield tangible results) is far preferable to the alternatives of indifference or, worse still, confrontation. The 1930s are a case in point. Indeed, when the need for cooperation in the economic and financial field was more generally recognised – as was the case in the Western world in the 1950s and 1960s – central bank cooperation as fostered by the BIS contributed significantly to a better understanding, and reduced areas of conflict, among different nations and thereby to positive spillover effects on the global economy as a whole. In any case, effective international cooperation is never to be taken for granted.

The central banks and the BIS can look back with some pride at several successes in this cooperation. Achievements such as the European Payments Union are given due recognition in Toniolo's work. It can be argued, however, that it is the frank and open exchange of views, the comparison of experiences, and the formal and informal meeting opportunities under the auspices of the BIS that have immeasurably helped the central banks execute their responsibilities, with due regard to the international environment in which they operate and with due attention to the implications of their actions for others.

As far as the BIS is concerned, it is encouraging to see that – by remaining small, flexible, and free from political interference – the Bank has, throughout its history, succeeded remarkably well in adapting itself to evolving circumstances. Thus, the BIS has transformed itself in recent years from a predominantly European organisation into a global forum for discussion reaching out to the entire community of central banks. Moreover, in addition to its focus on "traditional" monetary policy issues, the BIS has become ever more deeply involved in supporting the efforts of central banks and financial supervisors to fulfil their joint responsibilities in the area of financial stability.

Since the financial industry has grown rapidly in size, complexity, and sophistication, it is widely recognised that nurturing the right incentives for sound financial behaviour and for managing risks and returns in a global and competitive world requires close cooperation among central banks and between them and other financial authorities. The BIS has an important role to play in the general monitoring of the global financial system, but it is especially in the areas of banking regulation, market functioning, and the payment and settlement infrastructure that central banks and other financial standard setters have relied on the services of the BIS and the committees it hosts. A prominent example of this is the recent formulation of a new capital adequacy framework for banks ("Basel II").

The ability to adapt when change is required and to always place the needs and requirements of its constituency centre stage is also the main reason why I am convinced that the BIS still has a long and fruitful future before it.

It gives me great pleasure to commend Gianni Toniolo's history of the BIS to the widest possible audience of interested readers.

Malcolm D. Knight   Basel
General Manager of the BIS   November 2004

Preface

One early December night I woke up in North Carolina feeling uncomfortably cold. I reached for the light switch but the room remained dark. Still half asleep, I crept downstairs to check on the fuses, and I became aware that all around me was white and that it was still snowing heavily. I soon found out that there was nothing wrong with my fuses: no light came from any of the neighbours' windows, and the street lamps were out. In the following hours, battery-powered radios informed us that more than a million people in the area were cut off from power supply. Light, cooking facilities, heating, and running water were all gone. The network had collapsed. Under the weight of the snow, tree branches had broken off, disrupting the intricate web of electrical wires that connect individual houses with the local power lines as well as the latter with the main ones. It took several days of round-the-clock work by electrical engineers – and the cooperation of teams from neighbouring states – for light and heat to be restored to homes, schools, and offices. In the meanwhile, life was reduced to basics, if in a rather pleasant way. Most of the time was spent hunting for food and water, checking on friends, and sharing the heat in the houses of those lucky enough to possess such archaic items as coal- and wood-burning stoves.

At first, I was surprised at how easily, in twenty-first-century North America, a banal snowstorm could bring a large, sophisticated urban area back to the nineteenth century. But it soon occurred to me that one should be more surprised by the day-to-day functioning of a complex power distribution network than by its occasional failure. Our civilisation is largely based on network technology, which – though now developed to high degrees of sophistication – remains intrinsically vulnerable. Failure at just one of the connecting nodes is bound to incapacitate large segments of the net. An act of God or man can only too easily disrupt the flow of energy, information, fuel, merchandise, and people so vital to our daily life, as is routinely observed in large areas of the world.

The payments system is yet another complex network technology, one based upon sophisticated technical tools, market mechanisms, and institutional arrangements. We take it for granted that our cheques clear, that ATMs instantly provide cash anywhere in the world, that imports are paid for in the required currency, and that the desired amount of liquidity is available to us at any time at the lowest cost. But all this is far from being a given, far from being put in place once and for all. In fact, as with the power grid, we should marvel at the ordinarily smooth working of the international payments network rather than be surprised at its occasional malfunction.

In the wake of the 11 September 2001 attacks on the Twin Towers, the main central banks of the world issued a joint statement pledging unlimited supply of liquidity for international settlements. It was an exemplary display of prompt cooperation that was aimed at pre-empting a scramble for liquidity that would impair the payments network. Such swift cooperative action has not always been taken in past emergencies. Although central banks cooperated effectively in reorganising Europe's international settlements in the 1950s and in maintaining dollar–gold convertibility in the 1960s, their prewar record is much less shining. They were unable to prevent or mitigate the financial crisis of 1931 and the subsequent unravelling of the international payments system.

This book is about the successes and failures of central bankers in cooperating to maintain the stability and promote the efficiency of that delicate network that constitutes the system of international payments, of which they are the ultimate custodians. Since 1930, the main locus for multilateral central bank cooperation has been the Bank for International Settlements (BIS), which has provided central bankers with a venue for regular and discreet meetings, with research on issues relevant to international payments, and with a collective financial arm (as the "central banks' bank"). This book is therefore also an institutional history of the BIS from the time of its foundation in 1929–30 to the end of the Bretton Woods system in 1971–73.

The chapters follow a chronological sequence: I know of no better historical narrative than that which takes time seriously. Within each chapter, however, the material is organised to a large extent by subject matter, dealing separately with the most relevant issues in central bank cooperation and with the Bank's internal development and organisation. The first section in each chapter provides a general historical background to the events in the BIS history to be discussed in subsequent sections. The first and the last chapters do not follow the same paradigm as the others. Chapter 1 is designed to offer a brief introduction – based more on history than economic theory – to the themes of international payments and central bank cooperation. Chapter 12 deals with two topics not previously touched upon: the early moves towards cooperation among the European Community central banks, and the meteoric rise of the eurocurrency market. The reason for dealing separately with these two topics is found in their relevance for the development of central bank cooperation beyond the period covered in this book.

The analytical narrative stops in 1973; the reader interested in the subsequent history of the BIS will only find a concise chronology of the main events. There is more than one reason why the end of this book should coincide with that of the Bretton Woods system. On the one hand the book, and its underlying research effort, seemed to have already taken on considerable dimensions; on the other hand, 1973 marked a discontinuity not only in the history of international payments but in that of the BIS as well. However, the main reason for pausing in the early 1970s concerns the availability of primary sources, which generally are subject to the 30-year disclosure rule of the main archives visited for this research. In particular, the BIS archives – explicitly protected by the Bank's Statutes – were opened to the public in 1997, but only for records older than 30 years.

This book was largely written in Basel, a pleasant and lively city that I learned to enjoy. For a few years it became almost my second home. The Bank for International Settlements provided me with an exceptionally friendly and stimulating work environment, a most comfortable office, and all the research assistance I could dream of, but at the same time it granted me absolute freedom of research and writing. General Managers Andrew Crockett and Malcolm Knight could not have been more encouraging and supportive while simultaneously respecting and protecting the independence of my research. The views expressed here are thus my own and do not necessarily reflect those of the BIS management and member central banks.

In researching for and writing this book I accumulated a huge debt of gratitude to the large number of people who in various capacities and ways provided support and intellectual input to my work.

Piet Clement went far beyond the duties of a technically competent and intellectually refined research assistant. The chapters dealing with the London Economic Conference, the Second World War, the 1960s, and the EEC governors' meetings would probably not have seen the light of day without his essential contribution (which, however, does not imply any responsibility on his part). Piet's involvement was also invaluable in archival research, all over the world, and in bridging my German and Dutch language gap. The friendship we developed over the years is yet another gift coming from this project. Piet's wife, Greet Van Malderen, also deserves my gratitude for sharing with him the burden of his research.

Edward Atkinson provided superb archival assistance, was indispensable in organising my life in Basel, and contributed the Dramatis Personae (Annex E). I also enjoyed his proverbial English wit. Relevant and competent research input was provided by Michelangelo Van Meerten on the origin of the BIS and Stefano Battilossi on the eurodollar market. Kazuhiko Yago offered insightful comments and materials on matters pertaining to Japan. Leandro Conte and Marina Sorrentino served ably as research assistants at an early stage of the project.

My special thanks go to the friendly and supportive staff of the BIS Library and Records and Archives teams, and in particular to Maria Friesen, Arwen Hopkins, and Johannes Koch. Unobtrusively behind the scenes, Alan Mortby quietly made sure that I enjoyed all the support I needed. I am also grateful to the BIS Secretarial Service, Language Services, and print shop as well as to current and former staff members from other services for comments and assistance – in particular, Frederick Adelmann, Stephan Arthur, Joseph Bisignano, Paul Bridge, Raymond Fin, James Freis, Angela Maramag, and Jozef Van 't dack. Nigel Hulbert patiently and efficiently took care of the first round of editing of the manuscript.

Research at the BIS was extensively supplemented by a considerable number of other archival sources, in particular those of the main central banks and of several governmental institutions. This additional research was made both possible and agreeable by the professional and friendly assistance of Walter Pluym and Christa Asselman (National Bank of Belgium); Rolf Herget and K. Fitzner (Deutsche Bundesbank); Henry Gillett and Sarah Millard (Bank of England); Roland Rölker and Mascha Steinecke (European Central Bank); Mme. Cavillon-Troadec, Frédérik Grélard, and Fabrice Reuze (Bank of France); Olivier Feiertag (Historical Mission of the Bank of France); Gabriella Raitano and Sergio Cardarelli (Bank of Italy); Floris Joustra, Joke Mooij, Corry Van Renselaar, and Rian Beex (Netherlands Bank); Rosemary Lazenby and Joseph Komljenovich (Federal Reserve Bank of New York); Teresa Tortella (Bank of Spain); Mira Barkå (Sveriges Riksbank); Patrick Halbeisen (Swiss National Bank); Frau von Boeselager (Auswärtiges Amt, Berlin – Politisches Archiv); Martin Steinmann, Franz Gschwind, and Tamara Rodel (Basel University Library, Handschriftenabteilung); Brent Svertloff (Harvard University Baker Library); Herr Roeske (Bundesarchiv Berlin); Frau Oldenhage (Bundesarchiv Koblenz);

James Boughton (IMF); the staff at the Public Record Office (Richmond, U.K.); Mr. Guindi and Bernhardine E. Pejovic (United Nations Library and Archives, Geneva); and Wayne De Cesar (NARA, College Park, USA).

Renato Filosa, André Icard, and Bob Sleeper read the entire manuscript, providing valuable comments and saving me from many mistakes. Marten De Boer contributed a reconstruction of the main time series in the BIS balance sheet. Gunter Baer, Claudio Borio, Peter Dittus, Mario Giovanoli, Guy Noppen, Günther Pleines, Philip Turner, and Bill White either read parts of the manuscript or provided input of various kinds. My old friend Pierluigi Ciocca was immensely supportive throughout. Ignazio Visco was generous in advice, as were Peter Lange and Bob Keohane.

A number of actors and witnesses of the BIS history shared memories and recollections with me: André Bascoul, Robert Chaptinel, Richard T. P. Hall, Pierre Mangeney, Helmut Mayer, Warren McClam, Günther Schleiminger, and, most of all, Michael Dealtry, who also wrote extensive comments on early drafts of some of the chapters.

A number of colleagues made detailed comments on a first draft of the manuscript. They include three extraordinarily competent anonymous readers for Cambridge University Press and a panel of specialists in the field who spent a whole day with me in Basel in June 2004 discussing every chapter in detail. The panel was composed of Michael Bordo, Forrest Capie, Pierre-Cyrille Hautcoeur, Carl-Ludwig Holtfrerich, Jaime Reis, and Herman Van der Wee. I am most grateful for their comments and suggestions, which proved to be of great help in revising the manuscript. Needless to say, the standard academic disclaimer applies to them all.

Cambridge University Press was constructive and helpful as always. Thanks are specifically due to Scott Parris and Simina Calin. Matt Darnell put on a splendid editorial performance.

A special thought goes to the memory of Paolo Baffi, who would have written this book much better than I did; for many of us in Italy he remains a hallmark of civil passion and intellectual integrity.

My debt to Francesca Sanna Randaccio – the companion of my life and a superb economist – is *also* intellectual. Its full extent can be entirely appreciated only by the two of us. Paolo quietly understands that I owe him a lot.

The book appears at a time when, in a number of areas, the drive to strengthen multilateral international relations is at risk of losing momentum. I hope it will make a small contribution by showing that, in a tightly networked world, there is scarcely any better alternative to painstakingly seeking multilateral cooperation. The events of the 1930s serve to remind us that go-it-alone, autarkic, beggar-thy-neighbour policies are suboptimal for all and everybody. I also hope the book makes it clear how much patience, perseverance, and strength in weathering setbacks is required of the people – such as those who go on meeting regularly at the BIS in Basel – whose mission it is to build a more cooperative multilateral world.

Acronyms

ANB	Austrian National Bank
BCBS	Basel Committee on Banking Supervision
Benelux	Belgium, the Netherlands, and Luxembourg
BIS	Bank for International Settlements
BIZ	Bank für Internationalen Zahlungsausgleich (BIS)
BRI	Banque des Règlements Internationaux – Banca dei Regolamenti Internazionali (BIS)
C20	Committee of Twenty
CEEC	Committee of European Economic Co-operation
CGFS	Committee on the Global Financial System (G10/BIS)
COBRI	Comité d'Organisation de la Banque des Règlements Internationaux (BIS Organisation Committee)
Comecon	Council for Mutual Economic Assistance
CPSS	Committee on Payment and Settlement Systems (G10/BIS)
EC	European Communities
ECA	Economic Co-operation Administration
ECSC	European Coal and Steel Community
EEC	European Economic Community
EMA	European Monetary Agreement
EMCF	European Monetary Co-operation Fund
EMS	European Monetary System
EMU	European Monetary Union
EPU	European Payments Union
ERP	European Recovery Program (Marshall Plan)
Euratom	European Atomic Energy Community
FOMC	Federal Open Market Committee (U.S. Federal Reserve)
FRBNY	Federal Reserve Bank of New York
G10	Group of Ten countries

GAB	General Arrangements to Borrow (IMF/G10)
GATT	General Agreement on Tariffs and Trade
IBRD	International Bank for Reconstruction and Development (World Bank)
IADI	International Association of Deposit Insurers
IAIS	International Association of Insurance Supervisors
ICE	Independent Commission of Experts Switzerland – Second World War (Bergier Commission)
ICRC	International Committee of the Red Cross
IEPC	Agreement for Intra-European Payments and Compensations
ILO	International Labour Office
IMF	International Monetary Fund
IOSCO	International Organisation of Securities Commissions
MC	Markets Committee (G10/BIS)
MED	Monetary and Economic Department (BIS)
NATO	North-Atlantic Treaty Organisation
OEEC	Organisation for European Economic Co-operation
OECD	Organisation for Economic Co-operation and Development
RM	Reichsmarks
SDR	special drawing right (IMF)
UN	United Nations
UNCTAD	United Nations Conference on Trade and Development
UPU	Universal Postal Union
WP3	Working Party No. 3 (OECD)

ONE

International Payments and Central Bank Cooperation

1.1 A BIS View of Cooperation

The principal mission of the Bank for International Settlements (BIS), as
set down in its Statutes, is to promote the cooperation of central banks.[1]
The experts who in 1929 recommended the creation of the "International
Bank" wanted it to provide "an increasingly close and valuable link in the
cooperation of central banking institutions – a cooperation essential to the
continuing stability of the world's credit structure".[2]

Why central bank cooperation? Cooperation on what? With what objectives in view? How? These questions were asked by the BIS itself in
1935,[3] at a time when international economic cooperation lay in tatters,
only a few years after the high hopes raised by the Young Plan and the creation of the Bank. The failure of the London Conference of 1933 to revive
the international monetary system based on gold had left in its wake ac-
rimony, mistrust, and a myopic pursuit of national interests. Purposeful
world economic leadership was not in sight. Dark clouds were gathering
on the political and military horizons as Germany unilaterally repudiated
the military clauses of the Versailles treaty, Italy perpetuated its aggression
on Abyssinia, and Japan prepared to invade China. In this disheartening
context, the management of the BIS chose to engage in a definition of central bank cooperation, a concept often mentioned in public discourse but
seldom precisely articulated in its details and implications. It was a way for
the new international organisation to discharge one of its moral duties. In
the 1930s the BIS preached in the desert about the advantages of cooperation, but the intellectual contribution to the definition of the aims, scope,
and limits of central bank cooperation outlived the circumstances in which

1

it was made. It provides a useful starting point for the history of central bank cooperation as it unfolded in Basel between 1930 and 1973.

"For many", the BIS wrote, "central bank cooperation means only financial assistance". While mutual "financial aid is a spectacular evidence of central bank inter-relationship, nevertheless these exceptional measures, though useful, do not constitute the real kernel of central bank collaboration, which is or should be evident in continuous and daily practice rather than as an emergency manifestation".[4]

Why, then, central bank cooperation? According to the BIS, each central bank has substantially the same task – namely, "to regulate the volume of credit and currency with a view to lessening pronounced fluctuations in business activity, and to follow a policy designed to maintain fundamental equilibrium in the balance of payments in order to preserve some pre-agreed degree of stability in the international value of its national money, thereby facilitating trade and desirable capital movements from and to the country concerned".[5] But central banks operate in a world larger than their domestic sphere, if for no other reason than that each national currency is internationally traded and domestic policies are subject to influence from abroad. Their viewpoint therefore must necessarily face outwards as well as inwards. The interdependence of financial markets and the international nature and transmission of business fluctuations are such that the domestic policies of a central bank "may be rendered difficult or thwarted by the policy action of a neighbouring central bank". Thus, "far-seeing self-interest demands that banks of issue endeavour to work along parallel lines in the fulfillment of their independent duties, although measures taken to attain the common purpose need not be identical in different markets". According to the consistently held philosophy of the BIS, "long range national advantage and international well-being usually coincide in the desideratum that the credit and currency policy of the world's central banks be, as far as possible, uniform and through cooperation avoid being haphazard or mutually adverse".

The BIS saw a number of relevant matters on which central banks can usefully collaborate.

a. Evolving a common body of monetary doctrine in order to assure "the widest possible measure of common agreement on monetary theory, problems and practice, including agreement upon what the international standard is to be and how to maintain it".[6]

b. Gaining an understanding of the difficulties that confront neighbouring central banks. "The beginning of understanding", the BIS wrote, "in international affairs, whether in the political arena or in the economic and financial field, is the knowledge based on patient examination and sympathetic consideration of why the other nation adopts the measures which it does. Many of the difficulties which impede international rapprochement have their origin in inadequate acquaintance with all the facts of the situation, and in the lack of objective appreciation of the problems and reasoning of the other side. Even when the differences are irreconcilable, it is at least helpful to have them accurately defined".[7]

c. Learning how to avoid doing harm to one another, especially when one central bank is operating in the market of a neighbour, by the establishment of reciprocal banking, business, and personal relations.

d. Gathering and exchanging monetary and economic data. Such exchange of information is vital, according to the BIS, "with respect to the volume, movement and location of short-term balances and short-term foreign credits in general".

e. Improving inter–central bank practice in a wide range of technical matters.[8]

f. Assisting in the creation of new central banks as well as aiding smaller ones in "their efforts to follow a sound credit and financial policy and to maintain the international value of their local currency".[9]

g. Working out technical improvements to some of the features of the international monetary system.

What were, according to the BIS, the principal objectives of central bank cooperation? The first one was the maintenance of a stable system of international payments. In 1935 this meant "the general restoration of the gold standard and ... its successful working in the future". The second object of collaboration was "to attempt, as far as is possible by monetary and credit measures, to smooth out the business cycle, and to contribute toward a greater equilibrium in the general level of economic activity.... It is primarily by wise and prescient contraction or expansion of credit, as sound business conditions demand, that central banks acting in collaboration can do most to avoid undue fluctuations in the purchasing power of gold".[10]

How to cooperate? The BIS's own experience of the previous five years suggested "frequent meetings, visits, incessant exchange of information, common consultation and joint discussion, all to the end that at least mutual understanding may ensue, if not indeed harmonious action. In monetary matters", the BIS explained, "the psychological attitudes prevailing on the various markets are often factors of very great importance; to convey

a correct impression of elusive psychological influences is always difficult, but it can certainly be done most easily by word of mouth". With
some pride, the BIS added that "it is not generally realised how much
progress has already been made to promote greater contact between central banks", particularly since "the members of the BIS meet regularly ten
times a year".[11]

After explaining why central banks should cooperate and discussing the
areas, objectives, and tools of cooperation, the 1935 Annual Report concluded with a caveat: "Too much should not be expected from the cooperation of the central banks. It is not a panacea for economic ills, although
its realization would greatly contribute toward their prevention in some instances, or toward their alleviation in many others".

There are, the BIS noted, many reasons why central bankers find it difficult to cooperate: "the tradition and habit of secrecy", the desire to affirm
independence, "questions of prestige", "the spirit of nationalism". The
largest stumbling block, however, lies in the fact that "central bank cooperation is but one phase of international collaboration in general, and if that
is wholly lacking or if international relations are antagonistic, then central
banks, whose tasks are primarily of a technical order, have means inadequate to withstand the contrary tides".[12]

Such were the views on international monetary cooperation officially
held in 1935 by the BIS – created in 1930 as the first international financial
organisation – whose history from its origin to the end of the Bretton Woods
system is the subject of this book. The narrative will cover in some detail
the organisation and the operations of this institution. We shall deal with
people working at the Basel headquarters of the Bank or regularly gathering there from all over Europe, the United States, and Japan; at times we
shall even try to have a glimpse at their daily life. But the focus of the book
is on central bank cooperation as it unfolded in Basel over some forty-odd
years. Most chapters will open with a section aimed at providing a brief
background to the developments in the international monetary scene that
required the attention and intervention, successful or otherwise, of central
banks and their cooperative institution. Specialists may find these sections
redundant, but we trust that many readers, including historians and economists not specialising in international monetary affairs, will appreciate the
provision of a framework for specific cooperative (or uncooperative) actions
dealt with in subsequent sections of the chapter. Likewise, we felt it to be
appropriate, before beginning with the history of central bank cooperation
at the BIS, to provide a long-term perspective on monetary systems and cooperation. After outlining the evolution of international monetary systems,

we shall briefly spell out the reasons for international monetary cooperation and then discuss how much (and in what form) cooperation existed before the appearance of the BIS on the international scene.

1.2 International Monetary Systems, 1870–1973

One fundamental textbook classification of international monetary systems distinguishes between those supposed to work on the basis of market forces alone and those that require some kind of policy intervention. Systems based either on free-floating exchange rates or on pure (Hume-type) gold-standard–fixed rates belong to the first category. All other systems in between these two extremes are based upon a certain, though variable, degree of management by governments or ad hoc agents such as the central banks.

Such management postulates a certain, though variable, measure of co-operation. The latter can be informal (sometimes also called coordination) or formal. Informal cooperation takes place when each individual player (government or central bank, as the case may be) adheres to given rules of the game that – when autonomously followed by all participants – result in an efficient and stable international monetary system. Formal coopera-tion takes place when governments or central banks agree on ad hoc actions aimed at upholding or enhancing the efficiency and/or stability of the sys-tem. For instance, when every country participating in the gold standard lets changes in money supply reflect the inflow or outflow of gold resulting from balance of payments surpluses or deficits, an informal coordination (or cooperation) is taking place that maintains the viability of the system. When, to take another example, domestic political and social constraints make it difficult for a country to strictly follow the rules of the game (e.g., because the deflation required to maintain a stable exchange rate would create unacceptable levels of unemployment), then the system may be sta-bilised by formal cooperation in the form of loans (bilateral or multilateral) enabling the deficit country to overcome its temporary difficulties.

In the century that ended with the demise of the so-called Bretton Woods system during 1971–73, the international monetary systems linking the "core" countries of the world economy were based upon four different types of arrangements: (i) the classical gold standard, which ended in 1914; (ii) pegged exchange rates between 1914 and 1925 and again between the mid-1930s and the late 1940s; (iii) the gold exchange standard between 1925 and 1931–36; and (iv) the gold dollar standard of Bretton Woods from the late 1940s to the early 1970s. Each of these systems entailed interven-tions of some kind by the domestic monetary authorities – particularly those in the major countries – in order to maintain its efficiency and stability and therefore a degree of informal and/or formal cooperation.

In the early nineteenth century, three types of monetary standards[13] existed worldwide. A gold-standard bloc was formed by the United Kingdom (which converted paper money into gold at the price set in 1717 by Sir Isaac Newton), its colonies and dominions, and Portugal. A silver-standard bloc encompassed the Habsburg Empire, most of the German states, the Scandinavian countries, the Netherlands, and, outside Europe, Mexico and most parts of Asia (including China, India, and Japan). A third group of countries – which included France, Belgium, Switzerland, Italy, and the United States – adopted the bimetallic standard (whereby conversion was possible into either gold or silver, at a fixed rate between the two). The overall system proved to be rather stable owing to the free international flow of metal and to the fact that countries from each bloc tended to trade more intensively with each other than with those on different standards, thus also establishing long-lasting links that survived the end of the specific metallic regimes.[14]

By the 1860s, however, a general trend for monetary systems to converge on gold set in, encouraged by the fall in the relative price of silver induced by the operation of new mines in Mexico and Nevada, by the spread of gold coins as a result of rising incomes, by the economies of scale in the use of gold in international transactions, by the political defeat of the silver populist lobby in the United States, and by the new German Reich's adoption of the gold standard.[15] Most of all, the origins of the gold standard are deeply interwoven with the acceleration of international exchanges. Gold was favoured by the very fact that it was the monetary standard of the United Kingdom, the leading commercial and financial power, at a time of rapidly expanding international trade and capital movements due to falling tariff barriers (as sanctioned by the Cobden–Chevalier Treaty) and to rapidly decreasing transport and communication costs resulting from the expansion of the railways, steam navigation, and the telegraph. Whatever the reasons, by the early twentieth century almost the entire world – with the conspicuous exception of China – was on gold, the Russian and Japanese empires having joined in the last decade of the nineteenth century.

The "classical" gold standard, so called in retrospect to recognise its landmark character, was undeniably successful in providing the low-cost international liquidity needed to sustain an extraordinary period of growth of the world economy, now also termed the "first globalisation". Under the classical gold standard but not necessarily because of it, something quite close to price stability prevailed, exchange rates among the "core" currencies remained fixed,[16] and long-term interest rates converged. Scholars continue to disagree on the reasons for this success, which is likely to have depended on a host of favourable conditions both economic and political in nature. Fixed exchange rates remained compatible with medium-term balance of payments equilibrium owing to fairly flexible domestic labour markets and also to fairly free international movement of goods, labour, and capital. At the same time, the social and political conditions prevailing at the time – including low labour unionisation and limited suffrage – allowed monetary policy to target the exchange rate and governments to pursue orthodox fiscal policies without much concern for repercussions on the level of domestic activity and employment and attendant electoral backlashes. A certain amount of luck also helped in offsetting one of the drawbacks of the metallic standard: its dependence upon an exogenous supply of the metal. When, in the 1890s, the existing stock of monetary gold began to be inadequate to supply the desired amount of liquidity at the desired price, new sources of cheap gold came to be exploited in South Africa, defusing the danger of deflation.

For all its long-term success, the classical gold standard was not free from crises threatening the liquidity of the international payments system, foremost among which were those of 1890 and 1907. We shall discuss the role played by cooperation in dealing with these crises and, more generally, in the overall success of the classical gold standard.

During the First World War, gold convertibility was suspended. A floating exchange rate regime ensued, manipulated as far as possible by governments trying to peg their currencies or to let them slide as smoothly as circumstances allowed in the context of considerable financial and monetary cooperation amongst allies, particularly in the Entente camp. As inflation rates differed, however, the pegging was doomed to fail in the medium term, in spite of the hard currency expended in propping up the weakest currencies. Moreover, as soon as hostilities ceased so did inter-Allied financial and monetary solidarity, and each government was left to its own devices for the "defence" of the currency.

In spite of the huge efforts – both economic and political – devoted to orchestrating an orderly "return to gold", the fixed–exchange rate system introduced in the second half of the 1920s did not bear out the high hopes pinned on it. It neither provided a magical cure for most economic ills nor recreated the "belle époque", as some believed it would. In fact, it was short-lived and pretty much part of the problem rather than the solution to the economic troubles of the 1920s and 1930s. It took time for the political and bureaucratic elites, for public opinion, and for most academic economists and practitioners to realise that the First World War had wiped out the conditions associated with the vitality and resilience of the gold standard.

Universal conscription and the mobilisation of millions of people to fight shoulder to shoulder in the trenches for endless periods of time, sharing not only the same bread but the same fate of life or death, resulted in a huge increase in the political awareness of ordinary people. Immediately after the war, the widespread discontent in Europe was channelled into new ways of political mobilisation and action. Even if revolution failed everywhere except in Russia, governments could no longer overlook (as they somehow could in the nineteenth century) the need for mass popular support: universal male suffrage shifted the focus of fiscal and monetary policy towards domestic goals such as reducing unemployment. At the same time, better-organised labour movements and the coming of age of socialist parties increased nominal wage stickiness. Price flexibility was reduced by the globalisation backlash,[17] which had probably started before the war. Tariff barriers were raised everywhere, their effect amplified by the disappearance of large customs unions such as the Habsburg Empire. Cross-border movements of workers were only a fraction of the antebellum total. In short, the conditions that had previously allowed the relatively easy adjustment of the balance of payments and produced price equalisation under fixed exchange rates had all but disappeared by the end of the war.

One of the postwar concerns was the adequacy of supply of monetary gold.[18] It was particularly felt in Great Britain, where the shallow gold reserves cast doubts upon the role of the City as the world's financial centre.[19] Since London was an international repository for foreign exchange reserves, British experts proposed that banks of issue should be allowed to include holdings of key foreign convertible currencies in their official reserves.[20] The gold standard thus became a gold exchange standard. The flaw in the system was that it provided little incentive or constraint for central banks to hold a balanced composition of reserves. International liquidity was, therefore, to some extent at the mercy of central banks (such as those of France and the United States) that showed a high preference for gold rather than foreign convertible currencies. The postwar gold exchange standard, therefore, required a high degree of monetary policy cooperation.[21] In fact, as we shall see, central bank cooperation was indeed more explicit in the 1920s than it had been before the war, but it had to contend with the divisiveness of international politics and focused on the financial conditions for currency stabilisation rather than on overall, day-to-day, policy coordination. Then, in the early 1930s, it failed spectacularly: "unwilling to follow the rules or give up the standard, countries resisted steps to restore equilibrium real exchange rates. In retrospect, the breakdown of the gold standard seems inevitable; at the time, it seemed calamitous".[22]

The Great Depression finally convinced large segments of the elites and of the general public of the deflationary bias of the gold standard. However, the attraction of fixed exchange rates anchored to a solid metallic base was so strong that the gold exchange standard was resurrected by the Bretton Woods Agreements of July 1944, this time cushioned by a higher dose of international cooperation and formalised rules. The final demise of the gold anchor of the international monetary system came only in 1971. The gold exchange standard of the post–World War II period quickly developed into a gold dollar standard. Like its interwar predecessor, it harboured – as Triffin and others feared – a possible deflationary bias, but this did not materialise because of the underlying economic conditions and an unusual amount of international monetary cooperation under U.S. leadership. Social and political conditions as well as international relations again played a crucial role in sustaining the efficiency and stability of the international monetary system. It is commonplace in the literature to stress how the lessons of the interwar period were learned and mistakes avoided after 1945. Europe's "golden age" and the Japanese economic miracle were both the cause and the effect of rapidly increasing international trade in the context of stable exchange rates. The system ended, as we shall see in Chapter 11, when both the United States and Europe were no longer willing (or able) to bear their share of the cost of its continuation.

1.3   Reasons and Conditions for International Monetary Cooperation

Of the various international monetary systems briefly described in the previous section, some lasted longer and delivered more stability than others. The classical gold standard (1870s–1914) seems to have served the needs of international transactions longer and more efficiently than the arrangements that followed it in the first half of the twentieth century. Under the Bretton Woods system, international financial crises were fewer and milder than they were in subsequent decades. Historians and economists disagree on the extent to which these different historical records reflect the intrinsic technical merits of each system rather than the overall economic and political conditions prevailing in each of these epochs. The assessment of the impact of cooperation is part of this debate: was it more useful (or even necessary) in a given exchange rate system than in another? Did it crucially depend on the prevailing climate of international relations? These questions will, more or less implicitly, underlie much of the narrative and analysis contained in this book. Before moving on to that, it may be useful to say a few words about the rationale for international cooperation and, in the next two sections, to review the literature on central bank cooperation before the mid-1920s.

There exists a huge theoretical literature, in both economics and political science, about cooperative behaviour and the conditions for its success. In the ideal economist's world – with atomistic maximising agents, perfect competition both in the product and in the factor markets, and full symmetrical information – coordination is efficiently produced by market forces. In that same world, cooperation, because it entails agreements and commitments, actually stands in the way of competition and is likely to produce suboptimal outcomes. Some economists argue that, even when the real world is far from meeting the standard competitive assumptions, the pursuit of self-interest by individual agents (in our case, governments or central banks) produces a better coordination than cooperative behaviour. Market discipline, even if imperfect, they argue, will in the medium term reward monetary and fiscal virtue and punish vice, naturally creating a "sound" international monetary order. They also point to the inherent instability of cooperation among equal partners – given the high individual rewards to uncooperative behaviour – and to the dangers of rent-seeking inherent in cooperation induced by effective leadership.

Recent technical game theory literature yields mixed results on cooperation, depending on the assumptions made about the structure of the game, the relative dimensions and number of the players, their strategies, the payoff matrix, and other variables.[23] Yet one frequent result is that, in the presence of externalities (such as those deriving from a stable and efficient international monetary system), cooperative behaviour yields higher payoffs to all participants in the game. Another result is that in one-shot games (such as those of the standard Nash type) cooperation is superior to non-cooperation, whereas in the case of repeated games reputation and trust may substitute for explicit cooperation. Thus, as far as the international monetary system is concerned, one may argue that formal cooperation is definitely needed in dealing with major single shocks (e.g., financial crises) whereas the long-run sustainability of international monetary arrangements could rest on commitments made credible by reputation (yielding to informal cooperation, as defined in the previous section).

Political scientists, with the exception of extreme realists, tend to concur that international cooperation yields higher (if by no means equally distributed) payoffs to all participants. They therefore focus (and disagree) on how to achieve effective cooperation rather than on its desirability.

Extreme realism, an intellectual product of the Cold War, is based on the assumption that we live in an anarchic world where states fear for their survival and rely upon their relative strength to continue in existence. They thus do not enter into cooperative agreements that, while benefiting every-body including themselves, are relatively more favourable to others. This theory is worth mentioning because it may help us understand why in some circumstances, such as those of the insecure interwar years, cooperation was more difficult to achieve than in other circumstances such as those pre-vailing after the Second World War, when a hegemonic power provided the West with the public good of defence (while at the same time explaining why cooperation between the Eastern and Western blocs took place on such a low scale).

Robert Keohane, drawing also from Lindblom,[24] defines international co-operation as taking place "when actors adjust their behavior to the actual or anticipated preference of others through a process of policy coordination"[25] by adjusting their own policies to minimise their negative impact on other countries. In order to cooperate, states must have a set of goals to achieve and must be convinced that cooperative behaviour provides them with gains and rewards.[26] For our purposes, a useful political scientist's taxonomy of the ways in which cooperation may be achieved can be the following: it can be tacit, as some argue was the case with central bank cooperation before 1914; it can be negotiated, as it was in the interwar period (for instance, at the time of the creation of the BIS); and, finally, it can be imposed, as might have been the case after World War II.

The political science literature has provided a number of tentative hy-potheses about the systemic conditions under which cooperation may take place and may be sustained. "Recent theoretical reflection on the politi-cal economy of cooperation has shown that, short of recourse to force or to the enforcement services of a hegemonic power, international collective action requires a notion of reciprocity, whereby each member can be sure that there will be a balanced distribution (an ambiguous concept, though) of gains and losses deriving from the cooperative effort."[27]

The role of domestic policies in determining international monetary co-operation is often overlooked by economists[28] and political scientists. The issue, which will surface over and again in the following chapters, is impor-tant because national interests are determined by domestic preferences, be-cause domestic politics help to explain international strategies, and because international cooperation holds only as long as domestic lawmakers allow the continuation of negotiated agreements. It is unfortunate that no solid theory exists linking the domestic with the international political arena.

From this book's perspective, perhaps the most interesting explanation of cooperation sustainability "centers on the role of international regimes, which are defined as sets of norms, principles, rules, or decision-making procedures around which the actors' expectations converge".[29] Regimes aid in the decentralised enforcement of agreements, help in solving the defection problem, improve information about the behaviour of others, and reduce transaction costs in cooperating by reducing uncertainty. Regimes may be informal, as in the case of the classical gold standard, or more or less tightly structured with perhaps the creation of supranational bodies, such as the International Monetary Fund after World War II or (to a lesser extent) the BIS in the 1930s. It may be argued that the creation of a regime is difficult since it implies the prior decision by at least some states to cooperate; however, once created, regimes provide incentives both for members to remain in the agreement and for outsiders to join.

Regime creation leads us to the notion of international monetary systems as institutions. If we see these institutions as providers of a public good – such as a low-cost and stable supply of liquidity for cross-border transactions – then the question about why there is a need for international cooperation may receive a plausible answer. It is a fairly well-accepted result in economic theory that markets supply public goods in suboptimal quantity and that, under normal assumptions, the state (or an equivalent agent) may actually supply an optimum quantity of such goods. An international authority, endowed with powers of law-making and enforcement, might therefore produce an optimum quantity of an international public good such as stable money. In the absence of such an authority, its functions may be more or less efficiently performed by international cooperation via the creation of institutions approximating the functions of the international authority. Such institutions will definitely be less efficient than a supranational authority in the provision of the international monetary public good, but in some circumstances they may become strong and stable enough to supply the public good in close to optimum quantity. This is, at any rate, the not entirely unfounded expectation of the supporters of cooperation in the realm of international monetary institutions and policies.

Finally, it must be recalled that international cooperative institutions, formal or informal, remain viable only as long as they are seen as legitimate by those for whose benefit they are supposed to exist. By the early 1930s, for instance, the viability of the gold standard was undermined by the fact that workers, employers, and an increasingly large number of electors believed it to be detrimental to their own well-being. A viable international institution – in a world of independent, politically sovereign states – must be credible both in its ability to deliver an international public good and in its sustainability. Obligations arising from international conventions, customary laws, or treaties depend for their execution on the continued consent of the obligor countries, which in turn depends on their citizens' clear perception that "they have a long-run, broad-ranging interest to stick to [the contracted obligations], rather than to defect to pursue short-run gains".[30]

1.4 Central Bank Cooperation under the Classical Gold Standard

Let us now briefly turn to the scale and effectiveness of central bank cooperation prior to the launch of the so-called Dawes Plan (1924) that more or less settled the contentious issue of German war reparations, thereby removing the political obstacles to international capital movements and creating the conditions for the "return to gold".[31]

It must be recalled once again that the classical gold standard was not based on any formal international agreement or understanding.[32] All that was needed for a country to be a member of the gold club was for its bank of issue to commit itself to convert banknotes into gold at a fixed rate and to adapt domestic legislation, monetary policy, and financial practices towards the goal of making the conversion pledge credible.

In a textbook representation of the gold standard, the sustainability of the system simply requires national monetary authorities to cooperate by strictly adhering to the "rules of the game". In the presence of a negative balance of payments shock, the deficit country is supposed to raise its discount rate and the surplus country to lower it. If both comply, the combined effect of capital flows and changes in domestic activity and employment levels restores external equilibrium, keeps exchange rates stable, and maintains gold reserves in each country at the original desired level.

As clean, straightforward, and mutually advantageous as textbook tacit cooperation may appear under the gold standard, in practice it is difficult to achieve for two main reasons: (i) the domestic political cost of deflating the economy to maintain convertibility may be high or, amounting to the same thing, perceived to be high by policy makers; (ii) surplus countries have little incentive to inflate symmetrically (inducing upward price pressures) because their position within the gold standard club is not threatened: if anything, they may have an incentive to increase their gold reserves for future rainy days or just out of die-hard mercantilist prejudices. A cooperative and often superior alternative is for surplus countries to lend gold to deficit countries in order for the latter to restore external equilibrium over a longer time span, smoothing out the political and economic domestic costs of adjustment. Here again, however, the issue of incentives arises: in a nationalist and often confrontational world such as that of the nineteenth century, why should a country help out a neighbour rather than try to take advantage of its difficulties?

Economic historians are still divided over the issue of actual international monetary cooperation and about its role, if any, in supplying the international public good of adequate liquidity in a context of fixed exchange rates.

Marc Flandreau[33] lucidly summarised the options available to two central banks both threatened by a gold drain, that are facing a trade-off between exchange rate stability and output and are each affected by the decisions of its counterpart. They may pursue their targets independently, not relying on foreign cooperation, by raising interest rates competitively to attract gold. In this case both end up with identical gold reserves and low output, an outcome that is described in the game theory literature as competitive or Nash equilibrium. Alternatively, the central banks may cooperate by mutually adjusting their policies towards Pareto improvements that will bring them to a cooperative equilibrium, although this tends to be fragile because it may be to the advantage of each central bank to deviate from the agreed policy, thus reverting to the competitive equilibrium. A third possibility is that one central bank realises that lowering its discount rate (and thus letting gold flow out) will lead its counterpart to respond in kind. The fall in the foreign discount rate may compensate the benevolent central bank for the initial loss of gold. The trouble with this policy is that the bank initiating the move (the so-called Stackelberg leader) gains less than the one that follows, because the follower wins on all counts: it increases its reserves and reduces its interest rate. This may lead each central bank to try inducing the other to be the leader, again bringing the players back to the competitive equilibrium.

Which of these three situations prevailed during the pre-1914 gold standard? On the basis of documentary evidence from the Bank of England, the Bank of France, and the Rothschild Bank, Flandreau is drawn to the conclusion that cooperation was exceptional, never reciprocal, and that it always failed to be institutionalised. He finds that the attitude of central banks towards each other oscillated between hatred, neglect, and indifference. These conclusions (as Flandreau himself argues) should be qualified: not only is it hard to generalise on the basis of case studies, but he finds evidence that some cooperation did actually take place – which, however, he attributes to the self-interest of central banks, who seem to have helped each other only when this provided an immediate benefit to them, instead of mutually adjusting towards a long-run cooperative equilibrium. Moreover, the period is characterised, according to Flandreau, by cycles of more or less cooperative behaviour that were dictated by the overall provision and relative allocation of liquidity, by changing legal constraints on policy instruments, and by the balance of "monetary power" (i.e., the amount of gold held by individual countries), which somehow dictated central banks' behaviour with respect to their reserves and in turn gave rise to varying degrees of cooperation with their counterparts in other countries.

Flandreau's rather sceptical view of pre-1914 international monetary cooperation is not shared by other scholars. Eichengreen argues that "the credibility of the prewar gold standard rested on international cooperation": crises "were contained through overt, conscious cooperation between central banks and governments", which "discounted bills on behalf of the weak-currency country or lent gold to its central bank".[34] As the result of this cooperation, the pool of gold on which a country whose currency was under attack could draw far exceeded its own reserves, a fact that increased the credibility of the gold standard and therefore lowered the probability of speculative attacks and the frequency of actual mutual support. The latter, however, did not fail to materialise at times of major crises threatening the very existence of the system.

A textbook case of central bank cooperation is the Baring crisis of 1890, when a generous guarantee to the insolvent Baring Brothers organised by the Bank of England, compounded by rumours about difficulties in the City, drained reserves to such a low level that it seemed the Old Lady of Threadneedle Street would have to choose between the stability of the domestic banking system and the suspension of gold standard convertibility. To avoid forcing a choice that, however made, would have dealt a blow to the international monetary system, the central banks of France and Russia agreed to lend the Bank of England enough gold to prevent the occurrence of a run on gold.[35] In late 1906 and again in early 1907, an unusual amount of U.S. borrowing caused an outflow of gold from the United Kingdom that would have entailed an extremely large increase in interest rates in the absence of cooperation, which took the form of substantial purchases of sterling-denominated bills by the Bank of France, leading to a drain of gold from Paris, which did not raise its discount rate. Later in 1907 the U.S. stock market and banking crisis again drew gold from the United Kingdom, forcing its central bank to raise interest rates steeply. The measure, however, would not have been sufficient to defuse a threatening sterling crisis without international cooperation. In almost textbook fashion, "both the Bank of France and the Reichsbank allowed their reserves to decline and transferred gold to England to finance England's transfer of gold to the United States".[36]

The concern with national prestige, stronger at the time than it is now, somehow downplayed the request and provision of financial aid, as if not befitting great powers. Thus, there are hints that receiving loans may have been seen as humiliating, while granting support needed to be justified in the eyes of domestic public opinion by the pursuit of national interest. This may perhaps have obscured the cooperative language, even though actual cooperative behaviour did not fail to materialise at times of major crises.

If there is scarcely any doubt that cooperation took place at times of crises that threatened the very existence of the system, then two related questions arise: Was cooperation also necessary for the day-to-day operation of the system? What made cooperation possible? The answer to both questions is to be found in the conditions under which the classical gold standard operated. By credibly committing to gold and acting accordingly, countries made their most important contribution to the continuation of the system, which normally required only relatively minor adjustments in interest rates to work smoothly. This result was assured, in normal times, by the exceptional mobility of goods and factors of production and by a degree of labour market flexibility that characterised the forty-odd years before the outbreak of the First World War. At the same time, informal cooperation was maintained because its costs were perceived to be small in relation to the perceived benefits accruing to the national economy by the very fact of adhering to the gold standard (low international transaction costs, availability of low-cost financial capital, maintaining the long-term value of emigrant remittances, and the like). The output and employment costs of an increase in interest rates were possibly lower than they would be in the more rigid postwar commodity and labour markets but, most importantly, "there was scant awareness that defence of the gold standard and unemployment may be at odds".[37]

1.5   Central Bank Cooperation, 1914–1922

In the summer of 1914, amidst the uncertainty and confusion in the last hectic days before the actual beginning of military operations,[38] stock exchanges were closed and debt moratoriums declared (these included bank deposits, to pre-empt a run on the banks). Central banks all over Europe suspended gold payments, thus putting an end to the classical gold standard.[39]

Economic and monetary cooperation was a necessary corollary to military alliance. Needless to say, wartime cooperation was never idyllic: not only did national interests prevail at all times, but also prewar petty rivalries, jealousies, and idiosyncrasies were tenacious. Nevertheless, the very nature of the war – which, as it turned out, was won and lost more on the economic than on the military front – made financial cooperation unavoidable. Lending by the United Kingdom to France, Belgium, Italy, and the smaller Allied nations soon became a condition for their purchase of foodstuffs and raw materials from the British Dominions and from neutral countries, a flow of goods that German U-boats tried to stem and that eventually proved to be one of the key determinants of victory. After 1917 the United States stepped in to sustain inter-Allied financial aid, as the United Kingdom's available resources were almost exhausted. Wartime financial cooperation was most evident in the successive negotiation of sterling and dollar loans. But a degree of coordination of operations in the foreign exchange markets also took place in the attempts at the mutual pegging of currencies. Reasons of wartime propaganda were largely behind this type of cooperation. Since public opinion – friendly, enemy, and neutral – took the rate of exchange as a good predictor of military success and failure, moderating the exchange rate devaluation was seen as part of the common military effort.[40]

During the war central banks established, probably for the first time, formal bilateral links and agreements. Negotiations among Treasuries led to closer contacts between central banks. In 1916 a direct agreement between the Bank of France and the Bank of England resulted in shipments of gold from Paris to London as a loan guarantee. The two governors, Cunliffe and Pallain, set up a direct telegraph line between their respective offices to provide swift, regular communication.[41] In 1916, President Strong of the New York Fed spent almost three months in Europe, mostly between London and Paris, in order to establish formal agreements between the two central banks and the Federal Reserve Bank of New York for maintaining preferential[42] accounts with each, for the purchasing of bills, and for the earmarking of gold.[43] In 1917, the Bank of Italy opened an office in New York and entered into an agreement with the Federal Reserve Bank of New York for mutual representation.[44] It was during Benjamin Strong's wartime visits to London that he established the close personal relationship with Montagu Norman, then a member of the Court of the Bank of England, that was to provide intellectual leadership with regard to the development of central banking and lead to some practical cooperative results in currency stabilisation.[45]

Allied financial solidarity collapsed even before the ink on the armistice documents was allowed to dry. A major contradiction characterised the following five years as far as international monetary cooperation is concerned. The exhausted enemies transferred to the diplomatic and political sphere a good deal of the incomprehension and hate that had started the war in the first place, while conflicts of interest amongst allies erupted, no longer kept in check by the paramount interest of obtaining victory. At the same time, cooperation was explicitly discussed and even sought – albeit quite unsuccessfully – in the financial and monetary field. The history of central bank cooperation over this period of time is therefore more about talking than achieving.

Yet arguably, as we shall see throughout this book, the development of cooperative ideas among like-minded central bankers was not without long-term effects. It was in the immediate postwar period that Norman's ideas about the role of central banks in restoring a viable monetary system received wide attention and that earlier proposals about the establishment of an international bank found their way into official documents.

The floating exchange rate regime that replaced the wartime currency pegging was an unavoidable adjustment tool, given the enormous cross-country differences in wartime inflation rates. It also allowed monetary policy to try to accommodate the postwar reallocation of capital and labour and permitted the relaxation of wartime price and foreign exchange controls. At the same time it contributed to domestic inflation and so led to hyperinflation in Germany, Austria, and Hungary. Whatever the relative weight of the advantages and disadvantages of floating rates, the majority of European public opinion regarded them as an unmitigated disaster. An early return to gold was seen by many as a panacea for many ills, social and economic. Its advocates portrayed it as a symbol of the normal and happy prewar times that needed to be brought back as soon as possible.

In 1919 the U.K. Cunliffe Committee advocated the immediate return to gold convertibility, emphasising the role of the discount rate (known as the Bank rate) as a sufficient tool in promoting price adjustment, even at the cost of high unemployment.[46] In early 1919, Cokayne, the governor of the Bank of England, told its board of directors that he expected to raise internal interest rates so as to put the sterling exchange rate at about gold parity before the signing of the peace treaty.[47] "The men of 1919", Sayers noted, "believed that the best monetary system was that of 1913: a world gold standard centred on London, with the Bank of England controlling the system by manipulation of [the] Bank rate".[48]

A return to gold was also favoured by politicians, bureaucrats, and bankers in France, Belgium, and Italy, as well as in the countries that had remained neutral during the war. But even if dissent on the gold standard was rare, "each country sought a gold standard system that would meet the needs of its own economy and a route back to gold that would accommodate the specific problems posed by its own experience of inflation and currency depreciation".[49] Thus, countries whose currencies had depreciated far more than the pound envisaged a long march towards convertibility. Realising that sharp and prolonged deflation was unfeasible they leaned – in spite of lip service paid to the desirability of prewar parities – towards the position of Keynes, Hawtrey, Cassell, and others who recommended fixing the new gold parities at levels consistent with the current purchasing power of each national currency. National conditions and interests were so different that little cooperation was possible in the immediate postwar period to recreate a stable international monetary system; as Eichengreen observed, "so long as governments were at loggerheads, it was unlikely that national central banks could successfully collaborate".[50]

Even so, central bankers appreciated the necessity for international cooperation possibly more than others and, together with private bankers, they played an important part in the postwar negotiations and international conferences.[51]

Cooperative ideas developed from the close and friendly relations established between Strong and Norman during the war. When the latter became governor of the Bank of England in 1920, one of his priorities was to reassert the authority of the central banks and their independence from political interference after wartime subordination, an aim that he tried to achieve throughout the 1920s. One of the goals he later pursued in establishing the BIS would precisely be the creation of a safe haven where he and his peers could meet and do business away from political pressure.

Early in 1921, Norman issued a kind of central bank manifesto[52] outlining the main principles of central banking, which he circulated among a number of people[53] and wanted to propose for adoption by a conference of central bankers.[54] Norman stressed independence from national governments,[55] separation from (avoidance of competition with) commercial banks, banking supervision,[56] and cooperation.[57] The latter would consist of "confidential interchange of information and opinion", the conduct of foreign banking operations through the central bank of the country concerned, the mutual extension, "without undue regard to profit", of such facilities as "the custody of gold, monies and securities and the discount of approved bills of exchange". It is not by chance that an echo of Norman's specifications of cooperative behaviour will be found, though much expanded and more finely detailed, in the 1935 BIS guidelines mentioned in Section 1.1.

A first postwar economic conference, organised by the Council of the newly created League of Nations, took place in Brussels in 1920. It mainly discussed loans for the reconstruction of the European economies, but it also called for central bank independence.

A second conference, which eventually took place in Genoa in 1922, was not easy to convene. The U.K. prime minister Lloyd George, in the hope of re-establishing the United Kingdom at the centre of the world economy,[58] was keen on inviting Germany and Russia (now a union of Socialist republics). Germany was ready to seize the opportunity to make its comeback on the international scene but Poincaré, president of the French Republic, categorically refused to discuss the most contentious of all issues: German reparations. The opening to Soviet Russia also turned out to be unsuccessful. The United States refused to participate since the conference did not "meet American specifications"[59] about reparations and debt. Moreover, Benjamin Strong opposed the conference knowing that the British intended to discuss the gold exchange standard,[60] which he disliked, fearing it would tie the Fed's hands in pursuing monetary policy.[61] With such unpromising omens, the conference turned out to be a practical failure, one of many to follow. It did, however, have a lasting intellectual impact. "It was in Genoa", Rueff noted disapprovingly, "that the outline of the new policy took shape".[62]

A resolution of the Genoa Conference Financial Commission declared the re-establishment of a stable value of money to be essential for the economic reconstruction of Europe, but it left each country free to decide the timing of monetary stabilisation and the new exchange rates. At the conference, central banking was the subject of profound debates by economic experts, academics, and central and private bankers. Its resolutions mark the first uncompromising international recognition of the desirability of formal cooperation among central banks. In July 1929, during the negotiations on the establishment of the BIS, the British central banker Charles Addis said that the plan under discussion would "fulfill the dream of Genoa by the gradual development of the BIS into a cooperative society of Central Banks".[63] In fact, the ideas about an "international bank" that were openly debated in Genoa had been floating around since the 1880s.

1.6   The "International Bank": An Old Cooperative Idea

The idea of an international bank, discussed at the Genoa Conference, was not a new one. In fact, the principles upon which the BIS was to be based in 1930, as a body for central bank cooperation, evolved from a line of thinking that dates back to at least the 1880s.[64]

Luigi Luzzatti, a Venetian and a prominent Italian political figure, is largely credited with developing in 1907 the first ideas about an international body for central bank cooperation.[65] In fact, the issue had been on the agenda since the International Monetary Conference of 1881,[66] and in 1892 Julius Wolff, a professor at the University of Breslau, submitted at the Brussels International Monetary Conference a project for the creation of an international currency, to be used for emergency lending to central banks, backed by gold reserves contributed by the central banks themselves and to be issued by a joint institution based in a neutral country. Similar suggestions had been made in 1893 by G. François, who also wanted the creation of a gold clearing institution, and Raphaël-Georges Lévy, who suggested the establishment of an international central bank located in Berne.[67] But it was Luzzatti who gave these ideas both a more precise shape and wide publicity.[68]

Luzzatti was neither a utopian internationalist nor an abstract theorist: he drew his ideas from the observation of the actual – rather than textbook – working of the gold standard before the Great War. In a 1907 article in the Viennese newspaper *Neue Freie Presse*,[69] Luzzatti argued that the U.S. stock exchange slump of that year had been "complicated" by a liquidity crisis (he called it a "monetary famine") from which the main central banks had tried to protect their respective markets, scrambling for gold through competitive interest rate increases and other means. A "monetary war" of this kind was, according to Luzzatti, both detrimental and unnecessary: peace could be achieved through "cordial cooperation" by all markets in supplying gold to illiquid central banks. Cooperation, Luzzatti observed, was not impossible; after all, central banks previously had repeatedly come to each other's rescue (he cited the Bank of France lending to its U.K. counterpart and the central bank of Austria-Hungary providing gold to the Reichsbank). Rather than being occasional and dictated by extreme emergencies, Luzzatti argued, lending amongst monetary authorities should become the norm. An international commission endowed with "fiduciary powers" should coordinate action for the achievement of "international monetary peace". The initiative should be taken by such relatively marginal countries as Austria-Hungary and Italy, without large interests at stake, in order to win over the governments and the Bank of France, which Luzzatti saw as "the centre of the world's monetary power".

Luzzatti's article attracted considerable attention. Comments, both private and public,[70] came from various quarters and in various languages, focusing more on the practical difficulty of implementing the proposal than on its usefulness. The theoretical issue was, nevertheless, raised by Professor Lexis of the University of Göttingen,[71] who did not see anything warlike or even pathological in central banks responding to gold outflows by raising domestic rates. Luzzatti answered[72] that, in trying to retain "fleeing gold", central banks do not "behave tenderly" towards their customers and the public, "who receive right in their chests the blows of the international struggle for gold". Luzzatti was ready to acknowledge that central banks do not lend to each other out of fraternal feelings ("Gold does not have guts") but only out of their long-term self-interest. Politics, he argued, may get in the way of a clear vision of economic self-interest – hence the need for an international body, to be set up in normal circumstances, in order to provide for emergencies in a technical, apolitical way. International postal and telegraph unions, Luzzatti said, were not set up out of brotherly feelings but as a response to common interests. "There is no absolute remedy for financial crises", he wrote, "that are the consequence of human weakness, greed and imperfect forecasting.... What I simply ask for are agreements among experts capable of eliminating from inevitable crises those elements that are due to poor organisation of the banks of issue and treasuries or to the lack of agreements for mutual self-interested gold lending". In 1908, Luzzatti gave a lecture at the Institut de France suggesting the creation of an international clearing house.[73]

Amongst the most relevant reactions to Luzzatti's ideas were those of Cortelyou, U.S. Treasury secretary, who announced his intention of convening a European conference of central banks to better specify Luzzatti's proposal and create an "international gold certificate"; and of Wolff, who in the same vein proposed the issue of an international banknote.[74]

The idea of an international "settlements" organisation was discussed at a conference of central banks from small European countries held in Brussels in 1912, which explicitly referred to Luzzatti in a resolution for the establishment of a *Mitteleuropäischer Wirtschafts-Verein*.[75] Shortly afterwards Wolff published one of the more comprehensive studies on the needs of an international clearing house.[76]

Throughout the war, Luzzatti continued to preach his "monetary peace", participating in conferences of the Entente at Villa d'Este (Italy) in 1915 and in Paris in 1916.[77] During the war, Europeans also took great interest in the newly established Federal Reserve System of the United States, which many saw as an example of how an "international bank" might operate.

Soon after the war, Vissering, president of the Netherlands Bank, developed an original plan for the creation of an international currency that did not require recourse to lending or a common gold pool, partly foreshadowing the European Payments Union after the Second World War.[78]

Several of the ideas developed before the Great War resurfaced at the 1920 Brussels Economic Conference. The Belgian prime minister Léon Delacroix proposed the creation of an international monetary institution

that would issue its own banknotes.[79] Frank Vanderlip, former president
of the National City Bank, suggested reorganising the European central
banks following the model of the Federal Reserve System in the United
States.[80] The official U.S. policy stance, however, was against the creation
of a powerful international financial organisation. The conference, nevertheless, recommended that the League of Nations take the necessary steps
for the establishment of some kind of international clearing house.

   And so we return to the Genoa Economic Conference of 1922. This conference was mainly concerned with the economic and financial reconstruction of a war-torn Europe, but it also addressed, as we have seen, central
bank issues. It concluded that financial stabilisation would be facilitated
by central bank independence from "the influence of the political order".[81]
Most importantly in this context, the Financial Commission also passed a
resolution – apparently inspired by Hawtrey, Keynes, and Horne[82] – recommending the creation of "an association or permanent understanding for
cooperation amongst central banks, not necessarily limited to Europe, to coordinate credit policies, without detriment to the freedom of each individual
central bank".[83] In practical terms, the commission called for a conference
of central bankers and also suggested its agenda. The Bank of England
was entrusted with the task of organising this conference, where the idea
of continuous cooperation could be developed. Though this gave Norman
a mandate for convening the meeting of central bankers that he had wanted
in order to discuss his own "manifesto" of 1921, and though Strong was
not opposed to such a meeting, the conference was postponed indefinitely.
Norman apparently had a few substantive points of disagreement with his
colleagues and did not want to open the conference without previous agreement on the agenda and outcome.[84] Shortly after the Genoa Conference
closed, Luzzatti published a book summing up his ideas about international
monetary cooperation and the attendant debate.[85]

TWO

Gestation and Birth

2.1 The Background

On 11 November 1918, the Entente accepted Germany's unconditional surrender. Eight months later,[1] the peace treaty was symbolically signed in the Galerie des Glaces of the Versailles Palace, the very site where on 18 January 1871 the German Empire had been proclaimed. Then – defeated, humiliated, and stripped of Alsace-Lorraine – France had been saddled with 5 billion gold francs in reparations that were punctually paid within the next three years. Forty-eight years later, it was France's turn to recover lost territories and impose reparations. Over four long years, widows, orphans, wounded, and soldiers – trapped for months in the trenches – had all been promised that in the end "les Boches", as the Germans were derisively called, would pay; it was now imperative for the French government to honour its word. Public opinion in Belgium, whose neutrality had been violated in 1914, was equally keen on being repaid for suffering under occupation. Italy's grievances were mostly directed towards Austria-Hungary, but Italy was nevertheless determined to get its fair share of reparations, as was (if less confidently) the United Kingdom.

The blow stricken to Europe by the war was compounded by an ill-designed and ill-executed postwar settlement, one of the main causes for most of the ensuing international tension, economic instability, and depression as well as, eventually, another catastrophic war. The intricate web of postwar events does not need to be summarised here except for the issues

Background research for this chapter by Michelangelo Van Meerten is gratefully acknowledged.

most pertinent to the creation of the BIS: reparations and international monetary cooperation.

Besides security concerns,[2] politics and economics were inextricably intertwined with the other main postwar issues: war debts, reparations, and restoration of the international monetary system. The three questions were all related to each other: the Continental countries linked the repayment of war debts vis-à-vis the United Kingdom and the United States to Germany's reparation payments; the United States, whose Congress did not ratify the Versailles peace treaty, refused even to consider any link between debt and reparations,[3] yet made American investment in European countries conditional upon their settling inter-Allied war debts. At the same time, the free flow of U.S. investment to Europe was a necessary condition for the re-establishment of a functioning international monetary system. Thus, the three problems of debts, reparations, and international payments had to be solved simultaneously, a goal that only a high degree of cooperation could achieve. We have seen in the previous chapter that both central bankers and private financiers played an important part in postwar negotiations and international conferences,[4] but "as long as governments were at loggerheads, it was unlikely that [they] could successfully collaborate",[5] and the beginning of the 1920s was dominated by politics and by political rather than economic considerations.[6]

Politically, reparations were the most sensitive of the postwar economic issues,[7] so much so that it could be said that "the history of the reparation problem follows closely the course of the more general history of the postwar Europe"[8] and that they "set the agenda for the next twenty years".[9] Reparations would eventually also be the proximate cause for the creation of the BIS, so a brief survey of their intricate history is called for.

An important difference between the provisions of the Versailles treaty and previous peace settlements was that no sum was fixed for reparations in the treaty itself. A reparation commission was charged with setting the amount to be paid by Germany and deciding on the technical means for the transfer of payments to the Allies.[10] The Reparation Commission, chaired by Poincaré, did not come into existence until January 1920 and left experts to work for over six months. It was not until the following July that the German Chancellor and his Minister for Foreign Affairs first met an Allied ministerial delegation on equal terms at a conference in Spa. In a tense climate and under the threat of sanctions, the German delegation signed a protocol for the delivery of 2 million tonnes of coal monthly. The Spa Conference also set the percentages of the German reparations accruing to each

Allied power: France should receive 52%, the United Kingdom 22%, Italy 10%, and Belgium 8%, with smaller amounts going to the other Allies.[11]

On the more substantive issue of fixing the total amount of reparations, Spa was a failure. While a new conference convened in London was still sitting, on 8 March 1921, Allied troops led by Marshal Foch – the French wartime military leader – occupied Düsseldorf, Duisburg, and Ruhrort on the east of the Rhine on the pretext of Germany's failure to complete the preliminary reparation payment and carry out all disarmament provisions. The conference broke up and Simons, the German Foreign Minister, returned to Berlin to be welcomed as a hero by a huge crowd.[12] He made a public offer of payment of 20 billion gold marks, which the Allies rejected. In the meanwhile the exchange rate of the mark was plunging downwards and the country was heading towards hyperinflation.[13]

At the end of April 1921, the Reparation Commission finally set the amount of damage suffered by the Allies for which reparations were payable at 132 billion gold marks. A schedule of payments, divided into three classes of bonds (the so-called London schedule) was sent to Berlin and approved by the Reichstag by a tiny majority. At the end of 1921, however, the German government announced that it would be unable to meet its obligations for the following year and asked for a moratorium, which the Commission partly granted.

In August 1922, the U.K. government sent the Allied governments the so-called Balfour Note suggesting that the United Kingdom might renounce its share of reparations in return for a general settlement of both reparations and inter-Allied debts. The note did not win the approval of the Continental powers but set the basis for future U.K. policy: London would ask of Germany no more (and no less) than was necessary to pay its creditor (the U.S. Treasury). In France, by contrast, public opinion was outraged by the 1922 partial moratorium. Nonetheless, the German government, supported by a body of independent experts,[14] maintained that the country's economic situation did not leave room for reparation payments and so a moratorium was necessary. At the same time, the new Cuno government in Berlin proposed to issue a joint German–U.K.–French–Italian solemn declaration outlawing war; however, this was dismissed by the French as just a ruse to evade Germany's financial obligations.

In December 1922 Germany failed by a small margin to fulfil its commitment to reparations in kind (mostly coal). When the Commission met to discuss the situation, the French and U.K. positions appeared to be irreconcilable. The U.K. representatives withdrew from the conference and the French declared they had recovered full liberty of action for the execution of the peace treaty. On 11 January 1923, French and Belgian troops occupied the Ruhr basin in an attempt to secure the direct delivery of coal.

The nine months following this occupation of the Ruhr were the most dramatic period in the history of the reparations tragedy. They were also, as it happens, the beginning of the turning point on the way to a realistic approach leading to a more satisfactory, if still provisional, settlement.

The occupation was a political and economic disaster. On the political front it strained Franco-British relations to an extraordinary degree while playing into the hands of German hardliners, who also drew strength from unnecessary French mistakes.[15] The economic outcome of the occupation was the opposite of its declared aim: its cost to the French Treasury exceeded the revenue from coal and iron deliveries. Berlin reacted to the occupation by proclaiming passive resistance. Work ceased throughout the Ruhr and all reparation payments were suspended. Price inflation spiralled out of control. Social unrest increased. For over seven months, Cuno did not yield an inch in his policy of passive resistance. Poincaré, for his part, explicitly quoted the precedent established by Germany in 1871 for requesting reparation payment before his troops would evacuate the Ruhr. Belgium declared it would accept a reduction of the German debt only against a parallel reduction of inter-Allied debt, a link that the United States considered unacceptable.

The turning point in the postwar history of Europe began in September 1923 when a new German government, headed by Stresemann, took the unpopular step of declaring the end of passive resistance. An agreement was reached for coal to be mined again and transferred to France and Belgium. But the German economy could not resume reparation payments in significant amounts unless it could first import raw materials and foodstuffs, bring hyperinflation under control, and set its public finances in order, thereby regaining the confidence of international financial markets. In October, the United States was finally persuaded to cooperate with the U.K., French, Belgian, and Italian governments in trying to re-establish the conditions for peace and economic growth in Europe. Two ad hoc committees were created. The U.S. government did not directly appoint committee members but allowed American citizens to cooperate, formally in just a private capacity, inaugurating a procedure that would also be followed in the years to come with regard to the BIS. The most relevant of the two committees, charged with seeking methods of balancing the German budget and stabilising the exchange rate, was chaired by the retired American general Charles Dawes, founder and president of the Central Trust Company of Illinois.[16]

Though the heads of the main central banks were not members of the committees, they cooperated closely with them.[17] Thomas Lamont, partner at J.P. Morgan & Co., played an important part in the proceedings, as it soon appeared that the success of the German stabilisation would depend on the flotation of a substantial loan of 800 million gold marks on the international market. The Committee on Budget and Exchange Rate Issues had its first meeting on 14 January 1924 and on 9 April submitted a plan that, from the name of its chairman, became known as the Dawes Plan. This plan was discussed at a governmental conference convened in London on 16 July, and it was approved on 30 August.

Political changes in France played a crucial role in paving the way to reaching an agreement on the Dawes Plan. The elections of May 1924 resulted in a victory of the left. Poincaré was succeeded by Herriot, at the head of a radical government. According to Carr, "the date of this occurrence – May 11th, 1924 – may be taken as marking the end of the first postwar period of trying to establish peace by force. Some Frenchmen regretted afterwards that Poincaré's policy of enforcing the treaty at all costs was ever abandoned. But in 1924 it was recognised by general consent to have failed".[18]

The most important outcome of the Dawes Plan[19] was the rescheduling of German reparations, taking into account the country's capacity to pay. Reparations were to be paid in German currency, in the meanwhile anchored to gold, to an agent general for reparation payments seated in Berlin.[20] It was then up to the Agent General to manage the transfers into foreign currency.[21] French and Belgian troops were to evacuate the Ruhr area. The plan also took away the option for France to decide unilaterally on sanctions against Germany, but it left Germany under close supervision.[22] The Dawes Plan seemed to be an important step in the depoliticisation of the reparations issue. It was complemented by an international loan of 800 million gold marks (the equivalent of $190.4 million), maturing in 25 years and carrying an annual interest of 7%. The loan served two purposes: providing Germany a currency reserve and helping with the payment of the first annuity. The success of this loan marked the return of financial confidence. Issued in October, the Dawes Loan was soon oversubscribed: about half its total amount went to the United States, more than a quarter to the United Kingdom, and the rest to France, Belgium, Italy, the Netherlands, Switzerland, and Sweden.

The resolution of the reparations problem, in this new cooperative climate, also opened the way to solving another postwar problem – that of French security – with the Treaty of Locarno (October 1925), formalised in London soon afterwards. A few months later, in September 1926, Germany was allowed to join the League of Nations and to take a permanent seat on its Council.

The spirit of goodwill and optimism that emerged in 1924–25 favoured the resolution of other outstanding problems, in particular the settlement of inter-Allied debts and the reorganisation of the international monetary system under the gold exchange standard, described in Chapter 1. An agreement had already been concluded in December 1922 between the United Kingdom and the United States for the settlement of the war debt in 62 annual instalments. Then, following the Dawes Plan, agreements were concluded between the United States and the United Kingdom and amongst France, Italy, Romania, Yugoslavia, Greece, and Portugal for the repayment of wartime debts over a long stretch of time. The agreements entailed substantial reductions of the amounts originally due. They also lifted any remaining objection from the U.S. government for American capital to be invested overseas.

In 1925, the pound sterling was again made convertible into gold at the prewar rate of exchange. Italy, France, and Belgium also returned to gold over the next couple of years, albeit at different rates of exchange. Mussolini brought the exchange rate back to the level of 1922, the time of his "march on Rome" and seizure of power.[23] Poincaré was tempted by a "strong" franc but was stopped by Moreau, governor of the Bank of France, who wisely decided on an exchange rate close to the purchasing parity of the currency. Belgium, a small open economy, seized the opportunity of the return to gold for a competitive devaluation of its currency and fixed a new parity at about half that of Italy.[24]

Central bank cooperation was enhanced by currency stabilisations, particularly by the so-called stabilisation loans – organised and subscribed by a pool of central banks under the energetic leadership of Norman and Strong – that were made in order to strengthen the credibility of the conversion pledge. These official loans were also seen by the market as good-housekeeping seals of approval, opening the door to private capital flows to the countries involved in the currency stabilisation process.

The Bank of England and the Bank of France[25] shared information on a fairly regular basis,[26] but understanding between the two was made difficult by the postwar conflict in their policies towards Germany. The two central banks competed for influence in Central and Eastern Europe, where the French challenged the leadership of the Bank of England by taking an active stance in the stabilisation of Poland, Romania, and Yugoslavia. Both Norman and Moreau attached considerable importance to Central and Eastern Europe for the overall monetary and political stability of Europe,[27] but

Moreau was suspicious that the British were siding with the Germans and believed that, for security reasons, the area could not be left open to U.K. financial imperialism.[28] However, the main reason that central bank cooperation between Paris and London was not as smooth as circumstances in the 1920s would have required resulted from their diverging international monetary policy goals. "While the United Kingdom was seeking ways of economising on the use of gold, France was trying to acquire the metal as an instrument of power and to re-establish it as the sole monetary base."[29] In the second half of the 1920s, the tension between the Bank of England and the Bank of France stemmed mostly from the latter's policy of converting its sterling balances into gold.

Cooperation between the Bank of England and the Federal Reserve Bank of New York was "evident mainly at the time of changes in official discount rates, which were made only after consideration of the effects on the other country".[30] Collaboration between the two central banks was driven by their responsibility as issuers of reserve currencies, but it also owed a lot to cultural factors and to the excellent personal relations established (since the war) between Norman and Strong. In June 1927, for instance, in order to ease the pressure on the Bank of England, the head of the Federal Reserve Bank of New York bought gold against pounds from the Bank of France. The Federal Reserve policy during the mild recession of the summer of 1927 was also motivated by considerations about international cooperation.[31]

The Reichsbank was keen on regaining full acceptance in international circles, but it was more interested in cooperation on the provision of long-term capital, export credits, and (more generally) Germany's commercial penetration overseas than in issues directly related to central bank responsibilities. Excellent relations, based on mutual understanding and confidence, existed between Schacht, Norman, and Strong.[32]

In 1925, Norman first floated the idea of a central banks' club, which was eventually realised with the creation of the BIS. "I rather hope", he wrote in September of that year, "that next summer we may be able to inaugurate a private and eclectic Central Banks' 'Club', small at first, large in the future".[33] Strong soberly agreed that "a quiet meeting of some of the heads of the central banks" might be useful.[34]

Although the creation of the club was postponed by five years until the governors' meetings began to take place regularly in Basel, a first informal multilateral conference of the main central bankers was held at a friendly private home on Long Island (New York) on 1–6 July 1927. Strong convened the meeting out of concerns about the stability of sterling in a context of growing tensions between the Bank of France and the Bank of England.

The participants were Schacht, Norman, and Charles Rist, deputy governor of the Bank of France, as well as Strong himself. The Bank of Italy had hoped for an invitation, which did not arrive.[35] The conference addressed the issues of American and European interest rates, falling international commodity prices, and France's large short-term claims together with their impact on the pound and, more generally, on the stability of the system. The principal outcome of these discussions was Strong's renewed effort in support of sterling.[36]

The Long Island meeting was as high a degree of central bank cooperation as international politics allowed in the 1920s. A new meeting of central bankers in the Spanish town of Algeciras, not far from Gibraltar, was initially foreseen,[37] but Strong's deteriorating health prevented him from going. Strong's death in October 1928 is seen by some historians as a blow to central bank cooperation, but changes in the international economic climate mattered more than personalities. The Long Island achievement was short-lived. Both Strong and Norman had always known that "international cooperation could not run counter to domestic policy considerations".[38] From the beginning of their intense personal and institutional relations, they both clearly understood that national interests set a limit on cooperation. From late 1927 onwards it became ever more apparent that national interests diverged on both sides of the Atlantic and within Europe.

As Germany's economic growth picked up, the inflow of foreign (mostly American) short-term capital[39] appeared to be ever more vital for the country's capacity to simultaneously meet its international obligations and increase domestic private and public investment.[40] The situation was made more difficult by a provision of the Dawes Plan that linked the amount of reparations to a so-called prosperity index, so that economic growth resulted in increasing reparation payments. The flow of private American capital to Germany depended on an adequate interest rate differential between New York and Berlin, a differential that Strong had struggled to maintain even in the face of mounting domestic criticism. But by early 1928, low American rates had probably already ceased to be appropriate as far as domestic policy considerations were concerned. The mild 1927 recession reached its trough in November. The stock exchange boomed. In the first part of 1928, credit expansion continued to exceed the growth of output, and American gold flowed to France. In August 1928, the Board of Governors approved interest rate increases by the main Federal Reserve Banks.[41] The move reinforced a contraction in international lending that had started earlier the same year. This contraction "was accompanied by a phenomenon far more serious in its implications for the world stability – a diversion of lending from debtor countries. The superior attractions of the New York market from a speculative point of view diverted a portion of the reduced long-term capital exports of other countries to New York",[42] shattering the lending foundations of the international monetary system as it had existed since 1924.

A coordinated adjustment of exchange rates and/or monetary policies together with a downward revision of the reparation burden might have saved the international monetary system from the collapse it suffered three years later and might have cushioned the Depression. But the window of opportunity for cooperation that was opened in 1924 was rapidly closing: as Norman and Strong had anticipated, cooperation could not run counter to domestic policy considerations.

The last opportunity for cooperation rested on the converging interests in revising the Dawes Plan. This opportunity was seized with the so-called Young Plan and the creation of the BIS. The 1926 agreement between France and the United States for the settlement of war debts had to be ratified by the French Parliament before August 1929.[43] Failure to do so would compel France to pay the whole debt principal. The French were therefore interested in a settlement of reparations entailing a so-called commercialisation, whereby the German debt (or part of it) would be issued in the form of long-term bonds to be subscribed by international private banks and financial houses. The scheme seemed attractive not only because it would make fresh cash available to creditors but also because it seemed to promise to take much of the political heat off the reparations issue by turning it into a normal financial transaction. American financial firms were obviously interested, while depoliticisation looked appealing to Washington.[44] The Germans were also keen to reopen negotiations with a view both to alleviating the burden of reparations and to speeding up an early evacuation of the Rhineland by allied troops.[45] In 1927, Parker Gilbert, the Agent General for Reparations, had already expressed worries about a possible transfer crisis.[46] Cautioned by the major central banks and private financial houses about the hazard to the smooth functioning of the Dawes scheme that could result from the drying up of capital flows to Germany,[47] the Agent General officially stressed the urgency of coming to a final settlement on reparations in his fourth Annual Report, published in June 1928.[48]

Direct negotiations were opened between the German and French ministers of foreign affairs, Stresemann and Briand. Though the bilateral contacts and the meetings between Stresemann, Briand, and the French President Poincaré did a lot to ease tensions between the two countries, it was soon evident that there were too many obstacles in the way of a bilateral agreement.[49]

Against a background of a temporary easing of tension in Franco-German relations, Briand launched the idea of a conference of experts to study the commercialisation of the German debt.[50] On 16 September 1928, a statement by the Belgian, U.K., French, German, Italian, and Japanese delegates meeting at the League of Nations in Geneva signalled the opening of negotiations on an early evacuation of the Rhineland and affirmed the "necessity for a complete and definite settlement of the Reparations problem and for the constitution for this purpose of a committee of financial experts, to be nominated by the six governments".[51]

Both London and Paris declared that the experts should be independent and not bound by instructions from their governments. Because of the role of private American financiers lending to Germany, it was seen as highly desirable that nationals of the United States would sit on the committee.[52] The experts were charged with the task of drawing up a proposal for a settlement of the reparations, including the fixing of a sustainable amount for Germany's war indemnity.[53] The French delegation insisted that the experts also draw up a plan to commercialise German reparation payments, which was supposed to provide an incentive to continue transfers, since a default would cut Germany off from the international capital market. The Germans insisted that the settlement should lead to lower annual payments, less direct control by a reparations agent, and the evacuation of the Rhineland.

2.2   The Young Committee

The Committee of Experts, convened to work out a final settlement of German reparations, met on 9 February 1929 on the premises of the Bank of France in Paris and subsequently, for a total of 29 meetings ending on 7 June, at the hotel George V.[54] Each of the seven participating countries was represented by two experts.[55] The American banker Owen D. Young, whose prestige as a skilled financial diplomat had been established at the Dawes[56] Plan negotiations five years earlier, was elected president, as no agreement could be reached on appointing a European. Another American, Bate, served as secretary.[57]

The first meetings discussed reparations, their commercialisation and total amount, and Germany's capacity to pay. Progress was slow; the French wanted first of all to fix the amount and duration of payments, while Schacht "maintained that Germany's obligations should be determined on the basis of its capacity to pay and should accord with the spirit of the peace treaty, which had not intended to place a burden on Germany for more than one generation".[58] A tense debate followed on Germany's economic condition, which – the creditors argued – had improved tremendously since 1924, so much so that the country's standard of living was by then higher than that of some of its creditors. Reichsbank President Schacht replied by emphasising Germany's balance of payments deficit and the crisis in agriculture.

Since no agreement was reached on Germany's economic conditions and its capacity to pay,[59] the experts wisely moved on to discuss the organisation of transfers. According to Young, "Not until some cooperative machinery such as the International Bank was set up could there be a fair and intelligent talk about [reparation] amounts".[60]

The creation of an institutional innovation such as the BIS, Simmons persuasively argues,[61] responded to the need to improve the chances of future enforcement of contracts and to overcome information asymmetries as a way of facilitating the design of mutually beneficial lending contracts. It therefore responded to the needs of those who envisaged a large "commercialisation" of the reparation payments.

Enforcing repayment obligations of sovereign states is notoriously problematic: lenders know that borrowers have an incentive to break contractual commitments once the financing is secured. Well-designed international institutions could ease the enforcement problem in many ways. In the case of the BIS, the fulfilment of the debtor's obligations would be linked, as we shall see, to incentives such as the reinvestment in Germany of part of the proceeds from payments of interest and principal. At the same time, the international institution would facilitate collective creditors' actions in case of default. Asymmetry of information is also a problem in international lending to sovereign states: not only are debtors better informed than lenders about economic conditions affecting debt payment but, what matters most, they are insiders to their own policy-making information. International institutions can provide credible quality information on the borrower's economy and, if trust and confidentiality are developed, to some extent also on ongoing and future policy making. This is what the BIS tried to achieve through its Monetary and Economic Department and its central bankers' "club". Moreover, to the extent that international monetary cooperation could result in stabilising the gold standard, conditions for fulfilment of the debtors' contractual obligations would also be enhanced.

The idea of the so-called commercialisation of reparations was to give prospective private lenders a role in the Young negotiations even more relevant than the one they had played at the time of the Dawes Plan, and this contributed to the awareness of the usefulness of an independent, reliable, apolitical international institution to ease problems of contract enforcement and information. Thus, negotiations in Paris about the rescheduling of German reparation payments had to take into account not only the interests of the debtor (Germany) and of the official creditors (Belgium, France, Italy, the United Kingdom, and – indirectly via inter-Allied debts – the United States) but those of private lenders (holders and market makers of German bonds) as well.[62]

The work of the Expert Committee was soon divided among three subcommittees: on transfer safeguards (chaired by Stamp), on deliveries in kind (chaired by Perkins), and on commercialisation of the German debt (chaired by Lord Revelstoke).[63] It was this last group that undertook most of the preparatory work for the creation of the "International Bank". Besides Revelstoke, its members were Moreau, Morgan (assisted by Lamont), Francqui, Kengo Mori, and Melchior.[64] This subcommittee soon agreed that there should be two types of German annuity: an unconditional and a conditional one. Payment of the latter could be suspended for a period of up to two years in case of internationally certified adverse economic conditions in Germany.[65] Both types of annuity would be paid to a trustee that would take the place of the Transfer Committee established under the Dawes Plan.[66] The idea of an international institution that would take the form of a bank developed from reflections about the functions, powers, guarantees, and organisation of the proposed trustee.

The first draft of a project for an international bank for the commercialisation of the German debt was presented to the subcommittee by Francqui (Belgium) on 23 February 1929.[67] He envisaged a private bank, the capital of which would be underwritten by financial institutions from the creditor countries in proportion to those countries' shares in reparations. Financial institutions from neutral countries could also join. The bank would issue bonds to be serviced by the German transfers.[68] The trustee would be a separate company, seated in the United States,[69] with capital underwritten by major international banks.[70] A further memorandum on the "International Bank", incorporating French suggestions,[71] stated that its scope would be the settlement of reparations and, more generally, the economic recovery of Europe, thus introducing the notion that the new international organisation should not be limited to reparations only. Its capital, backed by German bonds, would be subscribed not only by creditor countries but by Germany as well. The bank should settle all reparations and provide a venue for European financial leaders to discuss mutual problems. In order to accommodate the German point of view, it was also envisaged that the bank should provide international long-term credit for the development of trade and for the promotion of growth in underdeveloped territories. It should be managed following the principles of a commercial organisation.[72]

A project for an international clearing house was presented by Schacht a couple of days later.[73] Schacht, obviously less interested than the creditors in the trustee functions of the new institution, drew on the earlier ideas about an international clearing house, which he proposed should be created by the central banks of the seven countries involved in the negotiations. In a revised version of his draft, Schacht replaced "Clearing House" by "International Settlements Bank",[74] which should be given an important role in providing credit to central banks, governments, and other borrowers, all under government guarantees. The Reichsbank was to enjoy the same statutory position in the bank as the other central banks. Schacht chose not to present his plan in the plenary session. Instead, he discussed it with Young, unfolding his ideas of the bank as an international institution providing substantial credit to enhance the development of less-developed nations, thereby providing export outlets for Germany's industries and facilitating the country's debt payments.[75]

Young took up Schacht's proposals and, in a series of private meetings, conveyed the idea that the trustee should be an institution carrying considerable weight: a large international bank performing clearing functions between central banks, settling reparations and war debts (including debts to the United States), providing credit on a large scale, and even issuing a sort of international currency. The aspect of this project most appealing to private bankers was that the bank would treat reparation debts as commercial obligations, removing the issue of reparations from the political sphere.[76] Young's ambitious plan met with mixed reactions. The general idea of a banking institution was largely shared, and the French interpreted the scheme's reference to debts to the United States as an acknowledgment of the link between reparations and war debts. The notion of long-term credit, on the other hand, was immediately labelled as "inflationary and disturbing both to commercial banks and banks of issue".[77]

Young asked W. Randolph Burgess of the Federal Reserve Board to sail immediately for Paris and entrusted him, together with Walter Stewart and Shepard Morgan, with the task of working out a plan for the international bank based on the parts of the Belgian and German schemes that met with general approval. The three American experts held discussions with the various delegates, in particular with Quesnay and Schacht, and presented a draft plan to the committee on 7 March 1929.[78] This plan, a compromise between the Francqui and the Schacht proposals, contained the main elements of the future BIS.[79]

The resources of the bank would come from subscribed own capital, deposits from Germany, proceeds of the sale of notes or securities issued as counterparts to German securities denominated in nonconvertible Reichsmarks, central bank deposits, and the rediscounting of bills.[80] The functions of the bank would be threefold. As trustee, it would receive, manage, and distribute Germany's reparation annuities (both unconditional and conditional). As a banking institution, it would facilitate German transfers by issuing bills, notes, and bonds as a counterpart to German bonds. Finally, it was envisaged that the bank would function as a central organisation for central banks, fostering central bank cooperation and providing services to them by granting them credit, accepting their deposits, and carrying out currency and gold operations on their behalf. The possibility of performing commercial operations to stimulate international trade was left open, subject to the condition that the bank would not constitute unfair competition for private financial institutions and that commercial loans would enjoy government guarantees.[81] The staff of the bank should be nonpolitical and its seat located outside the territory of a major power, yet in a country where it could obtain fiscal privileges.

On 10 March 1929 the project of the creation of a new international bank was announced to the press,[82] but the scheme was far from being finalised – not even the name of the institution had been agreed upon[83] – and the discussion continued. A number of drafts followed, incorporating also suggestions from other subcommittees.[84]

The French and the Italians opposed Schacht's idea of giving the bank wide lending powers to promote economic growth – which would have made it resemble the post–World War II IBRD (the so-called World Bank)[85] – as an inflationary artificial method of organising credit. Private bankers agreed, fearing unfair competition with commercial banks. Schacht tried as hard as he could to save the option for the bank to provide long-term credit, insisting on the need for Germany to obtain outlets for its exports, but he alienated some of the delegates by arguing that the loss of German territories in Europe and colonies overseas had weakened Germany's capacity to pay its debts. Eventually, Schacht managed to get a specific mention only of a possible role for the BIS in "opening new fields of commerce"[86] in the final draft of the Young Report.

On 12 March it was decided that the capital of the bank should be $100 million, one quarter paid up,[87] and that voting rights would be reserved for central banks, with each of the seven founding countries possessing equal weight. The latter decision was opposed by Moreau, who wanted representation on the board (and voting rights) to reflect each country's entitlement to reparations (where France had the lion's share). Morgan, on the other hand, suggested that representation should be correlated to the size of the countries' financial markets (in which case the United States and the United Kingdom would be in control of the bank). Both suggestions were finally rejected, but at Moreau's insistence it was decided that, until reparations had been settled in full, both France and Germany would have three directors each while the central banks of the remaining five founding countries would each have two directors. Five seats would have to be reserved for countries other than the seven represented in the Young Committee.

In the course of the discussion and consistent with his long-preached gospel, Norman insisted on the importance of establishing the BIS as an effective centre for central bank cooperation. Moreau loosely agreed on cooperation, but he was resolute on national central banks maintaining their full autonomy and not being tied down by common positions.

Because no official representative of the American government had sat at the experts' table, the issue of the link between reparations and inter-Allied debts was left unsettled, with most delegates implying that a link between the two issues would exist. In fact, keen on reaching an agreement, Morgan unwisely declared that the future bank would deal with all war-related debts, including Allied debts to the United States.[88] His remark had a negative impact on future relations between the BIS and the U.S. government, since it confirmed the belief of the U.S. State Department and Treasury that the bank was a political reparations institution, in which U.S. official participation was barred by the consistently held American policy stance on reparations.

The easiest part of the experts' work was concluded on 25 March 1929 with an overall agreement on the international bank, including statutes drafted by Sir Charles Addis.[89] The delegates then turned to their most difficult task: agreeing on the total amount of German payments, on the number of annuities (unconditional and conditional), and on each country's share in reparations. In the following ten weeks the discussion was often tense, with each delegate aware of his country's stakes in the outcome of the negotiations as well as of the repercussions of the debates on the domestic political scene. Schacht proved to be a shrewd negotiator, playing creditors off against each other to his advantage and using his real or supposed differences with the government in Berlin in order to reach advantageous compromises. All Young's diplomatic skills were called upon to avoid a dramatic rupture, to gain concessions from the various sides, and to conclude an agreement. The various phases of the proceedings in Paris regarding reparations need not concern us here: they have been masterfully summarised by Baffi, and the reader is safely referred to his book.[90] As far as the BIS is concerned, the discussion over reparations showed, on the one hand, that the experts envisaged the creation of an institution large enough to generate sufficient profits to allow some reduction in the overall reparations bill and, on the other hand, that the French were ready to grant a substantial reduction on the amount of reparations established by the Dawes Plan in exchange for the commercialisation of a major part of the reparations through the BIS.

The final agreement entailed an average annuity of 2,050 million Reichsmarks (of which 660 million was unconditional) for the period 1929–66, and a smaller amount for the period 1966–88, to match payments to the United States by Germany's creditors. The conference closed on 7 June 1929 with the signing of the experts' report – the so-called Young Plan – which also recommended establishing a BIS organisation committee, whose members would be appointed by the central banks of the seven participating countries.[91]

Given the advisory capacity under which the experts had operated, in order to become operative the Young Plan had to be submitted to the governments of the participating countries and then translated into an international agreement. Towards that end, a conference was called in The Hague, to which representatives of other former belligerents were also invited.[92]

2.3   The Baden-Baden Committee

The First Hague Conference met on 6 August 1929 and was chaired by Henri Jaspar, prime minister of Belgium.

Those who expected this conference to be just a ceremony for the ratification of the Young Plan could not have been more mistaken. The new U.K. Labour government, elected at the end of May, questioned U.K. acceptance of the reparation agreement. The electoral campaign had highlighted widespread discontent about taxation and thus Snowden, the new chancellor of the exchequer, was publicly committed to collect as much as he could from Germany. On the first day of the conference he argued that the Young Plan had given the United Kingdom too small a proportion of the annuities (in particular, unconditional ones)[93] and asked for a revision of the allocation of reparations among creditors.[94] The conference remained deadlocked over the issue until (i) French concessions about the evacuation of the Rhineland were reciprocated by Germany's commitment to increasing reparation payments and (ii) the Belgian, French, and Italian delegates agreed to lower their own share to accommodate most of the U.K. demands.[95]

The new U.K. government also had a different vision of the BIS: "Influential officials were sceptical of putting German payments on a commercial basis; they sensed an emerging alliance between central banks and investors in German securities that would press for future reductions in German payments. They were also sceptical of the Bank of England's claim that the BIS would be useful in securing central bank cooperation".[96] Moreover, relations between the Treasury and the Bank of England were not at their best, as the latter's role in the 1925 return to gold was about to be reviewed by the Macmillan Committee.[97] Snowden made it clear in The Hague that he wished governments to have a larger say in the operations of the BIS,[98] thus making the independence of the BIS a major theme for discussion in the Organisation Committee.

The First Hague Conference closed on 31 August with the signing of a protocol that accepted the Young Plan in principle,[99] leaving to seven committees the task of working out the technical details and reporting to a second Hague conference.

Three committees met in Paris, dealing with reparations in kind, reciprocal claims in respect of ceded properties, and the liquidation of liabilities of debtor governments under the peace treaties. Three other committees, charged with adapting German laws to the Young Plan, met in Berlin. The special Organisation Committee for the Bank for International Settlements was convened in Baden-Baden – the exclusive spa resort in the Black Forest where Tolstoy had set a scene in *Anna Karenina* – to keep it far from the spotlight of the press.

Because members of the Organisation Committee were to be appointed by the central banks, intensive consultations among them took place ahead of the meeting. Quesnay, head of the research department at the Bank of France, was particularly active in the pre-committee diplomacy. He visited the central banks of Belgium, Germany, Italy, and England,[100] discussing the statutes and functions of the BIS as well as its future seat. He argued that the bank would be governed only by its constitution, that it would not create credit, and that it should not resemble a "democratic League of central banks".[101] The U.K., French, and Belgian central banks all prepared their own drafts of the statutes of the future bank.

The Baden-Baden committee convened on 3 October and remained in session until 13 November 1929. The central banks of the six countries of the Young Conference had each selected two delegates.[102] The two American delegates were present in their private capacity only, even though their choice had been made in agreement with Harrison,[103] head of the Federal Reserve Bank of New York. One of them, Reynolds, was elected president.

The task of the committee was to draft the statutes of the BIS and the convention regulating its relations with the host country. Given the technical nature of the assignment and the advanced stage of previous preparations, it was hoped that the proceedings would be swift and smooth. But it soon became clear that the devil was in the details.

To start with, the delegates did not agree on how to interpret the scope of the committee's mandate.[104] According to Baffi, the two extreme positions were those of Beneduce and Schacht. The Italian delegate, backed by the French, maintained that the Young Report approved by the Hague Conference mandated central banks with the task of creating the BIS, which could well have been brought into life just by an initiative of central banks unconnected with reparations. It would then be up to the governments to entrust the management of reparations to the BIS after examining its statutes. According to Beneduce, the drafting of the statutes would be the sole responsibility of central banks, whereas a trust agreement should be negotiated afterwards with governments. Schacht, on the other hand, argued that the committee could not deviate from the Young Report as approved by the governments in The Hague.[105]

Behind the divergence on the extent of the mandate were differing views of the mission and organisation of the BIS. As an offspring of central banks, the new institution would be limited to their operational tasks. Yet as a governmental creature, the BIS could be entrusted with the functions advocated by Schacht and restated in a memorandum he circulated to the delegates, which read: "We envisage the possibility of a financial institution that should be prepared to promote the increase of world trade by financing projects, particularly in underdeveloped countries, which might otherwise not be attempted through the ordinary existing channels".[106] Schacht never abandoned his idea of a world bank *ante litteram*. The U.K. position was somewhere in between the "Latin" and the German theses. On the one hand, the Bank of England favoured the birth of Norman's central banks' club and disliked the idea of the BIS competing with commercial banks; on the other hand, the U.K. delegates had to reckon with Snowden's assertion of a governmental role in creating the new institution. This division over interpretation of the committee's mandate remained to the end, when disagreement over sending the final report (containing the statutes of the BIS) to the president of the Hague Conference was overcome by transmitting him a copy "for notification" only.

The impasse concerning the committee's powers was, however, momentarily overcome by a U.K. memorandum highlighting the different legal nature of the statutes and constitution of the BIS.[107] The constitutional act would deal with elements that were of direct interest to governments, such as arbitration, the composition of the board, and veto rights. Any change to the act would require the approval of the governments concerned. In its daily functioning and administration, the BIS should be free of government interference and should have the authority to amend its own statutes, although these could be subject to revision by governments at ten-year intervals.[108]

In discussing the general objective of the bank, all the delegates agreed (with some qualifications) that the Young Plan's mandate to "provide additional facilities for the international movement of funds" implied that the BIS's objective "went beyond the servicing of reparations to embrace other international financial operations and cooperation among central banks".[109]

On the bank's capital – fixed at the rather modest amount of $100 million – consensus soon emerged that it should be denominated in the currency of the country in which the bank was headquartered (behind the scenes, a discussion was simultaneously taking place about the location of the BIS). Quite predictably, the only dissenting view was expressed by the French, who insisted on capital being denominated in "grammor", expressed in gold weight to avoid competition with existing currencies, which would become an international settlement currency for transactions amongst central banks.[110]

Concerning the bank's operations, rather than listing all those that would be allowed, the committee opted for a formula that would simply give central banks of individual countries a right of veto on the operations carried out by the bank in their own markets.

Special attention was devoted to central bank deposits, particularly gold and convertible currency deposits, to be used also to settle international payments without going through the foreign exchange markets or actually moving gold between locations, thus giving the BIS the clearing-house functions envisaged by earlier proposals for an international bank.

As for the provision of funds, all except the British were inclined to allow the bank to issue bonds. On promissory notes, opinions were divided along lines that reflected the two main views of the functions and role of the BIS. The French opposed issuing promissory notes on the grounds that they would be equivalent to the creation of fiat money. For Schacht, promissory notes would permit the BIS to finance short-term lending operations. More generally, Schacht wanted to allow the bank to undertake a wide range of lending operations, including mortgage bonds, which he saw as directed mostly to Germany.

Dissensions were also conspicuous on the bank's governance. The granting of huge privileges to the directors appointed by the seven founding members, the French-inspired "aristocracy of the founders", prevailed against the opposition of Beneduce, Addis, and Schacht. A significant clash also took place concerning the creation of an executive committee, which some experts wanted to consist of persons – selected on professional rather than national bases – who would ensure a constant presence at the bank. Some delegates, however, argued that it would be difficult to find such qualified persons ready to leave their current occupations, while others feared that the limited powers of the board would reduce the governors' interest in attending its meetings. The French hostility to the executive committee derived from the desire to safeguard the prerogatives of the general manager, since their candidate for the job (Pierre Quesnay, of the Bank of France) was waiting in the wings. For the same reason, the French delegation proposed to give the general manager considerable autonomy and successfully fought against giving the "alternate to the president" the title and powers of vice-president.

Needless to say, the trustee functions of the bank and, more generally, its role in handling reparations – in particular with regard to their mobilisation (or commercialisation) – were also the subject of heated debate. The French insisted that they had made substantial concessions on the amount of reparations precisely in order to receive non-postponable mobilisable annuities. It was agreed that creditor governments could issue bonds in amounts corresponding to the capitalisation of all or part of the unconditional annuities due to them, either in their own market or in that of other countries, subject to the approval of the central bank of the country in question. The BIS could also directly issue mobilisation bonds.

"The discussion on the [official] language" of the statutes, Baffi wrote, "was marked by a mixture of pride, common sense and humor in which solemnity alternated with jocularity. All but the French were prepared to accept English as the official language, but Moret's insistence that the French text should be authentic as well led Schacht, Beneduce and even the Japanese Tanaka to request that the texts also be prepared and authenticated in the languages of their respective countries. Rather than have so many official texts in different languages, which would lead to confusion, Sir Charles Addis accepted that only the French text should be authentic: it was so decided, amidst thanks from Moret for the homage paid to the clarity of the French language and ironic remarks from the others".[111] Eventually, though, the Final Clause of the Hague Agreements of 1930 would accept both the French and English texts as authentic.

The choice of the seat of the BIS was long discussed informally before being dealt with officially. The Young Plan stipulated only that the BIS should be located in a country where it could "perform its functions with the requisite freedom and with suitable immunities from taxation".[112] There was broad agreement from the beginning that a location in Germany would not be appropriate. Other than that, there was no lack of candidate sites. The British had made no secret that they expected London to be picked: it offered excellent facilities and immediate access to the most sophisticated financial market in Europe.[113] Germany and Japan, both excluded from the choice, were inclined to support London. However, the French – who preferred Paris but realised that many of the objections to Germany applied also to France – were determined to prevent the choice of London for reasons of prestige and influence.[114] They therefore convinced the Belgian and Italian delegations[115] to join with them in arguing that no large country was suitable (on the grounds that it would be easy for it to exercise an influence on the BIS) and in proposing Brussels.[116] In retaliation, the Belgian capital was turned down by both the U.K. and the German delegations, a move that outraged the Belgians to the point that, on 7 November, they left Baden-Baden.[117] Amsterdam was then suggested, but it did not receive the support of the French and American delegations. The choice finally fell on Switzerland, a small neutral country with a buoyant financial market. Amongst the Swiss cities, Basel looked particularly appealing for its geographical position on the border of three countries and its easy railway access.[118] On 11 November 1929, President Bachmann of the Swiss National Bank travelled to Baden-Baden to open negotiations about locating the BIS in Basel.

The BIS Organisation Committee completed its task on 13 November 1929 with the signing of the Charter, Statutes, and Trust Agreement, copies of which were sent to the six central banks and to the Federal Reserve Bank of New York.[119]

At the Second Hague Conference[120] (3–20 January 1930), only a few changes were made to the Trust Agreement. After a crisis, on 13 January 1930, during which Schacht threatened that the Reichsbank would not participate in the BIS,[121] the Charter, Statutes, and Trust Agreement – together with a convention with Switzerland – were approved by the participating governments.

2.4   American Ambiguity

As we have seen, American bankers figured prominently in the process that led to the creation of the BIS. Yet the official U.S. position was constrained by its overall policy stance with respect to the postwar settlement. After the direct American involvement in a predominantly European conflict and the proclamation of the famous 14 points,[122] President Woodrow Wilson had been very active in the postwar diplomacy, including participation in the peace conference and the creation of the League of Nations. Congress, however, ratified neither the Versailles treaty nor American membership in the League of Nations.[123] Afterwards, the official U.S. policy was to avoid discussions, dealings, and conferences about reparations while at the same time insisting upon the payment in full of inter-Allied debts. This led to ambiguity in practical policy making. From a legal point of view, no link existed between reparations and debt payments, but the United States was fully aware that domestic political and economic conditions in the main debtor countries were such that the practical connection between the two issues could hardly be ignored. Moreover, private American capital was deeply involved in financing reparation transfers, Europe remained the main foreign market for American products and direct investment, and many considered its stability to be vital to American prosperity.[124] Thus, while the involvement of government officials was ruled out, private financiers and businessmen like Owen D. Young, Charles Dawes, Thomas Lamont, and J. P. Morgan were unofficially encouraged to take an active part in European negotiations on reparations and related matters. Their presence was prominent and crucial in the negotiations leading to the Dawes Plan in 1924, which opened the way to a flood of American loans to Europe.[125]

On the central bank side, Benjamin Strong, president of the Federal Reserve Bank of New York, had been an important advocate of central bank cooperation even though he believed in the self-regulatory mechanism of the gold standard. Following Strong's death in 1928, other Federal Reserve Banks challenged the leading position of New York in international financial diplomacy, which they wanted to be conducted directly by the Board of Governors. This weakened the position of Strong's successor, Harrison, himself a believer in international cooperation.[126]

Ahead of the Committee of Experts Paris meeting (February 1929), the State Department again feared that the conference would link reparations and wartime debts, presenting the United States with a united European front demanding a reduction or even cancellation of the latter.[127] It therefore refused to send a delegation. American private financiers, on the other hand, had every reason to welcome an initiative that promised to depoliticise the reparations issue and settle reparations in a way that would assist Germany in honouring its financial obligations.[128] Private lenders to Germany could only benefit from a reduction of official debt;[129] hence the ambiguity of American policy vis-à-vis the Young Plan. President Coolidge allowed and even encouraged private financiers to participate in the conference as independent experts, but he then tried to prevent an American from being appointed to the high-visibility presidential position.[130] The State Department, though officially absent, closely monitored the Hague Conference and requested detailed information about the negotiations from the U.S. experts in attendance.

In this context, the American delegates found themselves in an uncomfortable position, particularly as far as the link between reparations and Allied debts was concerned. When Young reported back home about proposals to split German payments into two parts, the first one to cover Allied debt payments to the United States and the other for outright reparations, Secretary of State Stimson reacted as if Young were an official American representative. "American delegates", he wrote, "have failed to maintain the position consistently taken by their government and their failure to do so may have unfortunate consequences in the future in so far as the protection of America's interests is concerned. If the settlement goes through as planned, the whole burden of the collection and transfer of reparation payments will fall on our shoulders and the allied debtor nations will have succeeded, by including Germany in their ranks, in creating a solid front which will exert continued pressure for the reduction and eventual repudiation of these debts".[131] However, when Young reacted by threatening to resign and pointing out the dramatic consequences of a complete failure of the conference, Stimson and new U.S. President Hoover moderated their criticism.[132] They remained, nevertheless, suspicious of the plans to create the BIS, a suspicion that – with various undertones – characterised the attitude towards the BIS of successive American administrations for the following twenty years.

American private financiers, on the other hand, saw the creation of the BIS as essential for the commercialisation of German bonds. The risk of issuing German bonds on a large scale was too high for a single firm to handle. They welcomed collective action through an international institution, which "would improve the chances of collecting reparations and protect individual firms from the risky business of managing the German debt".[133]

In their efforts to bridge the gaps between European experts, the Americans inevitably became involved in political statements. The already mentioned declaration by Morgan about the BIS,[134] hinting at a link between reparations and Allied debts, prompted a public statement by Stimson reiterating that the U.S. government did not wish to "directly or indirectly participate in the collection of German reparations through the agency of a bank or otherwise".[135] This declaration was the basis for the American policy in years to come, barring officials from the Federal Reserve System from serving at the BIS, labelled as an "international reparations bank".[136]

Under-Secretary of the Treasury Mills believed that the Bank "was nothing but a machine for the collection of reparations from Germany" and, since the U.S. government had never asked for reparations or indemnities from Germany, "it could not now properly authorise an official of the Government to become part" of the BIS.[137] Mills nevertheless admitted that "if neither reparations nor inter-Allied debts existed it would probably be advisable for the Federal Reserve System to participate in the organization and management of the international bank".[138]

President Hoover made it clear, on 18 June 1929, that the United States would not endorse the Young Plan: "our government is not a party to that agreement and therefore not a signatory to it".[139] Since, however, the United States did have claims on Germany resulting from the American expenses for maintaining troops in the Rhineland, a separate agreement on that portion of reparations was signed with Germany on 28 December 1929.[140]

The Federal Reserve Bank of New York was the one American governmental institution to nurture a keen interest in the BIS, for reasons that are easy to understand: (i) the New York banking community, the most outward oriented in the country, held by far the largest share of the U.S. foreign credits; and (ii) Strong's international and cooperative orientation was still pretty much alive. Since Washington ruled out the direct participation of representatives of the Federal Reserve System in the BIS, the New York Fed reluctantly opted for a second-best solution: friendly private bankers would sit on the BIS board.[141] Governor Harrison informed Moreau and Schacht that he himself would be available neither for the Baden-Baden committee nor for the future BIS board.[142] He nevertheless remained in touch with European central bankers in the run-up to the Hague Conference and followed both its progress and that of the Baden-Baden committee,[143] where he unofficially sent Jay E. Crane to assist Reynolds and Traylor and to keep him constantly informed.[144] Young, for his part, informed Under-Secretary of the Treasury Mills that Jackson Reynolds and Melvin Traylor would serve on the Baden-Baden committee, implicitly asking for his approval.[145] As president of the committee, Reynolds held a key position and was instrumental in steering it to a positive conclusion even though he was unable to create the business-oriented banking institution he had in mind,[146] accepting important limitations on the bank's activity in areas such as offering mortgage loans and accepting bills of exchange and promissory notes.[147]

Since the basis of the official policy was "not to involve the United States directly or indirectly in the machinery of the Young Plan and to avoid any possible future entanglement in the event of its breakdown",[148] the issue of BIS shares was also considered a political matter, falling under the jurisdiction of the State Department or the Treasury Department rather than the Federal Reserve.[149] Since the Federal Reserve Bank of New York was not permitted to own BIS shares and sit on its board of directors, a consortium of banks was formed – consisting of J.P. Morgan & Co., the First National Bank of New York, and the First National Bank of Chicago[150] – to subscribe the American tranche of the BIS capital and to appoint two Americans to the BIS board.[151] The names of Dwight Morrow and W. W. Stewart were initially suggested but then Young and Morgan proposed Gates W. McGarrah, at the time chairman of the Federal Reserve Bank of New York, and Leon Fraser, a member of the law firm of Ropes, Gray, Boyden and Perkins.[152] McGarrah, who had also been American representative at the Reichsbank, resigned from his position at the New York Fed on 27 February 1930.[153] Fraser, who participated in the negotiations of the Young and Baden-Baden committees, had previously been with the office of the Agent General for Reparation Payments.

2.5   The Legal Basis

The legal status of the BIS was laid down in the Convention respecting the Bank for International Settlements, signed at The Hague on 20 January 1930 between the government of the Swiss Confederation and the governments of Belgium, France, Germany, Italy, Japan, and the United Kingdom.

By signing the Convention, Switzerland undertook to grant the BIS a constituent charter and sanction its Statutes, both of which were appended to the Convention itself.[154] Approved by the Swiss Federal Council, the Convention and the Charter of the BIS obtained force of law in Switzerland on 26 February 1930. This cleared the way for the governors of the central banks of Belgium, France, Germany, Italy, and the United Kingdom – plus a representative for the Bank of Japan and one for an American banking group – gathered in Rome on 27 February to sign the instrument of foundation, thereby actually creating the Bank.[155]

It was no accident that, although the settlement of the reparations problem had been the immediate cause for setting up the BIS, the Bank's actual purpose was defined much more broadly by its Statutes: "to promote the co-operation of central banks and to provide additional facilities for international financial operations; and to act as trustee or agent in regard to international financial settlements entrusted to it under agreements with the parties concerned".[156]

Because there was no precedent for an international financial organisation created by international treaty, the legal status of the BIS broke new ground. On the one hand, the BIS was a bank structured as a limited-liability company. On the other hand, it had all the characteristics of an international organisation, possessing international legal personality and endowed with many of the privileges and immunities normally conferred upon intergovernmental organisations. This duality permeates the statutory arrangements of the BIS and had a lot to do with the Bank's specific institutional nature as a cooperative venture of the central banks.[157]

The BIS is an international organisation created by an international treaty signed by governments, but it was set up and controlled by central banks. The Bank's capital was set at 500 million Swiss gold francs,[158] divided into 200,000 shares of 2,500 gold francs each. The initial shares issue, on 20 May 1930, allocated 16,000 to each one of the five founding central banks and to the participating Japanese and U.S. banking groups, so that the founders would remain in control of the BIS.[159] Only 25% of the subscribed capital was paid up, with the Board retaining the right to call up the rest. The central banks or subscribing banking groups were free to offer their BIS shares for subscription to the general public.[160] However, the BIS could decline to accept a transfer of shares to a new owner, and the rights of representation and voting at the Bank's Annual General Meeting remained reserved for the central banks to whom the shares had originally been issued.

The Statutes[161] provided for the governors of the founding central banks to be ex officio members of the BIS Board of Directors. Each governor was entitled to appoint a second director of the same nationality – representing finance, industry, or commerce – thereby affirming the importance of the private sector in the creation and operations of the Bank. For the duration of the Young Plan, Germany and France appointed a third director each. Finally, the Board could elect up to a maximum of nine other directors from among the candidates proposed by other shareholding central banks. In practice, and until the early 1990s, the extension of the BIS Board of Directors beyond the founding central banks remained limited to the election to directorship of the governors of the central banks of the Netherlands, Sweden, and Switzerland.

Special provisions were made for the representation of the central banks of the United States and Japan on the BIS Board. Article 28 of the Statutes stipulated that if the governor of one of the founder central banks was not in a position to take up his ex officio seat on the BIS Board then he could nominate a substitute and, failing this, that the Board could invite a national of the country in question to become a member provided that his central bank did not object.[162]

The BIS's character as an international organisation was underlined by the special privileges and immunities the Bank was granted. Its senior management enjoyed diplomatic status. The Swiss authorities granted the Bank important tax exemptions.[163] Any dispute between the Swiss government and the other governments signatory to the Convention covering the legal status of the BIS was placed outside the competence of the Swiss courts and entrusted to the international Arbitral Tribunal established under the Hague Agreements of 20 January 1930. Similarly, Swiss banking legislation and supervision did not apply to the BIS.

One of the most far-reaching immunities granted to the BIS by its Constituent Charter[164] stipulated that: "The Bank, its property and assets and all deposits and other funds entrusted to it shall be immune in time of peace and in time of war from any measure such as expropriation, requisition, seizure, confiscation, prohibition or restriction of gold or currency export or import, and any other similar measures".[165]

All the aforementioned provisions made the BIS unquestionably an international organisation. Even if the texts of 1930 did not explicitly confer an international legal personality on the BIS, this status was subsequently confirmed by the Bank's de facto ability to conclude in its own right international treaties that fell under international public law.[166]

At the same time, though, the BIS was a limited-liability company, incorporated under Swiss law. The Statutes[167] enumerated the activities the BIS was authorised to carry out: buying, selling, and holding of gold for its own account or the account of central banks; buying, selling, and discounting short-term obligations of prime liquidity; buying and selling negotiable securities other than shares; opening and maintaining deposit accounts with central banks; and accepting deposits. The Bank was also allowed to act as an agent or correspondent of any central bank and to enter into agreements to act as trustee or agent in connection with international settlements.[168]

The Statutes also listed the activities the BIS was not allowed to undertake: issuing banknotes, accepting bills of exchange, making advances to governments, acquiring a dominant interest in any business concern, or owning real property other than as required to conduct its own business.[169] The listing of operations that the BIS was allowed or not allowed to carry out was meant to reassure private banks that the Bank would not become a competitor in their fields of activity.[170] The Statutes, however, did not explicitly rule out the possibility of the BIS undertaking certain credit operations. Last, but not least, the Bank was required to maintain sound liquidity.[171]

With regard to banking operations, some of the immunities granted to the BIS as an international organisation did not apply, and the Bank was made subject to the jurisdiction of the ordinary courts.[172] Thus, with respect to its normal business operations, the Bank could be proceeded against in any court of competent jurisdiction. This provision was made to facilitate BIS access to the financial markets and more generally to enhance its credit standing.

The character of the BIS as a limited-liability bank was important to the founding central banks for two main reasons. First, by making the BIS a technical and bank-oriented organisation modelled on their own domestic institutions, the central bank governors made it easier for themselves to keep politicians at arm's length. Second, the nature of the BIS as a bank allowed it to provide central banks with valuable banking services and, at the same time, to guarantee its own financial independence. In contrast with other international organisations (the League of Nations and later the UN, the OECD, etc.), the BIS would not be dependent on annual budgets voted by national authorities, since it earned its own living.

The distribution of profits was regulated as follows:[173] 5% of the net profits would be allocated to a legal reserve fund; out of the remaining profits, a dividend would be paid to the shareholders at the rate of 6% per annum on paid-up capital, and additional allocations would be made to a dividend reserve fund and a general reserve fund. After these allocations of profits, any remaining balance would be further distributed to (i) the governments or central banks in relation to the long-term deposits they maintained with the BIS in connection with the Young Plan and (ii) a special fund that in due course would be used to help Germany pay the last 22 annuities provided for by the Young Plan.[174]

In the final analysis, the Bank for International Settlements, although founded by an international treaty sanctioned by national governments, was very much tailored to the views and requirements of the central banks. To be able to fulfil its functions, the Bank was given broad powers – though perhaps not as broad as Hjalmar Schacht, for one, would have wanted. The founders made sure that the statutory arrangements for their new institution could not be easily changed. The key provisions of the BIS Statutes were declared "protected" articles, which meant that they could be altered only with the consent of all the signatories to the Convention. Finally, the 1930 Statutes[175] stipulated that the Bank could be liquidated only by a decision of the General Meeting supported by a three-fourths majority and in any case not before the totality of its obligations assumed in the context of the Young Plan had been acquitted.

2.6   High Hopes Are Raised: Comments on the Creation of the BIS

"It is very likely that April 22, 1930, will stand out in the future as one of the most important dates in the economic history of the world, for on that day the board of directors of the Bank for International Settlements held their first meeting at Basle."[176] Thus the U.K. magazine *The Banker* hailed the creation of the BIS. Several other financial and economic journals were equally, if more soberly, enthusiastic in their hopes that the BIS would contribute to international financial stability and peace. "We are happy", wrote a French commentator, "to see the birth of a new international institution of coordination which will bring about a better distribution of capital in the world and facilitate the settlements of international payments that in the past have given rise to so many difficulties and frictions between countries".[177] Or, as an anonymous author phrased it: "From whatever angle it is considered, the creation of the BIS is a major event in the history of mankind".[178] A number of people – including Mendès France, a future architect of the European Community – even saw the BIS as an important step towards European unity.[179]

During the Hague and Baden-Baden negotiations, however, enthusiasm had been far from universal. "Every banker in London, Paris, Berlin or elsewhere, admits that the Bank for International Settlements, as proposed by the Young Committee, will be an admirable instrument for facilitating international debt payments, but when it comes to discussing its functions as a bank pure and simple, if a sort of superbank, the inquirer discovers mixed feelings."[180] Particularly in the Anglo-Saxon world, many observers remained sceptical. A number of people in the City of London looked with suspicion at the creation of a "superbank" that they feared would compete in the area of commercial banking. "The reaction in London has been lukewarm to the international bank proposal, it being felt that the British have little to gain from it, and may find it a substantial competitor for business which has hitherto been handled by London."[181] "The British view, judging from statements made by certain London newspapers, is that the bank's activities shall be limited strictly to handling Reparations payments and war debt settlements, and that the 'commercial' functions of the new institution ... shall be quietly dropped."[182] *The Economist* was, from the beginning, a sober supporter of the BIS: "Those who regarded international co-operation in the use of gold as lying at the root of the solution of most other problems, and the avoidance of new ones, would see in the proposed bank for international settlements possibilities of the highest ultimate importance to the peace of the world".[183]

In spite of his general support, Sir Walter Layton, editor of *The Economist,* argued that ultimate responsibility for the success of the BIS would rest with governments. He even ventured the idea of putting the League of Nations in charge of the Bank. Considering him "the most responsible moderate critic at home", Norman invited Layton to become one of the U.K. members of the Baden-Baden committee.[184] As negotiations proceeded and the BIS began to take shape, fears of a commercial superbank eased and the U.K. press adopted a more reassuring tone, though doubts remained as to whether the BIS would really succeed in fostering central bank cooperation.[185] *The Economist* itself warned against overoptimism: "While popular opinion should not be encouraged to believe that in the BIS a panacea has been discovered for all the world's present difficulties in the realm of money and credit, we hope that ... Governments ... will generally approve the proposals now put forward and make it possible to launch an important and promising experiment".[186]

The influential financial commentator Paul Einzig, who later became one of the BIS's sternest critics, summed up 14 considerations to be taken into account when determining one's attitude towards the new bank, ranging from one's belief in international institutions to the possibility of the BIS assisting central banks.[187] He argued that the "International Bank" started with the tide, was the most suitable solution for reparations, and offered the advantage of central bank cooperation. Drawbacks in Einzig's eyes were the risks of political influence and credit inflation, but he concluded that for the sake of progress the world should be prepared to take some risk.[188]

The general feeling among the few informed observers in the United States was that the country did not need a "reparations bank". "America's large holdings of gold", the *New York Times* disconsolately wrote, "mean that we do not need this bank, so that for the present we shall have none of it, refusing the directorship offered to the Federal Reserve System. Thus one more effort at international cooperation must get on without official American help. It is something like the League of Nations story repeated".[189] For the *Journal of Commerce,* it was "difficult to see any excuse for the organisation of such an institution as a bank. The best plan undoubtedly would be to make it an accounting office and turn it over to the League of Nations".[190]

Feeling that information about the BIS was inaccurate, W. Randolph Burgess (who had participated in preparing the first draft of the BIS during the negotiations of the Young Plan) wrote an explanatory note[191] that formed the basis for an article by Jeremiah Smith, a Boston lawyer, in the *Quarterly Journal of Economics.*[192] Smith and Burgess expressed the hope that the new Bank would have the same positive effects on Europe as the Federal Reserve had had on the United States. "The most important benefit to be expected from the establishment of the Bank", Smith wrote, "lies in its furnishing a regular meeting place for the representatives of banks of issue.... The Bank should vastly increase the prospects for international cooperation in the field of finance". The article concluded that the BIS "undoubtedly [had] great possibilities for the future in exercising a steadying and stabilizing influence on international financial relations".[193]

Despite the official U.S. policy to refuse any official American involvement with the BIS, a number of American papers underscored the relevance of the Bank.[194] "International financial co-operation ... has had far-reaching results for the rehabilitation of Europe .... Such co-operation is necessarily personal and probably sporadic. Private initiative is too uncertain a reliance; it needs to be supplemented by a recognised and dependable agency, such as is contemplated in the International Bank."[195] "About the corridors of government buildings, and in private conversations, the opinion is frequently expressed that the United States cannot afford to keep out of the bank once it is formed."[196] The opinions of the American delegates at Baden-Baden received considerable attention: "In the mind of the general public", declared one of them to the *New York Times,* "probably the two most important questions are whether the bank will be a political organisation, and, second, will it be set up and will it operate so as to invade the field of private banking, that is to say, the field now handled by the joint stock banks and other private banks operating in international finance. I feel satisfied at the end of our session that I'm perfectly safe in answering 'No' to both of these questions".[197] A series of articles by George P. Auld in the *Herald Tribune*[198] gave a detailed account of the new institution, whose founding was saluted as "an event of the greatest moment".[199] Refuting U.K. and American scepticism, the article regretted the unofficial way the United States had chosen to participate in the "Bank of Banks". But, he added, "if an American banker is selected as head of the bank we shall again have reason for pride in the spectacle of our country taking a leading part *de facto* in a great movement for human betterment".[200] "As coordinator – especially in the all-important matter of operating a gold settlement fund to reduce gold shipments and stabilize the fluctuations of foreign currencies – [the BIS] has immense possibilities."[201] *Foreign Affairs* featured an article by Shepard Morgan, who advocated the BIS as an international institution for long-term credit.[202]

In France the BIS was welcomed mainly because it offered guarantees for reparation payments.[203] But opinions diverged on the other aspects of the Bank. For the political left the Bank incarnated the "wall of money" standing for the evil powers of international finance, ready to use credit to cut short any socialist economic experiment and capable of endangering the free development of European democracies.[204] Fears of the BIS as the guardian of American interests in Europe and instrument of the domineering "haute finance" were also voiced during the discussions on the BIS in the French Parliament on 28 December 1929.[205] Others, by contrast, saw the BIS as a counterweight to the dominating position of Anglo-Saxon financial institutions, despite some anxiety about "what will happen when twenty-four [central] bankers will decide on the financial life of Europe".[206] Others still hailed the wonderful opportunities the BIS would offer for developing world trade and prosperity, fighting business cycles and unemployment, and contributing through its emphasis on cooperation to the realisation of an economic United States of Europe.[207]

In the first phases of the Young Conference, "the Germans ... were, perhaps, the most enthusiastic supporters" of the new Bank.[208] As the outlines of the BIS became clearer, however, the initial optimism in Germany receded, giving way to scepticism.[209] Schacht himself contributed to this change. Increasingly disillusioned about the outcomes of the conferences in Paris, Baden-Baden, and The Hague, he resigned as Reichsbank president (March 1930) but continued to address the issues of reparations and the BIS in a number of highly publicised lectures and articles,[210] expressing the view that political pressures had resulted in much higher than affordable reparation payments and in scaling down the role of the BIS, particularly as far as long-term credit was concerned. In the German press, relief about the reparations settlement alternated with regrets about the limited possibilities for the BIS to provide credits and promote German exports.[211] The nationalist papers made much of the view that Germany had accepted an unfair settlement and too heavy a burden for the German people.[212] The press closer to the government, on the other hand, generally supported the creation of the BIS, even if it regretted the limited role the Bank would be able to play: this was in fact the criticism on which there was universal consensus in Germany.[213]

A critical review on the "Reparationsbank" jointly written by a number of prominent German economists[214] welcomed the ideas behind the creation of the BIS but concluded that the Bank was too small to have a real influence on world trade and too limited in its possibilities to grant credit. "The Bank will have the anomalous character of a Banking Institution charged with many political duties, with some economic duties, and with the fewest banking duties."[215] In the eyes of the German economists, the only positive aspect of the new Bank was its role in fostering international cooperation.[216] Central bank cooperation was also hailed by Governor Richard Reisch (of the Austrian National Bank) as the essential element of the BIS, the more so since central bankers would thus be less influenced by politics.[217] The importance of freedom from political pressure was also stressed by Elemér Hantos, former secretary of state of Hungary,[218] who saw central bank cooperation as an opportunity for a coordinated revival of the world economy.[219]

Whereas German economists seemed to be sceptical, their colleagues in Switzerland were much more optimistic. They welcomed the settlement of the reparations problem, and they hoped the BIS would be able to extend credit to the "non-capitalist world" and thus open new outlets for German exports, which in turn would allow an increase of American exports to Germany.[220] Also welcomed were prospects of central bank cooperation and gold clearing.[221] Needless to say, the Swiss press also acclaimed the choice of Switzerland and Basel, which was taken as international recognition of the Swiss tradition of neutrality and of the strength of its currency.[222]

2.7   Outlook and Expectations

On 23 April 1930, Pierre Quesnay, former head of the Bank of France's economic research service, was appointed general manager of the BIS.[223] The next day, he had a long interview with Norman on the future tasks and organisation of the international bank, which he afterwards duly summarised in a confidential memorandum.[224] The memo provides an interesting snapshot of the expectations concerning the BIS, of both the U.K. governor and his French interviewer.

The optimism of the recently appointed general manager contrasted with the slight disillusion detectable in Norman's words, even as they appear from the carefully edited transcript of his interview.[225] At one point, Quesnay even felt he should explicitly dispel the impression a reader might get that Norman meant to remain on the sidelines of the ongoing organisation process of the BIS.

Norman said he dreamed the BIS to be the realisation of his ideas, dating back to the 1920s, about the creation of an international monetary order through cooperation between strong and independent central banks, as free as possible from political interference. He candidly acknowledged that he first thought of being able to carry out this project all by himself, then tried to organise an international monetary centre around the League of Nations, and only later understood that "everything must gravitate around the BIS". Yet, he felt, there was too little about international cooperation in the BIS blueprint, to the extent that "conditions for getting started must be studied". Distrustful of reparations, Norman was wary of the direction the BIS was likely to take if it focused mostly on that issue.

Quesnay, on the other hand, showed little patience with regrets voiced even before the new institution had become operative. The current BIS, he said, had a great advantage over the one envisaged by Norman: it existed. Reparations were just an opportunity that he and others[226] had seized to create it. The rest would come in due time, and it was up to those involved to shape the new institution.

Norman saw the difficulties of the world economy as stemming from the bad organisation of international credit. The main task of the new Bank should therefore consist in addressing that problem. "We must work", he said, "to create the largest possible circulation of capital, to avoid capital scarcity in one country and abundance in another: this will be one of the Bank's tasks. It is possible to direct short-term capital towards long-term markets by coordinating the policies of central banks, their discount rates, and by increasing the control each of them has over its own market".[227] Quesnay pointed out that world economic difficulties were largely due to the "introduction of artificial elements in the organisation of production". The main issue, he said, was to avoid the accumulation of further stocks resulting from overproduction caused by prices kept artificially high by cartels, agreements, and the like. A true believer in the virtues of an unreformed classical gold standard, he saw the solution of many problems in letting it work according to textbook theory.

In stressing the need for new investments financed by long-term capital, Norman's position was closer to that of German than of French central bankers. He argued that the regulation of political debts, as carried out by the Young Plan, assumed a reorganisation of international credit. He agreed with Quesnay that by mobilising annuities the BIS might be able to produce a convergence of interest rates in Germany and elsewhere, but he again stressed not only collaboration but also the need for far-reaching reforms of the international payments system.

The two men only agreed that reforms were needed; they differed about their content. French purposes would be better served by the restoration of a *pure* gold standard that would enhance Paris as a financial centre, sitting as it did on a huge pile of bullion. The French therefore saw the BIS, and central bank cooperation through it, mainly as a facilitator of gold payments. On the other hand, Norman wanted to reform, not destroy, an admittedly anarchical gold exchange standard, a system he saw as better suited to the needs of the City. The BIS, he told Quesnay, may render better services than just economising on gold movements by creating a gold clearing system and rationalising the practice of earmarking. In his opinion, the Bank could rationalise the gold *exchange* standard. In particular, it should bring central banks that create credit on foreign exchange to count only on deposits with the BIS for their coverage of outstanding notes – that is, to count only on funds employed in each market with the accord of the relevant central bank. This would automatically enhance cooperation and reduce anarchy. He thought of the BIS as being capable of "creating a fashion" in the club of central bankers whereby only foreign exchange held with the BIS would count as reserves. To that end, Norman did not consider the creation of a research department, inevitably under the direct influence of Quesnay, to be sufficient. He also wanted the BIS to organise research groups that included members from all relevant central banks in order to prepare projects on the gold exchange standard, gold clearings, foreign exchange clearings, and the like to be submitted to the Board for discussion.

The difference in outlook and approach between the French and the British would continue in Basel throughout the 1930s, as we shall see particularly when dealing with the London Conference on gold. Nevertheless, these disagreements, however substantial, appear to be relatively modest when compared with the Reichsbank's approach to the new Bank. This approach was clearly outlined in a memorandum written on 8 April 1930 by Karl Blessing, future president of the Bundesbank (1958–69), then working in the Reichsbank's Statistical and Economic Research Department and soon to join the Central Banking Department of the BIS.[228]

The memorandum, entitled "Opinion on how the Reichsbank should conduct itself in the BIS", was meant to provide guidelines for the conduct of the German officials employed with the BIS. It opens by stating: "the Reichsbank should endeavour with all means at its disposal to gain as big a German influence in Basel staff as possible". Once at the BIS, German employees were advised to make sure that "no important business decisions are made without a German representative having knowledge of them or having had an opportunity to express their opinion". In this respect, Germany's attitude was no different from that of any other country: the existence of national delegations was, as we have seen, taken for granted when the BIS began to operate, and all were expected to report back home and to try to exercise as much influence as possible.

More peculiarly German were both the importance attached to the BIS itself by the author of the memorandum, as well as its political reasons.

"The fact that the reparation question has been delegated to a banking institution", Blessing's memorandum reads, "naturally turns this bank into a political institution, even if this is officially denied. The atmosphere, which in future will prevail in the Bank, will be decisive for the question of whether and under what conditions a revision of the Young Plan can be achieved. Consequently, it is of the utmost importance that Germany fills its leading posts in the Bank with first-rate personalities, i.e. with personalities whose power of judgement and expertise will match those of Quesnay, Siepmann and others. The post of Head of Section in the BIS is for Germany's foreign policy definitely as important as the posting of many ambassadors accredited with foreign governments". The main reason for gaining influence in Basel was to be as effective as possible in moving the BIS towards an early revision of the Young Plan. The latter was to be tolerated for the time being only because "every right-minded businessman knows that this Young Plan ideology was only invented to obfuscate the fact that an economically sound solution to the reparations question could not, or not yet, be found and that this ideology is therefore at loggerheads with the reality of things".

The advised strategy consisted of continuously stressing the arguments set forth by the German delegations in Paris, The Hague, and Baden-Baden. German officers "ought to refer time and again to the completely utopian objectives of the Bank; one could, for instance, regularly make specific requests for the BIS to guarantee export credits, even for high-risk business operations and even when it is obvious in advance that the Bank will turn them down. In addition, Germany should continuously stress that it must expand its exports at all cost – if necessary with the aid of state credit guarantees and other subsidy measures – in order to fulfil its obligations under the Young Plan, and, finally, that the success of this imposed, forced export-expansion policy is threatened by the resistance from Germany's trade partners.[229] By continuously drawing attention to this antagonism, it should be possible to gradually create an atmosphere in the Bank in which the anti-reparation bacillus finds fertile ground, in that the self-interest of the countries receiving reparations is affected through their own foreign trade interests. This, together with Germany's internal financial reconstruction, might prove to be the best possible revision policy".

"In addition", Blessing's recommendation continued, "the Reichsbank will point out in the BIS the impossibility of fulfilling the Young Plan thanks to foreign credits indeterminately. Especially in dealing with the Americans, it would seem appropriate to stress the dangers for the creditors of fulfilling the Young Plan obligations thanks to foreign credits, to make it clear to them that in the longer run payments must be covered through export

surpluses, and finally that an exceedingly high private debt level must unavoidably render either the private German foreign loans or the reparation
payments insecure. Of course, with all this, it should be made sure that genuine claims of the German economy for foreign credit are not jeopardised
and that German credit as a whole remains unshaken".

If one of the BIS's tasks – that of "reparation bank" – was, obviously,
radically contested, the second task – that of promoting central bank cooperation – was welcomed and upheld. "The Reichsbank", Blessing wrote,
"should cooperate loyally with the BIS as far as its objectives as bank of
central banks are concerned, since every improvement of the international
monetary and credit situation is beneficial for Germany as a large foreign
trading and debtor economy". As in the case of France and the United
Kingdom, however, Germany also saw cooperation as a tool for reaching
specific national goals. Whereas Quesnay wanted the gold standard to be
left free to operate, so that commodity prices could fall until a new equilibrium was reached, Germany had exactly the opposite objective. "The main
aim", Blessing said, "should be that the BIS manipulates the gold value in
such a way that international price levels remain as stable as possible. This
ought to be achieved through an appropriate gold distribution and credit
policy from the BIS". If Norman wanted to inject discipline into the gold
exchange standard by creating a convention whereby only foreign exchange
held with the BIS could count as central bank reserves, the Reichsbank suggested the "creation of credit, that could be used as a substitute for gold,
for instance by including it in the legal coverage of money in circulation of
the individual central banks".[230]

Most Germans in positions of responsibility shared the views on the
Young Plan and the BIS held by Schacht in Paris and Baden-Baden; his
departure from the Reichsbank, while depriving Germany of a shrewd negotiator and articulate advocate, did not result in a major policy revision.
When the U.S. stance is also taken into account, it appears once again
that each of the four main players in the supposedly cooperative game that
was about to open at the BIS perceived different payoffs and, accordingly,
pursued different strategies.

THREE

Organisation and First Operations

3.1 Off the Ground

The BIS was officially born in Rome on 27 February 1930.

The Bank could not begin to function until the required number of parliaments had ratified the Young Plan,[1] but at the same time the Young Plan could not be implemented until the Bank existed. Time, however, was running short; the first payments of the German annuities were due in June, and by then the BIS had to be ready to perform at least its reparation functions. It was Sir Charles Addis, vice-chairman of the Organisation Committee, who prompted a meeting of the ex officio and appointed members of the Board in order to take the necessary formal steps for the creation of the Bank, even though the latter could not operate until the conditions of the Hague Agreement had been met.

The Rome meeting began on 26 February and continued the following day. In attendance were Stringher, who took the chair as the most senior governor, Azzolini and Beneduce for Italy, Norman and Siepmann for the United Kingdom, Moreau, Moret, and Quesnay for France, Schacht for Germany, Franck and van Zeeland for Belgium, and Tanaka and Saito for Japan. The Italian capital was chosen out of deference to the ailing governor of the Bank of Italy, who found it painful to travel (he died the following December).

As a preliminary step, Board membership was completed by inviting two Americans to join. Harrison having declined,[2] cables were sent to McGarrah[3] and Fraser,[4] offering them the U.S. seats. In addition to that, the general bond for the Young Loan was approved in principle, and funds were allocated by each member central bank to cover the preliminary expenses of

61

the Bank prior to the first meeting of the Board of Directors.[5] Finally, the act establishing the official constitution of the BIS was signed.[6]

The Directors also heard a report by the Bank's Organisation Committee. A few days earlier, temporary premises had been found for the Bank in the city of Basel. The Grand Hôtel et Savoy Hôtel Univers was leased for a period of two years. Its location, adjacent to the Swiss railway station, was excellent, inter alia because of the direct connections to Geneva, Paris, Vienna, and Milan and because of its link with the German station in "Kleinbasel". The hotel served the Bank well, and for a much longer period of time than was originally anticipated.[7] "The many small rooms were well adapted for private offices. The dining room was remodelled and used as the Board room, while part of it served as the library."[8]

By mid-March, Fraser was at work, as alternate for the president, from the Paris headquarters of the Agent General for Reparation Payments, in rue de Tilsitt. McGarrah joined in April.[9] One of the issues to be dealt with concerned precisely the transfer of all the Agent's assets and operations to the new Bank. Other dossiers were also piling up on Fraser's desk. They included preparations for the issue of the Young Loan and of the Bank's shares. Staff had to be hired, but disagreement remained over Quesnay's appointment as general manager, and pending its resolution it was impossible to appoint the other managers.

On 22 and 23 April, the nominated directors of the BIS met in Basel for an informal meeting, again convened by Sir Charles Addis on behalf of the Organisation Committee, "for the purpose of saving time".[10] The original Board consisted of McGarrah and Fraser from the United States, Luther, Melchior, and Reusch from Germany, Moreau,[11] Brincard, and de Vogüé from France, Franck and Francqui from Belgium, Norman and Addis from the United Kingdom, Stringher[12] and Beneduce from Italy, and Tanaka and Nohara from Japan.

A number of major decisions were made at this first, unofficial meeting[13] and were afterwards validated "as decisions of a regular board meeting".[14] It was acknowledged that the Deed of Constitution, signed in Rome, had been promulgated by an ad hoc Swiss law and that the Bank was therefore duly constituted. The Statutes were adopted. Gates McGarrah was unanimously elected president of the Bank and chairman of the Board, with Fraser his alternate as president. Moreau, Addis, and Melchior were designated vice-chairmen "with equal rank". The Board also put an end to the long-standing and bitter quarrel over the appointment of the general manager. Quesnay was chosen, with Luther and the two other German members voting against "for serious reasons of principle".[15] The Bank also accepted in principle the functions of fiscal agent of the trustees for the Dawes Loan and adhered to the Trust Agreement regarding German reparations. The shares of the Bank were allotted to the original subscribers. A tradition-setting agreement was made that the ordinary meetings of the Board should take place in Basel on the second Monday of each month.

According to both McGarrah and Fraser, the climate at the Board meeting was most friendly, and several participants remarked on the spirit of cooperation. "Sir Charles Addis voluntarily stated he had no idea [things] would move so smoothly.... The whole atmosphere was that of a gathering of constructive businessmen and almost no political influence appeared." They felt "greatly encouraged and optimistic about the future".[16]

The first official meeting of the Board took place in Basel on 12 May. All members were present with the exception of Francqui, Melchior, and Nohara.

The Bank opened for business on 17 May, taking over the funds, accounts, capital, and records of the Agent General for Reparation Payments. On 20 May, with the public issue of the shares of the stock of the Bank, the long gestation period was over. The new international institution had been launched and was ready to sail.

3.2   People and Organisation

Once the appointment of the general manager had been made, it was possible to proceed with the other top appointments. To assuage the Germans and the Italians, Hülse (from the Reichsbank) was appointed assistant general manager and Italy's Pilotti as secretary general. These three people also headed the three departments into which the Bank was originally organised: Central Banking (Quesnay),[17] Banking (Hülse),[18] and General Secretariat (Pilotti). In addition to them, there were two other managers in an executive capacity: Rodd,[19] from the United Kingdom, and Marcel van Zeeland, from Belgium. Together with the president (McGarrah) and his alternate (Fraser), these five people made up the decision-making body that ran the Bank on a day-to-day basis. They met in McGarrah's office at 10:30 every morning to discuss the day's business and review the previous day's dealings.[20] Immediately below the managers, the Bank's hierarchy contained five people: Darton and Blessing in the Banking Department; Colenutt, Goodwin, and Sohet in the General Secretariat.[21]

Per Jacobsson joined in September 1931 as economic adviser.[22] Until his arrival, economic research was rather neglected: "For the present", Fraser wrote, "and probably for a long while we shall not indulge in publication of

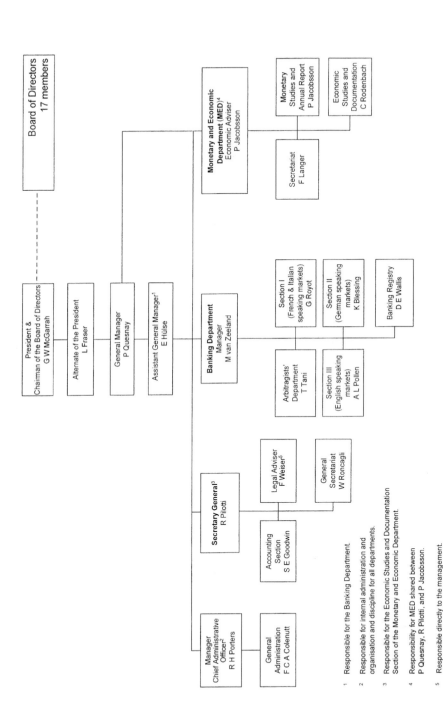

Figure 3.1. BIS "organigram", 1933 (reconstruction).

Board of Directors
17 members

President &
Chairman of the Board of Directors
G W McGarrah

Alternate of the President
L Fraser

General Manager
P Quesnay

Assistant General Manager[1]
E Hülse

Monetary and Economic
Department (MED)[4]
Economic Adviser
P Jacobsson

Secretariat
F Langer

Monetary
Studies and
Annual Report
P Jacobsson

Economic
Studies and
Documentation
C Rodenbach

Banking Department
Manager
M van Zeeland

Arbitragists'
Department
T Tani

Section I
(French & Italian
speaking markets)
G Royot

Section III
(English speaking
markets)
A L Pollen

Section II
(German speaking
markets)
K Blessing

Banking Registry
D E Wallis

Secretary General[3]
R Pilotti

Legal Adviser
F Weiser[5]

General
Secretariat
W Roncagli

Accounting
Section
S E Goodwin

Manager
Chief Administrative
Officer[2]
R H Porters

General
Administration
F C A Colenutt

1 Responsible for the Banking Department.

2 Responsible for internal administration and
   organisation and discipline for all departments.

3 Responsible for the Economic Studies and Documentation
   Section of the Monetary and Economic Department.

4 Responsibility for MED shared between
   P Quesnay, R Pilotti, and P Jacobsson.

5 Responsible directly to the management.

so-called economic information to be added to the overabundance of that commodity that already exists".[23] It was, however, soon realised that economic information on international monetary issues was less plentiful than at first thought, and that the BIS was in an excellent position to collect it from reliable sources, organise the material, and make it available in both official and confidential ways.[24] Moreover, the collection and dissemination of information of interest to central bankers stimulated their technical collaboration in an area deemed to be useful and, at the same time, of low political sensitivity. As we shall see, over the years, one of the reasons for the central bankers being so keen on paying their monthly visits to the BIS was connected with it being an excellent observation point.

The rest of the staff was drawn from three main sources: some were seconded by central banks, others were drawn from the dismantled office of the Agent General for Reparation Payments, and still others were hired directly out of no fewer than 13,000 applications received during the first weeks of the Bank's life.[25]

Those who came from the Paris and Berlin[26] offices of the Agent General were entrusted with more or less the same work as they had done before. The Central Banking Department was partly staffed with people from central banks. Many of them had gained international experience in the postwar reorganisation of banks of issue, with the League of Nations,[27] or in other capacities. According to an acute observer of the first months in the Bank's life, "only one or two had been in commercial banking. No one was a teacher, writer, or research worker in economics, except as this was part of an active role in financial life. Several were lawyers and had held official positions on regular or special commissions. In fact, a summary of the previous work of the personnel points emphatically to experience with special postwar problems and a wide international acquaintance rather than association with competitive banking".[28]

Salaries had to be fixed at a reasonably high level in order, as it was bluntly put, to make it for people "reasonably worth their while to go into exile, with their families, in Basel".[29] This applied to the top management as well: the president's salary was $36,000 plus $14,000 in entertainment allowance and director's fee. The general manager drew a total of $30,000, heads of departments between $15,000 and $20,000.[30] The fiscal immunity granted by Switzerland to the BIS and its employees constituted an additional incentive to move to Basel.

The first BIS organisation was a rather lean one. By the end of 1930 the staff comprised only 95 people,[31] including the seven members of the management.[32] Of the remaining, 23 were classified as officials and 64 as employees.[33] This was altogether a smaller staff than the one working for the Agent General for Reparation Payments,[34] even though the BIS carried out tasks other than those connected with reparations.

Besides the Swiss, who filled all the "minor staff" positions as well as most of the secretarial posts, the U.K. contingent was the largest, making up over a quarter of the total number of employees. The French presence was also numerous, totalling 17 people. The remaining nationality split was as follows: nine Germans, eight Belgians, seven Italians, four Americans, one Austrian, one Czechoslovak, and one Japanese.[35]

We have little evidence of the working climate at the former Grand Hôtel et Savoy Hôtel Univers. Eleanor Lansing Dulles, who spent a considerable amount of time in Basel in 1930–31, tells two apparently contradictory stories. The first conveys a picture of harmony and friendliness. "The desire to develop a well coordinated and harmonious organism made frequent conferences necessary. Those who had direct contact with the BIS at this time remarked on the friendly consultations and constant exchange of views between different departments. This was more notable because the men who were called together on such short notice came from different countries, had widely differing experiences, and had theories, which varied, often, in sharp contradiction. Some had known each other before, in Berlin or Paris, while some had met only occasionally or perhaps had no acquaintance with each other."[36] In her memoirs, on the other hand, Dulles describes a rather different atmosphere. There she recalls how she was at first warmly received, given a room and documents to work on, but two days later the arrangement was cancelled because, so Fraser told her, "he had received protests from the representatives of two member banks. They said they were not to permit a U.S. spy to report to the U.S. government and the Federal Reserve Board. I presume that the two were Japanese and German".[37]

There is, however, no contradiction between the two recollections by the same person about the climate prevailing in Basel during 1930–31. The animosity surrounding the choice of the general manager derived entirely from national rivalries and not from disagreements on the professional qualities of the individual candidates. If, over time, ill feelings were partly overcome, national allegiances remained. In a significant slip of the tongue, the minutes of the first unofficial meeting of the Board even refer to "national delegations". BIS employees such as Mitzakis and Pennacchio performed the semi-official role of liaison to their own countries' central banks. McGarrah and Fraser entertained regular confidential correspondence with U.S. authorities, in particular with Harrison, leaving no doubt as to where their first and foremost loyalty rested. In addition, the U.S. consul in Basel, Merle Cochran, made sure he was around whenever the governors met at the BIS, reporting back to the State Department in Washington on his numerous informal contacts with European central bankers and BIS staff.[38] Even the decision to allow as many as four languages[39] as the official ones for the Bank speaks of divisive national pride.

Yet evidence of national allegiancies and even rivalries does not entirely contradict the earlier observation about a friendly and collaborative climate. Considerations of national "politics" were probably confined to the higher echelons of the hierarchy, whose members nonetheless shared a common vested interest, personal and professional, in the success of the institution, thereby making for a good degree of collaboration in the day-by-day running of the Bank. Many of the immediately lower-ranking officials, on the other hand, were primarily interested in building a reputation as trustworthy international professionals. For all its divisiveness, the previous decade had seen the creation, as never before, of international organisations and emergency teams from which a core group of officials was drawn to the BIS. These were the people who created the esprit de corps that led Dulles and other visitors to report about friendliness and a collaborative attitude.

3.3 The Capital of the Bank

The authorised capital of the Bank consisted of 200,000 shares, each of 2,500 Swiss gold francs. The total of 500 million Swiss gold francs corresponded to the $100 million capital originally set by the Committee of Experts in Paris in March 1929.[40] When the Bank opened for business, 112,000 shares had been subscribed (in equal amounts) by the founding central banks and the proxy institutions of the United States and Japan. Out of an originally subscribed capital of 280 million Swiss gold francs, only 25% was actually paid up.[41] The balance could be called up at a later date at the Board's discretion.[42]

The five European central banks took up their respective shares on the understanding that they would be free to sell any amount of them on their respective markets,[43] while they retained the exclusive right to vote in the Annual General Meeting and to appoint two directors on the Bank's Board (three in the case of France and Germany, as long as reparations lasted).[44] Matters were not as simple in the case of the central banks of Japan and the United States: for different reasons, they were not allowed to directly hold shares of the Bank in their portfolios or in any other way participate in its capital.

In order to circumvent statutory impediments to the holding of shares by the Bank of Japan,[45] a group of 14 Japanese banks under the leadership of the Industrial Bank of Japan subscribed to the BIS's capital, while leaving to the central bank the right to appoint Board members.

In the United States, reparations, inter-Allied debts, and U.S. financial involvement remained politically sensitive issues – for reasons already discussed – and resulted in ambiguous relations with the BIS throughout the 1930s. It therefore took a little longer than in Japan to allocate the Bank's shares. The vehement attacks on the Bank staged by Louis McFadden, chair of the Committee on Banking and Currency in the House of Representatives, did not help the process.[46] By mid-June, however, the U.S. group of subscribers[47] had taken up the 16,000 shares allocated to the United States and to a large extent passed them on to a select group of clients.[48]

The issue of participation in the BIS's capital and Board of central banks from countries other than the signatory powers of the Hague Agreement had already been floating around for a while at the time of the first meeting of the Board, in April 1930. In particular, the central banks of three neutral countries – the Netherlands, Sweden, and Switzerland – had made it known, both privately and officially, that they were keenly interested in participating in the capital as well as in sharing in the administration of the Bank. Their interest, and insistence, derived primarily from the fact that they all presided over relatively large financial markets that would participate in the subscription of the Young Loan bonds. Moreover, Germany was indebted to the Swedish house of Krueger, and a swap of the latter's credit with Young Loan bonds was envisaged. Switzerland argued that – as the host country – it had an additional claim to early[49] participation. Bachmann, the chairman of the governing board of the Swiss National Bank, was explicit in stating that a quid pro quo for hospitality was expected. When the convention on the establishment of the BIS on Swiss soil was discussed before the Swiss Parliament, concerns had been expressed from various sides that the international bank would endanger the currency. "It was opposed to such apprehensions", Bachmann reminded his international friends in Basel, "that the Swiss bank of issue would be called upon to cooperate to the administration of the BIS and consequently there would be no ground to fear an interference with the Swiss exchange".[50]

In March and April, the two American Board members lobbied for an immediate invitation to be extended to the three central banks of the "financial countries" to participate from the very beginning not only in the capital of the BIS but on its Board as well. Norman, already sensing opposition and convinced that "unanimity at the beginning [was] essential for the future of the BIS", tried to convince McGarrah that the issue was not of immediate relevance: "if your neutral countries cannot be admitted at the beginning they may be admitted later".[51]

At the 23–24 April meeting, the three central banks from the neutral, "financial" countries were indeed invited to subscribe 4,000 shares each but on the explicit condition that "the invitation would be given without prejudice to the question of representation on the Board".[52] The latter had been unable to reach the desired unanimity as to which other countries should be asked to join. Applications for shares had also been filed by Romania, Poland, Yugoslavia, and Czechoslovakia, and many members felt that some of the central banks of smaller Central European countries involved in reparations should also be asked to join the Board. There was agreement in principle that such representation was desirable but disagreement about the actual choice.[53] For the time being, an invitation was extended to a total of twelve other central banks[54] to participate in the capital of the Bank, while a decision about Board membership was postponed. In June, it was decided to inform the central banks of Austria, Bulgaria, Czechoslovakia, Danzig, Denmark, Finland, Greece, Hungary, Poland, and Romania that they were welcome to subscribe up to a maximum of 4,000 shares each. A similar invitation to Portugal and Yugoslavia was approved in principle but put on hold until the stabilisation of their currencies was completed with the de jure introduction of the gold standard.[55] The central banks of the three Baltic states – Estonia, Latvia, and Lithuania – became shareholding members between October 1930 and March 1931.

Throughout most of the first year in the Bank's life, disagreement continued concerning enlargement of the Board, and the three neutral "financial" countries were kept waiting at the BIS's door. It was only on 19 May 1931 that Bachmann (chairman of the governing board of the Swiss National Bank), Vissering (president of the Netherlands Bank), and Rooth (first managing director of Sveriges Riksbank) were elected to the Board, joining the directors from the seven founding central banks or banking groups. From then until the early 1990s, membership of the BIS Board of Directors would remain limited to the representatives of these ten countries (with U.S. representation ending in 1935 and Japan's in 1945).

At the end of the first fiscal year, on 31 March 1931, a total of 165,100 shares in BIS capital had been subscribed by 21 European central banks and by the two banking groups in the United States and Japan. As a result, the Bank's paid-up capital amounted to 103 million Swiss francs.[56] The central banks of Albania, Norway, and Yugoslavia joined later in 1931.

3.4   Dealing with Reparations

On 17 May 1930, the day on which the BIS opened its doors in Basel, the Agent General for Reparation Payments transferred all reparation and Dawes Loan funds still in his hands to the newly established Bank. On 15 June 1930, the German government started to pay the monthly instalments due for reparations and the service of the Dawes and Young Loans directly into a BIS account. The disappearance from Berlin of the office of the Agent General was taken by many as marking the end of Germany's tributary condition and viewed as a good omen for improved international relations within Europe. It was followed, on 30 June, by the evacuation of the occupation armies from the Right Bank of the Rhine. Hopes were raised that the controversial "Reparation Bank" could, after all, perform its intended political task, precisely by depoliticising reparations and putting them on a more technical footing.

At this early stage, the tasks of the BIS with respect to reparations were twofold: leading the issue of the Young Loan and managing the receipt and redistribution of the German annuities (the so-called transfer function). At least in principle, both tasks could provide the basis for a reconciliation of the two functions of the Bank: promoting cooperation and acting as agent for reparations. Unfortunately, they soon turned out to be quite contradictory.

Immediately after being appointed and before the BIS officially opened for business, the top management began working on the Young Loan. In a letter to Owen Young, McGarrah summarised the reasons why negotiating the loan took more time than he had anticipated. Complications arose from the fact that the BIS had to "deal with the issuing bankers of nine different countries, with different laws and customs, with representatives of six interested Treasuries with conflicting desires and occasionally political antipathies, and finally with the German authorities, who were very careful about what they did".[57]

Intertwined with the institutional and political difficulties stressed by McGarrah were those connected with the condition of financial markets. In March, J.P. Morgan & Co. made it known that it considered the agreed amount of over $300 million to be too large for the markets to absorb at a fair price. If in the spring of 1929 it was reasonable to talk about issuing $400 million, Morgan argued that half that amount would make a realistic figure one year later. All foreign bonds were being "mercilessly" liquidated on the U.S. market, and an even greater distrust existed about German debt. Distrust was magnified by Schacht's repeated statements that the Young annuities far exceeded Germany's capacity to pay and by McFadden's campaign for financial isolationism.[58]

European bankers found it difficult to absorb the whole amount of the Young Loan bonds allocated to their markets, not only because of the overall conditions in mid-1930 but also because the bonds, issued in seven different currencies, were not easily interchangeable between different national markets.[59] Setting the issue price was not an easy task either. New York bankers favoured "a higher yield than the creditor governments wished. Differences with regard to internal taxation in some countries complicated the matter further".[60]

In this context, the BIS provided much-needed coordination, speeding up negotiations. At the beginning of May, a conference of bankers was convened by the BIS in Brussels to discuss the loan. McGarrah, Fraser, and Quesnay put pressure on the representatives of the most important banking houses and of central banks to reach an agreement. They stressed that it was imperative that the loan be subscribed before the summer because the first German reparation instalment, which the proceeds from the loan were supposed to support, was due on 15 June. The willingness of France to take the largest tranche of the loan made a favourable impression[61] and paved the way to a tentative agreement. The matter was taken up again by the central bankers gathered in Basel on 14–18 May. A committee consisting of Anderson, Luther, Masson, and Norman, meeting from 30 May to 3 June, finalised the details.

The so-called General Bond for the "German Government International 5½% Loan 1930", or Young Loan, was signed by Moldenhauer, the German minister of finance, on 10 June. The loan was issued immediately afterwards in Reichsmarks, dollars, belgas, French francs, sterling, guilders, lire, Swedish crowns, and Swiss francs. The total realised net amount of the loan turned out to be approximately 302 million gold dollars, out of a nominal 352 million gold dollars.

Two thirds of the proceeds of the loan were paid to the creditor governments in proportion to their respective share in the unconditional part of the reparation annuities, as laid down by the Young Plan. One third was paid to the German government for investment in the German Railway Company and the German Post Office and Telegraphs. The service of the loan, both interest and amortisation, was to be paid for two thirds out of the German unconditional annuities, backed by a collateral guarantee on specific tax revenues. The remaining third was to come directly out of the general revenues of the German government.

The BIS was appointed trustee for the holders of Young Loan bonds and put in charge of receiving and distributing the monthly instalments required for the service of the loan in accordance with the terms of the General Bond entered into between the German Reich and the BIS. The Young Loan bonds were issued at 90% below par, carrying a 5½% annual nominal interest and maturing in 35 years (1930–65).[62] As with the Dawes Loan, bonds were to be retired gradually by means of a sinking fund used to repurchase bonds whenever their price was at or below par or to redeem them at par by drawing if their market price was above par. In contrast to the Dawes Loan, where the U.S. issue was the only one for which the gold value of the bonds was explicitly guaranteed, the Young Loan carried a general gold clause.[63] The latter, as we shall see, would shortly provide ample material for litigation and put the BIS, as the trustee, in an awkward position.

The second task of the BIS with regard to the Young Plan consisted of handling reparation payments from Germany to the creditor countries. The German annuity had been fixed at 1,641.6 million Reichsmarks (about $410 million)[64] for the period 1 April 1930 to 31 March 1931. In addition, Germany still had to service the Dawes Loan of 1924, for which the BIS was now agent to the trustee.[65]

German payments went into a BIS account denominated Annuity Trust. They were then transferred to the interest-bearing accounts held by individual central banks with the BIS itself or withdrawn from the Bank. Central banks acted on behalf of their respective governments. From a technical point of view, these procedures did not differ much from those in force under the Agent General regime: "in fact the same person handled most of the exchange transactions before and after May 1930".[66] The BIS was, however, a better instrument for clearing the large amount of reparation funds. It operated in several money markets and could therefore offer a wide choice of exchanges to the recipients of the annuities. More importantly, arrangements had actually been made with a number of central banks "providing for the immediate conversion of one currency into another without passing through the open market",[67] thereby containing the impact of funds movements on exchange rates.[68]

3.5   The Banking Side

The BIS balance sheet as of 31 May 1930 totalled about 303 million Swiss francs (or $59 million); it rose to 1,901 million Swiss francs (roughly $370 million) by 31 March 1931.[69]

On the latter date the liabilities side consisted, besides capital, of a relatively large amount of long-term deposits (301 million Swiss francs, or 17% of total liabilities). These resulted directly from the Hague Agreement, which stipulated that all creditor powers and Germany should keep non–interest-bearing deposits with the BIS.[70] Hence, by virtue of the Hague Agreement, the Bank could count on long-term funds for approximately 404 million Swiss francs (long-term deposits plus paid-up capital). The remaining – and largest – part of the Bank's liabilities consisted of sight (demand) and short-term deposits, held by governments and central banks either for their own account or for the account of others.[71] Neither individuals nor private banks were allowed to make deposits with the Bank.

The availability of a large amount of resources, in the form of deposits by central banks, was crucial to the pursuit of the Bank's goal of maintaining confidence in the stability of the gold standard. Only an adequate amount of ammunition allowed the BIS to pursue its policy of "smoothing out exchange rate quotations" by increasing the Bank's holdings in currencies approaching "a low point between the gold points".[72] Ample resources were also essential to offer member central banks such services as rediscounting, currency and gold swaps, mobilisation of deposits, and the like. Interest rates on deposits were thus fixed at levels that rendered it advantageous for central banks to keep the largest possible amounts of their foreign currency reserves with the BIS, while at the same time guaranteeing great liquidity to their deposits.

There was another reason for showing large deposits. McGarrah and Fraser in particular were keen on reaching "a position that would take [the BIS] away from the accusation of being simply a reparation bank".[73] McGarrah also felt that his aggressive attitude in banking business had succeeded in winning the Bank of England back to the BIS cause.[74] In that respect, however, he was overly optimistic. Doubts persisted in London about the specific objective of the banking side of the BIS.[75]

The investment policy of the Bank was guided by the principle that it should maintain a high degree of liquidity. The first meeting of the Board passed a rather vague resolution about investment guidelines. A committee was appointed to "discuss with the management the principles to be observed in the investment and banking policy".[76] Following the committee's recommendations, the first balance sheet of the Bank showed only 2% of total assets invested in financial instruments maturing over one year and 10% maturing between six and twelve months. The rest was invested in time funds not exceeding three months' maturity (44% of the total), in commercial and treasury bills (32%), and in sight funds (10%).

It was obviously not easy to reconcile the policy of inducing central banks to keep relatively large deposits with the BIS (by offering an attractive remuneration) with an extremely liquid investment stance. Some risk had to be taken: high-yield German bonds made up most of the medium-term investments. As for short-term funds, Harrison did not hide his surprise at the BIS's aggressive activity in the U.S. market "in seeking new business and in competing for high interest rates".[77]

The statutory obligation to seek approval of the national monetary authorities whenever investing in a given market found a practical solution by placing funds almost exclusively through the central bank concerned.[78] This practice, however, did not apply to the Federal Reserve Bank of New York, since private bankers had objected to its monopoly of BIS business on the U.S. market.[79] In Japan, the BIS bought trade bills through the Yokohama Specie Bank.[80] As a rule, in the first year, the money received from various national sources was left in the markets from which it had originated. Interestingly, exceptions were made "to obtain experience of exchange operations, as soon as the necessary contacts have been made with the foreign centres notably London, Berlin and New York":[81] learning by doing was the rule for an institution that, in this as in other areas, had to invent itself from scratch.

In spite of British reservations, it must be reckoned that management was fairly successful in rapidly turning the BIS into a "true" bank, particularly as this accomplishment was neither guaranteed nor entirely anticipated by those who had set up the international bank at Baden-Baden.[82]

3.6   The Issue of Long-Term Lending

The issue of medium- and long-term credit had come up time and again during the discussions in Paris and Baden-Baden. It was, as we have seen, mostly raised by Schacht and the German delegation, but the United Kingdom had also shown an inclination to give it careful consideration. In the end, however, the Bank took the form of a short-term credit institution focused on preserving its own liquidity and that of member central banks, leaving the issue of long-term credit unaddressed. More urgent tasks occupied the first Basel meetings, informal and official, in the months immediately preceding and following the launch of the international bank; the issue of "middle term credit" came up again, in October 1930, only in the context of the guidelines for the Bank's investment policy. It was decided to appoint a committee to "study – in cooperation with the Management – ways and means of organising a system financing medium-term credit".[83] The committee consisted of Melchior (chair), Addis, and van Zeeland. They reported two months later with suggestions for the mobilisation of medium-term credits in the form of bills of exchange.[84] Given the BIS Statutes, the committee adopted a rather narrow definition of medium-term credit as bills maturing between three and twelve months. It was also suggested that the Bank should operate in this market only through the intermediary of central banks, without entering into direct contact with individual borrowers or markets. Only bills of a substantially self-liquidating character would be taken up in such operations.[85]

The problem of how to encourage long-term credit was first brought up by a memorandum written by Sir Robert Kindersley and sent by Norman to McGarrah in February 1931.[86] The document was sent to the BIS for consideration by the governors at their informal meetings, or even by the Board itself – even though, as Norman noted, BIS by-laws precluded contributing to what he called "a world scheme on a large scale". To Norman, the BIS was nevertheless the locus for international monetary cooperation and therefore the obvious intellectual and practical promoter of the plan.

The memorandum opened with an analysis of the causes of the "existing world crisis", the so-called maldistribution of gold that even now remains one of the mainstream explanations of the Great Depression. Accumulation of gold in the vaults of the French and U.S. central banks, Kindersley argued, first created "a boom and then collapse in the United States and restriction elsewhere", then impeded recovery as "the United States and France, instead of lending back to the world their surplus for a usable balance of payments, have been taking the surplus in the form of gold". The reason for the collapse in international long-term lending was seen in the fall in bond prices, which alarmed the general public in both the United States and France, an alarm compounded by "anxiety regarding the political situation in Europe, unwise and extravagant expenditure by certain borrowers", and the fall in commodity prices.

To remedy this situation, Kindersley proposed the "creation of some security which of itself is so good that in both these countries the public will be ready to purchase it". With this in view, it was suggested that an international corporation be created with a subscribed capital of between 25 and 50 million pounds. The corporation would then issue bonds for up to three times its subscribed capital. The money raised by the sale of the bonds was then to "be lent to such Foreign governments, Municipalities, Mortgage Banks, Harbour Boards, Railways and Public Utility Companies, as are in need of funds which cannot be obtained at the time through customary channels and are in a position to offer really good security".

The memorandum, only four pages long, was more a trial balloon than a precise plan of action. The reasons that this new international intermediary was expected to inspire more confidence than sovereign issues were not clearly spelled out. The fact that bonds would be secured for 30% of their outstanding amount by subscribed capital, only 10% of which would be called up, seems unlikely to have been sufficient to turn around the moribund international bond market. Much would depend on the reputation of the intermediary, and more needed to be said on how it could be established. Moreover, Norman's idea of a "world scheme on a large scale" was hardly upheld by the dimension of the envisaged operation. But before entering into details, the U.K. governor most likely wanted to wait for reactions from his peers.

Predictably enough, the Germans signalled a favourable disposition towards the proposed scheme, while the French reaction was substantially negative. According to Baffi, Luther's reaction was contained in a speech he delivered at the Leipzig Fair shortly after reading the Kindersley–Norman memorandum.[87] There the Reichsbank's president argued that Germany needed long-term credit not for new investments in manufacturing, where excess capacity existed, but to expand agricultural output and exports. It was also needed to lengthen maturities of external loans in order to end the "invisible occupation" by short-term loans.[88] As to the means to be used, Luther remarked in conclusion that "the Young Plan clearly gives the BIS in Basel a leading role in this connection".[89]

A long letter from Moret to McGarrah, which also enclosed a detailed appraisal of the original memorandum, expressed all French reservations about the project.[90] While pledging his wholehearted support to the aim of restoring worldwide financial confidence,[91] particularly on sovereign debt, the governor of the Bank of France felt that the means proposed in the plan submitted to the BIS governors were not satisfactory. His main objections were that the French market could not absorb fresh bonds in such a large quantity, that French banks were in any case about to create a long-term credit institution themselves (albeit on a much smaller scale), and that the BIS would not be "acting wisely by giving its patronage to an establishment" that it could not then administer, being forbidden from doing so by its own Statutes. The attached document was more explicit and took the shape of an actual counter-memorandum. It argued that those governments and public bodies with a clear credit record were still able to borrow "on reasonable terms"[92] while those who were unable to do so had only themselves to blame, as they did not always meet the "obligations freely subscribed to in favour of their creditors".[93] Not only the practical feasibility but the very usefulness of the scheme was challenged.

French opposition torpedoed the Kindersley–Norman project – much to the disappointment of Luther, who saw no other way of accepting the Young Plan except "in the context of a master design for international cooperation, one of the basic features of which would be the provision of long-term capital to Germany".[94] The March 1931 Board meeting managed to leave the door partially opened to BIS involvement in long-term credit by deciding to employ part of the long-term funds at its disposal in subscribing to bonds issued by the recently established International Mortgage Bank of Basel. The Board also requested management to submit "practical recommendations as to the manner in which the BIS might best assist in the revival of long-term financing".[95] Towards that end, an ad hoc committee was appointed, chaired by Francqui.[96]

The Francqui committee met in Brussels during May and June. The first meeting reached the unanimous conclusion that the BIS should act as the central organisation for the various long-term credit institutions existing in each individual country (eleven such institutions had been counted by the committee in six continental European countries).[97] The June meeting, dealing more specifically with the Kindersley–Norman memorandum, was unable to reach a unanimous conclusion. A majority resolution recommended the creation of an international long-term credit institution along the lines of the U.K. proposal. In an attempt to pre-empt French objections, an annex was added to the resolution, making explicit reference to the bold scheme proposed at about the same time by the French government to the Commission of Inquiry for European Union.[98] The majority quoted the official French government document as saying that capital should flow from surplus to deficit countries and that the French financial markets were immediately ready to operate in that direction.

Undeterred, Farnier (of the Bank of France) put on record his own minority dissenting position, reiterating Moret's arguments and expressing reservations as to the way the majority, and Francqui in particular, interpreted the "constructive scheme presented by the French government".[99] A few days later, the BIS Board could only "take note of the report of the committee" and vaguely recommend further study of how best long-term financing should take place, "without immobilising in the present circumstances the funds at the disposal of the BIS".[100] Other more pressing and momentous tasks were now requiring the close attention of the Board. The issue of international long-term lending surfaced again in the following years, in conditions even less propitious for international cooperation than those of the spring of 1931. To avail itself of an institution for long-term credit, the international community would have to wait until the World Bank was established by the 1944 Bretton Woods agreements.

3.7   The Peseta

During the early months of its existence, the BIS was requested to provide advice, and possibly financial assistance, to the Spanish authorities contemplating the introduction of gold convertibility.

In the 1920s, central bank cooperation under the leadership of Norman and Strong was to a large extent focused on the reconstruction of the international monetary system upset by the Great War. In its most visible form, this took the shape of collaboration in the so-called stabilisation loans to countries committed to reintroducing the gold convertibility of their currencies. This action was crowned by fairly large, if ephemeral, success: in 1930, the only large European country off gold was Spain.

After restoring budgetary equilibrium in 1926 and thereby producing a substantial appreciation of the external value of the peseta, Prime Minister Primo de Rivera had been in no hurry to embark upon the monetary deflation needed to introduce convertibility. In 1929, a consistent slide of Spain's currency on foreign exchange markets led to the creation of a national committee of experts to study the country's monetary situation. As in many other similar circumstances, the debate followed a chicken-and-egg pattern: would exchange rate stabilisation precede or follow gold convertibility? The former deputy governor of the Bank of France, Charles Rist – summoned from Paris to give his expert opinion – did not doubt that the immediate introduction of the gold standard was the only appropriate cure for the ailing peseta.[101] Others, more prudently, thought that stabilisation should precede convertibility. Moreover, a sizeable part of public opinion did not particularly miss the gold standard, abandoned in the 1880s. In the end, the experts adopted a noncommittal wait-and-see stance. For a while, after de Rivera's resignation in January 1930, more pressing matters took precedence over monetary issues. In August 1930, however, a new minister of finance, Wais, gave the peseta top priority in his programme. As a first step, he appointed his own under-secretary of state, Carlos Bas, as governor of the Bank of Spain and charged him specifically with establishing closer contacts with central banks abroad in order, as he put it, to "break the circle of our isolation"[102] and to see what should be done about the external value of the currency. It is in this context that the Spaniards approached the new international bank.

A delegation from the Bank of Spain held conversations in Paris on 16–20 October 1930 with McGarrah and Quesnay, as well as with Moret.[103] Bas's main message was that the Spanish government, which severely criticised the dictatorship's monetary policy, was now determined to stabilise the currency. A programme to that effect was under preparation for submission to the Cortes, convened for January 1931. The Spanish delegation said they were not seeking credit but rather wanted BIS advice and an introduction to the main central banks of Europe. The first advice offered by McGarrah and Quesnay was both political and economic, as it regarded the stabilisation level. They argued that a newly established democracy was unlikely to be aided by a policy of currency revaluation and suggested that convertibility should be established between 40 and 50 pesetas to the pound, or approximately at the ongoing rate.[104] They then suggested that a programme for the introduction of convertibility be prepared well ahead of the Parliament's meeting.

Bas insisted on a press release stating that the BIS and the Bank of France had promised a stabilisation loan. McGarrah and Quesnay were, however, adamant in asking that a stabilisation plan be prepared first; they would then submit it to the main central banks, and only upon their approval would credit be promised and organised. The BIS proposed, in other words, to follow the well-established pattern of the 1920s, with the new Bank in the role of broker and facilitator. A press communiqué was prepared along the lines suggested by the BIS, and a meeting was convened for the following day to work on the blueprint of the stabilisation programme. During the night, however, the minister of finance arrogated directly to himself the preparation of the plan and made it clear that neither a press communiqué nor detailed discussion with the BIS on the subject was desirable at the moment. McGarrah and Quesnay could therefore only insist on the importance of creating a favourable psychological atmosphere and then reiterate the BIS offer to assist unofficially in the drafting of the stabilisation plan. At this point, Bas, expressing doubts about the possibility of making progress with a serious plan during the following three months of an election campaign, asked for a credit – backed by gold – to peg the exchange rate of the peseta between 40 and 50 to the pound.

Bas and his party then crossed the Channel and met with Norman, the man most experienced in stabilisation processes. The governor of the Bank of England urged them to avoid at all costs the request for credit: the Bank of Spain was sitting on a rather enviable[105] bed of gold, which it should use for keeping the peseta within fairly stable limits pending the legislation on convertibility.[106] Neither Norman nor people in Basel, however, fully realised that Bas was requesting a line of credit, in spite of his bank's large reserves, because of the high political sensitivity of gold issues back home. In particular, conservative public opinion in Spain strongly objected to any shipment abroad of the yellow metal. There was also, as already mentioned, widespread opposition to gold convertibility. An advance in pounds on the security of gold deposited with the BIS in the name of the Bank of Spain would require no physical dislocation of the metal and attract little publicity. After all, this was precisely one of the tasks the new international institution was supposed to perform on behalf of central banks.

Quesnay travelled twice to Madrid and, in November 1930,[107] submitted to the Bank of Spain a report in which he argued that the country was in an excellent position to embark on a currency stabilisation.[108] He pressed for a conclusion while the markets were still betting on the peseta,[109] despite the difficult political situation and even rumours of revolution. Personally well received in Madrid, the BIS general manager recommended various measures to prepare for stabilisation: announcement of a pre-stabilisation, concentration of all foreign exchange dealings at the central bank, and mobilisation of part of the gold reserves to support the external value of the currency.[110] Quesnay tried also to convince his hosts of the advantages of keeping a substantial part of their gold on deposit with the BIS but stumbled again on the political objections to gold shipments abroad. He left, however, with an impression of mutual goodwill. Even the Spanish king let it be known that he "had been honoured" to read Quesnay's report.[111]

In the following weeks, however, the issue of gold shipments became the main bone of contention between Spain and the BIS. The latter refused to advance pounds against gold already deposited with it[112] unless the Bank of Spain made additional gold deposits. At the beginning of December the peseta again slid downwards owing to renewed political turmoil and the lack of ammunition to sustain its price on the London market.

The BIS took more time to decide about granting a loan of £2 million guaranteed by Spanish gold in London, and insisted on additional gold shipments.[113] In the meanwhile, Mitzakis was sent to Madrid to get first-hand information on the situation and to provide advice. In spite of his presence there, relations between Madrid and Basel cooled.[114] Bas, himself in a strained position between the government and the opposition, interpreted the pressures from Basel for swift action and additional gold shipments as manifestations of a lack of confidence in him and as an assault on his bank's independence. "You forget", he told Mitzakis, "that Spain is a great country. I do not hesitate to fight the Minister and my own Board, but I cannot tolerate the BIS telling me what to do when the whole country is trembling and I am the general defending the Bank against the communists".[115] To restore direct communications with him, McGarrah had to enlist the good offices of Dean Jay[116] to intercede with the Spanish ambassador in Paris.[117]

The overly active involvement of the BIS in Spain did not please Norman either. He strongly objected to a suggestion by Basel that a senior figure now be sent to Madrid along with Quesnay.[118] By sending over very senior people, Norman argued, there was a risk that the responsibility for whatever was done there would be thrown back on the BIS itself. "The responsibility over a long period prior to stabilisation", the governor lectured the BIS heads, "is a domestic and political question and, judging from past experiences, great difficulties are liable to arise and mistakes are liable to be made, which cannot be assumed by the BIS or anybody in that position. By and large the Spaniards have to work out their own salvation and if there are two factions I should be sorry for the BIS to be openly siding with one against the other".[119]

Around the middle of December, political developments in Spain[120] made BIS management "all the more apprehensive about the situation and all the more cautious in arriving at commitments".[121] At the same time, the Bank of Spain ceased its interventions on the currency market – a move Basel could hardly disapprove of, given the circumstances.[122] Quesnay postponed a new trip to Madrid until things simmered down. In the meanwhile, Mitzakis was very active in the Spanish capital. He advised on the reorganisation of the central bank, including the creation of a research department, and arranged for a couple of its future members to spend time in Basel for training.[123]

The advance of £2 million was finally arranged on 26 December after a dramatic meeting of the board of the Bank of Spain at which Wais, the finance minister, produced a "royal order" for the shipment of an additional million pounds in gold to London,[124] as requested by the BIS. The BIS now instructed their man in Madrid to persuade Bas to get the stabilisation plan onto paper. A draft of a "confidential declaration" on stabilisation was finalised at the end of December, with inputs from Mitzakis.[125] The idea was that Bas would hand it over himself to the BIS governors on the occasion of their next informal meeting in Basel. The document stated that Spain would reform its monetary system (formally still on a bimetallic basis) by adopting the "gold bullion standard", after a transitory phase on the "gold exchange standard", at a somehow devalued parity relative to the prewar period. A reorganisation of the Bank of Spain was envisaged, and a de facto stabilisation prior to the legal one was outlined.[126]

However, uncertainty remained, almost until the last minute, as to the advisability of a journey to Basel by the governor of the Bank of Spain. Fraser, possibly due to Norman's previous hard stance, was hesitant about encouraging the visit. He now feared BIS involvement in a plan whose outcome remained in doubt. Azzolini and Beneduce made Fraser change his mind, arguing that the visit would oblige Bas to "get down to realities" while the BIS could make "all the reservations as regards not assuming responsibility".[127] In Basel, Bas met informally with the governors, handed over his confidential memorandum, and had technical conversations with Simon and others. He stressed his confidence in central bank cooperation and in the BIS, underlining his refusal of the loans offered to Spain by private bankers.

Soon after his return to Madrid, Bas was involved in negotiations, initiated by the minister of finance, with J. P. Morgan and other private bankers for a short-term loan covering about half the amount of a large long-term loan to be floated by the state. The plan was put on hold by a Cabinet crisis[128] that also led Bas to offer his resignation.

The new government having confirmed Bas in his position, it seemed for a while that strict and cordial collaboration with the BIS would continue. Quesnay was again received in Madrid at the end of February 1931 and again offered Basel's services to foster the long-delayed stabilisation. Negotiations continued afterwards for an extension of the BIS advance in pounds. On 26 March the Bank of Spain signed a credit contract with J.P. Morgan & Co. and the Banque de Paris et des Pays-Bas worth £15 million. On the following day, the BIS renewed its advance and added a further million pounds to it. Spain's monetary authorities could now avail themselves of an adequate amount of foreign currency to try and keep the peseta within a narrow corridor in preparation for stabilisation, even though the BIS had contributed only a small part of that amount.

Then, in April 1931, Alphonse XIII abdicated. The end of the monarchy ushered in a difficult and tragic period in the history of the Iberian peninsula. It is pointless to speculate about a counterfactual monetary policy in the absence of such a momentous political break. But surely the introduction of the gold standard in the spring or summer of 1931 would have been either impossible or a gigantic mistake.

The BIS's involvement in the attempted stabilisation of the peseta highlights both the limits of the international bank, in the early stages of its life, and the lines along which it might have evolved in the absence of the disruption of 1931–33.

Once the media spotlight had been switched off, soon after its creation, it became clear that the BIS was for the moment neither to be welcomed nor to be feared as an already all-powerful supranational institution. In the early months of its life, the Bank lacked both the resources – financial and human – and the prestige to act authoritatively in its own right. The Spanish authorities understood that only too well and approached the BIS as an intermediary to the central banks, particularly those of England and France. The BIS managers themselves were ready neither to play an autonomous financial role nor to change the well-rehearsed pattern of previous monetary stabilisations, requiring the participation of the central banks acting in concert.

At the same time, however, it was not by chance that the Spanish government called upon the BIS to act as an intermediary. Spain was a large and proud country that for some time had been at the margin of the international community. It would have been a poor political move for its new leaders to appeal directly to France or England: an international institution was likely to be more palatable to public opinion. If it proved difficult for the BIS to provide advice and still be seen as respecting the independence of the Bank of Spain, it would have been impossible to do so for a large foreign power. Given time – both for learning by doing and to increase its own resources – the BIS, as it was then taking shape, might have developed an autonomous operative style and gained recognition as an independent body to which individual countries could resort without fear for their financial independence or, simply, their pride. But the turn of events – which began to unfold with the Credit-Anstalt crisis of May 1931 and soon spiralled out of control – changed the history of the entire continent and with it that of the BIS.

FOUR

The 1931 Crisis and International Lending

4.1   The Background

By the time the BIS became operational, in the late spring of 1930, the world economy was sliding into depression. In the United States, output and employment had been on a downward slope since late in the previous summer. The Wall Street crash had shocked the financial world and set European stock exchange indices on a sharp decline. Investment and international trade were weakening on both sides of the Atlantic. And yet, for most of 1930 it was still possible to believe – as did most governments, central bankers, and economists – that the crisis was just the disagreeable downswing of an ordinary business cycle. Given the extraordinary length and speed of the previous American expansion, many felt that an adjustment was not only acceptable but indeed salutary. The optimists among international observers could actually perceive "a general feeling in most countries that by the end of 1930 the worst phase of the business depression had probably been reached".[1]

During the greater part of 1930, the majority of observers worried mostly about the unprecedented fall in commodity prices.[2] The built-in instability of the international payments system and the dangers inherent in the combination of high debt ratios with falling prices were, at first, overlooked. The American banking crisis of autumn 1930 sounded a warning on both counts. "The winter of 1930–31 shattered the last defences of optimism; and serious people began to talk of the impending collapse of civilisation."[3]

The economic history of 1931 is an almost uninterrupted catalogue of disasters. It was, first of all, the year in which the crisis became global. When governments and public opinion realised that falling incomes, prices, and employment were universal phenomena and that a mechanism was in place for the international transmission of the crisis, they almost naturally and unanimously sought refuge in nationalism and autarky. Although much lip service was paid to it, economic cooperation was abandoned precisely when it was most needed.[4] The United States led the way with the Smoot–Hawley Tariff Act, signed by Hoover in July 1930 despite pressure from economists and businessmen alike to veto the measure.[5] In 1931, most countries resorted to an array of protectionist devices and introduced administrative measures reminiscent of a wartime economy in order to control capital movements. Even the United Kingdom returned to protectionism, after almost a century of free trade, in 1932.

In the 1920s – as a result of U.S. prosperity, often contrasting with unsatisfactory economic performance in the Old World – increasing numbers of Europeans came to admire and sought to emulate American values and culture. The Depression diminished the cultural influence of the United States on Europe. The flaws of the boom years were now exposed: the fragility of a system of international payments largely dependent on private loans, unprecedented levels of indebtedness (both domestic and international), and unequal distribution of costs and benefits. The Depression exacerbated such problems rather than easing them.

As Costigliola noted: "Aside from its economic and cultural impact, the Depression bred political and ideological tension. In much of the world, hard times hamstrung leadership and threatened upheaval. Hard-pressed taxpayers were less willing to sacrifice for war debts, reparations or tariffs. Frightened investors shifted their assets from one country to another, aggravating balance-of-payments difficulties, deflationary pressure, and political turmoil. Political paralysis at home and in international conferences undermined the liberal doctrine of solution through compromise and bolstered the extremists' appeal. Economic experts lost credibility even as expertise became more crucial".[6]

As already mentioned, the second half of 1929 – that is, the months of the Hague Conference and its technical follow-up – provided probably the last window of opportunity for a serious international cooperative effort. Even so, in 1930 optimists could still point to a few favourable omens. The London Naval Conference (January–April) ended in partial success. The Allied occupation force evacuated the Right Bank of the Rhine, and French Foreign Minister Aristide Briand even circulated a memorandum on the creation of a United States of Europe. But the grounds for pessimism outweighed those for optimism.

The quest for a revision of the Versailles treaty in the sensitive areas of disarmament and reparations continued to dominate and poison international relations after the Hague Conference.[7] During the campaign for the Reichstag elections of September 1930, Chancellor Brüning declared that no German accepted the Young Plan.[8] He also hinted that Germany might not be able to meet the Plan's financial obligations. The Nazi electoral propaganda on the Versailles issue was, however, much more radical than that of the chancellor, whose position was also weakened by the deflationary policies hitherto pursued by his government. When the votes were counted, the National Socialists won 107 seats in the Reichstag (having held only 12 previously). In October 1930, Schacht visited the United States, giving as many as forty lectures all over the country. He repeatedly aired his well-known view that reparations, the lack of colonies, closed overseas markets, and (more generally) the provisions of the Versailles treaty were responsible for Germany's economic problems.[9] He told Americans that only by ending reparations could they protect their investments in Germany and keep a friendly, moderate government in office. It was generally accepted in Germany that the country's economic difficulties were "to a large extent beyond German control" because, "unlike any other country, [it was] weighted down by an artificial burden".[10] Minister of the Interior Wirth, supposedly the government member most able to feel the country's pulse, declared at a cabinet meeting that foreign policy was not in tune with the thinking of the people.[11] From the last months of 1930 onward, German diplomatic soundings for a Young moratorium made it plain that ending reparations was now an explicit goal of Brüning's policy.[12]

Only a few months after the Young Plan machinery – including the BIS – had begun to work, the position of the German government and its diplomatic moves met with different reactions in the capitals concerned. For Paris, a revision of the treaty was simply out of the question. It strongly objected even to convening the special advisory committee contemplated by the Young Plan and made clear that unilateral rejection would entail reoccupation. Brussels and Rome were also opposed to any revision of the treaty, albeit less implacably. London, never a hawk on the reparations issue, feared for its own foreign exchange position, a concern that grew steadily until September 1931. It therefore did not rule out a moratorium on reparations, which it hoped would protect the City's private investments in Germany – provided it was coupled with a parallel step on inter-Allied indebtedness. Washington was thus the crucial element in the whole situation.

In the United States, the brief but severe crisis of autumn 1930 exposed the fragility of the banking system. The big eastern banks were not affected, but it was plain that they would be vulnerable to a German default on private loans, an eventuality that a well-designed and carefully executed moratorium on "political debts" could possibly prevent. The leading private bankers, accordingly, made it clear to the Hoover administration as early as in January 1931 that they favoured a moratorium on reparation payments.[13] By then, Hoover was definitely "aware of the house-of-cards condition of German–U.S. finance".[14] Brüning even hoped for a conference on the issue under U.S. leadership, "but Hoover ignored this proposal".[15]

A plausible case has been made that, by acting in 1930, the Federal Reserve could have mitigated the Depression at home through massive expansionary open-market operations without endangering gold convertibility.[16] The Federal Reserve did not act – not so much because it was constrained by legislation that it successfully lobbied to have removed in 1932 but rather owing to an absence of understanding of the dangers of the situation or to the "diffuse power structure" of the Federal Reserve System itself.[17] It is, however, difficult to say whether and under what circumstances such an early unilateral action by the United States might have also avoided the Depression in Europe and, most specifically, in Germany.

The question remains: What if action on war-related debts had been taken six or nine months earlier than it actually was? One may plausibly argue that it might have entirely altered the course of history. Economic historians such as Kindleberger[18] have speculated about the likely outcomes of larger, swifter, and better-coordinated international lending of last resort to Germany in the heat of the crisis (the late spring of 1931), and this remains the crucial counterfactual as far as the history of central bank cooperation is concerned. Yet it may very well be that in late 1930 and early 1931 world leaders, and Hoover in particular, held the key to an effective prevention of the crisis. They were surely aware of the fragility of the situation, both political and financial, and were discussing the moratorium option. They did not act mainly because, in domestic political terms, the time was not ripe. Public opinion was not yet prepared for debt forgiveness. As Bennett put it, "It was necessary to let the Young Plan lose some of its newness, and to convince the world that Germany had made a real effort to reform her finances and meet her obligations".[19] In other words, it was necessary for the crisis to become more acute, to be almost at the point of no return, in order to achieve sufficient domestic support for the moratorium. As it turned out, no action was taken until the point of no return had already been passed.

Postponing the revision of reparations did not buy world leaders more relaxed international relations. On the contrary, relations became ever more strained in the first half of 1931. Tension was raised by the disclosure of plans for a customs union (*Zollunion*) between Austria and Germany, another attempt by the German government to notch up a foreign policy success. The issue had been on the back burner since the war[20] as the second-best solution after an as yet impracticable *Anschluss*. When the plan was made public in March, it immediately met with French hostility. The United Kingdom was not as sternly opposed to the project as France but urged the two countries to suspend their negotiations, pending international approval. Italy – seeing the customs union as a first step towards political union – was also opposed, in spite of its strained relations with France. Washington, on the other hand, approved of the Austro-German proposal as a way to rectify one of the Versailles mistakes and as benefiting "people who are good customers of ours",[21] but it disapproved of the political implications with which the Germans had charged the project.

The issue of disarmament, ahead of the ad hoc conference of February 1932, also remained at the heart of the tension between Germany and France.

This, then, was the state of international relations in May 1931, when the Credit-Anstalt collapse triggered a crisis that even today can still be regarded as "the mother of all financial crises". In the following pages we shall briefly review the role of the BIS in the period from May to August 1931, when Austria, Hungary, Germany, Yugoslavia – the whole of central Europe – were all engulfed by a wave of banking and balance of payments crises. Italy, whose banking sector was as badly hit as that of the other countries, escaped without banking panic or excessive capital flight thanks to a cleverly planned and secretly executed massive injection of liquidity to the ailing banks. On 21 September, the United Kingdom was forced by a major balance of payments crisis to abandon the gold standard.

A few days earlier, on the night of the eighteenth, the Mukden incident gave the Japanese the awaited excuse for their occupation of Manchuria, which was completed by early 1932.

4.2   The BIS as International Lender: The Credit-Anstalt Crisis

On 8 May 1931, Austria's largest bank – the Oesterreichische Credit-Anstalt für Handel und Gewerbe – called upon the government for help: "its 1930 balance sheet had revealed a loss of 140 million schillings, amounting to about 85% of its equity".[22]

The Credit-Anstalt had been established by the Rothschilds in 1855 as part of their Europe-wide strategy to challenge the Péreire brothers on their own ground, that of branch banking and long-term credit to the manufacturing and construction industry. Over the years, the Credit-Anstalt grew into a large universal bank with wide-ranging interests all over the Habsburg Empire. After the war, its links with the economies of the so-called Successor States remained as strong and as ramified as ever. After its merger – under government pressure – with the Boden Credit-Anstalt at the end of 1929, the Credit-Anstalt's balance sheet accounted "for about 53% of the balance sheet totals of all 25 Austrian joint-stock banks".[23] Over two thirds of Austrian limited-liability companies did business with, and were in various ways connected to, the Credit-Anstalt. The bank enjoyed an extraordinary international reputation: its shares were listed on twelve foreign stock exchanges, 50% of its capital was held abroad, and international bankers sat on its board, presided over by Louis Rothschild. In the second half of the 1920s, it borrowed on excellent terms from over a hundred foreign banks.

According to Schubert,[24] the Credit-Anstalt was not a "normal bank". It was certainly not normal as far as its international standing was concerned; in all other respects, however, it was pretty much the archetypal large Central and Southern European bank. It is, in fact, impossible to fully understand the character of the Great Depression in continental Europe – the transmission of shocks from the financial to the real sector and from one country to another – without due regard for the postwar evolution of a financial system in which universal banking had a pivotal role. Closely knit links between banks and commercial enterprises were the rule rather than the exception throughout Central, Eastern, and Southern Europe. They entailed complex maturity transformations of short-term liabilities into illiquid assets, opaque markets for property rights, a concentration of decision making, and an implicit assumption of a too-big-to-fail doctrine. The last – together with an incredibly loose grasp of the modus operandi of the European banking system – was one of the main reasons behind the huge volume of lending at relatively low rates to European banks by their U.S. (and, to a lesser extent, U.K.) counterparts in the 1920s.

It is perhaps worth mentioning in this context that, by the time the Credit-Anstalt problem became public, the Italian government and central bank had secretly and successfully dealt with the liquidity crisis of the country's second-largest bank, Credito Italiano. A government-controlled holding company took over the bank's illiquid assets (equity capital in large manufacturing and utility companies, as well as long-term credits). At the same time, the central bank provided Credito Italiano with an injection of fresh liquidity, though the bank was henceforth restricted to operating in the short-term capital markets, forbidden to hold equity capital in nonfinancial enterprises, and, in general, required to behave like an ordinary deposit-taking institution. The same formula would be applied, on a much larger scale, in the October 1931 rescue of the most important Italian universal bank – Banca Commerciale Italiana – from a liquidity crisis of its own.[25] Both institutions were larger than the Credit-Anstalt. These swift and secret moves probably prevented a run on banks; allowed for continuity of operations and reorganisation of the major limited companies; stabilised the financial system by erecting firewalls between banks, other financial institutions, and commercial enterprises; and spared the country a balance of payments crisis and currency depreciation. The price of success on these fronts was, in the short run, a credit crunch hitting small and medium-sized companies and, in the long run, a pervasive state presence in the Italian industrial sector and banking system.

Events in Austria followed an entirely different pattern in which the BIS played a pivotal role as lender of last resort.

Over the weekend of 9–10 May 1931, representatives of the Credit-Anstalt, the government, and the Austrian National Bank held various sessions – often even changing the meeting location to preserve secrecy – to draft a "rescue" plan for the country's largest bank.[26] It was agreed that part of the losses, then estimated at a total of 139.6 million schillings, would be covered by the state (29.6%), by the Rothschilds (12.0%), and by the Austrian National Bank (8.9%). The remaining losses would be taken care of by a devaluation of the equity capital and by drawing on reserves. The state, the Rothschilds, and the central bank would then recapitalise the bank by subscribing a total of 89.4 million schillings of new shares.[27] Given that about half of the bank's shares were in foreign hands, the generous "socialisation of losses" implicit in the plan actually meant a subsidy by Austrian taxpayers to foreign capitalists. These measures were motivated by fears of a systemic crisis – affecting both the financial and the real sector – and of capital flight, which was likely to be followed by suspension of convertibility. It seemed a fairly reasonable course of action for a small, relatively open economy which less than a decade earlier had been saved from hyperinflation by international intervention *and* which had a relatively large foreign debt and was therefore dependent on its recently reacquired standing in foreign financial markets.

Once made public, on 11 May, the emergency measures agreed upon over the previous weekend were fairly well received abroad.[28] Austrians themselves proved to be more sceptical of the merits of the "plan" and began withdrawing funds from the ailing bank.[29] In the early days of the crisis, however, the Austrian authorities remained confident in their ability to control the situation. The national bank opened an almost unlimited discount window to the Credit-Anstalt, even though the latter's paper consisted mostly of de jure or de facto financial bills.[30] The government planned to finance its part of the rescue operation by issuing Treasury bonds on the international market. In the meanwhile it sought to obtain a standby credit of 150 million schillings (about $21 million) from international institutions.[31] The sum was believed to be ample enough to cover the Credit-Anstalt losses, then estimated not to exceed 140 million schillings,[32] even though doubts were already forming about this over-optimistic assessment.[33] Norman, who had been informed of the situation on 7 May,[34] ahead even of the Friday meeting of the Credit-Anstalt management with the Austrian authorities, referred the latter to the BIS.

The official reason given for this shift of responsibility from individual central banks to the BIS by the main architect of central bank cooperation was that an international institution now existed whose purpose was precisely to coordinate such cooperation better.[35] In fact, Norman was aware that the Bank of England's own vulnerability had already been perceived by the markets[36] and probably wanted to keep his powder as dry as possible. President McGarrah of the BIS immediately set about sounding out the main central banks about a loan to Austria while at the same time keeping in close touch with Francis Rodd, a Bank of England official seconded to the BIS, who had already been sent to Vienna.[37] The heads of the main central banks, including Harrison, were asked on 14 May whether they would be willing to participate in an Austrian loan. Most of them, including the Federal Reserve Bank of New York, reacted positively within one or two days.[38]

McGarrah's coordination task was made easier by the fact that a BIS Board meeting was scheduled for 18 May (a Sunday), to be followed on the nineteenth by the first Annual General Meeting of the Bank. President Reisch of the Austrian National Bank visited Basel ahead of the meeting to contact individual governors informally. The Board decided that "the BIS, both for its own account and as agent for central banks which were prepared to participate, should organise a credit to the Austrian National Bank of 100 million schillings secured by the discounted portfolio of that Bank, and guaranteed by it".[39] It was made clear that the loan was being made to the central bank, rather than to the government, and that the BIS would accept no responsibility for the reorganisation of the Credit-Anstalt.[40]

The loan was approved and broadly organised within a week of the outbreak of the crisis. This was no mean accomplishment. Why, then, did it take another two full weeks for the agreement to be actually signed and for the money to be made available to the Austrian National Bank? The question is not trivial. The BIS has been accused of being slow to act[41] and therefore partly responsible for the situation deteriorating to the point where only the imposition of administrative controls on foreign exchange dealings could stop the run on the Austrian currency.

As the central bankers were gathered in Basel on 18–19 May, the BIS received a cable from the Vice-President and the General Manager of the Austrian National Bank to the effect that the Credit-Anstalt management was getting in touch with the main international bankers – Morgan, Excellenz Bank, Lazard, Dreyfus, and others – asking them to urge the banks in their respective countries not to withdraw funds deposited with the Credit-Anstalt.[42] Towards the same end, the Austrian National Bank requested central bankers to exert moral suasion on the banks in their respective jurisdictions. The BIS was asked to "draw attention of central bankers to the enormous danger, which would result from credit withdrawals for the whole monetary position" of the country: coordinated action by all the Credit-Anstalt creditors was necessary, in their own interest. A "panicky credit withdrawal" would inevitably result in huge losses for everybody. At the same time, creditors were promised "every reasonable sort of control they may desire".[43] It was a thinly veiled request for a standstill agreement. On the following day, Simon, one of the experts sent by the BIS to assess the situation and provide advice, forwarded to Fraser an optimistic cable from the Credit-Anstalt, which believed that foreign banks, satisfied with informal guarantees from the government and the Austrian National Bank, would freeze their credits. A syndicate was in fact suggested, and further moral suasion and secrecy were requested of the BIS and member central banks.

However, inducing major foreign creditors to agree on the proposed six-month moratorium on their credits proved to be more difficult than the Credit-Anstalt had thought. Large foreign banks had already withdrawn deposits, declined to renew credit lines, and cancelled acceptances.[44] At the same time, as a result of its liberal rediscount policy, the Austrian National Bank was rapidly losing gold.[45] Note circulation was still amply covered, but gold losses made the BIS and the central bankers concerned about the proposed loan security. They demanded a guarantee from the Austrian government, which it was not prepared to give. Believing the situation to be highly emotional and driven by a lack of confidence not justified by the fundamentals, the national bank pressed the BIS at least for a statement "that the central banks of Europe would at all costs defend the Austrian currency from depreciation".[46] While these issues were being hotly debated, the Austrian National Bank asked the BIS to rediscount with it, for eight days, bills for up to 30 million schillings.[47] The BIS made the money available on 22 May.[48]

On 26 May, the Austrian government came very close to issuing a decree for a general moratorium on bank debts that was similar to the one issued in 1914. Leaked to nearby countries, the news generated considerable apprehension. Fearing that the Austrian decree would prompt foreigners to withdraw deposits from Hungary as well, the Hungarian government hastily prepared to declare a moratorium of its own. Immediately, Quesnay in Basel and Rodd in Vienna pressed the Austrian government for an alternative solution to the moratorium, the consequences of which they feared would be disastrous. They proposed, instead, that the government guarantee the deposits at all Austrian banks. To encourage this change in the government's policy, the BIS declared itself ready to announce at once the finalisation of the agreement for the 100 million schilling loan.[49] The agreement was finally signed in Vienna on 30 May 1931 by the BIS, both for its own account and for that of the participating central banks,[50] and by the Austrian National Bank. This was a typical syndicated loan putting up to 100 million schillings at the disposal of Austria's central bank, to be drawn in one or more instalments.[51] The agreement would be in force for three calendar months. The gold clause included a provision, of dubious legal value, against the possibility of a gold embargo imposed by the Austrian government.[52] The BIS suggested, or rather requested, that Bruins – a Dutch monetary expert who had served as League of Nations commissioner with the Reichsbank from 1925 to 1930 – be appointed "Foreign Technical Advisor" to the Austrian National Bank for the duration of the Credit-Anstalt crisis.[53] On 1 June, an international committee of the Credit-Anstalt's foreign creditors was constituted in London and van Hengel, another Dutch financial expert also suggested by the BIS, was given full powers to act on behalf of this committee.[54]

The finalisation of the loan agreement failed to reassure the markets. The Austrian National Bank soon exhausted the credit line opened on 30 May. At the BIS Board meeting of 8 June, a proposal by Bruins was discussed (and in principle accepted by the governors) for a further credit of 100 million schillings, tied to the issue of Austrian Treasury bonds on the international market. On 7 June, at the unofficial meeting of the BIS governors, Quesnay eloquently put the prospective loan, which he strongly advocated, into the broader context of the Austrian situation.[55] Having spent five years in Austria in the early 1920s as assistant to the League of Nations commissioner, Quesnay claimed to "have a certain knowledge of the Austrian mind". Based upon that knowledge, he made three points.

First, the Austrians trusted neither their banks nor their authorities: announcements were therefore useless; at best they produced positive effects for only a very few days. Quesnay argued that "It is only when, by a success of the floating of the contemplated loan, tangible proof will have been furnished that the guarantee of their Government is ... susceptible of being negotiated ... that confidence will be reborn in Austria". Second, the next step to be taken to restore the confidence of the Austrian public was – according to the BIS general manager – to convince foreign creditors to leave their deposits with the Credit-Anstalt for a given number of years. Such a step "will be sure to make for calm in general". Finally, a revival of confidence amongst the Austrian public, Quesnay claimed, would come if they felt "that behind their National Bank there are other powerful forces, viz. ten central banks of Europe associated under the auspices of the BIS". We have here, clearly spelled out by Quesnay, one of the possible justifications for international lending of last resort: signalling markets that the international community takes a positive outlook to the situation and, in any event, will not allow it to deteriorate. Quesnay's assessment was based upon his previous, quite unique, experience with the League's experiment of financial stabilisation in Austria, "a country to play with",[56] managed entirely from outside. Lack of credibility of domestic institutions, according to this view, implied tying their hands and replacing them with strong, credible, foreign or international institutions.

We shall never know whether – as many others, including Rist, believed – the swift granting of a new international loan would have restored confidence amongst the Austrian public, because the loan never materialised. As already noted, the new BIS loan was made contingent upon the flotation abroad of Treasury bonds for 150 million schillings.[57] Negotiations on the latter began in Paris with the Banque de Paris et des Pays Bas immediately after the BIS Board meeting of 8 June.[58] Difficulties arose at once concerning the nature of the securities required by Paris, which Vienna was unwilling or unable to provide. At the same time, the BIS insisted on a clearly spelled-out state guarantee regarding the internal schilling depositors of the Credit-Anstalt. On 12 June it seemed that the negotiations with the French bankers on the terms of the Treasury bond issue had been completed; only the final approval of the French government remained. On the following day, however, the news from Austria was so alarming that the bankers would not proceed without a guarantee from the main powers like that given for the 1924 loan. Moreover, the French were no longer prepared to subscribe to the whole amount and demanded London's participation. Precious time was thus lost.

The "alarming situation" in Austria was due mainly to foreign exchange withdrawals from the central bank by the five main Austrian banks. Since the committee of foreign creditors had already been formed, a good deal of the demand for foreign currencies was related to the transfer of assets abroad by Austrian citizens and companies – including, in all likelihood, by some of the banks for their own account. Unable to control the situation swiftly, the national bank was again pressing the government for an internal moratorium. The representatives of the BIS, supported by Sir Robert Kindersley of the Foreign Creditors' Committee, again impressed upon the Austrians all the dangers they saw in the moratorium, particularly that of contagion to neighbouring countries. For a moment, on 15 June, it seemed that negotiations in Paris and London were about to succeed, and the national bank put on hold its request for an internal moratorium. In the days that followed, however, the situation precipitated into confusion. The Austrian government, weakened by ministerial resignations, got wind that Paris was now making its assent to the loan contingent on some unspecified political conditions. Miscommunication between the BIS and its representatives in Vienna created uncertainty about Basel's request for a guarantee of internal deposits, which seemed no longer to apply. The central bank's request for a moratorium could no longer be delayed, since the publication of the midmonth reserve statement was due on 17 June and showed a further loss of 111 million schillings. At the eleventh hour, an agreement with the foreign creditors was signed, but then the cabinet resigned amid political turmoil.

Thus, when a note arrived from Paris spelling out the political conditions for proceeding with the loan, the Austrian government could only reply that, being no more than a caretaker, it was not in a position to accept those conditions. However, it is doubtful whether any Austrian government – or, for that matter, any government of a sovereign state – could have accepted what amounted to an ultimatum. The French government, in effect, required a declaration by Austria that "it would refrain from taking any steps which might modify the existing political and economic relations of Austria". This amounted not only to giving up the proposed customs union with Germany but also to an actual surrender of sovereignty.[59] At the same time, France had decided to send a committee of inquiry to the Central European countries, including Germany, and to request a study by the League of Nations on the Austrian situation.

The financial diplomacy so patiently and carefully crafted in the preceding weeks by the BIS officials in Vienna was in shambles. The second BIS syndicated loan was conditional upon the successful international flotation of Treasury bonds, which political vetoes now made impossible. Nothing further could be done by way of international cooperation. The moratorium again seemed inevitable. At this point, the Bank of England alone stepped in by offering an advance of 150 million schillings for seven days, renewable, as a bridge pending the flotation of an equal amount of Treasury bonds. This, however, proved ever more difficult to arrange as the Austrian external position continued to deteriorate. Negotiations with Société Générale de Belgique and some Swiss banks fell through "owing to the latter backing out".[60] Around mid-August, the Austrian government approached the League of Nations for advice and financial assistance,[61] again with little success. By that time, however, withdrawals both from commercial and savings banks and from the central bank had diminished substantially, and on some days even ceased altogether. By then, the BIS's main task had for some time been that of an adviser. It advocated higher discount rates and, during a mid-July emergency, even a general bank holiday. The new government and the central bank resisted both suggestions.

Repayment of the BIS loan was due at the end of August. At the same time, the Bank of England, itself under heavy pressure, now wanted to reduce its exposure in Vienna, having renewed the June loan for several weeks. London moved first, reaching an agreement on 15 August on repayment of one third of its outstanding balance by the end of August. The BIS at first tried to obtain an additional gold security on its own loan from the Austrian National Bank, but the request was received unfavourably by private creditors, who had reached an agreement on a very slow reimbursement of their own credits. They threatened to reopen negotiations. At this point, the BIS and the Bank of England decided to cooperate in proceeding step by step with the demobilisation of their respective loans, after a first repayment of 50 million schillings to London and 10 million to Basel. The two loans were renewed for the remaining amounts until 16 October 1931.

Austria continued to haemorrhage gold, although less rapidly than before. The fragility of the situation was reflected in the markets' reaction to an attempted putsch, which was "treated in the Vienna press as opéra comique"[62] and rapidly quashed by the government, but nevertheless resulted in the stepping up of gold withdrawals from the national bank.

The situation took a decisive turn only with the introduction of exchange controls on 9 October.[63] Immediately, the Austrian National Bank became more assertive with its foreign creditors, asking the BIS again to renew its credit, the repayment of which was due shortly. It claimed that the new foreign exchange regulations would "show their influence with an influx of foreign exchange". At the same time, it warned that "a negative attitude in the question of renewal of your rediscount must necessarily create a situation in which we could see no way out but [to] leave the gold standard".[64]

Slowly, a new equilibrium was reached. After losing 67% of its gold and foreign exchange reserves in 1931, the Austrian National Bank lost another 38% in 1932, to a level of just about $29 million (from $143 million at the end of 1930). The trend was reversed in 1933 and continued to improve thereafter.[65] In July 1932, the League of Nations sponsored an internationally guaranteed loan of 300 million schillings (about $40.5 million) to Austria. However, it took more than a year for the money to actually be raised, and then it was mainly used to pay back the 1931 short-term loans.[66]

4.3   Lending to Hungary, Yugoslavia, and Danzig

Besides Austria, during 1931 the BIS provided "crédit de secours"[67] to Hungary, Yugoslavia, Danzig, and, of course, Germany. Before turning to Germany, a brief assessment of the BIS's lending to smaller countries is in order so as to complete the picture of its role in that eventful summer.

In April 1931, on the occasion of Bethlen's tenth anniversary as head of the Hungarian government, Tibor Scitovszky wrote a paper praising the extraordinary economic progress made by the country during its short history as a fully independent state, considering its miserable conditions at the time of the Trianon Treaty. He pointed particularly to the following achievements: 500,000 hectares of land had been reclaimed; the production of cereals had increased by 40% and that of pig iron by 360%, the state budget was in equilibrium, and the gold standard had been maintained. Although Hungary was not immune from the international crisis, Scitovszky concluded, sound economic policies had saved the economic life of the country "from severer shocks".[68] The timing of these optimistic comments was, however, unfortunate.

In the second half of the 1920s, a considerable amount of foreign capital had flowed into Hungary, attracted by excellent returns. Already in 1928, however, the government reserved the right to approve and control lending by foreigners, a sign that the potential dangers of the situation had to some extent been identified. But for a while things continued as before, with little or no government regulation of capital markets. Predictably enough, in 1931, as soon as the difficulties of the Austrian Credit-Anstalt were made public, the demand on the central bank for conversion of pengös into gold or other currencies skyrocketed, threatening convertibility and requiring international attention. In the following months, events took a turn that in most respects followed the Austrian blueprint.

The National Bank of Hungary first turned to the Reichsbank, which provided a short-term facility of $5 million (28 million pengös). This line of credit was rapidly exhausted. On 4 June, the Hungarian central bank approached the BIS to obtain a line of credit of up to $8 million. The BIS acted immediately, ahead of the Board meeting, and on 5 June put $5 million at the central bank's disposal[69] while hastily dispatching R. H. Porters to Budapest. As the flight out of the pengö continued, the BIS organised a syndicated three-month loan of $10 million to Hungary.[70] This too was virtually exhausted even before it was issued,[71] and the BIS opened negotiations for yet another loan, which was intended as a bridge pending the international flotation of Hungarian Treasury bonds for $15 million. France, however, declined to participate. Eventually the loan, reduced to $11 million, was subscribed by five central banks and by the BIS itself.[72]

In July, the situation in Austria and the increasingly distressing news from Germany further heightened uncertainty about Hungary, as if its own problems were not acute enough. The country's most important bank, Ungarische Allgemeine Creditbank, was known to be in a precarious liquidity situation. Here too the main problem was a maturity mismatch between short-term liabilities, in large part external, and long-term (frozen) assets. As in the Credit-Anstalt case, the central bank could do nothing but discount bills that its own statutes did not allow it to rediscount.

On 11 July the government, having obtained full financial powers from Parliament, authorised the creation of a syndicate of local banks – led by the Pester Ungarische Commercial Bank – to float £7 million of Treasury bonds on the international market. The syndicate was also charged with the reorganisation of the ailing Ungarische Allgemeine Creditbank and with engineering a standstill agreement with the latter's foreign creditors. These measures did not have time to produce the desired effect. The news of the Darmstädter und Nationalbank crisis and of the German moratorium led to the proclamation of an extraordinarily long bank and stock exchange holiday in Hungary from 14 July to 14 August.[73]

The bank holiday bought precious time for the negotiation of both the international Treasury bond issue and a standstill agreement with foreign creditors. Neither yielded entirely satisfactory results. Only £5 million of Treasury bonds were subscribed, mainly in France. Negotiations with foreign creditors, complicated by rumours of currency devaluation,[74] were still under way when banks were allowed to resume business and dragged on afterwards.[75] Foreign exchange controls were introduced, while at the same time the government extended its own gold guarantee to foreign creditors.[76]

After the summer, the BIS-syndicated credits to Hungary were renewed periodically, as were those to Austria and Germany. In early September,

Hungary's outstanding debts to the BIS and the participating central banks were reduced by 20%. The remaining credit of $20.8 million was renewed to the end of the year,[77] and then several more times until June 1933, when negotiations began for consolidation. A final agreement was reached in October of that year.[78]

The financial situation in Hungary remained precarious. The façade of the gold parity of the pengö could only be maintained thanks to administrative controls on capital movements and foreign exchange transactions. A mission of the League of Nations sent to Hungary in September 1931 published a rather gloomy report on the financial and economic situation, only five months after the publication of Scitovszky's upbeat paper. According to the League's calculations, the cost of servicing Hungary's foreign debt was equal to about 10% of the country's national income.

In the summer of 1931, the BIS was also instrumental in arranging credit lines to Yugoslavia and to the free city of Danzig. The new Balkan kingdom was the last of the large European countries to introduce gold convertibility, in May 1931. In fact, the proceeds of the Yugoslavian stabilisation loan did not reach Belgrade until June. Yugoslavia's external financial situation was, however, less precarious than Austria's and Hungary's in that the flow of private capital had been relatively modest for most of the 1920s, also a result of exchange rate instability. Although the central bank's gold reserves were relatively slim, German reparations were by and large sufficient to cover the service of the external debt and the trade deficit. Hence it was the announcement of the Hoover moratorium that threatened a currency crisis and endangered the newly established gold convertibility.

A BIS representative, Bolgert from the Bank of France, was sent to Belgrade in early July to assess the situation. He recommended the granting of a credit to the central bank as a buffer to make sure that Yugoslavia would be spared contagion from the crisis in neighbouring countries.[79] Within a few days, the BIS and the Bank of France arranged a $3 million loan to the Yugoslav central bank, thanks to which its July statement could show a 37.8% gold coverage of circulation.[80] The BIS representative suggested strengthening the position of the dinar through a substantial increase in the discount rate. This proved to be politically impossible. The Hoover moratorium produced the expected negative effect on the balance of payments and the central bank's reserves. The withdrawal of deposits from commercial and savings banks, though steady, was not dramatic. Under the circumstances, the central bank applied for an extension of the BIS credit. The final reimbursement did not take place until April 1934.

A small credit (of only £150,000) granted to the free city of Danzig by the BIS and the Bank of England in July 1931 fared rather better: it was paid back a few days in advance of its due date.

4.4   The BIS and the German Financial Crisis

It is hardly surprising that an enormous literature exists on the 1931 German crisis. The implications of the most extreme counterfactual – that, in the absence of a crisis, Hitler might not have gained enough votes to become chancellor in January 1933 – are such that crisis management, both domestic and international, has attracted enormous scholarly attention.

Needless to say, even a cursory review of the events of that summer, let alone of their interpretation, largely exceeds the scope and aims of this volume. As in the case of Austria and the other countries, what follows is strictly confined to a summary of the circumstances that led to direct involvement by the BIS and the main central banks.

Albeit on a much larger scale, Germany's banking structure and financial position were in most respects similar to Austria's. Universal banking, with the attendant maturity mismatch of assets and liabilities, was the rule rather than the exception – especially (but not exclusively) in the case of large institutions. In the second half of the 1920s, banks had steadily increased their foreign short-term exposure, especially to the United States and the United Kingdom.[81] By 1930, Germany's total foreign indebtedness, as assessed by the Wiggin Committee (see Chapter 5) exceeded 25 billion Reichsmarks (RM), or about 35%–40% of the country's GNP. Of this, more than 10 billion RM was held short-term.[82] "Germany's transfer liability for interest on private debt had reached 1.4 milliard RM, not far short of the Young annuity".[83] Net withdrawal of foreign deposits began in 1930, contributing to an unwelcome contraction of the money supply,[84] but did not snowball until spring of the following year. It is impossible to know how far Germans themselves were behind the capital flight to the safer havens of Zurich and Amsterdam, but their contribution was surely far from negligible. Both Germans and foreigners felt the uncertainty created by the September 1930 Reichstag elections that had given one third of the seats to the extreme right and left, leaving an unmanageable majority in between that gave Chancellor Brüning no option but to rule by decree.

The Credit-Anstalt crisis added economic to political uncertainty.[85] Capital flight from Germany increased. By the last week of May, central bankers, concerned about the Austrian crisis, began to worry about Germany as well.[86] Matters did not come to a head, however, until 6 June, when Brüning declared that he doubted Germany's ability to meet the next instalments of the Young payments, due at the end of the month. Brüning's move was not unexpected: in the early months of 1931, New York bankers – increasingly concerned about a possible German move on reparations – had repeatedly tried to convince Berlin that default was not to be contemplated, since it would adversely affect Germany's creditworthiness.[87] The chancellor, however, was probably still convinced that he could get out of reparations while at the same time reassuring markets that private debts would be honoured to the last penny.

Despite Brüning's tight fiscal policy, the Reich's budget remained in deficit. New taxes were imposed and civil servants' salaries reduced, along with unemployment benefits. On 13 June the discount rate was raised from 5% to 7%. These measures did not stem the capital flight, and in June the Reichsbank lost about $250 million in gold and convertible currencies – over a third of its total reserves.[88] Worse still, a run on banks set in. In one month, the Darmstädter und Nationalbank lost almost 41% of its deposits, Dresdner almost 11%, and Deutsche Bank over 8%.[89] On 19 June, the Reichsbank introduced credit restrictions while Reichsbank Vice-President Dreyse telephoned London to sound out the Bank of England on the possibility of an international loan to Germany's central bank. He expressed "a preference for arranging such credit bilaterally between central banks rather than leaving it to the BIS".[90]

On the following day, 20 June, Hoover announced to the world his proposal for a one-year moratorium on all political debts (deriving from both reparations and wartime inter-Allied indebtedness). This so-called Hoover declaration possibly provided the last, brief window of opportunity for effective international cooperation to mitigate the disastrous effects of the German crisis. For a few days, Hoover's announcement eased the pressure on the German currency, buying governments and central bankers valuable time to arrange the necessary financial backing for the moratorium.[91] Unfortunately but not surprisingly, the opportunity was seized to only a limited extent.

On 22 June, Luther himself approached Norman for a short-term loan of $100 million to cover the minimum reserve requirement between 23 June and 16 July.[92] The Bank of England, itself walking on thin ice and concerned about a possible domino effect of the German crisis, gave a positive response. Its only condition was the participation of the Federal Reserve Bank of New York, which in turn required that France be involved.[93] On 23 June, the Board of Governors of the Federal Reserve Bank of New York approved the loan. At the same time, Harrison got in touch with McGarrah and the two agreed that participation of the BIS was desirable, in spite of Norman's scepticism.[94] A three-week $100 million credit was negotiated in London[95] by Vocke for the Reichsbank. The Bank of England, the Federal Reserve Bank of New York, the Bank of France, and the BIS each put up an equal share. The credit was repayable in three weeks (i.e., on 16 July).

The credit agreement was actually finalised only two or three[96] days after Luther's request. Considering the need to coordinate three central banks and to get the green light from their respective governments, it was a speedy move. After that, however, two crucial days were lost in coordinating the press communiqués to be issued by each participating central bank.[97]

The three-week credit was not announced in Basel until 26 June. By then, gold losses from Berlin had resumed owing to uncertainty about the French position on the Hoover moratorium.[98] The haemorrhage continued unchecked, so that by the end of the month the Reichsbank reserve ratio barely met the 40% legal requirement.

Franco-U.S. negotiations on the moratorium in Paris dragged on for more than two weeks after Hoover's declaration. Commenting on the situation, Norman told Harrison: "The delay in Paris is becoming critical in Berlin. The French can afford to wait, but Berlin cannot, as it is being bled to death in the meantime". Harrison felt that "Much of the good that could have been accomplished by Mr. Hoover's proposal is being lost by the delay and the resulting withdrawals from various countries in Europe, especially Germany – the country which Mr. Hoover intended primarily to help". As central bankers, both men had no doubt that in these circumstances speed was of the essence, but they felt powerless because details about the moratorium (which they regarded as marginal) were considered of great importance by the Treasuries.[99] On 5 July, Luther wrote to McGarrah that the international credit was completely exhausted, the reserve ratio had fallen below 40%, and Germany could not meet the Young payments due on 15 July. The Reichsbank therefore introduced further restrictions on credit.[100]

Only on 6 July did France finally agree to the moratorium, provided that the Young Plan obligations were not repudiated. A compromise solution was found whereby Germany would pay the unconditional part of the Young Loan, which would then be immediately re-loaned to the German Railways.

By the time the moratorium was finally agreed upon, the situation in Germany was getting out of control, mostly due to the eruption of a banking crisis that had long been simmering on the back burner. We shall discuss in the next section whether swifter, larger, and less politically conditioned international lending would have made a difference to the subsequent unfolding of events. In this brief chronology of Germany's summer of 1931, suffice it to say that – from this moment onward – the position of central bankers was more and more that of helpless onlookers than of significant players. They saw the reason for their being gradually sidelined in the increasingly political nature of the crisis and of its solutions. The illusion they naïvely nurtured at Baden-Baden of keeping politics out of the way was evaporating in the heat of the summer of 1931. But the intricate interplay of international and domestic politics was only one of the reasons why international central bankers no longer held the key to the solution of the crisis, if they ever had. The nature and dimension of the crisis were by then such that only Germany could help itself out of the mess. And it could do so by taking those very measures – such as bank holidays, debt moratoriums, and foreign exchange controls – that international cooperation was intended to avoid.

Speculation about troubled banks, in particular small savings banks involved in municipal finance and the large Darmstädter und Nationalbank (Danat), had appeared in the press since the beginning of June.[101] We have already mentioned the considerable size of deposit withdrawals throughout that month. Danat was targeted in particular because of its involvement with Nordwolle, a large and ailing textile group.[102] At the beginning of July, Danat's refusal to renew a loan to the municipality of Berlin fuelled new speculation about the liquidity of its assets.

While disclosing that it had discussed the problems of a major bank in difficulties, the "Reichsbank did nothing to make its credit rationing milder".[103] At this stage the central bank was still reluctant to take full responsibility for lending of last resort to large banks. According to James, both the German chancellor and the Reichsbank president worked on the assumption that the banking sector itself would take care of its weakest members and not allow a large credit institution to fail.[104] This was a gross misreading of the situation. As most similar cases (including the 1931 Italian banking crisis) suggest, stabilising action from within the banking system was unlikely to take place. In both the German and the Italian cases, a number of factors prevented emergency lending from private banks. Even under normal circumstances, in the absence of coordination or at least of freely provided information from a central institution, a Prisoner's Dilemma arises whereby individual banks do not supply needed liquidity to an ailing member of the system. And the 1931 situation was anything but normal. Liquidity was not plentiful and individual banks tried to conserve their resources, fearing further withdrawals of deposits. At the same time, while gambling with a systemic crisis, they actually stood to gain from the disappearance of a large competitor. Moreover, the Austrian case seemed to indicate that the

Credit-Anstalt's problems began precisely when it gave in to government pressure to step in and rescue the Boden Credit-Anstalt. The Austrian crisis also showed that forecasts about the total amount of a given bank's liquidity needs could be made, if at all, only from within the bank itself.

Whatever the reasons, help from within the system did not materialise. The run on banks intensified from the first week in July onwards, while capital flight continued. Gold drawn from the Gold Discount Bank, a dormant institution linked to the central bank, was soon exhausted. The Reichsbank's currency/reserve ratio dropped below the 40% statutory threshold,[105] in spite of its continuation with the policy of credit rationing. It is against this background that Luther undertook his well-known and well-dramatised tour of the European capitals to rally support from central banks and obtain new credit lines. Before leaving Berlin on 8 July, the Reichsbank president announced that a standby guarantee loan to the Gold Discount Bank had been arranged by prominent members of the German business community, conditional upon the help and cooperation of foreign central banks in the form of a new loan.[106] As Bennett puts it: "The Germans were serving notice that failure to meet their wishes would mean disaster – and they were thereby making disaster all the more certain if the failure took place".[107]

On 9 July, Luther flew to London just to meet Norman at Victoria Station on his way to the monthly meeting in Basel. The two men sat on the train discussing Germany's economic situation. According to Luther's account,[108] Norman was convinced that only negotiations between the governments could restore market confidence – leaving the impression that, as a central banker, he now felt powerless. He also hinted that the U.K. government might be ready to lend an ear to any request for help from the Reich's chancellor. He finally said that in his opinion only a further worsening of the situation in Germany would bring "the French to reason". On 10 July, Luther was in Paris to meet with Flandin and Moret, but he managed to secure a French commitment only to a renewal of the BIS central bank credit expiring on 16 July, to be discussed in Basel on the following days. For the rest, the French were adamant with their guest that only an improvement of the relations between the two countries could open the door to the granting of new credit lines.[109] In practice, they made credit conditional upon concessions regarding the proposed customs union with Austria, disarmament (in particular, abandonment of the project for the so-called pocket battleship), and the renunciation of German claims to the "Danzig corridor". At this point, instead of travelling to Basel as originally planned, Luther went back to Berlin, where the crisis was at any moment expected to explode into general panic and possibly revolution.

During an emergency cabinet meeting on 11–12 July, the German government again appealed for help in telegrams to Washington, London, Rome, and Paris. After a number of consultations, the U.S. authorities took the position "that Germany should first undertake credit restrictions" and "present a concrete proposal to the heads of the various central banks assembled in Basel".[110] The German government finally decided that Danat should close its doors while the government itself guaranteed its deposits. On the following day, a general bank holiday was declared.[111]

Luther, exhausted, had tried unsuccessfully to convince his central bank colleagues to move the BIS meeting to Berlin. On 13 July, he travelled to Basel but made a poor showing.[112] His fellow central bankers were, in any case, in a gloomy mood themselves. Norman felt that Germany needed "a credit but that the situation [was] so much political that he [questioned] how it [could] be handled". McGarrah, for his part, considered that there was nothing to be done at the moment but "await developments, especially until we can see what is being done in Berlin". Even before the meeting started, Norman was against "the Board of Directors of the BIS taking any action".[113] The only concession Luther was able to take with him from the BIS was a three-week renewal of the previous credit.

In the days that followed, the Americans and the French continued to press for tighter credit controls. The Reichsbank discount rate reached as high as 15% at the end of July, while the reserve ratio was allowed to drop below the 40% threshold.

As Germany continued to press for a large international credit, Hoover revived an earlier proposal and urged the British to summon a conference of ministers in London to try and overcome the deadlock. A hastily convened London conference (20–23 July) did not succeed in creating a more favourable political climate for cooperation. France offered a $400–$500 million loan as a quid pro quo for the aforementioned political concessions, to which no German government could possibly agree. At the end, "if none of the governments, excepting perhaps the American, could get its own way, at least they were able to block each other's path. And where U.S. aims succeeded, it was because they represented little but resignation, the least common denominator. When all was over, the situation had changed, but to no one's advantage. The Germans failed to get a credit, the French failed to get concessions, the U.K. Treasury failed to get permanent revision [of the Versailles treaty] and, one might add, the U.S. lenders failed to get their money back".[114] The only practical result to come out of the London Conference of July 1931 was a request to the BIS to convene a committee of experts, later known as the Wiggin Committee, to assess the actual economic situation in Germany and its capacity to pay and then to make recommendations accordingly.[115]

Brüning's later comment, with hindsight, was that the crisis of July 1931 – and, in particular, the steadfast attitude of his government in the face of adversity – did eventually yield positive results for Germany, as it ushered in the beginning of the end of reparations and made the world realise that Germany would not give in to political pressure, not even if sweetened by financial largesse; at the same time, a collapse of the German economy had been prevented.[116] There is more than a grain of truth in this, even though he should have mentioned the most crucial measure he took at the time: the introduction of administrative controls on capital movements. It is equally true that the crisis had to reach, or go over, the brink of the abyss before it was politically feasible to do what could have been done earlier at a much lower cost, and that recovery was engineered by the Germans without much support from the international community – but at the enormous cost of putting the country into Hitler's hands.

4.5   Assessing the BIS Experience as Crisis Manager

In 1931, the newborn BIS was at the heart of the first experiment ever of a multilateral attempt at managing an international financial crisis.[117] An overall assessment of this hardly successful experiment must be put in context, first of all by taking into account that Arnold Toynbee pronounced 1931, rather than 1914, as the century's *annus terribilis*.[118]

In retrospect, the impression of confusion and lack of direction one receives from observing international policy making in 1931 can perhaps be attributed to the fact that everything was in a flux in a year that turned out to be the watershed between two periods in interwar history. The year 1931 separated the 1920s, when attempts were made to re-create the pre-1914 open-market economy, from the 1930s, when faith was lost in the virtues of nineteenth-century capitalism and of internationally open markets. More than that, 1931 is the single year that most clearly illustrates the link between the two world wars. The depth and breadth of the financial crisis and the powerlessness of policy makers to prevent it, or mitigate its effects, stem directly from the mistakes made at Versailles. In many ways, everything that happened in 1931 is connected to 1914, or to 1919, in a sort of cast-iron "path dependence". The electoral success of the National Socialists was at least partly due to the frustration and humiliation felt by large segments of the German population as a result of the peace treaty in general and reparations in particular. Hitler's rising popularity created a climate of uncertainty that prompted capital flight from Germany, thereby jeopardising its ability to meet reparation payments and prompting further withdrawals of gold and foreign currency. Deflationary measures taken to reduce the haemorrhaging resulted in unemployment and social unrest that were at least partly responsible for the further electoral advance of the extreme right. The end result of this apparently unbreakable vicious circle was Hitler's final seizure of power and the introduction, almost universally, of some degree of autarky. The crisis of 1931, therefore, with its roots in the unfortunate settlement of the First World War, contributed in no small way to sowing the seeds of the Second.

If one takes such a broad view of 1931, the course of action pursued by the main central banks and BIS during the eventful months of May to September looks like a minor part in a drama where each player was acting according to a script written long before. France, the main culprit in much of the literature on the subject, was bound to pursue a policy, consistently maintained since 1919, of containment of German power. It was also the country that stood to lose most from the ending of reparations and that had least to fear from financial turmoil. The United Kingdom had lost its financial supremacy during the war – and with it its capacity for informal leadership. Moreover, the country was paying dearly for the mistake of overvaluing the pound in 1925. German democratic governments were pushed by a nationalist electorate to score a swift foreign policy success on the long-standing issue of reparations. The United States was also bound to act according to choices, made more than a decade earlier, that had lessened its influence on European affairs.

In these circumstances, all players made mistakes that have been pored over minutely by generations of historians and hence need not be reviewed here.[119] All in all, however, it seems hard to construct a counterfactual world where, in the absence of that single crucial mistake, history would have taken a different course. As mentioned previously, the last opportunities to mitigate the course of the international Depression were probably lost in 1930.

Against this background, it is not easy to keep the assessment of central bank cooperation, and of the BIS's action in particular, within the relatively narrow limits of the technical options open to these institutions. In the most authoritative history of the interwar economy to date, Eichengreen argues that only an extraordinary amount of international cooperation might have avoided the financial crises of 1931, since "the gold standard posed an insurmountable barrier to the unilateral pursuit of stabilizing action".[120] Adequate cooperation in this context meant not only the provision of enough international credit to offset the diminished credibility of the commitment to the

Table 4.1. *Central bank credits organised through or with*
the participation of the BIS, 1931

Austrian National Bank

Amount and date	100 million schilling syndicate credit, 30 May 1931.
Participants	BIS Sch. 40 mio.; FRB New York, Bank of England, Bank of France, Bank of Italy, and Reichsbank Sch. 7.7 mio. each; central banks of Belgium, the Netherlands, Czechoslovakia, Poland, and Greece Sch. 3.85 mio. each; the Swiss National Bank Sch. 2.25 mio.
Renewals	Nine renewals, normally for three months, between May 1931 and July 1933.
Reimbursement	Partial reimbursements in October 1931 (Sch. 10 mio.) and August 1933 (Sch. 50 mio.); reimbursement of remaining Sch. 40 mio. in September 1933.

National Bank of Hungary

Amount and date	$5 million BIS credit, 6 June 1931; $10 million BIS syndicate credit, 18–22 June 1931; $11 million second BIS syndicate credit, 8 July 1931.
Participants	BIS $9.1 mio.; Bank of England and FRB New York $5 mio. each; Bank of France and Bank of Italy $2 mio. each; central banks of Belgium, Czechoslovakia, the Netherlands, and Romania $500,000 each; central banks of Latvia, Poland, Bulgaria, and Greece, $900,000.
Renewals	Several renewals from 18 September 1931, normally for three months at a time.
Reimbursement	20% on all credits reimbursed in September 1931 ($20.8 mio. remains). Three credits consolidated as one for three years from 18 October 1933. Several renewals and partial reimbursements until January 1946. Remaining balance settled in January 1946.

Reichsbank

Amount and date	$100 million, 26 June 1931.
Participants	BIS, Bank of England, Bank of France, and FRB New York $25 mio. each.
Renewals	Nine renewals, each time for three months, between July 1931 and March 1933.
Reimbursement	Partial reimbursements in March ($10 mio.) and December ($4 mio.) 1932 and in March 1933 ($16 mio.); reimbursement of remaining $70 mio. on 13 April 1933.

Bank of Danzig

Amount and date	£150,000, 20 July 1931.
Participants	BIS and Bank of England £75,000 each.
Renewals	None.
Reimbursement	Fully reimbursed on 8 August 1931, before maturity date.

National Bank of Yugoslavia

Amount and date	$3 million credit, 31 July 1931.
Participants	BIS $1 mio. and Bank of France $2 mio.
Renewals	Ten renewals, normally for three months, between July 1931 and January 1934.
Reimbursement	Partial reimbursements in April 1932 ($2 mio.), January and October 1933 and January 1934 ($350,000); reimbursement of remaining $650,000 on 12 March 1934.

Note: "mio." = million, "Sch." = schillings.

Sources: BISA, 6.30 – *Granting of first credit of Sch. 100,000,000 to Austrian National Bank (May 1931)*; 6.31 – *Granting of credit to Hungarian National Bank (June 1931)*; 6.32 – *Granting of $100,000,000 credit to Reichsbank (June 1931)*; 6.33 – *Granting of £150,000 credit to Bank von Danzig (July 1931)*; 6.35 – *Granting of credit of $3,000,000 to National Bank of Yugoslavia (July 1931)*.

gold standard but also well-coordinated reflation. Action of this kind was beyond the power of even the most cooperative-minded central banks: it had to enjoy the full backing of governments for both political and technical reasons (the latter obviously relating to the need for coordination of fiscal and monetary policy). The central bankers of the time were perhaps not entirely able, intellectually and professionally, to comprehend the need for and the implications of wholesale policy coordination. However, they did come to realise that, from a certain moment (early to mid-July 1931), the key to the situation no longer rested in their hands and that governments had to take over. Nevertheless, central bankers had major responsibilities and opportunities in their own sphere of action that merit scrutiny regarding the BIS's first and only trial as international lender of last resort – or, if one prefers, crisis manager.

In assessing crisis management by international agencies, the timing, scale, and conditionality of the intervention must be examined.

The time component of international emergency lending is made up of two different dimensions: how early in the crisis assistance is offered, and how long it takes to be organised. As for the first, in the Austrian case there was no early warning of the Credit-Anstalt crisis, which nobody had anticipated. The offer of international support could therefore come only *post factum,* when the bank's predicament became known and credit was requested by the authorities concerned. The German case is more complex to evaluate in these terms. Capital flight had been plain for everybody to see for several months, particularly at times of electoral shocks, indicating that Germany's commitment to maintaining the gold convertibility of the mark was becoming increasingly less credible. Would an early international pledge to keep Germany on the gold standard have altered the course of events? Whatever the answer, it is clear that central banks – alone or through the BIS – could not have made a credible pledge of that kind, which would probably have succeeded only within a government-sponsored package that included some kind of reparation forgiveness. Moreover, the timing of intervention was conditioned by the need for all players to let the situation deteriorate to such a point that concessions on the Versailles treaty appeared unavoidable to their domestic electorate. This is the main reason why early action, which (as we have seen) was indeed contemplated, was in the end postponed until too late in the game. Technically, therefore, central bankers or the BIS can hardly be blamed for not moving to help Germany until June 1931: earlier intervention in the absence of full political backing would have been fruitless.

What about the other time dimension of international lending of last resort: the rapidity of its execution once requested by the relevant parties? Here again, on purely technical grounds, it must be recognised that the machinery of the Austrian and German loans was assembled quite swiftly. We have seen that the Austrian loan was agreed upon and organised by central bankers and the BIS in less than three days, and it took only a little longer to do the same for the much larger support offered to the Reichsbank. The existence of the BIS undoubtedly proved to be an advantage, in particular for the dissemination of information and coordination.[121] Any subsequent delays were of a political nature and only showed how illusory the idea of some of the BIS founding fathers had been that Basel would be a sanctuary where politics could be left outside the door. The renewal of the first credit lines was a more time-consuming business, but then timeliness was hardly essential. The granting of a second round of credits was caught up in political wrangling for which central bankers as such had little responsibility. When all is said and done, and taking into account that this was the first major experiment in multilateral crisis management, it is hard to find major shortcomings in the time dimension of its handling by central banks. In this particular respect, the existence of the BIS – inexperienced as it was bound to be less than a year after its birth – surely made a difference. This is especially true in the Austrian case. The BIS was instrumental in the immediate promise of credit facilities to the Austrian National Bank. Moreover, it was able to rapidly mobilise the time deposits of the Austrian National Bank, both those with the BIS itself and those with private banks (a technical function often overlooked but quite relevant in the early days of the crisis).

Was the quantity of ammunition supplied sufficient to successfully combat the crisis? Ex post the answer must be negative. Only credit lines several orders of magnitude larger than those initially made available to Austria and

Germany might have convinced markets of the credibility of the international commitment to the gold standard. In July, after the first emergency credits had been exhausted within a few days, new credits for much larger amounts did indeed become necessary. In the case of the Austrian loan, underestimation of actual needs was due mostly to an information gap. The main problems derived from the Credit-Anstalt's nonperforming or illiquid assets, and the BIS could at first rely only upon the information provided by the Credit-Anstalt's own management, the Rothschilds, the Austrian National Bank, and the government. All of them were responsible for the restructuring of the ailing bank and had large interests at stake; there was no reason to distrust the figures they provided. As soon as the emergency became known, the BIS immediately sent over experts to act both as fact finders and advisers (we shall discuss in what follows the merits of the advice provided). However, it took these experts a relatively long time to acquire first-hand information. The case of Germany was different. A balance of payments crisis due to capital flight had been under way for some time, and international credit to the Reichsbank had already been discussed (e.g., in the autumn of 1930); central banks should therefore have been in the picture as regards Germany's foreign indebtedness. In fact, the BIS and the central bankers concerned did not believe the June credit to be sufficient to restore market confidence. They saw it as an emergency bridge to buy time until the necessary political solution could be found.

No macro policy conditions were formally attached to the loan agreements, yet conditionality was clear, if implicit. Emergency (last resort) credit was arranged for the purpose of keeping the affected country on the gold standard. It was thus understood that the macro policy stance of the government and the central bank must be consistent with the aim of the loan. Informally, the central bankers concerned were not sparing with their advice. They consistently required the recipient countries to balance the state budget and increase the central bank discount rate. As Eichengreen puts it, policy advice was fettered by gold.

It has been argued that "ideology",[122] or the slavish adherence to the thinking of "defunct economists",[123] was the main reason for the gold obsession of central bankers during the Depression. And the cultural background and economic teaching with which policy makers had grown up undoubtedly played a role in shaping Depression policies. But there was a very good practical reason as well for doing whatever could be done, and being willing to pay whatever price was required, to maintain gold convertibility – namely, the protection of foreign private investments in Central Europe. High interest rates were consistent with the aim of avoiding inordinate capital withdrawals as much as possible, as were other informal conditions attached to the emergency credits. In particular, governments were firmly advised to refrain from imposing unilateral moratoriums and encouraged to offer their own guarantees for private bank liabilities, both old and new. The Austrian case illustrates the point well.

It is, however, at best questionable whether strict adherence to financial orthodoxy was the best self-interested advice to give in order to protect foreign short- and medium-term investments. Irving Fisher would shortly afterwards spell out the reasons why, even in a non-Keynesian environment, fighting deflation with deflationary policies was bound to be self-defeating.[124] In the case of Central Europe, the banking system structure made those reasons even more compelling. The fact that universal banks entertained long-term relationships with borrowers, through both lending and equity investment, implied a strict interdependence between banks and nonbank enterprises. The poor performance of the latter had a negative impact on the banks' balance sheets that would undermine depositors' confidence and threaten the banks' liquidity. The impact of deflationary policies on the corporate sector was therefore bound to compound the effect on the banking sector: higher interest rates might have had a perverse effect precisely on the depositors' confidence they were supposed to uphold.

The policy implications of the prevalence of universal banking in Austria did not escape some of the advisers sent to Vienna by the BIS. In a long report drafted on 2 June, Simon explicitly refers to the peculiarity (from an Anglo-Saxon standpoint) of Austria's banking structure.[125] Moreover, "In the case of countries whose mere existence is based on the confidence of foreign creditors, the country [can] hardly afford to leave an important private bank to its fate".[126] The reasons for "assisting at practically any cost and price a private bank" are even more compelling in the case of a bank that is "controlling and supplying with credit about three quarters of the Austrian industry and trade".[127] Simon argues that the failure of the Credit-Anstalt would have brought the Austrian economy almost to a standstill, "the more so as, in the panic that would have followed such a breakdown, the other private banks would not have been able to supply [the economy] with credit". Simon thus recommended that "in emergencies like the present one the central bank must not shrink from rapidly increasing the circulation in order to prevent the catastrophe of a big commercial bank", and argued that the BIS should offer its backing to that end.

A few days later, van Hengel, who represented the international committee of foreign creditors of the Credit-Anstalt in Vienna, provided a much more forceful and polemical analysis of the Austrian situation to both Norman and McGarrah. In explaining his reluctance to accept direct (as opposed to advisory) responsibility for the reorganisation of the Credit-Anstalt, he described the situation there in crude but realistic terms.[128] "The Credit-Anstalt problem is not the problem of reorganising a Bank under normal circumstances in the rest of the world .... Credit-Anstalt is much more a Holding Company of various enterprises than a Bank and the cleaning up is nothing less than re-organizing internal politics in Austria, foreign politics in Europe and stupid banking practices generally spread. Those practices were initiated and boomed by U.S. Banks with infantile knowledge of international banking and other conditions, and unhappily copied by a number of European banks, which thought that in the United States wealth brought wisdom along with it." But the problem was not Austria, or not Austria alone. "Finances now are the Western world over absolutely unsound because of the stupid financing by short term investments of long term capitalisation. This has led to a 'crise de confiance' [affecting] ... the whole of central Europe and probably the United Kingdom."

In van Hengels's opinion, there were only two ways out of the crisis: "a) Paying, which can be done by the respective Banks of issue parting with their gold and foreign exchange reserves .... None of those banks can meet 100% of the short-term indebtedness to foreign creditors, so that the BIS, and that will in practice have to be the United States and France, has to provide the balance .... If arrangements are half-hearted – of which I am pretty sure – withdrawals will continue. b) Stopping payments". Van Hengel's view was that agreements on debt restructuring had to be organised at once – not only for Austria, where the process was already nearing completion, but for Germany as well. Since German banks had no capital of any importance, "losses fundamentally ought to be borne by the creditors, even by foreign creditors. They may get State guarantees if they pay the price of acknowledging – in the shape of extension for long duration – that they invested long term and not for a short period". This was a reasonable (and not inequitable) proposal made early enough in the German crisis to have a chance of avoiding or mitigating the ensuing financial breakdown. But it was precisely the kind of advice that neither McGarrah[129] (nor Harrison behind him) nor Quesnay wanted to hear. Norman himself, who had the weakest position amongst the creditors, was not inclined to pay attention to suggestions of this kind. Moratoriums and standstills came a few weeks later, when the damage – economic and political – had already been done. In the end, private creditors lost most of their money anyway.

To sum up: Granted that the first experiment ever in multilateral crisis management by an international economic institution did not achieve its objective of protecting creditors by maintaining confidence in the international monetary system – mostly for reasons beyond the control of the BIS and the central banks involved – an assessment of the technical aspects of the experiment yields mixed results. The size of the resources available for emergency lending turned out, as many at the time predicted, to be utterly inadequate: only France and the United States could have provided enough ammunition to give a chance to the multilateral rescue of Central Europe but, for the reasons briefly outlined here, they stood aloof. For the rest, the timing component of the operation in assessing the situation and stepping in cannot be faulted: in fact, the existence of the BIS, inexperienced as it was, proved to be a valuable asset in speeding up the organisation of loans. On the other hand, the implicit conditionality attached to the loans (or, if one prefers, the policy advice provided by the BIS and the entire international financial community) was part of the problem rather than the cure. In this as in subsequent cases of international crisis management, the reasons for ill-advised conditionality were due partly to inadequate assessment of the situation, partly to faulty economic analysis, and partly to the weight of vested interests.

FIVE

The End of Reparations, the Gold Standard, and the 1933 London Conference

5.1   The End of the Interwar Gold Standard

Almost unnoticed at the time, the gold standard ended for practical purposes in Germany on 15 July 1931, when the Brüning government imposed its first administrative measures for "foreign exchange restrictions" – that is, limitations on the convertibility of the national currency into gold or foreign currencies. Hungary followed Germany five days later.[1] Foreign and domestic policy considerations advised against open devaluation, making it preferable to leave the government a large degree of freedom concerning whose money, and how much of it, was entitled to conversion. In the minds of their proponents, exchange controls also had the advantage of serving two purposes: the prevention of capital flight and the restriction of commodity imports.

Measures of the kind taken by Germany could not even be contemplated in the United Kingdom, whose political and legal tradition was, at the time, entirely alien to these German measures. Culture, politics, and the structure of the respective banking systems dictated the practical courses followed in the two countries to pursue the same aim: breaking their "golden fetters". As mentioned earlier, the pound had been under pressure from mid-1930 onwards owing to a weakening of invisible earnings – a traditional U.K. staple – and a slow but steady outflow of short-term capital.[2] The Austrian and German crises froze large amounts of U.K. foreign credits (bank deposits and reparation receipts): the debt crisis and the convertibility crisis were closely linked.[3] The option of applying the monetary and fiscal brakes was limited by the high unemployment rate that made such policies distasteful to the Labour government. International financial support – by then available only from the United States and France – came in the form of a small loan at the end of July 1931; further requests were politely declined by the Federal Reserve, "increasingly concerned about its own position".[4]

On 28 July, Norman collapsed from stress, took to his bed for a week, and was then ordered by his doctors to take a long holiday.[5] He remained abroad throughout the last phase of the sterling drama. At the end of August 1931, disagreement about how to handle the currency crisis led to the fall of the Labour government. It was succeeded by a national coalition government under the same prime minister (MacDonald) that included members of the Labour, Conservative, and Liberal parties. Plans for cutting expenditures (including unemployment benefits) and increasing taxes enabled the new executive to borrow a total of 400 million dollars in New York and Paris. But it was too late and probably too little to stop the capital flight. On his return voyage from Canada, aboard the *Duchess of Bedford,* Norman received from his deputies a puzzling cable stating "Old Lady goes off on Monday".[6] Only upon landing at Liverpool did he fully realise the meaning of the message: four days earlier, on Saturday 19 September, the decision had been made to suspend convertibility as of the following Monday. Some restrictions on capital movements were also introduced.[7]

As the BIS president later put it, central bankers around the world, and the BIS itself, "awoke to the realisation that the 'Gold Exchange Standard' was a misnomer; that in fact it was a 'foreign currency standard' concealing possibilities of grave financial losses. An embryo run was started on the Bank at Basel, which surrendered over 300,000,000 Swiss gold francs within a few days because central banks translated their reserves into metallic gold .... The policy of liquidity always followed by the Bank enabled it to meet the withdrawals easily".[8]

In the next weeks, and months, a number of countries followed the United Kingdom off gold, beginning – a few days later – with Norway, Sweden, Denmark, and Canada. In December, Japan suspended the gold standard, barely a year after its controversial reintroduction. Commonwealth and Latin American countries followed.[9] In December 1932, even the Union of South Africa, the world's most important gold producer, abandoned convertibility. Greece, Czechoslovakia, Yugoslavia, Latvia, Austria, Bulgaria, and Estonia did not formally devalue, following instead the German course of imposing limitations on capital movements: from the end of October 1931, the whole of Central and Eastern Europe, with the notable exception of Poland, had already de facto been off gold.

"At its height in 1931, 47 countries had been on gold. By the end of 1932 the only significant holdovers were Belgium, France, Italy, the Netherlands,

Poland, Switzerland, and the United States."[10] The last-mentioned, as we shall see, opted out in 1933. In the following two or three years, the "gold bloc" – led by France – held the banner of the old monetary regime alone.

By going off gold, individual countries regained control over their monetary policy. International coordination was no longer a precondition for reflation. To a fairly large extent, individual countries could move by themselves. Policy adjustment, however, was not instantaneous. Thus, "1932 may be styled a year of adaptation to changed conditions prevailing in the economic and monetary situation and one of some definite constructive effort".[11] In countries such as Germany, Italy, and the United States, the huge effort of reconstructing the banking systems was undertaken. The German financial restructuring involved the writing off of nonperforming assets and a substantial recapitalisation of the banks by the Treasury (ultimately by the Reichsbank). This accomplished, it was possible to reopen the stock exchange, which had remained closed for seven months. In Italy, similar results were achieved in January 1933 with the creation of the Institute for Industrial Restructuring (IRI). On 27 February 1933, the U.S. Congress passed the Glass–Steagall Act. The banking crisis, however, was not overcome until the new administration took office and its emergency measures were introduced.

Monetary policy responses to the new situation differed greatly from country to country. "Only in Denmark, Sweden, and Japan where the authorities moved decisively to expand domestic credit, and only in the United States, the Netherlands, and Switzerland, which were on the receiving end of international reserve flows, did monetary base raise between the end of 1931 and the end of 1932."[12] In most other countries, the opportunity for reflation was not seized immediately, either because the credit system first had to be restructured, or because of inflation fears, or because of inexperience. In fact, interest rates went down almost universally and continuously, but in most cases not far and fast enough to reflate the economy. Worldwide, prices and activity levels continued to decline throughout 1932.

In most countries, and in the world economy at large, the second half of 1933 marked the turning point in the recession. In the first months of the year, however, the gold standard produced its last major casualty in the form of a second and more severe banking crisis in the United States, after that of the autumn of 1930. As in most other cases, the banking and currency crises went hand in hand. The structure and organisation of the banking industry were partly to blame,[13] as were the diffusion and duration of the Depression. A liquidity crisis in Michigan drew funds from banks in neighbouring states, threatening their own liquidity position, and eventually spreading the contagion. As Eichengreen observed, "the Fed was sensitive to the banking system's need for liquidity. But by the beginning of March, its gold cover had fallen to 45%. Provisions for additional liquidity therefore threatened to breach the gold standard statutes and force the suspension of convertibility".[14] Insufficient lending of last resort to illiquid banks allowed the crisis to spread, thereby intensifying capital flight[15] and reducing the credibility of the gold-standard commitment. A vicious circle was established where expectations of devaluation exacerbated the liquidity crisis, further fuelling devaluation expectations. The long transition between the Hoover and Roosevelt administrations also contributed to market uncertainty. It had been known for a while that the newly elected president had refused to rule out devaluation explicitly as a tool for recovery and believed that a price increase of a considerable magnitude was needed to restore business confidence, particularly in agriculture. The banks' liquidity crisis came to a head precisely around the time of Roosevelt's inauguration. On 4 March the Federal Reserve banks closed all the leading stock exchanges. Two days later, Roosevelt issued a proclamation declaring a nationwide bank holiday to continue to 9 March, a deadline later extended.[16] A few days later, the president urged the Congress to pass emergency legislation "authorising him to regulate or prohibit the export, hoarding, or earmarking of gold or silver, and empowering the secretary of the Treasury to require the surrender of all gold coin, bullion, and certificates held by the public".[17] Abhorred "foreign exchange restrictions", so typical of financially weak Central European countries, were thus introduced in the largest and most market-oriented economy in the world. But they were at first used judiciously to avoid the impression that the gold standard had been de facto abolished. Licences to buy foreign currencies were granted liberally for "legitimate business purposes" and, for any purpose, to foreign governments and central banks, including the BIS. A degree of market confidence was actually restored: it was reassuring both to know that the executive now held enough power to act in a new emergency and to see that such power was used sparingly and judiciously. The banking crisis was halted. For a few weeks, gold actually flowed in again. Then a new confidence crisis arose in the second half of April, probably induced by market speculation on the president's intention to try and put an end to the Depression by raising prices to their 1929, or even their 1926,[18] level. Such a policy, if rigorously followed, was clearly incompatible with the convertibility of the dollar into gold. When legislation was introduced (the so-called Thomas Amendment) authorising "Roosevelt to stimulate inflation in a number of ways",[19] the dollar's slide accelerated and the president took the currency off gold by officially announcing, on 19 April 1933, that no further gold export licences would be granted.[20]

The participation of the BIS in the last chapter of the gold-standard history – the London Conference, the origin of the "gold bloc", its slow crumbling, and its eventual demise in 1936 – are the subject matter of the second part of this chapter and of much of Chapter 6. Before turning to gold again, however, we must see how the end both of reparations and of the gold standard affected the BIS (Section 5.2) and then go back to the summer of 1931 and see how the BIS became involved in the final stages of the reparations drama (Sections 5.3 and 5.4).

5.2   Facing the New Reality

The Hoover moratorium had a lasting impact on the BIS. A few months after its first anniversary, the new international financial institution was confronted with the collapse of one of the pillars of its very raison d'être. In the medium term, the end of reparations required a radical rethinking of the Bank's functions and role, a trimming of its staff, and an internal reorganisation. But it was probably the end of the gold standard, in 1931–33, that most affected the BIS's standing as well as its intellectual foundations.

The end of the complicated financial machinery of the Versailles treaty stripped the Bank of most of its financial functions as trustee and agent for reparations.[21] It was natural therefore for the Bank to emphasise that it had by no means exhausted its statutory objects, the first of which was defined in its Statutes as the promotion of "the cooperation of central banks and [the provision of] additional facilities for international financial operations".[22] The second Annual Report devoted a full chapter to "The Hoover moratorium and the Bank". It dismissed the impact of the moratorium on the regular business of the Bank – some 950,000 Swiss francs in forgone fees – as a "trifling sacrifice for the Bank to bear in the common effort to attenuate the burden upon the already overcharged exchanges of the current transfers".[23] More importantly, it claimed that "its effect upon the broader scope of the Bank's activities has been greatly to expand them".[24]

In the longer run this initial optimism was not to be entirely supported by the facts.[25] In the spring of 1932, however, the Bank had good reasons to believe that a lower volume of banking transactions would be more than compensated by an enhanced role as catalyst of international financial cooperation. "From a broader point of view," the report continued, "the real consequence of the moratorium was the utilisation of the Bank as a convenient centre to secure relatively quick action in the international financial sphere".[26] In fact, in 1931–33 the BIS was actively involved in setting up international committees and preparing economic conferences. The reasons for such activity, however, did not derive from a climate of international cooperation. On the contrary, they stemmed from the inability of governments to agree on meaningful collective action that resulted in deferring important policy issues to technical committees and further conferences. The end result of this situation, however, was favourable to the BIS insofar as it kept it in the limelight, showing the world that it still had important and new tasks to accomplish. In fact, the Bank's usefulness to the international community was never in dispute, especially as both reparations and the last-resort lending of 1931 left it with a number of delicate, if tiresome, duties to perform.

The London Protocol of 11 August 1931 provided the legal basis for the Hoover moratorium.[27] It contained a number of complex provisions related to the various loans and to the so-called unconditional part of the annuity[28] that required the trustee's attention, all the more so as tension and litigation ensued, complicated by currency devaluations.[29] As for the emergency loans of the summer of 1931, which had to be renewed several times, each of them required separate attention, both legal and economic, as well as a good deal of financial diplomacy.

The challenge posed to the BIS by the end of reparations was soon recognised and faced by the management of the Bank. Not so the subtler and potentially more dangerous threat to the very foundations of the institution: the end of the gold standard. In fact, the effects of the new international monetary conditions both on the BIS as an institution and on central bank cooperation at large cannot be overstated.

There were, first of all, legal and technical issues to be dealt with. As shown by the discussion in 1930–31 about new membership, the intention of those framing the Statutes of the BIS was that only central banks from countries on the gold exchange standard could be members of the Bank. At the time when the BIS became operative there were 47 such countries in the world, and the new international institution aimed at uniting as many of them as possible into a "gold club". If this was the guiding spirit of the Statutes, the letter was ambiguous insofar as they stipulated that new members should be from "countries whose currencies, in the opinion of the Board, satisfy the practical requirements of the gold or gold exchange standard".[30] It was, therefore, not necessary to amend the Bank's by-laws to adjust them to the new situation. However, de facto if not technically de jure, the new monetary regimes – based as they were upon floating rates and/or restrictions on capital mobility – were at odds with one of the fundamental provisions of the BIS Statutes. The technical problems to be dealt with after member countries came off gold were also numerous: the most important ones related to the exchange rates to be applied to transactions among central banks and to the gold clause, frequently not clearly specified in the loan agreements. In the end, solutions were found for the legal and technical problems, but they seldom fully satisfied all parties involved and at times contributed to the underlying tension in international relations that was inevitably reflected in the BIS Board and staff.

Ultimately, the major challenge posed to the BIS by the collapse of the gold standard was an intellectual one. Created to facilitate the smooth working of a system of fixed exchange rates and run by central bankers deeply convinced of the technical and ethical desirability of a gold anchor, the BIS was intellectually ill equipped to recognise, and come to terms with, the end of an epoch. While it dealt reasonably well with the technical implications of the new monetary regimes, it was slow in understanding the advantages of managed rates in the circumstances of the Great Depression, at least as a second best to fully fledged international economic cooperation. Basel remained the citadel of the gold preachers, increasingly isolated as the years went by.

The reluctance to relinquish gold intellectually made it difficult for the people gathering around the BIS to understand some of the important policy implications of the Great Depression and its aftermath. It possibly contributed to the delay in the adoption of needed reflationary policies, as in the case of the "gold bloc". It is nevertheless arguable that, by remaining firmly convinced of the desirability of fixed exchange rates, the BIS also provided some long-run positive externalities to international monetary policy making. Throughout the 1930s, fine minds in Basel continued to think, debate, and write on how best to improve and adapt to new circumstances a system of international payments based on gold. Some of these ideas, and some of the people who toiled on them, eventually contributed to the success of the Bretton Woods institutional arrangements. All this, however, lay in the distant future; in 1931–33, the history of the BIS is to a large extent the history of an institution striving to preserve the interwar gold standard in its existing form.

Central bank cooperation itself was made more difficult to achieve – and technically more complex to engineer – by the end of the gold standard. It was, in any case, an entirely new game. Poor international relations aside, the reasons that the years 1931–33 marked a watershed in central bank cooperation at Basel can be summarised as follows.[31] First, exchange rate management became the remit of governments, rather than central banks.

Soon after going off gold, a number of countries (notably the United Kingdom, the United States, France, Belgium, the Netherlands, and Switzerland) created exchange stabilisation funds aimed at limiting undesirable fluctuations of exchange rates. Such funds were managed either by the Treasury[32] or jointly by the Treasury and the central bank.[33] Since, given adequate resources, central banks can perform all the functions of exchange funds, it has been argued that their creation was "simply a recognition of the fact that the regulation of the currency, formerly a central banking function, [had] become a government function".[34] Moreover, the setting of the rediscount rate, and monetary policy in general, became a joint responsibility of governments and central banks. In this context, international monetary cooperation required, more than ever before, prior domestic coordination between governments and central banks.[35]

Second, the prestige of central banks, and even the kind of mythical aura that surrounded their power, did not emerge unscathed from the monetary debacle of 1931–33. This also meant a loss of independence and therefore of international bargaining power, as in many cases a great deal of that independence derived from the central bank's standing with the banking community and public opinion rather than from explicit legal provisions. Third, the very aim of cooperation was blurred. Whereas before 1931 it was clear, at least in principle, that the ultimate aim of central bank cooperation was the preservation of stable exchange rates anchored on gold, no such clarity of objective existed afterwards. Was cooperation aimed at reflating the real economy, or at affecting international price levels, or at obtaining exchange rate stability?

Finally, more substantively and most importantly of all, the end of the gold standard afforded individual countries more freedom in pursuing their own idiosyncratic monetary policies. Reflation could be (and was) pursued by individual countries even in the absence of cooperation from others. If, in principle, the coordination of economic policies was still as important for the overall recovery of the world economy, in practice it appeared to be less relevant to the welfare of individual countries. A "beggar thy neighbour" policy was always an option, and a temptation. But even countries that resisted it now had policy choices open to them that either did not require international cooperation or required it only to a relatively limited degree. Countries that, by using foreign exchange regulations, pursued domestic reflation through artificially low interest rates and import substitution could do so without any international cooperation. A second option, outright devaluation of the currency, would succeed better if other countries were brought to agree on avoiding a self-defeating race of competitive devaluations: cooperation was therefore desirable even if not strictly necessary. Small countries that pegged their currencies to that of the leader in their monetary area would take advantage from mutual coordination and some "understanding" from the larger player. Last of all, the few that remained on gold after 1933 – the so-called gold bloc – were bound to achieve effective cooperation not only amongst themselves but also with the largest capital markets outside the "bloc". As policies differed, so did the need for coordination and the forms it was supposed to take. In the new circumstances, a one-size-fits-all international cooperation policy of the kind implicitly envisaged at the time of the creation of the BIS would no longer apply.

5.3   The Wiggin Committee

Failing to find a reasonable compromise at the London Conference (20–23 July 1931),[36] the seven government representatives issued a declaration that was as vague as it was short. It stated, in the most general terms: (a) that the German financial crisis originated in a lack of confidence "not justified by the economic and budgetary situation of the country", and (b) that they were "ready to cooperate as it [was] within their power to restore confidence". The practical measures recommended, however, amounted to almost nothing: the renewal of the credit of $100 million to the Reichsbank, and measures aimed at maintaining the volume of the short-term credits already granted by private financial institutions to Germany. Further action was postponed until after the deliberations of a committee of experts to be set up by the BIS. Its task was "to inquire into the immediate further credit needs of Germany and to study the possibilities of converting a portion of short-term credits into long-term credits".[37]

This committee was put together speedily,[38] with members drawn from the private banking sector (except for a prominent newspaper editor and a representative of the Bank of Japan). It first met in Basel on 8 August. Albert Wiggin, chairman of the board of the Chase National Bank of New York, was elected to the chair. The committee delivered its report on 18 August.

Melchior, the German representative, was adamant in stating that short-term credit was no longer needed. The balance of trade was roughly in equilibrium, also due to the slack in domestic demand, as were public finances, thanks to "the drastic methods adopted by the German government".[39] Neither was "credit for increasing the foreign exchange reserves of the Reichsbank" required. "At the time of the London Conference there were", according to Melchior, "strong psychological reasons for maintaining a large reserve in foreign balances". Now, the acute crisis was over and "he did not think that an increase in these balances, obtained as a result of a rediscount credit from abroad, would have any special effect". On the contrary, it was Melchior's impression that "any such short term rediscount credit would be an embarrassment to the Reichsbank when it fell due".[40] He failed to mention that the situation had been improved drastically by exchange controls that were just then beginning to bite.

Germany had found its own way out of the financial crisis, once it became clear that international cooperation had failed. According to the German banker, what his country really needed were long-term credits that "would enable industrialists to give orders and so prevent an increase in unemployment".[41] In the discussion it was pointed out that "it was dangerous for Germany to borrow abroad to meet payments the credit for which should be supplied internally". To this, the German representative simply replied that "the situation of Germany was not normal, and that to-day it would be impossible to obtain internal credits".[42] Did the fact that foreign exchange controls would result in greater room for manoeuvre in managing domestic money and credit escape Melchior, as it seems to have escaped Brüning and Luther, or was he just making as strong as possible a case for an indefinite moratorium?

It was Sir Walter Layton who brought the committee's discussion closer to its agenda. The question about Germany's ability to finance its future economic development, after living above its means for at least seven years, was surely interesting but neither urgent nor strictly relevant to the immediate task of the committee.[43] Considering that net withdrawals of capital from Germany since the beginning of 1931 were estimated to be about 2.5 billion RM, a more pertinent question to ask was "what the consequences would be of not replacing it".[44] Less diplomatically, the Swedish member recalled that interested countries had convened conferences and expert committees "not only to assist Germany but also to protect themselves".[45] It was not in the creditors' interest to allow further deflation in Germany. In the same vein, Layton argued that the "replacement" – international or domestic, long- or short-term – of credit losses would not be inflationary but merely a desirable remedy "for the disastrous deflation of the past few months".[46]

Needless to say, reparations soon surfaced in the committee's deliberations. Moreau, supported by Beneduce, was not prepared to discuss the issue, "clearly outside the mandate of the Committee".[47] Layton, on the other hand, found it difficult to discuss Germany's credit needs within a context that did not include reparations. While he agreed that the Wiggin Committee was not empowered to discuss reparations, he felt that it could recommend to the president of the London Conference to have its powers extended. Moreau, strongly opposed to the idea that the Hoover moratorium be extended beyond its agreed term of one year, objected that the London Conference "did not legally exist any more".[48] The president of that conference (the U.K. prime minister) thus had no powers whatsoever.

The political and legal dispute went on, with Layton saying that "the sole preoccupation of public opinion in the United Kingdom was to see the matter [of reparations] taken up urgently". Moreover he said that he had "hitherto hoped that on the publication of this Committee's report the German government would be able to point out to the President of the London Conference that the report was not conclusive and ask the latter to take the initiative".[49] This would include summoning of the special advisory committee provided for under the Young Plan.[50] From a technical point of view it was obvious that no serious assessment of Germany's credit needs and no recommendation thereon could be made without taking reparations into account. At the same time, nobody was under the illusion that a "technical" committee could achieve a political success where government representatives had failed a few weeks earlier.

Although it had to accept its political limitations, the Wiggin Committee was successful in speeding up negotiations for a standstill agreement on short-term debts. In this it could act pretty much on its own authority because most of its members, beginning with the chairman, represented large creditors in their own countries and had been selected by the BIS precisely for that reason. While the committee was sitting in Basel, negotiations about roll-over and consolidation of short-term private credits to Germany had made progress at parallel meetings held in Berlin, London, and elsewhere. Some of the issues debated in Basel – such as that of the securities to be required for new loans to Germany – clearly affected the standstill negotiations. The two groups thus had to proceed simultaneously, since their agendas were partly overlapping. Coordination, however, meant scarcely affordable delays. Hence the Wiggin Committee took the initiative of inviting representatives of the banking groups and the German banks to meet in Basel on 14 August to try to finalise a standstill arrangement[51] by working in close contact with the committee itself. In the following five days, the two groups held constant consultations and reached their results almost at the same time.

It was Wiggin who finally applied pressure for a swift conclusion of the deliberations. "The world", he emphatically stated, "wanted help and was waiting for [their] report".[52] Its drafting was entrusted to Sir Walter Layton. On 18 August, the final draft was ready for approval. However, it had to be made public almost simultaneously with the announcement of the standstill agreement, not yet concluded.[53] The majority was inclined to vote in favour of the creditors' proposals, which the chairman defined as "reasonable". Melchior, saying that he would have to abstain, "appealed to the Committee to be patient a little longer" to avoid spoiling the excellent spirit that had thus far characterised the discussion. A meeting of the Wiggin Committee was called for 8 P.M. on 18 August, but it was not until after midnight that it was reported that, in adjacent rooms, the final points of disagreement on the *Stillhaltung* had been substantially settled. The committee could thus proceed to approve its final report immediately. Disagreement remained as to whether or not the president of the BIS, to whom the report was to be addressed, should be required to submit the report itself to the president of the London Conference.[54]

As to the committee's first task – inquiring into the immediate credit needs of Germany – the report directed its attention to: (a) whether it was possible to prevent further capital withdrawals; and (b) whether it was necessary to replace from foreign sources part of the capital hitherto withdrawn.[55] It was argued that the standstill arrangements substantially assured that no further capital flight from Germany would take place. With regard to replacement of withdrawn funds, the report stated that it was advisable for Germany neither to liquidate all its remaining foreign assets nor to increase its trade surplus further. An increase of exports would mean "the sale of goods at very low prices", while the reduction of imports "would involve a low level of consumption in Germany".[56] Neither course of action was advantageous to the world economy in general and to Germany's creditors in particular. It was therefore suggested that some further foreign credit should be granted to Germany and that such credits "should be in the form of a long-term loan".[57]

The report then turned to address the question of the actual possibility of Germany raising another long-term loan. The inescapable conclusion was that, although the German government had "given proof of its determination", it was "impossible to raise any long-term loan on the credit of Germany alone".[58] In order to restore confidence, the "political risk" had to be removed and clarity assured about the exact amount of Germany's foreign liabilities. Only governments, the committee reported, were in a position to restore confidence if they would just "realise the responsibility that rests upon them". "We think it essential", the report stated, "that before the prolongation of credit [i.e., the Hoover moratorium] comes to an end, [governments] should give the world the assurance that international political relations are established on a basis of mutual confidence ... and that the international payments to be made by Germany will not be such as to imperil the maintenance of her financial stability". With these noble words – where Layton's influence is evident – the experts sent the ball back once again into the politicians' court.[59] It was the old dictum again: "*Faites-moi de la bonne politique, et je vous ferai de la bonne finance*".

The Wiggin Committee's report also briefly dealt with the standstill agreement on short-term credits to German financial institutions, simultaneously finalised in Basel between representatives of German and creditor private banks. The arrangement entailed the maintenance of the existing total amount of private short-term credits to Germany at about their existing amount (some 6.3 billion RM) for a further period of six months, beginning 1 September 1931. In that respect, the BIS was requested by all interested parties to set up an arbitration committee "for the adjustment of any differences which may arise as to the interpretation and execution of this agreement".[60] The BIS appointed Marcus Wallenberg,[61] T. H. McKittrick of Higginson & Co. and future BIS president, and Franz Urbig[62] as members of the arbitration committee.[63]

5.4   The Beneduce Committee and the Lausanne Conference

Unable to agree on almost anything, the government representatives convened in London in July 1931 had resorted to the time-honoured diplomatic device of an expert committee. The latter, as expected, sent the ball back into the governments' court by recommending that they "should concert together with respect to the necessary measures for economic restoration, and assistance to Germany".[64] Hectic diplomatic activity followed the delivery of the Wiggin Report to the interested parties. It was agreed to proceed with the appointment of yet another committee of experts, which was to prepare the ground for a new conference to be called before the Hoover moratorium was to expire in July 1932.

This time, however, the convocation of a special advisory committee meant that a step forward was made towards an agreement for the extension of the moratorium on official German debts. In fact, the Hague Convention of 20 January 1930 (establishing the Young Plan) explicitly contemplated,[65] in special circumstances, a moratorium on the conditional part of the German annuity payments. The moratorium procedure involved three steps: (i) a request by the German government, upon which (ii) the BIS[66] would convene a special advisory committee to establish that the German economy was under special stress, and (iii) action by the BIS as trustee or by the governments concerned according to circumstances.[67] The decision to resort to this procedure was in itself the result of a compromise between the French and U.K. positions. Paris wanted annuity payments to be fully resumed in July 1932 – upon the expiration of the Hoover moratorium – while London insisted on a thorough reconsideration of the entire issue of war payments as a precondition for recovery. By calling upon the provisions of the Young Plan, the governments involved reached a compromise by implicitly accepting that any discussion (and subsequent action) would be confined to the conditional part of reparations only.

In the official request for convocation of the committee, the German government rejected the very basis of the compromise. The letter addressed by the Reich finance minister to the president of the BIS on 19 November 1931 expressly stated that the conditions envisaged by the Young Plan for the request of postponement of payments no longer applied: "Since the New Plan was framed, the economic and financial situation in the world, and particularly in Germany, has been fundamentally altered by a crisis without parallel".[68] The German government was adamant that it was not acceptable to confine the discussion and the ensuing deliberations to just one part of the reparation payments. "The Committee", the letter went on to say, "must examine the situation in all its aspects".[69]

The tone of the letter notwithstanding, as soon as it was received in Basel, the BIS president consulted concerned members and proceeded to appoint the special advisory committee. This consisted of seven "ordinary" members – one for each of the central banks of Germany, France, the United Kingdom, Belgium, Italy, and Japan, plus the Federal Reserve Bank of New York – and four co-opted members. The banks appointed Melchior, Rist, Layton, Francqui, Beneduce, Nohara, and Stuart. Bindschedler, Colijn, Diouritch, and Rydbeck were chosen at the first meeting of the committee, held in Basel on 7 December 1931, which also appointed the Italian Beneduce to the chair.[70]

According to the well-established blueprint for expert committees, a discussion on the extent of the mandate slowed the proceedings during the first meetings until gradually discussion was directed towards examination of the German situation, beginning with an update of the statistics in the Wiggin Report.[71] There was, however, the danger of a narrow and technical conclusion focusing only on Germany that would leave little room for political manoeuvre at the envisaged conference. Beneduce, supported by the U.K. delegate, tried to steer the discussion towards the repercussions of the German crisis on the world economy at large as a means of dealing with the effects of a reparations moratorium on the capacity of Continental countries to pay back their war debts. Following a well-rehearsed script, the Americans objected to any discussion of war debts, while the French and the Germans wanted the advisory committee to remain within the guide-lines set by the Young Committee.[72] Privately asked by Beneduce why he now accepted the French stance, Melchior replied that Laval and Brüning had reached agreement that a declaration be made to the effect that it was only the conditional payments that Germany was unable to meet.[73]

Consensus was found on two main conclusions – namely, that (i) repa-rations were amongst the main causes of the world depression and (ii) Ger-many could not possibly pay the Young annuities as long as the depression lasted. Layton insisted on adding a paragraph about the need for lower customs duties, a quid pro quo his government intended to request at the conference for sterling stabilisation – another prerequisite, he claimed, for international recovery.[74]

While disagreement remained about unconditional reparations[75] and war debts, the Germans maintained an ambiguous attitude. At plenary meetings, Melchior would sit rather passively. Bound by his government's official pol-icy, he did not press for a full discussion of reparations beyond the Young Plan boundaries, leaving that task to the U.K. and neutral delegates. "Truth is", Beneduce noted, "that, by getting so much indebted, Germany has cre-ated so many interests in contrast with reparations, that she may well leave to those representing such interests (English, Americans, etc.) the task of solving the problem for her."[76] At subcommittee meetings, on the other hand, more junior members of the German delegation held the extreme po-sition that no room for further payments of any kind existed in the German economy, even under the most favourable future scenarios.[77] Therefore, conclusions reached in the subcommittees were closer to the German than to the French point of view, and also because the Italians were instructed by Beneduce to discreetly support the former rather than the latter.[78]

On 23 December 1931, the final report was signed. A few hours ear-lier, Beneduce wrote: "We are reaching an agreement on a Report formally close to the French position, but in substance much closer to the German one. Experts will say that next year Germany will not be able to meet the conditional part of reparations. They will say nothing about the uncondi-tional part. But statistics and, more generally, the whole context of the report will make it clear that they have in mind much broader conclusions involv-ing not only the whole set of German payments but war debts as well. The repercussions of cancellations of debts of one country on the ability to pay of another country will be made explicit in an ad hoc section of the Report, in spite of the continuing opposition of the U.S. delegate."[79]

In any event, the report turned out to be even more explicitly committed to putting an end to all payments than Beneduce had anticipated.[80] In fulfill-ing the task assigned to them under the Young Plan, the experts said it was evident that Germany would "not be able in the year beginning in July next to transfer the conditional part of the annuity". They went on to say that it was their duty to draw the "attention of the governments to the unprecedented gravity of the crisis, the magnitude of which undoubtedly exceeds the 'relatively short depression' envisaged in the Young Plan". Whereas the latter's provisions were framed in a context contemplating a steady growth of world trade and prosperity, the reality had been very different. Shrinking trade volumes and falling gold prices had added "greatly to the real burden, not only of German annuities but of all payments fixed in gold". "Transfers from one country to another on a scale so large", the report added, "can only accentuate the present chaos." The conclusion could not have been more clearly stated, in plain rather than diplomatic language. "The adjustment of all intergovernmental debts (Reparations and other War Debts) to the existing troubled situation of the world ... is the only lasting step capable of re-establishing confidence which is the very condition of economic stability and real peace."[81]

In spite of the experts' plea for speedy action, it took six months for governments to meet in Lausanne and deliberate on the Beneduce Committee's recommendations. In spite of the delay, the BIS welcomed the "fruits of Lausanne" as "unexpectedly rich".[82] Upon closer inspection, however, the "firm intention of helping to create a new order" proclaimed by the participating powers did not seem to be matched by the actual results of the lakeside town meeting. All the conference did was – acknowledging that the Depression had already de facto abolished reparations – proceed to abolish them de jure as well. A token lump sum payment of 3 billion gold marks, in the form of 5% redeemable bonds, was required of Germany, mostly as a face-saving device for the French government.[83]

The Americans refused to discuss inter-Allied debts, an election year being the least appropriate time for concessions that would cost the U.S. Treasury over $3 billion. Nevertheless, Lausanne spelled the end of wartime debts as well. In December 1932, the United Kingdom, with some hesitation, paid its debt instalment. The French government was inclined to do the same, but the proposal was rejected by the Parliament.[84] From then on, Paris discontinued war debt payments. London made token payments in 1933, just enough to avoid an open admission of default, until in 1934 new legislation in the United States put a final end to this kind of payment. Thus, "the year 1932 saw the last act in the confused drama of reparation and inter-Allied debts which had tormented the world for more than ten years. The Lausanne Conference buried them both in the same unhonoured grave".[85]

On U.K. insistence, the Lausanne Conference created another committee, which met at Stresa from 5 to 20 September 1932, to address the debt problem of Central and Eastern European countries. The Stresa Conference recommended the establishment of a monetary normalisation fund to help the countries in question redress their financial situation and restore monetary stability. The further study of the mode of operation of the proposed monetary normalisation fund was entrusted to the League of Nations' Commission of Enquiry for European Union. On 2 November 1932, the commission published a report on the monetary normalisation fund scheme, recommending that it be administered by the BIS, but the scheme itself was never implemented.[86]

Formally, the Lausanne Agreement – by which most of the provisions of the Hague Agreement of 1930 were abrogated (though not those related directly to the BIS) – never came into full legal force.[87] Nevertheless, the Lausanne Conference produced the desired effect: Germany's World War I reparations were buried once and for all, creating ephemeral hopes for international cooperation. Resolution 5 of the Lausanne Agreement called for the convocation, by the League of Nations, of a conference on monetary and economic questions to deal with the financial and economic issues responsible for the world crisis. "The necessity to restore currencies to a healthy basis" featured prominently on the agenda. This was to be the London Conference of June–July 1933.

5.5   Custodian of the Gold Standard

As we have seen (Chapters 2 and 3), the gold standard was embedded in the very DNA of the BIS. At The Hague and at Baden-Baden, in 1929–30, the continuation of the existing international monetary regime was taken for granted. The international bank was established precisely to act as a technical facilitator of the smooth functioning of the gold-standard machinery, not least in view of the large capital transfers contemplated by the Young Plan. The BIS Statutes were adamant: "The operations of the Bank for its own account shall only be carried out in currencies which in the opinion of the Board satisfy the practical requirements of the gold or gold exchange standard."[88]

The news that the U.K. government had taken the pound off gold came as a shock to the whole world; it exploded like a bombshell in Basel. Whereas previously it had been possible to turn a blind eye to Germany's de facto drifting away from gold convertibility, it was impossible to pretend that nothing had happened in London on 21 September 1931. The only viable position for the BIS to adopt was taking at face value the official U.K. claim that convertibility had been suspended only temporarily; hence the Bank's intellectual and political commitment to do whatever in its power to promote a swift re-enthronement of gold in international payments. The intellectual contribution consisted of studying what could be learned from recent experience in order to amend the system and make it more solid in the future. On the political side, the BIS acted as a magnet for all those who felt the gold anchor to be irreplaceable in international monetary transactions, and it spent the following years lobbying for a return to gold.

When London went off gold, Tom Johnson, former U.K. Lord Privy Seal, apparently remarked: "Nobody told us we could do that".[89] From then on, politicians in a number of countries – notably in the United Kingdom and Scandinavia – began to entertain doubts about the "natural" superiority of the gold standard as a basis for the international payment system. Cracks in the hitherto monolithic stance of academic economists began to surface.[90] Central bankers, on the other hand, did not waver. "The gold standard", wrote a U.K. observer, "has become a religion for some Boards of Central Banks in Continental Europe, believed in with an emotional fervour which makes them incapable of an unprejudiced and objective examination of possible alternatives".[91] He might have added that Lord Norman retained a no less emotional attachment to gold and that, for quite a long time, the Federal Reserve Board remained of the same persuasion as the other central bankers.

Given its history and the composition of its Board, a firm stance on gold came naturally to the BIS. Moreover, the Bank's sharpest economic minds – Quesnay and Jacobsson – were themselves among those who had little doubt, in theory or practice, about the superiority of the gold standard. Moreover, Quesnay (who held "une vision presque mystique" of international solidarity[92]) maintained that the cooperative mission of the BIS could bear fruit only within a system of international payments ruled by gold.

Among central bankers, L. J. A. Trip – governor of the Netherlands Bank and vice-chairman of the BIS Board – was particularly active in promoting the cause of gold in international circles. As a member of the League of Nations' Gold Delegation,[93] created in the summer of 1929,[94] he participated in the drafting of an interim report on the gold standard, issued in September 1930,[95] and of the final report,[96] which did not appear until 1932. Appointed to investigate the causes of the fall in commodity prices[97] (the most worrisome international economic phenomenon in 1928–29), the Gold Delegation ended up discussing the breakdown of the international monetary system – delivering possibly the most closely articulated, analytically sophisticated, and thoroughly researched official document on gold produced during the Great Depression.

The split between the majority and minority view of the Gold Delegation developed along lines that have since become standard in the interpretation of the Great Depression. According to the majority, the causes of the collapse of the international monetary system were mainly to be found in the exogenous shocks hitting the world economy during the war and its aftermath. Such shocks were seen as resulting in "maladjustment", or disequilibrium, between demand and supply in the various markets and countries. No major fault was found in the international monetary system based on gold convertibility as such, and its restoration was therefore recommended. Consistent with their orthodox stance, the majority members saw three preconditions for the re-establishment of the gold standard: (i) "the restoration of a reasonable degree of freedom in the movements of goods and services"; (ii) "a satisfactory solution for the problem of reparation payments and war debts"; and (iii) the adherence by central banks to the "guiding principles in respect of the working of the gold-standard system".[98]

The dissenting minority note in the League's report was signed by the two U.K. members, Mant and Strakosch, and by Albert-Edouard Janssen, a former minister of finance of Belgium. Gustav Cassel, who felt he could not sign the report, recorded his agreement with the minority's monetary view of the Great Depression's causes and consequences as far as the international payments system was concerned. They observed that, the United States and France aside, the world's monetary gold stock had decreased by 16% in the 18 months to 30 June 1930.[99] Over the same period of time, the United States and France considerably increased, but unfortunately sterilised, their gold inflows. Thus, in the minority's view, the fall in prices had been generated by a decrease in the overall money supply "caused by a maldistribution of monetary gold rather than by any shortage of the world's monetary stock of gold as a whole".[100] The use of monetary policy to reflate prices was therefore recommended in a context of cooperation, particularly among the "paper-standard" countries. Only when prices were stabilised, the minority argued, would it be possible to find new suitable exchange rates and gold parities.

In essence this was a restatement of the policy Keynes and Cassel had preached in the desert before 1925. "If restoration of the gold standard", the minority wrote, "is to be the ultimate aim, this involves tasks the accomplishment of which will require great efforts and much time".[101] Finally, Cassel's memorandum of dissent bluntly observed that "the value of gold has become exposed to so many incalculable influences that it is impossible now in any true sense to speak of gold as a fixed standard of value. The destruction of the gold-standard system has, in fact, gone much further than a temporary abandonment by some few countries would denote. We are faced now with the complete destruction of the essential quality that made gold an acceptable standard of value for an international system of money". He went on to say: "It is an open question whether it will be possible in the future to restore the gold standard as an international monetary system. It is quite possible that the difficulties will prove insuperable, and that the paper standard will attain such stability as to become generally acceptable".[102] Cassel saw more urgent tasks for international cooperation at the time than speculating about the future monetary system, starting with the achievement of exchange rate stability among paper currencies.

The report's minority view gained growing support as the months went by. "When the Report of the Gold Delegation was published last year", Leith-Ross (chief economic adviser to the U.K. government) candidly admitted, "many of us, including myself, read with considerable scepticism the source of the observations of dissenting members. But experience of the last year has led me, at any rate, to revise that opinion. I find that in my country more and more people, whether politicians, or economists, or members of business are coming round to the conviction that the restoration of the gold standard is not practicable and may not even be desirable".[103]

In the first part of 1932, while the League's report was being finalised, Trip was active in promoting with his colleagues in Basel the majority view of the League's Gold Delegation. To that effect, he circulated a note of the Netherlands Bank endorsing the report's conclusions and discussed it at length in a speech delivered at the governors' informal meeting of 10 May 1932.[104] During the same period of time, the BIS management instructed its Monetary and Economic Department (MED) to prepare a paper on international monetary policy. The immediate occasion was a declaration on gold issued at a conference of South American central banks in Lima on 12 December 1931,[105] which the MED was required to study and comment upon. The paper[106] turned out to be little more than a review of Trip's and Rist's notes circulated at the May 1932 governors' meeting and of the League's report, only briefly touching upon the Lima resolutions. Emphasis was placed on the BIS's role as that of "an agency through which a rationalised gold exchange standard system should be administered".[107] The paper's main conclusions stressed the importance of economising on gold and smoothing exchange rate fluctuations, envisaged at Baden-Baden as one of the main tasks of the BIS. The paper also endorsed the proposal made by the League's report that "it would be advantageous to reduce the [central banks'] reserve ratios from their present high levels".[108]

On 11 July 1932, the BIS Board felt it desirable for the Bank to "take up a definite attitude with regard to the gold standard ... to aid in forming public opinion in connection with the approaching monetary restoration". The Board, therefore, unanimously adopted a resolution to that effect.[109]

The document stated that the BIS Board was of the opinion that the gold standard remained "the best available monetary mechanism, and the one best suited to make possible the free flow of international financing". The resolution pointed to three main preconditions for a general return to the gold standard: (i) the restoration of "a reasonable degree of freedom in the movement of goods, services, and capital"; (ii) the completion of "the solution of reparations reached at Lausanne by a satisfactory solution of war debts"; and (iii) "equilibrium in the internal economy" of each individual country. A familiar blueprint was echoed in the conclusions: central banks were powerless "as long as the main outstanding problems [are] not definitely dealt with by the governments". Only after progress was made in governmental policies could "action in the monetary sphere ... also begin". At that point the BIS would be "available to the central banks to serve as their common agency in the task of monetary reconstruction". The Board also declared itself in substantial agreement with the majority conclusions of the report of the Gold Delegation of the League of Nations.

Both the declaration drafted for public consumption and the internal paper by the BIS Monetary and Economic Department are consistent with the positions taken by the BIS ever since July 1931. Then, after a brief but hectic spell of active involvement in support of a key currency, central bankers and the BIS realised they could no longer play an important part in the game. In the absence of active cooperative policies by governments, there remained little ammunition available to central bankers to foster a return to global gold convertibility.

By stressing their impotence, central bankers were also able to maintain a fairly united front that would have collapsed had they been obliged to endorse concrete policy measures. Central bankers came from an intellectual tradition and from policy experiences in the 1920s that bound them to agree broadly on the superiority of the gold standard over any other system of international payments, at least as far as theory was concerned. They were, however, neither blind to the shortcomings of the system in the prevailing extreme conditions of the world economy nor able to turn an entirely deaf ear to the more or less critical attitude of their respective governments and public opinions. Thus, whereas Moret and Franck – or Luther and Azzolini under the shelter of exchange controls – could endorse the gold standard knowing they were speaking for their governments as well, the same was not true of Norman, or of Harrison after April 1933. The claim that there was nothing for central banks to do until governments acted somehow downgraded such matters as the "rules of the gold standard" to issues of "purely ... academic interest". Governors could thus follow their inclination by subscribing to the BIS stance on gold while at the same time avoiding clashing with their governments on policies of immediate practical relevance.[110]

Throughout the 1930s, the BIS reiterated – in various forms – the conviction that the gold standard was the single best system for international payments. Second-best alternatives were never explored analytically, not even when it became clear (by the BIS's own reckoning) that the necessary political preconditions for a return to gold could not be fulfilled in the short run. Yet there was ample room for technical bodies such as the BIS and the individual central banks to discuss and work out cooperative solutions to the many problems posed by the diffusion of paper standards, as suggested for instance by Cassel. The fact that excellent minds in Basel were somehow locked in an ivory tower crippled much-needed research on how to adapt to the new conditions, as far as the Basel laboratory was concerned. But as we shall see, technical refinements to the system were suggested in and around the BIS that would turn out to be of interest at a later time, when fixed parities became a feasible proposition again.

5.6   The Preparatory Commission of Experts for the London Conference

The London World Economic Conference of 12 June to 27 July 1933 was the last in a series of intergovernmental conferences, starting with that of Genoa (1922), convened to try to redress the main imbalances in the international economy resulting from either war or depression. Overall, such conferences yielded rather meagre results, and insiders approached each new one with increasing scepticism. Informed public opinion, nevertheless, mostly continued to see international gatherings, *faute de mieux,* as anchors of last resort for international economic cooperation. The failure of the London Conference, taking place at such a critical time for the world economy, dispelled whatever hopes were still nurtured about multilateral coordination in general and on monetary matters in particular. From then on, international economic cooperation was, at best, a bilateral affair.

The failure of the London Conference was not due to improvisation or lack of preparation. As we shall see, competent technical work was carried out ahead of the conference itself. Unfortunately, the latter took place at the worst possible moment, during a phase of delicate transition from depression to slow recovery and from one monetary regime to another; had it taken place one year later, its outcome might not have been so disastrous. Preparatory work at an expert level started at the end of 1932 under unfavourable political omens.[111] As mentioned before, Lausanne had dealt with reparations but not with war debts. The ensuing default by a number of European countries outraged public opinion in the United States, threatening U.S. participation in the London Conference. The impasse was overcome by agreeing that war debt would not be included in the London agenda. Conditions for fruitful negotiations on tariff reduction, which everybody recognised as a preliminary step to the reintroduction of the gold standard, were also unfavourable. A few months earlier, the Ottawa Agreements had ended almost a century of U.K. free trade and endorsed the principle of "imperial preferences" amongst Commonwealth nations. The United Kingdom, hitherto the main preacher against discriminatory trade practices, had weakened its case by committing the same sin. The agreements "highlighted the conflict between Britain's desire to reconstruct the international economy and its ambitions to cultivate closer ties with the Empire".[112]

As for monetary matters, which were the primary concern of the BIS and of its member central banks, most of the technical discussion and the drafting of the agenda for the London Conference took place at a time when still only one major currency area was off gold. In the winter of 1932–33, the position of the Hoover administration was close to that of the French government.[113] Both agreed that the stabilisation of the pound, as a first step towards the eventual reintroduction of fixed rates within a suitably modified gold standard, was a prerequisite for world recovery. In principle, U.K. officials favoured stabilisation but were unwilling to peg the pound in the absence of a French commitment to reflate. In Paris, on the other hand, fear of inflation was still the dominating factor in monetary policy. Uncertainty about the monetary stance of the U.S. president-elect further complicated the proceedings of the Preparatory Commission of Experts.[114] The commission had already finalised its work, and its recommendations had been forwarded to individual countries for political approval at the highest level, when Roosevelt took the dollar off gold.

The devaluation of the dollar, in April 1933, put discussions on currency stabilisation on a different and more complex footing. "The dollar parity was the anchor on which all the schemes for currency stabilisation had been fixed ... [and] the sudden abandonment of gold by the United States threw everything into the melting pot."[115]

From April onwards, none of the three main central banks shared a common policy target. Moreover, they were not necessarily in agreement with their respective governments. In April, a meeting in Washington of Herriot, MacDonald, and Roosevelt came to nothing. The two Europeans rejected, for different reasons, a U.S. offer to stabilise the dollar at a level 15% below the previous parity. The three agreed only on a monetary truce for the duration of the conference that would open in June. It soon appeared, however, that there was no agreement even on the truce itself. When the French explored the possibility of a de facto stabilisation at the current level of exchange rates, Harrison seemed willing to go ahead with the suggestion but Norman "was chary about it", as he thought "London would lose a lot" (of reserves).[116] Harrison's plea for collective responsibility in avoiding "disturbing fluctuations of the principal exchanges in which the world's trade was carried on"[117] failed to convince Norman. Gone were the days when he preached the same cooperative gospel, satisfied as he now was with the United Kingdom's ability to enjoy the advantages of both cheap money and a floating currency.[118] The three main central banks agreed only to inform one another of their intentions in the monetary field.[119]

The BIS played a major role in the preparation of the London Conference. As requested by the Lausanne Conference,[120] the Bank appointed two representatives – Trip and Fraser – to the preparatory Subcommittee on Financial Questions.[121] Trip was also the Chairman of the whole Preparatory Commission of Experts (of which the Subcommittee on Financial Questions was a subdivision).[122] The commission included Beneduce, Francqui, and Vocke – all members of the BIS Board, even if they were nominated in other capacities.[123] The commission of experts held its first session in Geneva from 31 October to 9 November 1932, during which time the Subcommittee on Financial Questions mostly discussed the conditions for an orderly return to the gold standard. Jacobsson was present from the beginning and was behind much of the drafting of the subcommittee's documents.[124] The commission met again in January 1933 and finalised its recommendations to the governments about the agenda for the World Economic Conference.

Shortly before leaving Basel for Geneva in October 1932, Jacobsson wrote a lengthy paper for internal BIS consumption, reviewing the most pressing international monetary issues.[125] Trying to make his arguments as widely acceptable as possible, Jacobsson came to a hardly contentious conclusion: in normal circumstances, and over the long run, international monetary stability favours the flow of goods and capital, which in its turn facilitates "the international division of labour between nations, with a consequent increase in general prosperity. Monetary stability", he said, "could be obtained either by the gold standard or by a system of international paper money managed by 'a single international body'". He then went on to argue that, since the latter was "outside practical politics under present day conditions", the gold standard remained the only viable system to avoid the ongoing disruption of trade and capital movements with the attendant loss

of production and employment. Jacobsson was convinced that public opinion in most countries was overwhelmingly in favour of the gold standard
and that there was trust in the "fund of experience gained in working this
system".

The disadvantages of the gold standard were also discussed. Jacobsson
reckoned that "the increasing lack of elasticity in the modern economic
system" made adaptation to price shocks more difficult than under prewar
circumstances and that, in the time needed to find a new equilibrium, "great
losses may be sustained through unemployment and other ways". He also
pointed to the loss of monetary sovereignty by individual countries and to
the cost – estimated to be around $300 million for the entire world – of a
system that kept resources immobilised in unproductive gold. The paper is
possibly the most interesting and acutely argued on the gold issue produced
by the BIS in the early 1930s. Its line of reasoning was carefully built to
command consensus from all central banks: it made the case for gold in the
long run while also allowing for deviations in the exceptional circumstances
of the Great Depression. It set out the blueprint for the "Basel consensus"
on gold.

The formal task of the Preparatory Commission of Experts was to draft
an agenda for the conference. In order to do so, it had to accommodate the
opposing views of the U.K. and French delegations, the persisting dissatisfaction of Germany (even after the Lausanne settlement), and the uncertainties of the Americans on almost every issue except for war debts, which they
wanted left out of the discussion. As mentioned previously, in monetary
matters there was broad common ground in paying perhaps more than just
lip service to the principle that, in normal circumstances, a gold standard
of some kind was preferable to other monetary arrangements. However, as
soon as it came to assessing circumstances or discussing the main features
of a viable international monetary system, opinions diverged sharply.

The British saw an early restoration of the gold standard as scarcely practicable and possibly not even desirable. And while praising a system that
had worked extremely well in the past, they observed that "the countries
which are still attached to gold [did] not realise the dangers" of the system as it existed in 1933. "The machinery is not working. Some essential
parts seem to be missing, radical reconstruction is required, involving perhaps a reversal of existing policies."[126] The French, on the other hand, were
convinced that early restoration of the gold standard was essential and that
"artificial" monetary interventions should be ruled out. They even saw the
gold exchange standard as a compromise solution to be abandoned as soon
as possible in favour of the "proper" gold standard.[127]

Germany followed its own path, siding with neither position. Its delegate, Posse, paid his own formal tribute to the gold standard, stressing that his country had not abandoned it and was even ready to lift restrictions on capital movements, provided that some essential conditions were met. The latter included the stabilisation of the pound, the acceptance by creditor countries of payments in kind together with their lifting of trade barriers, and a permanent solution to standstills on private credits.[128] Beneduce, the Italian delegate, vaguely stressed cooperation as well as the essential role played by the BIS in that domain, and declared himself a believer in cheap money – adding, however, that he was sceptical about monetary measures taken in isolation.[129] Given Japan's experience with gold, one would have expected it to side firmly with the United Kingdom. As it happened, delegate Tsushima was very cautious, pleading for a general agreement on future improvements to the gold system and, in the meanwhile, for leaving each country free to decide if and when gold convertibility could be restored.[130]

Questions of principle aside, one of the main policy issues around which most others revolved in the discussions within the Subcommittee of Experts on Financial Questions was how to reconcile exchange rate stability with economic reflation. The latter entailed a rise in the gold price of commodities. The issue compounded the divergence between the U.K. and French standpoints, rooted as much in their respective economic cultures as in the political and economic predicaments of the two countries. A compromise solution – most likely worked out by Jacobsson – found its way into the final draft of the agenda. It consisted of suggesting that the legal gold cover ratios of outstanding circulation by central banks be lowered considerably, thereby reconciling adherence to the rules of the gold standard with the contingent necessity of reflating the world economy.

The final document of the commission of experts opened with a preamble, drafted by Beneduce and Day, that combined the high-principled rhetoric of the American with the elaborate metaphors of the Italian. "In essence", it said, "the necessary programme is one of economic disarmament. In the movement towards economic reconciliation, the armistice was signed in Lausanne, [and] the London Conference must draw up the Treaty of Peace."[131] As far as monetary matters were concerned, the proposed agenda included: (1) conditions for a restoration of a free international gold standard; (2) currency policies prior to such restoration; (3) functioning of the gold standard; and (4) silver. Other items dealt with prices and the resumption of capital movements.[132] More generally, a joint Anglo-French document was agreed upon indicating four areas of government policy: settlement of intergovernmental debts; greater freedom of international trade; improvement of world prices; and the abolition of exchange controls and restoration of an effective international monetary standard. "If the Conference is to succeed", Leith-Ross and Rist wrote, "we believe that the governments of the world must make up their minds to achieve a broad solution by concerted action simultaneously on the whole field."[133]

In the presentation and discussion of the individual items on the agenda, particularly as far as the gold standard was concerned, the final documents by the commission of experts reflected what might be called the "Basel consensus" on gold.[134] The latter had begun to emerge in previous years but took on a more precise form during the deliberations of the commission, of which so many BIS people were members in one capacity or another.[135] The proceedings in Geneva were closely monitored from Basel, and as soon as the first session was adjourned a special meeting of the governors was convened for a broad discussion of gold-standard issues.[136] Prior to that governors' meeting, BIS management discussed what role the Bank should have in the preparation of the second session of the preparatory commission, scheduled to meet in January. Management ruled out covering such general subjects as the overall conditions for the return to gold, "for events between now and the Conference will certainly exert great influence on the conclusions to be arrived at in this field".[137]

On the other hand, it was deemed useful to deal with technical problems.[138] The ensuing preparatory papers for the governors' meeting included a note by Jacobsson drafting six resolutions on the reduction of gold cover ratios of outstanding paper circulation[139] and a broader aide-memoire for the discussion.[140] The latter is of particular interest as far as the formation of a "Basel consensus" was concerned. It opened by saying that "the great problem with which the World Conference will be faced is the question by what measures of international cooperation individual countries can be helped in their effort to restore – and then to maintain – equilibrium in their financial and economic position. These measures are not of an altruistic character because the restoration of equilibrium is indispensable for world recovery". It then reiterated the by then well-established Basel position that "it [was] the governments in the first place that should take things in hand", while central banks and the BIS could and should assist "to a very considerable extent".

After stating that the general aim of financial and monetary action should be the "return to the free international gold standard", probably preceded by a period of de facto stabilisation, the aide-memoire produced a list of targets for national and international policies. The former included sound conditions in public finances and "in the internal money and capital markets, flexibility in domestic markets". Not surprisingly, the issue of central banks' freedom from "government interference and political influence" was also taken up. It was basically the reiteration of the standard policy stance taken by central banks from the early 1920s onwards, stated in a general enough way to make it acceptable to all participating governors. International measures recommended included the solution of the war debt problem and the vexed question of price levels. Rejecting "budgetary inflation" and doubting that monetary policy could bring about a rise in prices, the document plainly said that such a rise might not be desirable, as it would maintain "by artificial means ... an excessive production apparatus, and thereby further hamper the unavoidable process of adjustment". Here central bank governors definitely parted company with the opinion of government experts in various countries, including those participating in the preparatory commission. Finally, the document dealt with the means to ensure a better working of the gold standard in the future. These also reflected the high degree of orthodoxy still prevailing among central banks, and therefore in Basel, in that it recommended that gold be allowed to move freely and that open-market operations be allowed only in order to "strengthen the effects of gold movements". There were, however, technical suggestions for improving the performance of the gold exchange standard. In particular, it was recommended that investment of foreign exchange reserves be made "only with the BIS or with and through other central banks" and that the latter abstain from foreign exchange operations having "the sole object of making a profit".

As soon as the preparatory commission had finalised its draft annotated agenda for the London Conference, Trip pressed for an endorsement by all governors of his document on "Rules of the Gold Standard".[141] The issue was discussed at the governors' informal meetings in February and March 1933.[142] "It would prove extremely useful for the restoration of the gold standard", Trip said on that occasion, "if it were possible for central banks to arrive at unanimity in the enunciation of the principles destined to govern the working of the gold standard in the future."[143] The proposal met with a mixed reaction. Fraser, fearing for the independence of central banks, wanted them to take the initiative to "prevent other infinitely less qualified entities from interfering".[144] Luther and Norman agreed in principle on the usefulness of a joint declaration that would supplement the one issued by the Board in July 1932. Franck spoke out vehemently against any form of declaration.[145] Beneduce found such a declaration to be unwise and likely to upset markets, since it would amount to an announcement of further deflationary measures.[146] The decision was postponed, as disagreement arose also on the content of the document.

The first part of Trip's paper followed the lines of previous BIS positions, and particularly of the aide-memoire for the discussion circulated in December 1932.[147] The second part of the note dealt with monetary policy in the areas specifically entrusted to central banks. There was little that was new with respect to the "Basel consensus" then emerging, but an effort was made to treat the matter in a systematic way.[148] Trip's proposal was for an international monetary system shadowing as closely as possible the prewar gold standard, or rather the way it was supposed to operate. "The primary guides for central bank policy should be gold movements", which must be left to market forces. However, this restatement of old-fashioned principles was not entirely politically harmless because it urged a symmetry of behaviour between surplus and deficit countries and between countries with large and small gold reserves. Moret expressed his not-so-veiled reservations by saying that he endorsed only a conditional use of open-market operations and that he objected in principle to the gold exchange standard.[149] Azzolini – saying that Trip's text formed merely a useful basis for discussion – suggested that a distinction be made between temporary (acceptable) and permanent (unacceptable) gold movements.[150] He also wanted foreign exchange reserves held with the BIS to count as gold reserves. Shimasuye, transmitting the comments of the governor of the Bank of Japan, agreed on the proposed rules but urged they be made to sound less strong and binding.[151] Surely central bankers could understand each other and agree much more than their respective governments,[152] but convergence on an entirely shared view was another matter.

Subsequent Board meetings in April again decided that further discussion on Trip's text was needed. The latter was finally approved at the governors' meeting of 7 May, which took place after suspension of the gold standard in the United States. The new text[153] was preceded by an introduction referring back to the BIS Resolution on Gold of July 1932. The introduction also said that it was "impossible for all the rules of application enunciated in the present memorandum to be made formally binding" and stressed central bank cooperation. On the latter issue, the necessity for consultation among central banks was balanced by the statement that, in case of disagreement, each had to act "on its own judgement of the situation". The fact that disagreement was possible (and actually pervasive) was acknowledged by substantially amending the last part of Trip's text that dealt with the BIS itself. In the final version the BIS was defined as "an essential agency for central bank action designed to harmonise conflicting views and for joint consultations", while Trip's note read: "The BIS constitutes a new agency for central bank action on common lines and for joint consultations". The end of the gold standard, now highlighted by Roosevelt's action, was producing cracks in the "Basel consensus". Nevertheless, central banks' opinions on monetary matters remained far more harmonious than those held by their respective governments. Upon arriving in New York in late March 1933, Fraser professed to journalists his firm belief in "the reestablishment of the gold standard in most countries within five years".[154] But it was governments, according to the central bankers, that held the key to the world economic recovery.

5.7   The BIS at the London Conference

The World Monetary and Economic Conference opened in London on 12 June 1933.[155] It was the largest assembly of sovereign states on record, with 65 countries represented by over a thousand delegates. As already mentioned, high hopes were pinned on this conference: "It was a striking tribute to the still persistent faith in the collective wisdom of mankind".[156]

The conference was organised in two committees: monetary and financial, and economic,[157] with the former divided into two subcommissions. The first was to discuss the "monetary truce", officially "immediate measures for financial adjustment"; the second subcommission dealt with "permanent measures for the re-establishment of an international monetary system". Two subcommittees were established within the second subcommission, one to deal with silver and one with the technical monetary problems connected with the working of the gold standard. The BIS was institutionally involved in the latter.

It was on immediate measures that the attention of most participants, of the media, and of public opinion was largely focused. And it was by this yardstick that the conference's results were mostly judged by contemporaries, as they are still judged by historians.

If high hopes were raised but little accomplished on several of the topics on the agenda, this was particularly true of exchange rate stabilisation. Discussions in the months prior to the opening of the conference yielded no agreement, not even for a short-term stabilisation of the relative value of the three main currencies. In May, soon after the suspension of convertibility of the dollar, a so-called Warburg plan for exchange rate stabilisation was for a while at the centre of discussions between Washington, London, and Paris.[158] In a positive reaction to the plan, the French government sent a note to the United States requesting the reopening of negotiations for the stabilisation of exchange rates ahead of the London Conference. The Bank of France suggested exploratory talks of central bankers that would not commit governments but could nevertheless pave the way for a "stabilisation agreement at approximately the present levels".[159] Washington, however, did not want to commit itself and allowed the matter to drag on in Harrison's hands until it was too late for a fruitful meeting to be convened before the conference. At that point, given uncertainties about the intentions of the Roosevelt administration, France and the United Kingdom were also reluctant to enter into any commitment. They argued that "before technical measures can be taken in cooperation there is a great need of clear understanding of the policy of the American government".[160] The matter, in other words, rested with the governments and there was little that "technical" central bank cooperation could accomplish in the absence of a wider political agreement.[161]

The issue of exchange rate stabilisation, at least for the duration of the London Conference, still hung undecided when Harrison and his party sailed for London aboard the S.S. *Olympic* on 2 June.[162] Talks were resumed on 9 June, as soon as the U.S. representatives had reached London. Once again it quickly became apparent that opinions were split not only between different countries but also between Treasuries and central bankers. The division was particularly sharp within the U.S. group. Harrison remained strongly in favour of stabilisation, while Sprague "was inclined to go slowly", fearing that stabilisation might retard recovery.[163] Norman, personally inclined towards some sort of pegging of the pound to the two other main currencies, was reluctant even to discuss the issue "until the governments had made up their minds what they were going to do".[164] Moret had the easiest job among leading central bankers because he was in agreement with his own government. It was easy for him to point to the inconsistency in the positions of the other two delegations that seemed to try and do "two things at the same time, namely, to get the benefits of inflation and yet have exchange stability".[165] Rumours, heard from time to time in New York, that France might abandon gold during the conference did not help negotiations,[166] nor did the poor flow of information between the U.S. delegation and Washington.[167] Finally, on 15 June, a scheme was agreed upon for fixing the price of sterling in terms of both dollars and gold for the duration of the conference. The technicalities of the agreement, worked out by Norman, included the allocation of $100 million for interventions on foreign exchange markets, together with an understanding that the agreement would be revised once the fund was exhausted. This was the high point of the conference: optimism could still be maintained.

The agreement had a perverse effect on exchange rates. Owing inter alia to inadequate communication between London and Washington, markets anticipated stabilisation at a relatively high level, for a short while pushing the dollar upwards relative to the pound and the franc. At the same time, discounting a tighter monetary stance, stock and commodity prices fell. Sensing the danger to his reflationary stance, on 17 June Roosevelt sent the U.S. delegation in London a clear message defining as "untimely" any measure of temporary stabilisation.[168] Even so, as the dollar resumed its fall the U.S. delegation in London yielded to U.K. pressure and opened fresh negotiations on currency stabilisation.[169] A new draft of the Norman plan – contemplating stabilisation only for the duration of the conference – was agreed upon. Professor Raymond Moley, one of Roosevelt's advisers, approved it on 30 June.[170]

Again the president intervened, disavowing the agreement, this time with a message to Secretary of State Hull, who headed the U.S. delegation. The message, made public on 3 July, is known as the "bombshell" declaration, and it sent the whole conference onto the rocks. "I would regard it a catastrophe", the message said, "amounting to a world tragedy if the Great Conference of Nations, called to bring about a more real and greater prosperity to the masses of all nations, should, in advance of any serious effort to consider these broader problems, allow itself to be diverted by the proposal of a purely artificial and temporary experiment affecting the exchange rates of a few nations only."[171] The rest of the message outlined, in a nutshell, Roosevelt's far from revolutionary economic doctrine based upon sound fiscal policies at home and open international markets for goods and capitals. By targeting "the old fetishes of so-called international bankers", Roosevelt's message explicitly aimed at, and succeeded in, burying the gold standard.

Roosevelt's "bombshell" message acted as a catalyst to the formal creation of a "gold bloc" whose identity had become ever more apparent as the conference proceeded. From the beginning, Beneduce (Italy), Bachmann (Switzerland), and Trip (the Netherlands) had fiercely opposed the proposition, floated by Chamberlain, that the conference should formally endorse a pledge by participating countries to avoid deflationary policies in the future.[172] The French, engaged in the tripartite negotiations for exchange rate stabilisation, had taken a less belligerent attitude. As time went by, the gold camp became increasingly uneasy about the usefulness of their presence in London.[173] Once it became clear that there was no hope of an early revival of negotiations, let alone of a general return to gold, the French government took the lead in the creation of a bloc of countries committed to the gold standard. On 3 July, soon after Roosevelt's message was made public, the governments of France, Italy, Switzerland, Belgium, the Netherlands, and Poland issued a communiqué confirming their "formal commitment" to maintain the gold standard in their "respective countries at the on-going parities and within the existing legal monetary framework".[174] The resolution ended by calling upon the respective central banks to "remain in strict contact" for the practical implementation of the policy outlined in the declaration.[175]

On 8 July 1933, the governors of the central banks of the six gold bloc countries gathered in Paris. The official communiqué mentioned the immediate application of the "technical arrangements laid down and decided upon at the meeting",[176] which had taken the form of a secret cooperation agreement.[177] The six governors pledged to assist each other in fighting speculative attacks and to intervene appropriately, each in his own market, in maintaining the parity of the currency of other member countries, in agreement with the concerned central bank. As a token of good will it was decided that no commission fee would be charged for operations on foreign exchange markets carried out in execution of the cooperation agreement.

For a number of reasons, the BIS management regarded developments leading to the formation of the gold bloc with great interest. There was, first of all, an institutional reason for that: the gold bloc countries included the majority (five out of nine) of the BIS Board members at the time. Second, the BIS had consistently argued that the gold standard was, at least in principle, the most desirable system of international monetary payments. There existed, on this issue, a genuine "Basel consensus" (or doctrine) shared by all the main central bankers, regardless of their contingent position on short- and medium-term exchange rate policies. At the London Conference, however, no agreement was found on most of the Basel positions: it was therefore natural for the BIS to see the formation of the bloc as at least partly vindicating the validity of its long-standing position. A third reason why the BIS top management felt free to show its support for the gold bloc initiative was that it knew that, privately, leading central bankers of countries outside the bloc still looked at it with a favourable, perhaps envious, eye and praised at least some aspects of the scheme.[178] Finally, the secret cooperation agreement signed in Paris explicitly pledged the six central banks concerned to seek the cooperation of the BIS in all matters pertaining to its statutory mission.[179] The presence of Fraser, president of the BIS, at the Paris meeting was acknowledged in the official communiqué.

We must now briefly account for the official participation of the BIS in the London Conference. The League of Nations asked the BIS to appoint

two representatives in a consultative capacity as well as to provide technical assistance to the conference secretariat. Trip and Fraser were appointed
to represent the Bank but the former declined, fearing a conflict of interest
with his other duties as governor of the Netherlands Bank. The president
was therefore the sole official representative of the BIS at the conference.
He performed the role of rapporteur of the gold-standard subcommittee.
Jacobsson headed the BIS staff seconded to the secretariat[180] that included
Blessing and Rodenbach.[181]

At the subcommittee meeting of 29 June, Fraser submitted the BIS note
on "General principles of the working of the gold standard", prepared in
Basel during the spring of 1933 (Trip's "rules of the game"), as a resolution
for adoption by the committee.[182] But discussions on the re-establishment of
an international gold standard quickly got bogged down, owing chiefly to the
reluctance of American delegates to commit their government's monetary
policy: U.S. delegates insisted that the BIS text should state that the obligation to convert into gold should be left to the discretion of each individual
central bank. On 3 July 1933, as a reaction to Roosevelt's "bombshell" declaration ruling out an immediate dollar stabilisation, the French delegation
suspended further participation in the subcommittee's deliberations.[183] On
12 July, an attempt to reactivate the work of the gold-standard subcommittee
in London failed and, a few days later, Kienböck (chairman of the second
subcommission) proposed winding up the committee's work.[184] The lack
of concrete results was manifest in the subcommission's final report. The
gold-standard subcommittee had not been able to reach any conclusions
with regard to methods of saving gold or of redistributing gold reserves.
The question of a gold exchange standard was referred back to the BIS
for further study. The resolutions on the working of the gold standard, as
submitted by Fraser, were adopted by all governments represented on the
subcommittee except for the United States, "which considered discussion
of the question at this time premature".

The final report dealt, in rather general terms, with two issues on which
the BIS had presented draft resolutions. The first concerned central bank
independence, a question still very dear to Norman;[185] the second covered
central bank cooperation as well as the role the BIS was supposed to play
in that regard.

Appreciation came from various quarters for the technical competence
shown by the BIS in London,[186] even though some thought that central
banks – with their precommittal position in favour of exchange rate stabilisation – had contributed to the eventual failure of the conference.[187]
And some asked why the BIS had risked its reputation on the matter of
the gold resolution. The insider's answer was, basically, that people in

Basel sincerely believed that the future of the international monetary system hinged on gold.[188]

A true believer in international cooperation, Jacobsson tried hard to salvage something from the overall failure of the conference.[189] Back in Basel, he summarised in ten points his view of the conference achievements.[190] He credited the London meeting for making possible a de facto cancellation of war debts, for improving economic relations between the West and the Soviet Union, for fostering a tariff truce, and for solving the silver problem. More generally he felt that, by finally putting issues related to the peace treaties behind and by basing discussion upon "each country's opinion with regard to future monetary policy", the conference "contributed to a better understanding of the position of the various countries". Moreover, Jacobsson valued the London Conference as "the occasion for establishing closer collaboration between the gold standard countries", a development that he regarded as being "in the general interest".

Ultimately, the failure of the World Monetary and Economic Conference did not deter the BIS from trying to reach a consensus on the need to restore the gold standard, even if in a distant future. Gold remained at the centre of the Bank's monetary doctrine for a number of years to come.

The governors' meeting on 23 July 1933 discussed the problem of the gold exchange standard, agreeing that – on a restricted basis and given the necessary reforms – it could serve to hasten the return of some countries to an international monetary standard. The next day, the BIS Board took note of the resolutions on monetary policy adopted by the London Conference and decided, in view of the U.S. position, to invite the Federal Reserve Bank of New York to participate in further discussions. The lukewarm response from New York, as well as the hangover from London and the divergence of views within Europe, prevented any progress from being made.[191]

The "Basel consensus" remained confined to the very general goal of restoring a free gold standard sometime in the distant future. Substantial divergence remained between central banks on the practical measures to be taken and on the mode of implementation of policies. One of the main bones of contention regarded open-market operations. The Bank of France insisted on the unacceptability of such operations as devious devices for price manipulation, while the United Kingdom and the United States increasingly clung to them as powerful policy tools.

5.8   The Bank's Role as Trustee and the German Transfer Crisis

The failure of the London Conference was, in Clavin's words, "as damaging to the future of economic diplomacy between the former allied powers as it was encouraging to the German Reich".[192] Germany drew strength from the economic divisions between France, the United Kingdom, and the United States, as they seemed to vindicate its own choice for autarky and bilateralism. In the following years, the Nazi government was bent on further exploiting these divisions to its own benefit in all areas, including in the financial field and beginning with external debt service, since this was seen as an obstacle to the country's internal recovery and rearmament. The so-called German transfer crisis came to a head in the spring and early summer of 1934, when Germany invoked a lack of foreign exchange reserves as justification for drastically reducing further service on its medium- and long-term external debts. This affected the BIS directly as trustee of the Dawes and Young loans.

By January 1933, when Hitler came to power, reparation payments had effectively ceased and a large part of foreign short-term credits held in Germany was frozen (standstill agreement). Only medium- and long-term commercial external debts continued to be serviced, including the Dawes and Young loans, which enjoyed special privileges guaranteed by international treaty. The Nazi government, however, soon set out to undermine the last remaining vestiges of the Versailles settlement in the form of servicing the Dawes and Young loans. These loans were considered not only a political liability but also an unacceptable burden to the Reichsbank's foreign exchange reserves because of their high interest rates (7% for the Dawes and 5½% for the Young Loan), which had become even harder to bear as a result of the deflationary policies of the early 1930s.

A first step taken by the German government was to tackle the gold clauses applying to the Dawes Loan (U.S. tranche) and the Young Loan (all tranches). This clause had been applied when the pound and the Swedish crown left the gold standard: the coupons of the U.K. and Swedish Young bonds due up to December 1932 were paid on the original gold value basis. When the United States abandoned the gold standard in April 1933, the new German government was put in an unfavourable exchange position, as over half of the outstanding Dawes bonds and nearly a third of the Young bonds were denominated in U.S. dollars and protected by a gold clause.

On 8 May 1933, the German Finance Ministry notified the BIS that the gold clause would no longer apply and that the service of the U.S. Dawes bonds – as well as the U.S., Swedish, and U.K. issues of the Young Loan – would henceforth be settled at the current exchange rate. The BIS replied that as trustee it could not agree to this unilateral change and reserved all the rights of the bondholders.[193] In practical terms, however, the trustee had little choice but to inform the paying agents about the German decision and to arrange for the payment on 1 June 1933 of all Young bond coupons falling due at their current value.[194]

Having repudiated the gold clause, the Reichsbank then called a meeting in Berlin of Germany's foreign creditors to discuss "the question of further continuation of transfer of foreign exchange for debt service" in view of Germany's precarious reserve position.[195] The BIS was not invited to the meeting, and in Basel this omission was taken as a sign that the Reichsbank had no intention of imposing transfer limitations on its service of the Young and Dawes loans. Nonetheless, Fraser asked Norman to take a tough stance with Schacht, stressing the "special position" of the two loans. Fraser rightly feared that the Reichsbank president would use the disgruntlement of Germany's other long-term creditors concerning the preferential treatment given to the Dawes and Young loans as a pretext for cutting all payments.[196] In fact, on 2 June the Reichsbank announced that Germany's gold and foreign exchange reserves had fallen to such a low level that the service of external debts could no longer be guaranteed in full. No explicit mention was made of the Dawes and Young loans. During a private dinner that same evening, however, Schacht made it quite clear to Fraser that he himself was in favour of continuing full service of the Dawes but not of the Young loan, which he considered to be "immoral".[197] A few days later, the same opinion was reiterated before the central bank governors gathered in Basel for the BIS Board meeting of 5 June.[198]

After the meeting of foreign creditors at the Reichsbank had come to an end, the German authorities moved swiftly. On 9 June 1933 a law was promulgated suspending transfers in foreign exchange with respect to most German external liabilities. German debtors were to pay the equivalent of the amounts of their foreign currency–denominated debts in Reichsmarks, at the going Berlin rate, into a newly established *Konversionskasse*. The pace and timing of the release of foreign exchange to external creditors were to be determined exclusively by the Reichsbank and the German Minister of Economics. Soon afterwards, the Reichsbank again convened the committee of representatives of long-term creditors from the Netherlands, Sweden, Switzerland, the United Kingdom, and the United States for further negotiations on possible exemptions to the new transfer law. This time, the BIS – as fiscal agent and trustee of the Dawes and Young loans – was invited to participate. The discussions took place in London at the end of June on the fringes of the World Monetary and Economic Conference. There, cracks again emerged in the creditors' front: whereas the legal transfer priority of the Dawes Loan was recognised by all participants, the status of the Young Loan remained controversial.[199]

On 30 June 1933, the Reichsbank published the terms of application of the transfer law for the period up to 31 December 1933. All foreign exchange transfers for amortisation purposes were suspended,[200] with the sole exception of amortisation payments for the Dawes Loan. The sinking fund instalments on the Young Loan would be paid in Reichsmarks into a blocked Reichsbank account opened in the name of the trustee.[201] For all practical purposes, amortisation of the Young Loan bonds was ceased.

As trustee, the BIS formally objected to this unilateral violation of the General Bond securing the Young Loan. Recognising Germany's difficult position, however, the Bank agreed to abstain from legal action – provided it was not requested to do so by a substantial proportion of the Young Loan bondholders it represented.[202]

Faced with reduced payments on the loans granted to Germany, in terms both of amortisation and interest,[203] the front of the long-term creditors crumbled. Those markets where the bondholders of the Dawes and Young loans represented only a small minority of long-term creditors to Germany, such as the Netherlands and Switzerland, had questioned the transfer priority granted to the Dawes Loan and (especially) the Young Loan from an early stage. They now began to look for alternative solutions to satisfy the holders of other German bonds in their markets through separate, bilateral agreements with Germany.[204] Since Schacht had consistently pointed to trade restrictions as the main cause for Germany's inability to earn sufficient foreign exchange to satisfy its foreign creditors, both the Netherlands and Switzerland proposed raising their import quota for German goods. In exchange, they required Germany to increase transfers related to the service of German debts held in their respective markets. The Bank of England also tried to come to a separate arrangement with Germany, but in this case with the express intention of safeguarding the transfer priority attached to the Dawes and Young loans. In January 1934, Norman secretly travelled to Berlin. There he proposed to Schacht that the Bank of England advance the Reichsbank a sum in sterling sufficient to settle all coupons on German bonds, other than the Dawes and Young bonds, held in the London market and maturing over the next one to two years. The idea was stamped on by the U.K. chancellor as soon as he got wind of it.[205]

While this parallel diplomacy was developing in the background, the Reichsbank called a transfer conference of the long-term creditors' committee in Berlin to discuss the extension of the transfer moratorium after 30 June 1934. Since Germany's official foreign exchange reserves were dwindling ever further (by 30 April 1934 they stood at a paltry 5.8% of outstanding circulation), it was generally expected that the transfer moratorium would be further tightened. This was confirmed in plain terms by Schacht during a private conversation with Fraser, Norman, Trip, and Bachmann at the BIS governors' meeting on 12 March 1934.[206]

In an attempt to agree on common positions in advance of the Berlin Transfer Conference, the various national committees representing Germany's long- and medium-term creditors, urged on by Norman, called a preliminary meeting at the BIS from 6 to 10 April 1934. Although the BIS did not officially participate in the discussions, the meeting was timed to coincide with the Bank's regular governors' meeting of 9–11 April, thus providing the opportunity for informal contacts. The creditors' representatives met with Schacht, who remained noncommittal. Despite Norman's efforts, the Basel meeting did not succeed in aligning the different positions.[207] The United Kingdom desperately wanted to avoid the breakup of the creditors' front, but at the same time it was anxious to maintain the transfer priority for the Dawes and Young loans. The Dutch and Swiss representatives, and to some extent the United States, were flatly opposed to any priority whatsoever. As the Swiss delegate Jöhr put it, the privileged treatment of the Dawes and Young loans constituted "a very essential discrimination to the profit of certain nations and to the detriment of others".[208] The Swedish representative fell in with that view, arguing that if the Dawes and Young loans enjoyed transfer priority, then so too should the 1929 Krueger Loan. The meeting broke up without any tangible result. As BIS Assistant General Manager Hülse remarked in one of his regular letters to the German Ministry of Finance: "The real battle will be fought at the plenary Conference in Berlin".[209]

The Transfer Conference, hosted by the Reichsbank, lasted a full month, from 27 April to 29 May 1934. It was chaired by BIS President Leon Fraser. He had at first maintained that he would only chair the Berlin conference on the understanding that the existing transfer priority for the Dawes and Young loans would not be up for bargaining. But he gave in to pressures from Norman and others, in spite of the fact that Schacht was unwilling to give any explicit guarantees to that effect.[210]

The discussion in Berlin followed a familiar script. The Reichsbank blamed international trade restrictions and quotas for its critical reserve position. Creditors found the forecasts about Germany's potential to earn foreign exchange to be based on overly gloomy assumptions.[211] Moreover, they argued that the intensive use of blocked and registered Reichsmarks as well as restrictive foreign exchange regulations seemed "rather calculated to deter the German businessman from doing any exports business".[212] It was, nevertheless, recognised that a case could be made for granting Germany further transfer concessions. A proposal was discussed to grant Germany a complete transfer moratorium on both capital and interest for one year, after which interest payments in foreign exchange would be resumed at 50% of the sums due.

In the end, no agreement could be reached. The conference broke down on Germany's insistence that all medium- and long-term credits, including the Dawes and Young loans, should be treated equally. Schacht yielded, at least partly, to the tremendous pressure from his colleagues in the Nazi government who wanted to put an end to the Dawes and Young loans, the last remnants of Versailles.[213] Skilful politician and psychologist that he was, Schacht played out the pressure that he was under to the good effect of attaining his long-standing goal of a substantial reduction in Germany's external liabilities. Thus, in his characteristically dramatic style, he wrote to Thomas Lamont: "Whether you may threaten me with death or not will not alter the situation because here is the plain fact that I have no foreign valuta, and whether you may call me immoral or stupid or whatever you like it is purely beyond my power to create dollars and pounds because you would not like falsified banknotes but good currency".[214] At the same time, Schacht remained uneasy as to Germany's international standing should it default completely on its external obligations. Apparently, the stress of the circumstances took its toll: Fraser told Parker Gilbert that the Reichsbank's president had "aged 10 years within the last 4 months".[215] The second reason for the failure of the Berlin conference lay with the creditors themselves: their divisions only made Schacht's task easier.

On 7 May 1934, while the Berlin conference was still in session, German Minister of Finance Count Schwerin von Korsigk had already warned the BIS that the German Reich would not be able to continue its service of the Dawes and Young loans after 30 June 1934.[216] After the conference, the German government announced a complete transfer moratorium for all Germany's medium- and long-term debts, including the Dawes and Young loans, driving their prices down at the major stock exchanges.[217] On 1 July, the transfer mechanism of the Dawes and Young loans – in which the BIS had played such a pivotal role – ground to a final halt. The BIS reacted by protesting against the German government's unilateral action and expressly reserving all rights and privileges of the Young Loan bondholders.[218] There was, of course, no illusion about the practical utility of any complaints. They were filed merely for future record, "to show", as Fraser put it, "that the Trustees were not asleep at the switch, and to demonstrate the thoroughly arbitrary way in which the German government has disregarded its engagements".[219]

As the full moratorium became a reality, the Dawes and Young bondholders went into a frenzy, flooding the trustee (through their respective issuing houses) with their protests. At one point, J. P. Morgan even suggested that the BIS lay a legal claim on German funds held in Switzerland.[220] Soon, however, bondholders in different markets saw their demands partially satisfied through bilateral clearing arrangements negotiated by the German government with their respective national governments.[221] Germany had successfully dismantled the remaining international machinery of the Dawes and Young plans, sidelined the BIS, and put its financial obligations on a purely bilateral basis. As *The Economist* observed: "one unfortunate consequence of the need for separate negotiations between Germany and her creditors is that the functions of the Bank for International Settlements as agent for the Dawes and Young Loans are being short-circuited. Another and wider consequence is that Germany's trade and finance are being divided up into a number of water-tight compartments".[222]

What was the position of the two Reich loans after 1 July 1934? The Dawes Loan had been serviced fully (both interest and principal) for nearly ten years. After 1 July 1934, the BIS had sufficient reserves left on its Dawes Loan account to pay up to 50% of the coupon due on 15 October 1934. At that date, the Dawes Loan had been redeemed for nearly half as far as the dollar bonds were concerned but for less than one quarter in the case of all other bonds. The Young Loan had not been fully serviced for three years when, in July 1933, the sinking fund instalments were interrupted. On 1 July 1934, the Reichsbank stopped all further payments on the Young Loan to the BIS as its trustee, so that the interest coupon falling due on 1 December 1934 could only be serviced to one sixth, out of the Young funds remaining on the BIS books. All in all, at the time of the German default, fewer than 7% of all the Young bonds issued had been fully redeemed.

As the BIS role as paying agent was finished, payments on maturing interest coupons were made directly by the German Clearing Office or the Reichsbank to the main issuing house in each of the markets where the Reich loans had originally been subscribed. Because different arrangements were in place with individual countries, the BIS could no longer monitor the service of the two Reich loans. Nevertheless, the Bank continued to send regular statements and payment reminders to the German Finance Ministry with respect to both loans. In turn, the Reichsbank notified the BIS of the status of the blocked Reichsbank account to which the sums in Reichsmarks required for the service of the Dawes and Young loans were credited and of what payments were made in the context of the different clearing agreements. The final chapter in the history of these two loans would be written

Table 5.1. *Receipt and distribution of German funds for reparation payments and loans service, 1930–34*

	June 1930 through March 1931	April 1931 through March 1932	April 1932 through March 1933	April 1933 through March 1934	April 1934 through June 1934	After June 1934
Reparations, unconditional part	510,000,000	207,052,474	1,484,565	0	0	0
Loan, German railways[a]		404,947,526				
Reparations, conditional part[b]	858,000,000	251,725,000	0	0	0	0
Total reparations[c]	1,368,000,000	863,725,000	136,872,041			
to France	750,583,333	242,739,115				
to United Kingdom	305,666,667	102,956,718				
to Italy	130,000,000	51,004,042				
to Belgium	81,833,333	25,650,000				
to others	99,916,667	36,427,599	1,484,565			
loan, German Railways		404,947,526	135,387,476			
Service, Dawes Loan[d]	72,761,748	80,235,440	71,408,888	57,342,113	12,672,071	0
Service, Young Loan[e]	55,195,071	65,646,420	64,418,105	44,660,982	10,069,788	0
Total German transfers	1,495,956,819	604,659,334[f]	137,311,558[g]	102,003,095	22,741,859	0

Note: All amounts in Reichsmarks (parity up to March 1933: RM 4.2 = $1 U.S.).

[a] Hoover moratorium (London protocol, 11 August 1931): unconditional part of reparations converted into a loan to the German Railway Company made on behalf of the creditor governments.

[b] Hoover moratorium (London protocol, 11 August 1931): conditional part of reparations suspended for the duration of one year as from July 1931.

[c] All further reparation payments suspended from July 1932 (Lausanne Agreement, 9 July 1932).

[d] Amortisation and interest payments through the BIS (fiscal agent to the trustees of the Dawes Loan 1924) suspended as of July 1934.

[e] Amortisation payments suspended as of July 1933, and all interest payments through the BIS (trustee of the Young Loan 1930) suspended as of July 1934.

[f] Not including RM 404,947,526 in unconditional reparations converted into a loan to the German Railway Company.

[g] Not including RM 135,387,476 in unconditional reparations converted into a loan to the German Railway Company.

Source: BIS Annual Reports, 1931–35.

long after the Second World War, and it would again (as we will see) involve the BIS.

Was the German transfer crisis of 1933–34 inevitable? Schacht for one has done everything he could to present it that way. Germany's external reserve position was no doubt extremely weak, and improving it substantially in the protectionist climate prevailing after the failure of the London World Conference would certainly have been no mean feat. On the other hand, as Ritschl has argued convincingly, a transfer and debt moratorium was not the unavoidable, predetermined outcome of Germany's turbulent course since the late 1920s. In the circumstances of 1933 – freed of reparations and with the Reichsbank's gold reserves already largely vanished – Germany might as well have devalued, thereby restoring its balance of payments and enabling it to continue servicing its external debts.[223] However, Hitler's government had no intention of taking this route.[224]

5.9   Emphasis on Cooperation

We have argued that of the two pillars on which the BIS originally rested – reparations and the gold standard – it was the latter's demise that had the most lasting impact on the Bank's life. The end of reparations affected the Bank's balance sheet negatively and left an unpleasant and cumbersome heritage of legal duties related to its trustee functions, but it did not otherwise affect the Bank's life adversely. On the contrary, it probably improved the climate at the Basel meetings, for instance by removing Schacht's original objections to its very existence and, in general, by making both the Germans and the British more at ease at the BIS. The end of the gold standard dealt a more serious blow to the Bank as originally set up and organised.

There was, of course, a material side effect to the end of the gold standard as well. "For an institution directed by its statutes to deal for its own account in currencies 'on the gold or gold exchange standard', the secession of sterling, the dollar and the many currencies influenced by them, acutely limited its field of action. Except for continued operations in the gold bloc currencies, and in other exchanges 'for the account of others', the bank became a sort of international investment trust, husbanding its funds and waiting for a brighter day."[225] But those who worked at the BIS were mostly concerned with the implications of the end of the gold standard for the policy and intellectual life of the Bank.

Almost by default, emphasis was placed, starting with the Annual Report, on the statutory mission of the Bank unaffected by the crisis: central bank cooperation. Capitalising on the ad hoc resolution of the London

Conference, some hard thinking was devoted to the cooperative nature of the Bank, particularly by Per Jacobsson. The latter's mind was more pragmatic than Quesnay's, who had always believed that the gold standard and cooperation went hand in hand and whose intellectual loyalty now leaned towards the gold bloc countries, led by France.

Persuaded neither by Keynes nor by his own fellow countryman Cassel, Jacobsson remained a believer in the gold anchor; he nevertheless endeavoured to conceive ways of putting central bank cooperation at the core of the BIS's daily life. He argued that, though important in emergencies, lending of last resort was not the kernel of the collaboration between central banks, for this collaboration should be "evidenced in continuous and daily practice".[226] A number of issues provided the scope for day-to-day cooperation, such as: "the evolution of a common monetary doctrine; the interchange of opinions in council; the avoidance of action that might harm another central bank; the interpretation by a central bank for the benefit of its neighbours of the trend of events in its own country; the formulation of a central bank practice regarding the fineness of gold bars and earmarking of gold; the provision of assistance and technical advice to countries establishing new central banks; concentrated action to eliminate the demonstrated effects of the gold exchange standard".[227] This patchy list found its way into the Annual Reports, in particular that of 1935 referred to in Chapter 1.

Luzzatti's and others' grand schemes for an international superbank, guiding and supervising individual central banks, was far from being on the horizon in the autarkic and nationalist context of the 1930s. The BIS could not even aspire to become the "rediscount bank for central banks, as the Federal Reserve System does for private banks in the United States" advocated by Fraser.[228] With plans for the BIS's role in international monetary matters brought down to earth, the best hopes for cooperation were pinned on "the continuous personal contacts at Basel of financial leaders from the various countries".[229] It was perhaps too little not only to the utopians but also to those who engineered the international bank at Baden-Baden or worked to set it up in 1930–31 – yet those meetings continued uninterruptedly to draw busy people from all over Europe to Basel once a month. The pudding must have been found tasty if it continued to pass the proof of eating for such a long period of time.

SIX

An Autarkic and Divided World

6.1　Strained International Relations

As we have seen, whatever favourable climate for economic cooperation had existed at The Hague in 1929, it could not be re-created in London four years later. By then, economic indicators in several countries were beginning to show signs of slow recovery. However, this was (or seemed to be) the result of independent domestic policies rather than of coordinated efforts. Credit for the improvement was given to devaluations, tariffs and quotas, clearings, controls on international capital movement, and the managed allocation of lending. More was to come in the following years; autarky – in varying forms and degrees – was to remain the keynote of the international economy for the rest of the decade. In 1933, the volume of international trade was down about 30% from its 1929 peak, while its value was only 40% of the 1929 figure.[1] In 1937, while world industrial output was about 9% above its 1929 level, the volume of international trade remained 5% below.[2]

E. H. Carr noted that: "In 1933, the first rift in the economic clouds coincided with a fresh darkening of the political horizon. Political preoccupations – the withdrawal of Germany and Japan from the League and the imminent breakdown of the Disarmament Conference – once more dominated world affairs and, though themselves in large measure due to economic causes, caused purely economic aspects of the crisis to take a subordinate place in men's thoughts".[3] It is difficult, and certainly beyond the scope of this book, to disentangle economic from political factors in the deterioration of international relations, let alone to establish precise causal links. International economic relations in the 1920s were poisoned by the politics of Versailles, while at the same time international capital movements and monetary stabilisation affected domestic policy making. Over the following decade, autarky postulated an extension of the domestic "economic space" by the creation of areas of financial and commercial influence abroad or, as in the case of Japan and Italy, by outright military conquest. In both cases, the adverse effect on international political relations was bound to be enormous. More generally, the spread of economic nationalism brought forth a grass-roots culture indifferent or even hostile to international cooperation. The League of Nations, as the organisation designed to "produce the maximum possible intergovernmental cooperation at any given moment",[4] was increasingly marginalised by the political consequences of economic nationalism in the 1930s.

The main events disrupting whatever cooperative international relations existed in the late 1920s are well known. In September 1931, Japan embarked on its conquest of Manchuria, completed in less than four months. It took one year *post factum* for the League of Nations to vote the ambiguous Lytton Report containing a mild condemnation of the aggressor and no mention of sanctions. This kid-glove treatment, however, did not prevent Japan from leaving the League. The episode marked a return to power politics and treaty repudiation that was to characterise the 1930s up to that fateful September 1939.

On 30 January 1933, Hitler became German chancellor. In October of the same year, Germany withdrew both from the Disarmament Conference, which had been dragging on inconclusively for the previous twenty months, and from the League of Nations. To counter the re-emergence of German power, France moved towards an alliance with the Soviet Union and sought to improve its relations with Italy. This did nothing to make Germany feel more secure. The year 1935 probably marked the point of no return beyond which normal, peaceful international relations became impossible. Soon after securing victory in the Saarland plebiscite, Hitler officially repudiated the military clauses of the Versailles treaty, making way for open rearmament. In October, Italian troops entered Abyssinia, prompting the League of Nations to impose sanctions against the invader. In March 1936, Germany reoccupied the demilitarised zones of the Rhineland. A few months later the Spanish Civil War broke out, dividing Europe into two bitterly opposed camps. In July 1937, Japan resumed its undeclared war with China. A few months later (March 1938), Germany annexed Austria; the Munich Agreement on Czechoslovakia (September 1938) held for only a few months.

Needless to say, international economic relations were deeply affected by the succession of political and military crises, by the formation of blocs or simple alliances, and by the dwindling prestige of the League of Nations. But, in addition to political shocks, economic developments themselves were responsible for strained international relations. In principle it may be argued that a system based on managed floats – as opposed to textbook pure floating exchange rates that have never existed in history – requires at least as much cooperation as the maintenance of an international monetary system based on fixed exchange rates. In the 1930s, cooperation should have meant above all coordinated reflation. After 1931, however, the environment proved to be less conducive to cooperative behaviour than at any time in the 1920s.

The events of 1931–33, touched upon in the previous chapters, led to the formation of at least five economic and currency blocs. The policy targets and tools of each proved to be seldom compatible with those of the others. The Ottawa Conference of 1932 drew the United Kingdom closer to its Commonwealth and away from continental Europe, the aim of the so-called imperial preferences being the creation of a trade zone where manufactured goods would be exchanged for agricultural produce and other commodities. After the devaluation of the dollar, the United States concentrated on domestic reflation. Germany did the same, with the additional aim of creating enough resources for rearmament. The German government resorted more rigorously than any other to exchange controls, managed allocation of credit, discriminatory tariffs, and quotas, clearing agreements to stimulate domestic demand and allocation of resources to "planned" objectives, while at the same time avoiding open inflation and official devaluation of the currency. The enlargement of the Reich's area of economic influence through trade agreements and foreign direct investment, particularly in Southeastern Europe, complemented the strategy of autarkic reflation. A similar strategy was pursued by Japan, the core of the fourth economic bloc, but in conditions that were more favourable than Germany's. Tokyo had to worry neither about formal adherence to the gold standard – abandoned in 1931, a few months after its hesitant adoption – nor about the absorption of large numbers of unemployed.

Finally, there was the gold bloc, where reflation could take place only within the constraints of gold convertibility. However, in this respect as in others, the gold bloc was far from being a homogenous entity. France, the leader of the group, could afford better than its partners the costs of remaining on gold. Its large gold reserves allowed some room for manoeuvre, although this became narrower as the years went by. In any case, the country could sustain better than others the political costs of deflation, as a large portion of the unemployed consisted of nonenfranchised immigrants.

Among the principal benefits of France's gold policy was that of maintaining Paris as an international financial centre. The same costs and benefits applied, to some extent, to the Netherlands. Belgium's export industry, on the other hand, having exhausted the advantages of the low parity established in 1926, grew increasingly restless, forcing the country off gold in 1935. Italy tried for a while to maintain convertibility with the aid of foreign exchange controls – mild at first, then increasingly restrictive. In 1935, however, preparations for the military adventure in Abyssinia drove Italy's economic policy nearer to Germany's than France's, and only the façade of the gold standard was kept in place, mostly for domestic political purposes.

Both in principle and in the light of subsequent events, economic policy coordination would have been a rational course of action for all the main international players in the 1930s. But things turned out very differently. "France managed its substantial gold and foreign exchange reserves independently, the United Kingdom, whose dollar reserves increased rapidly after the abandonment of the gold standard, made arrangements to invest directly on the U.S. market and to concentrate the sterling balances of the British Empire countries in accounts held directly in London, and Germany was progressively sealing itself behind the walls of a system of exchange controls."[5]

Against such a negative background and unfavourable odds, the ambitious plans made in 1930 for central bank cooperation had to be scaled down. Cooperative efforts, both bilateral and multilateral, were nevertheless made throughout the 1930s. In what follows, we shall discuss what kind of cooperation in monetary matters proved to be feasible in the autarkic world of the 1930s, around the focal point of the BIS (Sections 6.2–6.4), while also accounting for the Bank's life and operation (Sections 6.5–6.9).

6.2   Central Bank Cooperation in an Autarkic World: An Oxymoron?

On 11 November 1935, President Trip opened the monthly meeting of the Board of Directors by mentioning the sixth anniversary of the completion, by the experts at Baden-Baden, of their proposal for the BIS Statutes. He went on to say that, "although all the hopes raised at the time had not been fulfilled, the Bank had succeeded in promoting close collaboration between central banks".[6]

To what extent was this self-congratulatory remark also self-consolatory? What was the reality of central bank cooperation behind such an encouraging but general statement? A first answer to these questions was indirectly provided at the same meeting by one of the directors,[7] who, replying to the president, added that "These results were due largely to the excellent co-operation between the leading personalities of the Bank. It was hoped that this cooperation would be further extended and would develop into closer collaboration between the various markets and countries".[8] From the very beginning of their monthly meetings in Basel, central bankers believed that they were much readier to cooperate than their respective governments. The corollary to this postulate, particularly in Norman's opinion, was that a higher degree of central bank power and independence would result in more extensive and effective international cooperation in monetary and financial matters. In the 1930s, according to this view, the scope for monetary policy coordination had been reduced, not only because governments had grown more nationalist and litigious, but also because they had taken over functions (notably, foreign exchange management) that had hitherto been the domain of central banks.

To Norman, the end of the gold standard was to blame for all evils, including "a redistribution of authority and responsibility, which deprived the Bank of some of its essential functions".[9] In his gloomiest moments, therefore, he felt that, as "the central banks [were] pretty much in the hands of their governments [it was] impossible to do anything by way of cooperation".[10] The notion that the end of the gold standard per se reduced central bank independence and thus the scope and effectiveness of international cooperation is not easy to understand in pure economic terms. It is true that the gold-standard automatic adjustment mechanism existed in theory only and that the system, particularly in its post-1925 version, entailed a good deal of management by central banks, yet it is also true that it always retained some elements of automatism and some rules of play. The absence of a commodity anchor requires more rather than less central bank independence if price stability is to be preserved. Likewise, maintaining an efficient and stable system of international payments demands more rather than less central bank cooperation if large and erratic exchange rate fluctuations are to be avoided.

It is difficult to believe that these considerations escaped Norman's intuitive mind: when he said he missed the gold standard, he implied that he missed a system of which he and a few others were the high priests by virtue of their intimate knowledge of an intricate liturgy. He truly believed that those rituals kept outsiders at bay: governments, trade unions, manufacturers, the press. Norman was nevertheless correct in arguing that monetary policy coordination alone could not deliver balance of payments equilibrium and exchange rate stability in the presence of the panoply of administrative measures almost universally enacted to control the international flow

of goods and factors of production. Without a return to more open conditions in international trade and capital movements, as well as to multilateral
settlements, central bank cooperation was crippled. Cooperative autarky is
plainly an oxymoron.

There can be little doubt that the monetary events of 1931–33 affected
central bank cooperation negatively. According to Beyen,[11] from 1933 to
1936 the BIS was "a centre for consultation for monetary authorities whose
governments were no longer guided by a common purpose".[12] The policy
targets of the gold bloc countries were different from those of Washington, London, and Tokyo, to say nothing of Berlin. The gold bloc's share of
world output and trade was relatively modest, but its member countries happened to be over-represented in Basel. Beyen's judgement that there was
no longer a common purpose in using the BIS as an instrument of international cooperation[13] is probably too extreme. There remained, as we shall
see, areas where collaboration was possible and fruitful. It was nevertheless
true that the gold standard provided policy guidelines that vanished in September 1931. At the unofficial governors' meetings, views diverged sharply
about future policies. Representatives of the gold-standard countries now
found themselves in disagreement with and opposed by the Governor of
the Bank of England. It became harder to find common ground for cooperation. Moreover, as noted by an insider, it was no longer the case that a
common "monetary doctrine" of the four largest central banks could exert
a positive influence on the governors of the second-ranking central banks
gathered in Basel.[14] This too was a loss, as the provision of both leadership
and support in monetary matters to some of the small countries in Europe
had hitherto been the area where central bank cooperation and the BIS itself
had possibly been most successful.

What, then, was the cooperation referred to by Trip at the November
1935 Board meeting? He was specifically referring to exchange rate stabilisation after the devaluation of the Belgian franc in March 1935.

After July 1933, exchange rate stabilisation did not cease to be one of
the policy targets of governments and central banks, although it was subordinated to domestic policy goals (it was, after all, precisely to reappro-
priate their monetary sovereignty that London and Washington had gone
off gold in 1931 and 1933). In the second half of 1933, Roosevelt's priority was "to raise agricultural prices which were badly out of adjustment"
and he was therefore noncommittal about exchange rate stabilisation. Only
at the end of the year did the president begin to consider "the situation
in the farm area less acute", indicating that "he might be satisfied for the
present with the existing level of exchange rates".[15] He would, however,

still avoid any long-term commitment. London was likewise reluctant to let the pound appreciate. In June 1932, the U.K. government had created an exchange equalisation fund, placed under the control of the Treasury, the aim of which was to maintain the external value of the pound at desired (but unspecified) levels. In the first twenty months of its existence, this fund operated mostly to avoid an appreciation of the pound while at the same time increasing gold reserves. The U.K. currency was by then in demand,[16] given markets' doubts about the future of the gold bloc and uncertainties about Roosevelt's stance.

The exchange rate policies of Washington and London, and particularly their noncommittal attitude, were at odds with those of Paris, which had chosen the hard way of maintaining gold convertibility. In the second half of 1933, France lost some 800 million gold francs, and capital outflows continued in the first months of 1934 amid rumours of devaluation. When Roosevelt finally stabilised the dollar at $35 per ounce of gold in January 1934 (a 59% devaluation of the dollar compared to the pre-March 1933 parity), the governors of the gold bloc countries were appalled. At a secret meeting at the BIS on 12 February 1934, they seriously considered declaring an embargo on gold shipments to the United States.[17] All in all, gold losses were not particularly worrisome (in the second half of 1933 the Bank of France lost only about 6% of its huge reserves), but they obliged the authorities to stick to a politically costly domestic deflation. In mid-1934 capital flows were reversed, due among other things to the formation in France of a large coalition government. It was then the pound's turn to feel the pressure and for Paris to lose interest in exchange rate stabilisation, since it was recovering most of the previously lost gold. In particular, capital was flowing in from Belgium, where a looming banking crisis, scandals, and deep political divisions[18] threatened the convertibility of the franc.[19]

On 8 October 1934, the central bank governors of the gold bloc countries met at the BIS, ahead of a conference convened in Brussels[20] by the governments concerned, to discuss the bloc's problems. The meeting was in itself a manifestation of the failure of cooperation, as the main players outside the bloc were not even invited. The same governors reconvened in Basel on 12 November and discussed the ineffectual protocol approved by the conference,[21] which basically advocated bilateral action and had no impact on gold outflows from Belgium. These dried up briefly only in the wake of the Theunis government's formation and soon resumed under the weight of budgetary, banking, mining, and export problems.[22] In March 1935 – after a dramatic meeting in Paris with the French government that did not result in the hoped-for lifting of import quotas on Belgian goods – a royal decree introduced exchange controls. A new Cabinet of "national unity" was formed, headed by Paul van Zeeland, a director of the national bank.[23] A substantial number of the new government's members favoured devaluation. Unable to stop a renewed outflow of gold, van Zeeland finally decided to suspend convertibility and devalue the currency.[24] A well-paced monetary expansion accompanied devaluation, as a result of which "industrial production grew more rapidly between March 1935 and March 1936 in Belgium than anywhere else in the western world".[25]

Belgium's exit from the gold club did not stop the turmoil in the foreign exchange markets. The capital flight that continued from France, the Netherlands, and Switzerland affected gold reserves, although these remained well above the legal requirement thanks to continued deflation. From a technical point of view, the gold standard was far from being undermined: the threat to convertibility was political rather than economic, as opposition to deflationary policies within the remaining gold bloc countries gained strength. The politically explosive fact was that output and employment were by then rising almost everywhere in the world, while "only the members of the gold bloc failed to share in this world-wide recovery".[26] In Switzerland a ballot proposal for the suspension of convertibility was defeated narrowly in June 1935; in France and the Netherlands both, governments were made and dissolved over the gold (or rather the deflation) issue.[27]

It is against this background that in May 1935 a request by the Bank of France for a $200 million facility – to withstand the demand for U.S. currency in anticipation of the fall of the moderately reflationist Flandin government[28] – met with sympathy from both Roosevelt and Morgenthau. As we have seen, talks about cooperation on a de facto currency stabilisation between the United States, the United Kingdom, and France had been going on intermittently ever since the spring of 1933. Still, domestic policy considerations had always prevailed and, moreover, "Roosevelt was not opposed to de facto stabilisation, but neither was he excited about it".[29] In the spring of 1935, however, world recovery was under way and many felt that domestic prices in most countries had by then adjusted to the prevailing exchange rates. With the realignment of purchasing power parities of the main currencies,[30] exchange rate stabilisation seemed to make sense again from both the political and the economic point of view. Such authorities as Viner in the United States and Keynes in the United Kingdom supported stabilisation. Washington's support of the franc in May 1935 came as a first tangible sign of renewed cooperation, even though London was for the moment sitting on the sidelines in gloomy self-imposed isolation.

Trip's remarks about fruitful cooperation at the BIS Board meeting in November 1935 probably hinted at the U.S. loan to France and at the continuation of stabilisation talks, this time including the United Kingdom, in the second half of the year. It is true that these accomplishments, small as they were, resulted from bilateral (or at best trilateral) financial diplomacy rather than from multilateral central bank cooperation, but there was the feeling in Basel that "the close contact maintained had facilitated de facto currency stability".[31] It was argued that "close collaboration between central banks" had been able "to suppress speculation" and that "this example of central bank collaboration provided further proof of the validity of the monthly meetings of the Board". The actual meaning of these statements is not clear. In the context, however, they seem to imply (a) that bilateral cooperation was enhanced by a multilateral discourse of the kind that took place in Basel, and (b) that the substantial backing given by central bankers to the maintenance of or return to gold convertibility sent the right signal to the markets.[32]

That the BIS continued to be regarded as a valuable locus – if not for actual cooperation, then at least for the exchange of information and opinions – is witnessed by the eagerness of Merle Cochran to travel to Basel and to keep in touch with BIS officials when not there. Cochran, stationed in Paris, was the U.S. "Treasury liaison to the central bankers of Europe"[33] and played an important (albeit behind-the-scenes) role in the negotiations leading to the Tripartite Agreement.

6.3 The United States and the BIS

When Leon Fraser stepped down as president of the BIS at the end of June 1935, he also resigned his seat on the Board.[34] He did so for personal reasons: after a long spell in Europe he was anxious to settle in his homeland.[35] McGarrah, who had retained his seat together with the title of Honorary President, also tendered his resignation. After the stepping down of the two Americans who had served with the Bank since its creation, no U.S. citizen was to be officially present at BIS Board meetings until the appointment of McKittrick as president of the Bank at the beginning of 1940.[36]

As we have seen, while the U.S. government had consistently vetoed an official U.S. presence in Basel, the appointments of both McGarrah and Fraser had nevertheless enjoyed Washington's unofficial blessing. As BIS presidents, these two bankers were perfectly suited to act as liaisons between the BIS and high-ranking U.S. central bank officials. In particular, they kept in constant touch with Harrison at the Federal Reserve Bank of New York, providing an effective communication channel across the Atlantic. Occasionally, when bilateral relations were cool, Basel acted as a link between New York and a European central bank.[37] After the two men left the BIS, transatlantic communication began to falter, which was due also to the absence of Americans amongst the BIS staff.[38] Most of the issues previously dealt with by top management were thereafter taken care of impersonally by lower-ranking officials.

Why did the United States – which had masterminded both the Dawes and the Young plans and taken so much interest in the early development of the BIS – end up abandoning Basel altogether? To a large extent, the answer to this question can be found in domestic policy making and in a clash of bureaucracies.

Because overseas investment was largely concentrated in the hands of New York investment houses, the Federal Reserve Bank of New York had, almost naturally, taken upon itself the task of running U.S. central bank diplomacy, for which it possessed both skills and connections. Benjamin Strong had been an ideal partner for Norman's currency stabilisation strategies in the 1920s. Strong was probably one of the few Americans to recognise, soon after the war, that their country's newly acquired financial and economic might carried with it the unavoidable burden of new international responsibilities, and "he attempted the difficult task of meeting these responsibilities without sacrificing domestic objectives".[39]

Strong's monetary policy, favourable to the flow of U.S. capital to Europe and thus to the recovery both of Germany and of transatlantic trade, has been judged in two opposite ways. On one side are those who go as far as to argue that his untimely death[40] was a tragedy of worldwide dimensions, in the absence of which many of the rigours of the Great Depression might have been mitigated. The opposite view maintains that cheap money led to too much short-term credit being granted to European banks who in turn transformed it into long-term assets – with the resulting maturity mismatch as the main cause of financial instability and eventual crises. In the 1930s, the latter opinion was firmly held in influential quarters both at the Federal Reserve System Board of Governors and at the Treasury. And it coloured the overall assessment by Washington of the links with Europe maintained by the Federal Reserve Bank of New York and of its virtual monopoly of central bank diplomacy. No one dared openly challenge Strong when he was alive. But he was succeeded by George Harrison (less of a heavyweight than his predecessor), and many in Washington felt he should not be allowed the same room for manoeuvre overseas as that enjoyed by

Strong.[41] Thus, U.S. participation in the BIS Board was, to a large extent, the victim of a conflict between New York and powerful quarters in Washington about who should run day-to-day overseas contacts.

As we have seen, the official policy of the U.S. administration was that none of its members should serve in the BIS because of the institution's involvement in reparations. The ban included officials of the Federal Reserve System member banks and of the Board of Governors. In fact, McGarrah resigned from the board of the Federal Reserve Bank of New York upon his appointment as BIS president, which was informally cleared with the State Department. Harrison, however, was advised to avoid Basel when visiting European central bankers. As a result, Harrison and McGarrah had little direct contact with each other, a situation that was felt both as an embarrassment and a loss by the head of the Federal Reserve Bank of New York.

A consensus existed from the very beginning within the Federal Reserve Bank of New York about the desirability of U.S. participation in the BIS. The reasons given at the time reflected the heritage of Strong's thinking about the role of the United States in European affairs. "Some experience of international encounters ... leads us to believe that American participation exercises a moderating influence upon threatened European conflict, serves to quiet European fears born of manifestations of provincialism in Congress, and is generally superior in inventiveness and resourcefulness to European participation, despite a tendency to apply misleading simplification to phenomena which are often, psychologically and historically, highly complex."[42]

Upon his return from a trip to Basel in 1931, Antony Burgess, Harrison's deputy, was required to report to the Federal Reserve Board, which knew little about the BIS. He was extremely appreciative of the usefulness of the monthly unofficial meetings[43] and summarised his view by saying that he had come "away with the conclusion that the BIS is doing a very useful job, and that it is questionable whether any other institutions would have been able to mobilise funds to meet the various situations which have arisen, as rapidly as it did".[44]

In the spring of 1931, Harrison secured approval from the president, the State Department, and the Treasury Department for a visit to Basel. The relaxation of the previous ban was intended to enable the two banks to establish mutual business relations, but it did not alter the original stance against official U.S. participation in the "organisation and management" of the BIS.[45] Two years later, however, Harrison felt that the grounds for the original U.S. position on the BIS no longer applied. In May 1933, he wrote to Secretary of the Treasury Woodin asking whether – now that the issue of German reparations had become relatively unimportant – the Federal Reserve Board would have any objection to his accepting the position of director of the BIS.[46] At the Federal Reserve Board meeting of 10 May, Woodin stated that "it was his feeling that the matter is of considerable importance and, in view of the present situation, such service is inadvisable and action upon the request should be deferred".[47] The Board was unanimous in sustaining the Treasury secretary's stance. Harrison, however, did not demur. In November he told Norman, who was equally eager to bring him over to Basel, that he had talked to Roosevelt, who "was more anxious than ever" to have Harrison become a director of the BIS. "The question", he added, "was now resting with the Federal Reserve Board who would have to approve".[48] Yet difficulties again came from that quarter. In November, after further consideration of the issue, the Board reiterated its earlier "conclusion that he [Harrison] should not accept the appointment and that the Board was not willing to grant permission for such a step".[49]

Undeterred, the New York Federal Reserve governor went on lobbying for the position in Basel. In May 1934, Governor Black reported to the Federal Reserve Board that he had talked to Roosevelt, who was keen to have Harrison go to Basel for the Annual General Meeting of the BIS.[50] The prospect of his taking up a seat on the BIS Board nevertheless remained uncertain.[51] In the end Harrison did not attend that meeting, but he travelled to Europe in the summer and was at the BIS on the occasion of the July Board meeting.[52] He was somewhat disappointed with the visit and for a while did not attempt to have the Federal Reserve Board agree on the BIS appointment, but in early 1935 the matter acquired new urgency because the time was approaching when both Fraser and McGarrah would leave Europe for good. The plan for a second trip to Basel, scheduled first for July[53] and then for October,[54] had to be postponed indefinitely pending approval from the Federal Reserve Board.[55] On that occasion, Morgenthau told Harrison that he could "advise the Board not only that he and the President did not object to [his] taking up [his] position on the board of the BIS, but that they very definitely and affirmatively wanted [him] to do so".[56] This endorsement notwithstanding, Eccles – the governor of the Federal Reserve Board[57] – authorised him only to make the trip to Europe but not to accept the BIS directorship, as there was still opposition to that in the FRB.[58] The stalemate dragged on in 1936.[59] It seems that after 1937 Harrison did not renew his request: he is likely to have reached the conclusion that opposition from within the Federal Reserve Board would never be overcome.

The friction between Washington and New York produced a stalemate that resulted in neither institution appointing a BIS Board member. Nor was it possible to implement the second-best solution suggested by some European central bankers: the appointment of private individuals to replace McGarrah and Fraser.[60] The BIS was thus deprived of the essential U.S. presence, with consequences that were deeply felt in the years that followed.

What were the reasons for the tenacious opposition of influential Federal Reserve Board members to Harrison's appointment at the BIS? They were certainly strong enough to overcome the apparently favourable stance of both the White House and the Treasury on the issue. As mentioned earlier, these reasons can be traced back to the long collision over the reshuffling of powers between Washington and New York, particularly after the approval by Congress of the 1935 Banking Act.[61]

Harrison's claim to the BIS seat was grounded both in tradition and in the BIS Statutes. The two actually went together. European central bankers, accustomed in the 1920s to dealing with the Federal Reserve Bank of New York, considered it as their U.S. counterpart for all practical purposes. Thus, when the BIS Statutes were laid down, the ex officio seat was granted to the governor (later president) of the New York bank. This situation resulted in Harrison taking it for granted that, should a U.S. official be allowed to take up the seat, there would be no question about him being nominated. He therefore concentrated his efforts on providing valuable arguments about the advisability of an official U.S. presence in Basel. Such arguments were twofold. On the one hand, Harrison maintained that the BIS was a lively and valuable institution, that the monthly meetings enhanced cooperation, and that the United States could not afford to be cut off from Basel – for its own good as well as for that of Europe. On the other hand he argued that, after the Hoover moratorium, the BIS's involvement with reparations had become marginal and that therefore the original reasons for abstaining from official participation no longer applied. Moreover, U.S. foreign policy vis-à-vis international organisations seemed to have changed in 1934, when Congress authorised participation in the International Labour Office. Harrison argued that the BIS was much more of a technical, "apolitical" institution than the ILO, an offspring of the League of Nations.

At the Federal Reserve Board in Washington, two different camps emerged on the issue: one opposed U.S. participation altogether; the other argued that the chairman of the Board of Governors, rather than the president of the Federal Reserve Bank of New York, should be nominated. Both camps were critical of the role played thus far by New York in international financial diplomacy. Explicit reference was made to a speech made by Senator Glass during the Senate discussion on the Banking Act of 1933. "For a period of six years", Glass said, "one of the Federal Reserve Banks has apparently given more attention to 'stabilising' Europe and to making enormous loans to European institutions than it has given to stabilising America".[62]

A lengthy internal memorandum to the Board of Governors by a member of the Federal Reserve system staff spelled out in crude isolationist fashion the bottom-line reasons why Harrison should not be permitted to take up a seat at the BIS. The document singled out the monopoly enjoyed by the governor of the Federal Reserve Bank of New York in contacts with European central banks as being responsible for the alleged mistakes of the 1920s. In those years, it was argued, monetary policy was "formulated not in view of maintaining sound credit conditions in this country but with the view of restoring European countries to the gold standard and stabilising their currencies. Being the only official of the Federal Reserve System in constant contact with the heads of foreign central banks and the only official of the Federal Reserve System familiar with banking conditions in Europe, the governor of the Federal Reserve Bank of New York, through the force of such information and the power and prestige it gave him, was able to induce the other eleven Federal Reserve banks and the board of governors to adopt an easy money policy in the summer of 1927 which impartial observers[63] now regard as one of the principal contributing causes of the inflation and speculation which this country experienced during the years 1928 and 1929."[64] According to the same memorandum, in 1930 the administration vetoed Federal Reserve participation in the BIS not because of the latter's connection with reparations but as a response to "the growing public resentment against the involvement of this country and its banking system in European affairs". Again quoting Senator Glass, the argument against Harrison's case was that the Federal Reserve Bank of New York "should be brought within the actual jurisdiction of the central authority here in Washington".[65] Although this was an extreme position, it must be said that Harrison was viewed with some suspicion even in more moderate quarters for being "notoriously susceptible to U.K. influence",[66] and his requests were probably less well supported than he imagined.

Those arguing that "any action which might involve the United States or the Federal Reserve System in the affairs of the BIS might produce a very unfavourable public reaction"[67] maintained that central bank diplomacy would be best carried out on a bilateral basis. If necessary, they conceded, the governor of the Federal Reserve Bank of New York or another official of the Federal Reserve System could always visit Basel, provided the trip avoided the need to visit individual European capitals. In any case, the proponents of this course of action argued that there was "no reason for believing that [the United States] will encounter any difficulty" in securing "full discussion with the heads of European central banks" as they "need the cooperation of this country much more than this country needs theirs".[68]

The second camp within the Federal Reserve Board, while equally distrustful of the Federal Reserve Bank of New York with regard to foreign diplomacy, took a more positive line on central bank cooperation and on the BIS itself. A memorandum of October 1935 argued that "The extent to which the price level can be controlled by monetary and credit action still remains for the future to reveal, but experience points to the belief that if the maximum degree of control possible is to be secured, action by the monetary authorities of different countries must be coordinated. There need be nothing binding in this coordination, it should be voluntary and informal ... but if it is not present in some form and if different countries continue, as they for the most part have in the past, to pursue contradictory policies, then the scope for monetary control of the price level would appear to be limited." Towards that end, consultations of one kind or another were deemed to be indispensable. "Frequent consultation provides the basis for successful cooperation which most of those having practical experience in this field agree, is necessary if the two main objectives of monetary policy, namely stability of the currency in terms of prices and in terms of exchanges, are to be adequately attained."[69]

Those who held this view were not only impressed by the services rendered by the BIS in the field of central bank cooperation,[70] they also envisaged an expansion of its role: "In the BIS there is available an agency through which the monetary authorities of the different countries can arrange for such coordination of policy as from time to time may seem to them desirable." In particular, in pursuing exchange rate stability, the BIS was well placed to render great service in: (a) providing essential information on both short- and long-term capital movements; and (b) devising instruments "for counteracting the effect of vagrant capital movements on the losing and receiving markets", possibly through a "central equalisation fund made up of contributions from the nations interested and operated by the monetary authorities of these nations acting in concert through a central agency which might very properly be the BIS". Therefore, the 1935 memorandum continued, "the question may be asked if the prospects for the continuance of these favourable conditions would not be improved by official U.S. representation on the Board of the BIS".[71]

If cooperation was important and the BIS a proper instrument to that end, the issue of U.S. participation could not be avoided. The 1935 Banking Act required the Board of Governors to supervise relationships between individual Federal Reserve banks and foreign credit institutions. Since the Board had thus far developed little first-hand knowledge of the situations abroad and was obliged to rely upon the Federal Reserve Bank of New York, it was suggested that the "Board contacts might be widened and enriched to such a point that its knowledge of foreign situations would match that of the New York bank". In fact, it was argued that the simple refusal to permit Harrison to join the BIS, while making foreign contacts less effective, still left "the New York Bank in possession of the field". The Board should build up its own foreign contacts, and the BIS offered "the most convenient means to secure that". In practice, it was proposed that one member of the Board of Governors be appointed a BIS Board member: he would make two six-week trips to Europe every year, participating in four Board meetings and visiting individual central banks in between. "Having a job to perform and working relationships with foreign central banks would be of inestimable assistance towards developing the member of the Board of Governors whose particular duty it would be to keep the Board familiar with significant situations in the world's financial centres. Such a member could match personal experience against personal experience when it came to passing judgement on proposals of the New York bank." The chairman of the Board of Governors, who could not afford long absences from Washington, would participate in the BIS's Annual General Meeting, while an American residing in Europe would be appointed as second Board member.[72]

Some minor legal changes were required on both sides of the Atlantic in order to implement this plan. The BIS Statutes had to be amended so as to make it clear that, in the case of the United States, "central bank" should mean the Board of Governors of the Federal Reserve System. Amendment of the 1913 Federal Reserve Act might also be contemplated, where it stipulated that no member of the Board of Governors could sit on the board of any other banking institution.[73] While it was clear that in spirit the proviso did not apply to the BIS, such an amendment might be advisable as a pre-emptive move to any legal challenge to the proposed plan. Ad hoc legislation, of course, would require overcoming "Congressional distrust of international cooperation". To that end, the matter should not appear to be one of "internationalism vs. isolation, but of New York vs. the Washington authorities. On this issue, the Congress has seldom failed to decide in favour of Washington".[74]

Finally, if legal or political implications made the Board of Governors reluctant to utilise the BIS as its tool for central bank cooperation, the proponents of active foreign involvement by the Federal Reserve advocated ad hoc visits to overseas central banks as the second-best solution. The latter would be "more time consuming, [while] the incentive of regular scheduled meetings would not exist nor the atmosphere of business contacts. There would be no continuing job to work on", but it would still be better than nothing. "The one thing that does not appear possible for the Board is to isolate itself from personalities and situations abroad and at the same time discharge its responsibilities under the Banking Act of 1933. Isolation leaves it dependent upon the New York Bank not only in its work of supervision over that bank but also in the broader formulation of Federal Reserve policy whenever foreign situations play into that policy."[75]

Frank Tamagna[76] quotes Chairman Eccles as stating, on 5 February 1937, that he "did not wish the by-laws of the BIS changed in order to admit American members. After all, the question of international finance is the Treasury's problem and if the Treasury does not want the Federal Reserve to have representation on the BIS, the Federal Reserve is ready to drop the entire matter. Our thought was that the BIS would simply become a listening post where various central bankers would go once a month and exchange gossip". By 1937, the deeper reasons for central bank cooperation did not carry much weight with the Board of Governors. This is likely to have been the last time the question was discussed in the United States before World War II.

In the context of the relations between Basel and the Federal Reserve Bank of New York, mention should also be made of the latter's account at the BIS in the 1930s.[77] In the hectic months of the 1931 Central European crisis, the Federal Reserve Bank of New York – though not reluctant to participate in the international lending – felt that it was not in a position to promptly evaluate the creditworthiness of the central banks concerned. The BIS seemed to be the right agent in such circumstances.[78] Towards that end, the Federal Reserve Bank of New York opened a deposit of $10 million with the BIS on the understanding that it would be used to purchase bills endorsed by the BIS itself. In January 1932, Governor Meyer of the Federal Reserve Board advised the closing of the account. The BIS reacted strongly to the idea of the U.S. funds being withdrawn, pointing to the necessary continuation of financial assistance to several European central banks. Harrison was of the same opinion but had to yield to the Board in Washington. The withdrawal considerably irritated McGarrah, who did not fail to point out the contrast between the cooperative spirit in New York and the opposite disposition in Washington.[79]

6.4   The Tripartite Agreement

On 25 September 1936, a communiqué issued separately by the governments in Washington, London, and Paris stated that France would "readjust" its currency and that the three governments would collaborate in avoiding "as far as possible any disturbance of the basis of international exchanges resulting from the proposed readjustment".[80] The next day, both the Swiss franc and the Dutch guilder were devalued. Whatever had thus far survived of the interwar gold standard was buried forever.

The Tripartite Agreement, so called because it involved the three main financial powers, is something of a watershed in the history of the BIS. Created to facilitate the management of the international gold exchange standard, in the early 1930s the Bank had somehow to reinterpret its own role as an international organisation. It remained, however, a sort of high priest of the gold standard, preparing for its forthcoming reincarnation, and in the meanwhile it turned for support towards its remaining prophets, the gold bloc countries. The persistence of a small number of gold-convertible currencies provided the BIS with the opportunity to offer technical service to its members and to study how best to reform the gold standard in order to make it universally acceptable again. After 1936, the BIS had to forge its new role in a reality that no longer contemplated gold as a monetary anchor.

The Tripartite Agreement[81] was an extreme, if generous, attempt at international economic cooperation. It sought to mitigate the shock to the international monetary system caused by the devaluation of the "franc Poincaré". The agreement was negotiated at the governmental level, with central banks providing technical expertise and advice. The BIS was not called upon to offer its services, and *post factum* it gave a hint of dissatisfaction at being left on the sidelines. Having said that, one must nevertheless add that the existence of the international institution in Basel was not entirely without consequence. Triangular diplomacy could not entirely ignore the likely reactions of other countries, particularly those still on gold that were likely to be affected by the French devaluation. On this as on previous occasions, Basel proved to be a valuable source of information on facts and opinions as well as a convenient place for informal financial diplomacy with the parties not directly involved in the negotiations.

At the time of the Tripartite Agreement, Mussolini's invasion of Abyssinia and Hitler's reoccupation of the Rheinland[82] had brought the interests of the three large democracies closer together. Little could be done, however, in terms of exchange rate adjustment as long as Laval, a staunch supporter of gold, was prime minister in Paris. When the French elections brought to power Léon Blum's Popular Front (May 1936), it seemed at first that nothing would change in exchange rate policy: the Left, too, had pledged to keep France on gold.[83] But the new government was soon confronted by both capital flight and social discontent over steady deflation. The only policy alternative that would satisfy the needs of both remaining on gold (at least nominally) and increasing employment was the introduction of a left-wing version of the policies of exchange controls that had gained Hitler and Mussolini considerable domestic support. But those policies were not equally popular abroad; was it wise for France – asked those in favour of devaluation – to alienate the sympathies of the two other large democracies at a time when dictatorships were becoming increasingly assertive and even aggressive? This was the argument used by Monick to convince Blum. A diplomat who was well connected and respected in Washington and London, Monick understood that a wild devaluation of the franc would be of little help to the French economy – as the pound would follow suit – while at the same time creating havoc in the international monetary system with likely undesirable political consequences.[84] By the end of June, Monick had already secured Roosevelt's consent to a plan of concerted devaluation of the franc. For the rest of the summer, the joint diplomatic effort of Paris and Washington was directed at bringing London on board. Here the difficulty was that the French government's plan was to devalue "but then to return immediately to a gold standard at the new rate, though with extraordinarily wide gold points".[85] This meant not only convincing the British to refrain from a competitive devaluation of their own but also to stabilise the pound against both the dollar and the franc – in practice, a return to the gold standard. The U.K. government could not go as far as that.

Thus, in mid-1936, a coordinated devaluation and subsequent stabilisation seemed to offer the best hope for achieving "monetary peace". There were, however, other angles to consider, including the likely German reaction. Formal devaluation, let alone floating exchange rates, was not contemplated in Berlin.[86] In fact, when Schacht visited Blum in late August 1936,[87] a few weeks before the announcement of the Tripartite Agreement, little time was spent on discussing exchange rates. Schacht's perspective was – and always had been – broader: he tried to impress upon the French prime minister the idea that the only alternative to Göring's autarky was trade expansion and overall financial cooperation (by which he meant the resumption of Western lending to Germany). Schacht proposed an international conference for the creation of a new international order based on the burial of the Versailles treaty, and he mentioned trading the restitution of German colonies for disarmament.[88]

The other delicate issue concerned the likely reaction of the minor powers, with the attendant implications for international relations. In this respect the BIS proved to be of some value to negotiators. By 1936, as we have seen, there was no U.S. representative on the BIS Board, and the exchange of first-hand information on financial matters between Europe and the United States had undoubtedly suffered. However, this difficulty was mitigated by the presence at the U.S. Embassy in Paris of Merle Cochran, a "magnificent type of civil servant" whose task was that of keeping Morgenthau abreast of European developments. He played a minor but indispensable role throughout the negotiations by keeping in close touch with the Ministry of Finance and the Bank of France as well as with other central bankers. To this end, he travelled to Basel whenever the governors were assembled there and communicated frequently by telephone with Trip, Beyen, Schacht, Quesnay, Jacobsson, and many others. His long cables to the State Department and the Treasury provide detailed information on how the situation was viewed by these people.

Cochran's cables to Washington indicate that Basel had become a centre of international financial diplomacy in at least two ways. The first and most obvious one had to do with the simultaneous presence, once a month, at the BIS of central bank governors and of some of their more trustworthy collaborators and advisers. By going there, a skilful diplomat like Cochran had the opportunity both of letting his government's views be known to persons in authority in different countries and of gathering first-hand factual information and assessments. His contacts with Trip, in his dual capacity as head of the BIS and of the Netherlands Bank, proved to be particularly valuable. Trip's assessments of the situation in France and the United Kingdom during the summer of 1936 often proved correct. More important still, he hinted to the Americans through Cochran what his country would do after the inevitable devaluation of the franc. "When action comes it will consist in the Netherlands leaving the gold standard and then holding the guilder around a certain rate vis à vis the sterling .... Trip is not willing to tie the guilder definitely to gold at a new rate until he sees what other currencies do and particularly the sterling."[89]

The French could not count on Dutch solidarity if they returned to the gold standard after devaluation: Trip sided with those people in France, such as Monick, who argued for a managed float after leaving gold. He made it clear that he was even "willing to forgo his departure from the gold standard if ... the French were willing to devalue in concerted arrangement". If, on the other hand, France resorted to exchange controls, Trip let it be known that he "would feel free to tie independently to sterling".[90] The same position was taken by Switzerland: Bachmann agreed with Trip and indicated he would "tie the Swiss franc to sterling in the event the French franc leaves the gold standard".[91] By making their position unequivocally clear, the heads of the central banks of two small but financially important countries contributed to steering the direction of a concerted devaluation.

Besides the opportunities for financial diplomacy offered by the monthly meetings, there was a second way in which the BIS proved to be of service to international negotiations. In spite of its shortcomings and unfulfilled hopes, the BIS had acquired authority in its own right thanks to its links with the various central banks, to the invaluable statistical and economic information it gathered and disseminated, and to the acknowledged competence of its top staff. The latter, particularly Quesnay and Jacobsson, enjoyed the confidence of central bankers, who valued their opinion as able economists with inside knowledge of international monetary matters. As such, they played a minor role in the negotiations, as when Jacobsson was asked by both the U.K. Treasury and the Bank of England "whether he thought England would suffer any bad results from agreeing not to let sterling decline below a certain point provided the French franc were not devalued beyond a certain limit".[92] The BIS economist not only told them they could safely accept the scheme but "even suggested that it be made sufficiently generous to permit the franc to go down as far as the pound and the dollar".[93] By now, Jacobsson – himself a believer in the virtues of gold – and most of his colleagues at the BIS were convinced that co-ordinated devaluation of the French franc was by far the lesser evil and communicated their views to all those willing to listen. Jacobsson was also concerned about Germany, which he felt should still be considered "a key country in any international stabilisation scheme".[94] He reportedly argued that, if the United Kingdom and the United States wanted countries with low reserves to join in a new currency stability pact, then they "must open their markets to such foreign borrowers, notwithstanding their lack of sympathy with rearmament projects and religious persecution".[95]

In the summer of 1936, the position of the French franc improved slightly owing to tourism and the purchase of domestic goods by exporters who had hoarded foreign currencies as long as they could. This momentary easing of the pressure, together with the staunch opposition to devaluation of the communists in the Blum government, seemed to indefinitely postpone hopes of a coordinated currency realignment. Since this prospect increased the likelihood of exchange controls, the Netherlands and Switzerland reviewed their previous positions and considered independent action. By the end of July, the Blum government was beginning to realise the futility of its efforts. With the impending seasonal ebb of foreign tourists, the path of expansionary, easy-money policy followed thus far looked increasingly narrow. It could not coexist with the gold standard for long. Erstwhile gold worshippers such as Rist were mounting a domestic campaign for devaluation, which they saw as the lesser evil given that exchange controls were the only available alternative. Internationally, France risked – if not isolation – at least a cooling of relations with Western democracies at a time when the Spanish situation required as much unity of purpose as possible. Official contacts with London and Washington, which had ceased after Monick's missions two months earlier,[96] did not resume, even though (as we have seen) unofficial diplomacy such as Cochran's and Jacobsson's continued.

At the beginning of August, Labeyrie, the new governor of the Bank of France, left Paris for Berlin and Amsterdam. He would have preferred discussions in the seclusion of the BIS offices, but no Board meetings were scheduled until October. In fact, the trip attracted so much unwelcome publicity that Labeyrie soon came to appreciate "the advantages offered central bankers through assembling periodically at the BIS practically free from press".[97] The meetings revealed that there was still uncertainty in France about the appropriate course of action. At the end of August, gold outflows again reached alarming proportions. On 4 September the French Minister of Finance Auriol finally handed Cochran a draft for an agreement to facilitate French devaluation within a context of international cooperation to stabilise exchange rates.[98] This draft was still unacceptable to both Washington and London, since it called on them to maintain their prevailing rates while France was devaluing. Moreover, "it cited as the final objective of the contracting parties a general return to the international gold standard".[99] While this clause was meant for French public consumption, it was clearly unacceptable to the other two countries. There followed long triangular negotiations. Cochran, by virtue of his being a frequent visitor at the BIS and therefore "exceptionally welcome among central bankers", played "an important part" in the final stages of this episode.[100] On 19 September a final draft of the agreement, approved by Roosevelt, reached London and Paris. According to Morgenthau, the French at that point accepted the U.S. draft "in toto without changing a word".[101] The United Kingdom, having obtained an acceptable degree of devaluation, finally gave their approval. The Tripartite Agreement was concluded on 25 September, a Friday, and announced that same night.

The agreement[102] contained four main points: (1) acceptance of the French devaluation, (2) the policy goal of maintaining "the greatest possible equilibrium in the system of international exchanges", (3) a pledge to relax

import quotas and controls on capital movements, and (4) the understanding that "no country will attempt to obtain unreasonable competitive exchange advantage".[103] No mention was made of a return to gold: the three
governments merely announced their intention to use their reserves to avoid,
as far as possible, major exchange rate fluctuations. As the French negotiator Fournier put it to Cochran a couple of days later: "ni accord, ni entente,
uniquement co-opération journalière".[104]

Belgium, after its devaluation of March 1935 and its return to gold at the
lower parity in March 1936, had no difficulty in immediately acceding to
the agreement. Italy devalued – or rather "realigned", as it was termed – the
lira on 5 October, bringing its exchange rate against the pound and the dollar back to its pre-1931 and pre-1933 levels, respectively. The government,
however, reserved the right to lower the exchange rate by decree, a decision
that did not matter much anyway as exchange controls were by then very
tight. For the same reason, Germany did not move. Neither country ac-
ceded to the agreement: the level of their reserves allowed no commitment
to stabilise the exchange rate nor to relax exchange controls. Moreover,
and more importantly, the latter had become a useful tool in domestic policy making and resource allocation. The Netherlands and Switzerland, left
out of the final negotiations, immediately went off gold but did not join the
agreement until the end of November.

The reception given to the agreement in Basel was understandably cool.
At the Board meeting of 12 October 1936, President Trip officially merely
"referred to the monetary upheaval which occurred since the last meeting
and which had brought about the end of the so-called gold bloc". He then
added that "facts must be accepted and discussion seemed idle". The Board
voted a brief resolution drawing "attention to the urgent necessity of securing general stability of exchanges".[105] On their way home, the governors
learned of an addendum to the Tripartite Agreement issued on 13 October. It informed the world that, under new regulations, the Treasury of the
United States was ready to exchange gold for dollars and vice versa at a
fixed rate "with any country which gives reciprocal facilities to the United
States". The statement added that "the British government have arranged
for such facilities to be afforded in London to the United States authorities" and that "similar arrangements have been made with the Bank of
France". The explicit intention of these arrangements was to "provide for
effective cooperation between the three countries".[106] Needless to say, the
"resident officers of the BIS and particularly the German assistant General
Manager Hechler were quite provoked to learn ... that the three powers had

consummated a further agreement of interest to central bankers"[107] without the latter, gathered in Basel, getting wind of it.

The Tripartite Agreement does not stand out in the eventful economic history of the late 1930s. International relations in the three years leading up to the Second World War were such that the agreement could not possibly deliver exchange rate stability. Without political backing, central bank cooperation was reduced to personal courtesy among central bankers. Moreover, no amount of sound reserve management and technical coordination of efforts could possibly have avoided the transmission to exchange rates of the political and military shocks to the world economy from the events of 1935–39. The French franc traded more or less steadily at around 105.5 to the pound for about five months after the Tripartite Agreement. From March 1937 onwards, nothing could stop its depreciation. By the end of the year, the franc had fallen to levels not seen since the confusion of 1925–26, before Poincaré took over.[108] The pound/dollar rate remained more stable in the long run but was not free from fluctuations.[109] If stabilisation was its primary objective, the agreement failed to deliver.

Even so, the action undertaken by the three leading Western countries in 1936 cannot be entirely dismissed as irrelevant. Sayers rightly pointed to the change in attitude signalled by the negotiations leading up to the declaration of 25 September. There was then, he said, "widespread acceptance of the notion that rates of exchange were matters of multilateral instead of unilateral consideration and that there could be useful international action falling short of actual stabilisation".[110] Another important element was the end of Roosevelt's economic isolationism and his willingness to take the lead. Moreover, as emphasised by Bordo and others,[111] the agreement had a long-lasting intellectual impact: with its emphasis on key currencies, it was the predecessor to the French and Williams Bretton Woods plans and influenced the thinking of Keynes and White, both supporters of the agreement. For these three reasons, one can trace in the Tripartite Agreement many of the seeds that would bear fruit at Bretton Woods.[112]

As far as central bank cooperation is concerned, the Tripartite Agreement dealt the final blow to Norman's dream of a world where international monetary affairs are conducted by central bankers, independent from their respective governments and free to act according to their best judgement and deep understanding of the technicalities of the game. The agreement was negotiated by governments and meant primarily cooperation between governments rather than central banks.[113] Central banks were brought into the picture, as in the French case, more as government agencies than in their own right. The message was, as we have seen, received gloomily in Basel.

6.5   People and Organisation

The disintegration of political and economic cooperation after 1933 and the collapse of the gold standard system left their marks on the BIS. Two main trends characterised the BIS as an organisation in the late 1930s. On the one hand, it increased its already strong European emphasis as far as personnel, style, and outlook were concerned. On the other hand, it became less operations based and more intellectual.

As we have seen,[114] McGarrah and then Fraser ensured an influential (though unofficial) U.S. presence at the very top of the BIS until June 1935. After that time, the links with the United States became more tenuous and relations more impersonal. Gates McGarrah held the presidency, both of the Board and of the Bank, until May 1933, with Leon Fraser as his alternate. In 1932, Beneduce and Trip took over as vice-chairmen of the Board from Charles Addis and Carl Melchior. In May 1933, McGarrah resigned from the two presidential positions and was made honorary president while retaining his seat on the Board. It appears that, among other things, McGarrah was not entirely happy with living in Basel: witness also his lobbying for moving the BIS to London.[115] The issue of location was, in fact, discussed between 1932 and 1933 in a context that also involved the question of the desirability of a European presidency, with the English ready to concede moving to Brussels and appointing Jean Monnet.[116] Nothing came of it: Fraser, an American highly regarded by both the BIS directors and senior staff,[117] was appointed to succeed McGarrah in May 1933 and the BIS remained in Switzerland.

Two years later, for reasons discussed earlier,[118] appointing another American president was out of the question. The choice of Trip, the head of the Netherlands Bank, commanded sufficient consensus: he enjoyed an excellent technical reputation and came from a medium-sized country committed to the gold standard.[119] The problem with his appointment lay mainly in the difficulty of combining two full-time jobs. For a while, Trip considered resigning his position in the Netherlands. He honestly felt that "in order to develop, at the earliest possible moment, the task and position of the BIS in the right direction, the Central Banks may have to make some concessions in respect to their national policy".[120] Eventually, however, the strong opposition of the Dutch government to losing the services of a competent central banker prevailed. Fraser, however, was keen on having Trip as successor. With the help of Niemeyer, he engineered a compromise solution. He argued that, while "the Presidency of the institution [required] at least the appearance of a full time job", the current situation of the Bank hardly required such dedication, and a presence of two days a week would suffice.[121] Trip would hold both positions (in Amsterdam and Basel) while another Dutchman, J. W. Beyen, would carry on routine business on a daily basis in Basel, as alternate to the president.[122] Two years later, in 1937, Beyen was appointed president of the Bank while Sir Otto Niemeyer took over as chairman of the Board. Beyen stepped down at the end of 1939, Niemeyer in May 1940.

The general manager was the other key position at the Bank – probably the most important of all – and was held by Pierre Quesnay, who was just 35 at the time of his appointment. Quesnay was without doubt a brilliant mind, with ambitious ideas as to what the BIS might achieve.[123] Through his work for the League of Nations mission in Austria in the early 1920s and at the Bank of France after 1926, he was well connected with key people in Europe and the United States.[124] It made him a typical exponent of that first post–World War I generation of truly internationally minded technocrats. Quesnay was also quite restless and sometimes rash, an attitude that did not always go down well with his colleagues and with the central bankers.[125] He died in a drowning accident in September 1937. For his succession, Norman and Niemeyer favoured Hechler, a German, who had succeeded Hülse as assistant general manager in May 1935. When Hechler's candidacy failed to win the necessary support, there was some speculation that Hjalmar Schacht might be persuaded to leave Berlin to take up office in Basel.[126] France's candidate was (needless to say) another Frenchman, Fournier. Fearing that France might withdraw from the BIS while holding about 30% of the Bank's deposits, the Bank of England finally yielded on the issue of appointing a French citizen but, to save face, required that a different candidate from the original one be chosen. In December the Board appointed Roger Auboin, who had won his spurs as adviser to the National Bank of Romania and had recently been admitted to the General Council of the Bank of France.[127] He remained in office for the following twenty years.

The Italian Pilotti served as secretary general from the foundation of the Bank until 1951. Besides the aforementioned three positions, there were originally, as we have seen, two other managers at the Bank: Marcel van Zeeland of Belgium, who retired in 1962, and the Englishman Porters. When the latter resigned in 1936, Norman did not suggest a replacement. It seems that the governor of the Bank of England, dissatisfied with the organisation of the BIS, intended to signal his desire for reorganisation and for doing "away with distribution of posts on national basis".[128] However, the only result was that Porters's position remained vacant until after the war, when the number of managers was raised to six.

It was, in fact, almost impossible to do away with the practice introduced with the establishment of the Bank that the four largest European
central banks should each have the unwritten right to appoint one of the
managers. If the BIS were to be a privileged "listening post", then each
wanted to have its own "listener" as high up as possible in the hierarchy. If
the BIS were to produce and disseminate information, first-hand access to
both functions was deemed essential. Moreover, governors liked the idea
of being met by well-positioned friendly faces at the time of their monthly
congregation in Basel – so much so that, besides the appointed manager,
some central banks kept a "permanent liaison" at the Bank. One such person described his work as being carried out more in the Bank's corridors
or off its premises than in the office, stressing the importance of being on
friendly terms with the presidents and managers.[129]

The decrease in the BIS's activities and budget, from its peak in the first
two years of its existence, forced a reduction of its personnel and an overall rethinking of its organisation. Salaries and related personnel expenses
declined from 2.8 million Swiss gold francs in 1931–32 to about half that
figure in 1938–39, as both staff numbers and remuneration were cut.[130]

6.6   The Banking Side

In an internal note dated May 1934, van Zeeland highlighted "the inevitable
regression of the BIS banking activity", ascribing it to three main "exogenous circumstances": the end of reparations, the crisis of the gold standard,
and the development of clearing arrangements.[131] The monetary and financial transactions conducted by the BIS in the 1930s reflected the changes
in its functions (as the agent for reparation payments and as a central
banks' bank) brought about by deterioration of the political and economic
environment.

The "exogenous circumstances" referred to by van Zeeland had a negative impact both on the Bank's net income and on the amount of its available resources. Published net profits declined from 15.2 million Swiss gold
francs[132] in 1931/32 (the first full financial year) to 8.6 million in 1938/39.[133]
Assets were sharply reduced in 1931–33 and remained at a relatively low
level for the rest of the decade. As we have seen, even at their peak in the
early months of 1931, the BIS's resources were inadequate for its ambitious
goals of exchange rate stabilisation and international lending of last resort.
The reduction of central bank deposits in the early 1930s left the BIS with
fewer available resources for the rest of the decade. In 1931, BIS assets
were about 2.2 times those of Sveriges Riksbank and 77% of those of the

Swiss National Bank. In 1938 these ratios had dropped to 47% and 27%, respectively.[134]

As trustee and agent for reparations, the BIS was supposed to receive, manage, and distribute to creditors the sums paid by Germany, Bulgaria, Hungary, and Czechoslovakia under the terms of the Hague Agreement of January 1930. It was also expected to receive and make payments for the service of the international German loans of 1924 (the so-called Dawes Loan) and 1930 (the Young Loan) as well as of the international Austrian loan of 1930. In connection with these operations, creditor governments maintained special (guarantee) deposits with the Bank. In the first fiscal year (1930/31), the BIS fees for these services amounted to about 2.2 million Swiss francs. As circumstances changed, the fees derived from the BIS's original function as trustee and agent for reparations declined considerably.

Reparation-related fees, however, accounted for only 14.5% of the Bank's gross income in 1930/31. Most of its income was derived from the investment of its own capital and of depositors' funds. As we have seen, deposits could be received only from central banks and their governments; they were employed almost exclusively in the money market or in short-term securities.

Central banks' deposits were made in convertible currencies, in their national legal tender regardless of convertibility, and in gold. Over the 1930s, currency deposits held by central banks on their own account (i.e., unrelated to reparations) declined from 869 million Swiss gold francs in August 1931 to 132 million at the end of 1938, reaching as low as 48 million in August 1939. The share of deposits made by central banks in their own currency rose from about 6% on average in 1931–32 to over 80% in 1935, and it remained well over 50% for the rest of the decade.[135] This increase was related to the development of clearing agreements that often required the extension of credit in a partner's currency;[136] it was also the result of an active BIS policy of encouraging central banks to make deposits of this nature.[137] A total of 31 central banks kept currency deposits with the BIS during the 1930s; they were all European with the exception of the central banks of the United States, Japan, Turkey, Ethiopia, and Nicaragua.[138]

Until 1933, the BIS paid a single rate of interest for each category of deposits (sight, term) regardless of the currency in which they were denominated.[139] Since transactions were carried out only in convertible currencies,[140] no provision was made for exchange rate risk. The very idea of the BIS as the association of gold-standard central banks implied that the Bank's transactions were assumed to be conducted not in individual currencies but in the gold content they represented. This policy did not go unquestioned within the BIS,[141] as market interest rates for different currencies actually diverged (not all gold parities happened to be equally credible, even before September 1931).[142] Yet the BIS maintained its single interest rate policy after the devaluation of the pound and for a few months after that of the dollar. In November 1933 a special (lower) interest rate was established for deposits denominated in French francs, and shortly afterwards different interest rates on the dollar and the pound were introduced. By 1936, the BIS applied different interest rates on deposits in each currency.[143]

There were two kinds of gold deposits: bank deposits and earmarked gold. The first category was included in the Bank's balance sheet whereas earmarked gold was held off the balance sheet.[144] Bank deposits in gold were made for the first time in 1933 and were never particularly significant: at their peaks, in early 1934 and again in the second half of 1936, they did not exceed 14% of total deposits by central banks on their own account.

On the other hand, operations related to earmarking became increasingly important during the 1930s.[145] The BIS held a collective gold account in its own name with the Bank of England and the Federal Reserve Bank of New York. This account was divided into subaccounts representing earmarked gold in the name of the BIS for the account of central banks, which were the actual owners. In theory, the depository banks did not know which subaccount belonged to which central bank and executed orders only upon instructions from the BIS. "Transfers from sub-account X to sub-account Y were made by the BIS if and when a central bank owner of sub-account X wanted gold transferred to another central bank owner of sub-account Y."[146] Earmarked gold, therefore, allowed for cheap and confidential transactions between central banks, as the transfer of property merely entailed a book-keeping change by the BIS. Movements on earmarked gold totalled over 1,121 million Swiss gold francs in 1935–36 and over 1,512 million in 1938–39.[147] Other gold operations conducted on behalf of central banks included buying, selling, and transporting the yellow metal.

Capital and reserves increased from 110.2 million Swiss gold francs in 1931 to 191.2 million in 1934, levelling off at around 175 million in 1935–39. Dividend payments increased slightly in the first three years and remained constant at 7.5 million up to 1942 (6% annually on invested capital). In the early 1940s, BIS shares were held in more than 42 countries:[148] two thirds were in the hands of central banks, the rest with the public.

As we have seen, the BIS adopted from the outset an extremely liquid investment stance.[149] The Bank was not allowed investments in securities maturing in more than two years. The purchase of securities with no more than two years to run was allowed "in order to improve the yield on the capital held by the Bank, with a view to meeting administrative expenditure or dividend payments".[150] Funds at sight could possibly be employed in the various national markets, with the assent of the central bank concerned, by purchasing bills or acceptances on condition that the central bank agreed to their rediscount at any time. The BIS could make short-notice and fixed-term (one- to six-month) deposits only to the extent that their maturity matched that of the deposits received by the Bank itself.

From the beginning, these rules posed problems for an efficient allocation of BIS funds. The demand for the latter tended to be medium term and in local currencies, whereas the provision of funds was short term and to a large extent in dollars. As long as the gold standard existed, it was possible for the BIS to overcome, if not the maturity problems, then at least those connected with the conversion of one currency into another. Agreements were made with a number of central banks that allowed immediate conversion without going through the market.[151] The devaluation of the pound drew people's attention to exchange rate risk: hedging, hitherto not allowed, was introduced. With the end of the gold standard and the introduction of exchange controls, there was a tendency for central banks to reimburse BIS placements on their markets, while the BIS itself found it more difficult to lend because borrowers would not accept a gold guarantee clause. The Bank was therefore obliged to keep idle relatively sizeable sums, mostly in dollars. As we have seen, the issue of medium- and long-term loans was debated, and somehow dealt with, in the early months of the Bank's life. A medium-term placement of about 150 million Swiss francs, through the intermediation of central banks, was authorised at the end of 1930. The bulk of these placements took place in 1931. In some cases, liquidation proved difficult: investments for which there was an implicit assurance of rediscount or mobilisation remained in the Bank's portfolio indefinitely.

The banking operations of the BIS were supposed to be an instrument of – or at least consistent with – central bank cooperation. When designing the rules for such operations, the Board had accepted that "the important thing for the Bank is not to earn money on deposits at fixed term, but to have at its disposal the funds which it requires for its action as regulator".[152] The illusion of being able to play an important role as international monetary "regulator", if it was ever nurtured, was definitely dispelled by the events of 1931–33. The question then arose in the 1930s concerning the extent to which the BIS banking operations, on the relatively limited scale of those years,[153] could perform "a task of a nature more in connection with [the Bank's] functions as a club of central bankers".[154] It was recognised that financial assistance to central banks (i.e., international lending of last resort) "could never constitute a regular business of the BIS" and, when needed, could only be part of a general coordinated effort. A regular task could only be "in the line of the daily management of an international monetary standard, e.g. in the line of those transactions, which can smooth out seasonal and incidental fluctuations in the exchange rate of the respective currencies".[155] Even this task could not be fully performed after 1933 in the absence of a generally accepted international monetary standard. Nevertheless, the daily BIS banking business, it was argued, should be conducted in such a way as to be consistent with the Bank's cooperative nature. In this regard, the most useful accomplishments of BIS banking activity in the 1930s were probably (i) the use of deposits from central banks in their own currency to facilitate international trade settlements, and (ii) the development of a free gold market between central banks themselves. Beyen explained the latter as follows. Since London was then the only free gold market, central banks had to make their transactions there, buying and selling at rather widened points. "That means that if the central bank of Czecho-Slovakia has gold to sell and the Austrian National Bank has gold to buy and if – as usual – they do not find each other directly, they have to do their business via another central bank and have to pay or to lose the difference between parity and selling–buying price. It is there that we step in, when we can."[156]

The efforts made by the BIS in the last part of the decade to increase the volume of its banking business were, on the whole, not particularly successful. In 1937, it was observed that "central banks were making use of the services of the Bank in increasing measure", particularly as far as exchange transactions and deposits were concerned.[157] In June and September of that year, central banks' deposits reached their highest level since June 1933 and, while slowly diminishing afterwards, remained unusually large until the second half of 1938. Off–balance sheet earmarked gold deposits reached their prewar peak in March 1938.[158] All banking operations declined in the following months.

6.7 Clearing Agent for the Universal Postal Union

The Universal Postal Union (UPU), founded in 1874, had adopted the gold franc of the Latin Monetary Union as its unit of account. At its Madrid congress in 1920, the UPU decided to stick to its prewar unit of account, now embodied in the Swiss franc.[159] The respective claims of the different postal administrations were cleared through the international bureau of the UPU in Berne. Net debtors settled their bilateral balances at regular intervals in a gold currency. This international payment system worked relatively well before 1914, as most currencies traded at a fixed gold parity with the gold franc. In those years, the major problem for international settlements among postal administrations were the long delays between the cheques being drawn and cashed. Quite often, especially in the case of remote territories, this could take weeks if not months. This drawback was seriously compounded, both during and after the war, by exchange rate fluctuations (until the currency stabilisations of the mid-1920s) and again by the 1931–33 devaluations.

In 1933, the Swiss Postal Administration called on the BIS to explore the possibility of settling international postal payments by opening gold franc accounts in its books.[160] The proposal was backed by a resolution adopted by the UPU Cairo congress (March 1934). Fraser saw the initiative as opening "an interesting new field of activity for the Bank". He was hopeful that it might "be extended to include the settlement through the Bank for International Settlements of further international claims in connection with other semi-public funds, such as telegraph, telephone and railway charges. This would be of advantage both to the Bank for International Settlements and to the central banks concerned for it would be the means of concentrating these funds under the control of the central banks".[161]

The BIS was, however, reluctant to open gold-denominated accounts for the purpose of postal settlements and offered instead accounts and payments in any currency of the customer's choice. The scheme would speed up payments considerably. In May 1934, the new system was inaugurated by the Swiss and German postal administrations. By early 1935, postal payments were being effected by the BIS through currency transfers for the account of Australia, Belgium, Danzig, Denmark, France, Germany, the United Kingdom, the Netherlands, Norway, Sweden, and Switzerland.

All in all, the success of the new scheme was limited. The volume and value of postal payments effected through the BIS remained small. Moreover, in the second half of the 1930s, an increasing number of countries resorted to bilateral clearing agreements covering all international payments, including postal payments, thus bypassing the BIS altogether. It soon became apparent that the scheme was moribund.

After the devaluations of September 1936, the Swiss Postal Administration sought to revive the scheme. The BIS, which in the meantime had abandoned its reluctance to open gold sight accounts, sent UPU member administrations a new proposal[162] whereby central banks of the interested countries would keep an account in gold francs with the BIS to be used for the settlement of postal transactions.[163] Each central bank would then deal with its respective postal administration in national legal tender. It was not until the spring of 1938 that the system finally got off the ground, when the Finnish and Swedish central banks opened gold sight accounts with the BIS, paving the way for other central banks to join the plan. The Norwegian and Danish central banks followed shortly thereafter, as did the German Reichsbank and, before the end of the year, the Estonian and Swiss central banks. A critical mass was thus reached to get the system started. The first transfers between gold sight accounts under the new postal payments system were carried out in November 1938. The system developed very slowly over the following months.[164] Throughout 1939, the volume and value of transactions and the number of central banks involved remained fairly constant.[165] At the same time, a limited number of central banks continued to settle payments for their respective postal administrations through the old system of transfers between foreign exchange accounts held at the BIS. For this specific purpose, the Bank of England maintained a sterling account while the central banks of Hungary and Turkey maintained dollar accounts.

The UPU episode, in itself marginal in the history of the BIS, was yet another instance of how difficult cooperation had become in the autarkic environment of the 1930s. The idea of making the BIS the clearing agent for postal payments made sense: facilitating international financial transactions was one of the Bank's main statutory objectives, for which it had developed both the necessary network of central banks and refined technical skills. No other institution could have performed international clearing tasks more rapidly and cheaply than the BIS. Moreover, international postal settlements after World War I were in a state of considerable disarray and needed to be put on a more efficient footing. The whole issue was intrinsically technical, with little or no political undercurrent. And yet, notwithstanding the potential benefits of the scheme, it proved extremely difficult to induce a sufficient number of central banks and postal authorities to support it. By 1938–39, administrations in every country were reluctant to embark upon even minor ventures of international cooperation. Convertible foreign exchange was so scarce that it could not be spared even in small amounts, and international postal communication was hardly a national priority. The network of clearing agreements put in place by most countries seemed to offer a viable substitute for multilateral clearing.

6.8 The Monetary and Economic (Research) Department

The organisation of the BIS in the 1930s was reshaped mainly by increasing the emphasis on research.

From the outset, Norman had envisaged that the BIS would develop into a kind of research centre for central bank cooperation. He wanted issues such as the gold exchange standard, gold clearing, or foreign exchange clearing to be studied by consultative committees, which would then submit proposals for agreements between central banks to the BIS Board.[166] Consistent with this scheme was the idea, also floated by Norman, of releasing experts from the central banks for temporary posting to the BIS. They would breathe in the atmosphere of international monetary cooperation in Basel, improving the liaison between their respective central banks and the BIS once they returned to their mother institutions.

These ideas were taken up and discussed time and again during the 1930s, but practical results at first remained patchy and fairly limited in scope and impact. Though candidly admitting that he did "not really know what the expression central bank collaboration means", Fraser was particularly disappointed at the slow progress made in developing the BIS Central Banking Department.[167] He envisaged a department acting on three fronts: as an internal service providing information on market developments; as a "planning and thinking section" on central bank cooperation; and as a focal point for central bank contacts, in particular for their economic and statistical services. In these three fields of activity some limited progress was made during 1931. The small staff of the Central Banking Department organised its work thematically. Simon was given the task of studying questions related to "the creation of credit by private banks" and "relations between central banks and their markets". Rodenbach was entrusted with the study of "gold problems", and Philippovich devoted his time to "foreign exchange holdings of central banks" and "balance of accounts movements".[168]

The department thus began the collection of information relevant to central bank policy making, thereby laying the basis for an information hub at the service of both member central banks and the BIS itself. This was done (a) by creating a proper library; (b) by collecting economic and monetary information on individual countries as well as statistical material from the member central banks; and (c) by the BIS producing relevant information of its own. A compilation of gold and foreign exchange regulations effective in the different countries was published in 1931 and updated regularly thereafter. As early as 1930, the BIS started producing and distributing to its central bank members a series of research papers and background notes on monetary and economic topics.[169]

Needless to say, the 1931 crisis affected the direction of research in the Central Banking Department. The department was hard-pressed to cope with the increased demand for up-to-date information on the situation in

Central Europe. Rodd, Simon, and Blessing, as we have seen, were dispatched to Vienna to assist the Austrian National Bank.[170] Later the department offered research support to the Wiggin and Beneduce committees.

At the end of 1931, the Central Banking Department was renamed Monetary and Economic Department (MED), an internal reorganisation was carried through, and its main tasks became better defined. The MED was required "to provide information for the management and Board of the BIS, both as regards the economic and financial position in particular countries and as regards general tendencies affecting a number of countries". Also, "certain distinct problems, as for instance the gold exchange standard, the problem of short term credits, [and] problems connected with gold movements" had to be studied. Moreover, the MED was supposed "to contribute to the collaboration between central banks by making a certain amount of information, and the result of particular studies, available to the member banks".[171]

Supervision of the Monetary and Economic Department was initially shared between Quesnay and Pilotti, the Bank's secretary general. In the spring and early summer of 1931, U.K. economist Walter Stewart had served for a brief spell as economic adviser. In August 1931 the position was offered to Per Jacobsson,[172] a Swede. He joined the BIS a month later at the age of 37, coming from experiences of economic advising with Krueger and the League of Nations.[173] However, it was not until after the war that Jacobsson, always de facto in charge of the MED, formally became head of the department, while keeping his title of Economic Adviser.

In 1932, much of the work done in the MED related to reparations, in the preparation of the Lausanne and Stresa conferences, and to the gold standard, ahead of the London World Monetary and Economic Conference.

After the failure of the London Conference, the focus shifted towards research into capital movements, prices, international trade, and gold production as well as country studies. International statistics, neither plentiful nor accurate in the 1920s, grew steadily in coverage and quality during the 1930s. It is one of the great merits of the League of Nations to have pioneered the field. Its statistical yearbooks and monographs, some of them drafted by leading economists of the time, are a model of intelligence and accuracy. The BIS was second to the League in the provision of first-rate quantitative information on the international economy, particularly in the fields of specific interest to central bankers: money and exchange rates.

The quality and size[174] of the BIS Annual Report grew steadily, and it was the showpiece of the publications produced by the MED. Per Jacobsson was the main intellectual force behind it. The BIS Annual Report,

Keynes wrote, "is now the leading authority for certain statistics, not easily obtainable .... It is particularly useful because it goes beyond the published statistics and ventures on certain estimates and opinions which can only be based on information not generally available.... It is reasonable to suppose that the Report will not contain any statement which the representatives of the Central Banks know to be wide of the mark. The Staff of the Bank for International Settlements are much to be congratulated on the high interest of their Report. It is to be hoped that they will persevere in the regular collection and even extension of these vitally important statistics, which it is so difficult for the outsider to obtain in any reliable or comprehensive form."[175]

Beginning in 1936, the Annual Report adopted a standard format whereby, before providing the necessary information about the Bank's activity, it devoted a lot of space to developments in the international economy. It opened with a long introduction reviewing and interpreting the most relevant economic events of the previous twelve months and then went on to deal in detail with exchange rates, prices, international trade, gold production and movements, international capital flows and short-term indebtedness, rates of interest, and current trends in central and commercial banking.

Two themes run almost constantly through the BIS Annual Reports in the 1930s: the need for close international monetary cooperation, and the desirability of gold convertibility as a prerequisite to sound monetary policy. It has been argued that the Annual Reports "kept the tradition of the use of monetary policy alive" in alleged "sharp contrast with the discovery and prominence given fiscal policy in the 1930s".[176] This proposition is hardly tenable in the face of the contributions to monetary theory made in those years by Keynes, Fisher, Hawtrey, Ohlin, and Sayers, to name but a few,[177] and of the fact that monetary policy was constantly debated and implemented by the relevant policy-making authorities. It is true, however, that the Annual Reports carried a consistent re-proposition of the most traditional monetary theory, still intellectually dear to central bankers. Jacobsson was surely not a follower of Keynes. Even if, in the circumstances of the 1930s, the pursuit of an orthodox monetary policy (as favoured by the BIS) produced undesirable effects on the real economy, as shown in the case of France, the BIS's intellectual contribution in the quest for a reformed gold standard was not lost and bore fruit in more normal times. Some of the ideas developed in Basel, such as the demonetisation of gold for private individuals and the restriction of gold transactions to central banks, were later incorporated in the Bretton Woods agreements.

In 1933–34, the MED suffered as much as any other department from the cutbacks in staff and resources. Blessing, Darlington, and Philippovich left without being replaced. Jacobsson was left with Conolly as his only assistant. Credit for the MED's revival and further development into a full-fledged research centre for the BIS and its member central banks is largely due to Beyen. Immediately upon joining the BIS, Beyen called for the development of the Bank "as a source of general economic and monetary information to its constituents", for instance by producing "comprehensive and comparative economic and financial statistics for each of the major economies".[178] By the summer of 1935, a renewed expansion of the MED was under way.[179] Country studies and comparative statistical analysis were added to the research agenda. Norman's idea of encouraging the secondment of central bank experts to the BIS for temporary assignments in the MED, thus far applied on a limited scale, was pursued more forcefully. In 1936, member central banks were again invited to send expert staff to Basel to participate for a limited period (usually two or three months) in the work of the MED. The scheme was received favourably and continued in the following years.[180] The central bank staff sent to Basel remained on their central bank's payroll, while the BIS provided a daily allowance and the necessary research facilities. Good use was made of this system during 1936–38 by various central banks, including the Bank of England, the National Bank of Belgium, the Swiss National Bank, and the Norwegian, Polish, and Bulgarian central banks.[181]

6.9   The Governors' Unofficial Meetings

Given the reduced scope for effective cooperation in monetary matters, it is somehow surprising that the Basel meetings, both informal and formal, went on regularly and well attended throughout the 1930s. "Basel", one of the participants later recalled, "must have been important not only for me but also for other Governors. Otherwise they would not have been willing to devote so much time to their monthly visits. One left one's own country on Friday afternoon or evening and returned home on Tuesday morning".[182] The presence of towering personalities – such as Norman, Schacht, and the BIS's Per Jacobsson – must have been an additional attraction. As Merle Cochran reported to the U.S. State Department in late 1933: "The Directors prefer to view the BIS as a long-time proposition, and insist that its field of usefulness need not be analyzed or altered with every shift in world monetary and economic conditions. The Directors make the trips to Basel faithfully, absences even of the leading Governors being rare. Now that Dr. Schacht is a Director and is so powerful in the Reich, one of my Italian friends assured me that all of the other Directors could be counted on to attend the meetings, to watch Dr. Schacht, if for no other reason".[183]

A U.S. occasional observer spelled out the reasons why such meetings might have looked particularly appealing to participants. "The BIS as it exists at the present may be described as essentially a meeting place where monetary authorities from different countries can gather and discuss their problems. For this purpose it is admirably adapted. The quietness of Basel and its absolutely non-political character provide a perfect setting for those equally quiet and non-political gatherings. The regularity of the meetings and their almost unbroken attendance by practically every member of the Board make them such that they rarely attract any but the most meagre notice in the press.... The harmful speculation that might result from special visits of the monetary authorities of one country to those of another is thus through the agency of BIS entirely avoided. It is understood that the new President of the Bank is laying special stress on the 'Central Bankers' Club' aspect of the Bank's work since its purely banking functions are now so reduced."[184]

Participation in the official Board meetings on the second Monday of each month was often just an excuse for the trip. The discussion and approval of the Bank's routine business could be (and often was) left to the alternates, and – after the end of reparations – the occasions for formal decision making on truly relevant matters became few and far between. The true reason for regularly bearing the discomfort of long displacements from home was the participation in the informal meetings.[185] Saturday evenings and Sunday mornings were normally devoted to one-to-one encounters, business lunches, and socialisation at dinner parties. "In the twos and threes", as described by Schacht to Sayers, "they would have their meals over the weekend, perhaps listen to some music, get to know one another better".[186] Each governor enjoyed the facility of a private office within the Bank's premises, which he employed for his confidential conversations. At times, however, doors were left open so as to allow both Board and staff members to enter freely for occasional greetings and exchanges of information. The unofficial meeting of the governors, no minutes taken, took place at about four on Sunday afternoon and was followed by tea.[187] On the occasion of the monthly gatherings, high-ranking staff members (and their wives) residing in Basel were busy hosting receptions and dinners for large groups as well as for limited numbers of guests.[188]

A typical Sunday, when governors were in Basel, followed the pattern described by Jacobsson in one such occasion: "Day of Governors' meeting. At the Bank 11. Saw Nathan (Italy) .... Talked to de Jong about my observations on Trip's rules of the gold standard game. De Jong went to see Trip who asked me to come and see him. I went over all the points with

Trip, who took it all very well – he is an easy man to work with. Rooth was very nervous again. His wife was with him. I gave him my observations on Trip's rules. In the afternoon a walk with Cochran .... He was delighted about the measures taken by Roosevelt to bring about budget stabilisation and particularly about the work of the new Director of the Budget .... Dinner at our house: Rooth's, Trip, de Jong, Bachmann, Cochran. Trip was rather doubtful about Schacht."[189] We can easily imagine that all participants were engaged in an equally busy round of meetings and discussions. Information and gossip were exchanged, people got to know each other, personal ties were established and kept alive. As one of the participants put it: "The monthly meetings in Basel enabled us to keep in very close touch personally without too much travel around Europe, thus both saving time and avoiding the publicity and the rumours sometimes arising from visits to other capitals."[190] Another attraction was the presence at Basel of a competent international staff who would provide first-hand information and statistics. The strengthening of the research department in the 1930s was probably both a cause and an effect of the continued interest of governors in their monthly visits to Basel.

Norman was the most convinced advocate of the relevance of the informal meetings. His regular attendance[191] testifies to this conviction: "only ill health, and eventually the war, kept him away".[192] From the very start, Norman saw the BIS as the governors' club: the divisions of the 1930s and the reduction of cooperation in so many fields only reinforced his belief in the usefulness of face-to-face informal meetings, away from both the press and the governments. But there were other, subtly psychological, reasons for Norman's faithfulness to Basel. No longer the unchallenged *dominus* of monetary affairs at home, he cherished the overwhelming prestige he still enjoyed with his European peers at the BIS. According to Boyle, "Basel became to Norman in the thirties what New York had been in the twenties: a spiritual home away from home". And, as the archpriest of the religion of central bank cooperation, he undertook the journeys to Basel "in a spirit of earnest pilgrimage: by then there were few enough shrines left in the wilderness".[193]

For all the importance participants attached to the unofficial Basel meetings in their written or oral testimonials, it is not easy to pinpoint the actual reasons why they were deemed to be so relevant and, what matters most, what those meetings actually accomplished. How and to what extent did they enhance central bank cooperation? Little record was kept, or remains, of the unofficial Sunday afternoon general meetings, let alone of the one-to-one conversations in private offices, over lunch, during concert intervals, or in the course of walks along the Rhine or in the Black Forest. Personal diaries, occasional notes, and reports from BIS officials to their own governors (whenever the latter did not attend) convey the impression that the meetings' most valuable object was the dissemination of information, both facts and opinions. Internationally comparable and reliable economic statistics were neither plentiful nor easily accessible: the League of Nations and the BIS provided most of the state-of-the-art material in the field. The staff of the Bank were on hand to produce the latest results of their work in progress, as yet unpublished. More relevant still was the information gathered in Basel about ongoing policies within individual countries and about who did what, and why. Only insiders such as the governors and their closest collaborators were reliable sources for the latter kind of information, which was given out rather freely on the understanding that it would be disseminated only within the circle of central bankers. Needless to say, however, the most important information to economic policy makers relates to expectations. Facts and opinions are equally important in economics, as today's opinions influence tomorrow's facts. What scant evidence we have about the kind of information exchanged at the monthly meetings indicates that much of it was about opinions rather than established facts. In particular, governors were anxious to know what informed circles in the various capitals thought about developments in financial markets, in domestic politics, and in international relations.[194] This meant that the most fruitful intercourse took place on a one-to-one basis. When the Swedish Governor Rooth, a newcomer, complained that he found the meetings "humbug" – particularly since no information was given about the United States – Jacobsson explained "that very little was known [on the United States] outside the papers, and that the real opinion could only be told by people between four eyes".[195] Later on, Jacobsson observed: "It was good for Rooth to be in contact with BIS circles."[196]

The occasional U.S. visitor was impressed by the way those meetings allowed participants to see current affairs in a broader perspective. "These people have been concerned with their own problems without regard for the rights of anyone else. As they sat down around the table for two days you could almost see their point of view change as they began to realize the effects of their own actions .... The greatest use of the BIS is not in the specific action it may take but in the opportunity which it may afford for the gathering together of these central bank people and the development, as it were, of social pressure upon them to appreciate the problems of other countries." Such visitors left convinced that the most important result of the monthly unofficial gatherings was that the governors came "to those meetings, each thinking of his own protection, and [went] away with a broader feeling".[197]

Indirect evidence of the importance attached by central bankers to their monthly reunions in Basel can be drawn from Harrison's interest in acquiring first-hand information about discussions there, particularly at critical times in the financial markets. Kept away from Basel against his wishes, the governor of the Federal Reserve Bank of New York nevertheless made the BIS his main listening post in European affairs. He would, of course, telephone various people at the Bank of England, but his relationship with Norman never developed into the kind of intimacy enjoyed by Strong; moreover, by the mid-1930s, Washington's financial rapprochement with Paris did not make relations between New York and London warmer. The easiest way for Harrison to keep abreast of overall developments in Europe was to telephone Fraser in Basel. Typically, Harrison would ask Fraser "what news he had picked up yesterday at his Board meeting",[198] which both men regarded as the best barometer on the situation. On one occasion, for instance, when asked by the governor "whether he had any suggestion regarding action from this side of the exchange problem", Fraser postponed his advice by saying "that he might have a clearer picture after talking to central bank governors over this weekend".[199] When the meeting was over, Fraser duly returned Harrison's call, reporting opinions gathered over the weekend on the reasons for the weakness of the pound, on the gold bloc people being "bitter and angry with Norman", and on a private conversation with Tannery about a proposed joint Franco-American credit to the United Kingdom. A touch of gossip was added by recalling that "a great deal of time was spent in annoying Norman by praising the Americans".[200]

After May 1935, with Fraser back in the United States, direct contacts between the Federal Reserve Bank of New York and the BIS became less frequent. Still, some degree of liaison was maintained, mainly at the operational level but also through Merle Cochran of the U.S. Embassy in Paris, who continued to frequent Basel at the time of the governors' meetings. In talking to Cochran, the governors did not hesitate to seize the opportunity of making their views known across the Atlantic. Thus, in February 1936 Cochran reported: "Governor Norman talked to me about the United States. He asked me when we were going to begin walking the straight and narrow orthodox path in financial and monetary matters.... He said that such a system as we are operating could not properly be called a gold standard and that there was positively no chance of the world returning to an international monetary standard based on gold until United States policy is more clearly defined.... He said that the United States has all the trump cards and no matter how it plays its hand it will come out on top".[201] Or one month later: "With respect to the declaration of the U.S. Secretary of State in regard to international stabilization no one was optimistic for the near future. Most of the BIS people prefer to think of stability rather than stabilization".[202]

If, in the 1930s, the main and most useful tasks of the monthly meeting were the dissemination of information and the provision of a quiet and secluded forum for the exchange of opinions, their usefulness in central bank cooperation did not end there. By promoting a better understanding of the problems at hand, extended face-to-face discussions also helped smooth differences of opinion and ruffled feelings. Participants became more aware of each other's point of view, better able to see the complexity of most situations, and less prone to petty dispute. More important still, those discussions made it easier for participants to appreciate the overlap in their respective interests. An entry in Jacobsson's diary from May 1933 provides an example of the beneficial effects of the meetings on mutual understanding: "De Bordes rang up from Geneva and wanted to know how our meeting had gone. I told him that: a– Finland, Norway and Sweden happier than before; b– Eastern countries very pessimistic when they came – less so when they went for they had seen somebody was trying to carry on".[203]

Most governors and their alternates kept going to Basel right up until the outbreak of war. Schacht made his last official visit in January 1939, shortly before being relieved of his post; the Normans were travelling with him from Berlin, where they had attended the christening of Schacht's grandchild. In July, the two men met again in Basel, this time secretly since by then Schacht already feared for his life.[204] On that occasion, it was Norman who paid his last official visit to the BIS.

SEVEN

Wartime

7.1 Neutrality and Cooperation

The situation in which the BIS managers found themselves at the beginning of September 1939 had no precedent. Committed as they were to the survival of the institution, they knew that it could be achieved only by maintaining the strictest neutrality among countries that, while retaining their membership and decision-making powers in the Bank's Board, were at war with each other. At the same time, they were under no illusion: the institution would survive only as long as it was deemed useful by both conflicting sides. Treading the narrow path between neutrality and performing useful services to both sides proved to be extremely difficult for the BIS as the war progressed. Mistakes were made even before the war began, and numerous misunderstandings were created. Although some of the blunders can hardly be justified, even taking the extreme circumstances of the epoch into account, other aspects of the BIS wartime conduct that aroused suspicion or prompted condemnation at the time look in retrospect less erroneous than they did then. This chapter accounts for the life of the BIS during the six longest and most dramatic years in the history of the twentieth century against the background of the often ambiguous legal and practical constraints of neutrality – a stance unanimously chosen by the shareholding central banks in the conviction, shared by belligerents from both sides, that their Basel institution should be preserved for a time when peace would come again.

From a legal point of view, the situation of the BIS as the war began had no parallel; it was one of *jus condendum*. Norms and practices regulating neutrality were designed to apply to sovereign states: there were no previous instances to draw upon as far as international institutions were concerned. In 1939 the main source of neutrality norms was the Hague Convention of 1907. Neutrality was defined as the legal situation of a state that declares itself noninvolved in a given international conflict. Relations between belligerent and neutral states were regulated by the *jus belli,* which imposed a series of obligations mainly aimed at making sure that neutrals did nothing to increase the strength of one of the belligerents. In particular, neutrals were not allowed to provide belligerents with troops,[1] weapons and ammunition, or loans and financial subsidies. Nor could they allow movements of belligerents' troops across their territories or the installation of communication devices.[2] Belligerents, for their part, were barred from using neutrals' territories for military operations but enjoyed the right to inspect, and if necessary capture, neutral vessels carrying contraband goods and to block enemy coasts to all ships, including neutral ones.[3] These rules, all stemming from the general principle of the neutral's strict impartiality, were devised for sovereign states and had to be adapted to apply to the BIS.

The principles of international law on neutrality, hard as they were to define and apply to given circumstances, were anyway disregarded from the very beginning of the war. It was immediately apparent that neutrality would be respected only as long as it was useful to both camps; neutrals therefore found themselves fighting for their very existence, just like any belligerent. Principles and norms were bent, adjusted, and abandoned in response to the overriding necessity of survival.

The very concept of neutrality became irrelevant as it appeared that, from a military point of view, neutrals could be either a net asset or a net liability to the belligerents. They could not be indifferent (i.e., neutral).[4] Only the usefulness of neutrality to both warring sides assured the maintenance of a given country's neutral status. Norway, Denmark, the Netherlands, and Belgium were more useful to Germany as occupied territories than as neutral nations. Sweden and Switzerland, the latter after an initial German hesitation, were deemed useful as neutrals to both camps. Germany, therefore, did not occupy them and the Allies did not cut them off from the supply of vital raw materials and foodstuffs. "Neutral trade", notes Milward, "survived because it was in the interest of both camps, and in surviving it thwarted effective economic warfare against Germany".[5]

Germany imported enormous quantities of iron ore from Sweden, "which in 1939 and 1940 provided 40 per cent of her total iron supply (measured by iron content). Although the proportions dropped thereafter to about 25 per cent because of the German conquests in Western and Eastern Europe, the contribution of Swedish ores to a central segment of Germany's war economy is obvious".[6] Sweden went even further in accommodating Germany. It allowed "hundreds of thousands of German troops to move across its territory to and from different parts of Norway" and permitted "tens of thousands to move across to attack the Soviet Union".[7] As for Switzerland, it imported essential coal from Germany, being thereby shielded from Allied pressures, and substantially increased its exports to the Reich, which included arms and ammunition.[8] In the financial sphere, a clearing agreement signed in August 1940 between Germany and Switzerland opened a large flow of credits for Swiss exports to Germany. A subsequent agreement, of July 1941, was even more favourable to Germany.[9]

As it appeared, "the neutrality exercised by countries such as Switzerland or Sweden was far from any traditional concept of that word".[10] Unsurprisingly, their foreign trade was governed by German political intervention of the most pressing kind: the Reich's sweeping victories in the first phase of the war had left Switzerland completely surrounded by Axis territories, while German naval forces had total control over Sweden's seaborne trade. Only by maintaining a heavily biased neutrality could the governments in Berne and Stockholm spare their countries from the universal bloodshed, grant their citizens a decent standard of living, and guarantee their own survival. Whether – from a moral point of view – adherence to this kind of neutrality "was justified in the face of a political and social system so threatening as that of National Socialist Germany is another question".[11]

This context, both legal and factual, must be taken into account when surveying the wartime history of the BIS and its relations with the main central banks of Europe. In the autumn of 1939, the latter made the crucial decision to keep the BIS alive during the war, and not merely in a dormant state.[12] Throughout the following years, for a number of reasons discussed in this chapter, central banks – both belligerent and neutral – stuck to their original decision. In a very meaningful way, they effectively (if indirectly) cooperated in keeping their creature alive and well, as circumstances allowed. They stood by the BIS even when, after the summer of 1944, it was seriously threatened with dissolution.[13]

The circumstance that the Bank had previously been, and still remained, almost entirely a European institution did not help relations with the United States, which became increasingly strained in spite of the fact that an American was at the helm in Basel throughout the war. Washington – which even before the conflict understood and cared little about the BIS – saw its neutrality as coming close to siding with the enemy. To what extent was the accusation grounded in the BIS's actual behaviour? Or did it, rather, originate from lack of first-hand information? In answering these questions, the difficulties generally experienced by all neutrals in steering an impartial course during the Second World War cannot be overlooked.

In principle, the BIS's neutrality meant that no operation should have been undertaken that would be found questionable by any of the belligerent countries.[14] However, practical conditions for survival, as in the case of sovereign states, depended upon each side finding it more advantageous to keep the BIS alive than to close it down. The constant support of central banks, together with the peculiarly resilient legal structure of the Bank, proved to be its most effective survival kit. Governments, however, were not all of the same persuasion as their central banks. This was particularly true in the case of the United States and Germany. Whereas the former did not pose an immediate threat, the latter potentially did. The BIS headquarters were just a stone's throw away from the German border. The geographical and military situation made access to the BIS easy from Axis countries and almost impossible from the opposite camp. Moreover, due to its Young Plan origins, at the beginning of the war the BIS still had conspicuous investments in the German market. For these reasons, both personal contacts and business were bound to be biased towards Germany. These circumstances were not such as to make Caesar's wife always above suspicion, particularly when seen from the distant transatlantic perspective.

7.2   The Czechoslovak Gold Affair

One single episode affected, more than any other, the Bank's wartime reputation and loomed large in its historical conscience thereafter: the transfer in March 1939 to Nazi Germany of the Czechoslovak gold deposited with the BIS. Thus, even though the so-called Czech gold affair took place before the war's outbreak, it clearly belongs to the wartime history of the relations among central banks within the BIS framework.

To appreciate the emotional and political impact of the surrender by the BIS to the Reichsbank of a large part of the Czechoslovak gold reserves, it is useful to take a brief step backwards to the time of the creation of the Czechoslovak Republic out of the postwar dissolution of the Dual Monarchy. In its early years, the Republic did not possess a central bank. Most of the latter's functions, notably currency issue, were carried out by a bank office set up with the Ministry of Finance. The office also managed the Republic's gold reserves. These, initially small in size, increased considerably over time. "The source of the relatively rapid and large-scale accumulation of gold reserves was not, however, simply state-organised purchase of the metal. It also owed much to a broad public campaign that elicited gifts from firms and institutions, and above all, in 1919 and 1924, to organised collection among the population."[15] This fervent patriotic campaign was part of the broader drive to build statehood pride based on the Czechoslovak national and cultural identity. In this context, a much-publicised "Gold Treasure of the Czechoslovak Republic" came to be created, which was entrusted to the Czechoslovak National Bank (*Národní Banka Ceskoslovenská*) at the time of its establishment in 1926.

In the second half of the 1920s and throughout the 1930s, Czechoslovak gold reserves continued to increase, reaching a total of 94,772 kg at the time of the Munich Conference (September 1938).[16] By that time, as a precautionary move in response to the aggressive attitude of Germany, the Czechoslovak National Bank had quietly transferred most of its gold abroad. Part of it was deposited with the BIS and held in a BIS gold account at the Bank of England in London. Only 6,337 kg remained in the Bank's own vaults in Prague at the time of the annexation by Germany of the border areas (the so-called Sudetenland) following the Munich agreements.

On 23 February 1939, Berlin sent an ultimatum to Prague for the surrender of an amount of gold supposedly equivalent to the backing for the outstanding currency circulation in the occupied territories.[17] The Czechoslovak government yielded to the threat of invasion, and at the beginning of March 1939 the Czechoslovak National Bank requested the BIS and the Swiss National Bank to transfer to the Reichsbank 2,048.16 and 12,488 kg of gold respectively.[18] Immediately afterwards, invasion came anyway. On 14 March, President Hacha of the Republic of Czechoslovakia was summoned to Berlin and obliged to sign a convention putting the destiny of his people "in the hands of the Führer of the German Reich".[19] On the following day – one year almost to the date after the seizure of Austria – the Third Reich's troops marched through Prague, and Germany proclaimed a protectorate over Bohemia and Moravia.

On 18 March 1939, a special commissioner of the Reichsbank attached to the command of the German occupation forces appeared at the Czechoslovak National Bank's headquarters and, threatening their lives, forced the two directors present to send out two different gold transfer orders.[20] The first one was addressed to the BIS and was received in Basel on 20 March. It requested the transfer to the Reichsbank's gold account held with the BIS at the Bank of England in London of 23.1 tonnes of gold bars to be drawn from the gold account of the Czechoslovak National Bank, also held with the BIS at the Bank of England.[21] The second order, sent to the Bank of

England, contained instructions for the transfer to the BIS's own gold account with the Bank of England of about 26.8 tonnes of gold held by the Czechoslovak National Bank in its own name in London.[22]

The second order was never executed, since the Bank of England abided by the government's instructions blocking all Czechoslovak assets in London.[23] The BIS, on the other hand, carried out the transfer order it had received, crediting the Reichsbank's earmarked gold account in London with 1,845 bars (23.1 tonnes) of Czechoslovak gold on 22 March. In the following days, the Reichsbank swiftly emptied this account.[24] A total of 1,332 bars were exchanged with the National Bank of Belgium and the Netherlands Bank against gold held in Brussels[25] and Amsterdam.[26] Forty bars were exchanged with the BIS against gold held in Brussels,[27] and 473 bars were sold to the Bank of England.[28] In early April, the gold thus acquired by the Reichsbank was physically moved from Brussels and Amsterdam to the Reichsbank's vaults in Berlin.[29] The timing and details of these operations are essential for the understanding of this carefully planned and skilfully executed action by Germany in anticipation of the war. As a result of it, large quantities of Czechoslovak gold came in the possession of Germany, frustrating the precautions taken earlier by Prague to move abroad – mostly to London's safe haven – the bulk of its bullion reserves.

The transfer of Czechoslovak gold almost immediately became a major political issue in France as well as in England, and it remained a source of long-term embarrassment to the BIS.[30]

In a memorandum sent in 1941 to Cobbold, of the Bank of England, President Beyen of the BIS retraced the sequence of events that took place at the BIS on 20 March 1939, just after the fateful transfer order had been received. People in Basel were of course aware of the dramatic events that had taken place in Prague the preceding week, but not of the circumstances under which the directors of the Czechoslovak National Bank had been forced to sign the transfer order.[31] "I discussed the matter thoroughly with the Bank's legal adviser.[32] He held the view that no legal grounds could be cited against compliance. In his opinion", Beyen went on,

a plea of "duress"[33] could only be brought before a Swiss court by the persons who had acted under duress; and it was extremely unlikely that the two Directors of the National Bank would do this. To refuse to carry out the instructions, or even to hold them up, would therefore appear to be, not an act of administration, not an act implementing the policy of the Board, but rather an act of general policy.[34] It therefore was clear to me that I could not undertake such an act outside the Board. Normally I should have put the matter before the Chairman of the Board, Sir Otto Niemeyer. He was on his way to Egypt however and was therefore out of reach. The French General Manager M. Auboin, was not present at the conference.[35] He telephoned to me in the morning. From what he told me, apparently the governments of both London and Paris knew about the order. Subsequently it became known that the National Bank, whose instructions were implementing a clause in the agreement concluded between Berlin and President Hacha, had informed the French and Belgian Legations in Prague. M. Auboin said that M. Fournier, the Governor of the Bank of France, had discussed the matter with him and wanted to know what the BIS was going to do. I told M. Auboin what our legal adviser thought, and asked him to tell M. Fournier that I would be obliged to carry out the order unless I received advice that M. Fournier has sent me a telegram saying that, in the event of such instructions being received, he desired the execution of them to be deferred until the Board had taken a decision thereon. I said that I would defer execution pending an answer. At 6 p.m. M. Auboin telephoned to me stating that M. Fournier had discussed the matter with the English parties and that neither he nor they would be taking any action, because they felt there were no grounds for action. It was only some months later, after the matter had been raised in the English and French parliaments that, at the Governors' meeting preceding the meeting of the Board, M. Fournier protested – not against the carrying out of the instructions as such – but against the fact that they were carried out without the previous knowledge of the Board. I then reported my telephone conversation with M. Auboin, and expressed my astonishment that the one man who could have had the Board deal with the matter, and who had me expressly informed that he desired to take no action, should now be protesting. Of course M. Fournier made no rejoinder to this, he simply reiterated his protest at the official meeting of the Board.[36]

At the same meeting, however, Beyen received full support from Niemeyer. The latter told Fournier that the transfer "was a current banking operation with a client which formally still exists … and that as an international institution [the BIS] could not concern [itself] with political questions".[37] This was the position held by the Bank of England throughout the heated debate on the affair.

For many years afterwards, Beyen deeply resented the indignity suffered by the BIS and by himself personally as the result of the Czechoslovak gold affair. He felt it to be entirely undeserved and laid the blame on the political climate of appeasement prevailing in the spring of 1939.[38] But the formal, strictly legal position taken by the BIS management and by the Bank of England did not rise to the challenge posed by Hitler's unlawful occupation of Prague. The decision to authorise the transfer of Czech gold to Germany was first of all of a political nature. By seeking just one legal opinion – given impromptu by the Bank's own legal adviser and based only upon Swiss law – and refusing to "concern [themselves] with such momentous political questions", Beyen acted as if the BIS were only subject to commercial banking practices, forfeiting its moral obligations as an international organisation.

Beyen, however, had good reason for resenting being subsequently held as the main culprit of the hardly justifiable swift execution of the transfer. An essential point in the whole story of the Czechoslovak gold affair is that, on the crucial day when the BIS decided to honour the transfer order, the U.K. and French central banks and Treasuries had knowledge of it and did nothing to prevent it being carried out. Fournier might even have had some advance intelligence if it is true that, in warning his Czechoslovak colleague of the impending German menace, the French ambassador in Berlin explicitly said that the Nazi government was after Czechoslovak gold.[39] Fournier, though against the execution of the order, would not take upon himself alone the responsibility of stopping it. He actively sought U.K. cooperation. Fournier telephoned the Bank of England on 20 March and again on 22 March. He tried first to have Norman intervene with the BIS, then to "move the [British] Treasury to join with the French Treasury in formally requesting the BIS to part with no Czech assets lest they should fall into German hands". Norman's reaction to Fournier's request typically reflected his long-standing concern to shield the BIS from politicians' interference: at this eleventh hour he still nurtured the illusion that business could go on as usual. "I can't imagine", he wrote in a private note, "any step more improper than to bring governments into the current banking affairs of the BIS. I guess it would mean ruin. I imagine the Germans would never have paid any more interest to the BIS and at the Board we would then likely have found the Germans, Italians and Japs standing together! A nice kettle of fish for future smooth working".[40]

The reaction of the U.K. Treasury was initially cautious. They told Paris[41] that they "did not believe that this incident, however important it might seem, would lead HM Government to depart from their policy of not interfering with BIS matters which are outside their sphere and indeed outside their cognisance".[42] In fact, it is not clear what information the Treasury and the Bank of England shared at this early stage. Certainly, on 24 March, the U.K. government got its own independent information from Prague that "the [Czechoslovak] National Bank wished it secretly be conveyed to the Treasury without being quoted as the source of information that the 28,309 kilograms of fine gold lying at the Bank of England in the name of the BIS was the property of the National Bank".[43]

In the first days of April, Jacques Rueff travelled to London as a representative of the Bank of France to support his government's position that the Czechoslovak gold transfer should not be allowed to take place. Rueff told Cobbold, of the Bank of England, that "although the Central Banks [were] in theory independent, they could not be allowed to disregard the vital interests of their countries, and to hand over reserves which might be used by Germany in a few days for aggressive purposes". He also suggested a legal way out of the impasse. "Czecho-Slovakia", he said, "was now split up into three parts and the BIS could easily say that they could not act on the request of the Bohemian authorities without having agreement also from Slovakia and Hungary".[44]

By 24 March, as we have seen, most of the Czechoslovak gold had been transferred to Reichsbank accounts in Brussels and Amsterdam, and on 3 April this gold was already in Berlin. Yet, it seems that only a few people were informed that effective action could no longer be taken to prevent Germany from gaining possession of the Czechoslovak gold. Technically, the Bank of England was not supposed to know the owners of the subaccounts in the earmarked gold account held with it by the BIS, and this was one of the reasons given by the Bank for its inaction. In fact, they well knew whom the gold belonged to and when it had left the Bank, so much so that in early April Cobbold privately informed the Treasury that "the bird [had] already flown".[45]

Yet the few people who knew that the bird was out of the cage kept their mouths shut. In the following days and weeks, participants in the discussion that took place, both behind the scenes and in public, about the Czechoslovak gold continued to assume that it was still possible to save the "Gold Treasure of the Czechoslovak Republic".

The hope of keeping an altogether embarrassing affair away from the scrutiny of the press soon vanished. On 19 May, Einzig's *Financial News* and the *Daily Telegraph* published articles asking whether the Czechoslovak gold had already been released to the Germans and, if so, why the Treasury had not stopped a transfer that was clearly in violation of the so-called Czechoslovakia Act restricting transactions on Czech financial assets in London.[46] This triggered a debate in the House of Commons,[47] in the course of which Churchill provided a typical example of his anti-appeasement rhetoric: "We are going about urging people to enlist, urging them to accept new forms of military compulsion. If at the same time our mechanism of Government is so butter-fingered that 6 million pounds of gold can be transferred to the Nazi government ... it stultifies altogether the efforts our people are making in every class and in every part to secure national defence."[48]

Asked by Chancellor of the Exchequer Sir John Simon for detailed information on the affair, the Bank of England stuck to its official stance that it did not and could not know for whom the BIS held gold on its London account.[49] This left the chancellor in a most uneasy position.[50] He gained time by saying he would request the opinion of the government's lawyers on whether or not the Treasury could block the notorious transfer orders, and report such opinion to the House.

In the following days, the differences between the Treasury and the Bank of England on the Czechoslovak gold issue took on more and more of the nature of a debate over principles: should the central bank overlook its statutory obligations in the face of an immediate danger to national security? The chancellor told Norman that "the point on which some of the more serious criticism turned was that if the Governor knew that Germany was going to acquire large additional financial strength through the operations of the BIS, could not the Governor have warned His Majesty's Government?" To this Norman replied – untruthfully, it must be added, in order to cover his own position – that "in point of fact he did not know of the transfer, though he was very doubtful that he would have thought it his duty, as Director of the BIS, to make a statement about its transactions to the British Government".[51]

In a statement to the House, Chancellor Simon reiterated that the Bank of England was not aware whether gold held by it in the name of the Bank for International Settlements was the property of the Czechoslovak National Bank. He added that, according to his legal advisers, there was no validity in any of the suggestions made in the debate that the Bank of England would be entitled to refuse to obey the instructions given to it by the BIS. Moreover, the government was precluded by terms of the 1930 Hague Agreement and the 1936 Brussels Protocol from taking any steps, even by means of legislation, to prevent the Bank of England from obeying the instructions given to it by the Bank for International Settlements to transfer gold.

The result of this defence of the Bank of England's behaviour on strictly formal grounds was to shift the attention, and the blame, to the BIS. During the debate in the House of Commons, some members questioned the overall usefulness of the institution; others went as far as to demand the withdrawal of the United Kingdom from the Bank. If Norman saw no reasons for changing his stance on the BIS,[52] the debate sowed some doubts in the minds of Cabinet members, starting with the chancellor himself. The latter was unhappy that he had been forced to resort to legal explanations in order to "defend in Parliament a position in which [he had] no responsibility and no possibility of control". The result of the whole affair, as Chancellor Simon saw it, was the diffusion of a "vulgar view that His Majesty's Government, by refusing to interfere and disclaiming responsibility, [had] been handing

Czech gold to Germany".[53] It is not surprising, therefore, that the chancellor asked for a full review of the BIS position, including the possibility of winding it up.[54]

The political fallout from the management of the Czechoslovak gold affair, quite aside from its general political implications, was altogether devastating for the BIS.[55] It put the Bank in an unfavourable light in the eyes of the public. It exposed, even before war was declared, the potential for ambiguity and contradiction in its pledge to maintain neutrality, even when adhered to according to the strictest legal standards. Moreover, the debate on Czechoslovak gold resulted in explicit consideration being given for the first time to the "winding up" of the BIS by the government of one of the signatory powers of the Hague Agreements. From then on, the option of liquidating the Bank kept resurfacing in policy debates, particularly in the United States, until the time when it was formally recommended by the Bretton Woods conference in 1944 (see Chapter 8).

The swift execution of the order for transfer of the Czechoslovak gold to the account of the Reichsbank is one of the least commendable episodes in the history of the BIS. Neither the legal opinion that the management had to proceed according to standard banking practice nor the wavering of the French and U.K. board members appear to be good enough excuses for management's behaviour. The situation in Prague, both exceptional and patently illegal, not only justified but also mandated that prudent bankers – let alone international civil servants – delay action pending a more careful appraisal of its various aspects.[56] In fact, as we shall see, when subsequently faced with similar cases, the BIS refused to carry out the instructions received.

That being said, it should be added that the Czechoslovak gold affair – for all its blunders, misunderstandings, and hypocrisies – was also the offspring of the prevailing climate of appeasement: a mix of Realpolitik, hopes, illusions, and sincerely held ethical principles. Realpolitik determined the Munich agreements, which gave Germany a free hand in the Sudetenland in exchange (it was hoped) for peace or at least for a respite before the beginning of hostilities. Neville Chamberlain truly hoped that Hitler would stop territorial acquisitions after being allowed to reunite "Germans abroad" with their homeland. These hopes were shared by many. Harold Macmillan recalls how "Chamberlain came back [from Munich] in triumph, to a concentration of applause and even adulation hardly ever granted to any statesman in our history".[57] Daladier, the French Prime Minister, was received in similar style in Paris.[58] The British Dominions were enthusiastic. Roosevelt sent a message of praise and approval. In the following months, a programme of

Anglo-German economic cooperation was discussed. On 6 December, the French and German foreign ministers (Bonnet and Ribbentrop) signed in Paris a declaration "solemnly" recognising as permanent the existing border between the two countries, proclaiming pacific intentions, and pledging mutual consultation.[59] Later that month, meetings were held between the United Kingdom and the German Federations of Industry. Schacht visited London as the guest of Governor Norman and met with Chamberlain.[60] A climate of hope, or illusion, continued through the winter of 1938–39. In January, a coal agreement was signed between the two countries. In February, further economic cooperation was discussed in Berlin between Ribbentrop and Henderson, the U.K. ambassador. At the BIS Board meeting in Basel in March, Funk (Schacht's successor at the helm of the Reichsbank) spoke to Norman about Hitler's wish for good relations with the United Kingdom, and Norman agreed to the need for "fundamental appeasement between nations".[61] Munich seemed to be yielding such positive fruits that, only five days before the German invasion of Prague, Chancellor Simon declared to the Commons that he foresaw "five years of peace".[62]

Besides those who pursued what they honestly believed to be the best Realpolitik or nurtured hopes and illusions, there was also an influential minority of people whose pacifism was based on more general ethical grounds. Keynes, for one, like most liberals, "regarded peace as an almost overriding good". He held that "governments had no right to risk war for a principle without popular support", and such support did not exist in the first months of 1939. Moreover, he argued that, while on ethical grounds war can be justified only if "we know that it will make a future peace sufficiently better than the existing peace …, this kind of knowledge is rarely available"[63] and therefore war was seldom morally justifiable.

There were, of course, also those for whom appeasement was both bad politics and bad ethics. Churchill was the most prominent among them. After Munich, a member of the U.K. Cabinet (Cooper) resigned his post. Paul Reynaud and Georges Mandel in France did likewise. Others, in politics and in the civil service, voiced their opposition. But they were a minority in both countries. It is hardly surprising that the members of the BIS Board did not belong to that minority.

Even after the invasion of Czechoslovakia by Germany and, a few weeks later, that of Albania by Italy, not all were persuaded of the futility of appeasement.[64] If the guarantees given by the Western powers to Poland and the introduction in Britain of a conscript army signalled a policy change, many did not lose all hope of a negotiated peace. And Germany's Blitzkrieg

in Poland brought new recruits to the party that saw no alternative to negotiated settlement.

7.3   Neutrality Declaration and Policy

The Czechoslovak gold affair epitomised, even before war was declared,
the difficulties the BIS was to experience in following the path of neutrality,
inevitably seen as ambiguous by both sides.

On 1 September 1939, German troops crossed the Polish border. Two
days later, France and the United Kingdom declared war on Germany. The
outbreak of hostilities presented the BIS management with a strategic dilemma.[65] Should the BIS maintain its investments in the various markets
and try to remain as active as possible, or should it reduce them systematically in order to remain dormant for as long as the war lasted? Actual
liquidation, on the other hand, was considered neither desirable nor practically feasible.

Since it was impossible to convene the Board, its members were consulted individually by Beyen, the president of the Bank. The unanimous
response of the governors was against any systematic liquidation of BIS
assets; they concurred that the BIS should be kept alive as a valuable instrument for the postwar financial reorganisation.[66] The rejection of the option
of keeping the BIS dormant for the duration of the war implied that the
Board directed management to remain as active in international financial
markets as was compatible with the strictest neutrality. This was a momentous decision: for good or ill, it set the course of the Bank's life for the
following six years.

On 22 September Niemeyer, the chairman of the Board, asked Beyen to
cancel the forthcoming October meeting of the Board. Beyen then sounded
out the principal members about the attitude to be taken with regard to future meetings and about setting up decision-making procedures. Azzolini
(governor of the Bank of Italy) and Galopin (BIS Board member for the
National Bank of Belgium), whose countries were still neutral, insisted on
the continuation of the meetings. Neutrals only would participate, carrying proxies to vote for belligerents. The Germans favoured this solution,
which was opposed by France and the United Kingdom. Exchanges of letters went on for a while until it was agreed to discontinue the actual meetings
and to endorse management decisions by postal vote for the duration of the
war. Fournier (governor of the Bank of France) insisted that only the BIS
president, a neutral, be entrusted with powers to engage the Bank legally,

given that the other managers, belonging to belligerent countries, "would not have the moral authority to make decisions acceptable to all parties". He also wanted the positions of the managers from belligerent countries to be temporarily put on hold, so that only neutrals should run the Bank.[67] In the end, nothing came of this proposal: both the French general manager (Auboin) and the German assistant general manager (Hechler) retained their full functions in Basel.

The cessation of regular Board meetings meant that Board members had to be informed about management decisions and the Bank's business operations by mail.[68] At the Annual General Meetings, voting took place by proxy given by the member central banks either to the president – from 1 January 1940 the American Thomas McKittrick – or to one of the remaining neutral Board members who was able to make the journey to Basel.[69] This arrangement continued throughout the war, even though it increasingly appeared to be unsatisfactory, particularly in the Allied camp. In fact, by the spring of 1941, ten countries whose central banks held over a third of the votes on the BIS Board had fallen under Axis control, which – together with the votes held by Germany, Italy, and Japan – gave the Axis the majority of voting rights in the BIS.[70] Thus, throughout the war, Germany's enemies continued their membership in an international institution where their voting rights were largely outnumbered by those of the opposing side. Little wonder that this "anomaly", which initially went largely unnoticed, in time contributed to the suspicion with which the BIS was looked upon in influential Allied circles, particularly in the United States.

In shaping and defining its neutrality policy, the BIS had to consider two objectives. On the one hand, it had to ensure the preservation of the special privileges granted by the Hague Agreement. The latter stipulated that, even in time of war, the Bank's assets and deposits should be exempt from any measure of confiscation, expropriation, requisition, or import and export restriction.[71] On the other hand, the BIS had to make sure that none of these privileges was used to effect operations that would be harmful to any of the member countries, now at war with each other. Neutrality guidelines were envisaged to make these two objectives mutually compatible.

The Bank's eleventh Annual Report, published in June 1941, spelled out the general aim of its neutrality policy as consisting of confining its "activities strictly to transactions whereby no question can possibly arise of conferring economic or financial advantages on any belligerent nation to the detriment of any other".[72] In order to achieve that, the Board members had, already in the autumn of 1939, agreed on four main policy guidelines.

(1) No operation of the BIS should be such as to grant credit to a belligerent central bank. (2) When operating on a neutral market, the Bank should make sure that a belligerent country did not directly or indirectly profit from such operations. (3) The BIS should refrain from making decisions implying the recognition of territorial changes not unanimously accepted. (4) All the Board members should be granted free access to information on the Bank's operations and to have a say on the issues of principle raised by them.[73]

On 18 December 1939, the BIS issued a public statement defining its neutrality policy. The declaration, approved by all Board members, specified the first two of the points just mentioned, making explicit the self-imposed rules of conduct already observed by its management since the beginning of the war.[74]

The BIS neutrality declaration listed the following operations from which the Bank would abstain during the war, regardless of its rights under the terms of the Hague Agreement. (i) "Transactions the result of which would be to carry out, directly or indirectly, for the account of the central bank (or other institution) of a belligerent country, a financial operation in the market or in the currency of another country with which the former is in a state of war." (ii) "Disposing of its assets on a market of a belligerent country for the purpose of making or facilitating any payment to or on behalf of a country with which the former is at war." Such pledges to avoid making financial transactions or payments in the market of a belligerent country in favour of or on behalf of its enemies were of limited relevance. Enemy assets would in any case be frozen and payments across the front line reduced to trivial amounts. It was nevertheless important to leave no doubt as to the BIS's rule of conduct on the subject. It was, on the other hand, implicitly clear from the declaration that the BIS felt free to execute payments and any other transaction – on neutral markets – on behalf of belligerents from both sides.

Furthermore, the BIS declared it would not (iii) hold "in its own name for the account of the central bank (or other institution) of a belligerent country gold under earmark or other assets on the market of another country with which the former country is at war". It would no longer, for instance, keep gold under earmark for the Reichsbank on the London market. Finally, the BIS said it would (iv) take "all suitable measures", and in particular require appropriate statements of its correspondents, to make sure that individual transactions "would not fall directly or indirectly within the categories indicated above".[75]

The BIS soon came to realise that loopholes remained in the declaration, leaving the door open for questionable transactions from the belligerents' point of view. In January 1940, the Bank clarified its position with regard to the gold transports that it was then organising on behalf of central banks. The BIS said it would buy and transport to New York only gold that, before 3 September 1939, already belonged to a neutral central bank or had been acquired from another neutral institution since that date.[76] More generally, in a memorandum to the U.S. consul in Basel, McKittrick spelled out the "working rules" of the Bank's neutrality policy. They basically consisted of making sure that "no client can, by working through the BIS, obtain facilities which are not available to him directly and in his own name". This rule, known inside the BIS as the "no bypass" principle, meant that "the BIS [would] not support attempts to evade or circumvent the financial regulations of any country".[77]

Later in the war, the Allies made more explicit their point of view on the limits to financial neutrality. On 5 January 1943, the United Nations issued a formal warning to individuals and institutions in the neutral countries regarding the disposal by the Axis powers of looted property originating from the occupied countries.[78] As a result, the BIS Banking Department reformulated, in an internal memorandum, the rules of neutrality as applied to BIS financial transactions.[79] In addition to what had already been stated, the memo underlined the following guiding principles: (i) the Bank declined to undertake transactions between central banks of belligerent nations, even if they fought on the same side, or between a central bank of a belligerent and one of a neutral country, that could be undertaken as easily between the two counterparts directly; and (ii) the BIS declined operations that could not be settled entirely within the confines of either the Allied or the Axis zone (in order to prevent circumventing the reciprocal economic blockades). If strictly adhered to, these guidelines would have probably spared the BIS future accusations and misunderstandings. At the same time, strict adherence might have brought the BIS's activity virtually to a halt. Hence the Bank added, *in cauda venenum,* that such restrictions would not apply to transactions undertaken strictly for the account of the BIS itself with regard to the BIS's own commercial obligations (i.e., interest payments on BIS investments in foreign markets or BIS dividend payments to central banks and private shareholders). This loophole was essential for the survival of the BIS but it would cause the Bank political problems, misunderstandings, and bad publicity – particularly from 1944 onwards.

We shall see later how the BIS's self-imposed neutrality rules were applied as far as the financial and gold operations of the Bank were concerned.

As for the application of the Bank's policy of avoiding any action implying the recognition of territorial and government changes not universally
accepted, the lesson taught by the Czechoslovak gold affair was not forgotten. When similar instances arose after the outbreak of the war, they
were dealt with more prudently and correctly than in the unfortunate earlier
case. The first one again regarded Czechoslovakia, now the German protectorate of Bohemia and Moravia, whose central bank – now called the
Bank of Bohemia and Moravia – requested on 9 October 1939 the disposal
in favour of the Reichsbank of part of its remaining gold still earmarked
with the BIS. The order bore the customary legally valid signatures. This
time, however, the chairman of the BIS Board (Niemeyer) rushed a letter
to Basel urging that the operation not be carried out. The amount of the
requested transfer was trivial, but its execution would have implied recognition of political and territorial changes that Britain and France did not
recognise and would therefore have been in violation of the BIS's neutrality. "The Bank of Bohemia and Moravia did not press the matter and its
assets remained as they had been at the outbreak of the war."[80]

On 29 December 1939, Bank Polski (the Polish central bank) notified the
BIS that its headquarters had been moved to Paris, following the occupation of Warsaw by German troops and the partition of the country between
Germany and the Soviet Union.[81] No objection was raised to the continuation of business with this institution by the BIS, since it did not fall outside
any of the neutrality guidelines; in particular, it did not imply the recognition of any territorial changes.

In April–June 1940, German troops occupied Denmark and Norway, two
neutral countries.[82] The headquarters of the Norwegian central bank were
first moved to the city of Tromsö and then transferred to London. From
there its management sent an order to the BIS regarding the settlement of
an operation in Norwegian crowns. The BIS checked the validity of the signatures with the Norwegian embassy in Berne and executed the order. A
few days later, it received another order, concerning the payment of the dividend on the BIS shares, from the management of the Bank of Norway who
had remained in Oslo. The BIS was thus, for the first time, faced with the
existence of two managements of the same member institution, both claiming exclusive legal rights as its representatives. On this occasion, the BIS
set a precedent for its action in similar future instances by declaring it beyond its competence to decide the questions of law and fact involved in the
situation. Consequently, it said that for the time being it would not allow
any disposal of the assets of the Bank of Norway, including dividends ac-
crued, which were therefore blocked.[83]

A similar issue arose with the National Bank of Belgium, one of the BIS founders and a permanent member of the Board. On 28 May 1940, after a brief brave fight,[84] the Belgian army surrendered unconditionally to Germany. The government repaired to France and later to London, while King Leopold III chose to remain in the country as a prisoner. George Janssen, governor of the national bank, first followed the government but later, with the latter's agreement, returned to Brussels. On 23 July 1940, the BIS was officially informed that the head office of the national bank in Brussels had been reopened and Janssen had resumed his duties as governor there. However, Janssen's death on 9 June 1941 upset this arrangement. On 16 July 1941, the administration in Brussels, which operated under German control, nominated Albert Goffin to succeed Janssen as governor. Initially, this transition seemed to take place smoothly, but on 27 November 1941 the Belgian government in London appointed Georges Theunis as governor of the National Bank of Belgium and declared that the Bank had its official seat in London, not Brussels.[85] In reaction to these developments, the BIS reiterated its neutral stance, notifying both Brussels and London that it was in no position to decide in favour of either of them. The question of who legally represented and held the vote for the National Bank of Belgium on the BIS Board of Directors remained in abeyance. An element of pragmatism, however, was preserved in the BIS's attitude towards the National Bank of Belgium, and relations were not entirely broken off. Certain banking transactions were continued on condition that the BIS would not be called upon to "dispose of property held in custody for the National Bank of Belgium" either by Brussels or London. In particular, dividends to private shareholders resident in Belgium continued to be paid through the offices of the national bank in Brussels. In early 1944 an agreement was reached, which met with the approval of London, for the liberation of accumulated dividends to the national bank itself (Brussels office) in exchange for a partial reimbursement by the national bank of Belgian Treasury bills held by the BIS, which had not been redeemed after maturing in May 1940.[86]

A second gold affair threatened when, in the middle of June 1940, the Red Army occupied the three Baltic States (Lithuania, Estonia, and Latvia), arranging for their formal incorporation into the Soviet Union. On 12, 13, and 15 July the BIS received telegrams from the three central banks requesting their gold be placed at the disposal of the State Bank of the USSR. The gold was held for their account by the BIS under earmark in London, New York, and (for a trivial amount) in Berne. Contrary to the Czechoslovak case, the BIS management this time took external legal advice. Professor Schindler, an authority on international law from the University of Zurich, concluded that, given the circumstances, the BIS could not permit the disposal of the assets of the three banks.[87] Despite pressure from the Reichsbank – Germany was still allied with the Soviet Union – the transfer order was not executed. When, in June 1941, it was the turn of the Third Reich's army (on its way to Leningrad) to occupy the Baltic countries, the BIS management quietly congratulated itself on the decision it had made a year before, when it had created a precedent for not having to comply with new transfer orders now sent out by the central banks of the Baltic States under German control.[88]

The safeguarding measures taken in the cases of Norway and the Baltic States were also applied to Yugoslavia. On 5 April 1941, the National Bank of Yugoslavia instructed the BIS that, in case the country found itself involved in a war, all its accounts with the BIS should be converted into dollars and deposited with the Federal Reserve Bank of New York. The cable carrying these instructions was received in Basel on 7 April, on the same day that the BIS learned of Yugoslavia's entry into the war. The BIS immediately carried out the instructions by depositing $2.7 million with the Federal Reserve Bank of New York for the account of the National Bank of Yugoslavia. After this, the BIS lost contact with the central bank of Yugoslavia until the summer of 1941, when it received both from Belgrade (occupied by the Germans) and from London (where the Yugoslav government had taken refuge) communications about the disposal of the national bank's assets. In conformity with the policy already adopted, the BIS blocked the assets of the National Bank of Yugoslavia and froze the dividends that would have been paid to it.[89]

Unlike the aforementioned cases, the occupations of the Netherlands and France did not give rise to questions of recognition of territorial changes, as the authority of the respective central banks did not come to be disputed. Queen Wilhelmina and the Dutch government took refuge in London after the Dutch surrender on 15 May 1940, but the Netherlands Bank soon afterwards resumed its activities in Amsterdam with the blessing of the exiled government. In this case, the BIS had no problem in maintaining official contacts with the central bank in question and recognised its voting rights and dividend claims.[90] The Bank of France was in a similar situation. After the occupation of Paris on 14 June 1940, the head office of the Bank of France was moved to Chamalières (near Clermont-Ferrand) in unoccupied France and resumed operations there. The BIS recognised the Bank of France in Chamalières as the legitimate BIS shareholder and Board member.

7.4   Enemies under the Same Roof: Wartime Daily Life at the BIS

Ever since the origin of the Bank, the BIS staff had formed a small community of expatriates working more or less harmoniously in the relatively confined premises of the former Savoy Hôtel Univers. Not many of them were well integrated into Basel society, itself a rather closely knit network. Each month, the governors' meeting marked the high point in the community's social life, as managers and higher-ranking officials opened their houses for dinner and tea parties. In between meetings, travel was frequent, particularly (if by no means exclusively) to the home central bank of each individual BIS official. The feeling of "living in exile"[91] was therefore mitigated by the frequent visits from outsiders and by the equally frequent and free opportunity to travel back home and abroad.

The war brought about an abrupt change in daily life at the BIS. Until May 1940, Basel was a neutral enclave between two countries at war with each other. The city boundaries almost coincided with the Franco-Swiss border west of the Rhine and with the German-Swiss border north of the river; both borders were about three kilometres away from the Bank's headquarters. After the occupation of Paris, Axis-dominated or -friendly territories surrounded the BIS on two sides. Not only travel but also postal and telephone communications, particularly with the Western powers, became difficult and slow, at times even dangerous. The small community of BIS officials found itself increasingly isolated from the outside world at a time when the war between the respective countries of origin strained many personal relations.

At the outbreak of the war, citizens from neutral countries largely outnumbered those from belligerent ones among the high-ranking officials of the Bank: the president (Beyen) was a Dutchman, the secretary general (Pilotti) an Italian, another manager (van Zeeland) a Belgian, and the economic adviser (Jacobsson) a Swede. Only the general manager and the assistant general manager, Auboin and Hechler, came from countries at war with each other. There was, at the time, no U.K. subject amongst the BIS executive officers: Goodwin was chief accountant, and Colenutt and Conolly were number two under Pilotti and Jacobsson, respectively. Things changed with the opening of the Western Front, the invasion of Belgium and the Netherlands, and Italy's entry into the war (May–June 1940): Jacobsson and, until the end of 1941, McKittrick (the new president) remained the only citizens from neutral countries to hold senior posts at the BIS.

McKittrick had been elected president in June 1939 at Niemeyer's suggestion. He replaced Beyen when the latter retired from office at the end of the same year.[92] Thomas McKittrick, a midwestern, Harvard-educated American, had spent most of his professional career in Europe. Unlike all his predecessors, he had no experience in central banking, government, or international bodies, except for membership in the German standstill agreement Arbitration Committee created in 1931 (see Section 5.3). Though well introduced in the banking communities on both sides of the Atlantic, he was out of touch with the administration in Washington; in time, this proved to be a liability both to the Bank and to McKittrick personally. The other senior positions at the Bank were filled by people who had joined the BIS from the beginning or, in the case of Auboin, had already acquired considerable experience there. They all enjoyed the trust of the central banks and governments in their respective countries, kept in constant touch with them, and acted as liaisons. For these highly valued services they all had been exempted from conscription at home.[93] Aware that this was a potentially explosive situation, McKittrick wrote to the staff members from belligerent nations to express the management's expectation that they would confine themselves "strictly to the work of the Bank and would not undertake political activities of any sort whatsoever on behalf of any governments or national organisations".[94] If this was wishful thinking, it was nevertheless worth putting on record.

In May 1940, the community of international civil servants at the BIS was hastily removed from Basel to Château d'Oex, a small village in the Pays d'Enhaut, in the canton of Vaud. Over the previous winter, informed by the Swiss authorities about an evacuation plan for the population of Basel, the BIS management made its own contingency plans – including standby transportation – to assure the rapid removal elsewhere of both personnel and business records should the need arise.[95] In April, when military activity was stepped up, the sound of heavy gunfire constantly accompanied the life of the hitherto quiet border city, increasing the already high level of tension among the Bank's staff. It was thus decided to hasten preparations for removal to a quieter location. Gstaad, Interlaken, and Kandersteg were considered until the choice fell on Château d'Oex. There, the six-storey Grand Hôtel du Parc was rented in haste by the BIS when the situation looked to be set for the worse.

The Swiss authorities had, in fact, every reason to worry. Not only had they observed the fate of other neutrals, but they had also got wind that their country was next on Hitler's annexation list. As soon as the armistice between France and Germany went into effect on 25 June, the German high command issued orders for the final preparation of operation "Green" – later renamed "Christmas Tree" – for the partition of Switzerland between

Germany and Italy.[96] Even though the operation was eventually postponed until the time when Germany had defeated its European enemies, great uncertainty and concern permeated the Swiss Confederation's life in the spring and summer of 1940. Defence preparations, particularly plans for blowing up key railway tunnels, were stepped up.

On 14 May, German troops were spotted near the Swiss border at Basel, and the U.K. consul advised all citizens from Allied countries to leave the city at once. That evening, McKittrick and Auboin – the two officials with authority to dispose of the Bank's assets – repaired to Berne. On the following day it was decided that the Bank could not function normally in Basel, and all the personnel and their families were ordered to move to Château d'Oex. On 20 May the BIS began its first regular working day in the new headquarters.

At first, the relocation to Château d'Oex had a favourable impact on the morale of the staff. As the summer drew to an end and the neutral status of Switzerland seemed to be stabilised, however, the inconvenience of living in a small village began to outweigh the advantages of security in the minds of the staff and their families. Good houses for the winter were in short supply[97] and school facilities less than adequate. There were none of the amenities of a larger city to which the staff had grown accustomed.[98] Moreover, life in a small village obliged citizens of enemy countries to undesired proximity. As McKittrick later put it: "There was only one movie house in town, and if a Frenchman and his wife went to the movies and a German and his wife went to the movies, and they walked into each other, it was an embarrassment for all concerned. People were coming to hate each other".[99] There was also uncertainty about tax exemption, as the agreement signed with the canton of Basel did not apply to the canton of Vaud. Therefore, by early September, the vast majority of the employees were in favour of moving back to Basel. The BIS left Château d'Oex in early October 1940.

Back in the enclave city, the sense of seclusion remained for people used to free cross-border movement on diplomatic laissez-passer. If Jacobsson "was restless at weekends because his beloved golf course was in France" or disappointed at the cancellation of a series of lectures on gold he was supposed to deliver at the London School of Economics,[100] the sound of planes and anti-aircraft guns was a sad reminder to citizens of countries at war of the uncertain fate of their families and friends back home. Refugees came over the borders and, needless to say, agents from every side slipped in and out with whatever information they could gather: "life had some aspects of a spy thriller".[101]

Some travel was, nevertheless, possible to those holding neutral pass-ports. Immediately upon taking office, McKittrick visited Funk in Berlin, Azzolini in Rome, Fournier in Paris, and Janssen in Brussels. He later travelled adventurously to the United States.[102] Jacobsson was on a ship, travelling from Lisbon to New York in December 1941, when he heard of the Japanese attack on Pearl Harbor. He also made various trips to Sweden, Germany, and France. Thus, Jacobsson was in Berlin to give a talk at the Reichsbank in December 1942.[103] He was again in Berlin in June 1943 to discuss the Keynes and White plans for postwar monetary organisation.[104] Auboin travelled a few times to Paris and Chamalières (where the Bank of France had relocated).

At the same time, while the usual meetings could not be held, the pres-ident and managers encouraged governors and their staff to pay individual visits to the BIS. Fournier and his successor de Boisanger, as well as Az-zolini and Puhl (number two at the Reichsbank) were among the regular visitors. A few other European central bankers either came or sent rep-resentatives once or twice a year. More rarely, commercial bankers also called, as did the members of the diplomatic corps in Berne. The BIS re-mained an excellent listening point at a time when economic information was both vital and not as plentiful as it had been before the war.

As the Bank's activity shrank and the cost of living increased, manage-ment felt it necessary to dismiss some of the staff in order to reduce the total wage bill and allow pay increases for those remaining.[105] Needless to say, this policy – perhaps necessary in the circumstances – had its cruel side in that those laid off had to return to their war-torn countries and face much more difficult living conditions than those in neutral Switzerland.

In spite of the layoffs, the decreasing level of banking activity and re-strictions on travel meant that some of the staff found themselves not as fully occupied as they had been before the war. Some of their time was ap-propriated by Jacobsson to increase the level of research work. The Mone-tary and Economic Department continued to collect and publish statistical and economic information. The Annual Report, which never ceased to be published, almost trebled in size over the wartime years.[106] It covered at length foreign exchange and trade regulations, price changes, production and movements of gold, public finances, and central banking, as well as spe-cific topics such as international debtor–creditor relationships, lend-lease operations seen from both the U.K. and the U.S. side, and whatever eco-nomic data were available from the Soviet Union.

Towards the end of the war, the BIS activity was at such a low point that management, in order to find useful outlets for the Bank's underemployed intellectual capital, engaged in historical research on the Bank's first 15 years of life. The research project, referred to as "BIS reconsidered", yielded a number of internal papers summarising the business activities for each financial year as well as topical papers on the Bank's capital and shareholding structure.[107]

7.5   Belligerents' Diplomacy: McKittrick's Reappointment

In January 1941, sensing – as he put it – that his country's neutrality had worn thin, McKittrick wrote to Montagu Norman to propose strengthening "the Bank's neutrality by a closer association with the Swiss".[108] Feeling that deviation to either side would be fatal to the chances of the BIS surviving the war, the president proposed the creation of an executive committee, under Article 43 of the BIS Statutes,[109] to be composed of himself and Ernst Weber, president of the Swiss National Bank. In addition, Professor Bachmann (former president of the same bank) would be asked to act as a one-man advisory committee, under Article 44 of the Statutes.[110] For about one year, there was no follow-up to this scheme, but then the matter required urgent attention when, with the Axis declaration of war on the United States in December 1941, the BIS no longer had a neutral president.

In the delicate negotiations that followed, often conducted by proxy or through the intermediary of a neutral colleague, the main central bankers once again showed their determination to keep the BIS alive, with an eye to the postwar resumption of formal cooperation. In order to do so, they resorted to an informal, indirect way of wartime cooperation that entailed both skilful diplomacy and a degree of arm twisting with their respective governments.

The state of war between the United States and the Axis powers naturally made it uncomfortable for the Reichsbank and the Bank of Italy – the Bank of Japan was by then little interested – to have McKittrick as president of the BIS. Left to themselves, the two central banks would have been satisfied to leave matters as they were, but the German and Italian political authorities were less complacent about allowing the BIS to be managed by a citizen of an enemy country. In particular, the German Ministry of Foreign Affairs saw little reason for the continuation of the Reichsbank's membership of an international institution presided over by a citizen of a hostile nation and in which other enemy countries participated. In its view, either McKittrick should be forced to resign or Germany had to sever its links with the BIS. The Reichsbank gained time by recommending the Ministry of Foreign Affairs adopt a "wait and see" attitude, given that McKittrick's term in office would in any case expire at the end of 1942. The ministry agreed but insisted that an attempt ought to be made to replace McKittrick with a "neutral personality" at the earliest possible moment.[111]

In order to meet German reservations about voting for (and openly communicating with) a citizen of an enemy country, Azzolini proposed a revision of the earlier scheme devised by McKittrick.[112] The BIS directors would vote Weber, the president of the (neutral) Swiss National Bank, as chairman of the Board, empowering him to appoint the executive president of the Bank. The scheme would also allow for a neutral figure to keep a communication channel open between the BIS president and the members of the Board.[113] In fact, McKittrick, a citizen of a belligerent country, could not write directly to enemy authorities: not only would such communication be unacceptable to the authorities concerned, it would also expose McKittrick to harsh criticism, if not to criminal charges, in the United States.[114] However, neither London nor Berlin received Azzolini's proposal with any enthusiasm.

To the renewed objections of the German Foreign Ministry, the Reichsbank – that is, Vice-President Emil Puhl and their "man in Basel", Paul Hechler – responded that it was best to maintain McKittrick, whom they described as an easily manageable figurehead, rather than risking the appointment of another person. Puhl and Hechler praised the American president for being "professional and loyal" and maintained that "neither his personality nor his manner of conducting business have been cause for any criticism whatsoever".[115] On the other hand, they argued, the appointment of a different person as U.K. or U.S. representative in the BIS management would almost certainly upset the "until now smooth functioning of the BIS and its use by us for conducting gold and foreign exchange transactions".[116] Upholding Azzolini's scheme, Puhl and Hechler told von Ribbentrop, who insisted on McKittrick's immediate replacement by a neutral personality,[117] that – since the BIS Statutes vested the administration in the Board of Directors[118] – the actual control of the Bank's business would fall upon Weber, acting on behalf of the Board. McKittrick's influence would be reduced to a mere go-between between the Board and management.

In London, Norman was quite unhappy at the prospect of appointing Weber, a person he had little familiarity with, to the position formerly occupied by Sir Otto Niemeyer. At the same time, there was no question that it was essential to the Bank of England's interests that McKittrick, their own choice for president back in 1939, should remain at the head of the BIS.[119] In 1942, the Bank of England's continued participation in the BIS was debated on a number of occasions in the House of Commons. The

U.K. government's defence of the BIS centred on the argument that, with McKittrick at the helm in Basel, Allied interests were safeguarded.[120] Still unsure about whether or not they could trust Weber to stick to the agreement once appointed chairman of the Board, Norman and Niemeyer turned to McKittrick himself for reassurance. "We would agree to Weber's becoming Chairman of the Board", they wrote, "provided it is definitely understood that in consequence you would be reappointed President of the Bank. This proviso is essential and must be certain before we support the election of the Chairman".[121]

Towards the end of August 1942, the two camps were close to reaching a consensus on electing Weber as chairman and putting the issue of the presidency in his hands with authority to settle it, on the definite understanding that he would reappoint McKittrick. The practical question then arose of who would approach the candidate and the Board members to implement the scheme. Rooth, governor of Sveriges Riksbank, was the only director qualified for the task; by then, only two neutral directors remained on the Board, the other being Weber himself. In implementing the scheme Rooth[122] found that the Reichsbank was meeting with further difficulties in securing the assent of the German government. A statement by the U.K. Chancellor of the Exchequer in the House of Commons – to the effect that the management of the BIS was entirely in the hands of the president – did not make things easier in Berlin.[123] Eventually, as soon as it became clear that the other leading Board members did not object to this arrangement, the German Ministry of Foreign Affairs gave up its resistance and agreed that McKittrick could remain in function for the time being.[124] Once all the Board members had given their consent in writing, Ernst Weber was elected chairman of the BIS Board as of 1 December 1942. Under the authority conferred upon him, he renewed McKittrick's appointment as president of the Bank effective 1 January 1943, on the understanding that the position would be placed at the disposal of the Board as soon as it was able to resume its normal meetings.[125] McKittrick remained in office until June 1946.

7.6   The BIS and the Axis[126]

There was, as we have already seen, no room in Germany's global war strategy for respect of neutrality. Neutral countries were ruthlessly invaded and occupied, according to need or convenience. Besides the two Iberian dictatorships – one of them decidedly pro-Axis – only Sweden and Switzerland managed to escape occupation and to retain their independent neutral status. The option of ending their neutrality by occupation was indeed contemplated by Berlin but eventually discarded. The cost of occupying two additional countries, whose relatively strong armies had been trained for prolonged guerrilla resistance, outweighed the benefits of laying hands on their resources. Sweden was in any case willing to sell its high-grade iron ore to the Reich. As for Switzerland, there was of course the temptation to seize its large gold reserves. By 1940, however, nearly two thirds of the latter had – as a precaution – been shipped to New York and London.[127] A neutral Swiss financial market, on the other hand, might provide valuable service to the Reich's war effort. It is in this context that Germany's interest in the BIS must be considered.

The wartime German-Swiss financial relations have been well described by the so-called Bergier Commission.[128] In the 1930s, Nazi economic policy, while successful in absorbing unemployment, did not attain the goal of economic self-sufficiency. Despite the political pressure brought to bear on the negotiation of bilateral clearing agreements, many of them maintained a balance unfavourable to Germany, which had to be settled in hard currencies or gold. The war only intensified the need for imports of armaments and raw materials such as oil, iron ore, tungsten, and manganese, which were mainly supplied by Romania, Portugal, Sweden, Spain, and Turkey.[129] All this required both the availability of means of payment and the existence of an efficient market for financial transactions.

As early as 1933, in anticipation of the war needs, Schacht had begun a secret accumulation of gold reserves, which grew over time to be almost three times as large as the published reserves.[130] At the beginning of September 1939, the gold available to the Reich, which included the former Austrian and Czechoslovak reserves, was worth $256.7 million.[131] During the war, Germany acquired an additional $603.5 million worth of gold, only about 5% ($29.5 million) of which through lawful transactions. The largest amount ($483 million) was seized from the central banks of occupied neutral or formerly allied countries. The rest was brought to the coffers of the Reichsbank by actions belonging to the darkest pages in the history of the twentieth century. Gold worth $88 million was confiscated from citizens of Germany and the occupied territories. About $3 million worth derived from the infamous "Melmer gold", named after SS Captain Bruno Melmer in charge of shipments from the extermination camps.[132]

Out of a grand total of $860.2 million worth of gold available to the Reichsbank during 1939–45, $532.6 million was shipped abroad to settle debts arising from the delivery of goods and services and from interest and dividend payments. More than 77% of the latter amount went to Switzerland.

Whereas private banks played a nontrivial role in German war finance during 1914–18, this was not the case in the Second World War, when monetary and financial management was (to a large extent) entrusted to the Reichsbank. Schacht held the positions of minister of the economy and of president of the Reichsbank until 1937, when Walther Funk was appointed to the former post. From the beginning of 1939 onwards, the two posts were again filled by the same person: Funk himself. The wartime Reichsbank president, in spite of his previous appointment as Hitler's economic adviser, was more of a party bureaucrat than a financial expert.[133] He therefore left most of the central bank's business and its foreign relations in the hands of his vice-president, Emil Puhl.

A relatively young[134] gold and currency specialist, Puhl was an ambiguous figure. In Berlin he kept links with the SS Central Office for the Economy and Administration to which the Reichsbank rendered several important services, both at home and abroad,[135] while turning a blind eye to the origin of gold delivered by the SS to the Reichsbank. On the occasion of his numerous visits to Switzerland, on the other hand, he became "an expert in alluding to his scepticism vis-à-vis the national socialist regime and to posing as a competent specialist and an agreeable person in conversation".[136] He was an esteemed guest in Berne as well as in Basel, where Jacobsson entertained him in long conversations. As the Bergier Commission put it: "in an almost exemplary way, Puhl's character indicates how dubious it was to pursue *business as usual* with the Reichsbank".[137] Yet, to the BIS, he was a friendly German face and the man who convinced his own foreign ministry to let the Bank survive.

As already mentioned, governments from both camps had qualms about the little-understood international bank, sitting on neutral soil and staffed by experts from warring sides. In Germany, however, the issue of its relevance was apparently never raised until 1942, on the occasion of the discussion about McKittrick's reappointment, which provided the opportunity for a reassessment of the usefulness of the BIS to the Reich. In September 1942, Puhl, with the political backing of Funk, visited the Ministry of Foreign Affairs to plead for the BIS, forcefully arguing that the Bank was most important to Germany's war effort. On that occasion, Secretary of State Weizsäcker was impressed, as well as puzzled, by how strongly the Reichsbank took the issue of the continuation of the BIS to heart.[138] This made him wonder where the real importance of the BIS for Germany's interests lay.

According to the Reichsbank, the BIS had rendered Germany "valuable services" since the beginning of the war. They consisted of "a great number of important gold and foreign exchange transactions" (one memorandum talks about "concealed" transactions), providing the Reichsbank with "the necessary means of payment for the import of war-critical goods".[139] In addition, it was claimed that the BIS had proved extremely useful as the Reichsbank's "only listening post for issues of international finance and for the observation of financial transactions carried out by the enemy".[140] All of this, Puhl argued, was made possible thanks to the internal staffing of the BIS. In Basel, the Reichsbank could count not only on Assistant General Manager Hechler but on a group of excellently trained high-ranking Reichsbank employees as well. They guaranteed confidentiality in banking transactions and provided the Reichsbank with information that could not be obtained anywhere else and that had already proved valuable. Of course, Puhl added, the BIS offered these same advantages to the Allies. The British and Americans, however, had access to numerous alternatives to the BIS that were not available to the Reichsbank. The latter, having the sole responsibility for Germany's external finance and lacking foreign branches of its own, would suffer much more than its enemy counterparts should the BIS be closed down. Puhl went as far as to say that the BIS could be considered the Reichsbank's "only real foreign branch".[141]

Per Jacobsson, after visiting the Reichsbank in Berlin in December 1942, had good reason to write in his diary: "I knew full well to what extent the future of the BIS depends on Puhl's possibilities of holding the fort in Berlin".[142] In the end, however, the argument that most convinced a sceptical Ministry of Foreign Affairs was the realisation that the Italians were backing the Reichsbank's position rather than the genuine belief in the BIS's prime importance for the German war effort.[143] The reasons for the Italian support to the BIS were, however, quite different from those of the Reichsbank. Apart from McKittrick's excellent relations with Rome (he had started his European banking career with the National City Bank in Genoa), the Bank of Italy had reasons of its own to uphold the BIS. Governor Azzolini did not share Funk's idea of the uselessness of the international bank in a German-dominated postwar Europe. On the contrary, he saw in the BIS a potentially countervailing force to Germany's overriding monetary and financial influence.[144] It was mainly for this reason that in 1939–40 the Bank of Italy insisted on the wartime continuation of the BIS activity and, in 1942, stood by McKittrick's reappointment as president, lest the whole edifice collapse.

The Reich's Ministry of Foreign Affairs yielded more to the desire of pleasing its Italian ally in what was, after all, a relatively minor issue than to the persuasiveness of the Reichsbank's argument that the BIS was "indispensable" (*unentbehrlich*) in the provision of the necessary means to pay for war-critical imports. Even if everything helps in a war, it is indeed difficult to substantiate the Reichsbank's claim that the disappearance of the BIS would have made any material difference to the Reich's capacity to pay for its imports. Although (as we shall see) a few wartime BIS trans-actions favouring Germany or of a doubtful nature can be identified, these were not of paramount importance. Significantly enough, the Reichsbank itself, for all its rhetoric aimed at convincing the Ministry of Foreign Af-fairs of the BIS's crucial contribution to the German war effort, singularly failed to provide specific examples. The "great number of important gold and foreign exchange transactions" conducted through the BIS in favour of Germany was actually less impressive than the Reichsbank wanted the Ger-man government to believe. The fact is that the Reichsbank had reasons of its own in pleading the BIS's case with the Ministry of Foreign Affairs.

There were a number of reasons why, particularly after 1942, the Reichs-bank continued in its defence of the BIS, using the only argument acceptable to the government: its contribution to Germany's victory. The central bank had, first of all, to be consistent with its own past actions: if the Reichsbank had so far been satisfied with its collaboration with Germany's enemies in Basel, it had to provide some good reasons to justify this behaviour to the Nazi government. In the second place, one must not forget that the Reichs-bank was run by career central bankers and that the involvement of its pres-ident (Nazi minister Walther Funk) in actual day-to-day management was negligible. These professionals cared both for their own international rep-utation and for the survival of their institution in the long run. They were, as a result, more interested than the Nazi politicians in upholding their own and their institution's respectability within the central banking community. For some of them there remained a genuine commitment to the prewar ideal of central bank cooperation, based upon the trust established with the other central bankers within the BIS. Considerations of this kind probably go quite a long way in explaining why the Reichsbank continued to honour its prewar financial obligations to the BIS at a nonnegligible cost (albeit par-tially settled in looted gold; see Section 7.10). Finally, the Reichsbank may have interceded with the German government on behalf of the BIS with an eye to the future. By maintaining as much as possible civil relations with the other central banks – in particular (but not only) with the neu-tral ones – the Reichsbank professionals hoped to increase their country's chances of participating in Europe's postwar financial reconstruction in the case of Germany's defeat, which to informed people looked to be almost a certainty from 1942 onwards. When Jacobsson visited Berlin in June 1943, the official reason given was that he came to discuss the reorganisation of the German banking system. In reality it was to talk to a select group of Reichsbank officials and commercial bankers about the Keynes and White plans on a new postwar monetary system. It was thought best to conceal the real purpose of the visit, as "it would not look well to indicate interest from the [German] banks in the Anglo-saxon currency plans,... especially as Funk had in the autumn of 1941 issued a prohibition against consideration of postwar questions".[145]

The BIS's relations with the third Axis member, Japan, were of less consequence. Before the war, Japan had regularly sent its representatives to the Board meetings; but ever since the 1931–32 dispute with the BIS over the gold value of its Japanese investments, business relations with the Bank had shrunk to almost nothing. In 1940, the Bank of Japan – in order to secure a channel of payments to and from continental Europe – entered into negotiations with the BIS about increasing its deposits and opening a new account in the name of the Yokohama Specie Bank. The latter was refused by the BIS, as was a subsequent (1941) request for a long-term loan backed by gold stored in the Far East. The Bank of Japan never substantially increased its deposits with the BIS: all in all, wartime transactions between the two institutions were negligible.[146]

During the war, Japanese members of the BIS Board paid frequent visits to Basel. One of them was Yoneji Yamamoto, the Bank of Japan agent in Berlin, whom Jacobsson valued for being intelligent, cool, and "not a nationalist".[147] For most of the war years, Japanese interests were represented by Hisaakira Kano of the Yokohama Specie Bank, who in 1939 had been appointed vice-president of the Board. In 1944 he was succeeded by Kojiro Kitamura, who moved from Rome to Zurich. It was Kitamura who, through the Japanese BIS employee Yoshimura, approached Per Jacobsson in early July 1945 to enlist him in an attempt to mediate a peace settlement with the Americans. On the Japanese side, the initiative was supported by Kitamura, Kase (the Japanese minister to Switzerland), and General Okamoto, formerly the imperial military attaché in Berlin, who had direct contacts in the Japanese government and general staff. On the American side, Jacobsson was in touch with Allen Dulles, European director of the Office of Strategic Services (OSS), who held an open communication line to President Truman's office. Throughout July, Jacobsson met secretly with Yoshimura and Kitamura to discuss the conditions for a surrender. Communication to and from Tokyo was assured by the Imperial Embassy in Berne via coded telegraph. Above all, the Japanese were keen on retaining the 1890s constitution, with the emperor as head of state; also, for reasons of honour and prestige, they signalled great difficulties with the Allied demand for "unconditional surrender". In the end, precious time was lost (mainly through Japanese hesitations) and the initiative floundered. A month later, after atomic bombs had been dropped on Hiroshima and Nagasaki, the Japanese government sued for peace via Moscow. It was later hinted from Tokyo that the cables coming from Berne in July 1945 had at least strengthened the position of the peace party within the Japanese Cabinet.[148]

7.7   The BIS and the Allies

As already mentioned, one of the results of the Czechoslovak gold affair was to cast the BIS in an unfavourable light in the eyes of the U.K. public. A hitherto almost unknown institution, the BIS came to be noticed by the press almost exclusively for its transfer of Czechoslovak gold from London to Berlin. Needless to say, the government – and most particularly the Foreign Office – were anything but pleased about the bad publicity they indirectly derived from the affair. Such an unfortunate start notwithstanding, the BIS enjoyed the support of both the Bank of England and the Treasury throughout the war, and their influence played a vital role in rescuing the Bank at Bretton Woods in spite of the often lukewarm attitude of the Foreign Office.

One of the BIS's staunchest opponents in London was Paul Einzig, who back in 1930 had rather coolly welcomed the birth of the Bank. Throughout the war his articles in *The Banker* and in *Financial News* never ceased to accuse the BIS of being entirely under German influence and of all sorts of un-neutral behaviour.[149]

The Bank of England continued to pay close attention to the BIS's fortunes, its top officials remaining in close contact with Basel throughout the war. It was Otto Niemeyer who in the summer of 1939 first suggested McKittrick's appointment to the presidency, as a neutral citizen trusted by the Old Lady of Threadneedle Street. Niemeyer also took the initiative in drafting the BIS neutrality guidelines, which he then personally took to Paris for approval from the governor of the Bank of France, Fournier, and the French government.[150] The willingness of the U.K. authorities to cooperate with the BIS allowed the latter to easily obtain the necessary "navicerts" to ship neutral gold from Europe to New York through the Royal Navy's Atlantic blockade.

Sir Kingsley Wood, chancellor of the exchequer in Churchill's National Government formed in May 1940, did not change his predecessor's policy of commitment to continued wartime U.K. participation in the BIS, and more than once he told the Commons that this was the official stance of the

Cabinet. On 13 October 1942, Wood declared to the House that the president of the BIS was a U.S. citizen who enjoyed the government's "full confidence". Shortly afterwards, upon being reappointed president, McKittrick travelled to London to make his personal acquaintance with the chancellor, to thank him for his confidence and support, and to visit the Bank of England. Wood and Norman were respectively replaced by John Anderson (September 1943) and Lord Catto (April 1944), who followed their predecessors' policy regarding the BIS and stood by it at Bretton Woods.[151]

Unlike those with London, the BIS's relations with Washington went from bad to worse as the war progressed. At the beginning, when the United States was still neutral, the main reasons for friction were the same as those of the 1930s; these stemmed from the lack of understanding in Washington of the BIS in particular and of European financial policies in general. Yet New York bankers, under the influence of the Federal Reserve Bank, maintained a friendly attitude, which – in the wartime circumstances – was at best a mixed blessing for the BIS.

On 10 April 1940, the U.S. government issued an executive order[152] introducing the obligation for nationals of a number of belligerent countries to apply to the U.S. Treasury for licences regarding each transaction affecting assets held by them in the United States. In June, the Treasury ruled that the executive order would also apply to the BIS, considered to be "national of one or more of the foreign countries named in the executive order".[153] The BIS disputed this interpretation, arguing that it was "a corporation under Swiss law and must be considered Swiss if nationality needs to be specified".[154] To no avail: henceforth, all transactions carried out on accounts held by the BIS in the United States were subject to licensing by the U.S. Treasury. Annoying as this was, initially the Bank had little difficulty in carrying on with its U.S. business conducted exclusively on behalf of neutral countries. The Federal Reserve Bank of New York managed to obtain a general licence for the BIS, which allowed all transactions on BIS accounts that the Federal Reserve Bank considered to be "normal" or "routine" to be executed without delay. In June 1941, however, the Treasury revoked the BIS general licence.[155] As a result, executing banking transactions for third parties became extremely cumbersome. In addition, the BIS also faced increasing difficulties in reinvesting its funds held in U.S. capital markets. Finally, in October 1943, the Treasury Department severely limited the sale of Treasury bills and securities to individuals or institutions located in a country whose assets were blocked in the United States.[156]

In 1941–42, Per Jacobsson travelled to the United States, arriving a few days after Pearl Harbor. He lectured at several places, saw a number of leading economists, and visited the Federal Reserve Bank of New York. His interests were macroeconomic policy issues and postwar reconstruction. He did not take the opportunity of his visit to explain to the federal authorities the ongoing operations and neutrality policy of the BIS. His lectures, containing undisguised criticism of the New Dealers, pleased his European friends – Machlup, Haberler, and von Mises[157] – but did not gain him, or indirectly the BIS, the confidence of people closer to the government.

Whereas Jacobsson's visit to the United States was merely a missed opportunity for much-needed dissemination of information about and propaganda in favour of the BIS, McKittrick's definitely made a negative impact.

The president of the BIS had made it clear to his sponsors on both sides that he would accept reappointment only on condition that he would be granted a long "leave of absence" back home.[158] The official reason he gave was the understandable desire to be reunited with his family, but McKittrick was also keen on giving the Washington authorities a full account of BIS wartime conduct. He felt confident that the provision of first-hand information would improve the relations between his own country and the Bank. McKittrick left Basel in November 1942 and travelled through southern France to Madrid and then Lisbon. From there he flew to London, where he spent two weeks waiting for a flight across the Atlantic, in the meantime discussing BIS business with Norman, Niemeyer, and other officials at the Bank of England. The rest of the journey was quite long and adventurous. The complexity and length of the Atlantic crossing might indeed have been part of the acute communication and understanding problems between Washington and Basel, quite aside from the more substantive policy issues. McKittrick took off from the mouth of the river Shannon, in Ireland, on a Pan American hydroplane or "flying boat", as it was then called. The plane took him back to Lisbon, from there to Portuguese Guinea, then to Liberia and, finally, across the Atlantic to Brazil. It took him another five days to reach New York via Trinidad and Puerto Rico. Once there, he spent four months in the United States.

McKittrick's long visit to his homeland did nothing to improve Washington's understanding of the BIS, let alone change the U.S. policy with respect to the Bank. His negotiations on a relaxation of the blocking of the BIS funds in the United States were unsuccessful. "All I can show for it", he wrote to Niemeyer, "is a consent on [the Treasury's] part, after initial refusal, to review the application for permission to pay last year's dividend to shareholders resident in the United States from existing dollar balances".[159] McKittrick complained that – besides former BIS president Fraser and the Federal Reserve Bank of New York – nobody had any clear idea of what the BIS was doing, who ran it, or how in fact it managed to survive. More generally he was struck by the "general confusion and misinformation" about Europe.

McKittrick visited a number of government departments – Treasury, State Department, Board of Economic Warfare, Department of Commerce, Board of Governors – and claimed to have clarified a number of issues and shown that the BIS had "something to contribute" both to the war effort and to the postwar settlement. However, the one meeting he had with Secretary of the Treasury Morgenthau did not go well at all. McKittrick began by explaining the technical difficulties the BIS was encountering in paying its dividend to U.S. shareholders, in recouping its investment in Belgian Treasury bonds, and in servicing a dollar debt to the Swiss National Bank. After only twenty minutes, Morgenthau abruptly broke off the interview, saying that such questions should be discussed with the Treasury experts.[160] As a result of the BIS president's "diplomacy", the Washington establishment remained, at best, sceptical. While McKittrick was still in the country, Congressman Voorhis introduced a resolution in the House calling for a congressional investigation of the BIS.[161] It was, if anything, poor publicity. That aside, the official government attitude did not change and the BIS funds remained blocked until 1948.

It was ironic that the U.S. government's long-standing distrust of the BIS increased to the point of challenging its neutral stance while an American was at the helm of the institution. But McKittrick was a very poor choice, as far as placating Washington was concerned. Having spent the previous twenty years of his life in Italy and England, McKittrick was not well known in American government circles. Moreover, he deeply disliked the U.S. wartime administration, and such feelings are invariably reciprocated. Twenty years after the end of the war, in 1964, he still spoke bitterly of Morgenthau and White, in sharp contrast with the pleasant recollection of his being received in Rome as if he were "the king of something"[162] on his way back from the United States to Basel. Little wonder that, with an ambassador like this, the BIS cause – already compromised by a long history of misunderstandings – stood little chance of gaining the trust of wartime U.S. policy makers.

7.8   The BIS, Switzerland, and the Other Neutrals

The Swiss franc, which remained convertible, quickly established itself as the most important currency in intra-European payments, and Switzerland came to play a pivotal role in European foreign exchange and gold transactions. The Swiss National Bank's policy was determined as much by internal financial and economic goals as by foreign policy considerations.[163] Maintaining the franc's convertibility and a high level of economic activity and prosperity were, of course, worthy aims in their own right, but what mattered the most was that they were essential tools in preserving the independence of that small country, entirely surrounded by Axis-held territory. In 1940, Reichsbank Vice-President Emil Puhl unambiguously stressed this point in the course of a conversation with the BIS management, which was duly reported by Per Jacobsson to Weber, the Swiss National Bank president. "I said", Jacobsson wrote, "that it was of great importance to Europe that the Swiss currency should remain a free currency so that we would have on this continent one strong currency in which we could deal freely when the war was over. Herr Puhl immediately said that he agreed fully with this point of view and he added: 'That the Swiss do not introduce exchange restrictions is important also from a political point of view, for it constitutes a reason for leaving Switzerland free' ".[164]

Thus, the Swiss franc remained convertible, although external payments came to be increasingly centralised and controlled in the context of bilateral clearing agreements. In September 1941, a gentlemen's agreement concluded between the Swiss National Bank and Swiss commercial banks stipulated that the former would henceforth buy U.S. dollars from the commercial banks at the official rate only if they originated from export surpluses settled through official clearings. The BIS, however, retained much of its freedom of action when it came to foreign exchange transactions. As late as August 1942, it was confirmed that the BIS, by the immunities granted to it by Article 10 of the Constituent Charter, was exempt from the obligation to report external payments to the Swiss clearing authorities.[165] Its exchange transactions against the Swiss franc remained unrestricted.

In contrast to foreign exchange transactions, the Swiss National Bank imposed a number of restrictions on gold dealings. The main trigger for this was the U.S. executive order of 14 June 1941 by which all Swiss assets held in the United States were blocked, immobilising about two thirds of the Swiss gold reserves. In these circumstances, the national bank became concerned with the gold transactions between the German Reichsbank and Swiss commercial banks lest they result in net exports of gold from Switzerland, further reducing the freely disposable gold reserves. In the autumn of 1941, the Swiss National Bank asked the Reichsbank to bypass the commercial banks and to settle all gold transactions directly with the Swiss central bank.[166] The Reichsbank obliged, although this meant that it had to content itself with the lower official gold price offered by the Swiss National Bank. Having thus concentrated most of the commercial banks' gold transactions with the Reichsbank into its own hands, the Swiss National Bank was not particularly worried about those undertaken independently by the BIS, even though the latter purchased and sold gold at more competitive prices than the official ones. For one thing, the volume of the BIS gold transactions was relatively small. Moreover, the Swiss National Bank in any case preferred transactions to be settled through the BIS rather than in the free market. As Swiss National Bank Director Schnorf put it in December 1941: "The National Bank has no objections to raise against these transactions, in view of the fact that in this way the BIS is helpful in avoiding gold sales by foreign central banks on the free market".[167] This was, after all, one of the original purposes of the international bank, as envisaged by its founding fathers.

Less than a year later, however, the situation had changed and the Swiss National Bank took a much firmer stance with regard to the BIS's gold transactions. On 9 September 1942, BIS Assistant General Manager Paul Hechler met with the Swiss National Bank board of directors to discuss BIS operations on the Swiss market. The board made it clear that it could tolerate gold transactions between the BIS and foreign central banks only on condition that these remained limited and were settled at prices equal or close to the official ones.[168] The BIS argued that the volume of its transactions was already very limited and that the Swiss National Bank could monitor all the movements, since they were settled exclusively through the BIS's gold accounts held in Berne. Nevertheless, in order to maintain its good relations with the Swiss National Bank, the BIS agreed to widen the margin between its gold purchase and sale prices in order to bring them more into line with the official prices. In addition, the BIS would henceforth buy or sell gold only on condition that its central bank counterpart, when acting as a seller, committed itself to use the proceeds exclusively to settle payments obligations in Switzerland or, when acting as a gold buyer, declared that the Swiss francs used to buy gold from the BIS originated from export surpluses or other freely disposable sources. Under these conditions, which were similar to those regulating the behaviour of Swiss commercial banks, the Swiss National Bank agreed to the continuation of the BIS's gold transactions.[169]

The Swiss National Bank's policy of moral suasion and gentlemen's agreements soon revealed its limitations as far as satisfactorily stabilising the gold market. Hence, in December 1942, the federal government – at the insistence of the Swiss National Bank itself – resorted to formal regulation. Thereafter, gold could be imported or exported only with the express consent of the central bank, while a maximum price was fixed by law. Although the Swiss franc remained legally convertible, gold trade and gold prices were now under the strict control of the Swiss National Bank. The impact of the new regulations on the BIS's gold transactions was limited.

Of the other neutrals, Sweden was the one more interested in, and closer to, the BIS. Rooth, the central bank's head, had been actively involved in the BIS Board before the war and maintained his ties with Basel throughout the hostilities. As we have seen, he played a role in managing McKittrick's reappointment. Links between Basel and Stockholm were also maintained by Per Jacobsson, who travelled freely through Germany to his home country.

In the Iberian Peninsula, after its civil war Spain was never interested or involved in the BIS. Likewise, the Bank of Portugal was not a shareholding member of the BIS, and prewar contacts between the two institutions had been sporadic. But they became more frequent and closer during the war. In June 1940, the BIS contacted the Bank of Portugal to find out whether it would be possible to ship gold from Europe to the United States via Lisbon (the preferred route via Genoa had become impractical because of the war circumstances).[170] These soundings resulted in a first shipment from Switzerland to Portugal of 799 kg of fine gold, which the BIS undertook for its own account.[171] After that, the Bank of Portugal used the services of the BIS on a number of occasions, almost exclusively for the gold transactions described later in this chapter.

7.9   Wartime Business Activity[172]

The outbreak of the war had a considerable impact on the Bank's balance sheet. A run on the Bank's deposits took place between August and October 1939, reducing the overall volume of sight deposits from 82.6 million to 19.9 million Swiss gold francs and of medium-term deposits from 35.7 million to 2.7 million. Gold deposits also diminished from 14.4 million to 10.6 million Swiss gold francs. Long-term deposits, on the other hand, declined only slightly, mainly as a result of the withdrawal by France in October 1939 of the French Government Guarantee Fund. Overall, during the first months of the war, the BIS's total available resources (including capital and reserves) shrank by about 20%: a substantial but not dramatic amount, given the circumstances. The Bank's high degree of liquidity allowed it to meet these withdrawals without problems, thus enhancing its reputation as a prudent and trustworthy international monetary institution.

By the end of 1939, the haemorrhage stopped and, for the rest of the war, the balance sheet totals remained remarkably stable, oscillating between 458 and 496 million Swiss gold francs (the bulk of this amount consisting of the Bank's own funds and of long-term deposits tied to the execution of the Young Plan, which had been effectively frozen since 1931–32). As for business activity, the BIS remained involved in the type of transactions with central banks it had undertaken on a regular basis before the war – that is, the movements on deposit and gold accounts and gold and foreign exchange transactions. The number and volume of such transactions, however, was dramatically reduced, especially after the end of military operations in Western Europe in July 1940. By the summer of 1941, the business volume had fallen to less than a tenth of the average for the last three prewar years, and by 1943 it stood at less than 5%. In particular, foreign exchange transactions remained sizeable in number and volume during the first months of the war but dwindled rapidly thereafter. They averaged 45 million Swiss gold francs per month in 1938–39, falling to 23 million in the following year and to 5.1 million in 1940–41. Over the rest of the war (June 1941 to May 1945), the BIS carried out, on average, foreign exchange transactions for a mere 0.87 million Swiss gold francs per month.

The financial transactions of the BIS shrank to negligible amounts because, in the wartime international financial environment, central banks had little business use for an institution typically designed to facilitate the clearing of international payments in a context of currency convertibility. The very fact that most central banks had sharply reduced their sight and medium-term deposits with the BIS left limited scope for foreign exchange transactions and international settlements. Moreover, everywhere – even in neutral countries – monetary and financial markets came to be controlled by the state to a much greater and generalised extent than had been the case in the already tightly regulated markets of the 1930s. Central banks were turned into payment and financial agents of their governments, mandated to economise scarce gold and foreign exchange. Their international operations consisted to a large extent of payments to neutral suppliers, while inter-Allied transactions were mostly based upon bilateral credit schemes. Axis-dominated Europe basically inherited Germany's rigid system of credit restrictions and bilateral clearing agreements, which stifled much of international financial business. In addition, the BIS, like all other financial institutions, was affected by the increasingly stringent restrictions imposed by the neutral and Allied countries on their financial markets. The most important of such markets – and one of the few initially open for BIS investments – was the U.S. market, where (as we have seen) authorities stepped up financial regulation, deeply affecting BIS operations in their markets.

That being said, the BIS continued to be of service in foreign exchange transactions to a limited number of customers. Among such operations was the transfer, whenever possible, of dividend payments to the Bank's shareholders. Some of the payments to German-occupied or satellite countries made through the Reichsbank, which could thus avail itself of the foreign

Table 7.1. *BIS gold shipments, June 1938 to June 1940*

Customer	Amount	Destination	Amount
BIS own account	158.2 tonnes	New York	140.6 tonnes
Reichsbank	78.5 tonnes	London	54.0 tonnes
NB of Hungary	13.6 tonnes	Berlin	41.7 tonnes
Bank of Italy	10.5 tonnes	Berne	16.4 tonnes
Czechoslovak NB	5.2 tonnes	Genoa	12.5 tonnes
Bank of Norway	4.5 tonnes	Other destinations	10.9 tonnes
Other central banks	5.6 tonnes		
TOTAL	276.1 tonnes	TOTAL	276.1 tonnes

Source: Author computations from BIS records.

exchange involved or earn a fee for its services, raised more than one eyebrow in the Allied camp. Probably also objectionable from a strict neutrality standpoint was a series of foreign exchange transactions on the U.S. market in early 1940 on behalf of the Reichsbank for the benefit of the State Bank of the USSR.[173] The sums involved – $1.15 million from 23 to 29 May 1940 alone – were not negligible and may well have been connected to the settlement of German imports from Soviet Russia in the context of the Molotov–Ribbentrop pact.

Among the services offered to central banks by the BIS, gold shipments and gold location swaps became particularly important from the middle of 1938. As the probability of a European conflagration increased, many central banks called upon the BIS to help them secure a safe haven for their gold reserves. From June 1938 to June 1940, the BIS was instrumental in shipping over 140 tonnes of gold from Europe to the United States for safekeeping, for the account of central banks as well as for its own account. The BIS played a pivotal role in this preventive exodus because it offered the benefit of anonymity and of additional legal protection due to its Constituent Charter,[174] which granted immunity to the Bank's property, assets, and other funds in peace and in wartime. Moreover, thanks to its close contacts with many central banks (which themselves held gold on account with the BIS), the Bank was in an excellent position to offer its customers opportunities for gold location swaps or sales if desired.

The demand for gold transports out of Europe continued after the outbreak of war, and the BIS organised such transports until war circumstances made them impossible in the early summer of 1940.[175] Table 7.1 provides a detailed breakdown of the BIS gold shipments between June 1938 and June 1940. In reading the table one should keep in mind that, whenever the

BIS shipped gold for its own account, this was usually done for the benefit of an anonymous central bank client – prominent among them the National Bank of Belgium, the Netherlands Bank, and the Swiss National Bank – or to replenish the BIS's own gold holdings in New York. The latter could then serve to offer continental European central banks opportunities to swap their gold for gold held by the BIS in the United States. Indeed, during the period covered by the table, the Bank performed gold location swaps for a total of 105 tonnes. Of these, 39 tonnes were made available in London and 30 tonnes in New York.[176] The most important gold swap operations were performed for the Reichsbank (39.4 tonnes), the Netherlands Bank (25.6 tonnes), and the National Bank of Belgium (10.8 tonnes).

When cross-Atlantic shipments had to be discontinued, relatively small transfers of gold were undertaken on the Continent by the BIS. From 1 July 1940 until the end of the war in May 1945, the BIS shipped 21.3 tonnes of gold, mostly for its own account, with Berne (13.6 tonnes) and Lisbon (5.1 tonnes) as the major destinations.[177] Gold location swaps also dwindled to an overall total of 21.9 tonnes over five years. The BIS offered gold for exchange in Berne (9.2 tonnes), Buenos Aires (5.1 tonnes), and New York (3.6 tonnes) to the Swiss National Bank (5.8 tonnes), the National Bank of Hungary (5.3 tonnes), the Bank of Italy (3.2 tonnes), and a number of smaller customers.

Marcel van Zeeland, manager in the BIS Banking Department, spelled out the main reason why the BIS continued this type of operation throughout the war. "It is important", he wrote, "for the BIS to show its capability of being of service [to its customer central banks] despite the difficult times. The Bank is thus acquiring both experience and a reputation that are likely to be of great value at the moment of peace negotiations".[178]

If these were the Bank's motivations, some of the transactions carried out by the BIS produced quite opposite results from the ones desired. In serving its customers, the BIS was walking on thin ice, always at the risk of breaking – or being perceived as breaking – its self-imposed neutrality rules. When that happened, the operation in question dealt a blow to the Bank's reputation rather than enhancing it.

This was the case, for instance, with some transactions with the Bank of Portugal. After June 1941, when free gold transactions on the New York market became increasingly difficult, Portugal's central bank signalled to the BIS that it remained interested in acquiring gold. The Portuguese appetite for gold was easy to explain. The Portuguese trade balance ran a fairly large surplus, since the country supplied both Allied and Axis markets with substantial quantities of various goods. Not keen on accumulating huge amounts of unwanted foreign exchange, the Bank of Portugal sought to convert as many escudos as possible into gold on the few remaining free currency markets. These circumstances offered the BIS the opportunity to perform its typical clearing between the Bank of Portugal, eager to buy gold, and (in this case) the Bank of France, needing to provide importers with Portuguese escudos.[179] Thus, between September and November 1941, the BIS sold to the Bank of Portugal 1,634 kg of fine gold against Portuguese escudos, which were then paid to the Bank of France from which the BIS had acquired gold in the first place. At the request of the Bank of Portugal, the BIS transported the gold in question from Berne to Lisbon in three separate shipments. Besides obliging two customers, the BIS made a welcome profit on these operations.[180] Soon afterwards, the Bank of Portugal again called upon the services of the BIS to transport to Lisbon an additional 1,802 kg of fine gold that the Portuguese held in their own name at the Swiss National Bank in Berne.[181]

These transports, however, did not go unnoticed, and the Bank received a warning from Norman that authorities in London regarded these gold movements "with suspicion".[182] President Weber of the Swiss National Bank, himself in much the same predicament, told McKittrick that U.S. authorities were also displeased with the Portuguese–French gold transaction. Weber was explicit in stating that people were under the impression that "the BIS has been selling escudos to the Axis countries". Although formally neutral, Vichy was under strong German influence and the impression was a fair assumption unless proved unfounded. McKittrick could only reply that he had been given specific assurances by Auboin – the Bank of France man in Basel – that the escudos were for France's own use.[183]

As a result of these warnings, the BIS temporarily suspended further gold transactions with the Bank of Portugal. However, in October 1942 and again in February 1943, the BIS made two further gold shipments from Berne to Lisbon.[184] In the first case, the gold was bought from the Bank of France and then partly sold to the Bank of Portugal against escudos and partly deposited in the BIS's own gold account with the Portuguese central bank. The second shipment was for the BIS's own account. In all, from November 1940 to February 1943, the BIS transported – in eight separate shipments – a total of 5,076 kg of fine gold from Berne to Lisbon.

Another set of operations with a neutral country, Turkey, was also viewed with suspicion by both Washington and London. For most of the war, Turkey maintained a neutral stance while being strongly pressured from both sides to join their respective camps. Ankara had entered into an alliance with the Western powers on 19 October 1939, but it retained its neutrality in the conflict that had just broken out and maintained fairly close economic relations with Germany. In particular, Turkey was Germany's main source for chromium, an essential component of steel alloys for armaments. Only in August 1944 did Turkey give in to Allied pressures, breaking off diplomatic relations with Germany and discontinuing its chromium shipments.[185] In November and December 1939, the BIS entered into nine gold location swaps with the Central Bank of the Republic of Turkey for an overall amount of approximately 5,540 kg of fine gold. In each case, Turkey gave the BIS gold they held in Berne in exchange for BIS gold held in New York, Paris, and London. These operations were dictated by Turkey's desire to relocate part of its gold reserves to a more secure location.

More than four years later, three further gold swaps followed. Between 12 April and 8 July 1944, the Central Bank of the Republic of Turkey gave the BIS an overall amount of 3,173 kg of fine gold it held in London in exchange for BIS gold held in Berne. These swaps, involving only the BIS and a neutral country and therefore perfectly in line with the Bank's code of neutral conduct, nonetheless aroused the suspicions of the U.K. and U.S. authorities. An official at the U.K. Embassy in Washington drew the attention of the U.K. Ministry of Economic Warfare to the swaps, wondering whether the Trading with the Enemy Department had licensed the deals, especially in view of "the position taken early in the war that all BIS operations on its London holdings were to be regarded as possibly enemy tainted and therefore none should be executed".[186] This reopened the debate in U.K. governmental circles about the wartime activities of the BIS and the expediency of continued U.K. membership in the Basel institution. The controversy would be further stirred up by the resolution calling for the liquidation of the BIS adopted at the Bretton Woods conference in July 1944.

Some other gold operations in Southeast Europe involved two Axis countries, Bulgaria and Romania. During the first half of 1942 – that is, when Bulgaria was allied to Germany and Italy[187] – the BIS organised three gold shipments from Berne to Sofia on behalf of the National Bank of Bulgaria.[188] Moreover, in March 1943, the BIS sold to the National Bank of Bulgaria (acting as an intermediary for the French mining company Louda-Yana in Sofia) 49 kg of fine gold and shipped it to Geneva for delivery to the Banque Mirabeau there.[189] In spite of being carried out directly for the enemy, rather than for neutrals suspected of dealing with the enemy, these operations apparently raised no objections in London or Washington, possibly because they went unnoticed at the time.

During the war, the BIS also regularly performed gold operations with the National Bank of Romania. From October 1939 to December 1940, the

BIS bought 3,013 kg of fine gold, against Swiss Francs, from the National Bank of Romania. Most of these transactions took place when the country was still neutral.[190] After Bucharest joined the Axis, van Zeeland lured the National Bank of Romania into buying gold from the BIS rather than from the Swiss National Bank, as had previously been done, by offering more advantageous prices.[191] At the end of September 1941, the first of 15 gold deals between Basel and Bucharest took place, involving a total of 8,957 kg of fine gold until the end of the war.[192] The Romanians transferred most of the gold acquired from the BIS to various locations in Switzerland and to Romania itself.[193] The reason for these operations was the Romanian desire to convert their earnings in Switzerland (mainly Swiss payments for Romanian exports of oil and foodstuffs) into gold that could be used more freely to settle Romania's own payment obligations in Switzerland and elsewhere or to add to the Romanian reserves.

Finally, mention should be made in this context of the wartime operations conducted on behalf of the Red Cross. The BIS was first approached by the International Committee of the Red Cross (ICRC) and the League of Red Cross Societies in November 1940. These Geneva-based international organisations hoped to raise money with the national Red Cross societies all over the world in order to fund emergency assistance to civilian war victims in Europe, and they asked the BIS to act as banker for this operation.[194] The BIS accepted and asked its correspondent central banks to open in each country a special account for receiving such funds as might be collected by the local Red Cross societies.[195] This humanitarian project, however, did not produce the desired result, mostly because of national suspicions and the strict foreign exchange controls applying almost everywhere.

Even so, the BIS was able to carry out a number of exchange operations on behalf of the ICRC. In July 1941, the so-called Commission Mixte de Secours de la Croix-Rouge Internationale was established; it took over the deposit account that the BIS had opened earlier for the ICRC and the League of Red Cross Societies. During the following years, the Commission Mixte would use this BIS account as its current account for receiving funds and to make payments for deliveries of food, clothing, and medicine to war-stricken countries. From November 1940 until March 1946, transfers to and payments from the Red Cross account with the BIS exceeded 28 million Swiss francs, of which more than 22.5 million were spent on food, clothing, and medicine for civilian war victims in Belgium, France, Greece, Poland, Yugoslavia, the Netherlands, et cetera.[196]

All along, the BIS did what it could to be of assistance to the Red Cross. Regular banking charges were reduced or even waived, and starting June

1943 the BIS granted the Commission Mixte a somewhat higher interest rate on its deposits than was customary. The BIS also lent its assistance in setting up a system for the reimbursement of international telegram charges incurred by the Red Cross on behalf of several countries (for transmitting lists of names of prisoners of war).[197] On a number of occasions the BIS offered the Commission Mixte substantial bridging credits in order to facilitate the delivery of emergency goods to France.[198] In a few instances the BIS called upon the German Reichsbank for help in assisting the International Red Cross. This was the case when the Commission Mixte sought to change 140 million drachmas it had received in Greece into Swiss francs,[199] and again when the Reichsbank was called in to act as paying agent for the monthly subsidies the Red Cross transferred to a number of individuals in occupied territory.[200]

On several occasions the Red Cross explicitly thanked the BIS for its support in carrying out its humanitarian tasks. As a tribute of appreciation, Marcel van Zeeland, manager of the BIS, was appointed honorary treasurer general of the League of Red Cross Societies in 1948.[201]

7.10   Wartime Gold Transactions with the Reichsbank

Both during and soon after the war, the BIS's wartime gold transactions – particularly those with the Reichsbank – came under close scrutiny, and charges of improper behaviour were raised from some quarters, first and foremost in the United States. Given the relevance of the ethical implications of these gold transactions, even sixty years after the end of the Second World War, the issue must be carefully considered and covered in some detail. Piet Clement has recently punctiliously examined the issue.[202] What follows draws, at times verbatim, from his published and unpublished research.

Table 7.2 details the movements in and out of the gold deposit held by the Reichsbank with the BIS. The upper part of the table shows that, during the war, an overall amount of 21.5 tonnes of gold flowed through the Reichsbank's gold deposit account with the BIS. Of this total, 13.5 tonnes constituted new gold delivered to the BIS by the Reichsbank during the war. The rest was: (a) already on the Reichsbank gold account with the BIS from before the war (1.9 tonnes), (b) purchased by the Reichsbank from the BIS (6.0 tonnes), or (c) credited to the Reichsbank gold account with the BIS by other central banks (0.1 tonnes). The lower part of the table details the payments made by the Reichsbank out of its gold deposit with the BIS. The account served mainly two purposes: receiving German interest payments

Table 7.2. *Wartime movements on the Reichsbank gold account at the BIS*

Date	Transaction	Amount
Reichsbank wartime gold deposits with BIS		
1/9/1939	Initial balance	1,861.7
1/9/1939 – 8/3/1945	Deposits made by the RB to its BIS gold account (Berne)	12,016.6
12/4/1945	Deposit made by the RB for the BIS in Constance	1,525.6
Oct 1939 – Jan 1941	Gold purchased by the RB from the BIS	5,479.7
February 1940	Gold exchanged with other gold	499.9
Oct 1939 – June 1941	Gold credited to the RB by other central banks	88.5
	Total wartime RB gold availability in its gold deposit with BIS	21,472.0
Wartime withdrawals from the Reichsbank's gold deposit with BIS		
1/9/1939 – 12/4/1945	Interest payments on BIS investments in Germany	7,792.4
1/9/1939 – 12/4/1945	Payments for postal and railway services	6,017.9
Nov 1939 – May 1940	Withdrawn by the RB	5,809.0
February 1940	Swapped for BIS gold in Stockholm	502.7
Nov 1941 – Jan 1942	Sold to the BIS against Swiss francs	1,350.0
	Total wartime withdrawals from RB gold deposit with BIS	21,472.0
	FINAL BALANCE	0.0

Notes: Amounts listed are in kilograms of fine gold. "RB" = Reichsbank.
Source: Data from Clement (1998).

on the BIS's prewar investments in Germany (7.8 tonnes) and making payments to other central banks on behalf of the Reichsbank with respect to the international postal and railway settlements system operated through the BIS (6 tonnes). The remainder was either withdrawn by the Reichsbank from its BIS account early in the war (5.8 tonnes) or directly ceded to the BIS as a result of sale and exchange transactions (1.9 tonnes).[203]

Throughout the 1930s, the Reichsbank had held several gold deposit accounts with the BIS at various depository locations (Amsterdam, Berne, Brussels, London, and Paris). For obvious reasons of security, as in the case of the Czechoslovak gold held in London, most of these deposits had been emptied before the end of August 1939. Their contents were sold or – most frequently – shipped to the *Reichsbankhauptkasse* in Berlin. Consequently, at the outbreak of the war, the only gold deposits the Reichsbank still had with the BIS were held in Berne.[204] The balance of a small gold sight account, held in London and used for the transfer of international postal payments, was also transferred to Berne in October 1939.[205]

During the war, all Reichsbank gold that was newly deposited with the BIS was first sent to the German central bank's own gold deposit account with the Swiss National Bank in Berne to be transferred to the Reichsbank's gold deposits with the BIS at the same location.[206] There was only one exception to this procedure, in the very last days of the conflict. On 12 April 1945, the Reichsbank placed 1,525.6 kg of fine gold[207] at the disposal of the BIS at the *Reichsbanknebenstelle* in Constance (Germany), close to the Swiss-German border.[208] At this late stage of the war, the physical transport of this gold to Berne was refused by the Swiss authorities because of restrictions imposed on further German gold deliveries to Switzerland, following an agreement concluded with the Allies in March 1945. This gold, held under earmark in the name of the BIS in Constance, remained blocked there until after the war.

As mentioned previously, about a third of the gold in the Reichsbank's account with the BIS was used to settle Germany's interest payments to the BIS itself. These obligations had their origin in the Young Plan. In 1930–31, the BIS had made substantial investments in the German market that were directly linked to the final settlement of German reparation payments. These investments took place in the context of a commitment by the international community to reinvest in Germany part of the sums received as reparations in order to ensure the continuation of Berlin's capability to meet its financial obligations towards the creditor nations. When German reparation payments were suspended by the Lausanne Agreement, the BIS had to maintain its investments in Germany in order to preserve its own and the creditor nations' rights under the Young Plan, in view of a possible future settlement.

The BIS's investments in Germany consisted of (a) interest-bearing funds held at the Reichsbank and at the *Golddiskontbank* and (b) bills and bonds of the German Treasury and the German Railway and Postal administrations. The overall sum involved remained substantially unchanged after July 1931. At the end of August 1939, it amounted to 294 million Swiss gold francs ($96 million). Until March 1940 the interest due on these investments was settled by the Reichsbank through monthly payments in Swiss francs to the BIS.[209] Thereafter, however, the Reichsbank settled part of the interest payments due to the BIS in gold. This was the case for payments due between March and June 1940, in October 1941, and for all payments made between January 1943 and April 1945. As already mentioned, the main reason that the Reichsbank continued to honour its financial obligations with the BIS – in spite of the war – was its overriding concern to keep the Basel institution alive and to secure Germany's participation in it. Besides, the sums involved were comparatively small.

The suggestion that the Reichsbank make its interest payments to the BIS in gold instead of Swiss francs originated from BIS Assistant General Manager Paul Hechler.[210] After making a perfunctory protest, McKittrick felt he could not possibly refuse the gold. To do so, he argued, "would clearly give a pretext to discontinue transfer", while he felt that it was "clearly to the general advantage that transfers of interest should continue quite apart from whether they [were] made in devisen or gold".[211] After the war, the BIS stressed that it had had no legal basis to refuse German gold payments and that doing so "might have entailed a heavy responsibility for the Bank towards its own creditors under the Hague Agreements, particularly the French and U.K. Governments".[212] Throughout the war, the shareholding central banks – both Allied and neutral – were perfectly aware of these regular German gold transfers to the BIS and, as far as is known, did not object to them.[213] One should add that, from the point of view of the Bank's business operations, German wartime interest payments were its single most important remaining source of income. In the fiscal year 1940–41, interest earned on investments in Germany made up 70% of the BIS's total earnings (as against 50% before the war). Towards the end of the hostilities, the share of German payments in total earnings rose to about 82%. The BIS was, therefore, kept alive thanks to the uninterrupted flow of German interest payments. Deprived of this income, the Bank would have had to stop paying shareholders a dividend from the very beginning of the war.[214] To his U.K. and U.S. critics, McKittrick repeatedly answered that, after all, interest payments constituted a net drain of resources from Germany that could not be viewed as being detrimental to the Allied war effort.

The second most important item in the Reichsbank's gold payments to the BIS derived from postal dues. The Reichsbank participated in the clearing system for international postal payments set up by the BIS in the late 1930s at the request of the World Postal Union. In this system, sums due on account of international postal traffic were settled bilaterally between countries through gold sight accounts held by their respective central banks with the BIS. From September 1939 to January 1945, the Reichsbank instructed the BIS to debit its gold account for a total of 1,362.1 kg of fine gold for postal payments to Argentina, Belgium, Denmark, Estonia, Hungary, Finland, Norway, Slovakia, and Sweden. Payments to these countries were for relatively negligible amounts, comparable to what had been customary before the war, and do not seem to raise problems. More suspicious is the fact that over 70% of total gold payments for postal services made by Germany was transferred to the Hungarian National Bank in favour of the Hungarian Postal Service. The amounts involved were, by prewar standards, too high to be explained by Germany's regular postal service deficit with Hungary, even accounting for the presence of German troops there. More suspicious still is the fact that, apart from the international postal payments but following the same procedure, a total of 4,655.8 kg of fine gold was transferred from the Reichsbank's gold account with the BIS to the account of the National Bank of Yugoslavia in favour of the Yugoslav Railway Administration. These sums also seem too high to reflect the German deficit in Yugoslav railway traffic. Moreover, these transactions were carried out between June 1940 and March 1941, at the time of the most intensive Axis military build-up in the Balkans, and were discontinued after the German invasion of Yugoslavia and Greece in April 1941. The BIS archives record the technical execution of these transactions but remain silent on the motives behind them. Formally, these transfers may not have violated the BIS's self-imposed code of conduct of December 1939, but the context in which they took place and the amounts involved are such that they most likely concealed war-related payments.

The main problem with the German gold deposits – the one that raised the most serious ethical questions both soon after the war and more recently – regards the origin of the gold itself. Already during the war it was known that the Germans used on a massive scale gold looted from various sources to meet international obligations. Two Allied declarations, the first issued on 5 January 1943 and the second on 22 February 1944, warned all neutrals against accepting looted assets – and in particular looted gold – from Germany, as these assets would be reclaimed after the war with no entitlement to compensation.[215] Suspicions about the origin of the gold used by Germany in its international payments were routinely voiced in the international banking community on the basis of simple, back-of-the-envelope calculations. Before the war, the Reichsbank had been notorious for the small size of its gold reserves, officially amounting to no more than 40 tonnes at the end of 1938.[216] By these calculations, the absorption and confiscation of the Austrian and Czechoslovak gold reserves (88 and 30 tonnes respectively) could not account for the amounts of gold channelled abroad through the Swiss National Bank alone (roughly 345 tonnes), not to mention other central and commercial banks outside Germany.[217]

There were more specific warnings as well. In August 1943, Yves Bréart de Boisanger, the wartime governor of the Bank of France, travelled to Switzerland just to alert both the Swiss National Bank and the BIS about the fate of Belgian gold. In November 1939, the National Bank of Belgium had confided a large part of the Belgian gold reserves (more than 200 tonnes) to the Bank of France for safekeeping in the event of war. In the closing days of the German military campaign in France, this gold, together with French gold,[218] was put on an emergency transport to Dakar in

French West Africa, where it was stored. When, in late 1940, the Germans told the authorities of Vichy France that they would be held responsible for any loss of gold in case of a successful raid of the Royal Navy, the gold was moved inland, some 400 km from Dakar. The Germans then requested the Vichy government to deliver the Belgian gold to them in Marseilles. Governor Fournier tried to drag his feet, but he was replaced at the helm of the Bank of France in September 1940 by Bréart de Boisanger. Shortly afterwards, Vichy yielded to the German pressure. Formally, it was only the custody over the Belgian gold that was being transferred from the Bank of France to the Reichsbank, not the ownership. A first small shipment arrived in Marseilles by air in November 1940. However, flying the whole quantity of Belgian gold all the way from French West Africa to France proved too dangerous owing to the intensified presence of the enemy air force. The gold was thus transferred by train from its location in Kayes to Bamako, on the Niger river, and from there taken by boat and light truck all the way to Timbuktu and Gao. From there the gold crossed the Sahara either by truck or camel. When it reached the Moroccan border, it was again put on a train to Algiers and from there transferred by air to Marseilles. Each shipment took about 30 days to be completed. This adventurous transfer of Belgian gold from Africa back to Europe took much longer than anticipated, but by the end of May 1942 some 4,854 cases of it were finally stored in the vaults of the Reichsbank in Berlin.[219] The Reichsbank's "custodianship" was short-lived. In September 1942, the Belgian gold was requisitioned by the German government and put at the disposal of Göring, as Four-Year Plan Commissioner. The Reichsbank offered the National Bank of Belgium a token compensation in blocked Reichsmarks for its gold, which was refused by Brussels and later also by the Bank of France, which declared itself legally responsible vis-à-vis the Belgians. The purpose of de Boisanger's visit to McKittrick in August 1943 was precisely "to put the Swiss National Bank and the BIS on notice that, if any of the Belgian gold [is] found after the war in their possession or has passed through their hands, they may expect claims from the Bank of France for restitution".[220] At the time, McKittrick felt confident that all gold received by the BIS from Berlin bore the marks of the Prussian Mint and thus gave no indication of having ever been in Belgian possession.[221] Roger Auboin was not so sure. He advocated not only careful vigilance about the origin of the Reichsbank gold but also a rapid resumption of German payments in Swiss francs. "It is surely advantageous", he wrote, "to receive gold from the Reichsbank and sell it back to the National Bank of Romania, but in this matter profit is of secondary importance".[222]

As shown by subsequent events and findings, de Boisanger's warnings and Auboin's doubts were well founded. After being requisitioned by the Four-Year Plan authorities, the Belgian gold was sent to the Prussian Mint, where, between February and July 1943, it was melted down and cast into new bars bearing the Prussian Mint seal, new numbers, and false dates from 1934 to 1939. Thus concealed as prewar Prussian Mint bars, the Belgian gold was used by Germany for its external payments. More than half of it (109 tonnes) was paid into the Reichsbank's gold deposit with the Swiss National Bank in Berne. From there, 1.6 tonnes reached the BIS in settlement of the Reichsbank's monthly interest payments. Ironically, the Reichsbank started to use some of these "falsified" Belgian gold bars to pay the BIS just a few days before de Boisanger met with Auboin and McKittrick.

In spite of Auboin's reservations, the practice of accepting gold in settlement of Germany's interest dues was continued until a few weeks before the final surrender of the Third Reich. This is at odds with the behaviour of other "neutral partners" of the Reichsbank, who became more cautious towards the end of the war, when doubts no longer existed about which side would emerge victorious. In March 1944, Ivar Rooth, governor of the Swedish central bank, wrote to McKittrick about the Allied declaration of 22 February 1944 on looted gold. "I doubt", he said, "whether [neutral central banks] will continue to buy gold which may be regarded as looted or, even if not looted might lead to very unpleasant consequences for the buyers. Confidentially I can inform you that on principle we are no longer buyers of German gold".[223] McKittrick, however, while acknowledging that no specific agreement existed on the issue, remained confident that the Germans would deliver only "good" gold to the BIS. The reasons for his admittedly naïve confidence were rooted in the way he interpreted the Reichsbank's behaviour towards the Bank throughout the war. "It would be folly", said McKittrick, "for them to transfer interest to the BIS during the entire war period and then at the eleventh hour send gold which might seriously embarrass and discredit the institution which they have spent so much good gold and devisen to maintain".[224]

When the war was over, the Reichsbank and the Prussian Mint records captured by the Americans showed that the BIS had unknowingly received not only 1.6 tonnes of looted Belgian gold but also nearly 2.1 tonnes of looted Dutch gold. More recent research shows that, for its wartime payments, Germany also used gold looted from private citizens and concentration camp victims.[225] Some of this "victim gold" was delivered to the Prussian Mint and mixed with "monetary gold" when melting "new" gold bars. A detailed analysis of the available evidence and of the BIS's own records indicates that a limited number of gold bars delivered during the war to the BIS by the Reichsbank probably derived in part from the most tragic event of the twentieth century: the Holocaust.[226]

7.11   Italian Gold

No self-respecting institution can live without its own myths and legends; they enhance collective memories, shaping a strong esprit de corps. One of the BIS legends relates to the adventurous way in which part of Italy's gold reserves was spared the fate of being looted and taken to Berlin. As told by Jacobsson's daughter, the story has Pilotti – the Italian secretary general of the BIS – driving his own car full of gold across the Nazi-guarded Italian-Swiss border. At high personal risk he "had been able to pass himself off as just another private person going about his ordinary business".[227]

Reality was somehow less glamorous, if more plausible.[228] On 20 April 1944, a train arrived from Como, Italy, at the Swiss railway station of Chiasso, just across the border. With it came four freight cars holding gold from the Bank of Italy's reserves. Two of them were destined for the Swiss National Bank; the other two held 89 crates filled with 1,068 gold bars, or 12,605 kg of fine gold, for the account of the BIS. After the necessary formalities were completed, the gold was handed over to representatives of the BIS and the Swiss National Bank. The gold was then loaded on a Swiss freight train and continued its journey to reach the vaults of the Swiss National Bank in Berne. A few days later, on 25 April 1944, the Bank of Italy transferred an additional 3,190 kg of fine gold from its own gold account with the Swiss National Bank in Berne to the BIS gold account there.

Thus, at a time when the Allied armies were closing in on Rome and Mussolini presided over the puppet Social Republic in northern Italy, the Bank of Italy transferred to the BIS a total of 15,795 kg of gold. This transfer, together with that to the Swiss National Bank, was indeed intended to save part of Italy's gold from being taken to Germany.

The background on this transfer stretches back to the early 1930s. Shortly after its foundation, the BIS had invested considerable sums in the Italian market, just as it did in the markets of its other central bank members. These investments, in the form of short-term bills, were renewed regularly and earned the BIS a good monthly interest income. At the time of the outbreak of the Second World War, the investments on the Italian market amounted to 54.5 million Swiss gold francs.[229] They were covered by a gold guarantee from the Bank of Italy.[230]

On 25 July 1943, two weeks after the Allied landing in Sicily, Mussolini was removed from power and confined to a mountain resort in central Italy, while King Victor Emmanuel III appointed Marshal Badoglio to head a new Italian government. On 8 September, an armistice was signed after Italy's unconditional surrender to the Allies. By that time, the German army had taken up defensive positions throughout the peninsula and Mussolini had been freed by a German airborne commando and set up as the head of a puppet fascist republic in the north of Italy (the so-called Republic of Salò, from the name of the small town on Lake Garda that served as its capital). The southern part of the country, under Allied control, was governed by the king and Badoglio.

At the time of the fall of Mussolini, BIS Secretary General Pilotti happened to be in Rome for a meeting with Azzolini, governor of the Bank of Italy. A few days later, Hechler asked Pilotti to convince Azzolini to move the gold set aside by the Bank of Italy as a guarantee for the BIS investments in Italy (15,795 kg of fine gold in all) to safe custody with the Swiss National Bank in Berne.[231] The reasons given by Hechler for this request refer to the country's "uncertain future": he might personally also have feared that the Italian gold would shortly fall under Allied control. Azzolini replied that such a request was shameful, as nothing of the kind had ever been asked of other countries in similar situations, and Pilotti returned to Basel empty-handed. On the day after the announcement of the armistice, in September 1943, McKittrick reiterated the BIS concerns and urged the Bank of Italy to take all necessary measures to safeguard for the BIS the gold set aside against its investments in Italy.[232]

With the German occupation of Rome, Azzolini came under strong pressure – from both the Mussolini government in northern Italy and the German authorities – to leave the city and move the Bank of Italy's headquarters to the north. On 20 September 1943, anticipating that Rome would sooner or later be evacuated,[233] some German officers (including the notorious Major Kappler), accompanied by a special representative of the Reichsbank, turned up at the central bank's headquarters. They ordered the Bank of Italy to move its gold reserves to safe custody in German-controlled northern Italy. Azzolini was only able to avoid transfer by aircraft (which, he later said "would not have stopped in Milan");[234] to hide modest quantities of gold and silver; and to save the crown jewels. By the end of September 1943, about 119 tonnes of gold had been moved by train, under German military escort, to the Bank of Italy's vaults in Milan.

On 19 November 1943, when the news came through to Basel that the central bank's gold reserves had been moved from Rome to Milan, the BIS instructed the Bank of Italy to convert the totality of its investments into gold and to keep it ready to be sent to the Swiss National Bank in Berne.[235] Immediately upon receipt of this request, Azzolini informed the finance minister of the fascist republic.[236] Shortly afterwards, a similar request was transmitted by the Swiss legation in Rome on behalf of the Swiss National Bank.

Azzolini seems to have been at first inclined to delay complying with the BIS's and Swiss National Bank's requests. By the beginning of December, however, he had changed his mind. This was no doubt due to the attitude of the German authorities in northern Italy. At the end of November, Azzolini received a visit from Bernhuber, the Reichsbank representative for Italy, who conveyed the Reichsbank's wish that the part of the Italian gold reserves pledged to foreign creditors be moved to Berlin for safekeeping. At the same time, the German authorities were exerting pressure on the Mussolini government towards the same end. The Fascist government was able to resist the German demands by instead moving the Italian gold out of Milan to a safer location close to the German border, so that there would be no need to place it under formal German custody. On 19 December 1943, all the gold held in Milan was taken to Fortezza, an abandoned military fortress not far from the Brenner Pass border.

Anticipating that the gold's new location would be no more than a stopover to Berlin, Azzolini now fully embraced the demands of the BIS and the Swiss National Bank. He told the government that these were "debts of honour" and that Il Duce himself had always insisted on maintaining Italy's external credit position intact.[237] However, the finance minister's reaction was negative: he was adamant that not one ounce of Italian gold should be sent to Switzerland because the Swiss government had not recognised the Social Republic of Salò and, in any case, Italy's credit standing in Switzerland had become largely immaterial.[238]

The BIS and the Swiss National Bank, however, continued to work in the background to obtain the Reichsbank's support to break the deadlock. Hechler repeatedly called on Reichsbank Vice-President Puhl to use the Reichsbank's influence in Italy to obtain the release of the BIS gold.[239] The Reichsbank agreed to put its full weight behind the BIS request once it became clear that the Italians were not keen on shipping their gold to Berlin. In contrast to Mussolini's Fascist government, the German financial authorities still attached great importance to fulfilling Axis financial obligations to Switzerland and maintaining good relations with institutions such as the Swiss National Bank (SNB).

As in other wartime instances, central banks joined forces to achieve their specific policy aims, which differed from those of their own governments. On 24 January 1944, Reichsbank Vice-President Puhl met with Azzolini in northern Italy, where he had recently moved in response to German pressure.

Two days later, they paid a joint visit to Rahn, the German ambassador to Salò, and succeeded in obtaining the consensus of the German authorities in northern Italy for the gold shipment to Switzerland. This left only the Italian Fascist authorities to be won over. On 27 January 1944 Azzolini wrote to the finance minister, reiterating the BIS's and Swiss National Bank's request to send their gold to Switzerland and emphasising that the German authorities were now in favour of this transfer. No immediate reaction followed. In the meantime, however, the Fascist government and the Germans were negotiating a financial settlement that entailed the shipment of gold to Berlin. On 5 February 1944, an agreement was signed committing the Social Republic to the immediate release to Germany of 50.5 tonnes of gold from the reserves held in Fortezza as a contribution to the joint conduct of the war. Azzolini was informed about this agreement only on 25 February. On 2 March 1944, 49.6 tonnes of Italian gold reached the Reichsbank vaults in Berlin.[240]

At this point, the Fascist authorities gave up their resistance to the transport of the Italian gold pledged to the BIS and the SNB to Switzerland. On 17 April 1944, Azzolini wrote to the BIS and the SNB that all necessary authorisations had been obtained from the Italian and German authorities and that 23.4 tonnes of gold were being released for transport to Chiasso, in the canton of Ticino. There, as mentioned before, on 20 April 1944 it was taken into custody by the representatives of the BIS and of the Swiss National Bank.

This gold shipment, important as it was for the BIS, could not have taken place without the support of the German military and civilian authorities in Italy, which was obtained through the good offices of the Reichsbank. Azzolini played a similar role with the Fascist authorities. It was the joint efforts of the two central banks that succeeded in sparing part of the Italian gold the fate of being transferred to Berlin.

Only weeks after the BIS gold had safely reached Berne, Azzolini found himself in Rome at the time when the Allies captured the city. He was taken into custody and put on trial for cooperating with the German occupation forces and, in particular, for surrendering the Italian gold reserves to them. During the trial, Azzolini claimed that he had done his utmost in delaying the handover of the Bank of Italy's gold to the Germans. He also claimed credit for succeeding in sending part of the Italian gold to Switzerland, thereby keeping it out of German hands. During the trial, both McKittrick and Per Jacobsson sent a telegram to Rome pleading in favour of Azzolini.[241] This was not a smart move, since the message was taken as an undue interference by "foreign bankers" showing lack of respect for the High Court of Justice dealing with war-related crimes.[242] Here was another instance of how people at the BIS, while well meaning and loyal to their Board members, had remained out of touch with changing realities in Europe.[243]

7.12   Assessing the BIS's Wartime Conduct

Two years after the end of the war, the Federal Reserve Bank of New York produced a lengthy report on the BIS wartime activities. The report, written by the Bank's most loyal friend in the United States, concluded that "the charges against the BIS have never been substantiated by any documentary evidence of the bank's connivance with Germany. On the contrary, the British Government has repeatedly declared itself to be satisfied with BIS's neutrality, and the Bank of England did routine business with the BIS throughout the war; the central banks of the European Governments in exile in London concluded during the war arrangements with the BIS which they presumably considered satisfactory to themselves; and even the United States Department of State recognised the international character of the BIS when in 1942 it issued a passport to the president of the BIS, then on a visit to the U.S., for his return to Switzerland".[244] By 1947 (as we shall see in Chapter 8), the majority of policy makers concerned seemed to agree with this assessment, while public opinion had lost interest in the fate of the BIS. The Bank had resumed its peacetime activity, including the governors' meetings, was collaborating with the twin Bretton Woods institutions, and was helping to rebuild European financial cooperation. The issue of looted gold was about to be settled to the satisfaction of the then interested parties.

In later years, the BIS's wartime behaviour was again discussed by both pamphleteers and historians.[245] In particular, questions were raised during the 1990s about the BIS's gold dealings in the context of a more general inquiry into the international financial implications of the Holocaust. In the opinion of the Independent Commission of Experts Switzerland – Second World War: "A systematic examination of the BIS's abundant historical resources would shed light on the relationship between the Reichsbank, the BIS, and Swiss banks. However, no one has yet carried out a study of this kind".[246] Although we cannot claim to have conducted the "systematic examination" advocated by the commission – which would go beyond the aims of this general history of central bank cooperation in the BIS context – some conclusions about the BIS's wartime conduct can be drawn from the research embodied in this chapter.

The debate about the BIS's activities during the Second World War has mostly focused on two broad sets of issues, which are separate but somehow related to each other: looted gold and adherence to the neutrality rules of behavior.

Did the BIS receive gold looted from countries conquered by Germany and from private citizens or even from concentration camps? If so, did people in Basel either know or suspect where the gold came from? Did they do everything in their power to find out? As we have seen, there is no doubt – ever since the investigations of the Tripartite Commission[247] – that the BIS received looted Belgian and Dutch gold from the Reichsbank. We now also believe that some of the payments from Berlin were most likely tainted by small amounts of "victim gold". The fact that both types of looted gold amounted to a relatively minor share of total payments received by the BIS and are dwarfed in comparison to looted gold received by neutral central banks – in particular those of Switzerland and Sweden – cannot excuse the BIS for accepting this gold. Suspicions existed and warnings were heard loud and clear. They were, at best, overlooked in the naïve belief that the Reichsbank had no interest in betraying an institution that it went to such pains to keep alive. While this was the weak explanation provided by McKittrick at the time, it is likely that other and more relevant considerations tipped the scale in favour of letting the Reichsbank continue its gold payments up to the very end. The only way to make absolutely sure that the BIS would not receive a single gram of looted gold was to refuse any further payments from Germany. Yet because, by 1943, interest on German investments made up almost 80% of BIS income, it would have been impossible to stop the gold flow from Berlin without virtually closing the Bank. Years of work and of delicate diplomacy to preserve the BIS until the end of the war would have been jeopardised. Nobody in Basel or at the main shareholding central banks was prepared to risk that, and nobody seriously pressed McKittrick to stop Germany's gold payments.

Questions about neutrality are more difficult to frame, let alone to answer. Both the *jus belli* and accepted conventions allowed neutrals to trade with both sides provided they did not supply goods and services relevant to the war effort. To what extent were payment services of the kind provided by the BIS "relevant" to Germany's war effort? The most objectionable operations in this regard seem to be the gold transfers to Hungary and Yugoslavia on behalf of the Reichsbank. The very fact that these transactions were disguised under postal and railway payments signalled that they were sensitive and should be regarded with suspicion. Selling gold to Sofia and Bucharest was also questionable from a strict neutrality point of view. These were minor transactions, but they still amounted to the sale of services to one of the belligerent sides. Given the length to which governments went to preserve gold reserves, any transaction that helped in economising on gold could be seen as "relevant" to the war effort and therefore barred from correct neutral behaviour. Oddly enough, these operations (as far as we know) raised no eyebrows in London or Washington, whereas both objected to gold transfers performed on behalf of Portugal and Turkey, two neutral countries. Objections to the BIS acting as intermediary between Lisbon and Vichy, while formally not violating the Bank's own neutrality rules, rested on the assumption that the Pétain government was collaborating with the Axis rather than being neutral, as it officially claimed to be. It can be argued that in this case the BIS should have been more cautious than it was. It is, on the other hand, difficult to see why services of the kind provided to Turkey (gold transfers and swaps) should be considered objectionable from a "strict neutrality" point of view.

Besides the issue of looted gold, the most serious accusations against the BIS made during the war – at Bretton Woods and in the years immediately following the end of the conflict – concerned the Reichsbank interest payments and the Czechoslovak gold affair. In retrospect, the latter definitely looks to be the most serious war-related blunder made by the BIS. Even if the implication of the main central banks (particularly of the Bank of England) sets the affair in the post-Munich context of appeasement, this does not make it politically and morally excusable. Moreover, the affair ignited a devastating press campaign against the Bank and loomed large on its reputation throughout the war. It deeply annoyed friendly governmental circles and added to the suspicions of unfriendly ones. It provoked a call for revenge at Bretton Woods.

As for German interest payments, it must be said once again that they were a necessary condition for the BIS's wartime survival – much as the export of iron ore, machinery, and financial services was the reason why Sweden and Switzerland were allowed to remain free. For the BIS they generated essential income. For the Reichsbank, they were a price it willingly paid to attain its ultimate goal of maintaining the BIS alive as a viable instrument for international monetary cooperation and postwar financial reconstruction. McKittrick claimed that interest payments were a net drain of resources from Germany; however, the drain was in fact minimal, not only because payments were partly settled in looted gold but also because dividends to shareholders paid by the BIS went largely back to Axis-controlled territories. In any event, receiving interest payments from lawful investments and paying dividends to shareholders was not in breach of the Bank's neutrality.

To sum up, a number of mistakes were undoubtedly made by the BIS management in 1939–45. The most serious of them – swift transfer of Czechoslovak gold to the Reichsbank – took place even before the war began. Overlooking warnings about looted gold was also a serious error. Some of the gold swaps and payments on behalf of Germany to Axis-dominated countries probably breached the strict neutrality commitment. Other business that generated harsh criticism at the time – receiving German interest payments, paying out dividends, dealings with Portugal and Turkey – now look much less objectionable than they did during or immediately after the war.

The overriding priority given to the survival of the institution, a priority fully backed by the main Board member central banks, is largely responsible for the blunders Basel made before and during the war. Even the Czechoslovak gold affair can be explained largely by the desire to keep relations in Basel – if not harmonious – at least workable. Had the BIS not executed the order transferring the Czechoslovak gold to the Reichsbank, the latter would have possibly withdrawn from the Bank or assumed a hostile attitude. Another (though less significant) reason for some of the wartime mistakes made by Basel can be traced back to the isolation of its top management from the intellectual and political developments taking place in the West during the war, including the power shift in financial policy making from central banks to the Treasuries. This last point will be explored in more detail in the next chapter, which deals with the political outcomes of the BIS wartime conduct as perceived internationally – particularly in the United States – at the time.

EIGHT

Bretton Woods

8.1 The Road to Bretton Woods

In the BIS mirror, Bretton Woods may at first glance appear as no more than the conference that passed a resolution calling for the liquidation of the Bank. Yet some of the most relevant dimensions of that conference are traceable back to the political and intellectual issues behind the creation of the BIS in 1930, to its subsequent history, and to some of the people connected with it. The BIS was meant to be a response – but was one that eventually proved too timid and ineffectual – to the acknowledged mistakes made in the first postwar settlement and to the perceived flaws of the inter-war gold standard. In the same vein, albeit in a much more comprehensive way and in a more favourable political and intellectual context, the architects of the post–Second World War international financial institutions were driven by the determination to avoid past mistakes in creating a viable international monetary system. The lessons from past mistakes included the Great Depression, seen by many as largely man-made.[1]

The United Nations Conference at Bretton Woods, New Hampshire, is arguably the single historical episode known to every student of monetary or international economics. It took place in July 1944 at the Mount Washington Hotel at the foothills of New England's tallest and windiest peak. Forty-five countries debated and agreed upon a plan for the creation of a stable postwar international monetary system. The plan, presented to the public in April 1944 as "The Joint Statement of Experts on the Establishment of an International Monetary Fund", was supposed to be a compromise between the two brainchildren of John Maynard Keynes and Harry Dexter White. In fact, it was quite heavily biased towards the latter's proposals.

Morgenthau, the U.S. Secretary of the Treasury who presided over the conference, told delegates at the first meeting that their work "will shape to a significant degree the world in which we are to live".[2] And so it probably did, even though scholars disagree as to how far the monetary system in place until August 1971 actually resembled the one envisaged at Bretton Woods.[3] The conference ended on 22 July 1944 with the signature of an agreement creating the International Monetary Fund and the International Bank for Reconstruction and Development, better known as the World Bank. Soon after the end of the war, in early 1946, a conference was held in Savannah, Georgia, to adopt the regulations of the two institutions and to appoint the management.

Although there are a number of excellent studies on the intellectual and political road that led to Bretton Woods, the notion that the latter marked a major break with the past led most postwar economists and some historians to overlook the longer-run roots of the agreement. The issues discussed at Bretton Woods had been on the intellectual and political agenda since at least the beginning of the century, and many of the participants in the conference were the same politicians, scholars, and bankers who had researched, debated about, and acted on international monetary issues over the previous decades.

As we saw in the first chapter, the idea that central bank cooperation is a prerequisite for a stable and efficient international monetary system dates back at least to the end of the nineteenth century. The BIS provided as much formal and informal central bank cooperation as the international political environment allowed in the 1930s. Monetary cooperation was also at the core of the plan discussed at the Bretton Woods conference, where this time governments rather than central banks took the centre stage.

After the Great Depression and the failure of the London Conference of 1933, the debate about the future of the international monetary system moved along new lines. The BIS, while remaining a staunch supporter of gold, was actively studying and proposing reforms to the system that would allow the gold exchange standard to work. In tune with those who, like Hawtrey, still regarded the gold exchange standard as the best available system,[4] the BIS was convinced that it could only function if cooperation were stepped up. "The gross abuse of this standard", stated the 1935 Annual Report, "was largely due to the failure on the part of central banks ... to have a coordinated policy between one another".[5] Hawtrey also strongly advocated the establishment of an international lender of last resort of the kind the BIS was supposed but was unable to be. Besides cooperation, the main points stressed by Jacobsson and his staff had included the end of reparations, the lowering of tariffs, the abolition of exchange controls, and the introduction of measures for a better utilisation of central bank reserves. All these topics figured prominently on the Bretton Woods agenda.

At the same time, however, the failure of the supposedly built-in stabilisers to prevent worldwide deflation caused an increasing number of scholars and policy makers to lose faith in the gold standard.[6] The notion that more radical reforms were needed than just a change in the rules of the game within the gold standard was gaining political and intellectual currency.[7] The opinions of those, such as Cassel and Keynes, who were in the minority in the 1920s gained ground in the following decade. Some of the ideas floated at Bretton Woods had been outlined by Keynes as early as 1933: an international authority would issue "gold notes" to individual countries according to quotas proportional to their gold reserves.[8] The system, then seen as just a "qualified return to the gold standard", was supposed to allow for agreed changes in gold parities. In the 1930s, Keynes' main point of disagreement with the BIS – which he accused of living in an "unreal world"[9] – was about structural balance of payments disequilibria, which according to the Cambridge economist could be dealt with only by gold parity realignments.

The quest for a cooperative solution to external payments imbalances that would avoid competitive devaluations motivated the so-called Tripartite Agreement of 1936. The BIS initially gave this agreement a lukewarm reception but later advocated a more general adoption of its "principles".[10] The well-established BIS practice of offering central banks facilities for granting each other reciprocal credits in domestic currencies or gold was aimed precisely at increasing the liquidity available for international transactions and at minimising currency fluctuations and foreign exchange risk. In 1938, Paul van Zeeland proposed a revision and extension of the Tripartite Agreement to "help meet the threat to international trade posed by monetary disturbances", an issue central to the Bretton Woods agenda, by a large extension of the "method of reciprocal credits instituted by the BIS".[11]

Until the beginning of the war, the BIS was deeply involved in the debate on the practical innovations to be introduced in the system for allowing liquidity to grow along with international trade while at the same time guaranteeing price stability (both upward *and* downward) and avoiding shocks from external payments imbalances. While the BIS's perspective, shared by most central bankers, was one of reform rather than overhaul of the gold standard, the Bank shared the aims (if not the means) of the more radical reformers. It contributed superb statistical research and, most of all, unique experience and technical skill in monetary cooperation. It also provided a forum where unorthodox views, such as those of Schacht and Funk, could be heard. And Schacht undoubtedly influenced a number of U.K. economists, such as Henderson and Balogh, contributors to the magmatic cradle of ideas out of which eventually emerged the first formulation by Keynes of the "International Clearing Union" in the late summer of 1941.

In February 1940, a resolution calling for the establishment of an "Inter-American Bank" was adopted in Panama by the foreign ministers of several American countries.[12] The aims, functions, and organisation of this institution were modelled quite closely on those of the BIS: to promote currency stabilisation through direct settlements, to act as a clearing house for central banks, and to produce research and expert advice for governments and central banks. Harry Dexter White, assistant to the U.S. Secretary of the Treasury Henry Morgenthau, participated in the drafting of the Panama resolution. A U.S. Treasury official since 1934, White had been involved in pioneering the innovative use of the Exchange Stabilization Fund to stabilise the dollar not only against gold, as was the fund's original purpose, but also against other currencies.[13] From that experience and from the Panama negotiations, he drew his inspiration in framing the more comprehensive plan for an international monetary agreement that would go under his name.[14]

The Keynes and White plans, which eventually merged at Bretton Woods, originated independently of one another at about the same time. White gave thought to an international monetary agreement in the early part of 1941: "His ideas envisaged both an organisation to stabilise exchange rates and the means of providing the long term capital that would be needed after the war".[15] By the time the United States entered the war, the plan had taken quite a detailed shape, envisaging an "Inter-Allied Bank" and a "Stabilisation Fund".[16] A first mimeographed version of the White Plan dated April 1942 was produced with the collaboration of Edward Bernstein after it had received the unofficial approval of the State Department. The aims of this plan included: (a) a fixed–exchange rate regime; (b) the promotion of trade and productive capital flows; (c) the reduction or elimination of exchange controls, clearings, and multiple currency practices; and (d) the correction of the maldistribution of gold among countries. In addition, the White Plan considered the need to facilitate the settlement and clearing of international payments. Member countries would contribute gold and their own currencies to the stabilisation fund, from which (under certain conditions) they could then purchase the currencies of any other member. Membership in the fund entailed a number of commitments, which included maintaining fixed exchange rates, lifting restrictions on foreign exchange transactions, and ceasing preferential currency treatment. Export subsidies were not to be allowed without the approval of the fund, while capital movements would be subject to approval from the originating country. As already mentioned, an international development bank was to be established. On sending the plan to Roosevelt, Morgenthau indicated that it was the free world's response to Hitler's New Economic Order and suggested an international conference to launch the plan.[17]

Keynes's ideas for a clearing union originated in the summer of 1941 when he was discussing the Lend-Lease Agreement with the Americans.[18] Article VII of the draft proposal made it clear that, after the war, the United States expected the United Kingdom to avoid any discrimination in its transatlantic trade by dropping the system of preferential treatment for Commonwealth trade set up by the Ottawa Conference of 1932, clearing agreements and exchange controls. This was not readily acceptable to the U.K. establishment. The experience of the previous decade had convinced many in government, the media, and the economic profession that the existing panoply of controls on commercial and financial transactions was the only (if admittedly second-best) way to cope with balance of payments disequilibria without resorting to outright deflation. Not unlike Schachtian Germany, the United Kingdom sought to exploit its buyer's market position in agricultural products to "force" its own exports of manufactured goods by means of the "imperial preference" system or bilateral agreements. It was hard to believe that, after the war, net debtor countries would be able to pay for their essential imports in a free-trade environment in which the United States was expected to enjoy conspicuous competitive advantages for many years. Keynes nurtured no illusion that grants and loans – such as those under the Lend-Lease Agreement (or the Marshall Plan, which he did not live to see) – would be sufficient to solve the postwar international liquidity problem. He foresaw a dollar shortage. At the same time he knew that the United States was determined to create a postwar international economic environment based upon free trade and also had the strength to impose it. He saw his task as that of devising an international monetary system capable of accommodating free trade while at the same time avoiding both the deflationary bias of the interwar gold standard and the dangers of a dollar shortage. He called that an "ideal scheme".

If perhaps not quite "ideal", Keynes's international clearing union was one of his typically unconventional ideas, aimed at reconciling the U.S. quest for free trade with the United Kingdom's binding payments constraints while preserving – as far as possible – U.K. international economic influence. The union, in Keynes's original formulation, was an international bank "with the new unit of account that would be the basis for the issue of a new international currency",[19] aptly denominated "bancor".[20] The bancor's gold parity would be fixed but not unalterable. It was, in fact, a fiat money to be allocated initially to member countries according to a mix of indicators such as trade, population, and gold reserves. The union would put equal pressure on deficit and surplus countries to restore balance of payments equilibrium. Temporary deficits were to be financed by running overdrafts with the union, which would act as a clearing house for international payments. Overdrafts would become bancor balances held with the union by surplus countries, thus avoiding the accumulation (sterilisation) of such surpluses as in the 1930s. The clearing union would put pressure on both surplus and deficit countries to restore equilibrium by charging increasingly higher interest payments on their balances (either credit or debit) and, whenever necessary, by demanding simultaneous moderate revaluations and devaluations of their currencies. Unlike trade, capital flows would remain subject to limits and regulations. An international police force and a reconstruction and development organisation complemented the clearing union scheme.

Careful examination and comparison of the two plans in both London and Washington in late summer 1942 showed that they shared a number of common features. There were, nevertheless, also considerable differences: it took almost two years of discussion for the U.S. and U.K. governments to converge upon the joint proposal submitted to the Bretton Woods conference.

The main difference between White's stabilisation fund and Keynes's clearing union was that the former would operate in the currencies of the member countries while the latter would create an ad hoc international currency. The treatment of gold was also different, with the metal being relegated to a lesser importance with the union than with the fund. Here, however, the gap between the two visions was more apparent than real, as ultimately the currencies contributed by member countries to the fund were just as much fiat money as the union's bancor.[21] The two views differed sharply as to the burden of adjustment, which Keynes – mindful of the United Kingdom's and Germany's interwar experience – maintained should be shared by surplus and deficit countries alike. Some differences were more technical, such as the timing and method of international payments clearing; others concerned location and administration, as well as voting rights in the new international institutions. The latter issue was particularly sensitive – and contentious – because in Keynes's scheme voting rights were allocated in such a way as to allow the United Kingdom and the Commonwealth to outvote the United States jointly.

After a visit to London by White in October 1942, both plans were redrafted several times. Keynes insisted that the United States and the United Kingdom should reach a broad common view before circulating the plans to other parties: it was thus only in March 1943 that the White Plan was sent to the governments of 37 countries and, shortly thereafter, released to the press.[22] In June 1943 an informal discussion group, attended by representatives of 18 countries, discussed the postwar international monetary system in Washington. Suggestions coming from the participants in the debate were taken into account, and some were incorporated into the scheme for the stabilisation fund.

In September 1943 a U.K. team, which included Keynes, travelled to the United States for bilateral talks with the Americans. These were aimed at merging the two plans. "Keynes thought that he and White could settle all outstanding issues in a weekend's discussion."[23] In fact, he remained in the United States for six weeks, and it was not until 20 April 1944 that an agreement on principles was disclosed to the Congress and the press.[24] Even if the British had given up on calling the new institution "Union", a name apparently unpalatable to the U.S. Congress (though it was Keynes who eventually suggested naming it the International Monetary Fund), a gulf of differences remained. Some – such as the size of individual countries' quotas, the majority required for changes in the value of "unitas" (the fund's proposed unit of account), and the withdrawal procedure – were settled in Washington. Converging on the most important issues took another six months, during which time intensive economic diplomacy took place between London and Washington, also involving the Soviet Union and the main British Dominions. On most issues, the U.K. experts eventually accepted aptly reformulated U.S. proposals. On the role of gold, a compromise was found between the U.S. desire to maintain its pivotal role in the system and the U.K. preference to do away with it altogether. The new institution would buy gold at the current parity but, unlike central banks under the gold standard, would not be obliged to sell it at a given price. Many of the U.K. concerns about the role and value of the pound in the immediate postwar period were met by agreeing on a three-year transition period during which the fund's clauses would not be operative. At the time, a three-year period of grace was considered to be adequate; but as we shall see, the actual transition proved much longer.

After the April 1944 joint statement of principles, the wheels turned faster, even though it was necessary to gain the backing of Congress and Parliament. On neither side of the Atlantic were the respective administrations given an entirely easy ride. Representative Smith called the plan "the most un-American proposal ever presented to the people of this country".[25] In London, Lord Addison said the plan brought back the "horrid memories" of the interwar years during which time the "management of our fate, nationally, was largely in the control of the central bank".[26] Such was the mistrust of central banks that it was necessary to point out that the new body would be "an organisation between governments in which central banks only appear as the instrument and agent of their government". As we shall see, this intellectual and political climate was similar to the hostility encountered by the BIS at Bretton Woods.

Ahead of the conference at the New Hampshire resort, 16 countries (besides the United States) were invited to send representatives to a preliminary drafting meeting held in Atlantic City beginning on 23 June. The party then travelled by train to Bretton Woods, where proceedings began on 1 July.

The Final Act of the conference was signed by the representatives of each participating country on 22 July, the commitment being subject to ratification by the respective legislative bodies. The fund's ultimate aim was to "facilitate the expansion and balanced growth of international trade, and to contribute thereby to the promotion and maintenance of high levels of employment". Members' rules of conduct included collaborating in the maintenance of exchange stability at an agreed-upon rate and changing it only to correct a fundamental disequilbrium – with the concurrence of the fund. Member countries pledged themselves to make their currencies convertible after a suitable transition period, if so desired. Currency controls to effect trade discrimination were to be phased out and eventually eliminated, while controls of capital movements were permitted. Each member would subscribe its own membership quota in the fund, partly in gold and the rest in its own domestic currency. The sharing of statistical information and a generally cooperative behaviour were also required.

8.2 The BIS at Bretton Woods

The Bretton Woods Monetary and Financial Conference could not have been held at a more unfavourable time as far as the BIS was concerned. The Bank had long been subjected to a vituperative press campaign in the United States and accused of siding with the enemy by members of the Treasury Department and of Congress. At best ignored by the Federal Reserve Board of Governors, it was defended only by the Federal Reserve Bank of New York and by part of the banking community. The latter's support, however, was more a kiss of death than a blessing. Leon Fraser, former BIS president and now BIS champion, also led a group of bankers who opposed the international monetary reforms discussed at Bretton Woods.[27] On the European side, the French government in exile (under the influence of Mendès France) also adopted an unfavourable stance towards the BIS. The U.K. government – which was, besides the Dutch, the only one not to be prejudiced against the BIS – was divided on the issue.[28] Moreover, the fact that the conference took place at a time when the war was still being bitterly fought resulted in high passions as well as poor information. Most participants knew little, if anything, about the BIS and were ready to accept the U.S. view. When the issue of the dissolution of the BIS was brought up under these circumstances, not a single delegation came forth openly with an outright defence of the Bank as a respectable and useful institution. The BIS eventually survived because its enemies were divided about the means and timing of dissolution rather than about the ultimate end; because central bankers stood behind their creature; and, crucially, because the legal framework of its constitution proved difficult to unwind. Moreover, once the war was over and communications were re-established, it appeared that the BIS, for all its wartime faults, was not the criminal organisation depicted by the most radical press in the United States and the United Kingdom; further, postwar circumstances in Europe soon showed the usefulness of an experienced clearing institution.

On 10 July 1944, Commission III of the Bretton Woods conference[29] examined a recommendation submitted by the Norwegian delegation:[30] "Be it resolved", it proclaimed, "that the United Nations Monetary and Financial Conference recommends the liquidation of the Bank for International Settlements at Basel. It is suggested that the liquidation shall begin at the earliest possible date, and that the governments of the United Nations now at war with Germany appoint a Commission of Investigation in order to examine the management and the transactions of the Bank during the present war".[31]

Morgenthau and White, informed about the proposal ahead of its submission, endorsed it wholeheartedly. "McKittrick would be forced to resign", said White, "I would support the motion of the Norwegian delegate. I think it would be a salutary thing for the world".[32] However, both the U.S. State Department[33] and the U.K. Foreign Office, though either hostile to the BIS or indifferent to its long-run fate, thought it undesirable to discuss the issue at the conference. As soon as it received a report about the Norwegian resolution, the Foreign Office advised the U.K. delegation at Bretton Woods that "any resolution expressing opinion or suggesting action about [the] future of BIS or its liquidation would be improper".[34] The Foreign Office, inspired by the Bank of England, argued that the effect of the Norwegian resolution would be to encourage the enemy to suspend interest payments to the BIS, thereby improving the enemy's exchange position and harming that of the BIS, of which the United Nations countries were the principal creditors. In any event, the future of the BIS was a matter outside the concern of this international conference.[35] Edward Brown, a Chicago banker included in the U.S. delegation as representing "the tractable element of the banking community",[36] was also embarrassed by the virulence of the attack. His bank, at the request of the Hoover administration, had subscribed the BIS shares and distributed them to the U.S. public; the BIS, he said, ought to be dissolved but the conference was not the place to discuss the issue.

Furthermore, the U.K. government and the Bank of England regarded the proposal of a public inquiry into the wartime BIS dealings as inappropriate, at least for the time being. It must be said that both McKittrick and Beyen strongly supported the request for a full public investigation and continued to do so after the end of the conference. Beyen, who headed the Dutch delegation, found himself in the delicate position of defending the BIS against the accusation of misbehaviour in the Czechoslovak gold affair in which he had played such a crucial role. He therefore welcomed the investigation "as the only way for the people connected with the BIS to defend themselves against the scandalous slander that was irresponsibly carried out against them".[37]

It was only on 17 July that the resolution was discussed at a meeting of Commission III. In the days before, Keilhau (the Norwegian delegate) had ascertained that the U.K. and Dutch delegations were opposed to the resolution and that opinions were divided within the U.S. delegation. He therefore adopted a moderate stance, simply arguing that the BIS, created as the guardian of the gold standard, would henceforth be obsolete. Moreover, he said, some of its functions would be in direct competition with those of the fund. The original proposal was withdrawn and a new one submitted, dropping the call for an international investigation. The new draft recommended only "liquidation of the BIS at the earliest possible moment". The delegates from the Netherlands and the United Kingdom opposed the new resolution, suggesting that – while there was general agreement about the desirability of liquidating the Bank – the statement, as worded, was unsatisfactory. They maintained there should be some reference to the fund and to the inability of the two institutions to coexist, in order to avoid any impression of blaming the BIS for its wartime conduct. In view of the difficulty in reaching an agreement, the proposal was referred to a subcommittee.[38]

In the days that followed, the future of the BIS was the topic of lively private discussion within and between delegations. A new draft was proposed recommending "that at the date of the constitution of the Board of the Fund the necessary steps will be taken to liquidate the BIS". This text raised no objections from Keynes and the U.K. delegation. Annoyed that it had not been possible to pass the first Norwegian resolution, White opposed the new draft as an attempt to "give the BIS a clean bill of health", as the "public recognition, by forty-four nations, that the BIS is a good institution".[39] Moreover, he was convinced that the very existence of the BIS would make the start of the fund more difficult. Therefore, on 18 July, Luxford (a member of the U.S. delegation) proposed a parallel resolution,[40] which Commission III would ask Commission I (on the fund) to adopt. It recommended that a provision be included in the articles of agreement of the International Monetary Fund (IMF) "to the effect that the government of no country shall be eligible for membership in the IMF as long as the central bank of that country has not taken the necessary steps to foster the liquidation of the BIS".[41] This text was approved by the subcommittee, Dutch and U.K. objections notwithstanding. "Keynes", writes Skidelsky, "heard about it in the evening, and it put him into a towering rage. He stormed into Morgenthau's room, accused the Americans of double crossing the British and said that unless the U.S. resolution was withdrawn he would quit the conference".[42] The following day, Keynes wrote Morgenthau a letter. While reiterating his accord on the liquidation of the BIS, he could not agree to "write some specific agreement into the IMF [Articles]. For technical reasons this, whatever our wishes might be in the matter, would inevitably prevent us from participating either in the Fund or in the Bank until after the expiry of an indefinite period".[43] Morgenthau took Keynes's side against Luxford and White. On the same day, a joint Norwegian–Dutch resolution was presented to the press calling for the liquidation of the BIS "at the earliest possible moment". Beyen, the most outspoken paladin of the BIS at Bretton Woods, later said he went along with the resolution "not because he favoured it but to avoid a more extreme measure of excommunication, which had been proposed".[44]

According to Skidelsky, the excitement over this affair was such that it made Keynes ill – to the point that rumours spread on 19 July that he had suffered a heart attack. In fact, while always teetering on the edge of the precipice, Keynes recovered rapidly and, at mid-morning on 20 July, joined a meeting of the U.K. and U.S. delegations to finally settle the matter. "Morgenthau handed Keynes the proposal about liquidation 'at the earliest possible moment'. 'I don't quite know what the earliest possible moment is', said Mr. Bolton who accompanied Keynes. 'Not very early!' was Keynes's reply. He then came back to the proposal, which recommended the liquidation after the establishment of the Fund. 'The only difference', he said, 'is that that says it is contingent upon the establishment of the Fund. This says it shall be liquidated whether there is a Fund or not. I don't think we want to keep the damned thing alive, do we?' 'Amen, brother!', said Vinson."[45] It was agreed to support the Norwegian–Dutch resolution.

At the afternoon meeting of Commission III, Beyen made a statement to the effect that the Dutch delegation had always been willing to accept the resolution in its original form, considering the liquidation of the BIS as inevitable. Besides being incompatible with the IMF, the BIS, said Beyen, had statutes and a financial structure that were the "outcome of a situation that after the victory of the United Nations will no longer exist". He added that, while the conference might not be a suitable body to pass the original Norwegian motion, an investigation into the BIS could only be in the interests of future international cooperation.[46]

The recommendation for the liquidation of the BIS at the "earliest possible moment" was agreed upon by the Bretton Woods conference and included in its Final Act.

On 10 September 1944, the Berlin newspaper *Das Reich* gave a fairly long account of the BIS's vicissitudes at Bretton Woods, under the title: "The BIS under Fire".[47] According to the anonymous author, in the 1930s the BIS had been unable to reach the goals for which it was created, such as smoothly regulating reparation payments, promoting new financial deals, and favouring a sound monetary policy. It did, however, perform useful banking functions on behalf of central banks, particularly those of the smaller European countries. International monetary and financial relations, the article concluded, had become so complex that the postwar period would soon show again the necessity for an international clearing house. After the war, participants at the Bretton Woods conference would find that the IMF and the Bank for Reconstruction and Development could not perform clearing functions. Should they then be "unwilling to hear the unspeakable name of the BIS", they would be likely to create a new creature with a different name but much the same functions as the BIS.

8.3   After Bretton Woods

In spite of the unanimity with which the resolution about unwinding the BIS was passed at Bretton Woods, reservations remained in many people's minds about the advisability, and technical feasibility, of the decision.

Until after the end of the hostilities in Europe, positions on the issue continued to be much the same as those at Bretton Woods. The U.S. press remained as hostile to the BIS as it was misinformed about it. In Washington, both the Treasury and the State Department took it for granted that the BIS would be dissolved, but they could take no action as long as the war continued. Meanwhile, the Federal Reserve Bank of New York maintained its support for the institution in Basel and its contacts with it. London was less unanimous than Washington. The Foreign Office was inclined to side with the Bank of England in defending McKittrick's and the BIS's wartime conduct, while the Treasury was less supportive. The financial press was also divided: Paul Einzig's *Financial News* continued its anti-BIS crusade, while *The Economist* took a more favourable stance.

McKittrick, for his part, was furious and, a few days after the conclusion of the conference at Bretton Woods, demanded a full international inquiry into the Bank's wartime dealings. He wrote to the Bank of England that it was desirable "from the standpoint of the BIS, of associated central banks and of all persons concerned" that the institution's activities before and during the war "should be investigated". He wanted the investigation to be conducted by "a commission of unquestionable authority" and its find-ings to be published "by way of reply to repeated attacks and allegations based on misinformation and misunderstanding".[48] Lord Catto, who had succeeded Norman as governor of the Bank of England in April 1944, ad-vised McKittrick that for the chancellor "an enquiry would not be necessary or desirable", at least for the time being.[49] The Foreign Office concurred in thoroughly disliking the idea of an inquiry, likely to open a Pandora's box rather than to settle the matter for good. Two governors having repeatedly assured the government and the public that the BIS had done nothing during the war but routine business and had been scrupulously neutral, it seemed inappropriate to have an inquiry about whether or not they had been speak-ing the truth. Moreover, U.K. government officials nurtured few illusions about "uncontrollable" international committees.[50]

The Foreign Office policy was to play down the issue and gain time. "The BIS's only present supporters (for different reasons and in different ways)", stated an internal memorandum, "are ourselves, the Dutch and the Germans. Germany will be controlled by the Russians, the Americans and ourselves. The Russians will be at the least indifferent to the BIS, and the Americans (under the present Administration) are actively hostile to it". McKittrick was also part of the problem, as a man "long isolated in Switzerland" and "thoroughly out of touch with the way people are thinking nowadays".[51]

Isolation, however, was bound to end. Even before the war was techni-cally over, Basel was no longer cut off from the Western world, and the BIS officials became eager to catch up with events, ideas, and people. But "the fact that McKittrick, Jacobsson and company" were "emerging from their quarters and travelling over the wide world" threw the "U.S. Treasury into extreme anxiety".[52] "They felt", noted a U.K. observer, "that there was a plot here, though they do not quite know what and they are very anxious that these people should not turn up in America".[53]

In early May 1945, McKittrick wrote to the Treasuries of both the United States and the United Kingdom summarising the BIS position in regard to the Dawes and Young loans and stressing the Bank's own rights and obligations arising from the Hague Agreements. This prompted a request by Morgenthau to Anderson (the U.K. Chancellor of the Exchequer) to state what His Majesty's government was planning to do with a view to complying with the Bretton Woods resolution to liquidate the BIS.[54] Soon afterwards, however, Morgenthau was replaced by Vinson and Anderson by Dalton. The Treasuries in both Washington and London were now led by people who had not been as closely involved in the Bretton Woods negotiations as their predecessors.

The British took their time in replying to the new U.S. Secretary. The formal position was that the Bretton Woods recommendation was not binding on the governments and that the U.K. government thus far had neither accepted nor rejected it. On practical grounds, argued an internal Treasury memorandum, it would be wiser not to make a statement for the time being and to send Secretary Vinson a "very flat answer". On the margin of this memo, however, the new chancellor wrote: "But why don't we liquidate the BIS? It smells of the Schacht–Norman period! Who is now hesitating to take what action?"[55]

Dalton's reaction elicited another long internal memorandum, which – while taking liquidation for granted – again advised a delay in addressing the issue. There were several reasons that the matter was not considered to be urgent by top officials at the U.K. Treasury. First, the procedure would be complicated, the BIS being "unfortunately built to last", and more urgent tasks were then facing the Treasury. Second, it would in any case take years: a quick start would not yield quick results. Third, the last thing the U.K. government wanted was to "appear to be following the United States in this matter": the resolution was forced on the U.K. delegation "largely for reasons of [U.S.] internal politics", and HM government could not risk the appearance of throwing over their wartime BIS policy. The U.K. government did not want to put themselves in the wrong by appearing to accept "the American view of the BIS management".[56] Finally, the Bank of England stood to lose financially, to the benefit of the Germans, if the liquidation of the BIS were rushed. The Exchequer officials also noted that "for an institution which had no perceptible influence on the course of events for some years past, the BIS engenders an extraordinary amount of heat";

the Bank "should fade out rather than being suppressed in controversy and anger". The Exchequer also bore witness to the enormous political and intellectual changes that had intervened since the beginning of the war when it stated: "The fault of the BIS is to be old-fashioned to an extent which seems extraordinary after only 15 years of existence. That is a good reason for liquidating it, but not for blaming it".[57]

Around mid-September 1945, Dalton finally set out to write Vinson an official reply to Morgenthau's letter to Anderson, dated two months earlier. This letter signals a turning point in the official U.K. policy regarding the BIS. "It is plain", says Dalton in a first, partly handwritten, draft, "that the position of the BIS will have to be reviewed in the near future, and that it cannot continue to operate in the post-war period as it did before the war, but ... I have not yet had time to consider how we can best proceed to its liquidation, or its substitution by some more appropriate international institution". In the final draft of the letter, upon Lord Catto's suggestion, the last sentence reads: "or its adaptation, in some form, to present international needs".[58]

Soon afterwards, the Bank of England, rather than simply dragging its feet, came out explicitly against the liquidation of the BIS. To be sure, technical reasons were given to back this position,[59] but the most relevant ones related to the foreseen usefulness of the BIS in the postwar world. "What British interest is served by liquidation?" Catto asked Dalton. "We do not yet know when the Monetary Fund will be in effective operation: and in the meantime questions may easily arise *in Europe as an entity*[60] which would call for urgent solution. A purged BIS might be very serviceable in that event. It must not be forgotten that the BIS staff have had 15 years' experience on matters in which the Monetary Fund has none: and that it has in fact acquired a not inconsiderable influence over many of the smaller central banks of Europe, who will be much in need of counsel and have neither the entrée nor the understanding to deal with the United States, where they are completely *depaysé*. Europe's problems are by no means all world-wide and it is far from clear that a meeting place of European central banks is no longer required .... The Pan-Americans will certainly have their separate meetings: why should not the Europeans? Is it not much in our interest to aim at this?"[61] Niemeyer's influence is evident in this prose. The Bank of England now favoured a self-reform of the BIS, which would gradually withdraw from its past operations and become a sort of agent in Europe of the Monetary Fund's policies, "when those policies are sufficiently declared".

Privately, Dalton agreed with his U.S. counterpart that the BIS should be dissolved. In the margin of a letter from Vinson insisting on going ahead with the Bretton Woods resolution, the chancellor wrote: "I hate the BIS. It cumbers the ground. But the Governor of the Bank has views and should be consulted". Consultation with both the Foreign Office and the Bank of England advised a cautious reply, also suggesting a meeting with the French to settle the matter.

In the meanwhile, the Bretton Woods agreements had been ratified by a sufficient number of countries[62] to allow the IMF and the World Bank to open for business. The inaugural meeting of the board of governors of the two institutions took place in Savannah, Georgia, in March 1946. At the conference, the BIS was discussed only privately. The governor of the Bank of France, Monick, later recalled that he found both Vinson and White well disposed towards the BIS.[63] If they were not yet ready to yield on the issue, much of the animosity had faded away together with the priority previously assigned to the BIS's liquidation. Vinson had never been as sanguine about the Basel institution as his predecessor. White was, on the one hand, busy trying to become the first managing director of the IMF and, on the other hand, in a difficult personal situation: being secretly – and possibly unjustly – accused of being a communist and of passing on sensitive information to the Russians during the war. Moreover, in the previous year, the BIS case had been examined with more equanimity while the Bank was slowly getting reorganised to resume activity on a larger scale.

However, in May 1946, Dalton prevailed upon the Bank of England and asked the Foreign Office to include a clause in the peace treaty with Italy whereby the latter would accept in advance any decision taken by the Allies with respect to the Young Plan and the BIS.[64] This move was taken to make liquidation easier, whenever necessary, as a three-quarters majority in the BIS General Meeting was required to initiate the Bank's liquidation procedure. In any event, the treaty did not contain such a proviso, apparently because of Russian opposition to depriving Italy of its World War I reparation claims.[65]

The Italian peace treaty was the last instance when Dalton tried to impose his own view upon the Bank of England; the chancellor did not later change his mind about liquidation but decided he would not "force the governor".[66] In addition, the chancellor may have been swayed by Foreign Secretary Ernest Bevin, arguing in favour of the BIS for an entirely new political reason: "Since the end of the war representatives of the central banks of Central and Eastern Europe have come unobtrusively to the Bank for International Settlements at Basel to discuss their problems. Thus this Bank provides a window looking into a part of Europe to which we have no access and might well be a useful source of information about financial developments in that part of the world. I think, therefore, that while it is necessary to bring the BIS into appropriate relationship with the International Bank and Monetary Fund, it does not necessarily follow that the Bank for International Settlements should be liquidated .... I cannot feel that it is a good thing at present to do away with a going concern which has useful contacts in a part of the world where we are finding greater and greater difficulty in maintaining any contacts at all".[67]

Once Dalton had ceased insisting on liquidation, the game was only between Washington and London, with New York siding with the latter. In June 1946, the new U.S. secretary of the Treasury, Snyder, asked for a meeting with his U.K. counterpart to settle the matter. Dalton agreed in principle but only on the condition that his government did not have to commit itself in advance about an immediate liquidation. The two secretaries met at the IMF and World Bank meetings in Washington that September. Lord Catto and Eugene Meyer, President of the World Bank, also participated in the discussions. The positions of the two sides were by then rather crystallised, each repeating their well-rehearsed arguments.[68] Although the Washington meeting did not yield a definite result, Lord Catto reported that Snyder "seemed most receptive and very friendly".[69] In addition, the deadlock began to be overcome by an outsider's intervention. Maurice Frère, governor of the National Bank of Belgium and new chairman of the BIS Board,[70] made a fresh start with the Americans. By providing them with all the available, and sorely needed, information about the BIS he produced a very favourable impression on his hosts.

In the meanwhile, as we shall see, the Bank's activity was resuming. McKittrick left his Basel job at the end of June 1946, collaboration between the Bretton Woods institutions and the BIS was talked about, and preparations were under way for the first postwar meeting of the Bank's Board, which took place on 9 December 1946.

8.4   The Restitution of Looted Gold

Progress in making the Bretton Woods resolution obsolete proceeded in step with the quest for a satisfactory solution to the problem of looted gold accepted by the BIS in wartime payment for interest on its investments in Germany. The matter was pursued in the context of the Tripartite Commission for the Restitution of Monetary Gold, established by the Paris Reparations Conference of December 1945. The commission consisted of representatives of the governments of the United States, the United Kingdom, and France. The BIS offered its full cooperation with all central banks that might produce evidence concerning their looted gold.[71]

The settlement of all the claims on looted gold required a further two years to be completed, but the good start enabled negotiations to proceed in a cooperative fashion. To negotiators, the Bank soon appeared to have acted bona fide, given its readiness to collaborate fully and to restore whatever looted gold was in its possession to the lawful owner.

In June 1946, representatives of the Bank of France, to which Belgium's gold had been entrusted, met in Basel with BIS representatives and identified, to mutual satisfaction, 129 gold bars – about 1,607.4 kg – belonging to the looted lot in the possession of the BIS.[72]

In 1947 the Netherlands Bank claimed roughly 2,102 kg of gold, but it took quite a long time for them to provide, with the help of the U.S. Treasury, full evidence of their lawful entitlement to restitution of a slightly lower amount of gold (approximately 2,094 kg).

Two complications, regarding Hungary and Czechoslovakia, also stood in the way of a swift resolution of the gold issue. Part of the gold claimed by Belgium had been transferred, along with untainted gold, to the National Bank of Hungary in settlement of postal accounts.[73] A private agreement was negotiated by virtue of which Hungary's central bank undertook to recompense the BIS if it were established that some of the gold received by them had been looted and the BIS had to make restitution. Frère, who together with Auboin was negotiating with the Tripartite Commission, had the latter agree that 374 kg of Belgian gold transferred by the BIS to the Hungarian National Bank be included in the total amount for which the BIS pledged restitution.[74]

A more subtle legal point arose with respect to 2,031 kg of Czechoslovak gold received by the BIS in 1940 on deposit from the Reichsbank and later delivered to Yugoslavia.[75] The BIS asserted that this gold had been acquired by the Reichsbank under the terms of the Munich agreement and was therefore legally in Germany's possession. The first impulse of the U.S. representatives was to ask for restitution of this gold, arguing that – since Czechoslovakia had been admitted to the gold pool – any gold originating from that country should be considered as looted. This position raised a number of difficult and potentially embarrassing questions. Could the gold be regarded as looted if Germany had acquired it as the result of an international agreement? Was gold relabelled "looted" after the declaration of war and the subsequent recognition by the Allies of the Czechoslovak government in exile? Should examination of the whereabouts of that particular gold lot be extended to the central banks of the member countries in the Tripartite Commission that might indeed have received some of it between March and August 1939? It was eventually agreed to ignore the Czechoslovak gold transferred to Germany under the Munich agreements and to present the final settlement in the form of a lump-sum payment to the gold pool in order to avoid the embarrassing repercussions of producing a detailed list.[76]

The Americans also wanted an investigation into the gold deposit in the name of the BIS made in April 1945 at the Constance branch of the Reichsbank, since they had doubts about the bona fide character of the operation.[77] However, the U.K. and French representatives in the Tripartite Commission did not share the U.S. doubts. It was finally shown by the detailed examination of the BIS gold holdings in connection with the Dutch claims that none of the gold bars in Constance had been looted. The gold deposit was recognised as being received bona fide, as a normal transaction immune under the terms of the Hague Agreement of 1930.

Already in the second half of 1946 it was clear that, if nothing else, inertia and the sheer passing of time had made liquidation of the BIS unlikely. In October 1946, Maurice Frère, accompanied by BIS General Manager Roger Auboin, again discussed the BIS with the Treasury and State Department in Washington. In December, commenting on the forthcoming meeting of the Board of Directors, the U.S. consul general in Basel noted that "in well informed circles here it is generally understood that this bank will be 'saved'".[78]

By the time Frère and Auboin again visited Washington in March 1947, hints were coming from the U.S. Treasury, on the advice of the Federal Reserve System, that they would no longer take steps to press for the BIS's liquidation.[79] Any new official position by Washington as to the BIS's fate, however, had to wait for a final agreement on looted gold. Because of the mentioned complexity of the assessment process, it took another year for all the obstacles to be cleared.

Only when a final figure for looted gold in the possession of the BIS had been firmly established and accepted by all parties concerned did the U.S. authorities stand ready to bury the wartime accusations and misunderstandings officially. As Frère and Auboin arrived in Washington on 28 April 1948, an official statement was released to the press by the U.S. representatives at the IMF and the World Bank to the effect that the U.S. government no longer insisted on the implementation of the liquidation resolution.[80] A few days later, on 13 May 1948, a number of agreements were signed between the three governments represented on the Tripartite Commission and the BIS. They stipulated that the BIS would return to the commission, acting on behalf of the legal owners, 3,740 kg of looted gold received during the war.[81] At the same time, the U.S. Treasury unblocked the BIS assets held in the United States.

The agreements of May 1948 mark the watershed between the wartime and postwar history of the BIS. In practice, the latter may be seen as beginning six months earlier, when (as we shall see) the BIS was designated as the agent for the Agreement on Multilateral Monetary Compensation concluded between France, Italy, and the Benelux countries. Whatever the benchmark date, Frère and Auboin had every reason for self-congratulation on the accomplishments of their final diplomatic mission.[82] A month later, Maurice Frère was elected the first postwar president of the BIS, a position that had remained vacant since McKittrick's resignation in June 1946.

8.5 What "Saved" the BIS?

Success, unlike failure, generates many claims to paternity. The case of the BIS is no exception. Statements abound in biographies, memoirs, testimonials, and recollections claiming or assigning the decisive credit for rescuing the Bank from the edge of the precipice. Keynes is traditionally credited – lastly by his most recent and influential biographer – with saving the BIS.[83] At Bretton Woods his influence was definitely crucial but, afterwards, he equally definitely favoured liquidation.[84] Cobbold saw "the influence of the British Government on Snyder" as the critical factor.[85] But, as we saw, His Majesty's government was divided on the issue – with the Treasury favouring liquidation – a fact that led Baffi to regard U.K. Foreign Secretary Bevin as the actual saviour of the Bank.[86] Monick took a fair share of the merit when he said that, in Savannah, he convinced Vinson and White that the BIS should be kept alive.[87] Per Jacobsson credited Andrew Overby, assistant to the secretary of the Treasury, with saving the BIS in 1947–48.[88] But, of course, one should not forget the good offices of Maurice Frère and Roger Auboin in those years.

All these and other individuals contributed, to various extents, to the "happy end" of a story that, at the Bretton Woods conference, looked set to leave the BIS with little hope of survival. However, the main reasons that the Bank was able to weather the storm are the support it received from the main shareholding central banks and its own institutional resilience.

Hostility towards the BIS at Bretton Woods was rooted in a number of factors. One of these was the vague, if pervasive, feeling that the Bank was surreptitiously siding with Germany, a feeling that the management in Basel did not do enough to dispel. The seed of suspicion fell on particularly fertile ground as far as Morgenthau and White were concerned. That aside, there were two political reasons that the U.S. Treasury, engaged as it was in the creation of a grand scheme for postwar international financial reconstruction, was opposed to the very existence of the BIS. There seemed to be no place for the BIS in the framework envisaged at Bretton Woods. Moreover, in Washington's view, the new context was not compatible even with regional agreements of the kind that would see the BIS as just an agent of the European central banks. Domestic political considerations also played a role. The most important bankers' associations, and quite a few people at the Federal Reserve Bank of New York, were opposed to the administration's plans for postwar international financial reform. These same people were also the friends and main supporters of the BIS, which to many observers represented the bankrupt interwar monetary system. Finally, the 1930s had seen a considerable shift in power away from the central banks into the hands of the Treasuries, and the war had much accelerated the process. The shift was particularly visible within the U.S. and U.K. governments. At Bretton Woods the Treasuries dominated the political scene, with the central banks often confined to the role, albeit influential, of technical advisers.

Baden-Baden had taken place only 15 years before Bretton Woods, but it was as if a whole century had elapsed between the two international conferences: the BIS, and some of its Board member central banks, had not fully adjusted. They had certainly changed, but not enough – at least in the eyes of those who ran most of the show at the Mount Washington Hotel.

Against these unfavourable odds, the BIS could count on two solid assets: an institutional setting that made dissolution difficult to achieve by any single government, no matter how determined and powerful; and the unwavering support of the main European central banks.

The wise gentlemen who had drawn up the BIS Statutes at Baden-Baden had conceived an institution that proved difficult to unwind, protected as it was both by an international treaty and by Swiss corporate law. Moreover, they had been far-sighted enough to have the Hague Agreement explicitly contemplate the full protection of the BIS's assets and the continuation of its privileges in the case of war. The liquidation of the Bank required the approval of a three-quarters majority in the General Meeting. Moreover, liquidation could not take place before the Bank had discharged all its obligations under the Young Plan.[89] These obligations did not cease to exist as a result of the Second World War. A new international treaty was therefore necessary to eliminate the BIS. Thus, the Bank of England was able to draw the attention of the U.K. government to the complexity of the liquidation procedure in order to gain time, let wartime passions cool off, and shift the decision onto newly appointed government members not involved in the heat of the debate at Bretton Woods. Gaining time was also important to let information flow freely and for the BIS to reorganise and show that it possessed scarcely available expertise that could be of immediate use to the international community.

The second strength of the BIS was the unflinching support of its Board member central banks. While most governments neither knew nor cared about the BIS or had an almost instinctive hostility to it, central bankers remained loyal to their creature to the end. Between 1939 and 1945, the Bank of England, the Reichsbank, and the Bank of Italy used whatever influence they had on their respective governments to ferry the BIS across the troubled wartime waters. The Bank of France, saddled with serious problems of its own, needed some persuasion but eventually sided with its counterparts in supporting the BIS. The Federal Reserve Bank of New York also remained a loyal friend of the BIS. The generation of central bankers who were running the BIS at the outbreak of hostilities (and remained in charge until about 1944) were genuinely keen on seeing their cooperative creature (their club) survive the war. They tended to trust each other, drawing a line between enemy central banks and enemy governments. The common goal of preserving the BIS – in anticipation of the services it would provide for them in the postwar period – led central banks to a peculiar kind of informal wartime cooperation. Each of them, particularly those in London and Berlin, managed again and again to gain the consent of reluctant government officials to maintain links with the BIS. They approved the Bank's neutrality conduct rules and declared themselves satisfied that they were being followed thoroughly. They kept their men in Basel, worked out a compromise solution regarding McKittrick's reappointment, contributed statistics to the Bank, and made use of its research.

Having kept the BIS almost intact throughout most of the war, the European central banks concerned could not let it sink at the end of the conflict. In 1944–48 they brought their weight to bear in support of their creature. While the Old Lady of Threadneedle Street, and Niemeyer in particular, sustained most of the struggle, others were equally determined. The National Bank of Belgium played an important role after the end of the war, and the Netherlands Bank was strongly supportive, as was the Bank of France. Even the central bank of a country defeated and in tatters like Italy, a founding member of the BIS, provided all the support it could by appointing distinguished people to the Board and participating in the Board and general meetings as soon as they were resumed. The resumption of business and meetings soon after the war, even when the fate of the institution remained in balance, created a fait accompli that made dissolution ever more difficult to achieve. The new postwar generation of central bankers maintained their predecessors' support for the BIS as a useful and ready-made instrument for monetary cooperation.

That being said, one must add that the eventual survival of the BIS was to some extent of its own making. True, McKittrick had lost touch with developments and feelings in his own country and was (to a certain extent) responsible for the U.S. administration's misinformation about and mistrust of the BIS. However, if he was a liability in Washington he was an asset in London. More important, McKittrick shares with Auboin, Jacobsson, and the other managers the credit for the continued vitality of the Bank. Business may have been greatly reduced and meetings carried out only on a one-to-one basis, but research continued. The Annual Report grew in size and contained information to be found nowhere else. It is thanks to the fact that the organisation was kept alive and well, though smaller in size, that in 1947 the Federal Reserve Bank of New York could list the "valid reasons for the continued existence of the BIS. First", they wrote, "it is a convenient meeting place for European central bankers. Second, it possesses a certain amount of funds .... Third, it has 16 years of experience. Finally, it is in a position to carry out transactions from which the IMF and the International Bank are debarred by their statutes".[90]

NINE

Reconstructing Multilateral Payments

9.1   Europe's Reconstruction and International Settlements

The Bretton Woods conference was intended to design an ideal – "steady state", to borrow the economist's jargon – international monetary system that would last for a long period of time. The system's architects were under no illusion that their complex blueprint could be translated into a workable construct in a matter of months after the end of the hostilities. In particular, they knew that the central pillar of the new architecture, free currency convertibility, could not be erected overnight: in fact, achieving convertibility of the European currencies took even longer than most observers anticipated. The BIS played no small technical role in this process, drawing on its expertise in settling prewar international payments. Moreover, and more importantly, the BIS became once again the focal point of central bank cooperation at a time when international relations finally made such cooperation both possible and fruitful. Before we turn to central bank cooperation in the second half of the 1940s and the part taken by the BIS in the process, a brief background to the postwar international payments situation may be useful.

The economic efforts of one or two generations of Europeans were burned out in five years of fighting. In many countries the standard of living, as measured by per capita GDP, fell back to early twentieth or even late nineteenth century levels.[1] At the end of the war, not only the swollen number of poor urban workers but even the middle classes struggled daily, and at times unsuccessfully, to feed their families adequately. Yet Europe's potential for growth was largely intact. Human capital was undiminished. The damage inflicted to infrastructure and equipment was possibly less severe than theorists of strategic bombing liked to believe: some railroads were severely damaged but could be repaired relatively swiftly, upgrading quality in the process, while industrial capacity remained to a large extent intact.[2] Possibly the main constraints on Europe's rapid recovery were its foreign trade position and the level of its dollar or gold reserves. As Eichengreen put it: "Imported foodstuffs, raw materials and capital goods were desperately needed for sustenance and reconstruction. But given the scarcity of international reserves and credits, Europe's capacity to import was limited by its ability to export. Its ability to export was constrained in turn by the scarcity of imported inputs, in a classic Catch-22 situation".[3]

Both in the First and in the Second World War, the world's agricultural production shifted away from Europe. In 1934–38, the Old Continent (excluding Russia) produced about 43 million tonnes of wheat annually, as against combined production of 37.5 million tonnes for the United States, Canada, Argentina, and Australia. In 1945, Europe's production was down to 23 million tonnes, less than half the output of the four main exporting countries. As a result, huge amounts of wheat had to be imported in 1945–46 to satisfy basic food requirements.[4] Likewise, coal production fell short by about 30% of average 1935–38 consumption. The same was true for other foodstuffs and raw materials essential for survival and reconstruction. In normal conditions, gold and convertible currency reserves could be used to pay for essential imports, which would in turn generate exports, but Europe's reserves were largely depleted in 1945. The United Kingdom's gold reserves were reduced to virtually zero; France's were down 55% from the 1938 level; Holland's, 72%.[5] At the same time, private international credit markets were hardly functioning at all.

In this context, European governments had little choice but to keep in place the panoply of trade and exchange rate controls created in the 1930s and reinforced during the conflict. Many governments were inclined to do so regardless, as in most countries public opinion favoured state control of the economy over trade liberalisation and currency convertibility as a means of achieving full employment. In the absence of adequate means for international payments, barter reigned supreme: intra-European trade was largely carried on by bilateral agreements. The restoration of European trade required both an injection of dollar liquidity and European willingness to cooperate in moving from bilateral to multilateral settlements, and then to full currency convertibility as required by the Articles of Agreement of the International Monetary Fund. Aid and loans from the United States proved to be the decisive factor in starting the wheels of the Western European economy turning again: they allowed European countries to pay for essential imports while at the same time getting an intra-European multilateral payments scheme under way. The latter required cooperative behaviour that was forced upon the Europeans – fresh from their fratricidal struggle – by the United States, which made aid conditional on cooperation.

As noted by Milward, the postwar payments situation had, to a certain extent, "been forecasted by Keynes and others who had urged the United States at Bretton Woods to sustain the outward flow of dollars and gold at a higher level during the recovery period".[6] In fact, the immediate postwar outflow of dollars was far larger than anything these people had imagined. In the two immediate postwar years, through June 1947, the aggregate U.S. disbursement in Western Europe totalled over $10 billion (over 2% of the U.S. GNP at the time).[7]

The U.S. taxpayers' money siphoned to the Old Continent during this period was highly productive, judging from the speed of the European recovery. It was so fast that, in the summer of 1947, a dollar shortage emerged: demand for imports largely outstripped the supply of means of payment, which was due to unusually cold winter weather in 1946–47 and an exceptionally bad harvest.[8] Expectations were also shaken by the emergence of an unbridgeable gap between the western and eastern parts of the Continent and by uncertainty as to the political future of France and Italy. An ill-timed attempt by London to make sterling fully convertible,[9] in compliance with the 1945 loan agreement with the United States, was the main casualty of the shortage of international liquidity. The convertibility of the pound was suspended only 37 days after its introduction. It would take another eleven years for the experiment to be repeated – this time successfully, in tune with the main continental European countries.

The 1947 crisis gave impetus to implementation of the European Recovery Program (ERP), announced by Secretary of State Marshall at Harvard's commencement ceremony on 5 June 1947. In July, a conference of 16 countries convened in Paris drafted a European programme detailing their needs and commitments in relation to the ERP. Thus the Committee on European Economic Co-operation came into being, which would soon become a permanent organisation (the OEEC, from 1961 the OECD). In the autumn of 1947, the U.S. Congress granted "interim aid" of $522 million to Italy, France, and Austria. President Truman signed the Foreign Assistance Act on 3 April 1948.

The so-called Marshall Plan may well have originated, as Milward argues,[10] from a "mixture of national interest, prejudice, goodwill and misinterpretation of history"; it may perhaps have been based on economic theory that did not stand "up well to the test of further economic analysis or of historical practice"; it may possibly have availed itself of an intellectually unimpressive view of the economic effects of European integration. Yet it turned out to be "history's most successful structural adjustment program".[11] Even if the Marshall Plan – as Milward correctly points out – did not make a quantitatively significant contribution to investment growth in infrastructure or equipment, it certainly sped up Western European growth by altering the environment in which economic policy was made. In particular, the plan allowed governments to avoid "the harsh choice between contraction to balance their international payments and severe controls on admissible imports".[12] It also permitted the slow but steady "relaxation of controls that prevented markets from (efficiently) allocating resources and the opening of economies to trade".[13] De Long and Eichengreen probably overstate their case when arguing that, without the Marshall Plan, the pattern of postwar European political economy might well have resembled the over-regulation and relative economic stagnation of post–World War II Argentina. The market enzymes were too deeply rooted in Europe's history, its middle class was too enterprising, and its economy was too open and diversified for a comparison with Argentina to be convincing. It is nevertheless true that the Marshall Plan "should be thought of as a large and highly successful structural adjustment program"[14] without which currency convertibility, free trade, and a market-biased "mixed economy" would have taken much longer to materialise, with a considerable loss in productivity growth.

It is in this context that the BIS also "reconstructed" itself, once again to some extent reinventing its role to fit into the new international environment. In the process it made a contribution – at first modest but then of increasing relevance – to the organisation of Europe's postwar payments. This chapter deals first with the BIS's economic analysis of the postwar situation and policies. It turns then to the new (or not so new) role and organisation of the main central banks at the time when their representatives began once again to gather at their club in Basel. An account of the BIS's activities in the late 1940s follows. The chapter ends by discussing the first relevant postwar episodes of multilateral monetary and economic cooperation.

9.2   The Postwar Economy in the Analysis of the BIS

The wartime Annual Reports of the BIS provided invaluable (because otherwise unavailable) information on the world's main trends in output, prices, trade, labour markets, money, and credit. For some time after the war, information on the main variables in the world economy continued at a trickle, while decision makers, both in the public and in the private sector, increasingly thirsted for high-quality economic analysis of international trends. The two Bretton Woods organisations became operative only in 1946–47.[15] Although they soon set up research divisions and collected statistical information, the quality of their economic reporting did not initially match that of the BIS, which was based on longer experience and on well-tested channels for fact gathering. Thus, at least for a few years after the end of the war, the BIS Annual Reports offered the most comprehensive and best-quality information on the state of the world economy. The Annual Reports were, however, far from being just a collection of facts and numbers: the wealth of information supported an analysis of the postwar economy, and attendant policy recommendations, in quite striking contrast to the mainstream Keynesian orthodoxy of the time.

In the immediate postwar years, the BIS Annual Reports were almost single-handedly written by Per Jacobsson.[16] Now a full member of the BIS management – in his early fifties,[17] brimming with dynamism, an enchanting communicator – Jacobsson was more than ever the intellectual driving force of the Bank. He was by no means a theoretical economist; in fact, having left the University of Uppsala without completing a higher degree in economics, he always felt uneasy about the "difference between himself and the academic economist".[18] He was, however, widely read in many fields, including theoretical economics, his restless nature leading him ever wider rather than deeper to satisfy his intellectual curiosity. From 1917 onwards – when he fled to Stockholm, fearing to "petrify" in Uppsala, to work for Heckscher's Commission on Economic Preparedness – he found himself "driven away by nature from pure theory to the centre of action".[19] With a fast, intuitive mind and a fluid, clear pen, Jacobsson possessed to a high degree the gift of sorting relevant from irrelevant facts, for which he then provided economic explanations that fitted his policy prescription. His gift for languages and a career spent touring Europe and mixing with top policy makers endowed him with unmatched ability for comparative analyses, across countries as well as over time. All this is reflected in the content and style of the Reports relating the postwar developments in the international economy.

As for the underlying economic theory, neither Jacobsson's nor that of the majority of the central bankers slowly returning to Basel came anywhere near to the Keynesian revolution. Jacobsson claimed to admire Keynes as "the most gifted and most artistic man of [his] generation"[20] but did not understand his enormous stature as an economist. In trying to draw a distinction between Keynesians and Keynes,[21] Jacobsson saw the latter as the inspirer of economic policies he disagreed with, failing to grasp the essence and novelty of Keynes's theory. Drawing, without dogmatism, on the neo-classical tradition, Jacobsson's "special brand of practical, liberal inter-national political economy promoted belief in the self-adjusting forces of the market".[22] It provided continuity and coherence to the BIS's think-ing from the 1930s to the 1950s. The economics of the BIS both reflected and shaped the thinking in most central banks of continental Europe, but was otherwise in sharp contrast with the economic orthodoxy embraced by the Anglo-Saxon policy makers, by the Bretton Woods institutions, and by several Continental Treasuries.[23] At the time of Europe's reconstruction, Basel's economic analyses and policy prescriptions were conspicuously isolated and looked somehow old-fashioned. Today, as the philosophy un-derlying economic thinking and policy making has gone almost full circle to where it stood before the Great Depression, one cannot fail to note the "modernity" of the BIS's postwar economic thinking.

In the 1940s, "the BIS presented the strongest contemporary case among international organisations against the primacy of full employment and against downplaying the dangers of inflation when attempting to achieve that goal".[24] In a nutshell, the BIS's prescriptions for economic recovery were: aggregate price stability coupled with flexibility in individual prices (i.e., with the ending of price controls), enhanced competition in both the domestic and international markets, and an early return to international cur-rency convertibility. Only the achievement of these conditions would secure long-lasting full employment. For the BIS, monetary policy – rather than administrative controls on quantities and prices – was the most effective in-strument to check excess aggregate demand. Fiscal policy should maintain a relatively low level of taxation and balanced state budgets over the busi-ness cycle. In this last aspect, largely endorsed by commentators such as Jacob Viner, the BIS and the United Nations were on common ground.[25]

During and immediately after the war, fear of another depression was an overriding policy concern. Since deflation rather than inflation was ex-pected, the accepted policy prescription consisted in keeping interest rates low and stable. This would stimulate reconstruction investment while, if needed, price controls would quench inflationary pressures. The BIS thought differently. To make a convincing case, the 1946 Annual Report resorted to economic history. It discussed the depression of 1929–33 and argued that, although history did not allow forecasts, it was of interest to point out factors present in previous depressions that were unlikely to be operative in the postwar years.[26] According to the BIS, the large wartime pent-up demand meant that a cyclical downturn was not to be expected soon. When it did come, possibly by the end of the decade, domestic and international indebtedness would not be such as to create the kind of financial fragility that amplified the 1929 cyclical downturn. Private speculative borrowing was, by then, still unlikely to be of large proportions, while international lending – in contrast to the 1920s – was now of an official rather than private character, with repayments spread over a number of years. Second, conditions for agricultural overproduction, another factor in the Great Depression, did not exist after the Second World War: in the four main producing countries, acreage under wheat in 1945 was the same "as in 1929, while the demand for food had risen on account of population growth".[27]

Third, the Annual Report addressed the question, much debated between the wars, of whether a shortage of gold caused a secular decline in prices, contributing to the severity of the Depression. A long-run comparison of price behaviour after major wars showed that – whereas after both the Napoleonic and U.S. Civil War prices fell to below the level prevailing when the war started – in 1946 prices in the United States stood well above the 1939 level. Also, owing to the 1934 change in the dollar value of the metal, there was no reason to fear that global gold scarcity could generate deflation. As for the distribution of gold reserves, the Report recalled that "much of the gold which went to the United States in the thirties served as a vehicle for money flying from the war scares of Europe". Peace, it was argued, would bring about a more even distribution of monetary gold.[28] Finally, the BIS typically played down the risk of a "genuine lack of investment possibilities as compared with the propensity to save. The resolution now shown by national economic authorities to intervene in order to prevent mass unemployment" was quoted as a stabilising factor, but, the Report added, "there is no simple measure by which a depression can be overcome".[29] The conclusion of the long historical excursus contained in the 1946 Annual Report was an explicit warning against mechanical application of the recipes of the new Keynesian orthodoxy. Ironically, it was pretty much in line with Keynes's own warning against enslavement to defunct economists: "When a decline in business sets in", the Report stated, "this decline is likely to be different in some material respects from the depression which began in 1929.[30] There can be no simple repetition of the conditions then obtaining and, therefore, whatever means of action may be planned to cope with coming difficulties, they must not be slavishly inspired by what happened 'last time'".[31]

It is perhaps worth noting that, at the time of writing the first postwar Annual Report (recall that McKittrick was still at the helm of the Bank), people in Basel had an incomplete understanding of how the Bretton Woods system was supposed to operate. One could even detect a vein of nostalgia, typical of the interwar years, for the pre-1914 gold standard. "The currents of gold distribution", said the 1946 Report, "need to be carefully watched by the competent international institutions so that a disturbance of the equilibrium may be duly noted and remedial measures taken in time.... In meditating on these matters, it should not be forgotten that, as before 1914, the current gold production may be sufficient (then it was more than sufficient) to furnish the whole increase required in the volume of monetary demand".[32]

In 1947, concern about inflation acquired paramount importance in the view of the BIS, which stressed in particular its effects on the balance of payments and international trade. In Greece, Hungary, Romania, and Poland, runaway price increases threatened the complete collapse of the currency. In Italy, prices of commodities not subject to controls rose to up to forty times the prewar level, and in France the increase was over eight times. Prices more than doubled in several other countries, including Belgium, the Netherlands, Czechoslovakia, and Spain. "Inflationary issues for government purposes" and an "abundance of credit in the market" were characteristically singled out by the BIS as the standard causes of inflation.[33] Price controls, introduced by every European country as a politically acceptable means of keeping inflation somewhat in check, could not provide a stable solution. "It is not a counsel of perfection", the 1947 Annual Report bluntly wrote, "but basic common sense to emphasise the importance of bringing wartime inflationary methods to an end".[34] Jacobsson noted that "the imposition of controls has been very closely connected with the Nazi and Fascist regimes", a reason why he believed that people on the Continent were more keen "to return to the conditions of a free economy" than those in the Anglo-Saxon countries.[35] Only budget discipline and the control of the money supply would restore confidence at home and abroad.[36] Jacobsson took Belgium and Italy as examples of the success that could be obtained by discarding "cheap money".[37] Concerning the latter, the 1948 Report wrote: "In the course of 1947 there was a general lifting of price controls.... The fact that the price rise could not only be arrested but also reversed helped to restore the confidence in the currency. The reversal would not have occurred, had not stringent internal measures brought about a reduction in the budget deficit and limited the granting of new credits by banks and other financial institutions".[38]

"The time is ripe for a genuine overhauling of the methods of official intervention in economic life", the BIS wrote in 1948, precisely because "in parts of the continent there is still widespread hunger and distress, which lowers efficiency and is in itself a cause of further unrest". Price controls, intervention on capital markets to keep interest rates artificially low, and attempts at balancing foreign trade through controls had not produced the expected results. It was time, the BIS argued, for a return to market discipline, to control the total volume of monetary purchasing power, and to rein in government expenditure.[39]

On international economic issues, the Basel view was more consonant with that of the newly created Washington-based organisations. Characteristically, Jacobsson and the BIS saw foreign exchange controls as "meaning not only a loss of trade but a danger of moral isolation through reduced contacts, particularly regrettable at a time when Europeans ought to draw closer together".[40] Although the difficulties of the process and the time needed to complete it were not disregarded, free trade and currency convertibility were priority goals to be achieved at the earliest possible time. After the failure of the sterling convertibility experiment, the BIS regarded the new wave of aid coming from the United States as essentially a means to buy time for European countries to put their house in order so that, when the European Recovery Program expired, they would be ready for convertibility.

It goes without saying that the need for cooperation was constantly stressed in the BIS Annual Reports: governments were urged to "realise that, as was the case in the thirties, measures which hit world trade were really to the advantage of none and certainly delayed recovery".[41] By their very nature, "physical controls tend to intensify the trend towards nationalistic insulation. A wider application of appropriate financial controls[42] should permit the abolition of many existing hindrances and thus help to strengthen the ties of free international intercourse. Such application would, moreover, be consonant with the present-day orientation of ideas and action towards a system which combines close cooperation with the greatest possible freedom for the individual countries".[43]

9.3 Central Banks: *Plus ça change ...* ?

Many of the central banks whose governors attended the first postwar meeting of the BIS Board of Directors on 9 December 1946 had undergone considerable changes at both the personal and the institutional level since the previous meeting, more than seven years earlier.

Of the 15 gentlemen attending that last meeting on 10 July 1939, only five were in attendance in December 1946 (Niemeyer, de Vogüé, Weber, Brincard, and Rooth). The Board itself was reduced in size by the suspension of the German[44] and Japanese memberships, while a number of changes had intervened at the helm of central banks. Norman's long reign over the Old Lady had ended in early 1944 when a serious illness forced him to retire at the age of 72;[45] he was succeeded by Lord Catto of Cairncatto. Maurice Frère, the new head of Belgium's central bank, was elected chairman of the BIS Board in June 1946. Two years later he also became president of the Bank.[46] Holtrop had replaced Trip[47] as the Dutch Board member. Monick had taken over two years earlier (October 1944) from de Boisanger, the controversial wartime governor of the Bank of France. At the Bank of Italy – the only central bank of a defeated country allowed to retain uninterruptedly its statutory rights as a founding member of the BIS – Einaudi[48] was now governor, replacing Azzolini (who was on trial for alleged responsibility in allowing the Germans to seize part of the central bank's gold reserves). The changes in the BIS Board reflected the wartime and immediate postwar vicissitudes of each institution as well as the ordinary effects of the passage of time – namely, advancing age and deteriorating health. In the years that followed, Rooth,[49] Niemeyer, and Brincard assured a living memory of the prewar BIS tradition, while Weber[50] was soon replaced at the helm of his own institution and on the Bank's Board.

To what extent did the turnover at the head of most European central banks also reflect institutional and policy changes? Central banks are rather autocratic organisations, and any change at the top is likely to affect the style – and often even the substance – of their behaviour. But was there more than that? Did those time-honoured institutions actually change their skin as the result of the war? The answer to this question is pretty much a matter of emphasis. In most countries, institutional and political changes were deep and destined to last for decades to come. At the same time, however, one should not overlook the strong elements of cultural and operational continuity kept alive within central banks, particularly by their middle management.

The war, it must be said once again, simply catalysed a number of preexisting factors shifting part of the power in monetary and banking matters away from central banks in favour of the Treasuries. As in so many other political and social matters, in monetary policy making also the Great Depression was the actual watershed. Interest rate hikes in the face of rising unemployment did little to enhance the popularity of central banks, with politicians being held accountable by the electorate for the deeds of an "independent" body. Whether they had left it or remained on it, central banks had taken most of the blame for the failure of the interwar gold standard. The political result, as Norman put it, was "a redistribution of authority and responsibility, which deprived the Bank of some of its essential functions".[51] The Treasury rather than the Bank of England determined the exchange rate to be upheld by the Equalisation Account, even though

Threadneedle Street managed its day-to-day operations.[52] The high level of technical capability was precisely one of the reasons that the central bank retained a good degree of respect, among both politicians and civil servants, from which its remaining authority mostly derived. An even larger shift in power took place in countries that introduced exchange controls. Central banks had also largely failed in dealing with banking crises, and governments stepped into that area as well: this was typically the case of Italy, Austria, Germany, and Hungary.

It is not surprising, therefore, that a first wave of legislation making central banks somehow subordinate to governments had been introduced in the second half of the 1930s. Dictatorships led the way. The Italian banking law of 1936 provided for a soft nationalisation of the Bank of Italy[53] and gave the government formal powers of supervision over the banking system, even though the central bank remained the technical and the de facto supervisory body.[54] In this as in so many other matters, Hitler was more ruthlessly assertive than his southern former mentor: the German banking law of February 1937 ended the Reichsbank's legal independence from the government "and brought the bank formally under Hitler's control".[55] Less radical but nonetheless important changes were also introduced in the statutes of the Bank of France under the Leon Blum government. On 24 July 1936, the French Parliament passed a law that stripped its central bank's shareholders of the right to appoint 18 out of 20 members in the Conseil Général. Henceforth, 18 members would be chosen by public institutions. To borrow one of Napoleon's expressions, the French central bank "passed into the state's hands" while at the same time retaining its legal status as a private company.[56]

Immediately after the war, the two major victorious European democracies formally acknowledged the power shift that had occurred since the Great Depression by nationalising their respective central banks. In the United Kingdom, the Labour Party fought the July 1945 general elections with a manifesto that read: "The Bank of England with its financial powers must be brought under public ownership". When the plan was confirmed by the King's Speech at the opening of the new Parliament, Churchill, for the opposition, "declared that the national ownership of the Bank of England did not raise any matter of principle". Bipartisan consensus therefore existed on bringing "the law into accord with the facts", as Chancellor Dalton put it at the time.[57] The main features of the plan were by then also acceptable to the bank, which had quietly participated, over the previous couple of years, in preparing with the Treasury proposals for altering its own constitution while retaining a high degree of operational independence. The fact that central banks, in the United Kingdom as elsewhere, were called upon to contribute substantially to the drafting of the laws concerning their future status bears witness to the degree of influence and prestige they still retained. The Bank of England nationalisation bill received the royal assent on 14 February 1946.

The nationalisation of the Bank of France took place in the wider context of an overall reform that brought under state control the whole banking system, which since the Liberation had been under fire from the Left and the Confédération Générale du Travail, the main trade union. Banks were criticised for taking excessive risks in the 1920s, prompting the state to intervene to safeguard depositors in 1931, and more generally for exerting undue influence on the government itself. In this context the Bank of France was seen as systematically siding with the largest credit establishments at the expense of the local and regional banks. Only a full nationalisation of the central bank, it was argued, would allow the general interest to prevail.[58] On 2 December 1945, the Assemblée Nationale Constituante voted by an overwhelming majority (521 to 35) for the nationalisation of the Bank of France, of the five largest deposit banks, and of two *banques d'affaires*.[59]

A couple of years later, it was the turn of the central banks of Belgium and the Netherlands to change skin – or their make-up, as the case may be. On 14 May 1948, a law was passed whereby the entire capital of the Netherlands Bank passed into the hands of the state, even though the bank remained a limited-liability company. The law also regulated the relationship between the bank and the government, stipulating that the minister of finance was entitled to give policy directions to the central bank.[60]

The solution found in Belgium was only marginally different. There, too, the end of the war was followed by a debate on the role of the state in the postwar economy. The political outcome of the debate was the creation, by 1948, of a "mixed economy" aimed at maintaining equilibrium between public and private financial institutions.[61] The nationalisation of the National Bank of Belgium was also discussed; a compromise solution gave the state control of the bank without actually nationalising it. A law passed in 1948 provided for an issue of new shares in the central bank's capital, to be subscribed entirely by the Belgian state – which thus became the majority shareholder – while the rest of the capital remained in private hands (financial institutions and the public). For the rest, the 1948 law had little to change because a royal decree of 23 July 1937 had already increased the government's influence on the central bank and its monetary operations.

The other central banks that played a pivotal role in the first 15 years of the BIS's history were those of the three defeated Axis countries. At the beginning of October 1945, the U.S. authorities appointed Eikichi Araki as governor of the Bank of Japan, replacing Shibusawa, who became minister of finance. The new governor neither took up the Japanese seat on the BIS Board nor appointed a substitute.[62] The Bank of Japan did not rejoin the BIS Board until 1994.

At the end of the war, the Reichsbank ceased to exist. Its organisation was partly but not entirely disbanded: the offices in the Soviet zone were shut down, but elsewhere, particularly in the British zone, its organisation continued to function under Allied control – though in a muddled and ineffectual way. In March 1948, it was finally replaced by the Bank deutscher Länder.[63] Limited to the Western zones, the new central bank heralded the political division of the country, formalised a year later with the creation of two separate states. The Bank deutscher Länder became the central bank of the Federal Republic of Germany from the latter's establishment, in May 1949, until the foundation of the Bundesbank in 1957 (on the eve of the reintroduction of full convertibility of the Deutsche mark).[64] Formally independent from political influence, the Bank deutscher Länder was under Allied tutelage until the end of the Occupation. Its functions were those of a clearing house for the state-owned central banks of the various *Länder,* which appointed the members of the Bank's policy-making council. The first president of the directorate of the Bank deutscher Länder was Wilhelm Vocke, a former Reichsbanker, who was elected when other candidates – more compromised by their past – were rejected after arm-twisting by representatives of the U.S. and U.K. governments, themselves in disagreement about the degree of decentralisation of the new institution. Vocke was first invited to visit the BIS on the occasion of the Board meeting of December 1949.[65] Conversations followed about the reappointment of German representatives on the Board, as the Federal Republic was now replacing the Allied authorities in representing West Germany at international bodies such as the OEEC. A few months later, in April 1950, Vocke was appointed a member of the Board. A second German representative, Brinckmann, joined in June.[66]

In the case of Italy, no further institutional change in the relations between central bank and government took place after the "soft nationalisation" of the 1936 Banking Act. The latter was amended in 1947 to give the Bank of Italy independent supervisory powers over the banking system. An interim "commissioner" ran the Bank for some months in 1944[67] until a new governor, Luigi Einaudi, was appointed in January 1945. In 1947, Donato Menichella, the general manager, took over informally when Einaudi joined the government. A year later he was appointed governor upon Einaudi's election as president of the new republic.

With few exceptions, the people who resumed the journeys to Basel from December 1946 onwards were newcomers to the BIS. Did they also represent substantially changed institutions? The answer to this question must remain ambiguous. Nationalisations undoubtedly signalled a change in the official status of the central banks vis-à-vis the executive and law-making powers. And there is equally no doubt that, all over Europe, the intellectual and political approach to monetary policy making now emphasised the notion that final responsibility rested with elected officials, leaving the technical implementation of monetary policy to central banks. By and large, this was to remain the accepted wisdom throughout the reconstruction period and the long economic expansion of the 1950s and 1960s. It is, however, an exaggeration to say that "in practice, the central bank became a junior branch of the Treasury".[68] The situation in this respect varied from country to country, but in most cases central banks retained a fair degree of de facto independence – at the very least, in running day-to-day operations – which put them on a different footing from any government department. Governors were normally people of outstanding personality, capable of exercising moral suasion not only with bankers but with cabinet members as well. The high technical skills and integrity of their personnel put central banks in the position of providing invaluable advice to their governments as well as of efficiently carrying out tasks that the administration was often ill equipped to perform. The links with and services provided to the financial and business community also gave central banks a constituency of their own. More often than not, these circumstances afforded central banks considerable leverage and influence over government decisions, well beyond what could be expected from their subordinated legal status. In the end, personality mattered considerably. When the governor's prestige and intellectual power outweighed those of his minister, the central bank was only formally subordinated to the Treasury and so enjoyed a considerable degree of independence. When the opposite was true, the central bank was more dependent on the political power. This was not a postwar novelty: personalities mattered long before the turning point of the mid-1930s and the ensuing nationalisation wave. But within a legal framework giving the government the ultimate responsibility for monetary policy, the central bank's prestige and influence depended more than ever on the governor's intellectual, moral, and political stature.

To what extent did the allocation of the ultimate responsibility for monetary policy making to the Treasuries affect central bank cooperation? As argued in the sequel, the high degree (by previous standards) of international cooperation in the quarter century following the end of the hostilities depended to a considerable extent upon the overall conditions created by the United States' "consensual hegemony"[69] over Europe. However, it may be argued that international monetary cooperation was made easier by the fact that each country's players in the game, governments and central banks, now shared a single policy objective. This was often not the case in the 1930s, when it was common for central banks to more or less silently disagree with their governments' policy goals, with the former typically targeting the exchange rate and the latter unemployment. International cooperation suffered from the fact that a coordination problem among two independent authorities had first to be solved at home, especially in the absence of clear rules on how the solution should be found. After the war, whenever disagreement existed as to a single country's international economic policy, the government possessed the authority (at least in principle) to settle it.

9.4   Early Postwar Activity

McKittrick remained at the helm of the BIS for over a year after Germany's surrender. When he stepped down at the end of June 1946 to join the Chase National Bank of New York, the position of BIS president was left vacant. Maurice Frère became chairman of the Board on 1 July 1946.[70] Two years later he was also appointed president, reinstating the early 1930s practice of combining the presidency and Board chairmanship in one person (a practice followed at the BIS ever since). While (as we have seen) the Board of Directors was almost entirely renewed, the management assured continuity at the top. With the exception of Hechler, who died at the end of 1945 and was not replaced as assistant general manager, all the other executive officers of the Bank retained their jobs. Jacobsson's overwhelming intellectual influence was formally recognised by his joining the management as head of the Monetary and Economic Department while retaining his title of Economic Adviser. Marcel van Zeeland was appointed to head the Banking Department in 1947. The only new addition to the Bank's top positions was that of Oluf Berntsen, who had spent some years at the National Bank of Denmark in the early 1930s and became the number-two man in the BIS Banking Department.

The enormous uncertainty looming over European financial markets, the unclear status of the Bank's investments in Germany,[71] and the freeze on its assets in the United States affected the volume of BIS operations in the fiscal year ending on 31 March 1946, when – for the first and only time in its history – the BIS balance sheet registered a loss: the net income from capital and deposits did not cover administration costs. This was due primarily to the suspension of German interest payments, which had generated the bulk of BIS wartime revenues. There was a slight improvement in the following financial year, which closed with a small positive margin, even though the revenue from investment in Germany remained frozen. Deposits, however, totalled only 28 million Swiss gold francs as of March 1947 and the Bank's operations remained accordingly limited. Thereafter, BIS profitability improved. From the second half of 1947 onwards, as the reconstruction of domestic reserves proceeded in every European country, central bank deposits flowed again to the BIS; they totalled almost 500 million Swiss gold francs in 1950. The Bank, however, chose to build up adequate reserves before resuming dividend payments. It was only in 1951 that shareholders received their first postwar dividend.

Much time and effort were devoted to external relations. The most important issues dealt with by the management regarded the Bretton Woods liquidation resolution, looted gold, and the unblocking of BIS assets in the United States (discussed in the previous chapter). Maurice Frère, as we saw, proved to be an excellent ambassador to Washington. For the rest, the Bank's diplomacy was busy dealing with its functions as trustee of the prewar Austrian and German international loans and with the effects of regime and territorial changes on the property and voting rights of BIS shares. As far as the loans were concerned, immediately after the war the BIS wrote to all the governments concerned, recalling the rights and obligations falling upon the BIS as the result of the 1930 Hague Agreement and noting that the latter had never been abrogated.[72] The governments ignored the BIS's plea, and the Annual Report for many years recorded that no change or development had taken place as far as the BIS trustee and agency functions were concerned. It was only in 1953 that the London Agreement on German External Debts[73] provided for the resumption of servicing the Dawes and Young loans. A year earlier, servicing of the Austrian Government Loan of 1930 had likewise been resumed pursuant to an agreement signed in Rome.[74] In all three cases, the BIS continued to act as trustee or agent for the trustee.

Questions about the lawful entitlement to representation in the governing bodies of the Bank concerned – besides the cases of Germany and Japan referred to already – Austria, Albania, the three Baltic countries, and Danzig. The central banks of Austria and Albania were provisionally recognised as the lawful successors of their prewar institutions, while more caution was exercised in the other two cases.[75]

The first postwar meeting of the Board did not take place until the end of 1946. Once resumed, the meetings were initially less frequent than they had been before the war (only five were held in 1947), with alternates often sitting in for the governors. During 1946 and most of 1947, European central bankers had only a vague idea of what services the BIS – an institution with an uncertain future and modest financial means at its disposal – might provide to them in the coming years. Busy as they were with domestic matters such as monetary reforms, inflation, and paying for essential imports, the governors left to the BIS management the task of solving the problems inherited from the war and of making plans for the future.

This attitude changed at the end of the summer of 1947, when the dollar–sterling payments crisis signalled that Europe was far from ready for the kind of convertibility envisaged at Bretton Woods. The largely unforeseen speed of reconstruction was straining European import capacity, generating inflation in almost every country at a time when the European Recovery Program was beginning to take shape but not yet operative. The increasingly strained East–West relations accelerated changes in the U.S. strategic position vis-à-vis the Old Continent and, at the same time, demanded closer economic cooperation among Western European countries.[76] In this context, the BIS came to be regarded as a useful technical tool for international cooperation, and central bankers again allocated the necessary time for regular monthly visits to Basel.

The BIS's postwar operations were somewhat different from the prewar ones. Before 1939, the Bank's funds were invested in a comparatively small number of markets. Moreover, while formally short-term, a fairly large amount of the BIS funds – particularly those invested in Germany – were actually tied up for long periods of time. Obligations deriving from reparations no longer constrained the postwar activity of the BIS, which was therefore able to conduct truly short-term operations with a larger number of central banks than was previously the case.[77] Small countries like Finland were the first beneficiaries of BIS credit.[78]

The BIS's well-tested expertise soon proved useful to central banks for the execution of gold sales entailing forward repurchase and in exchanges of the yellow metal between markets, reducing physical transfers to a minimum. In particular, the Bank enabled European central banks to procure for themselves dollars against gold in Europe without physically shipping gold to the United States.[79] Pending the unfreezing of its assets in the United States, the BIS opened a new free account with the Federal Reserve Bank of New York, which allowed the resumption of its traditional policy of transferring into dollars a large part of its liquid resources. Small dollar credits were also granted to various central banks.

In the spring of 1948, as mentioned in Chapter 8, the diplomatic skills of Maurice Frère succeeded in settling the BIS's outstanding issues with the United States. One of the agreements concerned the unblocking of the Bank's funds in the United States, which were finally released and ex-empted from any restriction.[80] A few months later, the Federal Reserve Bank of New York obtained authorisation from the Federal Reserve Board to grant the BIS standby credits in dollars, required by Basel as a protection against any unusual drain on its dollar balances held against gold security.[81] At the same time, the BIS successfully encouraged European central banks to deposit with it as much as possible of their surplus funds in dollars. "A centralisation of such funds at the BIS" was considered important to place it "in a better position to respond to any demands made on the BIS as a centre of co-operation between the central banks in Europe".[82]

The early postwar investment and lending activity of the BIS, if limited in scale, was nevertheless welcomed by European central banks for its con-tribution to easing their dollar liquidity constraints. By the end of 1947 the Basel meetings had resumed the prewar monthly cadence; governors sig-nalled their renewed interest in the BIS by attending regularly. However, it took a longer time – even after the conclusion of the 1948 agreements – for the BIS to dispel a deeply entrenched diffidence and to gain respect in the United States. The BIS dollar deposits of European central banks raised the issue of whether the Bank was subject to the provisions of regulation Q, which did not allow interest payments on sight deposits. While arguing that it was not subject to the rules applicable to U.S. banks, the BIS preferred to quietly ask its customers to make time rather than sight deposits in dollars.[83] On more than one occasion, the Americans also suspected the BIS of less than fully complying with its own Statutes[84] in conducting dollar transac-tions without the formal approval of the U.S. monetary authorities,[85] who also complained about the unsatisfactory arrangements for informal com-munication with the BIS.

Personal contacts proved to be essential in improving relations between Basel and Washington. After Frère's and Auboin's visits to Washington in April–May 1948,[86] two representatives of the Federal Reserve Bank of New York (More and Rushmore) attended the 1948 BIS Annual General Meet-ing. In Basel, they examined the technical conditions upon which prewar relations were based with a view to restoring formal links between the two institutions.[87] The IMF and IBRD meetings in London and Washington, attended by BIS representatives, provided further opportunities for improv-ing personal relations and discussing issues of mutual interest. In July 1949 Auboin was received by Snyder, the United States Treasury Secretary, and handed him an information note dealing with current BIS operations.[88] Jacobsson, held in great esteem at the New York Fed,[89] was also deeply in-volved in fostering mutual understanding. An admirer of the United States, he was a true believer in face-to-face contacts and in the sharing of first-hand information, particularly at a time when economic, social, and political conditions were so much changed from the prewar period and yet personal contacts remained limited.[90]

Cooperation with the twin Bretton Woods institutions also contributed to improving relations with the United States. One of the motivations given at Bretton Woods for the liquidation of the BIS was its supposed overlapping with the functions of the new bodies. According to Knoke of the Federal Reserve Bank of New York, the BIS funds in the United States remained frozen pending "future developments, among them the question of future cooperation between the BIS and the World Bank".[91] In other words, it was up to the BIS to show that only the war and misunderstandings at Bretton Woods had led people to believe that its existence was incompatible with that of the Bretton Woods bodies. As it turned out, early postwar relations with the IMF remained confined to personal contacts and the exchange of visits. Cooperation with the IBRD, the so-called World Bank, took on a more operational character, also due to the latter's direct contribution to Europe's postwar reconstruction in 1947–48, which was "strategically important, though quite limited in quantitative terms".[92] Collaboration with the IBRD formally began in August 1947 with the opening of the latter's European mission, which the BIS both hosted on its premises and provided with technical support for the study of economic conditions in some European countries. In September of that year, President McCloy of the IBRD and Executive Director Black for the United States visited Basel and discussed future cooperation,[93] which a few months later materialised in the joint placement of the first IBRD bond issue in a currency other than dollars. The BIS negotiated the bonds' placement with a group of Swiss banks and then bought a good share of them for its own account, placing the proceeds in Swiss francs at the disposal of the Dutch government. The operation was regarded as a contribution to easing constraints on international payments.

9.5   The 1947 Agreement on Multilateral Monetary Compensation

The Committee of European Economic Co-operation (CEEC) opened its conference in Paris on 12 July 1947, only five weeks after General Marshall spoke at Harvard and announced the plan that subsequently went under his name. The U.S. State Department "wanted a European initiative in response to Marshall's speech and the creation of a 'European organisation'".[94] While the plan was still to be defined in detail before being submitted to Congress, Washington had already made it abundantly clear that

U.S. aid would be conditional upon cooperation amongst Western European countries. In particular, the U.S. government insisted on multilateral trade policies replacing bilateral agreements and exchange controls. The British Labour government, on the other hand, saw the maintenance of tight control over foreign transactions as a tool for its full employment policy. Moreover, "Washington's new policy seemed to be denying Britain's world role and the role of the sterling area"[95] with its attendant "imperial preferences", and this seemed to signal a weakening of the wartime special relationship with London. France, fearful that the envisaged multilateral cooperation within the Marshall Plan might entail an industrial revival of Germany and, more generally, jeopardise its status as a European great power, joined the United Kingdom in opposing the far-reaching policy goals of the United States. Besides these transatlantic divergences, differences emerged among the 16 countries participating in the CEEC. Belgium and the Netherlands were concerned about the future of the German economy, heretofore strongly integrated with their own economies. The Scandinavian countries, Greece, and Turkey had problems of their own.

Some scholars view the conference that took the name of Committee for European Economic Co-operation as the first step in the slow creation of a postwar integrated Europe.[96] To others it "did more to emphasise the lack of cooperation between European economies than their willingness to plan in harmony".[97] It is hardly surprising that, merely two years after the end of their "second Thirty Years' War", European governments were little prepared to discuss their common problems in a different context from that of the nineteenth- and twentieth-century "great power conferences" that in most cases yielded, if anything, ephemeral results. Most countries faced the hardest peacetime problems in living memory. The mental and political habit of preferring second-best autarkic solutions to the odds of untested international openness was deeply rooted. Century-old intractable issues, such as that of the Ruhr, loomed large in the talks. The details and implications of America's proposed aid remained unclear. The Paris conference highlighted Europe's mistrust of America's leadership and the latter's suspicions and disappointments about Europe. However, the very fact that it took place at all and that it did not end in a stalemate was in itself a success.

A first draft of the conference's final report showed that little progress towards planning economic integration of the various economies had been made and did not envisage a continuation, in any form, of a European co-ordination structure. Under pressure from the U.S. State Department, the executive committee revised the report to take into account America's desire for Europeans to take some steps along the road of economic integration as a condition for substantial aid. The final draft, presented to the press on 22 September 1947, contained the commitment of the European countries to form a permanent organisation, the future OEEC, once the U.S. Congress had approved the European Recovery Program bill. To the small minority of Europeans who dreamed of the swift economic (and political) integration of the continent, the conference looked like a failure. To those who believed that the initial steps invariably discount large amounts of inertia and that, at any rate, small steps are better than no steps at all, the conference appeared then, as it does with hindsight, to have been quite successful.

It was in Paris, during the proceedings of the CEEC, that the Belgian representative Alphand proposed to the former "gold bloc" – France, Italy, and the Benelux countries – the creation of a customs union within the coming five to seven years. This was not an entirely new proposal: Italy had already taken the initiative of sounding out France about a similar project – limited, however, to the two countries.[98] In the discussions that followed, Paris proposed some form of involvement of West Germany in the union and also suggested that Switzerland be part of it. The Italian government, for its part, took the opportunity to issue a statement to the CEEC in favour of a customs union amongst all the countries subscribing to the Marshall Plan as a first step towards a European union.[99]

It is within this general context that a much more modest (but immediately operative) decision was made by France, Italy, and the Benelux countries to enter into an agreement on multilateral monetary compensation, signed in Paris on 18 November 1947.[100] Member countries undertook to carry out, on the largest possible scale, "multilateral compensation operations between the balances resulting from the application of payments agreements already concluded between them".[101] Practically all countries participating in the European Recovery Program adhered to this agreement as "occasional members". While the five "permanent members" agreed to make automatic reciprocal settlements out of their respective balance of trade surpluses and deficits, "occasional members" would do so on a case-by-case basis.

The agreement was drafted by the Committee on Payments Agreements, which met as a technical subcommittee of the CEEC in September and October 1947.[102] The subcommittee requested the presence of a BIS representative at the October meeting, to help with the drafting of the agreement,[103] with the understanding that the Bank would be the agent in charge of carrying out the monthly compensations among member countries.[104] Experts from the latter were invited, even before the agreement was signed, to a technical meeting in Basel to examine the answers given by individual countries to a questionnaire about trade agreements and statistics and to draft the rules for the practical implementation of the multilateral compensations.[105] From 20 to 25 November, the BIS hosted a conference of the committee of delegates of the five signatory countries and of representatives or observers of Denmark, Greece, Norway, Sweden, Switzerland, and the United Kingdom. Observers from the U.S. Treasury and State Department as well as from the IMF were also present. The conference adopted the procedure concerning the compensation operations and drew up regulations for the application of the agreement. Some rough calculations were also made, on the basis of the data available to the BIS, about the extent of the possible compensation. Further meetings of the delegates followed in Brussels on 18 December and again in Basel on 7 January 1948.

At the meeting in Brussels, a resolution was passed inviting the central banks concerned to avoid carrying out the multilateral compensations deriving from the agreement directly, as these would be better and more usefully performed by the BIS. In any case, central banks were requested to inform the BIS of any direct transaction carried out as the result of the agreement.[106]

The compensation operations under the Paris agreement never reached a significant scale. At the end of December 1947, only $1.7 million of the $762.1 million outstanding bilateral balances had actually been offset. Only a total of $5 million in claims had been cancelled by the time the agreement expired.[107] In spite of the small quantities involved, however, the symbolic importance of this first multilateral payments agreement should not be overlooked. For the first time since the Great Depression a practical step was taken by the Western European countries acting in concert to ease, rather than tighten, the grip of bilateral settlements on trade and output growth. A path was opened that would soon lead to more encompassing agreements and to the European Payments Union. From a technical point of view, this first experiment was also important: data were collected and their reliability assessed, and the machinery of an international clearing house was set in motion again. As for the BIS, this was a tailor-made task owing to its links with the national central banks, to the accounts they kept with it, and to its prewar experience in managing currency and gold swaps. Its staff possessed skills for easing international settlements that existed in none of the new international institutions. Thus, the experience accumulated in the 1930s allowed the BIS to perform an indispensable technical task at a crucial time in the reconstruction of European payments. Central banks took notice of this development: more attention than in the previous two years was directed towards Basel, and thus was its network of contacts, exchanges, and visits revived.

9.6   The OEEC and the 1948 Agreement for Intra-European Payments and Compensations

The CEEC was converted into a permanent international body, the Organisation for European Economic Co-operation (OEEC), by virtue of a convention signed in Paris on 16 April 1948 by 16 European governments[108] and the representatives of the military governments of Germany and Trieste. Robert Marjolin, a Frenchman still in his thirties, was appointed secretary general of the Paris-based organisation. The United States saw the OEEC as the body that would allow Western Europeans to create a new society and economy, of which the Marshall aid would be the catalyst. In order to foster cooperation, the U.S. government made the OEEC responsible for: (i) making a formal recommendation for the allocation of ERP aid; and (ii) producing a common European plan for economic recovery over the envisaged duration of the Marshall Plan. By asking Europeans to fit the individual countries' requests for aid into a single, consistent, pan-European plan, the U.S. government – represented by Averell Harriman and Stanley Hoffman – actively sought to create a strong incentive to cooperation.

The U.S. government saw the creation of the OEEC as the first step on the road to rapid European economic integration.[109] The State Department was aware that "it would stick in the throats of Europeans that decisions so important to their economic welfare should be taken in international consultation",[110] but they were confident that, once forced upon Western Europe, economic integration would show its obvious advantages over autarkic nationalism. There was undoubtedly an element of naïvety in the U.S. belief that the Europeans would swiftly seize the opportunity, bury long-standing acrimonious divisions, and understand that national interests would be better served by pursuing Europe-wide welfare. A glimpse back to the long decades needed for reconstruction and healing after their own Civil War should have told Americans that Europeans too, like the citizens of the Union and Confederate states, would take time to heal their wounds and plan for a common future. Cooperation was, however, the only way for the Old Continent to overcome the "second Thirty Years' War" of 1914–45. And U.S. optimism and impatience, naïve as it looked to both contemporary observers and some later historians, was nevertheless salutary. In fact, European economic integration was slower than the United States thought desirable and proceeded along lines other than those advocated by the Marshall Plan architects. But the very fact that it took place – and that, judging from previous historical experience, it did so in a rather short period of time – is in itself a tribute to the early postwar U.S. visionaries.

Having said that, one must add that the first years of OEEC activity delivered much less than the Americans had hoped for. They had envisaged a truly supranational institution where collective decision making by a ministerial-level council would not be hindered by national vetoes. Reality turned out to be very different. The economic situation and needs of each individual country, as the BIS Annual Reports emphasised, were so different that it was almost impossible for collective decision making to harmonise them. Unanimity – that is, granting veto power to every country, large or small – was the only possible way for European integration to proceed. Whether or not this situation, to which one should add the United Kingdom's difficult relations with the United States and France's renewed fear of Germany, brought about a "collapse" of the OEEC (as argued by Milward) is largely a matter of definition. Like any other historical judgement, it ultimately depends on the eye and the expectations of the beholder.

The OEEC could neither live up to the high hopes pinned on it by the Americans nor satisfy the "planners" within each individual European nation state. In the end, it was unable to provide an encompassing framework for European reconstruction. Much of the Marshall aid turned out to be negotiated on a bilateral basis. Nevertheless, the Paris-based organisation was an innovative international institution. For many of the participants in the meetings, it proved to be a valuable experience. Milward himself observes that "throughout the first years of the OEEC the interest in and knowledge of what was being attempted in other countries greatly increased".[111] This was no small achievement, since information was scarce (Per Jacobsson observed that "neither the British nor the French travel[led] about in great numbers"[112]) at a time when it was no longer possible for anyone to rely upon past knowledge. Fresh information was indeed a most needed prerequisite for international cooperation. Moreover, if nothing else, it was within the OEEC framework that a new – more comprehensive if still unsatisfactory – accord to foster multilateral settlements was reached, a second landmark along the road that would lead to full currency convertibility and multilateralism ten years later.

The Agreement for Intra-European Payments and Compensations (IEPC), which had been preceded by months of careful examination of the problems involved and by much drafting and redrafting, was signed in Paris on 16 October 1948[113] by the 19 members of the OEEC (the 16 original European governments and the representatives of the U.K.–U.S. Bi-zone and the French zone of Germany, and of the Free Territory of Trieste).

The machinery of the IEPC was complex, reflecting the intricate web of bilateral trade relations within Western Europe. In essence, however, it rested on two basic principles. First, the European Recovery Program dollar allocation to individual countries was made in proportion to each country's estimated trade deficit with the "Western Hemisphere". Out of this amount, a "sub-allocation" of aid inside Europe was made under the IEPC scheme in order to meet forecasted "intra-European deficits". As far as the latter were concerned, each IEPC participating country either gave or received "indirect aid" in the form of "drawing rights", according to its trade position within Europe. Thus, surplus countries established "drawing rights" in favour of those expected to run the corresponding payments deficits. Second, an automatic offsetting of certain credits and debts was mandated by the agreement. Whereas under the previous (1947) agreement automatic settlements were limited to six countries only, now the provision applied to all the OEEC members.

A payments plan based on these principles required the active participation of the Economic Co-operation Administration (ECA), the U.S. organisation in charge of the application and supervision of the Marshall Plan (ERP). When goods supplied under ERP grants (as distinct from the part of the aid furnished in the form of loans) were available for sale in the recipient countries, the proceeds in national currency – called "counterpart funds" – were placed in a special account at the central bank, where they were earmarked for approved purposes. For the purpose of the payments scheme, it became necessary to establish a new form of ERP aid, neither loan nor grant, called "conditional aid" and also nicknamed the "Little Marshall Plan".[114] The condition was that, on receipt of the dollar aid, the countries concerned placed an equivalent amount of their national currency at the disposal of their debtors on current account of the balance of payments.[115] By creating "drawing rights", surplus countries could of course expand their exports beyond the limit set by the capacity of the trading partner to pay back an equivalent quantity of merchandise, as in the case of barter or "bilateral agreement".

"In the practical arrangement of the scheme", the BIS observed, "a high degree of co-operation was demanded, especially from the creditors. The 'Western Hemisphere deficit' and the allocation of dollar aid had been agreed upon before the intra-European payments plan was drawn up. 'Conditional' dollars for the intra-European payments plan were, therefore, not 'additional' dollars but part of the original aid they expected to get in any case".[116] Lacking an additional financial incentive, cooperation had to be based on an appreciation of the advantages of multilateral settlements. In any event, it did not easily take place, for a number of reasons. Individual countries were reluctant to abandon the well-trodden path of bilateral agreements and, in fact, over 200 new such agreements had been signed in 1947 alone. On the one hand there were countries, such as the United Kingdom, that believed they held a strong bargaining position due to the size of their overall trade and hence thought they would get better deals and balance their foreign accounts more advantageously through a web of bilateral accords. On the other hand, "planning" – with all its attendant emphasis on national needs and priorities – was, in various forms and degrees, the economic catchword of the time. There were good reasons for governments to lean towards dirigisme, given the ample evidence of market failures and the need to speed up reconstruction. And bilateral trade agreements, then as in the 1930s, were regarded as useful tools for resource allocation purposes. There were, needless to say, also not-so-commendable reasons why the overblown wartime bureaucracies favoured the use of bilateral arrangements. Lack of cooperation also resulted from the fact that the IEPC agreement did not provide for a system of large, centralised credit available to all participants.

Technical problems also contributed to the limited success of the IEPC. In particular, the allocation of "drawing rights" on the basis of forecasted deficits made the functioning of the system "as unpredictable and haphazard as that of the better known Monte Carlo roulette".[117] Moreover, for the plan to work smoothly, the "Western Hemisphere" deficit of any country, which set the upper limit for the "conditional aid" for that country, had to be larger than its European surplus; otherwise, the latter would not be fully covered by drawing rights granted.

"As the Marshall Plan approached its half-way mark, the walls of the bilateral trading fortress seemed capable of withstanding every assault. A proper system for promoting intra-European trade on a durable basis was still waiting to be born."[118] The European Payments Union (discussed in the next chapter), in which the BIS was deeply involved, would soon provide an acceptable alternative to and a politically viable road towards current account convertibility.

TEN

Achieving Convertibility

10.1 Europe's "Golden Age" and International Payments

By 1949–51, all major Western European countries had regained their peak prewar production levels.[1] The following two decades saw the most remarkable episode in the history of Europe's economic growth, so remarkable that contemporary observers – particularly in Germany and Italy, the two defeated countries and the fastest growers – did not hesitate to use the word "miracle".

During this "golden age", productivity growth in Western Europe outperformed that of the United States, finally engineering a long-awaited catching-up with the world's productivity leader. Not only was the rate of growth in Europe's real output almost double the secular trend, but cyclical fluctuations were extremely mild by historical standards, price inflation remained relatively low and stable, and external accounts seldom developed structural disequilibria. Full employment was the rule rather than the exception; in some countries it was achieved for the first time in recorded history. Poorer European countries grew faster than richer ones, resulting in a convergence of living standards across Europe.[2]

As is always the case with extraordinary and complex phenomena, the causes of the impressive postwar European growth were the subject of controversy among economists at the time. They are still hotly debated by economic historians.[3] Needless to say, opinions differed and still differ. Thus, at the time, Lamfalussy saw trade as the main engine of postwar growth,[4] for Kindleberger its main cause was an unlimited supply of cheap labour,[5] Kaldor emphasised dynamic economies of scale,[6] and Denison pointed to productivity gains from the reallocation of resources across productive sectors.[7] More recently, Boltho suggested that improved management of aggregate demand engineered the "golden age",[8] while Olson stressed institutional change.[9] The wealth of interpretations bears witness both to the extraordinary significance of this "golden age" and to its bewildering complexity.

Although single-cause explanations cannot fully account for this unique episode in the economic history of Europe,[10] the far-reaching international cooperation that took place – in sharp contrast to the 1930s – stands out as one of the main ingredients of Europe's postwar success.

As mentioned in the previous chapter, the leadership provided by the Americans after the war explicitly endeavoured to broker coordinated efforts for economic recovery. The Marshall Plan created the conditions for both international cooperation and the establishment of cohesive domestic institutions.[11] The OEEC was the main tool for the coordination of U.S. aid, but other bodies, such as NATO, were also instrumental to that end. The Bretton Woods conference set the standard for a cooperative international monetary system, even though this took longer to be fully implemented than anticipated in 1944 and also took quite a different shape from that envisaged by the founding fathers.[12] In the 1950s, Europe created its own cooperative institutions for intra-European payments: first the European Payments Union (EPU), and then the European Monetary Agreement when the EPU was dissolved.

In October 1947, 23 countries signed in Geneva the General Agreement on Tariffs and Trade (GATT). The main principles of the agreement were nondiscrimination (the most-favoured nation clause was to be extended to all signatory parties) and the dismantling of nontariff barriers to trade. A more ambitious plan for the creation of an international trade organisation foundered at a conference in Havana (November 1947 to March 1948) on profound disagreements over its charter, as the then-called underdeveloped (but also some European) countries rejected multilateralism and argued for the right to control international investment, create trade preferences, and impose import quotas.

In the 1950s, European trade was liberalised at a rapid pace, in striking contrast to the previous two decades. Whereas between 1929 and 1950 Western Europe's[13] merchandise exports had shrunk by 6%, between 1950 and 1973 they increased 6.3 times, twice as fast as domestic output.[14] By 1973, the region's GDP was almost four times as large as that of 1929, while its export trade was six times larger.[15]

Trade liberalisation and the free convertibility of national currencies into dollars (and thus into each other) were but two sides of the same coin. Not only were they jointly essential to the revival of the international economy, but neither of them could stand alone. Some limited progress had been made in the late 1940s to untangle the web of bilateral trade agreements and so loosen the grip of quotas and other physical constraints on trade, but the scarcity of international means of payment stood in the way of swift liberalisation. The Marshall Plan made a contribution to the reduction of the dollar gap (the shortage of dollars in Europe),[16] and so did the surge in U.S. imports caused by the Korean War. Nevertheless, in the early 1950s, the scarcity of dollars was still considered by most European governments as the major constraint on international trade policy. By setting up an efficient system of multilateral clearing and mutual credit, the EPU – in which the BIS played a crucial technical role – was a means to economise on dollars in intra-European transactions. It therefore allowed governments to reduce quotas and move from bilateral to multilateral trade agreements relatively free from the constraints of gold and dollar reserves, thereby making a major contribution to trade liberalisation. By 1955, about 85% of intra-European trade had been liberalised.[17] In the same year, the OEEC required member countries to liberalise 90% of overall intra-European trade by 1958. Most member countries met the target, and some came very close to full liberalisation.[18]

The relaxation of restrictions on European trade with North America proceeded at a slower pace. In 1953 only 11% of Western European imports from the dollar area were free from quantitative limits, compared with 71% of intra-European trade – an indirect confirmation of the impact of the EPU on trade liberalisation. In the early 1950s, the main problem in transatlantic trade was described as the "dollar shortage" or "dollar gap". It seemed that the U.S. economy was "producing goods which all countries wanted to buy, but scarcely needed to import anything in return".[19] Some observers feared this would be a permanent rather than a transitory state of affairs. European imports were thought to be price inelastic, making exchange rate devaluation a cure worse than the disease. At the same time, the lowering of U.S. import duties on European goods was deemed politically impossible. In the mid-1950s, however, the dollar gap disappeared as U.S. military expenditure abroad increased and U.S. capital found profitable outlets in low-cost Europe, close to rapidly expanding consumer markets. The OEEC countries moved to trade surpluses with North America and built up dollar reserves.[20] By the early 1960s, international payments problems derived from a dollar glut rather than a shortage.

This brief survey of Western Europe's economic cooperative achievements in the 1950s cannot be concluded without mentioning the Treaty of Rome, signed on 25 March 1957, which established the European Economic

Community (EEC) between France, Germany, Italy, and the three Benelux countries. The treaty, to be sure, drew its motivations and projected its ambitions far beyond economic matters, as would be indicated (in due course) by giving the EEC the more comprehensive name of "European Union". The original aim of overcoming economic nationalism was itself charged with substantial political objectives, which included avoiding further "European civil wars" and strengthening the postwar democratic regimes.

The main aims of the EEC were the abolition of trade barriers among member countries, the establishment of a common external tariff with the rest of the world, the liberalisation of service transactions, and the freeing of labour and capital movements. Common legislation prohibiting market-distorting government subsidies and private agreements for the restriction of competition was also envisaged. The treaty established the European Investment Bank similar in some respects to the IBRD.

The BIS emphasised the coordination provisions of the treaty that seemed to reflect the Bank's long-standing philosophy. "Member countries", read the 1957 Annual Report, "will be under a general obligation to pursue an economic policy aimed at the achievement of balance-of-payments equilibrium and the maintenance of confidence in the national currency. To this effect they will undertake to coordinate their respective policies and to ensure collaboration between their own administrative departments and central banks and those in the other countries".[21]

The Treaty of Rome became effective on 1 January 1958. One year later, the EPU achieved its aim when currency convertibility was declared by Western European countries, and it was therefore dissolved. With convertibility came profound changes in the ways of international monetary cooperation, which will be discussed in Chapter 11.

10.2   International Monetary Cooperation

"At the beginning of my career", Auboin recalled, "I knew the head of an exchange office who, when he ran short of foreign exchange, used to shut up the shop and go fishing. He felt that he was doing a useful job by 'saving' foreign exchange".[22] Nothing could be further removed from a modern perspective than such a characterisation of the currency markets. In fact, in university, when around the middle of the term the time comes to lecture the economics undergraduates on the intricate web of trade and capital-movement regulations enveloping the world in the 1930s and 1940s, they find the whole matter quite incomprehensible. This is due less to the cumbersome and tedious technicalities of the system than to the students' mindset. In today's domestic and international economic environment, it requires a lot of imagination for a young person even to conceive of a situation where trade was largely conducted on a bilateral basis and the transfer of monetary instruments across borders was subject to tight bureaucratic controls and authorisations. Equally, therefore, it is hard to make students appreciate both the extraordinary importance of the progress made after the war in creating a new multilateral environment and the enormous stumbling blocks that had to be overcome in the process. Yet it is perhaps not irrelevant, even today, to realise that the 1950s were one of the most fruitful periods in international economic cooperation. Cooperation in the 1960s may have been more intensive – within a better structured and functioning framework – than was the case in the previous decade, but the accomplishments of the 1950s are astonishing when the starting conditions, as briefly outlined in the previous chapter, are taken into account.

At the end of 1958, international monetary cooperation in Europe was crowned by the formal introduction of free convertibility[23] of Western European currencies into each other and into the dollar. Convertibility, now a concept largely taken for granted, was once defined as the "possibility to buy foreign currencies without previously asking a bureaucrat".[24] When joining the IMF, Western European governments pledged themselves to make their national currency convertible at a fixed rate, but none of them could honour the pledge. At the time, Europeans were all required to obtain official authorisation for foreign currency transactions. Multiple exchange rate regimes existed in many countries.[25] No one nurtured the illusion that full convertibility could be achieved swiftly. If nothing else, the short-lived 1947 experiment of the pound sterling had shown that sustainable unrestricted currency convertibility required more than ad hoc dollar loans reminiscent of the "stabilisation loans" of the 1920s.

In the immediate postwar period, free capital movements were allowed only between Switzerland and the United States, and even then funds transferred from the latter to the former were convertible at a "financial rate", which differed from the "commercial" one. With few exceptions, capital movements within the sterling area were also free at a fixed official exchange rate. In the rest of Europe, exchange controls insulated domestic financial markets.[26]

In the late 1940s, multiple exchange rates were phased out and official rates of exchange against the dollar were allowed to move close to the market rate, while at the same time foreign currency transactions were kept strictly under government control. The Multilateral Monetary Compensation Agreement and the Intra-European Payments and Compensations

Agreement, while politically important in breaking with the past, turned out to be quite irrelevant from a quantitative point of view:[27] in 1949, most intra-European payments were still settled on a bilateral basis.

From the standpoint of international monetary history, the 1950s began in 1949 with a spate of currency devaluations. Parallels were drawn at the time with the 1931 devaluation wave, but the only similarity between the two cases is in the role played by sterling.[28] For the rest, 1949 saw a degree of international coordination of exchange rate realignments unthinkable 18 years earlier. The new exchange rates were chosen cooperatively to reflect their projected purchasing power parity and thus to avoid competitive devaluations. The 1949 devaluations vis-à-vis the dollar (and realignments amongst European currencies) set the official exchange rates close to market equilibrium, as borne out in subsequent years by the stability of the new rates when exchange controls were progressively relaxed.

"The opening months of 1949", the BIS wrote a year later, "were characterised by quite a remarkable mood of optimism".[29] The gap between the quotations of the pound on the Swiss market and the official rate was narrowing. The foreign exchange position of several other countries, including large economies such as France and Italy, was also improving thanks to more effective fiscal and monetary policies. In the first part of the year, activity in most European countries continued to grow, as income levels were approaching prewar levels. At the same time, however, U.S. output growth was slowing down and primary product prices were falling. The reduction in purchases abroad by U.S. manufacturers hit the suppliers of raw materials, many of whom were located in the sterling area, putting pressure on the monetary reserves of the Bank of England. A number of emergency measures were taken by London in the summer of 1949, including a temporary halt to imports from the dollar area, prompting an intensification of the pressure for a devaluation of the pound that the United States had been applying for quite a while.[30] Since the beginning of the Marshall aid programme, the U.S. Treasury had felt that the foreign exchange rate of participating countries was no longer solely their own business but had become a matter of "grave direct concern" to the United States itself.[31] At the IMF, the U.S. executive director argued that "the Fund ought to be in a position where it could make positive suggestions to certain countries that their currencies were overvalued".[32] Moreover, Fund officials, beginning with Managing Director Gutt, now argued that, in the face of a rapidly recovering European economy, the immediate postwar constraints on trade no longer applied and that restrictions on current account foreign currency transactions should be relaxed.

By the summer, a degree of consensus was emerging at the IMF that an overall realignment of the official rates of exchange was desirable, beginning with a major devaluation of the pound. London, however, opposed any such move. Cripps [33] (the chancellor of the exchequer), most of the Cabinet, and Cobbold (the governor of the Bank of England) were all against devaluation. Dalton recorded in his diary: "Americans have now swung back to the mood of 1945. Convertibility and non-discrimination are now their principal aim – not helping Europe or resisting communism".[34] The Labour government, on the other hand, was inclined to deal with the situation by using the wartime tools of restrictions on trade and capital movements. It took the view that cutting government expenditure was not an option, particularly as elections were approaching, and that the suggestion of rising interest rates was "Montagu Norman walking again". "I thought", Dalton said, "we had buried all this stuff about Bank Rate".[35] Yet, as in 1931, it was the rapid drain of reserves that, around the middle of August, convinced the Cabinet and the governor, during a long illness of Cripps, that there was no alternative to devaluation.

Talks then followed in Washington about the extent of the devaluation and accompanying measures. In spite of mutual distrust, a cooperative stance prevailed. At first only Canada was involved in the discussions between the United Kingdom and the United States, but negotiations turned multilateral at the annual meeting of the IMF and the IBRD on 13 September 1949. A ten-point programme to improve the sterling-area dollar earnings was approved and made public, even before devaluation was officially mentioned. On the following weekend, the U.K. government proposed to the IMF a devaluation of sterling by 30.5% (from $4.03 to $2.80 per pound). Approval of devaluation was immediately granted and came into effect on 19 September. "A new situation had there and then been created for a great number of other currencies: and in the following days decisions were taken in various capitals in Europe and elsewhere, and devaluations were carried out, the approval of the IMF having, when necessary, been requested and obtained. Within a week, the currencies of some twenty countries had been devalued, these countries accounting for two-thirds of the total of world trade."[36] Austria devalued by as much as 53.2%, France by 21.9%, the Western zones of Germany by 20.6%, Belgium by 12.3%, and Italy by 8.4%.[37]

The currency realignments of 1949 brought official exchange rates close to the (Swiss) free-market rates, paving the way for a cautious replacement of trade and capital controls with fiscal and monetary policies as tools for maintaining external equilibrium.[38] More important still, in stark contrast to 1931, the 1949 devaluations were conducted within a cooperative context that was also heralding the dawn of a new era in international economic relations. True, cooperation was to a large extent imposed by the hegemonic power who held the purse strings, and it was mostly conducted on a bilateral basis with Canada as a go-between. But the outcome contrasted favourably with that of the Tripartite Agreement of 1936. Moreover, multilateral organisations were brought to bear (albeit at the end of a bilateral consultation process), establishing a meaningful precedent in coordinated exchange rate alterations.

Over the following nine years, the main aim of international economic cooperation consisted of repairing the damage suffered by the trade and payments network in the 1930s and 1940s. Completing the process took longer than many, including the BIS, had hoped. It has been argued that, by 1950, the "most obvious preconditions for the viability of current account convertibility" already existed. "A market-clearing exchange rate was within reach. Reserves were not grossly inadequate. Except in the U.K. and Ireland, monetary overhangs had been eliminated."[39] Yet the European governments acted cautiously in reducing administrative controls on commodity trade and international payments. Rather than moving fast on convertibility, they created the European Payments Union. One of the reasons for caution reflected concerns about the trade unions' behaviour and the evolution of unit labour costs as prerequisites for sustaining convertibility over the long term. Another reason for not rushing to dismantle controls on currency movements was the already-mentioned ideological opposition to monetary policy as a tool for exchange rate management. There were also more mundane, but nonetheless compelling, motivations: a swollen bureaucracy and sheltered sectors had a vested interest in maintaining a well-tested status quo rather than venturing into the uncertainty of international competition.

However, when all is said and done and when the starting point of the late 1940s is taken into account, the process of freeing intra-European trade and payments emerges as a remarkable success. It was heralded, as early as 1951, by the creation of the European Coal and Steel Community, a major institutional innovation.

The European Payments Union (EPU) was the main instrument for European monetary cooperation in the 1950s, leading up to current account currency convertibility. The BIS played a major role in this important, if relatively little known, international economic institution. Before reviewing the latter's history and assessing its impact, it may be useful to take a brief look at the daily life of the BIS during 1950–58.

10.3   The BIS in the 1950s

Immediately after the war, the staff of the BIS in Basel were busy ensuring the Bank's survival, while central bankers, preoccupied with pressing domestic issues, paid scant attention to their club by the Rhine. By the late 1940s, however, the governors' attendance at the monthly meetings had become more assiduous. By then, the BIS had overcome the Bretton Woods crisis and proven itself useful in granting technical assistance to the Agreement for Intra-European Payments and Compensations. In 1950, its role in managing a Europe-wide "clearing room" was hugely enhanced by the creation of the EPU. In the following years, the success of the latter had a positive impact on the BIS's visibility and reputation.

In 1955, the BIS celebrated its silver jubilee. The occasion was marked by the publication of a brief historical synopsis by Roger Auboin that appeared in the prestigious Princeton Economics Department *Essays in International Finance*.[40] Around that time, some soul-searching took place as to the future of the institution. Donald Macdonald, a fresh recruit to the BIS Banking Department, wrote: "The BIS is the child of central banks, but the child is 25 years old and even human parents get a little tired of making special efforts for their offspring after a certain time. On the other hand, if the child shows itself useful to its parents, they will usually be glad to do all they can in their turn for their child".[41] Convertibility, already in sight, would make the EPU redundant: what substitute services could the BIS provide to its "parents"? The answer to this question came almost naturally with the expansion of economic activity, also mirrored in the BIS balance sheet, and with the increased demand for cooperation generated by convertibility itself, discussed in the next chapters.

Between 1950 and 1959, total assets and liabilities[42] of the Bank increased 4.7 times, from 754.8 million to 3,528 million Swiss gold francs.[43] Gold deposits, almost entirely from central banks, expanded by more than a factor of 14 and currency deposits more than fourfold. Central banks, again acknowledging the usefulness of their creature, were certainly putting their money where their mouth was. Without calling up the unpaid capital,[44] the BIS could thus avail itself of a rapidly increasing mass of resources, about a third of which it held in gold bars and coins and the rest in short-term bills (including Treasury bills), acceptances, time deposits, and advances.

Gold operations were an area where the Bank had accumulated extraordinary expertise in both the official and the free markets. On the London gold market, which had reopened in 1954, it operated on very narrow margins,[45] endeavouring to secure for member central banks more advantageous terms than the official conditions of the Federal Reserve Board.[46] In 1957, a new dollar facility scheme was created with the agreement of the Federal Reserve Board, the basic idea of which was to provide dollars to central banks at interest lower than the market rate.[47] The remuneration of sight or short-term funds entrusted to the BIS was also attractive because of the Bank's operational skills on the volatile international money markets. At the beginning of the decade, the Bank encouraged member central banks to move from sight to "deposits subject to three months' notice, which enabled the Bank to grant credits to the best advantage".[48] However, with the passing of time and the steady growth of central bank reserves, moral suasion was no longer needed: the quest for better remuneration resulted not only in more funds being deposited with the BIS but also in a longer average maturity of the deposits.[49]

Besides offering central banks the best available conditions in the employment of their resources, the BIS also tried to serve them in other discreet ways. One such instance is worth mentioning by way of illustration. In 1955 the Bank deutscher Länder was ready to lend $100 million to the Bank of France but feared domestic criticism, in an election year, since it was already lending substantial amounts of dollars to the EPU. The BIS suggested that the German central bank place "100 million dollars on deposit with the BIS for two years, it being understood – but not mentioned in the contract – that the BIS should make an advance of a similar amount for a similar period to the Banque de France. In this case", the BIS argued, "the German authorities would not be making a loan but would merely be placing some of their reserves on deposit with the central bank's own central bank".[50] No political objection could be raised to such an operation.[51]

It was in the 1950s that the BIS first became involved with the process of European integration, albeit indirectly. As soon as the European Coal and Steel Community (ECSC) was created in 1951, Roger Auboin was sounded out about the BIS providing financial services to the ECSC, but nothing came of it.[52] Then, in 1954, when the ECSC High Authority negotiated with the U.S. government a $100 million loan, the BIS came into the picture. The loan was to provide the ECSC with the means to make advances for investment purposes to coal and steel enterprises within the Community. The major problem was that the U.S. government, acting through the Export–Import Bank of Washington, insisted on additional guarantees because the ECSC was regarded by the Americans as a possibly ephemeral supranational institution and unlikely to survive until the time when the loan would be fully redeemed. Therefore, the claims on the enterprises to which the loan was ultimately made, and the attendant guarantees, were set up as a separate portfolio serving as a pledge for the loan. The portfolio was then placed in custody with the BIS.[53] If the ECSC were to disappear, the enterprises would repay their debts to the BIS, which would then reimburse the original lender. Thus the BIS provided an additional security that allowed the ECSC to raise loans on good terms. The importance of this loan was political as well as economic: Jean Monnet was keen that the ECSC should borrow, as he wanted to show that the new Europe could obtain credit on the international capital market.[54] The same solution was applied the next year when the ECSC negotiated a 50 million Swiss franc loan with a syndicate of Swiss banks. Per Jacobsson intervened directly to win the Swiss banks over.[55] In all, between 1954 and 1961, the ECSC negotiated 16 different loans of this type – in markets as diverse as Belgium, Germany, Luxembourg, the Netherlands, Switzerland, and the United States – for a total amount of 817 million Swiss gold francs.[56] For all these loans, the BIS acted as depositary.

Enlargement of the shareholder base was actively pursued during the 1950s. Since it was deemed desirable that all central banks of the OEEC countries should also be members of the BIS, Portugal, Turkey, Iceland, and Ireland were invited to join.[57] In the second half of the 1950s the participation of Spain was also discussed, finally materialising at the end of 1960.[58] The BIS was also particularly keen on maintaining its links with member central banks from Eastern Europe. Hard currency credits were extended to the central banks of Czechoslovakia, Hungary, Poland, and Yugoslavia.[59] A policy was followed to promote contacts with representatives of these banks and of others that were not ex officio members of the Board, including defraying the cost of their return journey and paying a daily allowance to officials on visits to Basel.[60]

The appointment of a representative to take up the U.S. seat on the Board was discussed on several occasions but left open. Nevertheless, the debate over the issue reflected a friendlier attitude towards the BIS in Washington than had been the case in the 1930s, let alone in the immediate postwar years. Arguments against joining were now of a practical nature rather than of principle. In 1950, Washington approached Basel about the appointment of a director from the United States.[61] The Federal Reserve Bank of New York once again favourably assessed the case for participation in the BIS, arguing that the regional character acquired by the Bank since the war did not impair its usefulness to the international community. "With its strictly western European leadership and its great degree of flexibility and adapt-ability to changing circumstances, the BIS performs important functions in the present-day financial set-up."[62]

Federal Reserve System participation in the BIS Board was deemed ap-propriate for three reasons. First, a U.S. representative would have the opportunity of clearly stating, officially and unofficially, the Fed's "views on current monetary policy problems". Second, "under certain circum-stances the BIS might perhaps develop into the financial arm of the Atlantic Pact community". Third, participation "would serve a particularly useful purpose in case the System should extend stabilisation credits [in view of convertibility] to western European central banks".[63] The Cold War and the creation of NATO were also partly responsible for the more favourable perception of the BIS in Washington. According to Szymczak, a Federal Reserve Board governor, U.S. participation in the BIS was "likely to provide the most practicable way in which central bankers of the 'Atlantic commu-nity' could find regular occasions for informal discussions on matters that concern them as members of the community".[64] However, no action was taken about membership.

The issue resurfaced five years later on the occasion of the 1955 General Meeting of the BIS. In order to leave the door open for the Fed to join, it was agreed that Frère should be given proxy to vote for the U.S. sharehold-ers, so that the practice of inviting the First National City Bank could be discontinued.[65] Both Washington and New York now favoured joining, ar-guing that international monetary cooperation should be stepped up after the introduction of convertibility. The latter, it was argued, would make a pow-erful cooperative tool such as the EPU obsolete. The OEEC was also losing the relevance it enjoyed during the heyday of the Marshall Plan. The BIS, on the other hand, was there to stay: "from the point of view of finance, the arguments for its existence are not so cogent, but as a vehicle for providing monthly gatherings of central bank governors, and others, the arguments for it are overwhelming. The BIS is perhaps the most effective vehicle of co-operation amongst central banks in the world today". The Federal Reserve Bank of New York argued that the "Paris set-up" (i.e., the OEEC) was cre-ated to deal with "an inconvertible world whereas Basel is an ideal set-up for a convertible world. The dollar is at the heart of such a world and it is logical to think of us participating in Basel".[66] On the basis of the same ar-guments, however, the U.S. Treasury reached an opposite conclusion. If the purpose of formal representation on the BIS Board was to partake in infor-mal discussions with central bankers, then there was no need to change the existing informal arrangement of sending observers whenever needed.[67]

During the 1950s there was a gradual turnover in the top positions of the Bank, as most of those who had been in Basel before the war gradually retired or moved on. By the end of the decade, the only members of the old guard remaining in the management were Marcel van Zeeland and Frederick Conolly. Raffaele Pilotti, secretary general since the foundation of the Bank, retired in 1951. He was replaced by another Italian, Alberto Ferrari, still in his thirties and formerly a financial expert at the Paris International Reconstruction Committee.

In the summer of 1956, Burgess for the United States and Cobbold for the United Kingdom offered Per Jacobsson the position of IMF managing director, which he accepted in spite of the contrary advice of most of the BIS Board members.[68] His retirement became effective in October, by which time no replacement had yet been found to head the Monetary and Economic Department. Jacobsson's administrative functions were formally taken over by the general manager, and in reality by Rainoni, who had already performed most of this function under Jacobsson – notorious for being a poor administrator.[69] The intellectual supervision of the MED and the preparation of the Annual Report were entrusted to Paolo Baffi, seconded on a part-time basis from the Bank of Italy.[70] At the same time, Friedrich Lutz of Zurich University was hired as a consultant to the MED and required to be in Basel "whenever his university courses would permit".[71] With Jacobsson gone, some Board members expressed the view "that the value of the Report would be increased if it were shortened".[72] It was only four years later, in 1960, that the Bank appointed a new economic adviser, the U.S. economist Milton Gilbert.

In 1958, Auboin retired. It went without saying that his successor should also hold a French passport. The choice fell on Guillaume Guindey, a "normalien" with a previous career in the Ministry of Finance (where he was responsible for international affairs) and as president of the Mines de Cuivre de Mauritanie.

Maurice Frère, who in 1952 had been re-elected chairman of the Board and president of the Bank, resigned from the two positions in 1958, one year after the end of his governorship of the National Bank of Belgium.[73] Nevertheless, from 1958 to the time of his death in 1970 he retained a seat on the Board, and in 1964 he succeeded Niemeyer – the longest surviving Board member from the prewar generation – as vice-chairman. At the helm of the BIS, Frère was replaced by Marius Holtrop, president of the Netherlands Bank, described as "a man of great competence and high moral standing, of a certain Calvinist austerity, which contrasted with his predecessor's *goût de la vie*".[74]

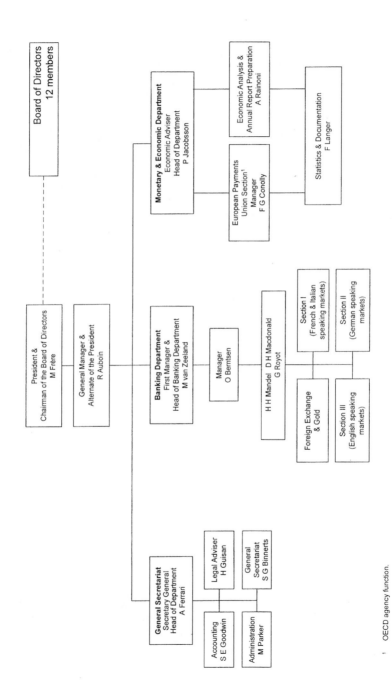

Figure 10.1. BIS "organigram", 1955 (reconstruction).

Board of Directors
12 members

President &
Chairman of the Board of Directors
M Frère

General Manager &
Alternate of the President
R Auboin

Monetary & Economic Department
Economic Adviser
Head of Department
P Jacobsson

European Payments
Union Section[1]
Manager
F G Conolly

Economic Analysis &
Annual Report Preparation
A Rainoni

Statistics & Documentation
F Langer

Banking Department
First Manager &
Head of Banking Department
M van Zeeland

Manager
O Berntsen

H H Mandel D H Macdonald
G Royot

Foreign Exchange
& Gold

Section I
(French & Italian
speaking markets)

Section III
(English speaking
markets)

Section II
(German speaking
markets)

General Secretariat
Secretary General
Head of Department
A Ferrari

Legal Adviser
H Guisan

General
Secretariat
S G Binnerts

Accounting
S E Goodwin

Administration
M Parker

[1] OECD agency function.

10.4 Economic Analysis

The preparation of the Annual Report remained the cornerstone of the Bank's research activity. The Report contained, as in the past, special sections devoted to such topics as the production and distribution of gold, currency markets, price movements, international trade, fiscal and monetary policies, and credit markets. The reviews of developments in individual countries and of various international agreements provided comparative information and analyses not otherwise easily accessible. In addition to the Annual Report, the BIS wrote a number of confidential position papers on various issues of interest to central bankers.[75] The Monetary and Economic Department also provided background material to lectures given by members of the management on the BIS itself, on monetary policy, on money and credit markets, and on international economic cooperation. Jacobsson, a great communicator, continued to enjoy lecturing worldwide, and other managers frequently accepted invitations to speak in public about the BIS and the international economy.

Research and its dissemination was traditionally regarded at the BIS as a tool for central bank cooperation. It created the basis for discussion amongst governors and central bank officials; it also provided an additional incentive to regular participation in the monthly meetings and for the secondment to Basel of promising young employees, particularly from small or peripheral central banks. Ad hoc research was also conducted at the request of individual central banks. Special studies were carried out on Italy, the Netherlands, France, Austria, and Germany as well as on the sterling area.[76] In 1953 the European Coal and Steel Community commissioned the BIS to conduct research into the financing of coal stocks in various European countries.[77]

In 1955, surveying the first 25 Annual Reports, it was easy for Auboin to detect "an unmistakable continuity of ideas and opinions".[78] Continuity ran along three recurring themes – free trade, "sound" money, and international cooperation – as seen through the prism of a nondoctrinaire practical brand of neoclassical orthodoxy. Policy prescriptions stemmed from blending such orthodoxy with a good dose of empirical common sense, drawn from the daily experience of central banking. This characteristically Jacobssonian approach did not change significantly when Baffi and Lutz took over the supervision of research at the BIS. Although both were more sophisticated theorists than Jacobsson, it is likely that neither (albeit for different reasons) was motivated to change the analytical framework underlying the Reports. Lutz, a distinguished German economist, nurtured no sympathy for any of the then-fashionable varieties of Keynesianism. Baffi, more open to the currents of theoretical novelty, was, by virtue of his profession, attracted to the practical policy side of economic analysis; in this respect – as in his endless curiosity, knowledge of several languages, and broad humanistic education – he was similar to Jacobsson. Whatever the reasons, the basic intellectual construction of the Reports did not change until Gilbert's arrival in Basel in 1960.

As mentioned in Chapter 9, the BIS, in a characteristically consistent way, opposed the postwar practice followed by most governments and central banks of holding discount rates constant at a low level. Mostly motivated by political considerations, this practice justified the use of administrative tools to control domestic prices, imports, and capital flows as well as to target inflation, the balance of payments, and exchange rates. The Annual Reports argued tirelessly against such policies as being detrimental to the efficient allocation of resources and thus to productivity growth. From the early 1950s onwards, monetary tools slowly regained their place in both economic thinking and policy making.[79] The change was heralded by the 1951 accord between the U.S. Treasury and the Federal Open Market Committee that ended "ten years of inflexible rates, following seven years of inactive and inflexible policies".[80] In the following years, central banks slowly rediscovered how to successfully operate monetary policy. It was, however, not until 1955 that the BIS declared that flexible monetary policies had "brought an end to the era of rigid credit conditions, which dated back to the depression of the 1930s".[81] Not only had changes to official discount rates become common practice by that time, they were also supplemented by open-market operations, changes in reserve requirements, credit ceilings, and moral suasion by central bankers. The BIS welcomed these developments as much on practical as on theoretical grounds: "Perhaps the greatest advantage of monetary policy is the flexibility with which it can be adjusted to a sudden change in the economic trend". The BIS noted that attempts made after the war to "regulate the economy by means of direct controls on the basis of long-range forecasts and annual plans" had often been upset by unforeseen changes. Moreover, "psychological factors operate too quickly and violently to be forestalled or counteracted by cumbersome methods". Therefore, the BIS argued, "only a more flexible policy, which can be altered, if necessary, several times a year, will give a chance of combining a measure of short-term stability with long-run economic progress".[82]

In the early 1950s, the BIS urged a swift reduction of trade barriers and administrative checks on international payments. It also promoted, primarily in the framework of the EPU, the extension of multilateral settlements.

As progress in both areas became apparent, however, the focus of the Bank's analysis shifted to monetary aggregates and to the danger of inflation.

Price stability, the BIS repeated year after year in its Annual Reports, was a prerequisite for long-term sustainable growth. But in the Bank's view, sound money recommended itself for a more general reason: it was the seal of a well-balanced economy and society. Sound money rested on equilibrium between output and wages, between saving and investment, and between imports and exports; it could not last without prudent and wise management of public finances. More generally, as Jacobsson put it, "great communities, including Athens, Venice and Florence, have always been most anxious to ensure that their currencies are held in the highest respect and are universally accepted".[83]

When Europe's reconstruction was by and large completed, the outbreak of hostilities in Korea triggered new concerns about price inflation. Commodity prices rose sharply in the world markets. In 1951, double-digit inflation was recorded in Japan and France and was alarmingly high (by peacetime standards) in the United States, the United Kingdom, and West Germany. In these circumstances, the BIS warned against the "fatal error to believe that the methods of financing and the controls which had been applied during the second world war could be usefully employed in time of peace, even if it were an 'armed peace' ".[84] The rearmament effort "should steer clear of inflation", which would "weaken the social and economic structure" – a loss of strength that, in the BIS's view, "free countries" could afford less than "those which adhere to a collectivist type of economy".[85]

During the 1955–56 expansion, the BIS again made the point that "economic progress could not have been achieved had not the authorities continued to apply flexible credit policies – which under the prevailing boom conditions meant credit restraint, including higher interest rates".[86] Needless to say, fiscal restraint was also recommended.

The focus on inflation expectations was quite uncommon at the time. Keynes' subtlest theoretical contributions were only superficially incorporated in the almost universally accepted new Keynesian orthodoxy. In a statement that was both remarkably clear and rare in contemporary economic analysis, the BIS noted: "Unfortunately there is still a widespread impression that prices are bound to go on rising. This inflation mentality must be extirpated".[87] A good dose of high interest rates and fiscal retrenchment – the Bank argued – in the presence of the "impressive increase in the supply of goods and services" would kill inflation expectations.

Ex post, the emphasis placed by the BIS and some central bankers on price inflation as opposed to most governments' concern with full employment may seem exaggerated. The system survived the 1950–51 "inflationary shock remarkably well. In the United States the price level was almost stationary for several years in the mid-1950s".[88] Average rates of inflation in Western Europe ranged between 2.5% (West Germany) and about 5% (France and Italy) per annum. When disregarding the inflationary effects of the Korea crisis, these figures were even lower (as low as 1.2% for Germany for the period 1953–59). Most importantly, there was no trend acceleration. Yet, insofar as the BIS reflected its members' opinions, the emphasis on inflation highlighted the feeling amongst central bankers that a return to a division of responsibilities between governments and monetary authorities was needed. Such a split was clearly spelled out at the time of the creation of the Bundesbank in 1957.

Other focal points of the BIS's economic analysis concerned exchange rate stability and international payments. The actual desirability of a fixed–exchange rate regime was never called into question. Milton Friedman's quite compelling intellectual case for floating rates[89] was not officially discussed. Nor was his point that a fixed but adjustable regime represented the worst of both worlds, as speculators were offered great profit opportunities in one-way bets. The point was made clear in 1957 by the huge loss of reserves in the fruitless defence of the exchange rate parity that preceded devaluation of the French franc. The BIS reported the event in a technical, matter-of-fact fashion without discussing its general implications.[90] This is hardly surprising: the desirability of fixed parities was part of the BIS's intellectual tradition, shaped by Norman's view of central banking. Moreover, and more importantly, the soon-to-be-reached convertibility at declared fixed parities within the IMF framework was then questioned by only a few academics, mostly in the United States, but never officially discussed in government circles.[91] National prestige came to be associated with the stability of the currency, and people like Jacobsson could hardly disagree with this view.

On the issue of the adequacy of international liquidity to the needs of rapidly expanding trade, the BIS somehow played down the dollar gap problem. The U.S. balance of payments with Europe was of course closely monitored, and the Annual Reports did not fail to draw attention to the benefits deriving from a reduction of the U.S. trade surplus. In a characteristic way, however, the BIS did not regard the U.S. trade surplus as an overriding problem. On the one hand, the BIS believed that the expansion of IMF reserves, the increase in monetary gold, and an efficient use of reserve currencies could go a long way towards maintaining an adequate level of international liquidity. On the other hand, consistently with its overall economic analysis, the BIS drew attention to the fact that the provision of liquid funds was ultimately a matter of efficient domestic and international credit markets. There were, of course, various technical improvements that needed to be made to financial markets, but these could not yield much fruit in the absence of freer trade, currency convertibility, and the full acceptance by governments in reserve currency countries of responsibility with respect to sound international money. Because international liquidity consisted of U.S. (and, to a small extent, U.K.) liabilities, the working of the system depended "to a large extent on the pursuit by these countries of economic and monetary policies aimed at maintaining the purchasing power of their monetary units, and so preserving confidence, at home and abroad, in their currencies".[92]

10.5   The Birth of the European Payments Union

As far as international payments are concerned, the European Payments Union (EPU) was the single most important, and successful, cooperative effort undertaken in the 1950s. "From 1950 to 1958 the EPU promoted multilateral settlements, encouraged the removal of trade barriers, and cemented the stability of exchange rates. Participating countries agreed to accept the currency of any other member in payments of exports, instantly unsnarling the suffocating tangle of bilateral agreements upon which [Western] Europe's trade had been based. Deficit countries were provided credits to finance temporary trade imbalances, obviating the need to restrict imports and, potentially, employment and growth."[93] The EPU ended with the declaration of current account convertibility for Western European currencies.

The agreement establishing the EPU was signed on 19 September 1950, effective retroactively from 1 July. It was followed, two weeks later, by the decision of member countries to liberalise up to 60% of their mutual trade. The EPU agreement was signed by 18 countries,[94] but its influence also reached out to the overseas monetary areas of the pound sterling, the French and Belgian francs, the guilder, and the escudo. Most bilateral agreements remained formally in force, since the EPU was created precisely as a tool for multilateral compensation of bilateral balances. There were five main technical innovations: (i) bilateral balances were automatically offset, so that each country had one single balance, debtor or creditor, towards the EPU rather than towards its individual members; (ii) balances were partly settled in gold or dollars by debtors to the Union and by the latter to the creditors; (iii) the Union extended credits to debtor countries, drawing from a fund created by surplus balances; (iv) a single unit of account, the U.S. dollar, existed for all payments and credits; and (v) the U.S. Treasury allocated $350 million as a start-up fund to cover temporary gold or dollar shortages in the multilateral settlement.[95] The Union operated within the framework of the OEEC, under the authority of the Council, and was run by a managing board; the BIS acted as agent.[96] The EPU terminated on 29 December 1958.

The first political initiative for the creation of the EPU came from Paul Hoffman, head of the Economic Cooperation Administration (ECA). In August and again in October 1949, Hoffman addressed the heads of delegation and Cabinet members of the OEEC countries in Paris, forcefully advocating "nothing less than the integration[97] of the western European economy [into] a single large market within which quantitative restrictions on the movement of goods, monetary barriers to the flow of payments and eventually all tariff barriers are permanently swept away". Hoffman also pleaded for fiscal and monetary policy cooperation. The resurgence of economic nationalism, he said, would nullify the efforts made under the Marshall Plan, given Europe's precarious dollar position and inadequate reserves.

Seizing the political momentum created by Hoffman, Richard Bissel, the ECA's assistant administrator for program, submitted to the OEEC a proposal for the creation of an intra-European clearing union. The proposal was the fruit of 18 months of drafting and redrafting and of discussion and dispute within the ECA and various U.S. government departments. It reflected U.S. impatience at the failure to find an acceptable formula for freeing intra-European trade from bilateral restrictions. According to Kaplan and Schleiminger, Bissel's proposal was an excellent diplomatic piece: while suiting U.S. purposes, it also accommodated "the divergent interests of the European governments".[98] A few days before submission of the U.S. plan, the OEEC secretariat in Paris also circulated a programme of its own to speed up the freeing of European trade. It proposed a mechanism for the free transferability of European currencies based upon the creation of a pool of such currencies, supplemented by a dollar contribution from the ECA. The money in the pool would be used to settle surpluses and deficits of each member within a certain amount (quota). Deficits exceeding a given country's quota were to be settled in gold or dollars.

Soon after Bissel's presentation, the U.K. government submitted in Paris its own, hastily assembled memorandum reiterating some long-standing positions of His Majesty's government: "retention of its bilateral payments agreements, minimal use of gold in intra-European settlements, the availability of sterling as the vehicle for transferring European currencies, and opposition to any new European institution with power to interfere in the internal policies of member countries".[99]

The OEEC proposal received little governmental attention until the submission of Bissel's memorandum. The latter, in fact, proposed a more effective system of incentives for both debtor and creditor countries to keep their external balance in equilibrium and to use macroeconomic policies towards that end. Moreover, to lure the European governments into the clearing union, the U.S. government offered to allocate ECA dollars in support. Bissel also privately suggested that some description of new trade and payments arrangements in the forthcoming OEEC Second Interim Report would positively impress the U.S. Congress on the eve of its debate on the third year's Marshall Plan appropriation.

A committee of experts[100] – led by Ansiaux, a director of the National Bank of Belgium – submitted on 21 January 1950 to the OEEC Council a draft proposal that took into account both the previous OEEC and Bissel memoranda but took little notice of the U.K. proposal. Besides suggesting that the new body be named the "European Payments Union", the experts proposed a management with strong discretionary powers and the appointment of the BIS as agent for the Union. The experts' system was "harder" than either the secretariat's or Bissel's and very much harder than the one proposed by the United Kingdom. (In the jargon of the time, "harder" meant "less credit".)[101] Moreover, the Americans found that the experts' report put too little pressure on surplus countries to adjust: an old, unresolved issue for fixed–exchange rate monetary systems. At the same time, the scheme asked debtors to assume gold obligations, thus reflecting a time-honoured French and Belgian monetary philosophy. The report, incorporated in the OEEC Second Interim Report, formed the basis for subsequent negotiations.

The main opposition to the EPU came from the United Kingdom, which was backed by the Scandinavian countries. From a pure economic standpoint, the United Kingdom's interests diverged from the Continent's in two main respects: (1) intra-European trade made up a relatively small share of U.K. total trade; and (2) the financial services industry, one of the U.K.'s main staples, was concerned with the role of sterling in international payments. More generally, the United Kingdom's geopolitical status and interests were perceived at the time as being only marginally linked with those of the Continent – a poor, war-torn area with an uncertain economic and political future. The U.K. position was clearly stated by Bevin in a personal message to Acheson: "The principal objective of our policy is to reconcile our position as a world power, as a member of the British Commonwealth, and as a member of the European community. We [therefore] cannot accept obligations in relation to western Europe which would prevent or restrict the implementation of our responsibilities elsewhere".[102] Their 1947 experience notwithstanding, the U.K. authorities were still flirting with the idea of making another attempt at sterling convertibility, which would make their participation in the EPU almost pointless. More important still was the belief that sterling should retain a role as a reserve currency, both for the flow of capital it assured to London and as a bond linking Commonwealth countries to the United Kingdom. Finally, even though London overlooked Europe's immediate economic prospects, concerns existed about competition from a resurgent Germany within a free and multilateral intra-European system.

It is now quite clear that, in the immediate postwar period, the U.K. elites both underrated the political and economic potential of the Continent and overestimated the capability of their country to maintain a leading role in global affairs while at the same time promoting prosperity at home. At the time, U.K. foreign policy, as stated by Bevin, went largely unchallenged – both politically and intellectually[103] – for reasons not difficult to understand. The U.K. public was rightly proud of how the country had emerged victorious from a mortal struggle in which, for 18 momentous months, it had stood alone against the German-led Axis. Why should the United Kingdom not win the peace as it had won the war? Moreover, the whole Commonwealth had closed ranks during the war under U.K. leadership: if colonial ambitions had to be scaled down, it could be hoped that common economic interests would cement political bonds. One must not forget that, at the end of the war, the sterling area – reinforced by the 1932 Ottawa Agreements – still accounted for almost half the world's trade. Even from a purely economic perspective, it was not at all obvious then that the burden of the sterling area would eventually outweigh its benefits. In the cultural and political climate of the time and with the information then available, it is not surprising that a bipartisan consensus existed as to the compatibility of domestic growth with an international monetary role. London was therefore reluctant to tie its future to that of the Continent and thus wanted the Union to be as loose as possible. The Scandinavian countries had long felt that their economic interests were inherently bound to the United Kingdom's, and they allied themselves to it throughout the EPU negotiations in the spring of 1950.

On the other side of the Channel, the main Western Continental countries were busy weaving closer bonds amongst themselves that would soon materialise in the creation of the Coal and Steel Community and, a few years later, in the Treaty of Rome. Each of the six countries had specific interests of its own, but none of them advanced major objections to the EPU project. Italy and Belgium were net intra-European creditors while running large dollar deficits. This was also the trade position of West Germany (the so-called Bi-zone) until the autumn of 1949, when the situation began to change. In any case, Germany's role in the negotiations was restrained while it tried to gain as much acceptance as possible in European circles.

Italy, which ran a substantial surplus with the United Kingdom, wanted to continue using its sterling balances to settle payments with those European countries with which it ran a deficit. Otherwise, "its political leaders were in the forefront of the European integration movement and sympathetic to the idea of a new European financial institution".[104] Belgium had already been obliged to extend credits to its bilateral trading partners in order to open foreign markets to its exports. Frère, the governor of its central bank, was quite suspicious of the EPU scheme, fearing that Belgium would be obliged to extend even more credit to Europe and thereby undermine the tight monetary policy he pursued even in the face of open U.S. criticism. On the other hand, Paul van Zeeland, the minister of foreign affairs, supported the whole idea of tighter European integration while at the same time appreciating – more clearly than Frère – Belgium's longer-run commercial interests in Europe. Ansiaux, the chairman of the experts' committee, was on van Zeeland's side; however, he negotiated a system entailing as little credit and as much dollar and gold payments as possible. France did the same, maintaining its time-honoured attachment to specie as the main basis for international settlements.

Throughout the spring and summer of 1950, negotiators at the OEEC headquarters in Paris were busy finding a workable compromise among diverging interests that would allow the swift launch of the EPU. Given the position of participating countries just outlined, the two main contentious (and connected) issues were the role of sterling and the desirable amount of credit to be extended to deficit countries. An agreement was found in a relatively short period of time. In sharp contrast to 1931, 1933, and 1936 – when the short-sighted pursuit of narrowly perceived national interests made agreement impossible or, as in the case of the Tripartite Agreement, volatile and short-lived – the EPU negotiations yielded a stable and efficient cooperative solution. This was due to a number of factors, the most important of which was the U.S. determination to make the Europeans agree. Hence the American government did not hesitate to wield all its influence at the negotiating table. At the time, there was broad consensus among U.S. policy makers that their country's interests would be well served by a strong Europe that was capable of buoyant growth after the end of the Marshall Plan. Towards that end they deemed it essential to create a cooperative environment, fully inclusive of Germany, in which trade and payments restrictions would be eliminated.

Negotiations, routinely conducted by an "inner group" of experts,[105] did not start until after the U.K. elections of February 1950, which confirmed the Labour Party in office. The starting positions saw the United Kingdom and the Continental countries on two opposite sides. The U.K. position rested on four main points: (i) maintenance of all existing bilateral sterling arrangements; (ii) settlement of balances primarily by credit, with gold being used only exceptionally; (iii) the right to impose discriminatory trade restrictions against structural creditors; and (iv) no interference by the EPU with U.K. domestic policies. Most Continentals, in contrast, were keen on giving gold payments a major role as a way of inducing balance of payments discipline. The division reflected not only the international position of the United Kingdom and the Continental countries but also the U.K. propensity to use a panoply of controls on trade and foreign exchange, rather than fiscal and monetary policy, in the pursuit of macroeconomic objectives. The United States, as we saw, was primarily interested in bringing an end to bilateral trade and payments agreements and trade restrictions while at the same time including the United Kingdom in the new arrangement. On gold and credit the United States took the middle ground between London and Brussels, the strongest advocate of gold settlements.

Readers interested in the technicalities of the debate are referred to the detailed account provided by Kaplan and Schleiminger[106] of the negotiations that took place in Paris during the "long, hot spring of 1950". Here it is sufficient to note that at a certain point it seemed necessary to create special rules for the United Kingdom that, for all practical purposes, would make it *not* a full member of the Union. Acheson, however, managed to convince Bevin to accept full membership. He assured his U.K. counterpart that the resumption of trade restrictions would be contemplated in extreme cases and that special provisions would be made for sterling balances. Moreover, the United States guaranteed a protection against U.K. gold losses. The issue of gold payments versus credit was solved by the United States granting Belgium more direct (rather than conditional) aid under the Marshall Plan. It was thus U.S. diplomacy, backed by U.S. money, that made the difference in producing a swift conclusion of the negotiations by the end of June 1950. This is not to say that the Europeans were unwilling to compromise for the sake of the common good. On the contrary, the result was also due to their skilful and bona fide participation in the negotiations and to their belief in the desirability of the EPU. Even so, in a game with so many players, a stalemate or a suboptimal outcome is the probable result in the absence of a broker able and willing both to compensate for individual losses and to guarantee the stability of the final compromise. The United States accepted that role and performed it convincingly, not shying from its responsibilities as leader of the Western world.

Gaitskell, a tough negotiator for the United Kingdom, eventually acknowledged that a new economic system had been created, "which is definitely going to make a difference, whatever they may say".[107]

10.6   Central Banks, the BIS, and the EPU

The BIS's attitude towards the EPU turned out to be fairly ambiguous. On the one hand, the EPU made greater use than did the earlier multilateral payment schemes of the technical skills and banking organisation of the BIS, enhancing the Bank's visibility as the locus for European monetary cooperation. On the other hand, the cumbersome settlement machinery of the Union was inconsistent with the free-trade policy preached by the BIS since the end of the war, which implied convertibility and nondiscrimination between trading areas.

Jacobsson, the tireless preacher of BIS's economic philosophy, was quite critical of the EPU. In a public lecture delivered in 1952 at Christ Church College, Oxford,[108] he listed the achievements and weaknesses of the EPU. Among the former he included the avoidance of trade disruption at the outbreak of the Korean War, the realisation by member countries of the importance of prudent monetary policy, and their willingness to submit their actions to policy review within the OEEC. It is interesting that he gave no credit to the EPU for being a second-best solution to convertibility via substituting multilateral for bilateral settlements. Among the Union's shortcomings, Jacobsson included its inability to deal with balance of payments crises, its being regional rather than global, and – interestingly – the fact that trade financing was "too much in the hands of central banks" rather than being provided by financial markets at large. Jacobsson's main conclusion was that "the EPU [was] not good enough as a permanent arrangement [and] ought to be replaced as soon as possible by a more international system based on free exchange markets and convertible currencies".[109] Auboin's view of the EPU,[110] though expressed in a politically more acceptable way, in substance coincided with Jacobsson's. General Manager Auboin was careful in saying that, while it was far from being a global institution, the EPU nevertheless incorporated the sterling and franc zones encompassing most of the international trade in raw materials. He also recognised the usefulness of the Union in virtually eliminating the shortcomings of bilateral agreements. At the same time, Auboin repeated Jacobsson's pleas for "sound" money and public finance, for free trade, and, most of all, for a swift introduction of free currency convertibility.

Over the years, and particularly after the end of the war, the BIS had developed an economic policy stance of its own quite independent from that of individual central banks, even if some of them were undoubtedly sympathetic to Jacobsson's economic precepts.[111] The BIS's assessment of the advantages and disadvantages of the EPU did not, therefore, necessarily reflect the prevailing view among the Board member central banks. Nevertheless, the initial reaction of the Board to the BIS's involvement in the new multilateral payments system was cautious: the Bank would be prepared to act as banker of the EPU but "could not accept responsibilities in the management of the scheme".[112] The implicit reference here was to the proposal aired by Ansiaux that the EPU be managed by a board consisting of eight central bank governors. "The governors bristled at the thought. They had a positive distaste for establishing a European monetary institution that they feared might become a permanent rival to the BIS."[113] Moreover, accepting managerial responsibilities would imply authority to censure policies of individual countries, an unthinkable break with the unwritten rules of their club and a threat to good working relations with governments.

At the informal meeting of the governors in Basel in March 1950, Auboin circulated a proposal that was well received by most participants: the idea was to maintain all existing bilateral agreements and to multilateralise only existing bilateral credits. The ECA contribution would pay for two thirds of debtor countries' deficits while the remaining third would be settled by whatever means of payment were available in the market. The system would operate for a maximum of two years. The scheme was only apparently in contrast with the BIS's economic policy stance favouring the end of government controls and free currency convertibility. By proposing a short-term solution involving a fair amount of free market settlements, Auboin and the BIS Board wanted to avoid the creation of an institution that might prove difficult to close, favouring instead a swift move to convertibility. Politically, however, the governors' proposal was a nonstarter. It would certainly have irritated the U.S. negotiators then trying hard to broker an agreement between the diverging interests of European governments. In fact, Auboin's document never reached the Paris negotiators' table.[114]

Eventually, a government-appointed board chaired by Guido Carli[115] took charge of running the EPU. Central banks and the BIS nevertheless played a substantial part in financing the scheme and making it workable. Conolly, as BIS representative, participated in the EPU board meetings in Paris. The monthly meetings in Basel provided convenient opportunities for discussing EPU matters, both technical and political. There were, as we shall see, frequent occasions for crisis management, in which central bankers and their institution in Basel became deeply involved. Convertibility also soon became the subject matter of many informal governors' meetings.

Besides providing its well-established forum for confidential exchanges among central bankers from the EPU countries, the BIS made a significant technical contribution to the success of the EPU. The Bank had by then accumulated unrivalled experience in performing trustee and agent functions, a nonnegligible part of its original mission.[116] In performing such functions for the IEPS, the BIS had established a system for cross-reporting by central banks of their own payments balances, which provided the technical basis for the EPU network.

Article 21 of the EPU agreement stipulated that the agent would report monthly on the "execution of the operations and the management of the fund" (i.e., the Union's assets). The agent was also responsible for the administrative and banking operations of the Union. "Administrative" referred to the clearing and settlement of bilateral balances, while "banking" consisted primarily of managing the liquid assets side of the EPU operations.[117] A small staff, separate from the ordinary Bank structure, was set up to take care of the agent's functions.[118] The BIS became the centre for operational instructions to the central banks and for the EPU accounting, while actual transactions were performed by the central banks themselves. The BIS also advised on the investment of the Union's liquid assets and on the many problems arising whenever changes were suggested to the Union's operating rules. Over the years, an excellent working relationship developed between the OEEC and the BIS.

10.7   The EPU in Operation

At its very first meeting, on 20 October 1950, the EPU managing board[119] was faced with a severe payments crisis involving the Federal Republic of Germany, created only a year earlier but already a major trading country in Europe. The combined effect of rapid industrial output growth,[120] trade liberalisation, and the payments facilities provided by the EPU itself had hugely expanded Germany's demand for imports. At the same time, a significant shift had taken place in the geographical origin of German imports in favour of EPU member countries.[121] It was thus clear to the EPU board that, at the current rate, Germany's deficit with Western European countries would soon exhaust the Federal Republic's quota of credit allowed by the Union's rules, in which case imports would have to be paid for in gold or convertible currencies.

Since the EPU board could not reach a consensus on how to manage the crisis, the chairman decided to seek a fresh appraisal of the situation. At short notice, two independent experts were invited to visit Germany and report on the situation to the next board meeting, in two weeks' time. The experts were Alec Cairncross and Per Jacobsson.[122] One could not imagine more different personalities than those of the ascetic Scotsman and the Swedish bon vivant.[123] A Keynesian,[124] previously an adviser to the U.K.

Labour government, and at the time economic adviser to the OEEC, Cairn-cross did not sympathise with Jacobsson's economics. Both men, how-ever, enjoyed well-established international reputations, and the EPU board hoped that the German government would be impressed by recommenda-tions supported by economists of opposite persuasions.[125] The board's trust turned out to be well placed. While their "respective methods of work dif-fered so greatly" that it took longer than anticipated to "come within sight of a completed document",[126] the two nevertheless reached unanimous conclu-sions. "This", wrote Cairncross, "was to some extent a fluke, since, in other circumstances, I could imagine a real difference in views. It did not seem to us, however, that credit restriction, liberalisation and increasing eco-nomic activity and employment would prove incompatible by the spring of 1951".[127]

The two experts came to the joint conclusion that the German economy was developing on a sound basis and that the balance of payments prob-lems derived partly from policy mistakes, not difficult to correct, and partly from accidental factors.[128] Jacobsson's appraisal was somewhat ideologi-cally charged, as he saw the opportunity for a test case of his conceptions about the use of monetary and fiscal policies. Cairncross simply regarded the situation as a straightforward liquidity crisis in an otherwise healthy econ-omy. However, they both predicted that, given appropriate policy measures and additional credit from the EPU, Germany's external position would get worse until January 1951 and improve thereafter. It was a bold gamble on which the two experts pinned their reputation, so much so that for a while Jacobsson felt nervous to the point of being "heart-broken".[129] In the end, however, the experts' analysis proved to be correct.

Urged on by Jacobsson, President Vocke convinced the German central bank council to raise the official discount rate from 4% to 6% – overruling Chancellor Adenauer, who exceptionally participated in the council's crisis meeting.[130] In addition, the German authorities increased the reserve re-quirements for commercial banks, placed a ceiling on credit, and imposed a cash deposit in Deutsche marks on importers requiring foreign curren-cies.[131] The experts' report to the EPU[132] board recommended that, given the policy measures already taken or promised by Germany, the Union should extend extra credit to the country, thus avoiding the reintroduction of trade restrictions that would hurt the whole European economy. Cairn-cross also stressed the political value of a cooperative European effort and the goodwill it would create in Germany. At the beginning of November the board conditionally[133] granted new EPU credit to the Federal Republic. It should be noted that it took only two weeks to complete the whole process of assessing the situation, finding a solution acceptable to a large group of countries, and granting international credit. What an extraordinary contrast to international lending in the 1931 crisis!

As anticipated, Germany's balance of payments deficit was not reduced at once.[134] Moreover, statistics were slow to come in and so the success of the manoeuvre remained in question until the spring. In February, the situation seemed so bleak that most feared that the special credit granted by the EPU, supposed to last to the end of May, would be exhausted by the middle of March. On the advice of the central bank, the German government temporarily suspended import liberalisation. Some EPU member countries even feared default on the credit thus far extended to Germany. In a situation not contemplated by the EPU rules, the OEEC stepped in to propose to the German government a scheme for granting new import licences accommodating the respective interests of the other member countries. At the same time, the EPU indicated its dissatisfaction with the implementation of German policies to restrict demand. Typically, a situation was developing where domestic authorities considered the measures too harsh and foreign creditors too mild, jeopardising international cooperation. At the BIS monthly meetings in February and March, the atmosphere was so tense that some participants did not even talk to Jacobsson. Friends begged him to reconsider his advice and "save his career and reputation".[135] Finally, at the end of March and exactly as Cairncross and Jacobsson had predicted, Germany's trade position within the EPU showed a surplus even before import restrictions had made an appreciable impact. Surpluses continued in the subsequent months and, by the end of May, Germany repaid the EPU special credit in full. At the beginning of 1952, Germany resumed its programme of trade liberalisation. German surpluses rather than deficits would be a European problem in the years and decades to follow.

The management of the crisis by the international community had a long-lasting favourable impact on Germany. "The senior civil servants", wrote Kaplan and Schleiminger, "had grown up in a Schachtian environment, with its emphasis on tough bargaining for bilateral advantages in trade. They were deeply impressed that Germany had been granted special credit – and astounded that it was permitted to reintroduce import restrictions without any retaliation from OEEC partner countries".[136] The successful management of a payments crisis at the very beginning of its existence also earned the EPU's young managing board and its chairman, Guido Carli, enormous respect.[137]

Apart from the German crisis, other storms threatened the EPU throughout its existence and particularly during its early years. The Korean War, which started in June 1950, had repercussions on trade flows, prices, and the allocation of Marshall aid. Rearmament was the new priority in order to

"close the gap" with the Soviet bloc. The ECA was renamed the Mutual Security Administration (MSA), and aid funds were partly redirected to buy
military equipment from Europe. World prices of raw materials increased,
fuelling domestic inflation. Swift reallocation of resources among sectors
took place. All this resulted in greater trade and balance of payments volatility, which the EPU was able to accommodate quite effectively. In fact, the
EPU mechanism was designed precisely to cope with large fluctuations in
trade surpluses and deficits. In spite of endless speculative rumours about
changes in exchange rates, none occurred during the first volatile years of
the EPU's life.

The management of the crises that followed that of 1950–51 highlighted
the cooperative spirit created by the EPU framework.[138] Cooperation was
not always effective and successful but, in retrospect, it can be said that Europe enjoyed more international monetary stability during the 1950s than
in most other decades of the twentieth century. One of the reasons for that
lies in the EPU mechanism, which somehow obliged its board to press for
adjustment both by deficit and surplus countries, as there was a limit to
the accumulation of credit by a single country within the European system.
Thus, by May 1952, the Netherlands' surplus was so great that the EPU board
applied its moral suasion to obtain a relaxation of the restrictive Dutch monetary policies, prompting a decline in the country's EPU surplus.[139] In the
same respect, Belgium presented a politically more delicate problem: it was
precisely its position as structural net creditor in intra-European trade that
had put its participation in the EPU in doubt up to the last moment. Having
achieved internal price stability earlier than most other European countries
(with the exception of Italy), the Belgian government liberalised trade and
lifted dollar-area import quotas sooner than others, while maintaining external payments equilibrium, at the cost of slower investment growth and
higher unemployment. Both the OEEC and the ECA felt that Belgium could
afford to grow faster, but Brussels turned a deaf ear to their recommendations. In the summer of 1951, Belgium was close to exhausting its creditor
quota within the EPU and requested that further surpluses be paid in gold
or dollars. The EPU board asked for a temporary increase in the quota, a
symmetrical move to the extension of temporary extra credit to deficit countries. From July 1951 to March 1952, the Belgian government reluctantly
acquiesced to the board's request, but neither party found the arrangement
satisfactory: it was clear that Belgium could neither extend indefinite credit
to its European trading partners nor expect to obtain substantial dollar payments from them. Following an all-too-familiar script, debtors argued that
Belgium should adopt a more expansionary domestic policy stance while

Brussels called for a curtailment of EPU credit to countries that failed to take adequate corrective measures for their deficits. Finally, a compromise involving an increase in gold payments to Belgium was reached when the EPU board found itself with more liquid assets in hand. Even if in this case the EPU's moral suasion did not succeed in getting Brussels to reflate, both parties were willing to cooperate and compromise – first by agreeing on a quota increase then on larger gold payments. A solution to the problem posed to the Union by Belgium's surpluses was found without trade disruptions or a slowing of progress towards intra-European trade liberalisation.

After the mid-1950s, the most complex problem of the EPU (besides decision making on convertibility, discussed in the next section) was France's continuous balance of payments difficulties. Initially, the situation dragged on with a mix of credits, including substantial ones from the IMF, and half-hearted domestic policy measures. By the end of 1956, France's deficit with the EPU exceeded $1 billion, and Paris increased trade restrictions. The EPU board met exceptionally at the BIS in Basel in June 1957 to discuss the measures taken by the French government and the extension of additional credit.[140] The Paris decision to suspend trade liberalisation was a matter of grave concern to the other EPU members. The Algerian question further aggravated the situation. At the informal governors' meeting at the BIS in April 1958, "everybody … was extremely gloomy about France, both politically and financially".[141] In May, General de Gaulle came to power. At the very moment that earlier policy measures, prompted by the EPU board, were beginning to take effect, the new government, advised by Jacques Rueff, adopted an even tighter fiscal and monetary stance.[142] The Rueff programme was topped by a return to trade liberalisation and a devaluation of the French franc by 14.8%. The devaluation took effect on 29 December 1958, the very day the EPU was officially wound up.[143] The BIS offered discreet support by making short-term facilities available to the Bank of France on a large scale.[144]

Private discussions among central bankers about the possibility that sterling might be devalued also took place from time to time during the 1950s, "but without indication that it had ever been seriously considered by the [British] government".[145]

10.8 Convertibility and the European Monetary Agreement

If the EPU was a substitute for early convertibility, was it really necessary? In its guarded and prudent central-banker prose, the BIS indicated that it was possible and advisable to move directly from the clearing system of the late 1940s to convertibility of Western European currencies. Once the EPU was created, the Bank remained convinced that its life should be limited and convertibility swiftly introduced.[146] It must be also added that membership in the IMF and OEEC entailed a general commitment to convertibility that many felt should be honoured as soon as possible. Forty years later, Eichengreen argued that "most of the conditions for the viability of current account convertibility appear to have been met when the European countries opted instead for the EPU".[147] If early convertibility was, under given circumstances, technically feasible, was it also politically possible? And was it, in any case, the best solution for Western Europe?

To answer the first question, let us briefly see how negotiations on convertibility proceeded in the 1950s.[148] The ink was still fresh on the EPU agreement when thoughts turned to convertibility in government circles in the United States and in the United Kingdom. Although U.S. diplomacy had played a key role in the establishment of the EPU, it was nevertheless clear to many in Washington that the European arrangement ran counter to the Bretton Woods philosophy and, more important still, that it protected local producers by creating discriminatory barriers to North American goods. The United Kingdom, on the other hand, had not abandoned plans for early convertibility of the pound and hoped to move independently of Continental countries, letting each of them follow at its own pace. London's main motivation was the re-establishment of sterling as a reserve and trading currency. Convertibility also gained favour on the Continent, although there it was mainly seen as a free-trade tool. Thus, while consensus existed about the desirability of convertible currencies, aims and priorities differed considerably.

The opening gambit came from Butler, the chancellor in the new U.K. Conservative government,[149] who in early 1952 proposed a rapid dash to sterling convertibility on a floating-rate basis.[150] If realised, the plan – codenamed "Operation Robot" – would have brought the EPU to an end before its second birthday. Churchill, however, took seriously his advisers' warning of the economic and political consequences of the plan, possibly reminiscent of those of the 1925 move to gold.[151] In February the Cabinet turned Robot down.[152] Butler himself admitted that killing the EPU would have damaging effects on the European economy and that the United Kingdom had more to lose than any other country. In mid-1952 there were no U.K. objections to the extension of the EPU for an additional twelve months. Later that year, the OEEC toyed with a U.K. proposal for an Atlantic payments union (APU), which attracted the interest of Secretary General Robert Marjolin, but "consideration in Washington was neither serious nor prolonged".[153]

A modified Robot plan, known as the "Collective Approach to Convertibility", was prepared for submission to the Commonwealth countries. It envisaged sterling convertibility for nonresidents of the sterling area, unbounded floating rates, and the involvement (besides the Commonwealth) of the United States, France, Germany, and the Benelux countries. Its name notwithstanding, the approach was not quite "collective" because London would be free to choose the date when sterling would become convertible. In spite of the improved balance of payments conditions, the implementation of the new scheme needed substantial U.S. and IMF support. A high-profile U.K. delegation[154] travelled to Washington in March 1953 but found it impossible to convince their U.S. counterparts that the time was ripe for sterling convertibility. The belief in the U.S. government was that the move was premature, given the overall conditions of the U.K. economy. Moreover, the administration felt that Congress would not grant the necessary resources. Back in Europe, the U.K. plan was presented to the OEEC, where everyone emphasised the objective of freeing intra-European trade, which would probably be jeopardised by early convertibility. Given the level of their reserves – equivalent on average to three months of imports – the Continentals were not ready to dispense with the EPU, which was successfully delivering trade liberalisation, their foremost priority.

The dash for early convertibility thus ended in frustration for the U.K. government. The move, however, was not entirely fruitless in that it put convertibility on governments' agendas as a proposition to be realised in the not-too-distant future. In June 1952, a panel of distinguished economists[155] told the OEEC Council that, if treated as a concern of practical policy and not put off until doomsday, convertibility would exercise a beneficial influence on domestic policy making. At the same time, the EPU managing board was mandated to study convertibility.

Over the following three years, study and negotiation were closely intertwined: a common path to convertibility was defined while at the same time the EPU's viability improved. The rapid growth of European output, employment, and trade, the building up of reserves, and the shrinking of the dollar gap all helped smooth the process.

Carli,[156] "a skilled economist with finely honed analytical powers", called a convertibility that tolerated widespread quantitative import restrictions a "caricature".[157] Doubts were also raised about the feasibility of confining convertibility to current account transactions. Both these propositions engendered reasonable doubt concerning whether convertibility was likely to occur in the immediate future; hence they were less acceptable to impatient, go-it-alone U.K. than to Continental board members, who favoured a gradual institutional approach. The two positions came closer when discussing fixed exchange rates, as both felt the IMF's narrow margins untenable. The entire board also agreed that it would be difficult for a convertible currency to remain in the EPU without adopting the Swiss double standard,[158] an arrangement that did not reflect what the United Kingdom appeared to have in mind.

At the end of 1952, the OEEC ministers instructed the EPU board to report on the renewal of the Union in mid-1953. In keeping with the majority's gradual approach, the board seized this opportunity to recommend improvements to the EPU that would also be appropriate in preparing for convertibility. Suggestions that imports from the dollar area should be gradually liberalised and that the role of gold and dollars in the monthly settlements be increased met with opposition from the United Kingdom,[159] backed by the Norwegian representatives.[160] At the November 1953 BIS governors' meeting in Basel "there was considerable misgiving about the British attitude", as all other governors felt that the United Kingdom's reluctance to increase gold settlements was inconsistent with its professed objective of convertibility.[161] A stalemate ensued that meant the renewal of the EPU in 1953 went through without substantial changes to its rules.

Towards the end of 1953, the deadlock began to be broken on the initiative of the creditor countries Germany, Belgium, and the Netherlands. Concerned about the magnitude of their credits within the EPU system, these countries proposed a system for repayment of long-standing debts that entailed, in essence, an increase in gold and dollar settlements within the Union. The creditor countries threatened to leave the EPU unless their demands were met. At the same time, they sweetened the pill by suggesting a complicated technical device by which countries that repaid debts and subsequently ran surpluses could in their turn be paid in gold or dollars.[162] France and Italy were vulnerable to the threat of EPU liquidation, since they would then be liable to repay their debts (of $300 million and $100 million, respectively) in three years. Italy, having liberalised 100% of its intra-European trade as early as 1952, also feared being forced to retreat from such a bold stance. The position of the United Kingdom was even weaker, as it would have to repay about $550 million.

The creditors' initiative got negotiations moving again. France and the United Kingdom offered repayment schemes over a period of seven years, obviously unsatisfactory to creditors. Discussion ensued at all levels – both bilateral and multilateral – within the OEEC, a forum preferred by the United Kingdom. Primarily, however, the matter fell back on the EPU managing board. The spring of 1954 saw European economic cooperation at its best. "The result was a continuous advance toward a broader package of EPU reforms. The Union was refurbished, as well as renewed. The eventual package went beyond the earlier patchwork of self-serving proposals, achieving a better balance of interests between creditors and debtors. In the process, emphasis was refocused on the viability of the Union itself rather than the interests of individual members. The end product was also a technically simpler arrangement." [163]

The final agreement contained a voluntary repayment scheme that was accepted by all creditors and debtors except for Greece, Turkey, and Iceland. Individual debtors agreed to repay in instalments from 60% to 90% of their outstanding debts, with substantial down payments. The EPU paid an additional amount of dollars to creditors out of its own assets, the net value of which still remained well above the original U.S. capital contribution. Towards the end of the negotiations, the secretariat secured, in the interest of the Union, an agreement that all future debts and credits would be settled on a flat fifty-fifty basis in gold and credit. Besides simplifying the Union's working mechanism, the decision assured its future liquidity. What mattered most, the increase in gold and dollar settlements was also a step towards convertibility. In fact, one year later in April 1955, on reaching an amicable agreement on a further extension of the EPU, the board almost unanimously recommended an increase in gold settlements from 50% to 75%.

In this cooperative climate, a compromise on convertibility could also be reached between the United Kingdom, still keen on moving fast, and the more gradual Continentals. In June 1955, upon renewing the EPU for a further year, the ministerial council of the OEEC decided that the Union could come to an end at any time upon request by member countries holding at least 50% of the quotas, subject to the condition that a European fund should then begin to operate. A European monetary agreement (EMA) for the creation of that fund was signed on 5 August 1955, to come into force upon termination of the EPU. [164]

The EMA provided for the creation of a European fund and a multilateral system of settlements, complementary to each other and aimed at maintaining economic cooperation among European countries upon the termination of the EPU. The fund, [165] modelled on the IMF blueprint, would supply short-term credit to member countries in temporary balance of payments difficulties in order to avoid trade-restricting measures. The OEEC would be given the role of making binding policy recommendations to countries seeking credit from the fund. Under the multilateral system of settlements, each participating country would assume three obligations: (i) establish buying and selling ratios for its currency in terms of U.S. dollars; (ii) grant interim finance to any other member within agreed limits; and (iii) settle debts and accept the settlement of claims within the system in U.S. dollars.

The new EPU rules and the EMA charted a smooth course to convertibility. The United Kingdom could now take the lead at a moment of its choosing, and most other OEEC countries would probably follow – encouraged also by the safety net provided by the fund to weaker currencies. The Continentals, aware as they were of the weakness of the U.K. economy, felt assured that the approach to convertibility would be collective and cautious. At the same time, they yielded to the metamorphosis of their cooperative institution, knowing that it would no longer make sense in a convertible currency world. The OEEC would necessarily become less important. The IMF and the GATT would take over as coordinating bodies in international payments, trade, and macroeconomic policies. The prospective loss of a valuable cooperative European institution was regarded with less apprehension in 1955 than it had been a few years earlier, as countries keen on closer economic integration were by then actively negotiating on the establishment of the Common Market.

It took another three years for convertibility to be realised. During that period, the EPU managed a few difficult crises, notably that of the French franc (described in the previous section). Finally, by midsummer 1958, the preconditions for sterling convertibility seemed to have been met. The stabilisation programme initiated a year earlier was finally bearing fruit. The U.K. fiscal deficit was shrinking. In 1958, a hefty balance of payments surplus was coupled with an encouraging 15% increase in the value of exports to the United States. Reserves, up 78% from 1957, now amounted to $2.85 billion, equivalent to over ten months' worth of imports.[166] Thus it seemed that the Bank of England's long-standing aspiration to open up foreign exchange markets in London could at last be satisfied. At the same time, by mid-1958, the step of officially proclaiming convertibility seemed to be mostly symbolic for countries like Germany, Belgium, the Netherlands, Switzerland, and Italy. The Continentals nevertheless remained cautious on political grounds. They preferred a continuation of the EPU for a while, with 100% gold settlements. In particular, Calvet for France and Carli for Italy argued that the replacement of the EPU with the EMA, a much less satisfactory cooperation tool, would further open up the divide between the Common Market and the rest of Europe. However, the U.K. government insisted on going ahead, and France – having decided on devaluation – finally supported the move. On 27 December 1958, the EEC countries and the United Kingdom officially notified the OEEC that they wished to invoke the termination clause of the agreement. The EPU board then took, on 29 December, the technical decisions necessary to liquidate the Union and transfer its assets to the European fund, mandating the BIS (as agent) to carry them out. At the same time, the board was reconstituted, with identical membership, as the Board of Management of the European Monetary Agreement.[167]

The EPU, a relatively little-known institution outside policy-making and academic circles, ended in triumph, a fate not shared by many other similar bodies. The hallmark of its success was the end of trade and foreign exchange discrimination in Europe, a goal that eight years earlier had seemed to many to be a generation away. Official currency convertibility was introduced in all the OEEC countries with the exception of Iceland, Spain, and Turkey. Only Germany and Belgium, however, allowed convertibility also for capital movements. In the other countries, "limited convertibility" applied, meaning that nonresidents were allowed to convert local currencies into dollars (but not into gold), at a given official price, for current account payments only.[168] But that was what IMF participation required: Bretton Woods allowed controls on capital movements and, for many countries, full capital account convertibility would be two or three decades away. When the EMA came into existence, the BIS assumed responsibility for the execution of all its financial operations until the agreement was terminated in 1972.[169]

Reverting to the questions asked at the beginning of this section, the long and complex negotiations – which encompassed almost the whole decade – indicate that an early rush to convertibility would have met with insurmountable political obstacles. Those within the U.K. establishment who were keen on reinstating sterling as a reserve currency, a goal for which convertibility was a necessary precondition, were long unable to overcome objections at home and stern opposition from the United States, while most Continental countries viewed the move with suspicion or scepticism. The latter was inspired by the apparent weakness of the U.K. balance of payments condition. Although Eichengreen is probably right in saying that the narrow technical conditions for convertibility already existed in 1950, most observers at the time did not seem to share this view. It is quite possible that technical judgements hid broader considerations inspired by prudence and by the desire to gauge the domestic and international repercussions of each step. If this was the case, it only reinforces the notion that the political economy of convertibility required all the time that the process actually took to yield fruit.

Whatever judgement one may form on the political feasibility of early convertibility, did the delay – whether or not politically justified – entail missed opportunities for Europe? How damaging was it to the Old Continent that its policy makers took such a long time to agree on convertibility?

The simplest answer to these questions is that early convertibility would probably have been a mistake if its viability had required either tighter monetary and fiscal policies than those pursued under the EPU umbrella or sizeable currency devaluations. In the first case, the counterfactual long-run benefits of sacrificing medium-term growth and employment on the altar of convertibility are not so obvious, and social costs might have been large. Devaluation likewise "implied a worsening of the terms of trade, reducing the size of the pie to be shared out among competing interest groups".[170]

The EPU worked like an embryonic customs union, at least as far as quantitative trade discrimination was concerned. As such, it both created intra-European trade and diverted trade to and from the rest of the world (mainly North America). In its first phase, roughly up to 1955, intra-European trade was rapidly liberalised while scarce dollars could all be used to buy U.S. goods. At the same time, an "infant industry" case can be made for protection of European manufacturers during reconstruction. Once the advantages of economies of scale had been reintroduced, Europe was ready for broader international competition, and extra-European trade was also liberalised in the second half of the 1950s. As for price distortions, Triffin, Eichengreen, and others argue that the scope for competition within Europe was so large – given postwar levels of protection of national economies and the size of the EPU area – that price distortions were relatively small. The EPU therefore created large opportunities for efficiency gains from arbitrage while at the same time delivering terms-of-trade benefits from stable exchange rates, made possible by trade discrimination against U.S. goods. Early convertibility, even if technically possible, was probably not in the best interests of postwar Europe.

Finally, the contribution made by the EPU to social cohesion in postwar Europe must not be overlooked. According to Eichengreen, "By turning terms of trade in Europe's favour, the EPU buttressed the contribution of the Marshall Plan, moderating the sacrifices in terms of living standards required to reach agreement on income distribution. Once this agreement was reached, macroeconomic stabilisation could follow and with it decontrol and deregulation. This made possible the continued operation of market forces, sustaining economic recovery".[171]

10.9   Eastern European Central Banks and the BIS

During the 1950s, the BIS's attention was mostly focused on Western Europe, but the Bank's prewar customer base in Eastern Europe did not entirely fade out of the picture. While these countries – Albania, Bulgaria, Czechoslovakia, Hungary, Poland, Romania, and Yugoslavia – either did not join or withdrew from the Bretton Woods institutions, their central banks retained membership in the BIS.[172] The BIS therefore offered one of the few available opportunities for direct contacts between Western and Eastern European monetary policy makers,[173] a fact that did not escape Western diplomats' attention, as witnessed by a June 1946 internal memorandum of the U.K. Foreign Office. The BIS, it read, "is a unique meeting place of East and West, and from our point of view might well become a valuable source of information about, and influence over, financial developments in Eastern Europe".[174]

For many years, the BIS Annual General Meeting was the most important event at which central bankers from centrally planned economies could meet with their Western counterparts, often on a bilateral basis. At the same time, the BIS provided Eastern European central banks with valuable services such as short-term deposit facilities, custody over gold holdings, and swap operations.[175]

During the 1950s, Comecon[176] countries also took an interest in the machinery of the European Payments Union, and the conclusion of the European Monetary Agreement led them to explore the possibilities of a multilateral compensation scheme between East and West modelled on the EPU. Such a scheme was discussed in 1955–56 in the context of the Economic Commission for Europe, based at the United Nations office in Geneva. In October 1956, a draft joint declaration on the multilateralisation of payments in intra-European (East–West) trade was adopted by a majority of the countries represented in the Economic Commission for Europe.[177] The multilateral compensation of trade balances would be the responsibility of the central banks involved. At the suggestion of some socialist countries (in particular, Hungary), the BIS was invited to act as agent for the scheme.[178] However, since a number of key Western countries had declined to endorse the joint declaration, the BIS thought it best not to become involved in East–West diplomacy and turned down the offer.[179] Eventually the scheme would be run – to little effect, it might be added – directly by the UN's Geneva office without any BIS involvement.

As with East–West trade, a bilateral rather than multilateral approach remained the rule for socialist countries' dealings with the BIS. Throughout the 1950s and 1960s, the Bank continued to arrange short-term credit operations, mainly for the central banks of Czechoslovakia, Hungary, Poland, and Yugoslavia.[180] In June 1956, the BIS Board of Directors decided to set ceilings for credit facilities granted to these four central banks, which were subsequently regularly increased.[181] Some credits were granted on an uncovered basis. In November 1960, in connection with the stabilisation plan for the dinar discussed between the Yugoslav government and the IMF, the

BIS Board of Directors raised the credit limit for Yugoslavia from 55 to 100 million Swiss francs, of which 30 million was on an uncovered basis.[182]

Bilateral contacts with the Eastern European central banks intensified from the late 1960s onwards, when a number of Eastern bloc countries implemented economic reforms designed to increase productivity growth, inter alia by stepping up the importation of Western technology and the international borrowing needed to pay for it. As East–West economic and financial diplomacy gained new momentum, representatives from the Eastern bloc central banks became regular callers at the BIS, not only soliciting further credit support but also to improve their staff's expertise in central banking and in operating on the gold and foreign exchange markets. Conversely, the BIS's top managers began to include the Eastern European capitals in their regular business trips.[183] However, when Eastern European central banks asked for a seat on the Board of Directors, they were firmly kept at bay.[184]

It should be recalled that, beyond the period covered in this book, cooperation between the BIS and Eastern European central banks became more systematic. From 1976 onwards, a regular meeting between the central bank governors from Eastern Europe and the BIS Board was organised in Basel twice a year.[185] The BIS extended loans to Hungary and Yugoslavia during the international debt crisis of the early 1980s.[186] In 1990, shortly after the fall of the Berlin Wall, a special service for Eastern European countries was set up at the BIS to assist central banks in the transition to a market economy.[187]

One issue in the relationship between the BIS and Eastern Europe remained unresolved until the 1990s: the participation of the Russian central bank in the BIS. In the 1930s, the central bank of Soviet Russia had not been considered for BIS membership, partly because of its idiosyncratic financial policies and partly because of the political stigma attached to the Bolshevik state, which at that time had not yet been officially recognised by a number of Western governments. After the Second World War, the USSR gained enormously in international standing both for its victory over Nazi Germany and for its influence over Eastern Europe. In addition, as far as the BIS was concerned, the Soviet Union looked interesting as one of the world's leading gold producers, a role that also gave it some leverage in international monetary affairs, particularly in the 1960s.[188] Nevertheless, since it was still unacceptable for Cold War diplomacy to seriously consider a closer integration of the Soviet Union into the international monetary system, the BIS remained reluctant to consider Russian membership.

In June 1958, the Moscow Narodny Bank, a Soviet bank based in London, enquired through the Bank of England whether the State Bank of the

USSR would be allowed to make gold deposits with the BIS and become a member of it. The Bank of England felt that this raised a difficult political issue – as well as an acute legal problem, owing to the gold of the Baltic States blocked by the BIS since 1940 (see Section 7.3).[189] In December 1961, on the occasion of the 150th anniversary celebrations of the Bank of Finland, BIS President Holtrop met informally in Helsinki with Korovushkin, chairman of the board of the State Bank of the USSR. Korovushkin brought up the issue of the Baltic gold deposited with the BIS, saying that he did not understand what prevented the BIS from handing it over to the Russians.[190]

In spite of Holtrop's refusal to discuss Baltic gold, a few months after the Helsinki meeting the president of the Banque Commerciale de l'Europe du Nord, a Soviet bank based in Paris, approached Guindey, the BIS general manager, enquiring on what conditions the State Bank of the USSR would be allowed to join the BIS. The matter was discussed informally by the governors during their July 1962 monthly meeting; the reply conveyed to the Russians was that the BIS was not at the moment considering an expansion in its membership and, if it did, only OECD and IMF member countries would be eligible.[191] However, the State Bank of the USSR did not take "no" for an answer, and the issue of Russian BIS membership was subsequently raised again – either by representatives of Soviet banks active in the West or by one of the Eastern European central banks.[192] Between 1968 and 1971, Zijlstra (then president of the BIS) convened three special governors' meetings to discuss Soviet admission,[193] all yielding the same result: Soviet membership was not deemed opportune, even though the State Bank hinted that it would accept a rather informal participation, much like the U.S. Federal Reserve's position.

The question of Russian membership would not be resolved until 1996, when the Central Bank of the Russian Federation became a BIS shareholding member. In the meanwhile, gold had been released to the newly founded central banks of the three Baltic States when they regained independence in 1991.

ELEVEN

The 1960s: Patching Up the Bretton Woods System

11.1   The International Monetary System, 1959–1973

It has been said that "the 1960s were the heyday of the Bretton Woods system".[1] More precisely, perhaps, one may say that the system only existed – albeit in quite a different form from its original conception – between 1959 and 1968. Before then, the lack of free current account convertibility of the European currencies frustrated the main purpose of the system itself, delegating its functions to a panoply of administrative (though quite efficient) measures. After March 1968, the erection of a firewall between the official and the free gold markets frustrated the gold-anchor element that the founding fathers had been keen on maintaining. During 1959–68, on the other hand, international transactions took place in a context of fixed-rate convertible currencies, with the few parity changes being carried out according to the rules.

The system soon revealed itself to be inherently unstable from both a political and an economic standpoint, and its sustainability required "a degree of management no one had foreseen"[2] that rested on a hitherto unprecedented dose of international cooperation. Even taking into account its eventual demise, however, the game of maintaining the system's viability for as long as possible was arguably worth the candle: the real economy boomed in Europe and, to a lesser extent, in the United States, sustained by and sustaining rates of growth in international trade not seen since the first decade of the century.

This chapter deals with central banks and their Basel joint venture as players in the great transatlantic cooperative game of the 1960s. The narrative will follow in some detail the unfolding of events – such as the management of the Gold Pool, the swap schemes, the support of the pound sterling – in which the BIS central bankers played a crucial role. It will also account for Basel's intellectual contribution to the debate on the reform of the system as well as highlight the role of the BIS in the "groups" and "working parties" that constituted the operative arms of cooperation. This section provides a brief background overview of the main events referred to in the following pages, drawing selectively from the huge literature on the subject.[3]

By the end of 1958, when current account currency convertibility was established, it was clear that the international monetary system operated as a gold dollar standard, with the pound sterling playing a minor – if problematic and destabilising – role. In reality, a system had evolved that, to some extent at least, betrayed the intentions of the Bretton Woods founding fathers.[4] The Bretton Woods conference of 1944, dominated by fears of stagnation, did not anticipate a booming postwar economy. It therefore paid little attention to the issue of international liquidity, assuming that new gold production and the provision for some increase in the IMF quotas would be sufficient to meet the main trading countries' need for international reserves. The agreement was essentially Wilsonian in that it "presupposed an identity of national interests in maintaining an open and harmonious international monetary system. Countries were assumed to be willing – and politically able – to accept the stern discipline of gold, for the sake of keeping their currencies convertible and their economies open".[5] For a number of reasons that need not concern us here, postwar reality turned out to be quite different: to a large extent, internationally accepted liquidity consisted of dollars. The gold anchor rested on the pledge by the U.S. Treasury to convert – on behalf of foreign monetary authorities only – dollars into gold at the fixed price of \$35 per ounce of fine gold, established by President Roosevelt in 1934.

As already mentioned, the 1960s were characterised by a rapid expansion of international trade, driven by continuous trade liberalisation and rapid output growth. The latter was, in turn, reflected in and sustained by booming international trade, within a virtuous circle that is part and parcel of the "golden age" story briefly outlined in Chapter 10. From the monetary side, the sustainability of the process required the creation of ever-increasing international liquidity, primarily in the form of central bank reserves. Insufficient means of international payments would obviously reduce trade and therefore output growth. Moreover, individual countries would proceed with a programme of trade liberalisation only if they felt comfortable with a level of reserves believed to be capable of cushioning the domestic economy from international monetary shocks. In fact, as noted by James, "inadequate reserves would be the most frequent reason given for a refusal to open trade, or for a willingness to contemplate higher levels of protection".[6] An adequate provision of international liquidity and its balanced distribution among trading partners therefore came to be considered by policy makers as an essential element in a process that was delivering prosperity at an unprecedented rate. Whether or not this view was entirely justified is another question.

With the dollar as the main reserve currency, the provision of international liquidity largely depended on the U.S. balance of payments deficit. The United States, therefore, enjoyed the privileges and suffered the limitations deriving from the status of international banker. As such, it benefited from seigniorage (i.e., the balance of payments deficits allowed Americans to permanently "live above their means") but was at the same time compelled to exercise discipline in the issue of money (i.e., in the size of its external deficits) in order to maintain confidence in the international currency.

Thus the system rested on an implicit pact, which Charles Maier defined as "consensual American hegemony".[7] The United States would supply international money, charging a fee for the service, in the form of continuous balance of payments deficits. Europe and Japan would gladly accept to pay the fee in exchange for international liquidity and for the stability of the payments system, which the United States would guarantee by a domestic economic policy consistent with its role as international banker, a policy that would maintain the external deficit within acceptable limits so that confidence in the dollar would not be undermined. The political understanding also included the provision by the United States of a military umbrella for Europe and Japan and direct investment in the two areas.[8]

Throughout the 1950s, this implicit pact upon which international relations rested was never seriously tested. A dollar shortage, rather than the opposite, characterised the first part of the decade, caused by the U.S. balance of payments surpluses of the time. When the dollar gap disappeared, U.S. deficits were narrow for a while, while gold production added to international reserves. European international payments were managed by the "visible hand" of the EPU in a context of limited convertibility. Europe and Japan were still relatively weak and dependent on U.S. loans and investments.

"Partly for economic reasons but more for political and strategic reasons, Western Europe and Japan agreed to finance the U.S. balance of payments deficit. United States' allies acquiesced in a hegemonic system that accorded the U.S. special privileges to act abroad unilaterally to promote U.S. interests. The U.S. in turn condoned its allies ... use of the system to promote their own economic prosperity.... As long as the bargain was sustained and not overly abused, the Bretton Woods system survived."[9]

From the late 1950s, the shifts in the relative importance of the world economies began to slowly erode the domestic policy conditions upon which the postwar "consensual American hegemony" had hitherto rested. The rapid expansion of Japan and Western Europe, their buoyant export trade, and U.S. overseas investments and military expenditure translated into larger U.S. balance of payments deficits. The United Kingdom also ran persistent external deficits, while West Germany, France, Italy, and Japan accumulated surpluses.

Even before these circumstances materialised, Robert Triffin lucidly noted that the system was inherently unstable and eventually doomed to fail.[10] For all its technical improvements, in particular those connected with IMF lending and convertibility limited to current account items, the system still rested on a gold anchor. New gold supply was therefore the ultimate source of international liquidity. On the basis of his own estimates of gold supply and trade growth, Triffin concluded that "the world's normal requirements for monetary reserves appropriate to the maintenance of convertibility by the major trading countries" were likely to exceed considerably over the 1960s "the contribution which might be expected from current levels of gold production".[11] Triffin therefore anticipated a deflationary outcome, also because of the legal obligation of the U.S. monetary authorities to keep a fixed minimum ratio between gold and note circulation. As far as international liquidity was concerned, Triffin saw an inescapable dilemma. Either the United States would keep its external deficit within limits compatible with maintaining confidence in the gold convertibility of the dollar, thereby inducing a deflationary bias in the world economy, or it would supply all the needed liquidity via ever larger deficits, thereby undermining the credibility of its gold pledge and opening the way to a flight from the dollar. Either way, the Bretton Woods system was doomed to fail in the medium term.

Policy makers, however, more or less consciously believed that the breakdown of the system could be postponed indefinitely, or that the system could be made to survive until a better substitute could be worked out, as long as the holders of dollars exercised restraint in converting them into gold. Two provisions of the Bretton Woods agreements helped in that direction: the limitation of gold convertibility of dollars to foreign monetary authorities; and the fact that individual countries were allowed to maintain administrative controls on short-term capital movements. What was required, then, was to find the most suitable ways for surplus countries to lend their dollars back to the United States (and to a limited extent to the United Kingdom).

No lack of technical instruments existed in the panoply of international finance in order to "recycle" surplus dollars back to the two main deficit countries: most of this chapter is devoted to outlining – sometimes in a quite detailed way – the ingenuity applied to find, in each particular case, the appropriate tools. However, what was needed first of all was the determination of the various players to use such tools in an effective way. In other words, propping up the system for an indefinite period of time required a commitment to cooperation for an equally indefinite period of time.

For a while, a cooperative commitment to refinance the U.S. (and U.K.) deficits made markets form the crucial expectation that the exchange rate of the dollar would not change. The assumed invulnerability of the dollar allowed the United States to run its monetary policy without too much regard for its impact on the balance of payments while at the same time keeping the entire world liquid. Confidence in the easy availability of liquid funds also allowed Western Europe and Japan to maintain an expansionary stance and to liberalise trade and capital movements without fear of short-term balance of payments problems. The system worked well precisely because domestic economic policies were not subject to balance of payments discipline. In any other circumstances it would have been politically impossible for the United States to maintain a fixed dollar parity and for other industrial countries to rapidly integrate in the Atlantic economy by doing away with trade barriers and administrative controls on capital movements.

The system therefore depended crucially for its functioning on a huge amount of international cooperation, which in turn rested upon the political relationship between the United States and the other major industrial countries that made the hegemony of the dollar acceptable. As long as this setting maintained credibility, markets would not challenge fixed exchange rates.

At the beginning of the 1960s, the rewards were such that cooperation in keeping the system stable appeared to be a positive-sum game to all the main players. Europe and Japan, while gaining strength, were still dependent, both economically and strategically, on the United States. They enjoyed an almost free ride in mutual defence and prospered from the ever closer Atlantic economic ties. The United States, for its part, was able to run its foreign policy largely on credit, avoiding paying the harsh domestic price of hegemony – a price that earlier in the century had proved too heavy to shoulder for the United Kingdom.

In a matter of a few years, however, cracks began to appear in the postwar U.S. construction that were due basically to the weight of its own success. As Western Europe and Japan rapidly caught up with U.S. living standards, their feeling of economic dependence on the United States diminished. The geopolitical environment was also undergoing considerable changes: the proximity of Russia and the rise of the Chinese giant, coupled with a growing sense of Europe's power and identity, pushed the main countries in the direction of a foreign policy less dependent on the United States, most particularly in the case of Gaullist France. At the same time, U.S. policy makers were increasingly weary of the constraints imposed on their domestic policy by their role of world bankers. During the Johnson administration, the twin commitments to Vietnam and the Great Society programme began to be perceived as inconsistent with the obligation of maintaining some sort of international monetary discipline. The publication in Paris, in 1967, of Servan-Schreiber's *Le Défi Américain* stands as a symbol of a fundamental change in transatlantic relations.[12]

In the second part of the 1960s, what had previously been regarded as a fair quid pro quo came to be interpreted differently on the two sides of the Atlantic. The United States maintained that its overall balance of payments deficit, in the presence of a trade surplus, was due to military expenditure for the common defence of the Western world and to the foreign direct investment by U.S. companies that transferred technology to and created jobs in the receiving countries. A sense of resentment at European "ingratitude" developed. On a more technical level, the United States argued that, in any event, the weight of adjustment should be borne equally by surplus and deficit countries. On the other hand, in some European circles and most of all in France, both U.S. military expenditure and overseas investment were now perceived as the tools of an aggressive foreign and economic policy that required containment. In economic terms this position translated into advocating as much as a return to a pure gold standard in order to impose monetary discipline on the United States: from this standpoint, surplus countries also felt they were in a stronger moral and political position than those in deficit. Inflation was blamed on the growing balance of payments surpluses.

International monetary problems also drove a wedge between the United Kingdom and the Continent, while at the same time enhancing the already close U.K.–U.S. ties.[13] Cooperation was strained as continental Europe tended to be ever more concerned with creating a reliable method to ensure that deficit countries rectified their balance of payments, while the United States and the United Kingdom sought to endlessly increase international liquidity, partly to take the burden off their shoulders. "In short, the Six [EEC] sought ways to force a reduction of deficits, the U.S. and the U.K. sought ways to fund them."[14]

Besides strained international relations, the Bretton Woods system was undermined by economic factors, precisely those stressed by Triffin a decade earlier. Unchecked U.S. deficits undermined the confidence in the gold convertibility of the dollar to an extent that cooperative international financial engineering found increasingly difficult to conceal. The accumulation of unwanted dollars in the reserves of the central banks of the Western world approached a critical level. In January 1965, the Bank of France made public its intention to convert part of its existing dollar reserves into gold and to do so for any future additions to its reserves. Inspired by experts such as Jacques Rueff, de Gaulle had become convinced that the gold dollar standard was doomed and that France had to act to provoke a radical rethinking of the international monetary system while protecting the value of its reserves in case the dollar should devalue. Shortly afterwards, at a press conference, de Gaulle explained his ideas on world monetary reform.[15] Stressing the undue benefit the United States drew from the system, he proposed a phased return to a gold-standard system in which the role of both sterling and dollar as reserve currencies would be eliminated. In a way, the Bank of France's policy was neither new nor much different from the contemporary practice of many European central banks. The novelty was that, instead of converting dollars discreetly in consultation with the U.S. Treasury and Federal Reserve, it now became a publicised policy creed.

The need to go beyond patching up to a major reform of the system had therefore become apparent. And in fact, as we shall see, reform came to be discussed in official international ad hoc committees – which, however, could only reproduce the different outlooks of the respective governments. A new international asset, the IMF special drawing right (SDR), was eventually created to complement gold and the dollar as international means of payments (some argued that it would also constitute a reserve asset, but it was never properly treated as such).

The SDR, introduced only in 1969, probably came too late and constituted too little an addition to international liquidity. The collapse a year earlier of the Gold Pool, a cooperative venture to arbitrage between the official and the free gold markets, signalled, after about a century of gold standards of various kinds, the final demise of gold as the anchor for the international monetary system. The failure of the Gold Pool actually marked the beginning of the end of the Bretton Woods system.[16] After that, the United States quietly adopted a stance of "benign neglect" of the dollar. The final act of the fascinating Bretton Woods story is discussed in the last section of this chapter.

Were the huge cooperative efforts put into patching up a system that was eventually doomed to fail worth their while? A broad historical answer to this question depends crucially on the value attached to gaining time and to the assessment of the longer-term costs of the eventual collapse of the system. Both judgements hinge critically on the observer's perspective.

From a European standpoint, the 1960s look like an extraordinary period of increasing prosperity and rapid catch-up with the world's productivity leader, characteristics that to a considerable extent were generated by a reversal of the policy stances adopted since the 1930s, by trade growth, and by freer labour and capital mobility. It is unlikely that such a favourable outcome could have been produced without the availability of ample international liquidity, the positive effects on long-term domestic and international investment generated by credible fixed exchange rates, the end of beggar-thy-neighbour policies, and the easing of domestic political constraints on trade liberalisation. Western Europe in 1971 was much richer and politically more mature than it had been in 1958, and it was therefore better able to cope with the social unrest, oil shocks, and inflation that characterised the 1970s. The European observer can hardly escape the conclusion that extending the life of the gold dollar system, even if with increasingly ad hoc measures, was on the whole highly beneficial. The same can probably be said from a Japanese viewpoint.

It is hard to say if the same conclusion applies to the United States. The international monetary system, as we saw, suited U.S. foreign policy, allowing for hegemony at relatively low cost. Whether or not it was also beneficial to the U.S. economy depends on the assessment of the effects of an adoption of floating rates sometime in the 1950s. A case can be made that the real exchange rate of the dollar was actually overvalued: if that were true then floating rates would have helped output growth, even though the impact might not have been large given the relatively "closed" nature of the U.S. economy.

11.2   The BIS in the 1960s

Before turning to the BIS's role in international monetary affairs in the 1960s, the Bank's institutional development must be accounted for. At the end of 1964, upon expiration of his mandate as chairman of the BIS Board, Sir Otto Niemeyer chose not to stand for re-election. He had been on the BIS Board uninterruptedly since 1932.[17] After the retirements of Auboin, Jacobsson, and van Zeeland,[18] Niemeyer was the last member of the prewar generation to leave the Bank. He was a living memory of the Norman–Schacht days and a symbol of the BIS continuity from then to the present. With Niemeyer's retirement, the longest-serving Board member was Maurice Frère, who had been at the BIS since the end of World War II. He served as vice-chairman until his accidental death while on a visit to Turkey in August 1970.

For the rest, the people who sat on the Board during the 1960s all belonged to a second generation of postwar central bankers that replaced those who had overseen reconstruction and the achievement of convertibility. Some of them served as ex officio Board members for the entire decade or most of it: Ansiaux of Belgium, Brunet of France, Blessing of Germany, Carli of Italy, and Åsbrink of Sweden. In the mid-1960s Lord Cromer was succeeded by O'Brien at the head of the Bank of England, and Schwegler by Stopper at the Swiss National Bank. Most of the other (appointed) members, besides Frère, also served for most of the decade: Deroy, Brinckmann, and Menichella. In 1964, Niemeyer was replaced by M. J. Babington Smith.

Holtrop, whose presence at the BIS dated back to the immediate postwar period, served as its president and chairman of the Board until his retirement as president of the Netherlands Bank in the spring of 1967. He was replaced in both capacities by Jelle Zijlstra, a former professor of economics and minister of finance as well as Holtrop's successor at the head of the Dutch central bank.[19]

Guillaume Guindey resigned from his post as general manager in November 1962[20] to take up a top civil service position in France.[21] The tradition of appointing a French citizen as BIS general manager, duly acknowledged by the governor of the Bank of France,[22] was not interrupted when the Board's choice fell on Gabriel Ferras. Interestingly, however, Ferras did not come to Basel directly from a position in France, as he had left the country ten years earlier,[23] but from the IMF, where he was then director of the European department. The coming of age of the new international financial institutions was at the time creating a large pool of competent international civil servants in a job market that had already existed before the war but had hitherto been quite thin. Five years before, Jacobsson had moved from the BIS to the International Monetary Fund, and now Ferras was hired from the IMF by the BIS. He was described as "a pale, melancholic, pessimistic, honest person", a "loyal friend" endowed with "a clear French brain, a nature focused on the essential, and a great humanity".[24] In U.K. eyes, Ferras enjoyed the rare advantage of "being French without being too French".[25] He died tragically in a car accident in December 1970. He was succeeded by René Larre, also a French citizen, a high-ranking civil servant at the Ministry of Economic and Financial Affairs who had previously represented France at both the IMF and the IBRD.[26]

In 1960 – after a four-year interregnum filled by Baffi and Lutz on a part-time basis and by Rainoni as acting head of the Monetary and Economic Department – the Board brought in Milton Gilbert from the OEEC (where he had been director of economics and statistics) to finally replace

Jacobsson as economic adviser.[27] Gilbert, an American[28] with a doctor-
ate from the University of Pennsylvania, had begun his career at the U.S.
Department of Commerce where, in the 1940s, he had headed the national
income division. Besides being an excellent economic statistician, Gilbert
had developed an early interest in international monetary affairs by participating in the Bretton Woods conference as a junior member of the U.S.
delegation, an interest that was sharpened during his time at the OEEC in
Paris. The fact that Gilbert was an American with a deep knowledge of Europe and an economist with sophisticated statistical expertise made him an
excellent choice to lead the BIS think-tank in the 1960s. He held this position until 1975, when he was succeeded by Alexandre Lamfalussy.

Secretary General Alberto Ferrari left office at the end of 1961. The appointment of Antonio d'Aroma, a former close collaborator of Italy's President Einaudi, also honoured the unwritten rule that the post should be filled
by an Italian citizen.[29] It was thus with an almost entirely new Board and
management that, in the 1960s, the BIS acquired a more important position
than ever among the main actors of international monetary cooperation.

In surveying the BIS's business activities during the 1960s, it should be
borne in mind that they were, then as before, part and parcel of its functions
as the center for central bank cooperation. Income derived from its banking
side provided the BIS with the resources to fund research and its dissemination, to support the mushrooming groups and committees working under
its auspices, and to organise meetings. Ferras, like his predecessors, also
indicated that profit making, while not the main consideration in the BIS
credit policy, was welcome in that it allowed "the Bank to be independent
of assistance and thus to avoid political interference".[30] Financial intermediation activity was also instrumental in developing first-hand knowledge
of international money markets, including the new eurodollar market, that
could not be gained by research alone. More important still, banking activities were the executive branch of cooperation in such areas as lending
amongst central banks, gold and currency swaps, syndicate loans, and the
like. Some of these were particularly relevant since they could not be carried out by other international financial organisations. The BIS was in an
advantageous position because it could act swiftly, without formalities and
in complete confidentiality, while at the same time remaining under the control of the central banks represented on the Board. For all these reasons, the
rapid growth of the BIS's banking activities in the 1960s can also be read
as an indication of enhanced central bank cooperation. In the 1960s, more
frequently than before, the BIS's operations also aimed at assisting individual central banks in controlling the volume of the domestic money supply,

either by increasing or by reducing the amount of national currency held by the banking system.[31]

The BIS balance sheet totalled 2.4 billion Swiss gold francs in 1957 (up from 499 million ten years earlier) and was almost ten times larger (23.8 billion) in 1971.[32] Net profits grew slightly more than proportionally; around the middle of the decade, they reached again the 1932 previous all-time peak of about 35 million Swiss gold francs. In 1971 the Bank's net profits came close to 100 million Swiss gold francs. As dividends were raised only parsimoniously, capital and reserves increased from 298.3 million Swiss gold francs in 1958 to 694.8 million Swiss gold francs in 1971.

To a large extent, the huge increase in the operations of the BIS Banking Department derived from the rapid growth of output and trade, particularly in Europe, accompanied by more than proportional increases in money supply, domestic credit, and international payments and lending, which translated into an equally swift expansion in central banks' assets, including gold and foreign currencies. Central banks found it advantageous to invest part of their growing assets with the BIS. In fact, about 90% of the latter's deposits came from central banks, which considered them attractive for a number of reasons: high liquidity[33] cum yields at the prevailing market rates, the protection of international immunities, and assurance that the funds would be invested in ways consistent with each central bank's monetary policy. The development of the so-called eurodollar market, discussed in the next chapter, also contributed to the increase in the activity of the BIS Banking Department.

In the 1960s, the share of gold in total deposits with the BIS reached its highest peacetime level. It was over 50% in 1960–63, reached 60% in 1965, and was still around 47% in 1968 when international support for the official gold price was discontinued. After 1971, with the end of the Bretton Woods system, the amount of gold deposits fell both in absolute terms and relative to the rapidly expanding currency deposits.

It was the Bank's long-standing practice to operate on the gold market almost exclusively on behalf of central banks. According to Ferras, "the BIS's principal concern in intervening on the gold market [was] to render service to the central banks that are its correspondents; thus it [kept] broadly in mind the objectives that central banks assign themselves in their common policy concerning the free gold markets".[34] As a general rule, the Bank did not take speculative positions in gold or currencies: all operations were hedged by spot or forward transactions in the opposite direction. Typically, the Bank bought gold forward against dollars, selling the same quantity of gold spot, again against dollars, and invested the dollars for the period up to the forward transaction at maturity. Gold was purchased from producer countries, from central banks, and on the free London and Swiss markets, and then sold to the market and to central banks.

The BIS also continued its traditional practice of holding earmarked gold (not shown in the balance sheet) as a service to member central banks and to the exclusion of all private bodies. In the 1960s, gold was held in six different European centres (London, Paris, Berne, Amsterdam, and Lisbon) and in two outside Europe (New York and Ottawa).

One legacy from the Bank's reparation origins, its 1930–31 investments in Germany, was finally settled in the 1960s. As we have seen, these investments were linked to the execution of the Young Plan and had been frozen, since the abrogation of the Young Plan by the 1932 Lausanne Agreement was never officially ratified. These BIS investments had been serviced by the Reichsbank right up to April 1945,[35] at which time they amounted to 293 million Swiss gold francs. After the war, the BIS's claim with respect to these investments was referred to the London Allied–German Debt Conference (1952–53). There the German government agreed to resume interest payments on condition that capital reimbursement be postponed until 1966. In late 1964, negotiations were reopened between a German delegation (headed by Hermann Abs of the Deutsche Bank) and a BIS delegation (which included Ferras, Macdonald, Guisan, and Frère) in order to establish the current value of the BIS's claim.[36] An agreement was reached in October 1965 whereby the BIS received in final settlement of its claim on Germany – which also included the looted gold the BIS had restituted to the Allies back in 1948 – the sum of 156 million Deutsche marks.[37] As a result of this agreement, the annuity trust account created at the BIS in connection with the Young Plan was closed. On the occasion of the 1969 revision of the BIS Statutes, all references to the Young Plan were deleted.[38] In the meantime, the BIS continued to act as trustee for the Dawes and Young loans. As a result of the 1953 Agreement on German External Debts, the service of these loans had been resumed through the issue of new, so-called conversion bonds. The last of these bonds were redeemed in 1980.[39]

In 1970–71, the BIS membership base was expanded for the first time since the Bank of Spain had joined in December 1960. In January 1970, the Bank of Canada and the Bank of Japan subscribed to 8,000 BIS shares each.[40] The Reserve Bank of Australia and the South African Reserve Bank followed in December 1970 and June 1971, respectively. This expansion was considered the logical outcome of the Bank's more "global" outreach and in particular of its role in the G10 framework. These four central banks became "ordinary" shareholding members of the BIS and were not invited to sit on the BIS Board. However, as we will see, the Canadians and Japanese cooperated closely with the central banks that did have a seat on the Board within the G10 framework.[41]

The BIS had always operated with a surprisingly small staff. However, owing to the enormous expansion in the volume of activities, the number of employees grew from about 160 in 1958 to 237 in 1971. By the late 1960s, therefore, it became clear that the old premises at Centralbahnstrasse 7 (the former Savoy Hôtel Univers) would soon be inadequate. Hence the Bank sent its architect, Martin Burckhardt, a preliminary estimate of office and other facilities requirements, asking him to come up with a design for new premises. Provision was made for a large number of visitors, for Board members – significantly including the Federal Reserve System – and for 50% more staff than existed at the time "even though such a large increase was [regarded as] unlikely".[42] A preliminary project for a circular tower was then produced for submission to the Cantonal Building Department, "with a view of obtaining its agreement in principle but without in any way committing the Bank to adopt the project".[43] The original project had to be revised because it violated a Basel rule stipulating that no building should look taller than the tower of the cathedral (Münster) when observed from Kleinbasel, across the Rhine. The building was also found objectionable by some Basel citizens, who asked that its design be submitted to a referendum. In this, however, voters expressed themselves in favour of the new construction by a majority of 32,000 to 14,000.[44] In 1971 the Board approved the purchase of a suitable site, just across the station square from the old premises, at Centralbahnplatz 2. The foundation stone of the new construction was laid in May 1973. The building, incorporating state-of-the-art technology, was completed in 1976, and the "Tower" was inaugurated in May 1977.[45]

For all the advantages of the new building, some governors missed the cosy atmosphere of the old premises. "In the old building", Leutwiler[46] complained, "we were all close to each other.... When I was in my office, I could hear the Governor of the Bank of England entering his own office, I knew he was there, I could go and see him ... next door".[47] Self-confessedly old-fashioned, Otmar Emminger also missed the former Savoy Hôtel Univers: "we could do our work just as well in those old-fashioned, cramped rooms, and they had a really intimate atmosphere.... In the old building, when I left my room I always happened to meet one or several of my colleagues, or I saw them when I arrived on Saturday afternoon because they were in the corridor, talking to each other".[48] According to some of the participants, the cosy atmosphere of the old building was part and parcel of the "Basel club" to which we now turn.

1. The former Savoy Hôtel Univers, Basel, seat of the BIS from 1930 until 1977 (picture 1931).

2. Meeting of the nominated directors of the BIS, Basel, 22–23 April 1930. From centre-front clockwise around the table: Reusch (Germany), Luther (Reichsbank), Melchior (Germany), Fraser (BIS), McGarrah (BIS), Francqui (Belgium), Franck (National Bank of Belgium), Addis (United Kingdom), Norman (Bank of England), interpreter, Tanaka (Japan), Nohara (Japan), Azzolini (Bank of Italy), Beneduce (Italy), de Vogüé (France), Moreau (Bank of France), Brincard (France).

3. Gates W. McGarrah, BIS President 1930–33.

4. Leon Fraser, BIS President 1933–35.

5. Pierre Quesnay, BIS General Manager 1930–37.

6. Left to right: Sir Charles Addis, Montagu C. Norman (Governor, Bank of England), and Hans Luther (President, Reichsbank), Basel, 22–23 April 1930.

In die Arena der Weltwirtschaftskonferenz

Die Staatsbankdirektoren: „Ave Cæsar!"

7. The 1933 London Conference: "These same gladiators meet each month in Basel". Central bank governors parade before Conference President Ramsay MacDonald. BIS management members are among the crowd (top right). Cartoon Derso & Kelen, London, 12 June 1933.

8. German directors of the BIS Board, mid-1930s. Left to right:
Reusch, Hjalmar Schacht (Reichsbank President), von Schröder.

9. Leonardus J. A. Trip, BIS President 1935–37 (right)
and J. Willem Beyen, BIS President 1937–39.

10. Roger Auboin, BIS General Manager 1938–58.

11. Thomas H. McKittrick, BIS President 1940–46.

12. Per Jacobsson, BIS Economic Adviser 1931–56.

13. The BIS's temporary seat at the Grand Hôtel
in Château d'Oex, May–October 1940.

14. Maurice Frère, BIS President 1948–58.

15. Lord Cobbold, Governor of the Bank of England 1949–61.

16. BIS Annual General Meeting, Basel, 13 June 1955.

17. Marius W. Holtrop, BIS President 1958–67.

18. Guillaume Guindey, BIS General Manager 1958–63.

19. Baron Ansiaux, Governor of the National Bank of Belgium 1957–70.

20. Paolo Baffi, part-time BIS Economic Adviser ad interim 1956–60,
Governor of the Bank of Italy 1975–79.

21. Gabriel Ferras, BIS General
Manager 1963–70.

22. Milton Gilbert, BIS Economic
Adviser 1960–76.

" I'm all for him making drastic economies as long as the children don't suffer."

23. 20 July 1966: after a renewed bout of weakness, pound sterling requires further international support, which is mainly arranged through the BIS. The U.K.'s European partners (de Gaulle, Erhardt, and Aldo Moro) want Wilson to make drastic economies but would not like to see the British Rhine Army nor the ELDO project (joint development of a European satellite launcher) suffer. Cartoon M. Mood, *The Times,* London.

The Economist

What the governor brought back

24. Bank of England Governor O'Brien stepping off the plane, straight from Basel, where he has clinched a deal for a second Sterling Group Arrangement. Front cover, *The Economist*, 13 July 1968.

25. Charles Coombs, Vice-President of the Federal
Reserve Bank of New York 1959–75.

26. Alfred Hayes, President of the Federal
Reserve Bank of New York 1956–75.

27. Karl Blessing, BIS staff member 1930–34,
President of the German Bundesbank 1958–69.

28. Jacques Brunet, Governor of
the Bank of France 1960–69.

29. Guido Carli, Governor of the Bank of Italy 1960–75.

30. Left to right: Jelle Zijlstra, BIS President 1967–81; Antonio d'Aroma, BIS
Secretary General 1962–77; René Larre, BIS General Manager 1971–81.

31. BIS Tower, Basel. Building started in 1973.
The Bank moved into the "Tower" in 1977.

11.3   The "Basel Club"

By the mid-1960s, the expression "Basel club" was commonly used by the press.[49] The phrase retained an arcane aura, as it loosely applied to the gatherings in Basel of the central bankers of the main industrial countries. In reality, the Bank often hosted larger groups and, on the occasion of the Annual General Meeting, the "club" included representatives of some fifty central banks and international monetary organisations.

As at previous times in the BIS's history, the focal point of the club was the monthly meeting weekend, which centred around the two key events in which the governors themselves participated: the Sunday afternoon informal governors' meeting (from 1964 this became the G10 governors' meeting) and the Sunday evening governors' dinner. These governors' meetings were the most secret of all, almost impenetrable even by historical investigation, as minutes were never officially taken and participants did not easily unbutton about the subject matters they discussed; in retrospect, most praised the informal chats at the club for being extremely fruitful. The Monday morning official meeting of the Board of Directors, on the other hand, was a purely formal affair, which often took no more than twenty minutes. In the 1960s, the club also became known for the number of official and semi-official groups hosted in Basel, for which the BIS provided secretarial, research, and intellectual support, in addition to frequent wining and dining. These groups originated from the extensive international monetary cooperation developed in the 1960s to support – or, more accurately, to patch up – the Bretton Woods system. The remainder of this chapter is devoted to the activity of these groups. Before moving on to those possibly more substantial and certainly better documented events, let us briefly try to peep furtively through the keyhole into the rooms hosting the informal monthly meetings.

Maurice Frère was not so keen on having the monthly gatherings gravitate around the governors' dinner, feeling that the focus should be on the formal Board meeting. Holtrop saw things differently and made the Sunday dinner of the governors the pivotal event of the two-day get-together. Regular participants in the "diners group" were the EEC governors, their counterparts from the United Kingdom, Sweden, and Switzerland, and the BIS general manager. Other governors who happened to be in Basel were usually invited. The head of Canada's central bank was a frequent guest, and it was in the 1960s that governors of the Bank of Japan again quite frequently (if informally) found their way back to the city on the Rhine. But perhaps the most important novelty in the informal meetings was the regular attendance by a U.S. "observer".

At the end of the 1950s the issue of the official representation of the United States in the BIS was still pending. In the 1960s, it remained on the agenda on both sides of the Atlantic and was occasionally debated, but nothing official came of it. One of the reasons why the issue did not find a formal solution was that both parties came to be satisfied with the informal ties that grew ever stronger with the passing of time. General Manager Guindey himself played down the need for a formal relationship, believing it "much more important that [the Americans] should come to Basel from time to time than that [they] should have a formal vote at the meetings".[50] Nonetheless, it was considered important that the U.S. officials going to Basel should be of the highest possible rank. At the end of 1960, as we shall see, the weakness of the dollar – between the election and the inauguration of President Kennedy – convinced both the Treasury and the Federal Reserve that a high-profile presence at the governors' meetings in Basel was desirable. Accordingly, Charles Coombs, vice-president in charge of the FRBNY Foreign Department, flew to Basel for the first time on the occasion of the December 1960 meeting.[51] From then on he was a regular invitee to the meetings, the flavour of which is found both in his published memoirs and his more confidential internal reports. In April 1961 Alfred Hayes, president of the FRBNY, attended the governors' Sunday afternoon informal meeting for the first time, though only after declaring that he understood the invitation to be "a goodwill gesture toward the United States which did not involve any change in the status of the [FRBNY] affiliation".[52]

Coombs found Basel to be "an ideal meeting place for central bankers seeking refuge for quiet and confidential discussion". The city, devoid of business travellers on the weekends, offered excellent restaurants "where waitresses consistently refused tips when service had been invisibly included in the charge". Accommodation – past the barely noticeable BIS doorway "squeezed between a pastry shop and a jeweler" – was spartan, but the former Victorian hotel allowed for numerous occasional meetings in the halls and corridors where people would stop "to shake hands in the continental fashion with any colleague going in the opposite direction". These private meetings, Coombs wrote, "were in themselves worth the trip: they provided not only a quiet testing ground for new ideas and approaches but also an early warning system when things were beginning to go wrong. The BIS weekends were what the French would call *sérieux*. However much money was involved, no agreements were ever signed nor memoranda of understanding ever initialed. The word of each official was sufficient, and there were never any disappointments.[53] The day's meetings over, the central bankers returned to their rooms in the Schweizerhof and the Hotel Euler, less than a minute's walk away, only to gather later on for their working dinners".[54]

Coombs found that, throughout the decade, Karl Blessing, president of the Bundesbank and a former BIS staff member, "played a towering role". "A cheerfully resolute man, Blessing was an unfailing source of strength and morale in all our Basel discussions."[55] Carli, at the time possibly the clearest analytical mind amongst the governors, also carried considerable authority[56] owing to his power of persuasion and also to the gold and dollar reserves on which he was sitting.

Deputy governors and executive directors in charge of foreign exchange transactions also organised, from 1961 onwards, their own informal meetings that were soon virtually institutionalised as the gold and foreign exchange experts' group. Amongst the regular participants were Coombs (Federal Reserve Bank of New York), Tüngeler (Bundesbank), Koszul (Bank of France), Iklé (Swiss National Bank), Bridge (Bank of England), Vandenbosch (Netherlands Bank), Ranalli (Bank of Italy), and André (National Bank of Belgium). They were joined, from 1964, by their counterparts from the central banks of Canada, Japan, and Sweden, turning it into a G10 group.

So the Basel club thrived in the 1960s. Members – senior and junior, permanent and occasional – became more numerous, all voting with their feet by habitually attending, month after month. Still, it is not easy for the historian to answer precisely two related questions: "Why were they so eager to come?" and "What did these regular informal meetings actually accomplish?"

To a large extent, the answer given to the first question by those travelling to Basel in the 1960s was quite similar to that of the 1930s,[57] in spite of the sea changes in the international context: they came first of all for an informal, relaxed, confidential, off-the-record, politics-free exchange of opinions, both bilateral and multilateral. Besides all that, Rasminsky,[58] governor of the Bank of Canada, found the meetings were not only "an invariable source of pleasure" but "served a therapeutic purpose" as well. For him, it was sometimes "like going to a psychiatrist and confessing one's self-doubts and hearing the confessions of others – a sort of group therapy".[59] The information value of the meetings was universally praised in the 1960s, as it was in the 1930s. "The most important aspect [of the informal meetings] is the general review of the state of the different economies", said a Swedish participant and later governor; "you [have] a certain picture in your mind's eye before you come and at the meetings you are able to assemble more pieces of the puzzle".[60] The background presence of a competent research staff, the active involvement of the members of the BIS management, and the regular attendance – besides the governors, their deputies and alternates – of experts from the individual central banks turned the monthly meeting into a conference on the state of the individual and international economies.

No other international organisation, with the possible exception of the OECD (which, however, mainly hosted government officials and risked being more politicised), offered the opportunity for such frequent, regular, and intensive exchanges of information among policy makers. With a single monthly trip one could keep abreast, almost in real time, of worldwide economic conditions and gather confidential information not found in the press. Certainly, there was much more institutional dissemination of information in the 1960s than there had been in the 1930s, if for no other reason than the existence of a larger number of international economic institutions. But at the same time, there was more need for information in the 1960s than ever before, precisely because of increased international interdependence. The latter also augmented the value of swift availability of first-hand knowledge, both of facts and of their most authoritative interpretations, and Basel turned out to be a cost-effective (particularly timewise) way of acquiring such knowledge.

Judging from one of the informal meetings and the subsequent dinner for which we possess detailed accounts (March 1969), information was shared not only about current events but also about future policy options.[61] The discussion opened with a report by Gilbert on the main points of the previous day's meeting of experts reviewing balance of payments conditions in the main countries. Each governor then made comments on his country's position and answered questions about his future policy intentions. Thus O'Brien asked Blessing if he "planned to take restrictive measures soon" in response to a foreseeable balance of payments deficit. The Bundesbank president replied that "he felt it necessary to damp down demand" but hoped that the Finance Ministry would cut the budget deficit, thereby allowing him to leave rates unchanged. Moving on to France, Stopper (Switzerland) asked Brunet "whether the Paris gold market could be closed and thereby reduce the possibility for the French public to speculate against the Franc" – to which the governor of the Bank of France replied that the gold market was "the thermometer not the cause of the fever". Ansiaux (Belgium) offered the cooperation of his banking system "in trying to stop the capital flight through banknotes", but Brunet replied that "if foreign banks would refuse to convert French banknotes, this would further weaken confidence in the franc and could topple the present parity". At that evening's dinner, the main topic discussed was the tightening of interest rates in Europe resulting from large-scale borrowing in the eurodollar market by U.S. banks seeking in their turn to ease the burden on their liquidity position imposed by tight U.S. monetary policy. It was one of those lose–lose situations in which international monetary policy coordination is most needed but that tend to degenerate into acrimonious debates, accusations and counteraccusations, second-guessing, and suspicions. And indeed, to use diplomatic jargon, the debate turned out to be very "frank". The high point was reached when Ansiaux said he did not understand why the United States could not stop U.S. banks from borrowing more from their foreign branches – implying, as the record states, "that the U.S. tight monetary policy was a deliberate way of bankrupting Europe".[62]

Yet, in the 1960s, the exchange of opinions and information was not the sole (and possibly not even the most important) function of the Basel club. International monetary cooperation was shaped and conducted in the various groups and committees, as discussed in this and in the next chapter. The matters dealt with often overlapped, as did participation – hence the desirability of some kind of informal coordination. Moreover, most of the work was carried out by deputies acting on broad instructions from their governors and reporting back to them. Instructions obviously reflected national interests, but these needed to be shaped into policies compromising with other national interests and framed into what may be defined broadly as financial diplomacy. The Basel club was a most effective locus of such diplomacy, much more so than publicised bilateral or multilateral ministerial meetings. Governors in Basel seem also to have been occasionally able to quietly defuse the disruptive potential of "matters of principle", or simply just protocol issues, that threatened to find their way into official communiqués.

According to Ferras, the discussion of domestic problems was aimed at policy coordination as well as information. "Coordination of monetary policies", he wrote, "is a quite informal matter which depends on various sovereign powers taking the action they consider appropriate in the light of their internal and external position. Discussion among Governors and other high officials of central banks contributes to such coordination, but there is no question of formal group decision concerning the action to be taken by individual countries".[63]

Among the governors interviewed on the occasion of the Bank's fiftieth anniversary, Carli was the most explicit in providing instances of monthly meetings that resulted in actual policy coordination and decision making. He cited the meetings of 1961–62 as being conducive to the establishment of the Gold Pool and the 1968 discussions on the sterling balances, which resulted in the agreement among central banks for the support of the U.K. currency. He also implied that the IMF General Arrangements to Borrow (GAB) and the G10 multilateral surveillance exercise originated at the Basel club, which also held parallel debates to those taking place at the IMF on the reform of the international monetary system.[64] An instance of how decisions were made informally comes from the aforementioned meeting of March 1969: O'Brien, governor of the Bank of England, "requested a renewal for another six months of the credit facilities that had been granted in November 1967" and "all present agreed to a 6-month extension of the 1967 BIS arrangements".[65]

An indication that the informal meetings were occasions when actual, if unofficial, decisions happened to be made also comes from the time and care devoted to their preparation by the U.S. participants. The U.S. case is particularly revealing because three institutions were involved: the FRBNY, the Board of Governors of the Federal Reserve System, and the Treasury. The Basel meetings were attended by a high-ranking FRBNY official (Coombs most of the time, occasionally B. K. MacLaury and John Ghiardi) who reported back to New York, which then informed the two bodies in Washington. Reporting would be enough if information had been the meetings' only purpose. In fact, however, trilateral exchanges took place ahead of the meetings – often soon after one of them, in preparation for the next one – when it was felt that discussion in Basel would result in some sort of informal understanding on decision making.[66] Procedural matters were discussed, such as the desirability of oral rather than written reporting at the meetings about sensitive matters like gold swaps[67] or the coordination role of the BIS general manager.[68] More substantial matters – such as the amount of U.S. participation in the sterling balances assistance,[69] interest rates to be charged,[70] the maturity of central bank dollar swaps,[71] and contributions to the Gold Pool[72] – were discussed ahead of the meetings in a way that leaves little doubt as to their relevance in policy framing.

The operational character of the BIS, which was called upon to participate in and/or to implement the various agreements made in the 1960s to keep the Bretton Woods system afloat, implied that a number of decisions had to be made by its Board and therefore agreed upon at the preceding informal meeting. Many such technical matters entailed broad policy implications.[73] Thus, according to Carli, in the 1960s the BIS played the dual role of decision maker and executive organ. Decisions were made "by the group who met on the afternoon and evening of the day before the Board official meeting". The operative side consisted in executing those decisions – for instance, in the case of the support to the pound and the Gold Pool.[74]

Carli's overall praise of the club's accomplishments, overly optimistic and oversimplified as it is, may perhaps be worth quoting because it gives sense of how the institution was seen by one of its members who reflected the opinion of many others. "The BIS was the only international organisation to behave like a national organisation. It was a true example of supranationality. It is one of the few international organisations that behaves like a single unit."[75]

11.4   1960–1961: The European Rescue of the Dollar

On Friday 3 March 1961, Guido Carli, governor of the Bank of Italy, arrived in FRBNY President Hayes's office at 33 Liberty Street, downtown Manhattan. Charles Coombs, vice-president for international affairs, was also present.[76] Carli came straight to the point. The Federal Reserve's weekly gold losses, he said, were frustrating a natural recovery of confidence in the dollar by seeming to challenge Kennedy's recent pledge to maintain dollar convertibility into gold. Believing it essential to stop the Fed's gold losses for a while to allow breathing space for the dollar to regain strength, he had come with an offer to sell the Federal Reserve Bank of New York 100 million dollars' worth of gold, sufficient to maintain its gold stock unchanged for a few weeks. "How soon do you need it?" Carli asked his hosts, who felt no embarrassment in answering that the following Monday would be soon enough. Having agreed on the deal and having exchanged "a few pleasantries, on which Carli generally wasted little time, he left for Idlewild to fly back to Rome".[77]

The world upside down? How could poor, war-torn, defeated Italy provide much-needed emergency financial support to the United States? In order to answer this question and to understand how the Bretton Woods system overcame its first serious crisis, a few steps back are needed.

Since the end of 1958, when convertibility was fully introduced in Western Europe, the region's current account surplus resulted in a considerable increase of its total reserves.[78] At the same time, the gold reserves of the United States were rapidly diminishing: in three years (1958–60), Fort Knox lost over 22% of its gold holdings. In 1960 alone, gold worth $1.7 billion (or 8.7% of the total) left its vaults for overseas destinations. The fact is, 1960 was an election year; besides the usual electoral cycle, the possible victory of a candidate like Kennedy, committed to expansion at home, did not encourage market confidence in the dollar. A perfect textbook illustration of Triffin's paradox, the situation of 1960–61 was the first serious test of the dollar gold exchange standard that evolved from the system created at

Bretton Woods. The U.S. balance of payments deficits were indispensable for supplying international liquidity, but the system rested on the understanding that creditors would increase their dollar balances rather than gold holdings. But they would do so only as long as the U.S. commitment to convertibility was credible.

In any event, a potential crisis that might have led to the premature demise of postwar international economic arrangements was defused by a good measure of cooperation, which included the creation of the Gold Pool, discussed in the next sections of this chapter. Deflationary measures in the United States were out of the question, as the country was confronted with both a domestic recession and an external account deficit, while at the same time the main surplus economies of Western Europe could hardly provide further stimuli to their booming economies, already close to overheating.

In the first part of 1960 the Americans were actively engaged in bilateral economic diplomacy aimed at persuading the governments of the main European surplus countries to fulfil their responsibilities in the adjustment process. In particular, the Europeans were urged to avoid sterilisation of their dollar inflows, to liberalise imports, and, most of all, to show their confidence in the system by steering clear of gold conversion. Germany and Italy, holding the second and fourth largest reserves, were forthcoming on the first two counts. The liquidity created by incoming dollars was allowed to exercise its effect on interest rates, which in Italy reached as low as 2%. Imports from the dollar area were further liberalised. The Bank of Italy exercised its strong moral suasion on the banking system for early reimbursement of short-term dollar debts.[79] The German authorities, unwilling to antagonise the Americans, also held back as much as possible on their gold purchases.[80] The Bank of Italy, probably to "avoid any semblance of putting pressure on the United States, turned quite heavily to the London free market for its purchases, pushing up the price there. However, when discreetly requested by the President of the Federal Reserve Bank of New York, it immediately suspended those purchases".[81]

At the late-September 1960 Washington annual meeting of the IMF, the U.S. delegation's official optimism could not hide the privately expressed concern about the future of the dollar.[82] The U.K. Chancellor of the Exchequer openly "called attention on the disquieting features of the international payments situation".[83] The possibility of a world monetary crisis akin to that of thirty years earlier was also evoked.[84]

Soon afterwards, in spite of the fact that central banks had ceased to buy gold, private demand drove the price in London to about $40 per ounce[85] following the decision by the Bank of England to let the market find its own equilibrium "without too much intervention".[86] In the last days of the U.S. presidential campaign, Kennedy stated that his administration would maintain dollar convertibility at the existing parity, thereby somehow easing the buying spree.

A few days later, on 6 November, the situation on the London gold market was discussed at the informal central bank governors' meeting in Basel. Governor Cobbold of the Bank of England reported that he was discussing the matter on a bilateral basis with the U.S. authorities. Hinting that the matter was mostly his own and U.S. responsibility, Cobbold suggested that central bank cooperation in this area should, for the moment, be confined to self-restraint in the gold market and to convincing agents that "the buying of gold at high prices [was] ... nonsense" and that devaluation rumours were "absurd". Holtrop (Netherlands) and Ansiaux (Belgium) supported Cobbold's position. Brunet (France) and Schwegler (Switzerland), on the other hand, expressed their utmost concern about the situation, which "cast doubt on the value of all currencies". Brunet suggested that "the European central banks should consider entering into a joint venture to sell gold in London in order to bring the price down to about $35". Cobbold objected that "European central banks would be unwise to think of reaching any formal agreements among themselves on this subject". He strongly felt that such a joint operation could be contemplated only if U.S. authorities themselves were to take the initiative, and could safely prophesy that "at some stage central banks might well find the burden [of selling gold on the market] too heavy: the result of starting on such a course and then being unable or unwilling to continue would be disastrous".[87]

As mentioned before, a U.S. representative informally participated in the governors' meeting held on 11–12 December 1960. It was not a coincidence that the U.S. authorities decided to send someone to Basel on a regular basis at such a difficult time. Coombs reported back home that "European central bankers were beginning to show signs of acute anxiety as to the future of the dollar. This anxiety was reflected in almost aggressive questioning as to the prospective policies of the new administration, and in a burgeoning of schemes – such as gold guarantees encouraged by the Bank of France – designed to protect their dollar holdings".[88]

The threat to dollar convertibility into gold at $35 per ounce bore some similarities to that faced by the United Kingdom in 1931. The available technical solutions were, obviously, also similar: devaluation (i.e., an increase in the dollar price of gold), floating exchange rates, and administrative controls on capital exports. The most straightforward course of action – the introduction of a policy mix aimed at balancing the external accounts of the United States – met with two objections. On the one hand, the country was in recession and the new administration could hardly contemplate tighter fiscal and monetary policies. On the other hand, as Triffin argued,[89] a reduction of the U.S. balance of payments deficit would be mirrored by a reduction in world liquidity with consequences that he feared would lead to a major depression. The dollar problem was thus a political hot potato for the incoming Kennedy administration.[90] Recognising the danger, the new president, in a move to reassure the markets, appointed Douglas Dillon (a Republican banker) as secretary of the Treasury and Robert Roosa (from the Federal Reserve Bank of New York) as his deputy.

As part of the same effort aimed at emphasising that the new administration ruled out dramatic novel initiatives, Alfred Hayes – president of the Federal Reserve Bank of New York – decided to attend personally, accompanied by Coombs, the January governors' meeting in Basel.[91] His presence was welcome and helped to create a more relaxed climate of opinion. Hayes pointed out that the new administration had no intention of departing from the previous basic financial policies: commitment to dollar–gold convertibility for central banks at $35 per ounce, avoidance of exchange and capital exports controls, and commitment to free trade. The European governors, for their part, felt reassured by the appointment of Dillon and Roosa. Blessing (Germany) and Carli (Italy) took a "philosophical view" of the U.S. deficit. The meeting touched on a number of subjects; the discussion was detailed and constructive, in a cooperative climate. European governors urged the U.S. monetary authorities not to "nullify European cooperative action by allowing interest rates to drop further". The only really contentious issue was raised by a memorandum prepared by the BIS on a gold guarantee for central banks' dollar deposits, a scheme that had been pushed for some time by the French. Schwegler (Switzerland) and Holtrop (Netherlands) also leaned towards some form of guarantee, which was firmly opposed by Cobbold (United Kingdom), Blessing (Germany), and Carli (Italy). Former Bank of Italy governor Menichella argued that the guarantee would create "a fatal obstacle to monetary and fiscal discipline" in the United States.

Taking it for granted that no drastic or novel measures for a permanent solution of the dollar–gold convertibility problem would be politically acceptable, even if technically feasible, all parties concerned felt it imperative to gain time in order to devise and implement measures that, while offering no permanent solution to the problem, would allow the system to remain reasonably viable for as long as possible. Thus, shortly before inauguration, Kennedy appointed a committee to "square the circle" by reconciling policies to increase the growth rate of the economy while at the same time reducing the external deficit.[92] Drawing on the committee's report, soon after inauguration, Kennedy made another public pledge to defend the present gold value of the dollar. He ruled out negotiations for a major reform of Bretton Woods without prior action by the United States to correct its balance of payments. The control of inflation was declared a priority. Other measures, mostly window dressing, were announced. The message apparently "rallied foreign confidence in the dollar, and the free market price of gold in London sank back toward the official $35 level".[93]

The climate at the 12–13 February 1961 Basel meeting was more confident about the short-term prospects of the dollar than it had been a month earlier, even though concerns remained over the threat of a deepening U.S. recession that might result in aggressive expansionary policies and so precipitate a new burst of speculation against the dollar.[94] No illusion existed that Kennedy's message was anything more than a holding action that could not be sustained long. The governors' interest focused on a proposal, contained in Kennedy's balance of payments message, to pay special rates on time deposits and Treasury securities held by foreign central banks. For different reasons, the governors (with the exception of Carli) were lukewarm about the proposal. Cobbold, Schwegler, and the BIS feared a transfer of central bank deposits from London, Zurich, and Basel to New York. Blessing was concerned about the market distortion induced by artificial prices.

In the following weeks, however, the Deutsche mark traded at its upper permitted limit against the dollar. In the face of persistent external account surpluses, the German authorities had attempted to limit the capital inflow by restricting nonresident short-term investment in Germany, by inducing commercial banks to roll over their short-term investments abroad, and by reducing the official discount rate in November and again in January, despite the high level of domestic demand. As these measures failed to affect the exchange rate, rumours of revaluation spread. When Carli showed up at Hayes's office to offer his gold swap on the first Friday of March, exchange markets were persuaded that the mark would very shortly be revalued. Since most agents expected a 10% revaluation, Carli knew that a smaller amount would not calm the storm. He thus came to offer ammunition to fend off the first attacks until better defences could be organised.[95] On that same weekend, a 5% revaluation of the Deutsche mark was decided, effective at the opening of the foreign exchange markets on Monday 6 March.[96] This 5% had turned out to be the political upper limit to the punishment the German government could inflict on its exporters for the sake of cooperation in the name of international monetary stability.

As expected, the revaluation was regarded as a "modest step" by central bankers[97] and considered by markets "as only the first in a series of similar steps".[98] Thus, "after two days of slightly lower quotations (though still well above the new par) the Deutsche mark returned to its upper limit against the dollar".[99] The Italian lira and the French franc also traded close to their upper limits. The three-month forward premium of the mark against the dollar discounted another 4%–5% revaluation. In the second week of March alone, Germany's monetary reserves rose by $200 million while U.K. reserves fell sharply.[100] It was now the turn of the Bundesbank to actively support the dollar: Blessing suggested that the FRBNY massively sell marks three months forward at a premium not higher than 1%; if, at maturity, the FRBNY could not cover them by spot purchases without incurring a loss, the Bundesbank promised to sell the Americans marks against dollars at the same rate specified in FRBNY forward contracts.[101]

When, on 11 March, the governors again convened at the BIS for their monthly meeting, they were aware that the German–American deal was in the wings (it was, in fact, finalised on the following Monday, during their last day in Basel). The European governors offered their own support by finalising the proposal made by the BIS to the FRBNY a few weeks earlier for a standby credit line of gold of up to $1 billion.[102] The BIS cooperative stance was duly acknowledged and appreciated in Washington.[103]

The remaining part of 1961 cannot be described as uneventful as far as currency markets were concerned, but the dollar was no longer under immediate pressure. The Bundesbank's support of the forward dollar market signalled that no further revaluation was to be expected in the short term, thereby steadying exchange rates. Around the middle of June, many short dollar positions were covered and the mark moved closer to its central dollar parity. In the meanwhile, a weak pound sterling received substantial short-term support from Continental central banks,[104] until London raised the Bank rate in the summer. The Berlin crisis and a sharp reduction in Germany's foreign account surpluses subsequently drove down the dollar–mark exchange rate.

Between the summer of 1960 and the early spring of 1961, the Bretton Woods system was put under severe stress as markets for the first time came to believe that the gold–dollar convertibility pledge might not be as solid as official statements claimed. The crisis was overcome by stepping up international monetary cooperation. European central banks and the BIS rose to the challenge. Surplus countries, in particular, did not shy away from partly shouldering their share of the burden in the adjustment process.

Coombs saw in the events of the early months of 1961 a refreshing "shift to a low-key, cooperative search for the right answers" after "years of thorough-going manipulation by the United States of international financial matters". He also saw this shift as shaping "the course of international financial co-operation for the [following] decade".[105] Gilbert at the BIS also praised the "spirit of trust and cooperation" created during the Kennedy administration, particularly through the "expertise, frankness and concern for the problems and opinions of other countries" of people like Roosa and Coombs. Yet from the vantage point of the 1970s, Gilbert – writing after retiring from the BIS – felt it necessary to clarify that "the defence of the dollar did not rest primarily on balance of payments measures. The dollar was defended, rather, by a variety of imaginative tactical arrangements and measures in the financial sphere".[106] To those arrangements we now turn.

11.5   Origin and Operations of the Gold Pool

As we have seen, at the November 1960 meeting the governors were much concerned about the price of gold on the London market,[107] which in the previous weeks had risen to $40 per ounce. Governor Brunet of the Bank of France cautiously suggested that European central banks pool some re-sources to operate in London in order to bring the gold price down. At the time, the suggestion was turned down by the other governors. Cobbold, in particular, was unwilling even to discuss the matter with his European col-leagues without prior agreement and consent from the United States.[108] In the following Basel meetings, the London gold market was monitored and discussed by the governors, but further proposals for joint intervention did not surface. This is largely because, from the beginning of March, gold prices on the free market fluctuated around the U.S. selling price[109] thanks both to measures taken by the U.S. Treasury on private gold holding[110] and to substantial Russian gold sales.[111] By early summer it became clear that the gold market's easy conditions could not be expected to continue. While U.K. gold losses continued, sales by the Soviet Union ceased when a satisfactory level of its dollar reserves was reached. Canadian and South African supplies to the free market also dwindled.[112] At the same time, the U.S. external deficit – hitherto considerably reduced – increased, and the building of the Berlin Wall in August created enormous geopolitical uncertainty.[113]

It is against this background that, on the occasion of the 21 September 1961 IMF meeting in Vienna, the U.S. secretary of the Treasury revived with the U.K. chancellor the idea of joint central bank operations on the London gold market.[114] They agreed that the other industrialised countries ought to share in the burden of keeping the Bretton Woods system viable. The Continentals, however, hardly needed to be convinced about the usefulness of a scheme that would protect the gold value of their dollar holdings. In fact, almost simultaneously, on 22 September 1961 Bundesbank President Blessing offered to make gold available to the Bank of England for interventions in the London market.[115]

Discussions on the Gold Pool scheme were first conducted at the governmental level. Dillon put his Under-Secretary for Monetary Affairs Robert Roosa in charge of first negotiating with the British and then bringing the other Europeans into the agreement. Roosa had to overcome a number of U.K. objections. First of all, London wanted to make sure that the special position of sterling as a reserve currency would be maintained. In particular, the U.K. government asked that its participation in a Gold Pool not preclude the Bank of England from buying gold from the U.S. Treasury in order to protect sterling's exchange position. The British also wanted to make sure that the proposal was not a first step in a broader strategy to limit and eventually close down the free gold market in London. After providing assurances on both counts, Roosa had to meet a final objection: Would the scheme hold? Cobbold's main objection to the French proposal of the previous year was reiterated to the Americans: if at any point in the future the Gold Pool scheme had to be abandoned or if the United Kingdom were forced to leave it, the psychological effects would be enormous and an irresistible run on gold would follow. This was, of course, a powerful argument to which the U.S. negotiators could only answer: "Is there a better alternative?" Finally, recognising that doing nothing was not an option and that apparently no better alternatives existed if the gold–dollar parity were to be preserved, the U.K. authorities agreed to the U.S. proposal – and also because, if the Continental countries joined the scheme, the United Kingdom could ill afford to be left outside of it.[116]

Then the Europeans had to be brought on board. Rather than going through governmental channels and engaging in laborious bilateral negotiations, the Americans were easily convinced by the British to turn to Basel's multilateral venue and present the scheme to the governors (gathered there for the monthly BIS Board meeting), whose countries – together with the United States – held nearly 80% of world gold reserves.

Given the significance of the topic to be discussed, Alfred Hayes travelled with Charles Coombs to Basel on 11–12 November 1961. The president of the Federal Reserve Bank of New York first discussed the Gold Pool proposal individually with the governors, some of whom had already been sounded out by the U.S. Treasury.[117] Not all governors were enthusiastic about the initiative. While they all shared an interest in the convertibility of the dollar, some were uneasy about losing their operational freedom in the gold markets and being drawn into an open-ended arrangement of which the ultimate outcome was uncertain and from which it would be difficult to disengage. Blessing (Germany) was among the most outspoken advocates of the Gold Pool, having previously yielded to U.S. pressure to keep a large share of the Bundesbank's reserves in dollars rather than in gold. Brunet (France) was rather lukewarm for the opposite reason. Cobbold (England), who had no option but to accept the scheme, was still not entirely convinced, fearing the Pool might undermine the hitherto unchallenged position of the London gold market and its privileged relationship with the main gold suppliers, in particular South Africa.

The BIS management had misgivings of its own about the scheme. As Macdonald, manager in the BIS Banking Department, put it in an internal memo: "We have long argued in favour of market forces and are now asked to participate in a scheme which aims at setting these on one side, so that the inconvenience of certain financial policies can be avoided. This may be justifiable at short term but in the longer term could be disastrous, not least of all for the U.S.". The BIS was also concerned that its own gold operations, mostly undertaken on behalf of the central banks, would be undermined. The Gold Pool, Macdonald wrote, "is [not] necessarily a good thing or equally favourable to all participants. Furthermore, the producing countries and the direct interests of the BIS suffer. This might well be judged to be worthwhile if the scheme would contribute to the maintenance of confidence in the dollar. There is, however, no guarantee that it will".[118]

Eventually, all major central banks yielded to the U.S. pressure, supported by Germany. At the governors' meeting it was agreed to give the scheme a trial run of one month. The contributions of the individual central banks were fixed at $35 million for West Germany, $25 million each for France, Italy, and the United Kingdom, $10 million for Belgium and the Netherlands, and $5 million for Switzerland. The United States would match the combined contributions of the others, so that a total amount of gold worth $270 million would be available for sales on the London gold market. These amounts were relatively modest, and the Europeans were glad that the United States was taking the largest share. The actual operations would be carried out on behalf of the Gold Pool by the Bank of England. The results of the operations would be monitored on the occasion of the next BIS Board meeting and at future meetings if the scheme were to be continued. The participating central banks agreed to abstain from buying gold on the London free market for the duration of the scheme. No publicity was to be given to these arrangements. By this time, the BIS network had engendered sufficient communality of purpose and mutual trust for the scheme to be agreed there and then, without a formal written agreement. At Hayes's insistence, the Gold Pool was activated immediately. This allowed the Treasury to ease pressure from Congress by discreetly informing members of its finance committee that the Federal Reserve, with support from the European central banks, was quietly acting on the London market to keep a lid on the gold price.

The BIS was also satisfied, because the Americans soon acquiesced in a resumption of its gold operations – as long as they did not run counter to the objectives of the Gold Pool and on condition that the BIS would report, on a monthly basis, all its operations to the members of the Gold Pool.[119]

The operations of the Pool were assessed at the governors' meeting of 9 December 1961.[120] Since the market had remained calm and sales by the Gold Pool had not exceeded $17 million, it was decided to discontinue interventions for the time being, while continuing to abstain from buying gold in the free market on an individual basis. However, because many European central banks were keen to replenish their gold stocks at the earliest opportunity, it was decided that the Pool would act not only as a selling but also as a purchasing syndicate.[121]

The running of the Gold Pool quickly settled into a routine pattern. The day-to-day operational decisions were left to the Bank of England as the Pool's agent in the London market. The Bank of England reported on a monthly basis to a group of experts from the participating central banks, who met at the BIS at regular intervals. The experts[122] not only monitored ongoing operations, they also discussed prospective developments on the gold market and prepared the ground for the decisions to be taken by the Gold Pool governors. The BIS was represented in both the experts' and governors' meetings by one of its managers: General Manager Gabriel Ferras, Head of the Banking Department Hans Mandel, or Economic Adviser Milton Gilbert. The BIS also provided secretarial services to the Gold Pool, under the direction of Michael Dealtry, feeding the group of experts with more complete and reliable statistical data on world gold production and consumption than had been previously available.[123]

Strictly speaking, the selling and purchasing syndicates were run as two separate entities. The former, with a ceiling of $270 million, was only to be activated by the governors in case of exceptional – and temporary – upward pressure on the market price of gold. The latter, formally activated by the governors in their Basel meeting of 12 March 1962, was to operate continuously whenever new supplies of gold outstripped private demand, allowing the syndicate to mop up market surpluses without exerting upward pressure on the price. The gold thus bought by the syndicate was then redistributed among its members on the basis of each central bank's share in the original sales syndicate. The Bank of England was allowed to set aside a reserve of some $30 million from the syndicated purchases in order to counteract temporary fluctuations on the market with targeted sales. As long as these fluctuations were part of the "normal" development of the market and could be offset within the limit of the reserves available to the purchasing syndicate, the experts saw no need to ask the governors to reactivate the sales consortium. After 1965, when the Gold Pool ran a permanent and fast-growing deficit, this distinction between selling and purchasing syndicate became purely academic.

The first important test of the Pool began on Friday 13 July 1962, when the Bank of England spent $20 million in calming the market. This scale of intervention on just one day had never been seen before, not even during the October 1960 crisis. As a result, the Americans pushed for a reactivation of the sales consortium, which was granted by the governors in August.[124] In September and early October, the demand pressure tailed off somewhat, only to flare up again after President Kennedy's television broadcast of Monday 22 October 1962 denouncing the Soviet deployment of long-range missiles in Cuba. On the following two days private buying on the London market reached $45–$50 million daily, all of which had to be provided by the central banks' Gold Pool. It was feared that the Pool's ceiling of $270 million might soon be broken. Actually, it did not come anywhere near that. As early as Thursday 25 October, the demand pressure eased as a negotiated outcome of the Cuban crisis became likely. By the following Monday, everything was back to normal on the London gold market. Oddly, it was the Russians who gave a helping hand in keeping a lid on the gold price. At the very moment that Khrushchev and Kennedy were arm-wrestling over Cuba, the Soviets sold huge quantities of gold to cover wheat imports following a poor harvest. From Wednesday 24 October onwards, as the superpower showdown lost some of its edge and market pressures abated, the Bank of England was able to buy most of the Russian gold on offer, thereby partly offsetting the losses suffered earlier that week.[125] By Tuesday 30 October, gold was being sold in London at $35.13 per ounce, the price quoted before the outbreak of the Cuba crisis. Thanks to the Gold Pool interventions and the providential Russian sales, the gold price had been successfully kept under control all along, rising to only \$35.20 at the height of the crisis in spite of hectic private demand.

In November the governors, upon the proposal of the Americans, decided to put the selling syndicate on hold again while continuing purchases. By the close of 1962, the Pool's net position had rebounded from an \$82 million deficit (end-October) to a \$53 million surplus. In their report to the governors of 12 January 1963, the experts sounded a moderately optimistic note: "There is reason", they wrote, "to hope that the gold market may be relatively easy during the coming months".[126]

An important element in the stabilising effect of the Gold Pool was the fact that its operation had become public knowledge. At the outset, the governors had instinctively opted for secrecy, feeling that attention should not be drawn to the central banks' concerns about the gold price. But confidentiality could not be maintained. In March 1962, press reports about the central banks' joint action on the gold market appeared in the *Journal de Genève* and were picked up by the London *Times*. On 24 July 1962 the *Journal de Genève* quoted the exact figures of the Pool's sales on the London market. Shortly after the Cuban crisis, *The Economist* was able to paint a fairly accurate picture of the Gold Pool's operations.[127] These press leaks were embarrassing for the central bankers involved and prompted the BIS to further restrict the number of distributed copies of the experts' reports.[128] *The Economist,* however, went right to the point when, after praising the Pool's job, it wrote: "The efficacy of the Pool might indeed have been still more spectacular if its activity had not been kept secret .... Even so, private buyers of gold are well aware that the central banks are not willing to let the gold price go above \$35.20 and they are consequently less ready to risk their funds in gold speculation. So the Pool appears to have established itself as an important part of the mechanism set up to protect and stabilize the Western currencies".[129] Faced with continuous leaks to the press about its activities, the Gold Pool finally adopted a more relaxed communication strategy, culminating in the publication of a fairly detailed account of its operation in the Bank of England's *Quarterly Bulletin* of March 1964.

In 1963 and 1964 the Gold Pool enjoyed a smooth ride. Increased output from the South African gold mines and regular Russian sales raised supply sufficiently not only to satisfy private demand but also to allow monetary authorities to add substantially to their reserves. For this purpose, the Gold Pool's purchasing syndicate remained active.[130] In the autumn of 1964, looking back on nearly three years of concerted action on the London gold market, the Gold Pool members showed satisfaction.[131] Once the Cuban crisis had subsided, the gold price had remained stable, mostly quoting below the \$35.0875 per ounce shipping parity.[132] At the same time, the participating central banks had been able to add to their official reserves more than \$1.2 billion of gold offered on the free market.

The regular experts' meetings in Basel became broader in scope, not only dealing with the Gold Pool operations as such but also reviewing developments in the exchange markets and sharing information on national economic and financial policies. In late 1964, participation in the group was extended to central bank representatives from Canada, Japan, and Sweden. It was thus transformed into the G10 Gold and Foreign Exchange Committee, which continues to play an important role in the BIS committees framework to this day (renamed in 2002, it is now known as the Markets Committee).[133]

11.6 Mutual Support: The Basel Agreement, Swap Networks, and "Bilateral Concerté"

In order to understand the other measures of mutual support undertaken in the 1960s, we must return to early 1961, when the bilateral support the Europeans extended to the dollar culminated in the revaluation of the Deutsche mark. This was the first exchange rate adjustment for a major Western currency since convertibility was introduced in January 1959 and, indeed, since the currency realignment of 1949.[134] The revaluation was regarded by the Germans as a cooperative gesture, going against the competitive interest of the country: a case in which the surplus partner took the adjustment initiative.[135] Karl Blessing, who had served on the BIS staff in the early 1930s and had succeeded Vocke as president of the Bundesbank in 1958, shared his predecessor's almost dogmatic opposition to unilateral changes of the mark's exchange rate. He was supported in this view by IMF Managing Director Per Jacobsson. In 1960, the restrictive credit policy adopted by the Bundesbank in order to dampen the internal economy backfired, as high interest rates attracted more foreign capital, further increasing the balance of payments surplus. The Americans had long argued that surplus countries such as Germany should contribute to restoring global equilibrium, if not by internal measures then by adjusting their exchange parity upwards. Otmar Emminger, a Bundesbank director, had already argued in favour of revaluation in numerous internal memoranda, but his remained an isolated voice.[136] However, the policy dilemma came to a head in late

1960 and increasingly pitched the Bundesbank against its own government. As President Kennedy's outspoken commitment to the existing dollar parity ruled out a generalised realignment of exchange rates, Blessing saw his hand forced and finally conceded to a 5% revaluation taking effect on 6 March 1961.[137]

The build-up to the Deutsche mark revaluation illustrates the engrained dislike for currency realignments among central bankers under the Bretton Woods regime, although the system did provide for the possibility of parity adjustments in case of fundamental balance of payments disequilibria. The immediate after-effect of the Deutsche mark revaluation did nothing to increase the central bankers' appetite for further experiments in this direction. The Dutch, taken by surprise, followed with a revaluation of the guilder.[138] Markets reacted nervously to the German move, anticipating further adjustments. Capital inflows into Germany and Switzerland continued, particularly at the expense of London.

The twin revaluations were discussed at the Basel governors' meeting on 12 March. Fellow governors conveyed to Blessing their disappointment at the lack of advance communication. The head of Germany's central bank, for his part, was adamant that further revaluation was "out of the question".[139] The meeting focused mainly on how to counter the speculative attacks on the pound sterling. A press communiqué drafted by Governor Cobbold read: "[The governors] are satisfied that the rumours which circulated last week in the markets about possible further currency adjustments have no foundation and they wish it to be known that the central banks concerned are co-operating closely in the exchange markets".[140] The co-operation referred to in the press communiqué came to be known, rather grandly, as the "Basel Agreement" or "Basel arrangements". It consisted of a series of ad hoc bilateral support deals between the Bank of England, on the one hand, and the other main central banks and the BIS, on the other.

At the BIS Annual General Meeting on 12 June 1961, the Bank of England reaffirmed its commitment to the $2.80 sterling parity, and Jacobsson (now at the IMF) stated that "there is no foundation whatever for the rumours that there are some new plans under international discussion for currency adjustment".[141] However, the Old Lady of Threadneedle Street requested further ammunition, to which the BIS contributed $154 million in gold swaps in June 1961.[142] The total assistance offered since March reached its peak at the end of June at $904 million. Pressure on sterling did not subside entirely until the announcement, on 25 July, by the U.K. government of emergency measures to reduce the external deficit. On 4 August the IMF agreed to make facilities available to the United Kingdom totalling $2 billion, the largest amount granted thus far by the IMF. The loan was partly used to repay the central bank assistance given under the Basel arrangements. The U.K. external position improved considerably, and throughout 1962 the exchange markets suffered no further disturbances.

In writing to Chancellor of the Exchequer Selwyn Lloyd, Cobbold, as governor of the Bank of England, hailed the Basel arrangements as "a most useful innovation, and ... a major factor in calming the storm". He added that "they may also prove, in conjunction with further developments in the IMF, to have opened a new chapter in international monetary co-operation".[143] The central banks had flexed their muscles for all to see. "The operation", Cobbold added, "is perhaps an example significant for the future of the power and the size of the resources which can be deployed by the leading monetary authorities when, as was the case on this occasion, they are in agreement about the aim to be pursued".[144] Cobbold was nevertheless not blind to the limits of international support operations, which he saw for what they were: "a short-term protective covering ... that does nothing to change any long-term trends.... Indeed", he said, "we cannot expect our partners to maintain these arrangements indefinitely unless we are able to show that our underlying position is responding to treatment".[145] The BIS was equally straightforward in its 1961 Annual Report: "While central bank co-operation, reinforced if necessary by other action, provides a strong basis for meeting speculative attacks on currencies, it is as well to be clear as to the possible scope of such measures. They afford temporary relief of a situation but they do not cure it. They take the strain off the exchange markets at moments of disorderliness but they do not make weak currencies strong. They afford time for adaptations of policies but they are not a substitute for such adaptations".[146]

The lesson central bankers took home from the attacks on the U.S. dollar and sterling in late 1960 and early 1961 was that, although the Bretton Woods exchange rate regime was vulnerable, effective central bank cooperation could deal with any threat to it – at least for the foreseeable future. The episode thus reinforced the consensus among central bankers with regard to the goals and means of international monetary cooperation. As Cobbold wrote Jacobsson, commenting on the March governors' meeting at the BIS: "I think the Basel talks were a great step forward and were very much in line with the talks we have been having in Washington – to the effect that we are all in the same boat, that threats in either direction to any currency are harmful to all of us, and that the dollar/sterling stability is the key-note of the whole thing".[147] Cobbold's call for unity was to be the rallying cry for the decade to come.

The Americans, for their part, wanted to exploit the constructive mood prevailing in Basel and take things one step further. In a letter to Governor Brunet of the Bank of France, McChesney Martin, chairman of the Federal Reserve Board, suggested that a small, confidential study group of senior central bank officials be established to look at "the problem of restraining or neutralizing short-term capital movements arising from interest arbitrage and speculation".[148] At the April 1961 BIS meeting the study group was set up, with experts from all central banks represented on the BIS Board and including the United States. The group discussed a wide range of subjects, setting much of the agenda for international monetary cooperation for years to come: the eurodollar market, the London gold price, and the role of the IMF and the BIS. Volatility on the foreign exchange markets was at the top of the agenda. Charles Coombs, for the Federal Reserve Bank of New York, suggested a formal agreement to make the facilities under the Basel arrangements available in the future.[149] The Europeans, however, opposed automatic short-term emergency support.[150] The episode once again underlined the difference in approach between an activist Federal Reserve bank – mirroring the activism of the new U.S. administration – anxious to take decisive measures designed to maintain the Bretton Woods status quo, and the more cautious European central banks, who wanted to keep their hands as free as possible.

The study group submitted its final report to the governors in May 1961. The document is of interest because it helped prepare the ground for the establishment of the Gold Pool later that year and for the discussion on the eurodollar market for years to come. It also contained an assessment of the role the BIS could play in "assisting central banks' efforts to maintain orderly exchange markets",[151] arguing that it should go beyond that of consultation and information exchange. It was suggested that, through its transactions with central banks, the BIS could play a more active role in the exchange markets. Although the Bank was bound to limit itself to short-term operations, it could act on its own, or as an agent for the central banks, or by arranging syndicate operations. This was indeed the direction the BIS was to take during the years that followed.

In the following months, some further thought was given to the procedure for possible future support operations. The most urgent practical problem was the coordination of information. In a context of bilateral support, the borrower alone had a complete overview of all transactions concluded with the different counterparties. As no established procedure for reporting existed, the participating central banks were not necessarily fully in the picture. This was felt to be unsatisfactory (and somewhat too easy on the borrower). In early 1963 an information procedure was agreed, in the context of the 1955 European Monetary Agreement, identified by the ugly jargon of "bilateral concerté". It introduced a duty to report to the BIS any support arrangements between one debtor and at least two separate creditors that went beyond the routine swap operations between two central banks. The BIS was then to keep all participants in the particular arrangement informed on the facilities made available by each central bank and on the drawings and reimbursements made by the borrower. The BIS would also prepare a full report on the matter for the EMA Board of Management.[152] When entering into the "bilateral concerté", European central banks made it clear that this did not automatically mean they were under an "obligation either to enter into discussions or to grant any form of short-term assistance".[153]

The new procedure was immediately put to the test. In early 1963, after more than a year and a half of relative calm on the exchange markets, sterling once again came under pressure. The main causes were the rejection by de Gaulle of the U.K. bid to join the EEC on 14 January 1963[154] – and the ensuing economic policy debate in the United Kingdom. Overall, reserve losses remained limited, but Chancellor Maudling decided to test the brand-new provisions for concerted bilateral assistance under the EMA anyway. At the end of March, the Bank of England borrowed $50 million each from the central banks of France, Germany, and Italy, while the Swiss National Bank put up $100 million.[155] The BIS duly notified all participants of the transactions undertaken by each one of them. The $250 million assistance allowed the Bank of England to easily weather the storm. By the end of June 1963, the sum had been fully repaid.

A second arrangement notified through the BIS under the bilateral concerté procedure came about in March 1964, in support of the Italian lira.[156] This particular operation, however, was not without controversy. By mid-1963, as the Italian economy was overheating, inflationary pressures had mounted while both the budget and the balance of payments had shifted into deficit. The exchange rate of the lira came under pressure. In September 1963, the Italian government undertook a combination of monetary tightening and fiscal measures to redress the situation. At the BIS meeting on the weekend of 10–11 November, Carli was still fairly confident that the Bank of Italy was not in any immediate need of assistance.[157] During the winter of 1963–64, as the balance of payments deficit increased further, the defence of the lira parity was eating more and more into the official reserves. Still, at the Basel meeting on 8–9 March 1964, the Bank of Italy's governor only vaguely referred to Italy's need for external assistance, without entering into details. The next day, however, he flew directly from Basel to Washington, where he negotiated a $1 billion package. This included a $100 million credit line provided by the Bank of England and a $150 million dollar–lira swap with the Bundesbank, both of which the Americans had insisted on negotiating on behalf of the Bank of Italy.[158] The press announcement of the arrangement on 14 March 1964 infuriated Italy's EEC partners, who felt that any joint support for the lira should have been arranged in Basel, or possibly Brussels (Monetary Committee of the EEC) or Paris (OECD).[159] The reason Carli gave for bypassing the Europeans was that he had left for the United States with the limited aim of extending an already existent swap arrangement between the Bank of Italy and the Federal Reserve Bank of New York. Heavy speculation against the lira during his stay in Washington had forced him to negotiate a much more far-reaching emergency package with his accommodating U.S. hosts, who, incidentally, had not forgotten Carli's support for the dollar back in 1961. At the BIS governors' meeting of 5–6 April, Carli was again unusually sharply criticised for bypassing Basel and the EEC and also for arranging emergency support not just to deal with a currency crisis but to address a fundamental balance of payments problem.[160] As it turned out, Carli was fully vindicated only a few months later. Almost immediately upon the announcement of the support package, speculation against the lira stopped, and by the summer of 1964 the Italian balance of payments again showed a strong surplus, thanks partly to the earlier government measures and partly to a boom of the world economy in 1963–64.[161] Of the $350 million support made available by the British, Germans, and Swiss, only $64.4 million had been effectively drawn.[162] In the end, the somewhat bitter aftertaste of this episode also helped to speed up the process of tighter monetary cooperation between the six EEC members: the first meeting of the Committee of Central Bank Governors of the EEC member states was held in Basel on 6 July 1964 (see Chapter 12).

The 1964 lira support operation underlined the growing importance of currency swaps as a technique for mutual central bank assistance. Swaps had been undertaken occasionally between central banks on an ad hoc basis as early as the 1920s. In essence, a currency swap was a bilateral agreement whereby one central bank opened in its books an account in its own (or occasionally in a third) currency on behalf of the other central bank and vice versa. An agreed amount of foreign exchange thus became available and could, for the duration of the agreement, be drawn at any time. One obvious advantage of this system was that a central bank did not have to maintain large amounts of many different currencies in its reserves for possible interventions in the exchange markets, but could instead activate its swap arrangements with other central banks to the same effect. Usually swap agreements were limited in time (generally for three months) in order to contain exchange risks and to avoid immobilising reserves for too long.

If, at the end of the agreed duration of the swap, no use had been made of it, it was either cancelled or put on standby for later reactivation.

Beginning in 1962, the U.S. monetary authorities developed this technique further. On 13 February 1962, the Federal Open Market Committee (FOMC) authorised the Federal Reserve Bank of New York to undertake foreign exchange operations on behalf of the Federal Reserve System "to help safeguard the value of the dollar in the international exchange markets".[163] Following this decision, Charles Coombs, responsible for foreign exchange transactions at the New York Fed, began weaving an intricate network of swap arrangements (or "reciprocal currency arrangements"), which would eventually link more than a dozen Western central banks and the BIS with the Federal Reserve in what Coombs called "the perimeter defence line shielding the dollar against speculation and other exchange market pressures".[164] The first such swap line was agreed between the Federal Reserve Bank of New York and the Bank of France for $50 million in 1962. A $100 million swap line between the Federal Reserve Bank of New York and the BIS, established in July 1962, was used to mop up a flow of hot money to Switzerland in June–July 1962. Under normal circumstances, the Swiss National Bank might have offered these dollars at the U.S. Treasury window to be exchanged into gold. Thanks to its swap agreement with both the BIS and the Swiss National Bank, the Federal Reserve Bank of New York was able to draw over $100 million in Swiss francs, which was immediately used to buy back the same amount of dollars from the Swiss National Bank, greatly reducing the dollar surplus of that bank.[165] Once market pressures subsided and the dollar strengthened, these swaps were reversed. From mid-1962, the Federal Reserve Bank swap network developed quickly. Total amounts available reached nearly $1 billion by the end of 1962 and more than $2 billion by the end of 1963.[166]

Besides the Federal Reserve Bank, other central banks also made use of swap agreements, which featured regularly in currency support operations, much in the same way as they had already been part of the March 1964 package in support of the Italian lira. Central banks also used currency swaps to offset seasonal foreign exchange pressures such as those caused by commercial banks' end-of-year window-dressing operations.[167]

The Federal Reserve swap network became a permanent feature of the international monetary system, surviving the Bretton Woods breakdown. It grew from $2 billion at the end of 1963 to $10 billion in 1969 and $30 billion in 1978. Coombs did not doubt that "within this defensive network, any government which is fully prepared to defend its currency should be able to mobilize sufficient financial resources to beat off any speculative attack".[168] Swaps, however, remained a short-term, emergency device, designed to address fluctuations of a relatively limited scope.[169]

The U.S. authorities used other financial techniques to protect U.S. gold reserves as well. From late 1961, the U.S. Treasury issued medium-term securities denominated in dollars or in other currencies. These so-called Roosa bonds – named after the U.S. under-secretary of the Treasury – were mainly offered to European central banks as an interest-bearing alternative to converting their dollar surpluses into nonperforming gold and to provide the United States with foreign currencies for market interventions or swap repayment. By the end of 1963, the total amount of outstanding Roosa bonds exceeded $750 million.

At the beginning of 1964, the BIS reviewed the existing array of short-term credit arrangements between central banks, concluding that "such arrangements seem certain to be a continuing feature of the system". These short-term facilities were essential in "absorbing or avoiding sudden and severe pressures on the foreign exchange market". While "a country should be able to provide for ordinary seasonal or other temporary fluctuations in its balance of payments out of its own reserves", the BIS reckoned that "with convertibility a currency may be more subject to pressures from movements of funds which cannot be met out of monetary reserves without the loss of reserves itself aggravating the situation". Thus, in the era of convertibility at fixed exchange rates, short-term credit arrangements were essential "to enable the monetary authorities to retain control over the course of events". Moreover, "the knowledge that concerted action will, if necessary, be taken is in itself a stabilising factor on the international monetary scene", and "the alternatives to cooperative credit arrangements are likely to include less freedom in trade and payments and more frequent exchange rate adjustments".[170] Here, then, was the basic philosophy underlying much of the cooperative efforts undertaken by the monetary authorities throughout the 1960s.

11.7   The Defence of Sterling

In the 1960s most policy makers believed that, in order to maintain the stability of the dollar's exchange rate, the sterling parity too had to be defended. As Milton Gilbert put it: "whenever sterling might be devalued, confidence in the dollar price of gold could be expected to evaporate and a large rise in the market demand for gold, as well as in central-bank conversions of dollars for gold at the U.S. treasury, could be anticipated".[171]

After the Second World War, the United Kingdom ran recurring balance of payments deficits. The causes for this were manifold. Throughout the

1950s and early 1960s, output and productivity growth were lagging behind those of the United Kingdom's main trade partners. Moreover, U.K. colonial and military commitments overseas, while being progressively scaled down, were still a major drain on the country's resources. Substantial capital outflows continued for direct and portfolio investment. The prevailing market feeling was that the pound remained overvalued, even after the 30.5% devaluation of 1949. The official reserves and external assets had been only very partially rebuilt after their wartime depletion. In these circumstances, unfavourable news on the British economy and its external position was likely to spark off, at any time, a run on the currency.

Owing to long-standing political, cultural, and economic links as well as to the still-shining reputation of London as a leading financial market, a large number of foreign banks and monetary authorities – particularly those in the former British Empire – held substantial sterling-denominated reserves. Thus, the pound sterling continued to play the role of a reserve currency, albeit almost exclusively limited to the Commonwealth sterling area.[172] While it is hard to say whether, on balance, the United Kingdom benefited from the reserve status of the pound, the existence of a junior reserve currency created an additional problem for the management of the international monetary system, particularly as – not entirely rationally – markets perceived a link between the dollar and sterling. Before 1914 and, to a lesser extent, between the wars, the Bank of England had run on thinner reserve ratios than the other European central banks, relying on the enormous liquidity of the London market (which it was able to manage effectively by small changes in the Bank rate) and on an outstanding reputation. After the Second World War, however, both conditions had weakened while at the same time the official reserves and foreign assets of the United Kingdom had been considerably depleted. At the end of 1962, overseas sterling net liabilities (the "sterling balances"[173]) amounted to £2.8 billion, while the United Kingdom's official reserves stood at barely £1 billion.[174] Hence the stability of the sterling–dollar exchange rate rested to a large extent on U.K. economic policy and a credible international commitment to support the pound.

In the early 1960s, as we have seen, the pound suffered two major bouts of weakness: in the first half of 1961, following the Deutsche mark revaluation, and again in early 1963. Each time the threatening crisis was defused by immediate international support. The improvement of the market's outlook on the pound, in March–April 1963, allowed Chancellor Maudling to launch his "dash for growth" programme, which included substantial tax reliefs. Maudling's declared purpose was to set the U.K. economy on a long-term path of higher, sustainable growth that would (it was hoped) also result in more balanced external accounts, with favourable effects on the exchange rate. His policy was also motivated by the more mundane electoral goal of enhancing the Conservative Party's re-election chances in the 1964 general election.[175] The programme did succeed in raising economic growth and reducing unemployment to record lows. It also led to a surge in imports and an increase in the external deficit.

By early 1964, the Bank of England started contingency plans for fresh international support for the pound. At the BIS meeting of 4–5 April 1964, which was largely devoted to the Italian lira, Governor Cromer tested the waters for a possible new central bank package to shore up sterling. Reassured by the governor's report that in case of need the Bank of England would have no difficulty in raising at least 200 million pounds, the Treasury felt – not least for reasons of speed and unconditionality – that "the balance of argument was distinctly in favour of looking to Basel assistance first, rather than going straight to the Fund to meet a speculative attack on sterling".[176]

In July 1964, estimates of the U.K. balance of payments deficit were revised upwards, and uneasiness increased on the exchange markets. In August, the United Kingdom obtained the renewal of an existing $1 billion standby credit from the IMF but did not draw from it. Instead, the Bank of England turned to Basel. During the last week of September, bilateral support arrangements were made with eight central banks for a total amount of $1 billion.[177]

The general election on 15 October 1964 returned the Labour Party to power with a small parliamentary majority. The first decision that Prime Minister Harold Wilson and his Chancellor of the Exchequer James Callaghan made was to hold to the existing parity of the pound, despite the fact that the balance of payments deficit for 1964 was estimated to be the largest in U.K. history. Labour, like most left-leaning parties in other countries, did not want its name to be associated in the public mind with devaluation. The knowledge that the United Kingdom could count on international assistance and borrowing facilities made the decision against devaluation easier to make.[178]

On 26 October, the new government announced a temporary import surcharge of 15%. In the absence of a more robust package, pressure on the sterling exchange rate mounted. At the meeting of the G10 governors in Basel on Sunday 8 November 1964, the European governors "concurred in the view that the programme so far announced had left an impression of weakness and reluctance to come to grips with the problem and that this would inevitably lead to the emergence of speculation in the exchange markets". The Gold and Foreign Exchange Committee also feared "a potentially explosive situation in the gold and foreign exchange markets".[179] Lord Cromer was urged by his colleagues to raise the Bank rate. This, however, was a government decision, and it met with considerable resistance in the Cabinet. Callaghan introduced his first budget on 11 November, two days after the Basel meeting, causing a flight from sterling due to the announced increase in social expenditure and the lack of measures targeted at the exchange crisis. The announcement of an increase in the U.S. balance of payments deficit contributed further to market nervousness. Faced with huge reserve losses, the Labour government finally increased the Bank rate from 5% to 7%. However, what only a few weeks before would have been seen as evidence of decisive action was now interpreted as an admission of failure. The markets were unimpressed and the flight from sterling accelerated.

On the morning of 25 November 1964, Lord Cromer, backed by the New York Fed's President Hayes, made a frantic round of telephone calls to his central bank colleagues in Europe. By 6:00 P.M. a $3 billion support package had been wrapped up. It was the largest operation of that kind in the history of monetary cooperation to that date.[180] It was also concluded in an incredibly swift manner. When, on the next day (26 November), Callaghan announced this support operation before the House of Commons, public opinion could not fail to be impressed by what central banks could do when acting cohesively.[181] In early December, the United Kingdom drew $1 billion under its standby arrangement with the IMF in order to repay the support received from central banks back in September, in the run-up to the general election. As a result of these measures, the sterling exchange rate improved immediately, although it continued to require substantial official interventions over the following few months.[182] Eventually, the $3 billion standby credit proved to be more than sufficient to steady the sterling rate.[183] "The central bankers retain their astonishing capacity for instant results. And if theirs is not the most desirable possible mechanism, geared always to short-term support of the status quo, it happens to be the only working one. By this new venture in ad hoc cooperation the central banks have indeed surpassed even their own past record."[184]

The sterling crisis was the main discussion topic at the BIS meeting of 13–14 December 1964. The feeling was that the United Kingdom was not yet home and dry. Participants recognised that, as Lord Cromer put it, some of the ground lost through the Labour government's "lack of knowledge and finesse" had been recovered.[185] However, Hayes's suggestion about a joint European statement endorsing the U.K. government's policy in order to restore confidence in sterling met with little sympathy. To most European governors, there was more the United Kingdom could and should do, particularly in terms of incomes policy. Some went further. Both in private conversations with Hayes and at the governors' dinner on Sunday evening, Holtrop – president of the Netherlands Bank and of the BIS – came out bluntly in favour of a sterling devaluation by about 10%. Hayes was appalled at what he considered irresponsible talk. He "expressed disagreement in the strongest terms with the idea of any sterling devaluation and told Dr. Holtrop that it would have disastrous consequences for the dollar and the whole international financial system". Nevertheless, at its meeting in February 1965, the Committee of EEC Governors began some discreet contingency planning for the event that the pound would be devalued.[186] The split between the Anglo-American view and that of most Europeans – ever present in the G10 discussions about reform of the system and within the Gold Pool – could not fail to surface on this occasion as well.

With hindsight, it is conceivable that, in the winter of 1964–65, the U.K. government might have overcome the economic policy stalemate by devaluing the pound – floating was not an option – and by implementing a more stringent budgetary and incomes policy. However, domestic policy priorities ruled out both devaluation and a tighter fiscal and monetary stance. The only available alternative – adopted by the Labour government for the next three years – was to rally international solidarity to shore up confidence in the pound sterling in order to gain time to gradually reduce the balance of payments deficit. With varying degrees of conviction, the world's leading central bankers lent their full support to this strategy. Even so, over the following three years and until the 1967 devaluation, the pound continued to navigate stormy waters. It may even be argued that the ready availability of international support to some extent contributed to the continued agony of the pound, as it cut short any serious consideration of devaluation and allowed the government to avoid a tougher domestic policy stance.[187]

In the summer of 1965 the pound sterling again came under pressure. The depletion of reserves was temporarily obscured from the public eye through the heavy use of IMF drawings and the Bank of England's swap line with the Federal Reserve Bank of New York, but by the end of August the United Kingdom's net reserve position (i.e., net of third-party credits and drawings) had fallen to no more than £516 million, leading the U.S. and U.K. monetary authorities to make an unusual and dramatic démarche. The scheme, suggested by Charles Coombs and the U.S. Treasury, contemplated concerted sterling purchases by the main central banks that would restore confidence "once and for all" and produce a "sterling bear squeeze" that would burn the speculators' fingers. The idea was that the G10 central banks would jointly issue a firm statement in support of sterling's parity and of U.K. government policies. Simultaneously, central banks would start buying sterling for an amount of up to 5% of their total reserves, steadying the sterling exchange rate and teaching speculators a costly lesson. It was hoped that, as a result, sterling would be in the clear for long enough to benefit from the improvement in the underlying fundamentals.[188]

Rupert Raw, adviser to Governor Cromer, visited the main central banks on the Continent to canvass support for the scheme. He met with a frosty reception. Many central banks felt it would be improper for them to give a public endorsement to an individual government's monetary and economic policy. Moreover, the sterling purchase scheme would "in essence" amount to a consolidation of "part of the sterling balances".[189] Immobilising part of their liquid reserves for an indefinite period of time would go against the statutory obligations of most central banks.

Reacting to his colleagues' negative stance, Lord Cromer hinted at the possibility that the U.K. government might resort to floating the pound, striking "a most serious blow to the international monetary system". It was agreed to call a secret meeting of the governors at the BIS on Sunday 5 September to discuss the sterling scheme further.[190] The atmosphere at the meeting was a mixture of gloom and irritation. "We are confronted with a clear and present danger", Hayes said, warning that "the penalty for failure in today's negotiations could be extremely severe: a floating rate for sterling would probably lead to a proliferation of protective measures which might quickly undo the progress of the last 20 years". Schwegler of the Swiss National Bank was persuaded that "devaluation would be a disaster of the first magnitude", and Governor Åsbrink of the Swedish central bank added that "a break in the sterling parity would probably destroy a system which had yielded good results and would set us adrift on an uncharted sea".[191] The proposed sterling purchase scheme was nevertheless categorically rejected. Carli, Ansiaux, Holtrop, and Åsbrink all called for a more systematic, long-term approach in tackling the sterling balances while at the same time offering a new round of short-term credits to the Bank of England. Lord Cromer accepted the offer from his European colleagues "with some embarrassment". In the end, only the Federal Reserve Bank of New York, the originator of the whole idea, promised to purchase sterling in substantial amounts on the market.

The new arrangement was announced on 10 September 1965, less than one week after the dramatic meeting in Basel.[192] The same day, Charles Coombs at the Federal Reserve Bank of New York and his counterpart Roy

Bridge at the Bank of England launched their attack – which the Europeans had chosen not to join – on the speculators. The combined effect was a decisive change in market sentiment; there was no need to draw on the standby facilities. As speculators ran for cover, funds flowed back to London. For the first time since early 1963, sterling was steady and comfortably above its par value on the markets.[193] Soon afterwards, the balance of payments also went into surplus, and the United Kingdom was able to repay some of its earlier debts. Thereafter, the pound remained firm well into 1966.

The governors took advantage of the return of calm on the exchange markets to look at the fundamental problems causing sterling's weakness. Upon their request, Gilbert produced a memorandum on "The problem of the sterling balances",[194] circulated at the BIS Board meeting of 13 December 1965. Gilbert's conclusions were (1) that "restoring a firm equilibrium in the external accounts of the United Kingdom [was] the immediate practical policy problem" while (2) "the slender U.K. reserves [should] be protected in some way from possible drawings on the sterling balances arising from conditions outside the United Kingdom and outside its control".[195] He suggested a new cooperative arrangement on the order of magnitude of a billion dollars to shield the United Kingdom from the threat of a sudden reduction in overseas sterling balances.

The proposal got a lukewarm reception at the December 1965 BIS meeting. The preliminary discussions on the Gilbert memorandum "did not go particularly well".[196] Some governors, in particular Brunet from France and Ansiaux from Belgium, were pessimistic about the United Kingdom's balance of payments and dubious about granting further assistance. Ferras used his Christmas holiday in Paris to try to win the Bank of France over to a cooperative effort.[197] He may not have been entirely unsuccessful because, by the time of the January 1966 BIS meeting, the principle that some collective arrangement should be worked out had been generally accepted, and now the discussion turned on the form this new type of assistance should take. It took the governors and their experts five more months and numerous meetings to reach an agreement.[198] The deadlock was broken in the April meeting when the Bank of France, "for the first time, indicated a positive wish to participate in the credit arrangements".[199]

The first so-called Sterling Group Arrangement was finalised in May and took effect on 11 June 1966. It consisted of a $600 million credit put up by a group of nine central banks and the BIS, with the BIS acting as the principal for the group (including the arrangement that the BIS contribution of $75 million would, in case of need, be drawn first and repaid last).[200] This credit was only to be drawn on by the Bank of England to offset a reduction in U.K. reserves caused by a contraction of the sterling balances held by sterling- and nonsterling-area countries. Initially limited to nine months, the Group Arrangement was subsequently renewed on an annual basis until it was liquidated by phased repayments between September 1969 and January 1971.[201]

This first Group Arrangement was a novelty on two accounts. For one thing, in contrast to previous support arrangements, it was not an ad hoc response to a sudden emergency situation but rather an attempt to provide a stabilising buffer for sterling, recognising that the latter's role as reserve currency burdened the United Kingdom with responsibilities it found increasingly hard to shoulder. In essence, the Group Arrangement tried to lessen the effects of the international role of sterling on the U.K. reserves position by sharing the weight of these responsibilities. The second innovation was the coordinating role played by the BIS. Whereas previous arrangements consisted of more or less closely coordinated bilateral agreements between the Bank of England and a number of individual central banks, the BIS now acted as the agent for a group of central banks. The combined facilities, made available by the participating banks, were administered centrally and put at the disposal of the Bank of England via a single BIS account (except for the contributions of the Bank of France and the New York Fed, which remained outside of the "group").

In the spring of 1966, it was clear that the restrictive measures introduced in 1965 had failed to curb demand, as unemployment remained at historical lows. If, on the real side of the economy, the British people "had never before had it so good", the external accounts suffered from upward pressure on wages and prices.[202] As the trade deficit increased, a rise in U.S. interest rates attracted funds away from London. Confidence in the pound once again weakened. On 20 July 1966, the government announced an austerity programme that included an attempt at controlling wages and prices as well as cuts in government expenditure. Nonetheless, the drain on the U.K. reserves persisted. The new governor of the Bank of England, Sir Leslie O'Brien, who had succeeded Cromer at the end of June, turned to the Americans for help. The Federal Reserve offered a substantial increase in its swap line with the Bank of England on condition that the European central banks, in their turn, agree to augment their swap lines with the New York Fed and put up at least another $400 million in new credits for the Bank of England.[203]

The matter was discussed at the Basel meeting of 4–5 September 1966, where debates at times became quite acrimonious. Holtrop and Ansiaux almost exploded with fury when Coombs pressed them to sign up to a new credit arrangement within the next week, implying that otherwise the Federal Reserve would no longer be able to support the United Kingdom.[204] In

Table 11.1. *U.K. reserves, sterling balances, and international support organised through or with the BIS, 1961–71 (millions of U.S. dollars at current prices)*

	Sterling balances (1)	U.K. reserves (2)	(2)/(1) (3)	International support via the BIS (4)		Support drawn (max.) (5)	Final repayment (6)
1961 March	10,399	3,021	29.1%	549	(Basel Agreement)	549	
June	10,349	2,772	26.8%	562	(Basel Agreement)	562	207
Sept	9,772	3,553	36.4%				789
Dec	9,929	3,318	33.4%				115
1962 March	9,607	3,452	35.9%				
June	9,845	3,433	34.9%				
Sept	9,654	2,792	28.9%				
Dec	10,816	2,806	25.9%				
1963 March	10,696	2,814	26.3%	250	(29/3/1963)	250	
June	10,850	2,713	25.0%				250
Sept	11,108	2,736	24.6%				
Dec	11,486	2,657	23.1%				
1964 March	11,953	2,660	22.3%				
June	12,228	2,705	22.1%				
Sept	12,491	2,540	20.3%	1,000	(21/9/1964)	1,000	
Dec	11,592	2,316	20.0%	3,000	(25/11/1964)		1,000
1965 March	11,371	2,330	20.5%			643	
June	11,057	2,792	25.3%				643
Sept	10,954	2,755	25.2%	925	(14/9/1965)		
Dec	11,407	3,004	26.3%				
1966 March	11,838	3,573	30.2%			50	50
June	12,001	3,276	27.3%	1,000	(1st SGA)		
Sept	10,931	3,161	28.9%	1,700	(13/9/1966)		
Dec	11,166	3,100	27.8%			150	
1967 March	11,676	3,259	27.9%				150
June	11,670	2,834	24.3%				
Sept	10,828	2,733	25.2%	250	(15/11/1967)	250	
Dec	8,856	2,695	30.4%	1,500	(22/11/1967)		
1968 March	8,954	2,722	30.4%	1,075	(21/3/1968)		
June	8,102	2,683	33.1%			680+	
Sept	8,112	2,717	33.5%	2,000	(2nd SGA)	275	
Dec	8,112	2,422	29.9%				
1969 March	8,426	2,470	29.3%				
June	8,599	2,443	28.4%				250
Sept	8,506	2,434	28.6%				275
Dec	8,942	2,527	28.3%				
1970 March	9,643	2,710	28.1%				680
June	10,049	2,791	27.8%				
Sept	10,068	2,666	26.5%				
Dec	10,128	2,827	27.9%				

	Sterling balances (1)	U.K. reserves (2)	(2)/(1) (3)	International support via the BIS (4)	Support drawn (max.) (5)	Final repayment (6)
1971 March	10,822	3,317	30.7%			
June	11,479	3,619	31.5%			
Sept	12,271	5,014	40.9%			
Dec	13,493	6,062	44.9%			

Sources and explanation.

COLUMN 1: "Sterling balances" = exchange reserves in sterling held by central banks and other official funds (including international organisations, but excluding IMF sterling balances) + private sterling balances ("other funds" or "banking and money market liabilities to holders other than central monetary institutions"), both in overseas sterling countries and nonsterling countries. Data from March 1961 to September 1962 taken from Bank of England, *Quarterly Bulletin*, vol. 3, no. 2 (June 1963), table 20, pp. 154–5. From December 1962, this series was discontinued and replaced by an improved series, resulting in higher total figures (hence the jump in sterling balances between September and December 1962). For more details on this change, see: Bank of England, *Quarterly Bulletin*, vol. 3, no. 2 (June 1963), pp. 98–105. Sterling balances figures for December 1962 to December 1971 are taken from "Overseas Sterling Balances, 1963–1973", in Bank of England, *Quarterly Bulletin*, vol. 14, no. 2 (June 1974), pp. 162–75.

COLUMN 2: "United Kingdom reserves" = official reserves (gold + convertible currencies + special drawing rights), as published in the statistical annex to Bank of England, *Quarterly Bulletin* (June 1962 – June 1972).

COLUMNS 4, 5, AND 6: BIS sources (see text); "SGA" = Sterling Group Arrangement.

COLUMNS 5 AND 6: figures for support drawn and repayments refer only to the contribution of the BIS group of central banks in these different support operations and are therefore not complete. The first and second Sterling Group Arrangements (June 1966 and September 1968, respectively) are not accounted for in columns 5 and 6.

EXCHANGE RATE: all amounts are in millions of U.S. dollars. Amounts originally in pounds have been converted into U.S. dollars at the prevailing official exchange rate: March 1961 to November 1967, £1 = \$2.80; November 1967 to December 1971, £1 = \$2.40. From March 1971 pound sterling appreciated considerably against the dollar, reaching a market rate of £1 = \$2.55 in December 1971; an official rate realignment was not implemented until the Smithsonian Agreement of 18 December 1971.

the end, O'Brien succeeded in defusing the tension. He expressed the hope that he was asking for assistance for the last time, "otherwise it would be a disaster". It took another week of intense negotiations over the telephone to reach a final agreement on a \$300 million new standby line to the Bank of England – consisting mostly of three-month currency swaps offered by eight European central banks – that came on top of the \$600 million increase in the swap line the Federal Reserve Bank of New York was already committed to.[205] The central banks concerned, including the BIS, also agreed to a substantial increase in their bilateral swap lines with the Federal Reserve Bank of New York. It then took a few more days, and all the diplomatic skills Ferras could muster, to agree on a statement announcing the new package on 13 September 1966.[206] Once again the markets were reassured, and they would remain relatively calm until the middle of 1967.[207] *The Economist* commented favourably on this display of timely crisis management: "Once more the central banks stepped in where governments clearly were not ready to tread".[208]

In early summer 1967, however, the trade balance of the United Kingdom again shifted into deficit because of slackening demand abroad and as a result of the Six-Day War in the Middle East and the closure of the Suez Canal. The announcement of the United Kingdom's second application to join the EEC provoked a public debate on the position of sterling within the Common Market. Finally, mild reflationary policies introduced in order to counteract rising unemployment were seen by the markets as a weakening of the earlier commitment to maintain the United Kingdom's external balance. At the Basel meeting of 8–9 July 1967, "there was a good deal of preoccupation with the worsening position of sterling".[209] At the meeting of the gold and foreign exchange experts in Basel on 9 September, Roy Bridge (Bank of England) noted: "Confidence is not at its best, everybody is looking over his shoulder, watching what the next will do".[210] The U.K. reserve losses from June until the end of August reached $1.3 billion. At the September 1967 governors' meeting there was some brief talk about a new support package, but nobody seemed keen to commit. However, Governor O'Brien had only just returned from Basel to his London office when he received a telephone call from Ferras, who told him "that there was a strong desire at the BIS to help the United Kingdom and that he had devised a scheme for doing so which he thought that BIS members would accept".[211] What Ferras had in mind was a much smaller package than before, totalling only some $250 million, that would allow the United Kingdom to make the last repayment on its IMF drawing of December 1964 falling due in December 1967. When informed by the governor about Ferras's démarche, Prime Minister Wilson and Chancellor Callaghan welcomed the scheme because it promised to buy them time to tackle the trade deficit and because it might prove useful in persuading the Americans to further increase their support for sterling. Unfortunately – but probably not by chance – the hammering out of the details took an incredibly long time, and the new facility was not announced until Wednesday 15 November 1967,[212] too late to save the day.

From mid-October the pound had come under renewed attack as the result of dock strikes in London and Liverpool and the publication of a European Commission report, which was read to imply a need for devaluation if the United Kingdom were to join the EEC.[213] But the U.K. Treasury still held out the hope that by means of a large, new international credit it might be possible to hold the line. The governors, meeting in Basel on 12 November 1967, were informed by O'Brien that the pound would have to devalue unless a large medium- to long-term support package could be guaranteed, since the Bank of England was already overburdened with short-term debt. This the governors could not pledge, and the only possible alternative seemed to be a $3 billion IMF standby commitment. In a secret memorandum to President Johnson, U.S. Secretary of the Treasury Fowler warned that the British were now on the brink of devaluation. While, Fowler argued, "it might seem tempting to settle this perennial problem now and let sterling go,... the risks for us are just too great to take this gamble if we can find another alternative".[214] However, the chances for another international rescue package were extremely slim. The U.K. request for a multi-government long-term loan of up to $3 billion was not feasible, and the Americans also objected to the IMF standby suggested from Basel because it would take weeks to negotiate and, more importantly, might use up all GAB resources, thereby jeopardising the chances for the United States itself to make a big IMF drawing if required. Given the negative outcome of these last-minute soundings, Wilson and Callaghan on Monday 13 November bowed to the inevitable. The formal decision to devalue the pound from its 1949 parity of $2.80 to $2.40, or by 14.3%, was taken by the Cabinet on 15 November. It was announced publicly and implemented on Saturday 18 November 1967. The two days between the decision and its implementation caused further reserve losses of nearly $1.5 billion.

From the perspective of international monetary cooperation, the sterling devaluation was handled fairly well. At the November Basel meeting, one week before the final decision was taken by the U.K. government, the G10 central banks had already been left in no doubt that a devaluation was almost certain and had been given an indication of the range the U.K. authorities had in mind. In contrast to the 1949 sterling devaluation, the 1967 one was not followed by a spate of devaluations elsewhere, so its effect on the United Kingdom's competitive position could be fully realised. Whereas the central banks had refused to put together a medium-term package to support the pound at its $2.80 rate, they immediately offered large-scale short-term assistance to support the new $2.40 parity. To this effect, at the end of November 1967, $1.5 billion was placed at the disposal of the Bank of England for a three-month period.[215] Together with a $1.4 billion IMF standby, this gave the United Kingdom enough ammunition to defend the new parity.

11.8   The BIS, the G10, and the Debate on Reforming the International Monetary System

Three lines of defence of exchange rate stability were set up in the early 1960s. Two of them – the Gold Pool and the swap network (mainly but not exclusively focused on the dollar–sterling rate) – have been discussed in previous sections. The third line of defence was highlighted by the General Arrangements to Borrow (GAB). The scheme was first proposed by Bernstein in a speech delivered at Harvard in 1958.[216] Anticipating that European currencies' convertibility would bring about much greater movements of international funds and fluctuations in reserve levels, Bernstein argued that large U.S. drawing rights from the IMF would be crucial to offset short-term adverse capital movements. But the IMF did not possess sufficient nondollar funds, even after the general increase in quotas that took place in 1959. The fact was, as Gilbert noted, that "it had not been anticipated in Bretton Woods that the United States might be an applicant for IMF credit".[217] Bernstein, Jacobsson, and others thus proposed "the creation of an additional facility by those industrial countries with an interest in preserving the functioning of the world reserve system".[218] The idea was to make advance arrangements in order to set up a mechanism of international lending of last resort to the United States to be used in times of crisis.

Fresh from his BIS experience, Jacobsson had long been convinced that for international stabilisation to succeed it was "sufficient that the leading industrial countries work together, i.e. United States, Great Britain, France, Germany and maybe Italy and Japan".[219] His consummate diplomatic skills were thus put to work to gain the endorsement of governments and central banks for the creation of a new standby credit facility available to the United States. As in the case of so many other proposals for international monetary cooperation, the problems in reaching consensus largely derived from the potential borrowers' desire to remain as free as possible from international constraints on their domestic policy and from the lenders' wish to make lending conditional on the borrower's compliance with agreed policy changes. To achieve consensus on the standby credit arrangement, the IMF managing director travelled extensively to Europe. In the summer of 1961 he visited London, Paris, Bonn, and Brussels and met with his old friends at the BIS Annual General Meeting.

In arguing for the setting up of an emergency facility at a time when there was no lack of international liquidity, Jacobsson knew he was speaking to an audience that still retained memories of the Great Crash of the early 1930s. "You will remember", he told his colleagues, "how many great financiers and economists declared in about 1929 that the financial problems were solved. And then in two years' time came the worst financial crisis the world has ever had in peace time. So one never knows".[220] He was not alone in raising the ghost of the early 1930s: Triffin, for one, feared a deflation induced by a liquidity crunch. But while using the same rhetoric, Jacobsson was not fond of "professors", as he somewhat dismissively called the authors of the various "plans" for the reform of the system.[221] "There is", he noted in his diary, "in the world a madness at the present, the Triffin Plan – the Stamp Plan – and don't know what. If there were a referendum, I suppose that 75% of the U.S. economists would favour some such plan – and perhaps something similar in England. And in France Raymond Aron told me that, if he were not a Keynesian, he would be a socialist – and there are many like him. God knows what students are taught". Aware that policy makers were equally suspicious of professors' plans, Jacobsson argued with them that the proposed borrowing arrangement was also a way to channel dangerous proposals "into some reasonable direction – into something countries can accept".[222]

The most contentious issue in the negotiations was the degree of control each lender should have over its own funds. The IMF favoured an entirely multilateral stance: the new facilities should be used according to the spirit and the letter of its Articles of Agreement.[223] The French insisted on semi-bilateral arrangements whereby each lender should decide whether its resources were needed and how they should be used.[224] The idea of a European fund, operated by the OEEC, that would lend to the IMF or directly to the United States and United Kingdom was also floated, as was the proposal of having the Monetary Committee of the European Community manage relations with the IMF.[225]

The compromise solution that eventually emerged provided for lenders' safeguards "by leaving the principal decisions in the hands of the lending countries".[226] In the guarded official language of the BIS, the GAB – finalised in December 1961 – was defined as an "agreement among a group of ten industrial countries[227] enabling the IMF to borrow supplementary resources under Article VII [of its General Agreement]. A sum of $6 milliard has been pledged on a standby basis, the purpose of which is to put the Fund in a position to aid a member of the group whose currency is threatened by a flight of short term capital. It is also intended to provide effective resources in the event of a large drawing by the United States or others in the group, without impairing the Fund's more usual operations".[228]

The fact that a special procedure was agreed upon for the use of the standby facilities that entailed cooperation among the ten participating countries somehow established the group (subsequently known as the Group of Ten or G10) "as an alternative and rival forum of international policy making".[229] It represented, in Harold James's view, "a major dent in the IMF's claim to universality".[230] The suspicion that in international financial cooperation some countries were more equal than others could not be avoided. Some members of the club, while often sceptical of its practical effectiveness,[231] tended to present themselves as the champions of stability, implicitly emphasising a divide between themselves and the less virtuous outsiders. Some of the latter even protested against their exclusion from the GAB. As for the BIS, it could hardly be embarrassed by the negative connotation the word "club" took on among nonmembers. Itself originating as the "club" of the main gold-standard countries, with core membership largely overlapping with the Group of Ten, the BIS held the view that responsibility for international monetary stability fell on the shoulders of the largest economies – a view, as we have seen, privately shared by its former economic adviser Jacobsson, now managing director of the IMF.

The events of the early 1960s that prompted setting up of the cooperative measures described in previous pages (the swap network, standby credits, the Gold Pool, and the like) signalled to policy makers the shortcomings of the system much more effectively than Triffin's papers and congressional hearings. Thus, at the IMF meeting in Washington in September 1963, the G10 decided to promote a study of the international monetary system.[232] This study, conducted by the Group's deputies (high-ranking Treasury or central bank officials), marked the beginning of the formal involvement of the BIS with the work of the G10. Robert Roosa, acting as chairman of the deputies' study group, asked the BIS to provide background information on the gold and eurocurrency markets and on short-term credit arrangements among central banks. The BIS assigned Milton Gilbert to participate in the study group's meetings with observer status.[233] The deputies' study group produced a report that was published in August 1964.[234] One of its recommendations, which was quickly implemented, was that the members of the Group would provide the BIS with statistical information regarding the means of financing their external accounts imbalances. The purpose of this "multilateral surveillance" exercise was to centralise and communicate in confidence to all the G10 central banks statistics on monetary reserves, allowing thereby for early warning of the likely use of the standby facilities created under the GAB.[235] The Americans disliked the "multilateral surveillance" idea, but they decided to go along with it in order to placate the Europeans and in particular the French.[236]

From late 1964 onwards, the traditional BIS governors' meetings on the Sunday afternoons and the Sunday night governors' dinners – in which the BIS general manager and economic adviser participated – effectively became a G10 forum as participation was broadened to include the governors of the Bank of Canada and the Bank of Japan. The BIS was also involved in the G10 study group on the creation of reserve assets, established as a follow-up to the August 1964 report and which, for a while, became the main forum for analysis and discussion of reforms of the international monetary system. The rest of this section is devoted to the BIS's contribution to that debate.

The August 1964 report of the deputies highlighted a sharp divide among participating countries about the functioning of the system and, therefore, about how to make it more stable. The crux of the dispute, as already noted, boiled down to conflicting views on the nature of balance of payments disequilibria. On the one hand, the United States and the United Kingdom argued that balance of payments deficits could be corrected only over a long stretch of time, particularly as surplus countries did not feel to be under any strong pressure to do their part of the job in the adjustment process. The United States and the United Kingdom saw neither the appropriateness nor the need to pay the domestic cost of the strong measures required to bring about a swift correction. On the other hand, some Continental countries – most particularly France – not only regarded deficit countries as too cautious in taking corrective measures but also felt they were paying a high domestic-inflation price for the continuation of their excessive surpluses. They concluded that strict limits should be imposed on borrowing facilities in order to create an incentive to reduce deficits. Neither faction was willing to contemplate substantial exchange rate adjustments seriously.[237]

The French government, under the influence of Jacques Rueff (who, as we have seen, had de Gaulle's ear), was the staunchest opponent of indefinite recourse to international financial engineering to finance the U.S. balance of payments deficit and prop up the dollar. Rueff's conviction that only a return to the gold standard could bring discipline and equilibrium back to international payments was shared by many in top government positions. Soon after leaving the post of BIS general manager to join France's civil service, Guindey wrote a government memorandum endorsing the gold standard. Since the war, he said, the French had been convinced that the IMF could not be "the centre of true cooperation among the countries that matter from a financial point of view, as it is too much under American influence". France, he added, "always favoured the use of the Basle Club and of the OECD for intimate European and Western joint work".[238] He also complained that France's Continental neighbours were too shy in supporting its views, with the exception of Belgium and Switzerland.

Everything in the BIS's history, intellectual tradition, and top-staff composition made the Bank naturally lean towards the position of the Continentals. However, the presence of Milton Gilbert – an American with a deep knowledge of Europe, and especially France – exercised a moderating influence, both political and intellectual, within the Bank itself as well as in the G10 deputies' debates. On the one hand he saw that a return to the gold standard was simply not an option; on the other, he was aware that financial engineering could not provide a permanent solution to problems of a structural nature.[239]

Gilbert's middle-of-the-road position is best summarised by the concluding remarks of a speech he gave in 1969. "In some quarters today", he said, "any favourable mention of gold brands one as a traditionalist who does not accept the 'new economics'. As for myself, I was convinced of the necessity of a managed economy while I was still a graduate student – and I have not changed. I just wish Congress believed in it as much as I do and was prepared to give the necessary flexibility to policy instruments. But some people seem to want all management and no economy. A managed economy in the domestic sphere does not mean that the money-creating power of the central bank should be subservient to the government. Similarly, in the international sphere, a managed system does not mean that the adjustment process should have low priority or that new means of payments should be created whenever it is politically convenient for one government or another".[240]

Three options, each with nuanced variants, were considered during the sometimes muddled discussions at the G10 deputies' meetings on the reform of the international monetary system. One group of countries, led by France, held that any workable reform would entail a permanent adjustment of the U.S. (and possibly U.K.) balance of payments. Indefinite accumulation of foreign debt was simply not sustainable in the long run. A corollary to this position was that – short of an outright return to the classical gold standard (which, amongst France's top civil servants, only Rueff and his followers seriously advocated) – the imposition of borrowing constraints on the United States was the only way to produce the right incentives to adjust. The proponents of this solution to the international monetary problems either said little about the role of surplus countries in the adjustment process or explicitly saw no reason why "virtuous" countries should give up domestic "discipline" in order to help profligate ones out of problems of their own creation. Exchange rate realignments received little attention or were ruled out as providing only a transitory benefit to the system. Moreover, proponents of the "structural" solution seemed to believe that the disappearance of the U.S. balance of payments deficit would also solve the liquidity-reserve problem by curtailing the amount of dollars that needed to be recycled in the system. In any case, the issue of reserve and liquidity adequacy did not receive particular attention within this framework.

The second view, endorsed primarily by the United States and United Kingdom, was diametrically opposed to the first one. It held that balance of payments adjustment, while certainly an aim to be pursued cooperatively in the long run by deficit and surplus countries alike, could not be contemplated in the medium term for both economic and political reasons. In the meanwhile, the U.S. deficit was deemed sustainable as long as international financial cooperation continued. Such cooperation, the U.S. representatives argued, was as much in Europe's interest as in North America's. Not only would the sudden disappearance of the U.S. external deficit plunge the world into a liquidity crunch, but the deficit itself derived mainly from U.S. military spending in Europe and elsewhere for Western defence, to which Europe made only a marginal contribution (some Europeans saw it otherwise: the United States ran a deficit to prop up its own hegemonic goals). Needless to say, the balance of payments and gold–dollar issues were interwoven with the strategic external policies of the United States in the 1960s.[241] This was nowhere clearer than in the so-called U.S.–German offset negotiations. In exchange for the presence of American troops in West Germany, the U.S. administration obtained from the Germans compensation in the form of military orders but also of large-scale purchases of U.S. Treasury bonds and, above all, the Bundesbank's commitment not to convert its dollar holdings into gold.[242] Technically, the difference between these two positions in the official G10 debate boiled down to a different assessment of the speed, efficiency, and domestic cost of the adjustment process. Holders of the first view felt that deficit countries were too cautious in using fiscal and monetary policy to promote balance of payments adjustment, the social cost of which they possibly overestimated. The other side believed that correction necessarily took a long time, particularly as surplus countries were not under pressure to assist in the adjustment; they also felt that the domestic cost of speedy adjustment in terms of output and employment would be unnecessarily high. Moreover, it would spread deflation internationally.

In between these two scarcely reconcilable positions was a third one, which saw the adequacy of liquidity supply as the cornerstone of any reform of the international monetary system. Gilbert and the BIS itself, together with the IMF, were the most ardent supporters of this approach. Two possible ways existed to increase international liquidity: an increase of the dollar price of gold, which had remained constant since 1934, and the creation of an ad hoc international reserve instrument issued by the IMF.

In December 1963, the BIS produced a memorandum for discussion at the G10 deputies' meeting on the prospective growth of gold reserves.[243] The Bank's gold production estimates, while slightly more optimistic than

Triffin's,[244] were (on the whole) consistent with the Yale professor's conclusion that, by the end of the decade, the stock of monetary gold would fall short of the world's demand for liquidity (reserves).[245] The G10 discussion of the BIS gold paper highlighted the already-mentioned split among its members.[246] The representative of Belgium (de Strycker) "did not think that there was any prospective shortage of gold or, therefore, that something else would have to be found in the place of gold". De Lattre (France) interpreted the BIS data likewise. Both of them were also critical of any suggestion that the G10 should ask member countries to exercise restraint in buying gold from the United States, as suggested by a parallel BIS paper on the Gold Pool.[247] In contrast, Roosa (United States) believed that "it was clear that substitutes for or supplements to [gold] should be found". The positions were split between those who wanted to keep gold at the heart of the system, and even enhance its role as an anchor, and those who held that current standby arrangements were for the moment enough to guarantee adequate liquidity while, in the longer run, the creation of a new reserve asset should be considered. In between stood the BIS's (Gilbert's) conviction that, while no credible substitute for gold was in sight, the current official price of the yellow metal could not be maintained without seriously risking a worldwide liquidity crunch.

All his life Gilbert remained convinced that an increase in the price of gold would have solved the problems that crippled the international monetary system in the late 1960s and, probably, would have allowed fixed exchange rates to survive well beyond 1971. Writing in the late 1970s after retiring from the BIS, he argued that raising the price of gold might indeed "have brought a permanent solution – if there is such a thing" to the extent that "the 1970s would not have thrown up the same problems if effective adjustment had been achieved in the 1960s".[248] Against the objection that by raising the price of gold the United States would breach a commitment to central banks holding dollar reserves, Gilbert argued that "dollar reserves earned interest and the United States was not obliged to give a gold guarantee in addition to paying interest. A central-bank Governor", he added, "naïve enough to believe he could enjoy the best of both worlds was in the wrong job".[249] Gilbert and the BIS, however, do not seem to have given much consideration to Triffin's most serious objections to gold revaluation (an argument that led him to favour the "internationalization of foreign exchange reserves"), in particular the need for periodic price changes (with the attendant built-in expectations), the excess liquidity that would for a time follow each revaluation, and the haphazard distribution of the benefits accruing from it.[250]

In the end, the 1964 report of the G10 deputies compromised on two concrete steps. In order to prop up international liquidity, the ten countries agreed to support an increase in the IMF quotas. The ensuing negotiations settled for a general increase of 25%, which took effect in 1965, as a compromise between the much smaller and much larger amounts favoured by the various participating countries. The Ten also decided that the so-called OECD Working Party 3 (WP3) should be put in charge of exercising multilateral surveillance over the financing of balance of payments deficits. This second step was taken to allay the fear of some Continentals (France and Belgium primarily but, to some extent, also Germany) that an injection of new liquidity into the system would further erode monetary and fiscal discipline in the deficit countries. Working Party 3 was to be helped in this new task by the BIS, which would both collect the relevant information and stimulate discussion on mutual surveillance at the governors' monthly meetings. On this, a sceptical Gilbert commented that "the 'multilateral' part of the exercise has proved to be much easier than 'surveillance'".[251] The consensus reached by the G10 deputies in August 1964 was made possible by sweeping the main contentious issues under the carpet or, rather, by entrusting them to two new study groups. One of them, chaired by Ossola, dealt with possible new reserve assets. A second group was charged with the ways and means of improving the process of balance of payments adjustment and became a fairly permanent discussion forum within the OECD.

In May 1965 the Ossola group sent the G10 deputies a report unambiguously stating that the world would soon be facing a liquidity shortage. As this group had not been mandated to find a common ground amongst participants, the report simply went through a careful review of the available options to meet such a shortage.[252] However, it took four more years – and creation of the two-tier gold market discussed in the next section – for an agreement to be reached on a new international reserve asset, the so-called special drawing rights (SDRs).

The reasons why it took so long to converge on a solution to the problem of international liquidity shortage have been best summarised by Harold James.[253] Besides the different positions within the G10, the insistence by nonmember countries that monetary management should be truly international must also be taken into account. In 1965, the developing countries produced a proposal of their own, through the newly born UNCTAD, that stressed long-term aid rather than the creation of new liquidity. The latter, it was argued, should be linked to development finance, and developing countries should be involved in the reform discussion. The IMF emphasised that international liquidity was its own business, while Schweitzer – who in 1963 had become managing director after Jacobsson's sudden death – warned against dividing members into "the reliable few and the less responsible many".[254]

About the same time (summer of 1965) came what James describes as the "partial conversion to Triffinism" of U.S. Treasury Secretary Henry Fowler, who called for an international conference to discuss improvements in the existing international monetary agreements.[255] This statement did not go down well with European central bank governors at their monthly BIS meeting. Divided as they were on substantive issues, they nonetheless all felt that the G10 was the more suitable, if informal, decision-making structure. The IMF, however, managed to establish itself as the appropriate forum for monetary discussion by arranging in 1966 joint meetings between the G10 deputies and its own executive board. This unorthodox initiative was accepted as a compromise by countries outside the G10; the IMF general manager stressed that the meetings were only intended to advance international understanding and that the IMF executive board did not meet in its capacity as the legal body of the Fund.

The first meeting took place in Washington in November 1966. Participation included the IMF executive directors and their alternates, and two deputies (one from the Treasury, the other from the central bank) from each of the G10 countries. Senior staff of the IMF also attended, as did representatives from the Swiss National Bank, the OECD, and the BIS.[256] The divisions within the G10 dominated the first joint meetings. Predictably enough, the French opening gambit was to deny the very purpose of the meetings: balance of payments adjustment should receive the greatest attention, while plans for the creation of new liquidity were secondary and would not solve any basic problem.[257] Parallel to the second joint meeting (held in London in January 1967), the finance ministers of the six European Community countries met in The Hague and requested their experts to study "ways of improving international credit facilities within the Fund". It appeared that France would consider the creation of some kind of "drawing rights" (the language was to omit any reference to "reserve") provided that the issue of such rights be approved by the IMF board of governors with an 85% majority, which would give the EEC countries a veto power.

At the two following joint meetings,[258] progress was made in designing the main features of the special drawing rights. The United States and the United Kingdom, however, insisted that the new asset should constitute the "front line reserve", while France asserted that it could not replace gold but would merely constitute an extension-of-credit facility. Eventually, France did not cast a vote for the SDRs in the IMF's board of governors, but the plan went ahead with only mild opposition from de Gaulle.

The BIS contribution to the SDR discussions was twofold. On the one hand, Ferras and Gilbert, as BIS representatives, regularly attended the G10 deputies' meetings. Gilbert in particular contributed actively to the debates and wrote several background papers. On the other hand, the monthly Basel meetings provided an opportunity for the G10 governors to informally discuss international monetary reform amongst themselves. Gilbert later noted that the most relevant issues were seldom touched upon in the open discussion at the governors' monthly meeting in Basel or at the WP3 meetings in Paris "because of their political sensitivity and the risk of leaks to the market. Such matters could be aired in limited confidential talks outside formal meetings. That the surveillance did not yield more positive results, therefore, was not for lack of information or opportunities for discussion; it was due to the political repercussions that strong measures could entail".[259] In such issues as the dollar price and assessment of the overall liquidity need of the system, the governors' opinions differed just like those of their governments.[260] Gilbert, in fact, complained to Holtrop that: "Although they have a special responsibility for the monetary system (without full power, it is true, to exercise it) central banks have not developed a common approach or exercised constructive leadership as a group in the discussion of the Ten. Yet, if the situation is allowed to drift into some sort of crisis – which is clearly possible – the general public is likely to put the onus for it more on the central banks than elsewhere".[261]

As for its direct participation in the G10 meetings, the BIS representatives supported the SDR scheme as "a good idea"[262] – an idea as good as others implemented in the same years, but not good enough to provide the solution to the international liquidity problem. Gilbert, who shaped and represented the BIS management's view, saw the SDRs simply as "a useful addition to the facilities of the system in supplementing reserves in gold and dollars and other facilities like IMF ordinary resources, the swap network, and the BIS".[263] In particular, he believed that a blurred definition of the SDRs (or "reserve units", as they were initially called), though politically expedient, obscured a fundamental issue. Would the SDRs be "an arrangement for automatic credit, similar in conception, though not in form to the EPU" or would they be conceived "as international money"?[264] In the first case, the issuing of units would not create additional reserves; in the second case, the question of trust should be addressed either by some form of gold backing or by strictly limiting the issue of SDRs. Either way, the creation of the new facility, although a good temporary measure, would not permanently ease the world's liquidity shortage. The goal, Gilbert never tired of repeating, could only be reached by a substantial increase in the dollar price of gold. The reasons why the BIS remained sceptical about the new facility's potential for becoming a full substitute for gold were entirely of a practical nature. They boiled down to one consideration, based upon experience: central banks would be reluctant to see the entire amount of growth in reserves derive from SDRs, much as they were unwilling to accumulate only dollars in their vaults. Therefore, the "tendency of gold to leave the United States and not to come back" would not be significantly altered by the introduction of the SDRs, which would simply be yet "another means of non-gold financing of deficits" without a permanent impact on reserve creation "unless other countries drastically changed their reserve-holding policies. As matters stand", a BIS report continued, "it is likely that the U.S. would have to run a large and prolonged surplus before gold would again move spontaneously in both directions. While this could happen, it would not be a happy solution of the problem from an international standpoint".[265]

The hectic succession of events in the gold and foreign exchange markets in 1968–69 may have contributed to the conclusion of an agreement on SDRs, the last attempt to patch up the Bretton Woods system before its demise in 1971–73. The amendment to the IMF's Articles of Agreement establishing the SDR facility came into force on 28 July 1969. The SDR was, in essence, fiat international money, allocated to individual countries in proportion to their IMF quotas and to the IMF itself. It had no backing and did not represent a claim on any other asset. In order to make it a more attractive instrument, a limit was placed on each country's obligation to accept SDRs. But, as anticipated by Gilbert, the mechanism ended up bearing more resemblance to a credit than a reserve instrument. In particular, restrictions existed on the obligation to accept it, a time limit was set for its partial repayment in the lender's currency, and it bore 1.5% interest. It was nevertheless officially hailed by the BIS as "potentially the most important new orientation of the monetary system since Bretton Woods".[266]

11.9   1968: The Beginning of the End

Starting in 1965, the debate on the reform of the Bretton Woods system acquired an added urgency because of adverse signals first transmitted through the gold market, a particularly sensitive gauge of market sentiment. As we have seen, the gold price on the London free market had remained stable during 1963 and 1964. Over that period of time, the demand from the central banks and the private sector roughly matched the producers' supply, so that the Gold Pool was able to purchase $1,262 million worth of gold, which was distributed among the central banks participating in the consortium.[267] Official reserves of European central banks kept growing,[268] with the notable exception of the United Kingdom. The only disturbing fact was the gradual increase in the ratio of foreign exchange to gold in most central banks' reserves, in spite of the gold purchases through the Gold Pool.[269]

Market sentiment began to change in late 1964 when private demand soared as a result of the pressure on sterling attendant upon the assumption of power of the new Labour government. Thus, at their meeting in Basel on 10 January 1965, the Gold Pool governors decided to reactivate the sales syndicate, which had been in abeyance since November 1962. In the following months, the publicity given by the Bank of France to its reserve policy – followed by de Gaulle's gold speech, the war in Vietnam, continued anxiety about the future of the pound, Chinese gold purchases, and tension between India and Pakistan – all made their contribution to keeping gold in high demand.

During the first three months of 1965, the Gold Pool sold gold for $200 million to prevent the London free price from rising above the level of $35.18 per ounce reached at the beginning of March. By April, demand pressures had eased and the gold price receded. At the gold experts' meeting in Basel on 6 March 1965, it was agreed that the Gold Pool operations should be continued. However, for the first time, this agreement was not unequivocally unanimous. The representatives of the National Bank of Belgium and the Bank of France (André and Lefort, respectively) did not join their colleagues in giving solemn assurances as to the medium-term continuation of Gold Pool operations. Charles Coombs made it clear that, in the event any Pool member wished to pull out, the Federal Reserve would step in to cover that bank's share in the Pool.[270] At the July 1965 Basel governors' meeting, it was reported that the cumulative deficit for the year stood at $149 million, leaving only $121 million available under the existing commitments for the support of the free gold market. Participants discussed what action should be authorised if the Pool became exhausted before their following meeting, scheduled for October. They decided, with the Bank of France governor reserving his position, that market support should not cease if the cumulative deficit of the Pool were to exceed the $270 million so far allocated to its operations. The deficit did rise to $238 million during August, but then Russian sales resumed and market conditions seemingly returned to "normal", so that the Pool was actually able to close 1965 with a $35 million surplus.[271]

In 1966, demand remained high owing to increased gold purchases by communist China, growing concerns over the slow process of international monetary reform, and mounting international tensions deriving from the escalated U.S. operations in Vietnam and the India–Pakistan conflict. The main problem, though, came from the supply side. So far gold sales, while highly volatile, had grown on average fast enough to keep pace with rising demand for both monetary and industrial purposes. In 1966 both South Africa and Russia failed to supply the London market with the gold quantity it had grown accustomed to in the previous years. Recovering from a balance of payments crisis, South Africa chose to rebuild its own gold stock rather than selling newly mined quantities to the market. Russia's sales behaviour had always been unpredictable. The country normally sold gold in the winter, the seasonally adverse period in its balance of payments, but these sales depended on the harvest and on other domestic conditions that were difficult to understand and forecast. In 1966 Russia sold virtually no gold in London. Under these conditions, Pool sales of gold in the first part of the year amounted to $166 million. At their 12 March 1966 Basel meeting, the experts discussed what answers should be given to governors questioning the advisability of sacrificing more official gold reserves to private hoarding.[272] In July, the governors' meeting – which took place amid renewed sterling weakness – again considered making contingency plans in case the Pool's sales breached the $270 million ceiling. All in all, however, they found good reasons to remain optimistic. Looking back on nearly five years of activity, the Gold Pool's track record appeared quite positive: the free market price of gold had been kept stable, and Pool members had added gold worth more than $1 billion to their reserves. Moreover, the amounts committed to the Gold Pool by each individual member were relatively small, leaving room (if needed) for a ceiling increase. Nonetheless, it was decided to discuss the matter again in September, while entrusting the Bank of England with the preparation of an ad hoc memorandum.[273]

O'Brien's report, though it gave technical reasons to assume that the deficit thus far incurred could be liquidated by the end of the year, did not rule out the need for further "temporary" contributions to the Pool. He did not shy away from recommending the continuation of an experience that seemed "to have worked well so far and to have achieved its objectives". "The knowledge of the existence of the Gold Pool", O'Brien added, "namely the fact that a powerful group of central banks are acting in consort in the gold markets, has had a stabilising and tranquillising effect upon world opinion and has enabled the London free market price to be kept within a range of $35.04 to $35.20 for over five years". He concluded that, even in the case of exhaustion of the resources available under the original commitment, "support of the market should not cease but should continue".[274]

Betting on a resumption of Russian gold sales, the governors, at their Basel meeting on 4 September, for the first time agreed on a $50 million increase in the Pool's resources.[275] However, no Russian sales materialised and by the end of 1966 the Pool's operational deficit had reached $260 million, perilously close to the original $270 million limit.

In order to understand the events leading to the end of the Pool and the splitting of the official and free gold markets, one must look at the structural break that seems to have occurred in the long-term trend in world gold production between 1966 and 1967. In the previous twelve years, world gold output had risen by about 70%, mostly as a result of the huge expansion of South African production due to the development of new mines. The opening up of new gold fields reached its peak in 1961–62 and stagnated thereafter.[276] "In 1967, world gold production ... registered its first decline since 1953."[277]

At the end of 1966 and during the first few months of 1967, calm returned once more to the gold market,[278] but the experts were aware of the fragility of a situation where – in the context of sluggish supply – any major political or financial crisis could lead to a run on gold.[279] At the experts' meeting in Basel on 6 May 1967, the prospect of running the Gold Pool at a continuous deficit gave rise to a fundamental discussion during which André of the National Bank of Belgium questioned the philosophy underlying the Pool.[280] During the second half of May 1967, pressure on the free-market gold price heated up as a result of growing tensions in the Middle East and the decision of the U.S. government to suspend silver sales for nonindustrial purposes. On 23 May, the Bank of England cabled the participating central banks that, as a result of heavy selling, the Gold Pool deficit had shot up to $282 million. The same day, Alfred Hayes, president of the Federal Reserve Bank of New York, called Gabriel Ferras, general manager of the BIS, with a request to arrange a further $50 million increase in the Gold Pool ceiling, above the $50 million agreed to in September 1966 (thus raising the limit to $370 million). Ferras consulted all participating central banks: with the exception of the Bank of France – whose governor, Brunet, requested some time for reflection – they all agreed to the proposed limit increase. A few days later, the Bank of France agreed to the increase in the Pool's resources but not beyond 31 July 1967, arguing that only a temporary increase was justified because of the situation in the Middle East. At the same time, Brunet made it clear that he would hesitate to continue Gold Pool participation if tensions on the gold market persisted after the end of the crisis, since this would highlight fundamental imbalances.[281]

The outbreak of the Six-Day War on 5 June 1967 strongly affected gold demand, prompting the Pool to feed the market with no less than $60 million in two days. At the instigation of the Federal Reserve Bank of New York, a further extension of the Pool ceiling to $420 million was arranged through the BIS on 5–6 June; the Bank of France declined to participate.[282] At the close of business on 9 June, the Pool's operational deficit reached $367 million. On 10 June, Mandel (head of the BIS Banking Department) called an emergency meeting of the experts in Basel. Different participants showed a different sense of urgency. Coombs, strongly supported by Tüngeler from the Bundesbank and Iklé from the Swiss National Bank, insisted on a firm immediate commitment on the continuation of the Gold Pool. For André (National Bank of Belgium) – strongly supported by Théron (Bank of France) – the highest priority was a change in strategy, entailing a radical rethinking of the Pool itself. Tüngeler, referring to the ongoing discussions on the introduction of SDRs, wanted the Gold Pool to continue to "hold the line until a new monetary system is evolved".[283] In the end, consensus was reached on continuing the Pool, provided that a fundamental discussion about its future took place once the current crisis had been overcome. At a governors' meeting later that day, McChesney Martin (chairman of the Federal Reserve Board) assured his European colleagues of America's absolute determination to maintain the gold price. While sounding pessimistic about the balance of payments deficit, he held out the prospect that the legal gold cover obligation would be removed soon, freeing up more reserves, which the United States intended to use "to the last bar" if need be in defence of the gold price.[284]

By the time of the following meeting of the experts group in Basel, on 8 July 1967, the Bank of France had officially withdrawn from the Gold Pool scheme. Its share was taken over entirely by the Federal Reserve Bank of New York. It was typical of the Basel atmosphere, though, that the French were not ostracised for their unilateral move and continued to be fully informed on the Pool's day-to-day operations. At the July meeting, Mandel and Gilbert of the BIS asked whether the time had not come to have the governors re-examine the basic philosophy and functioning of the Gold Pool.[285] However, because pressure on the London gold market had relaxed somewhat since early June, the experts decided against reopening this fundamental debate. Instead they recommended that the governors continue the Gold Pool as before, at least until the IMF meeting in September in Rio de Janeiro – which, it was hoped, would clarify the reform prospects of the international monetary system. The governors went along with this.

Heavy gold buying resumed in late July 1967 on rumours that the G10 talks on monetary reform were stalled. The BIS quickly arranged a further limit increase for Gold Pool sales, to $470 million. The market mood was now such that even the slightest rumour could set off a buying spree. Throughout the summer, private demand for gold remained high as a result of renewed pressure on the pound sterling and market nervousness in anticipation of the IMF meetings. In September, the IMF's executive board finally approved a draft outline for the creation of SDRs, which were aimed at meeting the world's liquidity shortage and easing the position of the dollar. But the fundamental debate on the characteristics and issue of SDRs went on for two more years; it was not until July 1969 that SDRs were actually activated.[286]

By the time of the experts' meeting on 9 September 1967, the Gold Pool deficit stood at $437 million. Their main preoccupation now was the continuous strain on sterling and the effect this had on the gold market. Two further extensions of the Pool ceiling were agreed on during September–October, bringing the available total to $570 million. Most governors were now getting seriously worried about the drain on their gold reserves and, taking up the BIS's suggestion, insisted that a special meeting should be convened to decide on the future of the Gold Pool. Heavy demand continued unabated, and on 8 and 11 November the Pool's ceiling was raised to a total of $670 million. Nonetheless, Charles Coombs tried to hold out brighter prospects at the experts' meeting in Basel on 11 November 1967, pinning his hopes on a quick implementation of the monetary reform programme announced in Rio, resolution of the Vietnam conflict in the next year or two, and a substantial improvement in the U.S. balance of payments thanks to a new presidential programme to be announced shortly. Realising that he sounded rather unconvincing, he backed up his plea for the continuation of the Pool with the assurance that the United States would take up the share of anyone who wanted to withdraw.[287] Most governors had indeed become eager for the experts to devise an elegant exit from their increasingly costly Gold Pool commitment. But, given the market mood, it was not easy to see how a retreat could be made without jeopardising what the Pool had been set up to achieve in the first place: exchange rate stability based on the fixed gold–dollar parity. In fact, the experts – and in particular the U.S. monetary authorities – had for some time been reviewing possible alternatives that ranged from gold movements and sales controls to the creation of gold value certificates.[288] All were rejected by the governors as being too complex, downright unworkable, or likely to produce undesired side effects. And so, for want of acceptable alternatives, the Gold Pool continued its operations in increasingly adverse market circumstances.

As we have seen, the devaluation of the pound, announced on 18 November 1967, did not have the hoped-for effect on foreign exchange markets. On Monday 20 November the London gold market was closed, but the demand pressure on other gold markets was such that the BIS was obliged to step in and temporarily assume the role of agent for the Gold Pool that was normally played by the Bank of England.[289] In just one day, the BIS had to sell 24.5 tonnes of gold, mostly to Swiss commercial banks, in order to maintain the price at $35.20 per ounce. This resulted in the need for a further emergency raising of the Gold Pool ceiling from $670 to $770 million the same day. On Tuesday, the news leaked to the press that the Bank of France had withdrawn from the Gold Pool arrangement back in June 1967,[290] triggering "the biggest gold rush in the history of the London market".[291] In the week following sterling devaluation, the Gold Pool ceiling had to be lifted to $1,370 million in order to cover sales of nearly $600 million.

To reassure the markets, Chairman McChesney Martin of the Federal Reserve Board asked the Gold Pool members to issue a joint statement of their unanimous intention to continue the Pool. In response, Bundesbank President Blessing convened an emergency meeting in Frankfurt. At long last, the time had come for the fundamental discussion on the future of the Gold Pool that the governors had been contemplating ever since the IMF meeting in Rio that September. The Frankfurt meeting of central bankers and Treasury officials on Sunday 26 November revealed a growing split between the Gold Pool members. Whereas the United States – supported by the Bank of England, the Swiss National Bank, and to a lesser extent the Bundesbank – pressed for continuation of the joint gold operations, the Bank of Italy, the National Bank of Belgium, and the Netherlands Bank indicated that they could not bear any further accumulation of dollars in their reserves resulting from the Gold Pool's sales. The meeting finally compromised on continuing Gold Pool operations for at least one more week and on issuing a press statement that reconfirmed the unanimous support for the existing exchange rate system based on the existing dollar–gold parity – without, however, explicitly referring to gold market interventions.[292]

The Frankfurt press communiqué succeeded in temporarily calming the gold market. In the following weeks, the Americans and the British agreed on a continuation of the Pool for at least one to three more months. The BIS Board meeting on the weekend of 9–11 December 1967 provided the opportunity to resume the discussion among all Gold Pool members where it had been broken off in Frankfurt. Its unintended outcome, however, was to spark a renewed wave of buying on the London gold market due to circumstances undesired and unsought by the BIS governors. The outcome of the Frankfurt meeting had left the U.S. Treasury concerned that various members of the Gold Pool were seriously contemplating immediate withdrawal. To better exercise moral suasion, the U.S. Treasury felt that a personal intervention from Under-Secretary Frederick Deming with the governors would carry more weight. Deming took the unprecedented step of inviting himself to the BIS meeting. The move ran counter to the institutional nature of the BIS and to the sensibilities of the central bankers. Ever since its foundation, the BIS had been exclusively central bankers' territory. The idea of a government official, and one with ministerial authority at that, breaking into the governors' meeting at the BIS headquarters in Basel was almost blasphemous, a violation of the inner sanctum of central bank cooperation.[293]

On the other hand, everybody was keen on reviewing the Gold Pool arrangement with one of its staunchest proponents. Besides, a member of the U.S. government could hardly be met with a diplomatic rebuff. A compromise was found. The gold experts were to meet first on the morning of Monday 11 December in the BIS building. In the afternoon they were to join their respective central bank governors for an ad hoc meeting with the U.S. delegation, headed by Deming, not on the BIS premises but on the neutral ground of the Hotel Euler – on the station square, three minutes' walk from the BIS building. Predictably, the news that the U.S. under-secretary of the Treasury was in Basel to meet the governors immediately became known in the press. It was widely assumed that this spelled changes in the gold policy of the world monetary authorities, possibly involving a change in the gold–dollar price or the closure of the London gold market. A new wave of speculative buying ensued, losing the Gold Pool another $550 million in gold and driving up its operational deficit to $1,949 million by the close of business on Friday 15 December. *The Economist* did not fail to note that Deming's trip to Basel had turned out to be "a pretty expensive plane ride".[294]

The outcome of the December Basel meeting was once more inconclusive. The discussion focused on immediate measures aimed at dampening gold demand. The introduction of a licensing system for "legitimate" gold purchases was rejected as too complex. Instead it was suggested that each central bank should impose a ban on forward gold transactions and step up moral suasion to limit gold demand to "legitimate" domestic purposes. The governors were under no illusion that these could be anything more than stopgap measures, with uncertain effects. On the more fundamental issue of the Gold Pool's future, Governors Ansiaux (Belgium) and Carli (Italy) came out forcefully in favour of creating a two-tier gold market. An "official" market, restricted to monetary authorities only, would continue to transact gold at the existing official price, next to a "free" market that was open to all other buyers and sellers, where the price would be determined by demand and supply. This idea had been circulating for some time but had always met with stiff resistance, in particular from the Americans, as leading to two different prices for gold (which could easily become untenable if they diverged too much) and as it would strengthen the bargaining position of the main suppliers, in particular South Africa.[295] Under-Secretary Deming reiterated the U.S. commitment to one gold price. Ansiaux pointed out that this could only mean that the Americans wanted an indefinite continuation of the Gold Pool, but, he said, the Americans "should understand that in Europe the central banks [are] at the end of their tether; they will not go on selling gold and accumulating dollars. The London market must be limited to supplying gold for 'legitimate' purchases or there must be two price levels. If we were to stop supplying everybody one day, why not today?" Carli, possibly with an intentional quip to Under-Secretary Deming, supported Ansiaux's sense of urgency by saying that "whilst his bank was still in control of the Italian situation, it might not be for much longer, since the politicians were moving into the monetary policy field".[296] The governors finally decided to ask the group of gold experts to report on the feasibility and possible effects of a two-price system. In the meantime, Gold Pool operations would continue.

Since heavy gold purchases on the London market continued after the Basel meeting, on 16 December the U.S. Secretary of the Treasury Fowler and Chairman Martin of the Federal Reserve Board issued yet another press statement, reaffirming their determination to maintain the $35 per ounce price of gold. The European central banks agreed to be associated with this statement, as the Americans reassured them that drastic action would be taken about the U.S. balance of payments. Once again, relative calm returned to the gold markets. Confidence was strengthened when, on 1 January 1968, President Johnson indeed announced a drastic balance of payments programme and legislation was introduced in Congress to remove the gold cover requirement for the dollar; this would free the entire U.S. gold stock, if necessary, for the defence of the dollar parity. The Americans, supported

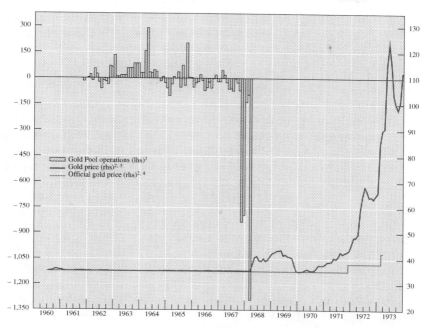

[1] In millions of US dollars. A positive (negative) value represents a purchase (sale).   [2] In US dollars per fine ounce.   [3] On the London gold market; monthly averages.   [4] Abandoned in April 1973.

Sources: Bank of England Quarterly Bulletins; BISA, 7.18 (16), box HAL2, f.01.

Figure 11.1. BIS Gold Pool operations and London gold price, 1960–73.

by the British, used this lull in the crisis to argue for a continuation of the Gold Pool and to shelve the plans for creating a two-tier market. The report on the two-tier system, which the experts were expected to deliver to the governors' meeting on 8 January 1968, was unceremoniously dropped.[297]

Throughout January and February 1968, gold demand on the London market remained at a relatively modest level, although the ceiling of the Gold Pool had to be raised two more times to reach $2,570 million at the end of February. Then, on 28 February 1968, a speech by influential U.S. senator Jacob Javits calling for cessation of the Gold Pool sparked off what was to be the Pool's final crisis. Speculative buying took on such proportions that the White House urged Chairman Martin of the Federal Reserve Board to attend the BIS meetings of 9–11 March 1968 in person. A hectic round of meetings followed. Everybody agreed that the game was up, and BIS President Zijlstra strongly advised burying the Gold Pool there and then. Nevertheless, Chairman Martin obtained one last reprieve both to allow congressional approval of lifting the gold cover requirement and so as not to compromise the U.K. stabilisation programme to be announced shortly by Chancellor Jenkins. On Sunday evening 10 March, the governors issued one more press statement expressing their continued support to the Gold Pool – which, however, failed to impress the markets. At the end of the Basel meeting weekend, on Monday 11 March, the operational deficit of the Gold Pool passed the $3 billion mark.

Now events moved quickly. Gold demand in London developed into a real haemorrhage for the Gold Pool. By Thursday 14 March, the operational deficit had reached $3,692 million. This was the last straw. Alarmed by the recent drain on U.S. gold reserves and in the certainty that the European central banks would accept no further reprieve, the U.S. Treasury advised President Johnson to discontinue Gold Pool operations with immediate effect. The president agreed that same afternoon. The Bank of England was immediately notified and asked to close the London gold market on the next day, Friday 15 March 1968.[298] An emergency meeting of the Gold Pool members was called in Washington for the weekend of 16–17 March.

On Friday 15 March, while the financial world was digesting the news of the sudden closure of the London market, a U.S. presidential aircraft was sent to Europe to pick up the Gold Pool central bank governors and fly them to Washington.[299] The discussions, at the Federal Reserve building in Washington on Saturday 16 and Sunday 17 March, were both excruciating and heated. It was "ten hours of meetings, drinking tea by the litre".[300] Besides the Gold Pool governors, Treasury officials from the United States and the United Kingdom participated, as well as Pierre-Paul Schweitzer, managing director of the IMF, and Ferras and Gilbert of the BIS. Chairman Martin of the Federal Reserve Board opened the meeting by reiterating the U.S. commitment to the gold–dollar parity. The day before, the U.S. Congress had narrowly voted the lifting of the gold cover requirement for the dollar, making additional reserves available to support the gold price. To all present, though, it was clear that even with this additional backing the Gold Pool could not be continued: a way out had to be found that would not disrupt the international monetary system.

In essence, two options were discussed: a substantial increase in the official price of gold, and the establishment of a two-tier gold market. The former was proposed by Governor O'Brien of the Bank of England and supported by Zijlstra and Ferras of the BIS. They argued that a higher official gold price would take pressure off the markets and buy time to work towards a more fundamental reform of the international monetary system through the creation of new liquidity instruments and the realignment of exchange rates. Milton Gilbert had long been advocating a substantial gold price increase, but without any success.[301] He later wrote that "other Governors, who confidentially believed that $35 was outdated, did not speak on the matter, as their governments, which had the power over the gold parity, were not willing to oppose the United States".[302] Martin, in fact, was adamant in rejecting the proposal on the grounds that it would be inflationary and would unduly reward the gold hoarders and gold producers, chiefly South Africa and Russia. Carli then repeated the proposal he had advanced at a previous meeting – namely, to create a two-tier gold market, an official one for central banks dealing among each other at $35 per ounce and a free market in which the monetary authorities would no longer intervene. Carli's proposal finally carried the day, as Martin felt that this was the lesser of two evils. The option of a free float for the dollar as well as the other currencies was raised but not seriously considered.

The drafting of the final press statement of the Washington meeting proved to be a difficult balancing act. Carli and Ossola of the Bank of Italy were largely responsible for the outcome. The communiqué noted that "the U.S. Government will continue to buy and sell gold at the existing price of $35 an ounce in transactions with monetary authorities. The Governors", it said, "support this policy and believe it contributes to the maintenance of exchange stability". The governors expressed their belief that "henceforth officially-held gold should be used only to effect transfers among monetary authorities" and thus announced their decision to no longer supply "gold to the London gold market or any other gold market". "Moreover", the press statement continued, in a hotly disputed sentence that the Americans had managed to push through, "as the existing stock of monetary gold is sufficient in view of the prospective establishment of the facility for special drawing rights they no longer feel it necessary to buy gold from the market".[303] A few governors observed that this pledge would make no sense unless gold were entirely demonetised. An appeal to all central banks by Under-Secretary Deming to show restraint in buying gold at the U.S. Treasury window raised more than a few eyebrows, but it nevertheless had a moderating effect over the following months. Finally, in order to forestall a breakdown of the foreign exchange markets upon the announcement of the dissolution of the Gold Pool, the governors agreed to a substantial increase in the existing swap lines as well as additional support to shore up sterling. They also invited "the cooperation of other central banks in the policies set forth above".[304]

The press statement issued at the end of the Washington conference got a better-than-expected reception from the financial press and the markets.

Stock exchanges remained calm and the pound relatively firm, thanks to a new austerity programme announced by Chancellor Jenkins on 20 March. The London gold market remained closed until 1 April. When it reopened, the price first settled at just below $38 per ounce. Over the following months the gold price fluctuated without a clear direction, but by early 1969 it hovered around $42–$43 per ounce. However, after the creation of SDRs in mid-1969, it fell as low as $34.75 in January 1970.[305] Two main reasons combined to keep the free gold price in relative check after the end of the Gold Pool: the reappearance of South African supplies, and the huge hoarding overhang accumulated in late 1967 and early 1968.

"With the two-tier scheme", Gilbert wrote, "the die was probably already cast for a monetary system without gold, though it was left to the next [American] administration to deliver the coup de grâce".[306] The demise of the Gold Pool undoubtedly marked the beginning of the end of the Bretton Woods system.[307]

An internal U.K. Treasury memorandum of late March 1968 asked: "Was our $220 million [i.e., the Bank of England's share in the Gold Pool net sales] worth it? I suppose the answer is we had no real alternative – and the operation as a whole was certainly worth trying".[308]

As with all the other cooperative endeavours put together in the 1960s to prop up the gold dollar system, an overall historical judgement of the Gold Pool depends on the value attached to gaining time. For those who believe that the exceptional output and trade growth of the 1960s partly depended on the relative stability of international monetary conditions, the Gold Pool was surely worth not only trying but having, in spite of its inevitable final breakdown.

During the first four years of its operation, the Gold Pool achieved its objective of stabilising the gold price on the London market with relative ease. From 1962 until the end of 1965, the Pool was able to distribute $1,310 million among its members to be added to their respective gold reserves. From early 1966, the fundamentals as well as the psychology of the gold market turned against the Pool, which nevertheless managed to keep the gold price under control until the very end of its operations. The Pool was discontinued because central banks were no longer willing to accept a further shift in the dollar–gold composition of their reserves.[309] By early 1968, the Gold Pool had largely become a one-man show, with the United States making up for about 80% of its gold losses; the participating central banks – with the exception of the Bank of England and the Bundesbank[310] – increasingly turned to the U.S. Treasury window to offset the gold losses suffered through the Pool.

From the outset, the Gold Pool was promoted and animated by the U.S. Treasury as one of the key elements in the ring of "outer perimeter defences" thrown up around the dollar.[311] The European central banks were enthusiastic participants in the Pool as long as it remained a useful device to share out the gold market surplus amongst themselves, avoiding a competitive scramble for gold. They dragged their feet after 1966, when they increasingly believed the gold cost of countering the underlying market forces to be too high. By March 1968 they were glad to abandon the scheme. The official exit from the Gold Pool was relatively well managed and the speculative wave soon subsided. In a way, March 1968 constituted a victory – albeit a short-lived one – for the United States.[312] A de facto dollar standard had been accepted by the main central banks as the only realistic alternative to a free float of the dollar, which was rejected by all, and the drain on the U.S. gold reserves had been halted.

11.10   The BIS Role in the Second Sterling Group Arrangement

The demise of the Gold Pool followed closely on the heels of the November 1967 devaluation of the pound, which had failed to put an end to the Bank of England's perennial concerns over sterling.[313] In particular, the high volume of sterling balances held by third countries remained worrisome. The 1966 Sterling Group Arrangement, up for renewal in early 1968, had primarily dealt with the impact on the U.K. reserves of temporary fluctuations in sterling balances held outside the sterling area. A paper written by the BIS's Michael Dealtry, however, recognised that a diversification of reserves by sterling-area countries themselves had also had "a considerable influence on the decline of total balances" and consequently a nonnegligible impact on the run-down of the United Kingdom's reserves since early 1966.[314] Given the amount of the total sterling balances,[315] a precipitous and massive move towards reserves diversification on the part of the forty-odd sterling-area countries was bound to have a major impact on U.K. foreign exchange reserves. In view of this, the Bank of England argued that something more was needed than an agreement dealing only with temporary fluctuations in nonsterling-area balances. Something on a much grander scale was required: a long-term loan to allow an "orderly retreat" from the legacy of sterling's once dominant role as an international reserve currency.[316]

Governor O'Brien began to prepare the ground with the governors at the Sunday dinner in Basel on 11 February 1968. As he spoke about medium-term financing to offset the expected diversification of sterling reserves,

broad agreement emerged among the governors that the instability of sterling balances posed a threat. Milton Gilbert stressed that failure to finance
the conversion of sterling balances "could lead to a floating pound rate,
which would be disastrous to everybody".[317] Although some governors were
of the opinion that this was rather an issue for the governments and the IMF
to deal with, it was nonetheless agreed that the Bank of England and the
BIS would prepare detailed proposals for further discussion.

A Bank of England paper on "The future of the sterling balances" was
sent to the BIS in March. It discussed two possible approaches: the first
using the IMF framework, the second centering on the BIS. The advantage
of going to the IMF was that this would signal that the sterling balances were
not just a U.K. or sterling-area problem but a global issue. There were also
drawbacks: negotiations would be cumbersome and lengthy and almost impossible to keep secret. Working through the BIS, on the other hand, would
guarantee speed, flexibility, and discretion. In fact, Governor O'Brien had
already made up his mind that Basel was preferable to Washington.

Over the following months, the Bank of England and the BIS worked together on the details of an arrangement that would meet the requirements
of the Bank of England and satisfy all central banks involved. At their May
1968 meeting,[318] the governors debated the scheme at length. The main
points of discussion concerned the long-term character of the proposed facility, which presented certain legal difficulties for some of the participating
central banks, and the need to create incentives for the sterling-area central banks to dissuade them from scaling down their sterling balances too
quickly.[319] The proposal was finalised on 20 June at a special meeting in
Amsterdam between Morse and Raw of the Bank of England on the one
hand and Zijlstra, Ferras, and Macdonald for the BIS on the other. The proposed amount of the "safety net" facility was pitched at $2 billion, as "there
would be no coming back for more!"[320] The facility, provided by twelve
central banks through the BIS, consisted of foreign currency swaps (made
available by the BIS) on which the Bank of England could draw during a
three-year period to offset reserve losses deriving from the conversion of
sterling balances held outside the United Kingdom.[321] To induce sterling-
area countries to slow down the conversion of their sterling balances, the
Bank of England offered them a dollar guarantee protecting the value of all
their sterling holdings above 10% of their total reserves. Sterling-area countries were asked to deposit at least part of their nonsterling currency reserves
with the BIS in order to increase the liquid funds available for the Group
Arrangement swaps. The terms of the second Sterling Group Arrangement

were broadly approved at the Basel governors' meeting on 7 July 1968 and were well received in the market.[322]

During the summer of 1968, negotiation teams from the Bank of England and the U.K. Treasury spread out from London on a whirlwind tour covering 41 sterling-area countries and territories – an awe-inspiring logistical and diplomatic tour de force. The terms for buying into the Basel arrangement had to be negotiated with each country individually. In the case of the most important holder of sterling reserves, Australia, Governor O'Brien himself flew out to broker the deal. By early September 1968, the Bank of England was able to announce in Basel that 30 countries which together held some 77% of official sterling-area sterling reserves had signed up. The remaining countries soon followed. This allowed the twelve participating central banks to give their final agreement to the scheme, although there was some last-minute bargaining on the respective shares as a result of the Bank of France's decision not to join.[323] The second Sterling Group Arrangement was officially announced by the BIS on 9 September.[324] BIS President Zijlstra and Governor O'Brien hailed it as "a most important act of international monetary cooperation". The arrangement came into force as of 23 September 1968. At the same time, the complete liquidation of the first Group Arrangement by early 1971 was also approved. Together with the tight budget (announced by Chancellor Roy Jenkins a few months earlier) and the steady reduction of the U.K. balance of payments deficit, the Group Arrangement contributed to a restoration of confidence.

In the end, the facilities provided by the second Sterling Group Arrangement were hardly used for their intended purpose. By the end of October 1968, the Bank of England had drawn $600 million but, in agreement with the governors, these funds were used to repay some of the previous short-term assistance.[325] The entire sum was repaid by September 1969, as the improvement in the U.K. balance of payments boosted the official reserves. The Bank of England made no further use of the second Group Arrangement facility. With the pound strengthening and most of the sterling-area countries in balance of payments surplus, the sterling balances rose from £3.4 billion in September 1968 to £4.2 billion at the end of 1970,[326] giving no reason for the Bank of England to draw on the facility. This outcome was not just the result of the stronger reserve position of the United Kingdom and the sterling area in general; it also owed to the individual agreements the Bank of England had concluded with each of the sterling area countries in the context of the second Group Arrangement. The commitment of these countries to maintain a fixed proportion of their official reserves in guaranteed sterling had meant that the increase in overall reserve levels also contributed to an increase in their sterling holdings. In that sense, the second Group Arrangement was undoubtedly a success.[327] As far as the BIS was concerned, the second Group Arrangement considerably expanded its customer base. Many sterling-area central banks from Asia and Africa – which had never before done business with the BIS – deposited part of their reserves with it as a direct consequence of their agreements with the Bank of England. These deposits reached a peak of over $500 million in early 1970, and many of the business contacts then established would be continued long after the end of the second Group Arrangement.

11.11   The French Franc and the Deutsche Mark

In 1969, the BIS Annual Report identified, somewhat provocatively, five "key sources of imbalance" to the international monetary system. Apart from the general issue of global reserve creation, these were the strains caused by the balance of payments and exchange rate positions of four individual countries: the United States, the United Kingdom, Germany, and France.[328] We now turn to the latter two, because developments in Germany and France in 1968 and 1969 were also relevant for the subsequent development of monetary cooperation within the BIS framework.

After the successful stabilisation of the French franc in 1958, France's external position had improved spectacularly. Between 1958 and 1967, France posted average annual real output growth of well over 5% while at the same time enjoying hefty balance of payments surpluses.[329] By 1967, official reserves, held predominantly in gold, had ballooned to nearly $7 billion and were the second largest in Europe.[330] It was from this strong gold position that, as we have seen, France challenged the gold dollar standard, even pleading for a return to a more symmetrical gold-standard regime.[331] Consistent with this strategy, from 1965 onwards the French government instructed the Bank of France to reduce its participation in joint central bank operations designed to support the pound and the dollar.

In May 1968, the unexpected outburst of social upheaval triggered by the students' revolt shook confidence in the French franc. Official reserves fell by more than $300 million in that month alone. In spite of reactivating the 1962 swap agreement with the Federal Reserve Bank of New York, the French authorities were compelled to close the foreign exchange market and to impose exchange controls for the first time since the introduction of convertibility at the end of 1958. The gold drain continued until a joint central bank support credit was announced in early July.[332] For a while, the announcement of the support package relieved the pressure, but heavy selling of French francs resumed in September as soon as exchange controls were relaxed, and they intensified in November as markets became convinced that the inflation triggered by the wage increases granted in the wake of the general strike – and the massive imbalance in France's external position – made devaluation unavoidable.

The overall nervousness of the exchange markets in the autumn of 1968 had as much to do with the French situation as with the continued weakness of the pound sterling and the seemingly uncontrollable strength of the Deutsche mark. German GDP was growing at a rapid pace in 1968, with a trade surplus and little sign of inflationary pressures, so that the mark traded at the upper limit of its parity.[333] After May 1968, the weakness of the French franc and the strength of the Deutsche mark were very much the two sides of the same coin. Capital fleeing France largely headed for Germany, forcing both the French and German central banks to intervene. In contrast to 1960–61, the Bundesbank this time quickly came to the conclusion that a revaluation of the Deutsche mark would be unavoidable and indeed desirable in order to safeguard domestic stability.

Behind the scenes at the BIS meeting of 17–18 November 1968, Bundesbank President Blessing and Governor Brunet of the Bank of France struck a deal whereby each would plead with their respective governments for a simultaneous 5% revaluation of the Deutsche mark and 5% devaluation of the French franc.[334] The German government, however, had thus far ruled out a revaluation, which it felt would constitute a unilateral concession forced on Germany with the sole aim of solving the structural problems of third countries; for its part, the French government had earlier rejected any notion of an imminent devaluation of the franc. As the onslaught on the markets continued, and in the hope of breaking the deadlock, an emergency meeting of the G10 ministers of finance and central bank governors was called to Bonn from 20 to 22 November. The Bonn meeting was later described by participants as "a shambles" and as "the most unpleasant monetary conference I ever attended".[335] Most participants had come to Bonn in the expectation of discussing the modalities of a Deutsche mark revaluation and French franc devaluation. However, on the day before the G10 meeting opened, the German government decided not to revalue but instead to impose a 4% tax on exports and grant a 4% reduction on import charges. This pseudo-revaluation was presented to the G10 meeting as a fait accompli. The final press communiqué of the Bonn meeting tried to strike a forceful and decisive tone in order to cover the lack of actual results. Even so, it was widely read to imply French franc devaluation, but again President de Gaulle decided against it. The only tangible outcome of the Bonn meeting was a $1.65 billion credit package to support the French franc, which was made available by ten central banks, together with the BIS and the U.S. Treasury, from January 1969.[336]

The Bonn communiqué also included a vague commitment to "examine new central bank arrangements to alleviate the impact on reserves of speculative movements". Nothing much came of it. At the BIS meeting of 8–9 December 1968, the governors discussed a rather general proposal for creating an "open-end monetary facility designed to offset international short-capital flows", originally put forward by Carli (Bank of Italy). However, in a statement published on 10 February 1969, the governors merely noted "that facilities between central banks, or with the BIS, have been established extremely quickly in case of need. If, at any time in the future, it appears that new arrangements are needed in order to cope with an unusually large movement of speculative funds, the central banks of the group declare themselves ready to meet together immediately, at the request of the President of the BIS, to arrange such additional facilities as the group may judge appropriate".[337]

The Bonn meeting had left the issue of exchange rate adjustments hanging in the air. Soon speculation against the French franc resumed and, at the Basel meeting of 9–10 March 1969, Governor Brunet (who was to be succeeded by Olivier Wormser one month later) appeared "worried and concerned".[338] The resignation of de Gaulle in April added to the uncertainty. At the beginning of May, the Bundesbank had to cope with the greatest inflow of foreign currency in its history. German government circles now came round to share the Bundesbank view that a revaluation had become unavoidable. Chancellor Kiesinger, however, had pledged to maintain the parity and would not budge. In the end, the French government made the first move. With de Gaulle replaced by Pompidou at the Elysée Palace, the French authorities took advantage of the relative calm in the exchange markets over the summer months to announce a surprise devaluation of 11.1% as of 11 August 1969. In Germany the elections of 28 September brought a new coalition to power, headed by Willy Brandt, which first let the Deutsche mark float upwards and then, on 24 October 1969, fixed a new parity at DM 3.66 per dollar, a revaluation of 9.3%.

11.12   The End of Bretton Woods

In 1968, the BIS Annual Report remarked that "developments came to pass which made the year 1967–68 the most disturbed for the international monetary system since 1949".[339] The end of the joint support of the gold price, the G10 discussions about international liquidity, and the difficulties met in reaching an agreement about the establishment of the SDR signalled a weakening of the cooperative climate that had prevailed in the first half of the 1960s.[340] At the same time, the parity adjustments in 1967–69 of the three main European currencies – the pound sterling, the Deutsche mark, and the French franc – reflected the stresses affecting the fixed-rate regime. Indeed, in October 1969 Germany had a taste, however brief, of floating rates.

The immediate causes of the end of the fixed-rate regime were economic, but the underlying forces were political: as noted in the introductory section, the "consensual hegemony" regime established at the end of the Second World War had become obsolete, largely a result of its own success. Prosperous Europe was increasingly weary of U.S. external deficits generated by military expenditure and direct investment, seen by many on the Continent as two sides of the same "imperialist" coin. American presidents – as Volcker noted twenty years later – "did not want to hear that their options were limited by the weakness of the dollar".[341] Unwilling either to embark upon restrictive polices to reduce the external deficit or to explicitly declare the end of the fixed-rate international monetary system, the U.S. authorities adopted a "do nothing" stance, also known as "benign neglect" of the dollar.

The first allocation of special drawing rights – on which so many hopes had been pinned – came too late and was relatively small in size. During 1970 and 1971 the IMF member countries were allocated SDRs for an amount equivalent to $6.5 billion, which was quite overshadowed by a parallel increase in dollar reserves, convertible into gold at sight, that amounted to $47 billion over the same period.[342]

In the BIS's analysis, the sparks that ignited the final run on the dollar originated in 1969 and were openly visible in 1970. Due to a tightening of U.S. monetary policy towards the end of 1968, U.S. banks borrowed heavily from their European branches (the so-called eurodollar market, discussed in the next chapter). Hence the net reserve position of the United States improved in 1969. However, U.S. banks "were not going forever to remain heavily in debt to their foreign branches. As monetary policy was eased in 1970, the banks began to reduce these borrowings, at first gradually and then rather rapidly from mid-year onwards".[343] The swing from restraint to ease in U.S. monetary policy was contrasted with an opposite shift in European (and particularly German) policies. In March 1970, when the Federal Reserve relaxed the squeeze, the Bundesbank raised its rediscount rate from 6% to 7.5%, thereby becoming the main recipient of the dollar outflow from the United States. The year 1970 thus witnessed a strong rebound for all major European currencies, with restrictive policies and high interest rates in most countries inviting a return of confidence and of capital flows. A major imbalance developed between Europe and the United States, where an easy-money policy and lower interest rates contributed to a significant weakening of the dollar. Things came to a head in the spring of 1971, when a new transatlantic currency crisis proved to be the prelude to the definitive collapse of the Bretton Woods system. Underlying the looming crisis, according to the BIS, was a lack of policy coordination, which "demonstrated what can happen when monetary policies of major countries are applied forcefully in opposite directions".[344]

It is not by chance that, around the turn of the decade, floating rates quietly found their way into the private discussions and memoranda of policy makers,[345] including the BIS, a long-standing bastion of gold and fixed parities.

Since the 1950s, Milton Friedman had challenged the prevailing fixed-rate orthodoxy. He traced his interest in floating exchange rates back to a period of time spent in Paris in 1950 as a consultant of the U.S. special representative to the ECA (the agency administering the Marshall Plan). The study of the Schuman Plan, he wrote, led him to the conclusion that "a common market would inevitably founder without floating exchange rates".[346] Another strong advocate for floating rates was Gottfried Haberler, who in the 1950s "made the case that European countries should remove their exchange controls and restore current account convertibility [by adopting] floating rates as had been done by Canada in 1950".[347] Friedman's[348] and Haberler's[349] work drew some attention from the academic world but, unsurprisingly, none from policy makers. "The world of the academic halls and the world of policy makers", Friedman observed, "very often seem to move on two wholly different levels with little contact between them".[350] This may indeed sometimes be the case, but the fact is that the majority of academic economists in the 1950s concurred on the desirability of fixed rates. Indeed, as we have seen, under the postwar arrangement and the EPU, floating rates were largely regarded as an interesting intellectual exercise and of little policy consequence. As circumstances changed, from the early 1960s onwards, and as the difficulty of clinging to fixed rates became ever more apparent, the floating option attracted renewed attention.

In 1966, Friedman, increasingly drawn into the public arena, made a plea for floating at a hearing before a congressional subcommittee devoted to international exchange and payments.[351] He also began to write a column on current affairs for *Newsweek,* alternating with Paul Samuelson and Henry Wallich. In 1968 he was an economic adviser to Nixon's successful presidential campaign and wrote an influential book on the balance of payments and monetary policy.[352] Though Friedman's radical exchange rate laissez faire remained an anathema to policy makers for most of the 1960s, the intellectual climate slowly changed. In 1970 Okun could write: "Research economists and academic experts today agree broadly, although not unanimously, that a greater degree of flexibility in exchange rates would be a desirable innovation".[353]

By the late 1960s, the floating option was discussed not only by academics but by policy makers as well. At the beginning of 1969, in a confidential memorandum for the G10 deputies, Otmar Emminger of the Bundesbank wrote: "Our international monetary system has become crisis-prone.... There is a strong feeling that major trading countries with balance-of-payments problems will resist with equal vehemence necessary domestic adjustments as well as the other alternative, i.e. a change in the par value of their currencies.... Indispensable adjustment measures (e.g. pound devaluation, two-tier gold market, U.S. tax measures, German and French measures of November 1968) have been forced upon unwilling countries by major international crises. Such a system of 'adjustment through crisis' is not very impressive, to say the least. The call for reform has become very wide-spread. It is usually directed towards the present exchange-rate system. Many people ask for greater 'flexibility' in the exchange rates. The favourite proposals are either wider margins for permissible exchange rate fluctuations of major currencies, or a gradual shifting of the parities in small steps ('crawling peg'), or a combination of the two".[354]

In January 1970, the BIS convened a meeting of high-level central bank officials from eleven countries on the possibility of greater flexibility of exchange rates. Under Gilbert's chairmanship, the experts discussed crawling pegs and the widening of fluctuation margins, ending up by rejecting both options.[355] Temporary floating, however, as recently practised by Germany, was seen to have some merits in particular circumstances.

Needless to say, the discussions about ways of increasing exchange rate flexibility were – like all previous ones on reforming the system – politically charged, reflecting the desire of most Europeans to curb a perceived U.S. hegemony. Giscard d'Estaing, the French Minister of Finance, advocated the creation of a "European pole, so as to establish, relative to the dollar pole, a more balanced system".[356] According to one U.S. observer, European central bankers were quite unanimous in expressing the desire to reduce the dollar's sphere of influence by taking a unified position in order to reduce their dollar holdings to a minimum sufficient only for intervention on foreign exchange markets. Unanimity ended, however, when means of achieving the shared goals were discussed. "Top officials", wrote the same observer, "of the central banks of Germany, Italy and the Netherlands have all proposed some form of exchange rate flexibility", which they regarded as a "means of curbing the dollar's influence, at least in the long run". Carli proposed "limited and controlled rate flexibility between European currencies to ease the integration within the EEC and to prepare the way for a system of flexible rates between Europe and the U.S.". The central banks of France and Belgium, on the other hand, "clearly expressed disapproval of any change to the fixed parity system". Only the latter, they argued, would oblige the United States to drink the bitter cup of monetary and fiscal discipline. In any case, capital controls were, for the French, preferable to exchange rate instability. The events of 1968–69 had not affected the long-standing positions of the various players – except perhaps for the United States, where the recent crises had produced a profound sense "that the U.S. dollar problem could not be addressed",[357] leading to a continuation of the "benign neglect" attitude of recent years.

In 1970 all European central bankers, whether accepting or rejecting greater exchange rate flexibility, still recognised that it was perhaps a useful but certainly insufficient means of resolving international monetary problems. As long as the dollar was the key international currency, efforts had to be made to solve the problems cooperatively. They also shared the view, as Emminger phrased it, that the predominant role of the U.S. currency put "a tremendous responsibility vis-à-vis the whole Western World on those who [had] to manage the dollar".[358]

The final crisis of the Bretton Woods system came when, as Harold James put it, "Germany abandoned the multilateral approach, because it transparently had failed to produce any change in U.S. policy or any substantial coordination in Europe, and went on an isolated course".[359]

At the end of 1970, the position of the U.S. current account balance was very weak, with the surplus all but disappeared. It was expected to weaken further as the economy gained speed. At the same time, the United States and Europe continued to pursue monetary policies that produced further flows of funds from the former to the latter. The previous year's exchange rate turmoil, the fact that the United States was perceived to be no longer in a position to afford further reserve losses, and – last but not least – the impact on expectations of the G10 discussions about the need for greater flexibility all added to the markets' belief that matters could get out of control at any moment.

The situation came to a head in the first few days of May 1971, when a further large inflow led the German authorities to close the exchange market.[360] According to the BIS, "the immediate causes of the crisis were two: the suggestion made simultaneously and publicly, by leading German economic research institutes, that the Deutsche mark be floated; and the knowledge that the Council of Ministers of the EEC was discussing the possibility of greater flexibility of the Common Market currencies vis-à-vis the dollar".[361] In fact Schiller, the joint economics and finance minister in the coalition government led by Brandt, tried to convince his colleagues in Brussels about the advisability of a common float against the dollar. When he failed, he went to the Bundesbank council to urge a unilateral shift to a floating stance. "A majority, led by President Klasen, opposed the idea, pleading instead for capital controls to deter inflows",[362] but in the end the government prevailed over the central bank, which was temporarily freed from its obligation of intervening on the currency market. The Deutsche mark was allowed to float freely as of 10 May. The Netherlands immediately followed suit, while Belgium introduced a separation between the official (regulated) and the free foreign exchange markets. The Austrian schilling was revalued by 5.05% and the Swiss franc by 7.07%. By early August, the Deutsche mark had floated upward to 8% above its previous parity with the dollar.

The U.S. reaction to the developments in Europe was typical: a flat refusal even to discuss a devaluation of the dollar. Connally, the new U.S. Treasury secretary, was adamant that trade and military expenditure overseas, not the dollar rate, were the problem. He threatened to revise mutual security and trade arrangements. Europe was now rich and well endowed with reserves: it should open its markets and make a larger contribution to its defence. "No longer", he said, "can considerations of friendship or need, or capacity, justify the United States carrying so heavy a share of common burdens".[363] Coombs noted that Connally had long been convinced "that the United States had for decades shown a woolly-minded disregard of [its] foreign trading interests and that the time had come to pound the table and set the accounts straight. He took a particularly harsh view of the Common Market and seemed to have written off Bretton Woods and the IMF as a total loss".[364] The U.S. Treasury secretary had become the leading spokesman for the doctrine of benign neglect, which translated into the popular slogan: "The dollar is our currency but your problem".

The float of the Deutsche mark for a while stopped the dollar inflow, allowing an improvement in the U.S. reserve position. But markets remained volatile. The final August crisis began on the sixth of the month when a U.S. congressional subcommittee report called for a general realignment of the exchange rate of the dollar against all the other main currencies – adding that, in the absence of such a move, the United States might have no choice but to suspend the convertibility of the dollar unilaterally. A new wave of dollar selling followed the report's publication. The final decision in that regard was taken at an emergency meeting called at Camp David for the weekend of 15 August 1971.[365] There, FRB Chairman Arthur Burns unsuccessfully tried to defend gold convertibility. He went as far as arguing that abandonment would signal the collapse of capitalism. Apparently, to Burns's arguments Connally replied: "So the other countries don't like it. So what?" – and when Burns added that they might retaliate: "Let 'em. What can they do?"[366]

On Sunday 15 August, Nixon made a televised speech asserting the strength of the U.S. economy and announcing a series of policy measures, including the unilateral closure of the gold–dollar window and a 10% import tax. Contrary to the letter and the spirit of the Bretton Woods Agreements, the IMF general manager had not been consulted and was merely notified a few hours prior to the announcement.

For a week after Nixon's speech, the main European currency markets remained closed while governments tried, and failed, to coordinate a joint answer to the U.S. move. On 23 August, markets were reopened amidst uncertainty and confusion. Two decades of painstaking, patient, and often only partly successful cooperative efforts lay in tatters.

The following year and a half saw a succession of rather half-hearted attempts to re-create a system of fixed exchange rates. The Europeans insisted that this would be possible only if the official price of gold were to be raised (i.e., if the dollar devalued), a solution long advocated by France as well as by Gilbert at the BIS. At the IMF meeting in September 1971, Chairman Burns of the Federal Reserve Board asked BIS President Zijlstra to sound out his colleagues about the feasibility and possible range of a negotiated realignment of exchange rates, in preparation for a G10 meeting scheduled for the end of November.[367] An intensive round of negotiations followed, partly in the margins of the BIS governors' meeting of 6 and 7 November 1971. The prevailing mood in Basel was one of "great concern" over the continuing state of uncertainty. Many governors believed, however, that the time was not yet ripe for a fruitful meeting on new fixed parities.[368] In his final report, Zijlstra stressed the need to act urgently because the prevailing uncertainty was "intensifying the recessionary trends".[369] He suggested a 5.5% devaluation of the dollar and a simultaneous revaluation of the other major currencies ranging between 3% and 9%. But the French franc, the lira, and the pound would not move.

Formal negotiations on the new parities took place at the end of November 1971. Finance ministers and central bank heads of the G10 met in

Rome to discuss the size of the realignment needed to bring the U.S. balance of payments into equilibrium. The meeting failed to reach an agreement. Only very few people, however, reconciled themselves to the idea that the era of fixed rates – inaugurated way back in the 1870s – had definitely come to an end, and a second attempt was made at a special G10 meeting convened at the Smithsonian Institution in Washington. The so-called Smithsonian Agreement of 18 December 1971 set the devaluation and revaluation amounts for each individual currency at significantly higher rates than those proposed by Zijlstra. The dollar devalued by 7.9% (or an increase in the official gold price from $35 to $38 per ounce). With most other currencies revaluing against gold, the net effect was a revaluation against the dollar of the lira (7.5%), the French franc and pound sterling (8.6%), the Deutsche mark (13.6%[370]), and the Japanese yen (no less than 16.9%).[371] The agreement was universally saluted as the beginning of a new period of stability.

The newly established fixed rates proved to be ephemeral. On 8 January 1972, scarcely three weeks after the realignment, the central bank foreign exchange experts meeting in Basel expressed their doubts that the agreement would mark a definitive return of calm to the markets.[372] And indeed, the markets almost immediately signalled that they did not believe in the stability of the new rate structure, especially as the dollar devaluation "had not been accompanied by any shift to domestic monetary and fiscal restraint".[373]

A statement issued by the governors, meeting at the BIS in March 1972, emphasised their determination to uphold the Smithsonian exchange rate structure and helped to calm the markets temporarily. However, in June 1972, the pound sterling came under renewed pressure and was eventually set floating. The Federal Reserve saw itself compelled to resume support operations for the dollar in the market and to reactivate the central bank swap network, both of which had been put on hold in August 1971. Finally, in February 1973 the dollar fell victim to a new speculative onslaught. A hastily decided new dollar devaluation of 10% failed to impress the markets,[374] and by the beginning of March the situation had deteriorated to the point that the Europeans decided they had had enough. The breaking point came on 1 March, when the Bundesbank had to purchase no less than $2.7 billion to support the dollar exchange rate. The exchange markets were closed, and on 12 March 1973 the EEC countries adopted a joint float against the dollar (with the exception of Ireland, Italy, and the United Kingdom, which adopted an individual float). Bretton Woods was dead. A new era in international monetary relations dawned, one characterised by the slow creation of currency areas and free floating amongst them.

"Between 1971 and 1974", Harold James wrote, "the international monetary system moved toward floating, not so much because this was an agreed solution, but because it emerged out of a failure to produce an agreed solution".[375] In the end domestic economic policy considerations prevailed over the perceived benefits of preserving a stable international environment of fixed exchange rates. Strictly speaking, it may be true that "The Bretton Woods system had been on life support since its inception" and that, "between 1958 and 1968, it had only been kept alive by a series of extraordinary measures that made little, long-term, macroeconomic sense".[376] But life support produced beneficial results: during this long decade of stable exchange rates and intense international monetary cooperation, the Western world enjoyed the highest economic growth rates in modern history, accompanied by full employment and relatively modest inflation.

The introduction of floating rates put central bank cooperation to a new test in an environment of slower growth and higher inflation. In many ways central banks regained greater freedom in controlling monetary aggregates and applying monetary policy instruments, but managing the international monetary system in a floating-rate regime soon appeared to be far from a smooth ride – as witnessed by renewed currency turmoil in the summer of 1973, partly caused by the Watergate scandal. As the BIS commented with a hint of nostalgia for the fixed–exchange rate regime: "This episode suggested the potential volatility of exchange markets under a regime of floating, where modest pressures can cause significant shifts in rates".[377]

TWELVE

Monetary Union and Financial Stability

12.1   At the Roots of the BIS's Future

The end of Bretton Woods marked a watershed in the history of international monetary systems, hitherto based on fixed exchange rates abandoned only at times of war or exceptional economic crises. From the early 1970s onwards, international settlements took place in a context of floating exchange rates, even if pegging within broad currency areas was more or less successfully attempted. Over the same period of time, international financial flows increased at a swift pace as a "second globalisation" – after the one that came to an end in 1914 – gathered momentum, spurred in part by technological advances. Restrictions on cross-border capital movements were relaxed and eventually abolished in most countries.

The end of Bretton Woods also signalled yet another moment in the history of the BIS when the Bank had to reconsider and adjust its own role in and approach to international monetary cooperation. Central banking was also deeply, if slowly, affected by the changes in the rules of the game regarding both exchange rates and international capital mobility. Moreover, in the last three decades of the twentieth century, innovations in the payments system produced, at least in some countries, a decline in the demand for traditional base money. The legal environment in which banking systems operated underwent major changes, as the various forms of financial repression hitherto prevailing in almost every country were gradually relaxed. At the same time, European financial integration and cooperation, at first rather neglected in the unification process, gathered momentum, beginning with the birth of the European Monetary System.

As at the time of previous sweeping changes in the international environment – the end of the gold standard and of reparations, the Second World War, the creation of the Bretton Woods system – the BIS was once again challenged to reinvent itself. While its traditional concern with the coordination of monetary policy was by no means abandoned, from the 1970s onwards the BIS developed two new major lines of activity. The first one entailed intimate involvement with the long process of European monetary integration, as the EEC central bankers chose Basel as the locus for their collaboration, with the help of a BIS-managed secretariat. The second important new direction taken by the BIS after 1971 concerned global financial stability, which drew the Bank into the field of financial regulation. This new area of interest also provided the rationale for extending BIS membership to include central banks from a number of emerging economies, and it prompted the U.S. Federal Reserve Board to finally take up – in 1994 – its seat on the BIS Board of Directors. In the 1990s, as the goal of European monetary union came eventually to be realised, the BIS also gradually shed its predominantly European character and acquired the features of a global international organisation.

In the early 1970s, these developments lay in the fairly distant future; their roots can nevertheless be traced back to the late 1950s and the 1960s. Therefore, although the most recent decades in the history of the BIS are not covered here and only summarily touched upon in the chronological appendix (Annex D), this last chapter deals with the committee of the EEC central bank governors and with the eurodollar market, both of which were at the origin of the new dimensions of the BIS's activity that characterised subsequent years.

In the 1960s, the central bank governors of the European Economic Community began to meet separately on a regular basis at the BIS, establishing the groundwork for future closer collaboration. The unravelling of the Bretton Woods system in 1968–73 acted as a catalyst for closer monetary cooperation among the members of the European Community: the Werner Report (1970) was the first serious attempt at setting the EEC on the path towards monetary integration. The role played by national central banks, and by the BIS, in this and other aspects of the construction of a unified Europe is still under-researched, but there is little doubt that it was significant.

Developments in the international money markets – beginning with the surge in the eurocurrency markets[1] – shaped much of the BIS's activity in the post–Bretton Woods era, now focused mainly on financial stability and prudential regulation. In the 1960s, the eurocurrency market had already faced central bankers with new questions about the likely inflationary effects of unchecked liquidity creation and about the systemic threats posed by un-regulated capital flows. The final demise of Bretton Woods and the onset of worldwide economic and financial instability highlighted the need for better cross-border banking regulation, or rather standard setting, which prompted the BIS to establish, at the end of 1974, the G10 Committee on Banking Regulations and Supervisory Practices. Now known as the Basel Commit-tee on Banking Supervision (or simply the Basel Committee), this body turned out to be one of the more significant developments in international financial cooperation during the last two decades of the twentieth century.

12.2 The EEC Governors' Meetings in the 1960s

"L'Europe", wrote Jacques Rueff in 1950, "se fera par la monnaie, ou ne se fera pas".[2] He did not have a single currency in mind, except in the sense that he saw the gold standard as a satisfactory approximation of it. Around the same time, Marius Holtrop, who was president of the Netherlands Bank and later also of the BIS, alluded to the guilder eventually being merged into one European currency.[3] But opinions of this kind were rare in the 1950s. Money did not feature high on the agenda of the first generation of architects of European unification.[4] The 1957 Treaty of Rome, establishing the Euro-pean Economic Community, spoke only vaguely about the coordination of monetary policy and even more vaguely referred to the member states' ex-change rate policies as being of common interest to the entire Community.[5]

The only practical action in the monetary field that followed the conclu-sion of the Treaty of Rome was the creation in February 1958 of the EEC Monetary Committee, meeting in Brussels, close to the EEC Commission. Each member government and the Commission appointed two members to sit on the committee, high-ranking officials from the respective Treasuries and central banks. Throughout the 1960s, the Monetary Committee was chaired by Emile van Lennep from the Dutch Ministry of Finance, with Calvet and then Clappier of the Bank of France and Otmar Emminger from the Bundesbank as vice-presidents. The EEC Monetary Committee was a purely consultative body whose tasks were to monitor financial and mone-tary developments in the member countries and to advise the EEC Council and Commission on such issues as the liberalisation of capital flows, ex-change rate policies, and balance of payments imbalances.[6] The ultimate goal was a closer coordination of monetary policies across the EEC, but it was nowhere clearly spelled out how this was to be achieved. In practice, the Monetary Committee was little more than a forum for polite information exchange. The revaluations of the Deutsche mark and the Dutch guilder in

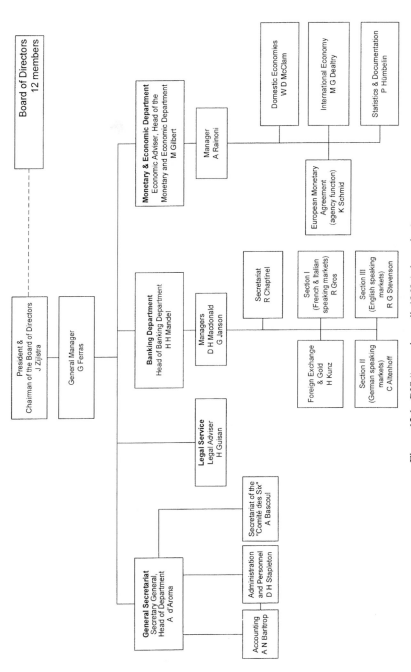

Figure 12.1. BIS "organigram", 1969 (adaptation).

March 1961, decided without any prior consultation, exposed the lack of monetary policy coordination within the EEC.

Although, at the beginning of the 1960s, money was not high on the agenda, the discussion among the EEC founder members ("the Six") about closer political cooperation gained momentum. In February 1961, a special committee was appointed to examine possible amendments to the Treaty of Rome with a view to introducing provisions for a mild form of political unification. In June of the same year, the Bonn meeting of the heads of state or government resolved to "give shape to the will for political union" and agreed to conduct regular meetings to try and arrive at a common outlook on the matter.[7] In February 1962, France's five partners put forward a plan for a political union to which de Gaulle responded by advocating a European confederation and by clearly stating that his country did not consider closer political ties desirable. This debate on political cooperation took place while the transitional period towards the common market was entering its second stage, as envisaged by the 1957 Treaty of Rome. In October 1962, the Commission presented an "action programme" for the implementation of stage 2 that, among other things, proposed a revision of the treaty to include monetary union as a goal to be achieved by 1969.[8] It was not by coincidence that monetary union was first made an objective of the EEC at a time when political cooperation was being hotly (albeit in the end inconclusively) debated: as we shall see, the question immediately arose about which should come first, political or monetary union.

In order to promote monetary cooperation, the Commission called for the establishment of a permanent council of EEC central bank governors to work alongside the Monetary Committee. On the occasion of the 1962 IMF meeting in Washington, Robert Marjolin, vice-president of the commission responsible for economic and financial affairs, sounded out the central bank governors of the Six about setting up such a council. He envisaged a committee – sitting in Brussels and chaired by a member of the EEC Commission – that would establish the practice of prior consultation on important domestic monetary policy decisions and define a common EEC position in international monetary affairs.

The EEC governors, meeting in Basel on 11–12 November 1962, rejected Marjolin's blueprint on almost all counts.[9] The BIS president, Holtrop, even suggested that the governors of the Six should not leave the initiative to the Commission and instead proclaim themselves there and then to be the official council of EEC central bank governors with its seat in Basel. Even if his more prudent colleagues did not take up the suggestion, it was nevertheless clear that the central banks would not accept the Commission's leadership.[10] On the occasion of the December BIS Board meeting, Marjolin travelled to Basel to see the governors of the Six and discuss the EEC's action plan, but he was unable to make them change their minds.[11]

In the following months, the Commission, already criticised by some member governments as being overly ambitious and centralist, climbed down from its initial position and over the next six years made only occasional official remarks on monetary policy guidelines.[12] With monetary issues out of the limelight, on 8 May 1964 the EEC Council of Ministers quietly approved the establishment of a "Committee of the Governors of the Central Banks of the Member States of the European Economic Community". The central bankers had largely got it their way. The purpose of the committee had been toned down considerably from the original Commission proposal. It now envisaged "consultations concerning the general principles and the broad lines of monetary policy" and regular information exchanges "about the most important measures that fall within the competence of the central banks, ... normally before the national authorities take decisions".[13] Instead of being chaired by a member of the EEC Commission, the Commission would "as a general rule, be invited to send one of its members as a representative to the meetings of the Committee". And, finally, instead of fixing its seat in Brussels, the governors made sure that the committee would as a rule meet at the BIS in Basel. Besides finding it logistically convenient to combine the new committee's meetings with their regular Basel weekends, the governors thus also signalled their intention to remain as independent as possible from the political centre of the EEC in Brussels.

The first official meeting of the Committee of EEC Governors took place in Basel on 6 July 1964. It was largely devoted to procedural issues. Marius Holtrop was elected chairman and Antonio d'Aroma secretary general to the committee; it was no coincidence that the two held the same positions at the BIS. The committee consisted of the five EEC central bank governors.[14] Each governor was entitled to bring a high-ranking official to the meeting. They were also joined by Robert Marjolin, the representative of the EEC Commission. It was decided that in principle the committee would meet every two months on the occasion of a BIS Board meeting. Although the BIS provided secretariat services to the committee, the committee's business was to be handled separately from all other BIS activities.[15]

The first two meetings of the Committee of Governors, in July and October 1964, highlighted the divergence of opinion between the central banks and the EEC Commission. In his opening remarks, Holtrop warned against "the sometimes exaggerated or false tendencies in favour of a European monetary union".[16] Marjolin, for his part, painted an optimistic picture of the level of economic unification already achieved among the Six and hinted at the Commission's feeling that the time had come for a more systematic approach to economic and monetary policy coordination. Towards that end, he said, the Commission was preparing proposals that would take the EEC along the path to monetary union. He argued that monetary union was possible even in the absence of political union, since the lack of the latter had not stood in the way of an economic union. Marjolin's passionate plea met with a cool reception. Both Holtrop and Blessing insisted that the Committee of Governors should limit itself to discussing the current monetary problems in the EEC. Monetary union, they said, was "a theoretical problem that should not figure among the priorities of the Six".[17] In the governors' view, monetary union was unthinkable without political union and the renunciation of national sovereignty. This remained the constant opinion of the EEC central bank heads throughout the 1960s and was defended most strongly by those of Germany and the Netherlands.[18] Any suggestions concerning the creation of an EEC pool of central bank reserves or of a common unit of account were seen as utterly premature.

During the first five years of its existence, the Committee of Governors consistently steered clear of any in-depth discussion of monetary union and, at least according to Marjolin, no substantial progress was made even on the less ambitious goal of monetary policy harmonisation.[19] What, then, did the committee achieve? For one thing, it acted as a forum for information exchange and helped enhance understanding of how monetary policy was defined and implemented in the six EEC member states. To Hubert Ansiaux, who took over as chairman of the committee from Holtrop in July 1967, its main contribution to the process of European integration during those early years was to stimulate exchanges of views on the situation in the different member countries, to encourage nascent consultations between economic and financial EEC leaders, and (last but not least) to greatly improve the comparability of statistics and reduce the publication lag for economic indicators.[20] Discussions in the committee on the economic and financial outlook for the Six were indeed based on increasingly sophisticated and timely analyses, which were prepared by the BIS's Monetary and Economic Department – under the direction of Antonio Rainoni – with inputs from all central banks concerned.

Beyond the exchange of information, the governors of the Six also used the committee to try to align their views on the reform of the international monetary system and on the sterling and U.S. balance of payments crises, as discussed in the BIS and G10 contexts. The absence of U.K. and U.S.

representatives at the committee meetings encouraged frank discussions on the consequences of the monetary policies pursued by the deficit countries, which often enough ended with one or the other governor stating bluntly that the U.S. authorities ought to swallow their pride and draw on the IMF to finance the U.S. external deficit.[21] However, the practical outcomes of these discussions were rather meagre. The Six agreed on the distribution of the burden for joint EEC participation in sterling support credits, but this was rendered ineffective by the Bank of France's refusal, from 1965 onwards, to be part of any further sterling support packages. Some degree of coordination was achieved in the participation of the Six in the central banks' swap network.[22]

Substantive discussions also took place on the role and composition of monetary reserves in the EEC member states,[23] on the creation of a centralised risk office, and on the desirability of interest rate convergence within the EEC. A note prepared by the Netherlands Bank led to the establishment of an experts' group, chaired by Rainoni, to look at ways of eliminating restrictions on short-term capital flows within the EEC.[24] However, none of these discussions led to positive action, let alone to the adoption of a common EEC monetary policy.

12.3 The Werner Plan and European Monetary Integration

In 1968, Raymond Barre, who had succeeded Marjolin, set out to revive some of the mothballed objectives of the 1962 action programme. By that time, the executive bodies of the EEC, ECSC, and Euratom had been merged into the European Communities (EC) and the customs union had been fully realised.[25] Barre's plans included the gradual elimination of the fluctuation margins between national currencies (allowed by the Bretton Woods fixed–exchange rate system), an automatic mechanism for mutual exchange rate support, the commitment to change parities only by mutual agreement, and the creation of a common European unit of account.[26] It was more pragmatic than the 1962 programme in that it stressed monetary "cooperation" rather than "integration".[27] At their summit in Rotterdam (September 1968), the ministers of finance of the Six requested the Committee of Governors, together with the EC Monetary Committee, to look into the feasibility of these proposals.[28] The disastrous G10 Bonn conference of November 1968, which failed to put an end to the French franc–Deutsche mark crisis, further convinced the European Commission that more energetic joint action in the monetary field was needed.

At the December 1968 EEC governors' meeting, Barre announced that the Commission planned a sweeping initiative to strengthen monetary co-operation. The Commission, he said, was working on the details of a rec-ommendation, to be put to the EC Council of Ministers, for "the creation of a permanent mechanism for monetary cooperation".[29] The governors' reaction was cool. Carli was "perplexed" at the notion of closer monetary cooperation within the EC, since the latter was no more than a customs union and certainly not a political or even an economic union. Blessing subscribed in principle to the ideal of a European federation with a com-mon currency, but he declared it unfeasible under prevailing circumstances. Brunet even refused to be drawn into the political question of monetary uni-fication. The points of view of the governors and the Commission seemed to be worlds apart, and Barre could only reassure the governors that closer cooperation did not necessarily mean the creation of a European currency or even of a common pool of monetary reserves.

In the following weeks, however, a good amount of water was poured into Barre's original wine. When it was submitted to the Council on 12 Feb-ruary 1969,[30] the plan's most far-reaching practical proposal was to insti-tutionalise a system of short-term monetary support credits that would be activated automatically whenever a member country's exchange rate came under severe pressure.

The monetary aspects of Barre's plan, which also entailed measures de-signed to achieve convergence of economic policies among the Six, were discussed at length by the Committee of Governors.[31] While initially cau-tious, the central bank heads soon realised that the proposed monetary in-novations were relatively modest. They let the Commission know that they agreed in principle to the creation of a short-term monetary credit mecha-nism between the EC member states – on condition that it would be preceded by more effective coordination of medium-term economic policies within the EC and by prior consultation on important economic policy decisions.[32]

The short-term credits envisaged by the governors would be limited in value and duration and would only be granted automatically in case of un-expected difficulties caused by a sudden deterioration of the balance of payments or by a strong divergence of the business cycles between member states. Granting of credit would immediately trigger a thorough review of the economic policies of the beneficiary country, followed (if necessary) by policy recommendations from the Commission. Governor Wormser of the Bank of France remarked that, under these conditions, the proposed mech-anism would be distinctly more restrictive and conditional than the many forms of unconditional, short-term central bank assistance already available through the BIS, the G10, or the New York Fed swap network. The EEC governors had no difficulty in accepting the mechanism proposed by the Commission precisely because it constituted no radical departure from the kind of mutual central bank assistance already practised on a broad scale in the 1960s. They nevertheless used the protracted debate between the Commission, the Monetary Committee, and themselves to press home their point that closer economic coordination should precede monetary coordination.

On 17 July 1969, the EC Council of Ministers accepted the principle of prior consultation on all important short-term economic policy decisions taken by a member state. At the same time the Council requested the Committee of Governors to work out the details for a short-term central bank credit mechanism along the lines of the Barre proposal. A group of central bank and EC Commission experts was duly constituted and reported to the Committee of Governors in November 1969.[33] On 9 February 1970, during a special session of the Committee in Basel, the agreement creating a system of short-term monetary support between the EC central banks was solemnly signed by the five governors.[34] The BIS was charged with operating the system as a common agent of the central banks.[35]

Willy Brandt once remarked that "the history of European integration is the history of its crises".[36] The currency crises of the second half of 1969[37] for the first time exposed as a fallacy the belief that economic integration could proceed regardless of monetary integration. On the occasion of the French franc and Deutsche mark exchange rate realignments, the EC Monetary Committee was briefed by France and Germany, but no prior consultation took place as envisaged by the EC Council decision of only a few weeks earlier.[38] Motivated by domestic considerations, the decisions made in Paris and Bonn strained relations within the EC. The currency realignments affected the EC's Common Agricultural Policy – as both contributions and subsidies were expressed in a fixed unit of account – and the devaluation of the franc was seen as providing an unfair competitive edge to French producers at a time when protective barriers were disappearing. There was concern that developments in the monetary field might begin to unravel the fabric of what had already been achieved in terms of trade liberalisation within the EC.

The 1969 currency crisis put the new political leadership in France and Germany to the test. Pompidou and Brandt, who had both come to power in mid-1969, met the challenge by taking a bold initiative in the monetary field. At their summit in The Hague (1–2 December 1969), the heads of state and government of the Six announced a plan for the creation of a full

Economic and Monetary Union (EMU). For the shorter term, they reconfirmed that "the development of monetary cooperation should be based on the harmonisation of economic policies" and agreed to discuss the creation of a European reserve fund.[39] A study group, chaired by Luxembourg Prime Minister Pierre Werner, was created to draw up the EMU blueprint.[40] The Committee of Governors was represented by its chairman, Hubert Ansiaux.

When the Werner committee began its work, on 20 March 1970, little consensus existed either on its final goal – the actual shape of the EMU – or on how it should be achieved. Two schools of thought soon emerged. One of them, represented by Germany and the Netherlands, held that closer monetary cooperation and eventual union would only be possible at the end of a process that first led to full economic and political union.[41] According to this view, the essential preconditions for monetary unification were the setting of economic policy goals at EC level, the longer-term convergence of such economic variables as interest and inflation rates, and a much more central role for the EC in budgetary matters. All of this presupposed a deeper political union among the Six and consequently a revision of the Treaty of Rome. The second position was expressed most consistently by France. It argued that – within the confines of the existing treaty – small, practical steps of monetary cooperation were possible and even desirable, which over time would gradually bring monetary unification closer.[42] The two positions came to be known as that of the "economists", insisting on economic convergence as a precondition for monetary union, and that of the "monetarists", giving priority to closer monetary cooperation. Theory was possibly on the economists' side, but monetarists had the psychological and political edge. The European Commission, keen to achieve practical results, tended to back the French position. So did the Belgians, who grew increasingly impatient with the preconditions the Germans and Dutch wanted to see fulfilled before agreeing to any practical steps in the monetary field.[43] The Italians often held a middle-of-the-road position.

The split in the Werner committee was reflected within the Committee of Governors. Its members consistently refrained from taking political sides, but the technical issues were contentious enough, in particular those related to the gradual reduction of the fluctuation margins between the EC currencies and to the creation of a so-called stabilisation fund. Both proposals were seen as the first practical steps towards the achievement of a monetary union.

At the instigation of the EC Council, the Werner committee entrusted a closer study of these two "technical" issues to the Committee of Governors, which to this end formed a group of experts chaired by Ansiaux (an avowed proponent of narrowing currency fluctuation margins) not only as a symbolic gesture to kick-start the monetary integration process but also as a statement of principle in the face of growing calls for greater exchange rate flexibility during the twilight years of the Bretton Woods system.[44] Under Ansiaux's effective chairmanship,[45] within two months the experts' study group sent the Werner committee a unanimous recommendation on the narrowing of the fluctuation margins of EC currencies vis-à-vis third currencies and on the establishment of a monetary stabilisation fund. As a concession to German and Dutch apprehensions, a statement was added to the effect that the reduction of margins would depend on parallel progress in the convergence of economic policies.

The final version of the Werner Report was submitted to the EC Council on 26 October 1970. It envisaged a full economic and monetary union – defined as an area with a single currency and a centralised monetary policy – to be realised in three stages, beginning in 1971 and ending in 1980. The conclusions of the report were adopted by an EC Council resolution of 22 March 1971, albeit in a toned-down form and without mentioning an explicit target date to complete EMU. It was agreed that, during the first stage towards EMU, which was to last three to five years, the central banks would limit the fluctuation margins between the EC currencies and that, on 1 January 1972, a mechanism for medium-term monetary assistance would become operational (in addition to the mechanism for short-term monetary support created in February 1970). Finally, the EC Monetary Committee and the Committee of Governors were asked to elaborate the functions and statutes of a European Monetary Cooperation Fund by 30 June 1972.

Immediately following adoption of the Werner Report, the final convulsions of the Bretton Woods system set in. In December 1971, the Smithsonian Agreement ephemerally restored the global system of stable exchange rates – by devaluing the dollar and widening (from 2% to 4.5%) the permitted fluctuation margins of other currencies against the U.S. currency – a move that went in the opposite direction from the Werner Report's recommendation on the narrowing of fluctuation margins.

In this new international monetary setting, the EC Council nonetheless decided, on 21 March 1972, to go ahead with reducing the fluctuation margins between EC currencies in order to move towards the first stage of the EMU. The Committee of Governors quickly settled on a mechanism, developed by an experts' group under the chairmanship of Théron (Bank of France), to reduce the maximum permitted fluctuation margins between the EC currencies to 2.25% while maintaining the new broader spread against the dollar of 4.5%. If the exchange rates between two EC currencies threatened to breach the limit, the two central banks concerned had an obligation to intervene symmetrically on the markets. This "Basel Agreement" was formally adopted by the governors on 10 April 1972.[46] It was referred to as the "snake in the tunnel", the "snake" being the narrow fluctuation margins among the EC currencies mutually moving up and down within the "tunnel" of broader fluctuation margins against the dollar.

For a little while, the Snake proved to be a popular animal among central bankers, yearning for stable exchange rates after the turmoil of 1971. The Six were joined in the arrangement by the prospective EC members Denmark, Ireland, and the United Kingdom, and later by Norway and Sweden. However, its success was short-lived. As early as 23 June 1972, the pound sterling, after a new speculative onslaught, left the Snake and was set floating. In February 1973 the Italian lira left as well, and soon after, in March, the "tunnel" collapsed as the dollar was floated and the Bretton Woods fixed–exchange rate regime was abandoned for good. From 19 March 1973 the remaining participants in the Snake adopted a joint float against other currencies. The withdrawal of France from the joint float in January 1974 dealt the joint EC exchange rate mechanism a final blow.

A second practical step towards EMU taken in the wake of the Werner Report – namely, the establishment of a European Monetary Cooperation Fund (EMCF) – scarcely fared any better than the Snake. This fund had first been suggested by Chancellor Brandt as a cooperative gesture and was included in the Hague declaration of December 1969. The purpose of the fund, as initially suggested, was to pool central bank reserves once sufficient convergence of EC economic and monetary policies had been reached. Upon the achievement of EMU, the fund was to be integrated into the envisaged European Community System of Central Banks. It was, however, only after the launch of the Snake, in April 1972, that the discussion on the implementation of the EMCF took off.

The Committee of Governors entrusted the task of elaborating a draft mandate and statutes of the fund to a group of experts under the chairmanship of Mertens de Wilmars, economic adviser of the National Bank of Belgium. From the outset the experts rejected the idea that the fund should pool central bank reserves at an early stage of monetary integration.[47] For the foreseeable future, central banks wanted to limit the functions of the fund to such technical tasks as management of short-term credit arrangements agreed between the EC central banks and multilateralisation of positions resulting from market interventions carried out in connection with the operation of the Snake.[48]

The fund became operational on 1 June 1973. The EMCF's status and functions were closely tailored to the wishes of the governors. There was no pooling of reserves. The composition of the board of governors managing the fund coincided with the Committee of EEC Governors. The latter successfully resisted an attempt by the EC Commission and the Luxembourg government to have the fund based in the capital of the Grand Duchy. Instead, the meetings of the EMCF board were made to coincide with the bimonthly meetings of the Committee of Governors in Basel, and the BIS was appointed as agent of the fund. The EMCF board meetings, in any case, did not take up much time because – until the creation of the European Monetary System (EMS) in 1979 – the fund was no more than "a book-keeping agency, virtually run as a sub-section of the Bank for International Settlements in Basle".[49] Thus the governors, privately sceptical about the feasibility of a European Monetary Union within the foreseeable future, managed to keep their meetings – and the attendant administrative and support activity – concentrated in Basel. They did so to economise on travel time and, what mattered most, to keep their increasingly intricate cooperative web as far as possible within the "club" and at arm's length both from governments and the Brussels Commission. By remaining loyal to Basel, the governors emphasised their role as autonomous authorities rather than government officials. "Furthermore", as Andrews has observed, "by conducting its business outside the territorial confines of the Community, the Committee underlined its relative independence from the orbit of the European Commission and from Community law. In short, the Committee was a strange hybrid: a Community body that was at the same time a central bankers' club".[50]

In March 1975, an EC Commission study group chaired by Robert Marjolin published a report that basically acknowledged the failure of the process started by the Werner Report: "Europe is no nearer to EMU than in 1969".[51] The timing of this first attempt at European monetary unification, at the climax of the crisis of the Bretton Woods system, had undoubtedly been unfavourable, even though the Werner blueprint was partly an attempt to provide the Six with shelter against the fallout from the Bretton Woods meltdown. In the 1970s the oil crisis, stagflation, and the accession of Denmark, Ireland, and the United Kingdom became more pressing priorities – for the EC and its member states as well – than monetary union.

By 1974, the first attempt at European monetary unification had petered out. Some lessons were, however, learned from that experience. Most importantly, it contributed to a gradual change in attitude among the main players. The French, always apprehensive about anything that smacked of supranationality, increasingly valued the rather informal approach of achieving monetary integration in a piecemeal fashion, partly through the Basel framework in which they had a large say. Whereas, before 1973, the Bundesbank was sceptical about closer monetary cooperation within the EC,[52] after 1973 it began to pay heed to its government's gradual switch to a more favourable stance, as in the "increasingly threatening international political economy [of the 1970s] German policy actors concluded that it was more costly for Germany to resort to unilateral monetary policies and much more attractive to pursue external monetary stability".[53] The Snake in particular had given its participants an instructive foretaste of what monetary unification would really mean. It was resuscitated, in a modified form, by the creation in 1978–79 of the EMS.

By the late 1980s, the time was ripe to relaunch the EMU project. The Delors Committee – entrusted by the EC Council in 1988 to again study the feasibility of economic and monetary union – began its work by looking back at what had gone wrong in the early 1970s. Apart from the unfavourable international climate, four intrinsic weaknesses in the process following the adoption of the Werner Report were identified: insufficient constraints on national policies, institutional ambiguities, excessive confidence in the ability of policy instruments to affect policy goals in a predictable way, and lack of internal political momentum.[54] The Delors Committee took these lessons into account when making its contribution to the 1991 Maastricht Treaty, which created the present-day European monetary union.

The contribution to European integration made by the Committee of Governors prior to the EC enlargement of 1973, when it was still a rather intimate group, was one of caution and realism. They saw, perhaps better than others, the political and technical difficulties of creating a monetary union at that early stage in the life of the EC. Their propensity for advancing in very small steps also reflected their own governments' concerns about the over-enthusiastic stance of the Commission. It is likely, but impossible to document, that a degree of legitimate self-interest in the preservation of the status and power of their own domestic institutions also coloured their opinions. The first ten years of the committee's life, however, were far from being unproductive. During this initial phase the committee created its own informal work practices, including the consolidation of its close link with the BIS, that became an "important source of informal rule creation".[55] Over the longer run and beyond the period covered in the preceding pages, the EC governors also developed their own consensus view on the unification process, particularly on monetary matters, and arguably succeeded in getting much of this view accepted as the basis for the political process.[56]

The Committee of EEC Governors has its place in the history of the BIS for two main reasons. The first relates to the strong institutional links between the committee and the BIS itself, which not only provided the secretariat to the Committee of EEC Governors but also acted as the agent for the agreement on short-term monetary assistance (1971), the EMCF

(1973–93), and the EMS (1979–93). The second reason concerns the very location of the committee meetings. The fact that they took place in Basel – rather than in Brussels, in the shadow of the EC Commission – affected the governors' contribution to the debate on monetary unification. In Basel the governors were part of the bigger picture. Their most important platform for monetary cooperation throughout the 1960s, 1970s, and 1980s was that of the G10 rather than the EC. In Basel, they looked at EC monetary policies from a more global perspective. For instance, before 1973 the issue of exchange rate stability between the EC currencies was closely linked to that of exchange rate policy vis-à-vis the dollar. It may be that, by starting out as a rather informal setup in the "Basel spirit", the committee affected (at least in part) the subsequent institutional development of European monetary union – especially if it is true, as Andrews argues, that some continuity exists between the informal institutional practices of the Committee of Governors and the organisation, rules, and norms of behaviour of the present-day EMU.[57]

12.4 The Eurocurrency Market

In the late 1960s and early 1970s, within the broad context of the Basel meetings, governors were less concerned with European monetary union than with the spectacular development of the so-called eurodollar markets, which some believed could weaken the effectiveness of domestic monetary policy and generate financial fragility.

In Milton Friedman's straightforward definition, eurodollars "are deposit liabilities, denominated in dollars, of banks outside the United States".[58] More generally, the eurocurrency market is defined as the market for short-term deposits and credits, denominated in a currency different from that of the country in which the deposit-taking and credit-giving bank is located.[59] In the financial jargon of the 1960s, eurodollars became the popular name for dollar-denominated, short-term wholesale deposits held by banks located outside the United States, including foreign branches and subsidiaries of U.S. banks, which in the 1960s made up roughly 80% of the estimated gross size of the eurocurrency market (which also included deposits denominated in Deutsche marks, pounds sterling, and Swiss francs). In the eurocurrency market, maturities usually ranged from call to one year, the median maturity being three months. Minimum size of deposits was in the region of one million dollars.

The prefix "euro-" derived from the fact that banks originally active in this market were located in European financial centres, first and foremost the City of London. Apart from London, sizeable eurocurrency business was handled from Luxembourg, Zurich, and (to a lesser extent) other Continental centres. However, the "euro-" prefix is partly misleading in that a sizeable "eurodollar" trade was carried out also by banks in Canada, Japan, and the Middle East (Beirut). In the 1970s the importance of eurodollar business in financial centres outside Europe grew rapidly, particularly in Singapore (the "Zurich of Asia", where the bulk of the Asian dollar market was located), Hong Kong, Manila, and offshore centres (Nassau, Cayman Islands, Panama, Bermuda).

Eurodollars per se did not amount to any significant financial product innovation in the 1950s. Operations in foreign currency deposits were well known in London before the First World War.[60] Bank transactions denominated in sterling and dollars had also been carried out in Berlin and Vienna in the late 1920s, only to be brought to an end by the 1931 crisis.[61] However, even if these were the direct antecedents of the eurocurrency system, the size of the operations was too small to influence foreign exchange and money markets and hence to be of concern to central banks and policy makers in general. What was new from the late 1950s onward was the scale on which banks took deposits in foreign currencies and used them for making loans to nonbank customers, the extent to which operations were taking place across national frontiers, and the degree of competition among banks for foreign currency deposits. "Also new, and really the essence of the Euro-currency market as such, has been the emergence of a large interbank market helping to channel liquid funds internationally from lenders to borrowers."[62]

According to the Federal Reserve Bank of New York, "The original impetus for the development of the Continental dollar market arose from the desire of several banks in Eastern Europe to leave their dollar balances with their correspondents in France and England rather than carrying them in their own name in the U.S. As these balances grew larger, these banks as well as their correspondents became interested in earning a return on them. They often offered these funds to foreign banks in need of dollar finance, especially in Italy, at rates somewhat lower than the borrowing banks would have to pay for credits from the United States banks.... By mid-1958 the market was well established but did not assume really impressive proportions until the end of that year when rates paid abroad for dollar deposits rose well above the interest that banks in the U.S. were permitted to pay for time deposits under regulation Q of the Board of Governors of the Federal Reserve System".[63] Others, like Johnston,[64] see the origin of the eurodollar market in the sterling crises of 1955 and 1957 that prompted the British authorities to place restrictions on the use of sterling in external payments, particularly for the financing of non-U.K. trade, while at the same time the U.S. current accounts turned into deficits, partly financed by the creation of dollar balances outside the United States. Schenk emphasises the role of innovative banks, such as Midland, which – rather than opening branch offices overseas – had an overseas office in London attracting business from foreign correspondent banks that found it convenient to rely on Midland for their business rather than locating in London and finding their own customers there.[65]

As already mentioned, an important drive for the market's rapid development came from the U.S. banking laws, in particular regulation Q. This regulation, dating back to the 1930s, imposed ceilings on the interest rates payable by U.S. banks on deposits held in the United States. Through their European branches or affiliates, U.S. banks were able to circumvent regulation Q and attract short-term deposits by offering competitive interest rates on dollar-denominated deposits. From 1964 onward the market's growth rate accelerated sharply when Citibank, Chase Manhattan, and Bank of America – rapidly imitated by a swarm of followers, both American and European – began systematically to tap the market through their London branches, attracting liquid dollar funds from all corners of the international money market.[66]

Whatever the proximate reasons for its first development – Russian fear of American confiscation, official ceilings placed on interest paid on U.S. deposits, American balance of payments deficits, British regulations, innovative banks – there were two conditions for the eurocurrency market to expand rapidly: the introduction of current account currency convertibility at the end of 1958 and the slow but steady lifting of controls on capital movement. Thus: "the Euro-currency business began to come into prominence in the latter part of 1958 and since the restoration of the external convertibility at the end of that year its volume grew practically without interruption".[67] Yet, at the beginning of the 1960s, the true impact and potential of the new currency market were not widely understood.[68]

Although the eurodollar trade was carried out in several financial centres, the City of London rapidly became the hub of the market for reasons that are easily understood: the presence there of large American banks with multinational scope and the technical sophistication of the market, which inter alia made it possible for banks to approach the market on their own terms and to maintain anonymity in the early stages of the dealing. One additional advantage of London was the permissive attitude of British authorities, namely the Bank of England, towards *entrepôt* bank business. Technological innovations in data processing and communications (transactions were arranged by brokers and banks' dealers over the telephone or by telex) played a critical role in the growth of the market by eroding information barriers and therefore lowering transaction costs. An efficient market thus came to be established.

Who were the players in this market? Prime depositors (lenders) were large corporations with international and multinational activities (among them many U.S. manufacturers that in the 1960s vigorously expanded their business in Europe), commercial banks located in the main financial centres of the Western hemisphere, and central banks (mainly outside the G10, but including the BIS). Final users (borrowers) were mainly large international corporations, which used short-term eurocurrency facilities as an alternative or complementary instrument to meet their short-term financial needs, particularly those arising from international trade.

The eurocurrency market was to a large extent an interbank market: a substantial amount of transactions took place through the redepositing of funds by one bank to another. It was common for a chain of several banks, in different locations, to serve as intermediaries between the original depositors and the final borrowers. The share of interbank transactions in total eurocurrency banking increased from some 30% in the mid-1960s to 50% in 1980; the percentage is even higher when considering the G10 countries alone.[69]

Starting in 1963, alongside the eurocurrency market for short-term credits, a eurobond market existed where multinational corporations and public entities issued (mainly in London and Luxembourg) long-term dollar-denominated bonds to be placed by international syndicates of underwriters with European investors.[70] The growth rate of both the eurocurrency and eurobond markets accelerated markedly from the mid-1960s onwards. The estimated net size of the eurocurrency market – based on reporting by the G10 European countries only – boomed from some $7 billion at the end of 1963 to more than $130 billion at the end of 1973. Over the same period, the annual volume of new issues on the eurobond market grew from a modest $140 million in 1963 to a record $6.9 billion in 1972 and $4.6 billion in 1973.[71]

12.5 Central Banks' Concerns about the Eurocurrency Market

The spectacular growth of the eurocurrency market during the second half of the 1960s was only in part the result of monetary policy in the United States. If regulation Q was a significant factor in the early growth of dollar deposits to foreign banks, the market continued to expand when in 1963–64 regulation Q was relaxed and the interest ceiling on short-term foreign deposits in the United States considerably increased.[72] From the mid-1960s onward, U.S. banks based in London were "utterly dominant" in the eurodollar market.[73] The American banks' expansion in Europe was spurred on by President Johnson's policies aimed at reducing the U.S. balance of payments deficit by restricting capital outflows. In 1965 the Voluntary Foreign Credit Restraint Program was introduced, which directed U.S. banks and corporations to reduce their deposits abroad and their lending to foreigners. One result was to encourage U.S. banks to handle international operations through their branches in London and other financial centres. The Foreign Direct Investment Program of the same year called for voluntary limits on U.S. corporations' capital exports. This programme, which was made mandatory in 1968, raised the need for these corporations to arrange financing abroad for their foreign expansion. As pointed out by Sylla, the incursion into Europe by U.S. banks in the 1960s was in essence their "escape from a stifling banking environment in the United States.... By invading Europe, the leading U.S. banks demonstrated how misguided in principle and how ineffective in practice were many U.S. banking traditions and regulatory measures handed down from the past".[74]

Unavoidably, the growth of the eurodollar market and the "invasion" of American banks, with their perceived dependence on U.S. monetary policies, raised a number of policy issues of direct concern to central banks. The issues that focused the attention of policy makers in the 1960s and early 1970s can be summarised under three main headings: the information gap, prudential issues, and domestic monetary policy concerns.

The information gap referred in the first place to the lack of consolidated data on the size and turnover of the eurocurrency market and on the sources and end use of eurocurrency deposits and credits. It also referred to the lack of a common understanding about what exactly constituted eurocurrency deposits and credits and of a common methodological framework to interpret the market's implications for the international financial system. It was thought that concerted international efforts would be the best way to fill the information gap. In this respect the BIS played a pivotal role.

The prudential issues were brought to the fore by the rapid expansion of the market, which in the early 1960s was already viewed with growing unease by some of the commercial bankers who were at the very centre of it.[75] Prudential concerns related mainly to a possible overexposure of certain market participants (especially given the amounts involved), to the fact that quite often the end users of the credits were obscured by the practice of redepositing funds between banks, and finally to an apparently growing mismatch in maturities between short-term deposits and short- to medium-term credits. These concerns were highlighted in 1963 by the heavy losses suffered in their foreign currency business by two companies of international standing, Stinnes and Ira Haupt. Later in the 1960s, once the eurocurrency market had become widely accepted as a permanent phenomenon, such concerns seemed to recede into the background – only to come back with a vengeance in the mid-1970s.

Finally, the monetary policy issues raised by the eurocurrency market had fundamentally to do with the fact that the cross-border capital flows engendered by the market were seen by some central banks as a potential threat to the effectiveness of domestic monetary policy. In essence, this debate was about interest rate–induced capital flows: commercial banks engaged in arbitrage, moving dollar-denominated liquidity across markets whenever the policy stance of individual domestic monetary authorities diverged, thus widening interest rate gaps. Any divergence between eurocurrency and domestic interest rates tended to translate into substantial short-term movements of dollar-denominated funds. As an important channel for sizeable international flows of short-term capital, the eurodollar market came to be seen with apprehension by some central bankers who feared it might make their discount rate policy a less effective tool in demand and exchange rate management. Some central banks, on the other hand, saw the eurocurrency market as a complement rather than a threat to their monetary policy.

Concerns about the impact of the eurocurrency market on domestic monetary policies came to dominate the debate among central bankers in the years 1965 to 1973, because interest rates in the eurodollar market were largely determined by U.S. monetary conditions, and this period was characterised not only by a divergence in monetary policies across the Atlantic but also (as we have seen) by conflicting views on how best to deal with the American balance of payments deficit in a context of fixed exchange rates.

On all three accounts – the information gap, prudential issues, and concerns about domestic monetary policy – there was clear scope for international coordination and, possibly, action. In all three areas the BIS played a pivotal role, achieving progress in some instances while failing to overcome the limits to international cooperation in others.

12.6   Filling the Information Gap

The rapid growth of the eurodollar market caught the attention of monetary policy makers as early as 1960. In November of that year, Alan Holmes and Fred Klopstock of the Federal Reserve Bank of New York published a study on the market for dollar deposits in Europe.[76] In May 1961, a study group of central bank experts meeting at the BIS discussed for the first time the eurodollar market and its role in cross-border short-term capital movements. On that occasion, Charles Coombs expressed some concern that this relatively new market might constitute a threat to monetary stability, but the Bank of England, with the City in mind, took a more sympathetic view.[77]

In early 1962, sensing that the eurodollar phenomenon was still uncharted territory, Milton Gilbert suggested that the BIS undertake a wide-ranging survey[78] to assemble data on the size, composition, and trends of this market. The idea was taken up by the governors, and a meeting of central bank experts was called at the BIS in October 1962 to discuss the eurodollar market. The BIS discussion note for the meeting stated that, "looked at strictly as a competitive phenomenon and as a service to both the lenders and borrowers who use it, the euro-dollar market would appear a useful development". The experts, however, were asked to focus on the potential "disadvantages or dangers" of this development, in particular whether it tended to counteract domestic monetary policies and whether it was "right for the central banks to leave the euro-currency markets without supervision or management".[79] If anything, the meeting showed that most central banks shared a desire to learn more about the volume of the market and "a genuine concern" about some of its potential dangers.[80] On the experts' recommendation, the governors decided to set up a regular statistical reporting system on eurocurrency operations, centred at the BIS; this, however, raised the sensitive issue of requesting commercial banks to report on the breakdown of their assets and liabilities to the central banks. The Bank of England, close to the nerve centre of the eurodollar market, was not convinced that this would be desirable or feasible.[81] In the end, the majority view of the other central banks prevailed: better statistical information was the necessary first step before the policy implications of the rapid development of the market could even be contemplated.

The setting up of the statistical machinery proved to be more difficult than anticipated. The main challenge, apart from collecting the relevant figures from the commercial banks, was to make a meaningful distinction between eurocurrency assets and liabilities held by resident and nonresident banks and those held by "other nonresidents" (central banks, public and private entities). By the summer of 1963, sufficient progress had been made for the governors to call a second meeting of experts in Basel, this time including representatives from the central banks of Canada and Japan as well as from the IMF. The meeting took place in November 1963 and focused on (i) definitions and the elimination of gaps and duplication in the statistical reporting and (ii) the market size, sources, and uses of eurodollars. The result was hailed by Gilbert as "a long step forward towards understanding the Euro-currency phenomena".[82] The governors welcomed the efforts to improve statistical reporting on the eurocurrency markets, while recognising that "in order to preserve good relations with commercial banks, central banks would have to be careful not to ask them for too many new statistics at this time".[83]

Shortly afterwards, in January 1964, a BIS paper on "The Euro-currency Market and the International Payments System" was submitted to the G10 deputies. It contained one of the first comprehensive estimates of the overall size of the market, then put at between 13 and 15 billion dollars on a gross basis (i.e., including interbank deposits), or $7 billion on a net basis, of which nearly 80% was expressed in dollars (the rest being mainly in Swiss francs, sterling, and Deutsche marks).[84]

Once a satisfactory quality in statistical reporting had been achieved, the question arose of whether the figures ought to be made public. The Bank of England favoured disclosure, preferably on a quarterly basis, which (according to Governor Cromer) would "increase public confidence about the composition of the market and the practices that prevail in it".[85] The IMF was also strongly in favour of "a break in the veil of secrecy that has crept up and that really doesn't do anybody any good".[86] In June 1964, the BIS devoted a special section in its Annual Report to the eurocurrency market, publishing for the first time summary figures of short-term liabilities and assets in eurocurrencies of nine countries' commercial banks. The question of whether a more detailed breakdown of the figures ought to be published on a more regular basis was further discussed at meetings of the eurocurrency market experts in July 1964 and again in February 1965. In March 1965, the governors finally decided against the publication of detailed statistics, mainly because only a handful of experts would be able to interpret them correctly and because in certain cases publication might make commercial banks more reluctant to contribute data. Henceforth, the BIS Annual Report remained the main vehicle for the publication of a summary overview and assessment of the development of the eurocurrency markets.[87] However, the BIS statistics were challenged by some London-based commercial banks (e.g., Westminster and the Bank of London and South America), who argued that estimates of the overall size of the market were inflated because of double counting of interbank deposits.[88]

In any case, there was broad agreement within the central bank community that "anything that grows by 25 to 40 per cent per annum warrants close attention".[89] By the mid-1960s, the annual meetings of the central banks' eurocurrency market experts had become a well-established feature on the BIS calendar. For the time being, fine-tuning the statistical output remained the primary concern.

12.7   The Eurocurrency Market and Monetary Policy

In 1962, the first discussions took place among central bank governors about possible policy implications of the eurodollar market. There was broad agreement that the problems it posed, if any, were in fact similar to those that could arise from any international short-term capital movements, which at the time every country regulated according to its international position and policy goals.[90]

One reason why most central banks at this point took a positive attitude towards the eurocurrency market was that it provided them with a flexible, liquid, high-yield investment outlet and a useful instrument to cover temporary liquidity imbalances. The BIS itself was a case in point, investing considerable funds in the eurocurrency market from the early 1960s.[91] An example of how the eurocurrency market could be helpful in financing balance of payments deficits was provided by Italy in 1962–63.[92] In November 1962, the Bank of Italy lifted the obligation for banks to maintain a balanced position in foreign currencies vis-à-vis nonresidents. This allowed them to borrow on the eurocurrency market, thereby alleviating the liquidity squeeze caused by the balance of payments deficit generated by an overheating economy. During the following twelve months, Italian banks borrowed more than $1 billion abroad, offsetting a payments deficit of roughly the same size.

The already-mentioned BIS paper prepared for the G10 deputies in January 1964 echoed the governors' opinion that there was no reason to be concerned about the development of the market: "The Euro-dollar market is today a substantial source of international credit. It brings many lenders and borrowers together on more favourable terms to both, and therefore more efficiently, than would otherwise be the case. Moreover, the impetus towards equalisation of money rates which it has given has been useful, not only to individual lenders and borrowers, but in the broader context of international monetary equilibrium". Only at the end of the paper did the BIS add a caveat about the future: "Maybe, because of its efficiency, the Euro-currency market has an exceptional potential for expansion which may create a special problem for monetary authorities in the future; but so far this does not seem to have been the case and on the whole it appears clear that the market has served a useful purpose".[93]

By the mid-1960s, the overall assessment of central banks – that there was little to worry about regarding the policy implications of the eurocurrency market – had not significantly changed.[94] At the annual eurocurrency market experts' meeting in July 1967, Roy Bridge (Bank of England) maintained that the eurocurrency market performed a useful function in the financing of international trade and proved to be "a natural market with a sensitive price mechanism" resistant to external shocks.[95] The English position was broadly shared by the other central banks, even though some of them warned that the flow of eurocurrency funds was beginning to have an impact on the effectiveness of domestic monetary policies, in particular in smaller economies. Gilbert actually argued that this was the case also for large economies, such as the United States and the United Kingdom, because in 1966 movements of eurocurrency funds out of London to the United States had weakened the effects of the U.S. credit squeeze and, at the same time, exacerbated the United Kingdom's external problems. Nevertheless, "there was quite general agreement among the participants that the sophistication of central-bank policy, both in the field of international co-operation and in domestic matters, has developed to a point at which the undesired side-effects of the Euro-currency market could be readily checked by means of ad hoc measures".[96]

In fact, central banks and the BIS were already intervening, if quietly, in the market to try to keep the differential between interests paid on eurocurrency and on domestic currency deposits within desirable limits. From 1965 onward the BIS itself, together with the Swiss National Bank, intervened in the market in order to moderate interest rate differentials caused by seasonal movements in and out of the eurocurrency market. In December 1966, for instance, the Federal Reserve Bank of New York and the Swiss National Bank made available to the BIS, through swaps, close to $500 million, which the BIS then channelled into the eurodollar market.[97] Such operations, which became more frequent and more important in size as the market grew larger, were not viewed with equal favour by all central bankers. To the Americans these operations were proof that the international money market needed a guiding hand. Coombs told his colleagues at the BIS gold and foreign exchange experts' meeting in January 1967 that the BIS was the ideal institution to maintain order in the international money market by intervening actively when needed, just like the individual central banks did in their domestic markets.[98] Johannes Tüngeler of the Bundesbank and most of his

Continental colleagues, on the other hand, believed that the eurocurrency market should be left to its own devices and that central bank interventions ought to be as limited as possible so as to avoid encouraging moral hazard by commercial banks, who would be led to downplay the risks they were running in the eurocurrency market.

The central banks' attitude of "benign neglect" of the eurodollar market began to change following the international monetary events of 1967–68. The Middle East war of June 1967, the sterling devaluation later that year, the gold crisis of March 1968, and the French franc crisis during the second half of 1968 all contributed to accelerate the pace of short-term capital flows, mainly through the eurodollar market. By the late 1960s the eurocurrency market, and in particular the eurodollar market, had grown to a mammoth size: the BIS estimated that over a period of scarcely two years, between the end of 1966 and the end of 1968, the net amount of dollar credits outstanding in the market had nearly doubled from $14 billion to $25 billion.[99] The eurodollar market remained heavily dependent on monetary conditions and policies in the United States, as concern spread about the effects on the American balance of payments of both the Vietnam War and President Johnson's Great Society programme. Whenever domestic interest rates in the United States came near the ceilings imposed by regulation Q, borrowing on the eurodollar market by U.S. banks increased, followed by a rise in eurodollar market rates. At such times, the huge short-term capital flows in and out of the eurocurrency market and sharply fluctuating interest rates began to make national monetary authorities more nervous than they had previously been about the potential impact of the eurodollar on the effectiveness of their monetary policy.

From 1967 onward, therefore, central banks became more active in the eurocurrency markets. This was particularly true of the Federal Reserve and the BIS. At the time of the Six-Day War in June 1967 and the sterling crisis later that year, the BIS activated its dollar swap line with the Federal Reserve and invested the proceeds in the eurodollar market in order to mitigate the interest rate hike.[100] Of course, as Gilbert noted at the experts' meeting in Basel in July 1968, such interventions – besides moderating interest rate fluctuations – also contributed to the further growth of the market by providing it with additional funds.[101]

The first half of 1969 was, in the words of BIS General Manager Gabriel Ferras, "the most hectic period in the history of the Euro-currency market" to that date.[102] A money squeeze in the United States led to a vast increase in the demand for eurodollar funds by U.S. banks. In addition, there was substantial eurodollar borrowing by French and Italian banks induced by domestic monetary tightening and, finally, a recurrent demand for dollars for conversion into Deutsche marks in anticipation of a revaluation of the German currency. As a result, the net volume of credit outstanding in the eurocurrency market at the end of 1969 was estimated at nearly $45 billion. Interest rates were pushed to unprecedented levels, reaching 12.5% in June 1969, when in just three weeks' time London branches of American banks alone sent $3 billion in eurodollars to their head offices in the United States.[103]

In this context, the possible effects of eurodollar flows on domestic monetary policies became a very sensitive issue. At the G10 governors' dinner at the BIS on 9 March 1969, Governor Ansiaux of the National Bank of Belgium acrimoniously accused the United States's tight monetary policy of bankrupting Europe by forcing U.S. banks to borrow heavily on the eurodollar market, thereby pushing interest rates to record highs.[104] Fears that the eurodollar market might spin out of control were further raised when (at the BIS meeting in April 1969) Charles Coombs announced, with "some embarrassment", that the Federal Reserve might be compelled to stop its traditional policy of feeding the eurodollar market at mid-year and year's end to ease pressures caused by window-dressing operations.[105]

In preparation for the annual meeting of the eurocurrency market experts at the BIS in June 1969, Gilbert asked the participants to reflect on the following questions: "Have euro-dollar flows helped or hurt management of domestic liquidity? Does the central bank have power to control the effects one way or the other? Have euro-dollar flows helped or aggravated balance-of-payments problems? Can central banks suppress the harmful and keep the helpful flows? Does this objective require direct controls over the banks' euro-dollar positions?"[106] The experts agreed that eurocurrency flows could indeed affect domestic monetary conditions and, in some countries, the balance of payments – but also that these undesirable effects could be largely neutralised by domestic monetary policy.[107] In fact, central banks had been quite successful in managing monetary aggregates even in the presence of a growing eurodollar market. In 1969, European central banks increased their discount rates and in many cases introduced direct controls on their commercial banks' foreign operations, while U.S. authorities announced in June a series of measures designed to curb incentives for U.S. banks to borrow in the eurodollar market.[108] As a result of these combined actions, taken after consultation, new borrowing on the eurodollar market tapered off during the second half of 1969 and interest rates fell.

"A 'monster' the Euro-currency market certainly is", wrote Emminger, "if one considers its phenomenal growth over the last decade and its present gigantic size".[109] Estimated at $45 billion at the end of 1969, deposits in the eurocurrency markets surpassed the combined currency reserves of all Western European countries. But was it "a benevolent or a malevolent monster?" Emminger believed that the increased mobility of short-term capital across borders was the natural consequence of currency convertibility and capital-account deregulation. The phenomenal success of the eurodollar market had only magnified an inevitable development – which, however, entailed a number of risks to international monetary stability. These included the potential repercussions of a breakdown in confidence (in particular, confidence in the dollar, "a contingency altogether too terrifying to visualize"), an inflation bias (if short-term lending and borrowing in the eurocurrency market led to an increase in the velocity of circulation, or, put differently, to "more credit being extended on a given monetary base"), and potential dangers from the high volatility of short-term capital flows ("every country has to consider a large part of the foreign short-term claims on its banks as a potential mortgage on its official reserves").

Because of these risks, prudent Emminger took a rather negative view of the eurocurrency market: "The huge international pool of liquidity which at a moment's notice is ready to flow hither and thither may, more often than not, undercut national stabilization or adjustment policies. Also, the balance-of-payments effect of such short-term money flows is likely to be more often destabilizing than stabilizing, because these flows conceal the real 'underlying' balance-of-payments deficit and blunt the automatic adjustment process, and because they are apt to inflate minor speculative flurries into major currency crises". Emminger was equally pessimistic about the chances for collective action to bring this "monster" under control: "Now and again it has been suggested that some of [these] risks and dangers might be lessened by a collective supervision of the Euromarket through a group of major central banks, acting, for example, through the Bank for International Settlements. Discussions among central bank experts have shown that such possibilities scarcely exist in practice. Supervision of the Euromoney market can only be exercised through the central bank responsible for the market place in which the individual Eurobank operates, or else through each and every central bank regulating the access to the international market by its own banks and corporations.... So each central bank is left to battle this 'monster' as best it can".

Emminger's pessimism was grounded both on the recent German experience and on the Bundesbank's monetary philosophy. In 1969 and 1970 the eurocurrency market flows seemed to work against German monetary policy. To counter inflationary tendencies deriving from an overheating economy, the Bundesbank raised interest rates, thereby attracting foreign short-term funds to Germany. It is not clear to what extent this capital inflow was determined by interest rate differentials rather than by the anticipation of a Deutsche mark revaluation, but Emminger believed that "German monetary policy had been largely undermined" by inward capital movements.[110] Capital inflows would have equally occurred in the absence of an established eurocurrency market – though perhaps not on the same scale – because of Germany's monetary and exchange rate stance, which was driven by its almost exclusive focus on inflation.

From the early 1970s onward, concerns about the eurocurrency market became widespread in the press as well as in international policy forums. At the IMF general meeting in Copenhagen in September 1970, Pierre-Paul Schweitzer hinted that "maybe the central banks could do something".[111] The BIS governors decided to call a special meeting of their deputies to discuss the possibility of joint supervision of the eurocurrency market; the meeting took place in Amsterdam in February 1971 and was followed, two months later, by a second meeting in Basel. The BIS background paper for these meetings highlighted a general concern about the monetary policy implications of the eurodollar market. Central bankers were uneasy, to say the least, about the preponderant influence of U.S. interest rates and U.S. domestic monetary policy on developments in the eurocurrency market that directly affected domestic monetary policy (as Emminger put it: "how to live in the same boat with an elephant?"). They also feared the supposed inflationary bias of the market.[112]

These were the concerns that led the G10 governors in April 1971 to the creation of the Standing Committee on the Euro-Currency Market, which still exists today under the name of Committee on the Global Financial System. The Standing Committee was to replace the traditional annual meeting of eurocurrency market experts and would hold more regular sessions. At the outset, it was broadly mandated "to consider policy problems arising out of the existence and operations of the Euro-currency market". In particular, since one variable over which the central banks had complete control was the investment of their own reserves, the committee was required to report "on the significance of the placing of central bank reserves in the Euro-currency market and the possibility of joint policy action by the BIS group of central banks in this respect".[113]

At the Standing Committee's first meeting, in May 1971, participants reported on details of their central bank's investment policy.[114] It was found that, among the G10 countries, only the central banks of Japan and Switzerland directly held deposits in the eurodollar market and in the relatively small amount of $140 million, but that much larger amounts were invested in the eurocurrency market indirectly through the BIS. The total of BIS eurodollar assets amounted to $3.1 billion (of which at least $2.5 billion was invested on behalf of the G10 central banks), representing a quarter of all official funds placed in the market,[115] which, in turn, made up only some 20% of the total size of the eurocurrency markets, then believed to be about $60 billion.[116]

Notwithstanding the relatively small size of G10 central bank funds in the market, it was felt worthwhile to try to reduce it. Charles Coombs at the Federal Reserve Bank of New York tried to work out various schemes that would offer central banks an alternative to eurodollar investments, such as special high-yield U.S. Treasury certificates or attractive money-employed accounts.[117] In the meanwhile, as an immediate measure, at their BIS April meeting the governors decided to freeze their direct and indirect (BIS) euro-dollar deposits. In June the BIS began to gradually reduce its eurodollar deposits by slowly transferring funds to the United States.[118] This self-restraining stance was not formally prolonged when the governors met in September 1971, shortly after President Nixon had closed the gold window, but there was "an understanding that the central banks would not rush back to the Euro-currency market".[119] At the same time, the Standing Commit-tee was given the mission to act as a watchdog, closely monitoring central bank activity in the market on a regular basis.

With the official component of the eurocurrency market brought more or less under control, the Standing Committee's attention shifted to the much larger private component. The governors put the following questions to the committee: Should the eurocurrency market be controlled? And, if so, how could this be effectively done? Means to control the growth of the market that were up for discussion included: domestic restrictions on the entry of eurocurrencies; establishment of reserve requirements for eurobanks; and adoption of a joint open-market policy on the eurocurrency market.[120]

Before tackling these questions, the Standing Committee undertook a detailed survey of practices and experiences in the member countries. The exercise revealed substantial divergences in policy approaches. In a coun-try like Germany, stringent regulations and reserve requirements applied to all transactions, whether in domestic or foreign currencies, on behalf of residents or nonresidents; yet in centres like London and Luxembourg, euro-currency operations were not subject to the restrictions that applied to the banks' domestic operations.[121] Continental European countries believed they suffered most from the development of the eurocurrency market. Germany in particular blamed much of the unsettling dollar inflows in 1970–71 on eurocurrency flows. These countries were thus more inclined to tighten surveillance and possibly even to intervene and introduce direct controls. Professor Kessler, a representative of the Netherlands Bank on the committee, argued that maintaining fixed exchange rates with an inconvertible dollar was possible only if "the Euro-currency market were controlled and monetary policies in the different countries co-ordinated".[122] Kessler was not alone in his belief that the eurocurrency flows posed a potential threat to the very survival of the Bretton Woods system.[123]

At the BIS March 1972 governors' meeting, Bundesbank President Klasen strongly pleaded for immediate policy measures, such as the harmonisation of interest rates and the introduction of joint open-market operations. The United States and the United Kingdom – the latter "thoroughly welcoming" the internationalisation of the City, as epitomised by the expansion of the eurodollar and eurobond markets[124] – argued that there was no reason for immediate concern and that further analysis was required before policy decisions concerning control of the eurocurrency market might be contemplated.[125]

During the second half of 1972, the Standing Committee discussed various possible approaches on the basis of detailed papers prepared by the Bank of England, the Bundesbank, the Bank of Italy, and the Federal Reserve Bank of New York, but the deadlock could not be broken.[126] When BIS President Zijlstra asked the experts to produce a summary report for the governors, all they could do was point out the different options and conclude that they had agreed to disagree. In a letter to René Larre (BIS general manager and chairman of the Standing Committee), Kit McMahon, the Bank of England representative, was explicit: "I have considerable reservations about the likely value of continuing the Committee's discussions.... It seems to me so improbable that we shall arrive at agreement on any scheme of control of Euro-currency banking that we should advise the Governors accordingly and discourage them from giving us any further mandate".[127]

The ball was back in the governors' court. At their May 1973 Basel meeting, they discussed the committee's progress report at length. Predictably, the same divisions that had appeared in the committee re-emerged among the governors. Klasen (Germany), Zijlstra (Netherlands), and Vandeputte (Belgium) insisted on introducing some form of control on the eurodollar market. O'Brien (Bank of England) retorted that he did not believe in international regulation and was in any case "not prepared to destroy the market in London to have it re-established in Singapore".[128]

The currency crisis of March 1973, which hammered the final nail in the coffin of the Bretton Woods system of fixed exchange rates, quite suddenly changed the parameters for the eurocurrency debate, now set in a context of floating rates and further internationalisation of financial markets.

Whichever way they assessed the effects of short-term eurocurrency movements, central bankers understood that speculative flows were easier to deal with in a floating– than a fixed–exchange rate environment. The adjustment burden could now be shifted from domestic monetary policy to the politically less sensitive exchange rate variable.

In any case, by the early 1970s concerns over the development of the eurocurrency market had largely shifted from the G10 to other countries. The huge amounts of petrodollars generated by the oil-surplus countries mostly found their way to the eurocurrency markets to be "recycled" by oil-importing countries borrowing in the same market to pay their oil bills.[129] The market now proved to be an efficient tool for channelling enormous funds smoothly from surplus to deficit countries.

In the 1970s, the source of the eurodollars' supply was increasingly out of the G10's control. On the demand side, too, the 1970s witnessed a clear shift away from the industrial to the developing world. Eurodollar lending to developing countries increased steeply, partly in reaction to a tightening of exchange controls on eurocurrency borrowing in several industrial countries[130] – thereby, incidentally, preparing the ground for the 1980s debt crisis. As a result of these developments, other international bodies, besides the BIS and the G10, also concerned themselves with euromarket policy issues.

In 1972, the IMF set up an ad hoc committee, the so-called Committee of Twenty or C20, to design a blueprint for the reform of the international monetary system. The C20 deputies, chaired by the Bank of England's Jeremy Morse, created a number of technical groups, one of which was to examine the problem of capital flows. The BIS was given observer status in the C20. In March 1973 it submitted to the C20 study group on capital flows a detailed report on the eurocurrency market.[131] Predictably, on this issue the C20 soon faced the same deadlock that the BIS's Euro-Currency Standing Committee had reached earlier.[132] Nevertheless, here too was a clear pointer to developments to come: the need for common international regulatory standards to help discipline cross-border capital flows gradually gained wider acceptance.

The Euro-Currency Standing Committee continued its work after 1974, mainly discussing the wider implications of market developments such as the recycling of oil surpluses in the 1970s and the international debt crisis in the 1980s. It also played a key role in the development of international financial and banking statistics, which since the 1970s have allowed a much better understanding of international financial markets and remain at the core of the BIS statistical work today.

12.8　Prudential Issues

In their first discussions of the eurocurrency market in 1962, central bank governors identified the fast-growing size of the market and the inadequate control of the creditworthiness of certain borrowers as potential risks for the stability of financial intermediaries. At the time, the governors were satisfied by Lord Cromer's absolute confidence that, by and large, banks were acting prudently.

In the following years, prudential issues – and in particular the potential overexposure of certain market participants – intermittently resurfaced in the governors' discussions, usually dominated by monetary policy concerns. In January 1965, the BIS invited central bank experts to a meeting in Basel to look into the feasibility of creating an international risk office with the task of centralising information on short-term credits to nonresidents. "The scope of the operation", an internal BIS memorandum stated, "will differ considerably depending on circumstances, for the information may be centralised either in the interest of the central banks alone or, if an international risk office were to be set up, for the benefit of the commercial banks themselves".[133] When the experts met in April 1965, however, it became clear that the creation of such an office was wishful thinking. Asking commercial banks to report on their international business to an international body raised insurmountable administrative and legal obstacles, not only in the countries where no national risk office existed but even in those where it did (Belgium, France, Germany, and Italy). The idea of establishing an international risk office was quickly dropped.[134]

Prudential issues disappeared from the Basel meetings' agenda until 1967, when central bankers discussed the credit risks implicit in the mismatch between short-term deposits and medium-term credits in the eurocurrency market. Some concerns were also expressed about the creditworthiness of certain ultimate borrowers, since their identity was often obscured because of the frequent interbank depositing and redepositing. It was argued that risks of a similar nature existed in most international credit transactions but were magnified by the phenomenal growth of the eurocurrency market.

Systemic risk was again discussed in 1969. The increasing maturity mismatch between borrowing and lending by banks engaged in the eurocurrency market was the cause of some concern, as it was argued that this would make the system more vulnerable to liquidity shocks. This was a controversial issue, but scholars and policy makers in the 1970s tended to agree that the extent of the mismatch in eurocurrency banking was indeed sizeable and increasing, mainly due to keener competition and declining margins, a general lengthening of credit maturities, and the expansion and diversification of medium-term lending to sovereign borrowers.[135]

Besides maturity mismatches, most central banks believed that a higher potential for financial distress existed in international than in domestic banking because of the size of the short-term capital flows, of a market structure where most operations involved either bank consortia or chains of intermediate deposits with multiple foreign banks, and of less stringent supervision by national authorities. It was argued that a deterioration in confidence could spread rapidly.

The BIS downplayed such concerns. In a speech given in December 1969, General Manager Gabriel Ferras stressed that most eurocurrency transactions were handled by the most solid and reputable banks in Western Europe and the United States.[136] The 1970s proved that the BIS confidence in the overall stability of the international banking community was fairly well placed. Little evidence exists of actual contagion effects, even during such major bank crises as the 1974 Franklin National collapse or the 1984 failure of Continental Illinois.[137] The dissemination of both theoretical and practical knowledge of the euromarkets and the resilience of the market itself throughout the financial turmoil of the 1970s induced participants to gradually downgrade the perceived risk. Institutional adjustment contributed to this process. After the Franklin National and Herstatt episodes of 1974,[138] most banks autonomously upgraded internal controls, and the responsibility of parent banks for their foreign branches was officially reaffirmed.[139] Hence, in this respect the markets rather than policy makers set the agenda for further international informal cooperation on prudential issues.

Immediately after the Herstatt failure, the BIS governors issued a multilateral declaration on the working of the international banking system that sought to calm concerns regarding the availability of lending of last resort in the euromarkets.[140] A wide-ranging survey of BIS member central banks led to a number of recommendations and a decision by the governors at their December 1974 meeting to create a new G10 standing committee, the Committee on Banking Regulations and Supervisory Practices. Chaired by Bank of England Deputy Governor Blunden, this committee met for the first time at the BIS in February 1975 and produced the so-called Basel Concordat of 1975, which advocated sharing supervisory responsibility for banks' foreign activities between host and home-country authorities. It took another decade of intense discussions before agreement could be reached on a "Basel Capital Accord". Issued in 1988, this introduced a credit risk measurement framework for internationally active banks that became a globally accepted standard. In June 1999, the (renamed) Basel Committee on Banking Supervision issued a proposal for a new capital adequacy framework to replace the 1988 accord. Known as "Basel II", it has been refined through a series of broad international consultations and is poised for implementation effective year's end 2006.[141]

Epilogue

1. Month after Month, They Always Returned

For three quarters of a century, with the exception of the war years, central bank governors and high-ranking officials have consistently made time in their busy schedules to travel once a month to Basel. Set on the banks of the Rhine – on the borders of Switzerland, France, and Germany – Basel is also endowed with wonderful cultural attractions: could they have been the main reason for such assiduous visits? If not, why did these people always return? The question, posed more than once in the preceding pages, was never answered in precise detail by those who made the monthly journeys. Generally disinclined to volunteer detailed explanations of their own behaviour, the governors made no exception as to the motivations for frequently meeting with their peers in Basel. When pressed to say what drove them regularly back to Basel, as on the occasion of the Bank's fiftieth anniversary,[1] central bankers hinted at the great value they attach to face-to-face encounters, bilateral or in a larger group, with colleagues from other countries. Lord Cobbold was adamant: "By far the most important activity in Basle ... was the private and informal talks between individual governors".[2] "The BIS", said Deroy, "provided every month a number of people in charge of monetary and financial affairs with the opportunity for frank exchanges of opinion favoured by the confidentiality of the environment".[3] Asked about the most important contribution made by the BIS to international monetary cooperation, Lord O'Brien answered: "I suppose ... the creation of an atmosphere of realism".[4] He went on to say that central bankers travelled to Basel "for discussion in private to test their own thoughts and opinions against those of their colleagues".[5] For de Strycker, "The contribution [of the BIS] to monetary cooperation consisted in the contacts it allowed

473

governors to establish with each other and of the information its staff was able to provide".[6] Emminger and Leutwiller were even disappointed with the new BIS "Tower" building, which they believed provided a less cosy atmosphere for informal conversations than the former Savoy Hôtel Univers.[7] Rasminsky candidly called the Basel meetings "a sort of group therapy".[8]

The focal point of the monthly weekends, sufficient to make the trip worth its while, was the informal governors' dinner, with its spontaneous discussions before and after, of which no record was kept. They put into practice Norman's idea that central bankers – until 1930 meeting occasionally, mostly on a bilateral basis, and often under an unwelcome limelight – ought to institutionalise their encounters in a continuous, multilateral, and confidential way.

When, in 1929–30, circumstances unrelated to central bank cooperation afforded the opportunity to create the international bank, its main promoters disagreed on its main functions and aims. The French wanted it to "commercialise" reparations, the Germans insisted it be a "development bank", the Americans focused on institutional protection for private lending to Germany, and the British – or at least their central bank – sought international support for the fragile gold exchange standard. On one single issue, however, they all concurred: more international monetary cooperation was desirable, and it should be entrusted to the new international bank – as had been envisaged by Luzzatti, Wolff, and others since the end of the previous century. Central bankers, once in charge of the BIS, almost naturally, without need for agreements and plans, translated the vague idea of "central bank cooperation" into a monthly fixture, for which the meeting of the Board provided just an excuse, its business being dealt with swiftly, on Monday morning, bags already packed. Unexpressed demand for regular institutional gatherings of central bankers was undoubtedly large given that, from the very beginning, the monthly Basel weekends became a well-attended routine, even when travelling from across Europe required spending at least a full night in the sleeping car each way.

The difficulty with the governors' monthly meetings in Basel, purportedly the kernel of international monetary cooperation at the BIS, is that – besides recording the participants' universal appreciation of their fundamental value, borne out by unwavering attendance – it is not easy to pinpoint exactly what these gatherings accomplished or what difference they made to international monetary affairs, given the vagueness of testimonies about their achievements and the absence of other direct evidence. One can, however, point to at least three main ways in which these meetings enhanced international monetary cooperation: the creation of institutional ties, the provision and dissemination of high-quality information, and actual decision making.

It has been plausibly argued that, in an "under-institutionalised international environment, the creation of common values, of confidentiality bonds, and of mutual respect is more important than the public announcement of binding engagements of high psychological impact but difficult implementation".[9] The international monetary environment in general and that of central banking in particular was virtually noninstitutionalised in the 1920s. Norman, the tireless advocate of central bank cooperation, was unable even to convene the governors' conference that figured high on his agenda and was endorsed by the Genoa Economic Conference of 1922. In such a context, even the 1927 gathering of the main central bankers elicited an unusual amount of attention, if for no other reason than that it was such an unheard-of occurrence. The world of central banking was so fragmented, with contacts at best bilateral, that only the strong exogenous push of the Hague Conference could create enough momentum for cooperation to be tentatively institutionalised, even if as a by-product of the reparations settlement. But once the prime reason for the creation of the BIS had ceased to exist, the central bankers' club nonetheless survived and thrived, having been institutionalised for good. We have abundant (if nonsystematic) evidence that common values, confidentiality ties, and mutual respect were built in Basel during the 1930s, the least cooperation-friendly of the peacetime decades. The cooperative philosophy expounded in the 1935 Annual Report[10] shows how far, in a relatively short period of time, the monthly meetings had succeeded in creating a common viewpoint on central bank cooperation. The same can be said of the perspective on the international monetary system: consensus was built in Basel that the gold standard should be reformed but not discarded and that domestic monetary policy should have as its prime goal price and exchange rate stability. A consensus view – turned into a shared value – also developed on the apolitical nature of central banking, setting its representatives above the fray as disinterested upholders of the national and international common good. This was a dangerous self-delusion, but it helped to cement the esprit de corps. Bonds and mutual respect were indeed created. Almost legendary is the friendship developed in Basel between Norman and Schacht, two towering intellects coming from cultures poles apart and representing opposing and confrontational national interests. Confidentiality was, from the very beginning, an essential ingredient in building a structured multilateral environment. The routine cadence of the meetings greatly reduced the interest of the public and the press in their proceedings.

The creation of a stronger institutional setting for central bankers to regularly exchange views, learn from and about each other, and nurture mutual respect could perhaps be regarded as a relatively minor achievement. Indeed, it was possible to see things that way in the 1930s. After all, the most significant multilateral attempt at monetary cooperation of the decade, the Tripartite Agreement, was negotiated and concluded to a large extent directly by the three interested parties. However, as Cochran's cables to Washington indicate,[11] almost unnoticed Basel had slowly built itself as an important centre of international financial diplomacy. And it was in the context of one of the BIS monthly meetings that the Netherlands and Switzerland were able to exercise their influence on the final outcome of the Tripartite Agreement. The common values developed in Basel during the uncooperative 1930s found their way into some of the Bretton Woods proposals and injected a healthy dose of anti-conformism into the postwar monetary policy debates. Moreover, and more important, when international relations became more cooperative, a consolidated tradition of institutional meetings, common values, bonds, confidentiality, and trust formed a robust foundation for further development in the 1950s and 1960s.

The monthly meetings also contributed to international monetary cooperation by disseminating high-quality information. Fraser, the second BIS president, was sceptical about "indulging" in the publication of economic information; he believed it to be already "overabundant".[12] Fraser was wrong: in the 1930s, precise knowledge of the monetary aggregates and policies in individual countries was relatively limited and its availability in comparable format was hard to come by. The League of Nations did a superb job of collecting and publishing economic statistics, but these suffered from three shortcomings: limited emphasis on monetary aggregates, lack of timely release, and difficulties in checking their accuracy. The BIS was able to overcome these shortcomings by having its member central banks as both contributors and final users of its statistical compilations. The availability of freshly produced statistical information and the possibility of discussing it with experts of Jacobsson's calibre was an additional magnet drawing the governors to Basel. The value of the BIS statistics is witnessed by the insistence with which the Federal Reserve Bank of New York asked to receive them by fast mail (after the end of American presence on the Board in 1935). It is, of course, impossible to measure the impact of information dissemination on international monetary cooperation. It is commonly observed, however, that a lack or asymmetry of information stands in the way of cooperation, particularly in areas that are not politically sensitive and constitute the bulk of day-by-day interaction amongst monetary authorities. Small countries stand to benefit most from good and swiftly available information about conditions elsewhere, and the BIS was also a catalyser of technical support to small central banks, particularly from Central and Eastern Europe.

The informal meetings were also on many occasions the actual locus for decision making. Carli's testimony is explicit: Basel was *the* place where important decisions were made "by the group who met in the afternoon or in the evening of the day before the Board meeting".[13] He was echoed by Ansiaux, who said: "on several occasions we put together in Basle, in less than twenty-four hours, three, four, five billion dollars to help this or that [BIS] member country".[14] Coombs described the "Basel credits" of 1961 to the Bank of England as being agreed upon – one of them over breakfast – during the governors' informal meetings.[15] Decisions about the Gold Pool and the 1968 Sterling Group Arrangement were likewise made at the informal meetings, which were also at the origin of the General Arrangements to Borrow and the G10 multilateral surveillance exercise. Chapter 11 provides several other instances of actual decisions made in the context of the Basel weekends.

2. The BIS Is Also a Bank

The fact that the BIS, as the first-born among international economic organisations, was set up as a bank (albeit of a special nature) owes much to its reparations role, even though at the time the idea of an international bank or clearing house had been floating around for about forty years. The end of reparations did not put an end to the banking activities of the BIS, which proved to be consistent with and useful to its remaining statutory objective: the promotion of cooperation among central banks.

Banking activity allowed the BIS to enjoy an unusual degree of financial autonomy among international institutions. By earning its own income, the BIS did not depend on appropriations by national parliaments or on members' subsidies. Out of the Bank's income came the resources supporting information services, research, expert and secretarial staff for the various committees, and the governors' monthly meetings themselves. In essence, the central bankers' club could avail itself of a sophisticated infrastructure it did not have to pay for. Moreover, the Bank's complex legal structure – the BIS was created by an international treaty and by a convention with the Swiss Confederation incorporating the Bank under its own law – enhanced its independence and, at the time of the Bretton Woods crisis, provided a shelter against dissolution. Besides these institutional advantages, as a bank the BIS was in a position to offer its shareholders a number of relevant services in settling multilateral payments.

The original idea was that the BIS would be able to facilitate the solution of the reparations transfer problem that had threatened the stability of the international monetary system and poisoned international relations. This was to be done mostly by reinvesting in Germany part of the reparation proceeds. The end of the entire scheme, slightly more than a year after its inception, makes it impossible to say whether the BIS could have provided a workable solution to the transfer problem – though its limited size casts considerable doubts on its ability to have done so.

The BIS received deposits, in various currencies and gold, from its shareholding central banks and invested them in liquid assets across different markets. In principle, this activity might also have been targeted at exchange rate stabilisation, but the relatively small quantity of the available funds, the constraints posed by the Statutes on their employment in national markets, and the need to provide depositors with hefty returns considerably limited the use of BIS resources in day-to-day exchange rate stabilisation.

Gold operations figured prominently among the BIS's activities. Central banks deposited gold for earmark with the BIS for a number of reasons: confidentiality (the centre where the gold was physically held – the BIS not having vaults of its own – was not informed about the identity of the ultimate proprietor of deposited gold), legal protection (international treaties granted the BIS privileges not granted to other gold deposit-taking institutions, which also made it attractive as a gold shipper), and income opportunities. The latter were connected to the gold–currency swap operations in which the BIS specialised from the first months of its existence. The opportunity of dealing with the BIS as counterparty in gold swaps increased central banks' flexibility in mobilising reserves. Fees and interest rates were extremely competitive, which was also due to the fact that the BIS did not necessarily have to maximise profits. These advantages were particularly appreciated by smaller central banks.

Gold deposits with the BIS were also used by central banks to settle reciprocal payments off-market, just by changing entries in the BIS's books. In some circumstances where multilateral payments were concerned, as in the case of postal settlements, the BIS acted as a clearing house for central banks participating in the scheme. At the time of the establishment of the BIS, it was imagined that its clearing-house functions would allow it to play a role in stabilising the gold standard. Events soon proved that the BIS was too minor an actor for such a big role. It was only in the late 1940s that the

BIS was called upon to perform a truly important clearing activity, which also required credit management, in the context of the slow reactivation of multilateral payments channels in Western Europe.

The banking resources and organisation of the BIS allowed it to play an autonomous, if relatively limited, role in international lending. At times of currency crises the Bank's own resources were employed (as a supplement to those made available by member central banks) within schemes orchestrated to sustain weak currencies, as in the case of the Austrian schilling and German Reichsmark in 1931 and of the pound sterling in the 1960s. The BIS participated in its own right in a number of other international support operations, the Gold Pool of the 1960s being one of the most notable. Thus the central bank community could draw not only on resources beyond its own (in cases when international lending was required) but also on the support of an institution that could coordinate international financial action. This potentially very effective tool was never allowed to acquire the quantitative dimension sufficient to act alone on behalf of the central bank community, each of its members preferring to maintain absolute control over the use of its resources for international support operations. Central banks never crossed the cooperation threshold (of more or less effectively coordinating their action and pooling resources for ad hoc operations) by entrusting their multilateral international operations to a single agent acting for all its members. That it was also a bank – which, incidentally, entailed first-hand experience in financial market operations – gave the BIS a character that set it apart from other international organisations such as (for instance) the OECD.

3. The "Above Politics" Illusion

The notion that central bankers could, and therefore should, set themselves outside the political arena loomed large in the attempts by Norman and Strong to institutionalise central bank cooperation in the 1920s. The same notion was nurtured at the BIS in the 1930s. One of the acknowledged magnets luring the governors away from their bustling capital cities to the quiet banks of the Rhine was the desire to get away from Treasuries, governments, and parliaments and to mix with their peers in a world above politics. Although Basel only exceptionally saw the presence of elected government officials, it is also true that whatever cooperative action was contemplated by the governors always took into account both domestic political constraints and the conditions prevailing in international relations. Cooperation bore fruit only when politics (domestic or international) was not an obstacle or, as was the case after 1945, actively promoted an overall cooperative environment.

Money, domestic and international, is intrinsically highly political. At least in the short run, monetary variables affect income distribution, and there is hardly anything as politically charged as changes in the allocation of income and wealth and of the power that goes with them. The politics of exchange rate stabilisation in the 1920s are an excellent case in point. International finance is thus also a foreign policy instrument, and a very powerful one at that, as shown on so many occasions during the period covered in this book: the crisis of 1931, the Tripartite Agreement, the reconstruction of Europe, the support of fixed exchange rates in the 1960s – to say nothing, of course, of the wartime years.

It must be added that international money became more politically sensitive after the First World War than it was during the era of the so-called classical gold standard. To be sure, financial diplomacy was part and parcel of international relations throughout the nineteenth century, but its impact on domestic policy was not then as strong and direct. After 1914, monetary policy trade-offs affected domestic politics more than had been previously the case. On the one hand, the structure of commodity and labour markets made the response of prices and wages to changes in monetary variables slower than it had previously been, thereby increasing the social cost of macroeconomic adjustment. On the other hand, the spread of (male) universal suffrage and the coming of age of mass political parties also increased the political cost of macroeconomic adjustment. All this made international action on exchange rate regimes – with the attendant balance of payments adjustment issues – much more sensitive to domestic politics than at any time before the Great War. In the 1930s, autarky resulted from the inability of world leaders to find solutions to international monetary problems that were compatible with the domestic policy equilibria in the major countries. Economic problems were also compounded by the security issues, assertive revanchism, and *Lebensraum* pretensions that plagued international relations.

Central bankers often blamed domestic politics and strained international relations for their powerlessness in achieving effective monetary cooperation. But they knew that their own propensity for and effectiveness in cooperation were also endogenous to the political environment. As authoritative members of their own domestic establishments they represented first and foremost national interests. Nevertheless, the myth – more carefully cultivated than intimately believed – of the apolitical nature of central bank activity and of those who engage in it was slow to die. It weakened after the Second World War but never entirely disappeared.

The fact is that cooperation under the aegis of the BIS proved to be effective only when a large enough number of countries agreed that a stable international monetary system would serve their national interests better than go-it-alone, nationalist, beggar-thy-neighbour practices. In the period covered by this book, the efficiency and stability of international settlements were, in the opinion of most policy makers, synonymous with fixed exchange rates. But after 1931–33, gold lost most of its lustre as the domestic costs of maintaining fixed exchanges at current rates looked extravagant to politicians in most countries, and internationally coordinated adjustment stumbled over the impossibility of agreeing on the distribution of its costs. After 1945, effective and far-sighted international leadership succeeded in making long-term international commitments look advantageous to individual countries and, therefore, in tipping the scale of domestic politics in their favour. The quality of the postwar national leadership was also crucial. The creation of domestic and international conditions conducive to cooperation on monetary matters was beyond the powers of central bankers, yet once the spirit of international solidarity prevailed over the forces of autarky there was much that a properly institutionalised setting for central bank cooperation could do in favouring the adoption of appropriate technical solutions to the problems at hand. It is only within these overall favourable conditions that Basel could become, as Carli saw it, the "brain trust of the system".

The international influence exercised by the governors' Basel club and the effectiveness of their cooperation were also affected – all other things equal – by the domestic and international standing of the central banks. If the twentieth century has been named "the era of central banks",[16] their role and prestige in monetary policy making were not constantly in the ascendent. At the time of the BIS's foundation, the main European central banks were formally private companies, regulated by the state because of their note-issuing privileges. In the second half of the 1920s, currency stabilisations and the reintroduction of convertibility enhanced their prestige and gave them a good degree of de facto autonomy from their governments that was due also to their claimed expertise in the arcane technicalities of the gold standard. During the Great Depression, however, central banks were (or were seen to be) unable to perform their main task: preserving confidence in the currency. Deflation, the end of the gold standard, and controls on capital movements all undermined the payments system of which central banks had hitherto been the jealous custodians. Both governments and the public lost part of the confidence they had thus far placed in central banks, with inevitable repercussions on their influence and prestige. Central banks came to be more tightly regulated and, around the war years, formally or de facto nationalised; some of their monetary policy functions were taken over by the governments. Even if strained international relations were the primary reason for the ineffectiveness of cooperation among central banks in the 1930s, it is likely that their diminished role and prestige also mattered. After the Second World War, the legal status of central banks remained pretty much subordinated to the Treasuries, but they did regain influence and a good degree of de facto independence, which also partly explains their more active and successful participation in international monetary cooperation.

4. The Pattern of Cooperation, 1930–73

The history of central bank cooperation at the BIS as narrated in this book can be seen in two distinct – though overlapping and connected – ways. The first is what can be termed the institutional history of the Bank. It consists of the build-up of permanent close relations between central bank governors, of the creation and development of an independent and competent staff of international civil servants, and of the Bank's international financial intermediation activities. The second strand in the history of the BIS is that of the success, or otherwise, of international cooperation in achieving the goals set before it. In shaping the BIS as an institution, central bankers enjoyed a large degree of autonomy, whereas the effectiveness of their cooperation depended (as already mentioned) not only on the central banks' willingness and capability but also on domestic and international political constraints largely beyond their control.

From the standpoint of its actual results, the pattern of central bank cooperation looks distinctly U-shaped. Let us briefly review what was achieved by central bank cooperation within the four periods into which the time span covered by this book can be usefully divided.

1929–30. The creation of the BIS was, in itself, a multilateral cooperative success – the result of the final international effort to come to grips with reparations, the most intractable of the post–World War I problems. The "International Bank" was made possible by the converging interests of Germany, its creditors, and private bankers in the "commercialisation" of reparations (i.e., in the conversion of part of the future flow of German payments into negotiable financial assets). Capitalising on the multilateral political effort to defuse the reparations time bomb, central and private bankers, in both The Hague and Baden-Baden, were able to iron out an agreement incorporating some of the long-established ideas about multilateral financial cooperation. This was no minor achievement, made possible by the skilful exploitation of the last window of opportunity opened in international relations before the ice age of autarky and war set in.

1931–46. Its founders expected the BIS to take up some of the international lending functions previously arranged between central banks on an ad hoc bilateral basis. Its ability to do so was unfortunately tested too soon and in the worst possible conditions when, in 1931, the BIS was called upon to provide and coordinate international lending to Austria and Germany. The BIS, central banks, and the international community at large conspicuously failed to overcome the causes or mitigate the effects of the crisis and its enormous long-term political and economic consequences. Much of the unnecessary damage wrought upon the German and the world economy was undoubtedly man-made. In its baptism of fire, the BIS did not live up to expectations. Besides being too small to effectively make a difference, the Bank sided with the rest of the international community in making loans conditional on measures that were part of the problem rather than the solution. This is even more unfortunate since, from a strictly technical point of view, the performance of the BIS was not unsatisfactory, particularly in the Austrian case. It swiftly dispatched experts to assess the situation, it coordinated the international loans, stepping up their delivery, and it effectively negotiated with the central bank concerned. The relatively good technical showing of the BIS makes its overall performance even more unfortunate, as it shows what a difference the BIS could have made had it been guided by sounder economic policies.

For the rest of the 1930s, the history of central bank cooperation is a history of failures at a time when cooperation was sorely needed and when, with the end of reparations, the BIS was left with the sole mission of promoting central bank cooperation. Strained international relations are largely to blame for this. Multilateral agreements were replaced by bilateral dealings; administrative controls over capital movements spread. But central bankers themselves are also to blame for their failure to achieve effective cooperation, particularly for their inability to free themselves from the straitjacket imposed on their behaviour by old-fashioned and mutually incompatible conceptual frameworks. Eventually, almost everywhere, governments took over the main responsibility for monetary policy; the autonomy of central banks was reduced, their prestige diminished. After 1933, cooperation at the BIS came to mean small, unambitious undertakings within the institutional domain of the Bank. Useful services were provided in the form of currency and gold deposits, gold–currency swaps, short-term investments, gold transport, and dividend payments. The quality and coverage of international statistics were improved, and research was upgraded. Central bank officers, particularly junior ones from small countries, were hosted and a body of international civil servants was trained and maintained in Basel.

All this was part of a more or less conscious attempt at keeping the institutional framework well oiled and ready for action in more auspicious times.

The instinct of self-preservation – shared by its main shareholders and its top management alike – is apparent in the BIS's long march in the wilderness, from 1933 to 1946. At first almost unconscious, the idea that the Basel organisation should be preserved for the future was more explicitly acknowledged as Europe slid towards the final tragedy. At the beginning of the war, central banks, in a last burst of informal cooperation, unanimously decided to keep the BIS alive as a tool for postwar resurrection of the monetary order. This decision allowed the BIS to survive but was also at the origin of the blunders made by the Bank during the war, blunders that almost led to its dissolution. It was this decision, implicit but unequivocal, that prompted its compliance with the infamous order for transfer of Czechoslovak gold to Nazi Germany. The same decision bore as its corollary the acceptance of German gold (in payment of interest for the BIS's investments) that so outraged the United States and ultimately contributed to the Bretton Woods resolution to liquidate the Bank. It was also, to a large extent, the central banks' determination to preserve their own cooperative institution that in the end nullified the Bretton Woods decision.

1946–58. The late 1940s and the 1950s were years of extraordinary transatlantic political, military, and economic cooperation. Spurred by the United States, European countries finally fell in line. The OEEC was the main locus of policy coordination amongst governments. The BIS was at first somehow sidelined, busy as it was adapting its institutional side to the new circumstances. The monthly governors' meetings, resumed in earnest in 1948, turned to their business of exchanging information, creating bonds, and improving mutual understanding. Economic analysis was enhanced and banking activity resumed. The BIS returned to centre stage with the birth, in 1950, of the European Payments Union (EPU), a striking novelty in international monetary cooperation. It was designed to reconstruct multilateral payments among Western European countries as a precondition for their full participation in the Bretton Woods system. Breaking with entrenched international trade and capital movement practices required all the political and administrative power governments could muster; the EPU was therefore first and foremost an intergovernmental affair, conducted within the OEEC. The BIS was called upon to contribute in its institutional capacity rather than as the central bankers' club. Its organisation and expertise were put in charge of running the complex system of the EPU's multilateral settlements and credits. The network of payments long established at the

BIS between central banks, each acting as the payment agent for its own country, proved to be what was needed in the circumstances. In the 1950s, the BIS performed to the full the function of international clearing house advocated by the early proponents of the "International Bank". Thus, the most successful cooperative task played by the BIS in the 1950s consisted in providing technical support to the OEEC in the day-to-day running of the EPU. The governors' club lived to some extent a parallel life without a major impact on the BIS's involvement in the EPU, paving the way for the much more intensive decision-making role it was to play from 1959 onward.

1959–73. In Carli's opinion, the BIS was, in the 1960s, "the brain trust of the [Bretton Woods] system. Its influence was as discreet as it was enormous".[17] This was the heyday of an international monetary system that was both successful and inherently unstable. Its relatively long stability was sustained by a hitherto unseen degree of management by the international visible hand, in which central banks came to play a larger role than at any time before and possibly since.

The reasons why central banks were so pivotal are to be found in the technical nature of the actions required to keep the Bretton Woods system afloat. The underlying political compromise implicitly assumed both that fixed rates with the gold dollar anchor should be maintained and that none of the main players should be required to pay a high domestic cost of balance of payments adjustment. The system's viability, therefore, required first and foremost a continuous refinancing of deficit countries by surplus countries, calling upon all the financial ingenuity central bankers could muster and thus putting them at centre stage. Standby loans, currency swaps, and mutual support schemes were the domain of central banking: governments assured the overall political backing but central bankers enjoyed a free hand in producing technical solutions. And, because all technical solutions were politically sensitive, central bank diplomacy flourished as never before. The 1960s would have been Lord Norman's dream decade.

Since the 1930s, Basel had been the preferred locus for central bank diplomacy. With cooperation-friendly international relations and charged by their governments with the mission of maintaining exchange rate stability at low domestic cost, central bankers could finally exploit all the advantages of the "International Bank" they had helped to create in the 1930s and made every effort to keep alive and well thereafter. The benefits the BIS could offer as a locus for central bank cooperation were now plain for all to see: its discreet "club" venue, its sophisticated international financial intermediary services, its research department, and its skilled support staff.

5. Conclusion

To sum up and conclude: the BIS was crafted to respond to the need, felt in some quarters since the end of the nineteenth century, for multilateral central bank cooperation aimed at softening the impact of international liquidity crises and, more generally, at improving the efficiency and stability of the gold standard. The advocates of cooperation were practical men, central bankers *in primis,* convinced of the desirability of fixed exchange rates anchored on gold yet also aware that the system would never work according to Hume's theory and that a modicum of visible hand would always be necessary. Once the BIS became operative in 1930, cooperation there took two main forms: frequent consultations amongst the heads of member central banks, and financial intermediation activities carried out by the "bank of central banks". Put to a test soon after its establishment, the BIS failed for reasons both exogenous and endogenous to its organisation and culture. In the divisive and autarkic environment of the 1930s, the BIS focused on research and on banking services to its members. At the monthly governors' weekends in Basel, multilateral cooperation was at least discussed if not practised. After the Second World War, the immediate availability of a well-oiled and experienced organisation for central bank cooperation somehow vindicated the views of those who had strived to preserve the BIS through autarky and conflict. Its service to the European Payments Union was essential to the EPU's enormous success as one of the most sophisticated devices for multilateral monetary cooperation. In the following decade Basel was one of the main centres, possibly *the* centre, for international monetary cooperation. Required by the peculiar features of the monetary system and sustained by effective (if declining) American leadership, international monetary cooperation saw central banks at centre stage, and the BIS was turned into an effective and flexible instrument for multilateral monetary cooperation.

What difference did the BIS make to international monetary cooperation during the first forty-odd years of its existence? The answer depends crucially on one's expectations. To take just one instance: the creation of the BIS in 1930 raised high hopes that were followed by disillusion. Cooperation was expected to forestall disaster; it failed, and the disaster was even larger than anyone had anticipated. Based on these expectations, the BIS's first showing was an unmitigated failure. On the other hand, one could argue that believing an inexperienced and undersized international institution could significantly affect the course of events in 1931 was utterly naïve. If such expectations existed, they were ill grounded. On this assumption, the BIS's performance in 1931 cannot per se be judged a failure.

A balanced historical judgement, taking the context into account, would probably view (i) the origin of the BIS as the quite unlikely outcome of divisive discussions about reparations and (ii) its subsequent adjustment to a sharp shock and changed circumstances as a minor but significant success. It would cast in a positive light the continuation in the 1930s of the multilateral meetings among central bankers, the financial services provided to shareholders, the enhanced statistical information, and the technical support provided to small central banks. These were hardly earth-shattering accomplishments but, in the context of international relations sliding to war, even a minor multilateral effort cannot be dismissed as utterly irrelevant – particularly so if one bears in mind that, during the long tunnel of autarky and war, the organisation was preserved for future fruition in a more auspicious international environment. If it had not already existed, the BIS would probably have been invented in the late 1940s.

The usefulness of the BIS to the international community in the 1950s and 1960s can hardly be doubted. It soon appeared to be complementary to its bigger twin siblings, the Bretton Woods institutions. It belonged to central banks rather than governments, it was a credit institution, it was lean and flexible. It was a European and, in the 1960s, a G10 organisation. Many saw the latter feature as a drawback from the point of view of international cooperation in a postwar world where an ever larger number of countries claimed or actually enjoyed an increased say in world affairs. But, as Jacobsson did not fail to point out, in the 1960s the fate of the international monetary system depended on cooperation among four, perhaps six, countries. That decision makers from these countries enjoyed a well-staffed, quiet, no-record-kept meeting place allowed for effective, swift multilateral action hardly possible in other contexts. If stretching the life of the fixed–exchange rate system at a time of rapidly expanding output and trade was, all things considered, a positive accomplishment (at least as far as Europe is concerned), then the BIS's contribution to the international community in the 1960s must be regarded as important.

There is another angle, rather than the broad perspective of international monetary systems, from which the BIS's track record can be assessed: that of its own founders and shareholders. As a multilateral central bank organisation the BIS was remarkably successful: it kept the banks in close relation and provided them with a technically competent tool to be employed in a number of common-interest tasks. Most of the services performed by the BIS for central banks were of a routine nature, each of them individually of no great consequence. The continuous flow of these services (the club, the bank, the provider of statistics, the payment settler) definitely mattered in the long run. Seen in this light, the BIS looks like a relatively small specialised international economic organisation – the first of its kind – that proved to be resilient and capable of reinventing itself in response to environmental changes. Such organisations often provide useful services to the international community that are little known to the general public. Moreover, in a world where the horizon of international relations is recurrently darkened by the clouds of go-it-alone policies, their technical accomplishments bear humble witness to the advantages and feasibility of multilateral international cooperation. A remark made long ago by Guido Carli is applicable to the whole period covered in this book: "The BIS is a relatively little known institution, whose role is bigger than the knowledge of it among the public at large".[18]

Notes

Chapter 1

1. Art. 3 of the BIS Statutes (1930): "The objects of the Bank are: to promote the co-operation of central banks and to provide additional facilities for international financial operations; and to act as a trustee or agent in regard to international financial settlements entrusted to it under agreements with the parties concerned". The latter mission of the BIS was in practice connected with the transfer of reparations imposed on Germany after the First World War and rescheduled in the so-called Young Plan (1929); it became obsolete in 1931, little more than a year after the foundation of the BIS.
2. BIS, *Fifth Annual Report,* Basel, 13 May 1935, p. 41.
3. Ibid., pp. 41–4.
4. Ibid., p. 41.
5. Ibid., p. 42.
6. Ibid.
7. Ibid., p. 43.
8. Among such matters, the BIS included: the size and weight of gold bars, rules for earmarking of gold, facilities for advances against gold deposits, clearings of central bank payments, gold swaps, and the creation of facilities for the secure investment and rapid mobilisation of funds of one central bank held by another.
9. BIS, *Fifth Annual Report,* Basel, 13 May 1935, p. 44.
10. Ibid., p. 45.
11. Ibid., p. 46.
12. Ibid.
13. In a system based upon convertibility, the monetary standard defines the unit of account in terms of a quantity of a given metal (into which banknotes can be converted at sight by banks of issue).
14. Flandreau (1995).
15. French reparations for the 1870–71 war were paid in gold.
16. The French, Belgian, and Swiss franc and the Italian lira all traded constantly around 25 to the pound sterling, while the latter was exchanged for 4.87 U.S. dollars.

17. See O'Rourke and Williamson (1999).
18. The resulting drop in world prices would affect the British efforts to regain its competitive edge by trying to reduce domestic prices. See Costigliola (1977), pp. 911–34 (in particular, p. 918).
19. De Cecco (1985), pp. 45–64.
20. Robert Hawtrey, Director of Financial Enquiries at H.M. Treasury, preferred a return to the gold standard at a later time and an exchange standard based on sterling, since "we do not want to smooth the way for New York to become the financial centre of the World": Hawtrey on 26 January 1920, quoted in Péteri (1992), pp. 233–58 (in particular, p. 251).
21. The need for cooperation was further increased by the fact that temporary suspensions were hardly credible and therefore did not provide an effective escape clause in times of acute crisis as they had done before the war. See Eichengreen (1995), pp. 99–118.
22. Meltzer (2003), p. 728.
23. For a review of some of the technical issues involved in modelling cooperation, see Canzonieri and Henderson (1991).
24. Lindblom (1965), p. 227.
25. Keohane (1985), pp. 51–2.
26. Milner (1991), p. 468.
27. Giannini (2002), p. 514.
28. A notable exception is Tabellini and his co-authors; see Tabellini (1990), pp. 245–65.
29. Milner (1991), p. 475.
30. De Bonis, Giustiniani, and Gomel (1999).
31. The period from 1924 to 1930 is covered in the next chapter.
32. An international conference was convened in Paris in 1867 "to discuss the practical transition to gold". However, it adopted a "laissez-faire approach to gold globalization", seen as a "recognition of the incapacity by policymakers to actually agree on a global stance"; Flandreau and James (2003), pp. 5–6.
33. Flandreau (1997), pp. 735–63.
34. Eichengreen (1992), pp. 7–8.
35. Clapham (1944), pp. 328–30; De Cecco (1974), pp. 92–4.
36. Eichengreen (1992), p. 51.
37. Ibid., p. 6.
38. Archduke Ferdinand was assassinated in Sarajevo on June 28. A month later, upon the expiration of its ultimatum, Austria-Hungary declared war on Serbia.
39. Throughout the war, however, efforts were made to preserve the forms of the gold standard and to constantly pretend that it was only temporarily suspended. See Brown (1940), pp. 48ff.
40. Governor Pallain of the Bank of France to Luigi Luzzatti: "If you could give the secret for restoring the exchange rate [to its gold parity] you would certainly be one of the great artisans of victory". Pallain to Luzzatti, 16 April 1916, IVSLA – *Pallain*, 31bis.
41. Mouré (2002), p. 148.
42. They were "free of charges and commissions except for out-of pocket expenses".
43. Chandler (1958), pp. 94–8.
44. Toniolo (1989), p. 50.

45. Strong and Norman first met on 18 March 1916. After dining at Norman's house, Strong wrote in his diary that his host "expressed very much the same feelings that [he] had felt, that the ease with which the mass Government short loans and currency note issues had been absorbed in circulation would lead to a lot of political quackery and financial heresies, especially with regard to fiat currency"; Chandler (1958), p. 95.

46. The Committee, appointed almost a year before the armistice, issued its first report as early as August 1918 (the final one is dated December 1919).

47. Sayers (1976a), p. 115.

48. Ibid., p. 111.

49. Mouré (2002), p. 51.

50. Eichengreen (1995), p. 160.

51. Smith (1929), pp. 713–25 (in particular, p. 716).

52. For the full text, see Sayers (1976a), Appendices, pp. 74–5. See also Clay (1957), pp. 284–5.

53. Schleidt (1931), pp. 80–3.

54. Mouré (2002), p. 151. Such a conference was, however, postponed indefinitely; see Section 1.6.

55. "Autonomy and freedom from political control are desirable for all Central and Reserve Banks"; Sayers (1976a), Appendices, p. 75.

56. "A Central Bank should have power to examine Banks which come to the Central Bank for credit assistance"; ibid.

57. "A policy of continuous cooperation is desirable among Central and Reserve banks"; ibid.

58. Costigliola (1984), p. 107.

59. Hoover to Harding, quoted in Costigliola (1984), p. 108. The United States did not want to be involved in multilateral discussions about reparations and debt. According to Costigliola, "American leaders found Genoa offensive".

60. Strong's opposition to the idea of the gold exchange standard would grow over time, and it would dampen his initial enthusiasm over central bank cooperation; Clarke (1967), pp. 37–9, 135. Similarly, the Bank of France did *not* amend its statutes in order to allow for convertible currencies to be included in its reserves. For Rueff the "gold exchange standard is a regime so Anglo-Saxon that it does not even have a French name"; Rueff (1963), p. 64.

61. Mouré (1992), pp. 259–79 (in particular, pp. 270–1).

62. Rueff (1963), p. 64.

63. Eichengreen and James (2003), pp. 515–48 (in particular, p. 522).

64. See: Argoud (1931), pp. 81–5; Mendès France (1930a), pp. 25–9; Mitzakis (1939), pp. 129–37; Schleidt (1931), pp. 24–6; Karamikas (1931), pp. 124–55.

65. Mendès France (1930a), p. 25.

66. Luzzatti participated in the conference as Italian representative and later observed that it was doomed to fail because it "aimed to codify a monetary utopia". *Corriere della Sera,* 12 December 1907, p. 3.

67. Karamikas (1931), pp. 126ff.

68. Mendès France (1930a), p. 26.

69. *Neue Freie Presse,* 15 November 1907.

70. See IVSLA, *Archivio Luigi Luzzatti,* b. 147: Questione Monetaria.

71. *Neue Freie Presse,* 28 November 1907.
72. *Neue Freie Presse,* 11 December 1907. See also IVSLA, *Archivio Luigi Luzzatti,* b. 154, fasc. iii, sez. B.
73. Luzzatti (1908).
74. Mendès France (1930a), p. 27.
75. Karamikas (1931), pp. 135–6.
76. *Das Internationale Zahlungswesen,* Leipzig 1913. Quoted in Dulles (1932), pp. 14–15.
77. Compte-rendus de la Conférence parlamentaire Internationale du Commerce – Paris, Palais du Luxembourg (Sénat), 27, 28 et 29 avril 1916: *La grande discussion sur la paix monétaire.* IVSLA, *Archivio Luigi Luzzatti,* GE.1922: 23–55.
78. Vissering (1920).
79. The claims on Germany would serve as a guarantee; see Mitzakis (1939), pp. 143–4; Eichengreen (1995), p. 156.
80. Mitzakis (1939), pp. 146–50; Schleidt (1931), pp. 62–4.
81. Ministère des Affaires Étrangères (1922), p. 151.
82. Eichengreen (1995), p. 158.
83. Ministère des Affaires Étrangères (1922), p. 151. See also Eichengreen and James (2003), pp. 515–48 (in particular, p. 520).
84. Mouré (2002), p. 151.
85. Luzzatti (1922).

Chapter 2

1. 28 June 1919.
2. In 1919–20, the United Kingdom and the United States reneged on their earlier promise to offer France a separate treaty, guaranteeing (among other things) the new Franco-German border. In so doing they exacerbated France's feeling of isolation in the face of any future German threat and consequently its determination to impose harsh reparations on Germany; see Jordan (1971), pp. 38–9.
3. The Americans feared they would be the only creditor facing a united European front of debtors pressing for a downscaling of allied debts. Costigliola (1984), pp. 104–5.
4. Smith (1929), pp. 713–25 (in particular, p. 716).
5. Eichengreen (1992), p. 160.
6. Cohrs (2003), pp. 1–32.
7. Keynes (1919) made an enormous contribution to alerting public opinion outside of Germany on the dangers – for the whole of Europe – of imposing too-harsh economic conditions on the defeated power.
8. Wheeler-Bennett and Latimer (1930), p. 41.
9. De Cecco (1985), pp. 45–64 (in particular, p. 47).
10. It was envisaged that the assessment would be made by 1 May 1921 and that meanwhile Germany was to pay on account a sum of 1 billion pounds sterling.
11. Wheeler-Bennett and Latimer (1930), p. 44.
12. Carr (1947), p. 54; see also Wheeler-Bennett and Latimer (1930), p. 45.
13. On the course, causes, and effects of the German postwar inflation, see Holtfrerich (1986).

14. The international experts were Brand, Cassel, Jenks, Keynes, Vissering, Dubois, and Kamenka. In November the exchange rate of the mark was 40,000 to the pound, as against 2,000 on 1 July 1922. Wheeler-Bennett and Latimer (1930), p. 48.
15. The French supported unpopular separatist movements; some prominent members of the local population were expelled or imprisoned for their participation in the passive resistance.
16. For the composition of the committees see Karamikas (1931), pp. 41–3.
17. Clarke (1967), pp. 47–8.
18. Carr (1947), p. 60.
19. For more details on the Dawes Plan, see Karamikas (1931), pp. 46–57.
20. The American Under-Secretary of the Treasury, Parker Gilbert, was appointed Agent General. Owen D. Young, who was Chairman of General Electric and had the favour of U.K. Prime Minister MacDonald and the French and U.S. presidents Herriot and Coolidge, took up this position on an interim basis during the first couple of months. Clarke (1967), p. 57.
21. Georges Barnich, director of the Belgian think-tank Solvay Institute of Sociology, proposed the commercialisation of the German debt by the Bankers Committee of the League of Nations as a solution to the reparations problem. Barnich (1923), pp. 226–9.
22. It is noteworthy in this context to recall that the Reichsbank was to be administered by a board of 14 members, half of whom (including the president) of German nationality and the remainder of U.K., French, Italian, Belgian, American, Dutch, and Swiss nationality.
23. Toniolo (1980).
24. Van der Wee and Tavernier (1975), pp. 183–208.
25. Moreau understood more than his predecessors the usefulness of international co-operation. He created a new department at the Bank for foreign relations and put Charles Rist and Pierre Quesnay in charge of it. An important novelty was also that the Bank acquired better legal and technical means to intervene on the foreign exchange market. Feiertag (1998), pp. 15–35 (in particular, p. 23).
26. Mouré (1992), pp. 259–79 (in particular, pp. 266–7).
27. Norman advocated a key role for central bankers in Central Europe because politicians seemed unable to prevent a collapse of the area: Péteri (1992), pp. 233–58 (in particular, p. 241).
28. Feiertag (1998), pp. 15–35 (in particular, p. 27). See also Sayers (1976a), pp. 183–201; Clay (1957), pp. 256–66.
29. Baffi (2002), p. 8.
30. Ibid., pp. 6–7.
31. Meltzer (2003), p. 174.
32. They are well documented in Clarke (1967).
33. Norman to Siepmann in September 1925, quoted in Kynaston (2000), p. 153.
34. Strong, quoted in Clarke (1967), p. 107.
35. De Cecco (1995), p. 126.
36. Clarke (1967), pp. 123–4.
37. Mouré (1992), pp. 259–79 (in particular, p. 271).
38. Meltzer (2003), p. 174.

39. For an analysis of the economic effects on the German economy of the inflow of U.S. capital, see Ritschl (2002), pp. 68–76.
40. Schacht (1953), p. 294. Also: Baffi (2002), p. 15; Ritschl (2002), pp. 68–76.
41. Meltzer (2003), pp. 228–30.
42. Brown (1940), p. 811.
43. James (1985), p. 64.
44. At the Long Island meeting, Strong told Schacht that a good time to discuss the German reparations would come at the end of the first five-year period of the Dawes Plan and after the 1928 U.S. elections. James (1985), p. 62.
45. The Rhineland had been occupied by Allied troops after the First World War, and its evacuation was foreseen by the Versailles Treaty after a period of 15 years, that is, in 1935 at the latest. Lüke (1958), p. 133.
46. On Gilbert's role, see Lüke (1958), pp. 143–53.
47. Simmons (1993), p. 377.
48. Weill-Raynal (1947), p. 405.
49. For more detail on the German-French negotiations, see Lüke (1958), pp. 136–42.
50. Weill-Raynal (1947), pp. 408–9.
51. Stopford and Menken (1930), pp. 132–3.
52. Wheeler-Bennett and Latimer (1930), p. 83. On American participation, see Section 2.5.
53. Schacht (1931), p. 73. It should be remembered that the Dawes Plan specified neither the total amount of German reparations nor the time span of the payments.
54. Copies of the minutes, drafted by Moret and Quesnay of the Bank of France, are in BISA, 7.12 – *Young Plan Experts' Committee,* box BR03.
55. Experts: Emile Francqui, Vice-Governor of the Société Générale de Belgique, and Camille Gutt, Belgian delegate of the Reparation Commission, for Belgium; Emile Moreau, Governor of the Bank of France, and Jean Parmentier, Governor of Crédit Foncier, for France; Hjalmar Schacht, President of the Reichsbank, and A. Voegler, General Manager of Vereinigte Stahlwerke AG, for Germany; Alberto Pirelli, of the Pirelli Group, Chairman of the International Chamber of Commerce, and Fulvio Suvich, member of the Financial Committee of the League of Nations, for Italy; Takashi Acki, of the Nagoya branch of the Bank of Japan, and Kengo Mori, member of the Japanese Diet, for Japan; Sir Josiah Stamp, Chairman of the London, Midland and Scottish Railway, Director of the Bank of England, and Lord Revelstoke, Chairman of Baring Brothers, Director of the Bank of England (the latter would be replaced by Sir Charles Addis, Chairman of the London Committee of the Hong Kong and Shanghai Bank, Director of the Bank of England), for the United Kingdom; Owen D. Young, Chairman of General Electric, Director of the Federal Reserve Bank of New York, and J. P. Morgan, Chairman of J.P. Morgan & Co. for the United States. Alternates: for Belgium, Baron Terlinden and H. Fabri; for France, Claude Moret and Edgar Allix; for Germany, Caspar Melchior and L. Kastl; for Italy, Giuseppe Bianchini and Bruno Dolcetta; for Japan, Saburo Sonoda and Yasumune Matsui; for the United Kingdom, Sir Charles Addis and Sir Basil Blackett; and for the United States, Thomas N. Perkins and T. W. Lamont. See *Report of the Committee of Experts on Reparations* (Young Committee, June 7, 1929) and Baffi (2002), p. 11.

56. Charles Dawes himself had become U.S. Vice-President and therefore could not attend the conference. Costigliola (1984), p. 210.
57. Baffi (2002), p. 11.
58. Ibid., p. 12. Unless otherwise stated, what follows is freely drawn from Baffi's work, which is based on detailed research in the BIS Archives.
59. On the never-ending and contentious issue of Germany's capacity to pay, see Ferguson (1998), pp. 395ff.
60. Simmons (1993), p. 380. Together with Baffi's, the work by Simmons is the most recent and innovative contribution on the foundation of the BIS.
61. Simmons (1993), pp. 361–405.
62. Ibid., p. 370.
63. "Comité des Experts Young Plan, Moret notes 00-00077, séance mercredi 20 février 1929", p. 2, BISA, 7.16(3) – *BIS History (Baffi papers)*, box RBL B9. See also: G. Royot, "Comité d'Etudes 1944, Extraits des comptes-rendus de M. Moret des séances du Comité des Experts du Plan Young, Paris, 23 février – 5 juin 1929", p. 2, BISA, 7.16(3) – *BIS History (Baffi papers)*, box RBL B13. From subsequent reports on the discussions in the subcommittee, it seems that Pirelli is also part of it.
64. Melchior is thus portrayed by Keynes (1972, p. 395): "A very small man, exquisitely clean, very well and neatly dressed, with a high stiff collar which seemed cleaner and whiter than an ordinary collar, his round head covered with grizzled hair shaved so close as to be like in substance to the pile of a close-made carpet, the line where his hair ended bounding his face and forehead in a very sharply defined and rather noble curve, his eyes gleaming straight at us, with extraordinary sorrow in them, yet like an honest animal at bay."
65. "Burgess report of trip to Europe February 23 to March 26, 1929 to Governor Harrison", p. 3, FRBNY, 797.3 – *Bank for International Settlements, 1934–1976*.
66. Baffi (2002), p. 15.
67. "Comité des Experts Young Plan, Moret notes, 00-00090 séance samedi 23 février 1929", p. 3, BISA, 7.16(3) – *BIS History (Baffi papers)*, box RBL B9.
68. M. van Zeeland, "BIS Reconsidered: Comité Young", pp. 4–5, BISA, 7.16(2) – *BIS Reconsidered*, box RBL2.
69. "Comité des Experts Young Plan, Moret notes, 00-00090 séance samedi 23 février 1929", p. 3, and "00-00098 séance lundi 25 février 1929", p. 6, BISA, 7.16(3) – *BIS History (Baffi papers)*, box RBL B9.
70. This had originally been Francqui's idea, which confirms his important role in the creation of the BIS claimed by Ranieri (1985), pp. 238–9.
71. Moret attributes the written version of the project to Moreau. "Comité des Experts Young Plan, Moret notes, 00-00101 séance mardi 26 février 1929", p. 1, BISA, 7.16(3) – *BIS History (Baffi papers)*, box RBL B9.
72. M. van Zeeland, "BIS Reconsidered: Comité Young, Memorandum No. 3 from 25 February 1929", pp. 6–7, BISA, 7.16(3) – *BIS History (Baffi papers)*, box RBL B13.
73. Schacht's Memo to Mr. Young, 25 February 1929, BISA, 7.12 – *Young Plan Experts' Committee*, box BR03. The draft was published by Lüke (1958), pp. 162–4.
74. In the second draft, the gold marks were replaced by Reichsmarks; Lüke (1985), pp. 65–76 (in particular, p. 72).
75. Schacht (1953), pp. 312–13.

76. "Comité des Experts Young Plan, Moret notes, 00-00118 – 00-00122 séance lundi 4 mars 1929", BISA, 7.16(3) – *BIS History (Baffi papers),* box RBL B9. See also Baffi (2002), p. 17.
77. "Burgess report of trip to Europe February 23 to March 26, 1929 to Governor Harrison", p. 3, FRBNY, 797.3 – *Bank for International Settlements, 1934–1976.*
78. "Burgess report of trip to Europe February 23 to March 26, 1929 to Governor Harrison", p. 4, FRBNY, 797.3 – *Bank for International Settlements, 1934–1976.*
79. G. Royot, "Comité d'Etudes 1944, Extraits des comptes-rendus de M. Moret des séances du Comité des Experts du Plan Young, Paris, 23 février – 5 juin 1929", pp. 8–14, BISA, 7.16(3) – *BIS History (Baffi papers),* box RBL B13.
80. Baffi (2002), p. 18.
81. M. van Zeeland, "BIS Reconsidered: Comité Young", pp. 17–19, BISA, 7.16(3) – *BIS History (Baffi papers),* box RBL B13.
82. M. van Zeeland, "BIS Reconsidered: Comité Young", annex I, BISA, 7.16(3) – *BIS History (Baffi papers),* box RBL B13.
83. In the reports to the Italian delegation to the government, it was called "Central Office for International Settlements". Pirelli to Mussolini, 15 March 1929, APAP, Pos. 35, Comitato Young, D/II/a/1, now in M. De Cecco, *L'Italia e il sistema finanziario internazionale, 1919–1936,* Laterza, Roma-Bari 1993, Doc. 95, pp. 651–3.
84. See: "Comité des Experts, Annexe 3 révisé le 12 mars 1929, by Fred B. Bates", BISA, 7.18(3) – *Papers Quesnay, papiers Comité des Experts,* box QUE3, 11; and "Committee of Experts, Annex 3 2nd revision March 18th, 1929, by J. C. Stamp", BISA, 7.16(3) – *BIS History (Baffi papers),* box RBL B6.
85. De Cecco (1993), p. 93.
86. *Report of the Committee of Experts constituted by the Geneva Decision of September 16th 1928,* Paris, 1929, pp. 18, 51.
87. "Comité d'Etudes 1944, Extraits des comptes-rendus de M. Moret des séances du Comité des Experts du Plan Young, Paris, 23 février – 5 juin 1929", p. 22, BISA, 7.16(3) – *BIS History (Baffi papers),* box RBL B13.
88. On the reaction in Washington to this suggestion, see Section 2.5.
89. "Rapport du Comité des Experts constitué en vertu de la décision prise à Genève le 16 septembre 1928", s.l. 1929, BISA, 7.18(8) – *Papers Royot,* box ROY6.
90. Baffi (2002), pp. 9–40.
91. *Report of the Committee of Experts constituted by the Geneva Decision of September 16th 1928,* Paris, 1929, p. 53.
92. The United States as observer, the British Dominions (Australia, Canada, India, New Zealand, and South Africa), and smaller European powers: Czechoslovakia, Greece, Poland, Portugal, Romania, and Yugoslavia. Dealtry and Baffi (1991), p. 32.
93. The amount to be received was set against the United Kingdom's payments to the United States. Wheeler-Bennett and Latimer (1930), p. 111.
94. Ibid., pp. 106–23.
95. Ibid., p. 115.
96. Simmons (1993), p. 389.
97. Sayers (1976a), Appendix 21. See also Kynaston (2000), pp. 193–202.
98. G. Royot, "Banque des Règlements Internationaux. Evolution de Juin 1929 à Octobre 1929", 21 juin 1944, p. 5, BISA, 7.16(2) – *BIS Reconsidered,* box RBL2.

99. The continuation of sessions was impossible owing to the opening of the assembly of the League of Nations. Wheeler-Bennett and Latimer (1930), p. 137.

100. G. Royot, "Banque des Règlements Internationaux. Evolution de Juin 1929 à Octobre 1929", 21 juin 1944, pp. 7–15, BISA, 7.16(2) – *BIS Reconsidered,* box RBL2.

101. G. Royot, "Du Comité des Experts à mai 1930 Dossier personnel annoté", BISA, 7.16(2) – *BIS Reconsidered,* box RBL2.

102. Louis Franck, Governor of the National Bank of Belgium, and alternate L. Delacroix, member of the Reparation Commission (upon his death he was replaced by Paul van Zeeland of the National Bank of Belgium), for Belgium; C. Moret, Vice-Governor of the Bank of France, and alternate Pierre Quesnay, head of the Research Department of the Bank of France, for France; Hjalmar Schacht, President of the Reichsbank, and alternate W. Vocke, member of the Directorate of the Reichsbank, for Germany; A. Beneduce, Chairman of Crediop, and alternate V. Azzolini, General Manager of the Bank of Italy, for Italy; T. Tanaka, delegate of the Bank of Japan in London, and alternate S. Sonoda, Manager of the Yokohama Specie Bank, for Japan; and Sir Charles Addis, Chairman of the London Committee of the Hong Kong and Shanghai Bank, Director of the Bank of England, and alternate Sir W. Layton, Editor of *The Economist,* for the United Kingdom. Following the recommendations of J. P. Morgan, the central banks co-opted the Americans E. Reynolds, President of the First National Bank of New York, and M. A. Traylor, President of the First National Bank of Chicago. Baffi (2002), p. 11.

103. G. Royot, "Banque des Règlements Internationaux. Evolution de Juin 1929 à Octobre 1929", 21 juin 1944, p. 5, BISA, 7.16(2) – *BIS Reconsidered,* box RBL2.

104. W. Roncagli "l'Oeuvre du Comité d'organisation de la Banque des Règlements internationaux", p. 13, BISA, 7.16(3) – *BIS History (Baffi papers),* box RBL B13.

105. Note from the German delegation at Baden-Baden of 21 October 1929, BISA, 7.18(3) – *Papers Quesnay,* box QUE4, f18.

106. Note from the German delegation at Baden-Baden of 21 October 1929, p. 2, par. 43, BISA, 7.18(3) – *Papers Quesnay,* box QUE4, 18. Similarly on p. 5, par. 166. The Bank is presented as a financial institution that "will be in a position to open up to trade new possibilities of development".

107. Memorandum from the U.K. delegation, "Reasons which prompted the British delegation to propose the separation of Constitution and Statutes", BISA, 7.18(3) – *Papers Quesnay,* box QUE4, f18.

108. Roncagli assumed this would open the door to regular supervision by the Financial Committee of the League of Nations, in which the British had a strong position. W. Roncagli, "L'Oeuvre du Comité d'organisation de la Banque des Règlements internationaux", p. 17, BISA, 7.16(3) – *BIS History (Baffi papers),* box RBL B13.

109. Baffi (2002), p. 47.

110. It may be recalled that Keynes's 1941 proposal for an international currency union entailed the creation of an international clearing bank issuing a currency denominated "bancor".

111. Baffi (2002), p. 57.

112. Synoptic table of statutes in English (proposed French draft with corresponding articles of the English draft, Belgian draft and Young Plan), 8 October 1929, BISA, 7.16(1) – *BIS Organisation Committee,* box RBL 1C.

113. W. Roncagli, "l'Oeuvre du Comité d'organisation de la Banque des Règlements internationaux", pp. 26–7, BISA, 7.16(3) – *BIS History (Baffi papers)*, box RBL B13.

114. Moret had received instructions from Paris that the Bank of France would not participate in the creation of the BIS if London were chosen. G. Royot, "COBRI Baden-Baden 3 octobre – 13 novembre 1929, lettres, notes et comptes rendus de conversations (Moret et Quesnay), compte rendu du 23 octobre 1929", BISA, 7.16(3) – *BIS History (Baffi papers)*, box RBL B13.

115. G. Royot, "COBRI Baden-Baden 3 octobre – 13 novembre 1929, lettres, notes et comptes rendus de conversations (Moret et Quesnay), compte rendus du 17 et 18 octobre 1929", BISA, 7.16(3) – *BIS History (Baffi papers)*, box RBL B13.

116. Brussels had already been mentioned at the Young conference as a possible candidate. Comité des Experts Young Plan, Moret notes, 16 March 1929, BISA, 7.16(3) – *BIS History (Baffi papers)*, box RBL B9.

117. G. Royot, "COBRI Baden-Baden 3 octobre – 13 novembre 1929, lettres, notes et comptes rendus de conversations (Moret et Quesnay), compte rendus du 7 et 9 novembre 1929", BISA, 7.16(3) – *BIS History (Baffi papers)*, box RBL B13.

118. Geneva dropped out because it hosted the League of Nations, Lausanne because it was too small, and Zurich because it hosted the Swiss National Bank and was considered too much under German influence.

119. Baffi (2002), p. 61.

120. Formally, it was just a continuation of the first.

121. Stopford (1931), pp. 495–528 (in particular, p. 515).

122. MacMillan (2002), pp. 495–6.

123. Ibid., pp. 488–92.

124. Costigliola (1984), pp. 140–57.

125. J.P. Morgan & Co. organised the banking group that distributed the Dawes Loan; Costigliola (1984), p. 146.

126. Clarke (1967), p. 151.

127. Wandel (1971), pp. 248–9.

128. M. van Zeeland, "B.I.S. reconsidered", 20 December 1945, p. 5, BISA, 7.16(3) – *BIS History (Baffi papers)*, box RBL B16.

129. Simmons (1993), pp. 399–400.

130. Wandel (1971), p. 238.

131. Costigliola (1984), p. 214. Also: Wandel (1971), p. 248.

132. The American experts should avoid "any bold statement" linking war debts and reparation; Costigliola (1984), p. 215.

133. Simmons (1993), p. 401.

134. See Section 2.2.

135. Official declaration from Stimson on 16 May 1929, quoted in Wandel (1917), p. 270. Also: Copies from FRBNY, Public statement May 16, 1929, BISA, 7.16(3) – *BIS History (Baffi papers)*, box RBL B1.

136. Baffi (2002), p. 38.

137. Copies from FRBNY, "Harrison report of a conversation with Undersecretary of Treasury Ogden Mills, of Saturday May 18, 1929", 23 May 1929, BISA, 7.16(3) – *BIS History (Baffi papers)*, box RBL B1.

138. Copies from FRBNY, Ogden Mills to Harrison, 19 June 1929, BISA, 7.16(3) – *BIS History (Baffi papers)*, box RBL B1.

139. Official declaration from Hoover on 18 June 1929, quoted in Wandel (1971), p. 271.
140. Germany was allowed, at any time, to postpone its payment to the United States for two and a half years. This necessitated readjustments at the Second Hague Conference where the Young Plan was discussed. The total annuities that the BIS was to receive from Germany had to be recalculated, and Germany was to assure that no priority would be given to the payment of reparations to the United States. For the full text of the agreement, see *Procès-Verbaux et Documents de la Conférence de la Haye, 1929–1930*, s.d., Annex H, paper no. 19, the German–American debt agreement. See also "Conférence Internationale de La Haye, Lettres échangées concernant l'Accord Germano-Américain", BISA, 7.16(3) – *BIS History (Baffi papers)*, box RBL B6; Wandel (1971), p. 271.
141. Copies from FRBNY, notes on the International Bank from L. Galantière to Governor Harrison, 13 July 1929, Appendix II, BISA, 7.16(3) – *BIS History (Baffi papers)*, box RBL B1.
142. Copies from FRBNY, outgoing cablegrams from Harrison nos. 795 to Schacht of 22 July and 797 to Moreau of 23 July 1929, BISA, 7.16(3) – *BIS History (Baffi papers)*, box RBL B1. In August Harrison informed them that he assumed the Federal Reserve Board could work with the BIS if it were to do business in the United States: copies from FRBNY, letters from Harrison to Schacht and Moreau of 13 August 1929, BISA, 7.16(3) – *BIS History (Baffi papers)*, box RBL B1.
143. Harrison stayed in touch with Moreau; Lamont with the British, as well as with Owen Young, J. P. Morgan, and Parker Gilbert. The latter also communicated the names of Reynolds and Traylor as members of the BIS Organisation Committee: G. Royot "Banque des Règlements Internationaux. Evolution de Juin 1929 à Octobre 1929", 21 June 1944, p. 5, BISA, 7.16(2) – *BIS Reconsidered*, box RBL2.
144. Copies from FRBNY, Harrison report of a conversation with Under-Secretary of State Joseph Cotton, 6 September 1929, BISA, 7.16(3) – *BIS History (Baffi papers)*, box RBL B1.
145. Copies from FRBNY, letter from Owen Young to Ogden Mills of 1 August 1929, BISA, 7.16(3) – *BIS History (Baffi papers)*, box RBL B1.
146. De Cecco (1993), p. 94.
147. W. Roncagli, "l'oeuvre du Comité d'organisation de la Banque des Règlements Internationaux", p. 35, BISA, 7.16(3) – *BIS History (Baffi papers)*, box RBL B13. Traylor wondered whether any banker would be willing to become a manager of a bank whose operations would be so restricted.
148. Under-Secretary of State Cotton to Wilson on 6 January 1930, quoted in Wandel (1971), p. 272.
149. Conversation between Cotton and Harrison on 18 April 1930, FRBNY, 797.3 – *Harrison papers*.
150. Weill-Raynal (1947), p. 571.
151. *Report of the Committee of Experts constituted by the Geneva Decision of September 16th 1928*, Paris, 1929, Annex I, p. 74.
152. Note by Young and Morgan of 10 January 1930, quoted in Baffi (2002), p. 66.
153. Letter from Governor Roy A. Young to Andrew W. Mellon, Secretary of the Treasury, 14 March 1930, FRBNY, 797.3 – *Harrison papers*.
154. "Convention respecting the Bank for International Settlements, with Annex, Signed at The Hague, January 20, 1930", in League of Nations, Treaty Series, vol. CIV,

no. 2398 (1930), pp. 441–71. See also *Accords conclus à La Haye en août 1929 et janvier 1930 en vue du règlement complet et définitif du problème des réparations,* Paris, Imprimerie Nationale, 1930, pp. 222–50. The current version of the BIS Statutes in Bank for International Settlements, *Basic Texts,* Basel, August 2003, and ⟨http://www.bis.org/about/legal.htm⟩.

155. See Chapter 3.
156. Art. 3 of the Statutes (1930).
157. For what follows we drew heavily on Mario Giovanoli's authoritative description of the BIS's legal status; Giovanoli (1989), pp. 841–64. Mario Giovanoli is Professor at the Faculty of Law, University of Lausanne, Switzerland, and has been General Counsel of the BIS since 1989. See also "The legal status of the BIS", *The Bank for International Settlements and the Basle Meetings, Published on the occasion of the fiftieth anniversary 1930–1980,* Basel, 1980, pp. 94–104.
158. The equivalent of 145,161,290.32 grams of gold; Art. 5 of the Statutes (1930). Krug (1932), p. 8.
159. At the end of the first financial year, the central banks of Belgium, France, Germany, Italy, and the United Kingdom – and the banking groups representing Japan and the United States – together held two thirds of the voting rights attached to the initial share issue. This proportion declined somewhat in later years as other central banks joined the BIS as shareholders, but it always remained well above 50%.
160. The entire American issue and part of the Belgian, Danzig, and French issues were sold on the market so that a minor part of the BIS's shares passed into private hands. More than seventy years later, on 8 January 2001, an Extraordinary General Meeting of the BIS would decide the compulsory withdrawal of all privately held shares; it was deemed that "the existence of a small number of private shareholders whose interest is essentially financial is no longer in conformity with the international role and future development of the organisation". BIS Press Release, 8 January 2001.
161. Art. 28 of the Statutes (1930).
162. This procedure was adopted in the case of Gates W. McGarrah and Leon Fraser, the American representatives on the BIS Board from 1930 to 1935. After 1935 and until 1994, the two seats on the BIS Board to which the U.S. central bank was entitled would remain vacant. In the case of Japan, it was the Governor of the Bank of Japan who appointed his substitute to sit on the BIS Board (often the permanent representative of the Bank of Japan or of the Yokohama Specie Bank in London). As a result of the San Francisco Peace Treaty of 8 September 1951, the Bank of Japan renounced its status as founder central bank of the BIS.
163. Art. 6 of the Constituent Charter.
164. Art. 10 of the Constituent Charter.
165. The scope of this provision was subsequently defined more fully in the Brussels Protocol of 30 July 1936, which was adhered to by most countries whose central banks were BIS shareholders.
166. For example: the Washington Agreement of 13 May 1948 with France, the United Kingdom, and the United States on the restitution of gold looted by Nazi Germany; or the agreements the BIS concluded with the Federal Republic of Germany on the settlement of prewar investments and debts in 1953 and 1966. The Headquarters

Agreement concluded between the Bank and the Swiss government on 10 February 1987 would confirm the Bank's international legal personality also de jure.
167. Arts. 20–26 of the Statutes.
168. Van de Burgt (1997), p. 291. Similar operations may be carried out with banks, bankers, corporations, or individuals provided the central bank of the country concerned does not object.
169. Schloss (1970), p. 12.
170. "The inclusion of a list of transactions from which the Bank is debarred ... shatters the dream of those few idealists who hoped that the Bank would issue international currency". Einzig (1930), p. 58.
171. Setting the minimum reserve requirement was left to the discretion of the Bank. "The Bank for International Settlements. A Commentary upon the Statutes", *The Banker*, 12(47), 1929, pp. 289–90. Einzig (1930, p. 58) thought it was unnecessary to require a minimum reserve ratio because the Bank was not a bank of issue.
172. Art. 57 of the Statutes.
173. Art. 53 of the Statutes.
174. "The Bank for International Settlements. A Commentary upon the Statutes", *The Banker*, 12(47), 1929, pp. 296–9. This distribution of profits secured a "fair remuneration of the capital invested, and a very conservative reserve policy".
175. Art. 55 of the Statutes.
176. "The Bank for International Settlements", *The Banker*, 14(52), 1930, p. 160.
177. Jaudel (1930), pp. 302–3.
178. "La B.R.I. Son rôle dans la vie économique mondiale", *L'esprit international*, 1 July 1930, p. 362.
179. See Mendès France (1930a); id., "Les premier bilans de la B.R.I., *Renaissance*, 30 August 1930.
180. "International Bank Test Engages Europe", *Wall Street Journal* (Paris Office), 25 July 1929.
181. *Journal of Commerce*, Washington, 26 July 1929.
182. *The Economist*, 14 September 1929, p. 471.
183. Sir Josiah Stamp's address to the Society of Incorporated Accountants, quoted in *The Economist*, 6 July 1929, p. 6.
184. Sayers (1976a), p. 354.
185. Karamikas (1931), pp. 170–1.
186. *The Economist*, 16 November 1929, p. 900.
187. Einzig (1930), pp. 107–8.
188. Ibid., p. 110.
189. "Young Regards Bank Chief Achievement", *New York Times*, 8 June 1929.
190. "Scope of the New Bank", *Journal of Commerce*, 8 October 1929.
191. Copies from FRBNY, W. Randolph Burgess to Governor Harrison, 10 July 1929, "The Bank for International Settlements", BISA, 7.16(3) – *BIS History (Baffi papers)*, box RBL B1.
192. Smith (1929), pp. 713–25. Smith sent a first draft to Burgess with a letter in which he said: "You will see that I have mangled your stuff a good deal, although I have used most of it in the body of this paper". Copies from FRBNY, letter from Jeremiah Smith to Randolph Burgess of 12 July 1929, BISA, 7.16(3) – *BIS History (Baffi papers)*, box RBL B1.

193. Smith (1929), pp. 713–25.
194. On the change of American interest in the project of the BIS, see Parker Willis (1929), pp. 193–202.
195. "Finding Flaws in the World Bank", *Journal of Commerce,* 15 October 1929. The article was a reaction against the negative, pessimistic view on the BIS from the Swedish economist Cassel, who denied the utility of the BIS in central banking cooperation (Karamikas 1931, p. 173) and considered that a central reserve bank for the world could not at the same time safely and properly "act on a grand scale as an investment institution". G. P. Auld, "America and the New Bank", *Herald Tribune,* 9 December 1929.
196. "Capital Views on World Bank", *Wall Street Journal,* 24 October 1929.
197. Traylor, quoted in: "Traylor Defends Reparations Bank", *New York Times,* 14 November 1929.
198. G. P. Auld, "The International Bank", *Herald Tribune,* 19 November 1929; id., "Control of the International Bank", *Herald Tribune,* 22 November 1929; id., "A Central Bank of Central Banks", *Herald Tribune,* 26 November 1929; id., "America and the New Bank", *Herald Tribune,* 9 December 1929.
199. G. P. Auld, "The International Bank", *Herald Tribune,* 29 November 1929.
200. G. P. Auld, "America and the New Bank", *Herald Tribune,* 9 December 1929.
201. I. Marcosson, "The Bank of Banks", *Saturday Evening Post* (Philadelphia), 11 October 1930.
202. Morgan (1931), pp. 580–91 (in particular, pp. 590–1).
203. "International Bank Test Engages Europe", *Wall Street Journal* (Paris Office), 25 July 1929.
204. Argoud (1931), pp. 72–3; Karamikas (1931), pp. 168–9.
205. G. Royot, "La Banque des Règlements Internationaux après Baden-Baden et jusqu'après la deuxième conférence de La Haye (novembre 1929 – fin janvier 1930)", 10 July 1944, p. 5, BISA, 7.16(3) – *BIS History (Baffi papers),* box RBL B13.
206. Caillaux (1929), pp. 61–5 (in particular, p. 65). According to Karamikas (1931, p. 168), Joseph Caillaux (French senator and former president of the Conseil) had actively contributed to limiting the scope and possibilities of the new Bank.
207. Argoud (1931), pp. 73–4, 213–14. Also: Karamikas (1931), pp. 167–8; Mendès France (1930a).
208. "It is easy to see why the German banker should be attracted to the idea. He is the banker more in need than all other bankers of foreign credit. His life is one long chase for it". "International Bank Test Engages Europe", *Wall Street Journal* (Paris Office), 25 July 1929.
209. Holz (1977), pp. 270–362.
210. See: "Dr. Schacht and His Successor", *The Banker,* 14(51), April 1930, pp. 15–19. See also Schacht (1929a,b; 1931a,b).
211. Karamikas (1931), pp. 171–2.
212. See: Holz (1977), pp. 270–362; also, W. Rosenberg (1933), *Die Bank für Internationalen Zahlungsausgleich,* Berlin, mimeo (copy in BIS Library), pp. 16–17.
213. G. Royot, "La Banque des Règlements Internationaux après Baden-Baden et jusqu'après la deuxième conférence de La Haye (novembre 1929 – fin janvier 1930)", 10 July 1944, pp. 2–3, BISA, 7.16(3) – *BIS History (Baffi papers),* box RBL B13.

214. Hahn et al. (1929).
215. Memorandum from L. Galantière, sent to Crane on 19 February 1930, p. 5, FRBNY, 797.3 (2) – *BIS General.*
216. Other authors also underscored the relevance for the future of promoting central bank cooperation: Lautenbach (1930), pp. 457–87 (in particular, p. 487).
217. Reisch (1930), p. 8.
218. "Die Reparationsbank – Ihre weltwirtschaftlichen Aufgaben", *Kölnische Zeitung,* 474, 30 August 1929.
219. Hantos (1931), p. 6.
220. Schleidt (1931), pp. 3–4.
221. See: Salin (1931), pp. 1–29 (in particular, pp. 26–7); Schleidt (1931), pp. 5–7.
222. "Freude der Schweiz über die Wahl Basels als Sitz der BIZ", *Wolff's Telegraphisches Büro,* 2320, 10 November 1929.
223. See Chapter 3.
224. "Conversations Quesnay avec le Gouverneur Norman, 24 avril 1930", BISA, 7.18(2) – *Papers McGarrah / Fraser,* box MCG3, 21.
225. The text was meant for confidential circulation to at least some of the members of the Board, since copies of it exist in central bank achives.
226. Quesnay cited (besides himself) Burgess, Stewart, and Shephard Morgan as those who jointly conceived the BIS.
227. "Conversations Quesnay avec le Gouverneur Norman, 24 avril 1930", p. 4, BISA, 7.18(2) – *Papers McGarrah / Fraser,* box MCG3, 21.
228. K. Blessing, "Gesichtspunkte für das Verhalten der Reichsbank in der BIZ", 8 April 1930, Bundesarchiv Berlin, R 2501 / 6735 – *Deutsche Reichsbank: Statistische Abteilung.*
229. The need to expand exports in order to be able to pay reparations had, of course, been a leitmotiv of German policy makers ever since 1919. See Chapter 14, "How (not) to Pay for the War", in Ferguson (1998), pp. 395–432.
230. All quotes on this and the previous page translated from: Blessing, "Gesichtspunkte für das Verhalten der Reichsbank in der BIZ", 8 April 1930, Bundesarchiv Berlin, R 2501 / 6735 – *Deutsche Reichsbank: Statistische Abteilung.*

Chapter 3

1. According to the provisions of the Hague Agreement of 20 January 1930, the Bank could not become operative until Germany and four of the five other signatory powers (Belgium, France, Great Britain, Italy, and Japan) had ratified the Agreement itself.
2. He gave, however, his unofficial blessing to the appointment of the U.S. members (see Chapter 2).
3. Gates McGarrah, Chairman of the Board of the Federal Reserve Bank of New York, had been a foreign director of the Reichsbank.
4. Leon Fraser had been, among other things, a counsel for the execution of the Dawes Plan.
5. "Proces-verbal de la réunion des Gouverneurs de banques centrales tenue à Rome à la Banca d'Italia le 26 février 1930", BISA, *Minutes of the Meetings of the Board of Directors.*

6. Giovanni Fumi, representative of J.P. Morgan & Co. in Rome, was empowered to sign the constitutive document on behalf of the U.S. banking group.
7. The BIS remained in its original premises until 1977, when it moved to a new building, nicknamed "the Tower", on the opposite side of the Basel Centralbahnplatz.
8. Dulles (1932), p. 66.
9. The two had not been appointed yet, but it was understood that they would take up their respective jobs.
10. "Minutes of the Meeting of the nominated Directors of the BIS held in Basel on the 22 and 23 April 1930", p. 1, BISA, *Minutes of the Meetings of the Board of Directors.*
11. Moreau soon resigned as governor of the Bank of France and was replaced on the BIS Board by his successor Moret on 25 September 1930.
12. Stringher died on 24 December 1930 and was replaced by Azzolini.
13. All members were present except Stringher, Reusch, and the two Japanese.
14. BISA, *Minutes of the Meetings of the Board of Directors,* 12 May 1930, p. 1.
15. "Minutes of the Meeting of the nominated Directors of the BIS held in Basel on the 22 and 23 April 1930", p. 1, pp. 3–4 and Annex A, BISA, *Minutes of the Meetings of the Board of Directors.* Luther argued that the Young Plan granted France and Germany "a position of preference [both had been given three directors each], but equal rights in the Bank" and that, in their opinion, "the election of Monsieur Pierre Quesnay as General Manager would not be in conformity with the aforementioned principle of parity" [ibid., Annex A].
16. McGarrah and Fraser to Harrison, Morgan, Young, and Reynolds, cable of 25 April 1930, BISA, 7.18(2) – *Papers McGarrah/Fraser,* box MCG7, f46.
17. The Department, initially called "Relations with Central Banks", then "Central Banking Department", and from 1932 on "Monetary and Economic Department" (or MED, as it is known to this day), was at the beginning left without formal organisation, pending contacts with the various central banks concerning their views on the matter and for them to appoint ad hoc officials "to follow the activities of the BIS". BISA, *Minutes of the Meetings of the Board of Directors,* 14 July 1930, Annex H.
18. The Banking Department consisted of an investment division (headed by Marcel van Zeeland) and a foreign exchange division (led by Takizawa).
19. Rodd was seconded to the BIS by Norman "for as long as may be necessary" after Siepmann, who had been closely involved in getting the BIS started, had declined to move to Basel for personal reasons. Norman to McGarrah, 20 May 1930, BISA, 7.18(2) – *Papers McGarrah/Fraser,* box MCG3, 22. Rodd returned to his job at the Bank of England in November 1931 and was succeeded by Porters.
20. Dulles (1932), p. 64.
21. BISA, *Minutes of the Meetings of the Board of Directors,* 16 June 1930, pp. 7–8.
22. Jacobsson (1979), p. 96.
23. Fraser to H. B. Elliston (Council on Foreign Relations, New York), 19 July 1930. BISA, 7.18(2) – *Papers McGarrah/Fraser,* box MCG7, f53.
24. In particular through the BIS's Annual Report, which quickly gained a solid reputation in the international financial world, but also through country reports and analytical studies on monetary policy issues produced at the BIS and circulated among member central banks (the Central Bank Publications series, BISA).

25. Dulles (1932), p. 57.
26. Among those who had been in Berlin were Goodwin, Colenutt, Bourgeot, and Blessing, the future president of the Deutsche Bundesbank.
27. These included Quesnay (who had spent many months in Austria), Simon, and van Zeeland.
28. Dulles (1932), pp. 59–60. This is a valuable source, especially since archival material on early staff, organisation, and working atmosphere is scarce.
29. Siepmann to Fraser, 3 May 1930, BISA, 7.18(2) – *Papers McGarrah/Fraser,* box MCG2, f14.
30. "Minutes of the Meeting of the nominated Directors of the BIS held in Basel on the 22 and 23 April 1930", p. 9, BISA, *Minutes of the Meetings of the Board of Directors.*
31. Excluding about 26 persons, classified as minor staff.
32. "Present salaries, Management and staff", in BISA, 7.18(2) – *Papers McGarrah/Fraser,* box MCG8, f59. The breakdown by departments was as follows: management, 14 (including seven secretaries); banking department, 17; central banking department, 7; general secretariat, 57; minor staff, 26.
33. BIS, *First Annual Report,* Basel, 19 May 1931, Annex II. The total number of employees recorded in the Annual Report is 94.
34. *Report of the Agent General for Reparation Payments,* Berlin, 21 May 1930, p. 19.
35. "List of staff grouped by nationalities", BISA, 7.18(2) – *Papers McGarrah/Fraser,* box MCG8, f59.
36. Dulles (1932), pp. 58–9.
37. Dulles (1980), p. 126. At the time, Fraser (writing to Eleanor's brother, future secretary of state John Foster Dulles) explained the incident by saying that he could not set a precedent that would have made it impossible "to refuse similar courtesies to those recommended by directors of other nationalities", adding that "the work of this bank, like that of any other, is in large measure confidential". See Fraser to J. F. Dulles, 14 October 1930, BISA, 7.18(2) – *Papers McGarrah/Fraser,* box MCG7, f53.
38. Merle Cochran was the U.S. consul in Basel in 1931–32. From January 1933, he acted as first secretary and financial attaché to the U.S. Embassy in Paris. He continued to travel to Basel on the occasion of the monthly Board meetings until the late 1930s. Cochran was extremely well introduced in the central bankers' world, meeting regularly with people like Norman, Schacht, Trip, and Francqui and with Fraser and Jacobsson of the BIS. Until late 1933 – that is, until shortly after the 1933 Monetary and Economic Conference in London, his detailed reports were sent directly to the U.S. Secretary of State, who shared them with the Secretary of the Treasury. After 1933–34, the reports diminished considerably in frequency and length. These reports provide valuable insight on the atmosphere in Basel and on the U.S. administration's thinking about European and monetary issues. They are preserved partly in: NARA, RG 84 – *State Department, Records of Foreign Service Posts, American Embassy Paris*; and NARA, RG 39 – *U.S. Treasury, Records of the Bureau of Accounts, Fiscal Relationships between the United States and the other Nations,* boxes 103–104. Thanks are due Harold James for drawing our attention to the second reference.
39. English, French, German, and Italian; thus only one of the languages of the seven signatory powers of the Hague Agreement (Japanese) was not included in the BIS official ones.

40. BISA, *Suggested Plan for the Bank for International Settlements,* 9 March 1930, Annex I, Section II.
41. BIS, *First Annual Report,* Basel, 19 May 1931, Annex IV.
42. Art. 8 of the BIS Statutes (1930).
43. In France and Belgium it was actually arranged for the general public to apply for shares. In the United Kingdom and Italy, the shares were retained by the central banks. See BISA, *Minutes of the Meetings of the Board of Directors,* 16 June 1930, p. 2.
44. Art. 15 of the BIS Statutes (1930).
45. Yago (2001).
46. McFadden was described as being "on a wild rampage about the Bank". His tirade against it in the House of Representatives on 10 February 1930 prompted Lamont to send him a letter detailing the factual mistakes contained in his speech. See Lamont to McFadden, 24 March 1930, BISA, 7.18(2) – *Papers McGarrah/Fraser,* box MCG7, f53. Undeterred, McFadden repeated his attack both in a radio broadcast and in a speech delivered in New York in early April; see Reynolds to McGarrah, 10 April 1930, BISA, 7.18(2) – *Papers McGarrah/Fraser,* box MCG6, f49. Louis T. McFadden, Chairman of the House of Representatives Committee on Banking and Currency (1920–31), later became notorious for his violent attacks in 1932–34 against "international bankers" in general and the Federal Reserve Board in particular.
47. J.P. Morgan & Co., the First National Bank of New York, and the First National Bank of Chicago.
48. McGarrah to Reynolds, 30 June 1930, BISA, 7.18(2) – *Papers McGarrah/Fraser,* box MCG6, f49.
49. Time was deemed a crucial factor because "the BIS is to start activity on Swiss territory, so that its relations with Switzerland will at once exert their effect, both as regards organisation and the operations". See Bachmann to McGarrah, 1 April 1930, BISA, 7.18(2) – *Papers McGarrah/Fraser,* box MCG6, f41.
50. Bachmann to McGarrah, 1 April 1930, BISA, 7.18(2) – *Papers McGarrah/Fraser,* box MCG6, f41.
51. Norman to McGarrah, 11 April 1930, BISA, 7.18(2) – *Papers McGarrah/Fraser,* box MCG3, f21.
52. "Minutes of the Meeting of the nominated Directors of the BIS held in Basel on the 22 and 23 April 1930", p. 5, BISA, *Minutes of the Meetings of the Board of Directors.*
53. In October, for instance, agreement seemed to exist about admitting as many as six new Board members. However, the Germans opposed a simultaneous membership of Czechoslovakia and Poland, while the French would only take Hungary (sponsored by Germany and Italy) if Czechoslovakia and Poland also were both admitted. See Pennachi a Azzolini, 22 October 1930, BdIHA.
54. Those of Austria, Bulgaria, Danzig, Denmark, Estonia, Finland, Greece, Hungary, Latvia, Lithuania, Portugal, and Norway. See BISA, *Minutes of the Meetings of the Board of Directors,* 12 May 1930, p. 6.
55. The National Bank of the Kingdom of Yugoslavia objected that, as the central bank of a country affected by reparations, it was not subject to the gold-standard rule for membership application under Art. 7(2) of the BIS Statutes. See BISA, *Minutes of*

the Meetings of the Board of Directors, 14 July 1930, p. 4. The Bank of Portugal would not join the BIS until 1951.

56. 165,100 shares at 2,500 Swiss gold francs (nominal capital 412.75 million Swiss francs, of which 25% or 103.18 million paid up).

57. McGarrah to Owen D. Young, 18 June 1930, BISA, 7.18(2) – *Papers McGarrah/Fraser,* box MCG7, f 53.

58. J.P. Morgan & Co. (NY) to D. Jay (Morgan Paris), cable of 17 March 1930, copied to Quesnay (for Moreau) and to McGarrah and Fraser, BISA, 7.18(3) – *Papers Quesnay,* Box QUE2, f 7.

59. Rooth to McGarrah, cable, 14 May 1930, BISA, 7.18(2) – *Papers McGarrah/Fraser,* box MCG6, f 40. Moreover, Rooth found the equivalent of $20 million allotted to Sweden to be "rather high", even though Krueger was assumed to take and hold as many as $15 million.

60. Dulles (1932), p. 364.

61. Ibid. In the end, however, the United States took a slightly larger share of the loan than France.

62. Interest was paid by presentation of coupons at one of the issuing houses on 1 June and 1 December of each year.

63. "The principal and interest of each bond shall be payable ... in the currency of the country in which it is issued, the unit of such currency being defined ... in all circumstances by the weight of fine gold determined by law as at present in force"; Article VI of the General Bond.

64. About 512 million RM were earmarked for financing programmes of deliveries in kind; the remainder could be converted into foreign currencies according to the Young Plan's provisions.

65. BIS, *First Annual Report,* Basel, 1931, p. 8 and Annex X.

66. Dulles (1932), p. 347.

67. BIS, *First Annual Report,* Basel, 1931, p. 5.

68. Moreover, the Young Plan allowed for more funds to be kept in Reichsmarks than was previously the case, and exchange rates benefited from this as well.

69. BIS, *First Annual Report,* Basel, 1931, Annexes III and IV.

70. France was required to keep an additional deposit to be held "on account of the Guaranty Fund which the French government is obliged to create in proportion to the mobilisation of the German annuities". BIS, *First Annual Report,* Basel, 1931, p. 3.

71. 71% of deposits had been effected in dollars, 11% in Reichsmarks, 9% in pounds sterling, and the rest in other European currencies. BIS, *First Annual Report,* Basel, 1931, p. 5.

72. Ibid.

73. McGarrah to Reynolds, 17 July 1930, BISA, 7.18(2) – *Papers McGarrah/Fraser,* box MCG6, f 49. It was, according to Merle Cochran, President McGarrah who gave "his co-workers 'money-sense' which they did not previously possess". Merle Cochran to the Undersecretary of State, 11 April 1933, NARA, RG 39 – *U.S. Treasury, Records of the Bureau of Accounts, Fiscal Relationships between the United States and other Nations,* box 103.

74. "Sentiment in England is decidedly more friendly, and the position of aloofness we immediately assumed when the Old Lady seemed inclined to hold back has resulted

in good cooperation". McGarrah to Reynolds, 17 July 1930, BISA, 7.18(2) – *Papers McGarrah/Fraser*, box MCG6, f49.

75. "To discover an objective for the Bank which will differentiate it from other financial agencies is, I should say, by no means an easy matter, especially on the purely banking side". Sprague to McGarrah, 5 September 1930, BISA, 7.18(2) – *Papers McGarrah/Fraser*, box MCG3, f21.

76. BISA, *Minutes of the Meetings of the Board of Directors,* 16 June 1930, p. 11; *Summary and Conclusions of the special committee with respect to the operations of the BIS,* 17 June 1930. The committee consisted of Moreau, Norman, Luther, and Beneduce, the Board's four most authoritative members.

77. Harrison to McGarrah, 12 September 1930, BISA, 7.18(2) – *Papers McGarrah/Fraser,* box MCG6, f48.

78. McGarrah to the governors of the BIS shareholding central banks, 6 May 1930, BISA, 7.18(2) – *Papers McGarrah/Fraser,* box MCG6, f47; BISA, *Minutes of the Meetings of the Board of Directors,* 12 May 1930, p. 7.

79. See Harrison to BIS, 24 June 1930, BISA, 7.18(2) – *Papers McGarrah/Fraser,* box MCG6, f47. Harrison, however, did not waive his right to object to BIS operations and asked to be informed of all such operations by "your passing any such funds through your account with us".

80. BISA, *Minutes of the Meetings of the Board of Directors,* 14 July 1930, Annex D, Report on the operations of the Bank, p. 6.

81. Ibid., p. 5.

82. One of them was Jackson Reynolds, who said: "When I was negotiating with the Treasuries in the Hague for [the BIS] compensation as Trustee, I was pretty pessimistic about the possibility of general business and permanent deposits with the Bank. It really quite amazes me to see the progress [the BIS is] making in getting away from the European conception of [its] functions of being simply a reparation bank". Reynolds to McGarrah, 2 September 1930, BISA, 7.18(2) – *Papers McGarrah/Fraser,* box MCG6, f49.

83. BISA, *Minutes of the Meetings of the Board of Directors,* 13 October 1930, p. 7.

84. BISA, *Minutes of the Meetings of the Board of Directors,* 8 December 1930, p. 5 and Annex XI/G.

85. Baffi (2002), pp. 88–9.

86. Norman to McGarrah, 2 February 1931, BISA, 7.18(2) – *Papers McGarrah/Fraser,* box MCG3, f21.

87. Baffi (2002), p. 90.

88. This was a theme often repeated by Luther in public addresses. He had borrowed the term "invisible occupation" (*unsichtbare Besatzung*) from Dr. Melchior; see Luther (1964), p. 112.

89. Baffi (2002), p. 91.

90. Moret to McGarrah, 4 March 1931; and "Projet de création d'une Banque Internationale de Prêts à des États et autres entités publiques", BISA, 7.18(2) – *Papers McGarrah/Fraser,* box MCG2, f11.

91. "I was very willingly among the first to express my agreement with the generous views by which Mr. Montagu Norman's proposal was inspired". Moret to McGarrah, 4 March 1931, BISA, 7.18(2) – *Papers McGarrah/Fraser,* box MCG2, f11.

92. "Projet de création d'une Banque Internationale de Prêts à des États et autres entités publiques", BISA, 7.18(2) – *Papers McGarrah /Fraser,* box MCG2, f 11, p. 3.
93. Ibid., p. 7.
94. Baffi (2002), p. 94.
95. BISA, *Minutes of the Meetings of the Board of Directors,* 9 March 1931, p. 6.
96. The other members were Beneduce, Farnier, Kindersley, and Melchior.
97. BISA, *Minutes of the Meetings of the Board of Directors,* 18 and 19 May 1931, Annex XI/G: "Report of the Committee created to examine the question of middle term credits", p. 1.
98. However, by that time, the Commission of Inquiry for European Union – set up in the context of the League of Nations to study Briand's proposals for the creation of a United States of Europe – was already performing its swan song. Walters (1952), pp. 430–4.
99. BISA, *Minutes of the Meetings of the Board of Directors,* 8 June 1931, Annex XII/D: "Report on the meetings of the BIS committee held in Brussels on 3 and 4 June, 1931".
100. BISA, *Minutes of the Meetings of the Board of Directors,* 8 June 1931, pp. 3–4.
101. Mitzakis (1939), p. 189. The book covers the BIS relations with Spain in a fairly detailed way, since Mitzakis was then the BIS representative in Spain. Facts in this section, whenever not covered by primary sources, are drawn from this book and from Aceña (2000).
102. Aceña (2000), p. 16.
103. What follows is drawn from the minutes of the meeting: "Conversations de Paris entre la Délégation de la Banque d'Espagne et les Représentants de la BRI, 16–20 octobre 1930", BISA, 7.18(2) – *Papers McGarrah /Fraser,* box MCG5, f 39.
104. The prewar parity was 25 pesetas to the pound. The external value was around 50 pesetas to the pound, while the Bank of Spain estimated wholesale prices to be 172 (1914 = 100), hence an estimated "internal" value of about 40 pesetas to the pound.
105. A 53% cover ratio of the outstanding circulation surely aroused Norman's envy.
106. Norman to Bas, 27 October 1930, BISA, 7.18(2) – *Papers McGarrah /Fraser,* box MCG5, f 39.
107. The BIS Board discussed the matter at its meeting of 10 November and authorised "the Bank management to continue the exchange of views with the Governor of the Bank of Spain regarding the stabilisation of the peseta". BISA, *Minutes of the Meetings of the Board of Directors,* 19 November 1930, p. 3.
108. Aceña (2000), p. 16.
109. The exchange rate had appreciated since the Paris meeting, and wholesale prices remained stable.
110. The concentration of all foreign exchange transactions in a single central office was achieved through the creation by Wais and Bas of the Centro Oficial de Contratación de Moneda (COCM). Quesnay also recommended that the Bank of Spain set up a research department to help determine and monitor the peseta's exchange rate. The Bank of Spain's Servicio de Estudios was created on 2 January 1931, closely modelled on the Bank of France's Service des Etudes Economiques, of which Quesnay had been the manager; Aceña (2000), pp. 15–19. Mitzakis seems

to hint that the suggestion for the creation of a research department came from him rather than from Quesnay.

111. Mitzakis to Quesnay, 16 December 1930, BISA, 7.18(2) – *Papers McGarrah/Fraser,* box MCG5, f 39.

112. A gold shipment for £2 million made in October had finally reached London and been put under BIS dossier for the Bank of Spain.

113. "We have been negotiating on the subject of the desired credit against the pledge of the gold now in London, but have subordinated any such credit to the shipment of further amounts of gold from Spain pursuant to a formal resolution of the Board of the Bank of Spain". McGarrah to Norman, 16 December 1930, BISA, 7.18(2) – *Papers McGarrah/Fraser,* box MCG5, f 39. Officially, the BIS insisted on pound drafts being covered by further gold shipments in order to leave enough free gold in London to defend the exchange rate of the peseta. Mitzakis, however, suggests that there were more substantial concerns, due to forward positions on the Spanish currency carried over from previous years, which could be easily covered (and eventually liquidated) only with an appreciation of the exchange rate of the peseta. Mitzakis (1939), pp. 197–9.

114. An advance of £2 million was offered by the BIS on 11 December 1930, but the Spanish answer was considered inconclusive and nothing came of it. Note by Fraser to Quesnay and Rodd of 17 December 1930, BISA, 7.18(2) – *Papers McGarrah/Fraser,* box MCG5, f 39.

115. Mitzakis to Quesnay, 16 December 1930, BISA, 7.18(2) – *Papers McGarrah/Fraser,* box MCG5, f 39.

116. The head of the Paris office of J.P. Morgan & Co.

117. "The Ambassador was able to re-establish direct communication between Governor Bas and the BIS". Jay to Fraser, 16 December 1930, BISA, 7.18(2) – *Papers McGarrah/Fraser,* box MCG5, f 39.

118. Fraser wrote to Norman suggesting the names of Siepmann, Beneduce, Paul van Zeeland, Walter Stuart, or "finally and distinctly last of all a Scandinavian named Jacobsson who, when connected with the League of Nations, went through many of their stabilisation projects, including the Portuguese". Fraser to Norman, 16 December 1930 and 17 December 1930, BISA, 7.18(2) – *Papers McGarrah/Fraser,* box MCG5, f 39.

119. Norman to Fraser, 18 December 1930, BISA, 7.18(2) – *Papers McGarrah/Fraser,* box MCG5, f 39.

120. Around the middle of December the Air Force seemed to be siding with the Republicans (they even dropped political leaflets on Madrid), and workers staged numerous protests.

121. Fraser to Norman, 16 December 1930, BISA, 7.18(2) – *Papers McGarrah/Fraser,* box MCG5, f 39.

122. "With petty revolutions operating on land and on sea and in the air, it is hardly the moment for the Spaniards to spend large sums in the hope of overcoming economic movements which are in fact the result of political reactions and affairs". Fraser to Norman, 16 December 1930, BISA, 7.18(2) – *Papers McGarrah/Fraser,* box MCG5, f 39.

123. Mitzakis to Quesnay, 11 December 1930 and 16 December 1930, BISA, 7.18(2) – *Papers McGarrah/Fraser,* box MCG5, f 39.

124. Mitzakis (1939), p. 200.
125. Mitzakis to Fraser, 30 December 1930, BISA, 7.18(2) – *Papers McGarrah/Fraser,* box MCG5, f39.
126. "Projet de déclaration confidentielle du Gouverneur de la Banque d'Espagne au Président de la BRI et aux gouverneurs des banques d'émission d'Europe, d'Amérique et du Japon", BISA, 7.18(2) – *Papers McGarrah/Fraser,* box MCG5, f39.
127. Fraser to Norman, 12 January 1931, BISA, 7.18(2) – *Papers McGarrah/Fraser,* box MCG5, f39.
128. 18 February 1931.

Chapter 4

1. National Industrial Conference Board (1931), p. 4.
2. BIS, *Second Annual Report,* Basel, 10 May 1932, p. 12.
3. Carr (1947), p. 139.
4. In early 1931, a committee of the League of Nations unsuccessfully attempted to draw up a plan for an overall lowering of trade barriers between European countries.
5. The repudiation of Hoover's former, more moderate policy of tariff revision in an election year did not yield the expected political benefit: the Republicans lost control of Congress.
6. Costigliola (1984), p. 223.
7. On the Hague Conference(s) and the Young Plan, see Chapter 2.
8. Costigliola (1984), p. 233.
9. Bennett (1962), pp. 18ff. Also: Schacht (1953), pp. 321–8.
10. National Industrial Conference Board (1931), p. 20. The paper was written or at least approved by such people as Franz von Mendelsson, Carl von Siemens, and Albert Voegler.
11. Bennett (1962), pp. 18ff. Also: Schacht (1953), p. 20.
12. Bennett (1962), pp. 24ff.
13. Ibid., p. 38. The Conference of the International Chamber of Commerce in Washington (May 1931) came to the same conclusion, which may have further prompted Hoover to take action. Rosengarten (2001), pp. 218–23.
14. Bennett (1962), p. 39.
15. Ibid.
16. Bordo, Choudhri, and Schwartz (2002), pp. 1–28.
17. Hsieh and Romer (2001), p. 44.
18. Kindleberger (1987), XV: "I believe that if the runs on Austria, Germany and Britain had been halted by timely international help on a massive scale, the basic recuperative powers of competitive markets would have prevented the depression from going on so long and so deep".
19. Bennett (1962), p. 25.
20. A *Zollunion* proposal had been discussed in 1918.
21. Stimson's words, quoted by Costigliola (1984), p. 235.
22. Schubert (1991), p. 7.
23. Ibid., p. 10.

24. Schubert (1991).
25. Toniolo (1980). In English: G. Toniolo, "Italian Banking, 1919–1939", in C. P. Feinstein (1995), *Banking, Currency and Finance in Europe between the Wars,* Clarendon Press, Oxford, pp. 296–314; and Toniolo (1994).
26. There are several contemporary accounts and later historical studies of the Credit-Anstalt and Austrian crises of 1931. Some of them will be quoted in this chapter. In what follows, I concentrate on the role played by the BIS and give a general account of the development of the crisis only in order to place the action by the BIS in its proper context.
27. Stiefel (1983); see also Schubert (1991), pp. 8–10. For more details see the Confidential Report sent to the BIS by G. W. J. Bruins on 9 July 1931. BISA, 7.18(9) – *Papers Rodd,* box ROD1, f1. Also: BISA, 6.30 – *Granting of Credit of 100,000,000 schillings to the Austrian National Bank, 1931.*
28. The legal basis for the execution of the agreement was provided by the Credit-Anstalt Law of 14 May 1931, no. 136.
29. According to Schubert (1991, p. 12), "in only two days the CA lost about 16% of its volume of deposits, and within two weeks about 30%".
30. Rodd to Fraser, 12 May 1931, BISA, 7.18(2) – *Papers McGarrah/Fraser,* box MCG1, f1.
31. Given the existence of two previous international loans sponsored by the League of Nations, authorisation from the latter was required for this additional placement overseas of Treasury bonds. The League's Control Committee authorised the issue on 18 May. "The placement then met with serious political obstacles"; Mitzakis (1939), p. 217.
32. According to the BIS's man in Vienna (see subsequent text): "The losses of the Credit-Anstalt are believed to be covered fully by a figure of 140 millions which is made up as to 60 millions by a hangover from the Bodencreditanstalt situation on account of bad bills and current accounts, 40 millions on own losses on current account and interest written off, and 40 million losses on portfolio. I am assured that the total figure represents the full ascertainable losses". Rodd to Fraser, 12 May 1931, BISA, 7.18(9) – *Papers Rodd,* box ROD1, f1.
33. "My experience suggests", Rodd continued in the above-quoted letter, "that the position may have been too optimistically regarded". Rodd to Fraser, 12 May 1931, BISA, 7.18(9) – *Papers Rodd,* box ROD1, f1.
34. Sayers (1976a), p. 234.
35. Schubert (1991), p. 159, quoting Kernbauer.
36. Sayers (1976a), p. 389.
37. Two other BIS men, Karl Blessing (originally from the Reichsbank) and Dr. Simon, were dispatched soon afterwards.
38. Clarke (1967).
39. BISA, *Minutes of the Meetings of the Board of Directors,* 18 May 1931, p. 1.
40. Among the reasons why the BIS, at this stage, was well disposed towards the National Bank of Austria was the fact that the latter was a net depositor with the institution in Basel. Moreover, "Austria was one of the first countries to follow the appeal to assist the BIS in its task of distributing over countries requiring funds any available surplus of its own resources. This attitude alone would have given Austria a moral title for expecting adequate support from the BIS even had the present

plight not made such a support imperative". "Report on Arrangements in Connection with the Austrian Situation", 8 June 1931, p. 3, BISA, 6.30 – *Granting of Credit of 100,000,000 schillings to Austrian National Bank, 1931*, vol. II, f1.

41. Kindleberger (1973), p. 131.
42. At the time, deposits by foreign banks with the Credit-Anstalt were estimated to total about $72 million (about 530 million Austrian schillings). Deposits by U.S. banks totalled $23.9 million and those by U.K. banks $26.76 million, with French, Dutch, and Swiss banks holding most of the rest. "Confidential Papers on Austria and Hungary by Mr. Rodd", BISA, 7.18(9) – *Papers Rodd*, box ROD1, f1.
43. Draft of a wire from Simon, 18 May 1931, not sent officially "for certain reasons" but telephoned to Rodd, to be communicated to the BIS management. BISA, 6.30 – *Granting of Credit of 100,000,000 schillings to Austrian National Bank, 1931*, vol. II, f1.
44. Simon to Fraser, 19 May 1931 and 20 May 1931, BISA, 6.30 – *Granting of Credit of 100,000,000 schillings to Austrian National Bank, 1931*, vol. II, f1.
45. From 12 to 29 May, the ANB lost 250 million schillings, bringing the gold-to-circulation ratio down from 80% to 50%. Krug (1932), p. 89.
46. Conversation between Siepmann and Rodd, 26 May 1931, BISA, 6.30 – *Granting of Credit of 100,000,000 schillings to Austrian National Bank, 1931*, vol. II, f1.
47. Simon to Fraser, 21 May 1931, BISA, 6.30 – *Granting of Credit of 100,000,000 schillings to Austrian National Bank, 1931*, vol. II, f1.
48. BIS to Devisenleitung, Vienna, 21 May 1931, BISA, 7.18(2) – *Papers McGarrah/Fraser*, box MCG1, f1. Also: Mitzakis (1939), p. 209.
49. The BIS, on the other hand, was not prepared to issue a declaration containing a wholesale commitment to the "maintenance of stability of the Austrian schilling", as requested by the ANB. Oesterreichische Nationalbank to BIS, 28 May 1931, BISA, 6.30 – *Granting of Credit of 100,000,000 schillings to Austrian National Bank, 1931*, vol. II, f1.
50. The Federal Reserve Bank of New York, the Bank of England, the Bank of France, the Bank of Italy, and the Reichsbank subscribed 7.7 million schillings each. The central banks of Belgium, the Netherlands, Czechoslovakia, Poland, and Greece each participated with 3.85 million, and the Swiss National Bank with 2.25 million.
51. Technically, the participating central banks, acting through the BIS as their agent, would rediscount bills or advance against the security of bills up to a total of 60 million schillings, with the rest of the sum being put up directly by the BIS.
52. The agreement stipulated that: "In no event will it be a good answer for the ANB to claim under the present agreement that the Austrian government has through embargo, prohibition of export of gold or currency, or any other form of interference, including the declaration of a moratorium, frustrated the carrying out of any of the obligations of the ANB". "Memorandum of Agreement between the ANB and the BIS", 30 May 1931, p. 2, BISA, 7.18(2) – *Papers McGarrah/Fraser*, box MCG1, f1.
53. Bruins to McGarrah, 3 June 1931, BISA, 7.18(2) – *Papers McGarrah/Fraser*, box MCG1, f1.
54. Telephone message (anonymous) from Vienna to BIS, 1 June 1931, BISA, 7.18(2) – *Papers McGarrah/Fraser*, box MCG1, f1.
55. "Short Resume of statement made by the General Manager, M. Quesnay, in the meeting of Governors held at Basle in the BIS on Sunday, 7 June, 1931, from 4 till

7.45 pm", BISA, 7.18(2) – *Papers McGarrah/Fraser,* box MCG1, f1. Quotations that follow are from this document.

56. The expression is borrowed from the title of A. Cairncross's book on post–World War II Germany; Cairncross (1951), pp. 19–34.

57. In a strict technical sense, the loan was actually granted (and the Austrian National Bank paid the attendant commission fees), but it could not be drawn before the successful international flotation of the government's issue. This position was re-iterated at two successive Board meetings in response to Austria's request that the money be actually put at its disposal.

58. The following account is based on an anonymous internal BIS memorandum, most likely by Rodd, dated Basel, 20 June 1931, BISA, 7.18(2) – *Papers McGar-rah/Fraser,* box MCG1, f2.

59. Bennett (1962), pp. 150–1.

60. "Austria", 8 July 1931, BISA, 7.18(2) – *Papers McGarrah/Fraser,* box MCG1, f2. The Swiss banks also refused to participate in the Credit-Anstalt creditor agreement and were withdrawing their funds from that bank.

61. McGarrah to Harrison, 18 August 1931, BISA, 7.18(2) – *Papers McGarrah/Fraser,* box MCG1, f2.

62. According to a report by Bruins to Rodd in Basel, dated 14 September 1931, BISA, 7.18(2) – *Papers McGarrah/Fraser,* box MCG1, f2.

63. "Foreign exchange payments were centralised at the ANB, and Austrians had to register all their foreign exchange holdings. The ANB had the right to buy any or all of them". Schubert (1991), p. 16.

64. Oesterreichische Nationalbank to McGarrah, 10 October 1931, BISA, 7.18(2) – *Papers McGarrah/Fraser,* box MCG1, f2.

65. League of Nations. Economic, Financial and Transit Department (1944), pp. 234–5.

66. Nötel (1984), p. 170.

67. The term is from BIS, *Second Annual Report,* Basel, 10 May 1932, p. 8.

68. Scitovszky (1931), p. 8.

69. Mitzakis (1939), p. 239.

70. Participants were the central banks of the United Kingdom, France, Italy, Belgium, the Netherlands, Czechoslovakia, and Poland, along with the Federal Reserve Bank of New York and the BIS itself.

71. The loan was made available to the National Bank of Hungary in two tranches, on 18 June and 22 June.

72. Participants in the new loan were the Bank of England and the Federal Reserve Bank of New York, for $3 million each, the Bank of Italy ($1 million), the National Bank of Romania ($500,000) and the Bank of Greece ($150,000). The remaining $3.35 million was put up by the BIS. BISA, 6.31 – *Granting of credit to Hungarian National Bank, June 1931.*

73. Mitzakis (1939), p. 243.

74. A plan was in fact circulated for a 20% devaluation of the currency through the in-troduction of a new currency called the *turul* with a gold parity equal to 80% of the gold weight of the pengö. Memorandum by E. Stein, General Manager of the Pester Ungarische Commercial Bank, 12 August 1931, BISA, 7.18(9) – *Papers Rodd,* box ROD1, f2.

75. Complications and misunderstandings arose between London, where individual agreements seemed to be preferred, and New York, which favoured a general standstill. Goodhue to Weiss, 24 August and 26 August 1931, BISA, 7.18(9) – *Papers Rodd*, box ROD1, f2.
76. Stein to Gannon (c/o BIS), 17 August 1932, BISA, 7.18(9) – *Papers Rodd*, box ROD1, f2.
77. Different types of gold guarantees were given. For details, see Mitzakis (1939), 244–5.
78. BISA, *Minutes of the Meetings of the Board of Directors,* 13 November 1933, p. 4.
79. Bolgert recommended a credit of $5 million; Mitzakis (1939), p. 251. Also: BISA, 6.35 – *Granting of credit of $3,000,000 to National Bank of Yugoslavia, July 1931.*
80. Mitzakis (1939), p. 252.
81. For an extreme but interesting view of the effects of American loans to Germany, see Schuker (1988).
82. *Report of the Committee appointed on the recommendation of the London Conference 1931,* Basel, 18 August 1931, pp. 2–5. Germany's total foreign debt (private and public) of 25 billion RM (or nearly $6 billion) at the end of 1930 represented 35%–40% of total national income at that time (estimated at 60–70 billion RM; Mitchell (2003), p. 910). This foreign debt was partly balanced by some 10 billion RM in foreign assets held by Germany, so that net foreign liabilities amounted to rather more than 15 billion RM. The real problems were the disproportionately high share of short-term credits, which were liquidated at an accelerating pace in early 1931 (between January and July 1931 no less than 2.9 billion RM – or nearly $700 million – in short-term foreign credits were withdrawn from Germany); and the high interest rates payable on this debt (5.5%–6% on average and often more), which was particularly harmful in the deflationary environment of 1930–31.
83. Schuker (1988), p. 51.
84. James (1986), pp. 293ff.
85. The fact that France's goodwill towards Austria was conditional on the shelving of the customs union with Germany provided an additional element of political uncertainty.
86. On 26 May 1931 Harrison cabled McGarrah: "I was somehow surprised at the sudden and substantial overnight drop of the German exchange below our gold point. I assume this may in some way be a reflection of difficulties in Vienna but would appreciate any views you might have with regard to it". The BIS President replied that he, too, felt that Germany was suffering from Austrian contagion. BISA, 7.18(2) – *Papers McGarrah/Fraser,* box MCG1, f1.
87. Schuker (1988), p. 56.
88. Clarke (1967), p. 187 (Italian edition).
89. James (1986), p. 302. According to James, "the initial foreign attack came from France".
90. Clement (2002), pp. 142–3. The reason given by Dreyse was that the Austrian precedent was not convincing (telephone conversation, Siepmann–Dreyse, 19 June 1931, in Bank of England Archive, OV 34/80). It is more likely, however, that the real reasons were political and pretty much the same as those behind Schacht's withdrawal

from Baden-Baden. The BIS was not popular in Germany because of its link with reparations.

91. Clarke (1967), p. 193.
92. Ibid., p. 191. Luther later claimed that he had initially pressed for a much larger credit, but this is not corroborated by the archival evidence. Luther (1964), p. 173.
93. Clarke (1967), p. 191. According to Clarke, the State Department was afraid that a loan to the Reichsbank would take the pressure off France to accept the Hoover moratorium.
94. Harrison's telephone conversation with Norman, 23 June, 10:45, FRBNY, *Harrison Papers,* 3115.2. Harrison suggested (after talking with McGarrah) that the BIS should be invited to participate. Norman said he "did not know whether they could or would do so and that they were so slow to act he was afraid there would be no time, but even so he agreed he would invite the BIS".
95. McGarrah let it be known that he was disappointed that the negotiations had taken place in London rather than in Basel and that the BIS had been involved only when the details had been finalised. According to McGarrah, that was "precisely the kind of credit which it is for the BIS to organise". Clement (2002), p. 143.
96. It is not clear from Harrison's close monitoring of the situation whether the final agreement was actually reached on 24 or 25 June.
97. Harrison's memorandum on his phone conversation with McGarrah, 25 June 1931, BISA, 7.16(3) – *BIS History (Baffi papers),* box RBL/B1.
98. Harrison's telephone conversation with Norman, 25 June 1931, 10:45, FRBNY, *Harrison Papers,* 3115.2. Norman said (for the second time in two days) that the loan had been arranged. Harrison complained that France was again against the Hoover proposal and that this was reflected on the markets.
99. Harrison's telephone conversation with Norman, 1 July 1931, FRBNY, *Harrison Papers,* 3115.2.
100. Luther to McGarrah, 5 July 1931, BISA, 7.18(2) – *Papers McGarrah/Fraser,* box MCG3, f18.
101. James (1986), p. 308.
102. In mid-June, the company had disclosed huge losses.
103. James (1986), p. 309.
104. Ibid.
105. As noted by Eichengreen (1992, p. 274): "The German Bank Law in fact permitted the General Council of the Reichsbank to reduce the cover ratio to less than 40% if the central bank paid a tax on the deficiency.... But to allow the cover ratio to fall beyond 40% while the gold standard remained in effect threatened to undermine the confidence in the future of convertibility and provoke a run on the Reichsbank's remaining gold".
106. Bennett (1962), p. 224. The guarantee was publicised through the device of publishing a letter from some of the prominent bankers and industrialists involved.
107. Ibid. Brüning claims in his memoirs that by this time he had become convinced that a state capital injection into the ailing banking system would be unavoidable, and that he was very sceptical about the chances of success (and indeed wisdom) of Luther's last-ditch attempt to obtain a large external credit. Pressure to replace Luther with his predecessor Schacht was already mounting, but Brüning decided against it, in part not to annoy Germany's creditors. Brüning (1970), pp. 306–9.

108. Luther (1964), pp. 185–8; Bennett (1962), pp. 225–6. The close personal bond that existed between Norman and Schacht was completely absent from Norman's relationship with Luther. Indeed, in his memoirs Brüning relates that Norman told him he could not stand Luther, whom he regarded as a "whinger". Brüning (1970), p. 307.

109. Bennett (1962), p. 230.

110. Ibid., p. 234.

111. James (1986), p. 314.

112. Harrison–McGarrah telephone conversation, 13 July 1931, BISA, 7.16(3) – *BIS History (Baffi papers),* box RBL/B1.

113. Harrison–McGarrah telephone conversation, 11 July 1931, BISA, 7.16(3) – *BIS History (Baffi papers),* box RBL/B1.

114. Bennett (1962), p. 249.

115. On the Wiggin Committee, see Chapter 5.

116. Brüning (1970), p. 309.

117. The financial "rescue" of Austria, in 1922–23, by a handful of countries under the auspices and authority of the League of Nations hardly qualifies as a precedent: the task then was to rebuild the public finances of a small, almost-failed state rather than stabilising the international monetary system by preventing the spread of contagion from a banking crisis. On the League of Nations and Austria, see Walters (1952), pp. 206ff.

118. Toynbee (1932).

119. Bennett (1962); Clavin (1996).

120. Eichengreen (1992), p. 286.

121. A memorandum by Simon, while praising the speed with which the BIS coordinated the organisation of the Austrian loan, noted that nevertheless a certain number of days were spent obtaining approval from all central banks concerned and suggested that, in the future, "it would seem useful to get ready in advance a kind of draft agreement". Dr. Simon, "Lessons of the Austrian Crisis", 2 June 1931, FRBNY, 797.36, p. 14.

122. Eichengreen and Temin (1997).

123. Keynes (1936), p. 383.

124. Fisher (1933), pp. 337–57.

125. Dr. Simon, "Lessons of the Austrian Crisis", 2 June 1931, FRBNY, 797.36.

126. Ibid., p. 1.

127. Ibid., p. 2.

128. Van Hengel to McGarrah, 11 June 1931, BISA, 7.18(2) – *Papers McGarrah/Fraser,* box MCG1, f1. The document refers to an almost identical letter sent a few days earlier to Norman. In early 1932 the board of directors of the Credit-Anstalt asked van Hengel again to take over the reins of the ailing bank. On this occasion, he accepted and became director general on 15 February 1932. By the time of his accidental death in 1936, he had succeeded in putting the bank back on the right track. J. P. B. Jonker, "Hengel, Adrianus van", in *Biografisch Woordenboek van Nederland,* vol. 6 (forthcoming). Advance publication: ⟨http://www.inghist.nl/Onderzoek/Projecten/BWN/lemmata/bwn6/hengel⟩.

129. Apparently he even refused to receive van Hengel, who finished his letter by "apologising for the frankness, perhaps even rudeness, in which I expose my views. As

an excuse I reiterate that you forced me thereto by your unwillingness to *discuss* matters with me". Van Hengel to McGarrah, 11 June 1931, BISA, 7.18(2) – *Papers McGarrah/Fraser,* box MCG1, f1.

Chapter 5

1. BIS, *Second Annual Report,* Basel, 10 May 1932, p. 13.
2. The year 1931 saw a net outflow of capital from the United Kingdom of about 103 million pounds, as against an average yearly net inflow of 105 million pounds for 1920–30. Net invisible items (financial services, etc.) also shrank by over 30% in 1931. Feinstein (1972), T82, T139.
3. Eichengreen (1992), p. 280.
4. Ibid., p. 283.
5. Boyle (1967), p. 267.
6. Ibid., p. 268.
7. They were lifted in March 1932.
8. Fraser (1936), p. 461.
9. The dates when individual countries either suspended convertibility or introduced foreign exchange regulations are listed in the BIS Annual Reports of 1932 and 1933.
10. Eichengreen (1992), p. 299.
11. BIS, *Third Annual Report,* Basel, 8 May 1933, p. 6.
12. Eichengreen (1992), p. 305.
13. Banks tended to be both "local" and "universal": their assets were neither sufficiently diversified nor, in many cases, sufficiently liquid.
14. Eichengreen (1992), p. 324.
15. The flight out of the dollar was overwhelmingly a domestic affair. Only 12.5% of the gold drawn out of the Fed's reserves in February 1933 was actually shipped abroad or earmarked in New York for foreign countries (data from BIS, *Third Annual Report,* Basel, 14 May 1934, pp. 22–3).
16. Brown (1940), pp. 1249–50.
17. Eichengreen (1992), p. 329.
18. According to Brown (1940, p. 1269), the restoration of the 1926 price level was "the announced goal of the administration" at the end of 1933.
19. Eichengreen (1992), p. 331.
20. "On 20 April, an Executive Order was issued prohibiting gold exports, except for gold already earmarked. The power of the Secretary of the Treasury to issue licences was restricted to such transactions as he deemed to be in the public interest, and then only with the approval of the President". Brown (1940), pp. 1254–5.
21. Arts. 3 and 4 of the BIS Statutes (1930). As we shall see, in fact a number of cumbersome and tedious duties as trustee and agent continued to weigh on the Bank's life and activity for many years to come.
22. Art. 3 of the BIS Statutes (1930).
23. BIS, *Second Annual Report,* Basel, 10 May 1932, p. 17. In fact, as the report itself pointed out, an important business consequence of the moratorium was the "gradual withdrawal by the creditor Treasuries of their balances on hand when the moratorium was instituted", reducing such balances to 68 million Swiss francs on 31 March 1932 as compared to 400 million on 30 June 1931.

24. BIS, *Second Annual Report,* Basel, 10 May 1932, p. 17.
25. See Chapter 6.
26. BIS, *Second Annual Report,* Basel, 10 May 1932, p. 17.
27. Ibid., pp. 17, 22–4.
28. As established by the Hague Agreement of 20 January 1930.
29. See Chapter 6.
30. Art. 7(2) of the BIS Statutes (1930). It was obvious at the time that the clause was phrased to bind future membership, as all the founding members were already on gold.
31. Details and instances illustrating each of the following points are contained in the rest of this chapter and, more especially, in Chapter 6.
32. Notably in the case of the United States.
33. Only in Switzerland was the Exchange Stabilisation Fund entirely managed by the National Bank.
34. League of Nations, Economic, Financial and Transit Department (1944), p. 158.
35. In this situation, it is possible to imagine international cooperation as a two-stage game requiring first domestic and then multilateral cooperation. In this setting, a stable equilibrium is known to be almost impossible to achieve, particularly in the absence of an international leader.
36. Conference of government representatives of Belgium, France, Germany, Italy, Japan, the United Kingdom, and the United States, convened at the insistence of President Hoover (see Section 4.4).
37. "The London Conference 1931, Declaration", BISA, 6.34 – *Committee set up by the BIS to investigate the credit needs of Germany.* Any international discussion on Germany's credit needs had to start out from an agreed assessment of the country's overall foreign indebtedness and its capacity to service it. This proved very difficult on the basis of the available statistical information, resulting in frequent revisions of earlier estimates. On this, see: James (1985), pp. 176ff; Ritschl (2002), pp. 107ff.
38. The committee included: Beneduce (Italy, Consorzio di Credito per lo Opere Pubbliche), Bindschedler (Switzerland, Crédit Suisse), De Groot (Netherlands, Amsterdamsche Bank), Francqui (Belgium, Société Générale), Layton (United Kingdom, editor of *The Economist*), Melchior (Germany, Warburg & Co.), Moreau (France, Banque de Paris et des Pays-Bas), Rydbeck (Sweden, Skandanaviska Kreditaktiebolaget), Tanaka (Japan, Bank of Japan), and Wiggin (Chase National Bank).
39. Financial Committee appointed on the recommendation of the London Conference 1931, "Minutes of the Second Meeting of the Committee held in Basel on 9 August 1931", p. 2, BISA, 6.34 – *Committee set up by BIS to investigate credit needs of Germany.*
40. Ibid.
41. Ibid., p. 3.
42. Financial Committee appointed on the recommendation of the London Conference 1931, "Minutes of the Third Meeting of the Committee held in Basel on 10 August 1931", p. 3, BISA, 6.34 – *Committee set up by BIS to investigate credit needs of Germany.*
43. Ibid., p. 4.
44. Ibid. Out of Germany's total losses of 3.5 billion RM since January 1931, about 1 billion RM had been offset by German withdrawals from abroad.

45. Ibid.
46. Ibid.
47. Ibid., p. 5.
48. Financial Committee appointed on the recommendation of the London Conference 1931, "Minutes of the Seventh Meeting of the Committee held in Basel on 16 August 1931", p. 5, BISA, 6.34 – *Committee set up by BIS to investigate credit needs of Germany.*
49. Melchior was of the same persuasion as Layton, arguing that "the opinion in Germany was that the London Conference was not finished". Francqui argued that "it was an illusion to believe that the President of the London Conference was in the position to take the initiative to submit proposals". Beneduce was adamant – and probably right on purely legal grounds – that "the Committee was appointed by the BIS and would make its report to the President of the BIS". Ibid., pp. 5–6.
50. See Section 5.4 regarding the so-called Beneduce Committee.
51. In fact, a number of representatives of private creditors to German financial institutions had been present in Basel from the beginning of the Committee's meetings, or had joined afterwards, in advance of 14 August. Financial Committee appointed on the recommendation of the London Conference 1931, "Minutes of the Fifth Meeting of the Committee held in Basel on 12 August 1931", p. 2, BISA, 6.34 – *Committee set up by BIS to investigate credit needs of Germany.*
52. Financial Committee appointed on the recommendation of the London Conference 1931, "Minutes of the Seventh Meeting of the Committee held in Basel on 16 August 1931", p. 6, BISA, 6.34 – *Committee set up by BIS to investigate credit needs of Germany.*
53. As is always the case, the devil was in the details. Disagreement remained as to the amount of Reichsmarks to be released in settlement of the credit balances and foreign contracts as well as on the date on which the *Stillhaltung* would become operative, with the German government against a proposed change from 3 July to 31 July. Financial Committee appointed on the recommendation of the London Conference 1931, "Minutes of the Eighth Meeting of the Committee held in Basel on 17 August 1931", pp. 1–2, BISA, 6.34 – *Committee set up by BIS to investigate credit needs of Germany.*
54. Financial Committee appointed on the recommendation of the London Conference 1931, "Minutes of the Ninth Meeting of the Committee held in Basel on 18 August 1931", p. 3, BISA, 6.34 – *Committee set up by BIS to investigate credit needs of Germany.*
55. *Report of the Committee appointed on the recommendation of the London Conference 1931,* Basel, 18 August 1931, p. 5.
56. Ibid., p. 7.
57. Ibid., p. 8.
58. Ibid., p. 9.
59. "The clearly defined technical investigation to which we have confined our attention", the experts concluded, "does not permit [us] to offer suggestions of a political character" – on which, they should have added, no agreement exists among them either – "But we felt it to be our duty to point out the reasons why it is impossible for the present to suggest definite plans for securing to Germany long-term credits". Ibid., p. 10.

60. Ibid.
61. Marcus Wallenberg, Sr. (1864–1943), board member, vice-chairman (1920–38) and chairman (1938–43) of Stockholms Enskilda Bank.
62. Franz Urbig, Berlin banker, director of Disconto-Gesellschaft, and chairman of the Deutsche Bank Supervisory Board.
63. BISA, *Minutes of the Meetings of the Board of Directors,* 12 October 1931, Resolution 175.
64. BIS, *Second Annual Report,* 10 May 1932, p. 19.
65. Art. 119 of the Convention.
66. See Art. 45 of the BIS Statutes (1930).
67. Young Plan, Art. 8(e), Paris, 7 June 1929.
68. It should be noticed that the exception taken by Germany to the Young Plan was reported in BIS, *Second Annual Report,* 10 May 1932, p. 19.
69. "Governo Germanico, Richiesta di istituzione del Comitato speciale consultivo", BIHA – *Rapporti con l'estero,* 96, fasc. 6.
70. Beneduce reported to the governor of the Bank of Italy that Francqui, put forward by the French, was not agreeable to the majority. Unanimity was found on the U.S. representative (Stuart), who declined "in view of the action he intends to take *vis à vis* his own government at the international conference that will follow the deliberations of the Committee". A unanimous vote was then cast in favour of the Italian delegate. Beneduce to Azzolini, cable of 7 December 1931, BIHA – *Rapporti con l'estero,* 96, fasc. 6.
71. New statistics were produced that substantially altered those published in the Wiggin Report. BIHA – *Verbali Comitato Beneduce, 9 December 1931,* B. 307, f1. See also James (1985), p. 178.
72. Beneduce to Azzolini, cable of 14 December 1931, BIHA – *Rapporti con l'estero,* 96, fasc. 6.
73. Melchior offered a rather Machiavellian explanation for his government's about-face, saying that the chancellor was not inclined to insist on a complete moratorium for fear that it would be taken as a guarantee that, once the moratorium expired, Germany itself should take the initiative to resume *all* payments. Beneduce to Azzolini, cable of 16 December 1931, BIHA – *Rapporti con l'estero,* 96, fasc. 6.
74. Beneduce to Azzolini, cable of 14 December 1931, BIHA – *Rapporti con l'estero,* 96, fasc. 6.
75. Melchior privately told Beneduce that he was now authorised to accept a committee declaration that Germany was unable to meet conditional payments only. Layton, on the other hand, said that MacDonald insisted on a committee position stating German inability to meet both the conditional and the unconditional commitments. Neutral delegates supported the U.K. stance. Beneduce to Azzolini, cable of 17 December 1931, BIHA – *Rapporti con l'estero,* 96, fasc. 6.
76. Beneduce to Azzolini, cable of 21 December 1931, BIHA – *Rapporti con l'estero,* 96, fasc. 6.
77. Beneduce to Azzolini, cable of 18 December 1931, BIHA – *Rapporti con l'estero,* 96, fasc. 6.
78. Ibid.
79. Beneduce to Azzolini, cable of 23 December 1931, BIHA – *Rapporti con l'estero,* 96, fasc. 6.

80. The report reviewed the German economic situation in the second half of 1931 (Chapter I), discussed circumstances that had led to the payments crisis (Chapter II), and surveyed the measures taken by Germany to fight the crisis itself (Chapter III). The conclusions (Chapter IV) conveyed the committee's political message. "Report of the Special Advisory Committee", Basel, December 1931, BISA, 6.40 – *Special Advisory Committee*.

81. All quotes from BIS, *Report of the Special Advisory Committee,* Basel, December 1931, p. 19–20.

82. BIS, *Third Annual Report,* 8 May 1933, p. 19.

83. The bonds were to be held for three years by the BIS as trustee. At the expiration of the three-year period, the BIS would float the bonds on the market at a price that should not be below 90% of par. (Acte Finale de la Conference de Lausanne, Art. 1). These bonds were never actually issued.

84. Renouvin (1958), p. 61.

85. Carr (1947), p. 149.

86. See BISA, 6.43b – *Stresa Conference.*

87. The creditor nations had made the ratification of the agreement subject to their first reaching a satisfactory settlement with their own creditors (i.e., the United States).

88. Art. 21 of the BIS Statutes.

89. Eichengreen and Temin (1997), p. 29. Ernest Bevin was one of the very few to voice a dissent (e.g., in the Macmillan Report) even before the pound sterling was taken off gold.

90. See Cassel's stance on gold in the subsequent text. For a general appraisal of the swing in economic orthodoxy that took place in the first half of the 1930s, see the collected essays in honour of Irving Fisher on the occasion of his seventieth birthday: Gayer (1937).

91. B. P. Blackett, *Planned Money* (Constable & Co., London, 1932, p. 71), quoted in Eichengreen and Temin (1997), p. 38.

92. M. Mitzakis to Lacour-Gayet, 14 May 1933, BFA, 1489200303/187 – *Liaison Banque de France – BRI.*

93. Beneduce was the other member of the BIS Board participating in the Gold Delegation, which also included Dr. Pospisil, the highly respected Governor of the Czechoslovak National Bank, and Mr. Sprague of the Bank of England. The other members were academics and private bankers.

94. By decisions of the Council of the League of Nations of 14 December 1928 and 17 June 1929, a special delegation was established to "examine into and report upon the causes of fluctuations in the purchasing power of gold and their effect on the economic life of the nations". This so-called Gold Delegation of the League of Nations Financial Committee held two sessions, in August 1929 and June 1930.

95. Copy of the interim report in BISA, 6.18 – *Gold, General,* vol. 1.

96. League of Nations (1932).

97. The phenomenon was officially termed "fluctuations in the purchasing power of gold"; ibid., p. 5.

98. Ibid., p. 24. The wiping out of reparations was, unsurprisingly, endorsed by Prof. Bonn (p. 58) and, surprisingly, by Guido Joung, who was soon to become Minister of Finance in the Mussolini government (p. 60).

99. Ibid., p. 65.

100. Ibid. In an interesting publication of 1936, the German Statistical Office would make the same case based on a detailed statistical survey for the years 1928–34 – contrasting the large gold holdings of the main creditor nations to the inadequate gold reserves held by the debtor countries. Statistisches Reichsamt, "Gold und Devisen in der Weltwirtschaft in den Jahren 1928 bis 1934", *Einzelschriften zur Statistik des Deutschen Reichs*, Nr. 33, Berlin, 1936, pp. 21–3.
101. League of Nations (1932), p. 72.
102. Ibid., p. 75.
103. League of Nations, Monetary and Economic Conference, Preparatory Commission of Experts, Exposé by Sir Frederic Leith-Ross, CP/Conf. M.E./34, Geneva, 9 January 1933, p. 3, BULH, NL 324 – *Nachlass Per Jacobsson*, f6103.
104. Rist and others also presented papers at the meeting, specially convened to discuss action to be taken to promote the reinstatement of the gold standard. BIS, "Note on certain international aspects of monetary policy as defined in recent statements", pp. 1–2, 15–16, CB Document no. 52, 30 June 1932.
105. BISA, 6.42 – *Conference of South American Central Banks held at Lima, Peru, December 1931.* The conference pleaded for a restoration of monetary stability through a return to the gold standard and for closer collaboration among central banks.
106. BIS, "Note on certain international aspects of monetary policy as defined in recent statements", CB Document no. 52, 30 June 1932.
107. Ibid., p. 15.
108. League of Nations (1932), p. 53.
109. BISA, *Minutes of the Meetings of the Board of Directors,* 11 July 1932, pp. 10–12.
110. At the time of the London Conference of July 1933, Governor Harrison was one who argued that – though he did not know what position Washington would take on the BIS document about the rules of the gold standard – he felt it to be entirely satisfactory from the point of view of his bank, since it was "of purely academic interest to us as we are not at the present on the gold standard". Harrison–Norman telephone conversation, 14 July 1933, FRBNY – *Harrison Papers,* 3114.4: "Harrison's conversations with M. Norman – 1933".
111. For an excellent overview of the issues related to the 1933 London Conference, see Eichengreen (1992), pp. 318–37, from which part of what follows is derived. Also: Clavin (1996), pp. 117–65.
112. Eichengreen (1992), p. 320.
113. Clarke (1972), p. 26.
114. Consider, for instance, the following assessment of the U.S. position with respect to the conference by Fraser: "In conversation with some friends in New York today over the telephone I enquired whether Williams and Day were coming [to the Preparatory Commission of Experts in Geneva] with any definite plan or programme, or were in a position to know or to say what the new Administration would be willing to back up at the coming conference. I was advised that Williams and Day had seen the new President ... but the impression of my informants (who ought to know what they are talking about) was that there was no definite programme and no definite decision as to just what could be done. In fact, there was general feeling that it would have been better to postpone the January meeting, and that the Americans were not ready to propose this in view of the War Debt

situation". Fraser to Trip, 30 December 1932, BISA, 6.43a – *World Economic and Financial Conference.*
115. Feis (1966), pp. 76, 116.
116. Norman felt that the current strength of the pound was due to transient factors and that, under a stabilisation agreement, the Americans and "the French would have to accumulate sterling in London in order to keep up the pound and that at the termination of the agreement [the United Kingdom] would have to pay the balance in gold". Harrison–Norman telephone conversation, 18 May 1933, FRBNY – *Harrison Papers,* 3115.4: "Harrison's conversations with M. Norman – 1933".
117. Ibid.
118. The exchange rate of the pound stood at about \$3.58 in April 1931. It steadily rose in the following months, reaching over \$5.10 (i.e., above the pre-September 1931 gold parity) by the end of the year. Federal Reserve System (1943), p. 681. Vis-à-vis the European currencies, however, the pound was rather weak, thereby giving British industry a welcome advantage over its Continental competitors.
119. "Confidential declaration Bank of England – Bank of France", 20 May 1933, BISA, 6.42a – *Gold Standard, 1 December 1932 – 31 October 1935.*
120. BISA, 6.43 – *Lausanne Agreement of 9 July 1932,* Resolution 5.
121. The appointment was announced on 25 July 1932. BISA, 6.43a – *World Economic and Financial Conference.*
122. There was also an economic subcommittee. The monetary subcommittee was in turn divided into three further (sub)subcommittees: money and credit, freedom of trade and capital movements, and public works.
123. For the whole group of BIS-connected members prior to the first meeting of the commission, see: Trip to Fraser, 20 October 1932, BISA, 6.43a – *World Economic and Financial Conference.*
124. Diary Per Jacobsson, 1 November 1932, BULH, NL 324 – *Nachlass Per Jacobsson,* Tagebücher – D.17.
125. BIS, "A– General Problems of a Return to a Common International Standard", CB Document no. 58, 19 October 1932; and BIS, "B– General Problems of the Gold Standard", CB Document no. 59, 20 October 1932.
126. League of Nations, Monetary and Economic Conference, Preparatory Commission of Experts, Exposé by Sir Frederic Leith-Ross, CP/Conf. M.E./34, Geneva, 9 January 1933, p. 3, BULH, NL 324 – *Nachlass Per Jacobsson,* f6103. A full set of documents related to the work of the Preparatory Commission can also be found in LNA, Geneva, carton R 4628, Section 10D – *Monetary and Economic Conference 1933, Preparatory Commission of Experts.*
127. Moret to Fraser, 5 December 1932, BISA, 6.43a – *World Economic and Financial Conference.* The Governor of the Bank of France praised the firm stance on gold taken in the two papers by the Monetary and Economic Department of the BIS, but he took exception to them as far as the endorsement of the gold exchange standard was concerned. "Je ne peux que regretter que la note de la BRI préconise à nouveau le système de la garantie-or. Cette question a fait l'objet de nombreuses discussions au cours des réunions de Bâle et, d'un commun accord, elle a été écartée en raison des difficultés d'application qu'elle soulevait…. Je ne puis, en effet, m'empêcher de penser que, quelque précaution que l'on prenne, ce système tendra toujours à favoriser une expansion illégitime de crédit…. Je ne me refuserais

... pas absolument à me rallier, pour quelque temps encore, à un système d'étalon de change-or, mais sous la réserve formelle que ce système ne s'écartera pas des principes posés dans le rapport de la Délégation de l'Or, c'est-à-dire qu'il sera d'un champ d'application très restreint et qu'il n'impliquera, sous quelque forme que ce soit, l'octroi d'une garantie-or". Moret also recalled that the League's Gold Report rejected open-market operations "comme absolument incompatibles avec le fonctionnement de l'étalon-or". At any rate, he added, such operations were only suited for certain markets, amongst which the French was not included.

128. League of Nations, Monetary and Economic Conference, Preparatory Commission of Experts, CP/Conf. M.E./2nd ss/ P.V.3, Geneva, 10 January 1933, p. 3; BULH, NL 324 – *Nachlass Per Jacobsson,* f6103.

129. Ibid., pp. 7–9.

130. Ibid., p. 12.

131. League of Nations, Monetary and Economic Conference, Preparatory Commission of Experts, Draft of Preamble, by Beneduce and Day. Geneva, 14 January 1933, p. 4; BULH, NL 324 – *Nachlass Per Jacobsson,* f6103.

132. League of Nations, Monetary and Economic Conference, Preparatory Commission of Experts, Sub-Committee I, Draft Agenda. C.P./Conf. M.E./ F./9, Geneva, 17 January 1933; BULH, *Nachlass Per Jacobsson,* f6103. Drafting of the detailed agenda was to a large extent the work of Per Jacobsson. See BULH, NL 324 – *Nachlass Per Jacobsson,* Tagebücher – D.17: entries 11–18 January 1933.

133. League of Nations, Monetary and Economic Conference, Preparatory Commission of Experts, II. General programme of the Conference. Draft submitted by Leith-Ross (U.K.) and Rist (France), Geneva, 16 January 1933.

134. As Merle Cochran, the first secretary at the U.S. Embassy in Paris, remarked: "If the work of the Preparatory Commission proves worthwhile, I believe that the BIS deserves much credit therefore". Merle Cochran to the Undersecretary of State, 23 January 1933, NARA, RG 39 – *U.S. Treasury, Records of the Bureau of Accounts, Fiscal Relationships between the United States and other Nations,* box 103.

135. Moreover, upon adjourning the commission's first session, President Trip called upon the BIS to provide further technical assistance in the preparation of the second session.

136. Fraser to Moret, Azzolini, Bachmann, Franck, Norman, Luther, Tanaka, Trip, and Rooth, 16 November 1932, BISA, 6.43a – *World Economic and Financial Conference.* The letter of invitation set out the following points for discussion for the meeting scheduled for 11 December:
   1. re-establishment of a common international monetary standard on a gold basis;
   2. understanding between central banks to secure a better functioning of the gold standard (fixation of gold points, movements of gold and their relation to the volume of credit on the respective markets, etc.);
   3. wider distribution of existing gold stocks and better use of present reserves for strengthening the credit structure of the world;
   4. alteration of reserve requirements, including safeguards against inflationary tendencies;
   5. using the BIS framework for coordinating the credit policy of the central banks (organisation of credits in connection with the stabilisation of currencies, closer contact in periods of currency reform, etc.);

6. reformed gold exchange standard system (limited, more centralised, controlled, and better secured);

7. excessive general short-term indebtedness, liquidation of the past (including standstill agreements, exchange restrictions, etc.), and the re-establishment of a sound system of international commercial credits;

8. excessive long-term indebtedness, including the suggestion that a panel of persons, who might be called upon to act as conciliators, should be set up.

"In addition, the Governors may wish to consider to what extent the BIS should assist in evolving methods of collecting information on the volume of international credits."

137. Note on the discussions at Management Meeting on 29 November 1932 (cover note indicates Jacobsson as author), BULH, NL 324 – *Nachlass Per Jacobsson,* steelcase 1.

138. Among such problems, it was decided that the BIS should pay special attention to the following. (1) "The question of to what extent it is possible to ask central banks to concentrate foreign exchange holdings with each other and with the BIS." (2) Methods by which foreign exchange holdings could be made more secure (gold clause, insurance fund, minimum deposits with the BIS). (3) The reduction of minimum legal gold coverage. (4) The collection of information and statistics about short-term indebtedness. (5) "Concrete suggestions for monetary action in relation to prices." (6) A general note on the work of the BIS.

139. Dated 8 December 1932, BISA, 6.43a – *World Economic and Financial Conference.*

140. Aide-memoire for discussion in governors' meeting on 11 December 1932, BISA, 6.43a – *World Economic and Financial Conference.*

141. McGarrah to Moret, Azzolini, Bachmann, Franck, Norman, Luther, Tanaka, Trip, and Rooth, 12 March 1933, BISA, 6.42a – *Gold Standard.*

142. Verbatim minutes of the informal governors' meetings of 12 February and 12 March 1933 are preserved in BISA, 7.18(4) – *Papers Hülse,* box HUL6, f.XI/34. These minutes were also forwarded to the New York Fed: McGarrah to Harrison, 20 February 1933, enclosing "Unofficial meeting of Governors of Central Banks preceding XXIX meeting of Board of Directors, 12 February 1933, 4–5:15 pm", FRBNY – *Relations with BIS.*

143. "Unofficial meeting of Governors of Central Banks preceding XXIX meeting of Board of Directors, Sunday 12 February 1933, 4–5:15 pm", p. 3, BISA, 7.18(4) – *Papers Hülse,* box HUL6, f.XI/34.

144. Ibid. What he meant by that is made clear in a letter to the Harvard economics professor Williams, one of the experts in the U.S. delegation to the Preparatory Commission. "Our general thought is that unless the central banks agree among themselves on some kind of a text, they may wake up and find something forced on them by the Governments when they meet in London – or is it going to be Washington?" Fraser to Williams, 15 March 1933, BISA, 6.43a – *World Economic and Financial Conference.*

145. "L'idée que nous, les Gouverneurs des Banques centrales, sommes à même de solutionner comme qui dirait par l'effet d'une baguette magique tous les problèmes angoissants de l'heure présente et de trouver des panacées contre tous les maux ne peut avoir germé que dans la tête d'un professeur hyper-idéaliste ou d'un pauvre

rêveur ignorant complètement de la vie réelle". "Unofficial meeting of Governors of Central Banks preceding XXIX meeting of Board of Directors, Sunday 12 February 1933, 4–5:15 pm", p. 7, BISA, 7.18(4) – *Papers Hülse,* box HUL6, f.XI/34.

146. "Une restriction monétaire ... qui se superposerait à la restriction économique exerçant déjà ses sérvices constituerait une veritable fatalité et renderait la situation générale du monde infiniment plus difficile et compliquée. N'y a-t-il pas déjà assez de méfiances de par le monde, à l'heure presente?" Ibid., p. 11.

147. The matter was to a large extent "outside the field of monetary policy as entrusted to central banks". Measures included in the agenda proposed by the Preparatory Commission were approvingly cited (war debts, freedom of movements of capital, goods and services, "sound" public finances, flexibility within the national economies).

148. "People", Jacobsson had noted earlier in his diary, "begin to find that Trip talks like a 'textbook'. Certainly Trip's danger is that he has not much experience about markets". Diary Per Jacobsson, 11 December 1932, BULH, NL 324 – *Nachlass Per Jacobsson,* Tagebücher – D.17.

149. Moret to McGarrah, 4 April 1933, BISA, 6.42a – *Gold Standard.*

150. Azzolini to McGarrah, 5 April 1933, BISA, 6.42a – *Gold Standard.*

151. Shimasuye to McGarrah, 8 April 1933, BISA, 6.42a – *Gold Standard.*

152. Unsurprisingly, Norman's suggested amendments to Trip's text were almost entirely terminological and grammatical. Norman to McGarrah, 20 March 1933, BISA, 6.42a – *Gold Standard.*

153. *General Principles on the Working of the Gold Standard,* Revised Text after Governors' meeting 7 May 1933, BISA, 6.42a – *Gold Standard.*

154. As reported by L'Agence Economique et Financière on 1 April 1933. See Merle Cochran to the Undersecretary of State, 3 April 1933, NARA, RG 39 – *U.S. Treasury, Records of the Bureau of Accounts, Fiscal Relationships between the United States and other Nations,* box 103. According to Cochran, Fraser's statement made a favourable impression.

155. Clavin (1996), pp. 117ff.

156. Carr (1947), p. 149.

157. Each participating country was represented on both committees. For the proceedings and documents of the subcommission dealing with the re-establishment of an international monetary system, see: LNA, Geneva, Carton R 4628, File 5383 – *Second Sub-Commission: reestablishment of an international monetary standard;* and File 5300 – *Monetary and Financial Commission, Sub-Committee II of the second Sub-Commission: technical questions.*

158. For details, see Sayers (1976b), pp. 276–9.

159. Harrison–Lacour-Gayet telephone conversation, 18 May, 1933, FRBNY – *Harrison Papers,* 3125.3: "Harrison's conversations with Mr. Lacour-Gayet, Bank of France, Director of Economic Research".

160. Sayers (1976b), p. 278.

161. In a subsequent telephone conversation, while reporting that the feeling in Washington was that it would not be feasible to arrange a meeting before the World Economic Conference, "The Governor added that personally he agreed with what Mr. Lacour-Gayet had said about the necessity for prompt exchange stabilisation and also as to the desirability of discussions being held jointly with governments

and central banks". Harrison–Lacour-Gayet telephone conversation, 26 May 1933, FRBNY – *Harrison Papers*, 3125.3: "Harrison's conversations with Mr. Lacour-Gayet, Bank of France, Director of Economic Research".

162. Diary of trip to London, June 1933, FRBNY – *Harrison Papers*, 3010.2: "Harrison Collection cables, Diary, misc. – Trip to London – 1933".

163. "Much of the improvement which we have had", Sprague said to an astonished French delegate, "[has] been initiated by the hope of inflation" (ibid.). Oliver Sprague (b. 1873) was an American economist and professor of banking and finance at Harvard. He acted as economic adviser to the Bank of England from 1930 to early 1933, and at the World Conference in London he was a member of the U.S. Treasury delegation. He returned to Harvard in November 1933.

164. Diary of trip to London, June 1933, p. 2, FRBNY – *Harrison Papers*, 3010.2: "Harrison Collection cables, Diary, misc. – Trip to London – 1933".

165. Ibid.

166. These rumours may partly explain the fanfare with which the birth of the gold bloc was subsequently announced.

167. Eichengreen (1992), p. 332.

168. Ibid., p. 333.

169. As late as 18 June, Jacobsson recorded an atmosphere of confidence and optimism. "18 June 1933 (Sunday)– Tea at Laytons. We came unfortunately late. Herbert Samuel there, as well as Hymans, Jung, Francqui, Beneduce, Cassel. Layton said the Conference had cleared certain corners during the first week: (1) Anglo American good relations maintained; (2) no serious break in the Conference – the Presidentship of the Fin. Cttee arranged amicably; (3) the Germans shown that they cannot have it all their way; (4) machinery arranged for de facto stabilisation [of] dollar etc., which may be used when desired; (5) McDonalds position strengthened". Diary Per Jacobsson, 18 June 1933, BULH, NL 324 – *Nachlass Per Jacobsson*, Tagebücher – D.17.

170. Strohl (1939), p. 186.

171. President's message to London Economic Conference addressed to Secretary of State Cordell Hull on 2 July 1933 and released to the press on 3 July 1933.

172. Strohl (1939), pp. 204–5.

173. "28 June 1933– Trip said to me: If this Conference is going to provoke speculation which threatens to drive us off gold, we better stop it the sooner the better." "29 June 1933– ... great commotion. The Gold countries threaten to leave the Conference if no assurance is given by Great Britain as to exchange stabilisation." Diary Per Jacobsson, 28 June 1933, BUCL, NL 324 – *Nachlass Per Jacobsson*, Tagebücher – D.17.

174. The initiative for issuing this communiqué to immediately counter Roosevelt's bombshell declaration was taken by Emile Francqui, member of the BIS Board of Directors and Belgian delegate at the London Conference. Van der Wee and Tavernier (1975), p. 258.

175. Resolution des Puissances Fideles a l'étalon-or à la Conférence de Londres, 3 juillet 1933. See Strohl (1939), p. 255.

176. "Communiqué issued by the meeting of certain central banks held in Paris on 8 July 1933", *The Financial Times*, 10 July 1933.

177. "Accord de coopération", BISA, 6.42a – *Gold Standard*.

178. Replying to Fraser, who had sent him "documents [about the Gold Bloc agreement], which I am sending to no other Governor in the world except your good self" (Fraser to Harrison, 9 July 1933), Harrison wrote: "Judging by the results as illustrated in the position of the gold exchanges since the accord was signed, I should say this was a first-rate job of central bank cooperation." Harrison to Fraser, 3 August 1933, BISA, 6.42a – *Gold Standard.*

179. Clause VIII.

180. Jacobsson recorded in his diary his boss's advice as to behaviour at the conference: "8 June 1933– Fraser gave advice: (a) keep careful, especially in the beginning, find out what people are coming with; (b) do not give the impression of being "in with" any delegation. Probably one's own delegation can give one a great deal of information. OK, but do not become part of it. Fraser himself would stay at another hotel than the U.S. delegation; (c) do not keep the impression that we are in London to push the BIS as the League fellows often do with the League. Point out what the BIS can do, but not in a way of fishing for it. Fraser confirmed that I was boss of the three people from BIS staff going to London". Diary Per Jacobsson, 8 June 1933, BULH, NL 324 – *Nachlass Per Jacobsson,* Tagebücher – D.17.

181. BIS representation at the London Conference was agreed by the governors at their informal meeting in Basel on 4 June. See: Notes on the BIS, The Governors' Meeting, Sunday 4 June 1933, BEA, OV5/8 – *BIS, Minutes of Meetings of Board of Directors*; and Avenol (Head of the Conference Secretariat) to Fraser, 27 May 1933, BISA, 6.43a – *World Economic and Financial Conference.*

182. Patricia Clavin (1996, p. 137) erroneously attributes the drafting of this resolution to Norman, on the basis of "a memorandum first presented by the Federal Reserve in New York". As we have seen, this resolution had been prepared at the BIS on the basis of Trip's original paper.

183. LNA, Geneva, Carton R 4641 – Section 10D – Monetary and Economic Conference 1933 – 5300, *Monetary and Financial Commission, Sub-Committee II* – Tenth Meeting, 3 July 1933.

184. LNA, Geneva, Carton R 4641 – Section 10D – Monetary and Economic Conference 1933 – 5300, *Monetary and Financial Commission, Sub-Committee II* – Twelfth Meeting, 19 July 1933.

185. "I wonder whether it is not desirable to secure from the Conference some definite pronouncement regarding the need of independent Central Banks to all countries.... a general blessing of Central Banks by the Conference would be very desirable and useful in the hands of a favourably disposed Government. I doubt whether it is desirable that the initiative in suggesting such a declaration should come from here, but there appear to be reasonable grounds to think that the BIS, being the centre most interested in the development of Central Banking institutions throughout the world, might be the proper originator." Norman to Fraser, 23 May 1933, BISA, 6.43a – *World Economic and Financial Conference.*

186. "Cox talked about the sub-Committee on technical questions and added that 'Fraser did do good work'. Ramsay MacDonald then said: 'Yes, I hear from all kinds of quarter what a very good man Fraser is'." Diary Per Jacobsson, 30 June 1933, BULH, NL 324 – *Nachlass Per Jacobsson,* Tagebücher – D.17. Cochran reported in the same vein to the U.S. State Department: "On all occasions ... Mr. Fraser ... has been most discreet and considerate in so far as American policies

are concerned, and his assistants have followed his example.... the men responsible for BIS management endeavour scrupulously to preserve the impartial and neutral position which is necessary for such an institution. I am sure that ... members of the American delegation were most favorably impressed by Mr. Fraser and his associates, and admired the thoroughness with which they had prepared for discussions of monetary problems". Merle Cochran to the Acting Secretary of State, 25 July 1933, NARA, RG 39 – *U.S. Treasury, Records of the Bureau of Accounts, Fiscal Relationships between the United States and other Nations,* box 103.

187. "Salter said that the Central Banks had spoilt this Conference by beginning with stabilisation – Central Banks could not endure that they were not in command, but by their action did then greater disservice." "Niemeyer said BIS had so far done very well at the Conf." Diary Per Jacobsson, 27 June 1933 and 1 July 1933, BULH, NL 324 – *Nachlass Per Jacobsson,* Tagebücher – D.17.

188. "Mr. Crick asked me why the BIS had risked its reputation by the issue of the gold resolution? I explained (1) that adherence for gold was not given for nothing: (a) conditions for a return involving also the settlement of international debts; (b) substantial acceptance of the Report of the Gold Delegation. (2) That it is better to be in advance of public opinion". Diary Per Jacobsson, 4 October 1933, BULH, NL 324 – *Nachlass Per Jacobsson,* Tagebücher – D.17.

189. "Lundvik asked me if there had been any results of this Conference. I said there are four: (1) the token payment without default by Great Britain to USA; (2) the settlement of the Anglo-Soviet dispute; (3) the Rumanian frontier-Bessarabia agreement – called a new non-agression agreement; (4) the contacts and consultations which no doubt have taught people a lot: the lining up of countries according to economic views without political attachments dominating. The strong collaboration between France and Italy. It is clearer now". Diary Per Jacobsson, 5 July 1933, BULH, NL 324 – *Nachlass Per Jacobsson,* Tagebücher – D.17.

190. "Some Results of the Monetary and Economic Conference", 25 July 1933, BULH, NL 324 – *Nachlass Per Jacobsson,* Box Lectures 18, F2.

191. BISA, 6.42a – *Gold Standard*; and 6.43a – *World Economic and Financial Conference.*

192. Clavin (1996), p. 196.

193. Exchange of correspondence in BISA, 4.2 – *German External Loan 1924, General,* vol. 2.

194. Incidentally, this decision was challenged in court by a Swedish bondholder, who argued that the money made available by the German government should have been pooled and distributed to all bondholders pro rata on a gold value basis. This challenge was dismissed by a ruling of the Swiss Federal Court of Appeal on 26 May 1936. BISA, 4.3o(1) – *Writ served on the BIS, Claim for payment at gold value of coupons of Swedish issue of German Loan 1930,* 2 volumes.

195. The meeting took place in the Reichsbank offices in Berlin from 29 May to 2 June 1933.

196. Cables, Fraser to Parker Gilbert, 17 and 19 May 1933, BISA, 4.3s – *Young Loan, Suggested interruption in payment of service moneys,* vol. 1.

197. Cable, Fraser to Parker Gilbert, 6 June 1933, BISA, 4.3s – *Young Loan, Suggested interruption in payment of service moneys,* vol. 1.

198. "L'atmosphère est plutôt sombre à la BRI depuis le dernier Conseil et la pénible déclaration du Dr Schacht", Michel Mitzakis wrote in one of his regular letters to Lacour-Gayet at the Bank of France; Bank of France Archive, 1489200303/187 – *Liaison Banque de France – BRI,* letter 6 June 1933.

199. The Swedish delegation, for one, was not prepared to recognise a transfer priority for the Young Loan over the $125 million Krueger Loan contracted in October 1929.

200. All other foreign exchange transfers for interest payments falling due during the second half of 1933 were reduced to 50%, except for interest payments on the Dawes and Young loans, which would continue to be met in full.

201. This special account was meant to serve as a collateral for amortisation payments once foreign exchange transfers were resumed, and it was to remain under the Reichsbank's control.

202. Letter, Leon Fraser to Hjalmar Schacht, 22 June 1933, BISA, 4.3s – *Young Loan, Suggested interruption in payment of service moneys,* vol. 1.

203. On 18 December 1933, the Reichsbank decided that foreign exchange transfers for interest payments other than on the Dawes and Young loans would be further reduced to 30% of the amounts falling due during the period from 1 January to 30 June 1934. Letter, Reichsministerium der Finanzen to BIS, 28 December 1933, BISA, 4.3s – *Young Loan, Suggested interruption in payment of service moneys,* vol. 1.

204. Cable, Reichsbank to Bank of England, 6 January 1934, BISA, 4.3s – *Young Loan, Suggested interruption in payment of service moneys,* vol. 1. Letter, G. Bachmann, President of the Swiss National Bank to Montagu Norman, Governor of the Bank of England, 5 March 1934, BISA, 4.28(5) – *Swiss-German Transfer negotiations.* Cable, Leon Fraser to J.P. Morgan & Co., New York, 26 March 1934, BISA, 6.51 – *Conference of Long & Middle-term Creditors of Germany.*

205. The idea was that the credit would have left the Reichsbank with sufficient reserves of its own to continue to service the Dawes and Young loans. Letter, Hülse, Assistant General Manager BIS, to H. F. Berger, German Ministry of Finance, 26 January 1934, BISA, 7.18(4) – *Papers Hülse,* box HUL1, I.7. Confidential cable, Leon Fraser to Parker Gilbert, 12 June 1934, BISA, 4.28 – *German External 7% Loan 1924 and German International 5½% Loan 1930, Suspension of payments after 30 June 1934,* vol. 1.

206. Cable, Schacht to Fraser, 24 April 1934, BISA, 6.51 – *Conference of Long & Middle-term Creditors of Germany.*

207. BISA, 6.51 – *Conference of Long & Middle-term Creditors of Germany.* Also: letter, Hülse to Dr. Berger, German Ministry of Finance, 18 April 1934, BISA, 7.18(4) – *Papers Hülse,* box HUL1, I.7.

208. Confidential memorandum of meeting of long-term creditors of Germany in Basel, BISA, 6.51 – *Conference of Long and Middle-term Creditors of Germany.*

209. "Der eigentliche Kampf wird in der Vollkonferenz in Berlin entbrennen", letter, Hülse to Berger, 18 April 1934, BISA, 7.18(4) – *Papers Hülse,* box HUL1, I.7.

210. Exchange of letters and cables between Fraser on the one hand and Norman, Harrison, and Schacht on the other, BISA, 6.51 – *Conference of Long & Middle-term Creditors of Germany.*

211. For instance, it was argued that Germany's estimated trade returns for 1934–35, as calculated by the Reichsbank, were based on the actual and substantial trade

deficits suffered in January–February 1934, which in the opinion of the creditors were exceptionally unfavourable. "Report of the Creditors' Subcommittee on Statistics", 2 May 1934, pp. 5–6, BISA, 6.51 – *Conference of Long & Middle-term Creditors of Germany.*

212. Creditors' Subcommittee on blocked Marks, etc., "Report to the plenary Conference dated 3 May 1934", BISA, 6.51 – *Conference of Long & Middle-term Creditors of Germany.*

213. As Fraser wrote to Dean Jay, Trustee of the Dawes Loan: "as the exchange position got worse and the agitation inside Germany for lower interest rates became more active, Schacht's attitude toward the Dawes Loan began to alter until he has now reached the extreme that the Dawes Loan has no priority whatever.... This evolution became pronounced in early March when, I am credibly informed, he had a talk with Hitler and advocated maintaining the special position of the Dawes Loan. Hitler opposed this because, it is stated, he considered the Dawes Loan was also tied in to reparations, and also because of the campaign to reduce interest rates.... The truth is therefore, in my judgment, that the trouble with these two Reich loans arises out of the politics and publicly announced policies of the Nazis, to whom Schacht has to bow and some of whose very extreme views he holds in check by making concessions." Fraser to Dean Jay, 28 June 1934, BISA, 4.28 – *German External Loan 7% 1924, German International 5½% Loan 1930, Suspension of payments after 30 June 1934,* vol. 1.

214. Letter, Schacht to Thomas W. Lamont, 20 April 1934, BISA, 4.28 – *German External Loan 7% 1924, German International 5½% Loan 1930, Suspension of payments after 30 June 1934,* vol. 1.

215. Cable, Fraser to Parker Gilbert, 12 June 1934, BISA, 4.28 – *German External Loan 7% 1924, German International 5½% Loan 1930, Suspension of payments after 30 June 1934,* vol. 1.

216. "Nach dem der Konferenz unterbreiteten Material über die deutsche Lage muss die Deutsche Regierung davon ausgehen, dass nach Beendigung der derzeitigen, bis 30. Juni d.Js. laufenden Transferperiode von der Reichsbank keine Devisen mehr für den Dienst der Auslandsanleihen zur Verfügung gestellt werden können und dass hierdurch auch der Transfer des Dienstes der Reichsanleihen betroffen werden wird." BISA, 6.51 – *Conference of Long & Middle-Term Creditors of Germany.*

217. Between 30 May and 20 June 1934, quotations on the London Stock Exchange for Dawes bonds fell from 75½ to 60 (down from 100 in early 1933) and for Young bonds from 54½ to 41½ (down from 92 in early 1933). See *The Economist,* 9 June 1934 (p. 1268) and 23 June 1934 (p. 1392).

218. BISA, 4.28 – *German External Loan 7% 1924, German International 5½% Loan 1930, Suspension of payments after 30 June 1934,* vol. 1.

219. Letter, Fraser to Dean Jay, 17 November 1934, BISA, 4.28 – *German External Loan 7% 1924, German International 5½% Loan 1930, Suspension of payments after 30 June 1934,* vol. 2. On 9 August 1934, Parker Gilbert had written to Fraser: "Norman always says, as you know, that the way to reach Schacht is through his affections, and though I have always found that quite impossible, I do believe that Schacht is a complex enough personality to have a capacity to rise to the occasion every so often if approached in the right way. Schacht has, I believe, made much of the present crisis by his debt repudiation policy, but I think he has gotten about

everything there is to get out of that policy, and he and Hitler will find themselves increasingly in a straightjacket unless they are prepared to reverse it. Schacht is quite capable of reversing it, and of doing so with quite a flourish, if he thinks that has become his destiny, and with Norman's help it is just possible that sometime in the next few months you might be able to persuade him that destiny calls him in that direction. I can't see any way out for Germany until there is such a reversal of policy. Hitler, and Schacht with him, are deadlocked, it seems to me, at every point, and on present policies Germany will continue to shrivel up and grow continuously more miserable. But if they are willing, as I believe they are able, to right about face, try to get on again with the rest of the world in business as well as political relations, and give evidence that they are trying again to make good on their debts instead of using them as clubs against their creditors, then I have no doubt that Germany will slowly but surely begin to recover again. The only way for them to give convincing evidence of sincere desire to meet their debts is to resume the service of at least the interest on the Dawes and Young Loans, for these loans are and will be the touchstone of German credit." Ibid.

220. Cable, J. P. Morgan to Fraser, 16 June 1934, BISA, 4.28 – *German External Loan 7% 1924, German International 5½% Loan 1930, Suspension of payments after 30 June 1934,* vol. 1.

221. In the course of the following few months, Germany indeed concluded comprehensive clearing agreements with the United Kingdom (4 July 1934), Switzerland (26 July 1934), France (28 July 1934), Belgium (5 September 1934), Sweden (5 October 1934), the Netherlands (13 October 1934), and Italy (16 April 1935). All of these agreements included arrangements for a resumption of reduced interest payments to the Dawes and Young loan bondholders in these respective countries.

222. *The Economist,* 14 July 1934, p. 70.

223. Albrecht Ritschl, *Deutschlands Krise und Konjunktur 1924–1934, Binnenkonjunktur, Auslandsverschuldung und Reparationsproblem zwischen Dawes-Plan und Transfersperre* (Berlin: Akademie Verlag, 2002), p. 191.

224. Years later, during one of his famous table-talks, Hitler recalled with relish how clever and irreplaceable Schacht had been at the time because of his gifts in fooling other people and his flair for financial hocus-pocus. Henry Picker, *Hitlers Tischgespräche im Führerhauptquartier 1941–1942* (Stuttgart: Seewald Verlag, 1963), pp. 286–7.

225. Fraser (1936), p. 461.

226. P. Jacobsson, "Bank for International Settlements", 26 June 1935, p. 4, BULH, NL 324 – *Nachlass Per Jacobsson,* steelcase 1.

227. Ibid., p. 5.

228. Fraser (1936), p. 464.

229. Ibid.

Chapter 6

1. League of Nations data reported in BIS, *Fifth Annual Report,* Basel, 13 May 1935, p. 12. See also Maddison (1995), p. 238.

2. See table in BIS, *Ninth Annual Report,* Basel, 8 May 1939, p. 37. Also: Hickman (1938), pp. 7–8.

3. Carr (1947), p. 152.
4. Renouvin (1958), p. 21.
5. Baffi (2002), p. 82.
6. BISA, *Minutes of the Meetings of the Board of Directors,* 11 November 1935, p. 1.
7. Unfortunately, a strict rule of anonymity about who said what is observed in the minutes of the BIS Board meetings.
8. BISA, *Minutes of the Meetings of the Board of Directors,* 11 November 1935, p. 1.
9. "When the gold standard was abandoned ... [f]oreign exchange became a Treasury matter, and perhaps it still remains to be seen what other responsibilities pass with it from Threadneedle Street to Whitehall". Speech to a gathering of Commonwealth bank governors, quoted in Boyle (1967), p. 287.
10. Harrison–Norman telephone conversation, 20 September 1934, FRBNY – *Harrison Papers,* 3115.5: "Conversations with Mr. Norman". Norman went on to say "that he thought the governments should be taking steps to free trade and loosen restrictions on trade whereas they appeared to be moving in the opposite direction by placing more and more restrictions". His concluding remark was that "on the whole,... he was distinctly gloomy about the outlook".
11. Appointed alternate to the BIS President in 1935.
12. Beyen (1949), p. 129.
13. Ibid.
14. Anonymous (but surely Pilotti's) report to Beneduce on the Board meeting of 8 May 1933, BIHA – *Archivio Beneduce,* 326, Beneduce.
15. Harrison–Lacour-Gayet telephone conversation, 15 November 1933, FRBNY – *Harrison Papers,* 3125.3: "Harrison's conversations with Mr Lacour-Gayet, Bank of France, Director of Economic Research".
16. In the second half of 1932, the Exchange Equalisation Fund operated to avoid an undesired appreciation of the pound. Mitzakis (1939), pp. 313–14.
17. Fraser was invited to attend the meeting and reported on it to McGarrah: "Norman had recommended [the gold bloc governors] an embargo on gold shipments to the United States. This they refused. Trip, however, wanted to have it decided and leak out that if the United States got naughty again and once more cut the gold price or dollar content, then there would be an embargo. This was voted down. The net of the discussion was that they would all proceed with business as usual, just as if nothing had happened, except that they would try to control credits in their markets and discourage any advances to speculators". Fraser to McGarrah, 13 February 1934, BISA, 7.18(2) – *Papers McGarrah/Fraser,* box MCG12, f68c.
18. The de Broqueville cabinet resigned owing to internal divisions about the efficacy and desirability of the continuation of deflationary policies.
19. The threat might have gone beyond devaluation. In swearing in the Theunis cabinet on 21 November 1934, King Leopold III warned the new government that public opinion was restless. "Vous représentez", he added, "à mes yeux le dernier espoir de sauver le pays par le jeux normal de nos institutions politiques". Ranieri (1985), p. 277.
20. At the end of the conference (20 October 1934), the gold bloc governments reaffirmed their intention to maintain the current gold parities. They advocated a trade increase between their countries but, characteristically, left to bilateral negotiations the task of finding the most appropriate measures to that end. "Protocol adopted by

the Conference of representatives of the gold bloc", BISA, 6.42b – *Conference of representatives of gold bloc.*
21. "Protocol adopted by the conference of representatives of the gold bloc", *Les Temps,* 22 October 1934.
22. Van der Wee and Tavernier (1975), pp. 272ff.
23. Brother of Marcel van Zeeland, manager at the BIS.
24. In March 1936, Belgium reinstated gold convertibility at the lower parity established a year before (−28%); Van der Wee and Tavernier (1975), p. 320. Belgium would remain on the gold standard until the outbreak of the Second World War.
25. Eichengreen (1993), p. 363.
26. Ibid., p. 378.
27. On the Dutch case, see de Vries (1994b), pp. 84–150.
28. Flandin fell on 31 May 1935 and was replaced by Laval, who was much more determined to stick to gold even at the cost of exacerbating both protectionist and deflationary measures.
29. Blum (1959), p. 132.
30. On the renewed intellectual efforts by the Bank of England and the BIS during this period aimed at better understanding and computing price relationships, see Sayers (1976a), pp. 473–5.
31. BISA, *Minutes of the Meetings of the Board of Directors,* 11 November 1935, p. 1.
32. BISA, *Minutes of the Meetings of the Board of Directors,* 17 June 1935, pp. 1–2.
33. Blum (1959), p. 136. On Cochran, see Section 3.2 (in particular, note 38).
34. BISA, *Minutes of the Meetings of the Board of Directors,* 17 June 1935, p. 2.
35. Fraser was probably ready to leave the Bank in the autumn of 1934 but was deterred by the reaction of the main central bankers, who "reacted violently against suggestion of [his] now quitting in the middle of [his] term". Fraser to Harrison, 23 October 1934, FRBNY – *Harrison Papers.* In January 1935, however, Fraser wrote in confidence to Harrison, informing him that he was going to work for the First National Bank of New York as from 1 June. Fraser to Harrison, 25 January 1935, FRBNY – *Harrison Papers.*
36. However, contrary to McGarrah and Fraser, McKittrick was not himself a director of the BIS. He was entitled to attend the meetings of the Board of Directors in his capacity as President of the Bank, but had no voting right. In any case, during McKittrick's tenure (January 1940 to June 1946), no Board meetings took place because of the war.
37. A good instance of this triangulation is provided by a telephone conversation between Harrison and Norman in March 1935. "Governor Norman said that while he had not talked directly with Governor Harrison for several months he had heard about him through Mr. Fraser and therefore felt that the gulf between them was not as wide as it would otherwise have been. Governor Harrison replied that he had also heard occasionally from Mr. Fraser about Governor Norman and that he understood that he (Governor Norman) was now the bad boy in the opinion of European central banks". Harrison–Norman telephone conversation, 18 March 1935, FRBNY – *Harrison Papers,* 3115.5: "Conversations with Mr. Norman 1936".
38. At the end of a letter containing a routine request for information, a BIS official apologised to his correspondent at the Federal Reserve Bank of New York by saying: "I hope I am not being too much of a nuisance to you but you will remember that we

have now no American in this bank to whom I can refer". Connolly to Galantière, 9 January 1936, FRBNY, Relations with BIS, BISA, 7.16(3) – *BIS History (Baffi papers),* box RBL/B1.
39. Chandler (1958), p. 478.
40. Strong died in October 1928 at the age of 56.
41. Meltzer (2003), pp. 259–60. The Banking Act of 1935 would formalise the shift of power and authority over the reserve banks to the Board in Washington. See also ibid., pp. 415, 470 ff.
42. Memorandum, Galantière to Harrison, 13 July 1929, FRBNY 290713, BISA, 7.16(3) – *BIS History (Baffi papers),* box RBL/B22 (letter Ms. Cumming to Baffi, 11 February 1986).
43. See Section 6.10.
44. Notes (not verbatim) taken on the statement made by Burgess, Deputy Governor of the FRBNY, at the meeting of the Federal Reserve Board on 30 October 1931 with regard to his recent trip to Europe. NARA, RG 82, *Records of the Federal Reserve System,* NWCH, box 13. Burgess noted that – while it was "too early to judge the effects of BIS on Germany, Austria and Hungary" – the BIS had "given us an instrument that puts us in the position at least to make an attempt without it being very expensive".
45. Harrison to McGarrah, 24 April 1931, FRBNY – *Harrison Papers.*
46. Harrison to Woodin, 8 May 1933, FRBNY – *Harrison Papers.*
47. Statement of Secretary of the Treasury Woodin at the Federal Reserve Board meeting of 10 May. FRBNY – *Harrison Papers.* I owe this information to an unpublished document prepared by Frank Tamagna for Paolo Baffi under the title: "Relations Between the Federal Reserve Bank and the BIS", 1985, BISA, 7.16(3) – *BIS History (Baffi papers),* box RBL/B35. On Woodin's position see Federal Reserve Board, "Legal and practical considerations affecting question whether governor of Federal Reserve Bank of New York should become a director of the BIS", 29 January 1936, p. 7, NARA, RG82 – FRS, box 14.
48. Harrison–Norman telephone conversation, 6 November 1933, FRBNY – *Harrison Papers,* 3115.5: "Conversations with M. Norman 1933".
49. Federal Reserve Board, "Legal and practical considerations affecting question whether governor of Federal Reserve Bank of New York should become a director of the BIS", 29 January 1936, p. 8, NARA, RG82 – FRS, box 14.
50. Ibid.
51. Harrison's conversation with Fraser: 6 April 1934, FRBNY – *Harrison Papers,* 3013.2: "Conversations with Mr. Fraser".
52. Harrison and Sproul (secretary to FRBNY) were at the BIS in early July 1934. As Fraser commented to the Board: "The visit of Governor Harrison has given rise to many unfounded rumours in the press". BISA, *Minutes of the Meetings of the Board of Directors,* 9 July 1934, p. 1.
53. Harrison's telephone conversation with Norman, 12 June 1935, FRBNY – *Harrison Papers,* 3115: "Conversations with M. Norman 1934–36".
54. Harrison's telephone conversation with Norman, 20 June 1935, FRBNY – *Harrison Papers,* 3115: "Conversations with M. Norman 1934–36".
55. Harrison's telephone conversation with Norman, 17 September 1935, FRBNY – *Harrison Papers,* 3115: "Conversations with M. Norman 1934–36".

56. Harrison's telephone conversation with Morgenthau, 15 August 1935, FRBNY – *Harrison Papers*, 2012.5: "Conversations with Morgenthau 1935".
57. As a result of the 1935 Banking Act, Eccles' title from 23 August 1935 was changed from Governor of the Federal Reserve Board to Chairman of the Board of Governors of the Federal Reserve System (as it still is today).
58. Harrison's telephone conversation with Morgenthau, 15 August 1935, FRBNY – *Harrison Papers*, 2012.5: "Conversations with Morgenthau 1935". In addition to the opposition by Board members, Harrison felt that Eccles had not given the matter enough consideration and was "considerably confused about the procedure".
59. Harrison's telephone conversation with Norman, 31 March 1935, FRBNY – *Harrison Papers*, 3115: "Conversations with M. Norman 1934–36". The Fed suggested that the BIS by-laws should be amended before a U.S. official sat there. Consideration of the matter was then postponed until after the autumn elections.
60. As early as 1934, Fraser had advised Harrison that "some of the directors here are dissatisfied with the present situation, because they feel that if you are not going to be in a position to accept the appointment, then we ought to appoint someone else.... If it then appears that the action of the Board in Washington is permanent rather than provisional, we must decide here what to do next". Fraser to Harrison, 19 January 1934, FRBNY, BIS Files (microfilm).
61. Meltzer (2003), pp. 415, 470 ff.
62. Federal Reserve Board, "Legal and practical considerations affecting question whether governor of Federal Reserve Bank of New York should become a director of the BIS", 29 January 1936, p. 15, NARA, RG82 – FRS, box 14.
63. Reference is made in the memorandum to *The Great Depression* by Lionel Robbins and to *Monetary Theory and the Trade Cycle* by Friedrich von Hayek.
64. Federal Reserve Board, "Legal and practical considerations affecting question whether governor of Federal Reserve Bank of New York should become a director of the BIS", 29 January 1936, p. 12, NARA, RG82 – FRS, box 14.
65. Ibid.
66. Blum (1959), p. 141.
67. Federal Reserve Board, "Legal and practical considerations affecting question whether governor of Federal Reserve Bank of New York should become a director of the BIS", 29 January 1936, p. 12, NARA, RG82 – FRS, box 14.
68. Ibid.
69. "Memorandum A – Benefits which the U.S. might be expected to derive from representation on the board of the BIS", 16 October 1935, NARA, RG 82 – FRS, NWCH, box 13.
70. See also Section 6.10 on the governors' unofficial meetings.
71. "Memorandum A – Benefits which the U.S. might be expected to derive from representation on the board of the BIS", 16 October 1935, NARA, RG 82 – FRS, NWCH, box 13.
72. All quotes are from "The Bank for International Settlements and the Board of Governors of the Federal Reserve System", 27 November 1935, NARA, RG 82 – FRS, NWCH, box 13.
73. An earlier version of the report noted that "The most recently created central banks, such as those of Canada, New Zealand, and Argentina, have special provisions for the BIS in their original statutes". "The Bank for International Settlements and the

Board of Governors of the Federal Reserve System", 12 November 1935, NARA, RG 82 – FRS, NWCH.

74. Ibid.

75. Ibid.

76. F. Tamagna, "Relations Between the Federal Reserve Bank and the BIS", Unpublished memorandum for Paolo Baffi, 1985, p. 18, BISA, 7.16(3) – *BIS History (Baffi papers),* box RBL/B35.

77. In what follows here, I have been helped by notes prepared by Frank Tamagna for Paolo Baffi. See "The Federal Reserve Bank of New York's account at the BIS in the interwar period", 1985, BISA, 7.16(3) – *BIS History (Baffi papers),* box RBL/B35.

78. Telephone conversation between McGarrah, Fraser, and Burgess, 24 July 1931, FRBNY, 797.3 – *Bank for International Settlements.*

79. McGarrah–Crane telephone conversation, 30 December 1932, FRBNY, 797.3 – *Bank for International Settlements.*

80. Sayers (1976a), p. 280 (the wording is from the statement by the British Treasury).

81. See, among many others: Clarke (1977); Sayers (1976a), pp. 475ff; Blum (1959), pp. 149–73; Eichengreen (1993), pp. 348–89.

82. In March 1936.

83. Vincent Auriol, the new Minister of Finance, was a strong supporter of the gold standard.

84. Monick is quoted as having said to Morgenthau: "We want this feeling of peace and not only for France but for the world that really this is monetary peace which is coming now". Blum (1959), p. 158.

85. Sayers (1976a), p. 478.

86. It is appropriate in this respect to quote Gottfried Haberler's remarks to Baffi when the latter was working on the history of the BIS: "Floating exchange rates would have made Schachtian policies unnecessary. But that is really from an economic standpoint, as we see things now. Actually floating at the time was out of the question. A change in the exchange rates would have been possible, but we have to keep in mind that Schachtian policies were also a device to bring pressure upon other countries. It would have been very hard for the Hitler regime to devalue the mark". Haberler to Baffi, 18 September 1984, BISA, 7.16(3) – *BIS History (Baffi papers),* box RBL/B22.

87. Transcript of the Blum–Schacht meeting, 28 August 1936, BISA, 7.16(3) – *BIS History (Baffi papers),* box RBL/B1.

88. The two men, both defeated in their political aims, would meet again in Dachau eight years later. Blum (1954), p. 534.

89. Cochran to Secretary of State, 8 June 1936, NARA, BISA, 7.16(3) – *BIS History (Baffi papers),* box RBL/B1, b.

90. Ibid. Trip was even ready, if the situation in France worsened and exchange controls seemed imminent, to take the lead in devaluing the florin in order to "help France to a wiser solution than exchange controls".

91. Ibid. On the same occasion, Cochran merely exchanged greetings with Norman and Niemeyer, who certainly did not need to be informed or to pass on information through him. He also saw Schacht, Beneduce, and Azzolini as well as Jacobsson. Referring to the abrogation of the trade treaty with Germany, the President of the Reichsbank typically asked Cochran how Americans "expected him to pay his debts

to the United States if we made it impossible for him to sell goods in our market or to gain foreign exchange through multilateral trade". Politics figured prominently in talks with almost everyone. According to Cochran, "Most Basel observers expect ... various neutral states to consider withdrawal from the League and the League to drift into a sort of political BIS where an expert staff would be maintained and international problems studied but more ambitious undertakings dropped".

92. Cochran to Secretary of State, 27 June 1936, NARA, BISA, 7.16(3) – *BIS History (Baffi papers),* box RBL/B1, b.
93. Ibid. The conversation was immediately reported to Cochran, who reported it back to Washington.
94. Cochran to Secretary of State, 8 June 1936, NARA, BISA, 7.16(3) – *BIS History (Baffi papers),* box RBL/B1, b.
95. Ibid.
96. Sayers (1976a), p. 479.
97. Cochran to Secretary of State, August 24, 1936, NARA, BISA, 7.16(3) – *BIS History (Baffi papers),* box RBL/B1, b.
98. Blum (1959), p. 160.
99. Ibid. On reading the Auriol draft, President Roosevelt – according to Morgenthau – reacted: "It's terrible! It gives me a pain!"; and on reviewing the section referring to a return to the gold standard, Roosevelt said " 'OUT!', with a very loud voice". Clarke (1977), p. 39.
100. Sayers (1976a), p. 479.
101. Blum (1959), p. 171.
102. In fact, the Tripartite Agreement consisted of three similar statements issued simultaneously by the governments of France, the United Kingdom, and the United States. The full text can be found in: BISA, *Seventh Annual Report,* Basel, 3 May 1937, Annex VII.
103. Sayers (1976a), pp. 280–1.
104. Ibid., p. 480.
105. BISA, *Minutes of the Meetings of the Board of Directors,* 12 October 1936, pp. 1–2.
106. Sayers (1976a), p. 281.
107. Cochran to Secretary of State, 14 October 1936, NARA, BISA, 7.16(3) – *BIS History (Baffi papers),* box RBL/B1, b.
108. The pound was exchanged in Paris for 148 francs one year after the agreement and for 178 a year later.
109. The British currency first appreciated by about 10% against the dollar (October 1936 – March 1938) but then lost about 13% in the following six months.
110. Sayers (1976a), p. 481.
111. Ikenberry (1993), pp. 164–6, 193. On the influence of the Tripartite Agreement on French plans for postwar international monetary reform, see Bordo, Simard, and White (1994), pp. 3–6.
112. As Clarke (1977, p. 55) puts it: "With the establishment of these arrangements, the first step was taken toward the rebuilding of an international monetary system".
113. Beyen observed that in the agreement "cooperation is formulated, not as a positive policy of coordination, but as a negative promise not to indulge in action that could disturb equilibrium". Beyen (1949), p. 112.
114. See Section 6.3.

115. Baffi (2002), p. 83.
116. Ibid. Baffi quotes a letter from Lamont to Morgan and a memorandum written by Siepmann in December 1932.
117. "[Members of the BIS staff] have frequently commented to me upon their pride and satisfaction in having Mr. Fraser as their Vice President and have revealed their hope that he might become the head of the institution". Merle Cochran to the Undersecretary of State, 14 February 1933, NARA, RG 39 – *U.S. Treasury, Records of the Bureau of Accounts, Fiscal Relationships between the United States and other Nations*, box 103.
118. See Section 6.3.
119. Trip has been described as always busy but at the same time exuding inner calm, and as being fair and tactful in dealing with people. See de Vries (1994b), p. 33.
120. Trip to Fraser, 23 January 1935, BIHA – *Archivio Beneduce*, 326, Beneduce.
121. Fraser to Trip, 24 January 1935, BIHA – *Archivio Beneduce*, 326, Beneduce.
122. On Beyen, who after the Second World War became Executive Director of the IMF for the Netherlands (1948–52) and Dutch Minister of Foreign Affairs (1952–56), see the forthcoming biography by W. H. Weenink. Weenink describes Beyen as a bright, sharp-witted man who felt like a fish in water in high society. He was a man of great thoughts, keenly interested in the big picture but less so in mundane, practical issues.
123. Already in 1929 Quesnay had argued that the BIS ought to create its own international unit of account, the "grammor". Partly under the influence of pan-Europeanists such as Count Coudenhove-Kalergi, the idea was still dear to him in 1934: "Je suis convaincu personnellement que s'imposera l'usage d'une monnaie de compte supranationale et j'ai toujours souhaité que la BRI devienne la Banque Centrale de cette unité poids d'or lors des reconstructions monétaires à venir". Quoted in Feiertag (2004), pp. 338–9.
124. He had worked together closely with, among others, Per Jacobsson (who noted in his diary on 6 May 1924: "Each time I meet Quesnay I become more enchanted with him. He is remarkable") and Harry Siepmann (Bank of England); Feiertag (2004), p. 336.
125. Merle Cochran reported in early 1933 on Quesnay's strained relations with his colleagues in the BIS management: "Through his aggressive attitude, M. Quesnay has made numerous enemies, and through his repeated errors in judgment, especially in connection with public and newspaper statements, Quesnay has frequently embarrassed the BIS". Merle Cochran to the Undersecretary of State, 14 February 1933, NARA, RG 39 – *U.S. Treasury, Records of the Bureau of Accounts, Fiscal Relationships between the United States and other Nations*, box 103.
126. See, for instance, "Kommt Dr Schacht als Generaldirektor der BIZ nach Basel?", *National-Zeitung*, 9 December 1937; and *Financial News*, 18 December 1937.
127. BISA, *Minutes of the Meetings of the Board of Directors*, 13 December 1937, p. 3.
128. Cochran to Secretary of State, 7 July 1936, FRBNY, BISA, 7.16(3) – *BIS History (Baffi papers)*, box RBL/B1.
129. Mitzakis to Lacour-Gayet, 28 November 1933, BFA, 1489200303/187 – *Liaison Banque de France – BRI*.
130. Salaries were reduced by 10% at the beginning of 1934. The size of the staff was then down to 78 from 115 in 1931. BISA, *Minutes of the Meetings of the Board of*

Directors, 13 November 1933, p. 1. Salaries were further reduced by 5% in 1936, when allowances of the members of the Board were also cut by 15%. BISA, *Minutes of the Meetings of the Board of Directors*, 6 April 1936, p. 3.

131. M. van Zeeland, "Activité de la B.R.I. évoluée", 2 May 1934, BISA, 7.18(8) – *Papers Royot*, box ROY1, f5.

132. In what follows, I shall refer to Swiss gold francs unless otherwise stated.

133. Comité d'études BRI, "BIS reconsidered: Travail final d'ensemble", partie II, January 1945, BISA, 7.16 – *BIS Foundation and History*, box RBL02.

134. Data for total assets of the Swedish and Swiss central banks from Mitzakis (1939).

135. Comité d'études BRI, "BIS reconsidered: Travail final d'ensemble", partie II, January 1945, p. 16, BISA, 7.16 – *BIS Foundation and History*, box RBL02.

136. BIS, "The Bank for International Settlements and the financing of international trade", BISA, *HS publications*, no. 45, 27 April 1937.

137. BIS Banking Department, "Remobilisation internationale des actifs B.R.I.", 20 February 1936, BISA, 7.18(8) – *Papers Royot*, box ROY1, f6.

138. Comité d'études BRI, "BIS reconsidered: Travail final d'ensemble", partie II, January 1945, p. 17-17bis, BISA, 7.16 – *BIS Foundation and History*, box RBL02.

139. The amount of the interest rate paid on deposits would be calculated as an average for all markets of the returns which the BIS itself "obtains for its deposits at sight and for the funds employed in investments which can be realised at any time". BISA, *Summary and Conclusions of the special committee with respect to the operations of the BIS*, 17 June 1930, p. 4.

140. To be accepted on deposit, individual currencies had to satisfy "the *practical* criteria of the gold or gold-exchange standard" (emphasis added). Arts. 21 and 26 of the BIS Statutes (1930).

141. See internal memos of the Banking Department (from December 1931 and 21 April 1932) arguing that the single interest rate policy would be acceptable only if the Bank did not take any exchange rate risk (and recommending, in any case, forward coverage).

142. See Sorrentino (1999).

143. Comité d'études BRI, "BIS reconsidered: Travail final d'ensemble", partie II, January 1945, pp. 29–31, BISA, 7.16 – *BIS Foundation and History*, box RBL02.

144. For the depositor there is an important difference. In the case of sight deposits he is entitled to receive back the same weight of gold, while in the case of earmarked gold he will receive back the same bars as originally deposited (I owe this clarification to Marten de Boer).

145. Earmarked gold in custody for central banks totalled 217 million Swiss gold francs at the end of 1934 and 272 million at the end of 1935. It reached 479 million in March 1938 and declined thereafter (to 237 million in March 1939). G. Royot, "Nomenclature des principaux événements ayant affecté la politique bancaire de la BRI", April 1945, BISA, 7.16 – *BIS Foundation and History*, box RBL02, f3.

146. Beyen (1949), pp. 136–7.

147. Ibid., pp. 13, 20.

148. As mentioned earlier, shares were originally (1930–31) issued in 26 countries. While most shares remained in the possession of the central banks, the entire American issue – and part of the Belgian, French, and Danzig share issues – were placed with the public. Over time, these privately held shares became scattered

geographically. Repartition of the BIS shares in 1930–32, 1939, and 1944 in: Comité d'Etudes BRI, "BIS Reconsidered: Travail final d'ensemble", partie II, January 1945, p. 7, BISA, 7.16 – *BIS Foundation and History,* box RBL02.
149. See Section 3.5.
150. BISA, *Summary and Conclusions of the special committee with respect to the operations of the BIS,* 17 June 1930, p. 2.
151. Comité d'Etudes BRI, "BIS Reconsidered: Travail final d'ensemble", partie II, January 1945, p. 36, BISA, 7.16 – *BIS Foundation and History,* box RBL02.
152. BISA, *Summary and Conclusions of the special committee with respect to the operations of the BIS,* 17 June 1930, p. 5.
153. In the mid-1930s, the BIS's "daily tasks as a business institution [were] confined to transactions in gold and foreign exchange for account of a relatively small amount of central banks and more or less seasonal credits to those banks". J. W. Beyen, "Memorandum on the development of the tasks of the BIS", part II, 27 August 1935, p. 13, BISA, 7.18(8) – *Papers Royot,* box ROY1, f5.
154. Ibid.
155. Ibid.
156. Ibid.
157. BISA, *Minutes of the Meetings of the Board of Directors,* 12 July 1937, p. 2.
158. It reached 479 million Swiss gold francs in March 1938 and declined thereafter (to 237 million in March 1939).
159. The Swiss franc, equal before the war in gold content to the French and Belgian francs as well as to the Italian lira, was the only currency of the former Latin Monetary Union to be restored to its prewar parity of 0.29032258 grams fine gold. The parity held until the devaluation of September 1936.
160. Letter, 13 June 1933, BISA, 6.48 – *International Payments under the World Postal Convention, Policy,* vol. 1.
161. BISA, *Minutes of the Meetings of the Board of Directors,* 12 March 1934.
162. "Settlement of international postal payments in gold francs through the Bank for International Settlements", 6 April 1937, BISA, 6.48 – *International payments under World Postal Convention, Policy,* vol. 1.
163. The BIS would charge no fees or commissions other than expenses incurred in carrying out the various transactions.
164. Charles Roches, "Règlements des soldes en francs-or par l'intermédiaire de la Banque des Règlements Internationaux à Bâle", *Journal des Télécommunications,* 12 December 1938.
165. The monthly average for 1939 was twenty transactions, resulting in a total of 40–50 kilograms of gold being debited and credited to the various gold sight accounts. See BISA, 6.48 – *International Payments under the World Postal Convention, Policy,* vol. 1.
166. "Conversations Quesnay avec le Gouverneur Norman, 24 April 1930", BISA, 7.18(2) – *Papers McGarrah/Fraser,* box MCG3, 21.
167. Mr. Fraser, "Note for Mr. Rodd", 14 January 1931, BISA, 7.18(2) – *Papers McGarrah/Fraser,* box MCG8, 58.
168. As a mere curiosity it may be mentioned that Thomas Balogh (later Lord Balogh) applied for a job at the Bank at the end of 1931. Nothing eventually came of it. He held a flattering reference from Burgess of the Federal Reserve Bank of New

York: "An economist from Hungary by the name of Balogh has written me that he is seeking a position with the BIS .... Balogh was in this country for a number of months doing some graduate work at Harvard.... He is a person of unusual ability, and would be very much worth considering if you are looking for an assistant for Jacobsson. He has worked in the Reichsbank, in a Hungarian commercial bank, and in the London market." W. R. Burgess to McGarrah, 18 November 1931, BISA, 7.18 (2) – *Papers McGarrah/Fraser,* box MCG9.

169. The series was called "Central Banking Studies" or CB series. Until the outbreak of the war in 1939, some 175 titles were produced. These studies were for internal consumption and for confidential circulation among the central banks. They covered a wide range of topics: analyses of the economic crisis and world trade developments (e.g., Pilotti, "La crise mondiale", CB Document no. 46, 1932; BIS, "Quelques considérations sur la situation économique mondiale", CB Document no. 118); surveys of gold production and gold and foreign exchange reserves held by central banks (e.g., BIS, "Holdings of gold and foreign exchange", CB Document no. 30, 1931; Blessing, "The gold exchange standard", CB Document no. 60, 1932; Jacobsson, "Notes on the gold problem", CB Document no. 100, 1937; Quesnay, "The superabundance of gold", CB Document no. 103, 1937); and individual country studies (e.g., BIS, "Analyse de la situation monétaire et économique de la France, 1925–35", CB Document no. 87, 1935; BIS, "Die Währungs- und Wirtschaftslage in Deutschland", CB Document no. 90, 1936).

170. Bank for International Settlements, *Service Note no. 45,* 1 June 1931. See also a note by Dr. Simon dated 15 July 1931, BISA, 7.18(2) – *Papers McGarrah/Fraser,* box MCG8, f 58.

171. BIS, Monetary and Economic Department, HS Series no. 18, *Note on the work of the Monetary and Economic Department,* 5 February 1932.

172. Official recognition and praise to the Swedish economist was repeatedly given at Board meetings. The President of the BIS said "that by far the greatest part of the Report itself was due to Dr. Jacobsson, the Economic Adviser of the Bank". BISA, *Minutes of the Meetings of the Board of Directors,* 13 May 1935, p. 5. "When the Report was referred to, one name above others must be mentioned, namely, that of the Economic Adviser of the Bank, Mr. Jacobsson". BISA, *Minutes of the Meetings of the Board of Directors,* 13 June 1938, p. 2.

173. Jacobsson (1979), pp. 84 ff.

174. The Annual Report's length, excluding budget annexes, rose from just 14 pages in 1931 to 157 in 1939.

175. Keynes (1934), p. 516.

176. Schloss (1970), p. 25.

177. For an excellent testimonial of the state of the art in monetary policy in the 1930s, see Gayer (1937).

178. Memorandum, 21 June 1935, BISA, 7.18(8) – *Papers Royot,* box ROY1, f 5.

179. "Note for Dr. Beyen: Reorganisation of Monetary and Economic Department", 6 August 1935, BULH, NL 324 – *Nachlass Per Jacobsson.*

180. "The system of inviting young economists from central banks for a period of a few months, which has been inaugurated at the suggestion of the Bank of England, had given good results and would be developed further". BISA, *Minutes of the Meetings of the Board of Directors,* 12 July 1937, p. 2.

181. BISA, 3.1(a) – *Trainees,* vol. 1, 1932–1969.
182. M. W. Holtrop's interview in BIS, *Personal Recollections and Opinions. Published on the Occasion of the Fiftieth Anniversary,* BISA, Basel, 1980, pp. 27–8.
183. Merle Cochran to the Undersecretary of State, 11 October 1933, p. 6, NARA, RG 39 – *U.S. Treasury, Records of the Bureau of Accounts, Fiscal Relationships between the United States and other Nations,* box 103.
184. "Memorandum A – Benefits which the U.S. might be expected to derive from representation on the board of the BIS, 16 October 1935", NARA, RG 82 – FRS, NWCH.
185. "It was indeed as a club rather than conference that Norman and others shaped the Basel meetings during those days". Sayers (1976a), p. 358.
186. Ibid.
187. "La séance officieuse des Gouverneurs se tenant à 4 heures et le thé étant servi ensuite, je vous propose de rester en tenue de ville pour le dîner"; McGarrah to Beneduce, 3 April 1933, BIHA, *Archivio Beneduce,* Cart. 326, Schacht.
188. Jacobsson's diaries abound with recollections of such events, records of which are also found in individual central banks' archives (mainly letters of invitation and thanks).
189. Diary Per Jacobsson, 12 March 1933, BULH, NL 324 – *Nachlass Per Jacobsson,* Tagebücher – D.17.
190. Lord Cobbold's interview, in BIS, *Personal Recollections and Opinions. Published on the Occasion of the Fiftieth Anniversary,* BIS, Basel 1980, pp. 55–6.
191. "Norman was ... the most regular attendant to [the Bank's] Board and meetings". Clay (1957), p. 367.
192. Boyle (1967), p. 281. In 1950, when the Bank of Iceland became a member of the BIS, Siepmann wrote to the Icelandic governor: "I know it is a long way from Iceland to Basle, but time spent on the journey is not as great as the time which Lord Norman spent, month after month, going to and fro by train and boat. If it were still possible to meet him there, it would be worth your while to travel three times round the world. But there are people who go regularly to Basle who knew him and have been influenced by him, and the tradition which he founded persists". Siepmann to Arnason, 15 March 1950, BEA, OV4 / 45 – *BIS General, 1950–52.*
193. Boyle (1967), p. 282.
194. These were the topics most frequently dealt with by high-ranking BIS officials when providing accounts of the meetings to governors who happened not to be present.
195. Diary Per Jacobsson, 12 March 1933, BULH, NL 324 – *Nachlass Per Jacobsson,* Tagebücher – D.17.
196. Ibid.
197. Notes (not verbatim) taken on the statement made by Mr. Burgess, Deputy Governor of the FRBNY, at the meeting of the Federal Reserve Board on 30 October 1931 with regard to his recent trip to Europe. NARA, RG 82 – FRS, NWCH. See foregoing text for other details on this testimonial.
198. Harrison's telephone conversation with Fraser, 9 May 1933. FRBNY – *Harrison Papers,* 3013.2: "Harrison's conversations with L. Fraser, BIS. 1933–35".
199. Harrison's telephone conversation with Fraser, 7 March 1935, FRBNY – *Harrison Papers,* 3013.2: "Harrison's conversations with L. Fraser, BIS. 1933–35".

200. Fraser's telephone conversation with Harrison, 11 March 1935, FRBNY – *Harrison Papers,* 3013.2: "Harrison's conversations with L. Fraser, BIS. 1933–35".
201. Cochran to Secretary of State, 11 February 1936, Washington, NARA, RG 84 – *Records of Foreign Service Posts,* 350/55/23/4: *American Embassy Paris, General Records 1936,* box 27.
202. Cochran to Secretary of State, 10 March 1936, Washington, NARA, RG 84 – *Records of Foreign Service Posts,* 350/55/23/4: *American Embassy Paris, General Records 1936,* box 27. Incidentally, at that same meeting, Schacht assured Cochran that "Hitler wants peace", and Norman told Cochran that he (Norman) "thinks Hitler is sincere.... He argues that the rest of the world is much better off with Hitler and Schacht in power than if they were out".
203. Diary Per Jacobsson, 11 May 1933, BULH, NL 324 – *Nachlass Per Jacobsson,* Tagebücher – D.17.
204. Boyle (1967), pp. 307–8.

Chapter 7

1. The situation of Switzerland had long been peculiar in that the country used to provide troops to any state willing to pay for them; the Constitution of 1848 put a stop to that practice.
2. "Neutralità", *Enciclopedia Italiana,* vol. 24 , Istituto dell'Enciclopedia Italiana, Roma, p. 703.
3. "Neutralità", Dizionario Enciclopedico del Diritto, diretto da Enrico Galgano, Cedam, Padova 1996, vol. II, p. 998.
4. Weinberg (1994), pp. 394ff, 402.
5. Milward (1987), pp. 322–3.
6. Weinberg (1994), p. 77.
7. Ibid., pp. 104–5.
8. Ibid., p. 396.
9. Frech (2001), pp. 129–46. In response to these agreements, the United Kingdom cut off the supply of raw materials to Switzerland.
10. Milward (1987), p. 324.
11. Ibid., p. 325.
12. "The option of a 'dormant' BIS was discarded from the beginning"; Auboin (1955), p. 15.
13. See Chapter 8.
14. Auboin (1955), p. 15.
15. Kubu (1998), p. 245.
16. Ibid.
17. Ibid., p. 246.
18. Since Czechoslovakia regarded the Munich agreement (which it called *Diktat*) as legally null and void, the return of this gold was part of the overall postwar Czech claim. Ibid.
19. Renouvin (1958), p. 167.
20. Kubu (1998), p. 246.
21. Original transfer order: Národní Banka Ceskoslovenská to BIS, 18 March 1939, BISA, 2.22e – *Statni Banka Ceskoslovenska, Gold Operations, Policy, 1932–1985.*

The total amount of the Czechoslovak gold deposit with the BIS in London at that time was 28,309 kg of fine gold – that is, more than a third of Czechoslovakia's total gold reserves (of which in March 1939 there remained some 74 tonnes of gold). The transfer order received by the BIS on 20 March concerned 23,087 kg of fine gold, so there remained 5,222 kg of fine gold (421 gold bars) on deposit with the BIS in London in the name of the (renamed) National Bank of Bohemia and Moravia. On 24 August 1939, this gold was sent partly to Amsterdam and partly to Berne. These 421 gold bars remained untouched, and after the war the re-established State Bank of Czechoslovakia took possession of them. "Czechoslovakia", BISA, *Gold Register – Accounts Closed*.

22. Národní Banka Ceskoslovenská to BIS, 18 March 1939, BISA, 7.16(3) – *BIS History (Baffi papers), Czechoslovak gold affair*, box RBL/B4.
23. The so-called Czechoslovakia Act, restricting operations on Czechoslovak financial assets in London, came officially into force only on 27 March 1939, but already on 15 March – the day of the German invasion – Chancellor of the Exchequer Sir John Simon had asked banks to block Czechoslovak assets held in the United Kingdom.
24. BIS subaccount no. 17 with the Bank of England. The precise reconstruction of the gold movements is due to the careful research conducted on the BIS's wartime gold operations by Piet Clement. Documentation is to be found in: BISA, 7.16(3) – *BIS History (Baffi papers), Czechoslovak gold affair*, box RBL/B4; and BISA, 7.18(5) – *Papers Hechler, Tschechoslowakei, Goldaffäre*, box HEC2, f 5.
25. 645 gold bars; the transfer took place on 23 and 24 March. In early April this gold was partly sent to the Reichsbank in Berlin and partly sold to the BIS against pounds.
26. 687 gold bars; the transfer took place on 23 and 24 March. On 3 April these bars were all moved from Amsterdam to Berlin.
27. Subsequently (3 and 6 April), gold bars were partly transferred by train to Berlin and partly sold to the BIS against pounds.
28. Transactions executed on 24, 30, and 31 March.
29. Official published gold reserves of the Reichsbank amounted to no more than 25.5 tonnes of gold in 1938. Some 88 tonnes of Austrian gold were added following the *Anschluss* in March 1938. The acquisition of Czechoslovakian gold in March 1939 added another 30.5 tonnes (transfers of March 1939 minus gold sold). Finally, the Reichsbank had accumulated since 1933 some 73.5 tonnes of gold in secret reserves, while German public banks other than the Reichsbank held nearly 11 tonnes. Thus, the grand total of German gold reserves just before the outbreak of World War II was some 228 tonnes of gold. Unabhängige Expertenkommission Schweiz – Zweiter Weltkrieg (2002), pp. 54–66.
30. For instance, T. S. Page of the U.S. Board of Economic Welfare wrote in 1943 that the transfer of Czechoslovak gold, seen as the "BIS only" recognition of German conquests, "probably impaired its 'acceptability' as an instrument [the BIS itself] to be used in the Allied reconstruction of Europe". Memorandum by Page, Economic Intelligence Division, to Knapp, Federal Reserve, 26 May 1943 – NARA, Reg. 20, FRBNY, box 14.
31. Josef Malík, one of the co-signatories of the transfer order, fled from the Protectorate of Bohemia and Moravia in August 1939. He then came to Basel to reveal the full facts of the case to the BIS management: "les fonctionnaires de la Národní

banka Ceskoslovenská ont été forcés de signer le 18 mars 1939 l'ordre en vue du transfert de l'or.... Cet ordre ... a été, à notre regret à Prague, effectué bien qu'on ait pu supposer que les fonctionnaires l'ayant signé, n'avaient pas agi librement, mais sous la contrainte exercée par les autorités allemandes et la Reichsbank". Josef Malík, Paris, to Beyen, President of the BIS, 13 October 1939, BISA, 2.22e – *Statni Banka Ceskoslovenska, Gold Operations, Policy, 1932–1985.*

32. Felix Weiser (1879–1944), an Austrian lawyer who after 1938 became stateless and in November 1942 obtained Swiss nationality, was the BIS's legal adviser from 1930 until his death in 1944.

33. Given the situation in Prague, it could not be ruled out that the two Czechoslovak directors who had signed the order, Peroutka and Malík, might have acted under duress.

34. Weiser outlined his legal arguments in a note he wrote in early June 1939, after the transfer had attracted public attention. Weiser, "Or Tchécoslovaque", 8 June 1939, BISA, 2.22e – *Statni Banka Ceskoslovenska, Gold Operations, Policy,* vol. 1. Weiser's conclusion reads: "Dans le cas du transfert de l'or, aucune question de droit public ne se posait, mais bien une simple question de pratique bancaire et d'application des règles du droit privé régissant les rapports entre déposant et dépositaire. La BRI n'avait donc pas d'autre alternative que d'exécuter, dans les délais requis par la pratique bancaire, l'instruction régulièrement donnée par son client".

35. He was in Paris.

36. Beyen to Cobbold, memorandum of 11 December 1941, BISA, 7.16(3) – *BIS History (Baffi papers),* box RBL/B4: "Czechoslovak gold affair – Italian Gold – Liquidation BIS, 1939–1946".

37. Niemeyer to Norman, 5 April 1939, BISA, 7.16(3) – *BIS History (Baffi papers),* box RBL/B4: "Czechoslovak gold affair – Italian Gold – Liquidation BIS, 1939–1946".

38. See, in particular, his autobiography: Beyen (1949), pp. 137–9.

39. Kubu (1998), p. 246.

40. This and the previous quote from a note by Montagu Norman, undated, BEA, copy in BISA, 7.16(3) – *BIS History (Baffi papers),* box RBL/B4: "Czechoslovak gold affair". The acid internal comment of the Treasury to Norman's entirely political stance was that he believed "it even more important to keep the Bank for International Settlements as a non-political body than to keep £6 million out of Hitler's hands". Handwritten note by SDW to Chancellor of the Exchequer, 1 April 1939, PRO, Treasury Papers, T160/1417 – *Proposed handing-over to the German Reichsbank of gold held by BIS for Czechoslovakia,* f1: 24 March to 8 June 1939.

41. Le Norcy, French attaché to H.M. Treasury, had conveyed to the British an urgent message from Bonnet and Reynaud that they strongly felt the transfer of gold to Germany should be opposed.

42. Memo on visit of Mr. Le Norcy, without date, PRO, Treasury Papers, T160/1417 – *Proposed handing-over to the German Reichsbank of gold held by BIS for Czechoslovakia,* f1: 24 March to 8 June 1939.

43. Telegram from Newton, Prague to Treasury, 24 March 1939, PRO, Treasury Papers, T160/1417 – *Proposed handing-over to the German Reichsbank of gold held by BIS for Czechoslovakia,* f1. As we have seen, the total deposited with the BIS in London was indeed 28,309 kg of fine gold, but of this total the transfer order received by the BIS on 20 March concerned only 23,087 kg of fine gold.

44. Note on a meeting with Mr. Rueff, Bank of France, for Sir Phillips, 3 April 1939, PRO, Treasury Papers, T160/1417 – *Proposed handing-over to the German Reichsbank of gold held by BIS for Czechoslovakia,* f1: 24 March to 8 June 1939.
45. Among the handwritten notes from the Treasury, dated 3, 4, and 5 April 1939, one reads: "Mr. Cobbold told me privately that the bird has already flown". PRO, Treasury Papers, T160/1417 – *Proposed handing-over to the German Reichsbank of gold held by BIS for Czechoslovakia,* f1: 24 March to 8 June 1939.
46. See note 23.
47. A first debate on the issue was held on 18 May; another followed on 26 May.
48. Gilbert and Gott (1963), p. 210.
49. In a reply to a request for information from Sir John Simon, Chancellor of the Exchequer, Norman simply explained how things stood from a strictly formal point of view: "I should explain", the governor wrote, "that the Bank of England hold from time to time amounts of gold in safe custody for the Bank for International Settlements. The Bank of England ... have no knowledge whether gold so held is in fact the absolute property of the Bank for International Settlements or is held by the latter in whole or in part for the account of others. It follows that the Bank of England are not aware whether gold held by them at any time in the name of the Bank for International Settlements is the property of the National Bank of Czecho-Slovakia." Norman to Chancellor of the Exchequer, 30 May 1939, PRO, Treasury Papers, T160/1417 – *Proposed handing-over to the German Reichsbank of gold held by BIS for Czechoslovakia,* f1: 24 March to 8 June 1939. A few days later, at a meeting with Treasury officials, "the Governor made it clear that it was not consistent with his duty as a banker to inform the Chancellor for publication what orders he had received from a customer to deal with the latter's account". Memo of meeting between Treasury officials (Sir Horace Wilson, Sir Thomas Barnes) and the Governor and Deputy Governor of the Bank of England on the supplementary questions raised by the Chancellor of the Exchequer, PRO, Treasury Papers, T160/1417 – *Proposed handing-over to the German Reichsbank of gold held by BIS for Czechoslovakia,* f1: 24 March to 8 June 1939.
50. "The Chancellor feels no doubts that the House would not be satisfied with the reply given by the Bank and that he would be placed in a very embarrassing position if he could not give the information". Note for F. Phillips, 1 June 1939, PRO, Treasury Papers, T160/1417 – *Proposed handing-over to the German Reichsbank of gold held by BIS for Czechoslovakia,* f1: 24 March to 8 June 1939.
51. Note by Chancellor Simon, 5 June 1939, PRO, Treasury Papers, T160/1417 – *Proposed handing-over to the German Reichsbank of gold held by BIS for Czechoslovakia,* f1: 24 March to 8 June 1939. On the same occasion, Norman reiterated his belief "that the continued existence of the BIS was of value as providing a means of contact between the various countries which would otherwise be wanting". "The BIS", he reminded Simon, "was created by a Labour Government and strengthened by the present National Government. It was true that its initial function of dealing with reparations had fallen into desuetude, but the Governor felt it would be a misfortune if it collapsed."
52. "In order to prevent misunderstanding", Norman wrote to Simon, "I should like you to realise that questions put by certain members in the House of Commons do not change my views on, nor my attitude towards, the Bank for International

Settlements.... It is possible that in one way or another the question of introducing political considerations into, or even of liquidating the Bank for International Settlements may arise ... the chief gainers in the event of liquidation would likely be the Reichsbank." Letter, Norman to the Chancellor of the Exchequer, 7 June 1939, PRO, Treasury Papers, T160/1417 – *Proposed handing-over to the German Reichsbank of gold held by BIS for Czechoslovakia,* f1: 24 March to 8 June 1939.

53. Memo, Chancellor Simon to Sir R. Hopkins, 9 June 1939, PRO, Treasury Papers, T160/1417 – *Proposed handing-over to the German Reichsbank of gold held by BIS for Czechoslovakia,* f1: 24 March to 8 June 1939.

54. Ibid. The review had to be conducted along the following lines: "a– What is the origin of the BIS?; b– Is it true that since the original purpose of the BIS was to facilitate reparations payments, the purpose of the Bank has ceased to exist?; c– Are there good and sufficient reasons why it should nevertheless continue and what are the pros and cons? In particular, what is the nature of the inconvenience we may have to face in the future if the present arrangements continue, or again if they do not?; d– Can we terminate our adherence to the Protocols? If so, would this in fact bring the Bank to an end, or would it involve the withdrawal of the British members of the Board? In any event, would it remove the difficulty which arises for HMG from the fact that Bank of England officials are members of the BIS Board though HMG has no duty or right to control them in any way?; e– Alternatively, what is necessary in order to wind up the BIS?"

55. Beyen (1949, p. 139) himself noted that "The BIS suffered gravely from the political opprobrium attached to the Czechoslovak gold".

56. Only weeks after the execution of the transfer order, the BIS adopted a much more prudent attitude in dealing with the central bank of the former Czechoslovakia. When informed by the Czechoslovak National Bank on 7 April 1939 that it had changed its name to National Bank of Moravia and Bohemia, the BIS immediately asked Professor Schindler of the University of Zurich for an independent legal opinion on the question of which central bank should be regarded the rightful successor to the Czechoslovakian National Bank and so be allowed to exercise the voting rights attached to the BIS shares originally subscribed by that bank. As a result of Schindler's opinion – which basically held that the voting rights ought to be split up between the central banks of the successor states of the Czechoslovak republic – the BIS suspended these voting rights because no satisfactory solution could be worked out between the parties involved. "Opinion Dr. jur. Dietrich Schindler", 5 May 1939, BISA, 7.18(5) – *Papers Hechler,* box HEC4, f6.

57. Macmillan (1966), p. 562. A few days earlier, when Chamberlain announced to the Commons that his peace efforts would shortly be crowned by a four-power peace conference, "all Members on both sides of the House stood up in honour of the Prime Minister". Only one of them remained seated, "his head sunk in his shoulders. It was Churchill". Ibid., p. 559.

58. Carr (1947), p. 271.

59. Renouvin (1958), p. 159. There followed, needless to say, contrasting interpretations of the declaration by the two governments, but public opinion at the time was further reassured by it.

60. Gilbert and Gott (1963), pp. 199–200. However, on that occasion Schacht intimated to the U.K. government his reservations regarding Hitler and clearly stated that it

was no use trying to influence the German leaders in the direction of cooperation. See: PRO, Treasury Papers, T188/227 – *Dr. Schacht's visit to London, December 1938.*

61. Marsh (1992), pp. 124–5, p. 298, note 20.
62. Renouvin (1958), p. 165.
63. Skidelsky (2000), pp. 28–9.
64. Two days after the invasion of Czechoslovakia, Chamberlain threw off his previous appeasement stance and issued a firm declaration stating that the freedom of the U.K. nation was threatened by Hitler's will to dominate the world.
65. See "Report of the management of the BIS to the Board of directors on the period since the last board meeting", 1 October 1945, pp. 4ff, BISA, 7.18(6) – *Papers Auboin,* box AUB2, f11.
66. See, for instance, Auboin to Fournier, 31 May 1940, BISA, 7.18(6) – *Papers Auboin,* box AUB4.
67. Conversation Auboin-Fournier, 13 November 1939, BISA, 7.18(6) – *Papers Auboin,* box AUB4.
68. The Board members were sent monthly reports on the operations of the Bank and quarterly reports on the development of the investments of the Bank on the principal markets. See BISA, 1.3(4) – *Report on BIS operations.*
69. After June 1940, these were either President Weber of the Swiss National Bank or Governor Rooth of Sveriges Riksbank.
70. Overall, the Axis controlled 134,858 (67.4%) of 200,000 votes.
71. Art. 10 of the Constituent Charter (20 January 1930).
72. BIS, *Eleventh Annual Report,* Basel, 9 June 1941, pp. 184–5.
73. R. Auboin, "Principes de gestion de la BRI pendant la durée des hostilités", 14 November 1939, BISA, 7.18(6) – *Papers Auboin,* box AUB4, f28.
74. "Circular letter to central banks having business relations with the Bank for International Settlements", 18 December 1939, BISA, 1.3(5) – *Board of Directors, Banking Policy during wartime (1939–1945),* vol. 1. See also M. A. Kriz, "The BIS wartime activities and present position", 11 June 1947, p. 6, FRBNY, 797.3 – *Bank for International Settlements* (recently transferred to NARA).
75. Ibid.
76. See, for instance, the letter of 14 February 1940 from the BIS to the Netherlands Bank: "to comply with the policy agreed with our correspondents since the outbreak of hostilities, we do not take over gold from Central Banks unless such gold was in their ownership prior to 3 September 1939 or has been acquired subsequently from neutral sources". Letter from BIS to Netherlands Bank, 14 February 1940, BISA, 2.21f – *De Nederlandsche Bank NV, Gold Operations, Policy,* vol. 1.
77. Memorandum McKittrick, 22 January 1941, HUBL, Thomas H. McKittrick Collection, series 2.2, carton 8, f32: *General personnel and office personnel, USA Legation, 1940–1944.*
78. "Inter-Allied Declaration Against Acts of Dispossession Committed in Territories Under Enemy Occupation or Control", 5 January 1943; see Slany and Eizenstat (1997), pp. 6–7.
79. BISA, 7.18(8) – *Papers Royot,* box 2, f12.
80. M. A. Kriz, "The BIS wartime activities and present position", 11 June 1947, p. 7, FRBNY, 797.3 – *Bank for International Settlements* (recently transferred to NARA).

81. The fighting in Poland had practically ended by the first days of October 1939.

82. To make sure that this time there would be no misunderstandings, on 15 April 1940 Norman and Niemeyer sent McKittrick the following telegram: "We presume that you would not in present circumstances release any Danish or Norwegian gold or other assets which you may hold". HUBL, Thomas H. McKittrick Collection, series 2.2, carton 8, f 1–2: *Correspondence Bank of England, 1939–1946.*

83. Cables and letters, BIS to Norges Bank, Oslo, of 25 June and 19 August 1940, and to Norges Bank, London, of 29 August 1941, BISA, 2.76d – *Norges Bank, Gold Operations, Policy, 1932–1985,* vol. 1.

84. On 10 May 1940, German troops had entered neutral Belgium, Luxemburg, and the Netherlands.

85. BISA, 2.6 – *Banque Nationale de Belgique,* vols. 1–2.

86. The BIS had originally subscribed 12.5 million Dutch guilders of these Treasury bills – issued through bank Mendelssohn & Co. in Amsterdam – as a short-term investment. Throughout the war, the BIS repeatedly pressed the National Bank of Belgium – both in London and Brussels – for reimbursement of these "Mendelssohn" bills, since their non-repayment immobilised a nonnegligible portion of the Bank's available liquid funds. BISA, 7.18(5) – *Papers Hechler,* box HEC1, f 1/5 and 1/7.

87. "Mit Bezug auf die baltischen Staaten bestehen somit gegenwärtig unabgeklärte Rechtsverhältnisse, sodass die Auslieferung des Goldes der bisherigen baltischen Zentralbanken an die russische Staatsbank die BIZ der Gefahr aussetzen würde, später von anderer Seite, d.h. von den bisherigen Eigentümern auf Herausgabe des Goldes belangt zu werden". Opinion Prof. Dieter Schindler, 19 August 1940, p. 18, BISA, 7.18(5) – *Papers Hechler,* box HEC1, f2.

88. BISA, 2.12d – *Bank of Latvia, Gold Operations, Policy, 1932–1985,* vol. 1; 2.20d – *Bank of Estonia, Gold Operations, Policy, 1932–1985,* vol. 1; 2.77d – *Bank of Lithuania, Gold Operations, Policy, 1930–1985,* vol. 1.

89. M. A. Kriz, "The BIS wartime activities and present position", 11 June 1947, p. 13, FRBNY, 797.3 – *Bank for International Settlements* (recently transferred to NARA).

90. However, in order to avoid any complications, the wartime governor of the Netherlands Bank, Rost van Tonningen – who had been appointed by the Germans in March 1941 and was a confirmed New Order man – was urged not to take the Dutch central bank's seat on the BIS Board of Directors. Instead, the previous governor and former BIS President L. J. Trip was persuaded to extend his tenure on the BIS Board. The BIS, through the Reichsbank, was instrumental in forcing this arrangement on Amsterdam. See: letter, Hechler to Puhl, 1 April 1941, BISA, 7.18(5) – *Papers P. Hechler,* box HEC1, f.B 1/3.

91. See Section 3.2.

92. Beyen's period of office was not due to expire until May 1940, but he asked the Board to terminate his appointment at the end of 1939. BISA, *Minutes of the Meetings of the Board of Directors,* 12 June 1939, p. 2.

93. General Manager Roger Auboin was mobilised, though only in February 1940 and with a special assignment to act as secretary general to the Allied Programmes Comité in the French Ministry of Finance. Even then he received a special dispensation that allowed him to return to Basel whenever his duties at the BIS required his presence there. Auboin was demobilised after the French capitulation at the end of June 1940.

94. "Rules of conduct to be strictly adhered to by staff in order to safeguard the neutrality of the Bank", October 1941, HUBL, Thomas H. McKittrick Collection, series 2.2, carton 9, f 23: *Miscellaneous notes, office personnel, 1939–46*.
95. R. Auboin, "Memorandum sur les circonstances qui ont conduit au transfert de la BRI à Château d'Oex", 22 May 1940, BISA, 7.18(6) – *Papers Auboin,* box AUB4.
96. Weinberg (1994), p. 174.
97. Not everybody was lucky enough to live, as McKittrick and the Jacobssons did, in the beautiful Château de Rougemont (graciously lent by an American friend of McKittrick), where a staff of seven was "a skeleton force compared with what was really needed". Jacobsson (1979), p. 141.
98. McKittrick to Janssen, 4 September 1940, HUBL, Thomas H. McKittrick Collection, series 2.2, carton 7, f 33: *Correspondence National Bank of Belgium, 1939–1946*.
99. R. R. Challener (interviewer), "A Transcript of a Recorded interview with Thomas McKittrick", 30 July 1964, Princeton University, Seeley G. Mudd Manuscript Library – *The John Foster Dulles Oral History Project*. Copy obtained by the BIS in October 1996. Erin Jacobsson provides a more charitable but less credible account of life at Château d'Oex, speaking of the "harmony in which the mixed international staff of the BIS managed to live side by side, in the closest of quarters, with no dissension". Jacobsson (1979), p. 141.
100. Ibid., p. 142.
101. Ibid., p. 144.
102. See Section 7.7.
103. On that occasion he also visited Karl Blessing, former BIS employee and future president of the Bundesbank, with whom he spoke freely about the course of the war and Germany's likely postwar position. At the end of the visit, Blessing remarked that what they had said "was undoubtedly 'lebensgefährlich' [fatal] had it been known by the Gestapo". Diary Per Jacobsson, 6 December 1942, BULH, NL 324 – *Nachlass Per Jacobsson,* Tagebücher – D.47.
104. See Section 7.6.
105. McKittrick to Goffin, 2 October 1941, HUBL, Thomas H. McKittrick Collection, series 2.2, carton 7, f 33: *Correspondence National Bank of Belgium, 1939–1946*.
106. From 137 pages in 1939 to 313 in 1944.
107. Preserved in BISA, 7.16(3) – *BIS History (Baffi papers),* box RBL/B16.
108. McKittrick to Norman, 16 January 1941, HUBL, Thomas H. McKittrick Collection, series 2.2, carton 8, f 1–2: *Correspondence Bank of England, 1939–1946*.
109. Art. 43 of the 1930 Statutes (currently Art. 42).
110. Art. 44 of the 1930 Statutes (currently Art. 43).
111. Letter from Weizsäcker, Staatssekretär Auswärtiges Amt, to Puhl, Vice-President Reichsbank, 3 January 1942, AAPA, Bestand Büro des Staatssekretärs, R 29847 (microfiche) – *Schriftwechsel Januar 1941 – Januar 1942*.
112. Puhl, Vice-President of the Reichsbank, informed McKittrick that the Reichsbank President did not wish to see McKittrick replaced as President of the BIS but that it was politically impossible for him to vote directly or even indirectly for an enemy national. McKittrick to Norman, 27 January 1942, HUBL, Thomas H. McKittrick Collection, series 2.2, carton 8, f 1–2: *Correspondence Bank of England, 1939–1946*.

113. "I should not write personally to the German and Italian members of the Board.... Weber of the Swiss National Bank should act as intermediary to forward communication such as I have formerly addressed to the directors". McKittrick to Norman, 27 January 1942, HUBL, Thomas H. McKittrick Collection, series 2.2, carton 8, f1–2: *Correspondence Bank of England, 1939–1946.*

114. Through the U.S. Ambassador in Berne, McKittrick had previously obtained Washington's green light for his continuation in the job "provided present conditions continue". McKittrick to Norman, 27 January 1942, HUBL, Thomas H. McKittrick Collection, series 2.2, carton 8, f1–2: *Correspondence Bank of England, 1939–1946.*

115. Letter, Puhl to Weizsäcker, 17 September 1942, AAPA, Bestand Büro des Staatssekretärs, R 29849 (microfiche) – *Schriftwechsel Juli–Dezember 1942.*

116. Wiehl, "Aufzeichnung betreffend Bank für Internationalen Zahlungsausgleich in Basel", 2 October 1942, AAPA, Handelspolitische Abteilung, Generalreferat für Wirtschafts- und Finanzfragen, R 106486, Band 3 – *Bank für Internationalen Zahlungsausgleich 1942–1944.*

117. Telegram Rintelen, 9 October 1942, AAPA, Bestand Büro des Staatssekretärs, R 29849 (microfiche) – *Schriftwechsel Juli–Dezember 1942*: "der Reichsaussenminister bemerkt, dass eine weitere Beibehaltung des Amerikaners McKittrick als Präsident der Bank nicht möglich sei.... Die weitere deutsche Mitarbeit an der BIZ unter der Leitung eines feindlichen Ausländers sei nicht angängig; ein anderer Standpunkt liesse sich auch mit den Gegenargumenten der Reichsbank nicht rechtfertigen."

118. Art. 27 of the 1930 Statutes (currently Art. 26).

119. "We certainly hope that means can be found for you to continue your Presidency of the Bank: indeed it is not too much to say that we regard it as *essential*" [emphasis in original]. Letter, Montagu Norman to McKittrick, 12 June 1942, HUBL, Thomas H. McKittrick Collection, series 2.2, carton 8, f1–2: *Correspondence Bank of England, 1939–1946.*

120. See, for instance, the statement by Chancellor of the Exchequer Sir Kingsley Wood before the House on 13 October 1942: "Since the outbreak of the war,... the conduct and control of the Bank have been and are today in the sole hands of the President of the Bank, an American citizen.... This gentleman has our complete confidence." House of Commons, *Parliamentary Debates, Official Report*, vol. 383, no. 110, 13 October 1942, columns 1595–1596.

121. Cable, Norman and Niemeyer to McKittrick, 4 August 1942, HUBL, Thomas H. McKittrick Collection, series 2.2, carton 8, f1–2: *Correspondence Bank of England, 1939–1946.*

122. The details of the proposal were communicated by Rooth to the "four leading members" of the BIS Board – that is, Montagu Norman, Governor of the Bank of England; Yves de Boisanger, Governor of the Bank of France; Walther Funk, President of the Reichsbank; and Vincenzo Azzolini, Governor of the Bank of Italy. Rooth to Norman, 17 September 1942, HUBL, Thomas H. McKittrick Collection, series 2.2, box 13, f1: *Sveriges Riksbank.*

123. McKittrick to John Norton (U.K. Minister in Berne), 2 October 1942, HUBL, Thomas H. McKittrick Collection, series 2.2, carton 8, f1–2: *Correspondence Bank of England, 1939–1946.*

124. Anonymous memorandum for the Minister of Foreign Affairs, 15 October 1942, "Aufzeichnung betreffend Bank für Internationalen Zahlungsausgleich in Basel", AAPA, Handelspolitische Abteilung, Generalreferat für Wirtschafts- und Finanzfragen, R 106486, Band 3 – *Bank für Internationalen Zahlungsausgleich 1942– 1944.* At the insistence of von Ribbentrop, Clodius (the German envoy to Rome) sounded out the Italian authorities on their position regarding the BIS presidency. The reply that came back was unequivocally in favour of the Reichsbank's position and must have made it easier for von Ribbentrop to give in with regard to McKittrick: "Giannini sagte mir darauf … nach Rücksprache mit den beteiligten Minister und dem Präsidenten der Banca d'Italia, alle zuständigen italienischen Stellen seien übereinstimmend der Meinung, dass wir die BIZ unbedingt in der bisherigen Form erhalten sollten". Geheimtelegramm Clodius, 16 October 1942, AAPA, Handelspolitische Abteilung, Generalreferat für Wirtschafts- und Finanzfragen, R 106486, Band 3 – *Bank für Internationalen Zahlungsausgleich 1942–1944.*
125. Extract from minutes of the action taken by the Board by correspondence between the 94th meeting held on 10 July 1939 and the 95th meeting held on 9 December 1946, Resolutions no. 932 and 933, in: BISA, 1.3(1) – *Board of Directors, Nominations–resignations,* vol. 1.
126. I am indebted, without implication, to Piet Clement for both archival research and insightful considerations on the subject matter of this section.
127. Unabhängige Expertenkommission Schweiz – Zweiter Weltkrieg (2002), pp. 95, 216.
128. The Independent Commission of Experts (ICE), chaired by Jean-François Bergier, was created by the Swiss Federal decree of 13 December 1996 to investigate the relations between Switzerland and Nazi Germany during the Second World War. The ICE was dissolved at the end of 2001. Its final report was published in March 2002: Independent Commission of Experts Switzerland – Second World War (2002), 597 pages. In addition, the ICE has published 25 studies on a wide range of subjects, such as Switzerland's wartime refugee policy, the armaments industry, trade policies, and the handling of dormant accounts of Holocaust victims after the war. Of particular interest in the context of this book is: Unabhängige Expertenkommission Schweiz – Zweiter Weltkrieg (2002).
129. Ibid., pp. 36–8.
130. What follows derives from Table 1 in ibid., p. 55. Conversion rate: 1 US$ = 2.479 RM.
131. The equivalent of some 228 tonnes of fine gold; ibid., pp. 54–66.
132. "It would be incorrect to believe that gold designated as 'Melmer' included all the gold stolen in the extermination and concentration camps". The quoted figure includes only the part that ended up at the Reichsbank. Ibid., pp. 60–1.
133. He had been state secretary in Goebbels' Ministry of Propaganda and was a confidant of Göring.
134. Puhl was born in 1899.
135. Unabhängige Expertenkommission Schweiz – Zweiter Weltkrieg (2002), pp. 38– 40.
136. Quotes in English are from the ICE's earlier interim report on Switzerland's gold transactions with Nazi Germany: Independent Commission of Experts – Second World War (1998), p. 19.

137. Ibid., p. 20.

138. Note, Weizsäcker, 23 September 1942, AAPA, Bestand Büro des Staatssekretärs, R 29849 (microfiche) – *Schriftwechsel Juli–Dezember 1942.*

139. "Die BIZ wird von der Reichsbank laufend als Vermittlungsstelle benutzt, über die jährlich eine grosse Anzahl umfangreicher Gold- und Devisengeschäfte läuft. Da sämtliche Gold- und Devisengeschäfte gegenwärtig ausschliesslich den Zweck haben, Zahlungsmöglichkeiten für die Einfuhr kriegswichtiger Güter zu schaffen, ist ein erhebliches kriegswirtschaftliches Interesse an der Aufrechterhaltung der BIZ gegeben" (anonymous memorandum for the Minister of Foreign Affairs, "Aufzeichnung betreffend Bank für Internationalen Zahlungsausgleich in Basel", 15 October 1942). "Die BIZ ist für uns während des Krieges unentbehrlich geworden für die Durchführung getarnter Gold- und Devisengeschäfte, durch die wir uns Zahlungsmöglichkeiten für die Einfuhr kriegswichtiger Güter schaffen" (Wiehl, "Aufzeichnung betreffend Bank für Internationalen Zahlungsausgleich in Basel", 2 October 1942). Both memoranda in: AAPA, Handelspolitische Abteilung, Generalreferat für Wirtschafts- und Finanzfragen, R 106486, Band 3 – *Bank für Internationalen Zahlungsausgleich 1942–1944.*

140. Wiehl, "Aufzeichnung betreffend Bank für Internationalen Zahlungsausgleich in Basel", 2 October 1942, AAPA, Handelspolitische Abteilung, Generalreferat für Wirtschafts- und Finanzfragen, R 106486, Band 3 – *Bank für Internationalen Zahlungsausgleich 1942–1944.*

141. "Der einzige Aussenposten der Reichsbank mit teilweise eigenem Personal ist die BIZ". Anonymous Reichsbank memorandum for the Minister of Foreign Affairs, "Aufzeichnung betreffend Bank für Internationalen Zahlungsausgleich in Basel", 15 October 1942, AAPA, Handelspolitische Abteilung, Generalreferat für Wirtschafts- und Finanzfragen, R 106486, Band 3 – *Bank für Internationalen Zahlungsausgleich 1942–1944.*

142. Diary Per Jacobsson, 21 February 1943, BULH, NL 324 – *Nachlass Per Jacobsson,* Tagebücher – D.46.

143. "Was die von der Reichsbank angeführten Gründe anlangt, so bin ich persönlich zwar nicht restlos davon überzeugt, dass tatsächlich die deutschen Finanzinteressen bei einem Aufhören der BIZ unabwendbar eine derartig weitgehende Schädigung erleiden würden". Wiehl, "Aufzeichnung betreffend Bank für Internationalen Zahlungsausgleich in Basel", 2 October 1942, AAPA, Handelspolitische Abteilung, Generalreferat für Wirtschafts- und Finanzfragen, R 106486, Band 3 – *Bank für Internationalen Zahlungsausgleich 1942–1944.*

144. Roselli (2001), p. 293.

145. Jacobsson and Hechler had already had an in-depth discussion on the Keynes and White plans with Reichsbank Vice-President Puhl and Director Hermann Abs of the Deutsche Bank on 1 May 1943 at the Hotel Baur en Ville in Zurich. At that meeting, Puhl said that he believed it would be necessary for Germany to join in the proposed new international currency order "in some form". Diary Per Jacobsson, June 1943, pp. 133–6 and 169, BULH, NL 324 – *Nachlass Per Jacobsson,* Tagebücher – D.45.

146. BISA, 2.7 – *Bank of Japan, Policy*; and 2.7f – *Bank of Japan, Gold Operations, Policy, 1937–1985,* vol. 1.

147. Diary Per Jacobsson, 22 September 1942, BULH, NL 324 – *Nachlass Per Jacobsson,* Tagebücher – A.43. Already in May 1941, Yamamoto had told Jacobsson that

he believed Japan would soon wage war against the United States (Tagebücher A.32, 19 May 1941). Also: Yago (2001), p. 7.

148. A detailed record of Jacobsson's Japanese peace mediation in July–August 1945 can be found in: Diary Per Jacobsson, "Japanese negotiations", July 1945, BULH, NL 324 – *Nachlass Per Jacobsson,* Tagebücher – A.55 and A.55bis. See also Jacobsson (1979), pp. 169–77: "Mediator between USA and Japan".

149. One such accusation was based on the fact that the BIS had published a 600-page text on German exchange controls while the equivalent U.K. pamphlet, also produced by the BIS, was only 68 pages long. *Financial News,* 24 January 1942.

150. R. Auboin, "Rapports de la BRI avec la Banque d'Angleterre pendant la guerre (Note confidentielle pour M. le Gouverneur de la Banque de France)", 17 November 1944, BISA, 7.16(3) – *BIS History (Baffi papers),* box RBL/B5, f.D.

151. See Chapter 8.

152. Executive Order no. 8389.

153. Telegrams, Federal Reserve Bank of New York to BIS, 25 June and 2 July 1940, BISA, 2.1 – *Federal Reserve Bank of New York, Policy,* vol. 2.

154. Telegram, McKittrick to Federal Reserve Bank of New York, 19 July 1940, BISA, 2.1 – *Federal Reserve Bank of New York, Policy,* vol. 2.

155. Telegram, Federal Reserve Bank of New York to BIS, 23 June 1941, BISA, 2.1 – *Federal Reserve Bank of New York, Policy,* vol. 2. See also: Note for the President: "Difficulties in connection with operations in USA", 18 July 1941, HUBL, Thomas H. McKittrick Collection, series 2, box 13, f2.

156. General Ruling no. 17, issued on 20 October 1943.

157. Jacobsson (1979), p. 161.

158. R. R. Challener (interviewer), "A Transcript of a Recorded interview with Thomas McKittrick", 30 July 1964, p. 22, Princeton University, Seeley G. Mudd Manuscript Library – *The John Foster Dulles Oral History Project.*

159. McKittrick to Niemeyer, 23 March 1943, HUBL, Thomas H. McKittrick Collection, series 2.2, carton 8, f2: *Correspondence Bank of England.*

160. On a personal level, McKittrick clearly did not hit it off with either Morgenthau or White. Back in Basel he told the BIS management that "Morgenthau well deserved his nickname in Washington – Henry Le Morgue" and that Harry Dexter White, with whom he had had a private meeting as well, "seemed to be a man who wants to order everything – at heart a totalitarian – a man keen on power, but able and knows what he wants". Diary Per Jacobsson, 10 May 1943, pp. 141–2, BULH, NL 324 – *Nachlass Per Jacobsson,* Tagebücher – D.45.

161. Resolution submitted on 26 March 1943, enclosed with: letter from Knapp, Board of Governors of the Federal Reserve System, to Knoke, Federal Reserve Bank of New York, 29 March 1943, FRBNY, 797.3 – *Bank for International Settlements* (recently transferred to NARA).

162. R. R. Challener (interviewer), "A Transcript of a Recorded interview with Thomas McKittrick", 30 July 1964, p. 35, Princeton University, Seeley G. Mudd Manuscript Library – *The John Foster Dulles Oral History Project.*

163. See in this respect Crettol and Halbeisen (1999).

164. SNBA, DDS, vol. 13, nr. 419, p. 1015.

165. See note: Henri Guisan (BIS legal counsel), 20 August 1942, BISA, 1.19 – *Banking Policy of the BIS,* vol. 1, 1930–1952.

166. Crettol and Halbeisen (1999), pp. 24–6.
167. Memo Telefongespräch mit der Schweiz. Nationalbank (Hechler-Schnorf), 8 December 1941, BISA, 2.14f – *Banque Nationale Suisse, Gold Operations, Questions of Principle,* vol. 1, 1930–1945.
168. "Die Nationalbank halte bewusst an der bestehenden grossen Marge zwischen ihrem Goldan- und -verkaufspreis fest, um zu verhindern, dass die Schweiz als Drehscheibe für Währungs- und Goldoperationen von andern Ländern benützt wird. Die Nationalbank sei auf Zusehen damit einverstanden, dass die BIZ weiter in bescheidenem Ausmass Goldoperationen mit ausländischen Notenbanken tätige, in der Meinung jedoch, dass sie sich an die Goldan- und -verkaufspreise der Nationalbank anlehne und diese in nicht allzu ferner Zeit ebenfalls zur Anwendung bringe." SNBA, *Direktions-Protokolle Nr. 644,* 9 September 1942, pp. 806–7.
169. "Telefonische Unterredung zwischen Herrn Hechler und Herrn Schnorf (SNB, Zürich) betreffend unsere Goldoperationen in der Schweiz", 26 and 28 September 1942, BISA, 2.14f – *Banque Nationale Suisse, Gold Operations, Questions of Principle,* vol. 1: 1930–1945. Also: letter from Hechler to Hirs, Director General SNB, 11 November 1942, BISA, 2.14f – *Banque Nationale Suisse, Gold Operations, Questions of Principle,* vol. 1: 1930–1945.
170. McKittrick to the Governor of the Bank of Portugal, 10 June 1940, BISA, 2.44d – *Banco de Portugal, Gold Operations, Policy,* vol. 1.
171. The gold left Berne by lorry (Gondrand, Basel) on 27 November 1940 to reach Lisbon, via unoccupied France and Spain, on 16 December. From Lisbon, the gold was shipped off to New York for the BIS's own account: 500 kg of fine gold on 27 December 1940 on the S.S. *Exeter*; the remaining 299 kg of fine gold on 31 January 1941 on the steamer S.S. *Excalibur.*
172. I am indebted, without implication, to Piet Clement for both research and insightful thoughts on the subject matter of this section.
173. BISA, Banking Archive – *Foreign Exchange Section Contract Book,* no. 12, 24 January 1940 to 7 July 1941.
174. Art. 10 of the BIS Statutes (1930).
175. By September 1939 the so-called navicerts had to be obtained from the U.K. and U.S. authorities for all cross-Atlantic shipments. In addition to that, insurance costs for war risks skyrocketed. With Germany's occupation of France and increased U-boat activity, shipments came to a halt (with the exception of the two smaller shipments organised from Lisbon to New York in December 1940 and January 1941 that were mentioned in the previous section).
176. For more details see BIS, "Note on gold shipments and gold exchanges organised by the Bank for International Settlements, 1 June 1938 – 31 May 1945", Basel, 9 September 1997. Available at ⟨http://www.bis.org/publ/bisp03.htm⟩.
177. The bulk of the gold transported to Berne came from Italy in 1944 as a reimbursement of BIS investments there (see Section 7.11). The gold transported to Lisbon was originally stored in Berne.
178. Memorandum, Marcel van Zeeland, 26 November 1941, BISA, 1.19b – *Banking Policy of the BIS, Gold Operations,* vol. 1: 1930–1959.
179. Cable, BIS to Bank of Portugal, 6 September 1941, BPAH, *Contabilidade c/Exterior, Movimento da Espécie Ouro, Correspondência trocada c/Banco Internacional de Pagamentos, 1941,* BPC EXT 12: "sommes approchés par institution

monétaire désireuse acquérir escudos en vue règlement opérations commerciales votre marché ".

180. Converted into Swiss francs, the Bank of Portugal was prepared to pay the BIS between CHF 4,955 and 4,986 per kilogram for gold delivered in Lisbon (as against the official price of CHF 4,920 the Bank of Portugal paid the Swiss National Bank for gold loco Berne). This allowed the BIS to buy gold from the Bank of France at a price fluctuating between CHF 4,881.5 and CHF 4,900 per kilogram of fine gold – that is, substantially higher than the official price of CHF 4,869.8 at which the French could sell their gold to the Swiss National Bank, which maintained a wide spread between its gold purchase price (CHF 4,869.8 per kg fine gold) and its sale price (CHF 4,920 per kg fine gold). Allowing for the freight and insurance costs for transporting this gold to Lisbon (approximately CHF 30–50 per kg fine gold), the BIS was still able to earn a profit of about CHF 30–50 per kg fine gold. BISA, 2.44 d – *Banco de Portugal, Gold Operations, Policy,* vol. 1.
181. 903 kg of fine gold were shipped on 3 December and 899 kg on 12 December 1941.
182. Cable in: HUBL, Thomas H. McKittrick Collection, series 2.2, carton 8, f 2: *Correspondence Bank of England.*
183. "Memorandum on conversation with President Weber on 11 March 1942", HUBL, Thomas H. McKittrick Collection, series 2.2, carton 11, f 7: *Schweizerische Nationalbank, 1940–46.*
184. They consisted of 841 kg of fine gold.
185. On 25 February 1945, Turkey declared war on Germany and Japan.
186. Telegram, McCombe to Bliss, 15 May 1944, PRO, Foreign Office Papers, FO 371/ 39029 – *Bank for International Settlements 1944.*
187. On 1 March 1941, giving in to German pressures, Bulgaria joined the Tripartite Pact and allowed German troops to take up positions inside Bulgaria. The German invasion of Yugoslavia and Greece in April 1941 was largely launched via Bulgaria.
188. In January 1942, the National Bank of Bulgaria expressed the wish to convert part of its currency holdings in Switzerland into gold. The BIS thus sold 1,045 kg of fine gold to the Bulgarians on 13 January 1942 (for this purpose the BIS had bought, on the same day, 1,050 kg of fine gold from the Reichsbank, loco Berne). The BIS then transported this gold by rail from Berne to Sofia in two shipments, leaving Berne on 12 and 25 March 1942 (527 and 518 kg fine gold, respectively). On 23 February and 11 March 1942, the BIS sold to the National Bank of Bulgaria an additional amount of 693 kg of fine gold, which was also transported by rail from Berne to Sofia on 13–17 April 1942 for delivery to the Banque de Crédit Bulgare there. Finally, in June 1942, the National Bank of Bulgaria asked for its annual BIS dividend to be paid in gold. The BIS agreed to convert the dividend, which was normally paid in the central bank's national currency, into gold and to send the 48 kg of fine gold resulting from this operation from Berne to Sofia for the account of the National Bank of Bulgaria (transport left Berne on 23 June 1942). BISA, 2.34 e – *Banque Nationale de Bulgarie, Gold Operations, Policy,* vol. 1.
189. This transaction was part of an agreement by which the mining company Louda-Yana was compensated by the National Bank of Bulgaria for ceding to the national bank the entirety of the gold produced by that company in Bulgaria. Letter, Banque

Nationale de Bulgarie to BIS, 1 April 1943, BISA, 2.34e – *Banque Nationale de Bulgarie, Gold Operations, Policy,* vol. 1.

190. At the beginning of the war, Romania found itself caught between a rock and a hard place as it was faced with Russian expansionist demands (Bessarabia and Vukovina) on the one hand and German economic interests (Plösti oilfields) on the other. On 14 October 1940, the Romanian government allowed German troops to take up positions inside the country, and a few weeks later it joined the Tripartite Pact. In the summer of 1941, Romanian troops participated in the German-led invasion of Soviet Russia, suffering badly even before the battle of Stalingrad. Soon afterwards, the war reached the home front. On 23 August 1944, the dictator Antonescu was placed under arrest by King Michael who, two days later, declared war on Germany.

191. In August 1941, BIS Manager Marcel van Zeeland discussed with I. V. Popesco of the National Bank of Romania the NBR's recent gold purchases from the Swiss National Bank. Van Zeeland alluded to the possibility that the BIS could sell the Romanians gold obtained from other central banks, thereby offering the benefit of "de prix nettement plus avantageux". Memo, van Zeeland, 9 August 1941, BISA, 2.40 – *Banque Nationale de Roumanie, Policy,* vol. 1.

192. Part of the gold the NBR bought from the BIS during the war (3,405 kg fine gold, to be precise) originated from the interest payments in gold the German Reichsbank had paid to the BIS previously.

193. On 19 January 1940, 3,183 kg of fine gold was transferred from the BIS to the NBR's own gold account at the Swiss National Bank in Berne. On 25 August 1942, the BIS, acting on instructions from the NBR, handed 3,001 kg of fine gold the NBR had recently purchased from the BIS over to Mr. I. V. Popesco at the Swiss National Bank in Berne for further dispatch to Bucharest. Finally, on 22 March 1944, 5,587 kg of fine gold was transferred from the NBR's gold account with the BIS to the UBS in Zurich. BISA, 2.40f – *National Bank of Romania, Gold Operations, Policy,* vol. 1.

194. Letter, ICRC to BIS, 8 November 1940, BISA, 2.118 – *Red Cross, Geneva.*

195. Letter, BIS to central banks, 23 December 1940, BISA, 2.118a – *International Red Cross, Account of BIS.*

196. For more details, see "Übersicht über die Bewegungen auf den Konten der Commission Mixte de Secours de la Croix-Rouge Internationale nach dem Stande vom 20. März 1946" and "Extrait d'une étude sur la Commission Mixte de Secours de la Croix-Rouge Internationale, publiée dans le numéro de mars 1945 de la Revue Internationale de la Croix-Rouge"; both in BISA, 2.118 – *Red Cross, Geneva.*

197. BISA, 2.118(4) – *International Red Cross, Agence Centrale des Prisonniers de Guerre, Compte télégrammes.*

198. See: letters, BIS, 6 January and 14 August 1942, BISA, 2.118 – *Red Cross Geneva.* In the end, this particular operation did not materialise.

199. The transaction did not materialise. See BISA, 2.118(3) – *International Red Cross, Conversion of drachmae 140 million.*

200. Mainly in Belgium; see BISA, 2.118(5) – *International Red Cross, Transfer of monthly subsidies.* The amounts involved were comparatively small.

201. BISA, *Minutes of the Meeting of the Board of Directors,* 13 September 1948.

202. Clement (1998), pp. 43–60.

203. For the precise details about each of the transactions summarised in Table 7.2, the reader is referred to Clement (1998), pp. 43–60. Also: Note on gold operations involving the Bank for International Settlements and the German Reichsbank, 1 September 1939 – 8 May 1945, Basel, 12 May 1997, at ⟨http://www.bis.org/publ/bisp02.htm⟩.

204. Deposit nos. 5, 7, 10, and 11 of the BIS gold deposit account at the Swiss National Bank.

205. Gold on "earmarked" accounts is allocated gold. The Bank's obligation with respect to gold held in such accounts is to place on demand at the disposal of its depositors, at the central bank where the deposit was constituted, the identical bars that had originally been deposited. Gold in "sight accounts" is unallocated gold. The Bank's obligation with respect to gold held in such accounts is to place on demand at the disposal of its depositors, at the central bank where the deposit was constituted, gold bars of the same type as it has received – up to the total fine weight standing to the credit of the account.

206. Also held at the Swiss National Bank in Berne, as the BIS never had vaults of its own at its premises in Basel.

207. The deposit consisted of 34 gold bars (418 kg fine) and 31 cases of gold coins (1,107.6 kg fine).

208. This gold was given in advance settlement of interest payments due by Germany to the BIS in the course of 1945.

209. Some 700,000 Swiss gold francs ($230,000) each month, or 8.4 million Swiss gold francs ($2.76 million) annually.

210. Letter, Hechler to Puhl, 16 November 1939, BISA, 7.18(5) – *Papers Hechler,* box HEC1, f.B1/1.

211. McKittrick to Niemeyer (Bank of England, Chairman of the BIS Board of Directors), 11 June 1940, HUBL, Thomas H. McKittrick Collection, series 2.2, carton 8, f1: *Bank of England.*

212. BISA, 95th Meeting of the Board of Directors of the Bank for International Settlements held in Basel on 9 December 1946, Annex 95/D(1), *Report of the Management to the Board of Directors on the period since the last Board meeting,* Annex XVII (c), p. 4.

213. See: HUBL, Thomas H. McKittrick Collection: McKittrick to Niemeyer (Bank of England), 11 June 1940, series 2.2, carton 8, f1: *Bank of England*; memorandum, McKittrick on conversations with Yves de Boisanger (Bank of France), August 1943, series 2.2, carton 8, f4: *Banque de France*; letter, McKittrick to Rooth (Sveriges Riksbank), 4 April 1944, box 13, f2: *Sveriges Riksbank.*

214. The last, slightly reduced, wartime dividend payment was made in 1944.

215. The Allied Gold Declaration of 22 February 1944 stated that the Allies would not recognise the transfer of title to looted gold that the Axis at any time held or had disposed of in the world markets. Slany and Eizenstat (1997), pp. 9–10.

216. Bank for International Settlements, *Ninth Annual Report,* Basel, 8 May 1939, p. 67. The figure given by the Independent Commission of Experts, based on calculations by the Swiss National Bank dating from 1939, is even lower at only 25.5 tonnes. Unabhängige Expertenkommission Schweiz – Zweiter Weltkrieg (2002), p. 54.

217. All figures are drawn from: Unabhängige Expertenkommission Schweiz – Zweiter Weltkrieg (2002), pp. 54–66. Reichsmark amounts are converted at the rate of 1 US$ = 2.479 RM; gold is valued at $1,125 per kilogram of fine gold.
218. Parts of the gold reserves of the Bank of France were also sent to (or already held in) New York, London, Dakar, Martinique, and Casablanca, but the bulk of Belgian gold was shipped to Dakar.
219. The story of the journey of these cases is told in more detail by Smith (1989), pp. 11–22; see also Rings (1985) and Truffaut (1997).
220. Note, McKittrick on conversations with de Boisanger, 11 August 1943, HUBL, Thomas H. McKittrick Collection, series 2.2, carton 9, f3: *Gold from Germany, 1943–46.*
221. Memorandum, McKittrick, 12 August 1943, HUBL, Thomas H. McKittrick Collection, series 2.2, carton 8, f4: *Banque de France, 1939–46.*
222. Note, Auboin to McKittrick, 9 August 1943, HUBL, Thomas H. McKittrick Collection, series 2.2, carton 9, f3: *Gold from Germany, 1943–46.*
223. Rooth to McKittrick, 23 March 1944, HUBL, Thomas H. McKittrick Collection, series 2.2, box 13, f1: *Sveriges Riksbank.*
224. McKittrick to Rooth, 4 April 1944, HUBL, Thomas H. McKittrick Collection, series 2.2, box 13, f2: *Sveriges Riksbank.*
225. Slany and Eizenstat (1997, 1998). Also: Foreign & Commonwealth Office (1998) and Unabhängige Expertenkommission Schweiz – Zweiter Weltkrieg (2002).
226. No precise figures can be deduced, because the gold bars in question paid to the BIS were part of a much larger batch of bars resulting from a series of melting operations undertaken at the Prussian Mint in which more than 22,000 kg of monetary gold was mixed with 82 kg of victim gold. Proportionally, this would put the amount of victim gold in the 1,407 kg of gold originating from these melting operations (and delivered to the BIS between March 1943 and July 1944) at approximately 5 kg fine gold. See Independent Commission of Experts: Switzerland – Second World War (1998), pp. 41–3. Unabhängige Expertenkommision Schweiz – Zweiter Weltkrieg (2002), pp. 69–71, and author calculations on the basis of BIS sources: BISA, 7.19(5) – *Looted Gold,* boxes OG1 to OG3.
227. Jacobsson (1979), p. 190.
228. F. Alfonso, *Azzolini e l'oro della BRI, Settembre 1943 – Aprile 1944,* Banca d'Italia (bozza preliminare), 1985 (copy in BISA, 7.16(3) – *BIS History (Baffi papers),* box RBL/B4). See also Cardarelli and Martano (2000), pp. 35–9.
229. They mainly took the form of bills of the *Consorzio per Sovvenzioni su Valori Industriali.* This was an institution created by the Bank of Italy in the wake of the First World War to finance manufacturing companies in their transition from wartime to peacetime production and then carried over throughout the 1930s. President of the Consorzio was Vincenzo Azzolini, the central bank's governor.
230. "En ce qui concerne les investissements représentés par l'escompte du portefeuille du Consorzio per Sovvenzioni su Valori Industriali,... l'or correspondant aux lire ainsi investies en Italie par la BRI (du poids et du titre de fin prescrits par le décret-loi du 21 décembre 1927) est toujours considéré par la Banca d'Italia, d'accord avec le Gouvernement Royal, comme indisponible, même dans le cadre du décret-loi du 21 juillet 1935, de sorte que la BRI peut, à tout moment, prélever et transférer

cet or, après réalisation des investissements y relatifs et versement des lire correspondantes". Azzolini to Trip, President of BIS, 8 August 1935, BISA, 2.5 – *Banca d'Italia, Policy,* vols. 1–2.

231. Hechler to Pilotti, 30 July 1943, BISA, 7.18(5) – *Papers Hechler,* box HEC2, f 7.

232. Letter and cable, McKittrick to Azzolini, 9 and 10 September 1943, BISA, 2.5 – *Banca d'Italia, Policy,* vol. 1.

233. The Allied troops, however, did not enter Rome until 4 June 1944.

234. Roselli (2001), p. 317.

235. Cable, BIS President to Banca d'Italia, 19 November 1943, BISA, 2.5 – *Banca d'Italia, Policy,* vol. 1.

236. Letter, Azzolini to Pellegrini, 22 November 1943, in F. Alfonso, *Azzolini e l'oro della BRI, Settembre 1943 – Aprile 1944,* Banca d'Italia (bozza preliminare), 1985, p. 34; copy in BISA, 7.16(3) – *BIS History (Baffi papers),* box RBL/B4.

237. Indeed, Azzolini provided Pilotti with the detailed gold bar lists of the Italian gold earmarked for the BIS. On learning about this breakthrough, on 22 December 1943 McKittrick wrote to Ivar Rooth, Governor of the Swedish central bank: "Quite unbelievably good news has come from Italy this morning.... This is the most striking instance so far of how it is possible for central banks to continue their activity even when almost all other business has become impossible". McKittrick to Rooth, HUBL, Thomas H. McKittrick Collection, series 2.2, box 13, f 1: *Sveriges Riksbank.*

238. Transcript of Azzolini–Pellegrini telephone conversation of 13 December 1943, in F. Alfonso, *Azzolini e l'oro della BRI, Settembre 1943 – Aprile 1944,* Banca d'Italia (bozza preliminare), 1985, pp. 46–8; copy in BISA, 7.16(3) – *BIS History (Baffi papers),* box RBL/B4.

239. Letters, Hechler to Puhl, of 29 September, 1 October, 15 and 24 November, 28 December 1943 and 19 January 1944, BISA, 7.18(5) – *Papers Hechler,* box HEC2, f 7.

240. A further shipment from Fortezza to Berlin of about 21.5 tonnes of gold took place on 21 October 1944.

241. McKittrick to government ministers Bonomi, Sforza, and Soleri, 8 September 1944, HUBL, Thomas H. McKittrick Collection, series 2.2, carton 8, f 11: *Banca d'Italia, 1940–46.*

242. Roselli (2001), p. 331.

243. In October 1944, Azzolini was convicted and sentenced to 30 years' imprisonment. On 28 September 1946, he benefited from a general amnesty and was released from prison. On 14 February 1948, the 1944 conviction was overturned and Azzolini was officially acquitted. See Roselli (2001), pp. 326–35.

244. M. A. Kriz, "The BIS wartime activities and present position", 11 June 1947, pp. 40–1, FRBNY, 797.3 – *Bank for International Settlements* (recently transferred to NARA).

245. Amongst the latter, the book by A. L. Smith, Jr. (1989) deserves particular attention. In Switzerland, something of a stir was caused by journalist G. Trepp (1993). More recently, McKittrick has been the subject of a rather tendentious book by Charguérard (2004).

246. Independent Commission of Experts Switzerland – Second World War (1998), p. 14; Unabhängige Expertenkommision Schweiz – Zweiter Weltkrieg (2002), p. 32.

247. See Section 8.4.

Chapter 8

1. On learning from the interwar experience in the United States, see Lary (1943).
2. Van Dormael (1978), p. 172.
3. Surely, the actual system was based much more upon the dollar and a direct relationship between the United States and Europe than the one envisaged at the conference. In one extreme view, Western Europe's postwar expansionist policies "provoked the 1947 payments crisis and destroyed the Bretton Woods agreements almost at birth". Milward (1984), p. 466.
4. He called the amended gold standard system as proposed at the Genoa Conference of 1922 "the ideal plan". Hawtrey (1932), p. 250.
5. BIS, *Fifth Annual Report,* Basel, 1935, p. 44.
6. Hawtrey (1950), p. 426.
7. For an excellent survey of the changes in the intellectual climate, see Cesarano (2000).
8. Ibid.
9. "When the Council of the BIS contemplate (as in their last report) a return to a regime of fixed gold parities, they are living in an unreal world, a fool's world". J. M. Keynes, "The Future of the Foreign Exchanges", *Lloyds Bank Monthly Review* (October 1935). Reproduced in Moggridge (1982), pp. 360–9.
10. BIS, *Seventh Annual Report,* Basel, 1937, p. 23.
11. Horsefield (1969), p. 9. In April 1937, Paul van Zeeland had accepted a joint invitation from France and the United Kingdom to inquire into the possibility of obtaining a general reduction of quotas and other obstacles to international trade in order to give effect to the principles laid down in the 1936 Tripartite Agreement. Paul van Zeeland, Prime Minister of Belgium from 1935 to 1937, was the brother of Marcel, one of the BIS managers.
12. The Inter-American Development Bank became operational only twenty years later.
13. Boughton (2004), p. 189.
14. Horsefield (1969), p. 11.
15. Ibid.
16. White's ideas were already fairly well developed when Morgenthau asked him to "prepare a memorandum and plan for setting up an Inter-Allied Stabilisation Fund" on 14 December 1941. White was made Assistant Secretary of the Treasury in 1945. Van Dormael (1978), p. 40.
17. Horsefield (1969), p. 25.
18. The most detailed account of the development of Keynes's "ideal scheme" is to be found in Skidelsky (2000), pp. 179–232.
19. James (1996), p. 36.
20. The "bancor" is reminiscent of the "grammor", which had been proposed by the French delegation and was strongly advocated by Quesnay back in 1929 as a new international currency unit to be used by the Bank for International Settlements. See: "Raisons qui ont amené la délégation française à proposer l'adoption du gramme d'or pur, grammor, comme unité de compte de la BRI", BISA, 7.16 – *BIS History,* box RBL/B6.
21. DeLong (2002), p. 160.

22. In fact, other more or less official proposals for monetary reform circulated around the same time. These originated from private U.S. citizens and from the U.S. Federal Reserve Board, Poland, France, and Canada; for details see Horsefield (1969), pp. 16–39. As mentioned in Section 7.6, immediately upon publication of the White and Keynes plans in the spring of 1943, BIS Economic Adviser Per Jacobsson was sought out by German bankers, headed by Reichsbank Vice-President Puhl, to discuss their implications for the postwar monetary system. Jacobsson had been in the United States from December 1941 to May 1942 on a lecture and information tour, during which he had been in close contact with many of the leading economists in Washington and New York.

23. Skidelsky (2000), p. 308.

24. Van Dormael (1978), pp. 109–26.

25. Ibid., p. 138.

26. Ibid., p. 146.

27. Opposition to the IMF was almost universal among U.S. bankers (who had no qualms, however, about the World Bank). James (1996), p. 64.

28. The Dutch position was strongly influenced by J. W. Beyen, former BIS president, a member of the Dutch delegation at Bretton Woods, future executive director at the IMF (1948–52) and Minister of Foreign Affairs in the Dutch government (1952–56).

29. The conference operated through three commissions: Commission I on the fund, chaired by White; Commission II on the Bank, chaired by Keynes; and Commission III on other means of international financial cooperation, chaired by Eduardo Suarez of Mexico. Horsefield (1969), p. 91.

30. It is not clear why the initiative was taken by the Norwegian Professor Keilhau. In his memoirs, Beyen gives the following explanation: the ground for the attack, he says, "was prepared by Harry White…. At international conferences it was not uncommon for big shots to make the small fry do their dirty work if they did not feel like sticking out their own necks…. The central bank of Norway was an old and trusted member of the BIS and there was no special reason for Norway to launch such an attack". See Beyen (1968), p. 165. Knut Getz Wold, Governor of Norges Bank (Norway's central bank), in a personal testimonial to Paolo Baffi dated 30 October 1980, wrote that the initiative was "taken by the delegation without reference to the Norwegian authorities in London. As a matter of fact, the Norwegian government in exile felt embarrassed because it wished to avoid being involved in a controversial question of this type".

31. U.S. State Department (1948), p. 333.

32. Van Dormael (1978), p. 204.

33. On Acheson's view, see ibid.

34. Foreign Office to U.K. Bretton Woods Delegation, cable 51, 14 July 1944, PRO, Treasury Papers T236/24 – *Overseas Finance Division: BIS liquidation, 1944.*

35. Lord Catto to Sir Richard Hopkins, 20 July 1944, PRO, Treasury Papers, T 236/24 – *Overseas Finance Division: BIS liquidation, 1944.*

36. Van Dormael (1978), p. 169.

37. Beyen (1949), p. 176.

38. Committee 2 of Commission III.

39. Van Dormael (1978), p. 205. Quotes of White's words are from the Morgenthau Diaries.

40. Skidelsky (2000), p. 354.
41. U.S. State Department (1948), p. 861.
42. Skidelsky (2000), p. 354.
43. Moggridge (1980), p. 97.
44. International Monetary Fund, *Draft Minutes Executive Board Meeting 382,* 12 November 1948, p. 12.
45. Van Dormael (1978), p. 206. The whole quotation is from the Morgenthau Diaries. Frederick Vinson was vice-chairman of the U.S. delegation to the Bretton Woods Conference. He was Secretary of the Treasury in 1945–46 and became the first Chairman of the Board of Governors of the IMF and World Bank in 1946.
46. U.S. State Department (1948), p. 915.
47. "Angeschossene BIZ. Die Hintergründe des Streites um Finanzkontrolle", *Das Reich,* 10 September 1944.
48. Cable, McKittrick to Bank of England (telegram Norton 3487 sent through British Legation in Berne), 26 July 1944, PRO, Foreign Office Papers, FO 371/39029 – *Bank for International Settlements 1944.*
49. Message, Catto for McKittrick (telegram 2717 sent through British Legation in Berne), 20 August 1944, PRO, Foreign Office Papers, FO 371/39029 – *Bank for International Settlements 1944.*
50. "Human judgement in general, and international human judgement in particular, are not infallible. It is quite conceivable that a committee would find that certain activities of the BIS had been improper, however far this may be from the real truth". Sir David Waley of the Treasury to Sir R. Hopkins from the Foreign Office, 2 August 1944, PRO, Treasury Papers, T236/24 – *Overseas Finance Division: BIS liquidation, 1944.*
51. For these reasons, a Treasury memo argued, McKittrick did not foresee "the anger which would be aroused if the BIS did pay a dividend out of income from a Germany which had not paid in full reparations". Note to Sir David Waley, 16 October 1944, PRO, Treasury Papers T236/24 – *Overseas Finance Division: BIS liquidation, 1944.*
52. "For reasons that can be felt rather than defined", observes the Foreign Office note: anonymous (probably Playfair's) memo to Rowe-Dutton and Jenkins, 24 April 1945, PRO, Treasury Papers, T236/25 – *Overseas Finance Division: BIS liquidation, 1945–46.*
53. Ibid.
54. Morgenthau to Andersen, 14 July 1945, PRO, Treasury Papers, T236/25 – *Overseas Finance Division: BIS liquidation, 1945–46.*
55. Note of Sir W. Edy to Padmore, 22 August 1945, PRO, Treasury Papers, T236/25 – *Overseas Finance Division: BIS liquidation, 1945–46.*
56. "The BIS do not deserve moral censure, nor do we for the backing we gave them in the past". Memorandum by Playfair to Sir Richard Hopkins, 6 September 1945, PRO, Treasury Papers, T236/25 – *Overseas Finance Division: BIS liquidation, 1945–46.*
57. Ibid.
58. Dalton to Vinson, 13 September 1945, PRO, Treasury Papers, T236/25 – *Overseas Finance Division: BIS liquidation, 1945–46.*
59. Many U.K. and French interests would be hard to unravel, and the liquidation procedure, beginning with the body to be put in charge of it, looked difficult to envisage

and execute ("the burial of an international institution is often even more difficult than its birth").

60. Emphasis added.
61. Lord Catto to the Chancellor of the Exchequer, 19 September 1945, PRO, Treasury Papers, T236/25 – *Overseas Finance Division: BIS liquidation, 1945–46.*
62. The agreements were supposed to come into force once a number of states having 65% of the total quotas had ratified the agreement. By the end of 1945, enough governments had confirmed ratification, and at the end of January 1946 the United States issued invitations to 34 governments to attend the inaugural meetings of the board of governors of the IMF and the World Bank.
63. Bank for International Settlements (1980b), p. 45.
64. Waley to Eady, 25 May 1946, and Eady's Note for the Chancellor's office, 27 May 1947, PRO, Treasury Papers, T236/25 – *Overseas Finance Division: BIS liquidation, 1945–46.*
65. Culpin to Waley, 24 June 1946, PRO, Treasury Papers, T236/26 – *Overseas Finance Division: BIS liquidation, 1945–46.*
66. Dalton's handwritten comment in the margin of a letter from the U.S. Secretary of the Treasury, 6 June 1946, PRO, Treasury Papers, T236/26 – *Overseas Finance Division: BIS liquidation, 1945–46.*
67. Letter, E. Bevin to James Byrnes, U.S. delegation at the Conference of Paris, 6 September 1946, PRO, Treasury Papers, T236/2735 – *BIS: liquidation.*
68. The only new idea floated at the meeting came from Dalton, who suggested that the BIS might be taken over – "cannibalised", he said – by the IMF.
69. Note, Waley to Hall-Patch, Foreign Office, 16 October 1946, PRO, Treasury Papers, T236/2735 – *BIS: liquidation.*
70. On postwar developments at the BIS, see Chapter 9.
71. It should be noted that the Tripartite Commission never looked into the question of the "victim gold" (gold taken from individual citizens and in particular from concentration camp victims). The issue was therefore never officially discussed with the BIS. The Tripartite Commission was officially dissolved on 9 September 1998, after the remainder of looted gold it had collected following the war and which had not been allocated to any of the claimant countries was donated to the International Fund for Needy Victims of Nazi Persecution. The archives of the Tripartite Commission, which had its seat in Brussels, have been transferred to the French Ministry of Foreign Affairs at the Quai d'Orsay in Paris (Archives diplomatiques).
72. BIS, *Minutes of the Meetings of the Board of Directors,* 14 June 1946, p. 12.
73. See Section 7.10.
74. Franks to Bevin, 5 June 1948, PRO, Foreign Office Papers, FO 371/68965 – *Economic, 1948.*
75. See Section 7.10.
76. Franks to Bevin, 5 June 1948, PRO, Foreign Office Papers, FO 371/68965 – *Economic, 1948.*
77. This gold had been deposited in Constance by the Reichsbank in advance settlement of interest payments due by Germany to the BIS in the course of 1945 (see Section 7.10).
78. Confidential note to the State Department by Walter H. Sholes, U.S. Consul General at Basel, "Bank for International Settlements and Bretton Woods", 4 December

1946, NARA, RG59 – *General Records of the Department of State,* 462.OOR 296: *BIS Decimal File 1945–1949,* box 1914, f4.

79. Niemeyer to Playfair, 16 May 1947, PRO, Treasury Papers, T 236/2735 – *BIS liquidation, 1946–1951.*

80. A. N. Overby, U.S. Executive Director to the IMF, to BIS, 26 April 1948, BISA, 7.16(2) – *BIS Foundation and Activities,* box RBL3, f1.

81. The Washington Agreement of 13 May 1948 was in the form of an exchange of letters between the BIS and the representatives of the three governments sitting on the Tripartite Commission for the Restitution of Monetary Gold. In accepting the 3,740 kg of fine gold restituted by the BIS, the three governments abandoned "toutes réclamations à l'égard de la Banque des Règlements Internationaux au sujet de l'or pillé qui lui a été transféré par l'Allemagne". BISA, 7.16(3) – *BIS History (Baffi papers),* box RBL/B5, f1.

82. On the same day, Frère and Auboin cabled to Basel: "Signé aujourd'hui accord définitif entièrement satisfaisant toutes questions". BISA, 7.16(3) – *BIS History (Baffi papers),* box RBL/B5, f.J.

83. Skidelsky (2000), p. 354.

84. Keynes to Catto, 2 March 1946, PRO, Treasury Papers, T236/25 – *Overseas Finance Division: BIS liquidation, 1945–46.*

85. Bank for International Settlements (1980b), p. 61.

86. Memorandum by P. Baffi, 17 June 1982, BISA, 7.16(3) – *BIS History (Baffi papers),* box RBL/B5.

87. Bank for International Settlements (1980b), p. 45.

88. Jacobsson (1979), p. 190. Not surprisingly, Overby came from the Federal Reserve Bank of New York.

89. Art. 55 of the BIS Statutes (1930).

90. M. A. Kriz, "The BIS wartime activities and present position", 11 June 1947, p. 44, FRBNY, 797.3 – *Bank for International Settlements* (recently transferred to NARA).

Chapter 9

1. In 1945, the per capita GDP of Austria had fallen back to its 1886 level, and that of France to its 1891 level. See: Crafts and Toniolo (1996), p. 4; Toniolo (1998), pp. 252–67.

2. Milward (1984).

3. Eichengreen (1993), p. 11.

4. BIS, *Sixteenth Annual Report,* Basel, July 1946, pp. 21–2.

5. Ibid., p. 51.

6. Milward (1984), p. 44.

7. This includes the 1945 U.S. loan to the United Kingdom, dollar credits to purchase U.S. property left overseas from the war, relief programmes for the occupied areas, and the UNRRA programme; ibid., p. 45. Disbursements of roughly $5 billion annually compare to the U.S. GNP figures for 1946 and 1947 of $212 and $235 billion (respectively) in current prices; Mitchell (2003), p. 766.

8. BIS, *Eighteenth Annual Report,* Basel, 14 June 1948, pp. 23ff.

9. Convertibility was declared on 15 July 1947 and suspended again on 20 August.

10. Milward (1984), pp. 57–9.

11. DeLong and Eichengreen (1991).
12. Ibid., p. 4.
13. Ibid., p. 5.
14. Ibid.
15. Both the IMF and the IBRD published their first annual reports in 1946, but these contained only official communications regarding bylaws, procedures, and the election of officials. In the following years the reports grew in size and contained more economic analysis and information, albeit limited to matters directly related to the mission of each institution: exchange rates and balance of payments in the case of the IMF, and development lending in that of the World Bank.
16. This conclusion is supported by BIS "oral tradition", by Jacobsson's daughter, and most of all by an even cursory textual analysis of the Reports and of Jacobsson's other writings: not only the arguments but the prose itself unmistakably reveal the same hand. Jacobsson (1979), pp. 194, 209.
17. Per Jacobsson was born in 1894.
18. Jacobsson (1979), p. 256.
19. Ibid., p. 19.
20. Ibid., p. 211.
21. See Jacobsson (1953), p. 4.
22. Enders and Fleming (2002), p. 249.
23. Economists at the United Nations were more cautious in espousing the Keynesian credo, "pointing to the dangers if policy-makers ignored the consequences of inflation"; ibid., p. 245. The International Labour Organisation, on the other hand, was primarily concerned with unemployment. See International Labour Organisation (1946; 1950).
24. Enders and Fleming (2002), p. 233.
25. Ibid.
26. BIS, *Sixteenth Annual Report,* Basel, July 1946, p. 44.
27. Ibid., p. 48.
28. Ibid., p. 50.
29. Ibid., p. 52.
30. This sentence was highlighted in the Annual Report; ibid., p. 53.
31. Ibid.
32. Ibid., p. 51.
33. BIS, *Seventeenth Annual Report,* Basel, 16 June 1947, p. 39.
34. Ibid., p. 167.
35. Jacobsson (1958), p. 257.
36. BIS, *Seventeenth Annual Report,* Basel, 16 June 1947, p. 167.
37. Jacobsson (1958), pp. 259ff.
38. BIS, *Eighteenth Annual Report,* Basel, 14 June 1948, p. 67.
39. Ibid., p. 164.
40. Ibid., p. 162.
41. BIS, *Seventeenth Annual Report,* Basel, 16 June 1947, p. 67.
42. The language here means control on aggregate money supply and government expenditure.
43. BIS, *Eighteenth Annual Report,* Basel, 14 June 1948, p. 165.

44. Funk, an active and outspoken participant in the July 1939 meeting, was being tried as a war criminal in Nuremberg. He served his sentence in Spandau. Suffering from gall-bladder cancer, Funk was released on humanitarian grounds in 1957.
45. Montagu Norman died on 4 February 1950.
46. The presidency remained vacant after McKittrick left at the end of June 1946 until Frère's appointment in 1948.
47. May 1946. Trip died in March 1947.
48. He served until 12 May 1948, when he was elected President of the Italian Republic. His seat on the BIS Board was filled by Donato Menichella when the latter was appointed Governor of the Bank of Italy in August 1948.
49. In December 1948, Rooth was replaced by Klas Böök as Governor of Sveriges Riksbank, and he retired from the BIS Board in March 1949.
50. Weber was replaced by Paul Keller as President of the Directorium of the Swiss National Bank and as BIS Board member in May 1947.
51. See Kynaston (1995), pp. 27ff.
52. Howson (1975), pp. 86ff.
53. The bank was transformed from a listed limited-liability company into an institution whose capital was held by state-controlled financial bodies (such as the nationalised insurance company and state-owned long-term credit institutions) and by the savings banks, over which the government retained both large supervisory powers and the right to make appointments in the management. See Guarino and Toniolo (1993).
54. Little changed in practice, as only the Bank of Italy possessed the expertise and the network of inspectors to supervise individual banks. In fact it can be argued that the central bank's de facto powers were increased by the introduction of more binding supervisory rules and standards. The fact remains that, legally, supervision now rested with the government. The situation was redressed in the immediate postwar period, when the bank's supervisory authority was fully restored.
55. Marsh (1992), p. 117.
56. Koch (1983), p. 40.
57. Fforde (1992), p. 7.
58. Koch (1983), p. 43.
59. Ibid., pp. 51–3.
60. See de Vries (1994a), p. 745.
61. Houtman-De Smedt (1994), p. 62.
62. The Bank of Japan renounced its BIS membership (and its status as "founder" central bank under the Young Plan) completely as a result of the 1951 San Francisco peace treaty; it only became a member again – without Board representation – in 1970.
63. Buchheim (1999), pp. 55–100.
64. In June 1948, the Deutsche mark replaced the Reichsmark as West Germany's currency.
65. For Vocke this was a kind of homecoming, as he had already been an alternate member of the BIS Board of Directors for the Reichsbank from 1930 to 1939. See Vocke (1973).
66. The legal grounds for the appointments were the subject of a debate. The right to appoint an ex officio member rested with the Reichsbank as the central bank of one of the six signatory powers of the Hague Agreement. It was uncertain whether the

Bank deutscher Länder could be considered as the lawful successor of the Reichs-bank (in particular, since two central banks existed in the territory of the former Reich). The appointments were therefore made under a statutory provision (par. 3, Art. 28[2]) allowing the other ex officio members to appoint someone of their choice if "for any reason, the governor [of the central bank of a signatory power] is unable or unwilling to serve as director".

67. Niccolò Introna exercised both the governor's and Board's powers from July 1944 to January 1945. A commissioner was also appointed in the North (the so-called Republic of Salò), but the BIS simply ignored this appointment.

68. Capie, Goodhart, and Schnadt (1994), p. 24.

69. See Section 11.1 and Maier (1988).

70. The position of Chairman of the BIS Board had been vacant since December 1945, when Ernst Weber of the Swiss National Bank had declined to accept a new three-year term.

71. Since April 1945, the Bank had not received information about its German invest-ments, which totalled some 293 million Swiss gold francs.

72. At the founding meeting of the association of the Young bondholders (London, Jan-uary 1947), an international lawyer, F. A. Mann, asked for an inquiry into the BIS's behaviour as trustee – to establish if damages could be claimed from the Bank. "Emprunt Young", 7 February 1947, BISA, 7.1(3) – *Board Secretariat Papers,* box Board 12.

73. Signed on 27 February 1953. For an assessment of this agreement, see Timothy W. Guinnane, "Financial 'Vergangenheitsbewältigung': the 1953 London Debt Agree-ment", Center Discussion Paper no. 880, Economic Growth Center, Yale University, January 2004.

74. BIS, *Twenty-Third Annual Report,* Basel, 8 June 1953, pp. 225–6.

75. Various memoranda dated 30 January 1947, BISA, 7.1(3) – *Board Secretariat Pa-pers,* box Board 12.

76. On the crisis of 1947 as a political and economic watershed, see Milward (1984), pp. 1–55.

77. BIS, *Eighteenth Annual Report,* Basel, 14 June 1948, p. 154.

78. A credit of $2,000,000 to the central bank of Turkey, a regular customer of the BIS since 1933, was considered in September 1947 but nothing came of it. Auboin to Knoke, 13 October 1947, BISA, 7.16(3) – *BIS History (Baffi papers),* box RBL/B1, f.D.

79. "We are buyers of gold against dollars from European Central Banks which are short of dollars. The gold thus bought we keep for our own account or sell it either to other central banks or to commercial banks, subject in each case to the agreement of the Central Bank concerned.... We are anxious to develop to a reasonable extent a gold market between European Central Banks, with the view of offsetting, as far as possible, the movements in their monetary gold reserves." Auboin to Knocke, 21 April 1948, BISA, 7.16(3) – *BIS History (Baffi papers),* box RBL/B1, f.D. One of the first such operations was conducted with the central bank of the Netherlands; dollar credits were granted in 1947 also to the Bank of Italy and the Bank of France. Knoke to Auboin, 2 August 1948, and Auboin to Sproul, 7 August 1948, BISA, 7.16(3) – *BIS History (Baffi papers),* box RBL/B1, f.D.

80. Only deposits with the BIS whose beneficiaries still remained blocked were put into a special account with the Federal Reserve Bank of New York and could not be drawn upon without the consent of U.S. authorities. The amount involved was, however, small.

81. "In our dealings with some of the central banks of Western Europe, we often have to reverse our position quite suddenly in order to carry out the services which we are asked to render. The selling and buying of gold in order to procure dollars for short periods is an expensive method. Therefore the said facility would be of great interest to us, even though we expect to have but little occasion to avail ourselves of it. We have in mind an amount of, say, $5 million with good will". Auboin to Knoke, 30 October 1948, BISA, 7.16(3) – *BIS History (Baffi papers)*, box RBL/B1, f.D.

82. Auboin to Knoke, 14 November 1949, BISA, 7.16(3) – *BIS History (Baffi papers)*, box RBL/B1, f.D.

83. Ibid.

84. Art. 20 of the BIS Statutes (1930) required that the BIS obtain the approval of national monetary authorities for operations conducted in the markets under their supervision.

85. L. Rounds (FRBNY Vice-President) to Frère, 7 August 1947, BISA, 7.16(3) – *BIS History (Baffi papers)*, box RBL/B1, f.E; and Knoke to Auboin, 2 August 1948, BISA, 7.16(3) – *BIS History (Baffi papers)*, box RBL/B1, f.D. On 4 November 1948, Knoke officially wrote to the BIS (as institution, rather than to Auboin), stating that "operations in this market by foreign central banks, including BIS, and foreign governments, should conform in a general way to our monetary policy". BISA, 7.16(3) – *BIS History (Baffi papers)*, box RBL/B1, f.E.

86. See Chapter 8.

87. Auboin to Knoke, 4 July 1948, BISA, 7.16(3) – *BIS History (Baffi papers)*, box RBL/B1, f.E.

88. "Note concerning the BIS", 14 July 1949, BISA, 7.16(3) – *BIS History (Baffi papers)*, box RBL/B1, f.E.

89. Knoke to Jacobsson, 7 November 1947, BISA, 7.16(3) – *BIS History (Baffi papers)*, box RBL/B1, f.E.

90. At that moment, Jacobsson wrote, "neither the British nor the French travel about in great numbers. It is no longer possible for any country to rely upon past knowledge, for there have been great changes". Jacobsson to Knoke, 18 November 1947, BISA, 7.16(3) – *BIS History (Baffi papers)*, box RBL/B1, f.E.

91. Knoke to Frère, 24 February 1947, BISA, 7.16(3) – *BIS History (Baffi papers)*, box RBL/B1, f.E.

92. James (1996), p. 73.

93. BIS, *Minutes of the 99th meeting of the Board of Directors*, 13 October 1947, p. 2. Also: BISA, 7.19(7) – *Cooperation BIS–IBRD, 1946–52*.

94. Milward (1984), pp. 63–4.

95. Ibid., p. 62.

96. Van der Beugel (1966).

97. Milward (1984), p. 70.

98. Ibid., p. 233.

99. Ibid., pp. 234–5.
100. The Bi-zone of Germany (i.e., the territory occupied by the United States and the United Kingdom) merged soon afterwards.
101. Art. 1 of the Agreement. See: BIS, *Eighteenth Annual Report,* Basel, 14 June 1948, p. 167.
102. The first meeting took place in London on 22–27 September 1947; the second one in Paris on 15–25 October 1947.
103. Frederick Conolly represented the BIS at the meeting. Having served as a senior official at the BIS since 1931, he was promoted to the BIS management in April 1948.
104. The BIS also acted as secretariat for the committee: in practice, the technical execution of the agreement was the responsibility of the Bank.
105. Dangelzer to Conolly, 28 October 1947, BISA, 3/10a – *Multilateral Monetary Compensation: Meetings of the Committee of Delegates.*
106. "Réunion du CCEE. Deuxième réunion du Comité des Déleguées, Banque Nationale de Belgique, Bruxelles, du 18 au 22 décembre 1947. Resumé des traveaux", Annexe I, BISA, 3/10a – *Multilateral Monetary Compensation: Meetings of the Committee of Delegates.*
107. Eichengreen (1993), p. 19.
108. Member countries were: Austria, Belgium, Denmark, France, Greece, Iceland, Ireland, Italy, Luxembourg, the Netherlands, Norway, Portugal, Sweden, Switzerland, Turkey, and the United Kingdom.
109. Ellwood (1992), p. 90.
110. Milward (1984), p. 180.
111. Ibid., p. 172.
112. Jacobsson to Knoke, 18 November 1947, BISA, 7.16(3) – *BIS History (Baffi papers),* box RBL/B1, f.E.
113. BIS, *Nineteenth Annual Report,* Basel, 13 June 1948, p. 200.
114. Eichengreen (1993), p. 21.
115. BIS, *Nineteenth Annual Report,* Basel, 13 June 1948, pp. 201–2.
116. Ibid., p. 202.
117. Triffin (1957), p. 153.
118. Kaplan and Schleiminger (1989), p. 27.

Chapter 10

1. Crafts and Toniolo (1996), p. 4.
2. In 1973, the ratio of the highest (Switzerland) to the lowest (Greece) per capita GDP was 2.9, down from 5.7 in 1950; ibid., p. 6.
3. For a comprehensive survey of the economic history of this period, see Van der Wee (1986).
4. Lamfalussy (1963).
5. Kindleberger (1967).
6. Kaldor (1966).
7. Denison (1967).
8. Boltho (1982), pp. 9–37.
9. Olson (1982).

10. Toniolo (1998), pp. 252–67.
11. Eichengreen (1996), pp. 38–72.
12. See Chapter 11.
13. Austria, Belgium, Denmark, Finland, France, Germany, Italy, the Netherlands, Norway, Sweden, Switzerland, and the United Kingdom.
14. Trade and GDP grew by 9% and 4.6% per annum (respectively) at constant prices. Data from Maddison (1995).
15. In 1973, Japan's export trade was about 27 times larger than it had been in 1950, and North American and Australian trade about four times larger. Developing regions, in particular India and Latin America, lagged behind in trade growth.
16. See Section 9.1.
17. BIS, *Twenty-Ninth Annual Report,* Basel, 8 June 1959, p. 161.
18. By 1 January 1959, Italy had liberalised 98% of its intra-European trade, the Benelux countries and Greece 96%, and the United Kingdom 95%; ibid., pp. 160–1.
19. Britton (2001), p. 136.
20. Between 1955 and 1960, Germany's and Italy's reserves (of gold and dollars) showed a threefold increase from $2.4 to $7.1 billion and from $1.1 to $3.1 billion, respectively.
21. BIS, *Twenty-Seventh Annual Report,* Basel, 3 June 1957, p. 163.
22. Auboin (1958), p. 7.
23. Convertibility was limited to current account transactions.
24. Jacobsson (1979), p. 246.
25. In France and Italy, a regulated foreign exchange market existed alongside an official free one. Exporters were obliged to sell only 50% of their foreign currency to the government at an official rate and could negotiate the remaining 50% on the free market. See BIS, *Eighteenth Annual Report,* Basel, 1948, pp. 88ff.
26. BIS, *Eighteenth Annual Report,* Basel, 14 June 1948, p. 101.
27. See Chapter 9.
28. As far as sterling is concerned, Cairncross and Eichengreen (1983, pp. 223–6) note the following common features of 1931 and 1949: (a) a recession in the United States; (b) a reserve level in the United Kingdom that was "inadequate in times of crisis"; and (c) the reluctance of governments to devalue at all (and hence delayed reaction).
29. BIS, *Twentieth Annual Report,* Basel, 12 June 1950, p. 150.
30. For a detailed, almost day-by-day reconstruction of the Washington–London economic diplomacy in the spring and summer of 1949, see Cairncross and Eichengreen (1983), pp. 112–39.
31. See Harold James quoting Treasury Secretary Snyder in James (1996), p. 93.
32. Ibid., p. 94.
33. In April 1949, Cripps even threatened to leave the IMF in the face of pressure to devalue; ibid., p. 95.
34. Quoted by Cairncross and Eichengreen (1983), p. 118.
35. Pimlott (1986), p. 452. Hugh Dalton had been Chancellor of the Exchequer at the time of the failed 1947 convertibility experiment.
36. BIS, *Twentieth Annual Report,* Basel, 12 June 1950, p. 153.
37. Ibid., p. 155. Ireland, the Scandinavian countries, Finland, the Netherlands, Iceland, and Greece devalued to about the same extent as the United Kingdom, as did all

members of the British Commonwealth with the exception of Pakistan (which did not change the value of the rupee) and Canada (which devalued by 10% only).

38. Soon after the devaluation, the U.K. government tried to signal a change in policy stance by announcing a 5% cut in government expenditure. The City, however, was unimpressed, since reserves were slow in building up again. "The Bank and the Treasury began to agitate again for higher interest rates, provoking from Dalton the classic expression of postwar monetary doctrine: 'You can't allow higher interest rates while resisting higher wage rates'". Cairncross and Eichengreen (1983), p. 139.

39. Eichengreen (1993), p. 62.

40. Auboin (1955).

41. Donald Macdonald, "Interest rates on our dollar deposits", 24 October 1955, BISA, 1/19 – *Banking Policy of the BIS,* Notes, 1953–1969.

42. Net of the funds invested in Germany before the war, which amounted to 297.2 million Swiss gold francs.

43. 1 Swiss gold franc was equal to 0.29032258 grams of fine gold.

44. Throughout the period, capital remained fixed at 500 million Swiss gold francs, of which only 25% was paid up.

45. BISA, *Minutes of the Meetings of the Board of Directors,* 4 April 1955.

46. BISA, *Minutes of the Meetings of the Board of Directors,* 7 December 1953, p. 2. Similar statement in: BISA, *Minutes of the Meetings of the Board of Directors,* 14 June 1954, p. 2.

47. The terms of the deal incorporated an option for the Bank to buy (or for the correspondent to sell) gold forward against dollars six months ahead at a premium of 0.5%. BISA, *Minutes of the Meetings of the Board of Directors,* 11 February 1957, p. 4.

48. BISA, *Minutes of the Meetings of the Board of Directors,* 8 February 1953, p. 3.

49. BISA, *Minutes of the Meetings of the Board of Directors,* 8 April 1957, p. 4.

50. Donald Macdonald, "Interest rates on our dollar deposits", 24 October 1955, BISA, 1/19 – *Banking Policy of the BIS,* Notes, 1953–1969.

51. In the end, the suggestion, made by the BIS to Vocke, was not taken up by Germany.

52. BISA, 6.38 – *European Coal and Steel Community,* General, vol. 1, 1951–54.

53. To that end, an Act of Pledge was signed between the High Authority of the ECSC and the BIS in Luxembourg on 28 November 1954. BIS, *Twenty-Fifth Annual Report,* Basel, 13 June 1955, pp. 201–2.

54. Spierenburg and Poidevin (1994), p. 313.

55. Ibid., p. 314.

56. BIS, *Thirty-Second Annual Report,* Basel, 4 June 1962, pp. 172–3. This was equivalent to some $270 million.

57. BISA, *Minutes of the Meetings of the Board of Directors,* 13 February 1950, p. 7.

58. BISA, *Minutes of the Meetings of the Board of Directors,* 9 November 1959, pp. 1–2.

59. BISA, *Minutes of the Meetings of the Board of Directors,* 11 July 1955, pp. 1–2.

60. BISA, *Minutes of the Meetings of the Board of Directors,* 8 April 1957, p. 2.

61. BISA, *Minutes of the Meetings of the Board of Directors,* 13 March 1950, p. 1.

62. Memorandum to Knoke, "Federal Reserve Participation in the BIS", 12 May 1950, FRBNY, 797.3 – *BIS–FRBNY Relationship*; and memorandum to Sproul, "The

Place of the BIS in the Present-Day International Financial Set-up", 8 June 1950, FRBNY, 797.3 – *BIS–FRBNY Relationship.*

63. Memorandum to Sproul, "The Place of the BIS in the Present-Day International Financial Set-up", 8 June 1950, pp. 7–8, FRBNY, 797.3 – *BIS–FRBNY Relationship.*

64. Szymczak to Sproul, 11 September 1950, FRBNY, 797.3 – *BIS–FRBNY Relationship.*

65. John Exeter, however, was sent as informal representative of the FRBNY. See: J. Exeter to A. Sproul, 10 May 1955, FRBNY, 797.32 – *Correspondence Files 1950–74, BIS Representation on Board of Directors*; and A. Sproul to H. Alexander, 25 April 1955, FRBNY, 797.32 – *Correspondence Files 1950–74, BIS Representation on Board of Directors.*

66. Exeter to Sanford, 16 April 1955, FRBNY, 797.3 – *BIS–FRBNY Relationship.*

67. Burgess to Martin, 28 July 1955, FRBNY, 797.3 – *BIS–FRBNY Relationship.*

68. BIS President Frère wrote to Burgess: "I am not sure that he would be the right man for the Fund.... Jac is certainly wonderful as an economist, but he has absolutely no administrative capacity and no interest for administrative problems". Frère to Burgess, 28 June 1956, BISA, 7.16(3) – *BIS History (Baffi papers)*, box RBL/B3, f.B. Niemeyer advised Jacobsson to turn down the offer, since heading the IMF could only end "in failure". Diary Per Jacobsson, BULH, NL 324 – *Nachlass Per Jacobsson,* Tagebücher – D.110: June–November 1956. See also Jacobsson (1979), p. 284.

69. "One can see from the papers on your desk that you are not an administrator", Lord Cobbold once told Jacobsson; ibid., p. 283.

70. He "would come to Basel for about a fortnight at the time of each Board meeting". BISA, *Minutes of the Meetings of the Board of Directors,* 10 December 1956, p. 2.

71. Ibid.

72. Ibid.

73. He tendered his resignation in October 1957 but agreed to remain in office until the 1958 Annual Meeting. BISA, *Minutes of the Meetings of the Board of Directors,* 14 October 1957, pp. 1–2. At the National Bank of Belgium, Frère was succeeded by Hubert Ansiaux.

74. Interview with Henry Deroy, in Bank for International Settlements (1980b), p. 67.

75. To list just a few examples: BIS, "Gold and Dollar Movements from 1945 to 1951", CB Document no. 227, 1952; Conolly, "Arbitrage in Foreign Exchange in Europe since October 1953", CB Document no. 247, 1953; BIS, "Monetary Stability and the Banking System (lecture Per Jacobsson)", CB Document no. 254, 1954; BIS, "Exchange Control Regulations in 11 European Countries", CB Document no. 301, 1959; Auboin, "Monetary Illusions Put to the Test", HS Document no. 281, 1952; Jacobsson, "The Position of Sterling", HS Document no. 349, 1955.

76. For example: BIS, "The Position in Austria at the End of 1952", CB Document no. 236, 1953; BIS, "The U.K.'s Foreign Trade with the Six Countries of the ECSC", CB Document no. 274, 1956; BIS, "Recent Trends in Germany's Balance of Payments", CB Document no. 281, 1957; BIS, "Italy. Monetary and Economic Situation, 1949–58", CB Document no. 299, 1959.

77. BIS, Monetary and Economic Department, HS Document no. 318 (1953) and no. 322 (1954): "The Financing of Coal Stocks".

78. Auboin (1955), p. 33.

79. A few countries – notably Belgium, France, and Italy – had already raised their discount rates above the wartime level in the immediate postwar period (1945–47) in their successful fight against potential runaway inflation.

80. Meltzer (2003), p. 712.

81. BIS, *Twenty-Sixth Annual Report,* Basel, 11 June 1956, p. 166.

82. BIS, *Twenty-Second Annual Report,* Basel, 9 June 1952, pp. 209–10.

83. P. Jacobsson, "Monetary improvements in Europe. Problems of a return to convertibility", Lectures given before the Royal Society for Economics, Cairo, 14 to 18 December 1950, mimeo, p. 38.

84. BIS, *Twenty-First Annual Report,* Basel, 11 June 1951, p. 251.

85. Ibid., p. 252.

86. BIS, *Twenty-Sixth Annual Report,* Basel, 11 June 1956, pp. 228–9.

87. Ibid., p. 229.

88. Britton (2001), p. 124.

89. Friedman (1953).

90. BIS, *Twenty-Eighth Annual Report,* Basel, 9 June 1958, pp. 171ff.

91. "In private, British officials, for example, as early as 1952, debated the case for floating the pound; but nothing of the kind could be said in public"; Britton (2001), p. 124.

92. BIS, *Twenty-Ninth Annual Report,* Basel, 8 June 1959, p. 243.

93. Eichengreen (1993), p. 1.

94. Austria, Belgium, Denmark, France, Germany, Greece, Iceland, Ireland, Italy, Luxembourg, the Netherlands, Norway, Portugal, Sweden, Switzerland, the Free Territory of Trieste, Turkey, and the United Kingdom.

95. For details see: BIS, *Annual Reports,* Basel, 1950–58; and Auboin (1954), pp. 39–60.

96. The deep involvement of the BIS in the origin and management of the EPU is witnessed, among other things, by the unusual initiative taken by the Bank to promote research on the history of the EPU. The result is an outstanding book that remains the standard reference on the subject: Kaplan and Schleiminger (1989). The narrative of the EPU's history contained in this section draws largely on the work of these two authors, one of whom (Schleiminger) was BIS General Manager from 1981 to 1985.

97. The first draft of Hoffman's speech read "unification"; it was changed to "integration" on Acheson's personal request. Ibid., pp. 29–30.

98. Ibid., p. 32.

99. Ibid., p. 36.

100. Among the committee's members were Guindey (the future BIS general manager), Keesing and Posthuma from the Netherlands, Ellis-Rees from the U.K. Treasury, and Malagodi and Ferrari (a future BIS secretary general) from Italy; Henry Tasca, assisted by Robert Triffin, represented the U.S. government.

101. Kaplan and Schleiminger (1989), p. 39.

102. Cabinet paper Annex B to CO (49) 203 (25 October 1949). Quoted by Kaplan and Schleiminger (1989), p. 29.

103. The "[British] government files show no studied analysis that might have warranted such a view"; ibid., p. 52.

104. Ibid., p. 57; see also Oliva and Stefani (2000).

105. The members of the inner group were Ansiaux, Ferrari, Guindey, Keesing, Posthuma, Tasca, and Triffin.
106. Kaplan and Schleiminger (1989), pp. 62–87.
107. Ibid., p. 87.
108. Jacobsson (1958), pp. 281–317: "Trade and Financial Relationship Between Countries".
109. Jacobsson (1958), p. 295: "Trade and Financial Relationship Between Countries". Guido Carli (the first chairman of the EPU managing board) later wrote that, since the Bank of England's view dominated at the BIS, the Bank had accepted the role of EPU agent reluctantly; Carli (1993), p. 93.
110. Auboin (1954), pp. 38–60.
111. It is perhaps an overstatement to say: "most central bank governors were heavily influenced by Jacobsson" (Kaplan and Schleiminger 1989, p. 64). However, they were surely more inclined than most of their governments to use monetary policy rather than administrative controls to keep prices and exchange rates within desired targets.
112. BIS, *Minutes of the Meetings of the Board of Directors,* 9 January 1950, p. 2. The discussion at the Board meeting was undoubtedly heated, with Cobbold – the Governor of the Bank of England – voicing his protest against the experts' proposal for the EPU.
113. Kaplan and Schleiminger (1989), p. 64.
114. A few weeks later, a softer version of the central bank governors' proposal was developed by Ansiaux and supported by the main Continental countries except for Germany; the United Kingdom and the United States opposed it, but for different reasons.
115. At the time, Carli was in no way connected with the central bank.
116. See Arts. 21 and 24 of the BIS Statutes (1930).
117. A full set of the Agent's Reports is to be found in BISA, 7.14 – *European Payments Union.* Further documents on the BIS's EPU functions are in BISA, 3.10(8) to 3.10(14) – *EPU.*
118. Conolly was the BIS representative on the EPU board throughout its existence, with Bruppacher serving as his alternate for the first six years and Schmid for the remaining period.
119. Voting members of the board were: Guido Carli (Italy), chair; Pierre Calvet (France), vice-chairman; Hugh Ellis-Rees (U.K.), vice-chairman; Sigmund Hartogshon (Denmark); F. A. G. Keesing (the Netherlands); Hans Karl von Mangoldt (Federal Republic of Germany); Paul Rossy (Switzerland); and Knut Getz Wold (Norway, joined in 1952). The board meetings were also attended by Hubert Ansiaux, chair of the OEEC Intra-European Payments Committee; Hubert Havlik, representative of the U.S. government; and Frederick Conolly as representative of the BIS.
120. An increase of 233% from the time of the monetary reform (June 1948) to November 1950.
121. See: BIS, *Twenty-First Annual Report,* Basel, 11 June 1951, pp. 45–53.
122. Both men were well acquainted with Germany's economic problem. Jacobsson, as we have seen, had been a frequent visitor to Berlin throughout the war and in its immediate aftermath. Cairncross had been involved in the Allied negotiations

on the level of German industrial activity following the Potsdam Conference on reparations of July 1945. See Cairncross (1987).

123. On their first meeting, Cairncross wrote: "[Jacobsson] proved to be suffering from severe oyster poisoning, so that it was by no means certain that he could take an active part during the first two or three days of the inquiry." A. Cairncross, "Report on visit to Germany 28 October to 3 November 1950", DBHA, N2/K3 – *Europäische Zahlungsunion,* Cairncross–Jacobsson Mission 1950, p. 1.

124. In his diary, Jacobsson wrote: "Dr. Vocke asked me whether Mr. Cairncross was a Keynesian and I replied that I would not call him a pronounced Keynesian; he was a very sensible economist". Jacobsson (1979), p. 237.

125. The BIS followed its standard practice of securing Germany's agreement before authorising Jacobsson's mission.

126. A. Cairncross, "Report on visit to Germany 28 October to 3 November 1950", DBHA, N2/K3 – *Europäische Zahlungsunion,* Cairncross–Jacobsson Mission 1950, p. 4.

127. Ibid.

128. Among the former, the experts cited the delay in adopting a tight money policy, of which a contributing factor was seen in "the strong local influences in the German central bank". Their recommendation was "to find ways of increasing the power of central direction exercised by the Bank deutscher Länder". OEEC, EPU, *Consideration of Germany's position,* 20 November 1950, p. 51.

129. Jacobsson (1979), p. 244.

130. In his talks with Vocke, Jacobsson was emphatic that the central bank should decide on an "impressive increase in the discount rate" and should do so immediately; otherwise, it would make "a lamentable impression". See Emminger (1986), pp. 52 ff. The German EPU crisis is dealt with in more detail by Holtfrerich (1999), pp. 333–41. An important side effect of this particular episode was that it considerably enhanced the authority and independence of the German central bank vis-à-vis its government.

131. BIS, *Twenty-First Annual Report,* Basel, 11 June 1951, pp. 49–50.

132. Given the need for rapid action, the report was at first verbally presented to the Board, the written version not being ready until November 20. See OEEC, EPU, *Consideration of Germany's position,* 20 November 1950.

133. These conditions were in substance those recommended by the experts and included, besides the monetary policy already implemented, commitments to avoid both a devaluation of the currency and fiscal deficits by the Federal and the *Länder* governments.

134. For a complete account of how the German economy evolved in 1950–51, see Cairncross (1951), pp. 19–34.

135. Jacobsson (1979), p. 244.

136. Kaplan and Schleiminger (1989), p. 114.

137. See Triffin (1957), p. 182. Von Mangoldt – German representative on the EPU board – was especially praised for the fairness and integrity of his actions, which assured his succession to Carli as chairman of the board in 1952.

138. See Kaplan and Schleiminger (1989), particularly Chapters 8 and 15.

139. Ibid., p. 138.

140. Ibid., p. 275.

141. Governor's note, "Basle 13–14 April 1958", BEA, OV4/52 – *BIS General, 1958–59.*

142. Per Jacobsson, now Managing Director of the IMF, had impressed upon de Gaulle the need to act on the French franc: "No country can gain international esteem if it has not a good currency. That the French franc has not been a strong currency has been very damaging to French prestige in recent years". James (1996), p. 107.

143. France could not miss the convertibility boat, since all its EEC partners and the United Kingdom were ready to take the step. This was certainly an added stimulus for the French government to speed up its reform plans. See also Bossuat (2003), pp. 723–52.

144. Governor's note, 22 December 1958, BEA, OV4/52 – *BIS General,* 1958–59.

145. Cairncross and Eichengreen (1983), p. 154.

146. As early as December 1950, Jacobsson wrote: "One great obstacle on the road to convertibility has been eliminated now that the United States has no substantial export surplus – or rather now that so large a part of the goods and services which other countries have to import can be obtained elsewhere than in the United States". P. Jacobsson, "Monetary improvements in Europe. Problems of a return to convertibility", Lectures given before the Royal Society for Economics, Cairo, 14 to 18 December 1950, p. 41, BISA, 7.18(11) – *Jacobsson Papers,* box JAC1.

147. Eichengreen (1993), p. 62. In particular, Eichengreen argues: that market-clearing exchange rates were within reach if European countries had been willing to coordinate the adoption of convertibility; that the overall level of reserves was adequate; that, with the exception of the United Kingdom and Ireland, monetary overhangs had been eliminated; and that the likely evolution of wage costs would not have undermined exchange rate stability.

148. A detailed account of these negotiations is to be found in Kaplan and Schleiminger (1989), pp. 157–228, from which the material for this section is drawn (unless otherwise stated).

149. The Conservatives returned to office in October 1951.

150. For an account of the proposal and its rejection, see Cairncross (1985).

151. While the Robot plan proposed floating rather than fixed rates, floating would be permitted only within a given range: Cherwell and McDougall, the prime minister's advisers, feared that an increase in the already high bank rate would be needed to keep the exchange rate from falling to the bottom limit, exacerbating unemployment.

152. The Bank of England tried to revive the debate that dragged on for some months.

153. Kaplan and Schleiminger (1989), p. 168.

154. Headed by Foreign Affairs Secretary and Deputy Prime Minister Eden and by Chancellor Butler.

155. Panel members were Robbins (chair), Bresciani-Turroni, Lindhal, Marget, Masoin, Rueff, and Schnider.

156. In October 1952, Carli yielded the EPU chair to von Mangoldt.

157. Kaplan and Schleiminger (1989), p. 186.

158. The Swiss franc was convertible into other convertible currencies, while exchange restrictions applied to all other transactions. It was argued that, in the absence of such a double standard, a fully convertible currency would become scarce within

the EPU (on account of its tendency to be converted into dollars) rather than spent within the EPU area.

159. The latter proposal was also backed by the Bank of England but opposed by the Treasury, probably for tactical reasons. Kaplan and Schleiminger (1989), p. 192.

160. The position of Getz Wold, the Board member from Norway, derived also from his belief that creditor countries should assume a major responsibility for correcting payments imbalances.

161. G. F. B. to the Governor, "Basle notes – EPU", 10 November 1953, BEA, OV4/47 – *BIS General, 1953–54.* The discussions in Basel had made it clear that Germany and the Netherlands were "greatly interested" in an early move towards convertibility but also that they felt that it was "no use London talking more on this subject".

162. Kaplan and Schleiminger (1989) rightly observe that this technical complication, known as the "gold sandwich *tranche*", helped engrain the notion that the EPU was a technical mechanism beyond the comprehension of the layperson.

163. Kaplan and Schleiminger (1989), pp. 201–2.

164. BIS, *Twenty-Sixth Annual Report,* Basel, 11 June 1956, p. 211.

165. The European Fund would have a capital of $600 million, deriving partly from the EPU's assets and partly from members' contributions.

166. Data from: BIS, *Twenty-Ninth Annual Report,* Basel, 8 June 1959, pp. 148–52.

167. Kaplan and Schleiminger (1989), pp. 317–19.

168. A. Ferrari, *Cooperazione Monetaria Internazionale,* Lecture at Ca' Foscari, The University of Venice, 23 October 1959, mimeo, p. 25.

169. Giovanoli (1989), p. 857. Whereas the EPU combined an automatic credit mechanism with compulsory clearing, the EMA only provided credit on an ad hoc basis and voluntary clearing for certain specified balances. During the 14 years of its existence (1958–72), the EMA's European Fund granted credit to four member countries only: Greece, Iceland, Spain, and Turkey. The total amount of outstanding credits never exceeded $150 million. See: BISA, 3.10 – *European Monetary Agreement, General correspondence, 1959–73*; and BISA, 3.10(11) – *EMA, Decisions of the Managing Board, 1958–72,* vols. 2–3.

170. Eichengreen (1993), p. 86.

171. Ibid., p. 121.

172. Czechoslovakia and Poland had joined the IMF from the outset, but Poland withdrew in 1950 and Czechoslovakia in 1955. Only Yugoslavia defied Moscow in this matter (as in others) and remained a member of the IMF. Horsefield (1969), pp. 116, 258, 363–4.

173. The State Bank of the USSR and the central bank of the German Democratic Republic were the only central banks from the Eastern bloc not to participate in the BIS.

174. Note on the future of the BIS for the Secretary of State, Foreign Office, June 1946, in PRO, Richmond, Treasury Papers, T 236/26 – *Bank for International Settlements: liquidation, 1946.* The same argument was reiterated by Foreign Secretary Bevin in defense of the BIS in a communication to the U.S. delegation at the Paris Peace Conference (see Section 8.3).

175. As early as 1946, the BIS placed a 4.5 million Swiss franc credit at the disposal of the National Bank of Hungary, and in June 1947 a 3 million Swiss franc advance was made available to the National Bank of Poland.

176. "Comecon" was the acronym for the Council for Mutual Economic Assistance, established in January 1949 with the aim of promoting trade and economic integration between the Eastern bloc countries.

177. United Nations, Economic and Social Council, Economic Commission for Europe, Committee on the Development of Trade, "Report of the Committee on the Development of Trade on its fifth session, 15–26 October 1956", E/ECE/TRADE/22, Annex II, BISA, 3.10g – *East–West Multilateral Compensation, 1956–58*.

178. Note, H. Mandel, "Conversation téléphonique avec la B N de Hongrie, Budapest (Mr. Fekete)", 3 May 1956, BISA, 2.32 – *Magyar Nemzeti Bank, Policy, 1930–1982*, vol. 1.

179. Letter, Roger Auboin to Gunnar Myrdal, Executive Secretary of the Economic Commission for Europe, 11 December 1956, BISA, 3.10g – *East–West Multilateral Compensation, 1956–58*. The following countries declined to endorse the joint declaration on East–West multilateral compensation: Belgium, West Germany, the Netherlands, the United Kingdom, the United States, and Turkey. The central banks and the BIS itself were opposed to the scheme: "There seems little doubt that, under the cover of proposals for increasing East–West trade exchanges, the Russians and their satellites are probing into the possibilities of setting up a payments organisation competitive with the EPU. The BIS staff are not in favour of entering into negotiations with the Iron Curtain countries regarding payment and clearing arrangements as, apart from the political repercussions, the BIS could not avoid granting credit on a large scale if an efficient clearing organisation were to be set up." Note, G. F. B. for the Governor, 15 November 1955, BEA, OV4/49 – *BIS General, 1954–55*.

180. These operations usually took the form of a Swiss franc or U.S. dollar credit, made available to the central bank in question for a period of three or six months (often renewable), arranged as a swap or against cover of that central bank's gold deposits with the BIS.

181. BISA, *Minutes of the Meetings of the Board of Directors,* Basel, May 1956 and 13 May 1963. On 13 May 1963, the Board doubled the overall ceiling for Czechoslovakia, Hungary, and Poland, plus Bulgaria and Romania, to $30 million (or roughly 100 million Swiss francs), of which half could be granted on an uncovered basis.

182. BISA, *Minutes of the Meetings of the Board of Directors,* Basel, 7 November 1960. Also: BISA, 2.10 – *Banque Nationale de Yugoslavie, Policy, 1946–88*, vol. 3.

183. Mandel, head of the BIS Banking Department, was in Prague in 1966, his deputy Macdonald in 1967. The visit in 1968 from Janson, manager in the BIS Banking Department, was postponed – because of the Soviet invasion in August of that year – but not cancelled. Mandel was in Warsaw in 1965, and BIS Secretary General d'Aroma visited Poland in 1969. Holtrop and d'Aroma were in Budapest in 1966; and Mandel visited the Hungarian central bank in 1967 and again in 1971. Royot visited Belgrade in 1961. Mandel was in the Yugoslav capital in 1967 and again in 1969. In between, in 1968, BIS General Manager Ferras had paid a visit to the Yugoslavs.

184. For instance, in June 1958 the National Bank of Poland approached President Frère with a request that one of the Eastern European countries be represented on the BIS Board. Note for Record, 11 June 1958, BEA, OV4/52 – *BIS General, 1958–59*.

185. "Meetings with the Governors of the Eastern European Countries", BISA, 7.1(3) – *Board Secretariat Papers,* box Board 32.
186. BIS, *Fifty-Third Annual Report,* Basel, 1983, pp. 164–6.
187. In that same context, from 1993 until 2004 the BIS participated – together with the IMF, IBRD, EBRD, and OECD – in the so-called Joint Vienna Institute, where central bankers, banking supervisors, and civil servants from the transition countries were offered intensive training courses in monetary policy issues and international finance.
188. Between 1962 and 1965, the Gold Pool was able to replenish its gold holdings partly thanks to Russian gold sales on the London market. In addition, between 1962 and 1965 the BIS bought, for its own account, no less than 830 tonnes of gold from the Russians.
189. Note, 12 June 1958, BEA, OV4/52 – *BIS General, 1958–59.*
190. Letter, Holtrop to Guindey, 29 December 1961, NBHA, 8.1/1830/1 – *BIS, Correspondentie General Manager, 1961.*
191. "Admission eventuelle de l'URSS à la BRI, Compte rendu de la réunion restreinte tenue à la BRI, le lundi 9 juillet 1962, après la réunion du Conseil", BISA, 7.1(3) – *Board Secretariat Papers,* box Board 29, f: "Possible USSR membership".
192. The Hungarian central bank was the most active in this respect, raising the issue on the occasion of the visits to Budapest by Holtrop in 1966, Ferras in 1968, and Zijlstra in 1969.
193. Meetings held on 9 December 1968, 17 November 1969, and 19 April 1971 (this last one in view of Zijlstra's impending visit to the Soviet Union). See: BISA, 7.1(3) – *Board Secretariat Papers,* box Board 29, f: "Possible USSR membership".

Chapter 11

1. James (1996), p. 157.
2. Ibid.
3. For a general overview see Van der Wee (1986), pp. 454–78. For an insider's view: Solomon (1982).
4. See for instance Milward (1995), pp. 135–51.
5. Van Buren Cleveland (1971), p. 42.
6. James (1996), p. 151.
7. Maier (1988).
8. On this subject see Gavin (2004).
9. Gilpin (1987), p. 136.
10. Triffin (1957); see also Triffin (1960), which reproduces two articles published in March and June 1959 in *Banca Nazionale del Lavoro Quarterly Review* as well as the statement rendered by the author to the Joint Economic Committee of the U.S. Congress in October 1959.
11. Triffin (1960), p. 70.
12. Zimmerman (2000), pp. 86–7.
13. Schenk (2002a), p. 353.
14. Ibid., p. 350.
15. See Rueff (1977), pp. 259–74; also, "Argument with Jacques Rueff", *The Economist,* 13 February 1965, pp. 662–5.

16. Holtfrerich (1999), p. 384.
17. He had also been Vice-Chairman of the Board since 1946.
18. Marcel (then Baron) van Zeeland, at the BIS since its foundation, retired as First Manager and Head of the Banking Department in March 1962. He was replaced by Hans Mandel.
19. Just before taking office as head of the Netherlands Bank and the BIS, Zijlstra had also briefly been prime minister of the Netherlands (November 1966 – April 1967).
20. However, he remained in office until the end of the financial year, in May 1963.
21. Guindey was later President of the Caisse Centrale de Coopération Économique and of the Compagnie Internationale des Wagons-Lits.
22. "The Governor of the Bank of France thanked the Chairman and the Board for having chosen another person of French nationality to the post of General Manager", BISA, *Minutes of the Meetings of the Board of Directors,* 12 November 1962, p. 3.
23. He joined the Bank of France in 1938, represented France at the OEEC and the EPU, and served as IMF director for France. In 1953 Ferras was appointed deputy director of the exchange restrictions department of the IMF and in 1956 head of the IMF European department.
24. "Entretien avec Antonio D'Aroma", January/September 1979, Bank for International Settlements (1980b), p. 190.
25. "Interview with Lord O'Brien of Lothbury", December 1978, Bank for International Settlements (1980b), p. 84. "His English was perfect", O'Brien said, "and he managed to keep an even balance between the Anglo-Saxon part of the organisation and the French, continental part".
26. BISA, *Minutes of the Meetings of the Board of Directors,* 19 April 1971, p. 2.
27. The post also entailed heading the Monetary and Economic Department. Gilbert took up his duties in November 1960. BISA, *Minutes of the Meetings of the Board of Directors,* 9 May 1960, p. 1.
28. At the beginning of the search, in 1959, the preference in Basel was definitely for a European to succeed Jacobsson. However, as it proved difficult to "find the right man" in Europe, the FRBNY was requested to obtain "biographical material" about suitable U.S. academics. Eventually the choice fell on Gilbert. See: Confidential Memorandum, BIS, 19 March 1959, FRBNY, 797.3 – *BIS Historical Documents: BIS–FRNBY Relationship.*
29. In the mid-1970s, d'Aroma was made Assistant General Manager and replaced as Secretary General by Günther Schleiminger, who was later replaced by another Italian, Giampietro Morelli.
30. G. Ferras, "The role of the BIS today", paper delivered at the Centre d'Etudes Supérieurs de Banque, 26 June 1967, p. 8, BISA – *Mimeo.*
31. Ibid.
32. See Annex B on the BIS balance sheet at the end of this volume.
33. On average, up to 85%–90% of the BIS deposits were either sight or at three-month maturity.
34. G. Ferras, "The role of the BIS today", paper delivered at the Centre d'Etudes Supérieurs de Banque, 26 June 1967, p. 5, BISA – *Mimeo.*
35. See Section 7.10.
36. Abs (1991), pp. 235–8.

37. This final payment by the German government of 156 million Deutsche marks, or 119 million Swiss gold francs, represented less than half of the initial investment of some 293 million Swiss gold francs. Of these 156 million Deutsche marks, 48 million compensated the BIS itself; the remaining 108 million were transferred to the creditor governments in compensation for the minimum deposits they had maintained on the BIS Annuity Trust Account since 1930. BISA, 7.8 – *BIS Funds in Germany,* box 12. Also: BIS, *Thirty-Sixth Annual Report,* Basel, 13 June 1966, pp. 165–7.

38. Extraordinary General Meeting of 9 June 1969, BISA, 1.4(6) – *Revision of the Statutes, 1968–69.* Compare Arts. 4 and 28 in the 1961 and 1969 versions of the BIS Statutes.

39. This was not yet quite the end of a long story. The settlement of interest arrears for the years 1945–52 had been postponed by the 1953 agreement until after the reunification of Germany. When this came about in 1990, new funding bonds were issued by the German Republic for the amount of €112 million, which are to mature in October 2010 – 86 years after the initial issue of the Dawes Loan.

40. The Japanese were already in the early 1960s probing for a renewed membership as shareholder of the BIS, a position they had given up as a result of the San Francisco Peace Treaty of 1951. See, for instance: Note, "Japan and the BIS", BEA, OV4/56 – *BIS General,* January–December 1962.

41. Since 1994, the governors of the Bank of Canada and of the Bank of Japan have been elected to sit on the BIS Board of Directors.

42. BISA, *Minutes of the Meetings of the Board of Directors,* 9 September 1969, p. 2.

43. BISA, *Minutes of the Meetings of the Board of Directors,* 12 January 1970, p. 2.

44. September 1971.

45. P. Clement, "The BIS – One Bank, Five Locations", *The Tower,* 11 October 2000, p. 9.

46. President of the Swiss National Bank, joined the BIS Board in April 1974.

47. "Entretien avec Fritz Leutwiler", April 1979, Bank for International Settlements (1980b), pp. 149, 155.

48. "Interview with Otmar Emminger", April 1979, Bank for International Settlements (1980b), p. 145.

49. G. Ferras, "Le rôle de la banque des Règlements Internationaux", Conférence donnée au Centre d'Études Supérieures de la Banque le lundi 26 juin 1967, p. 11, BISA, *Vorträge Ferras, 10 September 1969.*

50. Confidential Memorandum, BIS, 19 March 1959, FRBNY, 797.3 – *BIS, Historical Documents: BIS–FRNBY Relationship.*

51. Coombs (1976), p. 23.

52. Memorandum to Treasury Secretary Dillon and Assistant Secretary Roosa – "Relations with the BIS, 14 April 1961", anonymous but most likely by Coombs, FRBNY, 797.3 – *BIS, Historical Documents: BIS–FRNBY Relationship.*

53. Needless to say, such a climate of trust, a blessing as far as cooperation is concerned, is a curse as far as the historian's work is concerned.

54. Coombs (1976), p. 26.

55. Ibid., p. 28.

56. At the FRBNY he was nicknamed "our Italian Navigator"; ibid., p. 31.

57. See Section 6.10.

58. Not as Board member, Rasminsky attended the meetings "whenever he could" from the mid-1960s onwards.
59. "Louis Rasminsky, Speech delivered in January 1973", Bank for International Settlements (1980b), pp. 200–1.
60. "Interview with Carl-Hendrik Nordlander", April 1979, Bank for International Settlements (1980b), p. 165. Nordlander became governor of Sweden's central bank in 1976; before then he had, for 15 years, been a fairly regular visitor to Basel and an observer of the meetings.
61. J. F. Ghiardi, "Notes on Governors' meeting, March 9, 1969, Basel, Switzerland", 8 April 1969, FRBNY, 797.3 – *BIS, 1st File 1960–70.*
62. Ibid., p. 6.
63. "Interview with Monsieur Ferras", *The Banker,* 9 August 1966; and BISA, *Vorträge M. Ferras, 10 September 1969.*
64. "Entretien avec Guido Carli", April 1979, Bank for International Settlements (1980b), p. 109.
65. J. F. Ghiardi, "Notes on Governors' meeting, March 9, 1969, Basel, Switzerland", 8 April 1969, pp. 3–4, FRBNY, 797.3 – *BIS, 1st File 1960–70.*
66. Needless to say, a considerable transatlantic exchange of telephone calls also took place before sensitive meetings.
67. Hayes to Martin, Roosa and others, "Arrangements for reporting central bank mutual credit operations, July 1st, 1964", FRBNY, 797.3 – *BIS, 1st file 1960–70.*
68. Coombs to Hayes, "Conversation with Lord Cromer", 14 July 1964, FRBNY, 797.3 – *BIS, 1st file 1960–70.*
69. MacLaury to Hayes, Coombs, and Sanford, "Treasury view concerning sterling balance assistance", 10 February 1966, FRBNY, 797.3 – *BIS, 1st File 1960–70.*
70. Coombs to Ralph Young, Senior Adviser to the Board of Governors, 29 March 1966, FRBNY, 797.3 – *BIS, 1st file 1960–70.*
71. MacLaury to Coombs and others, "Swap arrangements maturities", 23 January 1967, FRBNY, 797.3 – *BIS, 1st file 1960–70.*
72. Coombs to Henry Fowler, Secretary of the Treasury, 27 February 1967, FRBNY, 797.3 – *BIS, 1st file 1960–70.*
73. "Entretien avec Guido Carli", April 1979, Bank for International Settlements (1980b), p. 109.
74. Ibid., p. 111.
75. Ibid., p. 112.
76. Charles Coombs had recently been appointed (April 1959) Vice-President of the FRBNY in charge of the foreign department.
77. Coombs (1976), p. 30.
78. BIS, *Thirteenth Annual Report,* Basel, 13 June 1960, table on p. 138; and BIS, *Fourteenth Annual Report,* Basel, 12 June 1961, table on p. 134. Japan's reserves were also increasing.
79. G. Carli, Appunto per Paolo Emilio Taviani, Treasury Secretary, 26 September 1960, BIHA – *Direttorio, Carli,* cart 69, fasc 4, sfasc 1.
80. On the intricate interaction between military defence, balance of payments, and monetary policy issues in the relations between West Germany and the United States in the 1950s and 1960s, see Zimmerman (2002).

81. The Bank was under direction from the Treasury to keep a given dollar/gold ratio in its reserves. G. Carli, Appunto per Paolo Emilio Taviani, Treasury Secretary, 26 September 1960, BIHA – *Direttorio, Carli,* cart 69, fasc 4, sfasc 1.
82. Ibid.
83. Triffin (1960), p. 155.
84. Ibid., p. 156.
85. "On 20 October, with the fixing price set as high as $36.55, prices broke loose and, with U.S. private buyers entering the market, as much as $40 per ounce was quoted for gold at one point. That was the peak of the rise, and after four days on which prices paid varied between $36 and $39 the fixing price was down to $35.71 on 27 October". BIS, *Thirty-First Annual Report,* Basel, 12 June 1961, p. 132.
86. Informal meeting of the central-bank Governors who are Board members of the BIS, 6 November 1960, BIHA – *Carte Baffi,* no. 275, fasc 1, p. 2.
87. Ibid., p. 3.
88. Report on visit by C. A. Coombs and T. J. Roche to February meeting of the BIS, NARA, RG 56 – *U.S. Treasury,* 69A-4707, box 111.
89. Triffin (1960).
90. Kennedy was "absolutely obsessed with the balance of payments". He told his advisers that "the two things that scared him most were nuclear weapons and the payments deficit". Gavin (2004), p. 59.
91. The account of the meeting comes from: "Comments on recent discussions with European central bankers", visit of Hayes and Coombs to the BIS and Bank of England, 6–9 January 1961, NARA, RG 56 – *U.S. Treasury,* 69A-4707, box 111.
92. The three-man committee included Allan Sproul, former president of the FRBNY, as chairman, Roy Blough of Columbia University, former economic adviser of Truman, and Paul McCracken, of the University of Michigan, former economic adviser of Eisenhower.
93. Coombs (1976), p. 19.
94. The account of the meeting comes from: Report on visit by C. A. Coombs and T. J. Roche to February meetings of the BIS, NARA, RG 56 – *U.S. Treasury,* 69A-4707, box 111.
95. Carli to Taviani, Secretary to the Treasury, 16 February 1961, BIHA – *Direttorio, Carli,* cart 35, fasc 66.
96. The Dutch guilder followed on the next day.
97. M. N. Trued to Coombs, notes on trip to BIS meetings, 11–13 March 1961, NARA, RG 56 – *U.S. Treasury,* 69A-4707, Box 111, p. 3. U.S. Under-Secretary of State George Ball's public comments on the revaluation being a "useful but modest step" contributed significantly to the continued nervousness of the exchange markets. Zimmerman (2002), pp. 129–30.
98. Coombs (1976), p. 32.
99. BIS, *Thirty-First Annual Report,* Basel, 12 June 1961, p. 149.
100. Ibid., p. 147.
101. Coombs (1976), pp. 33–4.
102. Macdonald to Coombs, 15 February 1961, NARA, RG 56 – *U.S. Treasury,* 69A-4707, box 111.

103. Roosa to Dillon, "My suggestion that the Federal Reserve comment publicly on BIS announcement of cooperation", 13 March 1961, NARA, RG 56 – *U.S. Treasury,* 69A-4707, box 111.
104. The scheme originated from the "Basel agreement", discussed in Section 11.6.
105. Coombs (1976), p. 29.
106. Gilbert (1980), p. 132.
107. The London market was traditionally the world's most important free gold market. It had been reopened in 1954 after a long wartime closure. Another free market for gold existed in Zurich.
108. Informal meeting of the central-bank Governors who are Board members of the BIS, 6 November 1960, BIHA – *Carte Baffi,* no. 275, fasc 1, p. 3.
109. $35.0875.
110. On 14 January, after another price hike, the U.S. Treasury prohibited persons subject to U.S. jurisdiction from holding gold outside the United States and ordered them to dispose of all existing holdings by 1 June 1961.
111. BIS, *Thirty-First Annual Report,* Basel, 4 June 1962, pp. 132–3.
112. BIS, *Thirty-Second Annual Report,* Basel, 12 June 1961, pp. 126–7.
113. The Berlin crisis unfolded after Khrushchev, meeting with Kennedy in Vienna in early June 1961, presented the West with an ultimatum: a peace treaty between East and West Germany (including "free city" or neutral status for West Berlin) must be negotiated by December. That deadline and then the building of the wall dividing Berlin in August 1961 raised East–West tensions to levels not seen since the Korean War.
114. D. H. F. Rickett, "Note for the record: meeting of the Chancellor with Mr. Dillon and Mr. Roosa at the British Embassy in Vienna on 21 September 1961", PRO, T 312/312 – *London gold market, schemes for co-ordinated purchases and sales of gold by central banks, 1961–62.*
115. D. A. V. Allen, "Note of a meeting in Sir Frank Lee's room on 27 September 1961", PRO, T 312/312 – *London gold market, schemes for co-ordinated purchases and sales of gold by central banks, 1961–62.*
116. "The broad position is that none of us can be sure about what the full implications may be later on if we agree to participate in the gold pool scheme. In short, we cannot be certain that we shall know what we may be letting ourselves in for. But despite this and despite the special position of sterling as a reserve currency based on gold, I am clear (and so is the Governor) that we cannot take the line that we must stand aside from the scheme if it commands general acceptance elsewhere". Sir Lee to Mr. Hubback for the chancellor, "U.S./European Gold Pool", 7 November 1961, PRO, T 312/312 – *London gold market.*
117. The Governor of the National Bank of Belgium, however, remarked that this was the first he had heard about the scheme. Note, J. Anson, "Gold", 15 November 1961, PRO, T 312/312 – *London gold market.*
118. Memo, D. H. Macdonald, "Gold Club", 11 January 1962, BISA, Basel, 7.18(16) – *Papers R.T.P. Hall,* box HAL 2, f01.
119. Note, Marcel van Zeeland, "Opérations sur or", 13 March 1962, BISA, Basel, 7.18(16) – *Papers R.T.P. Hall,* box HAL 2, f01.
120. Note, Rickett to Allen, "Gold", 15 December 1961, PRO, T 312/312 – *London gold market.*

121. The decision was made at a meeting held in BIS President Holtrop's office on 7 January 1962. Note, J. M. S., "Gold: talks in Basel 6/7 January 1962", PRO, T 312/312 – *London gold market.*
122. The heads of the gold and foreign exchange divisions of the central banks – such as Charles Coombs of the Federal Reserve Bank of New York, Roy Bridge of the Bank of England, and Johannes Tüngeler of the Bundesbank – normally participated in the meetings.
123. The first full report on gold production and consumption was submitted by the BIS at the experts' request on 30 November 1962. It was regularly updated with the latest figures after that.
124. Cable, Hayes to Cromer, Bank of England, 8 August 1962, PRO, T 312/949 – *London gold market. Scheme for co-ordinated purchases and sales of gold by central banks, 1962–64.*
125. Letter, Cromer to Blessing, 26 October 1962, DBHA – *Handakte Tüngeler*, B 330/08707: *Goldpool (Basel), 1962–68.*
126. "Co-ordinated gold operations, Report of the Group of Experts on the experiences of the past year", 12 January 1963, BISA, 7.18(16) – *Papers R.T.P. Hall,* box HAL 2, f01.
127. "How the Pool has worked", *The Economist,* 17 November 1962, p. 701.
128. See: "Co-ordinated gold operations by central banks on the London gold market, Report of experts meeting at the BIS, Basel, 9 February 1963", 10 February 1963, BISA, 7.18(16) – *Papers R.T.P. Hall,* box HAL 2, f01.
129. "Gold Pool's first year. Account balanced", *The Economist,* 29 December 1962, pp. 1293–4.
130. For the whole of 1963, the Pool was able to buy $639 million worth of gold. The end figure for 1964 was roughly the same: $623 million.
131. The Bank of England summed it up as follows: "The gold pool is not a rigid, cut and dried scheme. It originated to meet a practical need, developed in response to the behaviour of the markets and in accordance with the spirit of co-operation existing between a group of central banks whose interests lie closely together, and is operated in a flexible and informal manner. The underlying objective has been to avoid unnecessary and disturbing fluctuations in the price of gold in the free market, which might have, and probably would have, undermined confidence in stability of the exchanges, the maintenance of which is a common objective of all of the participants. The gold pool has done much towards achieving this objective.... there is little doubt that the knowledge that central banks were working together in the gold, as well as in the exchange, markets has helped to maintain public confidence in the existing international monetary structure". Bank of England, *Quarterly Bulletin,* vol. 4, 1 (March 1964), pp. 20–1.
132. See graphs entitled "London market gold price", BIS, *Thirty-Fourth Annual Report,* Basel, 8 June 1964, p. 105; and BIS, *Thirty-Fifth Annual Report,* Basel, 14 June 1965, p. 109. The shipping parity refers to the official gold price of $35 per ounce at which gold could be obtained at the U.S. Treasury gold window (although only by monetary authorities of IMF member states), plus shipping and transportation costs from New York to London. This means that whenever the London gold price exceeded the $35.0875 mark it became a profitable proposition to buy gold in New York, drawing on the U.S. gold reserves, and sell it in London.

133. The suggestion to open the Gold and Foreign Exchange Experts' Group to all G10 countries was first made by Charles Coombs at the meeting of the group in July 1964. None of these three newcomers joined the Gold Pool arrangement, since their own gold reserves were relatively small (in particular Japan's) and it was thus in their interest not to sell any gold and to maintain their ability to buy gold on the free market for their own account. See: note, 4 July 1964: "Réunion des Experts de l'Or", BFA, Sous-fonds Réparations et Banque des Règlements Internationaux, 1489200303/194 – *Collaboration entre les Banques Centrales, 1959–1966.*

134. The 1958 devaluation of the French franc did not constitute (strictly speaking) an adjustment of a fixed IMF exchange parity, since it was actually the occasion on which the French officially fixed such a parity for the first time since 1946.

135. See, in particular: Holtfrerich (1999), pp. 362–80; Emminger (1986), pp. 98–134.

136. See, for instance, Emminger's note of 20 January 1960 pleading for a 7.5% revaluation, DBHA, N2/00244 – *Akten Otmar Emminger.*

137. Interestingly, in the parliamentary debate on 8 March, Chancellor Adenauer made a point of referring to the move as a "devaluation of the dollar" rather than a revaluation of the Deutsche mark. Emminger (1986), p. 129.

138. The 5% revaluation of the guilder took effect on 7 March. Holtrop, President of the Netherlands Bank and of the BIS, was unreachable because he was on a visit to South Africa at the time. Jelle Zijlstra, who would succeed Holtrop in both functions in 1967 and was then the Dutch Minister of Finance, was instrumental in the decision to follow Germany's example. Puchinger (1978), p. 93.

139. "Top secret note, Governors' meeting at Basel, 12 March 1961", BEA, OV 44/34 – *Sterling Policy, 1961.*

140. Communiqué, 12 March 1961, BISA, 6/60 – *Monetary co-operation, 1961–1968.*

141. Dispatch, Clarence Hunter for Robert Roosa, 12 June 1961, NARA, RG 56 – *U.S. Treasury,* 69A-4707, box 111.

142. "Known assistance to the United Kingdom, 1961–1962", BISA, 7.18(21) – *Papers Helmut Mayer,* f: Assistance to U.K. and France.

143. Governor Cameron Cobbold to Chancellor Selwyn Lloyd, 28 April 1961, PRO, T 318/2 – *U.K. balance of payments: short-term assistance to sterling under the Basel arrangements, 1961–62.*

144. Bank of England, *Quarterly Bulletin,* September 1961, vol. I, p. 10.

145. Governor Cameron Cobbold to Chancellor Selwyn Lloyd, 28 April 1961, PRO, T 318/2 – *U.K. balance of payments: short-term assistance to sterling under the Basel arrangements, 1961–62.*

146. BIS, *Thirty-First Annual Report,* Basel, 12 June 1961, p. 156.

147. Cameron Cobbold to Per Jacobsson, 17 March 1961, BEA, OV 44/34 – *Sterling Policy, 1961.*

148. McChesney Martin to Brunet, 24 March 1961, BFA, 1489200303/196 – *BRI, collaboration entre les banques centrales, 1930–1961.*

149. M. Parsons, "Note on conversations in Basel, 10–11 April 1961", BEA, OV 44/34 – *Sterling policy, 1961.* Parsons noted that, when Coombs made his suggestion, "one could hear the shudders of the people around the table".

150. Parsons's record of the meeting continues: "I pointed out that what had happened last month was that the Governors had agreed amongst themselves the necessity of compensating action. Individual Central Banks had then taken an initiative in

offering assistance and the details both as regards amount and method had been decided between the operational departments in consultation as the situation developed. If it had been decided at the beginning of last month that we should sit down and reach a formal agreement in advance as to how the situation was to be handled in detail, we might have been sitting there still a month later and no nearer reaching an agreement. There were times when an attempt to be systematic could actually diminish the effectiveness of cooperation". Ibid.

151. Copies of the final report can be found in: BEA, OV 44/34 – *Sterling Policy, 1961*; and BFA, 1489200303/196 – *BRI, collaboration entre les banques centrales, 1930– 1961.*

152. However, it was left to the discretion of the central bank on the receiving end to decide the exact timing of the reporting to the EMA board, since "information passed on outside the participating group, even if on a confidential basis, might prove to be the equivalent of publication". F. G. Conolly to Charles Coombs, 13 March 1963, BISA, 7.18(23) – *Papers Milton Gilbert,* box GILB9, f: Bilateral concerté.

153. Minutes of the 252nd meeting of the Board of Directors of the BIS held in Basel on 11 February 1963, Annex 252 / D(1): *Proposed procedure for notification of support arrangements between central banks.* The BIS's Fred Conolly wrote to Charles Coombs on the new procedure: "The inspiration for all this comes rather obviously from the Basel arrangements of 1961 .... It is hoped quietly and unobtrusively to generalise this method of operating at a time when there is no great urgency to put it into action. As this all seems in line with U.S. policy, the Federal Reserve may feel able to regard it with benevolence .... You will, I think, agree that the scheme is tailored to your fashion; this was possible as it also fits the requirements of the main European central banks". F. G. Conolly to Charles Coombs, 13 March 1963, BISA, 7.18(23) – *Papers Milton Gilbert,* box GILB9, f: Bilateral concerté.

154. See Schenk (2002a), pp. 345–69.

155. "Known assistance to the United Kingdom, 1963", BISA, 7.18(21) – *Papers Helmut Mayer,* f: Assistance to U.K. and France. Also: confidential note, F. G. Conolly, "Support procedure, 7 May 1963", BISA, 7.18(23) – *Papers Milton Gilbert,* box GILB9, f: Bilateral concerté; and confidential note, K. S., "Support arrangements, 16 August 1963", BISA, 7.18(23) – *Papers Milton Gilbert,* box GILB9, f: Bilateral concerté.

156. For a full account of the 1964 lira support arrangement, see Fodor (2000), pp. 401–39, and Coombs (1976), pp. 84–5.

157. Note, W. Armstrong to Mitchell, 12 November 1963, PRO, T 318/93 – *U.K. balance of payments: short-term assistance to sterling under the Basel arrangements, 1962–65.*

158. A $100 million Swiss franc–lira swap with the Swiss National Bank was added in June 1964.

159. Copies of the press announcement in: BISA, 2.5 – *Banca d'Italia, Policy,* vol. 4, 1949–1982.

160. Fodor (2000), pp. 412–13.

161. BIS, *Thirty-Fifth Annual Report,* Basel, 14 June 1965, pp. 59–61.

162. The $100 million credit line provided by the Bank of England remained entirely untouched. See: "Table Banca d'Italia arrangements of March 1964", BISA, 7.18(23) – *Papers Milton Gilbert,* box GILB9, f: Bilateral concerté.

163. Coombs (1976), pp. 72–3.
164. Ibid., p. 90.
165. Charles A. Coombs, "Treasury and Federal Reserve foreign exchange operations", *Federal Reserve Bulletin,* vol. 51, 9 September 1965, pp. 1148–9.
166. BIS, G10, "Short-term credit arrangements among central banks and monetary authorities", 22 January 1964, BISA, 7.18(12) – *Papers Michael Dealtry,* box DEA14, f02: G10.
167. See, for instance: letter, Gabriel Ferras to Marius Holtrop, 2 December 1966, NBHA, 8.1/1830/6 – *BIS: Correspondentie General Manager BIS Mr. Ferras, 1966.*
168. Charles A. Coombs, "Treasury and Federal Reserve foreign exchange operations", *Federal Reserve Bulletin,* vol. 51, 9 September 1965, p. 1224.
169. For a theoretical assessment, see Howell (1989) and Howell (1993), pp. 367–80.
170. All quotations from: BIS, G10, "Short-term credit arrangements among central banks and monetary authorities", 22 January 1964, BISA, 7.18(12) – *Papers Michael Dealtry,* box DEA14, f02: G10.
171. Gilbert (1980), p. 135.
172. In the early 1960s, nearly a third of world trade was still being financed in sterling. This share would fall to less than one fifth by the early 1970s.
173. On the origins of the sterling balances problem, see Schenk (1994).
174. Bank of England figures are assembled in Cottrell (2003), pp. 787–803.
175. A critical assessment of the Maudling "experiment" can be found in Dell (1996), pp. 290–303.
176. Note, S. Goldman for Sir W. Armstrong, 8 April 1964, PRO, T 318/93 – *U.K. balance of payments: short-term assistance to sterling under the Basel arrangements, 1962–65.* In the context of United Kingdom's ambition to join the EEC, Governor Cromer also felt that "there was a certain amount of political advantage to be gained in using this largely European facility". The Treasury was in any case of the opinion that "the demonstration of central bank solidarity was a most important factor making for the steadying of opinion and the reinforcement of confidence".
177. The Federal Reserve Bank of New York put up $500 million, the Bank of Canada $50 million, and the remaining $450 million was split between six European central banks (the European contributions being reported through the BIS under the "bilateral concerté" procedure). The Bundesbank placed $150 million with the Bank of England, the Bank of France and the Swiss National Bank added $100 million each, the National Bank of Belgium and the Netherlands Bank $25 million each, and the Bank of Italy contributed a $50 million swap. See BISA, 7.18(23) – *Papers Milton Gilbert,* box GILB9, f: Bilateral concerté.
178. For this and what follows on the sterling crisis, see in particular: James (1996), pp. 183–91; Dell (1996), pp. 310–46.
179. This and the previous quote are from C. A. Coombs, "Notes on November 1964 BIS meeting", NARA, RG 82 – *Federal Reserve System, 550/01/19/3: BIS General, 1962–64,* box 18.
180. Holtrop, "Notitie voor de Directie", 30 November 1964, NBHA, 8.1/2796/1 – *BIS: centrale bank hulp aan Engeland, 1964–65.*
181. As by then customary, the support package consisted of a series of bilateral arrangements: mostly short-term credits, some currency swaps, and the odd medium-term

loan. The Americans contributed $1 billion, eight European central banks put up $1.3 billion, and the BIS itself $250 million. The remainder was contributed by the Bank of Canada, the Bank of Japan, and the U.S. Export–Import Bank. See: "Secret note: the international credits", December 1964, PRO, Treasury Papers, T 318/93 – *U.K. balance of payments: short-term assistance to sterling under the Basel arrangements, 1962–65.*

182. BIS, *Thirty-Fifth Annual Report,* Basel, 14 June 1965, pp. 126–8.
183. Of the $1.3 billion line of credit made available by the European central banks, no more than half was eventually drawn by the Bank of England. All of it was repaid by the end of May 1965. For details see BISA, 7.18(23) – *Papers Milton Gilbert,* box GILB9, f: Transaction tables, 1964–1971.
184. *The Economist,* 28 November 1964, p. 1042.
185. Swedish Governor Åsbrink even commented: "if all the measures that now have been taken, had been combined in a single package right after the Labor Government took office, all of us would have been very much impressed". This, and the following quotation related to the December weekend BIS meeting in: Hayes, "Notes on December BIS meeting", December 1964, NARA, RG 56 – *U.S. Treasury/OASIA,* 69A-7584, box 26.
186. At this meeting, the governors of the central banks of Belgium, France, Germany, Italy, and the Netherlands agreed that they would do nothing if the pound were to devalue by less than 10% ("give the English a chance to improve their situation"). A 10%–15% devaluation would be considered a danger zone, and anything above 15% would mean that the EEC countries – even Germany and the Netherlands – would have to follow. "Procès-verbal de la cinquième séance du Comité des Gouverneurs des Banques Centrales des Etats membres de la Communauté Economique Européenne tenue à Bâle le 8 février 1965", ECBA – *Committee of Governors.*
187. Cairncross and Eichengreen (1983), p. 167.
188. Coombs (1976), pp. 107–30. For the Bank of England, Coombs's suggested "sterling bear squeeze" was much less important than the attempt to obtain a strong joint declaration of support from the European governments and central banks that would be comparable, in the words of Roy Bridge, to the 1936 Tripartite Agreement. See Bridge to O'Brien, 2 September 1965, BEA, OV 44/125 – *Sterling support operation, the initiative 1965.*
189. Secret minutes of a meeting with Mr. Raw, and internal memo for the president, 31 August and 2 September 1965, NBHA, 8.1/2796/1 – *BIS: centrale bank hulp aan Engeland, 1964–65.*
190. As traditionally there were no BIS governors' meetings in August or September, there was some concern that this discreet gathering would attract unwelcome press attention. It was agreed that the governors would tell journalists that the meeting had been called to discuss the reform of the international monetary system in preparation for the annual meeting of the IMF later that month. G. Kessler, "Bespreking te Bazel op 5 september 1965", NBHA, 8.1/2796/1 – *BIS: centrale bank hulp aan Engeland, 1964–65.*
191. All quotes from Charles A. Coombs, "Report on special BIS Meeting, September 5, 1965", NARA, RG 56 – *U.S. Treasury/OASIA,* 69A-7584, box 26.

192. After the Basel meeting, a new support package was quickly put together via telephone. The European central banks contributed $370 million (the Bank of France did not participate).
193. BIS, *Thirty-Sixth Annual Report,* Basel, 13 June 1966, pp. 132–4.
194. Fforde and Raw of the Bank of England were quite satisfied that on the sterling balances problem "Gilbert had the right end of the stick" and that his judgement would "probably be favourable to our case". Note, Fforde, 15 November 1965, BEA, OV 44/152 – *Sterling policy, November–December 1965.*
195. Copies of Gilbert's memorandum in: BISA, 7.18(23) – *Papers Milton Gilbert,* box GILB4, f: Sterling balances, 1965.
196. Note on the governor's conversation with Sir William Armstrong, 15 December 1965, BEA, OV 44/152 – *Sterling policy, November–December 1965.*
197. Letter, Gabriel Ferras to Milton Gilbert, 22 December 1965, in BIS Archive, 7.18(23) – *Papers Milton Gilbert,* box GILB4, f: Sterling balances, 1965.
198. This very much to the frustration of Charles Coombs of the New York Fed, to whom it demonstrated "the evils of multilateral action" – especially since the strongest objections against the scheme came from the central banks of the smaller countries, in particular Belgium and Switzerland. T. P. Nelson at the U.S. Treasury, on the other hand, was probably more realistic: "Given the extensive background of assistance to the United Kingdom which has eaten up almost all of the U.K. medium-term resources and the continued poor performance of the United Kingdom in bringing about a fundamental improvement in their payments position, I do not myself think it surprising that negotiations have taken the turn they have and on balance am favourably impressed that the Europeans are willing to consider an institutionalized credit at all". Memorandum, T. Nelson to Under-Secretary Deming, 15 March 1966, NARA, RG 56 – *U.S. Treasury/OASIA,* 69A-7584, box 26.
199. Memorandum to the Secretary of the U.S. Treasury, 19 April 1966, NARA, RG 56 – *U.S. Treasury/OASIA,* 69A-7584, box 26.
200. The nine central banks in the "BIS group" were those of Austria, Belgium, Canada, Germany, Italy, Japan, the Netherlands, Sweden, and Switzerland. In two separate operations the Bank of France contributed $90 million and the Federal Reserve Bank of New York $310 million, bringing the total to $1 billion, the amount originally suggested in Gilbert's memorandum.
201. Drawings under the first Group Arrangement fluctuated in line with the fluctuations in the sterling balances; they peaked at $690 million at the end of 1967. For a detailed account of the drawings made under the first Group Arrangement, see BISA, 7.18(23) – *Papers Milton Gilbert,* box GILB4, f: 1st Group Arrangement, transaction tables.
202. The famous phrase "you've never had it so good" was Harold Macmillan's 1959 re-election slogan, but Wilson certainly felt it also applied to his term in office. On the balance of payments imbalance during the first years of the Wilson government, see BIS, *Thirty-Seventh Annual Report,* Basel, 12 June 1967, pp. 12–17.
203. Coombs (1976), pp. 138–44.
204. Holtrop, "Aantekeningen Governors dinner op 4 september 1966 te Bazel", NBHA, 8.1/2796/2 – *BIS: centrale bank hulp aan Engeland, 1965–66.*

205. The eight central banks were those of Denmark, Norway, Belgium, Germany, Italy, the Netherlands, Sweden, and Switzerland. Once again the Bank of France declined to participate.

206. BISA, 7.18(10) – *Papers Gabriel Ferras,* box FER11, f: Banques centrales, *England – Sterling balances and group arrangements.*

207. In early 1967, the Bank of England was able to repay most of the outstanding short-term drawings on earlier central bank facilities and to add modestly to its reserves.

208. "Those Currency Swaps", *The Economist,* 17 September 1966, p. 1161.

209. Alfred Hayes, "Notes on BIS meeting, Basel, July 8–9, 1967", NARA, RG 56 – *U.S. Treasury/OASIA,* 69A-7584, box 26.

210. Note, Tüngeler, "Besprechungen in Basel vom 9.–11. September 1967", DBHA – *Handakte Tüngeler,* B 330/08707: *Goldpool, Basel, Februar 1962 – Dezember 1968.*

211. A. J. C. Edwards, "Top secret note for the record, 'Support for sterling'", 13 September 1967, PRO, T 312/2313 – *BIS: foreign currency loan to U.K. in support of sterling, 1967–1969.*

212. Also, as Cairncross comments: "To some extent this help was counter-productive, since the smallness of the amounts involved was in striking contrast to the scale of assistance needed if the parity was to be maintained"; Cairncross and Eichengreen (1983), p. 188. For details on this facility, see BISA, 6.63 – *Refinancing arrangement for the United Kingdom, 1967–1971.*

213. Ironically, French President de Gaulle would veto the United Kingdom's second application for EEC membership just one week after the devaluation of sterling.

214. Henry H. Fowler, "Memorandum for the President", 12 November 1967, NARA, RG 56 – *U.S. Treasury/OASIA,* 69A-7584, box 22.

215. $700 million was put up by nine European central banks, the Federal Reserve Bank of New York added $500 million, the Bank of Canada $100 million, the Bank of Japan $50 million, and the BIS another $150 million. This facility was renewed for a further three months in February 1968. The contribution of the European central banks was then increased from $700 million to $975 million in March 1968. It was reduced again to $700 million in September 1968 and thereafter renewed for consecutive periods of six months until it was fully repaid by 23 March 1970. BISA, 7.18(23) – *Papers Milton Gilbert,* box GILB9, f: Transaction tables, 1964–1971.

216. Gilbert (1980), p. 133.

217. Ibid.

218. James (1996), p. 162.

219. 1960 entry in Jacobsson's diary, quoted by James (1996), p. 162.

220. Jacobsson (1979), p. 364.

221. Jacobsson once told Triffin that "if he had had any idea of what the IMF was doing he would never have put out his plan". Jacobsson (1979), p. 373.

222. Entry in Jacobsson's diary, quoted by Jacobsson (1979), p. 364.

223. Ibid., pp. 373ff.

224. James (1996), p. 163.

225. Jacobsson (1979), p. 366.

226. BIS, *Thirty-Second Annual Report,* Basel, 4 June 1962, p. 18.

227. The following countries (or their central banks) participated in the GAB: the United States, West Germany, the United Kingdom, France, Italy, Japan, Canada, the Netherlands, Belgium, and Sweden. Switzerland, not a member of the IMF, joined the GAB in 1964.
228. BIS, *Thirty-Second Annual Report,* Basel, 4 June 1962, p. 18.
229. Schenk (2002a), p. 350.
230. James (1996), p. 164.
231. Gilbert (1980), p. 134.
232. The G10 nurtured few illusions about the immediate impact of this initiative: "All our efforts face the twin risks of either upsetting those circles who fear that study implies a commitment to produce radical changes, or of offending those who suspect that study means instead a 'whitewash' of the status quo". Robert Roosa to Working Party no. 3 members, 11 September 1963, Bank of France Archive, 1489200304/59 – *Réunions des ministres des Finances et des Gouverneurs des banques centrales, 1962–1970,* f 1.
233. See Holtrop, "Note regarding conversation with Undersecretary Robert Roosa on October 4, Washington", BISA, 7.18(10) – *Papers Gabriel Ferras,* box FER7. The BIS's participation was formalised through a decision of the BIS Board of Directors of 14 October 1963.
234. Ministerial Statement of the Group of Ten and Annex prepared by the Deputies, "Examination of the outlook for the functioning of the international monetary system and of its probable future needs for liquidity", Paris, 10 August 1964. A copy in: BISA, 7.15 – *Group of Ten,* box G10/2.
235. BIS, *Thirty-Fifth Annual Report,* 14 June 1965, pp. 160–1. In a sense, the "multilateral surveillance" exercise was an amplification of the "bilateral concerté" procedure agreed between the BIS governors in 1963.
236. Gavin (2004), pp. 118ff.
237. It has been observed, inter alia, that "The acrimonious G-10 meetings discussions about the international monetary system revealed a deep schism between the U.K. and the Six over payments problems, which made it even more difficult to address these issues in the accession negotiations". Schenk (2002a), p. 346.
238. "Du côté français, on a constamment estimé depuis la guerre que le Fonds Monétaire International ne peut être le centre d'une véritable coopération entre les pays qui comptent au point de vue financier, car le Fonds est trop soumis à l'influence américaine .... On a toujours favorisé l'utilisation aussi grande que possible du Club de Bâle, de l'OCDE pour un intime travail en commun européen et occidental". Secret note, 21 November 1963, p. 13, BFA, 1489200304/1 – *Réflexions sur l'amélioration du système monétaire international.*
239. "It seems", Gilbert wrote, "that cooperation so far has been more successful in providing liquidity than in securing basic adjustments in both deficit and surplus countries. A greater effort to bring about and maintain international economic equilibrium would reduce the task of credit arrangements". BIS, G10, "Short term credit arrangements among central banks and monetary authorities", 22 January 1964, p. 17, NARA, RG 56 – *U.S. Treasury,* 56-75-101, box 131.
240. M. Gilbert, *The future of the international money system,* presented at the Symposium on International Monetary Problems sponsored by Model, Roland & Co., New York, 25 September 1969, p. 5.

241. Gavin (2004); Zimmerman (2002).
242. In early 1967, U.S. pressure was such that Bundesbank President Blessing reluctantly agreed to publish a letter in which he stated that for years the Bundesbank had refrained from conversion of dollars into gold and that the United States "may be assured that also in the future the Bundesbank intends to continue this policy and to play its full part in contributing to international monetary cooperation". Later, in 1971, after the currency turmoil of 1968–69 and the American retreat into a policy of "benign neglect", Blessing regretted his 1967 public statement of support for U.S. monetary policies. Zimmerman (2002), pp. 221–9.
243. BIS, G10, "The prospective growth in gold reserves", confidential, 3 December 1963, BISA, 7.18(12) – *Papers Michael Dealtry,* box DEA14, f01: G10.
244. Triffin (1960). Triffin's production estimates drew on work done by the IMF; his main contribution was to forecast demand for monetary gold and gold reserves.
245. The BIS paper did not attempt to forecast the world's demand for liquidity. However, since the Bank estimated an average annual addition to the stock of world gold worth about $1,450 million (as against Triffin's upper bound estimate of $1,350 million), and if we accept Triffin's estimate of the growth in international demand for liquidity, then the latter would exceed supply even if the more optimistic BIS projections were realised. Triffin, in fact, estimated that gold output should at least double in order to be consistent with rising demand for its monetary use.
246. Fairly detailed minutes of the meeting were taken by Dealtry. See: "Notes on the meeting of the Group of Ten Deputies, Friday 13 and Monday 16 December 1963", BISA, 7.18(12) – *Papers Michael Dealtry,* box DEA14, f01: G10.
247. BIS, G10, "The co-operation of central banks in the gold market", confidential, 3 December 1963, BISA, 7.18(12) – *Papers Michael Dealtry,* box DEA14, f01: G10.
248. Gilbert (1980), p. 219.
249. Ibid., p. 218.
250. Triffin (1960), pp. 80 ff.
251. M. Gilbert, "Problems of the international monetary system", paper presented at the International Industrial Conference, San Francisco, 14 September 1964, p. 3, BISA, H S 381 – *Mimeo.*
252. The report was published in August to coincide with the publication of the IMF annual report. G10, "Report of the study group on the creation of reserve assets", Washington DC, 1965, in BISA, 7.15 – *Group of Ten,* box G-10/2. In a foreword, Emminger (chair of the deputies) made it clear that the members of the study group were acting in their individual expert capacity only.
253. James (1996), pp. 165–74. For a more detailed chronicle, see Garritsen de Vries (1976), pp. 43–205.
254. Speech published as a supplement to: IMF, *International financial news survey,* vol. 18, 1966, pp. 141–4.
255. James (1996), p. 167.
256. Garritsen de Vries (1986), p. 88.
257. Ibid., p. 120.
258. Washington, 24–26 April, and Paris, 19–21 June 1967.
259. Gilbert (1980), p. 134.

260. See, for instance: Réunion des Gouverneurs du dimanche soir, 13 février 1966, à l'Euler, NBHA, 8.1/2794/4 – *BIS, G-10.*
261. Confidential memorandum, Gilbert to Holtrop, "The issue of the central banks in the Group of Ten negotiations", BISA, 7.18(10) – *Papers Gabriel Ferras,* box FER7, f10.
262. M. Gilbert, *The future of the international money system,* presented at the Symposium on International Monetary Problems sponsored by Model, Roland & Co., New York, 25 September 1969, p. 3.
263. Ibid.
264. BIS, G10, "Three questions about reserve units", Basel, 28 February 1966, p. 1, BISA, 7.18(10) – *Papers Gabriel Ferras,* box FER7, f.A34, f10.
265. Ibid., p. 5.
266. BIS, *Fortieth Annual Report,* Basel, 8 June 1970, p. 116.
267. O'Brien to Carli (and to all the other Pool governors), 11 August 1966, "The Gold Pool", BIHA – *Carte Baffi,* no. 275, fasc 1, p. 4.
268. In these two years, they grew by about 14%.
269. Disturbing in the sense that these burgeoning foreign exchange reserves could be offered to the U.S. Treasury – theoretically at any time – for conversion into gold. For now, the central banks refrained from taking this step. Indeed, Italy sold gold to the U.S. Treasury for $200 million in 1964 (and, as a result, the ratio of gold in its reserves dropped from 74% to 58%). BIS, *Thirty-Fifth Annual Report,* Basel, 14 June 1965, pp. 118–25.
270. "Gold meeting, 6 March 1965" (handwritten notes), BISA, Basel, 7.18(16) – *Papers R.T.P. Hall,* box HAL 2, f01.
271. O'Brien to Carli (and to all the other Pool governors), 11 August 1966, "The Gold Pool", BIHA – *Carte Baffi,* no. 275, fasc 1, pp. 4–5.
272. "Man muss daher damit rechnen, dass der Pool weiterhin zu Abgaben gezwungen sein wird, und es könnte eine Situation eintreten, bei der sich einige Zentralbanken fragen, ob es sinnvoll ist, Teile der Goldwährungsreserven für Hortungszwecke zu opfern". See "Besprechungen in Basel vom 12.–14. März 1966", DBHA – *Handakte Tüngeler,* B 330/08707 – *Goldpool (Basel), 1962–68.*
273. O'Brien to Carli (and to all the other Pool governors), 11 August 1966, "The Gold Pool", BIHA – *Carte Baffi,* no. 275, fasc 1, p. 5.
274. Ibid., pp. 7–8.
275. "Meeting of the Experts, 9 July 1966" and "Réunion, 3 September 1966" (handwritten notes), BISA, 7.18(16) – *Papers R.T.P. Hall,* box HAL 2, f01.
276. BIS, *Thirty-Seventh Annual Report,* Basel, 12 June 1967, p. 110.
277. BIS, *Thirty-Eighth Annual Report,* Basel, 10 June 1968, p. 110.
278. By early March 1967, the Pool's operational deficit had been reduced from $260 million to $217 million, largely because of the strengthening of sterling and increased South African supplies. (To counter sanctions taken by other African nations against the South African apartheid policy, the South African government had embarked upon a stockpiling programme for raw materials, selling gold to pay for it.)
279. "Es bestand allerseits Übereinstimmung darüber, dass die seit kurzem eingetretene Erleichterung der Lage am Goldmarkt nichts Grundsätzliches und den bekannten

Problemen (ständiges Ansteigen der nicht-monetären Nachfrage bei gleichzeit-
igem Stagnieren oder sogar Rückgang der Goldproduktion) geändert habe". See
"Besprechungen in Basel vom 11.–12. März 1967", DBHA – *Handakte Tüngeler,*
B 330/08707: *Goldpool (Basel), 1962–68.*

280. "Réunion, May 1967" (handwritten notes), BISA, Basel, 7.18(16) – *Papers R.T.P.
     Hall,* box HAL 2, f01.
281. Mandel, "For the record: Gold Pool", 24 May 1967, and Gabriel Ferras, "Pool de
     l'or", 29 May 1967, BISA, 7.18(16) – *Papers R.T.P. Hall,* box HAL 2, f01.
282. "Le Gouverneur de la Banque de France m'a indiqué qu'il aurait préféré ne pas
     avoir reçu ma demande et qu'il ne pensait pas pouvoir donner une réponse affir-
     mative, au moins pour le présent". G. Ferras, "Pool de l'Or", 7 June 1967, BISA,
     Basel, 7.18(16) – *Papers R.T.P. Hall,* box HAL 2, f01.
283. "Meeting, 10 June 1967" (handwritten notes), BISA, 7.18(16) – *Papers R.T.P. Hall,*
     box HAL 2, f01. For the SDR debate, see James (1996), pp. 165–74.
284. "Besprechungen in Basel vom 10. bis 12. Juni 1967", DBHA – *Handakte Tüngeler,*
     B 330/08707: *Goldpool (Basel), 1962–68.*
285. Note, 10 July 1967: "32ème Réunion à Bâle des Experts de l'Or et des Changes",
     BFA, Sous-fonds Réparations et Banque des Règlements Internationaux,
     1489200303/195 – *Collaboration entre les Banques Centrales, 1967–1989.* From
     January 1967, Mandel of the BIS had become the permanent chairman of the Gold
     and Foreign Exchange Committee (previously, the chair had been taken in turns
     by the committee members).
286. James (1996), pp. 170–1.
287. "Gold meeting, 11 November 1967" (handwritten notes), BISA, Basel, 7.18(16) –
     Papers R.T.P. Hall, box HAL 2, f01.
288. Coombs (1976), pp. 158–64.
289. "Gold Pool. Telephone conversations, Coombs-Bridge-Ferras-Macdonald, 20 No-
     vember 1967", BISA, 7.18(16) – *Papers R.T.P. Hall,* box HAL 2, f01.
290. Through an article by Paul Fabra in *Le Monde* on 21 November 1967.
291. "First, the Gold Rush", *The Economist,* 25 November 1967, pp. 867–8.
292. Treasury Historical Memorandum no. 20, "The Gold Crisis, March 1968", Janu-
     ary 1975, PRO, T 267/21 – *Treasury papers.* Also: Coombs (1976), pp. 162–3.
293. Puchinger (1978), pp. 163–4.
294. "Mr. Deming Drops a Brick", *The Economist,* 16 December 1967, pp. 1156–7.
295. The prospect of having to strike a deal with South Africa was further complicated
     by the fact that, on 13 December 1967, the United Nations adopted a resolution
     strongly condemning the apartheid regime and calling for global trade sanctions.
296. D. H. Macdonald, "Gold and foreign exchange markets, meeting of the Gover-
     nors and the U.S. under secretary of the Treasury, Hotel Euler", 11 December 1967,
     BISA, 7.18(16) – *Papers R.T.P. Hall,* box HAL 2, f01.
297. Note, Macdonald to Ferras, "Gold", 3 January 1968, BISA, Basel, 7.18(16) – *Pa-
     pers R.T.P. Hall,* box HAL 2, f01.
298. Coombs (1976), pp. 167–8. The closure of the London gold market required an
     Order in Council for which a meeting of the Queen's Privy Council had to be
     called in Buckingham Palace, just after midnight on 15 March. The episode led
     to the resignation of Foreign Secretary Brown, who felt he had not been properly

consulted by Prime Minister Wilson and Chancellor Jenkins on this sudden U-turn in the gold policy. See Dell (1996), pp. 355–6.

299. On 15 March the U.S. State Department had instructed the U.S. embassies in Europe to locate the central bank governors in question: "You must track down these men at all costs". Gavin (2004), p. 181.

300. Carli (1993), p. 238.

301. Gilbert (1980), pp. 141–9.

302. Ibid., p. 145.

303. The Washington Agreement of March 1968, and the understanding between the Gold Pool central banks to abstain from acting in the private gold market, would be officially revoked in November 1973 after the Bretton Woods fixed–exchange rate system had been abandoned.

304. BIS, *Thirty-Eighth Annual Report,* Basel, 10 June 1968, pp. 39–43. Full press statement of 18 March 1968 in: BISA, 7.18(16) – *Papers R.T.P. Hall,* box HAL 2, f 01.

305. As stated in the BIS Annual Report: "As regards the development of prices in the free gold market, 1969 came in like a lion and went out like a lamb". BIS, *Fortieth Annual Report,* Basel, 8 June 1970, p. 110.

306. Gilbert (1980), p. 149.

307. Holtfrerich (1999), p. 384.

308. Secret note, D. A. Bleach to Peterson, 26 March 1968, PRO, T 312/2041 – *Gold operations on behalf of the Basel syndicate, 1967–68.*

309. The final accounting outcome of the Pool was a deficit of $2,378 million, or (more accurately) the replacement in its members' reserves of $2,378 million worth of gold with dollars.

310. The Bank of England as a quid pro quo for U.S. support in defending sterling; the Bundesbank, at least in part, as a quid pro quo for continued U.S. military expenditure in Germany. See Zimmerman (2002).

311. James (1996), pp. 159–61.

312. Gavin (2004), p. 182.

313. For what follows, research was complemented by an interview that Piet Clement had with Sir Jeremy Morse on 3 February 2004. Morse was director of the Bank of England overseas department at the time of the events described here.

314. Confidential note, "Movements in sterling balances", 22 December 1967, BISA, 7.18(12) – *Papers Michael Dealtry,* box DEA13, f: Sterling Balances, 1967.

315. Calculated at more than £3 billion – or more than $7 billion.

316. A team headed by Jeremy Morse was set to work on a scheme for the long-term financing of official sterling balances. This would lead to the second Sterling Group Arrangement of September 1968.

317. B. MacLaury, "Notes of discussion at Governors' meeting on February 11, 1968, Basel", NARA, RG 56 – *U.S. Treasury/OASIA,* 69A-7584, box 26. It must be said that President Stopper of the Swiss National Bank was sceptical with regard to the claim that a floating pound would be a "catastrophe", adding that the international monetary system had survived the 1967 devaluation without any such catastrophe. Both Blessing and Hayes were quick to contradict Stopper, saying that with the devaluation of the pound "we had come too close to catastrophe for comfort". For insight into the Bank of England's approach see: note, J. C. Morse to Governor

O'Brien, "Briefing for Basel meetings", 9 February 1968, BEA, OV 44/159 – *Sterling Balances: Basel arrangements, January–February 1968.*

318. The meeting exceptionally took place in Amsterdam instead of Basel to mark the inauguration of the new head offices of the Netherlands Bank, BIS President Zijlstra's home ground.

319. See BISA, 7.18(23) – *Papers Milton Gilbert,* box GILB5, f: Sterling Balances, Jan–July 1968. The arrangement also raised a number of technical problems, which were resolved thanks to an ingenious scheme thought up by Macdonald, manager in the BIS Banking Department. Note, MacMahon to the governor, "The Macdonald Scheme", 10 April 1968, BEA, OV 44/160 – *Sterling balances: Basel arrangements, 1968.*

320. Note, Macdonald for the record, "Possible Second Group Arrangement", Meeting in the Netherlands Bank, 20 June 1968, BISA, 7.18(23) – *Papers Milton Gilbert,* box GILB5, f: Sterling Balances, Jan–July 1968.

321. Reimbursements were scheduled to be made between six and ten years after the coming into force of the arrangement. Central banks that could not enter into a three-year commitment would sign up for a briefer period of time while issuing a declaration of intent that they would renew their participation at the end of it.

322. See, for instance: "No Strength through Bankruptcy", *The Economist,* 13 July 1968, pp. 13–14.

323. Governor Brunet of the Bank of France declared that "In the French Government's opinion the problem at issue was of a governmental nature" and that therefore "The Bank of France was not allowed to enter into a commitment in this regard". BIS, *Minutes of the Meeting of Central Bank Governors,* 8 September 1968, BISA, 7.18(23) – *Papers Milton Gilbert,* box GILB5, f: Sterling Balances, 1968–1971.

324. Eventually, the contribution of the participating central banks was as follows: the Federal Reserve Bank of New York contributed $650 million, the Bundesbank $400 million, and the Bank of Italy $225 million; the Bank of Canada, the Netherlands Bank, and the Swiss National Bank put up $100 million each; the Bank of Japan $90 million, the National Bank of Belgium $80 million, the Austrian and Swedish central banks $50 million each, and the Danish and Norwegian central banks $37.5 million each. The BIS, finally, contributed $80 million of its own funds to make up the grand total of $2 billion.

325. In particular, the short-term support received in November 1967 after devaluation and in March 1968 following the suspension of the Gold Pool.

326. Bank of England, "Confidential note: Sterling balances", 5 November 1976, BISA, 2.2n – *Bank of England, Third Group Arrangement,* vol. 1: 1976–1977.

327. The Bank of England sought a renewal of the arrangement before it expired in September 1971, notwithstanding the fact that it had made no use of the facility since 1969. A two-year extension until September 1973 was granted at a meeting of the governors in Basel on 7 March 1971. Given the rising trend of sterling balances, it was not expected that during this period the Bank of England would draw on the facility. The sole purpose for the extension was to allow the Bank of England to renew its bilateral agreements on sterling balances with the sterling-area countries. See: "Aide-memoire, Second Group Arrangement, Summary of meeting in Basel on 7 March 1971 of the Governors of the central banks parties to the

above Arrangement", BISA – *Banking,* f: Second Group Arrangement, 1968–1972. The second Group Arrangement was officially terminated in September 1973. See: BISA, 2.2k – *Bank of England, Second Group Arrangement, Policy,* vol. 4: 1972–1982. With the de facto dissolution of the sterling area after 1972, in an era of generalised floating, the sterling balances issue receded into the background. It came back to haunt the United Kingdom as a result of the sterling crisis of 1976. A third – and final – Group Arrangement would be concluded at the BIS in February 1977, lasting until February 1979.

328. BIS, *Thirty-Ninth Annual Report,* Basel, 9 June 1969, p. 3.
329. Ibid.
330. BIS, *Thirty-Eighth Annual Report,* Basel, 10 June 1968, p. 128.
331. Bordo, Simard, and White (1994).
332. It consisted of a $600 million increase in the swap line made available by the Federal Reserve Bank of New York, of $600 million put up by France's partners in the EEC, and of another $100 million contributed directly by the BIS. The Bundesbank contributed $300 million, the Bank of Italy $200 million, and the National Bank of Belgium and the Netherlands Bank $50 million each. The $1.3 billion credit was initially limited to three months but extended twice thereafter. The maximum amount drawn on this facility was $1.1 billion during the third week of November 1968. The last drawing was repaid by the Bank of France on 21 May 1969. See: BISA, 7.18(23) – *Papers Milton Gilbert,* box GILB9, f: Transaction tables, 1964–1971.
333. BIS, *Thirty-Ninth Annual Report,* Basel, 9 June 1969, pp. 4–13.
334. Emminger (1986), pp. 141–2.
335. Expressions used, respectively, by U.K. Prime Minister Wilson and Bundesbank Chief Economist Otmar Emminger. On this and for a more detailed account of the franc–mark crisis of 1968–69, see: Solomon (1982), pp. 151–65; Emminger (1986), pp. 138–71; Holtfrerich (1999), pp. 384–90.
336. The Bank of France drew heavily on the facility in the spring of 1969, when a new speculative wave set in, and again in October of that year. The facility was to be fully repaid and terminated by 24 April 1970. See: "Aides à court terme mises à la disposition de la France entre mai 1968 et mai 1970", BFA, 1489200304/27 – *Coopération entre les banques centrales, 1966–71,* f 3.
337. The Carli proposal, dated 30 November 1968, in: FRBNY, 797.3 – *Policies and procedures, 1968.* Conclusions of the central bank governors of the Group of Ten and Switzerland on point 8 of the Bonn communiqué in: FRBNY, 798.3b – *First file, 1963–1983.*
338. John Ghiardi, "Notes on Governors' meeting, March 9, 1969, Basel", FRBNY, 797.3 – *BIS, 1960–1970.*
339. BIS, *Thirty-Eighth Annual Report,* Basel, 10 June 1968, p. 3.
340. Former BIS general manager Guillaume Guindey went so far as to state that from "1965 things began to happen that were gradually to reduce monetary collaboration among the Eleven almost to a façade". Guindey (1977), p. 37.
341. Quoted in James (1996), p. 211.
342. BIS, *Forty-Second Annual Report,* Basel, 12 June 1972, p. 23.
343. Ibid., p. 24.

344. Ibid., p. 25.
345. Leeson (2003).
346. M. Friedman, "Autobiography", Nobel e-archive:
⟨http://www.nobel.se/economics/laureates/1976/friedman-autobio.html⟩.
347. Bordo and James (2001), p. 30.
348. Friedman (1953), pp. 157–203.
349. Haberler (1953).
350. Friedman (1963), p. 23.
351. Friedman (1966).
352. Friedman (1968).
353. Okun (1970), p. 15; also quoted by James (1996), p. 213.
354. "Some remarks on possible reform in the exchange-rate system", Bundesbank, 9 January 1969, BEA, OV 53/40 – *International monetary reform, papers and comments, 1969.*
355. For the minutes of the meeting, see: BFA, 1489200303/193 – *Collaboration entre les Banques centrales, 1953–1989.* The Bank of England representative summarised the outcome of the meeting as follows: "A not particularly satisfactory two days' discussion took place on this complex subject". Meeting on exchange rate flexibility, Basel, 12–13 January 1970, BEA, OV 4/110 – *BIS: Bank of England notes following Basel meetings, 1959–1974.*
356. This, and the following quotes in this paragraph, from: C. A. Serpa, memorandum to S. V. O. Clarke, "European official views on international monetary problems", 22 June 1970, FRBNY, 260 – *BIS, 1969–1971.*
357. James (1996), p. 214.
358. C. A. Serpa, memorandum to S. V. O. Clarke, "European official views on international monetary problems", 22 June 1970, pp. 5–6, FRBNY, 260 – *BIS, 1969–1971.*
359. James (1996), p. 215.
360. Austria, Belgium, the Netherlands, and Switzerland also closed their exchange markets on 5 May.
361. BIS, *Forty-Second Annual Report,* Basel, 12 June 1972, p. 25.
362. Marsh (1992), pp. 189–90. See also von Hagen (1999), pp. 403–38.
363. James (1996), p. 217.
364. Coombs (1976), p. 219.
365. For a detailed account of the meeting, see Safire (1975).
366. James (1996), p. 219.
367. Solomon (1982), pp. 196–202.
368. D. E. Bodner, "Notes on BIS Governor's meeting on November 7 1971", FRBNY 797.3 – *BIS, 1971.* Also: David Bodner to Coombs, "The Current State of the Foreign Exchange Markets", 12 November 1972, FRBNY, No. 260 – *BIS, 1969–1971:* "The dominant theme at the last BIS meeting ... was the deleterious effect of uncertainty on trade and investment and the consequent urgent need for settlement of the [realignment of exchange rates] dispute".
369. Jelle Zijlstra, "Secret working paper", November 1971, BISA, 7.18(31) – *Papers Crockett.*
370. On 17 December the Deutsche mark – floating since May – had closed at 12.2% above par. Thus the realignment of 18 December of 13.6%, compared to the old

dollar rate, represented no more than a 1.4% increase over the prevailing market rate. BIS, *Forty-Second Annual Report,* Basel, 12 June 1972, p. 135.

371. Ibid., p. 30.

372. "Meeting of Gold and Foreign Exchange Experts", Basel, 8 January 1972, BFA, 1489200304/9 – *BRI, Euro-marchés, 1968–1985.*

373. BIS, *Forty-Third Annual Report,* Basel, 18 June 1973, p. 21.

374. Coombs later criticised this second devaluation as a failure that had only served to feed inflation. See: "Meeting of Gold and Foreign Exchange Experts", Basel, 16 June 1973, BFA, 1489200304/9 – *BRI, Euro-marchés, 1968–1985.* Coombs remained a staunch believer in fixed rates, also after March 1973.

375. James (1996), p. 234.

376. Gavin (2004), p. 185.

377. BIS, *Forty-Third Annual Report,* Basel, 18 June 1973, p. 26.

Chapter 12

1. Baer (1999), p. 352.

2. In an article with the same title published in *Synthèses,* Brussels, 4(45), p. 1950. Also reprinted in: Rueff (1963), pp. 123–9.

3. Wellink (1997), pp. 27–8.

4. For a comprehensive chronology of the European integration process after the Second World War, see Vanthoor (1999).

5. Arts. 105 and 107 of the Treaty of Rome.

6. Communauté Economique Européenne (1959), pp. 5–8.

7. Vanthoor (1999), p. 22.

8. EEC Commission (1962).

9. On 25 October 1962, the Bundesbank Council had agreed with Otmar Emminger that on technical and legal grounds an obligation to consult with the EEC partners prior to any major monetary policy decision was out of the question. Bernholz (1999), p. 744.

10. Pluym (2002), pp. 12–13.

11. JMS, "Note to the Governor on Common Market action plan", 17 December 1962, BEA, G1/940.3 – *Governors' files, BIS, 1950–64.* This report prompted Governor Cromer to write to Holtrop to give his views on the practical arrangements for the envisaged Committee of EEC Governors: "As I confidently hope that the U.K. will become a member of the EEC before long and that I shall, therefore, be joining in these meetings". Letter, Cromer to Holtrop, 21 December 1962, BEA, G1/940.3 – *Governors' files, BIS, 1950–64.*

12. Ansiaux and Dessart (1975), p. 47.

13. "Council decision of 8 May 1964 on co-operation between the Central Banks of the Member States of the European Economic Community" (64/300/EEC), *Official Journal of the European Communities,* 77, 21 May 1964, pp. 1206–64.

14. The Governor of the National Bank of Belgium also represented Luxembourg, which formed a monetary union with Belgium (BLEU).

15. Interview on 11 February 2004 with André Bascoul, who from 1965 assisted BIS Secretary General Antonio d'Aroma in writing up the committee meeting minutes

and organising the committee secretariat. Mr. Bascoul continued to perform these duties until 1988.

16. "Procés-verbal de la première séance du Comité des Gouverneurs des banques centrales des pays membres de la Communauté économique européenne tenue à Bâle le 6 juillet 1964", ECBA – *Committee of Governors*. The archives of the Committee of Governors were kept at the BIS in Basel until the end of 1993. Once the European Monetary Institute had been set up in Frankfurt am Main, the Committee of Governors archives were transferred there. They are now in the custody of the European Central Bank in Frankfurt am Main. Thanks are due to Dr. Roland Rölker and Ms. Mascha Steinecke for organising access to these files.

17. "Procès-verbal de la deuxième séance du Comité des Gouverneurs des banques centrales des pays membres de la Communauté économique européenne tenue à Bâle le 12 octobre 1964", ECBA – *Committee of Governors*.

18. See for instance Holtrop, supported by Blessing, in the committee meeting of 11 July 1966: "Il existe de telles différences de conjoncture [between the EEC countries], qu'il faut admettre des politiques monétaires différentes"; or Zijlstra in the meeting of 12 February 1968: "au stade actuel de l'intégration européenne, avec des politiques budgétaires autonomes, chaque pays membre est responsable de sa conjoncture et doit donc avoir une politique monétaire". "Procès-verbal de la treizième/vingt-troisième séance du Comité des Gouverneurs des banques centrales des pays membres de la Communauté économique européenne tenue à Bâle le 11 juillet 1966/le 12 février 1968", ECBA – *Committee of Governors*.

19. Marjolin (1986), p. 343.

20. Ansiaux and Dessart (1975), p. 56.

21. "Procès-verbal de la dix-neuvième séance du Comité des Gouverneurs des banques centrales des pays membres de la Communauté économique européenne tenue à Bâle le 10 juillet 1967", ECBA – *Committee of Governors*.

22. At the January 1967 meeting the committee decided to harmonise the starting and maturity dates of all EEC members' swap arrangements with the New York Fed. The move, designed to give the EEC central banks more leverage when negotiating future renewals or extensions of the swap network, took the Americans somewhat by surprise. "Procès-verbal de la seizième séance du Comité des Gouverneurs des banques centrales des pays membres de la Communauté économique européenne tenue à Bâle le 9 janvier 1967", ECBA – *Committee of Governors*.

23. "Procès-verbal de la onzième/treisième séance du Comité des Gouverneurs des banques centrales des pays membres de la Communauté économique européenne tenue à Bâle le 14 mars/11 juillet 1966", ECBA – *Committee of Governors*.

24. Agreement in principle that such restrictions ought to be lifted met with practical objections from those countries where certain of these restrictions were thought to be useful in combating imported inflation, such as the Netherlands. See the discussion on Rainoni's report on short-term capital movements in: "Procès-verbal de la vingt et unième séance du Comité des Gouverneurs des banques centrales des pays membres de la Communauté économique européenne tenue à Bâle le 13 novembre 1967", ECBA – *Committee of Governors*.

25. As of 1 July 1968.

26. Szász (1999), p. 11.

27. Dyson (1994), pp. 72–3.

28. Pluym (2002), p. 23.
29. "Procès-verbal de la vingt-septième séance du Comité des Gouverneurs des banques centrales des pays membres de la Communauté économique européenne tenue à Bâle le 9 decembre 1968", ECBA – *Committee of Governors.*
30. "Memorandum de la Commission du Conseil sur la coordination des politiques économiques et la coopération monétaire au sein de la CEE", *Supplément au Bulletin CEE,* no. 3, March 1969.
31. At this stage, a representative of the Monetary Committee, usually its President Van Lennep, participated on a regular basis in the meetings of the Committee of Governors.
32. Letter, Hubert Ansiaux to Jean Rey, President of the EEC Commission, 10 July 1969, ECBA – *Committee of Governors.*
33. One of the Commission experts was Giampietro Morelli, who was also a member of the EC's Monetary Committee secretariat. Morelli would become secretary general of the BIS in 1978.
34. Automatic support would be available for three months on the basis of quotas assigned to each participating central bank totalling $1 billion (with a possibility of being extended with a further $1 billion). "Compte rendu de la réunion des Gouverneurs des banques centrales des Etats membres de la Communauté économique européenne tenue à Bâle le 9 février 1970", ECBA – *Committee of Governors.* Attached to these minutes is the Final Act of the agreement setting up a system of short-term monetary support between the EC central banks.
35. The $1 billion ceiling was regularly increased thereafter. However, during the whole of the 1970s, this mutual support mechanism would be used only once: between March and December 1974, when the Bank of Italy drew the equivalent of $1.88 billion in credit. Bank for International Settlements (1980a), p. 74.
36. Brandt (1976).
37. As we have seen, in August 1969 the French franc was devalued by 11.1% and in October the Deutsche mark was first floated and then revalued by 9.3%.
38. European Communities, Monetary Committee (1970), pp. 12–13.
39. Szász (1999), p. 15.
40. For what follows see, in particular: Szász (1999); Pluym (2002); Werner (1977).
41. Bernholz (1999), pp. 746–50.
42. Bussière (2003), pp. 697–722.
43. According to Snoy, Belgian Minister of Finance: "Ce jeu de préalables abouti à ne jamais démarrer." Pluym (2002), p. 40.
44. At the meeting of the Committee of Governors in Basel on 13 April 1970, Ansiaux lashed out at the idea of wider fluctuation margins put forward by the IMF research department, which in his mind would inevitably lead to "un désordre et une absence de discipline dans le système monétaire international. Ces idées semblent orchestrées par les Etats-Unis avec la volonté de créer un système dans lequel des modifications de taux de change plus fréquentes et le plus souvent dans le sens de la réévaluation seraient possibles. De cette manière, le problème de la balance des paiements américaine, qui n'arrive pas à être réglé par le processus d'ajustement, serait réglé par des moyens artificiels. Ce serait une sorte de jeu sur les taux de change, le dollar restant immuable à 35 dollars l'once d'or et les autres monnaies devant se réévaluer par rapport à lui. Compte tenu notamment

du danger que présenterait pour la Communauté la possibilité de changer finale-
ment les parités, les Six doivent être fondamentalement en faveur du maintien de
la stabilité des taux de change". "Procès-verbal de la trente-huitième séance du
Comité des Gouverneurs des banques centrales des pays membres de la Communauté économique européenne tenue à Bâle le 13 avril 1970", ECBA – *Committee
of Governors*. For the IMF's role in the exchange rate debate in 1970, see James
(1996), pp. 213–14.

45. According to André Szász, Dutch member of the Ansiaux experts' group, Ansiaux
was particularly efficient in "quell[ing] all opposition and objections coming from
mere experts. This he did, complete with tantrums if deemed necessary". Szász
(1999), p. 37.

46. "Procès-verbal de la cinquante-huitième séance du Comité des Gouverneurs des
banques centrales des pays membres de la Communauté économique européenne
tenue à Bâle le 10 avril 1972", ECBA – *Committee of Governors*.

47. The proposal to pool central bank reserves at this early stage of monetary integration
was defeated for mainly two reasons: because it required a real transfer of national
sovereignty to a new Community institution (disliked by France among others), and
because it would make inroads into the "indivisible" monetary policy responsibility of the national central banks (central bank independence upheld most staunchly
by Germany). The idea of a European reserve fund can be traced back to Robert
Triffin's thinking of the late 1950s; see Maes and Buyst (2004), pp. 431–44.

48. The Committee of Governors transmitted its opinion to the EC Council and Commission in September 1972. Annex to: "Procès-verbal de la soixante-deuxième séance
du Comité des Gouverneurs des banques centrales des pays membres de la Communauté économique européenne tenue à Bâle le 11 septembre 1972", ECBA –
Committee of Governors. The EC Monetary Committee also delivered an opinion
on the EMCF on 5 September 1972. EC Monetary Committee, *Fourteenth Report
on the Activities of the Monetary Committee,* Brussels, 12 April 1973, pp. 32–6.

49. Szász (1999), p. 49.

50. Andrews (2003), p. 958.

51. Vanthoor (1999), pp. 72–3.

52. Dickhaus (1999), pp. 775–95.

53. Dyson (1994), p. 91.

54. The Committee for the Study of Economic and Monetary Union, "The Werner Re-
port Revisited", Paris, 1 September 1988, BISA, 7.18(19) – *Papers Gunter Baer,* box
BAE2. This reassessment was prepared by Gunter D. Baer and Tommaso Padoa-
Schioppa, who acted as the two rapporteurs of the Delors Committee. Subsequently,
Gunter Baer was the BIS Secretary General from 1994 to 2004. See also Padoa-
Schioppa (2000), pp. 113–25, and Maes (2002), p. 175.

55. Andrews (2003), p. 967.

56. In this connection see also Baer (1994), pp. 147–57.

57. Andrews (2003), pp. 956–73.

58. Friedman (1970), p. 275.

59. For the institutional and international aspects of the eurodollar market, see Bell
(1973). For an economic background, see Johnston (1983) and Gibson (1989). For
the origins of the market: Schenk (1998); Battilossi (2000), pp. 141–75; and Battilossi and Cassis (2002).

60. Einzig (1964); see also Battilossi and Cassis (2002), pp. 1–35.
61. Cottrell and Stone (1989), pp. 43–78.
62. Confidential paper for the Group of Ten, "The Euro-currency Market and the International Payments System", 20 January 1964, p. 1, BISA, 7.18(12) – *Papers Michael Dealtry,* box DEA14, f2.
63. FRBNY, "Continental Dollar Market" (no date but probably October 1960), see Coombs to Guindey, 17 October 1960, BISA, 2.1 – *Federal Reserve Bank of New York, Policy,* vol. 4: 1956–64.
64. Johnston (1983).
65. Schenk (1998), pp. 224–9.
66. Sylla (2002), pp. 53–73.
67. Confidential paper for the Group of Ten, "The Euro-currency Market and the International Payments System", 20 January 1964, p. 1, BISA, 7.18(12) – *Papers Michael Dealtry,* box DEA14, f2.
68. Kynaston (2002), pp. 268–72.
69. BIS, *Annual Reports,* 1965–1981; and Bank for International Settlements (1983).
70. Kerr (1984).
71. Figures taken from: BIS, *Thirty-Fourth Annual Report,* Basel, 8 June 1964, p. 130; BIS, *Thirty-Eighth Annual Report,* Basel, 10 June 1968, p. 58; BIS, *Forty-Fourth Annual Report,* Basel, 10 June 1974, p. 158; and BIS, *Forty-Fifth Annual Report,* Basel, 9 June 1975, p. 145.
72. BIS, *Thirty-Fourth Annual Report,* Basel, 8 June 1964, p. 136. Catherine Schenk (2002b, p. 90) downplays the impact of regulation Q.
73. Kynaston (2002), p. 324.
74. Sylla (2002), p. 71.
75. In late 1962, Sir Charles Hambro of Hambros Bank expressed his alarm to Bank of England Deputy Governor Mynors. Kynaston (2002), pp. 271–2.
76. Holmes and Klopstock (1960), pp. 197–202.
77. Kynaston (2002), p. 269.
78. Letter, Fred H. Klopstock to Milton Gilbert, 28 May 1962, BISA, 1.3a(3) – *Meeting of Experts, 1959–63,* vols. 1–2.
79. "Suggested questions for discussion at the meeting on the Eurodollar market", Basel, 6–8 October 1962, BISA, 1.3a(3) – *Meeting of Experts, 1959–63,* vols. 1–2.
80. Report, Ralph Young and Samuel Katz, "Euro-dollar meeting in Basel", 6–8 October 1962, NARA, RG 82 – *Federal Reserve System,* 550/01/19/3: *BIS General, 1962–64,* box 18. Comprehensive minutes of the meeting: "Réunion de représentants des banques centrales consacrée au marché de l'Euro-dollar", BRI, 6–8 Octobre 1962, BFA, 1489200304/26 – *Coopération entre banques centrales,* f2, *Soutien des monnaies, 1961–68.*
81. "The reluctance of the British delegation to supply figures was in marked contrast with the attitudes expressed by continental representatives". Report, Ralph Young and Samuel Katz, "Euro-dollar meeting in Basel, 6–8 October 1962", NARA, RG 82 – *Federal Reserve System,* 550/01/19/3: *BIS General, 1962–64,* box 18.
82. Milton Gilbert to the meeting participants, 4 December 1963, BISA, 1.3a(3) – *Meeting of Experts, 1959–63,* vols. 1–2. Oscar Altman of the IMF was satisfied that the statistical reporting was finally beginning to make sense: "I never would have thought two years ago that the data could have been improved as much as they have". Letter,

Oscar Altman to Milton Gilbert, 3 December 1963, BISA, 7.18(10) – *Papers Gabriel Ferras,* box FER8.

83. Letter, Gabriel Ferras to Masamichi Yamagiwa, Governor of the Bank of Japan, reporting on the governors' discussion in Basel, 23 January 1964, BISA, 7.18(10) – *Papers Gabriel Ferras,* box FER8.

84. Confidential paper for the Group of Ten, "The Euro-currency Market and the International Payments System", p. 19, BISA, 7.18(12) – *Papers Michael Dealtry,* box DEA14, f2.

85. Letter, Lord Cromer to BIS President Holtrop, 31 March 1964, BISA, 7.18(10) – *Papers Gabriel Ferras,* box FER8.

86. Letter, Oscar Altman to Milton Gilbert, 25 May 1964, BISA, 1.3a(3) – *Meeting of Experts, 1959–63,* vols. 3–5.

87. A. Rainoni to Fred Klopstock (Federal Reserve Bank of New York), 16 March 1965, BISA, 1.3a(3) – *Meeting of Experts, 1959–63,* vols. 3–5.

88. See M. Dealtry, "Note on a visit to London", 7 July 1965, BISA, 7.18(10) – *Papers Gabriel Ferras,* box FER8.

89. Baer (1999), p. 352.

90. On the widely different array of capital market regulations existing at the time in each individual country, see (besides the BIS Annual Reports for the years in question) Gilbert and McClam (1970), pp. 349–411.

91. By the end of 1962, the BIS was thought to hold $400 million in euromarket deposits in seven different locations. Bank of England figures quoted in: Schenk (2002b), p. 85. The BIS's euromarket investments provoked a somewhat sarcastic comment from the Bank of France's Calvet: "Je sais bien que la BRI doit gagner sa vie. Mais n'est-il pas piquant de constater que, comme banque, elle encourage les transactions en euro-devises, alors que, comme club elle s'en inquiète?" Note, Calvet for the Governor, 30 November 1963, BFA, 1489200303/188 – *BRI. Relations avec la Banque de France, 1929–85,* f5, *Dossier de Mr. Koszul, 1949–63.*

92. Ferras (1970), p. 97.

93. Confidential paper for the Group of Ten, "The Euro-currency Market and the International Payments System", p. 19, BISA, 7.18 (12) – *Papers Michael Dealtry,* box DEA14, f2.

94. As the BIS pointed out reassuringly, "there is no evidence that Euro-currency business has occasioned widespread departures from the canons of prudent banking". BIS, *Thirty-Fourth Annual Report,* Basel, 8 June 1964, p. 141.

95. "Meeting of Experts on the Euro-currency Market at the BIS", 6–7 July 1967, BISA, 7.18(10) – *Papers Gabriel Ferras,* box FER8.

96. Ibid., p. 7.

97. Letter, Ferras to Holtrop, 2 December 1966, NBHA, 8.1/1830/6 – *BIS Correspondentie General Manager Ferras, 1966.*

98. Note, Johannes Tüngeler, "Besprechungen in Basel vom 7.–9. Januar 1967", BHAH, B 330/08707 – *Goldpool, 1962–68.*

99. BIS, *Thirty-Ninth Annual Report,* Basel, 9 June 1969, p. 149.

100. On 6 June 1967, the day after the outbreak of the Six-Day War, the BIS invested $40 million in the eurodollar market in just one day. Note, David Bodner on telephone conversation with Mr. Mandel of the BIS, 7 June 1967, FRBNY, 797.3 –

BIS, policy and procedures, 1967. Also: BIS, *Thirty-Eighth Annual Report,* Basel, 10 June 1968, p. 145.

101. A. Hershey, "Notes on BIS July 8–9 1968, meeting of Central Bank Experts on the Euro-Currency Market, 22 July 1968", NARA, RG 82 – *Federal Reserve System,* 550/01/19/3: *BIS General, 1967–69,* box 17.
102. Ferras (1970), p. 99.
103. Kynaston (2002), p. 397.
104. J. Ghiardi, "Notes on Governors' meeting, March 9 1969, Basel", FRBNY, 797.3 – *BIS, First file, 1960–70.* See also Section 11.1.
105. T. P. Nelson, "Confidential Note for Undersecretary Volcker", 18 April 1969, NARA, RG 56 – *U.S. Treasury/OASIA,* 56-75-101, box 169.
106. Telex, Milton Gilbert to the experts' meeting participants, 28 May 1969, BISA, 1.3a(3) – *Meeting of Experts, 1967–71,* vols. 6–8.
107. As Ferras (1970, p. 103) summarised it: "The most important aspect of the relations between central banks and the Eurodollar market lies in the extent to which the market affects the ability of central banks to carry out monetary policies that are appropriate to conditions in their own economies. In a general way it can be said that the development of the Eurodollar market has diminished the freedom of central banks to use the conventional instruments of monetary policy for domestic purposes. The measures that central banks have taken at various times to try to isolate their financial circuits and their economies from the influence of the market are a clear indication of this. At the same time, the effects of these measures suggest that up to a certain point each country is reasonably well-equipped to deal with the problems that may arise for it in this field".
108. Monetary policy measures taken in individual countries were summarised in a bi-monthly BIS paper distributed to all central bank members: BIS, "Chronology of Financial and Economic Events", CB Document no. 324. This compilation – published at quarterly intervals from 1961 – also included data on the latest capital issues on the eurobond market. For the monetary measures taken in the first half of 1969, see Ferras (1970), pp. 101–2; for the United States, see BIS, *Fortieth Annual Report,* Basel, 8 June 1970, pp. 147–9.
109. In 1970, when writing these words, Otmar Emminger was Vice-President of the Bundesbank. All quotes in this paragraph taken from Emminger (1970), pp. 105–21.
110. Informal record of a meeting on the eurocurrency market held at the Netherlands Bank, 18th February 1971, p. 2, BISA, 7.18(23) – *Papers Milton Gilbert,* box GILB1.
111. Note, J. Zijlstra, "BIS Working Group," 17 February 1971, BISA, 7.18(23) – *Papers Milton Gilbert,* box GILB1.
112. There was, however, no consensus on the real impact of the so-called multiplier effect of the market. The debate continued over the years to come. In 1981 a paper published by the BIS concluded that: "the Euro-market's ... endogenous credit-creating ability is very small" but immediately added: "It is difficult to believe, however, that the state of Euro-market liquidity has no influence on Euro-bank lending policy or the expansion of the Euro-currency system. Independent multiplier effects may, therefore, still occur". Johnston (1981), pp. 49–50.
113. "Report of the President's ad hoc group on the Euro-currency market", 18 April 1971, BISA, 7.18(23) – *Papers Milton Gilbert,* box GILB1.

114. "Informal record of the first meeting of the standing committee of central bank officials on the Euro-currency market, held at the BIS on 8 May 1971", BISA, 7.18(23) – *Papers Milton Gilbert,* box GILB1.
115. Eurodollar investments by official bodies (mostly non-G10 central banks and, increasingly, oil-producing countries in the Middle East and Africa) were estimated at \$12 billion.
116. These and previous figures quoted in: "Informal record of the second meeting of the Standing Committee of central bank officials on the Euro-Currency Market, held at the BIS on 1 June 1971", BISA, 7.18(23) – *Papers Milton Gilbert,* box GILB1.
117. See the confidential memo from Charles Coombs to Under-Secretary Volcker and Governor Daane of 14 May 1971 as well as two confidential memos from Coombs to Federal Reserve Chairman Burns, dated 21 and 28 May 1971, FRBNY, 797.3 – *BIS General, 1971.*
118. BIS, *Forty-Second Annual Report,* Basel, 12 June 1972, p. 149.
119. "Informal record of a meeting of the Standing Committee of central bank officials on the Euro-Currency Market held at the BIS on 6 November 1971", BISA, 1.3a(3) – *Meeting of Experts, 1971–72,* vols. 9–11.
120. "Introduction to the second part of the Standing Committee's work: Euro-bank operations", 10 December 1971, BISA, 7.18(23) – *Papers Milton Gilbert,* box GILB1. Already in September, the BIS had prepared a detailed report – on "Compulsory reserve requirements and Euro-currency activity", BISA, 7.18(23) – *Papers Milton Gilbert,* box GILB1 – that compared such requirements in the G10 countries, highlighting the lack of harmonisation as well as the fact that in most countries no reserve requirements applied to foreign currency liabilities.
121. As Milton Gilbert put it: "Unfair competition has been established in favour of the Euro-dollar market, since the market [is] free from many restrictions to which the domestic banking sectors [are] subject. In [my] opinion, the equal treatment extended by the Bundesbank to the German banks' business, whether in domestic or foreign currency, [is] the right approach. Another question [is] whether the central banks can allow themselves such tremendous differences as they [have] in the recent past in the application of national monetary policies. [Do] they not have to have central-bank discipline in that respect, to prevent interest rate gaps opening up between countries? The central banks [have] tried to play God and they [have] not done it very convincingly". See: "Informal record of a meeting of the Standing Committee of central bank officials on the Euro-Currency Market, held at the BIS on 12 February 1972", p. 10, BISA, 7.18(23) – *Papers Milton Gilbert,* box GILB1.
122. "Informal record of a meeting of the Standing Committee of central bank officials on the Euro-Currency Market, held at the BIS on 8 January 1972", p. 9, BISA, 7.18(23) – *Papers Milton Gilbert,* box GILB1.
123. On the view that the eurodollar market contributed directly to the breakdown of the Bretton Woods system, see for instance James (2003), pp. 239–40.
124. Kynaston (2002), p. 286.
125. "Informal record of a meeting of the Standing Committee of central bank officials on the Euro-Currency Market, held at the BIS on 6 April 1972", BISA, 7.18(23) – *Papers Milton Gilbert,* box GILB1.

126. Papers in BISA, 7.18(23) – *Papers Milton Gilbert,* box GILB1. Whereas the German and Italian papers argued in favour of a system of international regulation – both through minimum reserve requirements and coordinated open-market operations – the Bank of England paper stressed the practical and fundamental objections to international regulation, concluding that "national controls are the appropriate first line of defence for dealing with capital flows which are harmful for a particular country".

127. Letter, C. W. McMahon to R. Larre, 27 February 1973, BISA, 1.3a(3) – *Meeting of Experts, 1972–73,* vols. 12–13.

128. "Summary of the discussion among the Governors on the Euro-Currency Market, 13 May 1973", p. 8, BISA, 7.18(23) – *Papers Milton Gilbert,* box GILB1.

129. James (2002), pp. 209–10.

130. BIS, *Forty-Fourth Annual Report,* Basel, 10 June 1974, p. 159.

131. "The Euro-Currency Market", Confidential report presented to the Committee of Twenty by René Larre, General Manager of the Bank for International Settlements, 3 March 1973, BISA, 7.18(23) – *Papers Milton Gilbert,* box GILB1.

132. One proposal involved "slowing down the growth of the Euro-currency market and … reducing inequalities in the competitive positions of domestic and Euro-currency banking" by applying reserve requirements to banks' foreign currency operations. However, the majority in this (C-20 technical) group came to the conclusion that "any attempt to impose coordinated restrictions on the market would either be ineffective because the market would be driven elsewhere or would jeopardize a useful and efficient capital market". James (1996), p. 250.

133. BIS memorandum, "The centralisation of information on bank credits to non-residents", 22 January 1965, BISA, 1.3a(3) – *Meeting of Experts, 1964–66,* vols. 3–5.

134. Letter, Gabriel Ferras to the governors, 24 May 1965, including "Note on the meeting regarding the centralisation of information on bank credits to non-residents", BISA, 1.3a(3) – *Meeting of Experts, 1964–66,* vols. 3–5.

135. See, for instance: Kane (1983), pp. 101–3; Heinevetter (1979), pp. 231–4.

136. Ferras (1969), p. 17.

137. See, for instance, Saunders (1987), pp. 196–232.

138. On the so-called Herstatt risk, see Galati (2002), pp. 55–65. It has been estimated that, over the three days following the collapse of Herstatt in June 1974, the amount of gross funds transferred through the New York multilateral net settlement system declined by 60%.

139. Heininger (1979), pp. 903–1034.

140. "The Governors had an exchange of views on the problem of the lender of last resort in the Euro-markets. They recognized that it would not be practical to lay down in advance detailed rules and procedures for the provision of temporary liquidity. But they were satisfied that means are available for that purpose and will be used if and when necessary". "BIS Press communiqué of 10 September 1974", BISA, 1.3a(3) – *Meeting of Experts, 1974–75,* vols. 16–17.

141. See ⟨http://www.bis.org/publ/bcbsc101.pdf⟩ for a brief history of the Basel Committee on Banking Supervision.

Epilogue

1. Bank for International Settlements (1980b).
2. Ibid., p. 55.
3. Ibid., p. 69.
4. Ibid., p. 88.
5. Ibid., p. 90.
6. Ibid., p. 128.
7. Ibid., pp. 145, 149
8. Ibid., p. 201.
9. Giannini (2004), p. 460.
10. See Section 1.1.
11. See Section 6.4.
12. See Section 3.2.
13. Bank for International Settlements (1980b), p. 111.
14. Ibid., p. 97.
15. Coombs (1976), pp. 36–7.
16. Giannini (2004).
17. Bank for International Settlements (1980b), p. 117.
18. Ibid., pp. 117–18.

Archives Consulted

AAPA	Auswärtiges Amt, Politisches Archiv Kurstrasse 33 D-10117 Berlin, Germany
APAP	Archivio Privato Alberto Pirelli, Milan
AN	Archives Nationales 11, rue des Quatre-Fils F-75003 Paris, France
ANBA	Oesterreichische Nationalbank, Bankhistorisches Archiv Postfach 61 A-1010 Wien, Austria
BAB	Bundesarchiv Deutschland, Abteilungen Reich und DDR Postfach 450 569 D-12175 Berlin, Germany
BAK	Bundesarchiv Potsdamer Strasse 1 D-56075 Koblenz, Germany
BEA	Archive Section Bank of England Threadneedle St. London EC2R 8AH, United Kingdom
BFA	Banque de France Service des archives Code courrier: 10-1069 39, rue Croix-des-Petits-Champs F-75049 Paris Cedex 01, France
BPAH	Banco de Portugal Arquivo Histórico Av. Almirante Reis, 71 1150-012 Lisboa, Portugal

BIHA	Archivio storico della Banca d'Italia
	Via Nazionale, 191
	I-00184 Roma, Italy

BISA	Bank for International Settlements Archive
	Centralbahnplatz 2
	CH-4002 Basel, Switzerland

BULH	Universität Basel
	Bibliothek, Handschriftenabteilung
	Schönbeinstrasse 18
	CH-4056 Basel, Switzerland

DBHA	Deutsche Bundesbank Historisches Archiv
	Wilhelm-Epstein-Strasse 14
	D-60431 Frankfurt am Main, Germany

ECBA	European Central Bank Historical Archive
	Kaiserstrasse 29
	D-60311 Frankfurt am Main, Germany

FRBNY	Federal Reserve Bank of New York
	Archives Section
	33 Liberty Street
	New York, NY 10045, USA

HAEC	Historical Archives of the European Communities
	Villa "Il Poggiolo"
	Piazza Edison, 11
	I-50133 Firenze, Italy

HUBL	Baker Library
	Harvard Business School
	Soldiers Field Road
	Boston, MA 021633, USA

IVSLA	Istituto Veneto di Scienze, Lettere e Arti
	Archivio Luigi Luzzatti
	Campo S. Stefano, 2945
	I-30124 Venice, Italy

LNA	League of Nations Archive
	United Nations Archives and Library
	Palais des Nations
	Avenue de la Paix 8-14
	CH-1202 Genève, Switzerland

MAEA	Ministère des Affaires Etrangères
	Direction des Archives et de la Documentation
	1, rue Robert Esnault-Pelterie
	F-75007 Paris, France

MAED	Ministère des Affaires Etrangères Centre des Archives diplomatiques de Nantes 17, rue du Casterneau F-44000 Nantes, France
MFAA	Archives of the Belgian Ministry of Foreign Affairs Archief van het Ministerie van Buitenlandse Zaken Kleine Karmelietenstraat 15 B-1000 Brussels, Belgium
NARA	National Archives and Records Administration College Park 8601 Adelphi Road College Park, MD 20740-6001, USA
NBBA	National Bank of Belgium Archive Boulevard de Berlaimont 14 B-1000 Brussels, Belgium
NBHA	De Nederlandsche Bank Historisch Archief Postbus 98 1000 AB Amsterdam, Netherlands
OFD	Oberfinanzdirektion Berlin Bredtschneiderstrasse 5 D-14057 Berlin, Germany
PRO	Public Record Office Ruskin Avenue Kew, Richmond Surrey, TW9 4DU, United Kingdom
PRSGM	Princeton University Seeley G. Mudd Manuscript Library 65 Olden Street Princeton, NJ 08544, USA
SAEF	Ministère de l'Economie, des Finances et de l'Industrie Service des Archives Economiques et Financières Centre de Savigny-le-Temple 9, rue de l'Aluminium F-77176 Savigny-le-Temple, France
SNBA	Schweizerische Nationalbank Archiv Börsenstrasse 15 Postfach CH-8022 Zürich, Switzerland

Bibliography

Abs, H. J. (1991), *Entscheidungen 1949–1953: Die Entstehung des Londoner Schulden-abkommens*, Mainz: von Hase & Koehler.

Aceña, P. M. (2000), *El Servicio de Estudios del Banco de España, 1930–2000*, Madrid: Banco de España.

Andrews, D. M. (2003), "The Committee of Central Bank Governors as a Source of Rules", *Journal of European Public Policy*, 10(6), pp. 956–73.

Ansiaux, H., and M. Dessart (1975), *Dossier pour l'histoire de l'Europe monétaire 1958–1973*, Louvain-la-Neuve: Vander.

Argoud, J. (1931), *La Banque des Règlements Internationaux dans le cadre de l'économie mondiale*, Paris: Duchemin.

Auboin, R. (1954), "La Banque des Règlements Internationaux et l'Union Européenne de Paiments", *Kyklos*, VII(1/2), pp. 39–60.

Auboin, R. (1955), *The Bank for International Settlements, 1930–1955* (Princeton Essays in International Finance, no. 22), Princeton, NJ: Princeton University Press.

Auboin, R. (1958), *Twenty Years of International Cooperation in the Monetary Sphere, 1938–1958*, Basel: Bank for International Settlements.

Baer, G. D. (1994), "The Committee of Governors as a Forum for European Central Bank Cooperation", in A. Bakker et al. (eds.), *Monetary Stability through International Cooperation: Essays in Honour of André Szász*, Amsterdam: De Nederlandsche Bank, pp. 147–57.

Baer, G. D. (1999), "Sixty-five Years of Central Bank Cooperation at the Bank for International Settlements", in C.-L. Holtfrerich, J. Reis, and G. Toniolo (eds.), *The Emergence of Modern Central Banking from 1918 to the Present*, Aldershot: Ashgate, pp. 341–61.

Baffi, P. (2002), *The Origins of Central Bank Cooperation: The Establishment of the Bank for International Settlements*, Rome: Editori Laterza.

Bank for International Settlements (1931a), *Report of the Special Advisory Committee*, Basel: Bank for International Settlements.

Bank for International Settlements (1931b), *Report of the Committee Appointed on the Recommendation of the London Conference 1931*, Basel, 18 August 1931.

Bank for International Settlements. Monetary and Economic Department. CB Documents.

Bank for International Settlements. Monetary and Economic Department. HS Series.

Bank for International Settlements (1931–1982), *Annual Reports,* 1930 through 1981, Basel: Bank for International Settlements.

Bank for International Settlements (1980a), *The Bank for International Settlements and the Basle Meetings: Published on the Occasion of the Fiftieth Anniversary 1930– 1980,* Basel: Bank for International Settlements.

Bank for International Settlements (1980b), *Témoignages et Points de Vue: Publication du Cinquantenaire 1930–1980* [Personal Recollections and Opinions: Published on the Occasion of the Fiftieth Anniversary 1930–1980], Basel: Bank for International Settlements.

Bank for International Settlements (1983), "The International Interbank Market: A Descriptive Study", BIS Economic Paper no. 8.

Bank for International Settlements (1997a), *Note on Gold Operations Involving the Bank for International Settlements and the German Reichsbank, 1st September 1939 – 8th May 1945,* Basel: Bank for International Settlements, available at ⟨http://www. bis.org⟩.

Bank for International Settlements (1997b), *Note on Gold Shipments and Gold Exchanges Organised by the Bank for International Settlements, 1st June 1938 – 31st May 1945,* Basel: Bank for International Settlements, available at ⟨http://www.bis. org⟩.

Bank for International Settlements (2003), *Basic Texts,* Basel: Bank for International Settlements.

Bank of England (1961), *Quarterly Bulletin,* I(3).

Bank of England (1964), *Quarterly Bulletin,* IV(1).

Barnich, G. (1923), *Comment faire payer l'Allemagne: Erreurs d'hier – Solutions de demain,* Paris: Ferenczi & Fils.

Basel Committee on Banking Supervision, ⟨http://www.bis.org/publ/bcbsc101.pdf⟩.

Battilossi, S. (2000), "Financial Innovation and the Golden Ages of International Banking: 1890–1931 and 1958–1981", *Financial History Review,* 7, pp. 141–75.

Battilossi, S. (2002), "Introduction: International Banking and the American Challenge in Historical Perspective", in Battilossi and Cassis (2002), pp. 1–35.

Battilossi, S., and Y. Cassis (eds.), (2002), *European Banks and the American Challenge: Competition and Cooperation in International Banking under Bretton Woods,* Oxford University Press.

Bell, G. (1973), *The Euro-dollar Market and the International Financial System,* London: Macmillan.

Bennett, E. W. (1962), *Germany and the Diplomacy of the Financial Crisis, 1931,* Cambridge, MA: Harvard University Press.

Bernholz, P. (1999), "The Bundesbank and the Process of European Monetary Integration", in Deutsche Bundesbank (1999), pp. 731–89.

Beyen, J. W. (1949), *Money in a Maelstrom,* New York: Macmillan.

Beyen, J. W. (1968), *Het Spel en de Knikkers: Een Kroniek van Vijftig Jaren,* Rotterdam: Ad Donker.

Blum, J. M. (1959), *From the Morgenthau Diaries: Years of Crisis 1928–1938,* Boston: Houghton-Mifflin.

Blum, L. (1954), *L'Oeuvre de Léon Blum*, Paris: Albin Michel.

Boltho, A. (1982), "Growth", in A. Boltho (ed.), *The European Economy: Growth and Crisis*, Oxford University Press, pp. 9–37.

Bordo, M. D. (1993), "The Bretton Woods International Monetary System: A Historical Overview", in M. D. Bordo and B. Eichengreen (eds.), *A Retrospective on the Bretton Woods System: Lessons for International Monetary Reform*, University of Chicago Press, pp. 3–108.

Bordo, M., E. Choudhri, and A. Schwartz (2002), "Was Expansionary Monetary Policy Feasible during the Great Contraction? Examination of the Gold Standard Constraint", *Explorations in Economic History*, 39, pp. 1–28.

Bordo, M. D., and H. James (2001), "The Adam Klug Memorial Lecture: Haberler versus Nurkse: The Case for Floating Exchange Rates as an Alternative to Bretton Woods", NBER Working Paper no. 8545.

Bordo, M. D., D. Simard, and E. White (1994), "France and the Bretton Woods International Monetary System: 1960 to 1968", NBER Working Paper no. 4642.

Bossuat, G. (2003), "La Banque de France dans les relations monétaires internationales de la France, 1945–1960", in Feiertag and Margairaz (2003), pp. 723–52.

Boughton, J. M. (2004), "New Light on Harry Dexter White", *Journal of the History of Economic Thought*, 26, pp. 179–95.

Boyle, A. (1967), *Montagu Norman, a Biography*, London: Cassell.

Brandt, W. (1976), *Begegnungen und Einsichten 1960–1975*, Hamburg: Hoffman & Campe.

Britton, A. (2001), *Monetary Regimes of the Twentieth Century*, Cambridge University Press.

Brown, W. A., Jr. (1940), *The International Gold Standard Reinterpreted 1914–1934*, New York: NBER.

Brüning, H. (1970), *Memoiren 1918–1934*, Stuttgart: Deutsche Verlags-Anstalt.

Buchheim, C. (1999), "The Establishment of the Bank deutscher Länder and the West German Currency Reform", in Deutsche Bundesbank (1999), pp. 55–100.

Bussière, E. (2003), "La Banque de France et les débats monétaires à l'époque de la première union économique et monétaire: la difficile émergence d'une identité monétaire européenne (1968–1973)", in Feiertag and Margairaz (2003), pp. 697–722.

Caillaux, J. (1929), "After The Hague", *The Banker*, 12(45), pp. 61–5.

Cairncross, A. (1951), "The Economic Recovery of Western Germany", *Lloyds Bank Review*, October, pp. 19–34.

Cairncross, A. (1985), *Years of Recovery, 1945–51*, London: Macmillan.

Cairncross, A. (1987), *A Country to Play With: Level of Industry Negotiations in Berlin 1945–46*, Gerrards Cross: Colin Smythe.

Cairncross, A., and B. Eichengreen (1983), *Sterling in Decline: The Devaluations of 1931, 1949 and 1967*, Oxford: Blackwell.

Canzonieri, M., and D. Henderson (1991), *Monetary Policy in Interdependent Economies: A Game-Theoretic Approach*, Cambridge, MA: MIT Press.

Capie, F., C. Goodhart, and N. Schnadt (1994), *The Future of Central Banking: The Tercentenary Symposium of the Bank of England*, Cambridge University Press.

Capie, F., and G. E. Wood (1995), "A European Lender of Last Resort? Some Lessons from History", in Reis (1995), pp. 209–29.

Cardarelli, S., and R. Martano (2000), "I Nazisti e l'Oro della Banca d'Italia, Sottrazione e Recupero, 1943–1958", *Collana Storica della Banca d'Italia,* Roma-Bari: Laterza.

Carli, G. (1993), *Cinquant'anni di vita Italiana,* Roma: Laterza.

Carr, E. H. (1947), *International Relations between the Two World Wars, 1919–1939,* London: Macmillan.

Cesarano, F. (2000), *Gli Accordi di Bretton Woods,* Roma-Bari: Laterza.

Chandler, L. V. (1958), *Benjamin Strong, Central Banker,* Washington, DC: Brookings Institution.

Charguérard, M.-A. (2004), *Le Banquier américain de Hitler,* Geneva: Labor & Fides.

Cipolla, C. (1957), *Moneta e civiltà mediterranea,* Firenze: Neri Pozza.

Cipolla, C. (1976), *Before the Industrial Revolution,* London: Methuen.

Clapham, J. (1944), *The Bank of England: A History,* vol. II, Cambridge University Press.

Clarke, S. V. O. (1967), *Central Bank Cooperation: 1924–1931,* New York: Federal Reserve Bank of New York.

Clarke, S. V. O. (1972), *The Reconstruction of the International Monetary System: The Attempts of 1922 and 1933,* Princeton, NJ: Princeton University Press.

Clarke, S. V. O. (1977), *Exchange-Rate Stabilization in the Mid-1930s: Negotiating the Tripartite Agreement* (Princeton Studies in International Finance, no. 41), Princeton, NJ: Princeton University Press.

Clavin, P. (1996), *The Failure of Economic Diplomacy: Britain, Germany, France and the United States, 1931–36,* Basingstoke: Macmillan.

Clay, H. (1957), *Lord Norman,* London: Macmillan.

Clement, P. (1998), "The Bank for International Settlements during the Second World War", in Foreign and Commonwealth Office (1998), pp. 43–60.

Clement, P. (2000), "The BIS – One Bank, Five Locations", *The Tower,* 11, p. 9.

Clement, P. (2002), "Between Banks and Governments: The Bank for International Settlements and the 1931 Reichsbank Credit", in T. de Graaf et al. (eds.), *European Banking Overseas, 19th–20th Century,* Amsterdam: ABN Amro, pp. 139–62.

Clement, P. (2004), "Central Bank Networking at the Bank for International Settlements, 1930s–1960s", in Dumoulin (2004), pp. 445–63.

Cohrs, P. O. (2003), "The First 'Real' Peace Settlements after the First World War: Britain, the United States and the Accords of London and Locarno", *Contemporary European History,* 12(1), pp. 1–32.

Communauté Economique Européenne (1959), *Premier Rapport d'Activité du Comité Monétaire,* Brussels, 28 February, pp. 5–8.

Coombs, C. A. (1962), "Treasury and Federal Reserve Foreign Exchange Operations", *Federal Reserve Bulletin,* 48(9), pp. 1148–9.

Coombs, C. A. (1965), "Treasury and Federal Reserve Foreign Exchange Operations", *Federal Reserve Bulletin,* 51(9), p. 1224.

Coombs, C. A. (1976), *The Arena of International Finance,* New York: Wiley.

Costigliola, F. (1972), "The Other Side of Isolationism: The Establishment of the First World Bank, 1929–1930", *Journal of American History,* 59(1), pp. 602–20.

Costigliola, F. (1977), "Anglo-American Financial Rivalry in the 1920s", *Journal of Economic History,* 37(4), pp. 911–34.

Costigliola, F. (1984), *Awkward Dominion: American Political, Economic, and Cultural Relations with Europe, 1919–1933,* Ithaca, NY: Cornell University Press.

Cottrell, P. L. (2003), "La Banque d'Angleterre, les Crises de la Livre Sterling et l'Europe, 1958–1967", in Feiertag and Margairaz (2003), pp. 787–803.

Cottrell, P., and C. J. Stone (1989), "Credits and Deposits to Finance Credits", in P. L. Cottrell, H. Lindgren, and A. Teichova (eds.), *European Industry and Banking between the Wars: A Review of Bank–Industry Relations,* Leicester University Press.

Crafts, N., and G. Toniolo (1996), "Postwar Growth: An Overview", in N. Crafts and G. Toniolo (eds.), *Economic Growth in Europe Since 1945,* Cambridge University Press, pp. 1–37.

Crettol, V., and P. Halbeisen (1999), *Monetary Policy Background of the Gold Transactions of the Swiss National Bank in the Second World War,* Zürich: Swiss National Bank.

Dealtry, M. (ed.), and P. Baffi (1991), *Chapters in the Early History of the Bank for International Settlements,* Basel: Bank for International Settlements.

De Bonis, R., A. Giustiniani, and G. Gomel (1999), "Crises and Bail-Outs of Banks and Countries: Linkages, Analogies and Differences", *World Economy,* 22(1), pp. 55–86.

De Cecco, M. (1974), *Money and Empire,* Totowa, NJ: Rowan & Littlefield.

De Cecco, M. (1985), "The International Debt Problem in the Interwar Period", *Banca Nazionale del Lavoro Quarterly Review,* 152, pp. 45–64.

De Cecco, M. (1993), "L'Italia e il sistema finanziario internazionale 1919–1936", *Collana Storica della Banca d'Italia, Serie Documenti,* vol. VI, Roma-Bari: Laterza.

De Cecco, M. (1995), "Central Bank Cooperation in the Inter-War Period: A View from the Periphery", in Reis (1995), pp. 113–34.

"Décision du Conseil du 8 mai 1964 concernant la collaboration entre les banques centrales des Etats membres de la Communauté économique européenne", *Journal officiel des Communautés européennes,* 77 (21 May 1964), p. 1206/64.

Dell, E. (1996), *The Chancellors: A History of the Chancellors of the Exchequer 1945–90,* London: HarperCollins.

DeLong, B. (2002), "Review of Skidelsky's 'John Maynard Keynes: Fighting for Britain'", *Journal of Economic Literature,* 40(1), pp. 155–62.

DeLong, J. B., and B. Eichengreen (1991), "The Marshall Plan: History's Most Successful Structural Adjustment Program", NBER Working Paper no. 3899.

Denison, E. (1967), *Why Growth Rates Differ,* Washington, DC: Brookings Institution.

Deutsche Bundesbank (ed.) (1999), *Fifty Years of the Deutsche Mark: Central Bank and the Currency in Germany Since 1948,* Oxford University Press

De Vries, J. (1994a), "The Netherlands Financial Empire" and "De Nederlandsche Bank", in M. Pohl and S. Freitag (eds.), *Handbook on the History of European Banks,* Aldershot: Edward Elgar, pp. 719–30 and 743–8.

De Vries, J. (1994b), *Geschiedenis van de Nederlandsche Bank; Dl. 5: De Nederlandsche Bank van 1914 tot 1948: Trips tijdvak 1931–1948, onderbroken door de Tweede Wereldoorlog,* Amsterdam: Nederlands Instituut voor het Bank- en Effectenbedrijf.

Dickhaus, M. (1999), "La Bundesbank et l'Europe 1958–1973", *Histoire, Economie et Société,* 18(4), pp. 775–95.

Dulles, E. L. (1932), *The Bank for International Settlements at Work,* New York: Macmillan.

Dulles, E. L. (1980), *Chances of a Lifetime: A Memoir,* Englewood Cliffs, NJ: Prentice-Hall.

Dumoulin, M. (ed.) (2004), *Réseaux économiques et construction européenne* [Economic Networks and European Integration], Brussels: PIE – Peter Lang.

Dyson, K. (1994), *Elusive Union: The Process of Economic and Monetary Union in Europe*, London: Longman.

The Economist, London.

EEC Commission (1962), *Memorandum of the Commission on the Action Programme of the Community for the Second Stage*, Brussels.

Eichengreen, B. (1992), *Golden Fetters: The Gold Standard and the Great Depression, 1919–1939*, Oxford University Press.

Eichengreen, B. (1993), *Reconstructing Europe's Trade and Payments: The European Payments Union*, Manchester University Press.

Eichengreen, B. (1995), "Central Bank Co-operation and Exchange Rate Commitments: The Classical and Interwar Gold Standards Compared", *Financial History Review*, 2(2), pp. 99–118.

Eichengreen, B. (1996), "Institutions and Economic Growth: Europe after World War II", in N. Crafts and G. Toniolo (eds.), *Economic Growth in Europe Since 1945*, Cambridge University Press, pp. 38–72.

Eichengreen, B., and H. James (2003), "Monetary and Financial Reform in Two Eras of Globalization", in M. D. Bordo, A. M. Taylor, and J. G. Williamson (eds.), *Globalization in Historical Perspective*, Chicago: National Bureau of Economic Research and University of Chicago Press, pp. 515–48.

Eichengreen, B., and P. Temin (1997), "The Gold Standard and the Great Depression", NBER Working Paper no. 6060.

Einzig, P. (1930), *The Bank for International Settlements*, London: Macmillan.

Einzig, P. (1964), *The Euro-Dollar System: Practice and Theory of International Interest Rates*, London: Macmillan.

Ellwood, D. W. (1992), *Rebuilding Europe: Western Europe, America and Postwar Reconstruction*, London: Longman.

Emminger, O. (1970), "The Euromarket: A Source of Stability or Instability?", in Prochnow (1970), pp. 104–21.

Emminger, O. (1986), *D-Mark, Dollar, Währungskrisen: Erinnerungen eines ehemaligen Bundesbankspräsidenten*, Stuttgart: Deutsche Verlags-Anstalt.

Enders, A. M., and G. A. Fleming (2002), *International Organizations and the Analysis of Economic Policy*, Cambridge University Press.

European Communities. Monetary Committee (1970), *Twelfth Report on the Activities of the Monetary Committee*, Brussels, 30 June.

European Communities. Monetary Committee (1973), *Fourteenth Report on the Activities of the Monetary Committee*, Brussels, 12 April.

Federal Reserve System (1943), *Banking and Monetary Statistics*, no. 173.

Feiertag, O. (1998), "La Banque de France et les problèmes monétaires européens de la conférence de Gênes à la création de la B.R.I. (1922–1930)", in E. Bussière and M. Dumoulin (eds.), *Milieux économiques et intégration européenne en Europe occidentale au XXe siècle*, Arras: Artois Presses Universitaires, pp. 15–35.

Feiertag, O. (1999), "Les banques d'émission et la BRI face à la dislocation de l'étalon-or (1931–1933)", *Histoire, Economie et Société*, 18(4), pp. 715–36.

Feiertag, O. (2004), "Pierre Quesnay et les réseaux de l'internationalisme monétaire en Europe (1919–1937)", in Dumoulin (2004), pp. 331–49.

Feiertag, O., and M. Margairaz (eds.) (2003), *Politiques et pratiques des banques d'émission en Europe (XVIIe-XXe siècle): le bicentenaire de la Banque de France dans la perspective de l'identité monétaire européenne*, Paris: Albin Michel.

Feinstein, C. P. (1972), *National Income, Expenditure and Output of the United Kingdom, 1855–1965*, Cambridge University Press.

Feis, H. (1966), *Characters in the Crisis*, Boston: Little, Brown.

Ferguson, N. (1998), *The Pity of War*, London: Penguin.

Ferras, G. (1969), "Le marché Européen du dollar", Conférence prononcée le 10 décembre 1969 à l'Institut d'Etudes Bancaires et Financières.

Ferras, G. (1970), "Central Banks and the Eurodollar Market", in Prochnow (1970), pp. 84–103.

Fforde, J. (1992), *The Bank of England and Public Policy, 1941–1958*, Cambridge University Press.

Fisher, I. (1933), "The Debt-Deflation Theory of Great Depressions", *Econometrica*, 1(4), pp. 337–57.

Flandreau, M. (1995), *L'or du monde: la France et la stabilité du système monétaire internationale, 1848–1873*, Paris: L'Harmattan.

Flandreau, M. (1997), "Central Bank Cooperation in Historical Perspective: A Sceptical View", *Economic History Review*, 50, pp. 735–63.

Flandreau, M., and H. James (2003), "Introduction", in M. Flandreau, C.-L. Holtfrerich, and H. James (eds.), *International Financial History in the Twentieth Century*, Cambridge: German Historical Institute and Cambridge University Press, pp. 1–16.

Fodor, G. (2000), "I Prestiti internazionali all'Italia del 1964", in F. Cotula (ed.), *Stabilità e Sviluppo negli Anni Cinquanta*, Vol. 1, *L'Italia nel Contesto Internazionale*, Rome: Editori Laterza, pp. 401–39.

Foreign and Commonwealth Office (1998), *Nazi Gold: The London Conference, 2–4 December 1997*, London: The Stationery Office.

Fraser, L. (1936), "The International Bank and Its Future", *Foreign Affairs*, 14(3), pp. 453–64.

Frech, S. (2001), "Der Zahlungsverkehr der Schweiz mit den Achsenmächten", in *Veröffentlichungen der Unabhängigen Expertenkommission Schweiz – Zweiter Weltkrieg*, vol. 3, Zürich: Chronos Verlag.

Friedman, M. (1953), "The Case for Floating Exchange Rates", in M. Friedman, *Essays in Positive Economics*, University of Chicago Press, pp. 157–203.

Friedman, M. (1963), *Post War Trends in Monetary Theory and Policy*, Athens: Center of Economic Research.

Friedman, M. (1966), "Free-Market Determination of Exchange Rates", in United States Congress, Joint Economic Committee, Subcommittee on International Exchange and Payments, *Contingency Planning for U.S. International Monetary Policy*, Washington, DC.

Friedman, M. (1968), *Dollars and Deficits: Inflation, Monetary Policy and the Balance of Payments*, Englewood Cliffs, NJ: Prentice-Hall.

Friedman, M. (1970), "The Eurodollar Market: Some First Principles", in Prochnow (1970), pp. 272–93.

Friedman, M. (1976), "Autobiography", Nobel e-archive: ⟨http://www.nobel.se/economics/laureates/1976/friedman-autobio.html⟩.

Furrer, R. (1938), "The Union Monetary Standard as Laid Down in the Universal Postal Convention", *L'Union Postale,* 63(12), pp. 352–87.

Galati, G. (2002), "Settlement Risk in Foreign Exchange Markets and CLS Bank", *BIS Quarterly Review,* December, pp. 55–65.

Galgano, E. (ed.) (1996), *Dizionario Enciclopedico del Diritto,* vol. II, Padova: Cedam.

Garritsen de Vries, M. (1976), *The International Monetary Fund, 1966–1971: The System under Stress,* Vol. I, *Narrative,* Washington, DC: IMF.

Garritsen de Vries, M. (1986), *The IMF in a Changing World, 1945–85,* Washington, DC: IMF.

Gavin, F. J. (2004), *Gold, Dollars and Power, The Politics of International Monetary Relations, 1958–1971,* Chapel Hill: University of North Carolina Press.

Gayer, A. D. (ed.) (1937), *The Lessons of Monetary Experience: Essays in Honor of Irving Fisher,* London: Allen & Unwin.

Giannini, C. (2002), "Pitfalls in International Crisis Lending", in C. Goodhart and G. Illing (eds.), *Financial Crises, Contagion and the Lender of Last Resort: A Reader,* Oxford University Press, pp. 511–45.

Giannini, C. (2004), *L'età delle banche centrali: forme e governo della moneta fiduciaria in una prospettiva istituzionalista,* Bologna: Il Mulino.

Gibson, H. D. (1989), *The Euro-Currency Markets, Domestic Financial Policy and International Instability,* London: Macmillan.

Gilbert, M. (1980), *Quest for World Monetary Order: The Gold-Dollar System and Its Aftermath* (with posthumous editing by P. Oppenheimer and M. Dealtry), New York: Wiley.

Gilbert, M., and R. Gott (1963), *The Appeasers,* London: Weidenfeld & Nicolson.

Gilbert, M., and W. McClam (1970), "Regulations and Policies Relating to the Eurocurrency Market", in Prochnow (1970), pp. 348–411.

Gilpin, R. (1987), *The Political Economy of International Relations,* Princeton, NJ: Princeton University Press.

Giovanoli, M. (1989) "The Role of the Bank for International Settlements in International Monetary Cooperation and Its Tasks Relating to the European Currency Unit", *International Lawyer,* 23(3), pp. 841–64.

Goodhart, C., F. Capie, and N. Schnadt (1994), "The Development of Central Banking", in Capie et al. (1994), pp. 1–231.

Guarino, G., and G. Toniolo (1993), *La Banca d'Italia e il Sistema Bancario, 1919–1936,* Roma-Bari: Laterza.

Guindey, G. (1977), *The International Monetary Tangle: Myths and Realities,* New York: M.E. Sharpe.

Haberler, G. (1953), *Currency Convertibility,* Washington, DC: American Enterprise Association.

Hahn, A., et al. (1929), *Die Reparationsbank: kritische Betrachtungen,* Frankfurt am Main: Frankfurt Societäts-Druckerei.

Hantos, E. (1931), *Die Kooperation der Notenbanken,* Tübingen: Mohr.

Hawtrey, R. G. (1932), *The Art of Central Banking,* London: Longmans, Green.

Hawtrey, R. G. (1950), *Currency and Credit,* London: Longmans, Green.

Heinevetter, B. (1979), "Liquidity Creation in the Euromarkets", *Journal of Money, Credit and Banking,* 11(2), pp. 231–4.

Heininger, P. (1979), "Liability of U.S. Banks for Deposits Placed in Their Foreign Branches", *Law and Policy in International Business*, 11, pp. 903–1034.

Hickman, E. (1938), *Statistisches Handbuch des Welthandels 1938*, Berlin: Verlag Hoppenstedt.

Holmes, A. R., and F. H. Klopstock (1960), "The Market for Dollar Deposits in Europe", *Federal Reserve Bank of New York Monthly Review*, 42(11), pp. 197–202.

Holtfrerich, C.-L. (1986), *The German Inflation 1914–1923*, New York: de Gruyter.

Holtfrerich, C.-L. (1990), "Was the Policy of Deflation in Germany Unavoidable?", in Jürgen Baron von Kruedener (ed.), *Economic Crisis and Political Collapse, The Weimar Republic 1924–1933*, New York: Berg, pp. 63–80.

Holtfrerich, C.-L. (1999), "Monetary Policy under Fixed Exchange Rates (1948–70)", in Deutsche Bundesbank (1999), pp. 307–401.

Holz, K. A. (1977), *Die Diskussion um den Dawes- und Young-Plan in der deutschen Presse*, Bd. I, Frankfurt am Main: Haag & Herchen Verlag.

Horsefield, J. K. (1969), *The International Monetary Fund, 1945–1965*, Vol. I: *Chronicle*, Washington, DC: IMF.

House of Commons (1942), *Parliamentary Debates, Official Report*, 383(110), 13 October 1942, columns 1595–6.

Houtman-De Smedt, H. (1994), "Le système bancaire en Belgique à travers les siècles", in M. Pohl and S. Freitag (eds.), *Handbook on the History of European Banks*, Aldershot: Edward Elgar, pp. 56–65.

Howell, K. K. (1989), *Central Bank Cooperation and the Role of the Bank for International Settlements in International Monetary Stability*, Lexington: University of Kentucky Press.

Howell, K. K. (1993), "The Role of the Bank for International Settlements in Central Bank Cooperation", *Journal of European Economic History*, 22(1), pp. 367–80.

Howson, S. (1975), *Domestic Monetary Management in Britain, 1919–38*, Cambridge University Press.

Hsieh, C.-T., and C. Romer (2001), "Was the Federal Reserve Fettered? Devaluation Expectations in the 1932 Monetary Expansion", NBER Working Paper no. 8118.

Ikenberry, G. J. (1993), "The Political Origins of Bretton Woods", in M. D. Bordo and B. Eichengreen (eds.), *A Retrospective on the Bretton Woods System*, University of Chicago Press, pp. 155–98.

Independent Commission of Experts Switzerland – Second World War (1998), *Switzerland and Gold Transactions in the Second World War: Interim Report*, Berne.

Independent Commission of Experts Switzerland – Second World War (2002), *Switzerland, National Socialism, and the Second World War: Final Report*, Zürich: Pendo Editions.

International Labour Organisation (1946), *Public Investment and Full Employment* (Studies and Reports, New Series, no. 13), Montreal: International Labour Organisation.

International Labour Organisation (1950), *Fourth Report of the International Labour Organisation to the United Nations*, Geneva: International Labour Organisation.

International Monetary Fund (1966), *International Financial News Survey*, 18 (supplement), pp. 141–4.

Jacobsson, E. E. (1979), *A Life for Sound Money: Per Jacobsson: His Biography*, Oxford: Clarendon Press.

Jacobsson, P. (1953), "Keynes: Costs and Controls", *Skandinaviska Banken Quarterly Review,* 34(4), pp. 81–5.

Jacobsson, P. (1958), *Some Monetary Problems, International and National,* Oxford University Press.

James, H. (1985), *The Reichsbank and Public Finance in Germany 1924–1933: A Study of the Politics and Economics during the Great Depression,* Frankfurt am Main: Fritz Knapp Verlag.

James, H. (1986), *The German Slump: Politics and Economics 1924–36,* Oxford: Clarendon Press.

James, H. (1996), *International Monetary Cooperation Since Bretton Woods,* Washington, DC, and Oxford: IMF and Oxford University Press.

James, H. (2002), "Central Banks and the Process of Financial Internationalization: A Secular View", in Battilossi and Cassis (2002), pp. 200–17.

James, H. (2003), "Eurodollar", *Oxford Encyclopedia of Economic History,* vol. 2, pp. 239–40.

Jaudel, P. (1930), *Les paiements internationaux,* Paris: Duchemin.

Johnston, R. B. (1981), "Theories of the Growth of the Euro-currency Market: A Review of the Euro-currency Deposit Multiplier", BIS Economic Paper no. 4.

Johnston, R. B. (1983), *The Economics of the Euro-market: History, Theory and Policy,* London: Macmillan.

Jordan, W. M. (1971), *Great Britain, France and the German Problem 1918–1939,* London: Frank Cass.

Kaldor, N. (1966), *Causes of the Slow Rate of Growth of the United Kingdom,* Cambridge University Press.

Kane, D. R. (1983), *The Euro-dollar Market and the Years of Crisis,* London: Croom Helm.

Kaplan, J. J., and G. Schleiminger (1989), *The European Payments Union: Financial Diplomacy in the 1950s,* Oxford: Clarendon Press.

Karamikas, C. (1931), *La Banque des Règlements Internationaux,* Paris: Editions Domat-Montcherestien.

Keohane, R. (1985), *After Hegemony,* Princeton, NJ: Princeton University Press.

Kerr, I. (1984), *A History of the Eurobond Market: The First 21 Years,* London: Euromoney.

Keynes, J. M. (1919), *The Economic Consequences of the Peace,* London: Macmillan.

Keynes, J. M. (1922), *A Revision of the Treaty,* London: Macmillan.

Keynes, J. M. (1934), "The Bank for International Settlements: Fourth Annual Report (1933–34), Basle, 1934", *Economic Journal,* 44(175), pp. 514–18.

Keynes, J. M. (1936), *The General Theory of Employment Interest and Money,* London: Macmillan.

Keynes, J. M. (1972), *The Collected Writings of John Maynard Keynes,* Vol. X, *Essays in Biography,* London: Macmillan.

Kindleberger, C. (1967), *European Postwar Growth: The Role of Labor Supply,* Cambridge, MA: Harvard University Press.

Kindleberger, C. P. (1987), *The World in Depression, 1929–1939,* London: Penguin.

Koch, H. (1983), *Histoire de la Banque de France et de la monnaie sous la IV République,* Paris: Dunod.

Krug, P. (1932), *La Banque des Règlements Internationaux et son rôle en matière de crédit*, Paris: Rousseau & Cie.

Kubu, E. (1998), "Czechoslovak Gold Reserves and Their Surrender to Nazi Germany", in Foreign and Commonwealth Office (1998), pp. 245–8.

Kuznets, S. (1967), *Modern Economic Growth*, New Haven, CT: Yale University Press.

Kynaston, D. (1995), "The Bank of England and the Government", in R. Roberts and D. Kynaston (eds.), *The Bank of England: Money, Power and Influence 1964–1994*, Oxford: Clarendon Press, pp. 19–55.

Kynaston, D. (2000), *The City of London*, Vol. III, *Illusions of Gold 1914–1945*, London: Pimlico.

Kynaston, D. (2002), *The City of London*, Vol. IV, *A Club No More 1945–2000*, London: Pimlico.

Lamfalussy, A. (1963), *The United Kingdom and the Six*, London: Macmillan.

Lary, H. B. (1943), *The United States in the World Economy, The International Transactions of the United States during the Interwar Period* (U.S. Department of Commerce, Economic Series, no. 23), Washington, DC: Government Printing Office.

Lautenbach, W. (1930), "Die Bank für Internationalen Zahlungsausgleich", *Deutsche Wirtschafts-Zeitung*, 27(20), pp. 457–87.

League of Nations (1932), *Report of the Gold Delegation of the Financial Committee*, Geneva: League of Nations.

League of Nations. Economic, Financial and Transit Department (1944), *International Currency Experience: Lessons in the Inter-war Experience*, Geneva: League of Nations.

Leeson, R. (2003), *Ideology and the International Economy: The Decline and Fall of Bretton Woods*, Basingstoke: Palgrave Macmillan.

Lindblom, C. (1965), *The Intelligence of Democracy*, New York: The Free Press.

Lüke, R. E. (1958), *Von der Stabilisierung zur Krise* (Basle Centre for Economic and Financial Research Series B, no. 3), Zurich: Polygraphischer Verlag.

Lüke, R. E. (1985), "The Schacht and the Keynes Plan", *Banca Nazionale del Lavoro Quarterly Review*, 152, pp. 65–76.

Luther, M. H. (1964), *Vor dem Abgrund 1930–1933: Reichsbankpräsident in Krisenzeiten*, Berlin: Propyläen-Verlag.

Luzzatti, L. (1908), *Une conférence internationale pour la paix monétaire: note pour l'Institut de France*, Paris: Imprimerie Chaix.

Luzzatti, L. (1922), *La Paix Monétaire à la Conférence de Gênes*, Roma: Libreria di Scienze e Lettere.

Macmillan, H. (1966), *Winds of Change, 1914–1939*, London: Macmillan.

MacMillan, M. (2002), *Paris 1919: Six Months That Changed the World*, New York: Random House.

Maddison, A. (1995), *Monitoring the World Economy 1820–1992*, Paris: OECD.

Maes, I. (2002), *Economic Thought and the Making of the European Union*, Cheltenham: Edward Elgar.

Maes, I., and E. Buyst (2004), "Triffin, the European Commission and the Project of a European Reserve Fund", in Dumoulin (2004), pp. 431–44.

Maier, C. S. (1988), *In Search of Stability: Explorations in Historical Political Economy*, Cambridge University Press.

Marjolin, R. (1986), *Le travail d'une vie: mémoires 1911–1986,* Paris: Robert Laffont.

Marsh, D. (1992), *The Bundesbank: The Bank That Rules Europe,* London: Heinemann.

Meltzer, A. (2003), *A History of the Federal Reserve,* Vol. I, *1913–1951,* University of Chicago Press.

"Memorandum de la Commission du Conseil sur la coordination des politiques économiques et la coopération monétaire au sein de la CEE", *Supplément au Bulletin CEE,* no. 3 (March 1969).

Mendès France, P. (1930a), *La Banque internationale, contribution à l'étude du problème des Etats-Unis d'Europe,* Paris: Librairie Valois.

Mendès France, P. (1930b), "Les premiers bilans de la B.R.I.", *Renaissance,* 30 August 1930.

Milner, H. (1991), "International Theories of Cooperation among Nations", *World Politics,* 44(3), pp. 466–96.

Milward, A. (1984), *The Reconstruction of Western Europe 1945–51,* London: Methuen.

Milward, A. (1987), *War, Economy and Society,* Harmondsworth: Penguin.

Milward, A. (1995), "The Origins of the Fixed-Rate Dollar System", in Reis (1995), pp. 135–51.

Ministère des Affaires Étrangères (1922), Documents Diplomatiques, Conférence Économique International de Gènes, 9 avril – 19 mai 1922, Paris: Imprimerie Nationale.

Mitchell, B. R. (2003), *International Historical Statistics: The Americas 1750–2000,* Basingstoke: Palgrave Macmillan.

Mitzakis, M. (1939), *Les crédits extérieurs: leur nature et leur rôle dans la défense des monnaies européennes 1920–1938,* Paris: Les Éditions Internationales.

Moggridge, D. (ed.) (1980), *The Collected Writings of John Maynard Keynes,* Vol. XXVI, *Activities 1941–1946: Shaping the Post-war World, Bretton Woods and Reparations,* London: Macmillan and Cambridge University Press for the Royal Economic Society.

Moggridge, D. (ed.) (1982), *The Collected Writings of John Maynard Keynes,* Vol. XXI, *Activities 1931–1939: World Crises and Policies in Britain and America,* London: Macmillan and Cambridge University Press for the Royal Economic Society.

Morgan, S. (1931), "Constructive Functions of the International Bank", *Foreign Affairs,* 9(4), pp. 580–91.

Mouré, K. (1992), "The Limits to Central Bank Co-operation, 1916–36", *Contemporary European History,* 1(3), pp. 259–79.

Mouré, K. (2002), *The Gold Standard Illusion,* Oxford University Press.

Mundell, R. (1972), "The Future of the International Financial System", in A. L. K. Acheson, J. F. Chant, and M. F. J. Prachowny (eds.), *Bretton Woods Revisited,* London: Macmillan, pp. 91–104.

National Industrial Conference Board (1931), *A Picture of the World Economic Conditions at the Beginning of 1931,* New York: National Industrial Conference Board.

Neal, L. (1990), *The Rise of Financial Capitalism: International Capital Markets in the Age of Reason,* Cambridge University Press.

Nötel, R. (1984), "Money, Banking and Industry in Interwar Austria and Hungary", *Journal of European Economic History,* 13 (no. 2, special issue), pp. 137–202.

Okun, A. M. (1970), *The Political Economy of Prosperity,* Washington, DC: Brookings Institution.

Oliva, J. C. M., and M. L. Stefani (2000), "Dal Piano Marshall all'Unione europea dei Pagamenti: alle origini dell'integrazione economica europea", in F. Cotula (ed.),

Stabilità e Sviluppo negli anni Cinquanta, Vol. 1, *L'Italia nel contesto internazionale,* Rome: Laterza, pp. 111–399.

Olson, M. (1982), *The Rise and Decline of Nations,* New Haven, CT: Yale University Press.

O'Rourke, K., and J. Williamson (1999), *Globalization and History,* Cambridge, MA: MIT Press.

Padoa-Schioppa, T. (2000), *The Road to Monetary Union in Europe: The Emperor, the Kings and the Genies,* Oxford University Press.

Parker Willis, H. (1929), "The United States and the New International Bank", *The Banker,* 11(43), pp. 193–202.

Péteri, G. (1992), "Central Bank Diplomacy: Montagu Norman and Central Europe's Monetary Reconstruction after World War I", *Contemporary European History,* 1(3), pp. 233–58.

Picker, H. (1963), *Hitlers Tischgespräche im Führerhauptquartier 1941–1942,* Stuttgart: Seewald Verlag.

Pimlott, B. (ed.) (1986), *The Political Diary of Hugh Dalton 1918–40 and 1945–60,* London: Jonathan Cape.

Pluym, W. (2002), *Vijfentwintig jaar rond de monetaire onderhandelingstafel: de rol van de Bank in de Europese monetaire samenwerking en integratie,* Brussels: Nationale Bank van België, mimeo.

Prochnow, H. V. (ed.) (1970), *The Eurodollar,* Chicago: Rand McNally.

Puchinger, G. (ed.) (1978), *Dr. Jelle Zijlstra: Gesprekken en Geschriften,* Amsterdam: Strengholt.

Ranieri, L. (1985), *Emile Francqui: ou, l'intelligence créatrice 1863–1935,* Paris: Editions Duculot.

Reis, J. (ed.) (1995), *International Monetary Systems in Historical Perspective,* Basingstoke: Macmillan.

Reisch, R. (1930), "Die völkerrechtliche Bedeutung der Bank für Internationalen Zahlungsausgleich", *Mitteilungen des Verbandes österreichischer Banken und Bankiers,* 1-2 (31 March 1930), p. 8.

Renouvin, P. (1958), *Histoire des relations internationales,* T. VIII, *Les crises du XXe siècle,* Pt. II, *De 1929 à 1945,* Paris: Hachette.

Rings, W. (1985), *Raubgold aus Deutschland: Die Golddrehscheibe Schweiz im Zweiten Weltkrieg,* Zürich: Artemis.

Ritschl, A. (2002), "Deutschlands Krise und Konjunktur 1924–1934: Binnenkonjunktur, Auslandsverschuldung und Reparationsproblem zwischen Dawes-Plan und Transfersperre", Beiheft 2, *Jahrbuch für Wirtschaftsgeschichte,* Berlin: Akademie Verlag.

Roches, C. (1938), "Règlements des soldes en francs-or par l'intermédiaire de la Banque des Règlements Internationaux à Bâle", *Journal des Télécommunications,* 12 (December).

Roselli, A. (2001), "Il Governatore Vincenzo Azzolini 1931–1944", *Collana Storica della Banca d'Italia,* vol. II, Roma-Bari: Laterza.

Rosengarten, M. (2001), *Die internationale Handelskammer: wirtschaftspolitische Empfehlungen in der Zeit der Weltwirtschaftskrise 1929–1939,* Berlin: Duncker & Humblot.

Rueff, J. (1963), *L'âge de l'inflation,* Paris: Payot.

Rueff, J. (1977), *De l'aube au crépuscule: Autobiographie,* Paris: Librairie Plon.

Safire, W. (1975), *Before the Fall,* New York: Doubleday.

Salin, E. (1931), "Die Bank für Internationalen Zahlungsausgleich", *Weltwirtschaftliches Archiv,* 33(1), pp. 1–29.

Saunders, A. (1987), "The Interbank Market, Contagion Effects and International Financial Crises", in R. Portes and A. K. Swoboda (eds.), *Threats to International Financial Stability,* Cambridge University Press, pp. 196–232.

Sayers, R. S. (1976a), *The Bank of England 1891–1944,* Vols. I and II, Cambridge University Press.

Sayers, R. S. (1976b), *The Bank of England 1891–1944,* Appendices, Cambridge University Press.

Schacht, H. (1929a), *Memorandum zum Young Plan,* Berlin: Druckerei der Reichsbank.

Schacht, H. (1929b), *The Paris Conference of the Experts: Address Delivered at a Meeting of the Deutsche Industrie- und Handelstag, Munich June 28, 1929,* Berlin: Druckerei Reichsbank.

Schacht, H. (1931a), "Die deutsche Wirtschaft unter dem Youngplan", *Deutsche Rundschau,* 57, pp. 177–81.

Schacht, H. (1931b), *Das Ende der Reparationen,* Oldenburg: Gerhard Stalling.

Schacht, H. (1953), *76 Jahre meines Lebens,* Bad Wörishofen: Kindler & Schiermeyer Verlag.

Schenk, C. R. (1994), *Britain and the Sterling Area: From Devaluation to Convertibility in the 1950s,* London: Routledge.

Schenk, C. R. (1998), "The Origins of the Eurodollar Market in London, 1955–1963", *Explorations in Economic History,* 35(2), pp. 221–38.

Schenk, C. (2002a), "Sterling, International Monetary Reform and Britain's Application to Join the European Economic Community in the 1960s", *Contemporary European History,* 11(3), pp. 345–69.

Schenk, C. (2002b), "International Financial Centres, 1958–71: Competitiveness and Complementarity", in Battilossi and Cassis (2002), pp. 74–102.

Schleidt, A. (1931), *Die Kooperation der Notenbanken,* Basel: Helbing & Lichtenhahn.

Schloss, H. (1970), "The Bank for International Settlements", *The Bulletin,* 65-66 (September), New York University Institute of Finance, 53 pp.

Schubert, A. (1991), *The Credit-Anstalt Crisis of 1931,* Cambridge University Press.

Schuker, S. A. (1988), *American "Reparations" to Germany, 1919–33* (Princeton Studies in International Finance, no. 61), Princeton, NJ: Princeton University Press.

Scitovszky, T. (1931), "The Economic Reconstruction of Hungary as a Result of Premier Count Stephen Bethlen's Economic Policy", in Hungarian General Creditbank, *Economic Report,* May.

Simmons, B. (1993), "Why Innovate? Founding the Bank for International Settlements", *World Politics,* 45(3), pp. 361–405.

Skidelsky, R. (2000), *John Maynard Keynes,* Vol. III, *Fighting for Britain: 1937–1946,* London: Macmillan.

Slany, W. Z. (ed.), and S. E. Eizenstat (coord.) (1997), *U.S. and Allied Efforts to Recover and Restore Gold and Other Assets Stolen or Hidden by Germany during World War II: Preliminary Study,* Washington, DC: U.S. State Department.

Slany W. Z., and S. E. Eizenstat (1998), *U.S. and Allied Wartime and Postwar Relations and Negotiations with Argentina, Portugal, Spain, Sweden and Turkey on Looted Gold and German External Assets and U.S. Concerns about the Fate of the Wartime Ustasha Treasury,* Washington, DC: U.S. State Department.

Smith, A. L., Jr. (1989), *Hitler's Gold: The Story of the Nazi War Loot*, Oxford, U.K.: Berg.

Smith, J., Jr. (1929), "The Bank for International Settlements", *Quarterly Journal of Economics*, 43(4), pp. 713–25.

Solomon, R. (1982), *The International Monetary System, 1945–1981*, New York: Harper & Row.

Sorrentino, M. (1999), "The Italian Lira in the Inter-War Gold Standard: Was the December 1927 Parity Credible?", Temi di Ricerca, 13 November 1999, Rome: Ente per gli Studi Monetari Bancari e Finanziari L. Einaudi.

Spierenburg, D., and R. Poidevin (1994), *The History of the High Authority of the European Coal and Steel Community: Supranationality in Operation*, London: Weidenfeld & Nicolson.

Statistisches Reichsamt (1936), "Gold und Devisen in der Weltwirtschaft in den Jahren 1928 bis 1934", *Einzelschriften zur Statistik des Deutschen Reichs*, 33, pp. 21–3.

Stiefel, D. (1983), "The Reconstruction of the Credit-Anstalt", in A. Teichova and P. L. Cottrell (eds.), *International Business and Central Europe, 1918–1939*, Leicester University Press, pp. 415–30.

Stopford, R. J. (1931), "The History of German Reparations: The Hague Conferences and the Bank for International Settlements", in A. J. Toynbee (ed.), *Survey of International Affairs 1930*, Oxford University Press, pp. 495–528.

Stopford, R. J., and J. Menken (1930), "The History of German Reparations from the Dawes Plan to the Young Report", in A. J. Toynbee (ed.), *Survey of International Affairs 1929*, Oxford University Press, pp. 111–66.

Strohl, J. H. (1939), *L'Oeuvre Monétaire de la Conférence de Londres (1933) et ses Conséquences*, Paris: Librairie Générale de Droit.

Sylla, R. (2002), "United States Banks and Europe: Strategy and Attitudes", in Battilossi and Cassis (2002), pp. 53–73.

Szász, A. (1999), *The Road to European Monetary Union*, Basingstoke: Macmillan.

Tabellini, G. (1990), "Domestic Politics and the International Coordination of Fiscal Policies", *Journal of International Economics*, 28, pp. 245–65.

Toniolo, G. (1980), *L'Economia dell'Italia Fascista*, Roma-Bari: Laterza.

Toniolo, G. (ed.) (1988), *Central Banks' Independence in Historical Perspective*, Berlin and New York: de Gruyter.

Toniolo, G. (1989), *La Banca d'Italia e l'economia di guerra, 1914–1919*, Roma-Bari: Laterza.

Toniolo, G. (1994), "The Rise and Fall of the German-Type Bank in Italy, 1894–1934", in P. Klep and E. Van Cauwenberghe (eds.), *Entrepreneurship and the Transformation of the Economy (10th to 20th Centuries): Essays in Honour of Herman Van der Wee*, Leuven University Press, pp. 433–44.

Toniolo, G. (1998), "Europe's Golden Age, 1950–73: Speculations from a Long-run Perspective", *Economic History Review*, 51(2), pp. 252–67.

Toynbee, A. (1932), "Introduction", in *Survey of International Affairs 1931*, London: Oxford University Press.

Trepp, G. (1993), *Bankgeschäfte mit dem Feind: Die Bank für Internationalen Zahlungsausgleich im Zweiten Weltkrieg: Von Hitlers Europabank zum Instrument des Marshallplans*, Zürich: Rotpunktverlag.

Triffin, R. (1957), *Europe and the Money Muddle*, New Haven, CT: Yale University Press.

Triffin, R. (1960), *Gold and the Dollar Crisis*, New Haven, CT: Yale University Press.

Truffaut, F. C. (1997), *Sauver l'or belge*, Tubize: Gamma Press.

Unabhängige Expertenkommission Schweiz – Zweiter Weltkrieg (2002), "Die Schweiz und die Goldtransaktionen im Zweiten Weltkrieg: überarbeitete und ergänzte Fassung des Zwischenberichts von 1998", in *Veröffentlichungen der Unabhängigen Expertenkommission Schweiz – Zweiter Weltkrieg*, vol. 16, Zurich: Chronos Verlag.

U.S. State Department (1948), *Proceedings and Documents of United Nations Monetary and Financial Conference, Bretton Woods, NH, July 1–22, 1944*, Washington, DC: Department of State.

Van Buren Cleveland, H. (1971), "How the Dollar Standard Died", *Foreign Policy*, 5(2), p. 42.

Van de Burgt, Th. G. J. M. (1997), *De "Bank for International Settlements" te Bazel 1930–1948: een historische synthese en analyse van bijzondere onderwerpen*, Doctoral thesis, University of Amsterdam.

Van der Beugel, E. H. (1966), *From Marshall Aid to Atlantic Partnership*, Amsterdam: North-Holland.

Van der Wee, H. (1986), *Prosperity and Upheaval: The World Economy 1945–1980*, New York: Viking.

Van der Wee, H., and K. Tavernier (1975), *La Banque Nationale de Belgique et l'histoire monétaire entre les deux guerres mondiales*, Bruxelles: Banque Nationale de Belgique.

Van Dormael, A. (1978), *Bretton Woods: Birth of a Monetary System*, London: Macmillan.

Vanthoor, W. F. V. (1999), *A Chronological History of the European Union 1946–1998*, Cheltenham: Edward Elgar.

Vissering, G. (1920), *International Economic and Financial Problems*, London: Macmillan.

Vocke, W. (1973), *Memoiren*, Stuttgart: Deutsche Verlags-Anstalt.

Von Hagen, J. (1999), "A New Approach to Monetary Policy (1971–8)", in Deutsche Bundesbank (1999), pp. 403–38.

Walters, F. P. (1952), *A History of the League of Nations*, vol. 1, London: Oxford University Press.

Wandel, E. (1971), *Die Bedeutung der Vereinigten Staaten von Amerika für das deutsche Reparationsproblem 1924–1929*, Tübingen: Mohr.

Weill-Raynal, E. (1947), *Les réparations allemandes et la France. 3. L'application du plan Dawes, le plan Young et la liquidation des réparations*, Paris: Nouvelles Editions Latines.

Weinberg, G. L. (1994), *A World at Arms: A Global History of World War II*, Cambridge University Press.

Wellink, A. H. E. M. (1997), "De Europese economische en monetaire samenwerking: van Rome naar Amsterdam via Den Haag en Maastricht", *Kwartaalbericht van de Nederlandsche Bank*, June, pp. 27–8.

Werner, P. (1977), *L'Europe monétaire reconsidérée*, Lausanne: Centre de Recherches Européennes.

Wheeler-Bennett, J. W., and H. Latimer (1930), *Information on the Reparation Settlement Being the Background and History of the Young Plan and the Hague Agreements 1929–1930*, London: Allen & Unwin.

Wolf, J. (1913), *Das internationale Zahlungswesen* (Veröffentlichungen des Mitteleuropäischen Wirtschaftsvereins in Deutschland, Heft XIV), Leipzig: A. Deichert'sche Verlagsbuchhandlung.

Yago, K. (2001), "Japanese Participation in the BIS: A note", mimeo, Faculty of Economics, Tokyo Metropolitan University.

Yago, K. (2002), "La BRI et les banques centrales au XXème siècle", Research Paper Series no. 29, Faculty of Economics, Tokyo Metropolitan University.

Zimmerman, H. (2000), "Western Europe and the American Challenge: Conflict and Cooperation in Technology and Monetary Policy, 1965–1973", *Journal of European Integration History,* 6, pp. 86–7.

Zimmerman, H. (2002), *Money and Security, Troops, Monetary Policy and West Germany's Relations with the United States and Britain, 1950–1971,* Cambridge University Press.

ANNEX A

BIS Statutes 1930

Chapter I
Name, Seat and Objects

Article 1. There is constituted under the name of the Bank for International Settlements (hereinafter referred to as the Bank) a Company limited by shares.

Art. 2. The registered office of the Bank shall be situated at Basle, Switzerland.

Art. 3. The objects of the Bank are: – to promote the co-operation of central banks and to provide additional facilities for international financial operations; and to act as trustee or agent in regard to international financial settlements entrusted to it under agreements with the parties concerned.

Art. 4. As long as the New Plan as defined in The Hague Agreement of January, 1930 (hereinafter referred to as the Plan) is in force, the Bank: –

(i) shall carry out the functions assigned to it in the Plan;
(ii) shall conduct its affairs with a view to facilitating the execution of the Plan; and
(iii) shall observe the provisions of the Plan in the administration and operations of the Bank;

all within the limits of the powers granted by these Statutes.

During the said period the Bank, as trustee or agent for the Governments concerned, shall receive, administer and distribute the annuities paid by Germany under the Plan; shall supervise and assist in the commercialization and mobilization of certain portions of the aforesaid annuities; and shall perform such services in connection with the payment of German Reparations and the international settlements connected therewith as may be agreed upon by the Bank with the Governments concerned.

Chapter II
Capital

Art. 5. The authorised capital of the Bank shall be 500,000,000 Swiss gold francs, equivalent to 145,161,290.32 gr. fine gold. It shall be divided into 200,000 shares of equal gold nominal value.

The nominal value of each share shall also be expressed on the face of each share in terms both of Swiss francs and of the currency of the country in which it is issued, converted at the gold mint parity.

Art. 6. The subscription of the total authorised capital having been guaranteed in equal parts by the Banque Nationale de Belgique, the Bank of England, the Banque de France, the Reichsbank, the Banca d'Italia, a banking group represented by the Industrial Bank of Japan acting in place of the Bank of Japan, and Messrs. J.P. Morgan & Company of New York, the First National Bank of New York, New York, and the First National Bank of Chicago, Chicago, the Bank may begin business as soon as a minimum of 112,000 shares has been subscribed.

Art. 7. (1) During the two years following incorporation the Board of Directors of the Bank (hereinafter referred to as the Board) shall arrange for the subscription of any unissued portion of the authorised capital.

(2) This unissued portion may be offered to the central banks or other banks of countries which have not participated in the original subscription. The selection of countries in which such shares shall be offered for subscription and the amount to be subscribed in each shall be determined by the Board by a two-thirds majority, provided that offers of shares shall only be made in countries interested in Reparations or in countries whose currencies, in the opinion of the Board, satisfy the practical requirements of the gold or gold exchange standard and that the amount issued in any one of these countries shall not exceed 8,000 shares.

(3) The seven Banking Institutions mentioned in Article 6 shall, in accordance with their several guarantees, subscribe or arrange for the subscription in equal proportions of any part of the authorised capital which at the end of two years remains unsubscribed.

Art. 8. (1) Twenty-five per cent. only of the value of each share shall be paid up at the time of subscription. The balance may be called up at a later date or dates at the discretion of the Board. Three months' notice shall be given of any such calls.

(2) If a shareholder fails to pay any call on a share on the day appointed for payment thereof the Board may, after giving reasonable notice to such shareholder, forfeit the share in respect of which the call remains unpaid. A forfeited share may be sold on such terms and in such manner as the Board may think fit, and the Board may execute a transfer in favour of the person or corporation to whom the share is sold. The proceeds of sale may be received by the Bank, which will pay to the defaulting shareholder any part of the net proceeds over and above the amount of the call due and unpaid.

Art. 9. (1) The capital of the Bank may be increased or reduced on the proposal of the Board acting by a two-thirds majority and adopted by a two-thirds majority of the General Meeting.

(2) In the event of an increase in the authorised capital of the Bank and of a further issue of shares, the distribution among countries shall be decided by a two-thirds majority of the Board. The central banks of Belgium, England, France, Germany, Italy Japan, and the U.S.A., or some other financial institution of the last-named country acceptable to the foregoing central banks, shall be entitled to subscribe or arrange for the subscription in equal proportions of at least 55 per cent. of such additional shares.

(3) No part of the amount not taken by the banks of these seven countries shall be subscribed in any other country unless it is interested in Reparations or at the time of issue its currency, in the opinion of the Board, satisfies the practical requirements of the gold or gold exchange standard.

Art. 10. In extending invitations to subscribe for capital in accordance with Article 7, paragraph 2, or with Article 9, consideration shall be given by the Board to the desirability of associating with the Bank the largest possible number of central banks.

Art. 11. No shares shall be issued below par.

Art. 12. The liability of shareholders is limited to the nominal value of their shares.

Art. 13. The shares shall be registered and transferable in the books of the Bank.
The Bank shall be entitled without assigning any reason to decline to accept any person or corporation as the transferee of a share. It shall not transfer shares without the prior consent of the central bank, or the institution acting in lieu of a central bank, by or through whom the shares in question were issued.

Art. 14. The shares shall carry equal rights to participate in the profits of the Bank and in any distribution of assets under Articles 53, 54 and 55 of the Statutes.

Art. 15. The ownership of shares of the Bank carries no right of voting or representation at the General Meeting. The right of representation and of voting, in proportion to the number of shares subscribed in each country, may be exercised by the central bank of that country or by its nominee. Should the central bank of any country not desire to exercise these rights, they may be exercised by a financial institution of widely recognised standing and of the same nationality, appointed by the Board, and not objected to by the central bank of the country in question. In cases where there is no central bank, these rights may be exercised, if the Board thinks fit, by an appropriate financial institution of the country in question appointed by the Board.

Art. 16. Any subscribing institution or banking group may issue, or cause to be issued to the public the shares for which it has subscribed.

Art. 17. Any subscribing institution or banking group may issue to the public certificates against shares of the Bank owned by it. The form, details and terms issue of such certificates shall be determined by the Bank issuing them, in agreement with the Board.

Art. 18. The receipt or ownership of shares of the Bank or of certificates issued in accordance with Article 17 implies acceptance of the Statutes of the Bank and a statement to that effect shall be embodied in the text of such shares and certificates.

Art. 19. The registration of the name of a holder of shares in the books of the Bank establishes the title to ownership of the shares so registered.

Chapter III
Powers of the Bank

Art. 20. The operations of the Bank shall be in conformity with the monetary policy of the central banks of the countries concerned.
Before any financial operation is carried out by or on behalf of the Bank on a given market or in a given currency, the Board shall afford to the central bank or central banks directly concerned an opportunity to dissent. In the event of disapproval being expressed within such reasonable time as the Board shall specify, the proposed operation shall not take place. A central bank may make its concurrence subject to conditions and may limit its assent to a specific operation, or enter into a general arrangement permitting the Bank to carry on its operations within such limits as to time, character and amount as may be specified. This Article shall not be read as requiring the assent of any central

bank to the withdrawal from its market of funds to the introduction of which no objection had been raised by it, in the absence of stipulations to the contrary by the central bank concerned at the time the original operation was carried out.

Any Governor of a central bank, or his alternate or any other Director specially authorised by the central bank of the country of which he is a national to act on its behalf in this matter, shall, if he is present at the meeting of the Board and does not vote against any such proposed operation, be deemed to have given the valid assent of the central bank in question.

If the representative of the central bank in question is absent or if a central bank is not directly represented on the Board, steps shall be taken to afford the central bank or banks concerned an opportunity to express dissent.

Art. 21. The operations of the Bank for its own account shall only be carried out in currencies which in the opinion of the Board satisfy the practical requirements of the gold or gold exchange standard.

Art. 22. The Board shall determine the nature of the operations to be undertaken by the Bank.

The Bank may in particular:

(a) buy and sell gold coin or bullion for its own account or for the account of central banks;

(b) hold gold for its own account under earmark in central banks;

(c) accept the custody of gold for account of central banks;

(d) make advances to or borrow from central banks against gold, bills of exchange and other short-term obligations of prime liquidity or other approved securities;

(e) discount, rediscount, purchase or sell with or without its endorsement bills of exchange, cheques and other short-term obligations of prime liquidity, including Treasury bills and other such government short-term securities as are currently marketable;

(f) buy and sell exchange for its own account or for the account of central banks;

(g) buy and sell negotiable securities other than shares for its own account or for the account of central banks;

(h) discount for central banks bills taken from their portfolio and rediscount with central banks bills taken from its own portfolio;

(i) open and maintain current or deposit accounts with central banks;

(j) accept:

(i) deposits from central banks on current or deposit account;

(ii) deposits in connection with trustee agreements that may be made between the Bank and Governments in connection with international settlements;

(iii) such other deposits as in the opinion of the Board come within the scope of the Bank's functions.

The Bank may also:

(k) act as agent or correspondent of any central bank;

(l) arrange with any central bank for the latter to act as its agent or correspondent. If a central bank is unable or unwilling to act in this capacity, the Bank may make other arrangements, provided that the central bank concerned does not object. If, in such circumstances, it should be deemed advisable that the Bank should establish its own agency, the sanction of a two-thirds majority of the Board will be required;

(m) enter into agreements to act as trustee or agent in connection with international settlements, provided that such agreements shall not encroach on the obligations of the Bank towards third parties; and carry out the various operations laid down therein.

Art. 23. Any of the operations which the Bank is authorised to carry out with central banks under the preceding Article may be carried out with banks, bankers, corporations or individuals of any country provided that the central bank of that country does not object.

Art. 24. The Bank may enter into special agreements with central banks to facilitate the settlement of international transactions between them.

For this purpose it may arrange with central banks to have gold earmarked for their account and transferable on their order, to open accounts through which central banks can transfer their assets from one currency to another and to take such other measures as the Board may think advisable within the limits of the powers granted by these Statutes. The principles and rules governing such accounts shall be fixed by the Board.

Art. 25. The Bank may not:

(a) issue notes payable at sight to bearer;
(b) "accept" bills of exchange;
(c) make advances to Governments;
(d) open current accounts in the name of Governments;
(e) acquire a predominant interest in any business concern;
(f) except so far as is necessary for the conduct of its own business, remain the owner of real property for any longer period than is required in order to realise proper advantage such real property as may come into the possession of the Bank in satisfaction of claims due to it.

Art. 26. The Bank shall be administered with particular regard to maintaining its liquidity, and for this purpose shall retain assets appropriate to the maturity and character of its liabilities. Its short-term liquid assets may include bank-notes, cheques payable on sight drawn on first-class banks, claims in course of collection, deposits at sight or at short notice in first-class banks, and prime bills of exchange of not more than ninety days' usance, of a kind usually accepted for rediscount by central banks.

The proportion of the Bank's assets held in any given currency shall be determined by the Board with due regard to the liabilities of the Bank.

Chapter IV
Management

Art. 27. The administration of the Bank shall be vested in the Board.

Art. 28. The Board shall be composed as follows:

(1) The Governors for the time being of the central banks of Belgium, France, Germany, Great Britain, Italy, Japan and the United States of America (hereinafter referred to as *ex-officio* Directors), or if any of the said Governors are unwilling or unable to hold office, their respective nominees (hereinafter referred to as substitute nominees).

The tenure of office of a substitute nominee shall be within the discretion of the Governor by whom he is appointed, but shall terminate in any case when that Governor vacates office.

Any *ex-officio* Director may appoint one person as his alternate who shall be entitled to attend and exercise the powers of a Director at meetings of the Board if the Governor himself is unable to be present.

(2) Seven persons representative of finance, industry or commerce, appointed one each by the Governors of the central banks mentioned in sub-clause (1), and being of the same nationality as the Governor who appoints him.

During the continuance of the liability of Germany to pay Reparation annuities, two persons of French and German nationality respectively, representative of industry or commerce, appointed by the Governors of the Bank of France and of the Reichsbank respectively, if they so desire.

If for any reason the Governor of any of the seven institutions above mentioned is unable or unwilling to serve as Director, or to appoint a substitute nominee under sub-clause (1), or to make an appointment under sub-clause (2), the Governors of the other institutions referred to or a majority of them may invite to become members of the Board two nationals of the country of the Governor in question, not objected to by the central bank of that country.

Directors appointed as aforesaid, other than *ex-officio* Directors or their substitute nominees shall hold office for three years but shall be eligible for reappointment.

(3) Not more than nine persons to be elected by the following procedure: –

The Governor of the central bank of every country, other than those mentioned in sub-clause (1), in which capital has been subscribed at the time of incorporation shall be entitled to submit a list of four candidates of his own nationality for directorship, which may include his own name. Two of the candidates on each list shall be representative of finance, and the other two of industry or commerce. From these lists the Board may elect, by a two-thirds majority, not more than nine persons.

The Directors so elected shall be divided by lot into three groups, as nearly as may be equal in number, of which one group shall retire at the end of the first, one at the end of the second, and one at the end of the third financial year of the bank. The retiring Directors shall be eligible for re-election.

At the first meeting of Directors in the second and succeeding financial years the Board may elect by a two-thirds majority not more than three Directors from a panel of candidates composed of lists of persons with similar qualifications to those specified in connection with the first election. the Governors of the central banks of every country, other than those mentioned in sub-clause (1), in which capital has at the date of such meeting been subscribed shall be entitled to submit a list of four persons to be included in the panel. Directors so elected shall hold office for three years, but shall be eligible for re-election.

If in any of the countries referred to in the preceding paragraph there is no central bank, the Board by a two-thirds majority may nominate an appropriate financial institution to exercise the right of submitting a list of candidates for election.

Art. 29. In the event of a vacancy occurring on the Board for any reason other than the termination of a period of office in accordance with the preceding Article, the vacancy shall be filled in accordance with the procedure by which the member to be replaced was selected. In the case of Directors other than *ex-officio* Directors, the new Director shall hold office for the unexpired period only of his predecessor's term of office. He shall, however, be eligible for re-election at the expiration of that term.

Art. 30. Directors must be ordinarily resident in Europe or in a position to attend regularly at meetings of the Board.

Art. 31. No person shall be appointed or hold office as a Director who is a member or an official of a Government, or is a member of a legislative body, unless he is the Governor of a central bank.

Art. 32. Meetings of the Board shall be held not less than ten times a year. At least four of these shall be held at the registered office of the Bank.

Art. 33. A member of the Board who is not present in person at a meeting of Directors may give a proxy to any other member authorising him to vote at that meeting on his behalf.

Art. 34. Unless otherwise provided by the Statutes, decisions of the Board shall be taken by a simple majority of those present or represented by proxy. In the case of an equality of votes, the Chairman shall have a second or casting vote.

The Board shall not be competent to act unless a quorum of Directors is present. This quorum shall be laid down in a regulation adopted by a two-thirds majority of the Board.

Art. 35. The members of the Board may receive, in addition to out-of-pocket expenses, a fee for attendance at meetings and/or a remuneration, the amounts of which will be fixed by the Board, subject to the approval of the General Meeting.

Art. 36. The proceedings of the Board shall be summarised in minutes which shall be signed by the Chairman.

Copies of or extracts from these minutes for the purpose of production in a court of justice must be certified by the General Manager of the Bank.

A record of decisions taken at each meeting shall be sent within eight days of the meeting to every member.

Art. 37. The Board shall represent the Bank in its dealings with third parties and shall have the exclusive right of entering into engagements on behalf of the Bank. It may, however, delegate this right to a member or members of the Board, or of the permanent staff of the Bank, provided that it defines the powers of each person to whom it delegates this right.

Art. 38. The Bank shall be legally committed *vis-à-vis* third parties by the signature of the President or by the signatures either of members of the Board or of members of the staff who have been duly authorised by the Board to sign on its behalf.

Art. 39. The Board shall elect from among its members a Chairman and one or more Vice-Chairmen, one of whom shall preside at meetings of the Board in the absence of the Chairman.

The Chairman of the Board shall be President of the Bank. He shall hold office for three years and shall be eligible for re-election.

Subject to the authority of the Board, the President will carry out the policy and control the administration of the Bank.

He shall not hold any other office which, in the judgement of the Board, might interfere with his duties as President.

Art. 40. At the meeting of the Board at which the election of a Chairman is to take place, the Chair shall be taken by the oldest member of the Board present.

Art. 41. A General Manager shall be appointed by the Board on the proposal of the Chairman of the Board. He will be responsible to the President of the Bank for the operations of the Bank and will be the chief of its operating staff.

The Heads of Departments, and any other officers of similar rank, shall be appointed by the Board on recommendations made by the President after consultation with the General Manager.

The remainder of the staff shall be appointed by the General Manager with the approval of the President.

Art. 42. The departmental organisation of the Bank shall be determined by the Board.

Art. 43. The Board may, if it thinks fit, appoint from among its members an Executive Committee to assist the President in the administration of the Bank.

The President shall be a member and *ex-officio* Chairman of this Committee.

Art. 44. The Board may appoint Advisory Committees chosen wholly or partly from persons not concerned in the Bank's management.

Art. 45. As long as the Plan is in force, the Board shall convene the Special Advisory Committee referred to in the Plan, upon receipt of the notice therein provided for.

Chapter V
General Meeting

Art. 46. General Meetings of the Bank may be attended by nominees of the central banks or other financial institutions referred to in Article 15.

Voting rights shall be in proportion to the number of shares subscribed in the country of each institution represented at the meeting.

The Chair shall be taken at General Meetings by the Chairman of the Board or in his absence by a Vice-Chairman.

At least three weeks' notice of General Meetings shall be given to those entitled to be represented.

Subject to the provisions of these Statutes, the General Meeting shall decide upon its own procedure.

Art. 47. Within three months after the end of each financial year of the Bank, an Annual General Meeting shall be held upon such date as the Board may decide.

The meeting shall take place at the registered office of the Bank.

Voting by proxy will be permitted in such manner as the Board may have provided in advance by regulation.

Art. 48. The Annual General Meeting shall be invited:

  (a) to approve the Annual Report, the Balance Sheet upon the Report of the Auditors, and the Profit and Loss Account, and any proposed changes in the remuneration, fees or allowances of the members of the Board;

(b) to make appropriations to reserve and to special funds, and to consider the declaration of a dividend and its amount;

(c) to elect the Auditors for the ensuing year and to fix their remuneration; and

(d) to discharge the Board from all personal responsibility in respect of the past financial year.

Art. 49. Extraordinary General Meetings shall be summoned to decide upon any proposals of the Board:

(a) to amend the Statutes;

(b) to increase or decrease the capital of the Bank;

(c) to liquidate the Bank.

Chapter VI
Accounts and Profits

Art. 50. The financial year of the Bank will begin on 1st April and end on 31st March. The first financial period will end on 31st March, 1931.

Art. 51. The Bank shall publish an Annual Report, and at least once a month a Statement of Account in such form as the Board may prescribe.

The Board shall cause to be prepared a Profit and Loss Account and Balance Sheet of the Bank for each financial year in time for submission to the Annual General Meeting.

Art. 52. The Accounts and Balance Sheet shall be audited by independent auditors. The Auditors shall have full power to examine all books and accounts of the Bank and to require full information as to all its transactions. The Auditors shall report to the Board and to the General Meeting and shall state in their Report: –

(a) whether or not they have obtained all the information and explanations they have required; and

(b) whether, in their opinion, the Balance Sheet dealt with in the Report are properly drawn up so as to exhibit a true and fair view of the state of the Bank's affairs according to the best of their information and the explanations given to them, and as shown by the books of the Bank.

Art. 53. The yearly net profits of the Bank shall be applied as follows: –

(a) Five per cent. of such net profits, or such proportion of five per cent. as may be required for the purpose, shall be paid to a reserve fund called the Legal Reserve Fund until that Fund reaches an amount equal in value to ten per cent. of the amount of the paid-up capital of the Bank for the time being;

(b) thereafter such net profits shall be applied in or towards payment of the dividend of six per cent. per annum on the amount of the paid-up capital of the Bank. This dividend shall be cumulative;

(c) as to the residue (if any) of such net profits twenty per cent. shall be paid to the shareholders until a maximum further dividend of six per cent. (which shall be noncumulative) is reached, provided that the Board may in any year withhold all or any part of this additional payment and place it to the credit of a special dividend reserve fund for use in maintaining the cumulative six per cent. dividend provided for in the preceding paragraph or for subsequent distribution to the shareholders;

(d) After making provision for the foregoing, one-half of the yearly net profits then remaining shall be paid into the General Reserve Fund of the Bank until it equals the paid-up capital. Thereafter forty per cent. shall be so applied until the General Reserve Fund equals twice the paid-up capital; thirty per cent. until it equals three times the paid-up capital; twenty per cent. until it equals four times the paid-up capital; ten per cent. until it equals five times the paid-up capital; and from that point onward, five per cent.

In case the General Reserve Fund, by reason of losses or by reason of an increase in the paid-up capital, falls below the amounts provided for above after having once attained them, the appropriate proportion of the yearly net profits shall again be applied until the position is restored.

(e) as long as the plan is in force any remainder of the net profits after meeting the foregoing requirements shall be disposed of as follows: –

(i) as to seventy-five per cent. to such of the Governments or central banks of Germany and the countries entitled to share in the annuities payable under the Plan as have maintained time deposits at the Bank subject to withdrawal in not less than five years from the time of the deposit or after four years on not less than one year's notice. This sum shall be distributed annually in proportion to the size of the deposits maintained by the respective Governments or central banks in question. The Board shall have the power to determine the minimum deposit which would justify the distribution provided for;

(ii) as to twenty-five per cent. as follows: –

If the German Government elects to make a long-term deposit with the Bank withdrawable only on the terms specified under sub-clause (i) above and amounting to the minimum sum of 400,000,000 reichsmarks, the said twenty-five per cent. shall go into a Special Fund, to be used to aid Germany in paying the last twenty-two annuities provided for in the Plan.

If the German Government elects to make such long-term deposit amounting to a sum below 400,000,000 reichsmarks, the participation of the German Government shall be reduced in proportion and the balance shall be added to the seventy-five per cent. referred to in sub-clause (i) above.

If the German Government elects not to make any such long-term deposit, the said twenty-five per cent. shall be distributed as provided in sub-clause (i) above.

The Special Fund referred to above shall carry compound interest, reckoned on an annual basis, at the maximum current rate paid by the Bank on time deposits.

If the Special Fund should exceed the amount required to pay the last twenty-two annuities, the balance shall be distributed among the creditor Governments as provided for in the Plan;

(f) at the expiration of the period referred to in the first paragraph of sub-clause (e) the disposal of the remainder of the net profits referred to in sub-clause (e) shall be determined by the General Meeting on the proposal of the Board.

Art. 54. Reserve Funds. The General Reserve Fund shall be available for meeting any losses incurred by the Bank. In case it is not adequate for this purpose, recourse may be had to the Legal Reserve Fund provided for in Article 53 (a).

These reserve funds, in the event of liquidation, and after the discharge of the liabilities of the Bank and the costs of liquidation, shall be divided among the shareholders.

Chapter VII
General Provisions

Art. 55. (1) The Bank may not be liquidated except by a three-fourths majority of the General Meeting. It shall not in any case be liquidated before it has discharged all the obligations which it has assumed under the plan.

Art. 56. (1) If any dispute shall arise between the Bank, on the one side, and any central bank, financial institution, or other bank referred to in the present Statutes, on the other side, or between the Bank and its shareholders with regard to the interpretation or application of the Statutes of the Bank, the same shall be referred for final decision to the Tribunal provided for by the Hague Agreement of January, 1930.

(2) In the absence of agreement as to the terms of submission either party to a dispute under this Article may refer the same to the Tribunal, which shall have power to decide all questions (including the question of its own jurisdiction) even in default of appearance by the other party.

(3) Before giving a final decision and without prejudice to the questions at issue, the President of the Tribunal, or, if he is unable to act in any case, a member of the Tribunal to be designated by him forthwith, may, on the request of the first party applying therefor, order any appropriate provisional measures in order to safeguard the respective rights of the parties.

(4) The provisions of this Article shall not prejudice the right of the parties to a dispute to refer the same by common consent to the President or a member of the Tribunal as sole arbitrator.

Art. 57. In all cases not covered by the preceding Article or by some other provision for arbitration the Bank may proceed or be proceeded against in any court of competent jurisdiction.

Art. 58. For the purposes of these Statutes: –

(1) Central bank means the bank in any country to which has been entrusted the duty of regulating the volume of currency and credit in that country; or, where a banking system has been so entrusted, the bank forming part of such system which is situated and operating in the principal financial market of that country.

(2) The Governor of a central bank means the person who, subject to the control of his Board or other competent authority, has the direction of the policy and administration of the bank.

(3) A two-thirds majority of the Board means not less than two-thirds of the votes (whether given in person or by proxy) of the whole directorate.

Art. 59. Amendments of any Articles of these Statutes other than those enumerated in Article 60 may be proposed by a two-thirds majority of the Board to the General Meeting and if adopted by a majority of the General Meeting shall come into force, provided that such amendments are not inconsistent with the provisions of the Articles enumerated in Article 60.

Art. 60. Articles 2, 3, 4, 9, 15, 20, 25, 28, 46, 53, 56, 59 and 60 cannot be amended except subject to the following conditions: the amendment must be adopted by a two-thirds majority of the Board, approved by a majority of the General Meeting and sanctioned by a law supplementing the Charter of the Bank.

Statutes

Amendments to the original text of the Statutes of 20 January 1930 were adopted by Extraordinary General Meetings held on 3 May 1937, 12 June 1950, 9 October 1961, 9 June 1969, 10 June 1974, 8 July 1975, 14 June 1993, 13 September 1994, 8 November 1999, 8 January 2001, and 10 March 2003. The amendments adopted in 1969 and 1975 were sanctioned in accordance with the conditions laid down in Article 1 of the Convention regarding the Bank for International Settlements.

BIS Balance Sheet, 1930–2000

This annex draws on a series of internal documents prepared by Marten De Boer, BIS manager (1985–2001) with responsibility for accounting and budgeting,[1] and it presents some salient facts regarding the operational side of the BIS's role as "bank of central banks". First, the Bank's unit of account during the period 1930–2003, the gold franc, requires some explanation. We then turn to the capital of the Bank and the long-term development of its balance sheet. Finally, we comment briefly on the BIS's dividend policy.

B.1   The Gold Franc

In the committee for the organisation of the Bank for International Settlements that met in Baden-Baden in October–November 1929, the French delegation suggested that the BIS should create its own unit of account, for which it proposed the "grammor" (that is, one gram of gold). This proposal was rejected and instead the Bank opted for the currency of its host country, the Swiss franc, as its unit of account. The Swiss franc was at the time freely convertible into gold at the fixed par value of one Swiss franc = 0.29032258 grams of fine gold.

On 26 September 1936, the Swiss franc was devalued by 30%, but the BIS decided to maintain the Swiss gold franc (GF) at its old parity as its unit of account. Thereafter the BIS's unit of account remained unchanged until March 2003. Up to that time, the Bank recorded its gold assets and

---

[1] In particular: "Dividend Policy", 11 April 2000; "The Bank's Capital", 20 June 2000; "Profitability and Provisioning", 3 October 2000; "Development of the Balance Sheet", 11 January 2001. BISA, 7.18(31) – *Papers Crockett*.

liabilities on the basis of the old gold–Swiss franc parity. Thus, one bar of gold with a standard weight of some 400 ounces, or about 12.5 kg, was recorded in the Bank's books as GF 43,055.

The conversion of currency assets and liabilities into gold francs at times gave rise to complications and entailed a series of modifications. Until mid-1936, the Bank's currency assets and liabilities were converted into French francs at market rates and then into gold francs on the basis of the Bank of France's selling price for gold. In 1936, the U.S. dollar was substituted for the French franc as the reference currency. All other currencies were first converted into U.S. dollars and subsequently into gold francs on the basis of the U.S. Treasury selling price for gold ($35 per ounce). This system remained in place until December 1971, when – as a result of the Smithsonian Agreement – the new gold parity of $38 per ounce was adopted as the basis for converting U.S. dollars into gold francs. In February 1973, the dollar was devalued again to $42.22 per ounce. This last reference basis was used until mid-1979, although in the meantime the official gold price used by the Bank had become increasingly farther removed from the market price. In June 1979, the BIS decided to adopt the market-related price of $208 per ounce for the conversion of U.S. dollar balances into gold francs, resulting in a fixed rate of 1 gold franc = $1.94149. This rate remained in place until March 2003.

In 2003, the Bank parted from the gold franc. As of 1 April 2003, the BIS's unit of account is the special drawing right (SDR), a basket of currencies defined by the IMF that is representative of the main currencies used in international trade and finance.

B.2   The Bank's Capital

Article 5 of the original Statutes (1930) fixed the authorised capital of the Bank at 500 million gold francs, equivalent to 145,161,290.32 grams of fine gold, divided into 200,000 shares of 2,500 gold francs each. The subscription of the Bank's capital was guaranteed under Article 6 of the 1930 Statutes by five central banks – namely, the National Bank of Belgium, the Bank of England, the Bank of France, the German Reichsbank, and the Bank of Italy – and by two banking groups, one acting in place of the Bank of Japan and another formed by three U.S. banks (J.P. Morgan & Co., the First National Bank of New York, and the First National Bank of Chicago). On 20 May 1930 these guarantor central banks and banking groups each subscribed 16,000 BIS shares, thereby underwriting the minimum of 112,000 shares required for the Bank to commence business.

In the two years following the opening of the Bank on 20 May 1930, most European central banks became shareholding members of the BIS. The Netherlands Bank, Sveriges Riksbank, and the Swiss National Bank took up 4,000 shares each on 20 May 1930. In June 1930, 4,000 shares each were taken up by the Austrian National Bank, the National Bank of Bulgaria, the Czechoslovak National Bank, the Bank of Danzig, the National Bank of Denmark, the Bank of Finland, the Bank of Greece, the National Bank of Hungary, the Bank of Poland, and the National Bank of Romania. Subsequently, between October 1930 and June 1931, the Bank of Estonia took up 100 shares, the National Bank of Albania, the Bank of Latvia, and the Bank of Lithuania 500 shares each, and the Bank of Norway and the National Bank of Yugoslavia 4,000 shares each. The remainder of 26,400 unsubscribed shares (out of the total of 200,000 shares of the first tranche) were subscribed by the seven founder central banks and banking groups in May 1932.

Thus, in 1932, the BIS shareholding membership consisted of 24 European central banks and two non-European banking groups (representing Japan and the United States). Thereafter, the number of shareholding central banks increased in three "waves". First, European representation became virtually complete when, in 1950–51, the central banks of Iceland, Ireland, Portugal, and Turkey joined, followed in 1960 by the Bank of Spain (at that time, in Europe only the central banks of the German Democratic Republic and the USSR were not BIS members). Second, in 1970–71, the BIS expanded its membership outside Europe. Towards this end, the authorised capital of the Bank was trebled to 600,000 shares, representing GF 1.5 billion (200,000 new shares were issued as bonus shares to the existing shareholders, and a further 200,000 were created to enable the Board to widen the membership of the Bank). The Bank of Japan, which had renounced its initial involvement with the BIS after the Second World War, rejoined in January 1970. The Bank of Canada became a shareholding member at the same time. Both central banks were already active in the G10 framework, which had begun to shape the BIS's activities from the early 1960s. Later in 1970 and in early 1971, the central banks of Australia and South Africa followed.

Thereafter, no major changes took place in the membership of the BIS until the third wave of expansion some 25 years later. Prior to that, in 1994, the governors of the Bank of Canada, the Bank of Japan, and the U.S. Federal Reserve System were elected members of the BIS Board of Directors, thus completing the representation of all G10 central banks on the Board. In September 1996, the BIS Board invited nine additional central banks, which had become increasingly involved in central bank cooperation at the BIS, to take up BIS shares: the Central Bank of Brazil, the People's Bank of China, the Hong Kong Monetary Authority, the Reserve Bank of India, the Bank of Korea, the Bank of Mexico, the Central Bank of the Russian Federation, the Saudi Arabian Monetary Agency, and the Monetary Authority of Singapore. In November 1999, the Bank again invited several central banks to become shareholding members, and the Central Bank of the Argentine Republic, the European Central Bank, the Central Bank of Malaysia, and the Bank of Thailand joined shortly thereafter. Finally, by September 2003, six additional central banks had taken up the Board's offer in May of that year to become members of the BIS: the Bank of Algeria, the Central Bank of Chile, Bank Indonesia, the Bank of Israel, the Reserve Bank of New Zealand, and the Central Bank of the Philippines. Thus, at the end of 2003, the BIS membership totalled 55 central banks and monetary institutions.[2]

On 31 March 2004, the number of the Bank's issued shares stood at 547,125, representing a paid-up capital of SDR 683.9 million.

When the Bank's initial capital was issued, the subscribing institutions were given the option of taking up the whole of their respective national issues of shares or of arranging for those shares to be subscribed by the public. The great majority of central banks chose to subscribe the shares themselves, but part of the Belgian and French issues and the whole of the American issue were subscribed by the public. This was also the case for part of the British, Danish, and Danzig issues, but the privately held U.K. shares were transferred to the Bank of England in July 1935, the privately held Danish shares were bought back by the National Bank of Denmark in 1953, and the entire Danzig issue was cancelled in 1979. The shares of the initial Japanese issue were held by a private banking group until 1952, when they were repurchased by the five founder central banks represented on the BIS Board.

All shares carried equal rights to participate in the profits of the Bank, but private shareholders had no right to attend or vote at the General Meetings of the BIS. Article 15 of the 1930 Statutes contained a special provision making the rights of representation and of voting independent of the ownership of the shares and reserving all voting rights for the central banks in proportion to the number of shares originally issued in their respective countries.

---

[2] At the time of publication, the legal status of the Yugoslav issue of the capital of the BIS was still under review following the constitutional changes in February 2003, which transformed the Federal Republic of Yugoslavia into the State Union of Serbia and Montenegro, with two separate central banks.

Although privately held BIS shares made up nearly a third of the total issued capital in the early 1930s, this proportion diminished thereafter and fell
below 16% after 1975, when the Bank made a voluntary share repurchase
offer to private shareholders. On 8 January 2001, an Extraordinary General
Meeting of the BIS decided henceforth to restrict the right to hold shares
in the BIS exclusively to central banks, as it was felt that the existence of a
small number of private shareholders – whose interest was primarily financial – had become increasingly inconsistent with the public international
role of the BIS and its future development. Consequently, the Bank undertook a mandatory repurchase of all BIS shares held by private shareholders.

B.3   Development of the Balance Sheet

The development of the BIS's balance sheet during the period 1930–2000
(see the figures later in this section) can be roughly divided into four periods: a very strong start (1930–31) followed by a sharp decline in activity
(1931–46), a slow recovery (1947–58), and finally a long period of strong,
almost uninterrupted expansion (1958–2000).

1930–31: A Strong Start
On 31 March 1931, the BIS closed its first financial year with a balance sheet
total of GF 1.9 billion ($680 million). At that time, the Bank's paid-up cap-
ital amounted to over GF 100 million and the BIS had received a number
of long-term, non–interest-bearing deposits (as foreseen in the 1930 Hague
Agreement) totalling over GF 300 million – in particular, deposits from the
creditor nations held in an annuity trust account, a German government deposit, and the so-called French Government Guarantee Fund. Apart from
these long-term deposits, the Bank also received much larger short-term
deposits from central banks, both for their own account (GF 810 million
on 31 March 1931) and for account of their governments (GF 650 million
on 31 March 1931). The deposits held with the BIS on behalf of the governments were partly related to the reparation payments under the Young
Plan, which were transferred by Germany to the BIS on a monthly basis but
generally disbursed by the latter to creditor nations only at half-yearly intervals. However, the bulk of the deposits made on behalf of governments
was maintained with the BIS pending outpayments abroad and also led to
the organisation of a clearing of intergovernmental payments.

A further increase in deposits took place during the first two months
of the second financial year, and the balance sheet total reached a high of
GF 2.1 billion at the end of May 1931. From then onwards the Bank faced
a sharp and prolonged decline in resources.

1931–46: Crisis and War

The events of 1931 profoundly affected the BIS's banking activities, liquidity, and balance sheet. First of all, the Bank was called upon to grant liquidity support in rapid succession to the central banks of Austria, Hungary, Germany, Danzig, and Yugoslavia. The interest margins earned on these emergency credits were substantial and contributed to a sharp increase in the Bank's profitability in 1931–32, but the related risks were also high – as evidenced by the credit to the National Bank of Hungary, which was not fully redeemed until 1946. Second, the Hoover moratorium (1931) and the Lausanne Agreement (1932) brought the reparations machinery to a standstill and thereby deprived the BIS of important sources of deposits. Thus the balances at the Bank held for the account of governments declined from GF 650 million at the end of the first financial year to GF 70 million on 31 March 1932. A further decrease occurred in the following two years, and these balances became of minor significance in the BIS balance sheet. Third, the 1931 financial crisis (and its longer-term repercussions) also led to a contraction of the short-term deposits held at the BIS by the central banks for their own account. Beginning in September 1931, when the United Kingdom suspended the gold standard, central banks withdrew their reserves held at the BIS on a massive scale because they needed liquidity to counter pressures on the exchange rate or sought to convert part of their foreign currency holdings into gold following the devaluation of sterling. From end-August to end-December 1931, central bank deposits at the BIS fell from GF 870 million to GF 465 million.

A further sharp decline in central bank deposits took place in April–June 1933 as a result of the devaluation of the U.S. dollar. The deposit business of the Bank suffered not only from the conversion of central bank foreign exchange holdings into gold but also from the statutory provision that the BIS was only allowed to conduct business in currencies that satisfied the requirements of the gold or gold exchange standard (Art. 21 of the 1930 Statutes). Since neither sterling nor the U.S. dollar fulfilled this condition after April 1933, the Bank's business in these currencies was gradually phased out. As a restoration of the gold standard became ever less likely, the Board decided in early 1936 to allow deposits and business transactions in currencies not satisfying the requirements of the gold standard, provided that an equilibrium was maintained between the assets and liabilities in each of these currencies.

By March 1934, central bank currency deposits at the BIS had fallen to GF 150 million (less than $50 million). Four years later, in March 1938, they stood slightly higher at GF 180 million. Two further runs on the Bank's currency deposits followed: at the time of the Munich Agreement in September

1938 and immediately after the outbreak of World War II in September 1939 (between end-July and end-October 1939, short-term currency deposits fell by 80%). At the end of the Bank's tenth financial year, in March 1940, the balance sheet of the Bank had declined to GF 470 million, of which GF 230 million consisted of the long-term deposits made under the Hague Agreements, GF 185 million was made up of the Bank's own funds, and only GF 35 million and GF 13 million (respectively) were currency and gold deposits held on behalf of central banks.

At the same time, during the second half of the 1930s, gold operations became an important part of the overall activities of the BIS, although this is not apparent from the Bank's balance sheet. The Bank opened "earmarked" gold accounts for central banks whereby gold was held in the name of the BIS but for the account of the customer in the vaults of a depository central bank. The amount of gold held in earmarked accounts rose from GF 120 million in March 1932 to GF 480 million in March 1938; these figures were not included in the balance sheet. In addition, from mid-1933, the BIS offered central banks a deposit facility expressed in a weight of gold. These gold deposit accounts, included in the Bank's balance sheet, were intended to permit book transfers of gold among central banks and thus avoid physical shipments.

The activities of the Bank were further reduced during the war years. The balance sheet total of GF 470 million at the end of March 1940 remained almost unchanged. By the summer of 1941, the business volume had fallen to less than one tenth of the monthly average recorded during the last three prewar years, and by 1943 it stood at less than 5%. Apart from a limited number of gold and foreign exchange transactions, the Bank largely confined itself to managing its long-term assets as conservatively as possible and paying interest on its deposits. Throughout the war, the Bank's main source of income was the interest paid by the German Reichsbank on the investments the BIS had made in the German market in 1930–31 in accordance with the Young Plan. These payments came to an end in 1945. In the financial year 1945–46 the Bank, for the first and only time in its history, suffered an operating loss.

1947–58: A Slow Recovery

After the war, the activities of the Bank resumed, showing a steady but relatively slow increase until the late 1950s. In fact it was only in 1955 that the balance sheet total again reached the level recorded at the end of the first financial year (GF 1.9 billion). The composition of the balance sheet was, however, quite different. Gold deposits amounted to some GF 0.5 billion in 1955 whereas in 1931 they had been almost nonexistent. On the other

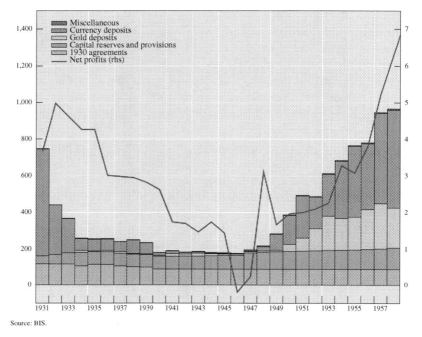

Figure B.1. Evolution of BIS balance sheet liabilities and net profits, 1931–58 (millions of U.S. dollars at current prices).

hand, short-term currency deposits were lower in 1955 than in 1931 (GF 1 billion and GF 1.5 billion, respectively). It was not until 1959 that the total of currency deposits exceeded the level reached in March 1931. The steady expansion in the balance sheet in the 1950s allowed the Bank to extend its practice of granting credit facilities to some of its member central banks, notably in Central and Eastern Europe.

The profitability of the Bank recovered slowly. Although the financial year 1945–46 had closed with a deficit, the Bank could again make modest allocations to its provisions in the following years. As a result, no net profits were reported until the end of the financial year 1948–49. This situation changed in 1950, when the Bank's accounts closed with a profit of GF 2.6 million. Thereafter the profitability improved further, and the reported net profits rose to more than GF 9 million ($3 million) in the late 1950s.

1958–80: Strong Expansion
The balance sheet rose steeply: from just below GF 2.5 billion in 1958 to more than GF 20 billion in 1970 and GF 100 billion in 1980. This expansion owed a lot to economic growth in the Western world and to certain

structural changes in the international monetary system, such as the return to convertibility of most European currencies in 1958, the liberalisation of cross-border capital flows, and even the eventual collapse of the Bretton Woods system of fixed exchange rates in 1971–73. The accumulation of U.S. dollars in the coffers of the central banks in Europe and Japan also benefited the BIS's business, as part of these additional holdings were placed on deposit with the BIS.

The gold deposits in the Bank's books started to rise sharply in 1959, and in the first half of the 1960s they were about equal to – or even higher than – the total of currency deposits. The background to this development was the strong rise in the gold holdings of several continental European countries (in particular France) that purchased gold from U.S. monetary authorities, while transactions with the IMF and on the market also led to an increase in their gold holdings (the Gold Pool was a net buyer of gold in 1962–65). Under these circumstances the gold operations of the Bank became important again, particularly since the BIS was often able to pay interest on time deposits in gold. Gold operations became less important in the 1970s, and the total of gold deposits with the BIS fell from over GF 6 billion in 1970 to GF 4.5 billion in 1980.

The decline in gold deposits during the 1970s was overshadowed by a rapid rise in currency deposits from GF 13 billion in 1970 to GF 92 billion ($36 billion) in 1980. The principal factor behind this increase was a sharp rise in world currency reserves during this period. The total of currency deposits with the BIS represented more than 8% of world foreign exchange reserves in 1980.

In 1964, the Bank started to issue its own Swiss franc notes in the Swiss market. The outstanding amount of these notes reached a high of GF 1.6 billion in March 1969. They disappeared from the Bank's balance sheet again in 1976. The issue of these BIS notes helped to reduce undesired liquidity in the Swiss market and enabled the Bank to buy Swiss franc–denominated bonds (so-called Roosa bonds) from the U.S. Treasury. The BIS holdings of Roosa bonds rose from CHF 300 million in May 1964 to CHF 1.1 billion in January 1969. The last Roosa bonds held by the BIS were repaid in early 1974.

Until the mid-1960s, a large part of the BIS's resources was invested in Treasury bills and other government paper while investments with commercial banks remained limited. The rapid increase in the Bank's deposits in the period 1965–80 gave rise to a substantial expansion of its placements in the interbank market. In the late 1970s such placements normally accounted for over 80% of the Bank's total assets. This change in the Bank's asset composition was related to the growth of the eurodollar market, which

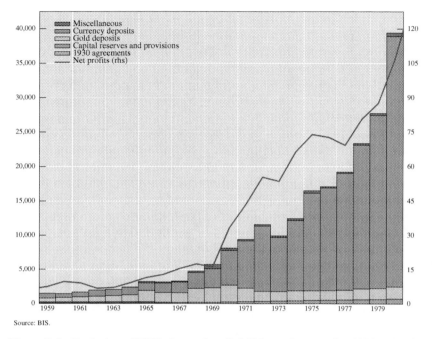

Figure B.2. Evolution of BIS balance sheet liabilities and net profits, 1959–80 (millions of U.S. dollars at current prices).

enabled the BIS to pay a higher interest rate on U.S. dollar deposits placed with it – representing some 75% of its total deposit base – than could be obtained in the U.S. domestic market. Investments by the BIS in the eurodollar market rose to more than $3 billion in early 1971 but were then temporarily reduced: the G10 central banks agreed to limit their own investments in the euromarkets out of concern about their extremely rapid expansion. The oil price shock of 1973 and the resulting balance of payments surpluses of the oil-exporting countries were major factors behind the continued expansion of the eurodollar market. The BIS also played a role in the recycling of petrodollar surpluses. Starting in 1974 the Bank attracted longer-term deposits from oil-producing countries, and these funds were used for investments in the oil-consuming countries. Besides granting advances to a number of central banks, the Bank also bought public sector bonds issued in oil-consuming countries.

1980–2000: Continued Growth

As noted before, in June 1979 the Bank made a drastic change in the presentation of its accounts by revaluing its unit of account, the gold franc, on the basis of a price of $208 per ounce of gold – that is, much closer to the actual market price of gold than the $42.22 per ounce used previously as the reference value. As a result, the balance sheet total for 1980 expressed in gold francs shrank dramatically, from GF 100 billion at the old parity to GF 24.4 billion after the revision. Twenty years later, in March 2000, this total had trebled to GF 74.8 billion ($145 billion).

Although the balance sheet rose significantly in the 1980s and 1990s, the increase in currency deposits held at the BIS lagged somewhat behind the overall increase in world currency reserves. At the end of March 2000 some 7% of these reserves were invested with the BIS, as against over 8% in 1980. This modest fall in market share reflected more active reserve management by the Bank's central bank customers, who became more return oriented as floating exchange rates lessened their need for liquidity. This tendency was reinforced when the introduction of the single European currency in January 1999 freed up reserves previously held for intra-European interventions in the exchange markets. The BIS adjusted to the changing preferences of its customers by introducing a tradable short-term instrument (1990) as well as a tradable medium-term instrument (1998). This, together with an increased remuneration on traditional short-term deposits, enabled the Bank to limit its decline in market share in a generally much more competitive environment. In times of market uncertainty, the BIS became something of a safe haven for short-term reserve deposits. The balance sheet total reached unprecedented highs of GF 89.5 billion at the end of December 1998 and of GF 87 billion at the end of December 1999, just prior to the introduction of the euro and the millennium date changeover (expected so-called Y2K problems), respectively. In both cases, these year-end build-ups of deposits were unwound in subsequent months.

Balance sheet growth in the period 1980–2000 reflects principally an increase in currency deposits. Gold deposits in the books of the BIS fell significantly, in particular in the 1990s. They declined from GF 4.5 billion in 1980 to GF 2.8 billion (approximately 820 tonnes) in March 2000. Over the same period, gold held for central banks off-balance sheet ("under earmark") also fell from GF 1 billion to GF 670 million. The 1990s were more generally the decade of central bank gold sales. Several G10 central banks with a long gold tradition and substantial gold stocks came to the conclusion that they were "overweight" in gold and started to shift part of their gold reserves into higher-yielding foreign exchange assets. The BIS handled many of these gold sales for its customers. When the succession of these sales led to uncertainty and lower prices in the gold market, a group of central banks announced in September 1999 that in order to calm the market they would henceforth coordinate their gold sales, which would

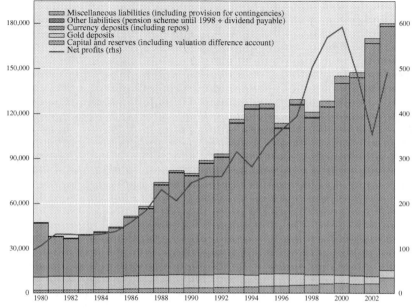

Note: For 2003, change in accounting policies for sales of own funds investments, provisions and retirement benefit obligations.
Source: BIS.

Figure B.3. Evolution of BIS balance sheet liabilities and net profits, 1980–2003 (millions of U.S. dollars at current prices).

be limited to a maximum of 2,000 tonnes over a five-year period. This agreement was signed by the central banks of the Eurosystem, the Bank of England, Sveriges Riksbank, and the Swiss National Bank, while the United States and Japan confirmed that they would maintain their policy of not selling gold.

On a number of occasions, the BIS put its resources to use in lending to individual central banks. In the early 1980s a debt crisis erupted in Eastern Europe under the impact of rising oil prices and high dollar interest rates. One of the countries affected was Hungary, and the National Bank sought BIS assistance in March 1982. In August 1982 the BIS, with the support of a number of major central banks, provided half of a $1.8 billion credit facility to Mexico. Further bridging loans, usually prefinancing the use of IMF resources, were arranged for Brazil, Argentina, Poland, Yugoslavia, and Nigeria. In the course of the 1990s the number of bridging loans declined sharply but the amounts involved became larger (e.g., a $13.3 billion facility granted to the Central Bank of Brazil in December 1998).

The lending activity of the Bank also remained fairly limited during the 1997 Asian crisis. With the support of a group of central banks, the BIS made funds available to the IMF on two occasions – an SDR 675 million facility in 1981 and an SDR 2.5 billion facility in 1984 – to bridge a possible liquidity gap in Fund resources. In addition to these multilateral credit facilities, the BIS frequently granted short-term advances to central banks on a bilateral basis. During the 1980s and early 1990s such advances were often linked to tensions within the European Monetary System, such as during the EMS crises of September 1992 and summer 1993.

From the mid-1990s, the Bank took a number of initiatives to strengthen its global character. Among them were the expansion of its membership base and the opening of two representative offices, in Hong Kong SAR (1998) and in Mexico City (2002). The BIS Office for Asia and the Pacific in Hong Kong commenced banking operations in October 2000, enabling the BIS to serve its Asian customers during their own trading day.

B.4   Dividend Policy

The 1930 Statutes provided that out of the net profit of the Bank – after the statutory allocation to the Legal Reserve Fund – a preferential, cumulative dividend of 6% per annum should be paid on the amount of paid-up capital. Of the remaining profit, up to 20% could be used to pay a supplementary, noncumulative dividend of a maximum of 6%. Up to the Bank's tenth financial year, ending in March 1940, the distribution of the net profit took place as foreseen in the Statutes. The Bank paid its shareholders the statutory 6% preferential dividend (GF 37.5 per share), while further amounts were credited to the Special Dividend Reserve Fund.

As a result of the low profitability of the Bank during the war, beginning in 1941 the annual 6% dividend to shareholders was paid by gradually drawing down and finally exhausting this Special Dividend Reserve Fund. From 1943 the dividend was reduced and in 1945 it was suspended altogether. Dividend payments were only resumed from 1951 onwards. In subsequent years the dividend amount was gradually increased, and the 6% level provided for in the 1930 Statutes was again reached in 1957–58. The nonpayment of a full 6% cumulative dividend from 1943 onwards led to the accumulation of dividend arrears. These were all settled in the period 1960–67.

Before and during the war, the dividend was declared in gold francs. Initially it was paid in the currency of the country in which the shares had been issued but from 1941 it was paid in the currency of the country of residence of the shareholder. For the period 1951–75 the dividend was still declared in gold francs while at the same time the Bank stated the current Swiss franc amount payable to the shareholders. From 1976 onwards the dividend was declared and paid in Swiss francs.

The statutory provisions regarding the dividend were changed in 1969, when the 6% preferential dividend was made noncumulative and the maximum rate of the supplementary dividend was reduced from 6% to 3%. At the same time, shareholders benefited from the increase in the Bank's capital, with 200,000 bonus shares being issued to existing shareholders on a one-for-one basis and paid for out of the Bank's own funds. In 1975 a further revision of the Statutes removed any ceiling on the dividend payout, thus leaving it to the discretion of the Board to decide on the annual dividend proposal to be submitted for approval at the General Meeting.

ANNEX C

BIS Board of Directors and Management, 1930–2005

C.1 Presidents of the BIS and Chairmen of the BIS Board of Directors

President of the BIS		*Chairman of the Board*
Gates W. McGarrah	April 1930 – May 1933	Gates W. McGarrah
Leon Fraser	May 1933 – May 1935	Leon Fraser
Leonardus J. A. Trip	May 1935 – May 1937	Leonardus J. A. Trip
J. Willem Beyen	May 1937 – December 1939	
	May 1937 – May 1940	O. E. Niemeyer
Thomas H. McKittrick	January 1940 – June 1946	
	December 1942 – November 1945	Ernst Weber
	July 1946 – June 1948	Maurice Frère
Maurice Frère	June 1948 – June 1958	Maurice Frère
Marius W. Holtrop	July 1958 – June 1967	Marius W. Holtrop
Jelle Zijlstra	July 1967 – December 1981	Jelle Zijlstra
Fritz Leutwiler	January 1982 – December 1984	Fritz Leutwiler
Jean Godeaux	January 1985 – December 1987	Jean Godeaux
W. F. Duisenberg	January 1988 – December 1990	W. F. Duisenberg
Bengt Dennis	January 1991 – December 1993	Bengt Dennis
W. F. Duisenberg	January 1994 – June 1997	W. F. Duisenberg
Alfons Verplaetse	July 1997 – February 1999	Alfons Verplaetse
Urban Bäckström	March 1999 – February 2002	Urban Bäckström
A. H. E. M. Wellink	March 2002 –	A. H. E. M. Wellink

C.2 Vice-Chairmen of the BIS Board of Directors

C. Addis and Carl Melchior	April 1930 – May 1932
Alberto Beneduce and Carl Melchior	June 1932 – May 1939 April 1930 – March 1933

661

Leonardus J. A. Trip	May 1933 – May 1935
Marquis de Vogüé	May 1935 – May 1939
Alexandre Galopin and Hisaakira Kano	May 1939 – May 1942
O. E. Niemeyer	December 1946 – December 1964
Maurice Frère	January 1965 – August 1970
Henri Deroy	November 1970 – January 1979
L. K. O'Brien	March 1979 – June 1983
Bernard Clappier	July 1983 – November 1985
Gordon Richardson	November 1985 – November 1988
Paolo Baffi	November 1988 – August 1989
Bernard Clappier	August 1989 – November 1991
Gordon Richardson	November 1991 – June 1993
Lamberto Dini	September 1993 – May 1994
Carlo A. Ciampi	July 1994 – May 1996
R. Leigh-Pemberton	June 1996 – June 2003
Hans Tietmeyer	June 2003 –

C.3   Members of the Board of Directors

Belgium

Governors:

L. Franck	February 1930 – December 1937
G. Janssen	January 1938 – June 1941
G. Theunis	November 1941 – October 1944
M. Frère	November 1944 – August 1957
H. Ansiaux	August 1957 – February 1971
R. Vandeputte	March 1971 – February 1975
C. de Strycker	March 1975 – February 1982
J. Godeaux	March 1982 – July 1989
A. Verplaetse	July 1989 – February 1999
G. Quaden	March 1999 –

Others:

E. Francqui	February 1930 – November 1934
A. Galopin	December 1934 – February 1944
C. Gutt	April 1945 – May 1946
A. E. Janssen	April 1948 – January 1952
	May 1954 – February 1956
J. Van Nieuwenhuyse	March 1956 – August 1957
M. Frère	August 1957 – August 1970
R. Vandeputte	January – February 1971
H. Ansiaux	March 1971 – January 1982
C. de Strycker	March 1982 – June 1989
J. Godeaux	November 1989 – September 1990
P. Wilmès	March 1991 – March 1999
A. Verplaetse	April 1999 –

Canada

Governors:

G. Thiessen	September 1994 – January 2001
D. Dodge	February 2001 –

France

Governors:		
	E. Moreau	February 1930 – September 1930
	C. Moret	September 1930 – January 1935
	J. Tannery	January 1935 – May 1936
	E. Labeyrie	July 1936 – July 1937
	P. Fournier	July 1937 – September 1940
	Y. Bréart de Boisanger	September 1940 – September 1944
	E. Monick	October 1944 – January 1949
	W. Baumgartner	February 1949 – January 1960
	J. Brunet	February 1960 – April 1969
	O. Wormser	May 1969 – June 1974
	B. Clappier	July 1974 – November 1979
	R. de la Genière	December 1979 – November 1984
	M. Camdessus	December 1984 – January 1987
	J. de Larosière	February 1987 – September 1993
	J.-C. Trichet	September 1993 – October 2003
	C. Noyer	November 2003 –
Others:	Marquis de Vogüé	February 1930 – March 1948
	Baron Brincard	February 1930 – June 1953
	H. Deroy	April 1948 – January 1979
	B. Clappier	November 1979 – November 1994
	H. Hannoun	November 1994 –

Germany

Presidents:		
	H. Schacht	February 1930 – April 1930
	H. Luther	April 1930 – March 1933
	H. Schacht	April 1933 – January 1939
	W. Funk	January 1939 – May 1945
	W. Vocke	April 1950 – December 1957
	K. Blessing	January 1958 – December 1969
	K. Klasen	January 1970 – May 1977
	O. Emminger	June 1977 – December 1979
	K. O. Pöhl	January 1980 – July 1991
	H. Schlesinger	August 1991 – September 1993
	H. Tietmeyer	October 1993 – August 1999
	E. Welteke	September 1999 – April 2004
	J. Stark	28–29 April 2004
	A. Weber	April 2004 –
Others:	C. Melchior	April 1930 – March 1933
	P. Reusch	April 1930 – January 1939
	K. Freiherr von Schröder	April 1933 – May 1945
	H. Schmitz	March 1939 – May 1945
	R. Brinckmann	June 1950 – July 1970
	L. Gleske	August 1970 – December 1975
	J. Schöllhorn	January 1976 – April 1989
	L. Gleske	May 1989 – September 1993
	H. Schlesinger	October 1993 – August 1999
	H. Tietmeyer	September 1999 –

Italy

Governors:	B. Stringher	February 1930 – December 1930
	V. Azzolini	December 1930 – June 1944
	L. Einaudi	January 1945 – May 1948
	D. Menichella	August 1948 – August 1960
	G. Carli	September 1960 – August 1975
	P. Baffi	August 1975 – October 1979
	C. A. Ciampi	November 1979 – April 1993
	A. Fazio	May 1993 –
Others:	A. Beneduce	February 1930 – May 1939
	F. Giordani	May 1939 – May 1945
	D. Menichella	June 1946 – August 1948
		November 1960 – December 1974
	P. Stoppani	November 1948 – November 1960
	P. Baffi	January 1975 – August 1975
	A. Occhiuto	October 1975 – February 1980
	P. Baffi	February 1980 – August 1989
	L. Dini	October 1989 – May 1994
	C. A. Ciampi	July 1994 – May 1996
	V. Desario	June 1996 –

Japan

Governors:	Y. Mieno	September 1994 – December 1994
	Y. Matsushita	December 1994 – March 1998
	M. Hayami	April 1998 – March 2003
	T. Fukui	May 2003 –
Others:	T. Tanaka	February 1930 – October 1932
	D. Nohara	February 1930 – May 1934
	S. Shimasuye	February 1930 – May 1934
	H. Kano	June 1934 – October 1943
	H. Munakata	November 1934 – September 1936
	S. Yanagita	September 1936 – October 1939
	F. Futami	October 1939 – February 1941
	Y. Yamamoto	February 1941 – October 1945
	K. Kitamura	October 1943 – September 1946

Netherlands

Presidents:	G. Vissering	May 1931 – December 1931
	L. J. A. Trip	January 1932 – March 1946
	M. W. Holtrop	July 1946 – June 1967
	J. Zijlstra	July 1967 – December 1981
	W. F. Duisenberg	January 1982 – June 1997
	A. H. E. M. Wellink	July 1997 –

Sweden

Governors:	I. Rooth	May 1931 – March 1933
		April 1937 – March 1949
	K. Böök	April 1949 – November 1951
	M. Lemne	October 1952 – May 1955
	P. Åsbrink	December 1955 – October 1973

	K. Wickman	December 1973 – November 1976
	C.-H. Nordlander	December 1976 – November 1979
	L. Wohlin	December 1979 – November 1982
	B. Dennis	November 1982 – December 1993
	U. Bäckström	January 1994 – December 2002
	L. Heikensten	January 2003 –

Switzerland

Presidents:
	G. Bachmann	May 1931 – May 1939
	E. Weber	June 1939 – May 1947
	P. Keller	May 1947 – May 1956
	W. Schwegler	June 1956 – August 1966
	E. Stopper	September 1966 – April 1974
	F. Leutwiler	May 1974 – December 1984
	P. Languetin	January 1985 – April 1988
	M. Lusser	May 1988 – April 1996
	H. Meyer	May 1996 – December 2000
	J.-P. Roth	January 2001 –

United Kingdom

Governors:
	M. C. Norman	February 1930 – April 1944
	T. S. Catto	April 1944 – February 1949
	C. F. Cobbold	March 1949 – June 1961
	G. R. Cromer	July 1961 – June 1966
	L. K. O'Brien	July 1966 – June 1973
	G. Richardson	July 1973 – June 1983
	R. Leigh-Pemberton	July 1983 – June 1993
	E. A. J. George	July 1993 – June 2003
	M. King	July 2003 –

Others:
	C. Addis	February 1930 – May 1932
	O. E. Niemeyer	June 1932 – March 1965
	M. J. Babington Smith	April 1965 – February 1974
	L. K. O'Brien	June 1974 – June 1983
	G. Richardson	July 1983 – June 1993
	R. Leigh-Pemberton	July 1993 – June 2003
	E. A. J. George	July 2003 –

United States

Chairman, FRB:
Others:
	A. Greenspan	September 1994 –
	G. W. McGarrah	February 1930 – June 1935
	L. Fraser	February 1930 – June 1935
	W. J. McDonough	September 1994 – June 2003
	J. B. Stewart, Jr.	June 2003 – December 2003
	T. F. Geithner	December 2003 –

C.4   Members of the BIS Management

General Manager:
	P. Quesnay	April 1930 – September 1937
	R. Auboin	January 1938 – September 1958

	G. Guindey	October 1958 – March 1963
	G. Ferras	April 1963 – December 1970
	R. Larre	May 1971 – February 1981
	G. Schleiminger	March 1981 – April 1985
	A. Lamfalussy	May 1985 – December 1993
	A. D. Crockett	January 1994 – March 2003
	M. D. Knight	April 2003 –
Assistant General		
Manager:[1]	E. Hülse	April 1930 – May 1935
	P. Hechler	May 1935 – December 1945
	A. d'Aroma	January 1975 – December 1977
	G. Schleiminger	January 1978 – March 1981
	A. Lamfalussy	March 1981 – April 1985
	R. T. P. Hall	May 1985 – January 1992
	R. Gros	February 1992 – December 1995
	A. Icard	January 1996 –
Secretary General:	R. Pilotti	April 1930 – December 1951
	A. Ferrari	October 1951 – January 1962
	A. d'Aroma	January 1962 – December 1974
	G. Schleiminger	January 1975 – May 1978
	G. Morelli	June 1978 – August 1994
	G. D. Baer	September 1994 – December 2004
	P. G. Dittus	January 2005 –
Head of Banking		
Department:	E. Hülse	April 1930 – May 1935
	P. Hechler	May 1935 – December 1945
	M. van Zeeland	June 1948 – March 1962
	H. H. Mandel	April 1962 – September 1972
	D. H. Macdonald	October 1972 – December 1973
	R. T. P. Hall	January 1974 – April 1985
	R. Gros	May 1985 – March 1995
	G. M. Gill	April 1995 – January 1999
	R. D. Sleeper	February 1999 –
Economic Adviser:[2]	P. Jacobsson	September 1931 – October 1956
	M. Gilbert	November 1960 – December 1975
	A. Lamfalussy	January 1976 – April 1985
	H. Bockelmann	May 1985 – April 1995
	W. R. White	May 1995 –
Legal Adviser:[3]	F. Weiser	April 1930 – March 1944
	H. Guisan	April 1955 – September 1974
	F. E. Klein	October 1974 – December 1986
	M. Giovanoli	March 1989 –

---

[1] Deputy General Manager since 2000.

[2] Economic Adviser, Head of Monetary and Economic Department since 1946.

[3] General Counsel since 1997.

ANNEX D

Chronology of Events, 1929–2005

Compiled by Michelangelo Van Meerten and Piet Clement

This annex chronicles the main events relevant to the history of the Bank for International Settlements. Major financial, monetary, and world events not directly related to the BIS are listed in italics.

1929

February–June	Committee of Experts (Young Committee), Paris.
7 June	Young Plan officially proposed.
31 August	First Hague Conference ends.
24–29 October	*"Black Thursday", "Black Friday", and "Black Tuesday" at the New York Stock Exchange (Wall Street crash).*
3 October– 13 November	Comité d'Organisation de la Banque des Règlements Internationaux (COBRI), Baden-Baden.

1930

20 January	Final Act, Second Hague Conference.
26–27 February	Central bank governors meeting in Rome: official foundation of the BIS, nomination of president and Board members.
8 March	Reichsbank President Hjalmar Schacht resigns over the Young Plan.
March	*Brüning cabinet takes office in Germany.*
22–23 April	First unofficial meeting of the nominated directors of the BIS in Basel.
12 May	First official meeting of the BIS Board of Directors.
17 May	BIS opens doors in Basel. Gates W. McGarrah, president; Leon Fraser, alternate to the president; Pierre Quesnay, general manager.
20 May	Founding banks subscribe first share issue.
17 June	*United States Congress approves Smoot–Hawley Tariff.*
October	Schacht tours the United States, speaking against the Young Plan.
24–25 November	Meeting of Committee of Exchange Experts at the BIS.

1931

January	Governor of the Bank of Spain visits BIS to negotiate peseta stabilisation.
April	BIS makes £3,000,000 advance to Bank of Spain to stabilise peseta.
11 May	Austrian government announces Credit-Anstalt crisis.
19 May	First Annual General Meeting (AGM) of the BIS.
30 May	BIS grants Sch. 100,000,000 credit to Austrian National Bank.
6 June	BIS advance of $5,000,000 to Hungarian National Bank.
18–22 June	BIS syndicate credit of $10,000,000 to Hungarian National Bank.
20 June	*U.S. government announces Hoover moratorium: one-year suspension of intergovernmental debts and reparations.*
26 June	BIS, with Bank of England, Bank of France, and Federal Reserve Bank of New York, grants $100,000,000 credit to Reichsbank.
6 July	*Franco-American agreement on implementation of Hoover moratorium.*
8 July	Second BIS syndicate credit of $11,000,000 to Hungarian National Bank.
13 July	Thirteenth BIS Board meeting: discussion of the German situation. In Germany, Danat Bank is declared insolvent.
14–15 July	*German banks closed for two days. Stock exchange closed.*
20 July	BIS grants £150,000 credit to Bank of Danzig.
20–23 July	*London Conference on German financial crisis.*
31 July	BIS and Bank of France grant $3,000,000 credit to National Bank of Yugoslavia.
8–18 August	Wiggin Committee enquiring into Germany's credit needs meets in Basel.
18 August	First German Standstill Agreement (six months from 1 September).
September	Per Jacobsson takes up position as BIS economic adviser.
21 September	*United Kingdom suspends gold standard.*
28–29 September	*Norway, Sweden, and Denmark suspend gold standard.*
September	BIS appoints German Standstill Agreement Arbitration Committee: Messrs. Wallenberg, McKittrick, and Urbig.
19 November	In a letter to the BIS, the German government requests that the Special Advisory Committee provided for in the Young Plan be convened.
November	Frère Plan for medium-term credits.
7–23 December	Special Advisory Committee, or Beneduce Committee, meets in Basel. Its final report recognises Germany's incapacity to resume reparation transfers.
17 December	*Japan suspends gold standard (to which it had returned in January 1930).*

1932

27 February	*Glass–Steagall Bill enables Federal Reserve Bank open-market operations to offset gold withdrawals and hoarding.*

February	*Bank of England discount rate reduction from 6% to 5% signals downward nominal interest rate movement in most of the world.*
February	*German Stock Exchange reopens, having been closed since July 1931.*
1 March	Second German Standstill Agreement (one year).
3 March	*United Kingdom abolishes the exchange restrictions introduced in September 1931.*
9 July	Lausanne Conference agreement on the suspension of reparations schedule (Young Plan). BIS invited to participate in preparatory committee for World Monetary and Economic Conference.
11 July	BIS Board issues public statement advocating restoration of the gold standard.
July	Keynes–Henderson plan proposes issue of an international note by the BIS. Ottawa Agreements on preferential trade within the British Commonwealth.
5–20 September	Stresa Conference for the economic reconstruction of Central and Eastern Europe proposes establishment of a monetary normalisation fund.
October–November	Preparatory committee for the World Monetary and Economic Conference meets in Geneva; Fraser, Trip, and Jacobsson represent BIS.
15 December	*France, Belgium, Poland, Hungary, and Estonia default on war debt instalment to United States.*

1933

January	League of Nations publishes agenda for the World Monetary and Economic Conference. BIS invited to designate two representatives to participate in the conference in a consultative capacity.
30 January	*Hitler appointed chancellor in Germany.*
4 March	*U.S. President Franklin D. Roosevelt takes office.*
6 March	*United States introduces embargo on gold.*
17 March	*Hjalmar Schacht returns as Reichsbank president.*
13 April	Full reimbursement closes Reichsbank emergency credit of 26 June 1931.
19 April	*United States officially suspends gold convertibility.*
8 May	Third BIS AGM. Leon Fraser succeeds Gates W. McGarrah as president and chairman of the BIS Board. Board discusses general principles of the working of the gold standard.
5 June	BIS Board meeting adopts resolution calling for independent central banks as prerequisite for gold standard.
12 June	*World Monetary and Economic Conference opens in London.*
3 July	*Roosevelt's "bombshell" declaration sounds death knell for early dollar stabilisation. Formation of the "gold bloc" announced: Belgium, France, Italy, the Netherlands, Poland, and Switzerland participate.*

8 July   BIS President Fraser attends first meeting of gold bloc in Paris.
September   Repayment in full of the BIS credit granted to the Austrian National
              Bank in May 1931.
14 October *Germany withdraws from the League of Nations and from the Geneva
              Disarmament Conference.*

1934

31 January *U.S. Gold Reserve Act fixes price of gold at $35 per ounce, a 59%
              devaluation of the dollar against gold. U.S. gold purchases and sales
              are restricted to transactions with central banks and governments.*
14 May   Fourth BIS AGM: adopts resolution on the gold standard.
April–May   Transfer conference at the Reichsbank in Berlin to discuss reductions
              in Germany's long-term debt service.
12 June   *The U.S. Reciprocal Trade Agreements Act signals first significant
              move towards tariff reductions.*
14 June   German finance minister announces suspension of further payments
              through the BIS for service of Dawes and Young loans as from
              1 July 1934.
8 October   Gold bloc governors meet privately at the BIS in preparation for the
              Brussels conference.
20 October *Conference of gold bloc representatives in Brussels adopts protocol
              with regard to the promotion of commercial exchanges and
              confirms commitment to gold parity.*

1935

11 February   Franco-German Saar Agreements signed at the BIS: final settlement
              of financial questions raised by the transfer of the Saar territory to
              Germany.
1 April   *First defection from the gold bloc: Belgian franc devalues by 28%,
              convertibility temporarily suspended.*
1 May   J. Willem Beyen takes office as alternate to the BIS president.
13 May   Fifth BIS AGM. Leonardus J. A. Trip succeeds Fraser as president
              and chairman of the BIS Board.
30 June   Resignations of Fraser and McGarrah end U.S. representation on the
              BIS Board.
October   *Italy invades Abyssinia.*

1936

13 February   BIS gives up discrimination against non–gold-standard currencies.
7 March   *Remilitarisation of the Rhineland by German troops.*
4 June   *Léon Blum's Front Populaire government takes office in France.*
30 July   Brussels Protocol signed by government representatives, giving effect
              to Art. X of the Hague Agreement protecting the BIS's property,
              assets, and deposits in time of peace or war.

25 September	*Tripartite Monetary Agreement between France, the United Kingdom, and the United States announced.*
25 September	*France suspends gold convertibility (franc devalues).*
26 September	*Belgium adheres to the Tripartite Agreement. Netherlands and Switzerland devalue currency and suspend gold convertibility.*
5 October	*Italy officially suspends gold convertibility (lira devaluation).*
24 November	*The Netherlands and Switzerland officially adhere to the Tripartite Monetary Agreement.*

1937

March	BIS accepts trustee functions for 4.5% French National Security Loan.
3 May	J. W. Beyen succeeds L. J. A. Trip as president of the BIS. Otto Niemeyer elected chairman of the Board.
8 September	BIS General Manager Pierre Quesnay dies in a drowning accident.
19 October	*Stock market crash in the United States marks new recession.*
13 December	Roger Auboin appointed BIS general manager.
December	BIS concludes agreement with Swiss National Bank on gold purchases at fixed prices.

1938

1 January	Roger Auboin takes office as new general manager of the BIS.
January	*Publication of the van Zeeland report on the possibility of removing obstacles to trade.*
12 March	*"Anschluss": German troops march into Austria.*
10 April	*Plebiscite in Austria sanctions the country's Anschluss with Germany.*
14 April	*Roosevelt administration promulgates recovery programme.*
25 June	Following the liquidation of the Austrian National Bank, the 4,000 BIS shares held by that institution are re-registered in the name of the Reichsbank.
30 September	*Munich Agreement: Czechoslovakia forced to cede Sudetenland to Germany.*
September	War scare in Europe provokes a strong increase in gold shipments from Europe to the United States organised by the BIS.

1939

20 January	*Hjalmar Schacht replaced as Reichsbank president by Walther Funk.*
15 March	*German troops enter Prague. Protectorate of Bohemia and Moravia proclaimed.*
21–24 March	BIS carries out transfer order of Czechoslovakian National Bank's gold to Reichsbank.
22 May	*"Steel Pact" between Germany and Italy signed.*
12 June	BIS Board meeting: Thomas H. McKittrick elected BIS president effective from 1 January 1940; discussion of execution of transfer order for Czechoslovakian gold.

10 July	94th BIS Board meeting, last Board meeting until 9 December 1946: discussion on the Bank's investment policy.
23 August	*Molotov–Ribbentrop pact concluded between Germany and the USSR.*
1 September	*Germany invades Poland.*
3 September	*France and Britain declare war on Germany.*
4 September	BIS suspends all new commercial credit operations.
18 December	BIS notifies counterparties of "rules of neutral conduct".

1940

1 January	McKittrick succeeds Beyen as BIS president.
January	McKittrick visits Berlin, Rome, Brussels, and Paris.
9 April	*Germany invades Denmark and Norway.*
8 May	Mandate of Sir Otto Niemeyer, Chairman of the BIS Board, expires. Position remains vacant.
10 May	*German invasion of the Netherlands, Belgium, Luxembourg, and France.*
20 May– 7 October	BIS seat temporarily moved from Basel to Château d'Oex.
10 June	*Italy declares war on France.*
15 June	*USSR occupies Estonia, Latvia, and Lithuania.*
22–25 June	*French capitulation (in southeastern France, the Republic of Vichy retains a semblance of independence under Marshal Pétain).*
July	BIS freezes accounts held by the central banks of the Baltic States.
July–October	*Battle of Britain.*
27 September	*Tripartite Pact, Germany-Italy-Japan ("Axis").*
7 October	BIS headquarters moved back to Basel.
28 October	*Mussolini invades Greece but suffers setback.*
20–22 November	*Hungary and Romania join the Tripartite Pact.*

1941

1 March	*Bulgaria joins the Tripartite Pact.*
6 April	*German troops invade Yugoslavia and Greece.*
22 June	*German army – joined by Italian, Romanian, and Hungarian troops – starts invasion of Soviet Union (operation Barbarossa).*
23 June	U.S. Treasury imposes obligation on BIS to apply for licenses for each banking transaction conducted on the U.S. market.
July–August	*German troops occupy Lithuania, Latvia, and Estonia.*
7 December	*Pearl Harbor, Japanese surprise attack on U.S. Navy. Japan and United States in state of war.*
10 December	*Germany and Italy declare war on the United States.*
December	*Japanese troops invade Malaya, Thailand, the Philippines, and Burma.*
December	Per Jacobsson visits the United States.

1942

June–July	*Germans launch second offensive in Soviet Union.*
27 October	McKittrick visit to the United States until 7 May 1943.
November–	
December	*Full-scale Russian counteroffensive.*
11 November	*Germany occupies southeast France.*
1 December	Ernst Weber, president of the Swiss National Bank, takes office as chairman of the BIS Board of Directors.

1943

1 January	McKittrick's mandate as BIS president renewed for three years.
5 January	*First Allied declaration on looted assets.*
31 January	*German army in Stalingrad surrenders.*
13 May	*Capitulation of German and Italian forces in North Africa.*
10 July	*Allies land in Sicily.*
25 July	*Italian king appoints Marshal Badoglio head of government. Mussolini deposed.*
August	Bank of France Governor Bréart de Boisanger visits BIS and Swiss National Bank, warning that Germans have requisitioned Belgian gold.
3–9 September	*Allies land in southern Italy. Badoglio government announces Italy's unconditional surrender.*
October	*Fascist Republic is set up in Salò, headed by Mussolini. German troops contain Allied advance in southern Italy.*
20 October	U.S. Treasury General Ruling no. 17 blocks most transactions on accounts held in the United States by (or on behalf of) residents of enemy and neutral countries (including Switzerland). BIS application for exemption is denied.

1944

22 February	*Second Allied declaration on looted assets (and looted monetary gold).*
20 April	Part of the Bank of Italy gold reserves arrive in Switzerland (BIS and Swiss National Bank).
4 June	*Allies enter Rome.*
6 June	*Allied landing in Normandy.*
July	United Nations Bretton Woods conference agrees on the creation of the IMF and World Bank. It also adopts resolution V, calling for the liquidation of the BIS "at the earliest possible moment".
July–August	*Russian troops re-enter Lithuania, Latvia, and Estonia.*
25 August	*Romania declares war on Germany.*
September	*France and Belgium liberated.*
5 September	*Soviet Union declares war on and invades Bulgaria.*
29 December	*Hungary declares war on Germany, but German troops hold Budapest.*

1945

19 February	*U.S. troops land on Iwo Jima.*
25 April	*Berlin encircled by Russian troops.*
30 April	*Hitler commits suicide.*
2 May	BIS President McKittrick sends out to central banks and Allied governments a letter explaining the BIS position and rights, and offers full cooperation regarding the restitution of looted assets.
8 May	*Unconditional surrender of Germany.*
6–9 August	*Americans drop atomic bombs on Hiroshima and Nagasaki.*
2 September	*Japanese surrender signed.*
6 December	*Anglo-American Loan Agreement signed, providing for sterling convertibility by 15 July 1947.*
27 December	*IMF's Articles of Agreement enter into force.*

1946

1 January	*Bank of France nationalised.*
14 January	*Paris Agreement on German reparations (Tripartite Commission on Looted Gold established).*
14 February	*Bank of England nationalisation bill.*
8–18 March	*Inaugural meeting of the IMF at Savannah.*
April	*League of Nations dissolved.*
14 June	Report by Bank of France experts on looted Belgian gold in BIS possession.
30 June	End of mandate of BIS President McKittrick. Maurice Frère elected chairman of the BIS Board.
9 December	First postwar meeting of the BIS Board of Directors.
December	German and Japanese participation in the BIS Board of Directors declared "in suspense".
18 December	*Initial par values agreed for the currencies of 32 of the IMF's 39 member countries.*

1947

5 June	*European Recovery Programme (Marshall Plan) proposed.*
15 July	*United Kingdom introduces sterling convertibility.*
20 August	*United Kingdom suspends sterling convertibility.*
18 November	BIS asked to act as agent for the Agreement on Multilateral Monetary Compensation (France, Italy, Benelux), Paris.

1948

January	*Benelux customs union comes into force.*
1 March	*Bank deutscher Länder established in Frankfurt.*
16 April	*Organisation for European Economic Cooperation (OEEC, Paris) established.*
April	*European Recovery Programme (Marshall Plan) enacted by U.S. Congress; Economic Cooperation Administration begins operations.*

13 May	Washington Agreement: BIS reimburses gold looted by Germany to Tripartite Commission; BIS assets in United States unblocked (see 23 June 1941 and 20 October 1943).
14 June	Maurice Frère elected president of the BIS while remaining chairman of the Board.
24 June	*Beginning of Soviet blockade of West Berlin.*
June	*German currency reform. Deutsche mark introduced.*
16 October	Intra-European Payments and Compensations Agreement for 1948–49; BIS appointed agent.
December	*State Bank of the People's Republic of China established.*

1949

4 April	*NATO Treaty signed by twelve countries.*
April	*Bank of Japan Law revised under U.S. supervision. Exchange rate of Japanese yen fixed.*
12 May	*End of Berlin blockade by Soviet Union.*
23 May	*Federal Republic of Germany proclaimed.*
7 September	Intra-European Payments and Compensations Agreement for 1949–50; BIS acts as agent.
7 October	*German Democratic Republic established.*
18 September	*Devaluation of the pound by 30.5% starts wave of IMF-approved devaluations.*
October	*Communists proclaim People's Republic in China.*

1950

3 April	Vocke, president of the Bank deutscher Länder, takes up seat on the BIS Board of Directors.
9 May	*Schuman proposes pooling European coal and steel.*
25 June	*Start of Korean War.*
August	*OEEC adopts Code of Trade Liberalisation.*
19 September	Agreement for the establishment of European Payments Union (EPU).
October	First meeting of the EPU managing board in Paris. Conolly represents the BIS (EPU agent).
October–November	Jacobsson–Cairncross mission to Germany (EPU). EPU special credit to Germany.
28 November	Central Bank of Iceland becomes BIS member.
5 December	Central Bank of Ireland becomes BIS member.

1951

10 January	Bank of Portugal becomes BIS member.
April	*European Coal and Steel Community (ECSC) established.*
24 May	Central Bank of the Republic of Turkey becomes BIS member.
8 September	San Francisco Peace Treaty between Japan and the Allied powers. Japan loses all rights it enjoyed under the 1930 Hague Agreement. Japanese participation in the BIS officially ends.
December	*Marshall Plan aid ends.*

1952

28–29 February	*U.K. government considers and rejects ROBOT (convertibility with floating rate).*
March	EPU short-term credit to France.
27 May	*France, Germany, Italy, and Benelux sign European Defence Community Treaty.*
13–14 August	*Japan and West Germany join the IMF and the World Bank.*
October	*Standby arrangements introduced by the IMF.*

1953

27 February	London Agreement on German External Debts, including settlement of the Dawes and Young loans, with BIS resuming duties as fiscal agent and trustee.
5 March	*Soviet leader Joseph Stalin dies.*
June	EPU renewed without change.
17 June	*Workers' uprising in East Germany; Red Army intervenes.*
27 July	*Korean armistice signed.*

1954

July	*France withdraws its troops from Indochina.*
August	*French Assembly rejects European Defence Community.*
1 December	*Central Bank of Israel established.*

1955

April	EPU special credit to Italy.
6 May	*Treaty establishing Western European Union (WEU) for economic, social, and cultural cooperation among Benelux, France, Germany, Italy, and the United Kingdom.*
1–2 June	*Conference of Messina: ECSC countries decide on a common market.*
5 August	European Monetary Agreement signed (to take effect after the end of EPU).

1956

17 October	*France obtains $262.5 million standby credit from IMF.*
October	Per Jacobsson resigns as BIS economic adviser to become managing director and chairman of the board of directors of the IMF.
4 November	*Soviet troops crush Budapest uprising.*
5 November	*French and British military intervention in Port Said/Suez.*

1957

January	With Jacobsson's departure, Paolo Baffi (economic adviser at the Bank of Italy) and Friedrich Lutz of Zurich University are

appointed part-time economic advisers to overlook preparation
of the BIS Annual Report. This arrangement will remain in place
until November 1960.

25 March	*EEC and Euratom treaties signed in Rome.*
July	*Deutsche Bundesbank replaces Bank deutscher Länder.*
10 August	*Devaluation of French franc by 16.7%.*

1958

1 January	*EEC and Euratom treaties come into force.*
18 March	*EEC Council resolution on the statutes of the EEC Monetary Committee.*
1 July	Marius W. Holtrop succeeds Frère as president of the BIS and chairman of the Board.
1 October	Guillaume Guindey succeeds Auboin as general manager of the BIS.
27 December	Announcement of the convertibility of all major European currencies for current account transactions.
29 December	*French franc devalues by 14.8%.*
31 December	European Payments Union wound up and replaced by European Monetary Agreement (EMA).

1959

1 January	*Fidel Castro's rebel army enters Havana.*
30 July	*Radcliffe Committee reports on the working of the U.K. monetary system, downplaying significance of monetary policy.*
November	*European Free Trade Association (EFTA) Convention signed.*

1960

May	*EFTA Convention enters into force.*
October	*Gold price in London temporarily reaches over $40 per ounce.*
1 November	Milton Gilbert takes up position as BIS economic adviser.
11–12 December	Charles Coombs, vice-president of the Federal Reserve Bank of New York, visits Basel on the occasion of the BIS Board meeting. From then on, Federal Reserve officials attend BIS meetings regularly.
28 December	Bank of Spain becomes BIS member.

1961

6–7 March	*Revaluation of Deutsche mark and Dutch guilder by 5%.*
12 March	BIS press communiqué on the close cooperation of central banks in the exchange markets: "Basel Agreement". Short-term credits from European central banks to Bank of England help support pound.

April	*OEEC Economic Policy Committee creates WP3 to study international payments system.*
17 April	*Failed U.S.-backed Bay of Pigs invasion of Cuba.*
13 August	*Berlin Wall built.*
September	*OECD replaces OEEC.*
12 November	Start of the "Gold Pool" aimed at stabilising the gold price through central bank market interventions.
December	General Arrangements to Borrow (GAB) are approved. Origin of the Group of Ten (G10).

1962

February	Swap network arranged by Federal Reserve, BIS, and nine other central banks.
February	The gold and foreign exchange experts of the central banks participating in the Gold Pool begin bimonthly meetings at the BIS.
7 April	*Van Campen report on EEC Monetary Coordination.*
August–November	*Cuban missile crisis.*
18 October	*First "Roosa bonds" issued in Switzerland.*
24 October	*IMF General Arrangements to Borrow (GAB) effective.*

1963

1 May	Gabriel Ferras succeeds Guillaume Guindey as BIS general manager.
5 May	*IMF Managing Director Per Jacobsson dies. Pierre-Paul Schweitzer succeeds him.*
September	*Study on the functioning of the international monetary system and its future needs for liquidity entrusted to G10 deputies.*
October	BIS invited to participate in the G10 study group's work.
22 November	*U.S. President Kennedy assassinated. Lyndon B. Johnson sworn in.*

1964

16 March	*$550 million swap agreements concluded between the Bank of Italy and U.S. Treasury and central banks.*
13 April	Formal establishment of the "Committee of the Governors of the Central Banks of the Member States of the EEC".
June	BIS starts publication of eurocurrency market statistics in the BIS Annual Report (eight European countries reporting).
6 July	First meeting of the Committee of EEC Governors at the BIS.
10 August	Publication of the G10 deputies' report on the functioning of the international monetary system and its future liquidity needs.
September–October	Experts from the central banks of Canada, Japan, and Sweden are invited to participate in the regular Gold and Foreign Exchange Experts' meetings in Basel, turning it into a G10 committee.

October– *November*	*Sterling exchange rate under pressure after the Labour election victory.*
26 November	Central banks' sterling support package of $3 billion announced.

1965

4 February	*De Gaulle press conference: plea for pure gold standard.*
10 February	*France announces it will convert all new accumulations of dollars into gold.*
1 July	*France suspends cooperation in EEC context (including Committee of EEC Governors).*
10 September	European central banks and BIS contribute $370 million to a new sterling support scheme; Bank of France abstains.
29 November	Agreement between BIS and Federal Republic of Germany on financial settlement of Young Plan–related BIS investments in Germany.

1966

29 January	*France resumes cooperation at EEC level.*
13 June	First Group Arrangement for pound sterling support.
13 September	New sterling support package ($900 million) announced.
December	For the first time in its existence, the Gold Pool ends the year with a sizeable deficit.

1967

5 June	*Israeli–Arab Six-Day War ends with Israeli victory.*
June	France withdraws from Gold Pool.
July	Jelle Zijlstra appointed president of the BIS.
14 November	BIS $250 million advance to enable United Kingdom to repay IMF credit.
18 November	*Devaluation of pound sterling by 14.3%.*
23 November	$1.5 billion central bank support package announced to defend the new sterling parity.
29 November	*IMF standby arrangement for the United Kingdom.*

1968

January– *February*	*Têt offensive: turning point in Vietnam War.*
15 March	Gold crisis climax: closure of London gold market. Washington meeting of central banks, with IMF and BIS representatives, on gold crisis.
17 March	Gold Pool operations discontinued. Central banks agree to refrain from buying and selling gold on the free market.
30 March	G10 meeting in Stockholm (with BIS).
May	*Student revolt and social unrest in France and elsewhere.*

31 May	*French decree re-establishes exchange controls.*
4 June	*France draws $745 million from IMF.*
19 June	*United Kingdom draws $1.4 billion from 1967 IMF standby arrangement.*
July	*EEC customs union completed.*
10 July	Bank of France short-term credit agreements with central banks and BIS.
20 August	*"Prague spring" crushed by Warsaw Pact troops.*
9 September	Second Sterling Group Arrangement announced.
20–22 November	G10 ministers of finance and central bank governors' meeting in Bonn.

1969

9 June	BIS Extraordinary General Meeting amends Statutes: capital is increased from 500 million to 1.5 billion gold francs, and all references to the Young Plan are deleted.
20 June	*IMF approves $1 billion standby arrangement for United Kingdom.*
20 July	*Apollo 11 moon landing.*
28 July	*IMF special drawing rights (SDRs) introduced.*
8 August	*French franc devalues 11.1% against dollar.*
19 September	*IMF approves $985 million standby arrangement for France.*
28 September	*Deutsche mark floated.*
24 October	*Floating of the DM rate ends with 9.3% revaluation.*

1970

2 January	Central banks of Canada and Japan become BIS members.
26 January	*EEC economic and finance ministers agree on measures for economic and monetary cooperation.*
9 February	Agreement on system for short-term monetary support between EC central banks signed in Basel.
26 October	*Werner Report on the creation of the Economic and Monetary Union submitted to the EC Council.*
23 December	BIS General Manager Ferras dies in car accident.
31 December	Reserve Bank of Australia becomes BIS member.

1971

9 February	*EC Council agrees on Economic and Monetary Union (EMU) to be realised by 1980.*
22 March	*EC Council of Ministers adopts the Werner Report on the realisation of EMU.*
18 April	G10 governors meeting in Basel establish Standing Committee on the Euro-Currency Market.
19 April	EEC Committee of Governors announces reduced exchange rate fluctuation margins effective 15 June.

1 May	René Larre takes up position as BIS general manager.
5 May	*Foreign exchange markets close in Germany, Austria, Belgium, the Netherlands, and Switzerland.*
9 May	Floating of Deutsche mark and Dutch guilder leads to postponement of reduced exchange rate margins planned for 15 June.
23 June	*Agreement on terms of U.K.'s entry into EEC on 1 January 1973.*
30 June	South African Reserve Bank becomes BIS member.
15 August	*President Nixon suspends gold convertibility of U.S. dollar.*
18 December	*Smithsonian Agreement: measures for monetary stability agreed by the G10 countries ("tunnel").*

1972

10 April	Basel Agreement for narrowing fluctuation margins between EC currencies adopted: the "snake" in the "tunnel".
23 June	*Pound sterling leaves the Snake.*
September	*First meeting of the IMF-sponsored Committee of Twenty (C20), set up to prepare a blueprint for the reform of the international monetary system.*

1973

1 January	*Great Britain, Denmark, and Ireland join the EEC.*
27 January	*Vietnam peace treaty signed.*
13 February	*U.S. dollar devalued by 10%. Italian lira leaves the Snake.*
March	*New currency crisis spells the definitive end of the Bretton Woods fixed–exchange rate regime.*
19 March	Switch to block floating: "tunnel" disappears but "snake" remains.
6 April	Regulation on the establishment of the European Monetary Cooperation Fund comes into force.
1 June	European Monetary Cooperation Fund becomes operational. BIS assumes function of agent.
6 October	*Arab–Israeli Yom Kippur War starts.*
10–17 October	*OPEC raises oil prices by 70%; start of first "oil shock".*
November	Central bank agreement to refrain from gold operations on the free market (Washington agreement of March 1968) officially buried.
December	Start of collection and publication of quarterly eurocurrency market statistics (or locational banking statistics) covering twelve European countries plus Canada, Japan, and the United States.

1974

17–18 January	*Committee of Twenty (C20) meeting in Rome: attempt at full-scale reform of the international monetary system abandoned. Generalised exchange rate floating.*
19 January	*French franc leaves the Snake.*
June	*Bankhaus Herstatt collapses: biggest bank failure in Germany since 1931.*

October	*Franklin National Bank (United States) collapses.*
December	G10 governors establish the Basel Committee on Banking Regulations and Supervisory Practices.

1975

8 March	*Publication of Marjolin Report on EMU and on institutional and structural disparities between EC member states.*
19 March	*Creation of European Unit of Account.*
10 July	*French franc rejoins the Snake at original parity.*
22 September	*Agreement in principle reached between Switzerland and the European Community on association of Swiss franc with the Snake arrangement.*
15–17 November	*Economic Summit of G6 at Rambouillet (France) endorses currency floating.*
20 November	*Swiss Parliament postpones indefinitely the possible association of the Swiss franc with the Snake arrangement.*
December	"Basel Concordat", adopted by the Basel Committee on Banking Regulations and Supervisory Practices, calls on host- and home-country authorities to share supervisory responsibility for banks' foreign activities.

1976

January	Alexandre Lamfalussy succeeds Milton Gilbert as BIS economic adviser.
7–8 January	*IMF agreement on use of SDRs.*
15 March	*French franc leaves the Snake.*
March–April	BIS takes up administration of the first European Community borrowing operations.
June	BIS, together with Group of Ten and Switzerland, provides a $5.3 billion six-month credit facility to the United Kingdom.
29 September	*Sterling crisis. United Kingdom requests a standby arrangement from IMF.*
18 October	*Exchange rate realignment within the Snake. Deutsche mark revalued by 2%.*

1977

3 January	*Two-year standby IMF credit for United Kingdom of SDR 3,360 million.*
10 January	Announcement at BIS of $3 billion sterling balances facility organized by seven central banks (third Sterling Group Arrangement).
4 April	*Further realignment within the Snake: devaluations of the Swedish, Norwegian, and Danish crowns, followed on 5 April by devaluation of the Finnish markka.*

| May | BIS completes move from the former Savoy Hôtel Univers to its new premises in Basel. The "Tower" officially inaugurated. |
| *28 August* | *Sweden leaves the Snake; further devaluations of Norwegian and Danish crowns.* |

1978

January	The "BIS Data Bank" of monetary and economic statistical time series becomes operational.
13 February	*8% devaluation of the Norwegian crown.*
16–17 June	*Jacques de Larosière becomes managing director of the IMF.*
16 October	*Realignment of the Snake: Deutsche mark revalued by 2% to 4% vis-à-vis other currencies.*
7 November	*IMF borrows from Germany and Japan to assist U.S. drawing of SDR 2.2 billion.*
December	*Iranian revolution and beginning of rise in oil prices.*
4–5 December	*European Council adopts the creation of European Monetary System (EMS), the Exchange Rate Mechanism (ERM), and the European Currency Unit (ECU).*
12 December	*Norway leaves the Snake.*

1979

13 March	Establishment of the European Monetary System (EMS), absorbing the Snake, and creation of European Currency Unit (ECU).
28 June	*OPEC decrees oil price increase by 24%. Second "oil shock".*
24 September	*EMS realignment: Deutsche mark revalued by 2% to 5% vis-à-vis other currencies.*
6 October	*Fed increases U.S. interest rates, convincing markets it will curb inflation.*
November	Publication of the first BIS Economic Paper ("Credit and Liquidity Creation in the International Banking Sector" by Helmut Mayer).
30 November	*EMS realignment: devaluation of Danish crown by 4.76%.*
24 December	*Soviet invasion of Afghanistan.*

1980

21 January	*Gold prices peak at $850 per ounce, a rise of 340% since November 1978.*
14 March	*U.S. credit controls imposed.*
2 April	*Prime rate of U.S. banks raised to 20%.*
17 April	*The People's Republic of China replaces Taiwan at IMF and at the World Bank.*
April	G10 governors entrust Euro-Currency Standing Committee with regular and systematic monitoring of international banking developments.
August	*Strikes in Gdansk, Poland, leading to the creation of independent union "Solidarnosc" on 22 September 1980.*

1981

1 January	*Greece joins the European Community.*
1 March	Günther Schleiminger succeeds René Larre as BIS general manager.
23 March	*EMS realignment: 6% devaluation of the Italian lira.*
October	First meeting at the BIS of the Group of Payment System Experts.
5 October	*EMS realignment: Dutch guilder and Deutsche mark revalue by 3% and 5.5% vis-à-vis other currencies.*
November	*Hungary and Poland apply for IMF membership.*
13 December	*President Jaruzelski imposes martial law in Poland, allowing for the dismantlement of Solidarnosc.*

1982

January	Fritz Leutwiler appointed president of the BIS.
22 February	*EMS realignment: devaluations of the Belgian franc (8.5%) and Danish crown (3%).*
March	Hungarian debt crisis; BIS provides emergency credit of $100 million to the National Bank of Hungary, followed by further BIS central bank assistance of $110 million in May and $300 million in September.
14 June	*EMS realignment: revaluation of German mark and Dutch guilder (4.25%); devaluation of French franc (5.75%) and Italian lira (2.75%).*
12 August	*Mexican debt crisis: Mexican Finance Minister Jesús Silva Herzog informs IMF and United States that Mexico's reserves are exhausted.*
18 August	Negotiation (IMF-Fed-BIS) of standby credit to Mexico of $1.85 billion, taking effect on 30 August; BIS provides half of the standby.
31 August	*Mexico imposes exchange controls and nationalizes its banking system; IMF subsequently organises banking consortium loan of $8.3 billion for 1983 conditional on structural reforms.*
6–9 September	*IMF and World Bank meeting in Toronto to address debt crisis of developing countries.*
8 October	*16% devaluation of the Swedish crown.*
16 November	*Bankers' meeting at the New York Federal Reserve to address the Mexican and Argentinian foreign debt problems.*
20 November	*Brazil requests a bankers' meeting to address its debt difficulties.*
December	BIS grants a $1.2 billion (increased later to $1.45 billion) bridging loan to the Central Bank of Brazil.

1983

January	BIS provides a $500 million credit facility to Argentina.
10 January	*15.5% devaluation of the Greek drachma.*
March	BIS provides $500 million assistance to the National Bank of Yugoslavia.

21 March	*EMS realignment: revaluations of the Deutsche mark (5.5%), Dutch guilder (3.5%), Danish crown (2.5%), and Belgian franc (1.5%); devaluations of the French (2.5%), Irish (3.5%), and Italian (2.5%) currencies.*
April	*Creation of the International Organisation of Securities Commissions (IOSCO).*
May	Basel Committee on Banking Supervision publishes "Principles for the Supervision of Banks' Foreign Establishment", updating the 1975 "Basel Concordat".
July	The BIS locational banking statistics (see December 1973) are complemented by worldwide bank lending statistics on a consolidated basis (bank claims with maturity and sectoral breakdown). From 1998 published as "BIS Consolidated Banking Statistics", these currently (2004) cover 30 jurisdictions, making up some 95% of international banking business.
30 November	*IMF quotas increased by SDR 29.2 billion, needed to meet the debt crisis.*

1984

1 January	*Creation of free-trade area between EC and EFTA.*
30 April	Joint BIS and 17 central banks twelve-month facility of SDR 2,505 million for drawings by IMF.
May	*Continental Illinois Bank collapses.*
25–26 June	*Fontainebleau meeting of European Council: agreement on reduction of British contribution to the Community budget.*

1985

7 January	*Jacques Delors appointed president of the European Commission.*
January	Jean Godeaux appointed president of the BIS.
12 March	Committee of EC Governors agrees on improving conditions of using and holding ECU.
14–15 April	EC Council of Ministers approves Committee of Governors agreement to pay market-level interest on ECU holdings.
1 May	Alexandre Lamfalussy succeeds Günther Schleiminger as BIS general manager. Horst Bockelmann takes up position as BIS economic adviser.
14 June	*European Commission publishes White Paper on the completion of the internal market; Schengen agreement on abolishing border controls signed by Belgium, France, Germany, Luxembourg, and the Netherlands.*
1 July	*Greece joins the EMS.*
22 July	*EMS realignment: devaluation of the Italian lira (6%) and revaluation of the other currencies (2%).*
22 September	*G-5 Plaza Agreement for concerted intervention to drive down the dollar.*
8–11 October	*Baker Plan to buy back debt at secondary markets.*
16–17 December	*Adoption of the text for the Single European Act.*

1986

1 January	*Portugal and Spain join the EC.*
25 February	*USSR communist party leader Gorbachev launches "perestroika" at the 27th party congress.*
21 March	Signature of Agreement between BIS and the ECU Banking Association (EBA) establishing the BIS as agent of the private ECU clearing and settlement system.
April	Publication of the report on "Recent Innovations in International Banking" by the Euro-Currency Standing Committee (Cross Report).
7 April	*EMS realignment: revaluation of the Dutch guilder and Deutsche mark (3%), as well as the Belgian franc and Danish crown (1%), and devaluation of the French franc (3%).*
June	*Mexican foreign debt default averted.*
August	The BIS takes up a $400 million share in an $1,100 million facility for the Bank of Mexico.
4 August	*EMS realignment: 8% devaluation of the Irish punt.*
October	BIS participates with $176 million in a $250 million facility for the central bank of Nigeria.

1987

12 January	*EMS realignment: revaluation of Dutch guilder and Deutsche mark (by 3% each) and of the Belgian franc (by 2%).*
16 January	*Michel Camdessus takes office as managing director of the IMF.*
26 January	*Gorbachev calls for "glasnost".*
10 February	Conclusion of BIS Headquarters Agreement with Swiss Federal Council. Creation of BIS Administrative Tribunal.
22 February	*Louvre Accord: G-6 finance ministers and central bank governors agree to stabilise and maintain exchange rates around their current levels.*
March	BIS provides $275 million of a $500 million bridging facility to the Central Bank of the Argentine Republic.
13 May	*Spain joins the EMS.*
1 July	*Single European Act enters into force.*
11 August	*Alan Greenspan succeeds Paul Volcker as chairman of the Fed's board of governors.*
12 September	Basel–Nyborg agreement on a comprehensive strategy and measures to strengthen the EMS.
19 October	*Black Monday: stocks drop by 22.6% on Wall Street.*
30 October	BIS provides $250 million of a second $500 million bridging facility to the Central Bank of the Argentine Republic.
10 November	*Portugal joins the EMS.*
November– December	*Bundesbank and other central banks ease their monetary policy in the wake of the stock market collapse.*
December	Basel Committee on Banking Supervision releases the document "Proposals for International Convergence of Capital Measurement and Capital Standards".

1988

January	W. F. Duisenberg elected president of the BIS.
June	BIS provides $200 million of a $250 million bridging facility for Yugoslavia.
24 June	*European Commission approves directive providing for full liberalisation of capital movements on 1 July 1990.*
27–28 June	Creation of Delors Committee ("Committee for the Study of Economic and Monetary Union") to examine steps leading to EMU.
July	Central bank governors endorse the Basel Committee on Banking Supervision's document "International Convergence of Capital Measurement and Capital Standards" or "Basel Capital Accord", to be implemented by the end of 1992.
July	BIS provides $250 million of a $500 million bridging facility to the Central Bank of Brazil.
October	BIS provides $190.5 million of a $500 million bridging facility to the Central Bank of the Argentine Republic.

1989

February	BIS Group of Experts on Payment Systems releases "Report on Netting Schemes".
15 February	*Last Soviet troops leave Afghanistan.*
10 March	*Brady proposals for reducing Third-World debt.*
12 April	Presentation of Delors Report on achieving EMU, outlining three stages and convergence criteria.
April	BIS conducts, with central banks, the first global survey of foreign exchange market activity.
19 June	*Spain joins ERM.*
August	BIS participation of $700 million in a $2 billion short-term credit support for the Bank of Mexico.
9 November	*Fall of the Berlin Wall.*
December	BIS participation of $300 million in a $500 million credit facility to the National Bank of Poland.
8 December	*EC Council decision to set up European Bank for Reconstruction and Development (EBRD).*

1990

5 January	*EMS realignment: devaluation and narrower margin for the Italian lira.*
March	BIS participation of $296 million in a $400 million credit facility to the Central Bank of Venezuela.
April	Basel Committee on Banking Supervision releases report on "Principles for the Supervision of Banks' Foreign Establishments", an amendment of the 1983 "Principles".
29 May	*Treaty signed establishing the European Bank for Reconstruction and Development (EBRD).*

11 June	*Bundesbank President Pöhl proposes achieving EMU in "a two speed process".*
20 June	BIS participation of $260 million in a $300 million bridging facility to the National Bank of Hungary and of $133.5 million in a $178 million bridging loan to the Bank of Guyana.
July	Creation at the BIS of a Service for Eastern European Countries and International Organisations in order to coordinate technical assistance to central banks in the region.
1 July	*Beginning of stage one of EMU: abolishment of capital movement restrictions.*
2 July	*Monetary union between East and West Germany.*
2 August	*Iraq invades Kuwait.*
3 October	*Political reunification of Germany.*
8 October	*United Kingdom joins the European Exchange Rate Mechanism (ERM).*
12 November	G10 governors announce establishment of permanent Committee on Payment and Settlement Systems (CPSS).
November	BIS releases report of the Committee on Interbank Netting Schemes of the central banks of the Group of Ten countries (Lamfalussy Report).

1991

January	Bengt Dennis appointed president of the BIS.
February	*UN coalition forces drive Iraqis out of Kuwait.*
7 March	BIS participation of $260 million in a $300 million credit facility to the National Bank of Romania.
14 April	*Inauguration of the EBRD in London.*
25 June	*Declarations of independence of Slovenia and Croatia from the Yugoslav Republic. Yugoslavia drifts into civil war.*
5 July	*Bank of Credit and Commerce International (BCCI) closed by central banks after allegations of fraud.*
19–22 August	*Communist hardliners attempt coup in Moscow that will lead to the break-up of the Soviet Union.*
20 August	*Re-establishment of independence of Estonia (Bank of Estonia recommenced its operations on 1 January 1990).*
21 August	*Re-establishment of independence of Latvia (Bank of Latvia created on 19 May 1992).*
September	BIS participation of 145 million ECU in a 300 million ECU bridging facility to the National Bank of Romania.
6 September	*Re-establishment of independence of Lithuania (Bank of Lithuania created in March 1990).*
17 September	*Declaration of independence of the former Yugoslav republic of Macedonia.*
9–10 December	*European Council agrees on draft Maastricht Treaty on European Union.*

1992

7 February	*Signature of the Treaty on European Union (Maastricht Treaty).*
3 March	*Declaration of independence of Bosnia-Herzegovina.*
6 April	*Portugal joins ERM.*
17 May	*Swiss referendum in favour of IMF and World Bank membership.*
1 June	*Russia joins the IMF and World Bank.*
2 June	*Danish referendum narrowly rejects the Maastricht Treaty.*
30 June	Reactivation of the BIS's shareholdership of the central banks of Estonia, Latvia, and Lithuania.
5 August	*Standby arrangement of SDR 719 million for the Russian Federation.*
14 September	*EMS realignment: Italian lira devalues by 3.5%; the ten other currencies revalue by 3.5%.*
16 September	*Italian lira, peseta, and pound sterling forced through the floor of the EMS. Sterling leaves ERM. Swedish discount rate temporarily at 500%.*
17 September	*Italian lira out of the ERM. Spanish peseta devalued 5%.*
20 September	*Referendum in France narrowly in favour of the Maastricht Treaty.*
September	Publication of the BIS Committee on Payment and Settlement Systems' report entitled "Delivery versus Payment in Securities Settlement Systems".
September	IMF, EC, EBRD, IBRD, OECD, and BIS set up the Joint Vienna Institute to provide technical training, mainly to officials from Eastern Europe, the former Soviet Union, and a number of Asian countries.
October	Euro-Currency Standing Committee (ECSC) publishes "Recent Developments in International Interbank Relations" (Promise I Report).
November	*Further devaluation of Spanish peseta and Portuguese escudo; Swedish and Norwegian currencies are allowed to float.*
6 December	*Referendum in Switzerland rejects ratification of the Agreement on the European Economic Area. Negotiations on Switzerland's accession to the EC suspended until further notice.*

1993

1 January	*Single European Market comes into force: freedom of movement for goods, services, persons, and capital.*
January– May	*Strains on ERM: devaluations of the Irish punt, Spanish peseta, and Portuguese escudo.*
1 June	*Czechoslovak Federation is dissolved and replaced with the separate Czech and Slovak Republics.*
14 June	The national banks of the Czech Republic and Slovakia become members of the BIS as successors of the Czechoslovakian central bank.
10 August	*ERM crisis: pre-emptive revision of the Exchange Rate Mechanism with the adoption of 15% floating margins for most currencies.*

September	Publication of the BIS Committee on Payment and Settlement Systems report: "Central Bank Payment and Settlement Services with Respect to Cross-Border and Multi-Currency Transactions".
1 November	*Treaty on the EU (Maastricht Treaty) takes effect.*

1994

1 January	Establishment of the European Monetary Institute (EMI) with a temporary seat at Basel; the BIS will function as agent for the EMI.
January	*International Association of Insurance Supervisors (IAIS) established.*
January	W. F. Duisenberg is re-appointed president of the BIS. Andrew D. Crockett succeeds Alexandre Lamfalussy as BIS general manager.
15 April	BIS takes up the function of collateral agent in connection with the restructuring of Brazilian external debt.
July	Publication by the Basel Committee on Banking Supervision of guidelines for the supervision and risk management of derivative business.
September	Release of the Euro-Currency Standing Committee's report: "A Discussion Paper on the Public Disclosure of Market and Credit Risk by Financial Intermediaries" (Fisher Report).
13 September	Federal Reserve System of the United States of America takes up the two seats in the Board of Directors to which it has been entitled since 1930. Governors of the Bank of Canada and of the Bank of Japan elected directors on the BIS Board.
November	European Monetary Institute (EMI) completes its move from the BIS in Basel to the Eurotower in Frankfurt.
November	Release of the Euro-Currency Standing Committee's report on "Macroeconomic and Monetary Policy Issues Raised by the Growth of Derivative Markets" (Hannoun Report).
December	*Fall of the Mexican peso by more than 50% – the country faces default.*

1995

1 January	*Austria, Finland, and Sweden join the EU and EMS; the World Trade Organization is launched as successor to the GATT.*
9 January	*Austria joins the ERM.*
February	Release of the Euro-Currency Standing Committee's report on "Issues related to the Measurement of Market Size and Macroprudential Risks in Derivative Markets" (Brockmeijer Report).
26 February	*Barings Bank crashes as a result of huge losses in derivatives trading.*
March	BIS Committee on Payment and Settlement Systems (CPSS) releases report on "Cross-Border Securities Settlements".
6 March	*Devaluations of the Spanish peseta and Portuguese escudo.*
15 March	BIS arranges short-term credit facility for up to $10 billion in favour of the Bank of Mexico.
April	BIS conducts first triennial central bank survey of foreign exchange and derivatives market activity.

28 April	BIS grants a $1 billion bridging loan to the Central Bank of the Argentine Republic.
May	Basel Committee on Banking Supervision issues "A Framework for Supervisory Information about Derivatives Activities of Banks and Securities Firms".
1 May	William R. White succeeds Bockelmann as BIS economic adviser.
15 May	Termination of BIS agency functions for the EMI.
1 July	*Schengen Application Convention comes into effect.*
October	BIS publishes report on the implications for central banks of the development of electronic money.
14 December	*Signing in Paris of the Dayton peace agreements, putting an end to three years of interethnic civil strife in Bosnia-Herzegovina.*
31 December	*Customs union between EU and Turkey comes into effect.*

1996

January	Basel Committee on Banking Supervision issues a formal amendment of its Basel Capital Accord.
March	BIS Committee on Payment and Settlement Systems publishes report on "Settlement Risk in Foreign Exchange Transactions".
15 May	*EMI council nominates Wim Duisenberg to succeed Alexandre Lamfalussy as president of the EMI on 1 July 1997.*
May	BIS publishes results of its first "Triennial Central Bank Survey of Foreign Exchange and Derivatives Market Activity".
August	The Committee on Payment and Settlement Systems and the Group of Computer Experts publish a report on "Security of Electronic Money".
October	Basel Committee on Banking Supervision issues a report on "Supervision of Cross-Border Banking".
14 October	*Finland joins the ERM.*
23 October	The International Association of Insurance Supervisors (IAIS) decides to locate its secretariat at the BIS.
1 November	The People's Bank of China, the Hong Kong Monetary Authority, the Reserve Bank of India, the Bank of Mexico, the Central Bank of the Russian Federation, the Saudi Arabia Monetary Agency, and the Monetary Authority of Singapore become shareholding members of the BIS.
24 November	*Italy rejoins the ERM.*

1997

14 January	The Bank of Korea becomes a member of the BIS.
March	BIS Committee on Payment and Settlement Systems publishes its reports on "Real-Time Gross Settlement (RTGS) Systems" and "Clearing Arrangements for Exchange-traded Derivatives".
25 March	The Central Bank of Brazil becomes a member of the BIS.
April	Basel Committee on Banking Supervision releases its "Core Principles for Effective Banking Supervision" and a "Compendium".

7 April	BIS takes up the function of collateral and escrow agent in connection with the restructuring of Peruvian external debt.
30 May	The national banks of Croatia, Macedonia, and Slovenia become members of the BIS.
8 June	First formal meeting of the Central Bank Governance Steering Group.
17 June	*Agreement on the Treaty of Amsterdam ("Stability and Growth Pact").*
20 June	*Creation of the Central Bank of Bosnia-Herzegovina.*
2 July	*Devaluation of the Thai baht after speculative attack in May and June.*
July–August	*Asian currency crisis: devaluation of the Philippine peso (11 July) and the Malaysian ringgit (14 July) and floating of the Indonesian rupiah (14 August).*
July	Alfons Verplaetse elected president of the BIS.
20 August	*IMF organizes a $16.7 billion rescue package for Thailand.*
October– *December*	*Asian crisis: $23 billion support package for Indonesia on 31 October, and an SDR 15.5 billion standby arrangement for Korea on 4 December.*
31 December	The Central Bank of Bosnia-Herzegovina becomes member of the BIS.

1998

1 March	BIS opens its archives to the public (30-year rule applies).
March	*EU launches enlargement process towards Central and Eastern Europe.*
31 March	BIS takes up the function of collateral agent in connection with the restructuring of the external debt of Côte d'Ivoire.
April	BIS cosponsors Year 2000 Round Table to help the financial industry prepare for the possible effects on information processing systems of the date changeover on 1 January 2000.
30 June	*Inauguration of European Central Bank in Frankfurt; W. Duisenberg first ECB president.*
July	Opening of the BIS Representative Office for Asia and the Pacific in the Hong Kong SAR. Host Country Agreement with China.
July	BIS Board decides to purchase the Botta building in Basel to accommodate its banking and IT services.
July	CPSS publishes "Reducing Foreign Exchange Settlement Risk: A Progress Report".
July	Creation of the BIS Financial Stability Institute (FSI).
20 July	*IMF finances an SDR 6.3 billion extended fund facility arrangement for Russia. Russia defaults on its GKO (government short-term bonds) debt and devalues the ruble in August.*
September	*Long Term Capital Management (LTCM) hedge fund nearly collapses.*
September	Joint report by the Committee on Payment and Settlement Systems and the Euro-Currency Standing Committee on "OTC Derivatives: Settlement Procedures and Counterparty Risk Management".
2 December	BIS coordinates a $13.28 billion standby arrangement for the Central Bank of Brazil.
31 December	After the euro's introduction, the BIS ceases to act as agent for the private ECU clearing and settlement system set up in 1986.

1999

1 January	*Launch of the single currency, the euro, for eleven EU member countries.*
January	BIS offers new medium-term instrument (MTI) to provide central banks with a longer-dated and liquid investment outlet.
February	Creation of Financial Stability Forum (FSF) by G7 finance ministers and central bank governors. BIS General Manager Crockett appointed chairman in a personal capacity.
February	The G10 Euro-Currency Standing Committee, established in 1971, is renamed "Committee on the Global Financial System" (CGFS).
24 March	*Nomination of Romano Prodi as president of the European Commission after resignation of the previous Commission on 15 March.*
March	Urban Bäckström elected president of the BIS.
March	BIS, IMF, World Bank, and OECD jointly publish, for the first time, creditor-based measures of countries' external debt.
April	The Committee on the Global Financial System issues recommendations for the design of liquid markets.
1 May	*EU Amsterdam Treaty enters into force.*
June	The Basel Committee for Banking Supervision releases a first consultative paper setting out a proposed reform of the 1988 Basel Capital Accord.
July	The Financial Stability Institute, set up by the BIS and the Basel Committee on Banking Supervision, starts its programme. Its purpose is to assist supervisory authorities in strengthening prudential supervision.
July	CPSS and IOSCO publish report on "Securities Lending Transactions: Market Development Implications".
September	CPSS releases report on "Retail Payments in Selected Countries: A Comparative Study".
26 September	Washington Agreement on Gold. European Central Banks announce they will limit gold sales for a five-year period to those that were already decided.
October	CGFS publishes "A Review of Financial Market Events in Autumn 1998" (Johnson Report).
October	Establishment of central bank governance network.
9 December	The European Central Bank becomes a member of the BIS.
24 December	The Central Bank of Malaysia becomes a member of the BIS.
31 December	"Joint Year 2000 Council" at the BIS coordinates efforts within the regulatory community and between the public and private financial sector to limit the impact on IT systems of the date changeover to 1 January 2000.

2000

1 March	The Bank of Thailand becomes a member of the BIS.
23 March	*Horst Köhler succeeds Camdessus as IMF managing director and chairman of the executive board.*

28 March	The Central Bank of the Argentine Republic becomes a member of the BIS.
22 September	*Joint action of ECB, Federal Reserve, and Bank of Japan to support the euro.*
September	CPSS publishes report on "Clearing and Settlement Arrangements for Retail Payments in Selected Countries".
October	Regional Treasury dealing room commences operations at the BIS Representative Office for Asia and the Pacific in Hong Kong SAR.
6 December	*IMF organizes $10 billion facility to support Turkey.*
7–11 December	*EU Intergovernmental Conference agrees on the Treaty of Nice.*

2001

1 January	*Greece becomes the twelfth member of the euro zone.*
8 January	Extraordinary General Meeting of BIS limits right to hold BIS shares exclusively to central banks and approves a mandatory repurchase of the privately held shares. Arbitral Tribunal in The Hague reconstituted.
15 January	BIS Committee on Payment and Settlement Systems publishes report on "Core Principles for Systemically Important Payment Systems".
16 January	Release of the Basel Committee's second consultative paper on the "New Basel Capital Accord".
March	Establishment of the BIS Asian Consultative Council (ACC) as a vehicle for communication between the Asian central banks and the BIS Board and management.
March	Release of the new-look BIS website: ⟨http://www.bis.org⟩.
April	Final Report of the Multidisciplinary Working Group on Enhanced Disclosure.
April	CGFS publishes "A Survey of Stress Tests and Current Practice at Major Financial Institutions".
11 June	Extraordinary General Meeting cancels the original Yugoslav issue of shares and issues new shares for the central banks of Bosnia-Herzegovina, Croatia, Macedonia, Slovenia, and Yugoslavia.
7 September	*IMF approval of SDR 16.94 billion standby for Argentina.*
11 September	*Terrorist attacks on the Pentagon in Washington and the World Trade Center in New York.*
11 November	*China becomes a member of the WTO.*
October–November	*U.S.-led coalition overthrows Taliban regime in Afghanistan.*
November	CPSS and IOSCO publish "Recommendations for Securities Settlement Systems".
December	*Argentinian government suspends external debt payment.*
December	*Enron default.*

2002

| *1 January* | *Introduction of the euro coins and banknotes in the twelve participating EU member states.* |

4 February	*IMF three-year standby credit for Turkey of SDR 12.8 billion.*
February	CGFS publishes "IT Innovation and Financial Patterns: Implications for the Financial System".
March	A. H. E. M. Wellink appointed president of the BIS.
May	The International Association of Deposit Insurers (IADI) decides to locate its secretariat at the BIS.
May	The G10 Gold and Foreign Exchange Committee (established in 1964) is renamed "Markets Committee" (MC).
6 September	*IMF approves Brazil's request for a 15-month standby credit of SDR 22.8 billion.*
November	Opening of the BIS Representative Office for the Americas in Mexico City. Host Country Agreement with Mexico.
22 November	Hague Arbitral Tribunal confirms the legality of the withdrawal of privately held BIS shares.
November	CPSS and IOSCO release assessment methodology used in "Recommendations for Securities Settlement Systems".

2003

January	CGFS publishes report on "Credit Risk Transfer".
1 February	*The Treaty of Nice (EU) enters into force.*
19 March	*Start of U.S.-led invasion of Iraq.*
March	CPSS publishes report on "Policy Issues for Central Banks in Retail Payments".
1 April	Malcolm D. Knight succeeds Andrew D. Crockett as BIS general manager.
1 April	The BIS changes its unit of account from the gold franc (in force since 1930) to the SDR (special drawing right).
29 April	The Basel Committee on Banking Supervision releases the third and final consultative paper on the New Basel Capital Accord (Basel II).
10 July	*The European Convention completes its work on a draft Constitution for Europe.*
28 July	The Bank of Algeria becomes a member of the BIS.
July	BIS entrusted with management of $1 billion Asian Bond Fund launched by the eleven members of EMEAP (Executives' Meeting of East Asia–Pacific Central Banks).
August	CPSS releases report on "The Role of Central Bank Money in Payment Systems".
13 August	BIS takes up the function of escrow agent in connection with the settlement of litigation in the United States related to the Lockerbie Pan Am flight disaster in 1988.
15 August	The Reserve Bank of New Zealand becomes a member of the BIS.
18 September	The Central Bank of the Philippines becomes a member of the BIS.
26 September	The Central Bank of Chile becomes a member of the BIS.
29 September	Bank Indonesia becomes a member of the BIS.
30 September	The Bank of Israel becomes a member of the BIS.
1 November	*Jean-Claude Trichet succeeds Wim Duisenberg as president of the ECB.*

2004

March	CGFS publishes report on "Foreign Direct Investment in the Financial Sector of Emerging Market Economies".
31 March	As a result of the entry of new members, BIS capital is increased to SDR 683.9 million.
1 May	*Estonia, Latvia, Lithuania, Poland, the Czech Republic, Slovakia, Hungary, Slovenia, Malta, and Greek Cyprus join the EU.*
7 June	*Rodrigo de Rato succeeds Horst Köhler as IMF managing director and chairman of the executive board.*
26 June	G10 central bank governors and heads of supervision endorse release of the "International Convergence of Capital Measurement and Capital Standards: A Revised Framework", better known as "Basel II", to be implemented by the end of 2006.
30 June	Launch of FSI Connect, a web-based information and learning resource for bank supervisors (with particular emphasis on the new Basel Capital Adequacy Framework).
November	CPSS and IOSCO publish "Recommendations for Central Counterparties".
17 November	*Euro exceeds $1.30 value for the first time since its launch.*
18 November	*New EU Commission chaired by José Manuel Barroso is approved by the European Parliament.*

2005

May–June	75th anniversary celebration of the BIS.

ANNEX E

Dramatis Personae: Biographical Sketches

Compiled by Edward Atkinson, BIS

ACHESON, DEAN (1893–1971) – Under-Secretary of the U.S. Treasury 1933; Assistant Secretary of State 1941–45, Under-Secretary of State 1945–47, Secretary of State 1949–53.

ADDIS, CHARLES (1861–1945) – Hong Kong and Shanghai Bank, in China 1883–1903, London Manager 1905–21; Director of the Bank of England 1921–32; Member of the Young Committee 1929; Vice-Chairman of the BIS Board 1930–32.

ANDERSON, JOHN (1882–1958) – U.K. Home Secretary 1939–40; Chancellor of the Exchequer 1943–45.

ANSIAUX, HUBERT (1908–1987) – Director of the National Bank of Belgium 1941–54, Deputy Governor 1954–57, Governor 1957–71; Alternate member of the BIS Board 1944–55, member 1957–82.

ÅSBRINK, PER (1912–1994) – Under-Secretary of State, Swedish Ministry of Transport and Communications 1951–55; Governor of Sveriges Riksbank 1955–73; Member of the BIS Board 1955–73; Member of the IMF Board 1973–76.

AUBOIN, ROGER (1891–1974) – Adviser to the National Bank of Romania 1929–37; Member of the General Council of the Bank of France 1937; General Manager of the BIS 1937–58, Alternate to the President 1948–58.

AZZOLINI, VINCENZO (1881–1967) – Director General of the Treasury 1927–28; Director General of the Bank of Italy 1928–30, Governor 1931–44; Alternate member of the BIS Board 1930, member 1930–44.

BABINGTON SMITH, MICHAEL (1901–1984) – Director of Finance, Supreme Headquarters of the Allied Expeditionary Force (SHAEF) 1943–45; Deputy Chairman, Glyn, Mills & Co. 1947–63; Director of the Bank of England 1949–69; Member of the BIS Board 1965–74.

BACHMANN, GOTTLIEB (1874–1947) – Director of the Swiss National Bank 1918, President of the Governing Board 1925–39, President of the Bank Council 1939–47; Member of the General Council of the Reichsbank 1924–30; Member of the BIS Board 1931–39.

BAFFI, PAOLO (1911–1989) – Bank of Italy 1936, Head of Research Department 1944–56, Economic Adviser 1956–60, Director General 1960–75, Governor 1975–79; External consultant for the BIS Annual Report 1956–60; Alternate member of the BIS Board 1960–75, member 1975–89, Vice-Chairman 1988–89.

BARRE, RAYMOND (1924–) – French Vice-President of the Commission of the European Communities, responsible for Economic and Financial Affairs 1967–72; Prime Minister and Minister for Economic Affairs and Finance 1976–78; Prime Minister 1978–81.

BAS VASALLO, CARLOS (1881–1938) – Senator for the province of La Coruña 1914–15; Senator for the province of Orense 1916–23; Governor of the Bank of Spain 1930–31.

BAUMGARTNER, WILFRID (1902–1978) – Member of the General Council of the Bank of France 1936–48, Governor 1949–60; Member of the BIS Board 1949–60; French Minister of Finance and Economic Affairs 1960–62.

BENEDUCE, ALBERTO (1877–1944) – President of the Consorzio di credito per le opere pubbliche; President of the Istituto per la ricostruzione industriale (IRI); Member of the BIS Board 1930–39, Vice-Chairman 1932–39; Chairman of Advisory Committee under the Young Plan 1931.

BERNSTEIN, EDWARD (1904–1996) – Assistant director of monetary research at the U.S. Treasury, 1941–46, Assistant to Secretary 1946; Director of Research at the IMF 1946–58.

BERNTSEN, OLUF (1891–1987) – Delegate of government at National Bank of Denmark 1932–36; Handelsbank Copenhagen, Resident abroad 1938–40; Société Générale New York 1939–40; Manager of the BIS Banking Department 1946–56.

BEVIN, ERNEST (1881–1951) – Member of Parliament (U.K.) 1940–51; Minister of Labour and National Service 1940–45; Foreign Secretary 1945–51.

BEYEN, JOHAN WILLEM (1897–1976) – Treasury of the Netherlands 1919–23; Alternate of the president of the BIS 1935–37, President 1937–39; Director, Lever Bros. and Unilever Ltd. 1940–46; Executive Director of the IMF 1948–52; Dutch Minister of Foreign Affairs 1952–56.

BISSELL, RICHARD (1909–1994) – MIT Assistant Professor of Economics 1942–48, Professor 1948–52; Economic Cooperation Agency's Assistant Administrator for programme 1948–51, Acting Administrator 1951; CIA Special Assistant to Director 1954–59.

BLACK, EUGENE R. (1898–1992) – U.S. Executive Director IBRD 1947–49, President 1949–62.

BLESSING, KARL (1900–1971) – Reichsbank 1920–31; BIS 1931–34; Adviser, Ministry of Economic Affairs 1934–37; Director of the Reichsbank 1937–39; Director of the Unilever Group in Germany 1939–41 and 1948–57, Chairman 1952–57; President of the Deutsche Bundesbank 1958–69; Member of the BIS Board 1958–69.

BLUM, LÉON (1872–1950) – President of the Council (Prime Minister of France) 1936–37; Vice-President of the Council 1937–38; President of the Council and Finance Minister March–April 1938; Ambassador Extraordinary of France 1946; President of the Council and Foreign Minister, Provisional Government December 1946–January 1947.

BOLTON, GEORGE (1900–1982) – Adviser, Bank of England 1933 and 1941–48, Executive Director 1948–57, Director 1957–68; Member of the BIS Board 1949–57; Chairman of the Bank of London and South America 1957–70.

BÖÖK, KLAS (1909–1980) – Deputy Governor of Sveriges Riksbank 1944, Governor 1948–51; Director of the Foreign Trade Department at the Swedish Ministry for Foreign Affairs 1947; Member of the BIS Board 1949–51.

BRÉART DE BOISANGER, YVES (1896–1976) – Senior member of the Council of State 1937; Second then First Deputy Governor of the Bank of France 1937–40, Governor 1940–44; Alternate member of the BIS Board 1937–40, member 1940–44.

BRIAND, ARISTIDE (1862–1932) – President of the Council (Prime Minister of France) 1909–11, January–February 1913, October 1915–March 1917, January 1921–January 1922, November 1925–July 1926, 1929; Joint winner of the Nobel Peace Prize with Gustav Stresemann 1926.

BRINCKMANN, RUDOLF (1889–1974) – Entered M.M. Warburg & Co. 1920, partner (later Brinckmann, Wirtz & Co. and M.M. Warburg-Brinckmann, Wirtz & Co.) 1938–1973; Member of the BIS Board 1950–70.

BRUINS, GIJSBERT W. J. (1883–1948) – First Professor and Vice-Chancellor of the Nederlandsche Handels-Hoogeschool, Rotterdam 1913–25; International Commissioner of the Reichsbank 1925–30; Adviser to Austrian National Bank 1931; Royal Commissioner of the Netherlands Bank 1926–43 and 1945–46; Executive Director of the IMF 1946–48.

BRUNET, JACQUES (1901–1990) – General Manager of the Bank of Algeria and Tunisia 1946–48; Chairman and Managing Director of Crédit National 1949–60; Governor of the Bank of France 1960–69; Member of the BIS Board 1960–69.

BRÜNING, HEINRICH (1885–1970) – Member of the Reichstag 1924–33; Reich Chancellor 1930–32.

BURGESS, W. RANDOLPH (1889–1978) – Entered Federal Reserve Bank of New York 1920, Deputy Governor 1930–36, Vice-President (title changed) 1936–38; Deputy to U.S. Secretary of the Treasury 1953–54, Under-Secretary of the Treasury 1955–57; Alternate Governor IMF 1953–57; U.S. Permanent Representative to NATO 1957–61.

BURNS, ARTHUR F. (1904–1987) – Chairman of the U.S. President's Council of Economic Advisers 1953–56; Member of the President's Advisory Committee on Labor–Management Policy 1961–66; Counsellor to the President 1969–70; Chairman of the Board of Governors of the Federal Reserve System 1970–78; Alternate Governor IMF 1973–78.

CAIRNCROSS, ALEXANDER (ALEC) (1911–1998) – Economic Adviser of the Board of Trade 1946–49; Professor of Applied Economics, University of Glasgow, 1951–61; Economic Adviser of the U.K. Government 1961–64; Head of the Government Economic Service 1964–69; Master of St. Peter's College, Oxford 1969–78.

CALLAGHAN, LEONARD JAMES (1912–) – Member of Parliament (U.K.) 1945–87; Chancellor of the Exchequer 1964–67; Home Secretary 1967–70; Foreign Secretary 1974–76; Prime Minister 1976–79; Leader of Labour Party 1976–80.

CARLI, GUIDO (1914–1993) – Member of the Board of Directors of the IMF 1947; Chairman of the Managing Board of the European Payments Union 1950–52; Minister for Foreign Trade 1957–58; Governor of the Bank of Italy 1960–75; Alternate member of the BIS Board 1959–60, member 1960–75.

CASSEL, GUSTAV (1866–1945) – Professor of Political Economy, Stockholm 1904; Member of the Gold Delegation of the League of Nations 1929–32; Swedish delegate to the World Monetary and Economic Conference, London 1933.

CATTO, THOMAS SIVEWRIGHT (1879–1959) – Director of Yule, Catto & Co., London 1919–40; Managing Director of Morgan Grenfell 1928–40; Director of the Bank of England 1940; Financial Adviser to the Treasury 1940–44; Governor of the Bank of England 1944–49; Member of the BIS Board 1944–49.

CLAPPIER, BERNARD (1913–1999) – Director of foreign economic relations at the Ministry of Economic Affairs 1951–63; Second Deputy Governor of the Bank of France 1963, First Deputy Governor 1966–72; Managing Director of Crédit National 1973–74; Governor of the Bank of France 1974–79; Alternate member of the BIS Board 1964–73, member 1974–94, Vice-Chairman 1983–85 and 1989–91.

COBBOLD, CAMERON (KIM) (1904–1987) – Entered Bank of England as Adviser 1933, Executive Director 1938–45, Deputy Governor 1945–49, Governor 1949–61; Alternate member of the BIS Board 1934–49, member 1949–61.

COCHRAN, H. MERLE (1892–1973) – Consul, Paris 1927–30; Consul, Basel 1930–32; Appointed Foreign Service Officer U.S. Embassy, Paris 1932; Adviser at 1st meeting of Experts' Preparatory Committee for International Monetary and Economic Conference, Geneva 1932, assisted at 2nd meeting, Geneva 1933; Deputy Managing Director of IMF 1953–62.

CONNALLY, JOHN (1917–1993) – U.S. Secretary of the Navy 1961; Governor of Texas 1962–69; Secretary of the Treasury 1971–72.

CONOLLY, FREDERICK GEORGE (1899–1972) – Bank of England 1919–31; BIS 1932–65, Manager of the Monetary and Economic Department 1948–65, representative Monetary Compensation Agreement, Multilateral Compensation Agreement, European Payments Union, European Monetary Agreement.

COOMBS, CHARLES (1918–1981) – Financial Adviser to Greek Government 1944–45; Federal Reserve Bank of New York, Economist 1946–51, Chief 1951–53, Manager 1953–57, Assistant Vice-President 1958–59, Vice-President in charge of the Foreign Function 1959–75.

CRIPPS, (RICHARD) STAFFORD (1889–1952) – Member of Parliament (U.K.) 1931–50; Leader of House of Commons 1942; Minister of Aircraft Production 1942–45; President of Board of Trade 1945–47; Chancellor of the Exchequer 1947–50.

CROMER, GEORGE ROWLAND (1918–1991) – Joined Baring Brothers & Co. Ltd. 1938, Managing Director 1948–61; Governor of the Bank of England 1961–66; Member of the BIS Board 1961–66.

CUNO, WILHELM (1876–1933) – General Manager of Hapag 1918; Reich Chancellor 1922–23; President of Hapag 1926.

DALTON, EDWARD HUGH (1887–1962) – Member of Parliament (U.K.) 1924–29, Minister of Economic Warfare 1940–42, President of Board of Trade 1942–45, Chancellor of the Exchequer 1945–47.

D'AROMA, ANTONIO (1912–2002) – Bank of Italy 1936–61; Office of the President of the Italian Republic 1948–55, Personal Assistant to President Einaudi 1949–55; Secretary General of the BIS 1962–74, Assistant General Manager 1975–77; Secretary General of Committee of Governors of Central Banks of the Member States of the EEC 1964–77.

DAWES, CHARLES GATES (1865–1951) – U.S. Comptroller of the Currency 1897–1901; Director of Bureau of the Budget 1921–22; Vice-President of the United States 1925–29; Ambassador to U.K. 1929–32; Winner of the Nobel Peace Prize 1925.

DEALTRY, MICHAEL G. (1925–) – Bank of England 1950–53; Monetary and Economic Department (MED) of the BIS 1954–90, Joint Secretary of the G10 Deputies, Manager of the MED 1981–90, Deputy Head of the MED 1986–90.

DE GASPERI, ALCIDE (1881–1954) – Italian Prime Minister 1945–54; Elected President of the European Coal and Steel Community 1954.

DE JONG, A. M. (1893–1969) – Director of the Netherlands Bank 1940–43 and 1945–47, Director's Secretary 1947–59.

DEROY, HENRI (1900–1979) – Secretary General of the Ministry of Finance 1940–43; Governor of Crédit Foncier de France 1945–55; Member of the General Council of the Bank of France; Member of the BIS Board 1948–79, Vice-Chairman 1970–79.

DE STRYCKER, CECIL (1915–2004) – Entered National Bank of Belgium 1945, Director 1958–71, Deputy Governor 1971–75, Governor 1975–82; Alternate member of the BIS Board 1956–71, member 1975–89.

DILLON, C. DOUGLAS (1909–2003) – Director and President of the United States and Foreign Securities Corporation 1936; Vice-President of Dillon, Read and Company, Director 1938, Chairman of the Board 1946; Ambassador to France 1953–59; U.S. Under-Secretary of State 1959–61; U.S. Secretary of the Treasury 1961–65.

DULLES, ELEANOR LANSING (1895–1996) – Research Associate with the Bureau of International Research (Harvard University and Radcliffe College), Switzerland 1930–32; Chief Finance Division, Social Security Board, Washington, 1936–42; Bureau of Economic Warfare 1942; Department of State 1942–62.

ECCLES, MARRINER S. (1890–1977) – Assistant to U.S. Secretary of the Treasury 1934; Governor of the Federal Reserve Board 1934–35, Chairman of the Board of Governors of the Federal Reserve System (title changed) 1935–48, Board member 1948–51.

EINAUDI, LUIGI (1874–1961) – Professor of Public Finance at University of Turin 1902–49 and 1955; Member of Senate, Kingdom of Italy 1919–45; Governor of the Bank of Italy 1945–48; Member of the BIS Board 1945–48; Constituent Assembly 1946–48; Senate of the Italian Republic April–May 1948 and 1955–61; Vice-Premier and Minister of Budget 1947–48; President of the Italian Republic 1948–55.

EINZIG, PAUL (1897–1973) – Paris correspondent, *Financial News* 1921, Foreign Editor, 1923, Political Correspondent 1939–45; Political Correspondent, *Financial Times* 1945–56.

EMMINGER, OTMAR (1911–1986) – Entered Bank deutscher Länder (later the Deutsche Bundesbank) 1950, member of the Board of Governors 1953, member of the Central Bank Council 1958, Vice-President and Vice-Chairman of Central Bank Council 1970; Executive Board IMF 1953–59; Chairman of Group of Ten Deputies 1964–67; Alternate member of the BIS Board 1969–77, member 1977–79; President of the Deutsche Bundesbank 1977–79.

FARNIER, CHARLES (1894–1980) – Principal Private Secretary to the Minister of Finance 1926–27; Second Deputy Governor of the Bank of France 1930–34; Alternate member of the BIS Board 1930–34.

FERRARI, ALBERTO (1914–1994) – First permanent Italian delegate of the Intra-European Payments Committee of OEEC 1948–50; Italian delegate at NATO committees (Paris and London); Secretary General of the BIS 1951–61.

FERRAS, GABRIEL (1913–1970) – Bank of France 1938; Alternate Representative for France in the European Payments Union 1953–63; Alternate Executive Director of the Managing Board of the IMF, Deputy Director of Exchange Restrictions Department, Director European Department; General Manager of the BIS 1963–70.

FOURNIER, PIERRE (1892–1972) – Second Deputy Governor of the Bank of France 1929–30, First Deputy Governor 1930–37, Governor 1937–40; Alternate member of the BIS Board 1934–37, member 1937–40; President of the SNCF 1940–46.

FOWLER, HENRY H. (1908–2000) – Director of the Office of Defence Mobilization, member of the National Security Council, 1952–53; U.S. Under-Secretary of the Treasury 1961–64, Secretary 1965–69.

FRANCK, LOUIS (1868–1937) – Member of Parliament (Belgium) 1906–26; Colonial Minister 1918–24; Governor of the National Bank of Belgium 1926–37; Member of the BIS Board 1930–37.

FRANCQUI, EMILE (1863–1935) – Chairman of the Banque d'Outremer 1915–23; Vice-Governor of Société Générale de Belgique 1923–32, Governor 1932–35; Minister without Portfolio (Belgium) 1926 and 1934–35; Member of the BIS Board 1930–34.

FRASER, LEON (1889–1945) – General Counsel, Dawes Reparation Plan 1924–27; Alternate of the president of the BIS and member of the Board 1930–33, President and Chairman of the Board 1933–35; Vice-President of The First National Bank of the City of New York 1935–36, President 1937–45.

FRÈRE, MAURICE (1890–1970) – Economic Adviser to Transfer Committee (Dawes Plan) in Berlin 1924–30; Adviser to Austrian National Bank 1932–37; President of Banking Commission 1938–44; Governor of the National Bank of Belgium 1944–57; President of the BIS 1948–58, member of the BIS Board 1944–70, Chairman 1946–58, Vice-Chairman 1965–70; Governor for Belgium of the IMF 1946–57.

FRIEDMAN, MILTON (1912–) – Professor of Economics at the University of Chicago 1948–82, Professor Emeritus since 1982; Member of Research Staff of the National Bureau of Economic Research 1948–81; Economic Columnist for *Newsweek,* 1966–84; Senior Research Fellow at the Hoover Institution (Stanford University) since 1976.

FUNK, WALTHER (1890–1960) – Head of the Reich Press Department then Permanent Secretary of the Reich Ministry for the Enlightenment of the People and Propaganda 1933–37; Reich Minister of Trade and Commerce and Plenipotentiary for the War Economy 1938–45; President of Reichsbank 1939–45; Member of the BIS Board 1939–45. Sentenced to life imprisonment at Nuremberg 1946; released from prison on health grounds 1957.

GILBERT, MILTON (1909–1979) – Chief of National Income Division, U.S. Department of Commerce 1941–51; Director of Statistics and Director of Economics at the Organisation for European Economic Co-operation (OEEC), Paris 1951–60; Economic Adviser and Head of the Monetary and Economic Department of the BIS 1960–75.

GLASS, CARTER (1858–1946) – Member of U.S. Congress 1902–19, as Chairman of Committee on Banking and Currency was patron and floor manager of Federal Reserve Bank Act in House of Representatives; Secretary of Treasury 1918–20; Senator for Virginia 1920–46.

GUINDEY, GUILLAUME (1909–1989) – Responsible for international affairs in the French Ministry of Finance 1943–53 (Algiers and Paris); President of the Mines de Cuivre de Mauritanie 1953–58; General Manager of the BIS 1958–63; President of the Supervisory Board of the Caisse Centrale de Coopération Economique 1965–72.

GUISAN, HENRI (1909–1994) – Assistant Legal Adviser and later Legal Adviser at the Caisse des Prêts de la Confédération Suisse à Berne 1935–41; BIS Legal Service 1941–74, Legal Adviser 1955–74.

GUTT, CAMILLE ADOLPHE (1884–1971) – Member of the Young Committee 1929; Belgian Minister of Finance 1934–35 and 1939–45; Minister of Economic Affairs 1940–45; Member of the BIS Board 1945–46; first Managing Director of the IMF 1946–51.

HABERLER, GOTTFRIED (1901–1995) – Lecturer and later Professor of Economics and Statistics at the University of Vienna; Expert attached to the League of Nations Financial Section 1934–36; Member of Faculty at Harvard University 1936–71.

HARRISON, GEORGE (1887–1958) – Federal Reserve Board, Assistant General Counsel 1914–17; General Counsel 1919–20; Federal Reserve Bank of New York, Deputy Governor 1920–28, Governor 1928–36, President 1936–41; New York Life Insurance Company, President 1941–48, Chairman 1948–58.

HAWTREY, RALPH GEORGE (1879–1975) – U.K. Treasury 1904–45; Director of Financial Enquiries 1919–45; special leave to lecture in economics at Harvard 1928–29; Price Professor of International Economics, Chatham House 1947–52; President of Royal Economic Society 1946–48.

HAYES, ALFRED (1910–1989) – Assistant Vice-President of New York Trust Co. 1946, Vice-President 1949–56; President of the Federal Reserve Bank of New York and Vice-Chairman of the Federal Open Market Committee 1956–75; Chairman of Morgan Stanley International Inc. 1975.

HECHLER, PAUL (1885–1945) – Reichsbank 1910; German Ministry of Industry and Commerce 1926–33; Reichsbank 1933–34; Member of German trade delegation to South America from July 1934 to January 1935; Assistant General Manager and Head of the Banking Department of the BIS 1935–45.

HOFFMAN, PAUL GRAY (1891–1974) – Federal Reserve Bank of Chicago 1942–49; Administrator of Economic Cooperation Act (Marshall Plan) 1948–50; Administrator of the United Nations Development Programme 1966–72.

HOLTROP, MARIUS WILHELM (1902–1988) – Managing Director, Royal Dutch Blast Furnaces and Steel Works, Ijmuiden 1939–46; President of the Netherlands Bank 1946–67; Member of the BIS Board 1946–58, President of the BIS and Chairman of the Board 1958–67; Alternate Governor of the IMF 1947–52, Governor 1952–57.

HÜLSE, ERNST (1881–1949) – Reichsbank 1906–30; Assistant General Manager and Head of the Banking Department of the BIS 1930–35; Alternate member of the BIS Board 1935–38; Member of the Board of Directors of the Reichsbank 1935–39; Reichsbank British Zone 1946–48; President of the Landeszentralbank Nordrhein-Westfalen 1948–49.

JACOBSSON, PER (1894–1963) – Member of the Economic and Financial Section of the Secretariat of the League of Nations 1920–28; Secretary-General to Economic Defence Council, Stockholm 1929–30; Economic Adviser of the BIS 1931–56, Head of the Monetary and Economic Department 1946–56; Member of the Irish Banking Commission 1934–38; Chairman of the Executive Board and Managing Director of the IMF 1956–63.

JANSON, GEORGES (1921–) – National Bank of Belgium 1946–55; OEEC/OECD 1955–61; Manager in the Banking Department of the BIS 1962–71; Director of the National Bank of Belgium 1971–88; Alternate member of the BIS Board 1971–88.

JANSSEN, ALBERT EDOUARD (1883–1966) – Director of the National Bank of Belgium 1919–25; Member of the Financial Committee of the League of Nations 1921–40; Expert for the Dawes Plan 1924–30; President of the League of Nations Commission for the Study of the Gold Question 1929–33; Belgian Minister of Finance 1925–26, 1938–39, and 1952–54; Member of the BIS Board 1948–52 and 1954–56.

JANSSEN, GEORGES (1892–1941) – Secretary General and then administrator and director of the Mutuelle Solvay 1928–31; Deputy administrator of the Société Belge de Banque

1932–35; Vice-Governor of the National Bank of Belgium 1937–38, Governor 1938–41; Member of the BIS Board 1937–41.

KELLER, PAUL VICTOR (1898–1973) – Professor of Social Economy, Commercial University St. Gallen 1930; Delegate for Commercial Treaties 1938; President of the Governing Board of the Swiss National Bank 1947–56.

KEYNES, JOHN MAYNARD (1883–1946) – Fellow of King's College, Cambridge 1909–46; Member of the Treasury's Committee on Finance and Industry 1929–31; Member of the Economic Advisory Council (EAC) created by Prime Minister Ramsay Mac-Donald to advise the U.K. government in economic matters 1930; Chairman of the EAC Committee of Economists 1930; H.M. Treasury 1914–19 and 1940–46; Editor of *Economic Journal* 1911–44.

KINDERSLEY, ROBERT MOLESWORTH (1871–1954) – Partner at Lazard Brothers 1906, Chairman 1919; Director of the Bank of England 1914–46; National Savings Committee 1920–46.

KITAMURA, KOJIRO (?) – Director of Berlin Branch of Yokohama Specie Bank; Member of the BIS Board 1943–46; Member of the Yokohama Specie Bank Board 1945–46; President of the Bank of Shiga.

KLASEN, KARL (1909–1991) – President of the Hansestadt Hamburg Landeszentralbank 1948–52; Member of the Norddeutsche Bank Board 1952–57; Member of the Deutsche Bank Board 1957–69 and joint spokesman of the Board 1967–69; President of the Deutsche Bundesbank 1970–77; Member of the BIS Board 1970–77.

KOSZUL, JULIEN-PIERRE (1903–1994) – General Manager Foreign Service, Bank of France 1955–64; Alternate member of the BIS Board 1959–64; Vice-President of Managing Committee, European Monetary Agreement 1962–64.

LABEYRIE, EMILE (1877–1966) – Revenue Court 1925–32; Public Prosecutor of the Revenue Court 1933–36; Governor of the Bank of France 1936–37; Member of the BIS Board 1936–37.

LAMONT, THOMAS W. (1870–1948) – Partner in J.P. Morgan & Co. 1911–40, Vice-Chairman of the Board and Chairman of the Executive Committee of J.P. Morgan & Co. Inc. 1940–43; Representative of U.S. Treasury on American Commission to negotiate peace, Paris 1919; Alternate delegate of Committee of Experts on German Reparations (Young Plan), Paris 1929.

LARRE, RENÉ (1915–1999) – Inspecteur des Finances 1945; Minister Plenipotentiary responsible for financial matters at the French Embassy in Washington, DC 1961–67; French Executive Director IMF 1964–67; Head of the Treasury Department, Ministry of Economic and Financial Affairs 1967–71; General Manager of the BIS 1971–81.

LAVAL, PIERRE (1883–1945) – President of the Council (Prime Minister of France) and Foreign Minister 1931–32, 1935–36; Deputy President of the Council and Minister of Information 1940; Foreign Minister 1940; Head of the Government, Foreign Minister, Minister of the Interior and Minister of Information and Propaganda 1942.

LAYTON, WALTER THOMAS (1884–1966) – Editor of *The Economist* 1922–38; Delegate to World Economic Conference 1927; Member of the Organisation Committee of the BIS 1929, of committee appointed as result of London Conference to inquire into Germany's credit position, and of advisory committee under the Young Plan (Beneduce Committee) 1931.

LUTHER, HANS (1879–1962) – German Minister for Agriculture and Food 1922–23; German Minister of Finance 1923–25; Chancellor 1925–26; President of Reichsbank

1930–33; Member of the BIS Board 1930–33; Ambassador to the United States 1933–37.

LUTZ, PROFESSOR FRIEDRICH (1901–1975) – Professor at Princeton University 1947–53; Professor of Economics at Zurich University 1953–75, Professor Emeritus from 1972; external consultant for the BIS Annual Report 1956–60.

LUXFORD, ANSEL FRANK (1911–1971) – Counsel's Office of U.S. Treasury 1935–39; Assistant Counsel for Foreign Funds Control 1942–43, Assistant General Counsel 1944; Chief Legal Adviser to the U.S. Delegation at Bretton Woods 1944.

LUZZATTI, LUIGI (1841–1927) – Professor of Constitutional Law at the University of Padua 1866–95; Member of Italian Chamber of Deputies 1871–1921; Senator 1921–27; Minister of the Treasury 1903–05 and 1920; Prime Minister 1910–11.

MACDONALD, DONALD H. (1908–1990) – Bank of England Overseas and Foreign Department 1939–48; Chief of U.K. Element, Allied Banking Commission for Germany 1948–52; Bank of England, Adviser 1952–54; Banking Department of the BIS 1954–73, Manager 1962–72, Head of the Banking Department 1972–73.

MANDEL, HANS HEINRICH (1907–2000) – Reichsbank Halle 1933–37; Diskontbank Berlin 1937–39; Wartime military service and then U.S. prisoner of war; Interpreter for U.S. occupation forces in Germany 1946; Bank deutscher Länder 1948–54; Banking Department of the BIS 1954–72, Manager 1956–62, Head of the Banking Department 1962–72.

MARJOLIN, ROBERT ERNEST (1911–1986) – Assistant to Professor Charles Rist 1934–37; Deputy General Commissioner of the "Plan de Modernisation et d'Équipement" 1946–48; Secretary General of the OEEC 1948–55; Vice-President of the Commission of the European Economic Community for Finance and Economics 1958–67.

MARSHALL, GEORGE C. (1880–1959) – U.S. Army officer 1901–1944, General of the Army 1944; Special Representative of the President to China with personal rank of Ambassador 1945; Secretary of State 1947–49; Defense Secretary 1950–51.

MARTIN, WILLIAM MCCHESNEY (1906–1998) – Assistant Secretary of the Treasury 1949–51; U.S. Executive Director IBRD 1949–52; Chairman of the Federal Reserve Board 1951–70.

MAUDLING, REGINALD (1917–1979) – U.K. Chancellor of the Exchequer 1962–64; Home Secretary 1970–72.

McCLOY, JOHN (1895–1989) – Assistant Secretary of War 1941–45; President of the IBRD 1947–49; U.S. Military Governor and U.S. High Commander for Germany, Frankfurt 1949–52; Chairman of The Chase Manhattan Bank 1953–60; Adviser to President Kennedy on Disarmament 1961; Chairman of the Coordinating Committee of the U.S. on Cuban Crisis 1962–63.

McFADDEN, LOUIS T. (1876–1936) – Member of Congress for Pennsylvania 1915–35, Chairman of the House of Representatives' Committee on Banking and Currency 1920–31.

McGARRAH, GATES W. (1863–1940) – U.S. member, General Council of the Reichsbank 1924–27; Chairman and Federal Reserve Agent, Federal Reserve Bank of New York 1923–25 and 1927–30; President of the BIS and Chairman of the Board 1930–33, Honorary President and member of the Board 1933–35.

McKITTRICK, THOMAS HARRINGTON (1889–1970) – with National City Bank of New York, Genoa, Italy, 1916–18; with Lee Higginson & Co., New York 1919–21, with Higginson & Co., London 1922–39, partner 1924–39; President of the BIS 1939–46;

Director of Chase Bank 1946–54, Vice-President of the Chase National Bank of New York 1946, Senior Vice-President 1949–54.

MELCHIOR, CARL (1871–1933) – Counsel, M.M. Warburg & Co., 1902, partner 1917; Member, German delegation to Paris Peace Conference 1919; German representative on the Young Committee 1929; Vice-Chairman of the BIS Board 1930–33.

MENICHELLA, DONATO (1896–1984) – Director General of the Istituto ricostruzione industriale (IRI) 1934; Director General of the Bank of Italy 1946–48, Governor 1948–60; Member of the BIS Board 1946–74.

MEYER, EUGENE (1875–1959) – Governor of the Federal Reserve Board 1930–33; Publisher and Editor of the *Washington Post* 1933–46; First President of the International Bank for Reconstruction and Development (IBRD) 1946.

MILLS, OGDEN L. (1884–1937) – New York State Senate 1914–17; U.S. Congress 1921–27; Under-Secretary of the Treasury 1927–32, Secretary 1932–33.

MITZAKIS, MICHEL GEORGES (1898–?) – Inspector Bank of France until 1933; seconded to BIS Central Bank Liaison Service 1930–33; Military Government of the French Zone in Germany, Representative at the Reichsbank and then Manager of the Foreign Exchange Office and member of the Allied Banking Commission 1945–49.

MONICK, EMMANUEL GEORGES MICHEL (1893–1984) – Inspector General of Finance 1920–45; Financial Attaché in Washington 1930–34, in London 1934–40; Governor of the Bank of France 1944–49; Member of the BIS Board 1944–49.

MOREAU, ÉMILE (1868–1950) – Governor of the Bank of France 1926–30; French member, Committee of Experts on Reparations 1929; Member of the BIS Board 1930; President of the Banque de Paris et des Pays-Bas 1930.

MORET, CLÉMENT (1885–1943) – with French Ministry of Finance 1908–28; Second Deputy Governor of the Bank of France 1928–29, First Deputy Governor 1929–30, Governor 1930–35; Member of the BIS Board 1930–35.

MORGAN, JOHN PIERPONT (J. P.), JR. (1867–1943) – Chairman of J.P. Morgan & Co. Inc., New York; Morgan, Grenfell & Co., London; Drexel & Co., Philadelphia; Morgan et Cie, Paris; Member of Commission to deal with German Reparations, 1929.

MORGAN, SHEPARD (1884–?) – Assistant Federal Reserve Agent for Federal Reserve Bank of New York 1919–24; Economic Adviser and later Finance Director Office for Reparation Payments, Berlin 1924–30; Vice-President and Chairman of Committee of Foreign Services, Chase National Bank 1930–49.

MORGENTHAU, HENRY, JR. (1891–1967) – Governor of the Farm Credit Administration 1933; Acting and Under-Secretary of the U.S. Treasury 1933–34; Secretary of the U.S. Treasury 1934–45.

NIEMEYER, OTTO ERNST (1883–1971) – Controller of Finance and Supply Services, Treasury 1922–27; entered Bank of England 1927, Director 1938–52; Member of the BIS Board 1932–65, Chairman 1937–40, Vice-Chairman 1946–64.

NORMAN, MONTAGU COLLET (1871–1950) – Director of the Bank of England 1907–44, Deputy Governor 1918–20, Governor 1920–44; Member of the BIS Board 1930–44.

O'BRIEN, LESLIE KENNETH (1908–1995) – Entered Bank of England 1927, Deputy Chief Cashier 1951–55, Chief Cashier 1955–62, Executive Director 1962–64, Deputy Governor 1964–66, Governor 1966–73; Member of the BIS Board 1966–73 and 1974–83, Vice-Chairman 1979–83.

OSSOLA, RINALDO (1913–1990) – Entered Bank of Italy 1938, Deputy Director General 1969–75, Director General 1975–76; Chairman of the Deputies of the Group of Ten 1967–76; Alternate member of the BIS Board 1975–76.

PALLAIN, GEORGES (1847–1923) – Ministry of Finance 1876–1884 (member of Léon Gambetta's cabinet 1881–82); Director-General of Customs 1884–1897; Governor of the Bank of France 1897–1920.

PARSONS, MAURICE (1910–1978) – Entered Bank of England 1928, Private Secretary to Montagu Norman 1939–43, Deputy Chief Cashier 1950, Assistant to the Governors 1955, Executive Director 1957; Alternate Governor for the U.K. to the IMF 1957–66; Alternate member of the BIS Board 1963–66; Deputy Governor of the Bank of England 1966–70.

PILOTTI, RAFFAELE (1885–1974) – Joined Italian Ministry for Agriculture, Industry and Trade 1912; Head of the Italian National Institute for Export 1926–28; Head of the general management of the Italian Ministry of Trade 1928–30; Secretary General of the BIS 1930–51.

PORTERS, R. H. (?) – Bank of England; Manager at the BIS 1931–36, Chief Administrative Officer 1932–36.

PRIMO DE RIVERA, MIGUEL (1870–1930) – Graduated from the General Military Academy in Toledo 1888, served as officer in Morocco, Cuba, and the Philippines; Military Governor of Cadiz 1915; Dictator of Spain 1923–30.

PUHL, EMIL (1889–1962) – Reichsbank 1913–45, Member of the Board of Directors 1934–45, Deputy President 1939–40, Executive Vice-President 1940–45; Alternate member of the BIS Board 1939–45. Sentenced to five years' imprisonment at Nuremberg but released from prison in 1949; Member of the Board of Directors of Hamburger Kreditbank.

QUESNAY, PIERRE (1895–1937) – Head of the Economic Analysis Department of the Bank of France 1926–29; Member of Young Plan Committee 1929; Expert at the Hague and London Conferences 1929–30; General Manager of the BIS 1930–37.

RAINONI, ANTONIO (1910–1978) – Bank of Italy, Private Secretary to Governor Einaudi 1945–46; Monetary and Economic Department (MED) of the BIS 1946–76, Research Sub-Manager working with Baffi and Lutz on the BIS Annual Report 1956–60, Manager 1965–76.

RASMINSKY, LOUIS (1908–1998) – Economic Section, League of Nations 1930–40; Entered Bank of Canada 1940; Member of the IMF Board 1946–61; Executive Director of the IBRD 1950–62; Deputy Governor of the Bank of Canada 1955–61, Governor 1961–73.

REYNOLDS, JACKSON (1873–?) – General Attorney for Central Railroad Co. of New Jersey 1906–17; President of First National Bank of City of New York 1922–37; Chairman of the Board of First National Bank 1937–39; Chairman of the Organisation Committee for the BIS, Baden-Baden 1929.

RICHARDSON, GORDON (1915–) – Chairman of J. Henry Schroder Wagg & Co. Ltd. 1962–72; Schroders Ltd. 1966–73; Schroder Banking Corp. Inc. (NY) 1968–73; Governor of the Bank of England 1973–83; Member of the BIS Board 1973–88, Vice-Chairman 1985–88.

RIST, CHARLES (1874–1955) – Economist; Deputy Governor of the Bank of France 1926–29.

RODD, FRANCIS JAMES RENNELL (1895–1978) – Bank of England 1929–32; Manager at the BIS 1930–31; Secretary of the League Loans Committee, London 1932; Joined Morgan Grenfell & Co. as partner 1933.

RODENBACH, CONSTANTIN (1892–?) – Reparations Commission 1919–29; BIS Central Banking Department (renamed Monetary and Economic Department) 1930–46; Secrétaire Général de la Conférence des Reparations Orientales, Paris 1933.

ROOSA, ROBERT V. (1918–1993) – Under-Secretary of the U.S. Treasury 1961–64; Partner in Brown Brothers Harriman & Company 1965; President, American Finance Association; Director, Prudential Insurance Company of America, American Express Company, Anaconda Company, Rockefeller Foundation, NBER, Council of Foreign Relations.

ROOTH, IVAR (1888–1972) – Governor of Sveriges Riksbank 1929–48; Member of the BIS Board 1931–33 and 1937–49; Managing Director of the IMF 1951–56.

RUEFF, JACQUES (1896–1978) – Member of Secretariat, League of Nations 1927–30; Deputy Governor of the Bank of France 1939–41, resigned; Judge, Court of European Communities 1958–62; President of Committee for Reform of French Financial Situation 1958.

SCHACHT, HJALMAR HORACE GREELY (1877–1970) – Reichsbank President 1924–30 and 1933–39; German member, Committee of Experts on Reparations 1929; Member of the BIS Board 1930 and 1933–39; Reichsminister of Economics 1934–37.

SCHLEIMINGER, GÜNTHER (1921–) – Alternate member of the Managing Board of the European Payments Union for Germany and Chairman of the EPU Group of Alternates 1952–58; Head of the division for European monetary questions at the Deutsche Bundesbank 1958–68; Executive Director for Germany at the IMF 1968–74; Secretary General of the BIS 1975–77, Assistant General Manager 1978–81, General Manager 1981–85.

SCHWEGLER, WALTER (1902–1994) – Swiss National Bank 1928–66, President of the Governing Board 1956–66; Member of the BIS Board 1956–66.

SCITOVSZKY, TIBOR (1910–2002) – Economics Department, Stanford University 1946–58; University of California at Berkeley 1958–68; Heinz Professor of Economics, Yale University 1968–70; Eberle Professor of Economics, Stanford University 1970–76.

SIEPMANN, HARRY ARTHUR (1889–1963) – U.K. Treasury 1912–19; Peace Conference 1919; Adviser to National Bank of Hungary 1924–26; Adviser to the Governor of the Bank of England 1926, Executive Director 1945–54; Alternate member of the BIS Board 1930–35.

SIMON, HANS (1887–?) – BIS Central Banking Department 1930–31.

SIMON, JOHN ALLSEBROOK (1873–1954) – U.K. Home Secretary 1915–16; Foreign Secretary 1931–35; Home Secretary and Deputy Leader of House of Commons 1935–37; Chancellor of the Exchequer 1937–40; Lord Chancellor 1940–45.

SMITH, JEREMIAH, JR. (1870–1935) – with American Mission to Negotiate Peace as Counsel to Treasury Department and adviser on financial questions; Commissioner General (League of Nations) for Hungary in charge of financial reconstruction 1924–26.

SNOWDEN, PHILIP (1864–1940) – Member of U.K. Parliament 1906–18 and 1922–31; Chancellor of the Exchequer 1924 and 1929–31.

SNYDER, JOHN WESLEY (1895–1985) – Director of Office War Mobilization and Reconversion, July 1945–June 1946; Secretary of the Treasury 1946–53; U.S. Governor at IMF and IBRD 1946–53.

STIMSON, HENRY LEWIS (1867–1950) – U.S. Secretary of War 1911–13; Governor General of Philippine Islands 1927–29; Secretary of State 1929–33; Secretary of War 1940–45.

STOPPER, EDWIN (1912–1988) – Director of the Trade Section of the Swiss National Economy Department 1961–66; President of the Governing Board of the Swiss National Bank 1966–74; Member of the BIS Board 1966–74.

STRESEMANN, GUSTAV (1878–1929) – German Chancellor and Foreign Minister August–November 1923, Foreign Minister until his death; Winner of the Nobel Peace Prize with Aristide Briand 1926.

STRINGHER, BONALDO (1854–1930) – Director General of the Bank of Italy 1900–28, Governor (title changed) 1928–30; Member of the BIS Board 1930.

STRONG, BENJAMIN (1872–1928) – Cuyler, Morgan & Company 1891–1900; Atlantic Trust Company, 1901–04; Bankers Trust Company, Secretary 1904–09, Vice-President 1910–13, President 1914; Governor of the Federal Reserve Bank of New York 1914–28.

TANAKA, TETSUSABUROU (1883–1974) – Entered Bank of Japan 1909, London Agency; Attended Versailles Peace Conference as member of the Japanese delegation 1919–20; Attended Hague and Baden-Baden conferences 1929; Japanese representative at London International Economic Conference 1931; Member of the BIS Board 1930–32.

THEUNIS, GEORGES (1873–1966) – First Belgian Delegate at the Reparations Commission 1919; Minister of Finance 1920; Prime Minister and Minister of Finance 1921–25; Minister of State 1925; President of the International Economic Conference in Geneva 1927; Prime Minister November 1934 to March 1935; Belgian Ambassador-at-large in the United States 1939–44; Governor of the National Bank of Belgium 1941–44; Member of the BIS Board 1941–44; Delegate to Bretton Woods 1944.

TRAYLOR, MELVIN A. (1878–1934) – Admitted Texas bar 1901; Appointed President of First Trust & Savings Bank, Chicago 1919; First National Bank (Chicago) appointed Vice-President 1919, President 1925; Member of BIS Organisation Committee, Baden-Baden 1929.

TRIFFIN, ROBERT (1911–1993) – Chief, Latin American Section of the Federal Reserve Board 1942–46; Director, Exchange Control Division of the IMF 1946–48, Chief Representative in Europe 1948–49; Alternate U.S. Representative, European Payments Union 1950–51; Professor of Economics at Yale University 1951–77.

TRIP, LEONARDUS J. A. (1876–1947) – President of the Netherlands Bank 1931–41 and 1945–46; Member of the BIS Board 1932–46, President of the BIS and Chairman of the Board 1935–37.

TÜNGELER, JOHANNES (1907–1989) – Reichsbank 1931–45, Reichsbank Director 1942; Head of Foreign Department of the Bank deutscher Länder 1948–53, Member of the Directorate and Head of Foreign Department 1953–57; Member of the Directorate of the Deutsche Bundesbank 1957–76; Alternate member of the BIS Board 1969–76.

VANDEPUTTE, ROBERT (1908–1997) – Lecturer and then Professor at the Catholic University of Leuven 1933–78; Acting Director of the National Bank of Belgium 1943–44, Regent 1954–71, Governor 1971–75; Member of the BIS Board 1971–75; Belgian Minister of Finance 1981.

VAN HENGEL, ADRIANUS JOHANNES (1886–1936) – Director of the Amsterdamsche Bank 1916–24 and 1927–32; Commissioner of the Rotterdamsche Bankvereniging

1924–27; Representative of the International Committee of Foreign Creditors of the Austrian Credit-Anstalt 1931–32; Director General of Credit-Anstalt, 1932–36.

VAN ZEELAND, MARCEL (1898–1972) – Manager of the BIS Banking Department 1930–47, Head of the Banking Department 1947–62, First Manager 1948–62.

VAN ZEELAND, PAUL (1893–1973) – Alternate member of the BIS Board 1930–35; Vice-Governor of the National Bank of Belgium 1934–35; Prime Minister of Belgium 1935–37, Foreign Minister 1935–36 and 1949–54.

VINSON, FREDERICK MOORE (1890–1953) – Member of U.S. Congress 1923–29 and 1931–39; Director of the Office of Economic Stabilization 1943–45; U.S. Secretary of the Treasury 1945–46; first Chairman of the Board of Governors of the IMF 1946; Chief Justice of U.S. Supreme Court 1946–53.

VISSERING, GERARD (1865–1937) – Secretary of the Dutch Stockbrokers' Association 1895–97; Director of the Amsterdam Bank 1900–06; President of the Java Bank 1906–12; President of the Netherlands Bank 1912–31; Member of the BIS Board 1931.

VOCKE, WILHELM (1886–1973) – Member of the Reichsbank Board of Directors 1919–39; Alternate member of the BIS Board 1930–38, member 1950–57; President of the Board of Directors of the Bank deutscher Länder 1948–57.

VOGÜÉ, LOUIS DE (1868–1948) – President of the Central Union of Agricultural Unions and the Society of French Farmers; President of the Suez Canal Company; Regent of the Bank of France; Member of the BIS Board 1930–48, Vice-Chairman 1935–39.

VON MANGOLDT, HANS KARL (?) – Chairman of the Managing Board of the European Payments Union, 1952–58.

VON PHILIPPOVICH, MAX (1892–?) – Austrian diplomatic service 1917–20; S Bleichröder (banking firm) 1920–27; Joined First National Corporation of Boston as representative in Europe 1927; BIS Central Banking Department 1930–33.

WEBER, ERNST (1881–1967) – Entered Swiss National Bank 1907, Member of the Governing Board 1925–47, President of the Governing Board 1939–47, Member of the Bank Council 1947–55; Member of the BIS Board 1939–47, Chairman 1942–47.

WEISER, FELIX (1879–1944) – Barrister-at-Law, Austrian Arbitrator of Anglo-Austrian Mixed Arbitral Tribunal 1921–29; BIS Legal Adviser 1930–44.

WERNER, PIERRE (1913–2002) – Governor of EIB 1958–74; Prime Minister of Luxembourg and Minister of Treasury 1959–74; Chairman of EEC Committee on Monetary Union 1970–71; Prime Minister, Minister of Treasury, and Minister of Cultural Affairs 1979–84.

WHITE, HARRY DEXTER (1892–1948) – Assistant Director of Research, U.S. Treasury 1934, Director of Monetary Research 1942; U.S. Executive Director of International Monetary Fund 1946–47.

WIGGIN, ALBERT (1868–1951) – Vice-President of Chase National Bank, New York 1904–11, President 1911–17, Chairman of the Board 1917–21, Chairman of the Board and President 1921–26, Chairman of the Board 1926–30, Chairman of the Governing Board 1930–33.

WOLD, KNUT GETZ (1915–1987) – Director General in the Norwegian Ministry of Trade 1948–58; Deputy Governor and Deputy Chairman of the Central Bank of Norway's Executive Board 1958–70, Governor and Chairman 1970–85; Chairman of EFTA's Economic Committee 1967–1971; Governor for Norway in the IMF 1970–85.

WOODIN, WILLIAM H. (1868–1934) – U.S. Secretary of Treasury 1933.

WORMSER, OLIVIER (1913–1985) – French Ambassador to the USSR 1966–68; Governor of the Bank of France 1969–74; Member of the BIS Board 1969–74; Ambassador to the Federal Republic of Germany 1974–77.

YOUNG, OWEN D. (1874–1962) – Vice-President of General Electric 1913–22, Chairman 1922–39; Chairman of the Radio Corporation of America 1919–33; Chairman of the Expert Committee on Reparations 1929.

ZIJLSTRA, JELLE (1918–2001) – Professor in Theoretical Economics, Free University, Amsterdam 1948; Minister of Economic Affairs in the Dutch cabinet 1952–59, Minister of Finance 1959–63; Prime Minister of the Netherlands November 1966 to April 1967; President of the Netherlands Bank 1967–81; President of the BIS and Chairman of the Board 1967–81.

Index

Okun, A. M., 431
organisation, of BIS: after end of Bretton
    Woods, *440*; and end of reparations,
    119–23; and first operations in early 1930s,
    63–7, *64*; and staff in late 1930s, 183–5;
    and structure in 1950s, *322*. *See also*
    Baden-Baden committee
Organisation for European Economic
    Co-operation (OEEC), 305–8, 310,
    339–46
Ossola, Rinaldo, 421
Ottawa Conference of 1932, 137, 161, 264
Overby, Andrew, 279

pacifism, and World War II, 212
Padoa-Schioppa, Tommaso, 606n54
Pakistan, and conflict with India, 411, 412
Pallain, Georges, 490n40
Parmentier, Jean, 494n55
Parsons, Maurice, 589–90n150
Perkins, Thomas N., 494n55
Pester Ungarische Commercial Bank, 98
Péteri, G., 493n27
Pilotti, Raffaele, 184, 193, 252, 253
Pirelli, Alberto, 494n55
Poincaré, R., 20, 27, 28, 29, 32
Poland: appeasement and start of World War
    II, 212–13; and BIS in 1950s, 319; and end
    of interwar gold standard, 116; and IMF,
    580n172; as shareholding member of early
    BIS, 69. *See also* Bank Polski
political science, and theoretical literature on
    cooperation, 10–11
politics: and "above politics" illusion of BIS,
    479–82; and appeasement policy during
    World War II, 211–12. *See also* autarky;
    foreign relations; nationalism
Pompidou, Georges, 428, 446
Porters, R. H., 98, 184
Portugal: and BIS during World War II, 238;
    invitation to join BIS in 1950s, 319
postal administrations, BIS and international
    settlements among, 189–91, 248–9
presidents, of BIS, 183–4, 224–6, 297, 321.
    See also Beyen, Johan Willem; Fraser,
    Leon; Frère, Maurice; Holtrop, Marius;
    McGarrah, Gates W.; McKittrick, Thomas
    H.; Trip, Leonardus J. A.; Zijlstra, Jelle
price stability, BIS advocacy of in 1950s, 325
Primo de Rivera, Miguel, 78
profits and profitability, of BIS. *See* balance
    sheet; capital; income

prosperity index, and reparations, 31
prudential issues, and eurocurrency market,
    456–7, 469–71
Puhl, Emil, 225, 228, 229, 236, 254–5,
    552n112, 555n145

Quarterly Journal of Economics, 54
Quesnay, Pierre: on common unit of currency,
    540n123, 563n20; and Credit-Anstalt crisis,
    93, 94; death of, 184; and establishment of
    BIS, 36, 40, 43, 56–8, 60, 61, 497n102; as
    General Manager of BIS, 62; and German
    reparations, 71; and gold standard, 132;
    and Monetary and Economic Department
    of BIS, 193; and organisation of BIS in
    late 1930s, 184; on Spanish currency
    stabilisation, 78–9, 80, 81, 82, 509n110

Rainoni, Antonio, 321
Ranieri, L., 495n70
Rasminsky, Louis, 365, 474, 585n58
Raw, Rupert, 393, 593n194
Realpolitik, and Czechoslovak gold affair,
    211–12
Red Cross, 244–5
refugees, and Switzerland during World War
    II, 222
Reich loans. *See* Dawes Plan and Dawes loan;
    Young Plan and Young loan
Reichsbank: and Bretton Woods, 281; and
    central bank cooperation in 1920s, 30;
    and Czechoslovak gold affair, 204–13,
    258; and German transfer crisis, 151, 152,
    153–4, 155; and gold transactions with
    BIS, 245–52, 258–9; Great Depression and
    German financial crisis, 101, 102, 103, 104,
    105, *108,* 111; and World War II, 224–5,
    227–31, 245–52, 258–9. *See also* Germany
Reisch, Richard, 56, 91
Reparation Commission, 25–6
reparations: and banking operations of BIS,
    70–2, 186; and economic difficulties
    of Germany in 1930s, 86; and German
    transfer crisis, 149–57; and Great
    Depression, 87–8, 129; and Lausanne
    Agreement (1932), 131; and negotiations
    at end of World War I, 24, 25–7, 28, 32,
    33–9, 45–7; reorganisation of BIS at end
    of, 119–23; and research of Monetary and
    Economic Department of BIS in late 1930s,
    193. *See also* Dawes Plan; Germany;
    international payments; Young Plan

Equalisation Fund, 165; and German
reparations after World War I, 25–7; and
German transfer crisis, 153; and Gold
Pool operations in 1960s, 375–81; and
Great Depression, 88, 105, 107, 109;
and international relations in 1930s, 161;
and London Conference of 1933, 137,
140, 145, 146; and response to creation of
BIS, 60; and sterling in 1960s, 388–99,
600–1n327; and Tripartite Agreement,
175–82; and World War II, 213,
232–3, 256. *See also* Bank of England;
London
United Nations, and financial neutrality during
World War II, 216
United States: ambiguity of on establishment
of BIS, 44–8, 53–4, 60; and banking
crisis in 1970s, 470; Baring crisis of
1890 and central bank cooperation, 15;
and Basel Agreement, 384; and bilateral
concerté, 387; and BIS operations in
postwar years, 299–300; and Board
of BIS in 1950s, 319–20; and Bretton
Woods, 268, 271–6, 428–36; and capital
of BIS in early 1930s, 68; and currency
realignments in 1949, 315; and discussions
on BIS representation in 1960s, 364; and
end of interwar gold standard, 117–19;
and eurocurrency market, 454, 456; and
European Monetary Agreement, 340–1,
345; and European Payments Union,
332; and European recovery in postwar
years, 285; and European rescue of
dollar in 1960–61, 369–75; and German
reparations after World War I, 25–7; and
German transfer crisis, 153; and gold
dollar standard in post–World War II
period, 9; and Gold Pool in 1960s, 375–81,
417; and Great Depression, 84, 86–7,
102, 105, 107, 109, 114; and international
monetary system in 1960s, 350–7; and
international relations in 1930s, 161; and
investments in early years of BIS, 74;
involvement with BIS in 1930s, 167–75;
and London Conference of 1933, 137, 145,
146; and OEEC, 305–8; policy stance on
reparations and establishment of BIS, 38;
relations with BIS at beginning of World
War II, 203–4; representation of central
banks at BIS, 49–50; trade with Europe
in 1950s, 311; and Tripartite Agreement,
175–82; and unofficial meetings of BIS

in late 1930s, 198–200; World War II
and relations with BIS, 214, 224, 233–5,
236, 240–1, 256. *See also* Federal Reserve
Bank of New York; Federal Reserve
System
Universal Postal Union (UPU), 189–91
Urbig, Franz, 127, 521n62

Van de Burgt, Th. G. J. M., 501n168
Vandeputte, Robert, 467
Vanderlip, Frank, 23
Van Hengel, Adrianus Johannes, 93, 112–13,
517–18n128–9
Van Meerten, Michelangelo, 24, 667
Van Tonningen, Rost, 551n90
Van Zeeland, Marcel, 61, 63, 74, 184, 185, 241,
244, 245, 297, 559n191, 583n18
Van Zeeland, Paul, 166, 262, 331, 497n102,
563n11
Versailles, Treaty of (1919), 24, 25, 86, 110,
119, 150
Victor Emmanuel III, King of Italy, 253
Vietnam War, 411, 412, 415, 462
Viner, Jacob, 166, 288
Vinson, Frederick, 275, 565n45
Vissering, Gerard, 22, 69
Vocke, Wilhelm, 102, 138, 295, 336, 497n102,
569n65
Volcker, Paul, 429
Voluntary Foreign Credit Restraint Program
(1965), 456
von Korsigk, Count Schwerin, 154
Von Mangoldt, Hans Karl, 578n137
Von Philippovich, Max, 192, 194–5
Voorhis, J., 235

Waley, Sir David, 565n50
Wallenberg, Marcus, 127, 521n61
Washington Agreement (1948), 278, 567n81
Watergate scandal, 436
Weber, Ernst, 224, 242
Weenink, W. H., 540n122
Weiser, Felix, 547n32, 547n34
Weizsäcker, G., 228
Werner, Pierre, 447
Werner Plan, 444–52
White, Harry Dexter, 182, 260, 263, 265, 268,
275, 556n160, 563n16
Wiggin, Albert, 123, 125
Wiggin Committee (1931), 105–6, 123–7
Wilhelmina, Queen of the Netherlands, 219
Wilmars, Mertens de, 449